D1231885

The Garland Library of War and Peace

The
Garland Library
of
War and Peace

Under the General Editorship of

Blanche Wiesen Cook, *John Jay College, C.U.N.Y.*

Sandi E. Cooper, *Richmond College, C.U.N.Y.*

Charles Chatfield, *Wittenberg University*

Oswald Garrison Villard

The Dilemmas of the Absolute Pacifist in Two World Wars

edited by

Anthony Gronowicz

GARLAND PUBLISHING, INC.
NEW YORK • LONDON
1983

These facsimiles have been made from material in the libraries of Yale University, Columbia University, and Harvard University.

Articles from *The Nation* are reprinted by permission.

Library of Congress Cataloging in Publication Data

Villard, Oswald Garrison, 1872–1949.
Oswald Garrison Villard, the dilemmas of the absolute pacifist in two world wars.

(The Garland library of war and peace)
Collection of articles, selected letters, excerpts from books, etc.
1. United States—Foreign relations—20th century—Addresses, essays, lectures. 2. United States—Military policy—Addresses, essays, lectures. 3. World politics—1900–1945—Addresses, essays, lectures. 4. World War, 1914–1918—United States—Addresses, essays, lectures. 5. World War, 1939–1945—United States—Addresses, essays, lectures. 6. Peace—Addresses, essays, lectures. 7. Free trade and protection—Free trade—Addresses, essays, lectures. I. Gronowicz, Anthony. II. Title. III. Series.
E744.V464 1983 327.73 82-6235
ISBN 0-8240-0504-X AACR2

Design by Alfredo Cruz

This volume has been printed on acid-free, 250-year-life paper.

Printed in the United States of America

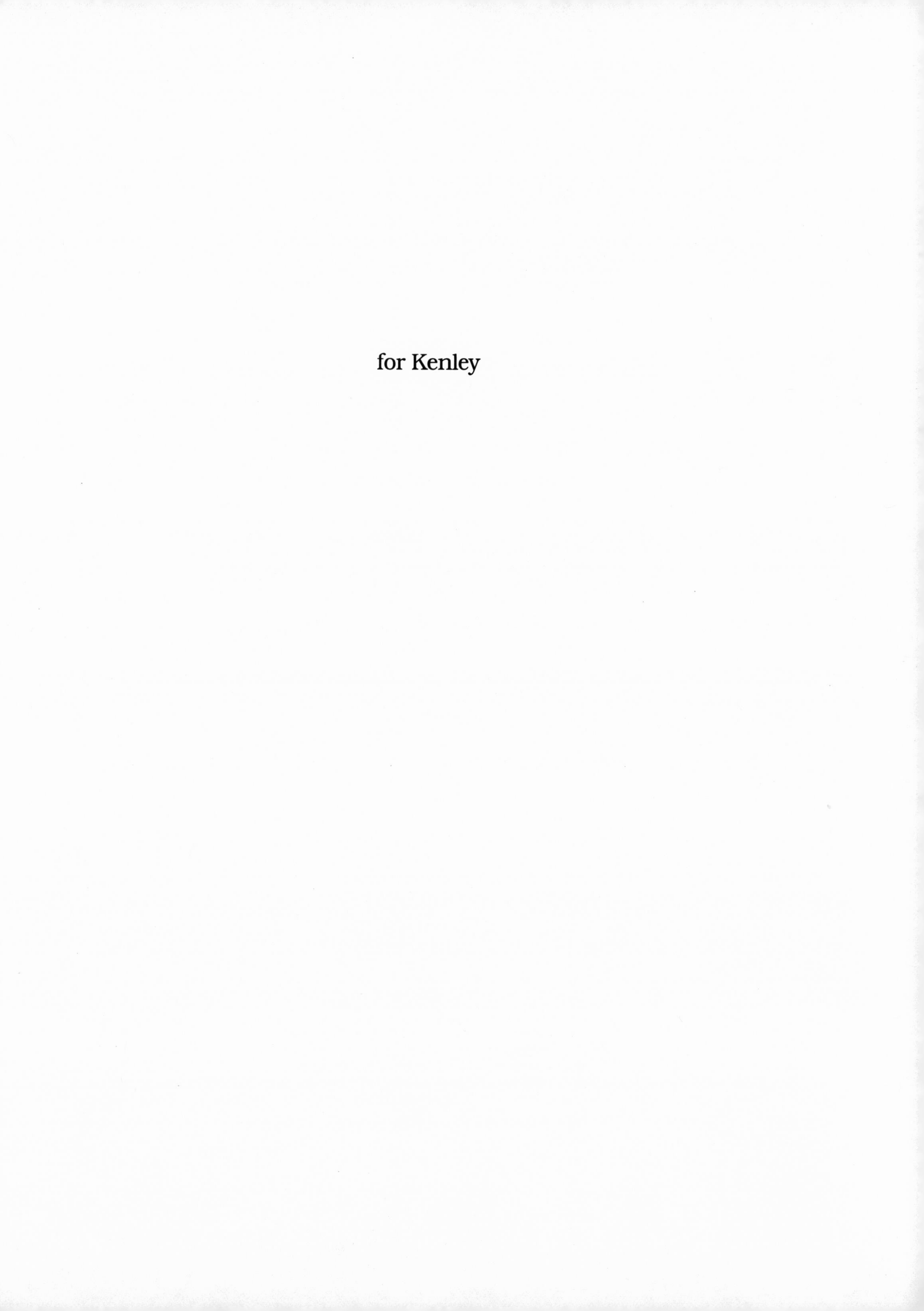

for Kenley

INTRODUCTION

Oswald Garrison Villard was owner and editor of the *New York Evening Post* and *The Nation* during the first half of the twentieth century. His career as a pacifist paralleled the buildup of the American military from a minor auxiliary of the state to the "military-industrial complex"[1] that dominates the economy of today.

The arms buildup began in the 1890's when private American enterprises encouraged government policymakers to develop a strong military, using the argument that national security required protection of foreign markets. Until that time, with the exception of the Civil War, the United States Army had never exceeded twenty-five thousand men. The United States was first industrially in 1880 and therefore possessed the economic capacity for such an endeavor. By the close of World War II the United States had the most powerful military in the world, while its forty-three percent share of industrial output was unsurpassed.

Villard fought against military expansion and conscription through writing and editing articles and books and by encouraging organizations such as the American Union Against Militarism. However, the United States economy was fundamentally strengthened by our involvement in the two world wars. No other country sacrificed so little and gained so much from these conflicts.

In his struggles Villard was assisted by a tradition that allowed him to place principle above expediency. His father had emigrated to New York after the 1848 German revolution to avoid facing combat against a Bavarian government set up by his uncle. As a reporter for the Lincoln-Douglas debates, he represented a German-language newspaper and later covered the Civil War for American journals. His favorable reportage brought him to President Lincoln's attention and led to his marriage to the daughter of the abolitionist William Lloyd Garrison. After the war northern big business flourished, and in 1881 Henry Villard acquired control of the Northern Pacific Railroad through the use of British and German capital.

Young Oswald's view of his father was rapturous:

> It was a precious heritage, indeed, to have a brave and handsome father, noble always in his integrity and his ideals.
>
> . . . in all those precious years he never heard from his . . . lips one selfish or self-seeking word, nor any expression or opinion that could be described as else than high-minded and liberal.
>
> He never urged that we should learn to make money; on the contrary he wished us to be professional men.[2]

In 1910 Villard dedicated a biography of John Brown to his father's "Beloved and High-Minded" memory.[3] He also drew inspiration from his maternal grandfather, who had been vehemently opposed to the American war against Mexico that led to the seizure of one third of that country in order to secure slaveholding Texas.

But it was to his suffragist mother that he attributed his heightened sense of vigor when under fire, and he was often under fire after 1910 for his negative views on war as an instrument of national policy.

> Always she was in her person a dainty aristocrat, dressing with exquisite taste and never with extravagance—an aristocrat in her fineness but entirely a democrat in her views and in her heart . . . One could hardly refuse that mother anything! . . . To modify any position she took for reasons of expediency—that was unthinkable; to shift her ground in order to gain a personal advantage, or to avoid unpleasantness, was as impossible for her as for her father . . . But her certainty of the correctness of her positions, and her taking it as a matter of course that everyone she met agreed with her, quite often led her into difficulties and into injuring the feelings of others she could have been the last to wish to hurt.
>
> These were the parents who gave me every opportunity in life, every benefit that wealth could bestow, and forged for me the tools that I used in my effort to mold the public opinion of my time.[4]

Villard's preference for a nonbusiness career was supported by his parents, and the difficulties his father encountered with members of his own class were transferred to his son.

> Father was never liked by the leaders in Wall Street . . . He never attended their churches—often very important from the business point of view—or belonged to their pet clubs. They did not like his being a free trader and an independent Democrat, or "Mugwump," and they held him at least partly responsible for Godkin and *The Evening Post's* vagaries.[5]

Though Villard emerged from the upper class with all the advantages that came with an 1890's Harvard education, he was not afraid of criticizing his peers whom he felt were responsible for destroying the liberal republican values that made this country admired the world over. His mother, father, grandfather, and uncle were all iconoclasts and exceptions to what they felt was the amorality of their class. They may not have understood the structural imperatives of the system, but they did regard certain moral imperatives as dear. Of his father and grandfather Villard wrote:

> Henry Villard and his father-in-law were alike in their fundamental beliefs and ideals, and approached life from the same point of view, although they could hardly have had more dissimilar upbringings . . . Both men were republicans to their finger tips, could conceive of no other defensible form of government, and passionately believed that it was possible to build the edifice of a perfect State upon American soil. Both held to the same social idealism, were complete liberals, were ardent internationalists in that they abhorred war, were devoted free traders, and believed in the brotherhood of man. Both were steeped in the doctrines of the Manchester school of British liberalism, and both personally knew and admired John Bright and Richard Cobden.[6]

Young Villard believed that opposition to war was a more noble *act* than being involved in military conflict, a curious inversion until we realize the importance Villard attached to setting a high moral standard for others to follow. So powerful was his need to be true to the principles of his maternal grandfather, so mutually reinforcing were his parents and the general circumstances of his upbringing that Villard could make a convincing case for condemning someone like John Brown for his actions while praising him for his beliefs.

> In Virginia, John Brown *atoned* for Pottawatomie *by* the nobility of his philosophy and his sublime *devotion to principle*, even to the gallows [my italics].
>
> It was the weapon of the spirit by which he finally conquered. In its power lies not only the secret of his influence, and his immortality, but the finest ethical teachings of a life which, for all its faults, inculcates many an enduring lesson, and will forever make its appeal to the imagination.
>
> For the Abolitionists, it will be remembered, he had nothing but contempt. Theirs were "but words, words;" yet it was by words, and words, embodying his moral principles, the theological teachings he valued so highly, the doctrines of the Savior, who knew no distinction of race, creed or color and by the beauty of his own peace and spirit in the face of death, that he stirred his Northern countrymen to their depths and won the respect even of the citizens of the South.[7]

Valuing word over deed led Villard to condemn American statesmen for engaging in violence and brutality in the conduct of foreign affairs.

> It was not until our conquest of Cuba and the Philippines, with its needless waste of life and, in the archipelago, shocking cruelties, that I arrived at my anti-war position.[8]

He did not consider the military an American institution and felt that our involvement in the Spanish-American War was a betrayal of American principles, rather than a reflection of them.[9] He was quick to condemn President McKinley for his role in this conflict:

> McKinley could have prevented war had he been sincere in his desire to do so . . . Spain had surrendered on nearly every point and had offered to submit to arbitration those on which she had not yielded . . . The blood of every American who died in that war and in the subsequent Philippine hostilities rests squarely upon the head of William McKinley.[10]

Theodore Roosevelt was excoriated for his "crass brutality and cave-man savagery."[11] Roosevelt, in turn, had once spiced a staid dinner with the remark "I *wish* that somebody would take Oswald Villard to pieces and forget how to put him together again."[12]

Even when critical, Villard savored such presidental recognition.

> I look back upon my relations with Mr. Taft with the greatest satisfaction. For a time his private secretary in the White House was Charles Dyer Norton, one of the most attractive and brilliant young men of his day, who had married at Thorwood [Villard's father's estate in Dobbs Ferry, New York] my cousin, Katherine Garrison, to whom I have always been bound in ties of especial affection. This gave me a particular interest in the Taft administration, so far as that was possible for one of my radically different political philosophy.[13]

Villard was committed to the principles of free trade and believed that a stronger military establishment would only serve to divert resources from socially productive ends.

> If I were dictator I should abolish every tariff because I know that the rapid rise of the three great industrial nations of modern times has been due chiefly to the fact that within their respective empires it has been free trade that has made them powerful and prosperous. Particularly I should say that this is true of the United States.[14]

These beliefs coincided with those of E. L. Godkin,[15] founder of *The Nation*, who had borrowed his notions of free trade from Cobden and Bright. Their ideas had helped shape the ideology of the Liberal Party, which came to power as England was attaining the height of its industrial and military power relative to the rest of the world. To those who ran the British Empire free trade was equated with progress and a free world.

Such views became more acceptable in American intellectual circles after the First World War had taken twenty million lives, and Villard's pacifism coincided with the isolationism of the 1920's. *The Nation* became a magnet for war-bred disillusionment, and into this spiritual vacuum he introduced the crusading values of free trade—his practical cure for war.[16]

Yet, the free trade principle had also been important to Woodrow Wilson, who thought it would resolve the market demands of a dominant and dynamic American corporate capitalism.[17] Free trade makes perfect sense for the capitalist power in a position of economic supremacy. The absence of trade barriers assists its large corporations in supplying certain advanced technologies for use by the elite native to a particular country. In return, this local elite allows its own people to be stripped of their raw materials, thereby preventing them from ever emerging as economic rivals to the capitalist nation. Exploitation of this cheaper labor power is at the expense of the worker in the dominant country, whose earning power can then be lowered to match that of the superexploited, less developed society. In addition, the more powerful and developed nation provides the international cartel or multinational corporation with legal protection at home and military protection abroad. In other words, free trade, as, for example, conducted by the United States in Latin America, coincided with the very "spirit of nationalism," which Villard maintained was the "greatest stumbling block" to its success.[18] Thus, Villard's promotion of free trade actually served to undermine his pacifist position.

The historical irony that Villard never integrated into his writings is that free trade among capitalist powers has only been possible when stronger nations are able to impose this policy upon the rest of the world through colonialism and imperialism. This relationship is inherently unstable as the larger capitalist countries are never satisfied with their rate of profits. As they become ever more dependent on foreign markets as a means of simultaneously relieving and enhancing their economies, they become more reliant on the military as a means of forcibly penetrating these economies. Rivalry among the capitalist powers intensifies and brings on conflict. Both world wars were conceived by American statesmen as wars for free trade. The United States entered these conflicts in order to prevent the Germans and Japanese from closing off vast areas of the world to our entrepreneurs and to dismantle the British Empire. It also acted to prevent the world's peoples from controlling their own markets and raw materials.

The correspondence that Villard makes between peace and free trade makes sense only if all countries of the world agree. Such concert can only be achieved when economies are fully developed and socialized. Villard never came to terms with the question of socialism. Although he considered himself almost a socialist, he didn't understand socialism very well:[19]

> I considered Socialism to be inevitable and that we are all more or less Socialists, even the conservatives.[20]

He did not grasp how the energies expended in class conflict could be redirected into "the nationalization of the masses" through war as was the case with fascist Germany, Italy, and Japan.[21] The coming of the First World War entailed such nationalization, as one social democratic party after another followed the lead of its nation's capitalists and bankers in supporting increased military expenditures and centralization of power in the federal government.

Villard wrote a series of articles for the *Evening Post*, later published in a pamphlet entitled *Preparedness*, in which he probed the crucial precedent that would be set if the United States were to involve itself in a European conflict of this magnitude.

> The European war will probably induce the coming Congress, under Mr. Wilson's guidance, to reverse our historic policy of a small army without reserves and to provide a still larger fleet. If this is the possibility . . . the tax-payers, who will have an enormous annual bill to pay, and the masses of our people generally, upon whose welfare the new departure will have such a far-reaching effect, should insist upon the laying down of certain national policies after the most careful debate and discussion. . . .
>
> But when . . . all the matters of military policy have been settled one way or the other, the great question still remains: *Should the United States, in the fevered disquiet of a world-crisis, alter the policy of its national life, and go in for large armaments?*[22]

Villard had been one of President Wilson's three closest advisors and supported him warmly in the editorial columns of his newspaper. When Wilson ran for president a second time in 1916, war had been raging in Europe for over two years, and Wilson's campaign slogan became "He kept us out of war." Villard felt that his arguments had carried weight with the president. Yet, a month after Wilson's inauguration ceremony American soldiers were fighting and dying on the European battlefield.

> It had long been inevitable but the blow was terrific none the less. It came nearer to unmanning me than anything in my life. For I knew, as I knew that I lived, that this ended the republic as we had known it; that henceforth we Americans were to be part and parcel of world politics, rivalries, jealousies, and militarism.
>
> From the moment war began the whole current of American life was changed and Mr. Wilson's great advances toward the New Freedom checked and finally stopped.[23]

Villard never had the grim satisfaction of knowing that the cruise ship *Lusitania* had a false bottom to carry arms when it was sunk with the loss of over eleven hundred lives[24] nor that the notorious Zimmerman Note, which revealed German plans for the takeover of Mexico, was a forgery concocted by British intelligence. More than any other pretexts these incidents acted as the Pearl Harbor for America's entry into World War I against Germany. These deceptions were not revealed to the American public until fifty years later, when the pressure of events no longer prevented their disclosure.

> When I arrived in Washington the day after the sinking of the *Lusitania* I found the capital in a state of excitement such as it has not known since the blowing up of the *Maine*.[25]

Villard was outraged by what he regarded as a personal betrayal by Wilson and used the *Post* to vent his anger. His staff protested, and Villard resigned to take over *The Nation*. From 1918 until 1933 as owner and editor-in-chief he transformed that periodical from a staid literary journal with a circulation of about eight thousand to a crusading liberal force in American letters with many times that readership. This was accomplished at a time when the forces of reaction were on the rampage; the Ku Klux Klan grew to five million members in 1925 while intolerance against Catholics and Jews was openly displayed by such public figures as Henry Ford. In the meantime, *The Nation* came to stand for social progress and human rights, especially with regard to Afro-Americans and women.

This new image of courageous and responsible opposition to congressional and presidential militarism gave *The Nation* a newfound prominence in national affairs. It also led to the confiscation of one issue by federal postal authorities for containing the observation that "the opinion of a Cornish miner or a Lancashire overlooker would help us more to an understanding of labor than any number of observations from Mr. Gompers [president of the American Federation of Labor]."[26]

In marked contrast the socialist press was systematically harassed, suppressed, and destroyed. It had dared to organize mass opposition to government policies and had millions of supporters, while *The Nation* aimed its appeal at a narrow, albeit significant, spectrum of the progressive intelligentsia.[27] To accomplish this objective Villard surrounded himself with a talented staff of writers and editors who contributed scorching probes of domestic injustice as well as American imperialism in Latin America[28] and Europe. His position on the First World War was generally shared by those who read and wrote for *The Nation*:

> We held firm not because we were egoists but because we knew that the great wave of national emotion was largely artificial: deliberately cultivated by the government propaganda; that it was an appeal to base human traits; that it could not . . . evoke great literary and artistic creations, and could only impoverish American promise.[29]

Thus did Villard attack Wilson's connivance with the European victors at Versailles:

> Great territories involving the lives of millions of black men were to be turned over to new masters, yet there was hardly a dark skin visible. Worst of all, for the first time in modern history, a great peace was to be written without a single representative of the defeated peoples in the council chamber.
>
> The calm way they go on carving up Europe without consulting the Russians, Germans, Austrians, Hungarians, etc. is beyond words.[30]

Villard welcomed the Bolshevik Revolution in Russia. Its former leaders had sent millions of citizens to their deaths in order to sustain a bankrupt and cruel regime. Though the seizure of political power by the Russian communists resulted in the loss of six lives, the foreign-inspired civil war and invasions by European, Japanese, and American forces killed over one million Russians.[31] Villard criticized American intervention because its soldiers ". . . had no personal quarrel with the Soviets or their subjects . . . [and were merely] . . . pawns of Woodrow Wilson in his illegal and unconstitutional war on Russia."[32]

To prevent future invasions Soviet leaders emphasized military preparedness. Unilateral disarmament would have meant national suicide as Hitler planned to murder or enslave all Slavic peoples and did manage to kill over forty million of them in the Second World War.

Villard did not accept this Soviet concern.[33] He found the Soviet war minister's military preparedness speeches ". . . as hateful to me . . . as when they come at home from talking generals of our own army, or from officials of the National Security League and the American Defense Society."[34] He did not appreciate the Soviet argument that war as an active instrument of foreign policy cannot be abolished until the class responsible is removed from power.

Villard's opposition to American involvement in the two world wars and his early support for the Russian Revolution led to accusations that he was a German agent. The same charge had been leveled against Lenin in the capitalist press as every effort to stop the slaughter short of total victory was labeled pro-German. Unfortunately, in his case some of Villard's sentiments lent credence to this charge:

> . . . the proudest and most powerful structure in all Europe lay in ashes, and the soldiers came marching home to moral and spiritual ruins more appalling than all the destruction in France . . . Those who had had such faith in their Kultur, their Germanic *Manneskraft*, their unequaled intellectual achievements, their extraordinary industrial successes had failed just where they expected to win—at the top. . . .
>
> How could God so have veiled his face to his chosen people?[35]

Although the final question is presented in the context of German self-appraisal, we cannot be absolutely sure that Villard does not accept this assessment, since nowhere in his other writings does he present a different analysis.

He wrote three books on Germany, the most on any one subject, placing its people's aspirations and accomplishments in the most sympathetic light. The important role that militarism and racism played in German life in the twentieth century is minimized. Yet when dealing with France, Villard cannot bring himself to say anything kind about that country or its people's achievements. In fact, his journalistic attacks on France persist past the official start of the Second World War:

> Plainly, it will be extremely difficult to hold the French in line for anything else than a peace which they trust will make forever impossible the domination of Europe by German armies. They have learned nothing and forgotten much.[36]

Emphasis on the treatment of German war victims far exceeds what little sympathy Villard is able to muster for the Russian, Yugoslav, Jewish, Polish, Gypsy, French, English, Belgian, and other victims of German aggression. No allusion is made to the over thirty million Russians killed in the two world wars—by far the worst civilian and military casualties in human history. In addition, World War II concentration camp horrors are scarcely mentioned except in such contexts as criticism of the American press for exaggerating American casualties in those camps.[37]

Villard was allowed to enter Germany to report on conditions there after its savage invasion of Poland in September 1939.[38] Though he condemned the Nazis, President Franklin Roosevelt's interior secretary, Harold Ickes, felt moved to characterize Villard as a "fellow traveler with Hitler."[39] His policy of turning the other cheek to the savior of the German industrialist alienated many progressives. They argued that pacifism was precisely what the führer desired of the big powers at that historical moment, since this would give him needed time to conquer smaller countries and integrate them into Germany's war machine in preparation for a massive attack upon the Soviet Union.

In the foreword to *Our Military Chaos*, written in 1939, Villard argued that if Germany were to wage war and win, it would not therefore become the automatic enemy of the United States, for "a conquered Europe would be too dangerous to it to warrant another war."[40] But since he also consistently maintained that the United States functioned best in a free-trade world, one that obviously could not survive in "a conquered Europe," a logical contradiction like this one gives rise to suspicions on the order of Ickes's.

Villard was also opposed to organizing to fight the Nazis: "Here again is the threat of civil war, of violence against violence which bodes no good to the German nation."[41] He warned American Jews who desired to fight Hitler that "they feel that if we do not get into the war Hitler will get over here and put them in concentration camps, so they are taking the direct road to anti-Semitism and militarism."[42]

Yet he proposed no realistic alternative course of action that would involve the organization of progressive elements within German or American society.

Villard also never fully accepted the notion that the roots of fascism lay in big business.[43] This greatly limited his ability to generate a politics relevant to the people's needs. However, his skills as a journalist did allow him to find the truth even if he wasn't able to follow through on his discovery: "For his [Hitler's] part he is not willing to apply nationalization to the heavy industries . . . [which], curiously enough, appear to have contributed to the Hitler treasury."[44]

After World War II Villard was politically isolated. His pro-German bias[45] was scorned by the left, and his failure to support American cold war policies led to his ostracism from the right. He interpreted the rush to transform the United States into a garrison state using the best of all possible reasons—fascist Germany and Japan—as leading to the economic ruin of the republic and the destruction of American idealism. The potential for nuclear holocaust led him to want to "save Jesus from Joseph,"[46] and he continued to write in opposition to this new imposed mass hysteria: "I could not put the signing of the North Atlantic Pact on my television last evening, for to me it marks the final blow to our beloved Republic, and the establishment of a complete military State."[47]

Ironically, Villard passed from the world scene just as German republican and socialist values were granted the historical opportunity to contribute to human progress. This possibility arose only after Germany had been soundly beaten in two world wars and was denied the national right to develop an independent military.

Villard was never able to make the connection in his writings between a beleaguered capitalism and militarism. He therefore declared the Second World War to be:

> . . . the result of a contest between idiocy on one hand and insanity on the other . . . 40 per cent of the blame for it rested squarely upon the last three British Prime Ministers.[48]

Although he recognized immorality and opportunism among capitalists, it was hard for him to analyze critically his own class position. He spent too much energy railing at individuals rather then fashioning concrete alternatives to the system that bred war:

> . . . forty-one years of responsible journalism have given me little respect for most of the men in high office in any country. Often I have said to myself: "Would that mine enemy could become President or Prime Minister." Nothing in my life has been more disheartening . . .
>
> . . . what most of us teach to our children, namely, that the highest honors in our national life go to men who have earned them by conspicuous service, is the veriest nonsense.[49]

Not able to bring himself to support mass organizations independent of the control of the nation's policymakers, he depended upon the power of moral persuasion to dislodge the war profiteers from power.

The faith that his ideas might win out also rested upon an unrealistic assessment of the potential political constituency for his views in the United States. At one point he quotes Montaigne to the effect that he was:

> "very fond of peasants—they are not educated enough to reason incorrectly." I have recorded my belief that I would rather trust the innate good sense and the judgments of five hundred Americans of the farms and villages than a similar number of more or less class-conscious college graduates.[50]

But certainly by the time Villard was writing these words American society had transformed itself economically and socially to the point where the kind of values generated by the rural American environment no longer had impact as so few Americans belonged to that sector of society. Yet the Jeffersonian ideal as embodied in the yeoman farmer was precisely what had yielded the unbounded optimism of Villard and other progressive interpreters of the American dream. Historically, even the political system had been constituted on this assumption, though the Civil War demonstrated the failure of the political system to resolve economic differences peaceably. It also destroyed once and for all the notion that the Jeffersonian ideal could ever triumph. In any case, this ideal had allowed itself to become monstrously perverted through plantation slavery and was therefore ripe for destruction.

Villard did not comprehend how completely the values of Hamilton had triumphed over those of Jefferson. He did not realize that his heroes of the 1920's—La Follette and Norris—political spokesmen for those who valued butter over guns—represented the last hurrah of the yeoman farmer. The Great Depression would become their grapes of wrath and would drive many of these midwesterners to California, where they would ironically secure jobs in World War II defense plants and unwittingly become defenders of the garrison state. The corporate capitalist system had broken their will and sense of independence and integrated them into the system through war-guaranteed economic rewards and media blitz. Those who remained outside the system stagnated or joined organizations like the Ku Klux Klan out of frustration.

Thus, though Villard's priorities were sensible and high-minded, his reliance on personal appeal rather than intense economic and political analysis and mass organization to stop war prevented him from developing a body of original theoretical work. Steeped as he was in liberal republican values of the German and American variety, he could not get beyond the concept of nationhood. His notions of brotherhood rested on outmoded and unconsciously self-serving economic notions like free trade in a capitalist world, though his strategic sense was sound.

> The whole nation has a profound interest in the question of whether we shall play a leading part in directing the trend of events towards disarmament, upon it may depend our own freedom from the crushing burden of military expenditure, which, largely by act of Mr. Wilson himself, this country began to assume in the panic and hysteria of last winter.[51]

His own assessment of John Brown can be applied to him, except instead of slavery Villard fought war:

> As inexorable a fate as ever dominated a Greek tragedy guided this life. He walked always as one blindfolded. Something compelled him to attack . . . and to that impulse he yielded, reckoning not at all as to the outcome, and making not the slightest effort to plan beyond the first blow.[52]

Anthony Gronowicz
Passaic County Community College

NOTES

1. A term that originated in President Eisenhower's 1961 Farewell Address to the American people.
2. Sydney Strong, ed., *What I Owe My Father* (New York, 1931), p. 157. Oswald Garrison Villard, *Fighting Years* (New York, 1939), pp. 17, 30.
3. Villard himself considered it "to be the only first-class job I have ever done." Villard, *Fighting Years*, p. 99.
4. *Ibid.*, pp. 21, 23.
5. *Ibid.*, p. 35.
6. *Ibid.*, p. 4.
7. Villard, *John Brown* (New York, 1910), pp. 586, 588, 589.
8. Villard, *Fighting Years*, p. 100. This intolerant, often savage treatment of minority peoples, a disturbing recurrent theme in American history, is best summarized in "American Justifications for Military Massacres from the Pequot War to Mylai," Blanche Cook, *Peace and Change*, III, nos. 2 & 3 (Summer Fall 1975). Long before Vietnam the United States military managed to exterminate 700,000 Philippine natives in the Spanish-American War.
9. Villard proved unable to precisely define his own political role. He was a liberal, but the closest approximation to definition is hinted at in the following excerpt:

   > Before I define a liberal, let me speak of Spain. When one beholds the horrible suffering there, the wanton butchery by rank outsiders . . . the damnable ruin of a historic people . . . one wishes there were a just and omnipotent God in heaven to behold what has come over those tired democracies. They cannot move. They cannot rouse themselves. They cannot damn as one man the foreign authors of that misery. [Villard, "What Is a Liberal?" *The Nation*, 11/27/37]
10. Villard, *Fighting Years*, pp. 134–135, 137.
11. *Ibid.*, p. 284.
12. *Ibid.*, p. 153.
13. *Ibid.*, p. 191.
14. Villard, "If I Were Dictator," *The Nation*, 1/20/32.
15. "One of his indictments of protection was that it was the mother of trusts and Socialism . . ." (Villard, *Fighting Years*, p. 122).
16. "When we fought for free trade we fought for labor . . ." (*Ibid.*, p. 121).
17. A path-breaking essay that integrated the entire range of Wilson's thoughts with his policies is Martin Sklar's "Woodrow Wilson and the Political Economy of Modern United States Liberalism," *Studies on the Left* (1960), pp. 17–47.
18. Villard, *Free Trade—Free World* (New York, 1947), p. 9.
19. His confusion is demonstrated in the following passage:

   > Denmark is to-day a more completely "socialized" state than Karl Marx

> dreamed of, and . . . France, Italy, and Sweden as well as Russia have practically Socialistic Governments or Socialists in control of administration. [Villard, "The Proper Attitude Towards Socialism," *The Nation*, 12/27/17]

20. Villard to Mrs. Crouch-Hazlett, 1/5/28.
21. George Mosse makes the most recent case for this position in *The Nationalization of the Masses* (New York, 1974).
22. Villard, *Preparedness* (New York, 1915), pp. 3, 19.
23. Villard, *Fighting Years*, pp. 324, 244.
24. "Germany's Biggest Blunder," *The Evening Post*, 5/10/15.
25. Villard, *Fighting Years*, p. 258.
26. The Espionage Act section prohibiting "'interference with the President's plan for a successful termination of the war'" was utilized "to ban anything that kept alive labor discontent." William Preston, *Aliens and Dissenters, Federal Suppression of Radicals: 1909–1933* (New York, 1963), p. 147 [based on his interpretation of DJ File 9-12-677-1].
27. William Preston provides the best documentation, culled from government files, of the government's attacks on citizen and immigrant dissent just after World War I. He counts twenty-nine separate occasions when the army suppressed radicals "without resort to constitutional procedures. . . ." Persons were arrested and held up to two years in jail without trial. Additionally, radicals could not:

    > lawfully conduct a defense. Postal office censorship excluded requests for contributions to the defense . . . it even prohibited the blank contribution forms themselves. [*Ibid.*, p. 116, 146]

    Villard reported:

    > They are sentencing men to fifteen years for passing a hand-bill urging a worker's protest against the intervention in Russia, and last week they gave six months to a man for sedition, whose sole offense was that he declared "Lenin to be the brainiest man in Europe", which is, of course, the truth as everybody admitted when I was in Paris and Berlin. [Villard to J. Howard Whitehouse, 1/19/20]

    Villard also claimed that conscientious objectors were tortured by U.S. army officers (Villard, *Fighting Years*, p. 335).
28. "We are witnessing deliberate warfare—another case where the American Executive has usurped the power of the Congress to make war, precisely as did Wilson twice in Mexico and also in Haiti and in Santo Domingo."

    "In the very week when our Secretary of State has published his correspondence with France urging an agreement to 'renounce' war between the two historic republics, we are sending the major general commanding the Marine Corps, with one thousand more marines and perhaps half a dozen warships, to Nicaragua" (Villard, "When Is a War Not a War?" *The Nation*, 1/18/28).

    "The atrocities are going to be glossed over and our occupation is to go on indefinitely" (Villard to Hobson, 12/29/21).
29. Villard, *Fighting Years*, p. 332. Villard was of the opinion that "the war making power has entirely gone out of the hands of Congress and in that way the Constitution has been nullified" (Villard to Houghton, August 22, 1927).
30. Villard, *Fighting Years*, pp. 386–387, 399–400.
31. "When the Russian revolution came along Franklin Lane calmly contemplated our spending a million lives to put it down, but that sacrifice, he said, will prove to us the value of law and order" (Villard, *Fighting Years*, p. 295).

Villard wrote the following on the international effort to do so in "The Crime Against Russia," *The Nation*, August 2, 1919 (see page 128 in this edition).

32. Villard, *Russia from a Car Window* (New York, 1929), p. 30.
33. "Communists with whom I have talked here share the belief prevalent in Russia that any economic boycott will be a prelude to a united military attack upon the Soviets. The suggestion is absurd today. With Germany in the hole in which it is industrially, agriculturally, and financially, a war is utterly out of the question. You not only could not enlist Englishmen for such an armed attack upon Russia, but I have pretty good evidence that the present British government does not intend to allow itself to be led into an economic boycott. . ." (Villard, "The New Drive Against Russia," *The Nation*, April 1, 1931).
34. Villard, *Russia From A Car Window*, p. 30.
35. Villard, *The German Phoenix* (New York, 1933), p. 4.
36. Villard, "Issues and Men: Collective Security Must Come," *The Nation*, December 23, 1939.
37. Villard, "The Shame Of The American Press," *The Progressive*, February 4, 1946.
38. His choice of words concerning the destruction of Poland, whose inhabitants suffered the highest wartime casualty rate of any country in human history—220 killed out of each 1000 inhabitants—is also revealing:

    Some horrible stories of the effects of the war upon Poland are naturally coming through—justified and truthful reports I believe, for you cannot wage war with the present high-powered killing weapons, airplanes, and such, without laying everything waste. [Villard, "Issues and Men: England, America, and the War," *The Nation*, September 30, 1939]

    Somewhat earlier he had concluded that "Germany will not be able for years to wage war against Poland, if ever" (Villard, *The German Phoenix*, p. 62).
39. Villard to William Allen White, April 29, 1941.
40. *Our Military Chaos* (New York, 1939), p. 4.
41. Villard, *The German Phoenix*, p. 106.
42. Villard to Lincoln Colcord, January 29, 1941.
43. Villard included a testimonial in *The German Phoenix* from a Nazi entrepreneur who felt that his compatriots had much to learn from their American counterparts:

    America has taught us how . . . America's political life is dominated by organizations representing economic interests. The organizations discuss the outstanding issues and adopt new policies. In Germany these questions are decided in the Reichstag. We must mend our ways and make our influence felt on the political parties . . . In order to carry out the ideas of our association money is needed. [pp. 131–132]

    The assistance offered German big business by American companies even after the Second World War had started proved invaluable to the development of Nazi Germany's military capabilities. These close, reciprocal relationships are examined in Gabriel Kolko, "American Business and Germany, 1930–1941," *Western Political Quarterly*, Vol. 15, No. 4, December 1962.
44. Villard, *The German Phoenix*, p. 129.
45. "In her brief existence (as a nation) she has made more positive contributions to knowledge and world-advancement than any other nation in the same period" (Villard, *Germany Embattled* [New York, 1915], p. 14).

    Later, in *The German Phoenix*, his evaluation of national character is rendered sadly inept by World War II events:

    German love of peace and order . . . [and] the sound German respect for the rights of individuals . . .

> This lack of solidarity, this inability of the Germans to subordinate any partisan motive in a grave emergency, indubitably arises from their remarkable individualism, their innate tendency to split up into endless groups of varying opinion. [pp. 23, 27]

46. Villard to Paul Hutchinson, June 16, 1947.
47. Villard to Irving Dilliard, April 5, 1949.
48. Villard, "Issues and Men: If This Be Treason," *The Nation*, February 3, 1940.
49. Villard, *Fighting Years*, pp. 524, 231.
50. *Ibid.*, p. 523.
51. *Evening Post*, "The Opportunity Before Woodrow Wilson," December 28, 1916.
52. Villard, *John Brown*, p. 586.

CONTENTS

Preparedness

By

Oswald Garrison Villard

President New York Evening Post Company

A Series of Eight Articles Reprinted from The New York Evening Post

Price 10 Cents

Introduction

HE following articles, written for the New York *Evening Post,* are an effort to show, first, the lack of any necessity for the extensive military and naval programme urged by the President of the United States, and secondly, that, unless a radical reform and overhauling of the army take place before any increase is made, the tax-payer will have less assurance than ever that he will receive his money's worth in military efficiency. Creating an army means something more than adding men or guns. In the articles that follow, facts are given as to the conditions in the army and navy which every American ought to know before he makes up his mind as to whether we need to enlarge our armaments, and what is needed if the policy of army increase is determined upon. Since these articles were written, Congressman Kitchin has given his word to the public, as a member of the House Naval Committee of years' standing, that our navy is twice as effective as the Japanese, and considerably more effective than the German. In fact, he quotes three of the highest authorities, Admiral Fletcher, Rear-Admiral Badger, and Admiral Winterhalter, all of whom testify that they would not have any fear in pitting the American navy against the German. He has further testified that in his judgment, if this programme goes through, it will no longer be a question of wondering whether we may become a great militaristic and navalistic power, but of recognizing that we have become one. Surely this alone, from a man of Congressman Kitchin's high standing as leader of the Democrats in the House of Representatives, ought to give the nation pause—at least until the European war is over.

O. G. V.

LIST OF ARTICLES

THE

Question of Preparedness

PREPAREDNESS—FOR WHAT?

Shall We Reverse Our Historic Policy of a Small Army Without Reserves?—Need of Defining Terms—Why All This Sudden Hysteria? —Enormous Difficulties of Invasion by Any Foreign Power

IT IS CONCEDED that a sudden burst of fear and anxiety as a result of the European war will probably induce the coming Congress, under Mr. Wilson's guidance, to reverse our historic policy of a small army without reserves and to provide a still larger fleet. If this is the possibility or probability, the taxpayers, who will have an enormous annual bill to pay, and the masses of our people generally, upon whose welfare the new departure will have such a far-reaching effect, should insist upon the laying down of certain national policies after the most careful debate and discussion, and above all upon the definition of many words and phrases relating to armament now so loosely used.

Many politicians are solemnly rising to assure us that they believe in "reasonable preparedness," a phrase that no one can define, certainly not to suit the advocates of large armies and navies any more than a "reasonable tariff". could be framed to suit both the protectionists whose pockets are lined by tariffs and the American people from whose pockets the dividends are drawn. Newspapers without number are also declaring that they favor "reasonable preparedness" without, however, the slightest effort to define these words for their readers. Some of them assure us that "reasonable preparedness" does not mean militarism, but if you offered them untold sums they could not draw for you the line which divides military preparedness from militarism. They do not know whether 250,000 regulars are one side of the line and 300,000 on the other; they cannot tell you if they would just when a military caste becomes a menace to a nation. They admit that it can be; they admit that in dealing with any militarism a nation handles the possible seeds of evil—our forefathers, who were familiar with British militarism, wished no inoculation of the virus no matter how diluted the dose.

They fall back, if hard pressed, upon the military experts, but here they are on still less stable ground because no dozen officers can be got to agree on any given proposal, and if they could be made to agree, they would not "stay put" because they would steadily be adding to the number of our possible or potential enemies and to the strength of each of those enemies, precisely as the British naval officers have shifted their ground in the last sixty years. Thus the latter long held that they must have the largest navy in the world to defeat any other single navy. Then they decided upon the historic "two-power standard," that is, one large enough to defeat simultaneously the two navies next strongest. This was the accepted policy, but just prior to the present war proposals were seriously made in naval circles that there be a three-power standard in order to take care at one and the same time of the German. French, and United States navies, the menacing growth of the last-named being avowedly the reason for this fresh demand upon the wealth of the British people.

WHAT IS "REASONABLE PREPAREDNESS"?

If "reasonable preparedness" is to be defined, there must first be a decision on certain far-reaching national policies. Thus: Are we to prepare merely for the defence of our shores or are we to adopt the military theory that often the best way to defend one's territory is to take the offensive and attack the other fellow upon his? This has been, as the present war has shown, the favorite theory of the German General Staff, which is still very proud of the fact that, barring Russian incursions into East Prussia, all the fighting has been on their enemies' territory in a war which every German is convinced is purely a defensive enterprise. If we are to pay the Germans the compliment of imitating them in this, as we are going to imitate them in many other ways if Mr. Garrison's plans are adopted, it means that we must have a far larger armada than for purely home defensive purposes. We must have ocean-crossing submarines, we must have hospital ships, and endless other auxiliaries, such as mine-laying vessels, "mother" craft for submarines and hydroaeroplanes, floating machine-shops for repairs, floating docks to be towed abroad as the British have towed theirs to the Ægean, and colliers by the hundred. The 183 war-vessels Mr. Daniels calls for would by no means meet the need. For if we send a fleet to defeat the Germans and to blockade Germany, vast quantities of coal and oil must be transported from the United States and transferred at sea, for there will be no friendly shelter in which to provision or repair or coal, and ordinary merchant vessels cannot be equipped with coal-transferring apparatus over-night. All of these problems become more intensive if the objective is Japan; and the Philippines—a great source of military weakness—would probably help us not at all.

Again, the question of a two-power or a three-power navy at once obtrudes itself, if we decide upon an offensive fleet. Already naval officers declare the Panama Canal not the great help it was expected to be, but a source of weakness, since it makes easy the splitting of the fleet. And it has a habit of being blocked. They, therefore, demand a Pacific fleet as great as the Atlantic one, and they want it all the more since, as any one can see who wishes to dream dreams and speculate as to the future, a joint combination of Japan and Germany against us is quite within the range of possibility after the present hatreds have died out. Nothing is impossible in view of what has happened in Europe, they say, and, therefore, we ought to prepare against *every* possible contingency. Is not China likely to arm now against us and Japan? At any rate, should we be any the less forehanded than the British? The enthusiasts of the Navy League, who are demanding an immediate bond issue of $500,000,000 to be spent on the navy alone, feel that we ought to arm against Great Britain, and have a navy larger than hers, no matter to what "power standard" she should go. They want, in their own words, a navy "capable of meeting any possible force from across the seas," i. e., a navy equal to that of

France, Germany, and England combined. And of course, if we are to arm against the British fleet, we must arm against Canada and fortify the boundary of whose defencelessness for a century we have been so proud.

Then there is the question of commerce—its destruction and protection. The United States, being practically a self-supporting nation, could behold with comparative equanimity all its merchant navy, none too large, blockaded in its own or neutral harbors. But naval officers do not like to contemplate this. Shall we not imitate the glorious careers of the Emden and the Karlsruhe? Is there any better way of protecting your own ships than by driving those of the other nations of the seas? Hence for our offensive navy we must at once create ocean-going submersibles, with an enormous cruising radius, particularly as we have taken the first step in that direction by authorizing the "fleet-submarine."

THE SIMPLER PROBLEM.

If, on the other hand, it is decided never to contemplate anything beyond a defensive navy, the officers admit that the problem is immediately simplified. They confess that much cheaper and smaller submarines and more of them can be constructed; that the huge auxiliary flotilla could be largely eliminated and the monitor type of coast-defence vessel, like those built for the Brazilian navy, which the British have found most useful on the shallow Belgian coast, can be greatly developed. The problem of mine fields could then be studied in coöperation with our land coast-defence forces, and the latter taken into account in the development of any purely naval-defence problem, particularly as our coast defences are considered impregnable by our leading ordnance and coast-artillery officers. The value of coast defences would seem to have been amply demonstrated in this war; the coast defences in the Dardanelles and along the Belgian coast have quite held their own in the contest with the floating gun. The British have not been able to land troops on the Belgian coast, despite the efficiency of their monitors. The question, then, would seem to be whether we have not a large enough fleet to make up the deficiencies, if any, in our coast defences, provided that we adopt as a fixed national policy the theory that we shall not send them abroad to wage war under any conceivable circumstances.

There was a time, and not so very long ago, when our military experts were certain that we could protect our coasts without any navy at all. This was the belief of the Endicott Fortifications Board, which drew up the present plan of our coast defences in the days before we had any navy worth speaking of. They undertook to do this for a comparatively small sum. Since that time we have spent $175,973,699.13, so that we ought to have something for our money.

WHY ALL THE HYSTERIA?

After the questions of policy are decided, would it not pay Congress and the American people to inquire calmly and quietly—and not in the stress of emotion of a world war—whether the present coast defences for which the builders vouch so unqualifiedly are not enough in connection with a large fleet of submarines to let us sleep o' nights?

The question is the more pertinent because no writer who favors greater preparedness seems to have any faith whatever in our present navy. If I were a naval officer, I should be deeply humiliated by the fact that every one of the dozens upon dozens of articles that I have read which explain why it is necessary that we should have a mobile army with reserves of no less than 500,000 men to stand behind our coast defences and to prevent the enemy from landing at Atlantic City or Montauk Point begins by taking it for granted that the fleet will be overwhelmingly defeated. I have heard learned Admirals make after-dinner speeches which began with the assumption—or the admission, if you please—that in any engagement our fleet in its present numbers would be smashed and sunk. They seem to have no confidence in themselves or their vessels unless they are given a complete preponderance in numbers. They have no belief in the possibility of a superior skill and morale to offset smaller forces.

So the civilian writers, even in the days before it was popular to run down the navy and to accuse Secretary Daniels of every crime in the category, including all the sins of omission and commission of all his predecessors, have no doubts whatever as to what will happen to our fleet in any possible action. To them, forsooth, any battle spells defeat, overwhelming, disastrous, complete defeat. They do not leave us even half a dozen submarines after it with which to harass any hostile fleet and the enormous aggregation of hostile transports and auxiliaries which will be necessary for any elaborate expedition against our shores, particularly if it should be a joint military and naval one. In all our military arguments we start on the theory and assumption that the worst conceivable is bound to happen; our fleet to the last destroyer and submarine goes down, and the enemy then chooses in all deliberation certain points well known to the magazine writers on our next wars, and the disembarkation takes place without the slightest molestation.

ENORMOUS DIFFICULTIES OF INVASION.

These writers are in no wise concerned with the fact that it is only with great difficulty that a landing of all the multifarious equipment of a modern army could take place anywhere without docks; that 42-centimetre guns, or even those considerably smaller, cannot be put ashore at Montauk without pontoons, lighters, cranes of great capacity, etc. One cannot land the modern field gun strapped across the bows of a couple of steam launches; but if one could, the process for a large army would be interminable. Certainly no foreign general in his senses would seek as his base a little harbor remote from a railroad which could not contain anything more than a fraction of the mighty armada an invading force must bring with it. Still less would he dream of landing on the open beach. It is true that Admiral Fletcher, when asked by a Congressional committee last winter whether an enemy could land on such a shore as that between Norfolk and Port Royal, where there are no anchorages for deep-draught battleships or any other craft, and a surf which so often becomes impossible in stormy weather for the stanchest lifeboats, replied that such a landing could be made.

Unfortunately no Congressman asked Admiral Fletcher what would happen to the people who landed, or how long they could keep in touch with their fleet, and how secure a base and source of supplies a fleet off the beach landing every round of rifle ammunition through the surf would be. Some of our Civil War veterans who spent three years rolling in the seas off those coasts in the blockading squadrons and tried so hard to stay at their posts in all weathers, could tell some interesting things about life under those conditions. Our commanding officers at Daiquiri in 1898, when we landed our troops on the beach, could also tell some stimulating facts about their own anxieties lest the transport fleet be scattered in every direction by a West Indian hurricane. Yet that was a trifling undertaking compared to any possible invasion of the United States. Gen. Shafter's army, for instance, had only 75 cavalry horses with it, and, of course, no heavy siege guns, aeroplanes, motor transportation, etc.

Merely to state the problems shows into what endless fields of speculation and of mere personal opinion one may be led. With all respect for Admiral Fletcher, his views—whatever they may prove in detail to be—can doubtless be offset by many other military opinions. Moreover, when it comes to guessing upon such matters as these a civilian opinion may be just as valuable as a military, certainly on the question of the transportation problem. One may doubt, however, whether Admiral Fletcher would deny the recent statement (New York *Times*, August 21, 1915) of Capt. Charles E. Kilbourne, of the Army General Staff, that no frontal attack by a fleet upon coast fortifications has ever been successful in modern times, Captain Kilbourne describing the naval attack on the Dardanelles as a "hopeless failure," as was the direct assault on Port Arthur by the Japanese ships. To this he might have added that even if the German fleet were out of the way the British navy would never dare to attack the German coast fortifications, protected as they are by mine fields, by the most treacherous shoals through which the most experienced pilot would take no ship if all the buoys and marks were removed, and the lighthouses extinguished. All of which merely reinforces the point already made that before any action towards further militarism is taken by the public the public should know precisely what our military problems are and what our real dangers. This knowledge should not be confined to the Army General Staff or to the Navy War College because those experts are bound to take counsel of their worst fears; they see darkly at all times, and, like all other military men the world over, never could be given enough men or ships or fortifications to satisfy them. If they could be thus satisfied, they would be unique in the history of militarism. If it is true, as Mr. Henry A. Wise Wood asserts, that there are documents in the War Department proving that 750,000 men could be landed on our Atlantic Coast in forty-six days, and 350,000 on our Pacific Coast in sixty-one days, both armies with sufficient supplies for three months, then the public ought to know it, for that involves again the admission that our fleet is of no value whatever and that our coast defences are not worth the vast sums spent upon them since we began to modernize them in 1884.

QUESTIONS TO BE SETTLED.

And then the public should be told whether besides the fleet the army must be raised to a three-power standard, that is, to a size capable of meeting the suppositious maximum fleet and landing forces of England, Germany, and France. This knowledge is very important, not only for Americans, but for the rest of the world. For if we plunge into armament on any considerable scale it will mean that the foreign countries will begin to count us in on their two- or three-power plan, provided always that the peace to come in Europe does not do away with the whole abominable and wicked system of armament with its frightful injustice to the working classes, upon whose bowed backs it binds such monstrous burdens. Proof of this is the discussion in the British Parliament and the Reichstag in recent years of the necessity of increasing the British and German fleets because of the growing peril from the American. The announcement that the United States had definitely decided on a policy, namely that of building a purely defensive navy, and of putting complete faith for defence in that and our unsurpassed coast defences, would at least free the European nations from the fear of aggression by us, just as the adoption by us of the reverse policy would cause the European war lords to take due notice and give them the excuse to wring more millions out of their oppressed subjects, and to draft more of them for the unholy profession of arms.*

For the United States there is still another decision possible: that we cling to our historic policy of being unarmed; that we go along as heretofore keeping free from the European entanglements in accordance with Washington's solemn admonition; that we instruct our Administrations to pursue the most pacific of policies, as President Wilson has but lately shown anew the power of the moral influence and the ideals of this nation to see us through a most difficult situation, and that we preserve our wealth for other and infinitely more valuable expenditures. For it must be clearly understood that, if we adopt either one of the other policies, we must at the smallest possible estimate increase our military expenditures to more than $1,000,000,000 during the next five years. To-day we spend, for military purposes, with pensions, 74 cents out of every $1 appropriated by Congress. We shall not only have to raise this figure to 90 cents, but vastly increase the number of dollars. Billion-and-a-half Congresses will be a matter of course. The income tax must go up and so must indirect taxes of every kind. We must also be prepared to starve education, the conservation of national resources, the development of rivers and harbors, of waste lands, and the betterment of social conditions in every direction. All as our tribute to the greatness of the German General Staff and the God of War!

*Since the above was written, Lord Rosebery, the English statesman, has publicly said: "I know nothing more disheartening than the announcement recently made that the United States—the one great country left in the world free from the hideous, bloody burden of war—is about to embark upon the building of a huge armada destined to be equal or second to our own."

WHAT IS THE MATTER WITH THE ARMY?

Injured by Political Interference from the Outside and Wastefulness and Sloth Within—Extravagance at West Point and Absurdity at Governor's Island—How We Misuse "Best Soldier Material on Earth"

IF THE advocates of peace were to run down the regular army as the advocates of greater preparedness have been decrying it during the last year, they would undoubtedly find themselves charged with being unpatriotic, if not traitorous, and certainly guilty of malicious hostility to our land-defence forces. The advocates of larger appropriations do not hesitate to denounce the army as being mismanaged and not up to its task, but they usually lay the blame upon Congress, which they say has "starved" the army, has insisted on the maintenance of forts of no earthly military value, built, like those at Helena, Mont., Cheyenne, Wyo., and Des Moines, Ia., for political purposes in order to placate certain powerful politicians, and perhaps thereby to purchase certain army reforms which could not otherwise have been attained. Senator Carter, of Montana; Congressman Hull, of Iowa, and Senator Warren, of Wyoming, were, in their persons, the "military necessity" for the construction of those three forts, which, like the one near Denver, ought long since to have been turned into civilian colleges and abandoned by the military.

But while politics has been the bane of the army, and Congress can be justly indicted for its treatment of the service, the faults in the army are by no means due to Congress alone. As any one who criticises the service and points out its shortcomings, except in order to ask that the taxpayers pour out more money for its aggrandizement, is sure to be denounced, let me say at once that the statements in this and other articles are obtained chiefly from army officers, and from twenty-five years of personal observation and study; that they are actuated by no spirit of hostility toward any individuals, though frankly written from the point of view of one who does not believe in a large army, yet has for a quarter of a century labored diligently to bring about the wise expenditure of 100 cents for every dollar appropriated by Congress, and has invariably defended the army against the politicians. It was an able Secretary of War who remarked to the writer that the trouble with the army was that its "survey-boards did not survey, its courts-martial did not court-martial, its retirement boards did not retire, and its promotion boards did not properly promote"—a condition of affairs that cannot be attributed to Congress, though its causes hark back to politics.

INTERFERENCE OF POLITICS.

Indeed, this very Secretary of War consented to the setting aside of sentences of courts-martial and actions of other military tribunals for personal or political reasons. During his incumbency we had some of the worst cases ever known of officers being jumped, through Presidential favoritism, over the heads of hundreds of others. Under this Secretary that order was first issued which Secretary Garrison is the first head of the War Department to enforce—that any officer using political influence should have it entered on its record against him.

But the politicians did not then stop going to the War Department; it was even carefully explained by officials to some of them that the order was issued merely to head off those who were not the Administration's favorites, or whose favor was not necessary to the Administration's success in Congress. Naturally, army officers stuck their tongues in their cheeks when this order was talked of and the old game of pull and politics went on as blithely as ever until the army discovered that Lindley M. Garrison meant business, and that the use of influence was being entered upon officers' efficiency records against them.

Now the corridors of the War Department are not visited by Congressmen and Senators, and there is at this writing but one case on record where Presidential favoritism has been used to the detriment of the army under Mr. Wilson—a rather flagrant case, too. How can one expect army retiring boards to retire adequately if the War Department sets aside their findings to oblige a Senator? The reason is known instantly, by the army grapevine telegraph, from Panama to Alaska and the Philippines, and the army guides itself accordingly.

It is only rarely that an officer is able to rise by merit. As soon as he enters the army, therefore, the young officer, if he is wise, marries the daughter of a Senator, or of a powerful newspaper owner, or of a millionaire contributor to campaign funds, and seeks to get ahead of his fellows not by superior diligence or ability, but by the free use of influence. It has been "the devil take the hindmost." When Congressman Hull, by reason of his being chairman of the House Military Affairs Committee, was able to land his son, a man of only mediocre ability, in a position as major, from which he rose in ten years to be a colonel and judge-advocate at the age of only thirty-seven, what incentive is there to qualify for such a position by legal study and practice? Again, when the war broke out in 1898 a lot of men, some good and some bad, were ordered to Fort Monroe to take the physical examination for commissions. A number of them failed, but they were all appointed just the same. President McKinley saw nothing out of keeping with his oath of office in appointing them, although they might break down at once in the war when capable officers were needed, or, if not, were certain to load up the retired list at an early age. But how could any Secretary of War expect that particular examining board to take its work seriously or to "find" candidates when it knew that its reports were utterly ignored?

SOME CONSPICUOUS INSTANCES.

Is it any wonder in view of this régime of politics that the soldierly spirit in the army is at a low ebb? Take the list of our present generals, and run over the reasons for their appointment to high positions. Gen. Wood was promoted to the rank of a regular brigadier because he was credited with having cleaned up Cuba—an excellent achievement, but not a military one, he being, moreover, a doctor without military training. Gen. Tasker H. Bliss earned the same rank by being an admirable collector of customs at Havana, jumping up from the rank of major for this worthy but non-military service. Gen. Frederick Funston won the same position because of excellent work as a volunteer colonel, for which a captaincy would have sufficed had not the Kansas delegation achieved more; Gen. J. J. Pershing jumped from captain to brigadier avowedly because of a successful expedition in the Philippines, but really because he was a son-in-law of the all-powerful Wyoming Senator. Gen. Albert Mills rose in a bound from captain to brigadier, thanks to Roosevelt's favor, because he had the good luck to be wounded, in the first skirmish in 1898, near the Rough Rider Colonel, and was a well-thought-of officer.

Two of the present brigadiers won their rank by act of Congress for excellent service on the Panama Canal; they merited reward, of course, but why should they, trained and practiced chiefly as engineers, be put into a position to command troops when one has never drilled more than a company in his life and the other commanded a volunteer regiment for four days only?

The rewards given by Congress for Panama work have been utterly disproportionate on the military side and merely drive home to the service the lesson that the way to jump from colonel to major-general of the line, as Col. Goethals did against his wish, is by *brilliant work along non-military lines*. Naturally, Major-Gen. Goethals is not interested in holding that rank or commanding troops when he is an engineer, and so he proposes to retire as soon as his canal work is done. The late Major-Gen. Frederick Grant was, of course, a purely political appointment; and so it goes.

RECENT APPOINTMENTS FOR MERIT.

Only recently have there been appointed generals who really merited the rank in the eyes of the service, and there again the credit lies with the Wilson Administration. That several of the others like Bliss, Wood, and Funston have made good as generals in the opinion of the service, does not, of course, weaken the fact that their original appointments were subversive of the interests of the army. Even the present Chief of Staff, Gen. Scott, an excellent man, of particular usefulness in Indian and Mexican negotiating, won his rapid rise under Mr. Wilson not by military exploits, but by non-military traits, his knowledge of Indians, their sign language, his skill as a plenipotentiary, etc.

This lack of the real soldierly spirit is the great weakness of the service today. By that is not meant that the army should acquire Prussian arrogance or embrace the spirit of Prussian militarism—though there are some officers quite ready to go the whole hog—but it ought to acquire German industry, German application, and German thoroughness. Judged by those standards a good part of the American army is lazy. Supposing every regiment of regulars were ordered to march out of its barracks and drill every day from 5 A. M. until eleven o'clock, as the German regiments do for months at a time—what would happen? There would all but be mutiny. The regiments would be depleted by desertions and most of the officers would think of resigning or would run to their Congressmen for help. Yet it is just such hard work that makes a fine army.

Foreign officers admire our West Point without exception; but there is no reason on earth, they say, why the excellence of drill attained there should not be the standard of the army. If it can be achieved in one place, it can in another. Yet the regular regiments that have passed through New York recently, notably the Thirtieth Infantry, have marched so badly and generally appeared so slack that in most foreign armies the colonel commanding would have been instantly cashiered or retired. Yet the physical material in that regiment was superb and the men looked wonderfully fit. Good marching on parade is not everything, and neither is soldierly appearance; but if they are worth the time and labor spent on them at West Point they are worth it in the service. Good shooting is worth far more, and so is the knowledge of how to care for oneself in the field, how to intrench, etc., etc. But as a matter of fact every real soldier knows that drill is at the foundation of discipline as the alphabet and reading are at the bottom of mental discipline.

The great trouble is that the newly graduated cadet finds the service slack, many poor colonels, and latterly far more interest in athletics than in purely military functions. There is no incentive to soldierliness, and no chance to advance oneself by rigid application to routine drills. Often a West Pointer, who was a model in his bearing at the Academy, slouches like any civilian appointee.

For this Congress is not responsible. Nor is it accountable for the gross extravagance in the service, and the constant lack of soldierly honor in dealing with the money Congress votes. If there ever was a wasteful branch of the Government, it is the army. I have myself seen it march away from manœuvre grounds and leave behind shower-baths and other facilities erected at a cost of thousands—for the near-by farmers to profit by.

A post surgeon recently requested, and his request was approved by the post commander, a $30,000 isolation hospital. The Secretary of War ascertained that there had been not one or two contagious cases in a year there; but that did not interest the surgeon. Another wanted a costly flight of stairs because the old one was worn out. A high official and three or four generals tested the stairs; they were perfectly sound, but being slightly worn, were offensive to the surgeon. Was not Uncle Sam's Treasury full? Why not turn to it?

But the classic example is West Point. If there ever was a colossal blunder, it was the reconstruction of West Point. It is architecturally beautiful; every conceivable comfort is provided. There is a power station there that is wonderful, and as spick and span as a cadet on full-dress parade. The gymnasium is superb, and, that the sons of Mars may know something about the Prince of Peace (though He was a Peace-at-any-Price man), there is a $450,000 Protestant chapel, which is one of the most beautiful church edifices extant. The post is lined with splendid officers' quarters, costing from $20,000 up, and the Superintendent has just asked for thirty or forty more, at $20,000 apiece. The administration offices are magnificent Gothic, and the cadets' quarters are quite beautiful compared to the plain ones that Sherman, Sheridan, Lee, and Grant occupied. What a lesson for the humble farmers' sons, the offspring of the plain American people! What a contrast to the real democracy with which the student body is recruited! What a complete reversal of the lessons of simple, hard living that a soldier ought to be taught!

But the officers who have controlled West Point care nothing for the example set by Kaiser Wilhelm I of Germany, who slept in his palace on his soldier's iron cot until the end of his life.

SOME WEST POINT EXTRAVAGANCES.

It actually costs $20,000, I have been informed in military circles, to educate a boy at West Point, as against $12,000 at

Annapolis. I do not vouch for the correctness of the figure, but give it as it came to me. It is said to cost Harvard $2,500 for each student. Of course, Harvard does not house or feed its students free of charge or pay them, but the disproportion is still far too great.

The Military Academy bill contains a provision of $17,700 in extra pay for officers, in addition to their regular salaries, and the Superintendent is asking $125,000 for a laundry which will wash several times as many clothes for the women and children of the Academy as for its cadets. What ideas as to what army posts ought to be will these cadets carry away with them? What are they to think when they see women living in costly quarters obtained from Congress on the plea that they were to be used only as bachelor quarters? What are they to think of the use of Cullum Memorial Hall for teas and social events of all kinds, as to which there is no reference in Gen. Cullum's will? Or of officers families boarding in a part of the costly bachelor officers' mess? Or that there are four and a half persons, chiefly women and children, at West Point to each cadet? That there are already 110 detailed officers in addition to civilian teachers to an average of 620 cadets, and many more are asked for? That the officers' quarters contain fine mahogany furniture, costing between $400 and $500 of the taxpayers' money? Can they take away any other idea than that an army post or school is erected primarily for the purpose of promoting the personal welfare and comfort of officers and their families, particularly their families?

The truth is that West Point is, because of its physical formation, not at all adapted for its purposes; but the fact that there is not enough drill ground now for 600 men in open-order tactics does not prevent the present Superintendent from asking that the corps be increased to 1,400 men.

ABSURDITY AT GOVERNOR'S ISLAND.

Of course, West Point is not the only place where one finds this waste of the public funds on the recommendation of army officers. What could be more useless than Governor's Island, the chief purpose of which is to provide a pleasant home for thirty or forty officers? Its garrison is needless, and no other army in the world would put a battalion of infantry on a little island where it could not march to save its souls. Hundreds of thousands of dollars would be saved if the place were closed up, the officers made to live on their allowances for commutation of quarters in the city of New York or Newark or New Rochelle, or wherever they pleased, just as the officers of German and French regiments find their own family quarters; no one cares where they live as long as they are on hand for duty. Surely, Gen. Barry, a real soldier among our generals, is entitled to great credit for holding down some of the extravagances at West Point, and particularly for preventing the waste of $25,000 for quarters there for the Secretary of War and the President of the United States (to be used once a year perhaps), for he was going directly against the popular current in the army.

Truly, if West Point is to be regarded as setting the tone of the army, then the tone of the service is one of unmilitary living, and needless extravagance, with the emphasis on anything but those ascetic and virile qualities and rigid, plain standards of living that go so far to make the true soldier. The cadets even go into camp in tents with permanent wood floors, electric lights, etc., and only once in a year do they leave the Point for a long march! Is it any wonder that a Bavarian general once said to me after seeing West Point:

"Your academy is splendid, your Corps of Cadets is magnificent, but, if I were the Superintendent, I would march them away from the academy and put them into camp in the hills behind the Point."

NOT STUDYING THE PRESENT WAR.

Is it surprising to learn that the large maps of the seats of war placed in the officers' mess at West Point at the outbreak of the war have been taken down because the fifty officers who resort to that mess are no longer sufficiently interested in the war to make it worth while to retain them?

I asked particularly the other day whether there were not weekly quizzes on the progress of the war there; whether the senior officers are not lecturing weekly on the strategy of the campaign as it is unfolded; whether they are not playing the war-game as it is presented in each one of the fields of operation, but I was assured that nothing of the kind had happened—incredible as it may seem—except a couple of lectures by a professor and some study by a little group of nine young officers, when the cadets, to say nothing of the officers, are supposed to be learning the art of war. That in itself is the most striking proof of the lack of the military spirit which is the chief evil in the army, and for which Congress is not responsible.

And what are cadets, and what is the public to think of the grave scandal which has just been developed at the trial of Lieutenant-Colonel Goodier now going on in San Francisco, at which officers have sworn that certain of their brother-officers of the Aviation Section have been drawing the 35 per cent. increase of regular pay, which is by law awarded to officers who are risking their lives by actually making ascensions, when they could not even handle an aeroplane? It was charged, under oath, that Captain Cowan, commanding the Aviation School at San Diego, had been drawing $113 a month extra pay since July, 1913, although not capable of taking a machine into the air alone, and Captain Cowan has admitted that he drew this unearned pay for twenty-five months! Does this not again suggest the need of a higher standard of conduct by officers towards their Government, or at least a new kind of preparedness for an officer's career?

The truth is that in many directions resources available are knowingly diverted from military to non-military purposes, as for instance in the matter of transportation; we have not modern military transportation, but plenty of money for busses and ambulances and non-military vehicles. They even run a bus line from one end of West Point to the other. Into the effect of all this upon the enlisted men of the army and their free use for non-military purposes, such as officers' servants, care-takers, etc., there is not space to touch in this article; but everyone who knows the army, knows what an abuse it is, and how it reduces the number of men available for military drills. It verges dangerously near the line of "honest graft," which reminds me that when the camp at Texas City of a whole division of our troops was broken up by the cyclone in August last, there were downright charges by a service journal that no worse place for military purposes could have been selected than the site of this camp, as to which this defender of preparedness declared there were grave rumors of real graft.

It is interesting to note, too, that the storm nipped in the bud as it were, the erection of several large dancing pavilions and club houses that were being built by the troops—military duty again—for the use of themselves some nights in the week, and of their officers the others. I have been trying my best to recall, if I ever heard of dance-halls being erected by French or German regiments, and I cannot remember that I ever did.

THE BEST MATERIAL ON EARTH.

Now the maddening thing about all this is that we can do a great deal better if we wish to, for we have the best material on earth out of which to build armies. No one surpasses the American in natural adaptability and the ability to think for himself. Take the story of Funston's Kansas regiment. It is exactly like that of hundreds of volunteer regiments in the Civil War, but it is an amazing tale of resourcefulness, of daring, dash, and Yankee ingenuity, and natural born soldiering, without much drill and next to no discipline. These fine qualities are there and available. Why do we not get them in peace times? Moreover, there are a number of able officers in our service who see the needs and deplore the whole present situation, and would do differently if they could, who do not believe in the Government's buying of polo ponies and foxhounds or running a lot of costly suburban communities, but would like to train real soldiers. Why is it that for an expenditure far out of proportion to what the German army costs—we have put, according to a statement of Chairman Hay of the House Military Affairs Committee, $1,007,410,270.48 into the army in the last ten fiscal years, 1905 to 1915, which is not so bad for a niggardly Congress—we do not get a regular army as good man for man as that of the German and the French?

Incidently, the taxpayer should ask himself whether he ought to heed the advocates of preparedness in adding more sums to the frightful waste that is going on, without the slightest assurance that he will have a bit more efficient or more military army than he has to-day. It is throwing good money after bad.

THE PRESENT MILITARY FOUNDATION

Defects in the Existing Organization of the Army—More Money Does Not Assure Greater Efficiency—Heaven-Sent Opportunity Neglected by President and Secretary of War

CONGRESSMAN HAY, Chairman of the House Committee on Military Affairs, recently wrote in the *Sunday Magazine* of the liberal $101,000,000 appropriated by Congress for the army for the fiscal year ending June 30, 1915, and declared:

"To say that the use of such money in the hands of officers of the United States Army does not make us efficient in a military sense, is to attack unjustifiably the ability of a set of men famous the world over for their contributions to military science."

What could be more preposterous? One might as well assume that because $200,000,000 a year is spent by such honorable and patriotic gentlemen as compose the Board of Estimate of New York for the city's upkeep, therefore every cent is wisely and economically disbursed! We know it is not; we know that it is honestly disbursed, but every one is aware that savings could be made; that legislative enactments require a good deal of expenditure that the city officials would never sanction; that bad business methods of the past take their toll, and that there are leaks and wastes in plenty which can only gradually be eliminated by that slow introduction of better methods adopted after most careful study and inquiry, which is now going on.

So in the army; every one knows that honesty prevails; that grafting is almost unknown and that an embezzlement among officers is of the rarest. Yet every one should also be aware that despite the enormous sums voted we have very small military results to show for the $100,000,000 which we have been spending annually, on an average, during the last ten years. In that period our army has averaged about 85,000 men. It cost, therefore, over $1,000 a man to provide the necessary arms, quarters, pay, supplies, fortifications, etc., for a force of that size, and the taxpayer is without guarantee whatever that his army is efficient. Pacifists, militarists, and Secretaries of War, all are united in saying that we do not begin to get what we pay for; that the army is wasteful and extravagant because of antiquated and red tape business methods, the slowness of disbursements, the extravagant expenditure characteristic of most Government bureaus, the placing of the emphasis upon luxurious accommodations and private comforts rather than upon absolute military efficiency, and particularly because of the interference of politicians. Under the circumstances, for Congressman Hay to point to his $101,000,000 and swear we are *therefore* militarily efficient is as absurd as to assume that if Congress votes $180,000,000 or $200,000,000 this year for further preparedness we shall get greater efficiency at the very hands and by the very methods that have been causing us waste and extravagance heretofore.

MORE MONEY DOESN'T GUARANTEE EFFICIENCY.

There is not the slightest reason to assume that we shall even get a greater degree of military efficiency. A poor army does not become a good army in any country because you vote it, or give it, more men, more guns, and more ammunition. Russia has demonstrated that, not only in this war, but long before this war hove in sight.

It is precisely here that Mr. Garrison and President Wilson have thrown away their great opportunity—an almost heaven-sent opportunity—to reform and overhaul the whole military establishment. If they had said to the country and to Congress:

"This whole thing is preposterous, because our methods are wrong and the real military spirit is lacking; we shall not recommend or ask the voting of a dollar additional until you overhaul the entire system, do away with the political forts, put a stop to the whole business of building extravagant suburban villages for our troops, and thoroughly investigate the entire military situation. When you have done this and cut millions upon millions out of our present Army bill, we shall recommend the additional defences which we think the seacoast needs."

It is a double blunder that they have committed, which smacks plainly both of short-sightedness and lack of statesmanship. In deciding to arm further at this stage of the world war without awaiting its outcome, they have in part thrown away the commanding position of the United States as the one great nation that was not arming, and, therefore, was in the best position to advocate universal disarmament at the close of the war; and they have neglected the best chance for a great internal reform, for the introduction of scientific management in one branch of the Government, that will probably ever come to them.

BUILDING ON BAD FOUNDATION.

With an unsatisfactory and out of date military foundation, never well built, as was conclusively shown in 1898, they are preparing to build upon that foundation an enormously costly additional superstructure which will inevitably partake of the weaknesses of the foundation. With the only bit of scientific management the army has ever known—that introduced into some of our arsenals by General Crozier, the chief of ordnance—practically ended by the dictation of labor unions, it is a crying shame that the Secretary and President did not unitedly stand for introducing this system throughout the army. The country would have listened to them as one man because it would have recognized at once that this is the first step, and the best step, toward national preparedness, if we really need any preparedness.

More than that, groups of fine young officers would have arisen in the service to coöperate and even to take the lead. The whole military spirit of the army would have been quickened and rejuvenated. It would have obtained an entirely new sense of its duty and responsibility to the Government if required to see to it that not only 100 cents are obtained for every dollar expended, but that at least 90 per cent. of that dollar is given to constructive military expenditure. Such a reorganization would have given the army new life and new pride in the service.

If Congress knows its business and is not stampeded into voting the President's programme, by the party lash; if it is actuated by purely patriotic considerations and really desires efficient preparedness, if it is not going to vote large sums under newspaper clamor with the quiet purpose of securing as large a part of that expenditure for particular political bailiwicks, it will itself insist upon such an overhaul and investigation. If that sounds too much like a counsel of perfection; if it is expecting too much of our Congress, so much the worse.

THE GREED FOR "PORK."

I was reliably told in Washington that Congressmen were already serving notice on Mr. Garrison that he would not get a dollar from them for preparedness unless they were assured that their especially pet political forts, or arsenals, or what not, were to be left undisturbed. Discouraging as that, if true, would be, and as the outlook for reform is, it is plainly the duty of Congress to inquire what has become of the enormous sums already voted. The German Kaiser is said to have remarked that his army and navy did not cost him more than ours, including pensions. This Congress ought to ascertain, and the reasons why this is so, beside the superficial ones that lie on the surface. Let it find out, for instance, whether many expenditures made, like that at Governor's Island, have not actually *hindered* the obtaining of real military results. Let it not vote two or three hundred millions more in the two years of its life without the most careful examination of the past and the most careful supervision of future expenditures.

It does not pay in this matter to trust to the experts. The writer was, perhaps, the first journalist in this country to advocate a General Staff, but that august body has been vastly more concerned with planning increases of the army (with unavoidable benefits in the way of increased rank to its members) than with pounding away in season and out of season upon the deficiencies in the service which would still stand in the way of anything like an efficient army if it were increased to 500,000 men to-morrow.

One of the ablest officers in the service, a graduate of West Point, of nearly forty years' service, who does not share the writer's views as to preparedness, says frankly that, as long as the army is "self-governed and self-inspected, it can never be trusted to govern itself well." He insists that there must be more stringent and direct civilian control by Congress; but he admits, of course, that heretofore Congress has declined to accept its responsibility in an unselfish spirit. He believes that no expert opinion, whether from the General Staff or any one else, should be accepted without the most rigid outside scrutiny. If, as he says, the inspections in the army are "usually farces, often overruled and restricted by order, so that they tend to degenerate into merely formal affairs carried on in order to see that the routine of the service is adhered to," there may well be reason to assume that the higher authorities in the army are not as keen to remedy any defects as they should be. Thus, Gen. Wood has been making hundreds of speeches in the past year, urging more troops and more reserves; I have read many reports of those speeches, but I have not found in one any reference to what is the matter with *the army itself.*

It is also suggested that, according to an army officer who ought to know, the first plan for an increase in the army that came from the General Staff to Secretary Garrison began with a provision for a full general and several lieutenant-generals, major-generals by the dozen, and brigadiers by the score. If this officer is correct, these were not recommendations that really aimed at increased efficiency.

DETAILS SHOULD BE SCRUTINIZED.

How important it is that the details of any increase scheme should be carefully studied, appears from the question how shall the army be enlarged. Supposing 30,000 men are to be added: Shall this be done by adding 30 more regiments of 1,000 men each? Most officers would say "yes." They would point out that regiments cannot be raised hastily in war-time, and quickly drilled, and would insist that we cannot have too many extra officers.

Probably most of the men giving this advice would not be consciously influenced by the fact that this would mean a promotion of 30 lieutenant-colonels, and 60 majors and 150 captains, and that therefore they would inevitably profit thereby; some might even, and probably would, regret that their own fortunes were tied up with the question.

But there is another side to the matter. European regiments number from 2,500 to 3,000 men; in Germany there are more than 200 men in a company in peace time so that a subaltern commands a "Zug" of about 70 men. We allow three officers to a company and the war time strength of that company is 112 and of a regiment approximately 1,300. Why should we continue to stick at this figure? The Civil War showed how rapidly regiments of 1,000 men thinned down to tiny battalions of 350. In one campaign, in 1864, a Connecticut heavy artillery regiment serving as infantry, shrank from 1,200 to 400 men in about six weeks time. The Canadian Princess Patricia Regiment is known to have been reduced to 135 in a fortnight at the front. In peace time our regular regiments are weak at a strength of 800, and few of them approximate that size. They usually average between 600 and 750.

Every officer knows that this is an inefficient number. In a recent article which appeared in the *Journal of the U. S. Cavalry Association*, Captain S. D. Rockenbach, 11th Cavalry, told some wholesome truths not often seen in print, at least by laymen, as to the present organization. He writes as follows:

"My testimony after nearly twenty-four years of commissioned service is that under the organization and system we have, it is impossible to make a troop efficient for war. If it is the overhead cost that counts, why can't we get the men to work with? Supposing we got the 41 [men of a troop] ready for combat without stunting their mental and physical growth, what would be left of them in a week's, a month's campaign, without a depot squadron to send up trained men and horses? We delude ourselves with the idea that we have a great excess of regular officers in time of peace; we must, but we must have something to train them with. I would have learned more in two years with a full troop, in a full squadron, in a full regiment, in a full brigade, in a full division, than I have in ten times that length of time under the existing conditions. Yet the American public expects the regular officer to be supertrained in the art and science of war practically."

INCREASE EXISTING UNITS.

There is no doubt that if Captain Rockenbach were asked what he would do with 30,000 more men for the army, he would put them into the existing troops, squadrons, regiments, brigades, and divisions. That would be real scientific management both from the point of view of the army and the point of view of the taxpaying public which is desirous of efficiency and does not want to be taxed for colonels and majors that add strength to the army only on paper. There could be no clearer illustration of the point that I have been trying to drive home in this entire article; that the foundation system of the army is wrong and that piling on more organizations without remedying the defects would be folly. Why is it not the proper thing to raise our regiments to 2,400 or 3,000 men at once if we must have more soldiers? It is interesting to note that some advance towards this policy appears in Mr. Garrison's plan to have three of the new regular regiments he proposes recruited to our war strength; but that is less than half the peace strength of some European regiments. If additional officers are needed, let Congress provide them separately to be used for detached service as are hundreds of officers to-day who are away from regimental work.

It is interesting also to note how Captain Rockenbach arrives at the figure of 41 men cited above, which he says could not be trained for a month under war conditions without needing reserves of men and horses. This is his very important analysis of an average troop of cavalry as it reports for duty in our army to-day.

Troop N, Xth U. S. Cavalry, has on the 24th of May:

Aggregate		81
Present and absent		78
Training remounts	18	
Charge of stables	2	
In quarters—1 mess sgt., 2 cooks, 2 room orderlies	5	
D. S., absent sick and furlough	6	
Recruits	1	
Sick	8	
S. D., veterinary hospital and exchange	2	
Machine-gun troop	2	
Headquarter troop	1	
Total absent from drill (combat)	35	
Total present for drill (combat)		41

The only criticism of this that most officers would make is that he does not allow sufficiently for detached service, for men on guard duty, acting as servants to officers, gardeners, etc. But as is the strength of the troop so is the strength of the regiment.

Everybody who has served knows the thrill and the inspiration that come from full ranks and large numbers. Is it any wonder that Capt. Rockenbach writes that "we do not admit that the regular army is inefficient, but, when we say that it is efficient, the American public should understand our mental reservations. It is efficient not considering any possible or probable use against modern troops, only up to 50 per cent. of its total strength, and it would not last a brief campaign against a modern army, even could we find one so small as to take us seriously and fight us. . . There should be no compromise, either a proper army or none at all, and once for all remove the delusion from the minds of the public as to their protection."

There are dozens of officers who share Capt. Rockenbach's feeling; there are dozens of problems, just like this one of where the proposed increase of men if voted should be placed, that ought not to be decided offhand either by President or Secretary or Congress, and the last persons whose advice should be taken as final in this matter are the men who are responsible in the army for the present system which Capt. Rockenback so clearly thinks a grave mistake.

If the system of the regular army is a mistake, or is inefficient in any degree, is it not absolute folly to graft upon it the reserve army of 400,000 men which Mr. Garrison and the General Staff have proposed and the President has accepted? What guarantee is there that the 400,000 reserves will be relatively even as efficient as our regulars? How can we avoid the conclusion that it is the duty of Congress to make our existing system modern, efficient, and really worth while before it adds one dollar to the one hundred millions it now blindly lavishes? The road to real preparedness, if we must prepare, leads no other way.

SOME OBSTACLES TO EFFICIENCY IN THE ARMY

Despite West Point Training and Ostensibly Rigid Examinations, Many Unfit Continue in Service—Shining Exceptions of the Ordnance Corps—Effects of Certain Social Conditions

WHY is it there is not greater military efficiency in our regular army to-day? The average layman can understand that politics has done serious damage to the service, and much money is wasted through the construction of costly barracks which are in effect costly suburban villages. He knows, too, that all Government departments are apt to be loosely administered as contrasted with private concerns organized to make money.

What the layman cannot understand is why there should not be among the officers of the service a high standard of professional efficiency. Are not 40 per cent. of the officers graduates of West Point? Have not hundreds of them attended the graduate schools in the army? Are there not examinations for promotion? Are not civilian candidates and those who would rise from the ranks rigidly tested? How can it be, therefore, that the army itself is inefficient?

To this the answer is: *Primarily because the individual officer is held practically to no standard of professional efficiency, and this despite examinations for promotion, efficiency records, etc.*

The law calling for the examination of all officers below the rank of major before they can be promoted to the next highest rank has, it is true, existed ever since 1891. At the present time there are under suspension for promotion for one year one captain and three first lieutenants who have failed in their first examinations, but during all these years since the law was passed only seventeen line officers have been dropped from the army for failure to qualify professionally. Fully nine-tenths of those suspended are passed on reëxamination, and in one case an officer who was discharged from the artillery arm and reappointed to the cavalry arm has been serving acceptably ever since.

Now, it would be most gratifying if we could assume that this record meant that the high professional ability of the officers of the army was easily demonstrable, for it would show that there is vastly less professional mortality among our officers than among a similar group of lawyers and doctors, to speak of only two other expert professions.

BUT MANY UNFIT SLIP THROUGH.

But every Secretary of War knows, and every officer knows, that the examining board is not nearly as rigid as it ought to be, and that many a man slips through who is professionally unfit to continue in the service. Either because the board does not set high enough standards or because it has become discouraged by political interference with the verdicts of other examining boards, or because out of a kind-heartedness toward a fellow-officer, which is one of the greatest weaknesses of the service, it sometimes gives a man a passing mark for the sake of his future and that of his wife and his children.

It is unfortunately the truth that there is no punishment for an officer who is professionally slack or lazy or who is unfit, precisely as there is no real reward for an officer who does his routine work zealously, studies incessantly to keep himself abreast of military development at home and abroad, and seeks in every way to fit himself for high command. There is a saying that to lose his commission an officer must either commit a crime or go far beyond the limits of toleration in bad personal habits. Let him be as dull as an ox, let him be temperamentally unfitted to command men, let him be so crabbed and narrow as to be a nuisance whenever he fills a position of independent command, he is still sure of his rank if his personal habits are exemplary—that is, if he does not drink, or steal, or offend against other commandments. Moreover, he will rise steadily in rank and retire with a handsome pension at the end of his service.

On the other hand, the man who has soldierly instincts, is devoted to his career, and is willing to work day and night for personal advancement and the benefit of the service—there are many such in the army—soon finds that nothing that he can do will advance him except in rare, exceptional cases. In the past, such an officer has needed political influence to get him ahead. It is true that at all times he won the esteem of those with whom he came in contact who valued a good officer. At times some bureau chief or some general during the Spanish War was able to pick out such an officer for temporary volunteer rank or for some important assignment. Such an officer, too, might find his way to the War College and the General Staff, but the chances have been that he must sit by and see an officer like Gen. Clarence R. Edwards jump from captain to brigadier-general, not because of any military service of distinction whatever, but because he was an excellent chief of the Bureau of Insular Affairs—non-military service again—and a warm personal friend of William H. Taft. Such an incident as that alone gravely discourages many a professionally zealous officer.

HOW EXAMINATIONS HAVE WORKED.

Yet high hopes were builded upon the examination for promotion when it was instituted. The examiners were given a wide latitude, and as it often happened that a man was examined far away from his regiment, it was hoped that social influence would be reduced to a minimum. But it hasn't worked that way, and the standards of examination have varied so much here and there—that is, an examining board at Manila might be so much more rigid than one at Fort Leavenworth—as to work an injustice to the service. Hence, for a time an effort was made to have all officers in continental America examined by one board in Fort Leavenworth. But this too has been abandoned and men are constantly passed upward who ought not to be advanced. Moreover, it is ridiculous to say that because a man has qualified as major, therefore he does not need to be tested as to his fitness for lieutenant-colonel or colonel or brigadier-general or major-general. There is no reason whatever why examinations should stop with the captain, but every reason that more and more severe tests should be applied, as officers rise higher in rank and assume increasing responsibilities for the welfare and discipline and efficiency of their subordinates in peace and for their lives, as well, in war time.

It seems to be generally admitted today that the German army is the most efficient in the world. It is the German army which is most rigid in its examination of officers and its elimination of men who are unfit. No major can become a lieutenant-colonel until he has demonstrated that he can fulfil the functions of a lieutenant-colonel under the eyes of a board of officers whose devotion to the service is so great that they do not hesitate to cut him off and end his career if he does not qualify. A German major is expected to show that he is fitted to be a colonel, and a lieutenant-colonel that he can, if necessary, take hold of a brigade. Social influence does not avail, neither does rank, and to a lesser degree the same has been true in France, but that it is in a lesser degree is brought out by the large number of French generals who have been summarily retired by Gen. Joffre.

When President Taft made Capt. Edwards a brigadier-general because he had been an excellent bureaucrat in Washington, he did not know whether Gen. Edwards really had the qualities of a general or not, because Capt. Edwards had never even commanded a regiment, much less a brigade. There was nothing to indicate that Gen. Edwards, if suddenly given command of a brigade in Mexico, would demonstrate that he had the capacity for the handling of masses of men, or had the personal quality of quick decision in emergencies which the successful general must have. Perhaps Gen. Edwards would prove to have these qualities. It is extraordinary how many of our haphazard generals have become valuable. But that is luck, or is due to American adaptability under responsibility, and is not because, but in spite of, as vicious a system of appointment as could be imagined.

GRATIFYING SIGNS OF REFORM.

Lately, it is gratifying to record, Secretary Garrison has adopted the policy of promoting colonels to brigadier-generals, not because of any conspicuous non-military service or in response to political pressure or social influence or friendship, but on the recommendation of the various generals, the General Staff corps, etc. But, gratifying as this departure is, it does not in itself give any assurances of stability, nor does it help to weed out the inefficients in the lower grades.

Among the officers who have been much stirred by this state of affairs is the chief of ordnance, Brig.-Gen. William Crozier. In season and out of season, on every occasion, he has urged that we introduce into our army a system of promotion, not by seniority, that is, longevity, but by selection, the selection of the worthy and industrious officers and the elimination of the unworthy. He aims, in other words, at the introduction of a merit system, and in principle every one must agree with him, particularly because, as will be shown later, he has applied those principles to his own, the Ordnance Corps. If it could be carried out without favoritism or social or political influence, it would make an ideal system. The difficulty is that in a republic it seems almost impossible to constitute a board of officers which shall be free from these hampering influences, and a system of selection which was influenced by other than purely military considerations would be more demoralizing than the present one.

FAILURE OF NAVY PLUCKING BOARD.

The experience of the navy's "plucking board" does not lead to the belief that the right kind of a board to promote by selection could be formed.

Mr. Roosevelt and many others were certain when this navy board was constituted in 1901 that it solved the difficulty in the navy, and that the board could be relied upon to do justice. Yet the last Congress abolished the board, whose decisions had in some cases caused the bitterest heart-burnings. For the army, none the less, it appears that for the present the best policy is elimination for military unfitness or incapacity. That is, by the slow process of improving the moral tone of the service the promotion boards, like the courts-martial, must be educated up to performing their functions without thought of anything but the interests of the service. As long as this is not done the army personnel will be far from the maximum of efficiency.

As long as it is *not done* all the money that President Wilson and Mr. Garrison may get from Congress for additional officers and men will not *in a single respect improve the morale of the army,* but will merely add to its numbers. It will in no wise give us a more efficient army than we have now, for true preparedness has much less to do with numbers than it has with the spirit and military efficiency of our army.

Now, Gen. Crozier is not merely an officer who preaches; he practices what he preaches, and the result is that the Ordnance Corps, over which he presides, is to-day the one highly efficient branch of the army. Why? Because he can eliminate unworthy officers and reward the worthy that come to his corps. This is due to the fact that, barring some permanent ones, the bulk of his officers are detailed from the line, after a most searching examination, for periods of four years. After these four years they must go back to the cavalry or artillery or infantry, whence they came, and serve two years with troops, before being again eligible for re-detail to the Ordnance. If an officer did not do well while with the Ordnance, Gen. Crozier simply forgets his existence; he has no right to demand a re-detail. If he is a good officer, Gen. Crozier keeps his eye on him and gets him back when the two years with troops are up.

Moreover, Gen. Crozier made his corps especially attractive by getting from Congress increased rank for the officers that come to him. That is, if a second lieutenant is detailed to the Ordnance, he gets the rank and pay of a first lieutenant during his four years of service; if a first lieutenant is detailed he gets the rank and pay of a captain; if it is a captain who goes to the Ordnance, he receives the rank and pay of a major as a reward for his ambition, for his zeal in volunteering for the Ordnance, and his industry in fitting himself for the searching technical examination.

RECOGNIZED BY PRIVATE INDUSTRIES.

I am one of those who think that the rush to secure Gen. Crozier's officers for civilian arms factories this year is in large part a tribute to the kind of men Gen. Crozier has secured by his merit system. Even in these boom times private concerns that have to earn dividends pick and choose their superintendents, and do not select military automata for responsible positions.

This is the only way to-day in the entire army in which an officer can advance himself in rank and pay by his own industry and merit! Surely, before it builds further upon the present unsatisfactory military foundation, Congress ought to inquire into the whole situation and ask Gen. Crozier and others why it is that this bit of scientific management cannot in one form or another be applied to the entire service.

A few years ago another device, which, if applied to the entire army and rigidly enforced, would do much good, was introduced into the Engineer Corps. It was provided by law that, when an officer was appointed to that corps as a second lieutenant from civil life, he should serve as a probationary officer for the period of one year, at the expiration of which he could be dropped for professional incapacity, moral unfitness, or, what is even more important, temperamental unfitness for the military profession. So far only two officers have been appointed under this law, and neither has been dropped. But the scheme is an admirable one, and, as has been urged by Lieut.-Col. Robert H. Noble, of the infantry, ought to be applied to all second lieutenants, whether appointed from the ranks, from West Point, or from civil life. There would be some considerable chance of this being enforced because a new officer has not formed any of those domestic ties which play so great a part in army life and in the decisions of its boards and courts. The War Department could withhold from such an officer permission to marry. It would all make the probationer walk a very straight line during his first year, and work very hard. While a choleric colonel might occasionally do an injustice in dropping an officer, the injustice would be slight compared to the good that would result if men were freely discharged when they failed to show industry, good character, and adaptability to the profession of soldiering. The Germans call some of their candidates for commissions "Offiziersaspiranten"—which tells the whole story.

Congress ought not to add thousands of additional officers to the army in the year 1916 without throwing this and other safeguards around their appointment, for nine-tenths of them will be inexperienced and with only the slightest military training, if any. Among them will be many temperamentally unfit or unable to exercise the power to command.

ATHLETICS AND DOMESTICITY.

There are officers in the army who think that athletics and domesticity are injuring the service to-day as much as whiskey did in the old days when the army was scattered over the plains. It is unquestionably true that the providing of homes for officers has become an almost unmitigated evil, and no survey of the causes of the army's inefficiency would be complete without a reference to it. I have already touched upon it, but it is worth while to record the fact that the American army is the only one that makes a practice of providing officers' families with residences. The custom grew up in the days of frontier duty and Indian-fighting when forts were forts and not barracks or cantonments. Now the most important posts are in or near cities so that the army could make vast savings if it allowed liberal sums for rentals and made the officers live in the towns. This might not be practical in Alaska or Panama or at certain remote coast artillery stations; but if the Government simply abandoned the policy of housing officers' families, it would save enough to maintain a number of regiments, besides doing away with a large amount of special "duty" as gardeners, servants, ice-suppliers, bus-drivers, postmen, etc., a detached service which, as already pointed out, leads to intense dissatisfaction among the enlisted men, besides depleting the strength of companies. In some cases it has led in fact to the abandonment of guard duty. To one familiar with the old army it is something of a shock to see the disappearance of sentries and the substitution of post policemen; for sentry duty, in the West at least, was one thing that was never slighted, and it has heretofore been deemed one of the most important functions of the soldier. But it is now disappearing as is the historic cavalry seat, which has been abandoned in our army in favor of the (for military purposes) abominable hunting seat.

EFFECT OF CERTAIN SOCIAL CONDITIONS.

Just what effect the suburban village type of barracks has upon the moral tone and social life of the army has often been set forth and never flatteringly. It is never good for a group of families to be thrown together constantly, any more than it is good for single men to live in barracks. Purely academic communities suffer in the same way as military posts, yet they are without the endless dissensions due to jealousies arising out of rank, precedence, etc., and are supposed to be absorbed in intellectual pursuits. It would be a gross libel on the army to accept Gen. Charles King's novels as a true picture of garrison conditions; but if one-fifth were true they would be an unanswerable argument for the simple system in vogue in England and all the Continental armies of letting army officers live like other folks and not apart from their own kind. It would do them infinite good to live among the people of the United States, for it would broaden them and render them less likely to consider themselves a caste, superior to all in civil life. There are plenty of officers who have sought detached service and been for years away from their regiments expressly to avoid the conditions of life in posts like Missoula, Benjamin Harrison, Logan, etc., just as there are officers who have served abroad who have earnestly urged the placing of all our regiments in barracks in cities as a step towards efficiency.

Why would it not pay Congress to inquire into all of this before it adds new regiments to our army? Is it the pork-barrel which prevents? Or is it the failure of the army leaders to point the way? Or is it both? The public ought to know. Incidentally, Congress ought to inquire into the mischief done by the constant transferring of officers of the fifteen regiments on foreign service, which makes regimental loyalty and *esprit de corps* impossible.

Let Congress look at the marines. This branch of the navy shines whenever contrasted with our soldiers. There are no West Pointers among its officers and only a few graduates of Annapolis and men from the ranks. The rest were green civilians when appointed. Five-sixths of its officers have entered the marines since 1898. It is a service to be proud of. Why? Is it wholly due to its connection with the navy, or its constantly seeing foreign service and going to sea? No; its admirable efficiency, the smartness, the neatness, and excellent set-up of the men and the *esprit de corps* of its officers, cannot be so easily explained. Some one ought to tell us why, some one like a committee of Congress. Would such a committee dwell on the fact that the Marine Corps provides no quarters at permanent posts—save here and there one at navy yards—for the families of its officers, in addition to some of the other differences between these two fighting forces?

LAND DEFENCES OF OUR COASTS

Why Are They, Like the Navy, So Lightly Ignored by the Militarists?—Their Adequacy Attested by Experts—Instance of the Dardanelles—Effectiveness of Mine Fields Shown in Present War—Difficulties of Invasion

NEXT to the navy officers, who in every discussion of national preparedness are brushed aside with the humiliating assumption that they will inevitably be defeated in any and every fleet action, it would seem as if our coast defences and their officers were the most shabbily treated by advocates of greater national preparedness. Thus I heard the president of the National Security League the other night dismiss our costly and elaborate system of coast defences with a wave of his hand and the remark:

"You know what our coast defences are. They may be good where they are, but anybody can land and walk around them."

His audience might surely have been pardoned for asking why, in that case, the fortifications were built at all. It was plainly merely scratching the surface of the subject. But Mr. Menken is hardly an exception to the rule; there are plenty of others who assume at the beginning of their plea for a greater army that our coast defences are no more of value than so many match-boxes. It is, therefore, worth while setting down a few little-known facts about them.

In the first place since 1888 there has been expended upon the seacoast defences of the United States proper no less than $126,112,068.50. There has been appropriated for all fortifications and related purposes in the United States and its insular possessions since 1888 a grand total of $175,973,699.13—rather a large sum if honestly spent, and it has been honestly spent, to wave aside as not worth considering. But, of course, large sums of money may be unwisely invested in an inadequate plant. Let us, therefore, see what the experts, to whom the Security League invariably turns for leadership, have to say as to the merits of the seacoast fortifications.

SOME TESTIMONY ON THE SUBJECT.

Testifying before the Sub-Committee of the House Committee on Appropriations in charge of the Fortifications Appropriation bill of 1915-1916, during February of this year, Secretary of War Garrison, in reply to a question whether in a broad sense our coast defences were adequate, replied as follows:

"Yes, sir; they certainly are adequate for the purpose for which they were placed there, qualifying only to the extent, that I do not mean to say that some guns may not be on naval ships that can shoot more effectively at extreme ranges, but when you come down to that you see how small a part that plays; those ships could not come in near the shore; they would have to lie out there and occasionally shoot, perhaps shooting on the hit-or-miss plan; and doing some damage or doing no damage."

Congressman Gardner and others having made much of this fact that the guns on the new Queen Elizabeth and other super-Dreadnoughts can outrange our coast ordnance, Secretary Garrison was asked what the War Department was doing as to this. He replied that he was asking for money to alter the mounting and elevation of the guns in the existing forts which would give them approximately the range of the guns on these new ships, and he suggested that in any new construction, guns equal or superior to any afloat should be installed. "But," he added, "there is no occasion to rush into that [the replacing of many old guns with new and larger ones], now, and to attempt to scatter 14 or 16-inch guns all over our continent would certainly result in our getting nowhere."

WHAT REAL SOLDIERS THINK.

Now, Secretary Garrison may be objected to on the ground that he is a civilian and not a military expert. Fortunately, there were military experts also in attendance upon this Committee. One of them was Brigadier-General Erasmus M. Weaver, Chief of Coast Artillery, whose duty it is, he said, to "be advised as to the character and sufficiency of our seacoast armament." In reply to a question, Gen. Weaver said:

"My opinion is that our system of fortifications is reasonably adequate for all defensive purposes which they are likely to be called upon to meet." A little later he again said:

"I have been a close student of the whole subject, naturally, for a number of years, and I know of no fortifications in the world, as far as my reading, observation, and knowledge go, that compare favorably in efficiency with ours."

Now, to make coast defences valuable something else is needed besides guns—properly trained officers and men. As to our Coast Artillery force, Gen. Weaver said:

"I think it is at least equal to that of any coast-defence personnel in the world."

In his annual report, dated Washington, September 19, 1914, Gen. Weaver had previously had the following to say about the efficiency of his men: "The work of the personnel has been maintained at a high standard of efficiency, as is evidenced below under the heading 'Instruction' and 'Target Practice.' Attention is particularly invited to the efficiency of gun and mortar practice at night. This is the second year that night practice has been attempted, and it is encouraging to note that the efficiency of both day and night gun and mortar, as well as mine, practice has been fully maintained. The effort has been, in both practices, to assimilate the conditions as closely as possible to those that would be met with in war."

GENERAL CROZIER'S TESTIMONY.

The greatest expert in this country on fortifications and guns, Gen. William Crozier, Chief of Ordnance, was also called by this committee. Being asked what, in his judgment, would be the condition in our fortifications after the alterations to which Secretary Garrison referred were made in the mounting and elevation of the existing guns in our forts, Gen. Crozier replied:

"I am of the opinion, Mr. Chairman, that they [our fortifications] will be of such power and will be recognized of such power *that naval officers would not put their ships up against them in a fight.* The 12-inch guns that we have mounted in our fortifications, after the alterations to which you have alluded, will have with this heaviest projectile a range of something over 17,000 yards, and I have not any belief that naval vessels, even when their guns will permit them to fire at a greater range than that, would stand off at a greater range and attempt to injure our fortifications by bombardment, because the chances of their inflicting injury would be so small that they would not consider the waste of the ammunition to be justified. Now, by another change, with the use of a lighter projectile, of 700 pounds weight, we could still further increase the range by 2,000 yards, or running up to about 19,500 yards for this old type of 12-inch gun. You have had some testimony before you to the effect that the claim had been made that after these changes these guns would be just as good as the best guns now being mounted on foreign vessels of war. Nobody that I know of has made any such claim, and I do not think anybody would claim that a modern 12-inch gun, no matter what you did with it, would be as good as a modern 15-inch gun; but in my opinion these guns, with the other advantages which land-defence fortifications have, will be adequate for maintaining a successful combat with vessels of war armed with any gun which is now under construction anywhere in the world, to my knowledge."

It would be hard to obtain a more positive statement as to what would happen if the Queen Elizabeth should appear off our coasts than this.

COAST DEFENCES STILL BELIEVED IN.

As has already been pointed out in a previous article, there has been nothing in this war to shake the faith of ordnance officers in coast defences. The German coast defences are protected by shoal waters and tremendous mine fields; navigation there is said to be so difficult that the most skilful pilot would not dare take a ship in when all beacons and lighthouses are extinguished and all the floating aids to navigation have been removed. As a result the British fleet has delivered no attack whatever upon the island of Heligoland or any other point of the land defences, thus indicating that there are other defences besides our own that naval officers will not, as Gen. Crozier said, "put their ships up against them in a fight."

In the Dardanelles we have had the Queen Elizabeth herself at work, and have witnessed her hasty flight to England just as soon as the German submarines appeared and torpedoed six of the Allies' battleships. American correspondents are among those who have testified that the guns on the British fleet did surprisingly little damage to the coast defences of the Dardanelles. A few guns were dismounted, but only one or two of the defences were, it is stated, actually put out of business. It is true that the guns of the ships made possible the landing (at a terrible cost of lives) of the Allied troops; but, once ashore, they have made little or no headway since, and, what is of greater importance in the discussion of our own defence problem, it is widely believed that as soon as the inclement weather sets in, about the 1st of December, the troops will have to abandon their positions and retreat to their ships, because in the absence of any harbor it will probably be impossible then to keep up communication with the troops. If this proves to be the case, it will be an interesting example as to what might happen to the enemy that is so blithely landed by the advocates of military preparedness on the open shores of Long Island or Atlantic City.

EFFECTIVENESS OF MINE FIELDS.

But a coast defence does not comprise only men and guns. There are other means of opposing an enemy. Of these the most important is the floating mine, which has taken such tremendous toll of ships and lives during the present war, that did such effective work during our Civil War in the rivers of the Confederacy, and, more recently, in the Russo-Japanese War. It will be remembered that when Admiral Beatty was victoriously pursuing the German battle-cruiser squadron he had to let the enemy escape with the loss of only one ship, because he found himself approaching German mine-fields and German submarines. He did not run on a mine, nor did a submarine, so far as known, attack one of his ships; none the less, he hauled off and started straight back for home, thus giving the best possible evidence of the respect that naval officers have for two methods of defending coasts.

The effectiveness of an individual mine has been many times illustrated but never better than by the sinking of the German cruiser Yorck, with a loss of three-quarters of her crew after striking one of the mines laid by Germans in their own waters. In addition to six Allied battleships submarined in the Dardanelles, two, the Ocean and the Irresistible, were sunk by floating mines, without the enemy's risking a man.. After this all the battleships disappeared.

Gen. Weaver has testified that the American defence plan involves submarines, especially in Puget Sound and San Francisco, in places where the water is so deep that mines cannot be used. One of the greatest submarine experts in the country writes me that with 200 submarines properly distributed "we should be secure from invasion." As long as there was a single American submarine afloat, any invading fleet would have a very uncomfortable time as it lay off our coast defences outside of the mine fields, with all lights out, with buoys removed and channels mined, and tried to put the fortifications out of business so that a landing could be achieved not on the open beach, but in a sheltered harbor.

Much is made by the advocates of greater preparedness of the fact, officially confirmed by Gen. Weaver in his testimony already referred to, that our coast defences are "open from behind." But so are all coast defences the world over; so they always have been since the day of the round masonry fort. This war has shown what a simple method of defence not only for the rears of coast defences but for forts, exists in the trench with barbed-wire entanglements. Gen. Kitchener's raw recruits have brought home the fact that they can hold off the German veterans in such trenches. Trenches have indeed saved the great line of French forts from Verdun to Belfort. Had the German siege artillery been able to approach near enough to these forts to hit them, they would have been smashed to pieces as rapidly as have been the Russian and Belgian fortresses that were deemed impregnable and the French forts that have succumbed.

AS TO SUPPLY OF AMMUNITION.

Finally, as to the supplies of ammunition available for coast defences, it is true that Gen. Crozier, Gen. Wotherspoon, and Gen. Weaver have testified that we have not the amount of ammunition on hand which those officers think necessary. Gen. Weaver considers that an allowance of two hours' supplies for each coast gun in the United States is sufficient, because of the possibility of transferring ammunition from one coast to another and one fort to another. Gen. Weaver testified that he had a full supply of ammunition on hand for the 10-inch and 12-inch rifles, but less than 50 per cent. in the case of the mortars. If, therefore, the advocates of preparedness wish to demand additional supplies for the larger guns and more for the mortars, they will be on sure ground and will have the hearty coöperation of these experts, particularly as the progress of events in Europe shows that far greater quantities of ammunition can be shot away in battle than any one had heretofore imagined.

Here again the question of policy comes up. If it is decided that we shall pursue the plan of defensive operations only, we can well afford, if we must have defences, to strengthen our coast defences, lay in all the mines we can possibly use, submarines in plenty, and dirigible torpedoes according to the plans of young Mr. Hammond, and any other devices that the Naval Inventions Board may work out. With a clear goal and definite problems assigned to it, the country should, with the coöperation of both services, be able to accomplish so much as to make it impossible for a foreign nation to consider the question of invasion and at the same time save ourselves from the cost of a huge fleet and army.

THE QUESTION OF AN OVERSEAS RAID.

As for this question of invasion, about which such utter nonsense has been written, still one more word is in place. Representative Williams, of Illinois, has estimated that it will require 1,000 transports, each conveying 1,000 men, with provisions, munitions, and arms and equipment, convoyed by 100 battleships, if Japan should seriously make an attempt upon our shores. Thirty-one transports and sixty-two war vessels were necessary to take the Canadian expedition of 33,000 troops to England at the beginning of 1915, and the 28,000 troops from Australia required forty ships. Germany could not do better. It is well worth while to quote in this connection what Representative Witherspoon, of Mississippi, said January 29 last on the Naval Appropriation bill about Germany's twenty pre-Dreadnought battleships:

> But what I want to call your attention to especially about these ships is that they ought not to be considered by us at all, for the reason that it is an impossibility for them to cross the ocean. They cannot carry coal enough to bring them across the ocean, not one of them. The maximum coal capacity of the first five of those German battleships is 1,050 tons. The maximum coal capacity of the next five is 1,400 tons. The maximum coal capacity of the next five is 1,600 tons, and of the other five is 1,800 tons of coal. You cannot get those ships across the ocean with that much coal. They can not carry enough coal to bring them, the largest of them, closer than within 500 miles of our shores, and I do not believe the smallest of them could get half-way across the ocean.

Even more striking is a statement in the brilliant book by a dissenting German, "I Accuse," in which he bitterly criticises his own Government from the beginning to the end. Speaking of a possible expedition from Germany to Great Britain, he says: "Notwithstanding all the admiration we may feel for the achievements of our heroic navy, it would be foolish to close our eyes to the fact that the gigantic superiority of the English fleet cannot be equalized by means of Zeppelins and submarines—of which latter, be it observed, England possesses a greater number than we do [in 1912 eighty-five, to which must be added ninety French]. And in all this we have to bear in mind the fact that the English fleet would be the assailant; the German fleet would be the fleet assailed, in so far as it managed to press forward to the Channel. The German fleet would, however, have to protect not only itself, but also clumsy cargo boats, incapable of self-defence, on which there would have to be transported to England a number of army corps, with the appropriate light and heavy artillery, cavalry, trains, pioneer troops, automobiles, and aircraft material. Is such an attempt at all conceivable? Is it possible that there are human beings who are prepared to expose to destruction at a blow on such a scale as this hundreds of thousands of their fellowmen?"

WHOLE EXPEDITION IN PERIL.

This mere statement of the problem would seem to show its impracticability.

As far back as February, 1909, a competent writer in the *Contemporary Review* pointed out that any fleet which could bring German troops to England could move only at a speed of six or seven knots an hour, the speed of the slowest vessel, and that these slow-going merchant ships, "crowded with men, would form an easy target for torpedo craft or mine layers, even in small force, and the sinking of a few would probably cause panic among the remainder."

The same writer pointed out that if 150,000 Germans were to be transported on 200,000 tons of shipping it would have to be "a force destitute of artillery, cavalry, and land transport." He also proved that 200,000 tons of shipping cannot be found lying in German ports at any one time, and that to gather them together would take days and probably weeks, and give due notice of their intention of moving. That it would take such an armada about three weeks to cross the Atlantic has recently been pointed out by Mr. Jonathan A. Rawson, jr., and this allows for fair weather and smooth seas all the way.

While it is true that the United States has not the overwhelming superiority of the English fleet, that does not alter the fact that an expedition to the United States, a distance of 4,000 miles from Bremen and Hamburg—and the Germans have no nearer base from which to operate—would be an undertaking so vastly more difficult than an invasion of England, that not even the Germans would contemplate it.

Surely there is nothing in the condition of our coast defences or in this problem of overseas invasion to make us give in to the sudden fears of the militarists!

SHALL WE PAY THE MILITIA?

Militia Pay Bill a Sop to the National Guard—Arguments Against the Proposal—Enormous Expense Certain to Grow, Even if the Beginning Were Moderate—Administration Preparedness Plan a Reversal of Historic American Policy

THE Administration plan for the enlargement of the regular army by the enlistment of a special reserve force in addition to the State militia is a radical departure in our history—first, because no such reserve has ever been undertaken before and, secondly, because it means the final abandonment of the plan to make of the existing National Guard a first-line reserve in time of war. As such it has served in several of our wars, more or less—generally less—successfully. But legal experts in the War Department and others have come to the conclusion that it cannot go any further in the Federalizing of the militia than it has now gone, without coming into violent contact with the Constitution of the United States. Hence the abandonment of the militia as a first reserve and the coming transfer of the affections and interest of the War Department to the new Federal reserve, provided that Congress shall sanction it.

That this will cause heart-burnings in the militia is obvious. That body has felt hurt because it was unofficially noised about that graduates of the publicity-achieving civilian camps of the past summer were to be regarded as in line for commissions as regular officers in war time. Militiamen, especially officers, who serve faithfully, put in much more time soldiering in one year than do those who spend a month at such a training camp. The drill is more trying and monotonous, and there is no glare of the lime-light about it.

Now, if it becomes known that the War Department will hereafter be only secondarily interested in the State troops, there is bound to be further disappointment, which cannot have a favorable effect upon enlistments, particularly in view of the fact that the new Federal Reserve will not have to drill throughout the winter, or to be in readiness for strike or riot duty, but will drill in summer time in the open. To offset this discouragement, the War Department again holds out the Militia Pay bill, this time as a sop, whereas heretofore it has been heralded as the one necessary step to make the National Guard the complete and efficient organization it ought to be.

WHAT THE PAY BILL OFFERS.

This pay bill is now a familiar one on the calendars of Congress, but not until last winter did it receive the sanction of the President, the War Department, and of the chairman of the House Military Affairs Committee, Congressman Hay, in addition to the National Militia Board, the National Guard Association, etc., or pass the House. Its object is simply to pay officers and men of the militia for all their drills in winter time; that is for service which, since the foundation of the republic, has been performed without remuneration as a patriotic free-will offering to the States and to the Union. The reason given for it is the assertion that greater efficiency and a better grade of militiamen can be secured by paying for the winter drills; that it costs men money to belong now; that many cannot, therefore, afford to, and that more serious and valuable recruits could be obtained if the militia could offer 50 cents a drill, or $2 a month, as compensation.

It is estimated that this bill will cost all the way from $8,000,000 to $15,000,000 a year. The more effective it might be, that is, the more it brought men into the ranks—if any—the higher would be the cost. It has been eagerly seized upon by certain State authorities whose slogan is: "Let Uncle Sam support the militia."

The proposal that if the militia is to be paid at all, it should be paid by the several States whose creation it is, evokes no enthusiasm whatever in the various State capitals. Hence the powerful militia lobby which has been working for the bill has wasted no time at home, but gone straight to Washington.

Even there, however, it has run upon some serious rocks. There are constitutional lawyers in plenty to point out that there is no provision in the Constitution which confers upon Congress the right to "support" or "maintain" the militia, and that the bill as drawn would make it possible for the President to strip a State of all its troops, leaving it powerless to suppress violence within its own borders or to enforce its laws, if he thinks occasion warrants his sending the entire militia elsewhere. In our recent border troubles, for instance, had this proposed law been in force, the President might have sent the entire New York militia to the Rio Grande on the ground of the "grave emergency" existing there, leaving the State bare of troops.

ARGUMENTS AGAINST THE PROPOSAL.

The arguments against the bill—arguments advanced not merely by captious civilian critics, but by some National Guard officers like Col. W. G. Bates, of the Seventy-first New York, and regular officers, and by others who have studied the question, among them a minority of the House Committee on Military Affairs —may be summarized as follows:

(1.) There is no guarantee whatever that the payments authorized will accomplish the desired end of increasing the *efficiency* of the militia.

(2.) The bill will create a new class of public servants to be paid out of the Federal Treasury for all time.

(3.) It will create another powerful military machine well organized, as its lobby shows, to bring pressure to bear upon Congress for further increases.

(4.) It is special legislation urged by men who will profit financially by its passage.

(5.) No reliable forecast whatever can be made of its cost, as is shown by the fact that the estimates vary by $7,000,000; that is, they run from $8,000,000 to $15,000,000 a year. One Congressman believes that it will go to $100,000,000 in a few years.

(6.) It makes possible a grave conflict of authority between a State and the Federal Government, and is a further blow at States' Rights.

(7.) The constitutionality of such a measure is more than dubious.

As to the first of these points, pay for the voluntary service now performed could only give us a better militia if the sole evil were non-attendance at drills and the money paid were sufficient to lure the men in the ranks to the armories on drill nights. Nor would it be a cure-all if the trouble were the quality of the men now enlisted. No pay of fifty cents or a dollar a night could tempt the men who compose the best-drilled and most efficient regiments such as the Seventh Regiment, Squadron A, the Twenty-third Regiment, and the crack regiments everywhere. As for the others—and the writer served in the ranks of an unfashionable regiment—they contain a good cross-section of the working classes of a city, very much the same kind of men who turn out in case of hostilities.

SUM MUST BE MUCH LARGER.

Undoubtedly they would be glad to have the United States give them real money for services they now render freely, but to most of them the sum would have to be far larger than is contemplated in order to induce them to enlist if there were no other motive. If there are some regiments in which the material is inferior, then the fault is largely with the officers; poor officers attract poor recruits, and make poor regiments. Well-officered and well-disciplined regiments, in which there is a good soldierly spirit, naturally draw recruits to them. There is the gravest doubt, moreover, whether the kind of men who would be lured into the service of the State by a bait of $2 a month, would be really worth having, as good, for instance, as the present material.

But if the whole trouble is with the officers, can better men be lured into the service by 20 per cent. per annum of the regular officer's pay? It is again doubtful, because in most States, officers are elected by the votes of the soldiers, who are all too apt to choose "good fellows," but weak disciplinarians, men rather of their own kind with whom they can be on terms of intimacy. So long as this system continues its evil workings will merely be intensified by the desire of officers in need of money, or pecuniarily ambitious, to intrigue with the men in order that they may succeed to the higher salaries of their captains or majors. The advocates of the bill ignore this point, but insist that regular pay will retain in the service "capable officers, many of whom might otherwise be compelled to resign," and enable "officers of moderate means to devote the time necessary to military duties and studies."

It is my observation that the bulk of the capable officers who resign do so because of pressure of business, that is, because of prosperity. Few officers of moderate means try to eke out their salaries by night work; hence, the drills do not interfere with securing of men of this class, and the pecuniary burden for uniforms, etc., is far less severe than is the demand for the time of an officer.

In our New York Guard troop, battery and company commanders, and some staff officers spend from three to five nights a week throughout the season at their armories. After a while the strain becomes too great or the officer's home life demands more attention. Not in one case in a hundred is the resignation due to inability to earn enough above one's living expenses to pay for the extra expense one is put to. It is the time demanded of the studious and ambitious officer that is the real stumbling block, and if officers of leisure can be found they are usually in no need whatever of 25 per cent. of a regular lieutenant's pay.

A LESSON FROM PENSION INCREASE.

As for the question of cost and the creation of a new political military machine, the former Adjutant-General of New York State, William Verbeck, in a twenty-six page pamphlet issued by him when in office, asked the question: "Will the National Guard, if the bill is passed, demand additional compensation?" He answered it thus: "This bill provides reasonable compensation and it is not fair to presume that the National Guard will undertake to make any unreasonable demands. By so doing, they would only injure the good reputation which they have already obtained. Unreasonable demands would be met by a just rebuke from Congress."

This was just what the country heard in the early days of the pensions after the Civil War. Did anybody say that the veterans of the Grand Army wished a pension for everybody? How scandalous to insinuate it, or to say that in a few years Government pap would be asked for skulkers, cowards, and camp-followers, or that more than a few millions would be! Yet we know what has happened in the last fifty years.

The minority of the House Military Affairs Committee on December 10, 1912, thus expressed itself as to the dangers that lurk behind this legislation:

> The minority making this report is convinced that the legislation proposed by the pending bill is not only unwise, but that it is dangerous in the extreme. Rather than enter upon a legislative course that will inevitably entail upon the general Government an enormous expense, which may be found in dire emergency to have been wasted, a course that will surely lead to the creation of a great military force that will become so powerful politically that Congress will be no more able to resist its demands than it has been to resist the demands of the far less compactly organized and manageable army of pension applicants and their friends, this minority would favor a reasonable increase of the regular army, leaving the States to maintain their own troops in their own way, and at their own expense, without any aid whatever from the United States. Objectionable as such an increase of the regular army would be, it would have the merit of assuring us the possession of an armed force that in time of war would, by its persistent training, be worth all of its cost, which undoubtedly would be cheaper in the end than the cost of the great semi-military, semi-civil organization, wielding tremendous political power, that will grow up as surely as the sun will rise and set if the course of legislation outlined by the pending bill is once entered upon.

CERTAINTY OF PROGRESSIVE DEMANDS.

Congressman Fitzgerald, of New York, Chairman of the Appropriations Committee in the last House, in speaking against the bill in Congress, after pointing out that the Federal Government is already paying out $4,000,000 annually for the equipment of the militia, said: "When men are put upon a basis where they receive 25 per cent. of the pay of an enlisted man, they will very quickly demand the compensation be increased to 50, to 75, and then to 100 per cent. of the pay of an enlisted man; and then, with this organized movement extending into every little hamlet throughout the country will come an irresistible demand that the pay of the enlisted men of the army be increased so that the militia may be the beneficiaries, and instead of imposing an annual charge of six or eight million dollars, as some well-informed persons predict, it will very easily result in a fixed charge of over thirty million a year . . . but now it is proposed that we change our policy, and, instead of relying upon patriotic motives that we rely upon selfishness and greed, and entirely upon a financial inducement for men to undertake service in the militia."

What the militia needs, if it is to be developed, is not pay, but popular encouragement, further advances along the lines of the last few years, during which it has made very great strides, notably in the East; the abolition of the election of officers; the freeing of its business methods from much of the regular army red tape, which often causes waste, and above all, its removal from the sphere of politics. It is politics and the lack of real military standards that have been the bane of the militia service. Of course, it is true that it needs greater efficiency, but it is getting this in a remarkable degree in these days—and wholly without the Militia Pay bill.

WHY CIVILIAN CONTROL OF THE NAVY?

Inherent in Our Theory of Government that Professional Soldiers and Sailors Shall Be Under Civil Authority—Blunders and Pride of Expert Opinion in the Navy's Past—Civilians Should Control Both Purse-Strings and Military Policy

WHY does the Navy need civilian control? Why should we not turn over the Navy Department, the navy itself, and everything relating to the service afloat to naval officers, making some Rear-Admiral the Secretary of the Navy, with a seat in the Cabinet? They do it in France and Germany and elsewhere. Why not turn over the whole business of the navy to the experts?

Primarily because it is contrary to the accepted Anglo-Saxon tradition, which has ever guarded most jealously the supremacy of civilian authority over the military. Our forefathers had been dominated by the military throughout their Colonial days; they were in no mood to exalt it after they had achieved their independence. They saw that even in the mother-country the control of the navy and army was kept in civilian hands, and they stuck to the principle not only in the administration of the Government, but in the safeguarding of the rights of the civilian individual from any interference by courts-martial—an echo of which we have just had in this State in the debate over the proposed Constitution. It is true that Washington appointed his old Chief of Artillery, Henry Knox, as the first Secretary of War, and it is a fact also that there is no law prohibiting the appointment as Secretary of War of a General on the active list or an active Admiral as the Secretary of the Navy. Generals Sherman and Schofield were two generals who acted as Secretary of War for considerable periods while also on the army's active list. Former officers in number have served as Secretary of War; fewer as Secretary of the Navy. But the principle that there should be complete civilian control has none the less been upheld by public sentiment and by tradition.

Indeed, President Wilson well stated the reason for it in his speech in New York on May 17, in which he defined the sphere of activity of our naval officers thus:

"The mission of America is the only thing that a sailor or a soldier should think about. *He has nothing to do with the formulation of her policy.* He is to support her policy, whatever it is, but he is to support her policy in the spirit of herself. And, the strength of our policy is that we, who for the time being administer the affairs of this nation, do not originate her spirit. We attempt to embody it. We attempt to realize it in action. We are dominated by it. We do not dictate it."

The reason for this is that the expert, however patriotic and highminded, cannot but look at things from a rather narrow and partisan professional point of view. When one thinks of the courtly and gentle Dewey, of Farragut, of C. R. P. Rodgers, and a host of other naval celebrities, to say nothing of the leaders of our present generation of naval officers, it is impossible to conjure up an American von Tirpitz, and yet it is true that there have been some men in high positions who seemed bent on subordinating everything to their own and the navy's aggrandizement. But even if this is exceptional, it is difficult for the men at the top in either the army or the navy to view things from the standpoint of the country as a whole. They have long been detached from civilian life, with the business side of which they may never have come into contact. Theirs is not the responsibility for raising funds, that is, for providing the ways and means for purchasing the armaments they desire. Their entire training leads them, moreover, to *fear* the oncoming of an enemy, and they habitually think of every possible combination that may be brought against them.

THE SOLDIER IS ALWAYS FEARFUL.

Hence, as already pointed out in these articles, no naval or military officer is ever satisfied with the forces at his disposal—at least, there is no record of such a one. The German General Staff was not—even after their levy upon the people of Germany in 1913, when they took a portion, not of the citizen's income, but of his property, in order to *defend* Germany against its menacing foes. No French or British general ever had enough men, and so it goes. Now, we are as a nation very certain, from the President down, that none of our officers of the army or navy will ever get into this frame of mind. Do we not all of us know Smith, Brown, and Jones, of the navy, and Robinson, Allen, and Tucker, of the army? Are they not peace-loving? Is there anything of the militarist about them? Well, the answer is that there is not individually, but that they are parts of a system and a machine which inevitably make for the subordination of everything civilian to the military. What other lessons can be drawn from the present experience of the world?

Is it not true that there have been French militarists, from the Louis down, as menacing to the world's peace as any made in Germany? True, under the Republic they have been held in check, but the Republic produced a Boulanger, and the Dreyfus trial, with its sickening revelations, also took place under it. Have we not even seen signs in one of the youngest of the great nations of the world, Japan, that its internal order was threatened by militaristic influences? Did not a Cabinet fall on the question of a naval increase or the refusal thereof? Were there not shocking stories of naval corruption from there a year ago, which proved to have been linked up with corruption in Berlin by agents of the German armament firms? "Since the war with China in 1894 brought in an era of huge contracts for supplies," says Robert Young, editor of the *Japan Chronicle*, "corruption in places high and low, in the army as well as the navy, has been a constant theme of the Japanese newspapers. . . . But the most fertile source of demoralization has been the temptation offered by huge contracts for armament material and the competition of rival firms." Rear-Admiral Fujii was arrested in 1914 for taking bribes aggregating $176,350.

Have we not got our own Navy League, headed by a former navy officer, which has just solemnly declared as its programme that we shall have not only the largest navy in the world, but one competent to meet and overcome the fleets of any three Powers that may be brought against us—say, Germany, England, and France? This is surely out-Bernhardiing Bernhardi! Yet this is solemnly urged by a rich and prosperous body of American citizens. If their policy were carried out, and there were a similar annual expansion of our land forces, is it too much to say that the business of preparing for war would take precedence over every other department of Government, whether concerned with education, or the development or conservation of resources, of water powers and waste lands, etc., etc.? Were that policy to be accepted by the American people, this country would become as much dreaded for its navalism as England has been, and it would be a standing menace to the peace of the world, however certain President Wilson and others may be that this country at this day and hour is not contemplating aggression, and never could think of aggression.

PERIL IS IN THE SYSTEM.

No, it is not the individual in the military and naval system that is to be inveighed against, but the system itself in which the individual is but a cog. The individual is swept along by the tide; he cannot help himself, and that tendency is best checked under free Governments by civilian control. More than that, is it not true, that in every walk of life the expert must needs be controlled, lest his absorption in his specialty make him subordinate everything to the development of that specialty? We have seen some curious evidences of this in the medical profession. Have we not had plenty of signs right here in New York city of the trend of certain medical men towards assuming autocratic control of the public? Do they not desire to vaccinate us by law, not once, but a number of times at once; do they not wish to pass laws demanding a rigid physical inspection of every individual at least once a year? Do we not find a conservatism as hostile to any departure from the old traditions as any one could find in the army or navy? Do we not find insanity experts who think that every individual varies mentally from the normal, and experts in other sad diseases who insist that 60 to 70 per cent. of the entire world is affected by them? Do we not find lawyers in plenty who look upon every problem that is presented from the point of view of the courts and the machinery of the law? The tendency of the expert to become absolutely absorbed in his subject is surely too obvious to need dwelling upon, and particularly when authorities confer upon him complete power, do we got excesses which serve to alarm the public.

But there is still another and a very particular reason why the control of the navy and army should not be completely handed over to experts. It is that the public does not get the best results when the experts are solely in charge. As to that, there could be nothing more illuminating than the history of the United States navy itself, in which is to be found instance after instance where professional conservatism and the pride of opinion of experts have combined to keep the service in a narrow rut and routine, and, therefore, prevented the adoption and development of new types of vessels and engines of war. It is easy to pick out a few historical instances.

CASE OF THE FIRST DREADNOUGHT.

For example, the first Dreadnought ever built was constructed, not in England, a dozen years ago, but in the United States in 1814. True, she was a wooden Dreadnought, but she was an all-big-gun vessel, and her vital parts were surrounded by an armor of oak exactly comparable to the armor of the battleship of to-day. This was the Demologos, or Fulton, built under the direction of Robert Fulton himself, and it was the first war steamship ever built. Besides having a wheel in centre, and the radical innovation of steam, her batteries of twenty long 32-pounders were reinforced by a submarine gun carrying a 100-pound shot. She measured 145 feet over all, and was built with two hulls separated from end to end by a channel 15 feet wide and 66 feet long, in which the waterwheel revolved absolutely protected from the enemy's shot. The main, or gun, deck, was protected by a parapet 4 feet 10 inches thick of solid timber, and on the upper deck many hundreds of men could have paraded. She had two stout masts and four rudders, so that she might go either way without turning. In addition, she had a furnace for hot shot, and could discharge an immense column of boiling water into an enemy's port-hole. She could have steamed through the British fleet from end to end unscathed, but, the war coming to an end, she was tied up in the Brooklyn navy yard, and there she lay for fifteen years, until she blew up. The navy made no attempt to improve upon her or to make use of Fulton's ideas, or to lead the world in producing war steamships. It was actually not until 1841 that two twin side-wheelers, the Mississippi and the Missouri, were finally built by the navy as its first steam cruisers, by which time war steamships were almost a commonplace abroad. Even as late as 1835, the famous Commodore Matthew Calbraith Perry nearly threw away his reputation when he asserted that a war steamship of 1,300 tons would be built to cruise the sea for twenty days at a time without accident.

The history of the Monitor affords still another bit of evidence. What difficulties Ericsson had in overcoming the conservatism of the Navy Department has been well pointed out in the admirable life of the inventor written by Col. William C. Church, the veteran editor of the *Army and Navy Journal*. Yet the Monitor, hastily built as it was, played a great rôle in revolutionizing warfare. The cause of its failure to become a dominating naval type was the lack of a proper ventilation system, the lack of any decks on which to parade the crew when at sea, and because the navy could not get used to the fact that water rolled over the deck while the Monitor was at sea. As soon as the war was over, the newest and best of the ships, the Dunderberg, etc., were sold to foreign governments. True, the Miantonomoh and the Monadnock cruised successfully, the one to Europe and the other around Cape Horn, but the navy stuck to the high-sided wooden ships until the new navy came, when it squarely turned its back upon this American invention and followed the British precedent in building the high-sided predecessors of the present battleships. These took, it is true, the principle of Ericsson's turret and armor, but abandoned some of the vital features which distinguished the Monitor. Curiously enough, to-day, in November, 1915, we have the British Prime Minister Asquith, lauding in the House of Commons, the service of the British Monitors as having been the most distinguished of any vessels since the war began, and praising Lord Fisher for his development and use of these boats which more nearly approach, if the fragmentary descriptions which arrive here are correct, the Ericsson Monitors than anything built since, with the exception of the two or three that the American Navy has constructed in modern times, only to abandon.

SO WITH TORPEDO BOATS AND SUBMARINES.

The history of the torpedo boat is the third illustration of the inability of our naval officers to become enthusiastic about new types of craft. The Confederates in the Hunley and David produced boats that brought us right up to the era of modern submarines. Cushing's torpedoing of the Albermarle, and the Confederate use of the torpedo and the near-submarine, were, despite the lapse of years, the step just preceding modern mine and torpedo developments. But the navy pressed not at all for the development of the torpedo boat until about 1890. It had in the seventies a torpedo ram, the Alarm, which like the Demologos was allowed to rust out in a navy yard. Its officers concerned themselves not at all with the study of the development of the floating mine, and for this the whole responsibility cannot be put upon the civilian Secretaries, for there were navy officers at the head of every bureau of the Department during these years. They could easily have slipped into the appropriation bills a few thousands for experimental torpedo boats, but they did not even protest very vigorously against the building in the late seventies of the Trenton and the Adams and other comfortable wooden ships of the old type that had been the rage before the outbreak of the Civil War, although in the seventies all of the rest of the world was going in for other kinds of vessels, and the modern mobile torpedo and torpedo boat were being developed soon after.

Even after the beginning of our modern navy, our officers were but little interested, Rear-Admiral C. McR. Winslow being one of the few to take a deep interest in this new type of torpedo vessel at the outset.

And so the story has been with the submarine, too. The first group of under-water boats was tied up in the navy yards! Only gradually was practice with them begun. Not until Secretary Daniels appointed Capt. A. W. Grant, of the navy, last May, to take charge of the submarine, was a separate organization for them deemed worth while. Indeed, the makers of these boats charge emphatically that a great deal of the trouble which has happened on these most delicate craft has been due to the fact that very young and inexperienced officers—ensigns, the ink on whose commissions was hardly dry—have been given charge, while officers of great skill and experience were demanded. All this is being remedied under Secretary Daniels's guidance, but the fact remains that the submarine was a step-child of the navy from the time that it appeared until the war abroad showed what others could do with it, and yet it was an American invention and the outgrowth of Confederate ingenuity and skill, as it had been, further back, the invention of Bushnell and Fulton. Indeed, the submarine has been but like numerous other American inventions which have had to find a market abroad because the designers could not interest the home authorities.

Surely, therefore, Secretary Daniels has done a great service in appointing a civilian board to coöperate with the navy, thereby not only bringing into touch with the service great talents, but creating a machinery that will examine and test all inventions offered and invite others, without professional prejudice, and put squarely alongside of the best navy talent a fresh civilian point of view untrammelled by red tape, precedent, routine, or traditions or customs. These are all practical reasons for the civilian control of the navy.

LESSONS OF THE PRESENT WAR.

Perhaps this new arrangement may lead to a reconsideration of our entire naval policy in the light of the European war. At present Secretary Daniels is asking for a little bit more of everything old and something new in the battleship cruiser, which in the opinion of many people has not yet demonstrated its worth. Nor has anybody yet really gauged the extent of the success of the German submarines, which at this writing are sinking merchantmen in the very narrows of Gibraltar right under the eyes of the fortress and in a passage-way so narrow that it would seem as if they could be guarded against there better than anywhere else, and the mystery of how they can operate hundreds or thousands of miles from a known base remains unexplained. We have not stopped to decide whether the battleship is on top or the submarine.

Least of all, as was pointed out in the first article of this series, have we really decided whether ours is to be an offensive or a defensive navy.

But after all, the prime reason for the civilian domination of the policy and management of the navy is that this Government is not warlike, that it places the arts and ideals of peace above those of war, and even above preparation for war. Those is control, therefore, must be men who are detached from any one interest, military or civilian, so that they may survey the whole field of the nation's development and ambitions, and proportionately divide the finances of the country between the various contending branches of Government. Moreover, the people in control must be those who are also charged with the responsibility fo raising the funds. This suggests one oi the dangers and weaknesses of the military programme in any country, for the officers of the General Staff can never be got to take any cognizance of the financial resources and needs of the Government; they not only demand the lion's share of the taxes wrung from a people, but they are absolutely indifferent to the starving of any other branch of governmental enterprises. We shall hear much, if the Wilson programme of preparedness goes through, about the next step, the formation of a committee of national defence to coördinate the functions of the army and the navy, and of all the civilian enterprises which it is now recognized must also be mobilized when war comes. If that committee is not supervised and controlled vigorously by Congress it will become a veritable Frankenstein monster, using all its influences to have the Government of the United States not only pour forth the bulk of its income for preparedness (the Japanese now pay one-third of their income in direct and indirect taxation), but to make preparation for war the chief business of this nation, as it has long been of France, Germany, Austria, and other countries.

THE REAL REFORM AND THE REAL PROBLEM

Never Was There Less Need for Haste in Military Measures—The Question One of Morale Rather than Enlargement—Present System Cannot Reform Itself—Warnings from Europe's Situation

IF THE ARGUMENTS and facts advanced in this series of articles are of any value, it must be plain that any haste in building up either army or navy will not result in real preparedness. To add to the navy before the lessons of the war are gleaned, may easily mean to squander millions in an inexcusably fatuous fashion. This is so self-evident that, across the water, the British astonishment at Mr. Wilson's programme has been thus voiced by the London *Telegraph:*

"We have the spectacle of the greatest democracy in the world, although separated from Europe by more than 3,000 miles, in such a hurry for more men of war that it has decided not even to wait for the lessons on construction and armament which the war may teach. Moreover, this decision has been reached by a party which came into power in opposition to the Rooseveltian policy of the 'big stick' and pledged itself to economy in armaments."

Similarly to build upon the present unsatisfactory and criminally wasteful military system will not result either in greater efficiency or better preparedness, with the exception of the matter of additional *matériel*—new fortifications and reserves of ammunition. All of which makes haste in arming absolutely inadvisable. Even if there were occasion for hurrying, an overhauling of our present army would seem the only wise policy.

NEVER LESS NEED FOR HASTE.

As a matter of fact, there never could be a time when there was less need of haste in arming. Every month that passes with the war in full blast increases the safety of the United States by further exhausting the combatants abroad. The President and Mr. Garrison themselves admit this, not only because they adduce no positive reasons which would warrant our preparing as if the foe were at the door, but because Mr. Wilson wishes to spread his naval programme over a period of five years, and Mr. Garrison desires Congress to take two years for the increase of the regular army. Would they delay thus if they felt that there were a grave crisis at hand? As a matter of fact, Mr. Wilson, barring political reasons, could perfectly well have repeated at the Manhattan Club the appeal of his message of a year ago—that the country keep calm and beware of changing the United States into an armed camp.

That men as sensible as President Wilson and Mr. Garrison have yielded to the latest argument of the militarists that at the close of the war we shall become the objective of robber-raids by Germany and Great Britain, because we shall be the only really prosperous nation, with large supplies of cash, is not to be believed. Munchausen never invented a more absurd fairy-tale. But if they did believe it, and were to convince Congress that something must be done, there is surely still time for a constructive procedure like the following. First, a decision as to what the policy of the United States shall be, whether defensive or offensive, and whether the country is to defend itself by its navy or primarily by its coast defences and mobile soldiery. How important this is appears from a letter I have just received from a high authority in the War Department, who states that every consideration of possible invasion *presupposes* the total loss of the command of the seas. That is, I take it, that every American submarine must disappear beneath the waves before our secondary defence on land will ever come into play, for it is impossible to conceive of an armada of a thousand ships crossing to our shores while there are still ten American submarines afloat. The British success in moving troops across the Channel, a two hours' run, affords no basis for comparison.

Secondly, Congress should inform the country specifically *against what possible foes* we are arming: There can only be three—Germany, Japan, and England. With France, Russia, or Italy the prospect of any hostilities is so absolutely remote as to be inconceivable; but if war did come, it could only be a question of naval combats. If there are only three probable enemies, the problem becomes at once greatly simplified, even from the point of view of the wildest military man, and we shall put an end to much loose talk about a possible European combination against us in the manner of the robber-barons of the Rhine in the Middle Ages.

A QUESTION OF MORALE.

Thirdly, Congress should itself show a realization of the fact that military values are not to be measured in terms of the size of fleets nor armies by their numbers. Morale, discipline, efficiency in shooting, and ability in high command are all determining factors. Examples of this are unending. Of what value to Russia was her fleet in the war with Japan, when her ships fired on each other at the Dogger Bank, and were so utterly unfit to combat the Japanese in the deciding naval battle? In the present war the Austrian army, for all its large numbers, was defeated by Servians and Russians until German efficiency took charge and competent German generals began to lead. Russia always has troops in great masses, yet in her whole modern history has never won in a conflict in which conditions were fairly equal, defeating the Turks in 1877 only because of Rumanian aid. What guarantee can Congress give to the country that the new Continental army Mr. Garrison asks will have any effective military value whatever? If Congress does realize that the question of efficiency is far more vital than that of mere numbers, it should begin its work by investigating the army from a purely military standpoint, unmuzzling every officer who appears before it, and giving him a guarantee that no criticisms of the service as it exists today will affect his future career. It would be impossible to exaggerate the startling character of the information that would come to it, from the younger officers in particular. It would demonstrate beyond question the existence of evils, which, however consecrated by years of growth and tolerance, are absolutely inconsistent with any efficient military service and work grave hardships to deserving and ambitious officers.

Such an inquiry would, of course, be compelled, if frank and honest, to place a large share of the blame upon politicians in and out of Congress. It would establish that there are economies to be effected, beginning with the present annual waste of $5,500,000 upon "political forts" which would not only result in increased efficiency but make possible a considerable enlargement of the army without additional cost. The most desirable outcome might even be the teaching of Congress how to make military appropriations so that it will not be induced to appropriate $17,700 in extra pay for officers engaged in the hazardous work of teaching cadets at West Point or to pay $1,500 every year for wooden floors for the tents of these cadets when they go into "camp"—youngsters who are to train men in real camps in the field living in electrically lighted tents with permanent iron frames and board floors! Such a committee of Congress, if really searching in its inquiry, would be particularly amazed at the army of civilians attached to our garrisons, while if they should put a stop to the free use of soldiers as "strikers," as gardeners, as drivers of ice-wagons, as servants and laborers of every kind and description, they would make the army vastly more attractive to worthy Americans.

Such a committee would speedily learn, among many other facts, (1) that general army appropriations lead to abuses and waste; that the exercise of discretion in expenditures in army posts and elsewhere leads to the precedence of the comfort of officers and their families over what would be of benefit to the public service; (2) that the lack of any actual supervision of the disposition of moneys appropriated or results obtained leads directly to inefficiency; (3) that reform from within is almost hopeless as long as there is no critical supervision from the outside, inspections by officers having less and less value; that there should be inspection by those free from army influences, precisely as we call in bank examiners to pass upon the condition of our banks—without any one feeling that that is a reflection upon the upright bankers; (4) that many of the army's faults are due to the carrying over into the military service, as reorganized in 1898, of customs like the building of homes for officers' families, which were not faults under the conditions controlling when the army was on the frontier and engaged in Indian campaigns; (5) that there is no better evidence of the necessity of a complete overhauling of the service than the so-called "Manchu" law passed by Congress itself in 1912, in order to put an end to favoritism and to absence on easy detached duty of many officers for long periods of years. This law requires that after four years of absence from his organization, an officer must be returned to his corps or else his pay will be taken out of the pay of the officer on whose order a violation took place. This law is a military monstrosity in that it is a direct interference of the Federal legislature with the management and disposition of the army's personnel. Yet the army welcomed it and believes that it adds not only to the officer's chance of getting a square deal, but to the efficiency of the service as well. None the less it stands as a grave indictment of the past yielding of the War Department to social and political pressure and of the military chiefs who permitted these grave abuses to go on and took part in them.

Once these facts were ascertained, Congress would have no difficulty in building up anew. The efficiency of the Ordnance Corps, and the Engineers along certain lines, the growing efficiency and ability of the Coast Artillery—which has made wonderful strides since the writer of this was drilled by officers of the old foot artillery in the days when an enlisted man in that branch might serve five years and never see a shotted gun fired—point the way. Congress could then strive for real preparedness by seeing to it that military neglect, indifference, and inefficiency are punished, and merit, zeal, and industry rewarded; that the political type of general forever disappears, and really capable generals be chosen who shall be kept so busy at their tasks that they shall not have the time to command divisions and departments and also make speeches all over the country in favor of more troops, more guns, and more reserves, with never a word as to the abuses that honey-comb the service. If Congress makes these changes it will put the army in a position where it can reform itself and it will find plenty of officers to respond and to take the lead for efficiency. For, as has previously been pointed out, we have many capable officers—as we have many shirkers and blatant self-advertisers—and the best soldier-material in the world since it is the most upstanding, self-reliant, adaptable, and intelligent.

MERE MONEY WILL NOT DO IT.

Unless this reorganization takes place Congress will have voted more men, yet have little more of any army and perhaps less efficiency, than at present. Certainly no one knows whether Mr. Garrison's proposed Continental army will have any military value whatsoever—which would suggest that before the raising of 400,000 men be attempted the experiment be essayed with say 40,000 to see if it is practical and whether Americans can be had for that sort of service.

But when all the details are discussed and when all the matters of military policy have been settled one way or the other, the great question still remains: *Should the United States, in the fevered disquiet of a world-crisis, alter the policy of its national life, and go in for large armaments?* It cannot be successfully averred that what Mr. Wilson proposes is merely an enlargement of the old policy. As Mr. Bryan has correctly pointed out, it is a complete break certainly so far as the army is concerned, in that thus far the army has been regarded as a national police and not as a body to prepare for invasion or war abroad. For more than a century the country has been unarmed and has never had a foreign war save of its own seeking. Even in the days when it was weakest, no one assailed it. Only since the days when we began to have a large navy have the rumors of war and the talk and gossip of war been abroad in the land to unsettle the public and to form the basis of militaristic appeals to Americans slavishly to imitate the military follies of the old world, to join the international alliance of the militarists who everywhere coin money out of the fears of the professional soldiers and keep the masses of the people in subjection by means of their armed fellows who are primarily instructed that they must kill their own relatives if the sovereign orders it.

What has been the pride of America—that we were free from a large professional soldiery, that the military and naval votes of our Congress could not, until recently at least, be used as the basis for increasing the burdens of militarism abroad and clamping still heavier loads upon the hard working peasantry, who, in the end, carry the soldiers on their backs—all this is now to be put aside without deliberation, without even the assurance that if the sacrifice is made the end sought will be achieved, and without, of course, waiting to put the issue squarely before the whole people a year hence. Is it any wonder that the President's words had but a half-hearted ring, or that foreign observers consider us the most volatile of people?

LIGHT-HEARTED DRAUGHT OF POISON.

It is, of course, partly due to the supreme self-confidence we have in ourselves, for which we are often criticised.

Those who with clean hands urge that we take far-reaching steps towards navalism and militarism believe, light-heartedly, that there is such a thing as a reasonable preparedness which would satisfy our generals and admirals. They, witnessing Germany's spiritual, moral, and now economic undoing through the poison of militarism, believe that we, too, can use the hypodermic syringe and escape the habit, indulge mildly in the drug, and profit only by its virtues, avoiding all its evil effects. That no one else has escaped the poison—not even democratic France—seems to count not at all in this hour, though every generation of Americans has thought differently until this day.

We are sure that with great armament works springing up about us like mushrooms over night, we shall escape the armament scandals of Europe, those due to international concerns like the Harvey United Steel Company, composed of British, German, American, French, and Italian companies, all of them engaged in booming the market for armor plates in their respective countries on the plea that each country needed to defend itself against the others; or the scandal of the Krupps, whose cannon and ammunition are now being used against Germany and the Germans that made them. But we, being satisfied with our experiences with the patriotic unselfishness of our trusts and our protected manufacturers, take no fear from the enormous transformation of peaceful American industries into those that make the supplies of war—we are beyond price and beyond temptation! We listen gravely to the assurances that we must increase our "national insurance" bill—now seventy-four cents on every dollar—as the only means to national safety, and forget that never have such large sums been spent in the way of national "insurance" as since 1900, and that never in any similar fifteen years in the world's history have there been so many or so terrible wars. We do not stop to ask whether a different kind of insurance is not needed; whether anybody else could be so utterly and hopelessly discredited as the militarists who raise this false cry have been by the events abroad.

Surely the way to true national preparedness for the genuine tasks of humanity, for the elevation of mankind, for the carrying on of the ideals of the great and unarmed American democracy of which we are so proud, lies elsewhere, along totally different lines!

GERMANY EMBATTLED

AN AMERICAN INTERPRETATION

BY

OSWALD GARRISON VILLARD

NEW YORK
CHARLES SCRIBNER'S SONS
1915

III

GERMAN MILITARISM AND DEMOCRACY

NINETY-THREE German savants who pledged their honor and reputation to the truth of their statements have recently declared that German militarism is one and indivisible with German culture. "Without it," they said, "our culture would long since have been wiped off the earth." From many other German sources come denials that Germany's militarism is a menace to the peace of Europe or to anybody else. It is defended, moreover, not only as a cultural but as a democratic institution. Germans are to-day thanking God for their militarism, on the ground that but for it Napoleon would never have been humbled and the German Empire would never have come to pass; that to its extent and thoroughness alone Germany owes her safety at this hour, when she is beset by the troops of nearly half the world, but has thus far carried on the war almost entirely on other people's soil. It is therefore worth while for Americans to examine this German institution carefully, particularly as we are already being told by certain soothsayers that the war convicts England of folly in not having resorted to universal conscription, and places upon us the duty of still greater military burdens, since by some occult reasoning it is apparent to them that if Germany wins we are to be the next victims of her aggrandizing ambition.

Like the nation itself, the German army is curiously two-sided, for it is both a democracy and an autocracy, but with the autocracy on top. It is a democracy because within its regiments are men of every rank and caste, of every grade of learning and every degree of poverty and wealth. It is democratic because it is compulsory and because it spares none. No amount of "pull" or power can free a German from his year or more of service; if he escapes, it is because the army's draft for the year when he becomes liable for service is so large that all

cannot be cared for in the existing organizations, or because some physical disability insures his exemption. Thus, when the call to arms came on the 4th of August it was literally an uprising of the people. The great wave of emotion which exalted the whole nation gained its impetus because men of every class went forth, singing, to die. Barriers of all kinds were levelled; in the enthusiasm of that tremendous hour, caste and rank were, for the moment, forgotten. The entire citizenship was drawn together by the levelling influence of devotion to a single cause. For the moment all Germany was a democracy, and democratic were the forces which stormed Liège, and swept like irresistible gray-green waves of the sea through Brussels, until they were nearly in sight of the defenses of Paris.

In the trenches to-day lie side by side, as common soldiers or non-commissioned officers, men who have made their mark in the field of learning, or science, or business, or the skilled professions. Some reserve regiments would seem to be a cross-section of the population. One of its lieutenants may be of humble origin, a minor official, let us say, in the Dresdner Bank;

serving with him may be a reserve lieutenant who drafted last year one of the most important bills ever laid before the Reichstag. A reserve non-commissioned officer who reports to them may be a survivor of the twenty-six Socialist deputies to the Reichstag who found the call of conventional patriotism far more compelling than the peace principles of their party. A lieutenant next to them may bear the plebeian name of Wilhelm Müller, yet be one of the ablest junior officials of the Colonial Office, for the moment bedfellow with a police officer of Berlin who has exchanged the pursuit of criminals for the pursuit of the French. Next in line may be a university professor of distinction, a painter for whom great things are prophesied, a musician of note, and with them may be serving apprentices, laborers, street-cleaners, conductors, hod-carriers — men from every humble and honorable walk in life. It is reported that the Kaiser recently met a soldier of the Landwehr driving a lot of hogs, whose presence on the road stopped the royal motor. To the Kaiser's delight, when he asked the spectacled herdsman whether he was a farmer in time of peace, he

answered: "No, your Majesty, I am a professor in the University of Tübingen."

There is similarly no discrimination among regiments when war is on; as far as this the General Staff's democracy extends. Whatever the prestige of a regiment in peace times, whether it be the Garde du Corps, the crack cavalry regiment, or the Death's Head Hussars, until lately commanded by the Crown Prince, or one of the Imperial Infantry Guards, it meets with no other consideration than that of the most plebeian infantry regiment when the fighting is under way. It makes no difference if every officer in it is of ancient and noble lineage. The Guards are reported to have been among the heaviest losers in the present war, precisely as at St. Privat in 1870, when five battalions lost every officer, and were fighting under their sergeants when the day was won. It is just the same with the Kaiser's younger sons; they have gone into the actual welter of battle exactly as if offspring of the humblest Westphalian peasant, Prince Joachim being wounded by shrapnel and Prince Oscar collapsing from exhaustion and heart weakness after a charge at the head of his regiment against Turcos, whose bullets laid low most of his regimental officers. The Crown Prince may be safe by reason of his being the nominal commander of an army, but his brothers are alive to-day only by the fortunes of war. Not unnaturally the German press has drawn biting contrasts between the sons of the Kaiser and the Prince of Wales, who, it was officially announced in England, was at twenty not sufficiently trained as a soldier to go to the front until three and a half months of war had passed. That the privilege of dying as the German General Staff wills belongs to princes as much as to anybody else is attested by the death of Lieutenant-General Frederick Prince of Saxe-Meiningen, a brother-in-law of the Kaiser's sister, and of other notables.

But the brief for the democracy of the German army does not end here. It enforces, so its adherents claim, a fine standard of personal conduct, of physical vigor, and of loyalty to King and country throughout the nation. The army takes the humblest conscript, however ignorant and lacking in self-respect, and turns him out a decent, healthy citizen with a fine

physique, excellent carriage, inured to heavy burdens, long marches, and absolute obedience. If he is a dull clodhopper from a Polish province, unable to speak German, the recruit is taught his King's language and how to write it; he learns, as Kipling puts it, to "wash behind his ears," how to eat, how to walk, how to keep himself scrupulously neat, and how to think for himself.

The great lesson of subordination to authority is thus learned, and in many cases self-restraint, as a result of methods which are applied just as rigorously to the son of a millionaire or of an aristocrat. The natural German love of outdoors and of exercise in the open is intensified by service with the colors; a genuine comradeship with men in all walks of life springs up, and with it comes the ability to feel as a German, to think in terms of the nation, whose patriotic songs one and all sing as they march, for singing is a wise requirement of the German military training. Certainly, as the English military reports have so generously attested, this training teaches men to face certain death for the Fatherland with a devotion never surpassed by Occidentals and equalling the stoical and fatalistic pursuance of death by Orientals. Again, the wonderful thoroughness of the military machine leaves its impress upon all who are for a time of its cogs, and to it is attributed some of that unequalled efficiency of the Germans to which the nation owes its extraordinary national rise and prosperity. The army is, in other words, regarded as a vital part of the great German system of education.

If this were all, to be said of German militarism, its case would be, perhaps, won. England and the United States might then be tempted to add a similar course to their educational system. But there is the other side.

It is hard to conceive of a closer corporation or a more autocratic body than the German General Staff; it *is* the army to which it gives the dominating note. It is a group of aggressive, hard-working, exceptionally able officers, envied by soldiers all over the world because the nation does as they tell it. In 1913, when they demanded one hundred and forty thousand more men, the war minister acted as their spokes-

man, and the Reichstag hardly questioned; the bulk of the Socialists, foreshadowing their desertion of their peace principles, acquiesced by a cowardly approval or dodged by a refusal to vote. For the first time, after this vote the tax-gatherer knocked at German doors not to take a share of the income, but some of the citizens' capital, and no one protested. To question the General Staff would be like questioning the Deity, a fact which explains why, the General Staff having declared that it was essential to invade Belgium, nobody in all Germany doubts that decision. One may start controversies over sacred theology in the Kaiser's domains, but not one as to the all-embracing wisdom of the General Staff, for on that there have never been two opinions since 1866 up to the time of this writing. When the deadly forty-two-centimetre guns were planned, the *Grosser Generalstab* asked the Reichstag for a large appropriation and obtained it without disclosing in any degree the purpose for which it was asked. It was enough that the war minister declared the *Generalstab* must have it for a purpose too secret and too important to be intrusted to the Reichstag committee on army estimates or to any but the inner ring of the army.

It is that inner ring which settles the fate of an officer after he has reached colonel's rank. Let one be overslaughed and he resigns at once. Let him blunder in the manœuvres and his "papers" go forward promptly; the General Staff sées to that. Physical efficiency is insisted upon as well as mental. An officer may be as dissipated as he pleases but he must be on hand with a clear head for the five-o'clock spring and summer march-out of his regiment. His habits and customs may be deserving of all sorts of censure, but if he studies diligently, passes his examinations well, has good efficiency reports, and is altogether *ein schneidiger Offizier* his superiors will say nothing. There is no age limit as in our army, as is evidenced by the prevalence of men approaching seventy in high positions to-day. Thus, Generals von Kluck, von Hausen, and von Bülow are sixty-eight; Generals von Moltke and von Emmich, the latter the capturer of Liège, are sixty-six; and Field-Marshal von Hindenburg is sixty-seven. But to hold their positions men like these must

be vigorous physically and mentally, agreeable to the General Staff, and absolute upholders of the existing military traditions and order.

By this we do not mean that each general must be a follower of Bernhardi. Many of the German generals probably never saw his book nor even heard of it. But they must subscribe fervently to the overbearing pretensions of the military clique, to the autocratic attitude of the army toward the civilian and the nation. They must carry themselves as members of an exalted caste whose adoration of their uniform borders on pagan worship Take the case of Colonel von Reuter, who commanded the Ninety-ninth Infantry, stationed at Zabern, in Alsace, and was acquitted in January of last year (1914) of the charges of illegal assumption of the executive power, illegal imprisonment of civilians, and the invasion of private houses in order to make arrests. This was at the time when his young officers, whom one could hardly accuse of being democratic in spirit, were sabring or persecuting the civilians, who were driven almost to revolt by the overbearing arrogance of the military. Colonel von Reuter himself openly and aggressively stated on his trial that if matters had gone any farther he would have turned his machine-guns, which stood ready in the courtyard of the barracks, on the populace. "Blood may flow," he had threatened at the crucial moment, "for we are protecting the prestige and the honor of the whole army and the gravely shaken authority of the government." "I was convinced that our government was allowing its reins to drag on the ground," he told the court, and so, in the name of autocracy, he assured the public prosecutor that "jurisprudence ends here," and declared martial law.

A court of high officers sustained Colonel von Reuter and his subordinates on the ground that a decree issued by the King of Prussia in 1820 — not a law — gave the military the right to intervene, without waiting for a request from civil authority, if they deemed the time had come to act. More than that, the army expressly upheld the arrogant acts of the officers, for whom the judge-advocate never asked more than a week's or three days' imprisonment as punishment! Colonel von Reuter is reported

to have won the Iron Cross; and the young officer who sabred the lame cobbler of Zabern is also at the front, but not, let us trust, in the name of democracy. In defending Colonel von Reuter, the minister of war, General von Falkenhayn, who has been acting as chief of staff during the recent temporary illness of General von Moltke, declared that, while the colonel might have exceeded his authority at times, his acts, nevertheless, saved his officers from the necessity of running their swords through the insulting civilians in order to protect the honor of the "Kaiser's Coat." This coat — hardly a democratic garment — thus inevitably recalls Gessler's hat; the General Staff means that there shall be no vital difference between the deference asked of Wilhelm Tell and that which the German civilian owes to the "gay coat" of the military. Officers have frequently been applauded and acquitted, or at most imprisoned in a fortress for a few weeks, for stabbing civilians or killing them in duels that are against the law but are often forced upon officers by decrees of the regimental courts of honor, whose ideals of conduct are direct inheritances from the days of Frederick the Great. If the full story of these courts of honor could be written, it would astound people everywhere.

In brief, the army is a narrow caste with professional ideals of a bygone time, scrupulously maintained in the face of modern progress by the ruling clique. From its highest officers, its General Staff, its Crown Prince, as well as its Kaiser, the army takes its tone as a bulwark of the privileged classes, to whom anything that smacks of democracy is anathema. It is the chief pillar of the great landlords, the *Junker*, and the aristocrats, as it is of the throne. When the Reichstag passed a vote of censure on the government because of the Zabern affair, an almost unheard-of thing, the government simply ignored the vote. Doubtless the imperial chancellor and General von Falkenhayn, the censured ministers, smile to-day if they think of this incident, and reflect how completely the war has placed the Reichstag, the Social-Democrats, and all the rest of the civilians in their power. There being no responsible ministry to fall in Germany, the fate of the nation has rested — less than a year after their

censure by the national parliament — in their and the Kaiser's hands. As for the Kaiser and the Crown Prince, who publicly upheld Colonel von Reuter, they may for the moment be democrats, but the only reason why they do not fear the Social-Democrats, whom a few years ago the Kaiser denounced as traitors to the country, is the existence of the army. General von Falkenhayn declared in the Reichstag, in December, 1913, that "without the army not a stone of the Reichstag building would remain in place." Is there any doubt that this democratic organization of eight hundred thousand men would close the doors of the Reichstag if the Kaiser so ordered? Did not the grandfathers of those now in the trenches in the Imperial Guard regiments crush out the republican uprising in 1848?

In this anti-democratic tendency the German army is not different from any other. The same trend toward caste and autocracy is noticeable, to greater or less degree, in every army; even a study of the social life of our American navy would prove this. If England creates a great standing army the same phenomena will be still more manifest than in her present regular force, which has been about the most undemocratic machine thinkable. The social, court, and petticoat influences that controlled the British service down to the Boer War have been known of all informed men. It took this present war, with its overwhelming need for officers, to break down the barriers of caste erected against the common soldier. Lord Kitchener did an unheard-of thing recently when he advanced one hundred and twenty-five sergeants and corporals to lieutenancies in a single issue of the official *Gazette*, yet no one would describe Lord Kitchener as an apostle of democracy. The nature of an army and its very organization are undemocratic; the whole basis is a hierarchy with the power centring in one head.

Of course, the autocratic nature of an army is not affected by the bourgeois antecedents of some of its officers. In Germany a man of plainest lineage, be he a good soldier, can rise to high rank. Of the active officers prior to the outbreak of war, 5.3 per cent were the sons of minor officials or of non-commissioned officers; that is, they came of families with no particular

social position. A number of the German corps commanders are to-day commoners who do not write *von* before their names. But they must have inherited or married means in order to hold their present positions, since German officers cannot live on their pay. To no regiment can an officer be appointed until he has been voted on by his future comrades, just as if he were entering a select club. This may make for harmony and for efficiency, but he would be rash who would assert that it smacked of democracy. Of the rest of the corps of officers, as it existed at the beginning of 1914, 9.7 per cent were sons of large landed proprietors, while 62.5 were sons of army officers, of civilian officials, of judges, and of members of the learned professions. Only 15.1 per cent were sons of business men; the remainder, comprising 6.3 per cent, represented a varied group of occupations.

Of course, many regiments are wholly closed to men without title. The bourgeois officers go to the least desirable regiments, and Jews are, of course, quite good enough to be reserve officers, and serve as *Kannonenfutter*, whenever the General Staff pleases. But none hitherto have been regimental officers, and none have risen to high rank in the staff departments to which they have been admitted as officers. Yet these are not the only undemocratic discriminations. Such newspapers as the Jewish *Frankfurter Zeitung* and the *Berliner Tageblatt*, as well as the Socialist *Vorwärts* — the *Frankfurter* and the *Tageblatt* are now unreservedly upholding the war and the army — have in the past filled columns upon columns with discreet criticisms of the military. When the army increase was voted last year certain Socialists took the opportunity to criticise the favoritism in regulations shown to the Imperial Guards. Of course, they accomplished nothing. Why should the General Staff pay attention to mere members of the Reichstag, and Socialists at that? In a democratic organization criticism of the organization is permitted; none is tolerated in the German army. When an exceptionally able military critic of the *Berliner Tageblatt*, Colonel Gädke, a retired officer, undertook to criticise the service, the military authorities tried to deprive him of his right to sign as "former colonel" of an artillery regiment. That he is not figuring

as a correspondent or critic now has perhaps some connection with this incident. Any effort to effect reforms in the army is certain to encounter grave obstacles. Did not the late General Bronsart von Schellendorf, one of the ablest war ministers Germany has had, fail utterly in 1893–96, despite his high office, in his effort to reform the army's court procedure and system of punishments?

If there is any atmosphere in which democracy does not flourish it is that of a Continental barracks. German discipline is unyielding as iron. The power of the officer is absolute and that of the non-commissioned officer little less so. The men in the ranks change completely every three years, but the non-commissioned officers are usually professional soldiers for a long term, who know the ropes well. The conditions are such that brutal ones among them can make existence a hell for any man they do not like. Just as it is hard to prevent some hazing at West Point, so there is always some in the German barracks. It is often almost impossible to checkmate brutality among the non-commissioned officers, because the presumption is always in favor of authority; so there are occasionally suicides in the barracks, frequently desertions, and sometimes trials of men finally caught in ill-treating subordinates. When Rosa Luxemburg, the fiery Socialist orator, declared at Freiburg last year (1914), in speaking of the case of a horribly abused soldier at Metz, "It is certainly one of those dramas which are enacted day in and day out in German barracks, although the groans of the actors seldom reach our ears," General von Falkenhayn, as war minister, prosecuted the "Red Rosa" for libelling the army. The case was promptly dropped when her counsel announced that they proposed to call one thousand and thirty eye-witnesses to such wrong-doing, mostly in the form of "slaps in the face, punches and kicks, beating with sheathed sabres and bayonets, with riding-whips and harness straps; forcible jamming of ill-set helmets on the wearer's head; compulsory baths in icy water, followed by scrubbing down with scrub-brushes until the blood ran; compulsory squatting in muscle-straining attitudes until the victim collapsed or wept for pain; unreasonable fatigue drill, and

so on. There were also abundant cases of absurd and humiliating punishments inflicted by non-commissioned officers, such as turning the men out of bed and making them climb to the top of cupboards or sweep out the dormitory with tooth-brushes." Now, single men in barracks are never plaster saints, as Kipling, the exalter of British militarism and hater of German militarism, has made quite clear to us. Sporadic cases of abuse happen in our own American barracks; but no one will, it is to be hoped, assert that in this phase of its existence the German army even faintly suggests a democracy.

This army has had its Dreyfus case, too, though the victim was not an officer, but a Sergeant Martin who on a second trial was found guilty, on circumstantial evidence, of killing his captain. The two civilian members of the court found him not guilty; the prosecutor asked only for imprisonment, but the military judges pronounced the death sentence in addition to imprisonment. They felt they must uphold their caste, right or wrong. A lieutenant stationed at Memel was found to have beaten a soldier so severely with a sword that his victim had to be dropped from the military service, compensated, and pensioned for injuries "incident to the service." Not that the other type of officer is lacking. As the writer knows by personal experience, there are plenty of kindly, gifted, and charming officers who are neither fire-eaters nor war-worshippers, who write no jingo books and do not subscribe to Bernhardi. They despise the intrigues, the narrowness, and frequent immorality of the small garrison, and the dissipation of life in the big cities. They recognize the antiquated character of the code of honor, but they are helpless to change it, and as they grow older the more ready they are to think an intense militarism the normal condition of society. If there are many officers of this type, particularly in the South German armies, the trend is, however, toward the overbearing arrogance of the Von Reuters, which is again merely saying that militarism unchecked and unsubordinated to civilian control will run to excesses everywhere. The note of Bernhardi has been more and more often heard with the cry that war is the natural state

of man and that the German army is for war. It is quite possible that the Kaiser, in the last moments before the war, was overborne against his better judgment by the General Staff clique with which he is surrounded, and signed the fatal order practically under compulsion. But there were thousands of his officers who went to the war exulting that the time had come at last when their years of devoted study and ceaseless training, unsurpassed in its comprehensiveness and its intensity, were to give way to the practical application of all they had learned as to man-killing.

The spirit of arrogance and aristocracy so characteristic of the extreme Prussian militarists has penetrated even further than into the South German armies. It has made itself felt in civil life in increasing measure, as is only natural. When men, by reason of the coat they wear, deem themselves sacrosanct and especially privileged, they are bound to have imitators in plenty, not only among those subordinated to them, but those whose garments are of the ununiformed multitude. The aggressive tone of the typical lieutenant is quickly caught, and so is his total lack of consideration for others. For instance, the rules of his caste make it impossible for him to carry a bundle or a bag for his wife, so she must lug it by his side, and there are many similarly odd customs. The habits of officers of the fashionable regiments do not help a young officer to a real respect for womankind, and the frequent marriage-à-la-mode for money to pay debts, or to support one's station in military life, does not tend toward morality or happiness. If he escape these perils, the young officer is in danger of becoming the conceited or silly snob whom the *Fliegende Blätter* satirizes so perfectly.

No one has yet, however, measured the whole effect of these tendencies upon the German nation. The roughness and the coarseness of the barracks and the supercilious attitude of the officers as a class are without doubt in part responsible for the arrogance and bad manners which are so often noticed by foreigners in German travellers, and are freely deprecated by the more refined and thoughtful Germans. One meets Americans and English in numbers abroad who can also be trying indeed; no country, alas, has a monopoly of purse-proud

travelling *nouveaux riches* or vulgar vacation-trippers; but many observers of Germany during the last three decades have been struck with the fact that German bad manners often go hand in hand with an assumption of superiority which is extremely trying, and may properly be connected with a similar military manner that an American often finds utterly unbearable. Among the masses, upon whom the three-year military service does have some excellent effects, their schooling under the overbearing non-commissioned officers is often to be traced by the spread among them of the unpleasant traits of the barracks. It may even be asked whether certain unsparing, roughshod methods of the nation's soldiers in Belgium, as well as the many offensive utterances in the press which have made so many Americans rub their eyes and say, "This is not the Germany that I knew years ago," are not due to a subconscious influence of the military spirit. Certainly, unchecked military authority invariably leads to an arrogant and tyrannical spirit which may be more or less inseparable from the military caste with its sharp social distinctions and clearly divided grades. Our own American army has often had to bear with precisely this sort of charge, and the allegation that it falls far behind the French in its lack of democracy and a due consideration by the officers for the enlisted men has also been made at times.

As for Germany, it may well be asked whether an army which by its very existence creates fear and militaristic rivalry, which forever talks war, can be either a democratic force or, in the long run, a sound educational influence. As an educational system it may have certain merits, but even German professors would hardly deny that it is bought at a heavy cost to the school system of the empire, and, lately, to the university world, for some of the greatest schools of learning find themselves hampered and pinched. If there are underpaid common-school teachers anywhere, they live in Germany, and particularly in Bavaria. The genteel poverty of these men who have to exist upon their pay is one of the great tragedies of life under the Kaiser. But the economic waste of the army is a chief stumbling-block to any betterment in their condition, precisely as the millions it costs prevent

reforms in many other directions. It would seem as if it would be better to have the Krupps earn less than twelve or fourteen per cent per annum and the school-teachers a little more. It would be better to be less efficient as a nation to the extent that that efficiency is created by the army, and for the masses to be happier, with a consequent decrease of a million or so in the Social-Democratic voters. As long as they can roll up four millions of votes and still protest against militarism, even though swept off their feet in war-time, all cannot be well with a culture founded on military force. That their voices and many others will again be uplifted to protest against war and armies when peace returns, is the one thing that is certain about this war.

In no such military and bureaucratic atmosphere as exists in Germany does democracy thrive! Instead, we have the tradition that as the German Empire is the army's creation so the nation's future is dependent wholly upon it. Imitating the ninety-three savants, three thousand German teachers in universities and schools of technology have put their names to the statement that there is no other spirit in the army save that of the nation; that the spirit of German knowledge and militarism are the same; that the German army and the German universities are identical in their aspirations, since both are devoted to science. They, too, apparently cannot understand that a culture which exists only by reason of the arms behind it is no more a normal, healthy growth than is an industry artificially created by a protective tariff, and kept alive solely by receiving part or all of its profits by the favor of a treasury. They belie their own culture, because it is a free growth while service in the army is compulsory, and compulsory service of the German type may be universal but it is not democratic. Again, this sudden assertion that Germany is wholly dependent upon her army for safety is the historic argument of decadent peoples relying entirely upon mercenaries. Is the German democracy of intellect so without any sources of strength within itself that it cannot flourish save by grace of the militarists? We believe that when the present *Rausch* (intoxication) of the German people is at an end their intellectual

leaders will be the first to deny this interdependence of their realm with another so materialistic, so mediæval, so autocratic, with such barbarous aims as conquest by blood and iron and man-killing by the hundred thousand.

When the sacredness of human life, upon which foundation every state is founded in time of peace, is so utterly disregarded, so basely violated, there can be no return to the older ideal save at a high price.

Beyond question, if the Kaiser triumphs it means a setback to every liberal democratic movement. War inevitably retards reforms wherever it is fought; the economic waste presses so heavily that a nation's shaken energies are usually absorbed for years in making good the losses. Then we may count upon declarations by autocracy and aristocracy that their militaristic policies triumphed, that the mailed fist on sea and land alone saved the country from completest disaster. Again, there is nothing in the Kaiser's record to lead any one to hope that if he wins he will seek to reward

the nation for its courage, steadfastness, and sacrifices by turning toward liberalism. But if he loses there will be a different story; only the defeat of the empire will afford hope that there will be rapid progress toward democratization, toward a responsible ministry, toward equality at the ballot-box in Prussia, toward elective rulers, toward the overthrow of the false gods of militarism and imperialism. Disaster will mean the real test of the Kaiser's greatness as it meant a supreme test of the spiritual qualities of both the Napoleons, to which neither of them reacted.

For human nature is so constituted that the public will begin to question and to find fault with its ruler if matters should go wrong. Then we should definitely learn if there are really great moral qualities and true spiritual leadership in the Kaiser; whether there is hidden in him any of that unshakable faith in the common people which exalted Lincoln in the hour of darkness. Surely without Lincoln's sympathy for and understanding of the masses he could never have led them through years of defeat and discouragement to final triumph.

Already we have been deeply affected by the war; we have been drawn into it spiritually by our sympathies, economically through our suffering and through the contributions of our granaries, our arms, and our powder factories; politically because of the appeals to us to act as judge of wrong doing. Shall the most extraordinary chance to lead the world back to the natural, peaceful status of man be allowed to slip by with no effort on our part? It is unthinkable, if there is any imagination left in the White House; if there is any response there to an overwhelming moral appeal. We know there is.

Here is a straightforward practical undertaking on behalf of peace to stir every man not

war-mad. Never was there a better vantage-ground for attacking the whole vicious system, because some of the oldest militaristic shibboleths have been shown to be utterly baseless. That hoary old falsehood that armies make for peace is as exploded now as is the assertion that training in arms alone keeps a nation from rotting out, from becoming craven and flabby. Hereafter militarism is in the open, to be defended, if at all, on the grounds that nobody is to be trusted; that mankind has not advanced during the centuries; that there is no way for any nation to live save with rifle on hip; that there is nothing in morality or national honor or Christianity. If militarism is to continue to exist, we must be frankly brutal, frankly cynical, and here in peaceful America we shall be urged by some fellow citizens to make the business of preparing to kill other peoples the supreme business of the nation.

The New York Evening Post
FOUNDED 1801

April 13, 1917.

Mr. Joseph P. Tumulty,
The White House,
Washington, D. C.

Dear Mr. Tumulty:

You have had my sincerest sympathy during these trying days, and I am glad to learn from your message through Dave Lawrence that you have not altogether forgotten me in this crisis. I know how you must have been suffering mentally and morally, and I can, I am sure, wholly enter into the feelings that must have been yours. To see your beloved chief congratulated by Henry Cabot Lodge, warmly endorsed and called upon by Theodore Roosevelt, and acclaimed with joy by every munition maker, every agent of big business and all the evil forces combined, against whom he has fought for American democracy until recently:- all this, I know, must have caused you profound concern and unhappiness.

As for the conscription proposal, of course you were good enough to prepare me for that. Do you remember our ride with Dave down to Mr. Burleson's office, when you assured me that the President would never, never sign such a bill? And do you remember my saying that you two were "the weakest links in the chain?" Remembering certain similar incidents in the past, I came back from Washington feeling convinced that the President would be won over to universal service before very long; and my reputation as a prophet has been enhanced.

Believe me, I am ready for any concentration camp, or conscription camp, or prison, but I am <u>not</u> at war and no one can put <u>me</u> into war, - not the President of the United States with all his power. My loyalty to American traditions and ideals renders that impossible.

We shall see what we shall see, but what I should like to know now is what shall we newspaper men say now who loyally supported the President's speech of January 22d, in which he said:

"It must be a peace without victory. It is not pleasant to say this ....I am seeking only

The New York Evening Post
FOUNDED 1801

to face realities and to face them without soft concealments. Victory would mean peace forced upen the loser, a victor's terms imposed upon the vanquished. It would be accepted in humiliation, under duress, at an intolerable sacrifice, and would leave a sting, a resentment, a bitter memory upon which terms of peace would rest not permanently but only as upon quicksand. Only a peace between equals can last............"?

As for myself, I am having these beautiful sentiments printed on a large card as a sort of loyalty pledge to the President.

As always, with warm personal regards to yourself as the most loyal and devoted of secretaries,

Faithfully yours,

Oswald Garrison Villard

Moving for Disarmament

THERE is nothing more striking about the peace discussions coming to us from Europe than the persistent recurrence of universal disarmament. It was foremost in the Pope's proposal. It was accepted without question in the German reply, and last week Count Czernin advocated it strongly on behalf of Austria-Hungary. Now we are quite aware that to most people to-day such a position on the part of Austrians and Germans will be viewed with distrust and suspicion. It will be said that the devil is sick and therefore a monk would be. It will be recalled that the Germans at the Hague Conference, as Mr. Choate frequently pointed out, were the chief stumbling-block to anything approaching the limitation of armaments; that when Mr. Churchill proposed the cessation for a year of the building of battleships by Germany and Great Britain, the Kaiser refused. Is it not, therefore, plain that, being defeated in their militaristic plans, the Germans are now suddenly become pious—until it suits them to begin anew? How can they ever be trusted again?

To this the reply is that if Germany, through its frightful losses and its evident defeat both in the field and in the court of morals, now makes confession, the fact suffices. To drive militarism out of Germany and Austria is a prime purpose of the United States and of the Allies. The German consent to disarmament is, therefore, to be welcomed and acclaimed, for it will make it easier for the Allies to dwell in the peace conference on the folly of it all, and to insist upon that complete disarmament which is the prerequisite to a reorganization of the world on sane lines and to the establishment of the League to Enforce Peace if that should prove to be the next step in doing away with war. No matter what the German motive to-day, it is a cause for devout thankfulness that there will be no need for long wrangling on this issue of disarmament when the peace envoys come together. The Entente is to-day definitely and officially committed to this programme, and it cannot now retreat from the position if it would.

But how can Germany be trusted? Easily enough. Disarmament is not a question of a treaty to be handled as a scrap of paper. It is a question of fact. It will be easy enough to require proofs of disarmament. A nation cannot disarm or arm save in the full light of publicity. In no country can military supplies be purchased save on a very small scale without an appropriation by Parliament or Congress. There can be no secret training of large numbers of men. If Germany is limited to an army of 50,000 men, it will not be possible for her to heap up war material for six millions, and there will not be the trained men to use it if it should by any means be acquired. It is easy to ascertain what orders are placed with the large ammunition plants of the world, and, moreover, there will be in every Parliament hereafter Socialists and pacifists to see to it that the nations live up to their word.

But far more than all this, disarmament will strike at the roots of the system which has made possible the mad militarism of to-day—universal military service. When the Prussians hit upon this scheme for providing a nation in arms in order to combat Napoleonism, they laid the foundations for the disaster of to-day and became responsible for the mad race for armaments which was impoverishing Europe before this war began. Disarmament means the ending of universal service. This is clearly recognized not only in the German statements, but in that of Cardinal Gasparri, who rightly sees in it the chief evil to be removed. It is universal service which has made the people of Germany playthings of the Kaiser and the General Staff, which has enabled the military caste to control that country, and has kept the Hohenzollern in power.

To our mind, except the restoration of Belgium and Servia and France, nothing is as important as this question of disarmament, because there alone lies the hope of avoiding such another calamity in the future. If disarmament does not come, the millions who have died in this war will have died in vain, and there will be a great question as to whether democracy has advanced and the cause of small nations has been safeguarded. The greatest enemy of democracy to-day is militarism, for that is merely a synonym for Czarism and Kaiserism. We do not agree with those who contend that militarism is merely the state of mind of a few men and that republics can arm to the teeth and in no wise become a menace to the world. It is the military system which makes militarists out of those who become part of it, and there is never a country where it should not be regarded as something to be got out of the world, together with the ammunition factories and armor plants.

The part that the United States should play in this is to us perfectly plain. It ought not to let leadership towards disarmament go to the Russians, the Germans, and Austrians. It ought to be guided by President Wilson's words that this noble America of ours "must never be turned into an armed camp." Secretary Daniels's assertion that we are to have the greatest navy in the world points absolutely the wrong way. In unworthy military competition lies economic ruin, as Count Czernin points out. His reason for urging disarmament is the enormously increased cost of armaments; if the world is to remain on the old basis, it must expend far greater sums for preparation for war than had been dreamed of up to 1914. No nation in Europe to-day can afford this and stagger under its burden of war debt as well. But, after all, the most powerful argument is the moral one. It is contrary to the teachings of Christianity, to the highest ethical doctrines by which the world is striving to progress, that nations shall go armed to the uttermost and rely on brute force as the only means of keeping the peace and preventing humanity from tearing itself to pieces. The United States will not be true to its institutions if it does not seek for itself the honor of leading in the abolition of military force.

The Proper Attitude Towards Socialism

OF the many inconsistencies in which the bulk of our press is wallowing nothing is more extraordinary than its treatment of our Socialists. At the very moment when Americans are eagerly longing for the news of the triumph of the German Socialists over the Kaiser, when they rightly see in the Liebknechts and Haases and Scheidemanns the one hope of a safe and sane Germany, free from the curse of its autocracy and its militarism, our Socialists at home are regarded with suspicion, charged with the Kaiserism they despise, and all too frequently lumped with I. W. W.'s and Anarchists. Every time the Government moves against the Socialists the press applauds. In the almost unparalleled intolerance of other people's opinions if they differ from the prevailing one, Socialists are treated as if enemies of society, a direful brood hatching something so new and so dreadful no one can quite define it. "Society" shudders, our politicians rage, and our leaders of industry declare that like the I. W. W. the Socialists ought all to be hanged.

Now in a benighted official like the Postmaster-General this sort of attitude is to be expected. He has the breadth of view of a small Texas town, and so he publicly declares that all Socialist newspapers are to be suppressed, "not because they are Socialistic, but because all Socialists are against the war and therefore seditious." His every utterance shows the provinciality of his point of view. It is perfectly evident that he is totally unaware of what has gone on in Europe; that there were over four millions of Socialist voters in Germany before the war; that Denmark is to-day a more completely "socialized" state than Karl Marx dreamed of, and that France, Italy, and Sweden as well as Russia have practically Socialistic Governments or Socialists in control of administration. Like our own too often ill-informed press, Mr. Burleson does not realize that Socialism has not anything in common with anarchy, that it is a widely supported economic theory of government, which, however faulty its economics, makes a tremendously powerful appeal because of its humanitarianism, its fellowship, its devotion to the cause of the workers, and its democratic trend. No cause can be wholly bad which enrolls millions of men under its banners of all classes in the countries where there is the suffrage. It is certainly not to be treated in 1917 as something entirely destructive and vicious, to be held down by force or by Government control, as Mr. Burleson essays to do—in utter ignorance that a bigger man than the Postmaster-General, namely, one Otto von Bismarck, tried this policy for some years, going to very great lengths to stamp out all Social-Democrats, only to find out that every time he struck one down a hundred arose in his place.

The extraordinarily bitter and narrow attitude of most of our leading newspapers, and of men as politically far behind the times as Mayor Mitchel and Theodore Roosevelt, is the more amazing because in the seven months we have been at war, we have taken the speediest and most far-reaching lurch into State Socialism recorded of any great country. It must be plain to every thinking American by this time that one of the prices we shall pay for our idealistic battling for democracy in Germany is a great swing towards radicalism. We must and shall have more democracy at home and greater popular control of governmental policies. It must be made impossible to plunge this country into war again in the precise way in which it was in April, 1917. But the reaction is likely to go much further than that. Shall we not see a retention of the price-fixing by the Government? Shall we not face permanent Governmental control of the necessaries of life as well as of mines, railways, the building and managing of steamships, warehouses, elevators, etc.? The whole trend is in that direction; the Non-Partisan League of the Dakotas is a sign of it as well as the great increase in the Socialist vote.

In view of this, how is it possible for newspapers which pretend to leadership to denounce those as traitors who advocate putting the Government in control of all business? When they talk thus, they indict their own President and their own Congress. They cannot cry out for a Government administrator of railways in war time and brand as seditious those who would have him in peace time. They cannot insist upon a tremendous concentration of power in the hands of the Government at Washington to beat the Kaiser and abuse those who think it a good thing when the Kaiser is beaten. They cannot say, as Mr. Roosevelt did, that a vote for Hillquit is a vote for treason when Mr. Hillquit merely wants to carry to the *n*th degree the policies which Washington now finds essential to the successful carrying on of the war. They will ere long, these militant journalists and politicians, have to treat with respect the views of those opponents of Socialism who sincerely believe that the price the United States will have to pay in the socializing of much of its political life is too great a sacrifice even for the privilege of breaking lances in behalf of the freedom of Germany from autocracy and militarism. The correctness of this point of view will still be challenged, but that it is a debatable position will be recognized before another year or two has elapsed.

As for the *Nation*, it sees nothing in the present situation to cause it to change its attitude towards Socialism. It is opposed to its economic doctrines as heretofore. It would again quote the words of its lamented editor, the late Hammond Lamont, who thus laid down in 1908 what ought to be the correct attitude of all opponents, whether in politics or journalism, towards the Marxians: "And as for other questions—we cannot believe that error will permanently prevail over truth. We are confident that individualism, in its main features, is the policy which has formed and which must preserve our institutions. But if we conservatives are mistaken, we cannot but welcome a discussion which shall open our eyes and set us right. Our attitude towards this topic, as towards any other which touches the vitals of our nation, must be that of readiness to defend our faith in open forum, to meet and conquer reason with reason."

But the *Nation* sees plainly that the time may be at hand when the Socialistic party may in the several States and the country as a whole be the radical party to which will flock in protest many hundreds of thousands of Americans who are wholly opposed to Socialism, precisely as many thousands of New Yorkers voted for Hillquit and Hylan as a protest against the war and the militarism of Mitchel, not because they believed in Tammany misrule or in the State as a controller of every function of life. It is too early to say, as Roger Sullivan has said in Chicago, that the time is already at hand to amalgamate the Republican and Democratic parties in the nation in a new line-up of conservatives against radicals. But it is quite possible to foresee a situation like that which would arise in New York if Governor Whitman and William Randolph Hearst should be candidates for the Governorship of the State next autumn. Many patriotic citizens who abominate the Kaiser and all his works, despise yellow journalism, and are outraged by the whole machine-type of wasteful and militaristic government which Governor Whitman typifies, would then feel themselves compelled to vote for a Socialist or some other third ticket as a patriotic duty and to preserve their self-respect, precisely as hundreds of thousands of Democrats who were opposed to most Republican economic tenets voted for McKinley against Bryan. When such a course as this is possible, it is time for press and public men to take a different attitude towards Socialism. That party is here to stay for long years to come and may serve an admirable turn as a club to compel the conservative parties to abjure reaction, to discard hypocritical democracy, and to devote themselves to a sane and sound democratic liberalism.

Some Reconstruction Proposals

By OSWALD GARRISON VILLARD

THE German peace proposals to the Bolsheviki, whatever their fate or their value, are compelling statesmen everywhere to reëxamine their positions. It seems apparent that until peace comes, whether that be now or next year or in 1919, the discussion of terms will steadily be in order. Lord Lansdowne's letter made it possible for anybody in the United States and in England to discuss peace conditions without being charged with treason. Mr. Asquith's speech and the German peace terms confirm this privilege. When it is remembered that as late as last August Americans were forbidden to discuss peace under any circumstances, under penalty of physical violence and Government denunciation, this progress towards rationality is highly gratifying. If by any chance those amazing men, Lenine and Trotzky, have really started an official interchange of views which will result in eventual peace, they will deserve well of the world, even if they should be doomed to fall to-morrow. Already by brushing aside diplomatic conventionalities they have obtained what Lloyd George and Clemenceau would not or could not get—a clear-cut statement of German peace aims.

But in the discussion of peace terms which is now going on so widely, is there not danger that because of the extraordinary range and variety of the problems which present themselves we shall lose sight of fundamental principles? When the war is over, we shall be facing what is practically the reconstruction of the whole world; no nation but will be profoundly affected by the inevitable readjustment. Every subject people and every nationalistic group seeking self-expression will appear before the peace conference asking for independence or self-government—the Finns, the Poles, the Hindus, the Ukrainians, the Armenians, the Persians, the various Balkan nationalities, the Zionists, the French-inclined natives of Alsace-Lorraine, the Algerians, the Egyptians, and endless others. If we turn to matters affecting international rights and policies, there will be the much-mooted freedom of the seas; the right of the *Hinterländer* to access to the oceans; the right of all the great Imperialistic Powers to approach the raw materials of Asia, Africa, and South America; the question of new sea laws; the matter of colonies. All of these things are formidable enough, yet they touch not at all upon the vital question of a new organization of the world, that is, disarmament, the question of a League to Enforce Peace or an International Parliament or a Court of Arbitration—the Hague Court expanded.

In such an overwhelming embarrassment of questions, issues, and problems, it would seem as if there were but one safe course for commentator or statesman, and that is to fall back upon certain broad, general principles. It is related of Wendell Phillips that, being asked by a slaveholder how he would reorganize the South after Abolition, and being assured that it was impossible to do so, that freedom meant chaos, anarchy, and a state of affairs in which no white woman or child could live, he replied: "In this matter I intrench myself upon the principle of human liberty and leave the working out of details to Almighty God"—a faith which time has eminently justified. Are there now any general principles upon which liberal-minded men who wish to make impossible either the running amuck again of Germany, or of any other nation which may have its day of militaristic madness, can agree at this stage of the discussion? The following are some that suggest themselves:

First and foremost: The disarmament of all nations, which includes the abolition of universal conscription; an immediate and radical disarmament which shall carry with it the establishment of small armed constabularies, but permit of the maintenance of no troops trained for war, and shall provide for the abolition of all navies and of the private right to manufacture arms and ammunition.

Secondly: The establishment of free trade and the abolition of all protective tariffs. This involves freedom of the seas and of trade to all peoples of the earth without fear or favor or special or preferential rights of any kind.

Thirdly: The acceptance of Abraham Lincoln's immortal saying that no man is good enough to govern any other man without that other man's consent as the only sound guiding principle for the readjustment of national, international, and racial relationships. It obviously carries with it a referendum in Alsace-Lorraine as to the future of those ill-treated provinces.

Fourthly: The establishment of an international parliament and an international court, to which latter shall be submitted all issues between nations, dropping once for all the phrase about causes which affect the honor of a nation, precisely as courts between individuals are not in the least affected by the individual honor as such of those who come before it.

Doubtless to many readers these four principles will seem so idealistic as not to merit much discussion. Yet I find many who believe that if any one of them fails of universal acceptance when the war is over, then by that much will the millions who have fallen in this war have died in vain. They are the clearest road to the advancement of democracy, and they cannot therefore be waved aside as wholly impractical. We have witnessed in the last three and one-half years more amazing things happen in the life of nations than any one could possibly have dreamed of. We who have seen Czardom collapse overnight ought certainly not to close our minds to any possibility. Sane men everywhere have a right to hitch their wagons to stars as never before. Can we not all agree that if none of these four principles is accepted when the war ends, then the unparalleled sacrifices of this war will have been largely for nothing? For we shall have smashed German militarism precisely as Napoleonism was crushed a century ago, and precisely as the causes of Napoleonism were left untouched we shall leave untouched the causes of this international catastrophe.

As to disarmament, that is all-essential. Militarism grows upon the exercise of the military habit, and no nation, in my judgment, can escape it which goes in for a large military or naval class. To say with certainty that our democracy can avoid it because it has never been militarized is, as ex-Secretary Fisher has pointed out, absurd because we have never tried the effects of having an enormous professional officer class, the permanent hundred and fifty thousand of military and naval officers which our militarists say is essential, if we are to have universal service. The danger of trifling with this issue, of talking *partial* disarmament, is comparable to the discussions of a partial freeing of the American slave by purchase or otherwise. Immediate and unconditional emancipation was what Abraham Lincoln found himself unwillingly driven to by the hard facts of war and the harder facts of absolute justice. It is now perfectly plain that the responsibility for this war rests primarily with the three General Staffs—the Russian, the German, and the Austrian—and the three Kaisers, who were the tools of their militarists—with the chief responsibility resting, before God and man, upon the Germans. If there is to be partial disarmament, we shall simply be confronted with the old fears which have built up nations in arms and placed the power to make war not in the hands of parliaments or of peoples, but in those of irresponsible sovereigns and still more irresponsible cliques of military men. Gradual disarmament appeals no more than gradual prohibition or the curing of the habitual drunkard by limiting him to one spree a week. With armaments must disappear the right of the private citizen to manufacture arms and ammunition, which should be reserved for the state alone.

Already there is among the Allies suspicion of disarmament because the Pope, Count Czernin, and to a limited extent the Germans, are for it. That is quite natural. After what the Germans have done, after the criminal character of much of their diplomacy has been revealed to us, it is not surprising that people look upon every suggestion that comes from them as upon Greeks bearing gifts. But in this case, a moment's reflection shows that it will be impossible for a nation that intends to disarm to go about the job in a way to deceive other nations. Modern war, as we now realize, means the heaping up of *matériel* whose cost is in the billions. It would be impossible for Germany, if it reduced its army to twenty-five thousand constabulary, to store supplies for two million men, for that would be known in a hundred ways. No Reichstag could vote a secret budget for military purposes disproportionate to the army in hand without being questioned at once by the Socialists as well as by foreigners. No General Staff could pile up thousands upon thousands of aeroplanes, huge guns, tanks, reserves of barbed wire, and all the rest without its becoming known.

But the best insurance for small forces is the abolition of universal, compulsory military servitude, for it was that devilish invention of the Germans which has made possible warfare on the present hideous scale, that is, the creation of "nations in arms." Abolish this and you abolish the ability to build up a military power to dominate the world, if only because universal service is unpaid service, and no nation could afford year in and year out to pay high wages to a professional establishment approximating that which the United States will have if it goes to universal service, or that which Germany had in 1914. If that seems an exaggerated statement, may I remind the reader that when in 1913 the Reichstag voted a further increase of the army and much additional equipment, it voted not a tax levy, but a levy on a portion of the property of the individual citizen—an example that British labor unionists are now following in their demand for a 25 per cent. capital levy at the close of the war. At any rate, it seems perfectly plain that genuine disarmament forbids any chicanery or deceit by nations who do not wish to play fair. Finally, there can be no trifling with this issue and no compromising, for if any large group of professional soldiers remains, the danger of conflicts will also remain.

The second principle, free trade, is hardly less important than the first, for behind the military men, and counting upon their aid and protection in oversea ventures, stand those who seek special privileges abroad or desire special trading or manufacturing privileges at home to be secured by building Chinese walls in the guise of protective tariffs around their countries. By no means enough has been said about the absolute necessity of free trade when this war is over if the world's financial recuperation is to be rapid. Yet it is a fact that wherever there is a special restriction on trade it is coming to the front now as a special grievance to be abolished by the peace conference. Of this, the Turkish monopoly of the waterways to Constantinople is the classic example. Free trade lurks in the background of the involved discussion of the freedom of the seas. Proclaim it and you do much to make plainer "the great illusion" that colonies and spheres of influence are worth fighting for, just as when you abolish navies you do away with the chief excuse for such wrongs as our conquest of Santo Domingo and Haiti—urged by our navy as a means of protecting the Panama Canal.

To this it is no answer to point out that free-trade England has been the nation above all others to develop spheres of influence and to seize naval bases. What guarantee, it will be said, is there that if all the nations were similarly wise and generous in their tariff policies as England has been since Cobden's days there will be less land-grabbing and less seeking after special positions and trade opportunities? There can obviously be no such guarantees if democracy of the secret and slimy kind remains the governing spirit of nations. But the very act of throwing down tariff walls would clear the atmosphere, end many rivalries, and enormously advance the feeling that the nations of this little earth must share it on a fair and just basis of competition. It would be worth while if only because it would be another blow at that old absurdity that trade follows the flag. Best of all, it will take another element of unmorality out of the world, for I am of those who believe that a protective tariff is a distinctly immoral affair. Nearly fifty years ago an American who won honors in the battle for humanity wrote thus upon this question:

> For the cause of human liberty covers and includes all possible forms of human industry and best determines how the productions thereof may be exchanged at home and abroad to mutual advantage. Though never handling a tool or manufacturing a bale of cotton or wool, he is the most sagacious political economist who contends for the highest justice, the most far-reaching policy, a close adherence to natural laws, and the removal of all those restrictions which foster national pride and selfishness. There is nothing intricate in freedom, free labor, free institutions, the law of interchange, and the measure of reciprocity. It is the legerdemain of class legislation, disregarding the common interests of the people that creates confusion, sophisticates the judgment and dazzles to betray. . . . Believing that the interests of the American people in no wise materially differ from those of any other country, and denying the rectitude or feasibility of building ourselves up at their expense by an exclusive policy obstructing the natural flow of material exchanges, I avow myself to be a radical free-trader. . . .

The very fact that the nations of the world have been

able to raise the necessary funds for carrying on the war when their revenue from imports has either ceased entirely or fallen off tremendously is a severe blow at the theory that we must at least have tariffs for revenue only. If we disarm, we shall remove the heaviest financial burden from every nation, make possible the steady reduction of the hideous debts of the war and the carrying of the enormous pension payments which will result from the struggle, and shall make impossible the excuse that we must tax imports in order to get money to carry on the Government. No one thing would do more to tie the nations together in bonds of friendliness than the adoption of the policy of free trade throughout the world.

As to Abraham Lincoln's immortal words, if we stop now to apply them to the map of the world, what miracles take place! From the ardent, never-surrendering Poles drops the shameful yoke of Prussian and Russian intolerance, and the once unconquerable Persians will fling off the bondage of Russia and England. Egypt may hope to govern herself once more. In Finland, in Russia, in the Near East, new nations will arise. Tripoli will send back across the Mediterranean those Italian troops whose conquest of her soil a few years ago is the blackest chapter in modern land-grabbing. In Palestine, in Arabia, nations already arising will stand alone. The German colonies will be purged of unworthy masters. To enumerate all the changes is staggering: it is all overwhelming in its possibilities, breath-taking in its magnitude—too great, most people will say too nearly the millennium, too radical, to be possible even at the price of eight millions of lives. Perhaps yes, but who can tell? Who would have thought that Russian revolutionist refugees would not only be dictating the fate of Russia to-day, but insisting to Germany that she state proper terms? With so extraordinary a fact as this confronting us who have seen things in three years that men would have been locked up as insane for predicting, can we sketch out events that are too vast, or formulate a programme that is really beyond the range of possibility?

As for my fourth principle, the establishment of international government, by the creation of a parliament of nations and a judicial tribunal of nations, to say nothing of a league of nations, the time has surely passed for either elucidating the proposal or advancing arguments in its behalf. Discussion to-day deals with those who shall be included in its membership, how great the police forces it will require, etc., etc. By this time it must be plain that these four principles merge themselves into one: we must establish, as the Pope has put it, "the fundamental point . . . that the material force of arms shall give way to the moral force of right," which means simply that right and justice and not might shall hereafter govern this world. How far it will be justifiable to maintain troops to enforce the decrees of the league of nations, each person must decide for himself.

Much will, of course, depend upon the spirit of those who have to make the new peace and to reconstruct the world. A peace signed in bitterness and hate and continued in that spirit will be of dubious duration. We ought to forgive our public enemies as readily as we forgive the individual who commits a crime against us, but there is an ethical duty for public opinion to exact proof of German recognition of wrongdoing and of sincerity of conversion before the sinner shall be received as one entirely cleansed of crime. The outraged public opinion of the world may certainly be counted upon to take care of this; its attitude and that of the peacemakers ought not to be that of men seeking to punish the greatest crimes in history by robbery or by the exaction of impossible penalties, but rather of the judges of modern penology, who desire to impose only that penalty which shall most speedily restore the criminal to society as a useful, safe, and worthy member. Are there four better proposals to accomplish a lasting peace than those enumerated above?

Socialism After the War

THAT the great conflict will leave the world a Socialistic world is admitted even by Socialists. This is not epigram, but matter-of-fact. Two years ago Socialists all over the world were holding funeral orations and post-mortems over the corpse of the Internationale. The demise was supposed to have occurred in the first week of August, 1914, which witnessed millions of Socialists in arms marching towards mutual slaughter, in spite of the international fraternity of labor, in spite of solemn discussions of the general strike as an automatic check upon war, in spite of the ancient slogan about the workers without a country and with no true cause but the class war. What more logical than the tragic inference that Socialism was dead because the war had uncovered its pretensions? What more justifiable than the prophecy that the betrayed and disillusioned masses would turn upon Socialism and rend it? Only it happened that the wailers over the bier erred just as much in being too logical with Socialism dead as they had been too vigorously logical in prophesying for Socialism alive. Were the mass of humanity really actuated by the laws of the syllogism, the Socialist Internationale should indeed have died. But the people of Russia were not logical when they rose to Socialism under the misery of three years of war; and the German masses have refused to be logical when they make the Socialist party the organ of their bitter discontent; and in Great Britain and in France and in this country people have chosen to forget how thoroughly Socialism "died" in August, 1914.

But if Russia, by a single miraculous gesture, has brought to life the Lazarus of revolutionary Socialism, there has been growing up, through the impulse of war, another, a milder, constructive Socialism. It is the Socialism of exalted state authority, of Government ownership and control, of taxation that before the war would have been regarded as confiscation. By its demand for unparalleled efforts and unparalleled sacrifices, the war has become altogether too big a task for the genius or will power of a man, or even a class. It has become a war of nations in the sense that it has mobilized virtually every man, woman, and child, but even more in the sense that it has mobilized not so much the nations' capacity for effort as their capacity for sacrifice. Thus something more than expediency will explain the astonishing equanimity with which people in this country not only accept the Government management of railways for the duration of the war, but speak of the state ownership of railways, mines, and public utilities after the war. An unformulated sense of justice enters into this state of mind. On the one hand, our present system of individual effort has proved unequal to the task imposed by the war. On the other hand, the masses have not only proved themselves equal to the task, but have met the emergency less through efficiency than through sacrifice. They have established a moral claim, as well as a practical argument, for what in general terms we call Socialism.

It behooves us to recall that once before prophecy based upon logic has failed in the case of Socialism. In the winter of 1914 Socialism, logically, was dead. In the winter of 1917-18 Socialism, logically, seems destined to carry everything before it. Aside from the peril involved in sweeping prophecy of any kind, doubts arise when we see the future of Socialism assumed so easily without any attempt at defining the kind of Socialism we mean. "Socialism" to-day means Government ownership of railways in the United States and the progress of Bolshevikism in Russia. But do people stop to compare the Socialism of Government ownership with the Socialism of Lenine and Trotzky? When we speak complacently of the breakdown of individualism and the advent of coöperation, do we compare the centralized coöperation of state ownership with the decentralized coöperation of the Russian communists?

Lenine and Trotzky are parcelling out the Russian territory and sacrificing national efficiency to local and individual liberty. The fact is that what we are now beginning to call Socialism, namely, the exaltation of the state, has long been denounced by radical Socialists as "State Capitalism." Not all the Government ownership in the world, according to this view, would be Socialism if government remained in the hands of the few. Hence the demand for the democratization of government, for the establishment of opportunities that should give the sons of the coal-digger and the mine-owner an equal chance to rise to the place of Director-General of Railways under Government ownership. But to Lenine and Trotzky even this "democratization" of Government is no guarantee. Wherever there is enormous concentration of power, whether in capitalistic ownership or Government ownership, the few will succeed in exploiting the many. The remedy is in the decentralization of power. Just as the Bolsheviki have found it necessary to shatter the discipline of the army in order to prevent the rise of a Napoleon, so they envisage the necessity of decentralizing the entire social and economic scheme to safeguard the interests of the common man. Between this Socialism and the Socialism to which we are reconciling ourselves in this country there is a fairly important distinction.

Progress Towards Free Trade

NOTHING is more important for future peace than development of free trade among nations. Happily, the prospects of trade liberalism have greatly improved during the year just past, and President Wilson signalized the coming of the new year with a courageous call for "the removal, as far as possible, of all economic barriers and the establishment of an equality of trade conditions among all the nations consenting to the peace and associating themselves for its maintenance." No wonder that our protectionists are startled. "What else can it mean," asks Senator Smoot, "than an elimination of all tariffs?" What indeed? As Senator Curtis truly remarked, "If the President had talked about the removal of political barriers or diplomatic discriminations, that would have been a different thing." Are the sentinels on the watch-towers of trade privilege justified in taking alarm?

A year ago the outlook for free trade seemed dark indeed. With Germany's Middle European scheme before their eyes, the Allies in the Paris resolutions of June, 1916, had pledged themselves after the war to refuse the Central Powers most-favored-nation treatment, to decline to sell them raw materials, to boycott their goods, and to prohibit their subjects from doing business in Allied countries. The Teutonic and the Allied scheme between them threatened to divide the world into two mutually hostile economic groups. Nor was this all. Rampant nationalism and imperialism, inflamed by war passions and reinforced by war's imperious financial demands, were threatening free trade in its one existing stronghold, Great Britain. The British protectionist movement, dead in 1914, had been called back to life; its leaders were looking confidently to protection and preference after the war. Indeed, the associated chambers of commerce of the United Kingdom had gone so far as to call for a tariff with four schedules of rates, rising progressively against the colonies, the Allies, the neutrals, and the enemy countries. Within the Government itself, Mr. Bonar Law, as Secretary for the Colonies, had put the Paris resolutions into effect on his own account by proclaiming, for a period of five years after the war, without the formality of Parliamentary sanction, an export tax on certain palm products sent out from the colonies, thus taking the first step in cutting off German materials.

During the past year the United States and the radical European labor movement have suddenly changed the whole aspect of things. The United States, for half a century the home of Bourbon protectionism, has now by the President's action been made the champion of trade liberalism. First, President Wilson expressed the universal Allied abhorrence of a militarist, economically exclusive *Mitteleuropa.* Then, in his reply to the Pope he served the Allied statesmen well by putting an effective quietus likewise on their pernicious Paris resolutions: "The establishment of selfish and exclusive economic leagues we deem inexpedient and in the end worse than futile." He has now gone beyond the reply to the Pope; for he not only opposes the creation of new barriers, but actually calls for the removal of existing ones. Seeking to draw the Central Powers after the war within the all-embracing net of mutual economic relationships, he throws out a clear hint of free trade as a foundation of the league of nations, and an implied economic threat against any outlaw state that does not consent to play its part in that league.

The wise statesmanship of the President has not hesitated to associate itself in this particular with the rising radical forces of Europe, just as he has joined with the Bolsheviki in the matter of general peace principles; for the British Labor party has now spoken out unequivocally for free trade and the open door, and for no discrimination against now hostile countries, as essential elements in a genuine peace. Evidently any fight for protection in Great Britain will thus have to be waged against a labor party united to defend the traditional policy. Join the radical labor element to the old Liberal free-trade group, and, now that the Paris resolutions are practically annulled, you have an excellent prospect for the maintenance of Britain's historic practice in matters of trade. Radical democracy everywhere is inclined to favor trade liberalism; and radical democracy is now reinforced by a widespread realization not only of the inequity of protective tariffs, but of their influence in breeding national animosities and so making for war. The peoples, as opposed to their rulers, are going to have little further patience with the things that make for war.

Again the President has chosen his alliances wisely.

In the United States there is as yet no radical or revolutionary force comparable with that which is staring every statesman in Europe in the face. Our trade liberalism comes from a different source. After a half-century of unbending protection, the United States in 1913 yielded to the desire of its manufacturers for foreign markets and took a long step towards freer trade. The war has aroused an intense spirit of nationalism here as everywhere in the world, yet our country has seen no real recrudescence of the protectionist propaganda. Meanwhile our export trade to South America and the East grows steadily, and out of our vast European war trade a permanent residuum is bound to be left. This very development of our export business is constantly increasing the influence of those business interests that desire trade freedom and not trade restriction. Purely commercial interests are beginning to dictate a liberal policy in the United States.

With the two great English-speaking democracies standing for trade freedom, and with the radical forces of the world coming to their support, the advocates of that policy, so essential to the peace and prosperity of the world, may well take courage. Hard battles are ahead. Doubtless the peace settlement can take little more than the first steps towards a league of nations with its twin requirements of disarmament and free trade. The protectionists will lose no chance to utilize existing hatred and suspicion for the further fencing of their preserves. It will be no easy task defeating them. Yet future generations may count it not the least of Woodrow Wilson's services that in a dark hour he recalled a mad world to sane ideas of trade relations, and dared in proclaiming those ideas to ally himself with the radical forces that are threatening the world with a new and strange epoch. What nineteenth-century middle-class liberalism failed to accomplish for the world at large, twentieth-century labor radicalism may yet bring about.

The Issue at Brest-Litovsk

INTIMATIONS have not been wanting that something besides gain or loss of territory has brought about the *impasse* between the Central Powers and the Bolsheviki. The Kaiser's insistence on the continued military occupation of Courland and the Lithuanian lands has been explained as not entirely arising from the intent to annex. These lands may conceivably be granted their political freedom. But what Germany is resolved upon is that these lands shall not be Bolshevikized economically. The proletarian revolution, with its appropriation of land and industrial capital, with its levelling of classes, with its ideal, according to Lenine's phrase, of the common peasant and workman giving orders and the former masters obeying, must not be allowed to flood into the new buffer states between an orderly Germany and a Russia headed for decades of turmoil. The Kaiser needs a great quarantine belt between himself and the Bolsheviki. As for the latter, their claims with regard to the disputed lands are obviously not claims of annexation. Courland and her neighbors are to be independent. But Trotzky, too, has his tactical programme. It is the reverse of the Kaiser's. He is determined that independent Courland and Lithuania shall be independent in the image of Russia. This is an end in itself, and a stepping-stone towards the conquest of all Europe for the Social Revolution. This is the mission to which the newly organized Red Army is dedicated. It is destined, not for the conquest of territory, but for the propagation of a faith.

Both sides at Brest-Litovsk have, therefore, recognized the principle of self-determination, and both sides have a string attached. On the German side there is reason to fear that the string is a good-sized cable which may at any moment be used to yank the newly emancipated lands into the arms of the Kaiser. On the Bolshevik side the cord is the less material one of historic affiliation, recent comradeship in the struggle against Czarism, and a community of economic interests, for even in the new Bolshevik system there must be some kind of economics or other. Sincerely enough the Bolsheviki, and for that matter their predecessors, the moderate Socialists of Kerensky, said to Poland, Finland, Ukraine, Courland, Lithuania, the Lettish lands, "Go in peace, free and independent sisters." But quite as strong was the expectation that these emancipated sisters would use their freedom of choice to remain around the old family hearth. And there can be little doubt that in the absence of outside compulsion all of the enfranchised lands, with the possible exception of Poland, would so remain. But precisely because the danger of such compulsion threatens from the side of Germany, the need has arisen for something like counter-compulsion from the side of the Bolsheviki. This is part of the meaning of the present internal struggle within Finland and within Ukrainia. If the bourgeois win in Finland, that country may gravitate towards Scandinavia. If the bourgeois win in Ukrainia, that country may swing into an Austro-Polish orbit. It is, therefore, as Russians as well as proletarians that the Leninites are waging a war of the Reds against the Whites in these border lands on the western edge of Russia.

Can it be that just a touch of the imperialist fever stirs even the blood in Bolshevik veins? Can it be that for all their professions of internationalism they cannot rid themselves of the ideal of Russia, different as possible from the Russia of the Czars, but still as big as might be? We need not assert this in order to believe that something of the forces which have moulded Russian history through the centuries still maintain their thrust. The Bolsheviki have definitely abandoned the age-long dream of Constantinople. They may not feel that thirst for the warm seas which drew on a "capitalistic" Russia eager for foreign markets. But an outlet upon the seas the Russia of the Bolsheviki must have if their federation of autonomous communes is not to sink back into the seclusion from which Peter the Great wrested the country. Even a Bolshevik Russia will have grain and flax and timber to sell, and will need ports to send them from. Yet what are the possibilities? Russia will have gone into the war to get a Mediterranean port and may emerge with no harbors at all, save frozen Archangel and distant Vladivostok. Finland takes Helsingfors, and may shut up Petrograd. An independent Courland takes away Riga. An independent Ukraine has claimed Odessa. All the windows looking out on western Europe may conceivably be walled up.

This factor, consciously or otherwise, must be present in the mind of Trotzky and his associates at Brest-Litovsk. There would be no occasion for worry if their ideal of a revolutionized and federated Europe could be guaranteed, a Europe with virtually no national boundaries, no customs frontiers, certainly no port restrictions. But Trotzky, in more candid moments, has admitted that the revolution in western Europe, with its powerfully intrenched bourgeois elements, is far from a certainty. He must face, therefore, the peril of a capitalistic Central Europe in direct or indirect control of Riga and Odessa. He must be content with the promise of trade concessions and freedom of the ports from a capitalistic Government. That is to say, he must be willing to leave Russia at the mercy of whatever commercial policies the future Germany and Austria may see fit to apply. The Bolsheviki cannot help thinking, too, of the internal problems which await them. Sooner or later the forces of reaction will assert themselves. We have the precedent of all history for that. The Russian people, in their moments of trial and despondency, will be asked to think upon what the Bolsheviki have done with a great heritage, with a nation which they found pressing forward steadily to the community of the open seas, and which they left crippled and isolated. It is for these reasons that the Bolsheviki cannot permit Germany to "determine" a barrier of new states between Russia and the rest of the world. The "self-determination" which the Bolsheviki have in mind for the disputed Russian lands is like the compromise established in the ancient debate between Free Will and Determinism. The border lands are to have freedom of choice, but it is to be exercised within a sphere determined by Russia's necessities as well as their own.

Russia and Democracy

RUSSIAN signatures have been attached to a treaty of peace at Brest-Litovsk, and the Allies confront a situation which calls for the highest wisdom, caution, and resolution. Not that we need special insight to understand the German purpose. This is now as plain as day. The disappearance of Russia as a military power is to be followed by the crushing of the Revolution. The Revolution is to be encompassed on all sides by fortresses of reaction garrisoned by German influence. German militarism has flung a challenge to the moral sentiment of the world.

With the military balance of power gone, there remains for the democratic nations, nay, there emerges more strongly than ever, the need of maintaining the moral balance against Germany, the balance of democracy against German militarist autocracy. Russia must be saved for the community of free nations. The healthy fruits of the Russian Revolution must be saved, not only for the sake of the great Slav people itself, but for the sake of the world. In combating the downfall of Russian liberty we should be fighting for ourselves. For just as truly as the destruction of Czarism sent a vivifying thrill through the free peoples of the world, the failure of the Russian experiment will spell reaction everywhere. The vista of a world democratically ruled, freed from the incubus of secret diplomacy, based on the self-determination of peoples, and granting a full measure of justice to the working masses, will disappear if the Russian Revolution disappears. The advocates of militarism in every free country will be justified in their words and works. It is for the Western democracies to say whether the vision of last March shall pass into history as only a nightmare.

In this sense, peace at the "expense" of Russia would be a monstrous thing. Lenine may argue that the surrender of Russian territories to German influence is not fatal; and that the problem is to "preserve as far as possible the revolution in Russia itself" until such a time as the war-weary nations shall join Russia in revolt. But the revolution in a dismembered Russia cannot live. It will have to face ultimately a reaction of national sentiment based on bitter resentment at the havoc wrought by the Revolution. It will be unable to carry out its programme in the isolation to which it has condemned itself. A barrier running from Finland on the Arctic to Rumania on the Black Sea will sever revolutionary Russia from the communion of the western world. Economic ruin confronts a country cut off from its principal ports—from Riga, Odessa, Helsingfors. But more than that, the Revolution in this truncated Russia must face the active enmity of the German power. The Kaiser has accepted the challenge of the Bolsheviki. They set out to infect the world with their ideas. Germany has set out to infect the Slavic world with its own ideas of "order." In that chain of border states which were formerly Russia, the Kaiser will have built up an active quarantine against the Russian Revolution. From Finland, Courland, Lithuania, Poland, the Ukraine, and Rumania the forces of reaction will play upon what remains of revolutionary Russia.

The German Government has set out to stifle the Russian Revolution for its own external interests and internal equanimity. The Allies must preserve the Russian Revolution for their own internal health and for the ideal of a community of free nations in which alone rests the hope of escape from such another agony as the world is now passing through. The mistakes of last year must not be repeated by the Allies. We must cut ourselves free from appraising the value of Russia to the world in terms only of her army.

The problem of the Allied governments and peoples is to seek for the elements of regeneration within revolutionary Russia. There is danger in looking towards Cossack or Japanese armies for the restoration of Russia to the western fellowship. Such methods at once raise in the hearts of the Russian people that dread of reaction which is still, and naturally, their most poignant fear. We must win back Russia by safeguarding her Revolution. We must search for those men and parties in Russia whose fealty to the Revolution can never be questioned, but who nevertheless stand for the unity of the Russian lands and against the German ideal of "order." For the time being they are submerged under the Bolshevik tide; but they exist. They are the men who, like Kerensky, envisaged the Revolution as working itself out in a Russia of federated republics, with every safeguard for national and cultural autonomy and self-determination, short of secession from the Slav brotherhood. They are the men and women of the Constituent Assembly, embracing the vast majority of the pioneers and martyrs of the long struggle for Russian freedom. To them the Allies should turn, with a pledge of their own national honor that the crusade is essentially one for the preservation of a free and democratic Russia.

The Press and the International Situation*

By OSWALD GARRISON VILLARD

TO-DAY international problems and duties overwhelm us. Abandoning for weal or woe our historic policy of concerning ourselves chiefly with the affairs of our own continent, we have plunged with high motives and altruistic zeal into international relationships and enmities which cannot but profoundly affect the life of the nation for all time. Domestic issues are completely overshadowed for the moment, or disappear altogether. Upon all leaders of public opinion is thrust the necessity of thinking internationally in terms to which Americans are almost wholly unaccustomed. How shall we meet these strange, far-reaching issues that imperiously compel our attention? More particularly, how are we of the American press dealing with them? We find ourselves literally overwhelmed by the volume of news that pours in upon us, to say nothing of the grave responsibilities of interpreting its foreign aspects. In the overwhelming magnitude of what is going on, editors seem able only to glimpse the striking and startling. Even then, few of the profession are rising to the duties of the day. The hours are too full of the making of history to allow time for constructive policy or suggestion. If we do find an editor who emerges from the hurly-burly to raise doubts, search after truths, and question policy out of wisdom and experience, we are likely to suspect him of being in sympathy with the enemy. The refusal of a large portion of the sober press to analyze events and public utterances in the light of past national policies and human experience, constitutes an alarming phenomenon. For the press to abdicate its function of guiding the formation of public judgment upon the basis of principles and facts is to serve the public ill. In war time a popular theory is that there must be complete abatement of independent thinking on the part of editors. Should independence lead them to differ in the slightest degree from opinions that have governmental sanction, a divided front might be presented to the enemy.

After a while, however, as the war has shown in every country, notably in England, this theory breaks down. There are speedily sharp differences of opinion as to administrative or military methods, and suddenly, by the act of a labor leader, or a beyond-the-seas aristocrat, or perhaps even of a United States Senator, there is a sudden loosening of pens and tongues, and lo, it is no longer treasonable to differ with authority. Plainly, therefore, history is against the theory that the press in war times shall either be speechless on foreign affairs, or merely the mouthpiece of the ruling powers. A press that is fully subservient to Secretaries of State or to Foreign Offices becomes, even in times of peace, a menace to its own country and often to the world—something to be scorned even by those who purchase it for their ends. A press that invariably approves every governmental act, quickly enough loses the public regard—as soon as the public realizes that it has abandoned the functions of a critic. Fortunately, we Americans have never witnessed any such governmental purchasing of the venal newspapers as has too often been the rule in Europe—of which the classic and horrible example is Bismarck using the "reptile press" at home for his frequently base aims and suborning journalists abroad by German gold.

On the other side, it is impossible to deny that the press, both in peace and in war, may have an unfavorable effect upon diplomatists and statesmen. For we have seen a yellow press in this country involve us in one war, and a metropolitan press throwing its entire power towards getting us into the present struggle; we have seen the London *Times* deliberately goad England into a wicked war upon the Boers. We see to-day an English newspaper potentate of unrivalled power making and unmaking Ministers and even dictating national policy. We behold his American counterpart deliberately seeking to embroil us in war with Mexicans and Japanese. Indeed, too often editors embarrass well-meaning diplomatists by frightening statesmen who are carrying on delicate negotiations into "taking extreme positions and putting forward impossible things, or in perverting history and law to help their case." It was Mr. Edwin L. Godkin's opinion that the press had influenced diplomatists disadvantageously in all except a few of the many cases he had observed during his long career. "Unhappily," he felt, "in times of international trouble the easiest way" for the newspapers to impress their readers always seemed to be "to influence the public mind against the foreigner." In 1895, after he had manfully stood up for reason and sanity in dealing with England in the matter of the Venezuelan boundary, he wrote that "until we get a race of editors who will consent to take a share of the diplomatists' responsibility for the national peace and honor, the newspapers will constitute a constant danger to the amicable relations of great Powers." Had he lived during the last five years, he would have had to admit a distinct bias towards war as the proper solution of international difficulties on the part of the bulk of the American press, and he would have been appalled at its positive ferocity towards those who maintain, even in war time, that there are nobler and higher ideals than the imposition of national policy by brute force.

What adds to the anxiety of those Americans who are aware of the waning of journalistic authority in this country is the widespread feeling that there are still other criticisms to be made of its conduct than those I have touched upon. No honest journalist can deny that our newspapers have steadily been losing ground on the score of accuracy, responsibility, and willingness to present all sides of the case in other matters than foreign affairs. It is widely alleged in every reform camp in the land that the press has become a class press-organization in place of a national journalism. The complaint is not new; only more intense as our underlying unhappiness as a people has increased of late. Thus, one finds many Americans to-day who feel that Mr. Gladstone's unanswerable indictment in 1876 of the London journalism of that day apropos of an international incident would apply to our own American journalism of 1918:

> There is an undoubted and smart rally on behalf of Turkey in the metropolitan press. It is, in the main, representative of the ideas and opinions of what are called the upper ten thousand. From this body there has never, on any occasion within my memory, proceeded the impulse that has prompted and finally achieved any of the great measures which, in the last half-century, have contributed so much to the fame and happiness of England. They did not emancipate the Dissenters,

*From an address delivered at the University o California, March 20, 1918.

Roman Catholics, and Jews. They did not reform the Parliament. They did not liberate the negro slave. They did not abolish the Corn Laws. They did not take the taxes off the press. They did not abolish the Irish Established Church. They did not cheer on the work of Italian Freedom and Reconstitution. Yet all these things have been done, and done by other agencies than theirs, and despite their opposition. . . Unhappily, the country is understood abroad mainly through the metropolitan press.*

The parallel is interesting, even alarming, for if public faith is further weakened in journalism as it has been shaken in the old-fashioned diplomacy and statesmanship now so utterly discredited, we shall surely be open to the danger of conquest by demagogues, by the vile spirit of foreign militarism, or by unintelligent revolutionists of the most radical stripe. In a world in chaos, it is essential that there should be something to tie to, something to which men may hold fast—even the power of the church has been waning under the stress of a world war. There must be some basis of accurate knowledge by which men may test events and shape the course of the nation. Our forefathers deemed the newspapers the chief bulwark of our liberties, and attempted to safeguard the rights of the press by a constitutional provision lately much honored in the breach. In order that the newspapers may exercise the corrective and critical influence which those wise statesmen considered essential, the gathering and presentation of news must be absolutely independent of politicians, officeholders, and censorships.

As an instance of the way the press takes everything for granted in foreign affairs, let us consider our recent adventure in Haiti and Santo Domingo. In those countries we have pulled down Governments, have refused to pay interest on a national debt, have closed up one Congress and placed absolutely autocratic military governments in charge, in direct opposition to the wishes of those people. I do not inquire here as to the justice, the morality, or the consistency of these acts. I only point out that, so far as I could discover, there were not more than five journals in this country which took the trouble to examine into the facts, or the reasons for the Government's action, or that sought for independent knowledge as to what led up to this development. There was the usual chorus of absolute approval. America could do no wrong; why inquire? That is a happy state of mind and a convenient one, in case this Caribbean policy should be reversed two years hence, when there would be the same chorus of journalistic approval. If the desideratum is a watchful, well-informed, intelligent, and independent press, bent upon preserving the liberties of ourselves and our neighbors, then truly are our newspapers sorely lacking.

The question before us is how to bring about moral responsibility in the moulders of our public opinion, and how to keep them free from governmental domination—nothing more and nothing less. Party journalism has long since outlived its usefulness in America; newspapers everywhere have learned that political independence in domestic affairs pays—not only in influence and public respect, but in dollars and cents as well. Yet, in 1884, nothing could have been more visionary than the belief that, within thirty years, the bulk of our newspapers would be free from party bondage. I can think of no higher duty for the profession to which I am giving my life, as my immediate forebears gave theirs—I celebrate in October the one hundredth year of consecutive journalistic service in America by the family to which I belong—than that it shall dedicate itself to the ideals towards which President Wilson now leads the world. There is the surest way for journalism to recover its lost prestige, to clear itself of the charge that it is a class press, that it is a commercial press, that it likes war for war's sake, that it lags behind in every reform. There is nothing in all the world so worth while as to search out some vital principle to which one can devote oneself heart and soul, through good repute and bad repute, through good times and evil times. It is the same for a profession as for an individual. In that exquisite introduction to his recently published "Recollections," Lord Morley writes: "The oracle of to-day drops from his tripod on the morrow. In common lines of human thought and act, as in the business of the elements, winds shift, tides ebb and flow, the boat swings, only let the anchor hold."

*Morley's *Gladstone*, Vol. II, p. 557.

The Peace Issue

. . . the German sword will win us peace. . . . The coming world peace will then, through the German sword, be more assured than hitherto, so help us God.—[Emperor William.

Our next duty is to introduce the policy of permanent preparedness. . . . After the war is over all these foolish pacifist creatures will again raise their piping voices against preparedness and in favor of devices for maintaining peace without effort. . . . It is a hundred times more important for us to prepare our strength for our own defence than to enter into any of these peace treaties.—[Theodore Roosevelt.

We are not going to give in—not until we have established the world on the new basis. Under the new basis let us have no more standing armies. . . . As long as you have militarism, as long as you have standing armies and these powers, poor suffering mankind will never see that development.—[Gen. Smuts.

THESE three statements, all laid before the American people within a period of forty-eight hours, present clearly the major issue that is to be determined at the end of this war—is there or is there not to be a new order? It is with no desire to score points, or to indicate disagreement at a time when unity is imperative, that we call attention to the agreement between the American ex-President and the German Kaiser, as against the South African warrior-statesmen, that peace in future must rest on the sword. The German sword would impose an unrighteous peace on an unwilling world; the American sword, needless to say, wielded by Mr. Roosevelt, would maintain solely a peace of righteousness—but both alike would rest on unconquerable force.

As opposed to these two champions of naked might we hear the piping voice of the foolish pacifist creature from South Africa, the creature that did not hesitate a decade and a half ago to draw the sword against the mightiest empire of the modern world, in behalf of what he believed to be the right, and who triumphed in defeat, who again drew the sword with the outbreak of the present struggle, and who now challenges his fellow-citizens of the British Commonwealth to stand fast till victory comes—to what end? That the British Empire may have the military power to make its righteous will effective throughout the world? That universal military service throughout the British dominions may make the Empire safe from attack? It is not thus that this warrior speaks. His talk is of moral principles, of adjustments based on self-government and freedom, of the abolition, not the reduction, of standing armies.

Trained in the school of war, of politics, and of diplomacy, this statesman yet believes in the possibility of a real peace, based on justice and fairness and mutual consideration among states. He may be wrong, but at least his career is not that of an impractical visionary. And if he is wrong then, no matter what else happens, Germany will have won this war, for she will have led the world to accede to armed might as the ultimate arbiter in the affairs of states.

After the agony of the years just past, the American people and all the peoples, we believe, if ever they clearly understand this issue, will not accept defeat; for the unsophisticated man is ready to believe with General Smuts that we see to-day "the agonies of a dying world," a world of force and violence that with increasing definiteness the peoples have willed to have no more—and woe to the statesman who stands in their way or fails to guide them to their goal. Two leaders, President Wilson and General Smuts, have seen the issue clearly and have reiterated over and over one idea—that the important thing is not to pile up military preparations to prevent the next war, but to strive with all our might to secure conditions of peace and world organization to make future wars impossible. President Wilson has used the resounding words justice, freedom, and self-government, but instead of making them a mere cover and front for the emotional state induced by a national crisis, he has striven, with growing definiteness and success, to give actual content to those words, to point out the application of those principles, as we see them, to concrete territorial and racial problems. And always he has kept in the forefront the question of world organization.

The President's diplomacy has not been working in isolation for a new world order. The Russian revolution, for all the disastrous accompanying military collapse and internal disorder, has yet removed from the world a militarist autocracy that was a constant threat to peace. British labor has set its face like flint against a British imperialistic peace and in favor of a real peace—organization, disarmament, and all. The world over, outside the Central Powers, the democratic forces appear on the whole to have been growing more definite in ideas and better organized in action for a real peace. Can we snatch it out of the welter?

President Wilson and General Smuts both believe in the possibility of a permanent, guaranteed peace. Both hold such a peace the only gain for which the democratic peoples can hope. Both realize that it is to be attained, if at all, only by a skilful composition of the mighty forces loosed by this earth-shaking war, a composition guided by understanding, faith, and vision. Against them are arrayed not only the terrific military forces of the German Empire, but the mighty moral and intellectual powers of imperialism and stupidity in the Allied countries. The German military caste have made abundantly clear to all of us the menace of Prussian militarism. But as Mr. Roosevelt's address makes clear, many of us have not the imagination or the faith to see any actual alternative to Prussian militarism after the war except an American militarism, a British militarism, an Allied militarism too mighty for its Prussian rival. They agree with the Kaiser that "when mankind changes these things also will change, but first mankind must begin to change."

That is the issue that we face. A whole-hearted faith in the vision of the American President and the South African Premier, and such a faith alone, we believe, can make us strong enough to win this war; for, as General Smuts has said, in words that we do well to recall with Germany thundering at the western gates: "This is not a war of armies; this is not a military war. In the end this war will be decided on the moral forces set going in this war, which are far stronger than any army, artillery, or munitions of war."

Has Germany Lost Her Reason?

PRESIDENT WILSON'S speech at Baltimore on Saturday had much to say of force. But there was in it also an appeal to reason—the reason of the German people, if they have not entirely abdicated it. The Kaiser's vainglorious threat to impose by the sword such a peace as he desires upon his enemies, the President meets with proud defiance. If it is the German contention that force and force alone must decide everything, the Allies, this country with its resources in men and money as yet scarcely tapped, will answer with a force greater than Germany can array. The official German press declares that the blows dealt by Hindenburg and Ludendorff are intended to make the French and English and Americans "submissive," so that they will accept the kind of peace which Germany will be gracious enough to offer them. To this there is but one reply possible, and President Wilson made it with high spirit. The free people of the United States will never submit or yield to brute force or a peace reeking with injustice.

Spokesman of this settled determination of his fellow-countrymen, Mr. Wilson also represents them in his reiteration of the nature of the peace which this country seeks, and with which alone it will be satisfied. Americans have nothing to gain from the war except their own security and a new world-order, in which weak nations will be established in their rights as firmly as the strong. A peace based on this principle has repeatedly been urged by the President upon the Central Powers. To it their statesmen have paid lip-service, but their military commanders have overridden or silenced the civilians, for the time being, and have shown what kind of peace by tyrannical oppression they really aim at. Their dominating and exploiting purpose has been made so plain to all the world that even Mr. Arthur Henderson, leader of the British Labor party, and warm advocate of peace by agreement, has cried out that the "cynical" sort of peace forced on Russia by Germany is intolerable because it is not "clean." Despite all this, the President took pains to reaffirm his readiness, even now, to "discuss a fair and just and honest peace at any time that it is sincerely purposed. This is not simply an appeal to German reason. It is good tactics at the present juncture. For the military masters of Germany, calling as they are for the sacrifice of thousands more every day on the battlefield, pretend that their enemies seek to crush and dismember the Empire. On Monday morning, we had the semi-official German statement, in comment upon the President's speech, that Germany now sees that she will lose everything unless she wins the war. But all that she would really be asked to give up, according to President Wilson, would be the purpose to impose her will upon Europe and the world by force of arms. In the very act of facing the rulers of Germany and telling them that their unholy ambitions can never be attained, Mr. Wilson sufficiently indicates to them the road to a righteous peace. The question is whether there is a remnant of reasonable men in Germany who will make their voices heard when it appears that all the added bloodshed which the inexorable army chiefs are demanding will be in vain, so far as concerns making Germany unquestioned conqueror.

There have been a few signs of late that a better mind is coming to some in Germany. Highly significant is the stir made by the publication of Prince Lichnowsky's memoranda, showing that, in his opinion, the war was not forced upon Germany, but, rather, deliberately brought on by her rulers. The former Foreign Minister, von Jagow, has been writing about the Prince's disclosures, and while he disputes and challenges some of the facts and conclusions, frankly admits that he can no longer adopt "the theory now widespread among us that England was the originator of all the intrigues leading to the war." Acceptance of this point of view by the Government—and, as the *Westminster Gazette* points out, von Jagow must have had official permission to publish what he did—would obviously put a new face on the old controversy, and would powerfully influence public opinion in Germany.

Unless reason has fled from that country, we may expect soon to hear utterances that have been held in abeyance while the great German offensive promised success. They will have something to say about President Wilson's speech. They will see its two great implications. It pronounces the doom of the Pan-German scheme to master the whole world. This is impossible of realization so long as Great Britain and the United States are alive and have an atom of strength with which to resist. The arrogance, the heaven-defying pride, of the German militarists will be met and defeated. But there is yet a way out for all. It is plainly stated by President Wilson. Let everything that has been done or attempted in the war—the secret treaties of the Allies, the peace treaties of Germany with Russia and the Ukraine and Rumania, the wrongs of Belgium, the claims of France, the question of the German colonies—let all be brought to a final world-settlement in a spirit of justice and fair dealing. The door to such a plan is still left open by the President. Is there reason enough left in Germany to see what must be done and to urge it?

Will Germany Disarm?

TO most Americans these words doubtless are as sounding brass or a tinkling cymbal. Yet the last number of the *New Europe* summarizes an article by Professor Delbrück cautiously urging disarmament from the standpoint of purely German interests. International arbitration and disarmament could have no place in the calculation of the statesmen before the war, says Delbrück, yet it is now possible with certain reservations to believe "that these derided notions, hitherto entertained only by persons of no account, are to be raised to the position of the ruling principle of our time." This astonishing confession of faith comes from one of Berlin's most respected thinkers.

Delbrück assumes, of course, that the "ring of iron" was deliberately forged by Germany's present foes for the purpose of crushing her. Given that assumption, his argument proceeds thus: The Russian Czardom was a constant menace to Germany. "Autocracy can never bring domestic peace"; hence foreign adventure as a means of relief for domestic evils. But Russian autocracy gone, the Slav peril disappears, and Germany can afford to consider disarmament. France, unsuccessful in this war, can never again summon to her aid in the work of revenge a coalition as formidable as the present one; therefore she, too, will be ready for permanent peace There remains Great Britain. The U-boat in a decade will be ten times more powerful than at present. Pacifism is Great Britain's sole hope of meeting domestic and imperial difficulties alike. But the Indian Empire rests on force, and Britain must likewise settle accounts with Japan. Given a settlement that will let these two states lay down their arms, military and naval disarmament alike will be attended with little risk to Germany. Summarizing, Delbrück argues that "Germany is the only one of the Great Powers which, both in domestic solidarity and in military power, has little or no reason to seek relief in pacifism, and for that very reason she has least to fear from disarmament and arbitration."

The financial burdens of armament constituted no weighty argument for disarmament before the war, says Delbrück, but that consideration has now acquired real force. Armaments do not bring wars, he avers; rather they are the instruments of policy. Disarmament and arbitration, then, are to be favored on three grounds: first, that without them the intolerable burden of debt and taxation will bring the world to a state worse than the present war; second, that "the war will create conditions in peace which will make peace itself worth preserving and easier to preserve"; and third, that "Germany has less to fear from a simultaneous limitation of armed force by sea and land than any other nation, and consequently dare not withhold the boon from the rest of the world."

In reading Professor Delbrück's essay, we must restrain our natural impatience with his erroneous assumptions concerning the causes of the war, his natural pride in the present military situation, and his rather patronizing attitude towards the rest of us. The important question is simply whether his ideas offer us any practical help in our efforts to bring the war to a righteous close and to insure a durable peace. The militarists have Germany by the throat, and undoubtedly their grip has been in many ways strengthened by the events of the half-year since Delbrück wrote. But it so happens that their further military progress only strengthens his argument. Unless we are to assume, as a large part of our countrymen honestly do assume, that the Germans have gone clean mad, then we are obliged to argue that no matter what the blindness of the war lords, the civil authorities and the great body of the people, who furnish the cannon fodder and pay the taxes, must appreciate the force, from the purely German point of view, of the argument for disarmament. We believe, in other words, in opposition to many current notions, that Delbrück is spokesman for an important body of opinion in Germany.

Why, then, it will be asked, have the German generals hitherto been able to command the support of this body of opinion? The common answer is, because the whole German people has been corrupted by militarist and imperialist ambitions. It is well to recall Lincoln's dictum, "You cannot indict a whole people." Reading no more than the scanty items of news that the censor allows to filter through, the fair-minded student realizes that the generals retain the support of the ordinary German citizen because he firmly believes that the very existence of his country, in face of greedy and covetous foes, depends on them. The idea appears to us Americans as so contrary to the facts that we cannot understand how any rational person can believe it; yet such is the German belief.

While the guns roar on the western front, and while we hurry to the support of our allies every man for whom we can find transport, let us at the same time try to understand the mind of those against whom we fight. To find that any of the Germans are even now prepared to accept one of the great fundamentals of a lasting peace must indeed be heartening to the President, who has steadily striven to raise the conflict above the level of a conflict for territory to the plane of a struggle for justice and permanent peace.

If Germany and all the nations are willing actually to disarm at the end of the war, the rest follows almost automatically. For disarmament implies as a condition precedent that limitation of national sovereignty which is involved in any scheme of world organization. It implies the adjustment of international relations on the basis of reason and not of force. It deprives the big states of their power to lord it over the little ones, and almost of itself carries with it to all peoples the right of self-determination. It puts an end to colonial exploitation and investment competition based on comparative military and naval power.

We do not mean to suggest that disarmament mechanically brings about these results—rather that it must rest on these conditions. When Professor Delbrück seriously suggests disarmament, let us welcome this German reinforcement to our cause, and continue still, along with our military efforts, the attempt to reach the reason and conscience of the German people.

Bedfellows of War

FEW, we are sure, can read the almost daily appointment of "Big Business" men to high office under the Wilson Administration without mingled feelings. To some, it is true, the calling in of captains of industry like Charles M. Schwab, Edward R. Stettinius, and John D. Ryan is a cause for unmitigated satisfaction; in Wall Street certainly their selection gives unqualified joy. In all business circles there is doubtless relief that practical men, conversant with large affairs, have been summoned to the nation's councils, for there has been an honest feeling of unrest that affairs involving billions should be in the hands of men who, like Secretary Baker and Secretary Daniels, were without experience in large business enterprises. There has been a belief that the Administration has been needlessly amateurish in a situation of a magnitude so staggering as to be literally overwhelming. Now, from the purely technical point of view, the placing of Mr. Schwab at the head of the country's shipbuilding is admittedly one of the greatest steps taken to defeat the Germans. His extraordinary energy, ability, and resourcefulness make him in the *Nation's* eyes the man best fitted to direct the construction of ships at this hour.

Yet we cannot deny that a feeling of amusement mingles with our satisfaction—amusement at the strange turn of affairs which the whirligig of fate has brought about, for this is the same Charles M. Schwab who has been portrayed to the country as a robber baron, coining such a large fortune out of the making of armor for the navy as to render it essential last year for Congress to establish its own armor plant in West Virginia without waiting to see whether the war would bring in its train disarmament or the scrapping of battleships. For more than a year Mr. Schwab refrained from going to the city of Washington lest his presence be misconstrued as an endeavor to lobby against the Administration, which he did, however, honorably oppose by costly advertisements in the newspapers. Moreover, Mr. Schwab is on both sides of the fence, for he is constructing three-quarters of our great new fleet of destroyers, and may even as a Government official have the awarding of new contracts to his own shipyards. If politics makes strange bedfellows, what shall be said of war? Here is the Wilson Administration, which, during its first term, positively declined to have any relations with anybody tainted by Wall Street, cheek by jowl with the men it fought and denounced for so long, opposition to whom was the platform which led to its being given charge of the nation's affairs. To have suggested in 1913 that the day would come when Henry P. Davison would be a welcome visitor in the White House on any matter would have been to write oneself down a lunatic or worse, for it is an open secret that in those days no member of the firm of J. P. Morgan could obtain an appointment at the White House no matter what his business. There is a story of a partner of the firm who complained bitterly that if he was to be denied the White House as a tainted person, the Government at least ought to put him on trial and prove wherein he was an enemy to the country; at any rate, he thought, the Treasury ought not to count upon his firm for any aid in matters financial. But that is long since forgotten; the old feuds which broke out when Mr. McAdoo took office are for the moment healed by the war and the necessity for financing it. Had anybody prophesied in 1914 that Mr. Wilson would turn over national supervision of aircraft production to John D. Ryan, who typifies to all reformers in Montana the most dangerous "Big Business" control of the State in the interest of the copper kings, he would surely have been in danger of police arrest. Similarly denounced would have been the suggestion that Bernard Baruch, one of the heaviest plungers in Wall Street, would bask in the high favor of the man who indited "The New Freedom" as a clarion call to the country to rid itself of the very sort of thing which Mr. Baruch and the others named have typified. But the fact remains that the President has now changed his policy, which was at one time so extreme that he would not permit any of these men to come into his presence.

Undoubtedly this is one of the results to have been expected. In every country in this war men of nearly every type have buried the hatchet to help the Government, and it is an interesting fact that up to this time it is the conservatives and reactionaries who have forged most rapidly to the front, patriotism being always one of their specialties. The President certainly could not deny to "Big Business" men their right to share in the responsibilities of the hour. As it is, he has not yielded grudgingly, but has cheerfully and freely called upon them to come and help, and he saw, *mirabile dictu*, nothing out of the way in selecting the senior partner of a Wall Street bond house to head the new finance committee appointed by the Government to deal with private financing during the war. Surely no one can accuse him hereafter either of discriminating against a set of business men, of turning his back on experts, or of being narrow-minded and cherishing his business dislikes.

A recent writer in *Collier's Weekly*, in discussing Mr. Wilson, prophesied that after defeating those critics who rallied around Senator Chamberlain in the attack upon him and Secretary Baker, the President would then promptly go ahead and do the very things his critics wished him to do. He fortified his prophecy by many illustrations to prove that this is part of Wilson's political philosophy, and he was right in both the prophecy and the illustrations. The President has acted as the writer said he would act. He is disarming his critics by doing in his own quiet way precisely what they wished to compel him to do by legislation. One of their cardinal criticisms was that theorists were in charge of the Government, and not practical business men who had employed labor by the hundred thousand. If any one rises now to make such a charge against the leader of the nation, Mr. Wilson has evidence to the contrary in plenty for their immediate refutation. As to the effect that this change of policy will have upon both our business life and our political contests after the war, time alone will show. But if any future Woodrow Wilson arises to write another "New Freedom," the captains of industry will have a forceful answer as they point to their patriotic and valuable service in war time. As to Mr. John D. Ryan, for instance, a ready defence will hereafter be, when he is assailed as the dominating tyrant of Montana: "How can that be when the President entrusted to me the task of winning the mastery of the air for the United States?"

The President and the War

THE President is, in some respects, on trial to-day as never before. We do not mean, of course, as the leader of democracy and of liberal opinion. There he stands by himself, far beyond all others in high office. It is as the Executive officer of the nation that he is being put to the test. He is now called upon to demonstrate that he is equal to administrative problems of a magnitude never before paralleled; that as manager of the country's affairs he is capable of administering them in a national crisis which far transcends in its difficulties and ramifications anything dreamed of heretofore. Is he a sufficiently capable business head? Can he, being but a single finite individual, accepting the enormous responsibilities placed upon him by Congress at his request, conduct the business of the hour with dispatch, compelling efficiency in every department?

It is this question, we are sure, which is worrying thoughtful men and women the country over. As a spiritual leader the bulk of the people trust the President and rank him high. But can he guide the nation's destinies through the maze of business complications which constitutes the greatest of wars? To-day he is possessed of every conceivable power short of absolute dictatorship. Congress has divested itself of all its powers save one large one—the control of the purse-strings. It has even bestowed upon the Postmaster-General the ability to crush any newspaper critic of the President whose opinion is interpreted to be a stumbling-block in the prosecution of the war. How will the President make use of this vast authority, greater, we believe, than that possessed by any king or kaiser? Will he build up a national war machine controlled by the ablest possible machinists and operated with the maximum of efficiency; will he take Congress and the public into his confidence; will he let duly authorized committees know what is going on, as is in some degree the case in England, and in far greater degree in France? Or is it to be a Government within four walls, self-satisfied, self-content, impatient of critics and of inquiry?

The happenings of the past fortnight lend sharper point to these queries than they have borne heretofore. The President last week indignantly refused, as he had refused before, to permit Congress to appoint a committee which might conceive its functions to be to inquire into and supervise the conduct of the war. In consequence, the Senate modified its pending proposal to an inquiry into the progress of aircraft and ordnance production and into the Quartermaster Corps. With the President's feeling that there should be no committee to supervise the conduct of the war everybody can sympathize; if he is to exercise executive control, he must exercise it undividedly. Yet Mr. David Lawrence last week reported from Washington the growing belief that some authoritative means must be provided for sifting popular complaints on their merits. It cannot be left to executive officers to investigate themselves or their fellows.

When anything goes wrong with the conduct of a campaign in Great Britain there is appointed a Parliamentary committee to investigate; for instance, when the Maurice scandal broke out, it seemed natural to Mr. Asquith to move for a special committee of inquiry. Even the Kaiser had to yield to the entirely novel demand for a Parliamentary committee to watch the progress of the war and keep in touch with executives when the Reichstag was not in session; hence we have the Reichstag Main Committee sitting all the time as a committee on the state of the nation. There *must be a check* upon officials, and not even President Wilson should be free from the necessity of having such a committee to prevent his subordinates from forgetting efficiency and neglecting the danger of graft and of waste.

The country is unhappy in regard to the airplane situation; the *Christian Science Monitor* is one of the powerful newspapers of the country which have been voicing this uneasiness and demanding that the country be informed what has been done with the money voted for the Aircraft Board. It insists that to describe Mr. Borglum as a knave or a fool or a genius is utterly beside the point; what it wants is the facts as to expenditures. To us it seems that the whole Borglum entanglement is proof positive of the need of a standing investigating committee for purposes of inquiry. The President blundered in appointing Mr. Borglum and giving him tremendous powers, which he had to revoke. We are glad that he has now called in Mr. Charles E. Hughes to investigate his investigator and to soothe the great popular uneasiness which has arisen. But that, to our mind, is not the way to do it; it is Congress which should investigate the failure of a department. Here it is that Congress has an opportunity of vast service to the country.

Mr. Balfour on Peace

IN marked contrast to the "bitter-ender" attitude of President Lowell, Mr. Taft, and others at the meeting of the League to Enforce Peace in Philadelphia, is Mr. Balfour's statement of last week that the door is open in England to any honest peace negotiation. "If any representative of any belligerent country desires seriously to lay before us any proposals, we are ready to listen to them," declared the British Secretary for Foreign Affairs. True, this statement has been made officially before, but there is something extremely significant in its being made again just now. Hitherto, since the offensive began, all the talk has been that the word "peace" must not even be mentioned until all danger from the German offensive is over. But the British Government is above any such intractable position; hence it gave full scope to an extraordinary peace debate.

Through Mr. Balfour, the Lloyd George Government has taken the only wise and humane course possible. People here, remote from the conflict, appreciating neither what its daily toll is nor how it is endangering the whole structure of civilization, may talk bravely of not discussing peace at all, but the Allies plainly feel differently. They were ready to treat with Sixtus. They are ready now to discuss "any proposals"—in the interest, of course, of a "fair and honorable peace." These words do not suggest a peace which will dismember Germany nor humble her beyond recovery. *Neither do they mean a German peace.* As the *Nation* has repeatedly pointed out, no peace proposals will be considered as leading to a "fair and honorable peace" which do not include the complete restoration and freedom of Servia and Belgium and the evacuation of all French territory. A complete reconsideration of the Russian situation must also be insisted on. That is the *sine qua non,* and that it is understood by the Central Powers is clearly shown by the terms Prince Sixtus was prepared to offer. No German need be misled by yesterday's debate or by Mr. Balfour's utterances; the will to fight on for these essentials of a peace is unchanged. But no really human statesman could possibly refuse to listen to any serious, decent offer of peace and be just or fair to the men who are hourly dying to crush the German menace and to establish a lasting peace.

With the light that is given us by Mr. Balfour it is now possible to understand clearly the whole story of the Prince Sixtus negotiations. On March 31, 1917, he presented the Hapsburg offer to President Poincaré. Its text was given out at Paris April 11, 1918. It provided:

(1.) France: "I will support by every means, and by exerting my personal influence with my allies, France's just claims regarding Alsace-Lorraine."

(2.) Belgium: To be entirely restored, including her African possessions, and compensation for losses suffered.

(3.) Servia: To be restored in her sovereignty, with access to the Adriatic, and "wide" economic concessions in Austria-Hungary.

(4.) Russia: "Events in Russia compel me to reserve my ideas with regard to that country until a legal, definite government is established."

This offer, according to Mr. Balfour's statement of last week, was for the sole knowledge of President Poincaré and George V and their Premiers, Ribot and Lloyd George. The detailed and apparently authentic account recently given by the Paris correspondent of the *Manchester Guardian* speaks of two visits by Prince Sixtus to England and of his return to Switzerland confident in the success of his mission; a state of mind which elicited a second letter from Charles I expressing his pleasure at "the substantial agreement" between himself and the British and French Governments, and pledging his influence with Germany in favor of reasonable Entente terms; and that in case Germany proved obdurate, Austria would accept the Entente terms for herself.

Like that other peace feeler which came some time in October, 1917, from German sources to Briand, and was by him transmitted to Ribot, who rejected it as a "trap," this offer from Charles I was rejected. But whereas the second approach was brushed aside by Ribot—then Foreign Minister in the Poincaré Cabinet—without consulting the Foreign Affairs Committee of the Chamber, an action which aroused protest in the Chamber, this direct offer from Charles I. as Mr. Balfour stated, was discussed by a committee of the French Chamber and rejected. On what ground? On the ground that the Hapsburg letter made no mention of Italy, and that therefore it must be regarded as an attempt to estrange Italy from the Entente. It was discarded not as a peace offer, but as a "peace offensive."

For the future as for the past, this question of sincerity in any proffer of terms from the Central Powers must no doubt determine the attitude of the Allies. After Brest-Litovsk it is inevitable that greater caution than ever shall be exercised by the Entente. But from this it is a far jump to the conclusion that henceforth only a deaf ear should be turned to any voice from the enemy camp. Mr. Balfour's expression of a readiness to entertain serious proposals was repeated by Mr. Asquith. Coupled with the plain affirmation that an enlarged Alsace-Lorraine—which the French have been seeking—could not enter into the British war aims, and was not, in fact, the settled policy of the French Government, this does hold the door open. Germany may speak and be listened to. But Germany also knows, we repeat, the irreducible minimum for a patient hearing, not only from the Allies, but from the United States. Mr. Balfour has placed the responsibility of continuing the war more than ever squarely upon Germany.

How Not to Help Russia

A MILITARY expedition to Russia has become the topic of heated discussion in the last few weeks. The advocates of this measure see in it a way of restoring Russia to "normal" conditions and of making her a fighting force. A military expedition consisting of English, Japanese, and American soldiers, it is argued, would rally around itself the sound and sane elements of the Russian people; the Bolshevist usurpers would easily be overthrown, and the prostrate country would awaken to new vigorous life.

That such a scheme should find even a moment's consideration only shows the extent of popular ignorance in matters concerning the Russian revolution, and the popular belief in quick remedies against fundamental social evils. The advocates of an expedition imagine the Bolsheviki to be an insignificant group of hot-headed agitators who tricked the country into disaster. Remove these pernicious individuals, they argue, and the social organism of Russia would quickly recover. The question, however, presents itself as to why the "better" elements of Russia have so little succeeded in counteracting the influence of Bolshevism, why the Bolsheviki have succeeded in holding their power far longer than any of the provisional governments after the downfall of Nicholas Romanov, and why the Bolsheviki have so easily defeated the conservative Russian generals, among whom were such popular leaders as Kaledine and Kornilov.

The obvious reason is that behind the Bolsheviki are the Councils of Workingmen, Peasants, and Soldiers, known as the Soviets, and behind the Soviets are the masses of the Russian people. The Bolshevist Government has proved to be the most stable since the collapse of the monarchy because the Bolshevist programme fitted best the ideas and inclinations of the Russian masses. These ideas may be erroneous, and many a wild Bolshevist dream has turned out to be an actual calamity for Russia. This, however, does not alter the fact that the Soviets are vitally connected with the bulk of the plain Russians. The Russian peasant, the Russian factory worker, and the other elements of laboring

Russia do not believe in Milukov and do not believe in Kerensky, but they do believe in their own Soviets.

If a military expedition were now to come and start a movement to overthrow the Soviets, it would amount to declaring war against the Russian masses. However liberal the promises of the Powers behind the expedition may be, the masses will not believe them. The masses will see in the expedition an attempt to destroy their freedom. Civil war under such conditions becomes imminent. Siding with the Allied military forces we should find many of the former landlords, Cossacks, factory owners, and other conservative elements, who form a minority of the nation. Russian radicals and Socialists of an anti-Bolshevik character would hardly lend their assistance to a military expedition destined to punish Russia for the excesses of her revolution, while the Soviets would certainly call the masses to resist Allied invasion. The outcome would be deplorable in every way. Russia would be plunged into a deeper chaos of misery and destitution. The work of reconstruction now planned by the Soviet administration would become impossible. German penetration of Russia would not be stopped, and the Entente Allies would have to be charged with preventing Russian democracy from working out its own forms of life.

The advocates of military intervention in Russia overlook the fact that it is not the Soviets that have destroyed Russian transportation and the normal course of Russian industrial production; not the Soviets that have caused the wearing down of machines, tools, and implements which cannot be reproduced in Russia; not the Soviets that have ruined the financial system, the currency, and the exchange. All this was inherited by the present Government from the old régime and is, primarily, a result of the war and the backward economic condition of the country. A military dictator would not be able to provide Russian railroads with locomotives and rolling stock, Russian peasants with scythes and threshing machines, Russian industries with the equipment and instruments which they used to import from England, America, and other countries. A Government headed by Milukov or Guchkov or Grand Duke Nikolai Nikolaievitch would be no less helpless than the Government of Lenine and Trotzky; it might be even worse off, being confronted with embittered millions who would meet its decisions with contempt, scorn, and resistance.

Military intervention in Russia is the worst of all possible ways to relieve the Russian situation. Back of the plan lies the conviction that the Russian masses are hordes of savages who can be driven at will by a masterful hand. The history of the present revolution proves the fallacy of this conviction. The Russian masses lack education, culture, and habits of organization; yet they have manifested a remarkable love of freedom and a conscious tendency towards realization of industrial democracy. We must give up the idea of solving Russian problems *for* the Russian people *against* the wish of the Russian masses.

Russia and Recognition

IT is now a little more than seven months since the Russian Maximalists ousted Kerensky from power and Lenine and Trotzky took over the direction of the Russian Government. From that moment, the question of the attitude which the Allies and the United States ought to take towards the Bolshevik régime became one of grave importance. Only three possibilities, apparently, presented themselves. One was to recognize the Bolsheviki, formally or informally, gain the good will of the new Russian democracy, and insure the continuance of Russian help, imperfect as it might be, in resisting Germany and winning the war. Another was to repudiate the Lenine-Trotzky Government and intervene by force to bring about either the restoration to power of Kerensky and his followers, or the establishment of some other Government with which the United States and the Allies could coöperate. The third was to wash one's hands of the whole business and leave Russia to follow its own devices, to go over to the German side if it must, or stew in revolution if it chose.

What the Allies and the United States have done is to adopt the third of these possibilities, while at the same time threatening to adopt the second. For months now, and increasingly during the past few weeks, there has been talk of intervention. The prominence which has been given of late in the press to advocacy of such a course bears all the earmarks of a powerful, well-organized, and amply subsidized propaganda. It has been no secret from the beginning that England and France favored intervention. Japan is for it, and with a special interest from the obvious fact that the military burden, in the present plight of the Allies on the western front, would devolve principally upon the island empire. The only thing that has prevented the beginning of Japanese or Allied operations in Siberia, with European Russia as the objective, has been the opposition of President Wilson. We see no reason to believe that President Wilson's views in the matter have converted either European or Japanese statesmen, or that the financial and business interests which naturally favor a "strong policy" with Russia share his opinion. But the United States holds the whiphand in the war; without the aid of the United States the Allied cause is lost; and what the Government of the United States proposes the Governments of the Allies and Japan must accept. We may rest assured that there will be no armed intervention in Russia until the United States consents, and President Wilson thus far declines to consent.

Russia, meantime, has been left to itself. Temporarily exhausted by war, its economic life thrown into extreme disorder, its transportation system broken down, its credit jeopardized or destroyed, and its political thought stirred to violent agitation by the overthrow of the old order and revolutionary experiments with a new, it has been left to grope its way to light and safety under difficulties without parallel in history. Neither from the Allies collectively nor from any of them singly has it received any assistance worth mentioning in meeting German aggression or reëstablishing its own internal life. Beaten, robbed, and left for dead, its former friends have passed by on the other side. The political ideas for which the Bolsheviki stand have been ridiculed, misrepresented, and denounced, and the press has had to submit to the censoring of Russian news. Such turning over of a great people to divisive forces within and without, on the plea that, since armed intervention is undesirable, no other policy save that of let alone could possibly be considered, is a spectacle which every true friend of Russia, as well as every generous believer in international unity, must view with humiliation and chagrin.

The one thing that seems pretty clear in it all is that we are not "helping Russia" in any tangible way. Neither by letting Russia alone, on the one hand, nor by continuing an active discussion of intervention, on the other, is the United States, whose policy in these respects is also that of the Allies, contributing anything of great moment to the rebuilding of Russia or its restoration to a place of influence among the nations. For President Wilson's steadfast refusal to sanction forcible intervention in Russia there cannot be too high praise, but the longer continuance of a negative policy of official non-intercourse with the present Russian Government is bound to produce, in the thousands of Russia's friends in this country, a feeling of disappointment and apprehension. Russia needs help, not neglect. Mr. Wilson has clearly made known his desire to help, and with that desire the American people, we confidently believe, are in hearty accord. But are we helping Russia in any tangible and satisfactory way by merely letting it alone?

The alternative of recognition of the present Russian Government undoubtedly involves serious questions of fact as well as of policy. Yet the present diplomatic situation is anomalous—one might almost say ridiculous. At Washington, M. Bakmetiev is still referred to as the Russian Ambassador, and informally is treated as such; yet he appears to represent, if he represents anything, only the repudiated Kerensky régime. Mr. Francis, meantime, remains in Russia as American Ambassador, and from time to time appears to have some communication with the Soviet Government; but the United States declines to recognize that Government by any kind of official act. We have, in short, no diplomatic relations, of a sort to enable us to transact any political business, with the only Government actually operating in Russia, while at the same time we keep up the farce of extending a quasi-recognition to a former representative of a Russian Government which for months has been dead, and which there is small reason to believe will ever be resuscitated.

Under these circumstances, we cannot but think that the American public is entitled to know the reasons which, it must be assumed, have seemed to the Administration to dictate this policy of long-continued let alone. A careful study of newspaper reports from Russia during the past two or three months appears to indicate that the present Russian Government, in spite of the enormous difficulties of its position, is gaining in strength and solidity. Be that as it may, the facts of the Russian situation, whatever they are, ought to be known at Washington. If they are not known, no further time should be lost in getting them. And if they are known, they ought to be published, in order that the public may see and understand the reasons for a policy which apparently gives no help to Russia and brings no credit to the United States. The very fact that we have taken a firm stand against intervention makes it morally incumbent upon us to secure for Russia, in other ways, the moral and material support in the rehabilitation of its national life which the advocates of intervention loudly insist should be extended. We cannot do that by treating as an outcast among the nations the only organized Government that Russia knows. The question of recognition is not one to be decided hastily, but it is also, we think, not one to be dodged. Sooner or later it will have to be met, and the answer ought to be given in the light of all the facts of the case. The thing to be sought first of all is the welfare of Russia; then, through a rejuvenated Russia, the defeat of Germany and the peace of the world. It is hard to see that, thus far, our policy towards Russia has done much for the attainment of either of those ends.

An Informal Peace Conference

IN spite of the discordant chorus of censure and approval which has greeted the recent speeches of Dr. von Kühlmann and Count von Hertling, the speeches themselves raise once more a question which has long troubled some of the most loyal supporters of the Allied cause. Why is it that, with each side professing an earnest desire for peace, no attempt is made to get together and talk things over? With the United States and England and Germany all announcing their peace terms, why has there not been at least an informal conference to discuss the matter? Granted that some of the claims on either side are, or are thought to be, extreme or dubious, and that neither party greatly trusts the other, are the reasons conclusive against a preliminary parley? No more in diplomacy than in business, in ordinary times, is it thought necessary to defer negotiations merely because all the demands of the parties concerned do not harmonize in advance, or because one side is suspected of sharp practice while the other has not fully disclosed his hand. On the contrary, such conditions frequently suggest that negotiations had best begin at once, even if nothing more is accomplished than clearing the air and letting in the light. Why do the warring nations, in spite of their professions, hold stubbornly to a different course?

Dr. von Kühlmann, for example, in his Reichstag speech, makes the significant admission that an end of the war "can hardly be expected through purely military decisions alone." Kaiser and General Staff to the contrary notwithstanding, Germany can no longer hope to defeat the Allies in the field. Here, certainly, is a hopeful opening for diplomacy. With regard to Belgium, which he views as "one question in the entire complex," he declines to offer "a prior concession" by making a statement which would bind Germany "without in the least binding the enemy." The Allies also regard Belgium as "one question in the entire complex," and are determined that, whatever else happens, the independence of Belgium shall be restored. Because, however, the question of Belgium cannot be compromised, is no reason why a number of other questions could not be discussed. "The absolute integrity of the German Empire and its allies," declares Dr. von Kühlmann, is now, as formerly, "the necessary prerequisite condition for entering into a peace discussion or negotiations." President Wilson and Mr. Lloyd George have both stated emphatically that they do not desire the destruction of Germany or its people. With the existence of Germany as a nation not an issue, a large ground for discussion is already cleared.

The Imperial Chancellor, Count von Hertling, goes further than the Foreign Secretary, and puts the question of opening negotiations frankly up to President Wilson. On February 10, it will be remembered, Mr. Wilson enunciated four principles which, he declared, must govern in the making of peace. To those principles Count von Hertling, on February 24, gave his assent "in principle," and stated that the four points "might possibly form the basis of a general world peace." This, assuredly, was promising. Everybody knows that, in weighty matters, agreement upon principles is the usual preliminary to agreement upon details. To the assent of the Chancellor, however, Mr. Wilson has as yet vouchsafed no reply, and his silence now provokes Count von Hertling into a repudiation of a peace league of which the enemies of Germany desire to be the kernel.

This tossing back and forth of protestations and charges

has become a farce. If we say that we desire peace, declares the Chancellor, our enemies call it "weakness," "impending collapse," or "a crafty trap." If, on the other hand, we assert our determination to defend ourselves against conquest, our opponents cry "militarism." Yet Mr. Asquith declares that no peace terms that are "unambiguous" will be ignored, and Mr. Balfour assures the House of Commons that any "sincere" offer will be carefully considered. Mr. Wilson has more than once spoken in the same strain. What is needed now is that the Governments which have been voicing these lofty sentiments should translate their words into acts. We agree with Dr. von Kühlmann that "far-going advances on the road to peace can hardly any longer be expected from public statements which we shout to each other from the speaker's tribune." If the Allies and Germany really desire peace, they ought now to find a way of getting together and discussing one another's terms.

This is not, in any sense whatever, the same thing as saying that the United States and the Allies must be prepared to accept a German peace. They desire nothing of the sort, and it will be their own fault if they are trapped into accepting one. They have certain demands which they cannot waive. They demand, for example, the restoration of Belgium and Servia, the return to France of the territory which Germany has conquered and devastated, the relief of small nationalities from political oppression, and assurance that such a war as is now going on will not occur again. If Germany will not accept these indispensable conditions, then let the war go on, if need be to its bitterest end. But we do not surely know that Germany, especially now that no victory at arms can certainly be descried, would not accept these terms; while in regard to a long list of other questions with which a peace settlement must deal, neither the Allies nor the Central Powers have yet made unequivocal declarations. There is moral compulsion, as well as happy circumstance, in the fact that the larger portion of the peace programme is still matter of debate even among the Allies themselves. Nothing is to be gained by reiterating the charge that Germany is insincere, and will not keep an agreement after one has been made. The conduct of Germany in the past has afforded, unhappily, only too much warrant for the charge. Nevertheless, her peace offers have been made, and the Allies may well give her an opportunity to confirm them, or else to repudiate them before the world.

Such a conference as has been indicated might well be, in every way, informal. It should be held on neutral soil, and might even be called by neutral Governments and participated in by their representatives. There need be no agreement to be bound by anything which the conference might do, nor any elaborate preparation of arguments or array of counsel and experts. It should be purely and simply an effort to discover, by frank discussion face to face, whether at this time a peace of any sort is possible. There need be no armistice; indeed, there should not be. Let hostilities continue in full vigor while the conference sits, as proof, if proof be needed, that the hand of America and the Allies will not be stayed until a righteous peace is assured. A conference under such conditions would be, to be sure, a proffering of both the olive branch and the sword; but so long as the leaders of the nations profess their earnest desire to receive the symbol of peace, it were better that it be proffered with arms than not at all.

A Pseudo-League of Nations

IT is at least an interesting coincidence that the Reichstag speech of Dr. von Kühlmann, the Imperial Foreign Secretary, on June 24, should have been delivered just at the moment when the question of a league of nations was being actively discussed in England and France. A few days before, Viscount Grey had stirred England by the publication of a pamphlet in which the menace of militarism, and the necessity of joint action of all nations to combat it, were impressively set forth. "There is more at stake in the war than the existence of individual states or empires or the fate of a continent," he declared. "The whole of modern civilization is at stake." A league of nations, if it is to contribute to the saving of civilization and the safeguarding of future peace, must embody two principles. The idea "must be adopted with earnestness and conviction by the executive heads of states," and the Governments which unite to form it "must understand clearly that it will impose some limitations upon the national action of each and may entail some inconvenient obligations."

The first of these conditions Viscount Grey finds "actually fulfilled" in the case of President Wilson, and also, actually or potentially, in the case of the heads of all the Allied Governments. On the other hand, Germany, so long as military rule continues, will oppose the formation of a league of nations. The German people, accordingly, must be convinced that "force does not pay," that the aims and policies of her rulers "inflict intolerable and also unnecessary suffering upon her," and that only through the abandonment of "sharp swords, shining armor, and mailed fists" is the peaceful development of Germany to be assured. Until Germany realizes these truths, such a league of nations as President Wilson contemplates is impossible.

Viscount Grey's frank admission that nothing is to be hoped for from a league of nations unless Germany is a member has evoked hostile comment from the French press. What France is inclined to favor, if the expressions of leading Paris newspapers are an indication, is, apparently, a league of nations against Germany, not a league in which Germany will occupy a place. That such a union would mean, in practice, nothing less than a division of the world into two armed camps, with neutral states occupying a precarious No Man's Land between them, must be obvious. It is disappointing, therefore, to find Earl Curzon, the Government leader in the House of Lords, in a speech in the House on June 26, advocating virtually the same thing. It is true, as Earl Curzon pointed out, that the formal or informal union of the twenty nations, with about two-fifths of the population of the globe, now allied against Germany, is a hopeful nucleus for a true league of nations, and that some machinery for joint international action already exists. When, however, on the ground that the admission of Germany to a league of nations is "impossible" until she has been "compelled by force of arms to abandon her world dream," he proposes the formation of two leagues, one of the Allies and the other of their enemies, he is practically on all fours with the reactionary opinion of the Paris press. No such scheme, as Viscount Grey declares in his pamphlet, meets in the least the conditions of such a league as President Wilson urges.

Such a proposal as that of Earl Curzon plays directly into the hands of Germany. Count von Hertling, speaking in the Reichstag on June 25, twitted President Wilson for failing to reply to the Chancellor's acceptance "in principle" of Mr. Wilson's four principles of peace, enunciated in February, and declared that it was no longer necessary to discuss a league of nations of which the enemies of Germany "would be the kernel." If the opinions voiced by the Paris press, and given concrete shape by Earl Curzon, really expressed the minds of those who have been most concerned to bring about a league of nations, the sneer of Count von Hertling would have been justified.

We do not believe that any such conception of an international league will be generally accepted. There can be no objection to the Allies forming among themselves such a union as will best enable them to defeat the German armies and crush German militarism. No union of that kind, however, should be allowed to masquerade as a league of nations in any such sense as has hitherto been connoted by that term. An essential element of a true league of nations is that all nations shall be members of it. So long as a militant Germany puts civilization in peril, Germany cannot enter a world league. What is necessary is, as Viscount Grey points out, for Germany to undergo a change of heart, if President Wilson's conception of international unity is to be realized. It is one thing to discipline a member of the league for misconduct, once the league is formed. It is quite another thing to attempt to form a world union with the one great disturbing Power among the nations left out. To adopt the latter course would be to put a group of nations in battle array and call it peace. With the object-lesson of the present war writ large before our eyes, the last end of a world so organized would be worse than the first.

Universal Military Service

WE are glad to print elsewhere Rear-Admiral Goodrich's letter favoring universal military training, not only because of the standing of the writer—long a valued contributor to the *Nation*. We cannot, however, abate one jot from the historic opposition of this journal to the introduction of universal compulsory military training whatever its form or whatever the system advocated, whether it be French, Swiss, or German. To that wicked Prussian device for militarizing a nation we attribute not only the utter moral downfall of the Germany of to-day; it has been the means by which Prussia has subordinated the Bavarians and other South Germans to her will, and is responsible for the whole modern phenomenon of "nations in arms."

So profoundly do we distrust the spirit which universal military service engenders in every country in which it is tried that we should oppose it even if we believed it accomplished everything that Admiral Goodrich claims for it. But we deny that as a peace-time institution—and we are discussing it here solely on that basis—it will necessarily make good American citizens or that it will banish class hatred and racial cleavages. That has not been the experience abroad, either in Russia or in Austria-Hungary. Were it such a wonderful melting-pot, it must long since have wiped out the racial rivalries which are to-day a chief hope for the collapse of the Dual Monarchy. In Germany it has not only not democratized the nation; it has been the most anti-democratic force at work there. The rich and educated serve one year, while the poor serve two. The various regiments represent every kind of social snobbishness, differentiation of rank, and aristocratic privilege—and there have been somewhat similar conditions in France, though there conscription in peace time bears its friendliest aspect. But even in France we have had the horrifying revelations of the Dreyfus case, the narrow escape from a military *coup d'état* engineered by Boulanger, and the changing by Presidential decree of railroad workers about to strike into reserve soldiers.

Now we are quite aware that in debating this subject any one who suggests that America might be militarized by universal service is met with incredulous smiles, if not by charges of pro-Germanism. Our correspondent shares the prevailing easy American optimism. But no less a person than Mr. Walter L. Fisher, a member of Mr. Taft's Cabinet and a believer in strong military preparedness, has pointed out that the past of America offers no analogy or security on this point. Because we were without militarism when we had a regular army of only 25,000 men and 2,200 officers, there is no logical reason to assume, he points out, that we shall not be militarized when we have 50,000 or 75,000 regular officers devoting all their time to teaching the art of war and preparing for its exercise. As for the discipline such involuntary and compulsory military service is alleged to bring about, we do not care for discipline acquired by the subordination of men's minds to military drill-masters. The best mental and moral discipline is acquired in other ways, else has our entire philosophy of life and education been wrong.

We must also confess ourselves heretics in the matter of the physical benefits to be acquired, and this despite the gains in health and vigor of our soldiers at the cantonments. But have France and Italy profited enormously by their universal training; are the Germans rated as physically supermen because of their drill-masters? This war has shown very clearly that the countries without universal service are not physically behind those that have it. As to Admiral Goodrich's challenge to name anything else as a substitute, we would remind him first that the leading American teachers of physical culture are opposed to military drill, and next that the British army turned to Swedish exercises as soon as this war began as the best and quickest means of preparing Kitchener's Mob for the trenches, abandoning their own old drills. We are more than willing to see the Swedish system made compulsory for boys and girls in all our schools, and we believe that all the non-military benefits which Admiral Goodrich desires and we desire can be obtained in this way without objectionable military features.

We must, however, say frankly that we regard the agitation of this matter now as detrimental to the conduct of the war and disadvantageous to the President and Secretary Baker. Mr. Wilson has nobly declared disarmament to be one of the fourteen peace terms for which we are striving; if we come out for universal service now as a permanent policy, it will cast doubt abroad upon his and our sincerity. Lloyd George has declared the abolition of universal service to be "one of our most important war aims," and the British Minister of Education, Mr. Fisher, has definitely pledged the Government not to introduce military drill in any British public school, no matter what the outcome of the war. In this vital matter we stand squarely with the powerful National League of Teachers' Associations, which on Independence Day sent a telegram of congratulation to Secretary Baker for his stand against universal service, expressing its warm approval of his "refusing to be stampeded into the endorsement and adoption of a permanent system of universal military training"—"that monstrous evil," they call it. They rejoice that, thanks to Mr. Baker, "we are in no danger of losing the chief end of the war before the war is more than well begun," and they assure him that his course "is well understood and is silently approved by the great American people."

The Latest Peace Offensive

WE commented briefly last week upon the extraordinary speech of the German Chancellor, Count von Hertling, in the Reichstag on July 11. Taken in connection with the equally extraordinary speech of the Austro-Hungarian Foreign Minister, Baron Burian, addressed to the Austrian and Hungarian Premiers on July 16, the character and scope of the latest "peace offensive" of the Central Powers are now clear. The two speeches do not, to be sure, cover exactly the same ground. Each speaker was expressing, in form at least, the views of his own Government, and much of what was said was doubtless intended in each case for home consumption. Each, however, was also addressing the Allies and the world; but while the incidents adduced are different, the point of view from which they are considered and the general tone of the discussion are, in all essential respects, the same.

The crucial point in Count von Hertling's speech is its reference to Belgium. Germany, we are told, has no intention of keeping Belgium permanently "in any form whatever." This declaration, if it could be taken by itself, would certainly be in the highest degree encouraging. If there is any one thing to which the United States and the Allies are committed, by moral obligation as well as by their own will, it is the restoration of Belgium to independence. But the Chancellor hastens to add qualifications. Belgium, although not to be retained permanently, is nevertheless to be used as a "pawn" in the negotiation of peace. What Germany expects to get for it is, first, a guarantee of protection, and, second, an assurance of economic advantage. Not only is Belgium not to be used by the Allies "for ground on which to deploy military forces," but it must also "be made to the interest of Belgium to secure close economic relations with Germany" in order that Germany may not be "isolated." By "attaining such an intimate commercial connection," a "political agreement" would result through which Germany would "secure the best guarantees against future perils from England and France by way of Belgium." In other words, the Belgian "pawn" is to become, politically and economically, a buffer state.

Baron Burian, naturally, is not concerned over Belgium, but over Austria-Hungary. He pays a graceful tribute to President Wilson as a genius to whom nobody would refuse homage, and whose coöperation nobody would decline. With the four peace principles enunciated by Mr. Wilson in his Fourth of July address, "apart from certain exaggerations," Baron Burian is in accord. The recent peace treaties concluded with Russia and Rumania need not disturb the Allies, since "none of the belligerent states need ever come into the position" of those hapless nations. "We are ever ready to enter into peace negotiations with all our opponents." Not, however, without qualifications. Austria-Hungary will not discuss any question affecting its own territory, nor will it permit its enemies to say how the peoples which make up the Dual Monarchy shall be governed. The "uninvited prescriptions" of the Allies regarding the creation of new states and the reconstitution of old ones, the apparent willingness that "one-half of Austria-Hungary may perish in order to make the other half happy," can never be tolerated. Austria-Hungary has its domestic difficulties, but so also have the Allies. "Sweep before your own door," exclaims Baron Burian.

If the words of Count von Hertling and Baron Burian have no other meaning than that which appears to lie open upon their face, the immediate outlook for peace, so far as any diplomatic advances by the Central Powers are concerned, must be adjudged dark. With Belgium a makeweight, the Russian and Rumanian treaties a finality, and the territorial integrity of Austria-Hungary a *sine qua non*, the discussion of peace suffers a well-nigh impossible handicap at the start. It is conceivable, of course, that the Chancellor and the Foreign Minister did not mean exactly what they said, or that at least they did not intend their words to be taken too literally. The fact that Count von Hertling's speech was promptly acclaimed in Germany itself as proof that the militarists and annexationists had triumphed over the liberals, and that the Kaiser and Ludendorff were now to have their way, may indicate that the Chancellor was not free to make an unqualified promise to restore Belgium, but felt compelled to hedge the assurance about with reservations vague enough to admit of later interpretation. One detects, too, in Baron Burian's acid remarks about the necessity of excluding from a peace discussion all reference to the alienation of Austrian territory or the reorganization of the Austrian state, an admission that outside criticism and propaganda have begun to tell. In neither case is it imperative to assume that these spokesmen for the Central Powers intended their words to be taken as a definitive closing of the door to peace negotiations save upon their own terms.

Nevertheless, it is just because the statements of Count von Hertling and Baron Burian are susceptible of more than one interpretation that they are so unsatisfactory. What was needed, above everything else, was clear speaking. The thinking world is sick of war. The appalling sacrifice of human life and efficiency, the incalculable waste of material resources and wealth, the jeopardizing of everything that has made modern civilization an achievement to be valued, holds no vision of beauty or reward to make men value it. What every friend of peace desires, what President Wilson, Mr. Lloyd George, and M. Clemenceau have declared that they were straining their eyes to discern even afar off, is some concrete and unequivocal proof that Germany is ready, on its part, to end a war which it criminally began, and that Austria-Hungary is of the same mind. What the spokesmen of the Central Powers offer, instead, is a profession of desire for peace so enmeshed in qualifications, prior claims, and vague implications as not only to afford no sure substance of which the Allies can unhesitatingly take hold, but also, what is worse, to cast doubt upon the sincerity of the profession itself. The Central Powers cannot in conscience complain if, after this latest exhibition of diplomatic unfrankness and bad faith, the United States and the Allies regretfully conclude that no other course is open but to go on with the war. If the way to peace is barred, the opponents of Germany are not the ones who have obstructed it.

It is admittedly a large task so to rehabilitate the German conscience that the word of Germany may be trusted. A long step will have been taken in that direction, however, when a statesman appears who will speak out without equivocation. Until the language of German diplomacy takes on greater frankness and truthfulness, the Central Powers must be content to see their peace overtures greeted only with suspicion. We say this regretfully because, in a recent editorial, the *Nation* expressed its belief that the holding of an informal peace conference would be opportune.

Russia and Intervention

FROM the beginning the *Nation*, as its readers know, has been opposed to military intervention of any sort in Russia. That opposition has not been based upon any extravagant notions regarding the aims or accomplishments of the Russian revolution, nor upon an overweening fondness for the principles or methods of the Bolsheviki, nor yet upon the imputation to the United States or the Allies of selfish and ignoble motives. We have realized to the full the gravity of the German menace and the desirability of enlisting Russia on the side of the Allies if Russia is to fight at all. Our opposition to armed intervention, regardless of whether the force be large or small, has had quite different grounds. We have from the first believed, and still believe, that the whole truth about Russia has not been told, that important facts unfavorable to the Allied view have been deliberately withheld, and that both the nature and work of the Soviet Government have been in important respects systematically misrepresented and discredited. More than that, we have felt that the appearance of an armed force in Russia, no matter with what professions of high purpose it might be heralded, was not only likely to help rather than hinder the German designs, but was almost certain to arouse, in large sections of the Russian people, feelings of deep and lasting resentment at the coercion to which the country was henceforth to be subjected.

The resort to military intervention is all the more regrettable because, as it seems to us, an opportunity for helping Russia in other more useful and sounder ways has in the meantime been lost. What Russia has needed for months past is the sympathy and forbearance of the Governments which were once its friends. Its efforts to reconstruct its society upon a democratic basis, novel and groping as some of those attempts apparently have been, have merited some better form of recognition than cold and critical neglect. The humiliating peace of Brest-Litovsk need never have been made had not the Allies and the United States, with amazing blindness, turned a deaf ear to the Russian appeal to be represented in the conference. The rehabilitation of Russian industry, agriculture, and commerce, without which Russia could not hope to regain a place among the nations, might at any time have been begun, and with small likelihood of thereby replenishing Germany's exhausted stores to any appreciable extent, if only the Allies had permitted foreign trade to be resumed. And even if the economic revival had been small, the supplies of food and clothing needed to cope with widespread hunger and nakedness, and the medical resources necessary to combat epidemic disease, might still have been introduced with beneficent results had not the American Red Cross folded its arms. This much at least a Christian civilization might have done without calling to its aid a single soldier.

Now, however, that armed intervention has begun, it is for the American and Allied peoples to wish it well. Whatever the mistakes of the past, they must now if possible be remedied. We have an unparalleled opportunity to put into practice, albeit on a vast scale and under complicated and difficult circumstances, the principles of disinterestedness and good will which the Allied Governments, in formal announcements, have proclaimed. If there is anarchy in Russia, it should now be replaced by order and the reign of law. If the Czecho-Slovaks turn out to be more concerned to win some political advantage for themselves or appropriate some portion of Russian territory than to fight the Central Powers on the eastern or western fronts, their spectacular career as a distinct force should be terminated without delay. There ought certainly to be no time lost in repairing and equipping the railways, reopening factories, restoring foreign and domestic commerce, distributing food and other necessaries, checking typhus and cholera, and opening the schools and the universities.

These are some of the material things for which the American and Allied commanders, backed by the sympathetic support of their Governments, ought now to pave the way. Great as they are, however, they are small in comparison with the task of political rehabilitation. Here, more than anywhere else, the disinterestedness of the Allies will be tested. If, in spite of the presence of a military force, there can now be brought about in Russia a free and full expression of political opinion in elections which are neither corrupted nor coerced, it will be an international achievement worthy of all praise. The difficulties, it must be admitted, are great. Precisely what form of government best suits the Russian needs is a question on which the Russian people themselves have not yet spoken with a clear voice. The temptation will be strong, with those who now have military force at their command, to cut the Gordian knot and impose upon Russia a form of government which will best suit some ulterior purpose of the Entente. There are powerful influences ready to restore Kerensky, and others equally ready to keep him from power at any cost. A cunningly contrived division of Russia into several states is a very real danger. All this, with international intrigues and secret schemes of every sort, the Allied Powers must resist if through their efforts Russia is to be free. The world waits for the first example in history of a great nation, upon which the fortunes of war have brought evil days, restored to liberty, health, and power, without force or fraud, by the unselfish help of a group of sister states. And while this good work goes on, let us have the truth, the whole truth, and nothing but the truth about Russia.

Higher Education and War

THE Federal Bureau of Education has taken official notice of the task which confronts the nation of keeping up the supply of technical and scientific knowledge necessary not only for the conduct of military operations, but for carrying on essential war industries. In a special report on the subject, just published, the Bureau calls attention to some of the more serious and difficult factors in the problem. The United States is now carrying on military operations of the first order 3,000 miles from its base of supplies and 4,000 miles from the centre of population. That is the task, defined in its simplest terms. Nothing like it has ever been attempted in the world, and the success thus far has been so notable as to fill Americans with imperishable pride. We have already met and overcome engineering difficulties far greater than those of any other nation engaged in the war. The average haul of men, munitions, and supplies is 4,500 miles by land and sea. Transportation alone is a stupendous enterprise, and behind it are the awe-inspiring processes of production. About everything else in connection with America's share in the war there may be two opinions, but there can be only one about the speed and efficiency of her organization to meet the great demand, and the unanimity and diligence of her people in their regimentation. But now, to keep up the steady and abundant flow of war material, we must have an ever-increasing number of men and women of highly specialized training. We are now trustees of the principal remaining source of supply of such specialists, and our centres of production are our educational institutions.

The Bureau reflects the anxiety that many have felt regarding the depletion of the colleges and universities by draft and enlistment. Doubtless the colleges should not actively discourage recruiting; but whether that be so or not, it would have been impossible for them to have done it, even if they had regarded such a course as the part of wisdom and true patriotism. Now, however, following the suggestion of the Board, they can make it clearer than they have hitherto been able to do, that young men and women who are qualifying themselves for engineering or other technical specialties are preparing for the country a possession of priceless value. There may be no general distinctions possible in the delicate matter of personal service, but unquestionably service in the line which each may desire will be worth more to the country than any other service that the same persons could render; and no more than this is necessary to make out a clear case. The natural instinct for values can here, as usual, be safely trusted. The best reason and judgment of most people instinctively turned against the idea of a Kreisler, for example, serving in the trenches. Not that Kreisler's distinction as a specialist entitled him as such to exemption as a privilege, but because it was felt, and rightly, that the Government might have made better use of him elsewhere. Similarly, it is only a distorted patriotism which insists that young men now training in technical lines should enlist for non-technical duty. We have too long followed this rough and indiscriminate method with college and university students, with the result of entailing a deplorable loss upon the efficiency of the nation.

It is both gratifying and reassuring to know, therefore, that the Bureau of Education is aware of the danger. The report just issued urges the maintenance of all the processes of higher education at their utmost efficiency, and particularly the development of an adequate supply of teachers. Institutions of learning are asked to make every effort to bring their opportunities within the reach of all suitably prepared men and women of college age. Where financial aid is needed, the Bureau recommends that it be extended; and it urges young people who possess the requisite qualifications to come forward "in increasing numbers to the task of preparing for the highest service of which they are capable." All this is as it should be. It is gratifying, too, to see that the Bureau is looking ahead to the period of reconstruction. The best minds in Europe have long been at work on that problem, but we, unfortunately, have been so preoccupied with the present, and our hands and hearts have been so full of the business of satisfying immediate and pressing needs, that we have only just begun to think of the things that are to come. What is certain is that, for a long time after the war, there will be urgent need for all the trained ability that is left in the world. The nation that has the most and the best-trained ability will come out best, whether the prevailing ideal of the reconstruction period be that of seeking or of service, of international competition or international coöperation.

The War Department also has had an eye on the effect of wholesale enlistment from the colleges. It proposes to organize a Students' Enlisted Corps, which shall offer to students an immediate military status and develop them as a military asset, "while at the same time preventing the unnecessary and wasteful depletion of the college through indiscriminate volunteering." The language is worth quoting as showing that Secretary Baker is well aware of the folly of grinding seed corn. The country is by no means so short of man-power as to require that students anywhere should suffer either distraction or temptation. An intelligent patriotism must see, with the Bureau of Education and Mr. Baker, how important it is that interruptions of every sort should be avoided; and it must develop a public opinion powerful enough to protect students against the foolish social pressure which has already driven so many of them out of the particular sphere of service which they are best fitted to perform. It is time that the patriotism which sees in "national service" only so many million men and so many million rifles and bayonets should give way to something more foresighted and sensible; and there is no place where such a reform can be more quickly and effectively worked than in the colleges themselves.

Least of all should the pursuit of general culture be neglected. The report of the Bureau of Education says less about this than sound patriotism could wish; still, it indicates the need, at least by implication, in instancing the demands which will inevitably attend the return of peace. The nation will then need, as never before, clear, objective, and abundant thought; and except through culture, the knowledge of the best that has been thought and said in the world, the needs cannot possibly be met. In the time to come cultured men will be indispensable; no array of skilled cataloguers of phenomena can take their place or do their work. It may be that the youth who to-day is diligently reading Plato, Homer, and Sophocles, quite out of the popular current and perhaps despised and rejected as a slacker, will in due time turn out to be the one who is best preparing himself to give the country distinguished service.

Civil Liberty Dead

It is estimated that in New York and near-by towns 75,000 men have been "arrested" in the last two days by the agents of the Department of Justice, assisted by soldiers, sailors, and patriotic organizations impressed for that purpose, and that fewer than 3 per cent. of those arrested were found to be "slackers" in fact. This means that over 70,000 citizens who had faithfully discharged their self-imposed obligations in the first selective draft were rudely seized in their goings to and fro, bundled into trucks and improvised patrol wagons, exposed in a helpless manner to the hoots and jeers of the populace, detained for hours in barracks and armories, and at last released without any possibility of redress. . . .

THUS speaks no pacifist or anti-war newspaper, but the Republican, intensely pro-war, "bitter-ender" New York *Tribune*. It errs on the side of mildness. Senator Johnson likened these raids to the application of the "Law of Suspects" during the Reign of Terror of the French Revolution. Senator Calder and other pro-war Senators were unrestrained in their denunciation, and even Senator Sherman asked: "Is there any material difference between this militarism and Kaiserism in Berlin and the bayonetting of innocent men about the streets of New York?" No more disgraceful or more lawless happening has occurred in the metropolis. These arrests without warrants, mostly by striplings in uniform and irresponsible agents of a volunteer, self-appointed protective (!) league, were an offence against the historic spirit of the nation, as they were a deadly insult to the men who had submitted to the draft, either joyfully or with patriotic resignation. It was Prussian militarism pure and simple, even if it emanated from the Department of Justice.

No wonder the President has ordered an inquiry. Men were torn from their wives' sides in the theatres, yanked out of street cars, pulled off milk-wagons and trucks of all kinds, which vehicles were left to stand where they were abandoned. Men from up-State and New Jersey—and there were thousands of them—who had no warning of the raid and had left their cards at home—were first taken to police stations and then to an armory, where everything was in utter confusion and where many spent the entire night upon their feet. Numbers were held by the police who showed their registration cards, but were without their classification cards, which have never been issued by the draft boards of many up-State towns. And always there was this Prussian spectacle of men with rifles in their hands surrounding groups like the curb-market brokers in Broad Street as if they were criminals. This not in Russia nor in the home of the "Beast of Berlin," but in America, the home of democracy, the land of the free.

The most amazing thing about it all is the long-suffering patience of the public. In England the Government has never since the beginning of the war seen the day that it dared undertake such a raid on the rights of its subjects, and, so far as we are aware, nothing like it has ever been attempted in France. How will it read when, with the inevitable exaggeration, it reaches the Berlin press? It was Oliver Cromwell who said: "There is but one general grievance, and that is the law." It really seems as if the Department of Justice intended the American people to feel similarly. Certainly nothing that the I. W. W. has ever done or dreamed of doing could make the draft so unpopular in a few short hours with so many supporters of the President and of the war as this act of the Department of Justice, or of its ill-advised agents. Do they share the opinion truthfully or untruthfully attributed to an English cynic, that one can put anything over on Americans, who wear the same clothes, think the same thoughts, and read the same newspapers?

But, after all, the worst feature of the affair is not the official anarchy. It is the fact that personal liberty and freedom have disappeared in America, and that the bulk of our vocal patriots thoughtlessly approve of it in the earnestness of their desire to win the war. At the very moment when the British Labor party and the Liberal party together have demanded of the Lloyd George Government that freedom of press and speech shall be restored at once—*now*, not when the war ends—when the French Socialists have just unanimously voted that, war or no war, there will be a general strike in France if Clemenceau again denies their passports to Socialists who desire to attend the long-planned Inter-Allied Socialist Conference—we in America are witnessing the suppression of the right of public meeting and of a free press, with almost no protests. The freedom with which the *Manchester Guardian*, the *Daily News*, the London *Nation*, and a host of other papers in England and Ireland criticise the Government for the Government's good is unknown here. Senator Johnson did not exaggerate when on Friday last he declared that the only place in the United States in which there is free speech to-day is the Senate in which he spoke. Both Democrats and Republicans denounced the New York outrage irrespective of party lines. But when so weak and ineffective a Senator as Mr. Sherman, of Illinois, begins to attack the Administration, as he did in a lengthy speech on the third of September, there is at least this much encouragement: it appears that there is the beginning of that Opposition in Congress the need of which has been so painfully obvious. If the Republicans are searching for an issue, they need look no further. If the American people could realize what has been done and is being done throughout the country in the name of liberty, they would emphatically demand and support an organized Opposition to the end that this government may again be a government of laws and not of men.

An official of the Department of Justice was privately asked this week why an American newspaper was denied the mails because it contained an editorial from the London *Nation*, passed as proper both by the British censor and the American Censorship Office; why the *Public*, a most devoted and loyal upholder of the war and of the President and Secretary Baker, has twice been denied the mails. He had no explanation to offer. What *is* the explanation of it? Why is it that a democracy that ought to be infinitely more jealous of its constitutional rights and prerogatives than a limited monarchy can thus in a year's time knuckle under to official bureaucracy and autocracy—without protest? What is the psychological explanation? Is it terrorism? Is it the all-embracing Espionage act, under which a man may go to jail for expressing an unfavorable opinion about the principle of a draft, or for saying that this is a capitalistic war? Is it the result of official propaganda, or of an over-cultivation of the narrowly nationalistic spirit? We cannot answer. But we are certain that if the war goes on much longer and Mr. Wilson wishes to retain such leadership of the world of liberalism as he has obviously won in the last eighteen months and to shape the outcome of the war, he has no time to lose in examining what is being done to make democracy unsafe in America.

The One Thing Needful

THE labor missions that we send abroad seem to be singularly unproductive of information. They go as propagandists rather than as reporters. Mr. Duncan has been abroad recently; Mr. Spargo and Mr. Gompers are there now. They went on a crusade, a salesman's drive, when every circumstance of the occasion indicated that if they were to go at all, their mission should be that of an explorer. The one thing needful at the present moment is that we should know the whole state of European labor. On its industrial side, our war programme must be based on accurate knowledge of the capacity and intention of European workers, and on its political side no less must it be adjusted to the power and purpose of the whole European proletariat. Nor is it enough that our Government should have this information; our people must have it. The old tripartite division of function in former wars, when an upper class planned and directed, a middle class found the money, and a lower class fought and labored, is no longer possible in any nation. Mr. Winston Churchill admirably describes this present war as a race with revolution; and whether the revolution be violent and bloody or "a revolution by due course of law" depends finally upon nothing but the opportunities permitted the several peoples to gain true knowledge of one another's conditions and purposes. No less grave than this is the matter which emissaries like Mr. Gompers have in hand. Mr. Duncan went to Russia; he was looked to for a full and authoritative report of the conditions of Russian labor. We know now, to our cost and discredit, what his observations were worth. Mr. Gompers will be looked to for a report on British and Continental labor. We can anticipate the formula. He will return to "an Atlantic port," where he will "express his confidence" in this or that, and then presently make his way to Washington to "assure the Administration" of this or that. Nothing more is to be expected. Mr. Gompers, like Mr. Duncan, goes abroad as neither an observer nor a prophet, nor has he the first qualification for either rôle. He is a salesman on a drummer's rounds. He went, as a New York paper grandly says, "to sell this country's idea of victory to the pacifist elements in Allied countries, especially England." When Mr. Gompers drops the sample case and mounts the tripod, therefore, the public will get from him at his best merely the kind of information that a sturdy partisan drummer, travelling continually in an atmosphere of sheer bagmanism, is able to furnish; and with all that the public can do nothing.

A belligerent people has no way of viewing foreign peoples simply as men and women of like passions with themselves, at work in a common world; and this is precisely the view it should by right have and must have in the present instance if our readjustments are not to be catastrophic. Americans have the press; but between terrorism and subsidy there are obvious reasons why our journalism may not even pretend to present a complete record of the European labor movement. We have the enterprise of Mr. Creel, but Mr. Creel, too, is a salesman, bearing the burden and heat of the day as he "sells the war" to his fellow-countrymen. Our diplomatic service has commercial attachés, the Department of Labor has agents in foreign service and gets out excellent reprints of European documents and statistics. All this, however, does not quite enable us so to follow the current of events as to make a dependable forecast of the future. Our military reports are of strategy, armies, positions, lines, but not of men. Our industrial reports are of goods, markets, ships, credits, but not of people. They do not help us to understand the swift and subtle play of forces between human beings; and knowledge of these is the essential knowledge that we must somehow get.

How, for example, are we to interpret the action of the British Trade Union Congress on September 4 when it adopted its peace resolution and demanded a voice in the peace conference? Will Mr. Gompers tell us its motive? Is he qualified to have a respectable opinion? If his report becomes to some extent the basis for American policy, shall we be justified in a sense of security? Mr. Spargo, only a few days before the resolution, had an article in the New York *Tribune* saying that no trade union in England could muster a decent pacifist minority. Is then the overwhelming repudiation of the bitter-ender Havelock Wilson a mere personal triumph for Mr. Henderson irrespective of his views and principles, the triumph of a pacifist but not of pacifism? How, again, shall we regard the attitude of French organized labor towards peace terms and intervention in Russia; its threat of a general strike if passports be not granted to delegates to international conferences; the triumph of the extreme minority Socialists in formulating a general platform? What took place at the recent conference of the Miners' Federation at Southport under the presidency of Robert Smillie; or at the secret session of labor at Perth, West Australia, attended by the Premier of Queensland? The resolutions adopted there mentioned President Wilson by name. The Premier of New South Wales called them "arrant nonsense," but even so it would be well to know what was in the minds of those who promulgated them. Does the red flag fly over the Trades Halls in Sydney and Melbourne, and, if so, what does it signify? What are we to think of a five-line item buried in the last page of an evening paper last Thursday, saying that extremists dominated the Socialist Congress at Rome, which passed strong resolutions against the war?

We have had one bitter and shameful experience in permitting diplomats, soldiers, corporation lawyers, and journalists to interpret a social and industrial upheaval in Russia instead of simply and sensibly letting the Russian people, who were chiefly concerned and presumably knew what they were driving at, interpret it themselves. Mark Twain said that while a naturalist's opinion about a bug was very interesting and valuable, he would a great deal rather get the bug's opinion about itself. Why not let European labor speak freely for itself? The opinion of a Cornish miner or a Lancashire overlooker would help us much more to an understanding of British labor than any number of observations from Mr. Gompers. Let Mr. Ramsay MacDonald help us further; let M. Longuet help us to understand the French laboring classes, and M. Graziadei the Italian. Let us hear freely from minorities as well as majorities, from the rank and file as well as from the leaders. Let us do all we can to promote the free interchange of opinion among international groups of every name, sect, and persuasion. If there are governmental arrangements that prevent this, let American labor see to it that they exist no longer. It is not a matter that concerns governments. Common understanding is essential to the coöperation of peoples; and without this coöperation no war can be won, no peace made permanent.

The Progress Towards Peace

SUCH we consider the three steps taken by President Wilson and the German Chancellor in the last seven days—progress towards peace. From the bulk of our fellow-citizens, who see in the President's second reply only war *à l'outrance*, we differ completely. The President has not closed the door; the long-distance negotiations or exchanges of opinion are certain to continue. Germany, if her plight is so serious as to induce her to swallow the President's fourteen peace terms with their vagueness as to Alsace-Lorraine, must continue with President Wilson the negotiations looking towards a settlement. That she will find it difficult to comply with his demand that the U-boats be called off and that the stripping and often wanton ravaging and burning of evacuated territory cease forthwith, goes without saying. But having herself imposed the harshest terms at Brest-Litovsk, Germany knows full well the bitter cup of which the vanquished must drink. Nothing, we are sure, will appeal to the American public as much as this insistence that atrocities on sea and land shall cease. The latest sea-horrors, the drowning of women from a Japanese vessel, the shelling and drowning of all but a few of the helpless crew of an American transport, and the sinking of a militarily insignificant Irish mail-boat with the loss of more than 300 lives—these are things that ought to cease in the name of common decency.

Yet, while we can heartily sympathize with the humanitarian impulse that distinguishes this portion of Mr. Wilson's message; while we feel that in the main, our jingoes to the contrary notwithstanding, the President is headed neither for war to the bitter end nor for a war of revenge, we cannot deny our disappointment at the lack of generosity and of definiteness in the second reply. Even when U. S. Grant insisted on unconditional surrender, he did it gracefully and generously; he handed back Lee's sword; he let the private soldier take his horse and rations with him. Wicked and barbarous as the German foe has been, no nation ever showed magnanimity and generosity without thereby adding to its own stature and increasing the humiliation of the enemy. What we should have liked to see in the President's answer is what might be called the "categorical imperative"—a clear-cut statement of exactly the points, a, b, c, d, in which the German answer was unsatisfactory and, 1, 2, 3, 4, what Germany must do to obtain peace. Sooner or later our terms must be definitely stated.

We are the more concerned about this because of the reactions from the President's second note. The jingoes whose praise Mr. Wilson ought to shun like poison are as sure now that he is their own as they were certain last week that he was to be abused as Mr. Roosevelt and the New York *Tribune* promptly abused him. Some Liberals see great hope and encouragement in the President's reply. This may be a tribute to the President's ability to please everybody on occasion, but it is extremely dangerous. Never before was Woodrow Wilson in so difficult a position; it is the crisis of his world leadership and of his moral influence which confronts him. His tremendous skill and ability are put to the completest test. The more regrettable is it, therefore, that there was vagueness in the second note which may return to plague him—as have returned upon Republican lips the vaguenesses of his peace terms.

Take, for instance, the final passage calling attention to the sentence in his Fourth of July address in which he laid down as one of the terms of peace: "The destruction of every arbitrary power everywhere that can separately, secretly, and of its single choice disturb the peace of the world." As to this Mr. Wilson now says:

> The power which has hitherto controlled the German nation is of the sort here described. It is within the choice of the German nation to alter it. The President's words just quoted naturally constitute a condition precedent to peace, if peace is to come by the action of the German people themselves. The President feels bound to say that the whole process of peace will, in his judgment, depend upon the definiteness and the satisfactory character of the guarantees which can be given in this fundamental matter. It is indispensable that the governments associated against Germany should know beyond a peradventure with whom they are dealing.

What does this mean? Jingo newspapers are interpreting it as the abdication of the Kaiser; others take a different view. Would it not be fair to those who have already brought about an amazing revolution in Germany by the admission of Socialists to the Cabinet and the establishment of a responsible ministry to tell them just what more is needed? How much of an interference in the inner concerns of Germany is actually intended? Mr. Wilson has already said of the United States: "She would disdain to take advantage of any internal weakness or disorder to impose her own will upon another people" (February 11, 1918). He has gone further: "Neither do we presume to suggest to her [Germany] any alteration or modification of her institutions" (January 8, 1918). Has the policy changed? If so, let us know it. Again, as to arbitrary power which may plunge a country into war. That power exists in every nation. Mr. Wilson used it at Vera Cruz; England has seen it exercised on numerous occasions. Would what Mr. Wilson has in mind be met by the Kaiser's divesting himself of the power to make war, which divesting so reliable an authority as the *Frankfurter Zeitung* declares to be coming? Do we not owe it to ourselves to define the "character of the guarantees" which we ask? Do we not otherwise run the risk of seeing the progressive German elements who are fighting our fight swept off their feet by a feeling that their country is being paltered with and that there is nothing left but to die in the last ditch? Is it not true that a hundred thousand American lives may hang upon this question of definiteness or indefiniteness?

Finally, we can only echo what we said last week, that a peace, honorable, just, definitive—one to satisfy all true Americans whose souls are not corroded with bitterness and hate and all those abroad as well who have fought the good fight—is in reach if we but desire it. We must not forget to think of those abroad, we who are still so fresh, so young in the war, so eager for sacrifice. Side by side with the quotations from Lord Northcliffe and the bitter-ender newspapers which the Associated Press carried on Monday of this week is this touching picture of last Sunday in London: "London streets, parks, and public places were crowded with people to-day. The crowds had an almost festive aspect. Such cheerfulness has long been unknown here. The people believe peace is near, and that it is peace with victory." Are these high hopes to be disappointed? In its issue of September 28, just received, the London *Nation*, commenting upon Senator Lodge's bitter-end speech, says that if his conditions are to prevail Germany and Austria "will, of course, resist their doom to the last. And we must remind Mr. Lodge that this Armageddon of his is to be fought out in Europe, not in America, and we, not he, will live amid the ruins it will have left us."

The Way of Peace

WHILE Senator Lodge and Mr. Roosevelt have been achieving notoriety abroad by their demand for unconditional surrender and war to the bitter end, significant indications of doubt or dissent have been cropping out in unexpected quarters. The New York *World*, which has certainly not been lax in supporting the war, bluntly asks "how many of the Americans who are shouting for 'unconditional surrender' know the meaning of the words they use," and deplores the demand as "thoughtless and irresponsible." Mr. Taft, who stands for unconditional surrender, nevertheless writes in the Philadelphia *Public Ledger* that Mr. Wilson's fourteen points are "very general," and declares that it will be "a negotiated peace," and one "depending on the honor of the Hohenzollerns for its maintenance." Professor J. Holland Rose of Cambridge University, one of the most distinguished of English authorities on modern history and international relations, writes in the New York *Times* that "the tide of events has swept on" since the fourteen points were drawn up, and that they do not fully cover the questions to be dealt with; while the Hon. Leslie M. Shaw, formerly Secretary of the Treasury, comes forward with an offer of $500 "to any reputable international lawyer" who shall give him "in terse and definite form the legal meaning of each of the fourteen points."

What Senator Lodge, Mr. Roosevelt, and the assertive advocates of unconditional surrender are doing is, of course, to urge the adoption of a Junker programme. It is a curious fact that the United States, having gone to war to abolish militarism and the rule of force, and with solemn declaration of its purpose to make the world safe, not for armies, but for democracy, should now be urged by Republican leaders to spurn all offers of peace in advance, overrun Germany with its armies, and dictate the terms of settlement at Berlin. This is Junkerism and militarism of the most approved German sort. However its particular object may be camouflaged by talk about freeing Europe from oppression, its spirit and method are essentially at one with those of the Kaiser and his supporters. With such a programme, discussion is of course quite out of the question; the peace for which the world yearns, the political freedom which Americans have believed was somehow the birthright of all mankind, is to be achieved only by smashing through to Berlin.

It is much to be regretted that Senator Lodge, in outlining the terms of peace which a military victory is to obtain, should not have been more explicit regarding the two main points. It is all well enough to talk about dismembering Austria, or adding to the territory of Italy, or driving the Turk out of Europe, or restoring Alsace-Lorraine. All these are complicated questions, it must be admitted; and they are very much more complicated than they were when the war broke out because of the positions which the Allies and the United States have taken with reference to the Jugoslavs, the Czecho-Slovaks, and the Poles. But they are not the crucial questions. What does Senator Lodge propose to do with Germany? Assuming that the German armies have been destroyed, the country occupied by an Allied and American force, and the Imperial Government helpless, what next? Is the Kaiser to be deposed, or the Empire destroyed or broken up, or the Reichstag remodelled? If so, how is the thing to be done? If Germany is to be parcelled out among its enemies, how are the shares to be apportioned? If it is to be preserved as a State, precisely how does Senator Lodge propose to reform it?

This is one of the chief points. The other is Russia. "What is the American policy with respect to Russia?" the New York *Globe* asked the other day. "No one seems to know. . . . Our Government seems unable to make up its mind. . . . There is the most painful evidence of lack of stability of view." After a year of revolution, the Administration has not yet taken the public into its confidence. It publishes documents whose authenticity rests under grave doubt. It seizes and segregates the papers of various persons who know Russia from the inside, and interferes with newspapers which champion the cause of the Soviet Government. It continues to recognize Mr. Bakhmetiev as Russian Ambassador, although we suspect that Secretary Lansing would be puzzled to determine what Government Mr. Bakhmetiev represents. In spite of the fact that nobody is at war with Russia, the troops of half a dozen nations are carrying on military operations in Russia and fighting pitched battles with the Soviet troops. One searches in vain in the threatenings and slaughters of the Republican Junkers to find how they propose to deal with this anomalous situation.

If Senator Lodge and Mr. Roosevelt really desire to help the country which they have served in high places these many years, they will take a different tack. They will cease trying to force the Administration to adopt the rôle of a Prussian Junkerdom, and address themselves to a study of the real problems involved in the negotiation of a peace. We do not speak unadvisedly when we say that some of those problems were never graver than they are at this moment. Nothing more than a reading of the English and French newspapers is needed to make clear that England is seething with labor disturbance, and France with political and Socialist agitation. A greater menace to the established order than Prussianism has grown great on the horizon, and that is Bolshevism. Only the other day Lord Milner, the British Secretary of State for War, declared in an interview that an armistice, if it guaranteed the military supremacy of the Allies, ought by all means to be attained if possible, and warned the Allies that an attempt at the present time to dictate drastic changes in the German Constitution would stiffen the resistance of the German armies.

We venture to think that there are three things which Mr. Wilson can do to help the present dangerous situation. The first is to come out with all his might against the Junkers, whatever their party affiliations, who are trying to force his hand. He will find the people with him when the issue is sharply drawn. The second is to ask the Soviet Government to say, clearly and fully, what it wants from the United States and the Allies, and, in particular, what it proposes to do with the Russian debt. The large holdings of Russian securities in France give that country a peculiarly vital interest in the future of Russia, and if the question can be cleared of its present uncertainty and apprehension, a material obstacle to peace will, we believe, have been removed. The third thing is to recognize the gravity of the social situation in every European country, and to take a few steps towards meeting Germany at the peace table before the great war shall have had time to become a war of revolution. Perhaps we shall soon hear that the good offices of Colonel House are being used in furtherance of these ends.

The Nation
EDITORIAL DEPARTMENT, 20 VESEY STREET
NEW YORK CITY
P. O. BOX 794 TELEPHONE BARCLAY 4200

Nov 8, 1918

Dear Mr. Tumulty,

I hope you will find time to read these articles. It is just because of these things which the President could at any moment have stopped that he is today without the liberal support he needs in this trying hour when the real victory of the war is still to be won. I am dismayed by the defeat, because you in the White House have not built up a liberal party there & permitted Burleson & Gregory to scatter & intimidate such liberal forces ~~as~~ have existed.

In this connection, the Nation has added 4,750 readers (without special effort) since I took hold July 15. It is not a personal following, but a spontaneous response to the liberal ideas we are preaching & our upholding of the President's 14 peace terms. As we, because of the paper famine, have undertaken no circulation campaign I consider this proof of the existence of a great body of liberal opinion waiting to be led. Shall it go to the Bolsheviki or the reactionary Republicans? That the President himself & no one else will decide.

Faithfully yours,

Oswald Garrison Villard.

Nov. 8, 1918.

November 12, 1918

Dear David Lawrence:

May I say to you how shocked I am by your dispatch in tonight's Evening Post? What you describe as coming from us is imperialism of the worst kind, which will make Prussian militarism a charming and attractive thing in comparison. What has come over you and those in Washington to blind you to the wickedness of interfering in the domestics concerns of Germany and of deciding what kind of a government they shall or shall not have? Why are you throwing over the principle of self-determination and self-government? Have you forgotten what Lincoln said, that no man was good enough to govern another without that man's consent? I had thought that we touched the bottom of degradation in what we are doing in Russia. But the policy you advocate in Germany is even worse and will make a mockery of our whole pretence that we stand for democracy, self-government and the right to develop along one's own lines, whether they spell Bolshevism or not. A people's right of revolution is one of the most sacred that there is and no outsiders have a right to interfere with it.

How glad I am that I am not owning the Evening Post, for I should either have to exclude many articles that you have recently written or to hang my head in shame.

You ought to take note of this week's Nation on the Russian situation. We are beginning to take the lid off some of our Government's action which will not bear the light of day.

Sadly yours,

Peace at Last

A HUMILIATING armistice signed on the enemy's terms, the Kaiser fallen, the throne lost to the Hohenzollern, Germany crashing to pieces in violent revolution—thus ends the war which has convulsed the world. The mills of the gods have ground exceeding small, albeit at terrible cost, and all too slowly since the pistol shot at Sarajevo which destroyed empires, created new nations and began what may prove to be the overturning of our whole social and economic systems. Never could it more truthfully be said of anyone than of the Kaiser to-day that he that taketh the sword shall perish by the sword—and this whether he is to come now to a violent end or to spend the remainder of his days in contemplation of the wreck that is his doing. No more fearful moral guilt ever rested on any one. The man who proclaimed that he was vice-gerent of God, and that he held his authority direct from the Almighty, has learned not only that might does not make right, but that there can be no partnership with the Almighty unless the aim be unselfishly to benefit and uplift mankind. From the moment of the invasion of Belgium, for those who have trust in the eternal verities, who know that the world does move forward, who still have faith in the divine possibilities of mankind, what is happening in Germany is merely what was as certain to take place as the world was bound to turn in its orbit. From that moment the Kaiser was doomed, whether he won on the battlefield or not; the only question was whether he was to fall through the legions of the Allies or through the acts of his own subjects.

And it is primarily through the acts of his subjects that he has fallen. The German Michel, long caricatured as the dullest of peasants, has decided that he has had enough. The infectious example of Russia, close at hand, told. So we see the almost incredible spectacle of the Kaiser unhorsed not by fiat of the Allies, but by the most despised of his political parties, the Socialists, and a regency proclaimed—with what kind of a head? Some prince, some King of Saxony or of Württemberg? Not at all; with Friederich Ebert acting as Chancellor—Ebert who was for years a common harnessmaker, who never had other than a common-school education, who has not even a *von* to his name! What could be more spectacular, what more dramatic and thrilling, than the Kaiser's abdicating to make way for a man from the ranks of manual labor, a Socialist agitator at that? Nothing could more clearly illumine the horizon of the future, nothing else could possibly be as significant of the overturn to come. There will be those to see in this passing of power from the rich and privileged only evil; who will interpret it as the ending of a golden age and the beginning of the end of civilization. For ourselves it spells a new and most hopeful human era.

For if the mills of the gods have caught and crushed the Hohenzollerns and Hapsburgs and the Kings of Bavaria and Bulgaria and what not, they have still much crushing to do. Every remaining king, whether well-meaning figure-head or despot, should and must go. But these are now few in number. Then, we agree with the German Socialists that no man who had anything to do with starting this war should remain in public life. In Russia, in Austria-Hungary, and in Turkey they are gone. We hope and trust that the spirit of revolution abroad will not die until all the makers of secret treaties are cast out, and with them, as among the worst enemies of mankind, the armament-manufacturers, the Krupps, the Creusots, the Armstrongs, the Whitworths, and our own lesser armor and gun-makers. We desire no end to revolution abroad until customs-houses everywhere have gone by the board. We wish no end to democratic ferment in Europe until the professional diplomat of the past has been ground flat, and with him those alleged statesmen who believe that the backward or sparsely-inhabited spaces of the earth exist only to be exploited. We wish no end to the revolution until there shall no longer be talk of developing hinterländer, spheres of influence, and colonies, but of some means of holding them in trust by joint international agreement for the benefit of those to whom the soil rightfully belongs. Thus we would have England retire from Egypt and Persia, the Italians from Tripoli, and Japan from Kiao-Chou, France from Cochin-China and Madagascar, and Belgium from the blood-stained Congo, while the United States sets the example by retiring from the Philippines, Haiti, San Domingo, and Nicaragua. We wish no limit to the spread of liberalism until the vicious doctrine that a country shall protect by the force of arms its citizens who invest abroad shall be forever discarded. For we are not of those who can see the mote only in the eye of our Allies or enemies. There are those in plenty—men like Taft and Roosevelt, preachers of reaction and hate—in this country for whom the mills of the gods are turning slowly—slowly, but with the terrifying, inescapable certainty which marks the progress of the glacier that no human agency can stay.

For the Kaiser is but the vilest flower of a system, and it is the system and the spirit which underlie it that must go. The battle against Prussian militarism is not yet won. Its first bloody phase is, thank God, at an end. But if this war has proved anything, it is that the spirit of Prussianism exists everywhere, in Paris, in London, in Rome—very strongly—and in Washington. Only in Moscow is it wholly crushed to earth. We shall neither have made this the last of wars nor safeguarded democracy, if we do not extirpate everywhere the spirit that would not only conquer other people's lands as Germany conquered Belgium and Servia, and Italy conquered Tripoli, but would enslave their souls and bodies as well. As long as it is left to a few men anywhere to decide whether nations shall go to war, as long as there are men abroad like Mr. Taft to say that just when we have crushed German militarism we must war against the Russians and Germans to see to it that the revolutions there result in precisely the kind of Governments that we prefer, just so long is the war to end war merely begun.

To-day, however, everybody must rejoice without stint that the last of the German Kaisers has gone. We are witnessing the greatest, the swiftest, the most dramatic tragedy the world has ever beheld. When one thinks of all the great things that Germany has accomplished for the world, its contributions to art, literature, music, and science, when one thinks of what Germany might have done for the world, but for her false leaders, one feels like echoing Capt. Philip at Santiago: "Don't cheer, boys, the poor devils are dying." Under our very eyes is dying the greatest of modern empires, in some respects the greatest nation of our times. May it be the last of the empires! And out of its bitter anguish and travail may there arise in the future, without foreign interference, a new, an honest, and a glorious democratic State to help point the way toward the goal of all mankind, liberty, fraternity, equality!

Hands Off in Europe

MR. WILSON'S lofty utterance in announcing to Congress the original armistice terms is well supplemented by Lloyd George's appeal for a peace of justice unmarred by the desire for vengeance. Certainly Allies whose cause has been crowned with such glorious military success have no reason to be either petty or revengeful. Moreover, Mr. Wilson and Mr. Lloyd George both declare that the idealistic aims they have declared to be those of the Allies shall be lived up to in the peace. If they so insist, the entire outcome of the war will be as gratifying as is that of its first phase. When one reads the dispatches and sees how complete is the collapse of autocracy and German militarism, —far more complete and thorough-going than anybody in either France, England, or the United States had dared to hope—one sees the reason for proceeding with a gentle hand. Mr. Wilson has already recognized the necessity of providing food.

Mr. Wilson is both a Southerner and a historian. In treating a fallen and defeated foe he surely cannot forget the treatment extended by the North to Lee, Davis, Johnston, and other unsuccessful Confederates. No more glorious page exists in our history than that which portrays the clemency and forgiveness extended to the Confederates in the face of a revengeful spirit in the North—about as vengeful, as is shown by the editorial from the New York *Times* of April 17, 1865, which we recently reprinted, as that which exists in certain quarters to-day against our late enemies. Had the North yielded to this feeling, had it shed the blood of the Confederate leaders, it would not only have made martyrs of them, it would long have delayed the reconciliation which has taken place. Yet those Confederate leaders were also accused of piracy, of wicked cruelties, of "wholesale massacres and torturings, wholesale starvation of prisoners." We cannot believe that any Allied statesman will seriously demand the trying of the Kaiser and his generals or insist that Holland violate the right of asylum. But it is well, nevertheless, to recall the wisdom of the North's treatment of the men who desired to destroy the American Government. The last thing to do with the Kaiser is to make a martyr of him.

But to mingle justice with charity is not all that we ought to do abroad. Nothing more discouraging has appeared in our press than the sudden demand that we go in and police Russia, Germany, and Austria against any possible manifestations of Bolshevism. The unabashed New York *Tribune* speaks of "Bolshevist Russia as the only armed enemy in the field. The Allies are still at war with her. She must be crushed as Germany has been crushed." The *Tribune* also thinks that Finland is our "covert enemy" and that her political and military status "leaves much to be cleared up." The *Tribune* has the unenviable distinction of being about the only American newspaper to regret that the war stopped when it did. As for Mr. David Lawrence, who so often writes as the mouthpiece of officialdom, he declares that if the Allies "fail to remove the elements that are making for anarchy inside of Germany, particularly the leaders of the proletariat who believe the way to get food is to introduce their own ideas of requisitioning or commandeering, the whole situation will require the presence of American armies in Europe for an indefinite period of time." Unless food is sent into Germany, he says, Germany is likely to fall into the hands of a German Lenine and Trotzky, and then, of course, we must take hold and intervene. In other words, we are to throw overboard Mr. Wilson's official assurances that we are not going to interfere in the internal concerns of the enemy countries.

Now we submit that if this policy is carried out it will do the grossest violence to our best American traditions. "What," we hear it asked, "do you approve of Bolshevism?" Not at all. The *Nation* never has approved and never will approve of reform by force. But it does believe that the right of revolution is sacred to a people, and that the very principle of self-determination which has been laid down as one of the objects of this war forbids us to interfere with political development in either Russia or Germany. That development is entirely the domestic concern of those peoples. If Bolshevism proves to be the desire of the majority in Germany, as it has done in Russia, and if it can maintain itself in Germany, as in Russia, for a year—or for a hundred years—then that is Germany's concern and hers alone. We shall not admire her taste in government; we shall profoundly deplore the resort to violence and the going to extremes. But we shall maintain with all possible emphasis that it must still remain her affair and not ours. We shall believe that she alone must purge herself of her past wrongdoing and false leadership, no matter what the cost; that reform from within will be the only reform worth while; and that any reform imposed from without by foreign force will hinder and not help. Foreign interference must by its very nature become hated and distrusted, even if it performs the rôle of the benefactor bringing order and food. It is a profound convulsion through which Germany is passing. It is searching out her very depths. What is going to come of it no man knows. But if democracy means anything, it means to-day: "Hands off, let them work out their own regeneration; give them food, give them sympathy, but under no circumstances compel them by our bayonets to adopt the kind of Government which we think they ought to have."

It is because of this belief that we so ardently hope soon to hear the news of the withdrawal of the Allied and American troops from Russia. Our war upon that country was excused on the ground that it was necessary to prevent the Germans from overrunning Russia. That excuse falls to the ground now; yet we hear that, with the war over, our fleet and that of the Allies are to force their way to Petrograd; that while everywhere else the hated "Hun" is being disarmed and demobilized, his forces in the western Russian provinces are to be used to "maintain order." Was there ever anything so topsy-turvy? What will the Russians say to the Allied use of Germans against them? And this further forcible action, be it remembered, is taken against a country with which we are not legally at war. Upon the desirability of going to war with the Russians Congress has never passed. Moreover if a new Government should arise without Lenine and Trotzky and under another name, though just as radical, it is possible that our fury to intervene would not abate. Be that as it may, however, we repeat that we shall be denying our democracy and going back upon our historic traditions if we continue to war upon the Russians and undertake to police Germany. What would we Americans have thought of any foreign nation which should have dared to police us in the days of our chaos and of our infirm Government during the trying and unhappy years 1781-1789?

The Armistice

OF the armistice terms imposed upon Germany by the Allies there are two texts. The first, dated November 11, was incorporated by President Wilson in the address which he read to Congress on the same day. A "corrected text," made public in the newspapers on November 13, contained textual or substantive variations from the first text in no less than eighteen of the thirty-five articles. Why the President of the United States used, or was allowed to use, in his communication to Congress, what seems to have been only a preliminary draft of the articles, or why it should have been deemed necessary to revise more than half of the articles within a few hours of the publication of the document, does not appear. The fact that the armistice was drawn up by Marshal Foch and the Supreme War Council, and not by Mr. Wilson, does not mean that Mr. Wilson was necessarily ignorant of the terms until the document was handed to him; the probability is that he was fully advised regarding the deliberations of the Council, and knew as well as did the Council what the terms were to be. If it is to be assumed, as Washington dispatches indicate, that the changes were made by Marshal Foch with the authority of the Council, it must also be assumed that such extensive and important changes were made in order to meet some new and grave situation.

The impelling motive, no doubt, was the rapid progress of the revolution in Germany and a sudden fear of danger from Russia. How far the armistice will pave the way for a wise and just treatment of either situation will depend upon the way in which the Allies use their power. So far as the armistice deals with the cessation of hostilities, the surrender of warships, artillery, munitions and supplies, the abandonment of pillage and wanton destruction, the evacuation of occupied territory in France and Belgium, the protection of the civil population, and similar matters, its provisions are beyond cavil. Some of the terms are severe, but they are not more severe than Germany deserves or should have expected. The Allies are determined that, whatever else happens, there shall be no renewal of the war on the part of Germany; and they have properly imposed terms which, so far as can be seen, will make such renewal impossible.

In two important respects, on the other hand, the armistice terms may well occasion anxiety. Not only are the German forces to retire from occupied territory on the left bank of the Rhine, but the Allies and the United States are also to garrison Mainz, Coblenz, and Cologne, together with a considerable area on the right bank of the river and "the strategic points of the regions." In other words, the Allied and American forces are to occupy, during the period of the armistice, an undefined portion of German territory which they have not conquered and from which the Germans are to retire in order that the Allies and Americans may enter. All other considerations aside, it is clear that no provisions of the armistice are so likely to stir the enmity of the German people as this presence of foreign soldiers within their borders. With Germany shaken to its foundations by a violent political and social revolution, the presence of an overwhelming Allied and American police, fully armed and ready for instant action, may well seem the very negation of the principles of democracy and self-determination which the opponents of Germany have proclaimed, and which the German people, in the troubled moment of a great defeat, are trying to apply to their own political condition.

The revised provision in regard to Russia is deeply significant. As the terms were announced by President Wilson, Germany was to withdraw its troops from any territory which before the war belonged to Russia. Under the revised terms, the withdrawal of German troops from Russian territory is to take place "as soon as the Allies, taking into account the internal situation of these territories, shall decide that the time for this has come." Why this change of front over night? One reason at least is clear. The Germans, instead of aiding the Bolsheviki, as the Allies and the United States have all along been asserting, are actually holding the Bolsheviki in check; and with the wave of Bolshevism now sweeping the Central Powers and threatening to reach every neutral state in western Europe, the Allies are in no hurry to see another flood let loose in Russia itself. German soldiers may be anathema to the Allies and the United States, but they are good enough to be used in stopping the Bolsheviki. Back of all this stands the dark spectre of an Allied and American invasion of Russia, already foreshadowed by the terms of the Austro-Hungarian armistice. The Dardanelles and the Black Sea are open; all Russian vessels seized by Germany in the Black Sea are to be handed over, not to Russia, but to the Allies and the United States, which are also to hold in trust, until peace is signed, the Russian gold which Germany has seized. Is it possible that the Allies and the United States are seriously contemplating the imposition of their own will upon the Russian people, not by their own strength alone, but with the help of German troops?

The Peace Conference

WHAT has been said in print thus far about the peace conference is, on the whole, either superficial or disappointing. It could not well be otherwise when the scantiness of the information which has been given out is considered. When one has said that there will probably be a meeting at Versailles some time in December of representatives of the Great Powers; that President Wilson proposes to attend; that Mr. Lloyd George, M. Clemenceau, and a number of other Premiers and Government officials, and of course Colonel House, will also be present; that the Jugoslavs, the Czcho-Slovaks, the unredeemed Greeks, and a considerable list of other aspiring nationalities are assuming that they will be represented, while labor, women, and Socialists are demanding that they shall be represented; that the Great Powers are trying to find some way of representing what they are pleased to call "Russia" or "the Russian people"; and that Mr. Creel and Mr. Sisson will be on hand to help with the news in the intervals of organizing democratic propaganda for Central Europe and South America, one has mentioned about all the facts concerning the conference that can be set down with assurance. How the assembly is to be constituted, what Governments and peoples are actually to be included and who their delegates are to be, and what principles are likely to be followed in dealing with the questions to be considered, are matters in regard to which a waiting world is still largely in the dark.

Now it ought to be clear—we believe that it is perfectly

clear—to every Government and to every thoughtful man or woman throughout the whole world, that nothing whatever about the preparations for the peace conference, or, after the preliminaries have been completed, about the proceedings of the conference itself, ought to be left in the dark. Everybody who desires a just and lasting peace must say over and over again, and keep on insisting, that the only guarantee of such a peace is open diplomacy, and that open diplomacy means openness about procedure as well as openness about results. It is, for one thing, a matter of very great importance who the delegates are to be. Mr. Lansing, for instance, is a capable diplomatic official; he knows all the precedents and may be expected to see, so far as his influence goes, that the established forms and proprieties are carefully observed. In almost any other country than the United States he would long since have found an honorable place as Permanent Under-Secretary of State for Foreign Affairs. But if his powers or his habit of thought fit him to deal wisely or sympathetically with such a revolutionary complex of national, racial, and class interests as now holds the attention of the world, the fact has not yet appeared; and if the peace conference is to be made up chiefly of delegates of his sort, or of such as have equally restricted vision of other kinds, the peace that will be made will satisfy nobody whose opinion now greatly matters.

Again, it makes a great deal of difference how widely the nations of the world are represented. One hears it said, for example, that neutral states will have only a restricted place if they are so fortunate as to be represented at all, and that Germany must not expect to be consulted until the completed terms are handed to it. Any such discrimination, we are confident, would be an injustice which the coming generation will repay in hatred, if not in blood. The war has been a world war. Not every nation, it is true, has been in arms, but there is not one anywhere that has not suffered deeply from the struggle, or that has not come out of the conflict with grievances to be redressed or ambitions to be pondered. The peace conference should be a world conference —victors and vanquished, belligerents and neutrals, small Powers and great, the nations still in travail as well as those already born and grown up.

Of the larger problems which will come before the conference, two have special interest for Great Britain and the United States. The first is the so-called freedom of the seas. Doubtless the question of maritime rights in general, and of the status of the seas in time of war more particularly, would in any event have been an important item in the programme of the conference; but Mr. Wilson's inclusion of a demand for "absolute freedom of navigation," in war as well as in peace, in his list of fourteen peace points, gives to the question a distinctly greater significance. Unfortunately, neither Mr. Wilson's message of January 8 nor any of his earlier or later addresses has sufficed to make clear precisely what it is that he is demanding, and there are already numerous indications of sharp difference of opinion in this country and Great Britain as to how the question should be settled. What there ought to be no difference of opinion whatever about, however, is that there will be no freedom of the seas worthy of the name so long as Great Britain and the United States go on planning for great navies against the eventuality of another war. All that will happen, assuming that the two countries do not quarrel, is that the seas will be free for the uses of those who speak English by preference, and for such others only as are willing to conform to the rules which the two English-speaking Governments choose to accept.

The second great question is composite, in part territorial and in much larger part political. There seems to be a pretty unanimous opinion among the Allies that the conquered German colonies will not be restored to Germany. English statesmen, on their part, have repeatedly intimated that Great Britain does not want them, although Mr. Hughes, the Australian Premier, would apparently be quite willing to see them in English hands. What is really involved, however, is the much larger question of self-determination of peoples. Why, to be quite frank, should there any longer be colonies at all, unless the people of a colony obviously prefer a colonial status to any other? It is easy to decide that there are backward peoples, that they ought not to be selfishly exploited, and that they must have protection and help during their progress upward. But how about the peoples who quite obviously are not backward, who feel no need of protection, and who want to be free? Is the peace conference going to acquiesce in the continuance of a dependent status for them, especially when they insist that they abhor it and will have no more of it if they can help it? We feel sure that if Great Britain and the United States really wish to join hands in making the world safe for democracy, they will not burn incense at the altar of the Jugoslavs and Czecho-Slovaks, and at the same time withhold independence, if independence is desired, from Ireland and India, Porto Rico and the Philippines. Self-determination is one of those "sapling truths," as Ruskin calls them, which it is dangerous to follow unless one is willing to follow it to the end; and the success of the peace conference will be gauged in large part by the frankness with which it recognizes this particular truth and the consistency with which it pursues it.

Crisis, Not Victory

THERE is no use in mincing matters in discussing President Wilson's annual message. Save in a few relatively unimportant respects, the message is disappointing. On none of the great issues which are before the country and the world, and in regard to which the attitude of the President is rightly looked upon as a factor of first-rate importance, has the message anything definite to say. Even the staunchest admirers of Mr. Wilson, the supporters who have stuck by him through thick and thin, must feel chagrin and humiliation that, in one of the greatest moments of our history, when it is supremely important that what is settled shall be settled right, the Chief Magistrate of the American people should on the one hand frankly confess that he does not yet know his own mind, at the same time that on the other hand he says nothing at all. Not even Mr. Wilson's unctuous insistence upon the rectitude of his own intentions, nor yet his frank intimation that, so far as he can see, the hope of a righteous outcome of the peace deliberations rests with him, will offset the clear indication that, so far as some of the most weighty domestic matters are concerned, he has no policy, and that on the weighty matter of peace his future course must be taken on trust.

Certain specific recommendations of the President, to be sure, are likely to meet with general approval. The immediate determination of the taxes that are to be levied for 1918, 1919, and 1920 will appeal to the business community and the public in general as wise and sound; and it is to be hoped that Congress will take the same view of it. The suggestion that Government control of food and shipping will have to be continued for a time after the peace, in order that the needs of suffering populations as well as the return of American troops from Europe may be provided for, is also beyond cavil. There will be no dissent, either, from Mr. Wilson's insistence that Belgium and France, the two countries whose industrial life has been most seriously shattered by the war, "should not be left to the vicissitudes of the sharp competition for materials and for industrial facilities which is now to set in." Of course the treaty with Colombia should be ratified, and that long-standing occasion of international irritation and misunderstanding removed.

These are not the supreme questions of the moment, however. The three issues which bulk largest in the public thought at this time, and the treatment of which will most vitally determine the course of American policy for years to come, are the railways, reconstruction, and the peace. On all three of these points the indecisiveness of Mr. Wilson's message is glaring. Ought we to have Government ownership of railways or not? "What is it right that we should do with the railroads," asks the President, "in the interest of the public and in fairness to their owners? "Let me say at once," he replies, "that I have no answer ready." The "only thing that is perfectly clear" to him is that "it is not fair either to the public or to the owners of the railroads to leave the question unanswered," and that it will become the President's duty to return the roads to their owners, "even before the expiration of the statutory period," unless "some clear prospect" of Congressional action presently appears. Congress will doubtless be grateful for the invitation to legislate, but what is to be thought of an executive leadership which, on the most crucial aspect of the wide question of Government ownership which has ever been presented to the country, offers no constructive suggestion even for debate?

So in the main, but with an important modification, is it with reconstruction. The one concrete proposal of the message is that public works, especially the reclamation of such public lands as are not now arable, may well be undertaken as a partial solution of the labor problem after the war. We are not at all certain that any large number of discharged soldiers will take kindly to the ditch-digging and stump-pulling which the Government is urged to offer them, even though the land is to be put upon the market on easy terms after it is ready for the plough. Beyond this particular alleviation, however, Mr. Wilson is not specific save in regard to administrative procedure. He makes it clear that reconstruction—the word itself is printed in quotation marks as if its connotation were dubious—is best to be carried on through existing executive agencies. This is plainly enough a repudiation of the suggestion of a reconstruction commission however constituted, and an indication of Mr. Wilson's purpose to keep the process of reconstruction in his own hands. What the goal is at which he is aiming, however, is not divulged.

It was everyway to be hoped that, on the all-important question of peace, Mr. Wilson's message would help somewhat to clear the air. What the President has to say, however, is more than disappointing. Not only does the message throw no new light whatever on what is likely to be done at the coming conference, but some of its statements raise disturbing questions. "The Allied Governments," Mr. Wilson declares, "have accepted the bases of peace which I outlined to the Congress on the 8th of January last," and "very reasonably desire my personal counsel in their interpretation and application." Is this the whole story? Have the Allied Governments ever accepted, in a way that any of them would regard as even morally binding, Mr. Wilson's fourteen points as anything more than an interesting statement of questions which may well be discussed? Have any of the Allied Governments ever expressed their "reasonable desire" for Mr. Wilson's "personal counsel" in the form of an invitation to attend the peace conference? Is it not rather the fact that Mr. Wilson goes to Europe at his own invitation, to save, if he can, some distinctive elements of his peace policy which are in jeopardy? If such is not the case, why does he dwell upon the transcendent importance of his mission, and his duty to see that the "bases" which he has laid shall have "no false or mistaken interpretation" put upon them?

Moreover, what are we to think of Mr. Wilson's unqualified endorsement of the programme for a huge American navy vastly too big for any purpose except war? Is Mr. Wilson to land at Brest whittling a big stick?

Mr. Wilson's message is the utterance of a great man with his back to the wall. The pressing issues of the war have left him no time to think of equally pressing domestic questions, nor has he been able to surround himself with the wise advisers whose ideas he might with propriety make his own. As to the future at home, accordingly, he has nothing of importance to communicate. His peace programme, on the other hand, framed before the United States entered the war, is apparently dividing the Allies instead of uniting them, and he must now throw his presence and his voice into the scale. The rhetoric of his message still wears something of its customary gilt and tinsel, but the substance which it ornaments is not victory, but crisis.

Justice to Russia

FROM the start the unfriendly intent behind Allied intervention in Russia was revealed by the frank though futile opposition of President Wilson. His objections gave the situation away; he admitted it to be a bad business before he became a partner in it, and his final surrender served only to emphasize the helplessness of benevolent intentions before the cynical determination of the controlling forces among the Allies. The excuses offered from time to time by the Governments engaged in crushing what the Germans had left of the Russian revolution were dishonest and hypocritical, but they served their purpose for the time being. They quieted the protests of timid liberals. They stilled the natural objections of those who pointed out that our armies had been enlisted to fight Germany, not to carry on military operations against Russian workingmen. But the propaganda of lies and suppression of facts was indeed a house built upon the sands.

Even to persons who had no way of knowing the flimsy stuff of which the building was made, the course of the Allies in Russia must sometimes have seemed perplexing. The newspapers talked of German arms and German gold, and autocratic rule in Russia, and disorder and terror, and the Czecho-Slovaks, but every man with sympathy and imagination must have seen something more. He must have seen a great people struggling with the hardest problems a nation has ever faced; struggling to build out of disorder and corruption a new untried society, struggling to demobilize without suffering and upheaval fourteen million war-sick men and to create fresh forces to defend the new-born revolution, struggling against German domination and intrigue and Czarist plots, struggling most fiercely of all against the horror of starvation—struggling, yet holding its head high and shouting its faith to an indifferent world. He must have seen with wonder the spectacle of "the great democracies of the West" picking up their weapons and trying to destroy that young faith with arms and lies and starvation.

He should have seen something of this. But if he failed to see before, surely he must see now; for the whole structure of falsehoods and excuses has collapsed. The "unstable" Soviet Government has lasted a year and a month in the face of all its trials and its enemies. The need of an Eastern front against Germany disappeared with the signing of the armistice. The duty of chasing the Germans out of Russia disappeared at the same time, and German troops were actually invited to stay in the invaded parts of Russia to help the Allies in "preserving order." The Czecho-Slovaks are discovered to have been offered by the Bolshevist Government free passage through Russia if they would return home in peace. Arms and materials of war are no longer in danger of falling into the hands of an Imperial Germany. The most hostile critics of Bolshevism are now loudest in their assertions of its complete hold upon the people of Russia. And as for the disorder and chaos and terror which have formed the most recent and widely-advertised Allied excuse, the *New Statesman,* always bitter in its opposition to the Bolshevist Government, is reported as saying in its latest issue: "Order is more thoroughly established in Russia now than at any time since the fall of Czardom. Food distribution is better organized than at any time during the whole war. Factories are rapidly starting up again as fast as raw material can be obtained. . . . Terror has ceased. It has been greatly exaggerated."

New voices are being raised in every country demanding the facts about Russia, demanding the reasons for intervention, demanding action by the peace conference. It looks as though Allied statesmen would be forced to listen, at least, and to answer. The latest reports from Paris indicate that the Allies do not intend for the present to undertake intervention on a large scale, but are to keep their troops in Russia to give "moral support" to those "orderly" Governments that are or may be in existence, and send forces into the Ukraine to relieve the departing Germans. This is the moment when the question is up for decision, when every word counts. Will the cry of the people be loud enough to carry through the padded walls of the palace at Versailles? The men who will gather there are commonly called statesmen; but they are also politicians, and politicians will always listen to the voice of the people if it is loud enough and speaks in no uncertain terms. Not as political partisans or "intellectuals" or "liberals," but as honest men of decent impulses, we Americans must tell the Government that represents us the only course that seems to us to accord with the principles of self-determination which it has proclaimed.

We ask the withdrawal, as rapidly as physical conditions permit, of all American troops from Vladivostok and northern and southern Russia, and meanwhile the complete cessation of hostilities. We ask that the plans announced for a military expedition into the Ukraine be abandoned. We ask the recognition of the Soviet Government and, as the immediate consequence of such action, negotiations leading to the establishment of commercial relations with Russia. We ask that diplomatic and other accredited agents of the Soviet Government be received and that Boris Bakhmeteff, the so-called Russian ambassador, be deprived of the diplomatic and financial privileges now accorded him. We ask that all unfriendly propaganda carried on by the Government of the United States or any of its branches immediately cease. We ask that the Government of the United States bring pressure upon the Allies to abandon their present policy in Russia and secure, under threat, if need be, of complete dissociation from their plans, the withdrawal of all Allied troops. We ask that representatives of the Soviet Government be admitted to the peace conference. We ask the prompt dispatch, in coöperation with the Soviet Government, of food and clothing and necessary industrial and agricultural machinery for sale or free distribution. We ask these things for the Russian revolution and the starving people of Russia; but even more we ask these things in order that the United States may for its own sake share in righting an intolerable wrong, that no man in this war shall have died for empty words and worthless phrases, and that from this time forth the world may be made forever safe for hopeful experiments and new adventures in democracy.

Foreign Correspondence

Peace Manoeuvres

(By Cable to the *Nation*)

London, January 4

THE putting out of a tentative programme for the peace conference and the announcement of Lloyd George's agreement with the President's policies have been the sensation of the week in London. Such action has the merit of letting in a little daylight. So far as it is a bit of open diplomacy it is to be welcomed. The public now knows what it had suspected, namely, that despite President Wilson's optimism, the battle for a clean peace is far from won. The President, in asserting that all was going well, played a bold game and a shrewd one, in the hope of holding the Allies to their promises. Perhaps, if he had not come to England, he could have reached the actual assembling of the conference without an explosion; but the spectacle of Lloyd George and Wilson assuring the world they had agreed and arranged everything was too much for Gallic pride. This was evidenced in Clemenceau's statement by the assertion that he himself won the war and his reference to France's being the battleground while England and America were not. It has long been known here that Clemenceau is most intensely jealous of Lloyd George's assertion that the latter won the war.

Despite the clouds, the skies have cleared somewhat, and there is a growing belief in the best-informed circles that some kind of league of nations will probably result. What kind, remains the all-important question, as to which no authoritative information is given. The British Labor party at its wonderfully effective Albert Hall meeting on Thursday made that perfectly clear, declaring that it wants no new Holy Alliance, but a league which will be a league of free peoples really determined upon peace, and not an imperialistic alliance of old-fashioned diplomats deciding, perhaps, what shall be the right form of government for Russia or Turkey or India. Ramsay Macdonald reviewed at some length the history of the Holy Alliance to show that we are to-day at just about the same point as the diplomats of 1815, and that President Wilson has not yet voiced a single thought that was not advanced at the time of formation of the alliance. Yet there were the most earnest and enthusiastic support of the President and a complete lack of confidence in the English leaders. The same feeling was also evident in the equally remarkable demonstration at Free Trade Hall, Manchester, on Monday, by an entirely different kind of audience, representing the best business and liberal elements of that rich and powerful city.

The Albert Hall crowd cheered to the echo the assertion that Wilson had reached a position of world leadership by sheer force of moral appeal and by the moral positions he has taken. Yet for all its belief in him the Labor party, which polled two and a quarter million votes in the last election, will not take from his hands a sham league or a mere paper affair. Its leaders will now hold similar meetings in all the provincial cities for the purpose of rousing public sentiment further and bringing pressure to bear upon Wilson to stand fast and upon Lloyd George to do the right thing. It is discouraging that anybody remains to desire, as Clemenceau does, and as such Tory organs as the *Morning Post* here do, the retention of the old fatal order of checks and balances. It would seem as if any sane Frenchman would realize the terrible price paid for the alliance with the bloodstained Russia of the Czar, without which France would probably never have been drawn into war—an alliance largely dictated, of course, by the enormous French investment in Russian bonds.

Clemenceau's announced attitude toward this—or the Allies' attitude toward it, if he speaks for them—is another proof of the slowness with which error is eradicated from the world. There is indeed little new under the sun. Why should an enlightened man believe to-day that the spread of Bolshevist ideas can be controlled by a ring of bayonets stationed in Posen, Odessa, Riga, and elsewhere, as Clemenceau would have us believe when he advocates the plan of a *cordon sanitaire?* One need only look back to the history of the French Revolution and the attempts made to prevent the spread of the magic words *liberté, égalité,* and *fraternité,* to realize that the cordon plan may have precisely the opposite effect of that desired. Fighting battles against a state of mind is one of the poorest games rulers can play, and yet that game is now in full swing against Russia.

It is admitted that considerable British forces being landed in Riga actually demanded that the wicked and contemptible Hun troops should stay at Riga and help them defend that city against Lenine and Trotzky. This is about the clearest proof we have yet had of the topsy-turvy state of the world. A certain section of the British still demand the hanging of the Kaiser, the return to Germany of all interned Germans, and no intercourse with them of any kind. I have seen shops here displaying signs forbidding the entrance of any German-born person, whether long naturalized or not. Yet at the same moment these abominable Hun troops in Riga are offered the high honor of becoming brothers in arms to the English against the Bolsheviki and there are indications that there may be similar appeals to them to be good fellows and help out in Poland.

As it is, there is every evidence that the Allies are getting deeper and deeper into Russia, and that the Pichon plan of arming Russians to fight the battles of the Allies will lead to complications no man can foresee. Yet I constantly hear, on the best of authority, that President Wilson expressed himself while here in London, as before leaving the United States, in opposition to the further use of American troops in Russia. On the other hand, it is part of the extraordinary contradictions that make it so difficult to judge the existing situation, that we hear persistent statements that more American troops are going to Russia. Sooner or later people must see that the best way to get rid of Lenine and Trotzky is to let them hang themselves and let them show just how long a Government like theirs can survive. The more strongly the cordon of foreign troops is placed around Russia the stronger, unfortunately, are Lenine and Trotzky likely to be; that is the opinion of all the liberal leaders here, both in and out of the press, and of numerous successful and unsuccessful candidates for Parliament with whom I have talked, who unanimously report the greatest interest in the electorate as to Russia, and the most direct opposition to military interference there. Shall we again see a Government embarking on a foreign policy against public sentiment at home? That is the question which people are asking here and on which we should soon have light.

OSWALD GARRISON VILLARD

Secrecy at Versailles

(By Cable to the *Nation*)

Paris, January 18

IF the American people could know in detail what has been going on here these last three days they would rightly be extremely proud, not of their peace commissioners, but of their press correspondents; for the latter, faced suddenly with the decision of the preliminary council to make utter mockery of Wilson's avowal of open covenants of peace openly arrived at, have taken up the gage, and at this cabling have achieved a substantial success. How the President could have yielded on this vital point is absolutely inconceivable, for it is fundamental, and essential to victory on other issues. His one hope of success lies in securing the continued support of public sentiment by letting the peoples who have so warmly acclaimed him since his arrival in Europe know just what is going on, that they may stand behind him. Behind closed doors he can be easily outvoted, and without stenographic minutes all sorts of stories may be freely circulated to his injury. This is so evident that the whole fate of the conference may obviously depend upon the stand taken now. Yet President Wilson was present when the fatal action was taken, and he seems neither to have protested nor to have seen the impropriety of rules of procedure for the conference being laid down by a totally different body.

Immediate action by the American correspondents has led to a considerable gain in that there will be three American, three British, three French, and three Italian newspaper men present, and three representing other countries—fifteen in all. A solemn document, defending this limitation, was read to the American newspaper men. Composed by a member of the American commission, it is characterized throughout by all the familiar methods of Metternich, Bismarck, and similar masters of the old game of secret diplomacy. It did not satisfy the correspondents, for it specifies these privileges only for the open sessions of the conference. A rumor that there are to be five secret sessions to one open one did not cheer the correspondents, who have not forgotten the President's pledges. They accepted these concessions and one removing the restriction forbidding all members of the conference to have any relations with any newspaper man, but are determined to fight on. They believe that the French correspondents, who were in all-night session, did not represent truly the French press. These Frenchmen wanted not only the complete exclusion of all correspondents, but the censoring of every line of copy sent by anybody, while our men demanded the abolition of all censorship—a demand not referred to in the reply to the Americans on Friday.

The Americans are now planning a conference of all correspondents here to fight still further. An account of this conference and the further results, if any, will probably be printed in the dailies before this *Nation* appears. But no cable can adequately describe the splendid spirit of the American committee headed by John Nevin, of the United Press, Arthur Krock, of the Louisville *Courier-Journal*, and Herbert Bayard Swope, of the *World*. In twenty-two years of journalistic experience, I have never seen a finer spirit or a keener appreciation of professional responsibility; for the whole group have realized that they were fighting for the freedom and integrity of our press in order to save President Wilson from the effects of his own lamentable blunder. They have felt that they were serving the interest of the whole country. American defeat here would be an incalculable disaster. Had the original plan, to which the President assented, gone through, the correspondents must have packed up for home, or if they had stayed they would have had to pick up stray crumbs of knowledge, often wrong, which would have made the peace conferrees waste much time in denying reports and rumors. This cloud overhangs and darkens the formal opening of the session. The affair has added to the friction and has made many see the advantages of holding such a conference in a neutral country. There was of course the usual ceremony attending the opening, and to this session the correspondents were admitted, but the fact remains that the work of the conference is being done in small private gatherings and that the big four completely dominate.

The conference met with no representation of Russia, Germany, or Austria. It is the first conference of the kind ever held in modern times at which the beaten side was not permitted to be present and to argue for its future. Unless the situation changes Germany will know nothing of her fate until she is told what it is to be, and the vast interests of a former Ally, Russia, may be wholly neglected.

It is certainly disappointing that Mr. Wilson has thus early resumed his old habit of compromising. The ancient excuse is advanced by some that the President, in yielding on this minor matter, is saving his trumps for the really big plays, like the League of Nations. The mistake of this is that there is no bigger issue than covenants openly arrived at, and that he who starts by yielding at the beginning is likely to yield in the middle and all the way through as a result of his early weakness. More than that, the President has so many cards in his hands and such marvellous popular support that he ought not to yield an inch. He has denied the report here sent to the New York *Tribune* that if he is thwarted he will take the troops out and go home. It was a pity to deny something that did him infinite credit. Of course the American correspondents here propose to continue fighting on for the President's peace terms; they can see their responsibility to their fellow countrymen in no other light, and they will be the first to acclaim Wilson if he wins and whenever he wins.

Meanwhile it is pleasant to report that in some directions at least the skies continue bright. There is a continued diminution of the talk of invading Russia, and it is encouraging that the note to the correspondents says that the conference realizes the necessity of making peace as rapidly as possible so that the armies may be mustered out soon. Yet it must not make peace so rapidly as to plant the seeds for future wars or do injustice through lack of adequate consideration of the endless problems involved. Among the managers of the conference there is keen appreciation of the need of saving Europe from Bolshevism, but apparently there is little realization that the surest way to continue unrest is to deny the fullest publicity to decisions affecting the fate of so many nations and peoples.

So the most important conference in the world's history opened at last this afternoon with a rather commonplace but fitting speech by Poincaré and tributes by Sonnino, Wilson, and George to Clemenceau. Mr. Wilson spoke gracefully as always but with unusual earnestness and restraint. The terrible responsibility resting upon the conference seemed to make itself felt and the gravity of this historic meeting, attended by all the correspondents, was emphasized by the absence of any applause, the only ripple of laughter being due to the error of an interpreter in translating a compliment paid by George to Clemenceau. The Tiger did not show his teeth, but declared that the programme of the conference had already been mapped out by Wilson, and, best of all, that the League of Nations would head the agenda of the next general meeting. So, with the fairest of words, was adjourned the first session of a body to which the eyes of all the world are turned, which contains more prominent dictators of governmental policies than any ever assembled before, but which numbers among its members no woman, scarcely a labor man, and no representative of the despised foe or the Russian democracy.

OSWALD GARRISON VILLARD

Two Cable Letters

I. The Private and the Premier

(By Cable to the *Nation*, delayed in transmission)

London, January 4

LONDON has this week witnessed extraordinary scenes —British soldiers marching upon the Foreign Office and the Prime Minister's residence, demanding their immediate release from service. The Prime Minister came back in a hurry to deal with them. They were cheered on their way by crowds showing the heartiest sympathy with what the *Morning Post* discreetly terms indiscipline. The *Daily News* declares editorially that the British army is seething with unrest. Nothing like this has ever happened in the history of the British army; the soldiers have shown themselves victors in this engagement with the Government, which has acceded to their wishes for speedier demobilization. Officers have everywhere shown good judgment and wisdom but have had to yield to the spectacle of the private soldier calling upon the Brigadier General. Another committee has obtained an audience with Sir William Robertson, which has naturally astounded London, already none too happy about the Soldiers' Councils elsewhere. The problem presented is one to put George to his trumps, for it has grave inherent difficulties. Soldiers obviously cannot be allowed to demobilize themselves, but the task of getting rid of an army which it took four years to create cannot be performed overnight. If it were possible the labor market would be glutted and serious results would follow. But the prompt action of the Government in modifying the conditions of discharge shows how nervous it has become and how great is the danger; if an unwise officer should attempt violent measures shots might easily follow which would naturally have an unpleasant echo abroad. Even in the navy there is unrest, for mine sweepers refused to go out until their pay was raised ten dollars a week for the most dangerous duty.

While the Government is entitled to some sympathy in view of the magnitude of the problem, it is none the less also to be criticised, the public feels, for not having made greater preparation to meet such an emergency. What shall the Government do under the circumstances? London and the nearby camps are full of men tired of drill, homesick, eager to return to their families. It is pathetic to watch the groups of Australian troops hanging around the offices of their respective Governments, in the Strand, gazing on pictures of home scenes. Transportation difficulties make it unlikely that they can be returned for a long time. They are certain that the war is over and are not the least bit alarmed over the possible re-entry of Germany into the war. They have too much commonsense to be worried by assertions of imperialistic military critics to the effect that large forces are needed for the occupation of Germany torn by civil strife and offering the spectacle of constant fighting in the streets of Berlin. A Paris newspaper declares that peace will not be signed for a year. These happenings in London give notice to the rulers that the soldiers do not propose to be kept away from civil life by any necessity of doing garrison duty in Germany for a period of a year or longer.

There is no doubt whatever that rumors of large forces being sent to Russia have had much to do with the scramble to get out of the army. There is also the fear that the best available jobs will be taken by discharged munition workers. This has had much to do with the announcements in the press that there are not large forces in Russia—only twenty thousand there now and none being sent, and that the British fleet which has been shelling the Reval coast and bringing refugees out of Riga has definitely left those waters. All this shows the nervousness of the Government but even more it shows the stern necessity which has confronted Lloyd George and forced him to adopt and announce a definite policy as to Russia. The demonstrations of the soldiers, if continued, will compel the British Government to make peace with Germany, which will not necessitate a long occupation. This is all the more necessary because the old British Regular Army has practically disappeared during the war and the voluntary enlisted men of 1914 and 1915 feel that they should be let out before the conscripts. There are, therefore, no long-enlisted men to be thrown into Germany. Everyone who has seen these lorries full of soldiers mutinying in the friendliest and most pacifistic spirit, but still mutinying, and who remembers what troops have done elsewhere when war was ended, asks "what next?"

There is no real cause for alarm, for the men have no general grievance, only an individual one, and they are reasonable and open to influence if convinced that the Government is moving as fast as possible. But it plainly serves notice on the Peace Conference (the opening of which has been delayed another week) to get down to business as rapidly as possible. Now that Wilson has returned from his Italian trip it seems as if business could and should be transacted as rapidly as possible, for it is obvious that he must return to America not later than February 15. This leaves a scant five weeks to deal with the most vital problems the world ever faced. More and more evident does it every day become that if the evil of militarism is not promptly removed from the world, civilization will collapse through the spread of violent Bolshevism. It is also becoming apparent that not only militarism must go but also the preparations for militarism and war. The whole hateful business must be done away with. There are many here who believe that this week's happenings have put an end to the possibility of conscription coming in England and that George or his successor will not dare to urge it in Parliament no matter what may be the peace terms. These people are too sanguine. What is plain is that we have been witnessing direct action of the clearest kind by men in uniform acting in unison and cheerfully taking the risk of the severest punishment. This example is especially not desired, coming as it does on top of threats made by the extremists in the Labor party to resort to direct action in their despair of achieving reform through efforts at controlling and reforming Parliament.

The next ten days will show whether the action taken by the Government will suffice to quell the trouble, but no one can deny that the Government has received a rude jolt from the quarter least expected. It has given color to the feeling that George's new Government may collapse quickly, not because of any adverse vote in the House of Commons but because of outside dissatisfaction. Lloyd George's position is not enviable and he must show now whether or not he is a statesman. Whichever way he looks there are situations which might stagger him, situations brought about by his lack of fair, above-board, and prompt dealing, and by his lack of wise, clear-cut policy.

People are asking here whether it was necessary to render Germany revolutionary by the continuance of blockade; they applaud the action of the American Government in Washington and elsewhere stating that it wished the blockade lifted. No sensible man to-day can continue to believe that humanity can be made to improve and prosper by brute force and bloodshed. The whole world cries out for a new order to be created at Paris along the lines laid down by Wilson.

OSWALD GARRISON VILLARD

II. Versailles and Princes' Islands

(By Cable to the *Nation*)

Paris, January 25

THERE is no Peace Conference—as yet. Wilson's speech at to-day's formal session was one of his most skilful achievements and constituted a real triumph. The only question now is how effective the league of nations will be, and whether the door will be opened to Germany. Even the committee on credentials has not met, though the Paris press has gravely assured us that its laborious task was holding back the next full session of the conference. Yet the week has been a wonderfully fruitful one because of the extraordinary action taken in regard to the Russian situation.

The American people, correspondents are assured by high authority, should realize that there is much confusion between actions taken by three bodies here—the Peace Conference which is not yet even organized fully, the Supreme Imperial War Council, and the heads of the various Governments here assembled. Probably most Americans think that the action in regard to Russia was taken by the Peace Conference or by one of its committees. Nothing of the kind. The conference proper had nothing to do with it. I should even be willing to wager that some of our peace commissioners knew nothing about it till they read of it in the papers.

The action in question was taken by the heads of the Allied Governments, and credit for it belongs squarely to Wilson. Of this every American may well be proud: An act so cheering, wise, and right-minded as to call for the highest praise to Wilson for originating and putting it through, and to the English and French for yielding their earlier positions. It is only fair to say that the English partly changed their policy a couple of weeks ago for reasons which I have twice vainly tried to convey to the readers of the *Nation*—but the censor has intervened. The English deserve the greatest credit, because it is only a few weeks since they were still denouncing Lenine and Trotzky as arch-fiends and swearing that they would never treat with them save as violators of every international and humanitarian obligation. It is easy also to recall the solemn denunciation of the Bolshevists given out by our State Department some time back. Nevertheless it is certainly the dawning of a new day in diplomacy when Governments are willing to come out in the open and admit that they were wrong and frankly to give up a position previously assumed. This still further enhances the favorable opinion of British policy and the British representatives that was already current. From two high sources in different departments I have just heard commendation of the British attitude in matters not directly concerned with making peace, and the same approval seems due in this Russian matter.

The President's manifesto is beyond all criticism as a statement of the correct attitude toward Russian internal affairs and conforms to his position that there should be no interference in the Russian people's business—from which attitude he departed when he landed troops in Archangel and Vladivostok. Ever since the peace mission got ready for work American unwillingness to take part in further invasion has been perfectly clear here. Some important American personages do not hesitate to say that they are convinced that American public opinion would never stand either for landing troops in Russia for a big war, or for financing and supplying food to the Allies to enable them to carry on such a war. But whatever motive induced Mr. Wilson to move, it was an action which has thrilled all lovers of democracy here and all champions of a new order. True, the French press is unhappy and so doubtless are the Tory organs in England, but the powerful Northcliffe press will surely support it. Had it been taken months ago millions of lives might have been saved. The remarkable thing is that the action was taken after two of the bitterest anti-Bolshevik diplomats had been heard, one of whom said it was no longer a matter of attacking Bolshevists but of defending Europe by force of arms from their attacks and their propaganda. Both counselled war. Interest now turns to Moscow. The men best informed about the Bolshevists are divided as to whether the latter will accept the offer and for the sake of internal peace abandon their war against Germany and Poland, and their determination to carry class war throughout the world, or whether they will put themselves in the wrong by refusing. The Russian camps here in Paris refusing to-day to participate are much upset by the positive announcement that the Allies will no longer finance or support any counter revolution. This leaves Kolchak, among others, beyond even the prayers of the American Defense Society.

There is no denying that it is a great moral victory for Lenine and Trotzky. This is irritating to some Americans here who represent the Lodge point of view. While it does not solve the problem, it at least brings it into the realm of common sense and kindly handling. At this stage, the situation parallels that of Mexico when the Niagara conference was called, and people here are careful to point out that even that gathering did not later prevent armed intervention in Mexico. We shall not be out of the woods until the trees are all behind us, but the end of the forest is certainly much nearer.

It is an extraordinary spectacle that we are now witnessing—the whole world being ruled from one capital by three men. If the delegates from minor countries do not like it they say nothing. Russia was to have been a concern of theirs. The question now is what else will be taken out of their hands by this volunteer self-appointed supreme council of an existing league of nations. The advantages involved, such as the possibility of quick and concerted action, are obvious, yet there are many who fear that this domination of the world by a handful of men will have a bad effect upon the effort to establish a world league. The danger that a few unscrupulous men might at some future time impose their will on the world is in reality another argument for disarmament; for when you strip nations of their weapons, the tremendous superiority of a country like ours over weaker nations largely disappears.

As regards the press, the unhappy situation still prevails. Cases of withholding and editing despatches have been laid before the commission, but without result as yet. The President could not get any correspondent here to testify that the promise as to publicity and full information, made to congress on December 2, has been carried out. On that occasion, it will be remembered, he said: "At my request the French and English Governments have absolutely removed the censorship of cable news which until within a fortnight they had maintained and there is now no censorship whatever exercised at this end except upon attempted trade communications with enemy countries." The correspondents can not learn, for instance, whether the Americans have a league plan or not. Some officials say they have seen a plan which was finished only last Sunday, the nineteenth, while others deliberately give the impression that there will be no plan offered on behalf of America, but that a composite of the Smuts, Cecil, and French plans will be worked out plus the American suggestions.

The lack of a labor man on the American delegation is keenly felt, since international labor problems are now coming up, and no proper spokesman for English or American labor is at hand to speak with authority. It is explained, however, that American experts are in hiding somewhere and may be produced in due season. To add to the difficulties of the correspondents, mail delays are maddening and several correspondents have been notified by their home offices that nothing has been received. One pleasant feature of the censorship is that the censor usually forgets to tell you what he has done with or to your message; but this week he notified the New York *Call* that an entire dispatch had been suppressed. We are all eager to see if this clear case will be made the basis of representations.

Wilson continues to deny himself to all pressmen. The grave problems before the conference are again illustrated by distressing news of massacres of Jews in Galicia by Polish soldiers. Now that the war to end war is over there seems to be no disposition to end the killing.

It is such news, as well as the deliberate attempts elsewhere to take additional territory by force, which has led to the emphatic warning here to-day that there must be prompt grounding of arms. This is another admirable step —but it is to be noted that it comes not from the Peace Conference but from the little inner group (President Wilson and the Premiers) who seem to have usurped the functions of the conference, meeting in that complete secrecy which Wilson, Lloyd George, and Clemenceau first desired for the conference itself. Secret covenants of peace secretly arrived at seem to be the rule with them, and one wonders whether the conference itself will ever have any other function than solemnly to ratify their action.

No peace conference is actually meeting here. Certainly no conference took the step concerning Russia which led Franklin Bouillon and André Chéradame, in the rooms of the French committee on foreign propaganda last Friday evening, to start a movement to undermine Wilson at home. Chéradame says nobody in the world approves Wilson's Russian plan. OSWALD GARRISON VILLARD

Paris, Feb. 5, 1919.

Dearest Love

I could not cable until last night that I am leaving Paris to-day for Bern, because I did not finally get my passport until five o'clock it having been held up again by the army intelligence bureau. Fortunately I had Col. House's authority to use his name and with the aid of letters from his secretary succeeded in finally getting through. What is more important I got it without any questions being asked or pledges exacted. If none is asked at the border, I shall be able to head northeast in about a week to what is the most interesting place in Europe just now. The only drawback is the fact that I shall be entirely without news from home for perhaps four weeks, but I think that through Emil Hilgard I can arrange for cables to keep you from worrying. Kautzky and others are at Bern and they will advise me as to best plan. Also the man I want most to see, Kurt Eisner from Munich. I am looking forward to the trip with the greatest eagerness and real excitement. Of course, I should like to have waited for another week here until Wilson started back, so as to have covered the whole phase of the first stay in Paris. But I have sent a despatch which will be good for next week and Lewis Gannett will send another to wind up if there is occasion. The news from Bern is quite thrilling so far as the debates as to the origin of the war is concerned and I wish I could have been there this week, but when I tell you that it has taken me more than two whole days' time, in fact nearly two and a half, to get the three visas necessary you will get some idea of how time is lost and wasted in Paris. I certainly would never do this again without bringing a private secretary along for the time lost in chores and errands and notes and travelling across town as you have to in order to send any despatch after 7.30 P.M. would enable one to see many people and write a lot more. I still feel that what I have done for the Nation is very poor but everybody else feels the same about his work which cheers me up a little. We are all agreed that it has been a most trying and difficult task, with no help whatever from Wilson who obstinately refuses to see newspaper men, while Lloyd

George and Clemenceau help their men and are helped by them. THe morning meetings with GeN. Bliss and Mr. White and occasionally Mr. Lansing are a farce.

Strunsky goes with me to-day but will return here, so that our association which has been almost constant, will end at Bern. He has worked hard but is dispirited, too, has not been very well and is anxious to get home as are all the men. A group of them goes to-day, quite disgusted. (Don't tell Mrs S. the above if you should meet her)

I am armed with an excellent letter from Gen. Smuts for use with any British officers, one from Minister Vandervelde, commending me to All Belgian officials and one from House's secretary which will help. I met so many interesting people during the last week of my stay here that things were beginning to open up. For instance Joseph Reinach of our I.R.S. advisory committee asked me to-dinner at his beautiful house where I met the Vanderveldes whom I had seen in New York soon after the war began, when they were pleading the cause of Belgium, Viviani, Lady Wemyss, wife of the First Lord of the Admiralty, who told extremely interesting inside things -the young and attractive Duchesse de la Romchefoucauld and others. Poor Reinach lost his only son on the 18th day of the war and his young daughter six days later, lost her husband and soon after her brother-in-law-all the young men those two poor people were especially interested in. It is no wonder that Reinach is pretty bitter against the Germans.

I took tea with Madame Vandervelde yesterday. She is quite Bolshevik and wishes that all the leading men of the Conference could be guillotined as she says that, except Wilson, they are all standing between us and a rational world. Their deaths she says would spare those of many others! Viviani she despises among others. She also reports that every where she goes there is nothing but scoffing at Wilson and derision for the league of nations and the system of mandatories for the colonies and this was the tone at Reinach's. The French are so certain of the folly of it all that they want to make Germany so weak as to forever remove the menace of German militarism. I find it very hard to see what the outcome of it all is to be and, strictly speaking, any conference which is no conference at all like this one, ought to fail. It is all being decided by the self-appointed committee consisting of Wilson and the prime and foreign ministers. Naturally the rest of the delegates are furious and especially those from the minor states who are asking why they were brought here. It is largely Woodrow's bad way of doing things. And the calm way they go on carving up Europe without consulting the Russians, Germans, Austrians, Hungarians is beyond words. No one knows how it will end, where or when it will end and everybody wonders how they can drift on this way much longer without serious troubles with peoples or armies. Heaven knows I wish they would strike. It is enough to make an anarchist out of anybody to see the world in such hands. But the fact is that, as I am cabling, we owe to Wilson everything that has been achieved and that if he had not come over this conference would have been the worst thing that ever happened in its disgusting thirst for the spoils. The Poles and Czecho-Slovaks, Italians and others have about as much idea of making this a better world and of ending war as the cows in New Jersey.

I have been twice to the theatre since I last wrote, once to the opera to see Thais and once to see the greatest French actor of to-day, Guitry, play a dramatization of the life of Pasteur. Miss Grace Abbott, Jan Addams's right hand man went with me to the latter nd enjoyed it as much as I. There is not a woman in the cast and it is really only a s succession of scenes out of the life of Pasteur but so wonderfully acted by Guitry as to be absolutely absorbing and at times so touching as where he succeeds with his first case of inoculation for rabies, as to bring the tears. yesterday a very interesting man, Sir Thomas Barclay, an old resident of Paris and Andre Chevrillon, the other member of my international section came to lunch with me and developed the most divergent views from the same facts! Margaret Mayo went with me to Thais which was well sung. Miss Mayo you may identify as author of Baby Mine, Twin Beds, and

Polly of the Circus.we met herin London through Foreman with whom she has just written a play.

I am leaving my trunk but have bought a little soldier's one which holds quite a lot. But I am down to bare bones and have stocked up only with soap for T.E. My plan is to come back here for a few dyas and go to the front and the battle fields. But I do not see how I can go home the 10th of March and accomplish what I wish to. I am as crazy as the rest of this homesick and sick crew of journalists to get back (the Chicago Tribune has, I just hear, recalled all its big staff save one and Probert who has been rooming with Lawrence is quite ill with pneumonia.) Montague Glass, author of Potash and Perlmutter who has been writing here and sails to-morrow says he never before has been in a place where they studiously treated him as if he were a servant. But I have little complaint. I have kept well have lost to my joy quite a little weight ad barring one attack of rheumatism, which lasted only two days, have felt splendidly. The exercise I have had has done me a world of good. You may hear from me first at Brussels or Coblentz.

I am sending a copy of this to F.G.V. at Berkeley. Your two letters Jan.10 and 14 gave me much joy and I am as proud as can be of Dorothea's, it is so well written and expressed and I am more delighted than I can say that she has been behaving so well. If I know anything it is that she is going to be a great joy to us. Her story of Ahba's seeing his Daddy in T.R.'s picture made me crazy to squeeze him! I am glad you went to see the office and thatxyou had a good time with Eddie Webster. I do envy him his motoring, but I shall be quite ready to settle down after this, for some time. Dorsis's letter was quite worth waiting for; apparently I lost her first. I shall be so mad if that long, long letter about our terrible voyage does not turn up.

With a heartful of love to the dearest of wives and best of mothers to her little flock, and hugs to all of them.

Ever your, Oswald.

Foreign Correspondence

On the Eve of the Conference

Paris, January 13

"IT'S a regular national convention of Americans," remarked William Allen White as he stood at the Place de la Concorde and beheld the never-ending stream of Americans passing back and forth. Paris is truly flooded by Americans; on the Rue de Rivoli one sees more American uniforms than French, and the prevailing language is so little that of Paris that the humorous are already suggesting that signs reading "Ici on parle Français" should be placed in the shop windows. There are really too many Americans here, far too many for Paris, far too many for their own good. As Bishop Brent said in his sermon yesterday, the French hearthstone has been trodden upon often enough these last four years; it is time strangers got out and left the French a bit to themselves.

But Americans are not the only ones here; every other nationality is represented on the streets. And then there are pitiful delegations of Lithuanians, Poles, Russians, Dodecanesians, and heaven knows how many more—pitiful because they seem so helpless, so at sea, yet so intensely bent upon somehow getting their case before the Allies and obtaining quick action. Quick action! With a Peace Conference not yet getting down to business; with the preliminaries not yet settled, with postponement after postponement and hope deferred making the heart sick; with the most difficult of problems in Poland, Russia, and Germany pressing for settlement or decision, and somebody postponing the Conference every day—Wilson, Clemenceau, Orlando, one after the other! Mr. Wilson's departure for home is only four weeks away. Men may die by the thousand and women and children starve if you please, but the Conference must be postponed.

But there are others here who impress me far more than the Americans and the English and the Italians and the groups representing all the new nations who have so suddenly been born into the world, some, perhaps, to die a-borning. When I stand upon the streets and see the long rows of captured German cannon, ghastly in their war paint, and behold the grateful helplessness of their silent captivity, I can only see and think of the dead who fought these guns and the thousands who fell when they belched forth. What of these dead? When I vizualize them I have a deep feeling of pity for Mr. Wilson. He has tasted a popular acclaim given surely to no other man in history. The honors bestowed upon him here in Europe are such as have certainly come to no one else, for they have come from the hearts of the people, who more and more are turning to him as their one hope. Yet how can any one envy him? Upon him rests the most terrible responsibility. The liberal opinion of the world declares him its spokesman; the plain, usually voiceless, people of Italy, France, and England have found speech to cheer him as they have never cheered any one before. From across the Rhine, the ignorant, deluded, beaten Germans look to him as the one man who may secure to them a future worth while. What if he disappoints victors and vanquished alike? I know that if he fails it will seem to all liberal thinkers in England as if the blackness of utter desolation and hopelessness were settling down upon the world. And what will the dead say? That thought will never down. Here in this city, in that heavily overornamented Louis XV room in which the Conference is to meet, will be decided whether the dead died in vain or not; whether this was really the war to end war or whether that phrase was the merest cant and hypocrisy. Is it any wonder that in these hours of maddening delay, of ignorance on the part of all the press representatives here as to most of what is going on, one thinks ever of the ghostly legions which must be marching up and down the Champs Elysées and mounting guard over the palace where sleeps Woodrow Wilson?

No one knows to-night all that is happening except a few insiders. Much they may be putting through, the little group of men who rule the world, but they alone can measure how much. I am told, by one who should know the truth, that the real business is being accomplished in these informal meetings; that when the Peace Conference meets it will be really only to record decisions, and that until the behind-the-scenes decisions are ready the Conference will mark time. "Open covenants of peace, openly arrived at!" What a mockery the phrase sounds here! Yet it is true that the position of the maker of that phrase has steadily improved during the last two weeks. His trip to Italy strengthened his hand enormously; the people simply could not be kept from him and there is no doubt that they worship him. The danger is that they really believe that like some magician he will produce for them, out of his hat, an entirely new world. It could be done, heaven knows. It could be done right here in Paris, here and now, in the year 1919. But we must be content, they tell us, with half a loaf—and happy if we get as much as that. The fear is that a *bon mot* of one of the Paris newspapers which runs, *"Après la guerre du droit, la paix du tigre,"* may come true.

We shall see what we shall see. Outwardly things are not going well. Mr. Lansing is not cutting a good figure before the correspondents; he fences in the daily parleys, instead of taking the men into his confidence, very much as he used in Washington, and there was a regular *émeute* at his conference yesterday. The English correspondents one hears are similarly unhappy; of our own, many are suffering from nostalgia and are eager to get home. Their restlessness is due not to the fact that they are not getting news to send out, but that they are not getting vital news to send out to the American people. They have become very eager to win the President's battle for him, but they are fearful that if they are not given the information they need they cannot prepare the ground in America in time for the seed to fall on fertile soil. It is interesting to see how these men have grown more liberal as they have become more and more familiar with the forces opposing the league of nations. They are beginning to realize, many of them, that the creation of the league is rightly the first thing upon the programme, not only for its own intrinsic value, but because of the necessity of having an instrument with which to deal with the vast number of problems of which Mr. Wilson in his address at Manchester declared that neither the Peace Conference nor any other single group of men could grapple with all at one time. They are despondent just now because the details of the President's plans for the League are not being given to them, and many of them believe that there is no such plan. In this they are mistaken unless my information is entirely at fault. Even some of the French press speak of the President's withholding his plan for strategic reasons until the Conference opens—perhaps to prevent concerted attacks upon it in advance.

But while the press correspondents are thus unduly concerned for reasons that do them honor and reasons over which they have no control, it is undeniable that the situation on the eve of the opening of the Conference is in some aspects a serious one. The note of M. Pichon of January 5, replying to the wise and sensible request of the British Government that the Allies invite all the parties to the Russian struggle to send representatives to the Peace Conference, rejected that humane proposal in language so vigorous and so violent that the reply of the other Allies is awaited with some anxiety. Again, there has been an unfortunate publication in *l'Humanité* of a statement on Poland given by Mr. Lansing in confidence to the American correspondents. It is not only that the publication appeared, but that it appeared in a newspaper hostile to Clemenceau under circumstances that made it seem as if it had been deliberately given out by our commissioners. More than that, it was a flat denial, in unqualified terms, of the inspired report published apparently by the Supreme Command, i. e., General Foch, that the Americans have agreed to invade Poland with the Allies. Any further use of such emphatic language by either side will undoubtedly engender dangerous heat—all the more dangerous because there is not that cordial spirit between the fighting forces which one had been led to expect, and which ought to exist. The war for justice, for liberty and civilization, is having some curious results!

But while the above report of the actual conditions on the eve of the fateful gathering sounds discouraging, the truth is, as I shall cable to the *Nation* this week, that the situation is not actually so discouraging as it has been. Four weeks ago the outlook for sanity on the Russian situation seemed dark indeed. Now it can be stated authoritatively that all danger of American as well as of British intervention in Russia is past. That is in part due to correct thinking and proper political instincts; it is also to be credited to the march of events. The recent sensational statement of the Swedish correspondent of the London *Times*, that the Lenine army is no longer a Bolshevist army but a Russian one, well armed and well officered and commanded by one of the ablest officers the old army produced, has put statesmen on notice that the task of unseating the Bolshevists is one to call for bloodshed on a large scale and for an expenditure of treasure which the United States alone can supply. We cannot expect to hear of the immediate withdrawal of our troops from Archangel because it is inaccessible now on account of the ice. But the Vladivostok troops may be homeward bound sooner than people at home expect.

What the Allies will do in that unhappy country nobody yet knows. It is quite possible that there may be some British and French military interference there. What the Lithuanian Committee is here to ask is that some twenty thousand American Lithuanians in Pershing's army be released to them, and that plenty of arms and ammunition be given to them as well—and while they seek audiences with the powers that be to obtain this and other help, the Bolsheviki are sweeping through the Lithuanian country at a rate that makes it obvious that it will have been overrun long before adequate military aid can arrive there. The difficulty of aiding Poland is increased by the fact that there are two would-be Governments of Poland, one of the Polish Committee in this city, which the French Government favors, and the other that under General Pilsudski, which has actually governed for the last two months under very trying circumstances. Again, there have been signs there as well as elsewhere that when you create a new state you are not thereby necessarily cleansed of all imperialistic ambitions.

The magnitude of the problems and their multitude are simply overwhelming. What of Persia, what of Albania and Syria and Armenia, and the three new republics in the Caucasus about which the American Commission to Persia has just brought authoritative information to Paris? One hears very little of them all. Mr. Wilson is rightly concentrating public opinion upon the league of nations, after which the question of disarmament ought to come to the fore. Too many men have been taught the use of deadly weapons, too many soldiers have learned the advantage of indirect attack, to make the world very safe for either democracy or autocracy at present. Certain monsters have an unhappy way of turning against their Frankensteins.

OSWALD GARRISON VILLARD

Our Weekly Cable Letter

Marking Time at Versailles

Paris, January 31

THE skies and omens continue favorable in this second week of the Peace Conference and we are assured of a third and interesting meeting on Saturday. While it is as hard as ever to obtain precise information, it seems to be agreed that Wilson has scored another point in winning the English agreement to the principle that all German colonies shall be treated as wards of the league of nations. While there may still be many a slip between cup and lip, and it is not yet clear that Lloyd George has won assent, it is evident to the correspondents that the American authorities are immensely pleased at the progress made. Wilson himself is reported to have shown his teeth at Wednesday's conferences as he had not done since his arrival and to have let it appear that there are times when he will fight. Lloyd George is not so happy as he was and is complaining that the Conference is slow and that he cannot see as much of the President as he would like in order to make things move. But if it be true that Wilson carried his point yesterday it marks a new era in the history of the backward nations and ends the possibility of dividing as spoils the captured German colonies. If so, it will be one of his greatest achievements.

We are still witnessing a curious spectacle—the doing of much of the work of the conference by bodies not officially connected with or having authority to act for it. It is rumored that Lloyd George was quite disconcerted when Wilson went on the committee to work out the detailed plan of the league, fearing he would be still more engrossed, but the committee has not as yet met. It is explained that sometimes these things can be as well done by informal conferences as by committee meetings. Yet so much depends upon the details of the scheme that it should engross all the time of those entrusted with the overpowering responsibility of creating it. We are still without an American plan for a league and are informed here that for strategical reasons no American plan as such will be given out. On the other hand those who have seen the English plan tell me that it is brilliant and extremely well worked out in its details. Whether this will be made public or whether a composite of all the plans will be laid before the conference for approval is not clear. But evidently there is no intention of using the American press to educate people in the details of the scheme before it is sprung upon the world. The uncomfortable fact is that the Conference is moving slowly and so much in the dark that public interest in its work may wane.

The growing unrest in various nations is reflected in Lloyd George's own feeling of impatience. Thus the British delegates to the Berne Conference (which despite difficulties bids fair to be an extremely interesting meeting) showed great concern, when passing through Paris, over the labor situation in Great Britain, notably in Glasgow. They say many capitalists will hold back the making over of plants or the taking up of new lines until they know the outcome of the Peace Conference. Meanwhile there are endless strikes and there is considerable unemployment. This is playing into the hands of the direct actionists. While greatly pleased that the Peace Conference is taking up international labor problems they fear that any action will have too much governmental flavor, especially since George Nicoll Barnes and Mr. Gompers will have so much to do with it. The report that President Wilson has ordered Mr. Polk to behave himself and be sensible in the matter of granting passports to non-governmental American Socialists gave great satisfaction here, but this is dampened by the additional gossip that Wilson has ordered Mr. Gompers to attend the Berne Conference, where he is not wanted. Indeed there are few non-governmental places where he is wanted. In the main, therefore, most nations are more encouraged this week.

The English camp, however, is somewhat discouraged and some therein begin to have doubts as to whether a peace conference representing only one-third of Europe can make peace for all of Europe. They are discouraged, too, lest the Prinkipos conference fall through. The leading Paris representative of Lenine and Trotzky is confident that the Bolsheviki will attend, now that the Archangel Government and other opposition groups have declined. It is gradually agreed here that the choice of a meeting place was not happy. What will happen if Prinkipos falls through no one seems to know. But the soldier opposition to more fighting is not waning. The conservative French press still openly opposes Wilson, being quite against his colonial policy. This, however, was Pichon's week for blowing hot and his interview with the correspondents with its implied rebuke to Foch was quite satisfactory.

What the people at home must realize is that the battle here will not be won until the final documents are signed, and no one knows when that will be. Meanwhile they must content themselves with general assurances that things are moving as well as could be expected considering the personalities and problems involved, and the curious method of transacting the real business outside the Conference. There is still sharp conflict of opinion, for there are plenty here to share Lodge's view that the league should come after peace instead of Wilson's opinion that it should come immediately.

OSWALD GARRISON VILLARD

The Victory the Allies Need

"GREAT BRITAIN never repudiates her treaty obligations." Such was the proud retort of Secretary Balfour when the radicals in the House of Commons clamored for the repudiation of the secret treaties. This attitude of the British Government was hailed at that time as the embodiment of honor and was contrasted with the "scrap of paper" position of militaristic Germany. The loyalty to earlier commitments revealed by the developments at the peace conference makes it clear that this position toward the secret treaties is by no means exclusively British. It is shared to the full extent by the other Allies. The loyalty of Italian statesmen to the secret treaty of London, for example, is quite as uncompromising as Mr. Balfour's. In fact, they denounce as a traitor any one who dares suggest that Italy in the interests of world peace should forego any of the provisions of that instrument. However edifying this devotion to treaty obligations, the maintenance of these secret agreements is a paralyzing influence at the conference. Indeed, it is safe to say that there will be no peace settlement at all if the Allies, big and little, persist in their loyalty to *sacro egoismo* and maintain all the claims based on secret deals.

It was the general assumption that by giving assent, however informally, to President Wilson's fourteen points as the principles of the peace settlement, the Allied statesmen automatically abrogated their secret agreements. The only thing still left for discussion, as the ordinary man understood the matter, was the application and interpretation of these principles. How remote was this understanding from the facts! Concerning the readjustment of the Italian frontiers, for example, President Wilson declared that it should proceed "along clearly recognized lines of nationality." But how does this square with the treaties? The imperialists, in Italy as elsewhere, have no desire to follow the lines of nationality. They think, not in terms of principles, but in terms of power. They uphold the sanctity of secret bargains, not the right of self-determination. The Paris correspondent of the New York *Times* in an illuminating statement of Italy's cause quotes three main grounds on which the Italian delegates "will contest for Fiume as well as everything promised to Italy by France, England, and Russia." The first ground is purely strategic: "The territory so promised is necessary to the future protection of Italy and therefore for the peace of Europe." The second is interesting: Italy should not be asked now to reduce her claims because "the territory promised by the Allies in 1915 is far less than what Italy asked at that time as her allotment when going into the war." Most amazing is the third: "Italy entered the war, agreeing to fight Austria in coöperation with Russia, but Russia collapsed, leaving Italy to do the work alone [the entry of the United States is not mentioned] so that the territorial compensation now should be at least as great as what was originally promised. . . . So Italy contends she did twice as much war work as first expected of her, but received much less than her original request and she balks at further reductions." Thus the principle of self-determination is replaced by "allotment for going into war" and the principle of nationality by "compensation for doing war work."

We instance thus fully the case of Italy only as a single illustration of the conflict between the principles of justice proclaimed by President Wilson and the bargains actually in effect. Italy stands by no means alone. In addition to the secret treaties earlier published, we have recently read the text of the Allies' agreement with Rumania, and have learned of the British-Japanese deal concerning the Pacific Islands. How many more of these sordid bargains remain unrevealed there is no means of knowing. What was the deal with the Czecho-Slovaks, what the bargain with the Polish National Committee in Paris? The Associated Press recently compiled a comprehensive summary of Allied claims. Reading this statement one gets the impression that it is only a new edition of the secret treaties, but it goes beyond any agreements that have as yet been made public. In introducing this catalogue of annexationist greed the Associated Press correspondent explains that it represents the "maximum of hopes." It represents, unfortunately, the maximum of cynicism as well. The difficulty which the correspondent sees lies in the fact that the aspirations of the Allies are "often overlapping," and the task of the conference is to adjust them into a "coördinate whole."

If the task of making peace were actually the adjustment of claims, this would be well enough. Difficult as the settlement of overlapping demands may appear, there is always room for compromise, and all the Paris dispatches joyfully announce that all the delegates are animated by the spirit of compromise and that every one is actuated by the principle of give and take. In their hope to take much, all the claimants have a considerable margin to give. The Czechs, for example, might perhaps be induced to give Lithuania and the Ukraine to Poland if they themselves were allowed to take Silesia, or to give Silesia to Poland and take German Saxony. The possibilities for the application of the principle of give and take are so varied that all claims might be coördinated. But all this annexation of German land, in accordance with secret deals, this Balkanization of eastern Europe, this proposed crippling of Russia, is the surest way to future wars and not to peace.

The most striking feature in the summary of Allied territorial ambitions is its negation of the principles proposed by President Wilson and accepted, as the world believed, by the Allies. The claims are apparently based on the following grounds: (1) The stipulation of secret treaties. (2) The securing of good strategic frontiers. (3) Traditional interest. (4) The forestalling of other greedy Powers. (5) Plain desire for expansion. The right of peoples to decide their own destinies is mentioned only twice.

Such is the spirit in which the various delegations have gone to Paris, and such are their commitments under the bargains they have made. They appear to be obsessed by the idea of power, by the right of victory, and by the instinct for spoils. Instead of a peace settlement based on justice and humanity we are witnessing a spectacle of claimants demanding the spoils agreed on as a reward for "war work." Such bargains are in flat contradiction of the principles of justice and self-determination enunciated by President Wilson and acclaimed by the peoples of the whole world. The President appears to be fighting with his back to the wall, unable so far as territorial claims go to make any headway amid the barbed-wire entanglements of secret treaties and agreements among the Allied Powers. The Allies have achieved a marvellous military victory, but their success will be vain if they fail to achieve a still greater victory—the victory over themselves, over the obsession of power, and over the instincts of imperialism.

A Forgotten Condition of Peace

The great task before the world, through the peace conference, is the healing of the nations, which means the welfare of all peoples. This can only come through world freedom made possible by economic freedom, which means economic peace. Now that the greatest of all wars is happily over, and the international spirit of freedom has vanquished national greed for world power, there must come the great peace which will first of all remove the economic, social, and political motives for future wars. If the new peace is not such a peace, the war will have been waged for naught and the sacrifices of millions of men have been in vain. For the first time in history there is an opportunity for the nations of the world to lay down their economic weapons along with their military arms and join in an actual brotherhood of humanity.

TO all of which amen! The distinguished group of American free traders from whose cabled memorial, addressed through Secretary Lansing to the peace conference, we have quoted the above paragraph, have given utterance to a profound even if self-evident truth, constantly forgotten. We hail their memorial as a welcome sign of returning sanity in a world where unreason and hatred have for four and a half years held almost undisputed sway. We note with satisfaction that the names of some of the chief apostles of hate are signed to this manifesto. With the dreadful strain of actual hostilities removed, human nature again begins to assert itself in the desire for the healing of the nations, and reason once more takes the throne as men seek the means of healing.

If the conduct of the representatives of the Governments at Versailles had thus far given any evidence of accessibility to such considerations, we should adjure them to give the most earnest attention to the arguments of this pronouncement. For we are of that number who do most honestly believe that peace among the nations is one of the great desiderata of human existence. Further, we believe, with Dr. L. P. Jacks, that war is the result, not of human nature, but of state nature, and we hold that in order to get rid of the greatest scourge of the race we must create conditions of freedom. We must let human nature function freely and coöperatively, instead of working within the limits of artificially created restrictions that set one man or group of men against another. Our grievance against the quarrelling and scheming diplomats who gather about the great table at Versailles or plot in the anterooms is just that they appear to give no thought to the creation of those conditions of freedom.

Specifically, so far as the peace conference concerns itself with peace—and peace seems to be a minor consideration with it—it appears to busy itself with the machinery of world order, and not at all with the attempt to create that unity of the spirit which is the bond of peace. We do not underestimate the importance of machinery, but all the machinery in the world will not make peace. The conference is discussing the creation of a league of nations, with elaborate paraphernalia of national representation, and courts, and sanctions, and "mandatories," and what not—but however essential is the creation of some organ for the management of super-national affairs, no man in his senses imagines that such a body can of itself keep the peace among men if Governments deliberately make it to the interest of certain of their citizens to bite and devour their neighbors, and teach the remaining citizens that it is their duty to support the enterprise, with the sword if necessary.

Economic greed has indeed been "the chief and most prolific source of modern wars," as the memorialists assert; "economic peace is the vital atmosphere of a league of free nations and involves freedom of trade in the mutual interest of all nations and to the disadvantage of none." We may create peace machinery until doomsday, and if we still use the power of Governments to create special opportunity for some groups and classes, denying it to others, if we give certain manufacturers and traders a special advantage because they belong in our country, withholding it from others because they belong in France or Belgium, if we throw special protection around investors in China or Mexico because they are Americans, denying it to others because they are Englishmen—if we use the power of Governments in this fashion, then we create the conditions precedent to war, and all the leagues we build cannot save us from its dread ravages. We care not one whit for the old political controversy between protection and free trade; we care everything for the progress of mankind toward freedom and peaceful coöperation. And as an absolutely fundamental condition of such progress, abundantly demonstrated to be such by hundreds of years of disastrous experiment with other and vain means of preventing wars, we press upon the attention of every thoughtful man the necessity that the power of Governments no longer be used to secure special advantage for special groups of citizens; we utterly repudiate tariffs, concessions, and the whole foul brood of pestilential war-making arrangements. Do the gentlemen at Versailles even dream of moving on this path to freedom?

Our Weekly Cable Letter

Wilson and the World

Paris, February 6

MORE than ever is it a battle of Woodrow Wilson against the field. More than ever the struggle goes on behind closed doors. Points are won. Great innovations in policy are announced as being accepted in principle, and yet there remains everywhere the greatest skepticism as to the outcome, except in the headquarters of the President himself. Wilson appears before the Chamber of Deputies, which cheers to the echo the daring speech in which he again warns the world that it is the people who are to be legislated for and not the Governments. Yet while man and speech are cheered to heaven, the opposition continues, and in all official gatherings, social or otherwise, there is unconcealed scoffing at Wilson and the league and its mandatories.

As the weeks pass, the weariness and uneasiness of the French intellectuals as to what is happening grow plainer and plainer. Never was man in a harder position than Wilson. He well knows the need of haste. If there were any doubt of it the events at Glasgow and Belfast would have settled that. Yet how can there be haste when one considers the extraordinary magnitude of the issues and problems? Wilson is between the devil and the deep sea. Much skepticism of eventual results is found in the American newspaper ranks in Paris. This discouragement is increased by the fact that while Lloyd George is in close relation with the British correspondents, the Americans are never permitted to see the head of our delegation and draw from him inspiration and encouragement. In short, what we are witnessing is the Wilson method and manner of governing, which has so irritated and often angered Congress and public men at home, applied to the world field. There is every evidence that people here do not like it either. There are open mutterings that this American Wilson is the greatest dictator the world has ever seen.

The rank and file of the conference are more and more irritated as it becomes plain that most of the work is being done by a self-appointed committee of President Wilson and the Prime Ministers and envoys. They have grown this week into a full-fledged court. Representatives of a country or group appear to state their case, and in some instances a decision is rendered without referring the matter to the conference at all. The conference has yet to hold its third full session, last week's having been postponed at the last minute without even the return of money at the box office or the offering of rain checks. Thus runs the complaint every hour. Yet the fact remains that if the American dictator were not here this would simply degenerate into the worst scramble for the division of spoils ever seen. If Wilson did not show this obstinate determination to have his way there would be no hope left for an embattled world, except outright revolution against the Governments here represented.

This is not to say that the only way to fight a battle is Wilson's way of fighting. He compels the admiration of the people for his courage, ability, and oratory, but the people near him are not drawn to him by ties of affection and personal devotion here any more than in the United States. Yet one wonders what will happen when he goes home, which will now be soon. Is the conference to mark time until he returns? Or is Colonel House strong enough to carry on for Wilson in his absence, or will it be the opportunity for the reactionary forces to proceed as they like? The leading men will not want to await his return. The outcry of peoples and armies who want matters settled will become louder than ever.

Some of the best French people insist that the terms for Germany must be laid down soon if the public is to remain patient. This unrest is also echoed in the report that this week will see the completion of the rough draft of the proposed league, so that Wilson may be able to show it when he returns. But no one here has any conception of what its final form will be. Obviously if the league plan is hastened in this way the best results cannot be obtained. Here again we have a conflict between the existing world situation and the need for deliberation. More than that, I cannot insist too strongly that details will mean everything. Take, for example, the question of mandatories. If the mandatory is merely to be told to take the ward and do with it as he pleases, there will be practically no change. The great victory won by Wilson in compelling Japan, Australia, and England to accept the mandatory system will be a Pyrrhic one if the duties and powers of the mandatory are not clearly defined. If territory is to be handed over to syndicates and trusts to be exploited as in the past, what will be the difference from the past except that the nations will not have direct title to the property? And there will indeed, presumably, be the possibility of appeal to a high court when there is misgovernment. But who, for instance, is to pay the bills of non-self-supporting colonies, the mandatory or the league itself? These and many other pressing questions begin to present themselves as the mandatory plan is studied. People in America should understand that we are but at the beginning of a long fight. Americans should be proud that America beyond all others is standing for the right, and that Wilson has won two vital points in principle.

Wilson is shouldering tasks no other man has essayed; perhaps no other could essay them. His defects and errors must be borne with and the world must be as patient as possible, particularly America and sorely tried France. The French may be right that it would have been better to decide Germany's fate at once and then settle down to a slow and careful creation of new world machinery. But Wilson is doing what seems best to him. It is true that he has been stupidly deprived of the aid of the American press and that he has consented to dealing in private—which privacy makes directly against him. But when all is said and done he still has the confidence of all the liberals here. He is the only hope that the outcome will be anything else than an utterly disastrous defeat for liberalism everywhere. It is a time neither for undue elation nor for pessimism, but for gratification that we have won what we have and a clear cut realization that there are tremendous difficulties and odds against us in the struggle for the right. At any rate people everywhere should realize that the present status of the world, however trying, is infinitely better than it was only three months ago. OSWALD GARRISON VILLARD

Foreign Correspondence

I. The Position of France

Paris, January 26

THE French have at last come to the plan of a league of nations—though they prefer to have it called the Society of Nations. Yet the rumors as to the extraordinary demands of the governors of the French Republic continue: Syria, part of Armenia, enormous war indemnities, the left bank of the Rhine, and perhaps the Palatinate as well. Failing this they want a neutral zone back of the Rhine. Most of all they want to dispose of the Bolsheviki and build up the eastern front. The explanation given by well-informed Frenchmen is that France is war-weary to a degree that no one but a Frenchman can appreciate. Though victorious it has much of the psychology of a beaten country so utterly worn down is it by its heroic struggle of more than four years. The one great yearning is that its eastern boundary be forever freed from German menace. The French remember how quickly they themselves recovered from the terrible events of 1870 and they are frankly afraid that their greatest enemy will recover with equal rapidity from what seems a much greater disaster. Theirs is the psychology of fear. That this is a mistaken attitude is the belief of the kindliest of foreign critics. Germany is far more completely crushed than the French realize. There is, of course, the possibility that there will some day be a restoration of the empire and the seating of a new emperor. But there are various ways of safeguarding the future. The Socialists believe that France should secure herself by socialistic government and the development of internationalism. The advocates of the league of nations insist that if the league takes vital shape, France will be sufficiently safeguarded without a neutral zone. Our own American high command is credited with the belief that the modern conditions of war—aerial torpedoes, long range guns, and deadly gases—are such that neutral zones are of little avail. Some of our military men have even come to believe that the only hope for the future is the control of armaments by a supernational authority or absolute disarmament. I have talked with one general who says that to know what brought on this war one need but remember that all concerned had weapons in their hands.

Why do we hear of no proposal to disarm Germany? Why do we not hear discussions of the limitation of Germany's army to a possible 25,000 men on a long-term enlistment basis? Is it unwillingness to relieve the German people of the terrible burden of taxation in support of armaments. Is it the fear of their falling prey to a Bolshevist army if they are not allowed a strong cordon of bayonets on their eastern frontier? The Allies demand the immediate cessation of the building of all submarines; why not insist that Germany pledge herself to build no warships and to transform such as may be of her present ones into merchant carriers and to sink the rest?

Germany could not complain of this, because Erzberger and Ebert have already talked of establishing a national militia in place of the army which, in their own interest, should have been demobilized much faster. Nor could Germany assert that this would leave her open to attack from other sources. The present European Allies are, of course, so spotless in their motives and so determined to make the world safe for democracy that any thought of aggression on their part would be entirely out of the question; besides which the league of nations will see that the Poles and the Jugoslavs and the other new nationalities do not cast covetous eyes upon their neighbors.

This is, I fear, too rational a solution to be accepted by this peace conference. Disarmament is the most important thing to be achieved. Therefore one hears less about that than about anything else. The word is not used. The limitation of armaments is urged by General Smuts though he is apparently unaware that the dictionary holds such a word as navy. On the other hand, the American who is perhaps best informed on the league of nations tells me that the leading British advocate feels there is no possibility of disarmament at present. This is grave news, indeed, for if the nations must go on with the mad race for armaments, burdened as they are with present war debts, the prospect of human happiness is dark. The most unpopular thing in the world to-day is the carrying of arms—about which I could tell some interesting things if the censor permitted.

I laid these proposals, as to German disarmament, before a high military authority here and found him in sympathy. He himself would have had the armistice require the complete disarmament of Germany on sea and on land and would have limited the terms to that. There would then have been no need for an army of occupation, and the Allies could have gone on with their plans for disarmament. But the remedy was too simple. Will the Allied military men try to prevent the complete disarmament of Germany to protect their profession? Not if they are like the veteran I have quoted. He is heart and soul in favor of the immediate limitation of armaments, and the absolute forbidding of compulsory military service everywhere. He said, incidentally, that there would never be universal military service in America unless America had gone mad. He then remarked significantly, "I should not be surprised if the Germans forestalled the peace conference by themselves abolishing universal service and substituting some form of national militia."

This would, of course, be the best answer to French fears. The French have had one man killed of every thirty souls living in France when the war broke out, and a similar number disabled—one in every thirty. A recurrence of such a catastrophe must, of course, be made impossible. But the question is which course will be more effective to this end—disarmament, or a retention of the military system which made the explosion of 1914 inevitable? Even with the menace of German militarism removed there are still territorial claims made by France which must be reckoned with.

It is not fear of Germany which made MM. Franklin-Bouillon and Chéradame begin their counter offensive to Mr. Wilson for his humane action in regard to Russia. It is not for the permanent safeguard of her eastern boundary that France lusts after Syria and part of Armenia, desires a controlling hand in the Balkans, and covets one of the two German cables to America. These matters stand in a different category. Some are championed by a few militarists, some by a handful of imperialists. Some of them are probably advanced as trading points, and are not to be taken too seriously. Yet it is undeniable that they bear seeds of possible discord between France, England, and America, and the sooner they are uprooted the better.

The Chéradame incident is disquieting because the atmosphere here is already so electric. A keen British observer said some time ago that during the first month of Mr. Wilson's stay in France he would be the most popular man who ever entered Paris; in the second month of his stay there would be mutterings and protests against his leadership; and at the end of three months he would be the most unpopular man in France. The first two prophecies seem to have been verified. All the more important, therefore, that the third should not be. It would indeed be a misfortune if any thing could mar the fine feeling between the two countries. If rocks are to be avoided, it is essential that we have a clear understanding of the attitude of France, which seems to onlookers grossly materialistic and imperialistic. Americans at home may perhaps judge more leniently and with greater appreciation than do many here, who feel that the French proposals make not for a better world but for a worse one. The only safety for France, as for all the world, is to do away with the weapons for human slaughter.

OSWALD GARRISON VILLARD

A Russian Policy at Last

THE disquieting news comes from Paris that the statesmen there assembled have definitely resolved to crush Bolshevism in Russia by force of arms. This news confirms the worst fears raised by the recent Allied abandonment of the Prinkipo Conference, and by the sheer hypocrisy of the statement issued in justification of that step. The impossible is to be attempted. Ideas are to be fought with machine guns. With the avowed object of stamping out Bolshevism at its source, the thing is to be done which will spread Bolshevism throughout the world. Our negative Russian policy, namely, a determination not to treat under any circumstances with the Soviet Government, has suffered a gradual metamorphosis in the furnace of white-hot political affairs, and now appears in its durable form as a positive policy, dominating the whole situation.

Sergius Sazonoff, the Czar's Foreign Minister in 1914, now Minister of Foreign Affairs in the Denikine Government, and holding also a mandate from the Omsk Government in Siberia, emerges as the leading figure in that group of diplomats who represent in Paris the anti-Bolshevist Russian factions. More and more, according to authentic report, he is the man to whom the Allies are looking and with whom they are dealing for the development of that policy which ostensibly is designed to "save Russia," but which in reality is calculated to destroy the Soviet authority. Lvov, Tchaikovsky, Bakhmeteff, and even Maklakoff, are hesitating amateurs in comparison with this old-line diplomat who speaks the full language of the Quai d'Orsay and retains no uncomfortable illusions. His is the plan for retrieving the Russian situation which is coming to be the generally accepted policy of the Allied statesmen.

The first tenet of this plan, as already stated, is a firm resolution to crush the Soviet Government in Russia. No more dallying with Prinkipo conferences and such-like compromise measures; they are too likely to play the boomerang. The Soviet authority is to be destroyed if it takes a term of years. Sazonoff sits in the Russian Embassy in Paris and outlines his plan openly to the newspaper men (though they do not send it to us, for some reason). He thinks that with 200,000 troops he can smash the Soviet Government in eighteen months, provided a rigorous economic blockade is meanwhile maintained against Soviet Russia. What sort of troops? British, French, and American, of course. And where will they operate? In the Black Sea region—this is the main feature of the plan. The Archangel venture was bound to be a disaster; we must be wise and practical this time. The Dardanelles are now open, the climate is milder in the Ukraine, and food is more plentiful; we must work up toward Moscow from the Black Sea as a base, consolidating the country as we go.

From a military point of view it seems like a sound plan, except that it will need 2,000,000 troops instead of 200,000. But from a political point of view, it is incredible that the diplomats of the Quai d'Orsay can still harbor such a notion. Yet the news is that they actually do harbor it. If they cannot read the signs in the sky, have they forgotten the march of Napoleon? If they cannot comprehend the daily and hourly events in England, France, Italy, and Germany, have they not yet discovered that the intervention of last August in Russia only strengthened the Soviet authority?

Foreign Correspondence

Personalities at Berne

Berne, February 7

THE hall in which I am writing certainly fits a gathering of representatives of the proletariat, in its plainness and bareness. Here are ninety-one delegates sitting at tables laden with literature of propaganda, resolutions of committees, and the printed records of proceedings. The air is thick with tobacco smoke despite large and threatening signs forbidding smoking. At the sides of the room are long tables at which are crowded the representatives of the press, who outnumber the delegates. There is not a lackey, not a uniform, not a decoration nor title; there is no guard of honor at the door, no formality, no ceremonial. There are no long lines of automobiles before the building, no waiters in dress suits to serve tea, no gilt, no braid, no candelabra! This is simply a hall in which plain men are meeting, and not the barbarously ornate hall on the Quai d'Orsay.

But there are greater differences than lie in the settings. For here is a real conference, in fullest publicity, with real debating, a conference of men and women, a conference of victors and vanquished alike, a conference not, it is true, without a President, for Kurt Eisner of Munich is here, but a conference which none the less is absolutely without official domination. Nobody in Berne is taking orders, and the gathering meets three times a day instead of twice in four weeks.

The wisdom of restricting the Conference to general lines speedily became apparent. To have attempted to settle all the territorial problems in a week's session was plainly impossible, so that the prime results of the Conference remain the burying of the hatchet, the interchange of opinions, the reconstitution of the Internationale, and the giving to the world of the first international charter of labor, and the various opinions expressed in the resolutions. But these results are well worth the effort.

It is strange to see that compared to previous meetings of the Internationale this is a conservative gathering. It no longer represents the extreme Left, as it did five years ago, but is actually scorned as too conservative by the Swiss Socialists, the Russian Bolshevists, who are as unrepresented here as at Paris, the Italian Minority Socialists, and, of course, the Spartacus group in Germany. What will the situation be a year hence? No one can mingle with the delegates without being profoundly impressed by their simplicity, their straightforwardness, their earnestness, their breadth of view, and their international aspirations for a just, a wiser, and a better world.

Though no Socialist myself, if I had the power to decide on which conference to rest the future of the world, I should unhesitatingly, and with real joy, decide for this simple conference with its plain membership. With profound respect for Mr. Wilson's achievements in Paris, I would take the whole making of peace out of governmental hands, out of those of the Clemenceaus, Lloyd Georges, and Orlandos, and place it here in the hands of a democratic gathering of democratic people, the real representatives of those who have fought, bled, and died for their countries.

The International Conference has brought together in one room a large number of the most interesting personalities in Europe. It was, of course, a source of regret that there were no representatives of the Swiss, whose guests the Conference in a sense was, and one would have wished to see the Italian group which opposed the war so uncompromisingly. While it was well, in the matter of German and French disloyalty to the Socialist cause, to let bygones be bygones, it was none the less good to meet and hear the men who had inflexibly lived up to their principles. There was no Liebknecht to receive the plaudits of the audience, but the rather noisy hall grew still whenever Ramsay Macdonald spoke. This was not only the instinctive tribute to his superb presence, but an appreciation of his steadfast opposition to the war, maintained at so great a cost.

In marked contrast to Ramsay Macdonald is another extremely interesting figure—Kurt Eisner. In his hirsute appendages and bald head President Eisner strongly suggests Lyman Abbott, even though he is not tall or thin; but he speedily made it clear that these were the only points of resemblance. He spoke without effort at oratory, with few gestures, with clear enunciation, and the Conference listened in rapt attention. There was no doubt that he was a man of absolute courage and frankness, yet one meeting him on the street would set him down as a typical German pedagogue, the absent-minded professor dear to *Fliegende Blätter.* One would never guess him to be president of a very considerable country, and a successful revolutionist. The story of his revolution is so extraordinary that one naturally expects the leader to be a fiery young man of the Carl Schurz or Gustav Koerner type. He had been known in Munich before the attempted revolution of January, 1918, chiefly as a feuilletonist and a frequenter of cafés. But it is said that when with a handful of men he stormed the Landtag in an impromptu manner the Government abdicated and royalty ran away with a speed incredible even in a comic opera. This may be true, but after all there is something about Eisner which explains his being the right man at the right moment. He was himself in doubt, when he left this morning, whether he would be President much longer. But his reception here did distinct honor to Bavaria.

Every time that Frederick Adler took his place on the platform a thrill ran through the audience. He has all the appearance of a dry-as-dust pedagogue with a tremendous head of hair, stooped shoulders, and as marked prison pallor as if he had but yesterday left the cell in which he had so long awaited the executioner. As the lady beside me remarked, "He would have been dead long ago if Austria had had the courage to carry out his sentence." The revolution freed him and he is now addressed by all the Socialist leaders as Comrade Adler.

Two days before the end of the meeting, in walked an old man whose face was familiar. It was Eduard Bernstein, so long head of the Socialist Revisionists in Germany. He was full of his adventures in coming to the Conference over the worn-out railroads of Germany, but he seemed to exert no influence whatever.

Kautsky, with his gentle, spiritual personality, is by far the most attractive figure among the Germans and Austrians. Troëlstra, from Holland, is an extremely interesting figure. His refinement and culture are as obvious as his ability. Though this was a Labor as well as a Socialist Conference, it was only in the English delegation that one found men who had plainly had workshop experience.

McGurk and Shirkie were unmistakably representative of the real sons of toil. Though inclined to be somewhat unreasonably obstreperous at times, they lent desirable color to the picture, for most of the Continental representatives were obviously of the agitator or Parliamentarian type.

The French delegation lent expected warmth and Gallic piquancy. Several of them talked too often, but they bore themselves well and generously, except for a professional Alsatian, and their violent roaring at one another was at times a joyous relief from the monotony of the double translations. (As every speech had to be delivered three times, as is usual at international gatherings, it is no wonder that Esperanto is regarded with growing favor.) There is no doubt, however, of the intense rivalry between Longuet and Renaudel which splits the French delegation.

On the platform sat Henderson, Branting, and Huysmans; the Englishman was gladly heard; the Swede with more reluctance, as he speaks three foreign tongues equally badly and as presiding officer let proceedings drag unnecessarily. Huysmans's keen, sensitive face was a delight to watch. His readiness to step in at just the right moment, with precisely the elucidating word or the exact compromise necessary stamped him as a most valuable secretary and leader. A Belgian with deep feelings, he is yet wholly without bitterness. Stuart Bunning also made two admirable speeches at critical moments. It was extraordinary how personal differences were set aside for the sake of the Internationale; under such circumstances it could not fail.

Chief among the women were the two from England, Mrs. Philip Snowden, and Margaret Bondfield, to whom Lloyd George denied a passport to go as a delegate to meet with the American Federation of Labor, despite her great services to the working women of England. Near the door, an interested spectator, sat Rosika Schwimmer, of Ford Peace Ship fame, temporarily Hungarian Minister to Switzerland.

Two interesting men from Germany were frequently in the audience: first, Professor Wilhelm Förster, who held his chair in the University of Münich despite his resolute opposition to the war and his insistence that Germany was in the wrong. He is a strikingly handsome man of great ability, and is now Bavarian Minister to Switzerland by appointment of President Eisner. The second, whose remarkable revelations did so much to prove to the world at large the full guilt of Germany—Dr. Muehlon. He begs me to tell the *Nation's* readers that the condition of the children in Germany is dire beyond words, so many of them are dying from undernourishment and actual starvation. He begs us to do what we can to help the little ones whose condition will be still worse if the Allies continue the blockade and delay the peace. This I am the more willing to do as Dr. Muehlon's services to the United States and the war were such as preclude undesirable propaganda.

It only remains to touch in this letter upon a subject which makes every American here thoroughly ashamed. I refer to the attack upon the Conference by Messrs. Gompers, Walling, and Russell, to which the Conference has officially replied through its officers, Hjalmar Branting and Arthur Henderson. It had seemed as if Mr. Gompers and his associates had done all that they could in the way of misrepresentation of those who do not agree with them as to policy, but in this attack they have clearly outdone themselves in vituperation and mandacity. It is a great pity that the United States should be unrepresented at this vital con-

OSWALD GARRISON VILLARD

The Darkening Outlook For Peace

MR. A. G. GARDINER, the editor of the London *Daily News*, is one of England's most accomplished journalists. What he says on any public question is listened to and quoted, not merely because he is the responsible editor of a great newspaper, but also because he has back of him a great body of liberal opinion which, while less radical than that for which the *Manchester Guardian* or the London *Nation* speaks, is perhaps on that account more likely to be accepted as the matured conviction of the thoughtful British public as a whole. When, accordingly, Mr. Gardiner launches so unsparing an attack upon the peace conference as appeared in the editorial columns of the *Daily News* a few days ago, we may be sure that the situation is at least as bad as it is painted, if indeed the failures and mischievous tendencies of the conference are not under rather than over stated.

The situation at Paris, set forth by Mr. Gardiner with no mincing of words, and confirmed in all essential respects by no less able a correspondent than Dr. E. J. Dillon, is such as to make every friend of a democratic peace sick at heart. The outlook is more than discouraging—it is humiliating. After two months of organized existence, there are still no terms of peace announced or known to have been practically agreed upon. Various committees and commissions have been created, and from time to time they have been reported to be at work, but if they have worked to any useful constructive purpose the world has not been informed as to what that purpose is. Yet the failure of the conference to produce thus far so much as a single article of peace might be forgiven were there any assurance that that body is in essential accord on the principles of peace or its larger details, or that no advantage was being taken of its procrastination to deepen the miseries or heighten the complexities which have followed upon the war. Unfortunately, the evidence is all the other way. Not only is the conference itself torn by dissension, but what is far worse, its member Governments, by the policy which some of them are pursuing, are as good as inviting the continuance and spread of the violent disorders which are sweeping Europe, while at the same time forging such potent material for racial, national, and class conflict in the future as to make the hope of long-continued peace hardly more than an iridescent dream.

What some of these evils are has been made clear, in language unwontedly frank, by Mr. Gardiner in the editorial to which we have referred. At the head of the list is the impossible treatment of Germany in the matter of indemnities. Germany, it appears, is to be asked to pay some $30,000,-000,000, at the rate of $600,000,000 annually for fifty years. This is in addition to new armistice conditions, the appropriation for an indefinite period of its merchant marine, and the demands of France for territorial acquisitions and guarantees which, if accepted and enforced, will go far to render Germany impotent as a military or naval power. These extraordinary demands, mainly the result of the stubborn insistence of the French Government supported by the prestige of Marshal Foch, upon reparation for the past and protection for the future, are rightly characterized by Mr. Gardiner as beyond reason, partly because they exceed the ability of Germany to pay, and partly because, being humiliating as well as excessive, they will fix in the heart of the German people an undying hatred of France and the Allies which will be certain to burst out in war at the earliest opportunity. And the conference which is dallying with peace is actually planning for war. Great Britain, which professes sympathy for a league of nations, is nevertheless asking for £440,000,000 for its army and £149,000,000 for its navy; France intends to keep up a large army; and the United States, the only professedly altruistic nation represented in the conference, holds in reserve a huge naval programme whose initial building cost aggregates $650,000,000,000. So far as the peace conference is concerned, the only disarmament in sight is the disarmament of Germany, and that, presumably, is to be accompanied by military occupation of the country while the indemnity is being paid. Does anyone in his senses imagine that this sort of thing will make for peace, or commend the league of nations to any country reluctant to join it?

So it is with the remainder of the dreary category. Nothing has been done by the conference to help Germany and Austria to accomplish the constitutional revolution which Mr. Wilson has demanded, or to reëstablish the industry out of whose surplus product alone can an indemnity be paid. The commissions which have been appointed to deal with Poland and to treat with the Russian factions contain hardly a single name of first-rate calibre, the disorders in Germany run daily a more violent course, and soldier outbreaks in England show how seriously the ferment is spreading. A brutal embargo upon food, declared by Italy and stubbornly persisted in, bade fair to result in the starvation of some millions of Jugoslavs and others in southeastern Europe, after which, presumably, the imperial designs of Italy will be easier of accomplishment, and it is not yet clear but that relief has come too late. With other millions starving in other parts of the world and exorbitant food prices everywhere, the Paris negotiators still wrangle over the question whether hunger shall be relieved by low-priced wheat from Australia or Argentina or high-priced wheat from the United States and Canada. Meantime Japan, a silent observer of the futile game, presses its demands upon China and prepares for an economic invasion of Siberia, while the brotherhood of man is to be cemented in the United States by the prohibition of immigration and the systematic deportation of aliens. Over all hangs the shadow of revolution, before whose grim advance the peace conference, like the nations which compose it, folds its hands in dull helplessness and awaits the wrath of the gods. Never has an international conference, summoned at the conclusion of a great war for the express purpose of restoring peace and making the world better, shown so little skill or piled up for the nations which it represented such mountains of difficulty.

If anyone ever really imagined that the proposal of a league of nations would bind together the spokesmen of the nations in unity of sentiment regarding the problems which confronted them, or repress the schemes of calculating selfishness which the years of war had stimulated, he must by this time have been undeceived. The world knows now, what it has been suspecting for some time, that, while it has gained a draft of the constitution of a league, it has as yet gained nothing else. The forces of selfishness and reaction appear dominant in the preparation of the document, as in the secret and disreputable bargains which it ratifies.

The End and the Means

ACCORDING to all the Paris dispatches, President Wilson has authorized the statement that the league of nations plan is to be an integral part of the peace treaty. If this be true, we regard it as a deliberate attempt to dragoon the Senate of the United States, and as such, a logical and fitting climax to the whole discreditable course of the Paris conference. It is the familiar trick of the "rider." The people of this country want the peace treaty signed and out of the way, the business interests being especially impatient of delay. At the same time, they are very imperfectly informed about the implications of the league covenant, and reluctant to wade through the diplomatic jargon which half-conceals its sinister purposes. Peace, too, is the immediate consideration; the matters canvassed in the covenant appear remote. If the Senate refuses to ratify a treaty of which the covenant is an integral part, it must carry a fearful burden of obloquy for obstructing peace; and this, apparently, is just what the manœuvres reported from Paris have in view. We may be quite sure, too, that every agency at the disposal of the Administration will do its utmost to manufacture and strengthen public sentiment against the opposition of the Senate; and this, again, is quite as it should be. It is quite appropriate that this measure should prevail, if it does prevail, wholly by force of false pretence, indirection, and dragooning, rather than only in part. This alliance of victorious Governments, masquerading under the pretentious lying title of a league of nations, organized for sheer economic exploitation, has nowhere in its constitution sincerity enough to make fitting one single inch of furtherance by aid of any honorable means whatsoever. It should continue and end under no other than the auspices of its beginning.

We must make it clear at the outset that we do not discuss the general idea of a league of nations. As to that, we spoke fully in our issue of March 8. We believe that a league of nations is inevitable, and that it will come automatically and spontaneously, by means which politicians do not contemplate. The removal of economic barriers and the restrictions now imposed by political governments upon industry and trade, would, we believe, at once effect the same free economic union among world states that now prevails among the United States of America; and we think that a free economic union is the only one that will have stability or permanency. What may be done by way of further political union, or closer political association, among world states, we do not know. While we are skeptical about it, we are aware that many able minds are in favor of trying it, in a belief that some good will come out of the attempt. We wish to refrain from any discouragement of this optimism; hence we must be understood as saying nothing unfavorable at this time about the general aspiration toward a league of nations. We merely wish to expose the character of the particular proposal which President Wilson brought back from France, and which he apparently intends, if he can, to compel the Senate to ratify. We do this the more freely because the very aspiration we mention, the pacific and friendly instinct of mankind, can be so easily perverted to support this proposal by reason of the fact that it bears the name of the thing aspired to. No trick of the politician is more common than this; this it was, for instance, which foisted a bogus reform of the nominating system on the people of New York State by calling it a "direct primary." This it may be, too, which will foist this alliance-contract upon the people of the United States, by calling it the "league of nations."

An equally insidious and undoubtedly more powerful appeal is made by this covenant also to the spirit of easy opportunism. Compromise is the rule of the world. Suppose it is not all one wants; still, it is something, and perhaps one should support it more or less on faith in its being a start in the right direction. But that is precisely what it is not. It has no quality or characteristic which essentially differentiates it from treaties that have hitherto bound the European states into competitive and predatory groups. The war has made the liberal spirit impatient of opportunism and compromise. If all the cost and sacrifice involved in a struggle to "make the world safe for democracy" have purchased nothing better than a rescript of old treaties, if it has not brought about the practical affirmation of a single essential democratic principle, we can not see any place for opportunism in judgment. Faith, under such circumstances, is not faith, but indolent, shirking credulity.

We have never discussed the proposed alliance-contract from the nationalist point of view, for those aspects of it are sure to be quite fully set forth by others. We agree with Mr. J. A. Hobson that "for America it would be an entangling alliance," and as such subversive of our best traditions—and indeed, as President Wilson himself admitted, subversive of certain elements of our independent sovereignty. These may be valuable or not; we think they are far too valuable to surrender. What interests us especially, however, is the kind of hands into which they are proposed to be surrendered; and here we find the terms of the covenant far from reassuring. Any proposal to surrender them into the hands of a group of gentlemen like those assembled at the Paris conference, for instance, to permit them to serve the purposes and carry out the motives which the Lloyd Georges, Clemenceaus, Orlandos, Balfours, Lansings, and Sazonovs have exhibited with unfailing regularity throughout their course of public life, appears to us absolutely inadmissible. But we are content to leave this view of the covenant to Senator Knox and his associates, knowing that they will say everything for it that can be said. We concern ourselves by preference with that special view of the covenant which may perhaps without prejudice be called the liberal view—and that without any inflated pretensions to being an organ of liberal opinion. We are simply in the very considerable number of those whom President Wilson, by keeping up his perpetual semblance of hitting the right nail on the head without ever really doing it, has bemocked and deluded; and in all we shall find to say about the league covenant, we speak only for ourselves and such of this number as agree with us.

The first half-dozen of the "fourteen points" were calculated to raise liberal hopes and stimulate liberal enthusiasm above measure. Understood for what they meant in the plain natural sense of language—and not for whatever Mr. Wilson's subsequent glosses might make them mean—they could reasonably be accepted, and by many were accepted, as a definite statement of the purposes for which the Allies were fighting—the purposes for which the United States, at least, was certainly fighting. Open diplomacy; freedom of the seas; freedom of trade; disarmament; the principle of self-determination; and the rights of small nations—such was Mr. Wilson's lofty bid for the liberal's toleration of the war. *Caesari appelasti, ad Caesarem ibis.* What we have gotten is a connivance hatched in impenetrable secrecy, a secrecy of which Mr. Wilson was himself among all the machinators present the most jealous; a connivance, further, which enables the carrying out of every execrable secret bargain laid down by the Allied Governments since the war began. So much for the first blandishment in Mr. Wilson's elaborate seduction of liberal opinion. If he has made good his professions with anything more substantial in respect to the other five points of promise, there is nothing in his proposed covenant to indicate the fact. Free seas, free trade, disarmament, self-determination, and the rights of small nations have now the precise status which they had before Mr. Wilson offered them his devotion; and his address of January 8, 1918, has the indelible indorsement of history as a "good-enough-Morgan."

What we have is a calm, arrogant, and ruthless formulation of a plan of world-domination by the five conquering powers, a device for causing the exploitable territories of the earth to stand and deliver without the risk and cost of war. Stripped of its verbiage and a cant that is matched perhaps only in the Act of Algeciras, this is the sheer fact of Articles xvi-xix inclusive. The Governments of the United States, Great Britain, France, Italy, and Japan are the league of nations; they are the executive council; they appoint the dummy directors; they pass finally on the qualifications of candidates; they are, in short, an absolute and irresponsible oligarchy. So far from recognizing freedom of the seas, freedom of trade, disarmament, or self-determination, their collusion precludes these possibilities. International commerce cannot be carried on except at their pleasure, under their jurisdiction, and, it is surely by this time superfluous to add, to their profit. Teleologically considered, we are offered an economic alliance which has as its primary object, in general, the exploitation of a propertyless dependent class the world over, and, as between nations, the exploitation of the vanquished by the victors, and of weaker nations by the stronger. It is an organization of what Mr. Frederic C. Howe calls "financial imperialism" raised to its highest possibility. It contemplates only a political peace, and that a *pax Romana.* Of economic peace it gives no hint; on the contrary, it contemplates the inaguration of unprecedented economic war.

This, then, is the ground of objection to the covenant upon which we choose to stand. We ask that the document be taken upon this ground and examined, with strict attention to the economic implications of every proposal, the possibilities of economic exploitation covered by every arrangement. Especially we urge this upon the propertyless and exploited class in all countries, for it is their chief concern. The past four years fortunately have given them some useful experience of the niceties of diplomatic language, and they now have the opportunity to turn it to most profitable account. They are, too, in a position where they may have something effective to say about the point-blank handing over of their economic destiny to persons or to groups that have hitherto shown themselves conspicuously dishonest in their administration of a similar trust; and they can say it none too soon. The nationalist interest of the document is for us all; its economic interest is peculiarly theirs. Let them consider what the six doctrines for which Mr. Wilson offered a casual and opportunist sponsorship in January, 1918, mean for them; then let them consider the proposals which he now sponsors and insists upon, and see which way their economic interest inclines them.

Germany Today

TWO CABLE LETTERS FROM THE EDITOR

I. Food or Chaos

(By Cable to the *Nation*)

Paris, March 21

I HAVE just returned to Paris after four weeks in Germany. It would be impossible to exaggerate the gravity of the German situation. While it is true that the Government by resorting to the harshest measures, has won a temporary victory over the insurgents in Berlin, Halle, Liepzig, and elsewhere, it has had to compromise by promising the permanent inclusion of workers' and peasants' councils in the new constitutional arrangements. It is announced that a much more extended and violent strike and uprising will take place on March 26. Whether the Ebert Government will be able to maintain itself then depends entirely upon the attitude of the troops and the speed with which the Allies and America rush in food. Even food is not certain to save the day for the Majority Socialists; for there is much evidence that the Allies have continued the blockade far too long, not only for Germany's good, but for their own. I believe to be correct the German estimate that in the Empire eight hundred die daily because of undernourishment and inability to resist disease; for I have made careful inquiries in Munich, Weimar, Dresden, and Berlin.

If humanitarian America could realize the actual state of affairs it would compel the Red Cross to push in food, milk, oils, grease, and soap. It is now agreed that food will be sent in, and fats too, but milk and grease as well are needed. I have seen infants in Berlin and Dresden hospitals with the shrunken limbs and swollen stomachs characteristic of famine sufferers, and I have seen that the midday meal for all patients in one hospital is simply a carrot soup —nothing else—for all ages and all conditions of disease. No special diets are possible and physicians are unable to build up their patients after fever or when the shock of operation is over. Most children now being born in Berlin are ten months infants, but the women are the greatest sufferers as they are denying themselves food for the sake of their children. No one can live on the rations allowed; all have to obtain food surreptitiously at terribly high prices. Workmen are getting high wages but have to spend all to get enough food to keep alive. One workman I saw earns a hundred marks a week, but has bought no clothes since the war began, and is literally in rags. His two children are dead and his wife is dying from consumption. Tuberculosis is increasing greatly, as is venereal disease brought in by returning soldiers. The week I was in Dresden not one pound of meat was distributed. There will be no bread there by April 15 unless relief from the Allies comes in time. Conditions in Munich are almost as bad. There will be positively nothing to ration there after May 5 unless aid comes.

What this means politically is that the moral superiority of the Allies is steadily waning and a bitter hatred, particularly against the French, which did not exist there at the time of the surrender, is rising in Germany. The result is there is now talk of revenge which was not heard before. Everything is uncertain in industry and business because of the delay of peace conditions, and the people are much stirred by the reports from Paris partitioning Germany and demanding immense wai indemnities. It is the universal belief that the Government will not sign any extreme peace terms, but will invite the enemies to enter and take over the country. The ministers say that the Ebert Government could not live a week if it should sign such a treaty as is being outlined. A council of one hundred and fifty leading business and professional men, called by Government, met last Thursday in Berlin, presided over by Bernstorff. They agreed that no terms would be acceptable that should compel the annulling of the German war loans or that imposed heavy indemnities; the bankruptcy now existing in everything but name would be preferable to that. The whole country is so aching for peace and longing to begin reconstruction that it may finally accept any terms, as the ships have finally been turned over to get food.

The German delegates will entrench themselves firmly upon Wilson's fourteen points and will declare anything contrary to these to be in violation of the armistice agreement. They will particularly insist upon the first of the fourteen peace terms—open covenants of peace openly arrived at—which was abandoned by Wilson on his arrival at Paris. So deep is the feeling that all classes say that if a Brest-Litovsk peace is forced upon them (such as their militarists, they now admit, fastened upon Russia) they will open their doors wide to the Russians and if Bolshevism comes either because of the peace or the duration of the blockade since the armistice they will pull Europe down with them. The spread of Bolshevism in Germany is remarkable. At least five hundred Russian agents in Berlin are known to the Government, which is honestly and deeply concerned about the presence of the Trotzky army on the frontiers. Berlin is full of forged Russian, English, and French money, to which rich Germans contribute on the curious theory that if the Socialists can be made to fight among themselves there will be a chance for reaction and the return of the former capitalistic régime. When I was in Munich the Soviet leader there received offer of unlimited sums from Berlin capitalists if they would go to the edge of the French zone of occupation to start propaganda in France. The feeling now being aroused makes against the hope of permanent peace and Wilson's plan. Whether or not it is now too late to relieve the mistake by food supplies; whether Ebert and Scheidemann can maintain themselves by the compromise of taking some independent Socialists into the Government, the next few weeks will show. But it now looks as if Senator Lodge were right—that peace should have been made first and the league afterwards, though not for the reasons which he wishes to further.

Many times during these four weeks when I have heard the shooting of rifles and machine guns it has seemed as if the whole bottom of present society were dropping out. All who do not belong to the proletariat are profoundly concerned by such a fact as that Bavaria has forbidden all further purchases of real estate pending the taking over of all lands and houses by the State. Communism is advancing by leaps and bounds. But the absence of strong leaders everywhere (the natural result of repression and the lack of democracy of the old Prussian régime) makes it extremely difficult to forecast just what will happen. But there will be no trains running in six weeks if lubricants are not received. I was wholly unprepared for the present extreme situation, believing with others in Paris that many reports had been circulated for effect; but when you stand in a group of public school children and notice how many of six and seven have the size of three and four years and how wan and ill they all look you realize that the talk of undernourishment and famine is not German propaganda. Fair minded Americans who saw what I have seen would agree that the punishment is now enough and that the continuance of the blockade simply means suffering and death for the most innocent. If it was desired by continuing the blockade to make the Germans realize what they did to the Belgians, that aim is now fully achieved.

What Americans must now decide is whether they wish Bolshevism to overrun Germany by the violent methods of Lenine and Trotzky. Local Soviets are here to stay and Brunswick is already practically a Soviet republic. Those who desire still further revenge on Germany will perhaps rejoice. But one cannot say where the spread of Bolshevism will stop, and whether it will not cross the German boundary and enter France and England, whence it would inevitably reach America. Ideas cannot be excluded by laws or bayonets. The only way that Bolshevism can be beaten is by proving that its teachings are harmful and do not help humanity towards better government. It may be that this can only be ascertained by widespread convulsions of society, but it is inevitable that the experiment will be tried. The United States Senate, which, according to press dispatches, believes that our Government can best be secured in its present form by the enactment of a new espionage act, would do well to take a trip to Berlin at once. The Senators would first send a hurry call to Paris for food for the masses within forty-eight hours, and they would also learn things which might lead them to alter their views on the peace treaties and the value of prisons as checks to the spread of new ideas, be they for better or for worse. They would see plainly that if Bolshevism does not sweep over Europe it will be because of the German dam. If they were in Berlin they would have to adopt a different attitude towards our late enemy; indeed they may soon be obliged to do so any way; just as many military men believe that in a sort time there will have to be a joint war against Lenine and Trotzky.

If the Senate is terrorstricken now we may imagine their alarm on finding that the Majority Socialists, who were the extreme radicals when the war began, are now the conservatives. The Senate has no time to lose in building a Chinese wall around America. I suggest that they forbid the coming of all news from Europe, beginning ten days hence—by which time I hope to be at sea!

It is only a few days ago since four of Noske's soldiers were killed on the Kurfuerstendamm in a fashionable district of Berlin at the exact spot where Rosa Luxemburg was thrown into the canal by some German officers who liked her ideas no better than does Senator Overman. I heard firing in Moabit as I walked through the Thiergarten. Sniping was then spreading all through the exclusive western section of Berlin. It is said that over one thousand were executed. Martial law is spreading over all Germany. One cannot tell nowadays just what the consequences of going to war will be, just when it will end, and just how safe for democracy the world can be made by this bloody means.

OSWALD GARRISON VILLARD

II. The New Mind

(By cable to the *Nation*)

Paris, March 22

THE morning that Eisner was assassinated I was in the Landtag, which was dissolved by revolver shots. After witnessing some fighting on the streets, and having seen something of fighting in Berlin, I am prepared to affirm that no one need have the slightest fear of Germans again starting anti-Allied hostilities. If such fear is responsible for keeping large armies of occupation in Germany, the troops may be sent home promptly, particularly the Americans. The demoralization of the German forces is complete, especially in Bavaria, where the last regiments are being mustered out and all trained officers are being rapidly sent away from the War Ministry. The troops, comprising half-fed, untrained boys, are as ragged as Falstaff's; all staff work is at an end, and everyone says it would be impossible to recruit ten thousand men to start up a new war. The workers are determined that the old conditions shall never return. One cause of dissatisfaction among workmen with the Ebert Government is the proposal for a new standing army. This feeling is intensified by Noske's brutalities. In Munich many officers of the old army are in flight, and in Berlin officers refuse even to show themselves, though they are armed at all times. There have been murders of officers in so many places that they are often afraid to appear in uniform at night in certain sections. I have heard most violent denunciations of their old officers by the soldiers on the streets, and as serious charges against them of immorality, theft, and cruelty as were ever made by the Allies.

Many questions are asked about the Germans' state of mind: Do the people understand what has happened to them, and how they are regarded by the rest of the world? This can best be answered by saying that the working people and soldiers are through with the old régime forever. Their instincts are truer and better than those of the more educated groups who have done much to educate the public to the realization of the real facts in occupied districts. I have also met many educated people, like Eisner, whose eyes were opened during the war after they got over the intoxication of the first war hysteria. It is surprising how one hears the frankest admissions in shops, on streets, and in railway trains, that the Germans were absolutely lied to. This is sometimes, though not always, considered adequate excuse for many things. Coming from Berlin I met two former officers in the train. One was denouncing one Allied army of occupation for its severity. The other at once spoke up and said: "We have no right to complain; they are only giving us a dose of our own medicine as we gave it to Belgium and France, and they are not making it as severe as we should have, had conditions been reversed. We have no business to complain and I for one propose to stand it like a man, with teeth clenched, knowing that we have no right to protest."

But not all are as sensible as this man. There are still officers who write silly letters. There are still men of the vicious type of Reventlow and not a few officers of all ranks who would like to see the old order back. It is disappointing, too, to meet many people who ought to be well informed but who are still threshing over the old straw and insisting that whatever the faults and crimes in the German method of carrying on the war, the blame for beginning it rests on others. It at once appears that these people have never seen Serbia's answer to the Austrian ultimatum and other documents of vital import. One Munich editor assured me that he went to war believing that Germany was assailed, but that official documents which passed through his hands as an officer convinced him that his people had been lied to and deceived. But with the smaller people—soldiers and shop-keepers—one finds unanimous feeling. There will probably always be some people who refuse to see the light, such as General Hoffmann (the author of the abominable Brest-Litovsk treaty), with whom I talked, who is certain that everything done was for the best. One hears at Weimar and elsewhere far too much talk in Prussian tone and some rattling of sabres. Perhaps it is too much to expect that all the reactionary elements should have disappeared overnight. But just now the mills of the gods in Germany are grinding exceeding small. Indeed the grinding process has just begun. No one will say a good word for the Kaiser or admit the possibility of his ever coming back. "Ausgeschlossen" is the one word everybody uses when that question is put. It is true that more than a hundred thousand signatures were obtained to a message of sympathy to the Kaiser, but that was done only by appealing to sentiment; and when one thinks how many of the old nobility and militarist crowd there were this seems an insignificant number. What is much more important is that the Independent Socialists have as one plank of their platform this sentence: "Immediate creation of a federal court with the duty of bringing to book those guilty of having helped to bring on world war and having prevented a timely peace"—a threat very much more likely to worry Ludendorff, Hindenburg, and others than would similar talk at the Paris conference. The Majority Socialists, too, are leaning toward an investigation of war guilt, but events follow one another so quickly that is is impossible to prophesy what will happen. The only certain thing is that if the laboring men had their say that court would be at work now.

One of the best services that could be rendered Germany, and one which I hope to see German-Americans undertake, is the preparation for circulation in Germany of facts about the crimes at Louvain and elsewhere in Belgium, the Von Papen, Boy-Ed, Luxburg, and Zimmermann notes, and also the submarine wickedness. Cheap editions of these, which everybody could buy, would greatly widen the gulf between the old régime and the new, and would make forever impossible the recurrence of anything like military caste. Meanwhile Germany is paying the penalty for the crimes of the old régime. But the plain people who had no part in the old Government cannot see why Americans in particular should wish to starve their women and children. They see that their defeat was the best thing that could happen and believe that a decent Germany will rise from the ashes of the old. They are willing to go through bankruptcy and face Bolshevism if this is necessary to their purging, but they want food, coal, oil, and other things to enable them slowly to build up again. So far as old Germany is concerned, it is wonderful how much has been sloughed off, even if it is disappointing that no strong new leaders have as yet arisen. Everything about the old régime made against this, and we may have to wait some time for new men.

The only reason the Ebert Government is in office to-day is that the opposition, while it has a programme, has no men to offer to the directorate as alternatives. If they had, Ebert and Scheidemann would go at once. Their weakness is that they had so much to do with the old régime that they are praised by the reactionaries and that the instinct of the people tells them that these men are back numbers. Yet it is a fact that at present people are rallying to them because of their belief that the alternative is anarchy. As soon as it appears that there is another alternative which is not Bolshevism or communism, these men will go. Indeed, the peace terms may be their undoing. The frame of mind of the property owner may be guessed, when one considers the taxing away of all war profits, the taking of a portion of every man's property for the current expenses of state, and the introduction of increasingly heavy inheritance, property, and income taxes, besides the annulling of all war loans, with certain exceptions. Some embattled capitalists have flown their property by aeroplane to Switzerland, and small motor boats have transferred large funds to Denmark and elsewhere, but this has to be done secretly because the Government takes one-third of all the property of those who emigrate. When it is realized that the fall in value of the mark results in great losses in changing money to foreign values, there is little to be saved even if passports can be secured. Like the Bavarian decree, the Independent Socialist platform forbids private ownership of all lands and houses in cities. Citizens having rooms unused in any house must turn them over to the city to be filled with anybody in need of lodgings.

Sometimes I think the difference between old and new Germany is best illustrated by the simple fact that the Bavarian Government has already begun altering royal palaces and villas, making them over into homes for working people. After that who will dare call this a fake revolution? When I left Paris, certain Northcliffe papers were calling the recent uprisings "cinema revolutions." The gentlemen who wrote these words would have found other adjectives if they had been present with me and seen the wonderful outpouring at Eisner's funeral, had watched the fighting in Munich, had seen the absolute disarmament of the bourgeoisie and the arming of every trade-union worker in Munich with an army rifle and many rounds of ammunition.

The first revolution overthrew monarchies; the second is purely a class revolution; the third—if it occurs—will establish straight Soviet republics. Against this the fight is being made; and it is hoped that the food now purchased from the Allies will prevent it. Germany is, however, in a vicious circle requiring more than food. Factories are shutting down for lack of coal and raw materials, and this adds to the army of unemployed, and swells the Bolshevist ranks. The steady deterioration of transportation prevents the carrying of coal even when it is available. Finally, repeated strikes further paralyze transportation and cut down coal production. Surely it needs a genius to save Germany.

Unfortunately for the Allies, the war has shown that war or social revolution in one big country affects all the world. The wall of bayonets with which Pichon wished to encircle Russia cannot prevent the spread of radical ideas to France, Belgium, and Italy. Pichon, by the way, says that if Germany does not sign the peace terms the war will go on. But it takes two to make a war. The Germans are skeptical, too, about the Allied desire to keep large armies in a country just now engaged in a class war, particularly when France, for instance, has a deficit in sight of four billions of francs for the current year.

OSWALD GARRISON VILLARD

Paris, March 30, 1919.

Dearest Love,

As I have cabled, I have been very well received since my return here. Whereas I felt very much out of things when I was here before, I have been very much in the swim since I turned up from Ger. All the newspaper men think that I have had the most interesting and exciting experiences of anybody; even the men who are just back from Russia envy me and I have been interviewed for the English, Paris and American papers. Mr. Lansing Gen. Bliss, Mr. White and Col. House all talked with me, Lansing especially being more cordial than ever before and it was he who told Lloyd George that he must see me. I was at once asked to breakfast and L.G. was so interested that he kept me for an hour and a half. I have also dined with Smuts and was also asked to dine with Lord Robert Cecil, with whom I had a long talk two days later. I was one of the speakers at a great dinner given to 36 visiting members of the Cleveland Chamber of Commerce at which I was most warmly greeted by Gen. Pershing who has given me a motor for a two-day trip to the battlefields of the U.S. army in the Argonne on which I start at 7 A.M. to-morrow. Indeed, I have been so much entertained that I could make this letter sound like one of Charles Gregory's epistles! Only Wilson did not send for me but sent me word, in characteristic fashion when Lansing insisted that I make the effort to see him, that he knew "all I had to tell him and more besides!" Was there ever such monumental egotism?

The changed tone here is quite amazing, as to the outcome of the conference. Many people think that there will be no peace made because they cannot make it. All pretence of its being a conference has passed and Lloyd George, Orlando, Wilson and Clemenceau are trying to work out something. AS a very important personage put it last night, they have been "fighting like hell " all the week and no one yet knows whether the victory has come or not. The French are simply mad with fear of the Germans and utterly rapacious and the Americans of all kinds who are on the boards and commissions are nearly worn out in fighting them. Hoover, for instance, is nearly a wreck. It took him from Dec. 9 until four days ago to get permission for the German fishing fleet to go to sea. The Americans all see that if Germany is not saved from starvation and Bolshevism all Europe will go down. The results of my observations are the same as theirs and hence the eager use they have made of me and my views. // Whether Europe can be saved now remains to be seen and will be decided soon, but I know people who are making their arrangements to get their families away by May first when they think revolution will come here. I never saw such pessimists as one meets here. I still believe that something will come out of it, but something so weak and poor that it will mean nothing at all. Meanwhile there is every possibility of fresh wars and bloodshed. If the Conference should go down, it would be the most remarkable moral happening in history for it was conceived in hypocrisy and falseness and carried on in a spirit absolutely at variance with the pretended objects of the war. It would prove that war cannot be ended by war and many other admirable things but when one thinks of the misery and disillusionment that will come if it fails, one hopes for its success. The Germans are daily getting into a stronger position because of the mistakes of the Allies and the delay and can kill the whole thing if they wish to by simply refusing to sign. Never was there such a bankruptcy of statesmanship as is to be seen here - chiefly because of W.W.'s old cowardice and insincerity. It can be written down now that whateever happens it will be such a miserable compromise as to avail nothing for the security of the world. Anything may happen but the belief grows that we may be facing the most terrible calamities the world has ever seen ever seen. Believe me that I have no more important business for the coming summer than to buy Dorothea's farm and I mean to do it. If you had looked revolution inthe face as I have and seen what I saw in Bavaria you would be looking for five acres and a house now.

Well, you dear old darling!, if you had been here the day last week when I succeeded in bribing a man to get me a berth on the Rochambeau you would have seen about the happiest man in Paris. They told me when I got here that I could not sail before April 24 and I was simply wild for I could not have stood waiting until then. Now they tell me that the ship may be delayed a couple of days and I do not like that, but I am counting on having my dear family about me on the fifteenth anyway—she is a nine day boat & due the 13th. Indeed if she sails on time this letter may only reach you a day or so before I do. Hurrah! I could go to Russia in a responsible position and do a whole lot of things, but home for me! I have had all I want of Europe for some time and only wish that you could have had a little of it for I fear that it will be a long, long time before it will be agreable to stay over here again.

With a heartful of love and most joyous anticipations,

Your ever devoted "man,"

O.G.V.

O.G.V.

War or a Righteous Peace

FOR a time after the preliminary draft of the constitution of the League of Nations was announced it seemed likely that the Paris Conference would contrive a peace treaty which by its superficial resemblance to the desires of America would pass hasty scrutiny. The Fourteen Points were not to be adhered to, and many questionable territorial amputations were to be sanctioned. But the treaty would have had the glozing of democratic rhetoric and would have received its vindication by the weary minds which put it together. And America, bewildered, to say the least, by the raucous European medley, would have been grateful to welcome its delegates home and to get back to business. But the prospect is wholly altered. The force of unexpected popular movements has, it now appears, involved us in the predicament of choosing to stand unequivocally by the principles we affirmed for the peace or to withdraw from the Conference.

The calamity of vengeance which France sought to visit upon the Central Empires has invoked the law of revolt. Not only was Germany to be starved until an indemnity had been paid, but her industries were to be kept idle until French mills were on a peace footing, and then were to be dependent for raw materials on the victors' whim. The German prisoners were to remain in bondage, as a post-bellum reprisal. The Saar basin was to be loot for French manufacturers. The Rhenish provinces were either to be annexed to France or to become an autonomous but dependent province. The Polish tories were to possess not only Poland but East Prussia and Danzig. The Czechs were to encroach upon regions where Germans were in the majority. Rumania was to incorporate innumerable Hungarians in a new empire that was to dominate the Balkans. Russia was to be invaded and made to pay her French debt. This intransigent French programme could not receive the consent of Great Britain, Italy, or America. The British and Italians themselves had prizes to claim, and empires to extend and fortify. But the French insistence was strong enough to enforce armistice terms which, originally as harsh as the demands of military security could reasonably require, were made vindictive and then predatory.

Thereupon something developed which the Paris delegates, burning in the heat of their own inflammation, had not deemed possible. The German people, conscious of the discrepancy between the Fourteen Points and the peace in preparation for them, determined to withstand it. And the Karolyi Government resigned Hungary to the Soviets.

The mood of Germany and Hungary has dispelled the confusion in Paris. The Conference had been a conflict between the clashing claims of the Allies, with little thought that the broken enemy could fail to grant what the victors might agree upon. Now the problem is of another description. It is a question, not of deciding what concessions the Allies and the United States are willing to make to one another, but of finding whether or not peace can be made for the world. Either a meeting-ground must be found with the peoples of Central and Eastern Europe, or a new war must be initiated.

The latter alternative is by no means so obscure as it was a few weeks ago. The Scheidemann Government cannot survive if it consents to carry out provisions of any treaty which is not the substantial fulfilment of the pledge the Allies and America gave in the armistice. And the only Government likely to succeed Scheidemann's is an even more radical one. The bourgeoisie is not too inferior, numerically, to set up a Cabinet, but it probably would prefer the socialization programme to national humiliation. The Soviet principle has been passed favorably by the Constitutional Convention at Weimar, and the menace of Allied occupation to enforce a long term of economic serfdom and the expropriation of German provinces would do more to make communists of property-owners than a century of propaganda. Furthermore, the door is open to a formidable East-European alliance. Russia and Hungary would immediately join. The Soviet revolution is expected any day in Vienna. The Czecho-Slovak Socialists have already delivered an ultimatum to the Prague Government. The Polish reactionaries, never representative of the majority, can remain in office only as purveyors of Allied food and as imperialists whose empire is guaranteed by an Allied dictatorship. A German-Russian accord would overthrow Paderewski even more expeditiously than he was installed.

The alternative of war has already been chosen by the chauvinist press of Paris; and the Northcliffe papers, after a few months of pseudo-liberalism, are quoted as advising a campaign against Russia. For such tories in England and France the case is pellucid: better more fighting than Soviets at home. And they undoubtedly think to rejuvenate the jaded armies by talk of rescuing the half-million Allied troops east of the Rhine, and by anti-anarchist phrases. The peace delegates are moving more cautiously. The influence of the Americans is being used on behalf of an understanding with Russia, and our arguments have the authority of the facts which Mr. Bullitt brought from Moscow. But we can hardly hope to change the character of French policy, especially as Clemenceau would prefer war to bankruptcy.

The severity of the armistice terms and the inhumanity of the blockade have invited catastrophe, but the highway to peace is not absolutely barricaded and the road is one which America can show. Our power at this moment, if we are honest enough to employ it, is perhaps greater than ever before. We can veto and direct. We can marshal the liberals of England, France, and Italy and compel the acknowledgement of our disregarded principles. There can be no war without our consent, for we alone possess the means to finance it, with the fresh armies for invasion. The key to peace today, however, is to be sought, not in Moscow or Budapest, but in Berlin. There need be no new intrenchment of a belligerent Europe if Germany accepts the peace treaty. But we are dealing, not with monarchs, but with a nation which through its parliamentary leaders entered into an undertaking to uphold the Fourteen Points. A democracy cannot be coerced to submit to an infringement of such elemental rights as were set forth in that undertaking. Yet the Allies, who are committed by it, have revoked their word. Mr. Lloyd George won his election by a promise to do so. M. Clemenceau is a *Realpolitiker.* Most of the debates at the Conference have been in discussion of arrangements beyond the limits of the agreement. And the secrecy of the negotiations is the confession of their nature.

All of President Wilson's utterances have expressed a belief in the practicability of the moral conduct of human affairs. It is a belief which he may by this time have learned to practice, if only by the bitter lesson of Russia. Does he ever ask himself what America gained by intervention? Did it in the least enhance his prestige for the greater task of Paris? Did it facilitate the finer peace? But even this compromise, and many others, may conceivably even now be retrieved. "Only a peace between equals can last. Only a peace the very principle of which is equality and a common participation in a common benefit." If such a peace be made with Germany and Russia, there will be no renewal of bloodshed. It is the President's hour; the course of world affairs has given him the mandate. We are not sanguine that he can exercise it and remain in Paris. If it should develop that coöperation with the Allied plenipotentiaries there means participation in a disaster, the call of loyalty to them would be a poor call to heed. A distinction may be drawn these days between the French Government and the French people; Lloyd George apparently does not represent the majority in England; Orlando is not Italy. The ethics of humanity are better than the practices of the Quai d'Orsay. To European liberals Mr. Wilson is still the leader, and if he ever summons their support after taking a courageous stand he will rally a mightier host than his opponents. These are the words that accompanied the announcement of the Fourteen Points; they remain our promise:

> We do not wish to injure her [Germany] or to block in any way her legitimate influence or power. We do not wish to fight her either with arms or with hostile arrangements of trade if she is willing to associate herself with us and the other peace-loving nations of the world in covenants of justice and law and fair dealing. We wish her only to accept a place of equality among the peoples of the world—the new world in which we now live—instead of a place of mastery.

The Grave Situation at the Peace Conference

(By Cable to the *Nation*)

Paris, March 28

NOT even the decision to cut down the committee of ten to the Big Four and so hasten the making of peace reveals to the full the shock which the Peace Conference has sustained from the sudden surrender of Hungary to Bolshevism. But it is undeniable that some people here now see the handwriting on the wall. I am struck by the great change in the feeling in Paris in the last six weeks. The optimism that was universal when I left is now found only in the highest circles. Veteran journalists are saying openly that anything may happen, particularly as M. Clemenceau's position no longer seems as secure as a week ago; one journalist has cancelled his sailing for America, which was scheduled for this week, fearing a collapse of the Conference. For this change other things besides the delays are responsible. For what progress has been made the world has the Americans and the English to thank. Our representatives have from the first realized the Bolshevist danger and the need of feeding the Central Powers as well as the other countries, but delegates of the other Powers have resisted every such effort. The lifting of the German fishing blockade this week crowns the effort started by Americans as far back as early December. All that has been accomplished has taken infinite patience on the part of both Americans and English. The differing views of the French have often seemed to us fatal to the purposes of all. In every committee and subcommittee there are differences of opinion.

The Committee on the League of Nations has its work well in hand and has made numerous changes this week and will make more. But the question is whether we shall get any league and any peace at all. I have talked to some people at the Hotel Crillon who have given up all hope. For one thing, the attitude of Germany is causing profound concern. Germany has hit upon the most dangerous weapon in the world—non-resistance. It is needless to say this is not from any ethical reasoning or any sudden conversion to the practicability of the teachings of Jesus, but becaus the Germans see in the lack of aggressive constructive statesmanship in Paris an opportunity to defy the Allies to go back upon the Fourteen Points in any respect, and they shrewdly suspect that the Allies have no desire to put any more troops into Germany to be exposed to the risk of Bolshevist infection. All Germans who have considerable property interests are eager to have the Allies walk in and uphold the old order. In this point of view they are at one with the Government leaders who declare that they will under no circumstances give up German territory east or west. All the dispatches from Germany which have appeared this week have borne out the reports I have made to the leading British and American authorities since my return, as to the rapidly growing antagonism in Germany to the signing of any treaty of the kind now being proposed. Yet no one suggests a return to fighting. It would be impossible to recruit 20,000 Germans to go to war again. What is planned is a simple refusal to accept any treaty which goes beyond a reasonable indemnity for Belgium and Northern France, the abolition of the army and navy, and the loss of colonies and of Alsace-Lorraine. The Germans may then say to the Allies: "What are you going to do about it?"

I have tried to find out what the policy of the Allies would be in case this should happen and can only learn that the food blockade would immediately be restored. But I get no reply when I ask the men who suggest this if they think that the humanity of the Allies will stand such a strain, especially in view of the recent refusal of General Plumer's British soldiers to stand guard over starving women and children. Personally I am not convinced that Germany will refuse to sign, if that means the death of from ten to twenty millions of people, for I cannot conceive any men being so Spartan as to take that attitude. I cannot forget, too, how many Germans told me they would never give up their fleet, and yet how readily they gave it up when the time came.

But what the situation calls for is the immediate conclusion of peace, and that is not in sight, despite the rumor of its coming next week. The Peace Conference as a whole disappeared long ago, and all semblance of a conference organization as well. The Committee of Ten has now gone; will the Committee of Four do any better even in view of the Hungarian warning? That collapse, incidentally, is laid by some American officials squarely at the doors of Senator Lodge and of our Senate, for amending the Hoover food bill so as to prevent the giving of food to any former enemies. Karolyi, in his letters to Paris, has been begging for food and foretelling just what would happen. His appeals were in vain, and there is the most intense anxiety lest what has happened there be repeated in Slovakia, Italy, and especially in Austria, where Vienna is now considered as surely doomed as Petrograd. I have talked with one of the ablest American observers just back from Italy. His word is that the situation there is very serious. Indeed, there are enough sad prospects to intensify the gloom of those who see nothing ahead but the collapse of Europe. But this is not the time to despair or take counsel of the hopeless. We shall learn in the next few weeks whether the world's statesmanship is or is not completely bankrupt. There is little doubt that if Germany refuses to sign, the League of Nations is dead. Therefore it all depends upon President Wilson now whether or not the precious months lost in talk will prove the wrecking of the enterprise.

We are witnessing here the solving of one of the greatest ethical problems ever faced, and the testing of the political philosophy that good can come out of evil, or that the world may be redeemed by carnal weapons and the slaughter of millions. The entourage of the President is reported to be still very hopeful, but it is interesting that no one here any longer speaks of making the world safe for democracy, in view of the rapidity with which Bolshevism is making Europe highly unsafe for the kind of democracy we Americans have hitherto deemed best.

Men of all opinions in Paris are greatly concerned at the failure of the American press and public opinion to understand what the situation here is, and to realize that the world is changing as we watch week by week. We read the *Times*, the *Tribune*, and the *Post*, and marvel at the state of mind and the utterly different world which they represent. Perhaps we are too near and too discouraged to be able to judge. The unanimous opinion expressed yesterday, however, by a group of American officials (who have been reflecting the greatest credit upon their country by their labors here) is that there will be a sorry awakening for America when she realizes how far from the actual truth have been her conceptions of world conditions.

A few more shocks like the news from Hungary would cause a grave crisis here. It is not surprising that one hears talk of an early peace with Lenine and Trotzky on condition that they will promise that there shall be no more proselytizing either by insidious official propaganda or by force of arms. There is reason to believe that this might be acceptable to them on account of the terrible famine conditions now existing in Russia.

OSWALD GARRISON VILLARD

Foreign Correspondence

I. The Swiss Situation

Zurich, February 15

AT this distance one wonders whether the American public realizes what it means to Europe to have the signing of peace so long delayed. Switzerland, for instance, has suffered gravely by the war—the enormous expense of keeping so large a part of her army mobilized, the necessary food restriction, and the serious lack of clothing and coal. So long as the actual peace is deferred Switzerland must keep men on her frontiers, if only because of the thousands of interned invalid prisoners. The prisoners from the Allied countries have been returned, but soldiers of the Central powers are still carefully guarded. If the interned could be sent home, it would help in the distribution of food. Rations of bread, cheese, sugar, fats, and milk are still carefully apportioned, and it is expected that there will soon be two or three meatless days a week. The Swiss obey the food laws exactly. You cannot cross the boundary until you have shown your passport and then you receive your first food tickets. When leaving the country you must turn in what tickets you have left; if you have been giving coupons away you are fined on the spot. This makes endless work for a sorely-tried but very efficient Government.

Despite the fact that Switzerland is so harassed by her economic conditions, she is already seeking new ways in which to help suffering humanity. She has been a great international post-office for all nations; she has made room for thousands of sick and wounded, many of whom she has harbored at cost, or less than cost; and she has been a refuge for political exiles of all the countries. Now she is seeking particularly to aid the starving city of Vienna. A report lies before me, of the distribution of the Swiss supplies in that stricken city. The poverty is beyond words; the lack of food and under-nourishment—especially among children—is heartrending. According to this report and that of the British Red Cross, 500,000 families go daily to the free kitchens of the municipal Red Cross.

Beyond Switzerland are nations begging for a settlement of their fate. Thus the German Austrians and Bohemians, left unattached by the collapse of Austria-Hungary, are most eager to unite with Germany. Bohemian Germany is overrun by the Czechs, who lay claim to the most important parts. Every day's delay at Paris adds to the disorder and discouragement. The same is true of Hungary, where the Slovaks are showing an imperialistic earth hunger. Holland, like Switzerland, has performed many helpful offices for all the warring nations. She, too, ardently needs the relief that peace will bring, including the return of the rest of her shipping that was "borrowed" by the Allies against her will. From Belgium there is reported such utter prostration and such difficulty in getting people to work again that the task of reconstruction seems almost appalling. There must be unrestricted railroad communication as soon as possible as the first step. At present there is only one train a day from Paris to Brussels, and it is an all-day run, though before the war it took only five hours. Little Luxembourg, too, awaits her fate. Shall she revert to her former status or be joined to France or Belgium? There is still an uncomfortable ferment which has led to one change of rulers since the armistice and may lead to another.

The Allies face an extremely difficult problem in hastening the peace. If they make a quick peace there will be a tremendous demand for the immediate discharge of large forces, which would be considered undesirable by labor circles on both sides of the ocean. All countries are now living under the fear of Bolshevism—even Switzerland has its Bolshevist menace.

OSWALD GARRISON VILLARD

Revolutionary Germany

I. When Eisner Was Shot

Munich, February 22

"YOU will find," said my friend, "that the Baseler Hof is the quietest hotel in the quietest street in Munich—but it is very convenient." Just at this moment, as I sit in my room in the aforesaid Baseler Hof, the machine guns in the quietest street in Munich are rumbling, and the crack of rifles is incessant. I dare not open my window to look out, for every time I have tried it someone calls out: "Head in, or I'll shoot"—and the head comes in. But I can see out of my window. The firing party is just beyond my vision, but I can see the flashes. Civilians come running by for cover. A street light shines right down upon as picturesque a group of reserve soldiery as ever a De Neufville painted. The quietest street in Munich, and not two hundred yards away men are being killed by their brothers!

The day began well. My impudence in calmly walking in and demanding a seat in the journalists' gallery of the Landtag met its just reward. A representative of the American press at this historic opening session of the first democratic Landtag in Bavaria—"Well, really, mein Herr!" The session was just about to begin, the journalists' box was already more than filled—and what papers had mein Herr with which to identify himself? "Here is my American passport, here my Paris pass as a Peace Conference correspondent, here my visiting card." "But what is there to show that you are connected with the *Nation?*" I try to explain a rather intimate connection; suddenly it is unnecessary. Something about the name on the passport attracts. Is it possible that I am my father's son? Yes, indeed. "Well then, of course," he says, "here is a ticket to the box and good luck. I used to live in the Pfalz, where your father did."

The gentlemen in charge of the box are equally amazed. A colleague from America? Well, he will have to be content with standing-room. He was well content with standing-room and in a minute was in the journalists' box directly opposite the "tribune" or dais upon which the officials sit, looking down upon the gathering representatives. The correspondent of the *Frankfurter Zeitung* kindly pointed out the various dignitaries. That Minister there on the right was a locksmith's apprentice only a little while ago. Timm, the Minister of Education, on the left, is a tailor's son and was long a public school teacher. There is Auer, the Minister about whose head the storm is raging. He is the son of a sewing-woman—and left school at eleven to be a herdsman for eleven years. Yet this is aristocratic Bavaria. Then there is Rosshaupter, Minister of Military Affairs, to whom the Independent Socialists and Bolshevists are as much opposed as to Auer; he is charged with having been too kind to the officers of the old army. Several woman delegates come in. "Think of that in Bavaria," adds my coach; "woman suffrage in hidebound, priest-ridden old Bavaria. Then there is Professor Quidde, the chief of the Bavarian pacifists, of whose efforts to stop the war you must have heard in America. Now they are all here except the President, Kurt Eisner."

A moment later a very young man as pale as a sheet walked quite feebly to the platform. "That," said the voice by my side, "is Fechenbach, Eisner's secretary. What is wrong? Something must have happened to Eisner." At that moment a soldier dashed into the journalists' box. "Kurt Eisner is murdered," he called in a voice that startled the whole house; "Kurt Eisner has been shot"; and to prove it he held up the bloody eye-glasses of the Liberator of Bavaria.

I cannot exaggerate the shock to the Landtag. Everybody cries out: "Shame!" The galleries are more excited than the Landtag. Even the journalists join in. "Adjourn, adjourn!" they cry. Then comes the news that the assassin is the young Count Arco-Valley. The temporary president calls the meeting to order, and in a cool, calm voice announces the assassination of the President, and declares the meeting adjourned for an hour. Everybody goes out. The gravity of the situation is recognized at once. Eisner had intended to resign that morning, as soon as the Landtag should be organized, from the office he had held ever since leading the revolution in November. Now the bitter hatred of him cherished by the middle classes, the aristocracy, and the officials, big and little, and carefully fanned by the capitalistic press, had vented itself. That the murderer was a count only made it worse. More than one declared that there would be bloodshed that night, and that Bolshevism would come to Bavaria. "I pity the anti-Eisner press tonight," said one. "There will not be a stone left in the building of the *Muenchener-Augsburger Zeitung.*" "You had better get away," declared my Frankfort friend to his wife; "things are likely to happen here."

Just at this point my newspaper instinct failed me. Remembering a noon engagement, I went out to telephone that I could not keep it. When I came back in five minutes the way was blocked. Journalists' passes were no longer of any avail, as others besides myself learned. We stood about disconsolate. But a representative from Vienna thought we should miss nothing and went off advising us all to stay indoors that night. "Tonight blood will flow." I was left wondering what would happen next. Only two days ago, on my arrival in Munich, I ran right into the attempt of six hundred sailors to take the city by surprise in the interest of the reaction, and saw some of the fighting around the railway station. From what I witnessed at that time it was clear enough that four years of warfare had not been without their effect in accustoming all classes to the method of attaining their ends by violence; and now, with the hero of the people shot down by a member of the hated old ruling class, I could not help asking myself what was to be the result of this dastardly crime on the relations between Bavaria's rulers and her hungry and embittered population. What next in quiet Munich?

The answer came quickly enough. An officer dashed out of the Landtag crying out, "Auer is assassinated, Auer is assassinated—and Osel!" The news spread like wildfire. What happened, my friend of the *Frankfurter Zeitung* described later. "You may thank your lucky stars that you were not there. The Landtag had hardly assembled again and listened to a couple of tributes to Eisner, including one by Auer, when a man walked in and fired point blank at Auer. An officer dashed at him but was shot down. Then they began shooting from the galleries all around us. Osel was killed outright, and a clerk as well. Auer is not dead, but wounded. We journalists crawled out of that box on our hands and knees! I have seen terrible things and witnessed two attempts to assassinate kings, but I never saw anything like the panic and terror and flight and the general promiscuous shooting." I myself could add a little to the tale, for as I stood at the door, there came out a man with staring eyes and pale face, who gathered the soldiers at the doors about him. I moved nearer to hear what he said. He kindly remarked as he saw me, "There's another chap we ought to get." Two soldiers urged me away. "Better go home. Something might happen to you here." The man walked off quietly with four soldiers. As he did so another came to me excitedly and said, "See that man? He's the fellow who just shot Auer and the others, and they are letting him run away!"

The news of Eisner's death went through the city as if on wings. The effect was instantaneous. No one needed to be told that trouble was to come. The street cars stopped running, disappearing as if by magic. The restaurants on the main streets hastily closed, and the shops one and all pulled down their heavy roll shutters. As I went out to lunch I met long processions of workmen—pale and gaunt and lean—so over-worked, starved, and hungry-looking as to move any heart. They had laid down their work and declared simultaneously without consultation a three-day general strike. To every well-dressed man they cried out, "We'll get square with the aristocrats who killed our Eisner." In less than three hours the stage was all set for civil war. It was in the air.

Proclamations came thick and fast: first one from the Council of Workmen, Soldiers, and Peasants declaring that the revolution was in danger and that a three-day strike was ordered. By four o'clock aeroplanes were flying over the city dropping proclamations: bits of white paper proclaimed that everybody must be indoors by seven o'clock; bits of blood-red paper declared a state of siege; anybody found on the street after seven o'clock would be arrested. Still another proclamation declared that anybody who stole or pillaged would be shot on sight. Troops were soon moving in every direction. There were no laggards in getting home when seven o'clock came. By seven-thirty there was firing under our windows, and now they are at it again.

There are no newspapers, the telephone has stopped, the postmen are in the strike, and the telegraph offices are closed. There were three killed and eighteen wounded in the fighting last night near us, and more elsewhere. Our street is guarded like a fortress; the machine guns that spoke last night are on guard still, but are silent. The Regina Palast Hotel across the Promenaden Platz got off pretty well, but the Bank for Industry and Commerce was well peppered, and the great plate glass windows of stores are riddled or altogether smashed. It is impossible to enter the railway station, and there are no cabs, no taxis, no cars. Everywhere are excited groups, talking over the events of the night and exchanging the latest rumors. But it seems to be true that twenty prominent men of the bourgeoisie and military have been seized as hostages. It is announced that they will be shot at once if another attempt is made upon any member of the present Government. I walked to the newspaper quarter. Every newspaper office is in the hands of troops, and publication has been forbidden. Great placards on some of the offices read: "Comrades! Don't shoot. This building is in the hands of the Councils." Most serious are the placards demanding that the bourgeoisie disarm at once under heavy penalties, and announcing that every workman who is over twenty years of age and is a member of a recognized trade union will be armed forthwith. Soldiers are raiding all the gun shops and entering private houses in search of arms. All day great wagons and trucks rumble through the quietest street in Munich bringing arms, food, cartridges, and huge bundles of straw for the soldiers to sleep on. The Landtag building is to be one of the chief fortresses. Other auto trucks, with their exhausts wide open, are patrolling the streets; machine guns are mounted upon them and the trucks are filled with soldiers wearing trench helmets.

This afternoon we were allowed to receive a newspaper edited by the combined *A. B. & S. Räthe*, as they are styled (*Arbeiter, Bauer und Soldaten*), which are now ruling Bavaria. It is a commentary upon human nature that when the reformers are in they promptly imitate some of the worst habits of the Outs. This revolutionary paper is as one-sided as the others have been, but we are promised that freedom of the press will be restored in a few days under a more or less permanent censorship "to prevent the overthrow of the revolution and to insure the spreading of truth by the capitalistic press." These Bavarians have still much to learn about real democracy, but the extreme leaders do not want real democracy; they are frankly working for the domination of the middle classes by the proletariat. This is a class war. The class which has been exploited for centuries is determined to do all the ruling for the future and is more than ready to down the middle classes and to exterminate the rich. How little did those who initiated the world war imagine that they were likewise beginning a class war whose outcome might well be the complete overthrow of the old order.

There is no doubt that Arco-Valley's shot will have many serious consequences for Bavaria. It is already plain that Kurt Eisner, who was a plain journalist little known outside his profession, will go down in Bavarian history as the Lincoln of his time, even though it is only three and one-half months since he emerged from obscurity, and with a handful of followers proclaimed the republic, thus sending the royal family scurrying away before he could even urge them to go. The spot where Eisner fell, just around the corner from the quietest street, is heaped with flowers, and there is a guard of honor, while a sign reads: "Proletarians, hats off before the blood of Kurt Eisner." All day women and children have been coming and laying little handfuls of flowers upon the sidewalk, and every man uncovers as he passes. I have seen three men roughly handled, beaten till the blood came, for having expressed pleasure at Eisner's death. What infuriates the people is the knowledge that in the clubs, at the university, and in all the well-to-do sections of the city, men and women of property are freely saying that Eisner ought to have been shot, that he was nothing but a Galician Jew anyway, and never was a Bavarian. What right had such a man to come here and upset the existing order? Such critics admit that he may have been a man of peace himself and may even have meant well, but in their opinion he released the terrible forces which are now threatening to engulf all society and destroy civilization itself. It is evident that such will never judge him aright, and that the working people will speedily build around him a tradition of growing beauty. One gets everywhere a wonderful feeling that the people on the street have lost something infinitely dear.

But the guns are going again tonight; we have just had a heavy explosion like the discharge of a mine thrower, and rifle firing is clear enough. What will the morrow bring forth?

II. Who Shall Inherit the Power?

Munich, February 26

TODAY all the working folk of Munich have turned out to bury Kurt Eisner—and the proletariat has shown that it knows how to honor its dead. The long procession through the city, the great crowds, the masses of flowers, the aeroplanes flying overhead, the funeral music of military bands, above all the wonderful solemnity and dignity of the crowds themselves, have been profoundly impressive. There have been those who feared disturbances, and others who were certain that we should behold outbursts of rage. Nothing of the kind occurred; the city has been as safe today as any one could wish. Tonight the auto-truck patrols are more numerous than ever, but they are not needed. During the day there has been only a small proportion of policemen and soldiers in the crowds. The services at the chapel in the cemetery were without prayer or religious ceremony. Gustav Landauer, one of the Soviet leaders, pronounced the oration, and brief speeches were made by representatives of the most important delegations which had brought the great wreaths that lay in masses on the chapel floor. Then the coffin was carried to a neighboring building for cremation, and Kurt Eisner had indeed passed into history.

Is it without significance that the family and chief mourners and the chief officials of the temporary Government drove home in the royal carriages, denuded of their silver trappings and royal crests? It was Kurt Eisner himself who altered the aspect of these carriages last November, but one wonders what will happen to them and to all Bavaria now that he has gone. He wanted to lay down his office; he wanted to go back into opposition, which was his *métier*. But he was counted on to keep people from going at one another's throats, for he was a pacifist, and his own revolution was bloodless. So the question is still, what will happen to Bavaria? The first result has been the announcement that the various Socialist factions have come together. Fechenbach, Eisner's secretary, is credited with that accomplishment, and it is announced on every wall as "Kurt Eisner's legacy to Bavaria."

But there is much more to be done than that, and even when one reads that staring proclamation one wonders how long the Bolshevist lion and the moderate Socialist lamb can lie down together. For it is characteristic of the Bolshevist that he is a rampant person, aggressive to a degree, and absolutely bent on getting his own way. At the other end of the town, there are the wholly conservative elements, completely cowed, deprived of every means of self-defence, routed out of bed at all hours by searchers for arms and sometimes by plain marauders. I talk with these people, and more than ever I feel that history is repeating itself, that just as we have had a parallel with the Napoleonic Wars and are now getting a new Holy Alliance at Paris, so the aristocrats and capitalists in Munich are now realizing how the French aristocracy felt when the bottom dropped out of their world. The people who used to rule here are utterly stunned. They cannot comprehend the situation; they have no explanation as to why they are being ruled by former herdsmen and journeyman-apprentices and peasants and labor leaders. They cannot understand that there is no longer a royal court in Munich, that their army is at an end forever, and that their sons, its officers, are turned adrift in the world with three months' pay and no other profession to turn to. Their anger and sense of injustice, that these wild, hungry workmen should be the only persons armed, is equalled only by their general inability to understand the downfall of Germany. "What happened?" they ask. "We seemed to be winning the war, we *were* winning the war, and then everything seemed to go to pieces overnight." It is hard to tell them that they had to lose the war because they were eternally in the wrong, and it is still more difficult to make them see that they deserved to lose their tremendous power, their complete control of the Government. They cannot bring themselves to realize that the gaunt and violent workmen they meet on the streets are of their own creation, that if they had governed well there would be no men to look like this and talk like this, to come out suddenly into the light of revolution. Nor are the leaders happy who are now trying to form the new Government which the Landtag was to have appointed, had not the bullets of a butcher and his accomplices driven it away in fear. They believe that by taking hostages and arming the proletariat, by driving out Prince Joachim, the son of the Kaiser, as soon as they discovered that he was in Munich disguised as a simple count, and by holding the troops in line, they have prevented any further reactionary moves like the one last Wednesday that gave me my first insight into what street fighting looks like. But their real danger lies today in their own associates of the extreme left. Will they hold to the pledge to work together? Will they be content to bide their time before attempting to force a straight Soviet republic? The Catholic Church was compelled today, much against its will, to ring for an hour all the church bells in Bavaria as a requiem for the man who has just done the terrible thing of separating Church from State. Will the peasants, controlled as they are by the Church, stand for more radicalism, or have they had their fill? Above all, have the present Ministers the constructive force within themselves necessary for this great emergency? These are the questions still to be answered. Thanks to a chance friendship, I have been able to meet many of the eager spirits that are trying to build the perfect state here in Bavaria. It was the new and able Minister of War, but lately a sergeant in the old army, who brought me back from Eisner's funeral today in his automobile—I mean the late Crown Prince's superb motor. Even the War Minister is depressed tonight. Things are not going well. The death of Eisner has not cemented factions as was expected.

Friday, February 28

Fridays are dangerous days in Munich. Did I not feel quite as much of a fool as if I were personally concerned in the affair when a dozen men this afternoon rushed into the Landtag room and made everybody hold up his hands at the point of a revolver? I shall never think any motion picture "hold-up" untrue to life after this. The session today of the Councils-Congress, composed of delegates from the Soldiers', Workmen's, and Peasants' Councils through the country, which was to have yielded its revolutionary control to the dispersed Landtag, was quite exciting in itself. Suddenly from the left there burst in armed men, yelling *"Hände hoch!"* For a moment we journalists failed to take it all in, until we were covered from the dais below and told to be quick about it. Some of these invading gentry had a revolver in each hand, and as everybody recalled the tragic events in this room just a week ago there were shouts of "Don't shoot, don't shoot!" The spectators had all been searched for arms, but we wondered, none the less, as it soon appeared that the object of the raid was the seizure of the Bolshevist leaders, whether shots would not be fired, especially by the guard behind us. There are usually about eight guards to keep us in order, but when it occurred to me to look for them they had absolutely vanished. Dr. Levien and Kurt Mühsam, the two chief radicals, were seized at once. Levien was roughly thrown from his chair and beaten. The members of the Government present were as much in the dark as everybody else until the leaders of the party announced that the garrison of Munich, headed by my friend, the Minister of War, and by the commander of the city and the chief of police, had decided that the Councils-Congress should be no longer kept from doing its work by any group of Bolshevists. The blunder was apparent at once. It certainly ends the career of the Minister of War. Fortunately, one of the youngest leaders was quick to see that if this Congress was to survive it must at once right the wrong against its parliamentary immunity. On his motion a committee was sent to demand the return of the seized members. In half an hour they were back, with Dr. Levian there—his head bound up, one hand rather swollen cheered and applauded as he entered, even the extreme right. "But, gentlemen," he said, very earnestly, "one does not applaud a man who has just been beaten as I have been beaten. I hope we shall now go on with the order of the day." It was a magnificent exhibition of calmness and coolness. It is commonly said that he could proclaim himself dictator of Bavaria tonight if he wished.

March 1

Calling upon a young physician last night, I found Dr. Levien there—his head bound up, one hand rather swollen—and heard from his own lips what happened. They took him out into the hall, held revolvers to his breast and forehead, and told him to prepare for his end. By his coolness he probably saved his life. From others it appears that in twenty minutes he had talked his captors into lowering their weapons and that by the time he was reached by the committee from the Landtag he had been freed by his guards, whom he had so thoroughly convinced of being misled that they pointed their revolvers at their own leader. Thus this *coup d' état* came to naught.

Levien is the first real Bolshevist I have seen at close range. He is coarse, but obviously extremely able. He wears high Russian boots, and a torn and battered uniform (he served in the German army during the war), and has no income save his pay as a member of a soldiers' council. With his stained bandages he looks a pirate chief. Yet, unattractive as his personality is, his power attracts and fascinates. There was a typical young Russian woman-student literally kneeling at his feet. Levien was educated at two universities, has his Kant and Hegel at his fingers' ends, is master of three languages and three German dialects, at least, and has a splendid library (his sole possession, he says) in Switzerland, where he was studying when the war began. He knows exactly how to speak to the masses, and it is fortunate, indeed, that the young physician, who is also an old friend of Levien's, succeeded in getting him to promise not to excite the workmen. He did speak to them moderately on leaving the Landtag building in the "quietest street in Munich" yesterday. "Why do you not make yourself dictator?" one of those present asked him. "I should need four strong men to see me through," was the reply, "and they are not to be had." He put his finger on the sore spot. There are no strong men standing at the front here; that is the great difficulty. I had already come to the belief that Levien's is the strongest personality here, unpleasant as it is. He can well afford to sit back and wait. There is still no sign of any strong Government being formed, or even of a weak one, which knows just what it wants and how to get it. "If only Eisner were here," is what many are saying, except at the other end of town, where people still rejoice, quietly, that he is dead.

One thing sounds familiar to my ears—the denunciation of the press, which is called wholly unrepresentative of the plain people, and is held responsible for the murder of Eisner by its deliberate falsification of his Berne speeches. It is proposed to curb this press at once, by censorship and by establishing a state monopoly of advertising, and compelling the press to print advertising at cost, so as to remove all possibility of private profit from journalism. How similar are the problems of the several nations! When I left New York the radicals there found in the capitalistic press their real enemy. Good liberals, not extremists, in London filled my ears with indictments of the rich and powerful press of England; the same complaint, but little altered, is the special grief of the French radicals. The editors of our American dailies would do well to take note of these currents of popular feeling in Europe and elsewhere.

Dr. Muehlon, whose Krupp revelations and contributions to the history of the war are known to American readers, was asked to come here from Berne in charge of the Bavarian Foreign Office, but after talking matters over he declined. The general strike is ended, but the state of siege is not. Without a pass one cannot get out at night, and it is considered none too safe at that because of the numerous thieves and plunderers. I am often stopped and cross-questioned, but I say, "I am an American," *civis Romanus sum.* I get a military salute and the right of way at once. Being out without my pass, two nights ago, I was seized by the guard in this street on my way home. An officer came on the run. "Oh, it's that *Amerikaner,*" he said, "let him go." It is quite amazing the way people tell me all their troubles as if I were not a frank critic of their war misdeeds. But it makes one proud of being an American to hear from all sides nothing but praise of our troops, both as fair and square and brave fighting men and as the kindest and most gentlemanly of invaders. The most interesting talks I have had here have been with men on the street, particularly on those first two nights before the state of siege, when the reactionary elements had tried to capture the public buildings. Then I stayed out most of the night, wholly fascinated by the street gatherings. How these soldiers denounce their former officers! Stealing is one of the least of the offences they charge against them. It is no wonder that no officer of the old régime dares show himself upon the streets in uniform and that many have fled. The fact that Arco-Valley, Eisner's murderer, was a boy lieutenant in the war is the final straw.

I have spent this morning at the Food Bureau. If the people of the United States knew what the figures show—that there will be absolutely no food here in three months—they would denounce the blockade. The officials showed me the ration for twenty-four hours. It would not keep a chicken alive. Naturally everybody has to get more by hook or by crook. Such wan, sickly faces as one sees whenever there is a queue at a tobacco store or a butcher's or at the market! I went to early market the other morning.

There was literally nothing to be had save roots which one would hardly feed to animals in America. It is the underpaid official and professional and clerical classes with fixed incomes that suffer most terribly. They are so weak, many of them, as to be practically useless.

But on the pillars there are placards signed by the soldiers, denouncing the extremists. Aeroplanes have been flying over the city from an army corps headquarters located in Würzburg, begging the Munich garrison to rid the country of radical pests and disturbers. There was heavy firing again last night. Whither? Whither?

III. Perplexities at Weimar

Weimar, March 5

WHY is there no longer interest in Germany in the National Constitutional Assembly? And why in Weimar itself is it sharply criticised? Primarily because it has shown itself so long-winded. The prolonged debates have too often given evidence that party spirit still survives; and the Assembly has often proceeded as if there were all the leisure necessary for discussions *ad infinitum.* There has been little to show that the members understood that Germany was on the edge of complete chaos and ruin, and that speed was essential. The result has been that the Spartacan movement has been greatly reinforced by the outspoken fault-finding of many who felt that the Assembly should have shown prompt results. Some of these complaints are not well founded. Rome was not built in a day, and what is left of the German Empire cannot be constituted anew in a couple of weeks, particularly when the long-drawn-out negotiations in Paris leave the whole German people in the position of a criminal waiting for sentence. Many of the complainants are angry merely because the Convention did not at once proclaim a Soviet republic; nothing else would have satisfied them. Others are indignant that the process of socializing all German industries has not already been carried out—as if this were possible.

None the less, there has been just ground for criticism, both of the Ebert-Scheidemann Government and of the Constitutional Assembly. The faults of the one are largely the faults of the other. In the first place, the Assembly is composed largely of old men or of men who were more or less closely connected with the old régime. While there are, of course, new men, and the Assembly as a whole is as representative in its make-up as any one could wish—there are peasants and workingmen of all kinds, as well as counts, ex-officials, professors, writers, and editors galore—the *Journal de Genève* is not far wrong when it describes this Assembly as "a sister of the defunct Reichstag." It is a great pity that the leadership could not at once have gone to men of an entirely new type, men who, like Dr. Muehlon, were entirely opposed to the old Government. It is not fair to say of Ebert, as the Geneva paper does, that he is using precisely the language of Wilhelm; yet it is undeniable that the presence here of men like Dr. David, of Count Posadowsky-Wehner, of the notorious Dr. Dernburg, and of many others of the old school gives ground for popular uneasiness. My journeyings thus far have given me the impression that the truth about the war and the responsibility of its authors is much better understood among the returning German soldiers and the "plain people" than among the wealthy and the well educated, who ought to know better but who are too set in their opinions or still too illinformed. There is much truth on the side of those who say that radicalism (not Bolshevism) has swept over Germany so fast that the political waters have rushed by and gone far beyond this Weimar Parliament.

Certainly the Assembly makes no great impression of vigor and force upon the casual observer. It was to have adjourned last week, for a month or so, in order to let the Constitutional Committee work out the Constitution, but it is holding brief daily sessions out of fear, some say, lest an adjournment at this critical time of general strikes be misconstrued. A pleasant feature is the daily questioning of the Government, as if it were a permanent legislative body and not a temporary one. This custom has already brought out, among other things, some extremely interesting facts about the reasons for the German move for an armistice, and has fixed upon Hindenburg and Ludendorff the burden of asking it. An attack upon the Government for its alleged failure to act with sufficient vigor in the matter of the fresh Polish outrages on the frontier, despite the recent Allied drawing off of both parties to fixed lines, gave Erzberger an opportunity to answer effectively and vigorously, and to add a biting truth, that if the Germans had but treated Poland better when she was in their grasp there would be neither so keen a desire for revenge nor so much anti-German bitterness. It was curious to hear the old stories of terrible outrages upon women and children, bobbing up again upon this side of the line from this new field of war. The enemy always makes it his special business to outrage women and butcher children—no matter who the enemy is.

One action of the Assembly has pleased many and yet I am glad to be able to report that several persons whom I have met regard it as a great mistake. I refer to the vote to raise at once an army of about 190,000 men to be composed largely of the volunteers who have been acting at various places, notably Berlin. It is a temporary measure, and its execution is subject not only to further consideration by the Ebert Government and the Parliament within a couple of years, but also to revision by the Allies in the peace terms. Those who support this measure point to the presence of some thirty or forty thousand troops of various kinds in Berlin today, defending it from the attacks of the Spartacans and the plunderers who are taking advantage of the general strike to rob and murder, as proof that a strong force is needed to keep order during this trying time of readjustment. The opposition believes that in a force as large as this lies the germ of a new and dangerous militarism, and they point to the speeches of Noske, the Minister of War, as proof that the old spirit of militarism is abroad in the land. Both are right. German men are now so accustomed to killing that it seems to many the desirable way to settle disputes. They have become hardened to bloodshed—indeed nothing impressed me more in Munich than the quiet way in which the people took the killings that went on while I was there.

For the present, accordingly, a very strong police force is desirable—but not an army. If Noske arms troops, not for the purpose of restoring order but to intrench the present Government, there can be only one outcome. It is not a pleasant spectacle that we have here at Weimar—a supposedly democratic Constitutional Assembly meeting in a town garrisoned by hundreds of troops brought here from Berlin together with many Berlin policemen. The town is so closely guarded that you cannot enter it without showing a permit—indeed you cannot buy a ticket for Weimar at any town without showing an official *laissez-passer.* Naturally, the Independent Socialists and Spartacans have made the most of this state of affairs by asserting that it is in itself a confession that the Assembly and the Government would fall of their own weight if troops were withdrawn.

But one thing the debates have brought out, and that is that nobody here desires the return of the old military system—and particularly that of universal military service. This they are quite willing to leave to America, though they cannot see why America should be so foolish as to wish to take it up. If the Allies are really going to insist upon the complete wiping out of the German fleet and the limiting of the army to a police force, there will be a hearty amen from nearly the entire German people. The veterans will never stand for the old order, and it is even specified in the new act that the troops shall elect their own officers, which shows clearly how complete is the break with the old order of things. Even here, where there are the best-looking troops that I have seen, where the officers wear swords and have some of the old smartness to their get-up, the soldiers rarely salute them.

If there has been no sign in Weimar of any big new men coming to the front, there are some new issues. I refer particularly to the proposal of Minister Preuss, who drew up the provisional Constitution, that Prussia shall be cut up into several small republics. The Assembly is in fact facing some State-rights problems not unlike those which made the beginnings of our American Government so difficult. Herr Preuss is a theorist, a university professor far too remote in his thought from the actualities, so that he has drawn a scholarly proposal which looks well upon paper, but pays little regard to existing political conditions, traditions, and jealousies. If there is a natural wish on the part of the smaller states to see to it that Prussia shall not have the dominating influence which it wielded during the old régime, it is on the other hand going quite too far to throw away all of the Prussian tradition, which certainly had some value, even where there was so much that was bad and mistaken. Germany will unquestionably be much weakened if she re-forms herself into a number of small states and increases the administrative machinery and the bureaucracy. Over-administered she has always been; there is probably no other nation where the class of civil servants is so large. What Germany needs is real union, but it is one of the evil results of the war that old antagonisms like that of Prussia and Bavaria have broken out again.

This, I am solemnly told by some, is due entirely to Entente intrigue and money, and to the republican movement furthered, by Americans particularly, from Switzerland. Of course, there are other and far more weighty reasons; the antagonism is historic. All through these last two weeks there has been visible in Munich much nervousness lest the Prussians try to intervene, and notice was solemnly served by the Soviet, or rather by the ruling powers of the moment, that any move to intervene on the part of the Ebert Government would be bitterly resisted. On the other hand, the Federal Minister of Justice, Wolfgang Heine, in discussing the proposal to break up Prussia, rightly declared that any serious dividing of Prussia would weaken the whole nation. The jealousy of Berlin is noticeable in the proposal to make of the capital a separate state, which would put a heavy financial burden upon the rural sections of Prussia, which now profit by the large taxes of Berlin. But it is singular that a proposal which has so often been mooted in New York, when it has seemed so hard to reconcile the differences of city and State, should find its echo here. Alas, the difficulty of reconciling city and country dwellers is adding another to the already almost unbearable burdens which the collapse of Germany has fastened upon its people, as a punishment for years of servility, blindness, and worship of false gods.

To return to the Constitutional Assembly, however, what one Minister has said to me here is perhaps true. It would possibly have been better not to try to frame an entirely new Constitution in these terrible times, but instead to alter the old one just enough to make it conform in important points to the new demands, and then to go ahead with the election of a new Reichstag and tackle immediately some of the problems of socialization and reform. For an outsider it is hard to judge. What has been done here has not been adequately set before the people, however, or it would not have been necessary for the Ebert Government hastily to placard the whole country with big signs reading, "Die Socializierung ist da!" and then describing the agreement to socialize at once all the mines. The Ebert Government gets on as well as it does because the opposition parties, except the Independent Socialists, have no programme to offer, and not one of them has any better men to put forward. But before these lines appear in print there may be events to undo all the work of the Weimar Assembly. That depends in part upon the Allies; here the situation may be helped a little by the announcement that the Workmen's, Soldiers', and Peasants' Council will be embodied in the new Constitution—a long step toward the Russian Soviet system.

IV. Civil War in Berlin

Berlin, March 13

HOW does it seem to be in a great city with a general strike and civil war going on? If you had landed at the Potsdamer Bahnhof in Berlin any day this week your first impression would have been that some holiday was being observed. There were enormous crowds on the streets because the underground and surface cars were not running. It was, therefore, the opportunity of the fakirs and street vendors, of whom there are more than ever here because many discharged soldiers find this the quickest way to begin making money. The presence of every kind of vehicle that can be put into service as a jitney adds to the holiday aspect. The only dissenting notes are struck by the little patrols of soldiers, wearing their trench helmets, passing from time to time, and the auto-trucks with machine guns prepared for service, the crews ready for instant action. These trucks, familiar in Munich, are here varied by an occasional armored car with startling skull and bones painted upon it. As the week has progressed, these patrols have been even more ready for service, particularly the crews of ordinary motor cars. The rebels captured and murdered the military passengers in two cars without giving them a moment to recover from the surprise of the attack upon them.

Noske, the Minister of Defence, who is apparently the one forceful—brutally forceful—member of the Ebert Cabinet, has proclaimed that any insurgent caught with arms in his hands will be shot at once, and already there are reports of many such executions. Noske's excuse for this rests on the stories which emanate from Government sources of the brutalities and wholesale murders of the Spartacans. Some of these, like the account of the shooting in cold blood of sixty-two occupants of the Lichtenberg police station, are already becoming dubious. It will be as impossible to certify who began these outrages as it was to run down most of the stories of war outrages. The Spartacans declare that Noske invented these stories of massacres to excuse his resorting to "the white terror." The Spartacans moreover deny that their name should apply at all to the forces which are doing the fighting. They declare in their newspapers—which Herr Noske has suppressed for a few days—that they are opposed to bloodshed, and that the fighting is being done by disorderly elements and unemployed soldiers and sailors for whom they are not responsible. To this the Government newspapers make the effective answer that if that is the case the Independent Socialists and Spartacans are morally guilty in not denouncing the resort to arms more effectively and in attacking Noske every time he makes one of his bloodthirsty speeches at Weimar. Noske desires, quite openly, to be as thorough in his work of cleaning up Berlin as were the Germans at Louvain; they were certain that if they only burnt enough of that city and killed enough of its citizens there would be no further trouble in Belgium, and that the Belgians would love them for their thoroughness and efficiency. He proposes to cut out root and branch all armed opposition to the Government, and to spare no one. He is upheld by most people who believe that if Berlin does not have the "white terror" now it will inevitably get the "red terror" of Lenine and Trotzky later.

How this policy will succeed remains to be seen. At this end of town it is hard, indeed, to realize that the bloody work is going on every day and that hundreds are being killed, wounded, and captured. Not a sound of the firing is to be heard here in the Potsdamer Platz, although they have used heavy guns and *Minenwerfer* on both sides. It is as it would be if there were fighting in the Bronx; life in lower New York would be going on much the same save that in the newspapers there would be much fuller and better accounts of what is happening than we are allowed to get here. From the vagueness of the reports the battle might be back at Ypres. But when one goes over to the Lichtenberg district, there are enough sights and signs of war to please anybody. Just before I left New York, I heard an American woman bemoaning the fact that the armistice had come so soon before more German women and children had been killed. If this good, kindly Christian had been with me last Sunday morning I think that her desire would have been quite satisfied in the region around the Alexanderplatz. There she would have learned that many of the victims have been women and children. It is surprising to see other women and children walking about quite freely in the zone in which the troops are operating. Yesterday a shell exploded by accident in a group of some thirty persons who at a corner were watching the shells that flew past them toward a barricade a couple of blocks beyond. That shell sent some thirty to the hospital, while an airman killed and wounded fifty by dropping a bomb upon a group which he doubtless supposed to be made up of soldiers, but which consisted of spectators in front of a wrecked house. The curiosity of the children is not to be balked. Just after we passed a corner a gentleman insurgent leaned out of a window and took a shot at a sentry in the middle of the street. We all went back to observe the remainder of the proceedings and three little tots were quite upset when told by the grown-ups to go home. Shots cracked around one all the time, yet the streets were full of people, and nobody seemed to be hit while we were there. Those of us who were not inhabitants of these districts naturally jumped a little at first, but it was speedily plain that this was not at all *comme il faut*. You are only supposed to look back without stopping to observe; it is also distinctly bad form to cast a careful eye up at the roofs in search of snipers.

The truth is that these people are so deadened to killing by four years of war, and so enervated by starvation and long-drawn-out undernourishment, that most of them have lost the capacity to feel very deeply. They have a helpless, fatalistic air. They say it is *schrecklich* and *entsetzlich*, and then go their way. It is dreadful, it is almost terrifying to see the ruin of this part of the city—the wrecked houses, the gaping windows, the great department stores from which millions of Marks' worth of goods have been plundered, and the shell scars everywhere. After ten days of fighting the Government troops have not yet got the upper hand. It is another fearful indictment of human society that it has so administered its great cities everywhere that there are great bodies of underfed, underpaid, suffering, and brutalized men and women who think that the only way to better their lot is by committing crimes and killing hundreds of their fellows. Taking the Spartacans at their word, it is the evil underworld that is doing the murdering. But whose fault is it that there is a criminal underworld? Can the disease be cured by Noske's methods? The general strike is over, but already it is announced that there will be a worse one by March 26 that will cover all Germany. One feels that this thing can go on indefinitely, despite Noske. Certainly there is no more difficult and trying kind of fighting than this hand-to-hand work in a great city where your enemy escapes over the roof while you are coming up the first flight. Already the damage in this outbreak is estimated at 40,000,000 Marks in addition to the January losses, and after one has seen this quarter, this amount does not seem an overestimate. This is a nice sum for an already overburdened municipality to pay.

It is the same condition of nervous exhaustion and of endless waiting for the worst to happen which also explains the extraordinary phenomenon that all Berlin has been dancing mad. There is a cartoon upon the hoardings and advertisement pillars representing a woman dancing with a skeleton, and underneath is the legend: "Berlin, do you not see that it is Death that is your partner?" But there is nothing more natural than that men who have been for four years deprived of all rational enjoyments should be turning to them frantically. The concerts are crowded; one has to buy tickets at least a week in advance, and the same is true of the theatres. Men say to me frankly that they do not know where it is all to end or what is to happen to them and their families, whether there will not soon be anarchy, and whether they will be allowed to have any money two years hence. Having just come back out of the jaws of death, they propose to enjoy themselves till the crash comes. I am inclined to think that nature knows what she is about, and that Noske does not in forbidding dancing until further notice. Were I in his boots I should be asking myself whether with that outlet for the desire for innocent amusement closed those who are excluded from the dancing halls will not find much worse things to do and whether a great deal more blood will not flow in consequence. It is undeniable, of course, that there has been a great moral relaxation in Germany. From the land of the best order, it has become one of the most lawless. That is the natural result of war and also the natural reaction from a state of affairs in which every citizen was regulated to the last degree by officialdom with its endless signs, *Es ist verboten.* I am told that during the war the various Government bureaus issued thirty thousand orders or new regulations, violations of which were punishable by fine and imprisonment. There were so many that the attempt speedily broke down, for nobody could possibly keep himself informed as to what he could or could not do. Now the reaction is emphasized by the new-found freedom of the revolution.

So Berlin wears a singularly unkempt air. The public buildings and walls are covered with bills and proclamations, appeals to the electorate, and warnings against Bolshevism. The neatest city in the world has dirty streets, many of which, like those of New York, are torn up because of new underground railways. The people look neat but seedy; no one may buy a dress who has more than two dresses already. German women have always dressed badly, and the effect is heightened by the wearing of old clothes. One of the greatest causes of suffering is the lack of soap, which makes it impossible to keep clean, and compels the wearing of linen much longer than usual. People are obliged to wash the children with potash water, and their skins suffer—but the Allies apparently think that giving the Germans soap and letting the German shipping fleet put to sea will adversely affect the settlement, or the League of Nations, or the boundaries of Jerusalem, or prevent their taking the place of the Lord as the dispenser of vengeance. This lack of cleanliness the German women feel keenly, for whatever their faults they were a clean people. More than that, the inability of the poor to purchase underwear results in a sad state of affairs for the children, as I was informed at a crêche. The worst sufferers are by no means the laboring classes, but what is known as the middle class, which comprises the great group of small officials, and Germany is the land of small officials. I have talked with a number who described to me their utterly desperate conditions—some of them get much less than a tram driver, who today receives in Berlin more pay than a captain in the army. Every one of these men shows a loss in weight and admits what the superiors say, that there is a marked loss in their mental efficiency and alertness. A typist in the Dresden Foreign Office told me she was appalled at her own inability to do a day's work, and a distinguished Berlin physician, who not only used to work all day at the curing of nervous disease but also devoted his evenings to research, tells me that he has to rest for two hours every afternoon and that he cannot even read at night because of exhaustion. He attributes much of the rioting to purely nervous reasons and says that he prophesied during the war that the worst effects from the strain of being under fire would come after the men went home. The soldiers find it hard, indeed, to get down to work when they can find it. They like the few Marks a day paid to the unemployed, and from idlenesss drift into insurgency. Most of the soldiers whom one sees never got to the front, but are callow youths, pale and weak, who can scarcely carry a pack. The men from the front feel the shortness of food more than anybody else, because they were well fed in the army until the collapse began about July last, and they simply cannot live on the prescribed rations.

Oswald Garrison Villard

The Truth About the Peace Conference

IT has, of course, been everything but a peace *conference.* So far as the word is concerned, it is a palpable fraud upon the world. A small executive committee, first of ten men, then of five, then of four, has been parcelling out the globe in sessions so secret that their closest associates, the members of their own delegations, have not known what was going on. The very existence of this committee is the result of an arrogant, unauthorized assumption of power, for never and nowhere did the conference endow Messrs. Wilson, Orlando, Clemenceau, and Lloyd George with the authority to transact all the business and come to all the decisions. The Germans need not complain if they are arbitrarily summoned to Versailles and told to take the treaty and sign it without discussion. They are only in the same category with all the various Allied delegates to the "Conference," except four. The Allied delegates, too, will be told, in the language of one of our captains of industry to his stockholders, to "vote first and discuss afterwards." Of all the groups of unemployed workers in France, none is so deserving of sympathy as the lesser delegates. Statesmen like Venizelos—and there are a few statesmen in Paris whatever the appearance to the contrary—have been graciously permitted to appear as expert witnesses whenever the question of the boundaries of their countries was to be considered, but not otherwise. They are now informed that the treaty will be published on April 24, and that a complete copy will be handed to the Germans on April 28. Between those dates the puppets who are officially styled delegates will be given a chance to ratify the treaty, but that is all. They are to bow to the superior knowledge of the Big Four with the same obedience, the same abnegation of their reasoning faculties and of their consciences, as if they were the willing tools of a Tammany Hall.

How is it possible to produce a democratic peace or a lasting one under such conditions? A democratic peace, frankly, it can never be; a lasting peace it can be only if heaven shows an unexampled favor. When the Conference assembled, eleven wars were going on in which heavy cannon were being used; at the beginning of April, it was jestingly said at the Hotel Crillon (the American headquarters) that it was quite fitting that the wars had grown to fourteen, because there was thus one to each of the fourteen peace terms. But if the wars have multiplied, the fourteen peace terms have steadily grown less. One by one they have been abandoned by their originator until their very names are almost forgotten. Who hears today in Paris of the freedom of the seas? Who, when he reads of the Saar basin, recalls the fine phrase about "no punitive indemnities or annexations"? Actually, we seem to have progressed but little since Napoleon. If there are today four Napoleons setting up new Governments and re-drawing the map, at least the great Emperor spared the world the hypocrisy of clothing his acts in language to charm—and to be discarded at will. And while the Big Four have wrangled, argued, reargued, and fought, Europe has come to the very edge of the abyss. It is civilization itself that is now trembling in the balance.

That Mr. Lloyd George, at least, sees this is at last apparent. In his speech last week in the House of Commons he boldly declared that a new and more terrible enemy than the Germans has arisen in Europe, namely, hunger; but he forgot to explain why the menace of hunger, communism, and anarchy is so terrifying today as to overshadow everything else, or who is responsible for its growth to such vast proportions. It is the Big Four upon whom this terrible responsibility rests. The Big Four took from November until the end of March to lift the food blockade of Germany, and meanwhile Hungary and Bavaria, and now Vienna, have surrendered to communism or anarchy. It took them until April to decide that Russia should have food, thus trying a pacifist policy where the policy of imposing their will by bayonets had utterly and deservedly failed. Poland, Czecho-Slovakia, Rumania, Italy, these are a few of the Allied states that are on the verge of revolution or collapse, either because they are hemmed in by the blockade of Germany on the one hand and of Russia on the other, or because they are in such desperate need of a reëstablishment of normal conditions in social and industrial life. One of the ablest American correspondents, with twenty years of international service to his credit, arrived in Paris three weeks ago from Poland, Czecho-Slovakia, and Italy. When asked his opinion of the situation in those countries he shook his head. "What is needed even more than food is the mail, the uncensored telegraph, the cable, the commercial traveller, the through express, the breaking down of all the barriers that war erects between states," he said emphatically.

Nevertheless the barriers remain, and Lloyd George would fain have us believe that there was no other way. Peace, he declared, could have come no sooner, and his excuse is the magnitude and the multiplicity of the problems involved. Never was there a greater falsehood uttered. A quick and satisfactory peace could have been obtained by the fifteenth of January, or earlier, had there been no travelling about, had there been a real desire for a quick settlement or a sincere adherence to the fourteen peace terms. An acceptance of Mr. Wilson's original terms would have permitted the Allies to go at their leisure into the questions of new nations and new boundaries. Such a peace, to which the immediate signature of Germany could have been obtained, might have been drawn up in twenty-four hours. It would have included an agreement to form a league of nations, the cession of Alsace-Lorraine, the taking over of the German colonies on joint account pending a detailed settlement, the seizure of the entire German war fleet, the reduction of the German army to a gendarmerie for the preservation of order, the immediate razing of the fortifications on the Rhine, and a pledge by Germany to make good the destruction in France and Belgium. With this preliminary treaty out of the way, the blockades could then have been lifted forthwith. Food would have flowed into Bavaria, Austria, and Hungary, and perhaps even Italy could have been saved. With normal intercourse restored throughout Europe, rasped nerves would have been soothed, immediate needs of food supplied, the militant and vengeful revolutionary spirit checked if not entirely banished. Further, the safety of the Allies would have been guarded.

Here lies the crux of the matter. Tell the average American that his representatives at Paris have been working with might and main to get food to the Central Powers as well as to Northern France, Belgium, Serbia, and Poland, and he mutters something about its being incredible and pro-German. It is quite as hard for him to see that our Lansings and Hoovers and Houses and McCormicks and Davises and Baruchs have been just and wise in insisting that the enemy must be fed, as it has been for Clemenceau to realize the same necessity. These American officials who have conferred so much honor upon our country abroad, are to be suspected neither of pro-Germanism nor of undue sympathy with the enemy. They have simply had the prevision to see that the Central Powers were the key to the European revolutionary situation; that if Bolshevism was to be checked it must be checked at the boundaries of the Central Powers. But others did not see this, despite ample warnings, and so Bavaria and Hungary have been communized, and a mischievous and vacillating Russian policy has been followed under which Lenine has won one victory after another in the field of diplomacy and in that of arms. The fight which American officials have made at Paris to save Europe despite the Allies has been the one bright chapter in the dismal story of chicane, intrigue, selfish aggression, and naked imperialism which has given the lie to most of the high-sounding phrases with which the Allies carried on the war, and to which the secrecy of the whole proceeding has rendered staunch aid.

As for the League of Nations, some of our foremost representatives in Paris have lost all interest in it, not merely because it has been the particular property of the President, or because it is a weak and dangerous proposal as it now stands, but also because they can really think seriously of nothing save the terrible plight in which all Europe finds itself. Of what use will a League of Nations be if Europe is to flare up in a revolution in which all the states east of the Rhine will be joined in a veritable league to impose their extreme social policies upon the rest of the world? When sober men of long political experience are face to face with the possibility of a Europe relapsing into another Dark Age, they find it hard to take interest in a League of Nations which is foredoomed to failure by the insincerity of many of those who have accepted it, by the exclusion from it of the representatives of two-thirds of Europe and all of the black races, and which holds out few attractions to the small and the neutral nations. The strongest advocates of the League in Paris, men who have worked for a real league with all their strength, offer no argument for the Paris plan save that it is a half or a third of a loaf. "Try it," they say, "and out of it may come something worth while."

Something good may indeed come of it, but so may, and with more certainty, a good deal that is evil. Already by an autocratic counting of votes the League is to come into being without recognizing the equality of the citizens of all of its members; and this at once will kill all Japanese interest in it. If the League is actually formed under the present draft, it will be in fact only another Holy Alliance. It will be a continuation of the present Entente with enormous power vested in the very men who are at present in the position of having brought Europe to the edge of the abyss while they talked and talked. There is in the League the possibility of a world dictatorship so odious as to make a revolution in Russian style seem almost tolerable. Even a third of a loaf may be of no value to a starving man if its ingredients are uneatable or poisonous; and if Mr. Wilson is now actually ready to agree to the giving of special guarantees to France by Great Britain and the United States, he has dealt the *coup de grâce* to his own creation and it is **no longer worth discussion by serious minded Americans.**

But there is more to the case than that. While the indefensible delay at Paris has raised everywhere the spectres of revolution and famine, it has also placed the Germans in a position where they can trump any move the Allies may wish to make by simply refusing to sign the peace treaty. The chances are against their doing so, but that does not mitigate the danger of their refusal, for if they decline to sign, the League of Nations is dead and most of the work done at Paris goes for naught. Moreover, even if the Ebert Government accepts, there is the gravest question whether it will not collapse at once, and give way to an extremist Government ready to make common cause with Lenine and Trotzky and to denounce the treaty. This danger would not have arisen had such a peace as is outlined above been submitted by the Allies early in the year, before the Bolshevist forces had gained headway, before starvation in Central Europe had become acute, and before the universal belief had become fixed that the Entente intends nothing else than the deliberate destruction of Germany and of the former Dual Monarchy.

As for Mr. Wilson, it is not easy to describe exactly the part he has played. Without him the Peace "Conference" would have degenerated into an orgy of land grabbing and imperialism. His idealism has been the saving grace if such saving grace there be. He has been the only one of the Big Four who has really desired to create a better world. But the old defects of his public character—his unwillingness to take counsel, his colossal egotism, his inability to hold at any cost to a principle which he has laid down, his readiness to compromise—together with his inability to translate beliefs into fact and action, and his refusal to take either the press or the public into his confidence, have forced him into the position of playing a lone and secret hand, and have already cost him the wondrous and all but overpowering confidence of the plain people of Europe which at first was his. When Mr. Wilson goes so far as to overrule a majority vote because it does not result as he wished, he need expect only criticism commensurate with the adoration which was his, beyond any other man's, a few months ago.

Yet it is far more than a test of the real moral force and character of President Wilson which we are witnessing. It is a far-reaching test of the value of war as the creator of moral values. Entered into on the part of the American public with the highest idealism, and with the confident belief that it was to be a war to end war and to make the world safe for democracy, the war thus far has made the world less safe for democracy than it has been at any previous period in modern times, and in addition has brought a brood of actual wars and the threat of others in its train. The struggle is ending at Paris with bitterness and hatred as well as with colossal hypocrisy. It is ending with the whole modern order of society on trial for its life; for nothing is plainer than that if the four men who have become the dictators of the world can not produce a peace that is real, one that shall not only end war but also do away with armaments, a deceived and disappointed world will try other ways and means. Can war be cured by more war, or is it to be cured by frankly trying to apply the doctrines of Christianity and the brotherhood of man? This is the question which is to be answered at Paris. Beside it the new Holy Alliance misnamed the League of Nations sinks into insignificance.

OSWALD GARRISON VILLARD

The Communists in Bavaria

By OSWALD GARRISON VILLARD

I MET Dr. Max Levien, the Russian Communist who has been one of the leaders in the establishment of a Bolshevist Government in Munich, on the night of the 28th of February. It was on that afternoon that a group of men entered the Landtag building and made all of us who were attending the meeting of the Workmen's, Peasants', and Soldiers' Council stand with our hands in the air, at the point of revolvers, while they took Dr. Levien, Erich Muehsam, and one other out to beat them with revolvers and to threaten them with death. So stupid was this procedure that it was perfectly obvious that the reaction must give Levien increased authority and power. There is no doubt that he could have declared a Soviet republic that day and won over the working men to him had he felt himself strong enough to do so. As I watched this singular personality after he had had his bandages renewed, I could not but feel that, repulsive as he was to me, he had only to wait to have the situation play into his hands. I had just telegraphed that afternoon to Colonel House and Herbert Hoover that a Bolshevist dictatorship would be established in Munich in April if food were not forthcoming at once, and the more I studied Levien the more certain I was of the correctness of the prophecy, which time has completely justified, for the dictatorship was set up on the fifteenth day of April.

Of the other Bolshevist leaders, perhaps the two most interesting were Muehsam and Gustav Landauer, both journalists. It was the latter who made the address at the funeral of Eisner. Both are long-haired visionaries whom Eisner alone could have held in check. I heard a man say that instead of beating Landauer and Muehsam or arresting them they could be shorn of their power, like Samson, if their long locks and beards were removed and their picturesqueness destroyed. But there was no doubt of the ability of Landauer. He spoke well at the meetings of the Soviet which I attended, and so did Muehsam, who was as calm and collected as Levien after the extraordinary experience to which they were subjected on the 28th of February. The truth is that these men were more determined and united and more aggressive than any other group. They could have been held in check then had the other side had any leadership, but the curse of the situation was that with the death of Eisner there was no man left upon whom the moderates could unite. It was just because of this that the assassination of Eisner was so utterly stupid from the point of view of the propertied classes. It left the way open for men with the brute force of Levien and the fanaticism of Landauer and Muehsam to seize the leadership.

What I cannot understand, however, is how they have been able to bring to their extreme point of view others who were quite opposed to them at the beginning of March. There was Ernst Toller, for instance, a young idealist, whom I first met at the Internationale in Berne, where he was thoroughly dissatisfied because that body was not as radical nor as sympathetic with the Russians as he wished. Toller's opportunity came after Eisner's death, when he made some excellent addresses counselling calmness. When the attack was made upon Levien and Muehsam it was Toller who insisted that these men must be brought back, that the Parliamentary immunity of the Soviet must be preserved at any cost, and he was of the committee that went out to bring them back. He was himself a pacifist and absolutely opposed to the use of force, and yet he whole heartedly joined the extremists who have brought about the present terrible conditions in Munich, and was for two weeks with Dr. Neurath, the brains of the Communist Government, until he fled the city. I am astounded, too, that an officer like Major Ernst Paraquin, who, with his brother, fought all through the war, should now be one of five officers of the old army who are drilling and organizing the Red Guard. While both brothers are Socialists, they have the highest social connections, and they were both utterly opposed to the Bolshevist idea. Whether they have yielded to the inevitable, or whether they have been convinced that there is nothing left to do but join those in power and serve, as far as possible, as moderating influences I do not know. One of the bourgeoisie said that he did not expect any of his class to be alive within two years.

Early in March the conservatives were counting upon the peasants to save the day for Bavaria. There was a certain Herr Gandorfer, a man of striking personality and obvious force and power, who was the leader of the peasants in the Soviet, in which body he often spoke out in opposition to the views of the extremists. "As long as Gandorfer sticks we are safe," was the remark on every side; and later, in Berlin, I was again told that the Communists could get no hold on Bavaria because the peasants with their small landholdings would inevitably be opposed to communistic doctrines. This I could not believe, for I had already seen a dispatch, too startling to print, in the office of one of the Berlin newspapers, which reported that the peasants in Württemberg, up to that time the quietest portion of Germany, were "entirely undermined" by the Bolshevist doctrines. It has already appeared that Gandorfer went over to the opposing camp with his large following. This is all the more remarkable because the peasantry of Bavaria is devotedly Catholic, and the church influence has been steadily against the Bolshevist movement, in fact against the revolution. One of the first acts of Eisner was to separate church from state, and when he was killed the Soviet compelled every Catholic church, as well as every Protestant, to ring its bells for an hour during the funeral of Eisner, in honor of this Jew who had dealt the church such a blow. Where the Catholic authorities refused to obey, the populace blew down the church doors with hand grenades and rang the bells themselves.

Why should Bavaria, the most conservative and most reactionary of the German States, have been with the exception of Brunswick the first to go to such extremes? It is a difficult question to answer. The greater the repression, the more violent the reaction when the explosion comes, and there is no doubt that Bavaria was sufficiently repressed and quite too strongly controlled by its priesthood. It had long had the highest percentage of illegitimate births of any State in the German Empire, because of the difficulties thrown by the church and the state in the way of marriage. But, next to this, one comes back invariably to the fact that the Soviet leaders are what the Germans called *tatkräftige Menschen*, that is, men "capable of deeds."

The Week

THE Peace Conference apparently ends in a final series of compromises. As the Chinese have been sacrificed to Japan, so Belgium is to be propitiated by most-favored-nation treatment in the matter of indemnities, upon which she insisted under threat of withdrawing from the Conference. Then the Italians seem to have been lured back by what appears to be a typically Wilsonian compromise. Fiume, if press reports are correct, is to be autonomous for two or three years and then go to the Italians, another port being perhaps built on the Dalmatian coast for the Jugoslavs. Thus does Mr. Wilson turn another complete somersault, for only a few days ago (April 29) he wrote that "there would be no justification, in my judgment, in including Fiume, or any other part of the coast line to the south of Fiume, within the boundaries of the Italian Kingdom." Now, it seems, these words should read: "No justification, in my judgment, *for a period of two years*, in including Fiume within the boundaries of the Italian Kingdom." By the time this issue of the *Nation* is printed, the Peace Conference will be practically over and the treaty—which the Germans will now probably sign—will be spread before the world. Whether the good in the treaty outweighs the evil remains to be seen, but history must record that a more despotically undemocratic treaty was never written and that the Conference ends with the delegates, more than ever pitiful puppets, meekly assenting while the Big Three throw all principles and "peace points" to the winds in a mad scramble to end up the business somehow and get the thing over with. A treaty has been achieved, but the gods must none the less weep when they consider how the opportunity really to reorganize the world on a sound, humane, generous, democratic, and Christian basis has been flung away.

THE honest pleasure with which liberals everywhere greeted the stand of President Wilson in the matter of Fiume must be tempered by more than one consideration. It is only too easy, as Mr. Wilson himself has remarked in another connection, to become so engrossed by the sideshows that one misses the circus. The diplomatic skirmish over Fiume raised much noise and dust—enough, it would seem, to blind the people of the world to the fact that a whole battle was being lost on another front. Fiume, specifically granted to Croatia by the terms of the Treaty of London, will now, following the discovery of a new "formula" of compromise to satisfy Italian aspirations, be reserved to the Jugoslavs under a temporary arrangement. So much for President Wilson's courageous skirmish. Meanwhile the remainder of the secret Treaty of London, quite intact, quite as cynically unjust as it ever was, quite as opposed to the principles for which four million men were sent to die, apparently takes its place as another accomplished fact. England and France are pledged to the support of the Treaty and have never indicated any intention of repudiating it. Perhaps it is well for the Peace Conference and the President that the skirmish of Fiume so successfully drew attention from these other unpleasant incidentals. With China despoiled and the Saar Valley torn from Germany, with the Allied armies crushing the life out of the new Hungarian republic, the less the attention of Mr. Wilson's "plain people everywhere" is focused upon the ruins of the Fourteen Points and the triumph of the old diplomacy, the better for the future of cautious and official liberalism.

IN few instances has the old diplomacy triumphed so easily and so thoroughly as in the decision regarding Japanese demands in China. Here was no pretence that Japan had racial claims to the province of Shantung, no suggestion that Kiaochow or Tsingtao desired annexation to Japan. The case rested upon the simplest ethics in the world, the ethics of "having 's keepings." Japan, with admirable freedom from cant, demanded the former German concessions in Kiaochow on the basis of private promises extorted from China, and a manifest ability to hold on to what it wanted in any case. The situation was so plain and undisputed that it left the Allies quite unable to fling around their acceptance of the Japanese demands any of the rosy-hued mists of words in which most of the transactions of the Peace Conference have been draped. The Council of Three simply, as the Reuter correspondent phrased it, "arrived at the conclusion that the Japanese demands must be satisfied." Lest the League of Nations be still-born and a dangerous anti-Entente alliance spring into being, another "principle" was abandoned. The promised physical return of Kiaochow to China can hardly be considered a triumph for democratic diplomacy. Japan had previously agreed to return the territory, and, according to Baron Makino, "there is no example in history of Japan breaking her word." So Japan has entered into the complete possession "without reservation" of all former German concessions in Kiaochow, undertaking in the fulness of time voluntarily to restore sovereignty in the Shantung peninsula to China, retaining there mere "economic privileges"; and the situation in the Far East is only a little more complicated and inequitable than it was before the Council of Three took up the matter.

THE Japanese delegates appear to have sold their country's birthright of equality for the gratification of imperialistic and commercial ambitions. It is a matter for doubt whether a port on the peninsula of Shantung and a tighter economic strangle-hold on China will as truly satisfy the aspirations of the common people of Japan as would a public recognition from the world of their equal place among its peoples. The time has passed in Japan when the will of the people can be either ignored or identified with the will of their rulers. The rice riots last summer were more than a protest against high prices and scanty fare. They indicated, as all Japanese observers have admitted, a deep distrust of the economic and political rulers of the country. No Ministry would have resigned in deference to a mere spasmodic protest against the cost of living. The rice riots were a manifestation of deep-seated political and social unrest. The present Ministry, all but two of them commoners, have secured the passage of an electoral reform bill almost doubling the number of voters in Japan. The campaign preceding the passage of the bill was notable for the active propaganda carried on by the advocates of more radical measures for the enfranchisement of students, and for universal suffrage without property qualifications. Intellectuals and working men joined in the fight, and even woman suffrage had its open supporters. The moderate Government measure was plainly a concession to a growing democratic opinion that must be recognized and clearly distinguished from the hard imperialism of the ruling groups in Japan.

AS the crisis of the Peace Conference approaches, the veil that hitherto has covered the face of our Russian policy seems to be lifting. A change of tone is noticeable in the Russian propaganda in our newspapers. There is less talk of idealism and more of practical common sense, less of argument and explanation and more of flat decision. Every day the statement that Kolchak is to be recognized by America and the Allies appears in some imposing form. The State Department recently issued a warning to American commercial interests against entering into trade arrangements with Soviet Russia, stating that such arrangements could not hope to receive the protection of the American Government. The War Department has announced that 8,000 men will be recruited immediately for service in Siberia. Most important of all, however, was the frank admission of Mr. Lloyd George in the House of Commons two weeks ago, in which, after referring specifically to "Kolchak, Denikine, and Kharkov," he stated that "they raised armies at our instigation and largely at our expense," and went on to say, "we are not sending troops, we are supplying munitions." This, of course, is the primary question; the diplomatic recognition of the Kolchak régime is a relatively unimportant matter. It would be merely official acknowledgment of an actual condition that had existed for some time. It would perhaps be a more honest proceeding for America and the Allies to recognize the Siberian Government and have it over with; but recognition of Kolchak would wake up a good many sleeping dogs, while under the present arrangement Kolchak is getting all that he needs, and the reign of "law and order" is being forwarded in a most satisfactory manner.

WHAT is the actual status of the reported Franco-American alliance which we have been hearing about for the last few weeks in the newspapers? The first news of it came with a hint of authoritative information. A little later President Wilson, through Secretary Tumulty in Washington, officially denied that he had entered into any agreement with the French Government. But after four months of the Peace Conference, men have grown cynical concerning official statements, and have begun to pay attention to facts and events. The French had a plan, said to have been sponsored by Marshal Foch, for permanently garrisoning the Rhine. This plan they have been willing to modify. Something has evidently quieted their fears as to the future security of France. And on the second of May we had a press dispatch from Paris stating that "coincident with publishing the peace treaty on Tuesday it is believed that Premier Clemenceau will announce the terms of the Franco-American understanding," and continuing as follows: "It is officially declared that this agreement already is reduced to text and that it insures American

troops for France in the event of German attack." Is this the familiar method of propaganda in advance of the event, or is there actually some fire behind the smoke? The President, of course, has constitutionally no power to enter into such an agreement with a foreign Government. At the same time, he actually has power to do almost anything which conforms to public opinion; but we do not believe that an alliance such as has been suggested conforms in any measure to public opinion. If Premier Clemenceau has the text of a Franco-American agreement, we hope that he will publish it.

AT no time have the enemies of Hungary shown much regard for the terms of the armistice forced by them upon that unhappy country. Oppressive as they were, these terms imposed obligations which the Czechs and Serbs and, more especially, the Rumanians, with the apparent sanction of the French military command, have calmly ignored. The humiliating terms and their ruthless violation marked the doom of the moderate Karolyi Government many months before its actual fall. Now, it appears, the entire armistice has gone the way of all other inconvenient agreements between nations. A Rumanian army, said to be led by French officers, is surrounding Budapest, and apparently aims to overthrow the Government, to which, only a few weeks ago, the Peace Conference sent a distinguished envoy. It is reported that the Hungarian Government has offered territory in exchange for peace and freedom from assault and destruction, but the invaders refuse to be satisfied with a mere peace of Brest-Litovsk. They drive on over a helpless people toward a victory of subjugation. The responsibility for this wanton act of aggression cannot be laid at the feet of the disorganized Governments of the new states surrounding Hungary, nor even of the French officers in charge of the invasion. The government of the Allied world is today in the hands of three men, and to them must be given credit or blame. It seems fair in this connection to put before the Council of Three certain questions regarding which the whole world must be in doubt. Are all Soviet Governments, whether orderly or chaotic, friendly or aggressive, destined from their birth to be destroyed by Allied arms? Need armistice terms no longer be regarded as binding upon the victor? May war against nations hereafter be carried on without the formality of a declaration of war, and without the sanction of the Governments involved? These questions deeply concern the people of the United States in their relations with more nations than one.

Trying the Kaiser

OF all the decisions made by the Peace Conference, none is likely to prove more momentous or fraught with more far-reaching consequences for the peace of the world than the decision to try the Kaiser. It is always unfortunate when an action, whether public or private, that violates the most elementary principles of justice and fair play concerns the treatment of a person whose character is bad and whose conduct has been despicable. Few persons today, either in Germany or in any other country, would care to apologize for the conduct of the Kaiser in bringing on or in prosecuting the war. If ever a theory of government, or a method by which the ambitious designs of a ruling class and its subservient followers were to be spread throughout the world, has been utterly repudiated by the deliberate judgment of civilized peoples, that theory and policy are those to which the Kaiser and his supporters were committed. Yet it must be pointed out that, however contemptible and wicked the course of the Kaiser and other German leaders may have been, the action which the Peace Conference has taken is morally and legally wrong, and that the plea of international morality urged in its defence is a ghastly sham. The one redeeming feature in the whole deplorable business is the staunch opposition of the American delegation to this worse than criminal folly—an opposition for which there cannot be too high praise, or for which the men who have courageously voiced it could be better entitled to grateful remembrance.

What are the legal and moral facts to which this madness of the Peace Conference stands opposed? Fortunately, they are neither technical nor complicated. From the standpoint of public law, the Kaiser was not a person, but an institution of government. While he enjoyed certain rights of private persons, such for example as the right to hold property in his own name, his status as a private individual was almost entirely overshadowed by and merged in his character as head of the German state. To discriminate between his acts as an individual and his acts as head of the German Empire, so far as his political or other official conduct is concerned, is practically impossible. Any trial of the Kaiser, consequently, for his course or motives in bringing on or prosecuting the war, is in fact a trial, or an attempted trial, of the executive branch of the German Imperial Government. Such a trial, even if it conformed to any known rules of international law, which it does not, as our delegates have steadily pointed out, becomes in effect a trial of the German nation and its people, and a scandalous addition to the already portentous list of burdens, punishments, and discriminations which the peace treaty is to impose. If anything could add to its unrighteousness it is the requirement, incorporated in the peace treaty, that Germany itself shall aid in furnishing the evidence upon which its former ruler is to be tried.

Moreover, even granting without reservation the truth of all the weighty charges of bad conduct lodged against the Kaiser, to whom is he responsible? There is only one answer. The Kaiser is responsible to the German people. He was their Kaiser; the Government of whose executive powers he was the embodied representative was their Government; and they, if they choose, may try him on any charge they please to lodge against him, and may imprison him, or exile him, or kill him, or impose any other punishment upon him, as they may see fit. If they try him unjustly, that is nevertheless their affair. But he is not responsible to the United States, or Great Britain, or France, or Italy, or to the Powers combined, any more than the rulers of any of those Powers would have been responsible to Germany for their misconduct if Germany had won the war. There is no rule or principle of international law known to the world under which the head of a state which is a recognized member of the family of nations can be made criminally responsible for his public acts, however heinous they may have been, to the states which have beaten him in war. There is not a nation represented at the Peace Conference which would not have cried out at the shocking evidence of German political immorality had Germany, during the war, announced its purpose to try for high crimes and misdemeanors the heads of the Allied states or any of them in case it were victorious.

This is not all, however. The decision to try the Kaiser involves a violation of principles of justice, good faith, and freedom which every one of the Allied Powers recognizes as part of its own Constitution, and any departure from which, in the case of their own nationals, is rightly regarded as a violation of fundamental rights and a menace to liberty. Until the Conference spoke, no civilized state failed to admit the righteous rule that crimes were somewhere to be defined, that the law was to be certain, that the court which tried an offender must have competent jurisdiction, and that men were not to be punished for acts which were not recognized offences when they were committed. The Peace Conference has thrown these principles to the winds. Although *ex post facto* laws and proceedings are hated and banned in every state, the Kaiser is to be tried by *ex post facto* procedure. Although no law is in existence under which he can be tried, he is to be tried under laws specially framed for the purpose, or, failing such, on general principles. Although no court of competent jurisdiction exists or can exist, a tribunal of some sort is nevertheless to be set up. Although the worst criminal may nowhere be compelled to testify against himself and is entitled to the judgment of an impartial court, the German people are to be compelled to furnish evidence against a branch of their own Government, and to submit it to a court whose bias is known in advance. And over the whole mad business is to be thrown the sanctimonious mantle of a League of Nations, an organization which had no existence when the Kaiser's acts were committed and which has none now, and of an alleged international morality which, even if it yet possessed either accepted definitions or recognized sanctions, would be discredited forever by the international crime which is now to be committed in its name.

The Kaiser will be tried if the Allies insist, laws and Constitutions and morals to the contrary notwithstanding. Having been tried, he will probably be convicted. Whatever his fate, the world will have another culprit whom many, at least, will thenceforth esteem a martyr and to whose memory will rally the reactionary forces, still strong, of autocracy, militarism, and class pride, to vex the course of democratic progress for a generation. How long can the Big Three go on straining at the pillars of the temple without bringing the structure of democracy toppling upon their heads? If the wreaking of vengeance under the guise of international justice is to prevail, how long will it be before the peace treaty brings peace and righteousness to the world?

The Madness at Versailles

IT was not to be hoped that there would be a generous peace. The wickednesses of the German armies were too obvious, the bad faith of the German Imperial Government had been too clearly demonstrated to admit of any settlement which did not impose heavy penalties and exact specific and ample guarantees. The temper of the victorious Allies as a whole was too harsh, and that of the French in particular too strained with nervous dread, to make possible a peace under which Germany would have much power to recuperate rapidly. Moreover, official reports and unofficial intimations from Paris, although dealing for the most part with scattered details rather than with larger or connected topics, have been sufficient to indicate that the Peace Conference was little disposed to make concessions, and increasingly inclined to be drastic. For a rigorous peace, in short, the world was already somewhat prepared. But it was not prepared for a peace of undisguised vengeance, for a peace which openly flouts some of the plainest dictates of reason and humanity, repudiates every generous word that Mr. Wilson has ever uttered regarding Germany, flies in the face of accepted principles of law and economics, and makes the very name of democracy a reproach. In the whole history of diplomacy there is no treaty more properly to be regarded as an international crime than the amazing document which the German representatives are now asked to sign.

Only as one keeps in mind the high professions with which the war was conducted—professions of which Mr. Wilson, more than any one else, was the polished and unctuous mouthpiece, and which the Allies by their applause impliedly accepted—is the enormity of what has happened to be fully comprehended. The world was to be made safe for democracy. German militarism was to be crushed, and the German Constitution itself was to be so changed as to emancipate the German people from autocratic rule and make impossible the repetition of such a war as this one had proved itself to be. The German people, who, it was repeatedly affirmed, had had no part in bringing on the war, and who at the worst were the helpless instruments of its prosecution, were to be freed from tyranny and given a chance to take their place among the peoples who love liberty and practice righteousness. Again and again, in the rhetorical documents in which Mr. Wilson expounded to a waiting world the divine order of human society, he declared that America, at least, had no quarrel with the German people, that it begrudged them no greatness which their industry and intelligence might attain, and that a victorious peace, if it meant punitive damages or harsh restraint, would be worse than useless as a world settlement. And for the attainment of these ends and their sanctification a League of Nations was to be set up, with Germany itself, if it would cease to do evil and learn to do well, as one of its members.

How have these generous professions, honorable alike to those who made them and to those who trusted them, been carried out? The treaty affords only one answer. Germany and the German people are virtually to be destroyed. The burdens which the treaty imposes are heavier than any people can bear and progress. To begin with, German territory is to be diminished. Including Alsace-Lorraine, Silesia, Posen, the Saar Basin, and other areas, Germany is to lose 35,175 square miles, in addition to 8,572 square miles in Schleswig and East Prussia which will presumably have to be parted with in consequence of referendum votes on the question of allegiance for which the treaty provides. Even conceding that the whole of Alsace-Lorraine ought to be restored to France, and that the inhabitants of the designated portions of Schleswig and East Prussia should be allowed to determine their allegiance, the loss of territory still aggregates 29,575 square miles. In addition to deprivation of territory in Europe, Germany is to renounce in favor of the Allies and the other so-called associated Powers all its overseas possessions, including not only its colonies but its rights and property in China, Siam, Liberia, Morocco, Egypt, Turkey, and Bulgaria. The destruction of Germany's military and naval power is virtually complete; its army is reduced to 100,000 men, its navy is cut down to a handful of vessels, conscription is abolished, the further construction of wireless stations is forbidden, and most of its cables are appropriated by the victors. Within a zone of fifty kilometres east of the Rhine all fortifications are to be destroyed.

All this, drastic as it is, forms only the opening chapter. There are to be reparations, indemnities, and strangling economic punishments as well. What the aggregate amount of indemnities and reparations is to be has not, apparently, yet been determined, but, whatever it is, Germany is to go on paying it for thirty years, beginning with an initial payment within two years of a billion pounds sterling. At the same time it is required to devote its economic resources directly to the restoration of the invaded regions of Belgium and France; to deliver annually for ten years to those countries and to Italy great quantities of coal (one of its principal coal fields, the Saar Basin, having in the meantime been surrendered); and to grant to the Allied and associated Powers preferences and concessions in trade which will go far toward destroying German competition in any branch of industry. As if deliberately to add insult to penalty, the victors further propose to exact from Germany most-favored-nation treatment for their own vessels in the German fishing and coasting trade, and even in towage; while as a guarantee that the requirements of the treaty will be met, German territory west of the Rhine, together with the bridgeheads on that river, is to be occupied by Allied and associated troops for fifteen years, unless in the meantime the requirements of the treaty are fully complied with.

Nor is this all. The provisions for the disarmament of Germany, which might easily, had the victorious Powers so chosen, have been made a beneficent illustration of how a great state might live in peace and happiness without an army or a navy greater than the needs for a police, are wholly negatived, so far as moral value is concerned, by the failure of the treaty to provide for any measure whatever of disarmament on the part of the Allies and their associates. As the treaty stands, Germany is to be stripped of its means of defence as well as of offence, while its conquerors hover about it fully armed. If there were still need of proof that the League of Nations, as a device for insuring world peace, is only an alliance of three great Powers to enforce their will upon all the others, the treatment accorded to Germany at this point should furnish the demonstration. Further, what is to be said for a treaty which requires Germany to "hand over to the associated Governments, either jointly or severally, all persons" accused of "having committed acts in violation of the laws and customs of war," together with "all documents and information necessary to insure full knowledge of the incriminating acts, the discovery of the offenders, and the just appreciation of the responsibility," one of the alleged offenders being the former Kaiser, now outside of German territory; to concede in advance the validity of treaties yet to be made with Austria-Hungary, Bulgaria, and Turkey, including the decisions which may be made regarding their territory; to recognize in advance any new states that may be formed out of the territory of the three Powers mentioned, with such boundaries as may be agreed upon; to accept in advance the decisions of prize courts of the Allies regarding ships or goods; and to admit the jurisdiction of a League of Nations of which it is not a member, and which it cannot enter save with the unanimous consent of the Powers which are seeking its destruction?

Such are the terms to which the representatives of Germany are asked to set their hands without demur. Such is the treaty which is to end a war fought to overthrow autocracy and militarism and to enthrone democracy and peace. Such is the settlement to which the President of the United States has given his approval, and which the Senate of the United States will be asked to ratify. The heinousness of its offending, the calculating harshness of its demands and impositions, the gross repudiation of moral obligations and good faith which it involves, its gross injustice to the Allied peoples themselves and to their moral standing, become only the more apparent as its terms are studied. It is a peace of vengeance, not of justice. It will not restore Germany to the family of nations; it will destroy Germany as a Great Power. What will be the fate of Germany if the treaty prevails is, however, quite the least important aspect of the matter; the great and startling question now is what will be the fate of democracy, of political and economic liberty, of morals and ideals? How stands it with the peoples at this grave moment in the world's career?

It would be idle now to mince words. The meaning of the treaty is obvious. After nearly five years of strenuous effort and high expectancy, the hopes of the peoples have been destroyed. The progress of democracy as either a theory or a practice of social righteousness has been suddenly and forcibly checked. The great reforms which were to substitute the rule of peoples for the rule of Governments, abolish war as a means of aggression or of settling international disputes, break down alliances and balances of power, put secret diplomacy under the ban, do away with discriminating tariffs, establish the right of self-government for all peoples who desired it and were fit to exercise it, and bind the nations in a world league in which all would enjoy equal rights and equal opportunity, have been checked in their progress. In place of these helpful things of which patriots had dreamed, and which the peoples of the world for one brief moment imagined they were about to grasp, there has been enthroned at Versailles an arrogant and self-sufficient autocracy of five Great Powers, two of which are practically at the mercy of the other three; an autocracy owning no authority save its own will, deliberating in secret, parcelling out privileges and territory as best serves its own interests, turning a deaf ear to protests and closing its eyes to facts, observing no sounder principles than those of political compromise, and ordering all things by its own self-centred notions of how the peoples may best be controlled. It is this Versailles autocracy which, in crushing Germany as a world Power, has itself assumed the rôle of world dictator. That it is vindictive as well as powerful, that its resources are immense, and that it intends to have its way with the peoples and their aspirations, no one now need cherish any doubt whatever. Progress henceforth is to go by favor, and the favor will be that of the Big Three.

History, perhaps, will some time tell us how, among the men who have dominated the proceedings at Versailles, the responsibility for this state of things should be apportioned.

None, surely, who have had a hand in the determinations of the Peace Conference can go unblamed, save as they may have been overborne by the weight of authority. Yet the verdict of history will not, we think, be incorrectly forecast if the larger blame for the check which liberty and democracy have received is laid to the charge of Woodrow Wilson. To Mr. Wilson, more than to any other man who has ever lived, it fell to voice the aspirations of the world's peoples and to receive their homage. The times and the opportunity were alike supremely great. The stream of revolt against privilege and privilege-begotten wealth, the demand for the abolition of autocracy and the substitution of a political and economic régime in which the people should rule in fact as well as in name, had risen to the point where all that was needed, apparently, was wise and inspiring direction to make it an instrument of the greatest gains for human welfare that the race had ever known. It was Mr. Wilson's achievement to give to this great yearning of the world's masses, not indeed constructive leadership, for he has builded nothing that will endure, but a winning exposition and a moral unction which caught the imagination of peoples everywhere, riveted their attention upon him as the one man living who sounded their motives and voiced their aspirations, and made him their idol as well as their guide and friend. The trust which the peoples gave him, the appeals which they fondly directed to him, and the high expectations with which they hung upon his words, were as pathetic in simplicity as they were imposing in weight and mass. He was the hope of democracy, and the fear of his enemies was the confidence of his friends.

How Mr. Wilson has repaid the confidence which the peoples gave him, all the world now knows. The one-time idol of democracy stands today discredited and condemned. His rhetorical phrases, torn and faded tinsel of a thought which men now doubt if he himself ever really believed, will never again fall with hypnotic charm upon the ears of eager multitudes. The camouflage of ethical precept and political philosophizing which for long blinded the eyes of all but the most observing has been stripped away, and the peoples of the world see revealed, not a friend faithful to the last, but an arrogant autocrat and a compromising politician. And with the loss of the robes which gave him sanctity goes also the loss of all liberal and ennobling support. There will still be many to applaud the treaty, and to join hands with Mr. Wilson in remorseless effort to push vengeance to completion, but they will not be the liberals who long acclaimed him as their leader nor the masses who once saw in him a second Providence. Those who stand with him now—strange transformation when one recalls the years of his ascendancy—are the staunch supporters of power and privilege, the controllers of great wealth and dictators of social favor, the voluble champions of the established order against every form of revolution, the preachers of hate and prejudice, and the timid and dependent whose souls are not their own. These are the ones who now do Mr. Wilson honor.

It is well that the line should at last be clearly drawn, for with the publication of the German treaty the real battle for liberty begins. All that has gone before—the overthrow of Czardom in Russia, the constitutional struggle in Germany, the establishment of a Soviet Government in Hungary, the revolt against tyranny or constraint in all quarters of the globe—are only the preliminaries of the great revolution to whose support the friends of freedom must now rally everywhere. Less and less, as that struggle widens, will the world have place for either liberals or conservatives: Versailles has forced men into two main camps, the radicals and the reactionaries. Heaven grant that the revolution may be peaceful, and that it may destroy only to rebuild! Whatever its course, it is the peoples who have been deluded and ignored who will play the leading part, for with the appalling example of Mr. Wilson and the Peace Conference before their eyes, the peoples will have small use for any leadership save their own. This is the scene which the moral collapse at Versailles opens to the world, this the promised land toward which the peoples of the world will now press with all their strength. With Germany crushed and autocracy enthroned, with the strong hand of power at the throat of liberty, the battle opens which is to make men free.

June 10, 1919.

Mr. Clayton R. Lusk, Chairman,
Joint Legislative Committee on
Investigation of Seditious Activities,
Murray Hill Hotel, New York City.

My dear Sir:-

A friend tells me that the attention of your Committee has been attracted to a false report of testimony given by me before the New York State Reconstruction Commission in Brooklyn some weeks ago. According to a report in the New York Tribune I was made to say that I favored the Soviet form of government for America. This is precisely the opposite of what I did say as the stenographic notes of my testimony show. Not that I can conceive it would be improper in any way to advocate the introduction of the Soviet by peaceful methods if anybody knew enough about it to decide whether it is a governmental device of value to the world or not. That we shall not be able to find out for many years to come in all probability and not until the present determination to confuse the European Soviet, a system of government, with the brutal and bloody acts of the men in Bavaria and Russia who have been operating as Soviets has come to an end.

I had the good fortune to see the Bavarian Soviet at work and reported to the Peace Commission in Paris the result of my observations, for which I received the thanks of the Secretary of State.

If I have any information of value on this or any other subject I hope that the Committee will not hesitate to call upon me.

I hear your detectives are coming to hear me speak next Thursday night at the Pennsylvania Hotel. Unfortunately, I am not going to speak about Russia, and will only give to the audience there the report I made on food conditions in Germany to Mr. Hoover, Mr. Lansing and Mr. Lloyd George. But if your detectives still plan to come, I shall be glad to have them ask for me at the door and I will see that they are given front seats.

Yours very truly,

V-R

Defeat the Treaty!

THE revised peace treaty handed to the Germans on Monday constitutes a distinct victory for liberal and radical opinion. On May 10 the Germans were told in these words that it was a case of take it or leave it: "They (the Allies) can admit no discussion of their right to insist upon the terms of the peace treaty *substantially* as drafted." Of the treaty itself a chorus of approval arose from imperialists everywhere. It was the promised peace of justice—"terribly severe but just"—according to the *New York Times*, while the *Evening Post* even went so far in its awed admiration of this commixture of hypocrisy, bad faith, and imperialism, as to speak of its being like a "voice from heaven"—in the justice, we presume, of its rigid sentencing. But to liberals everywhere it sounded only like a voice from another region, condemning the world to another era of imperialism, secret diplomacy, ill-will, and international hatreds, if not to anarchy and chaos. The voices of protest raised everywhere had their effect upon the self-appointed parcellers of the world. The take-it-or-leave-it policy was abandoned and after eighteen days of wrangling, of compromising, of further bargaining in secret, the revised terms of the "perfect treaty" are before us. This time the Germans are told that they can make only a yes or no reply.

The revised terms are correctly described as involving no change in principle—or spirit, we should add. They are accompanied by a most effective and truthful rehearsing of the crimes of the Germans plus the familiar upbraiding of the German people for not revolting sooner. Despite Mr. Wilson's repeated assertions that we were warring, not on the Germans, but on their rulers, the former are again judged guilty, and their judges once more veil their own land-grabbing, their deliberate violation of the Fourteen Points upon the basis of which they concluded the armistice, by regrets that the nature of the case necessitates the judgments imposed. As for the modifications of the terms, they are to be welcomed—notably the plébiscite for Upper Silesia, restoring to respectability in this case the unhappily violated principle of self-determination. For the rest, the Big Four explain that their language did not mean what it said; that the Germans quite misunderstood this point and the other, and that, by the grace of God, they are to be admitted to the League of Nations not now but soon, if the stability of their government warrants it and if they properly carry out a treaty which cannot be carried out. There is no recession from the theft of the Saar Basin; the outcry against the abominable outrage upon the Chinese of Shantung goes unnoticed. Assurances there are that the gracious Allies do not mean economically to cut the throats of the vanquished, but simply to go through their pockets. The Germans may even constitute a reparation commission of their own to be in touch with the Allied body whose members are to be the real rulers of Germany for fifteen years. And this is the final reply; this the final proof to the world of the unselfishness, of the love of justice of the Allies; the final proof that this was a war for liberty and humanity, for the rights of nations, for the freedom of the seas; the final proof that this was a war to make democracy safe and to end war itself. On Monday, Andrew Bonar Law in the House of Commons declared that there were *twenty-three* wars going on in the world—all as a result of the war to end war. Thus have the Allies restored peace and the Council of Four made mock of unselfish aims.

So the deed is done, so far as Paris is concerned. But the anger of the supporters of this wicked pact, who do not see that it does far more injury to the morale of the Allies and their standing at the bar of history than to the Germans, continues unabated. Our metropolitan press is turning upon the liberals who have compelled the modification of the treaty but will still have none of it, and seeks to shoulder upon them the responsibility for the failure of the treaty, if it fails in Washington. The Big Four are guiltless; it is only those who refuse to compromise with their consciences and to remain silent when this glorious opportunity to make over the world is flung away in hypocrisy and greed, who are guilty. Patriotism, we are told, should drive liberals into condoning wrong-doing, into forgetting the nation's pledges, into turning their backs upon the ideals which Mr. Wilson set up for the nation when it entered the war. Liberals will do nothing of the kind. They indignantly repudiate the idea that the responsibility is theirs. Who was it who all through the war championed the President and upheld those ideals? Who were the men and women in England and France and Italy who bowed down and worshipped him when he came to Europe, but the liberals of those countries and the masses of the peoples? Why are these persons, who wanted nothing so much as to uphold him, all against him today? Because they know that he has sold them out and because they will not connive in silence. Their loyalty is a higher one than to Woodrow Wilson and his confederates in Paris; it is, as Mr. Wilson has so often declared, to humanity itself, and, we would add, to sincerity, to truth telling, to honesty, and to common decency as well.

But now Mr. Wilson is speedily to return and go upon the stump at home in order to convince us once more that black is white and white is black. We are doubtless to hear that the Fourteen Points prevail wherever applicable. We are to be told again that the half loaf of the covenant is not what he wanted, but that we must gratefully accept it as the best we can get because it is the basis for the whole treaty. The *Nation*, for one, cannot compromise one iota of its opposition to the treaty. The possibilities of evil in it and in the sham league are so great that it wants both rejected and a simple declaration by Congress that the state of war is at an end. But, the argument runs, do you not see, that you are throwing yourself into the hands of the most reactionary Republicans; you are striking hands with a Nelson and a Lodge? Liberals have no use for the Nelsons and Lodges. It was Maria Weston Chapman who during the Abolition struggle marvelled that the good Lord used instruments in that cause which she would not touch with a forty-foot pole. Sixty feet we always wish between us and Mr. Lodge. But our concern is not with him. If he were upholding the treaty with the *New York Times* we should still be opposing it. We have no present interest in the treaty as a political document; we are interested in it as an index of integrity and good faith. There is only one question for liberals: is the treaty just, in keeping with our national honor; will it achieve peace and righteousness? And just because honest men must answer *"No!"* liberals will continue to oppose the treaty and the League to the limit of their powers, leaving the responsibility where it properly belongs—upon the perpetrators of this crime against the men who died in France for something else.

American Militarism Waning

MOST gratifying are the signs that come from various directions of the abating of the militarist mania in America. Particularly is there reason for profound thankfulness in the attitude of the returned soldiers. There is every evidence, despite the lawlessness of many men in uniform on May Day, that our troops have returned from overseas with a stomach-full of soldiering, with no love for the trade and none too much for their officers, with the greatest eagerness to get out of uniform, and with the minds of many open to new ideas. We meet on every hand returned men who insist that no future emergency could get them into uniform again, and we have even heard of a captain who, after having gone to France with the intention of becoming a professional soldier, recently forfeited a two week's leave with pay in order to take his discharge immediately; he would not wait fourteen days to don civilian clothes.

Such incidents as these might well be mere straws, if there were not so many of them. Thus the *San Francisco Call* reports that the sentiment of the Seventy-seventh Division, in which there were many Western men, was largely opposed to universal military service and to parading; they wanted to get through with the whole thing. The *Call* is convinced, as a result of its observations of the returned soldiers, that "we shall not, and cannot have universal military discipline" until America is radically changed. Indeed, so great is the reaction from universal military service that the National Security League is really in despair about it. In a very frank letter to the *New York Tribune* its publicity director reports that in all high school and college debates the proponents of universal military service were "defeated at the ratio of practically two to one." He adds: "The League considers the results in these debates and the comments thereon most illuminating as an exposition of an enormous sentiment against universal military training which will have to be overcome." To the *Tribune* he makes a touching appeal: "We trust that you will keep up the fight," but the stony-hearted editor answers in the headline: "Let the League do it." This deliberate abandonment on the part of the *Tribune* of the one thing indispensable to keep the Hun and all future Huns from our shores, is certainly amazing, but not more so than the complete calm with which the country has received the news that the army estimates have been cut so severely by Congress that in place of an army of 509,000 men asked by the War Department we are to have the beggarly one of 300,000, upon which we are to spend $718,000,000, instead of $1,100,000,000, and that after all we are not going to have the greatest fleet in the world.

It is interesting, too, that the army's recruiting campaign by means of appeals to meetings and groups of citizens has absolutely broken down; it is the gossip in Washington that returned soldiers have interfered. So the army has resorted to a new device—advertising! Some two hundred thousand dollars are to be expended in proving that military service is not a military affair at all—bless your innocent heart, no!—but really a university extension course under most experienced teachers. The first page-advertisements which have appeared in the dailies—needless to say the dailies think very highly of this procedure—inform us that "being a soldier of the United States is the finest business in the world." It is surely obvious that the drafted men do not think so, or else it would not be necessary to advertise now for men to take their places; but perhaps they were not aware of what the advertisement tells us, that the soldier "meets agreeable people *including lots of nice girls*, at Hostess Houses, et cetera [very much et cetera]. He goes to dances, if he wants to. In fact, he usually has a better time than a civilian." Comment is surely superfluous save that Secretary Baker, who has told Congress he approves this girl-bait, has plainly reached the silly stage of his career.

Most gratifying of all is the decision of the American Legion, which refused to be stampeded into endorsing universal service at its St. Louis convention, to do away with all titles. Its members declare they will not make the mistake of the G. A. R.; for them every member, whether he be a young Roosevelt or plain Jim Smith, will have the title of Mr. and nothing else. Satisfactory as all this is, it is not time to declare that all danger is over. The universal training bills are still before Congress and are to be pushed with all possible speed. Efforts are being made, moreover, to inculcate the spirit of militarism among the young boys, despite the fact that the New York State Reconstruction Commission has come out squarely against universal military training in the schools. It has been a military failure in New York as it has been these many years in Massachusetts. Nevertheless, Secretary Baker has yielded to the demand for universal training for high-school and college students, and the lobbies of the army and navy and National Guard are still at work. It behooves all opposed to Prussianism in America to fight vigorously all such proposals.

The Peace That is No Peace

"WE have made a peace, but it is not *the* peace," wrote Clarendon in 1856. It is not *the* peace which has been made this week in Paris; it is merely a stage which we have reached in the progress of those terrible forces which have been unleashed by the war. No peace so wicked, so hypocritical, so contrary to every Allied pretence, can endure—of that there can be no doubt whatever, least of all in Paris. That the Germans would succumb to *force majeure* this journal has had no doubt whatever. In Berlin in March last it was as plain as a pikestaff that any treaty would have to be signed, that despite all protestations, despite the correctness of their assertions that they have been tricked and betrayed by Mr. Wilson's promise of the Fourteen points, the Germans were themselves so bankrupt in moral power and righteousness, so exhausted physically and nervously, and so destitute of unselfish moral leadership or of leadership of any kind, that the acceptance of any peace was inevitable. It would have taken rare moral steadfastness, a Spartan courage, a readiness to see millions of their fellow-citizens die of hunger before their eyes because of the brutal and inhuman blockade of the Allies, in order to say no to Versailles. The Germans should have said no. They owed it to themselves and to the world to do so. It would have taken them a long step toward the restoration of their own self-respect and manhood—but it was beyond their moral power.

And so they will continue to pay the price for the wickedness of their former leadership and of their own conniving at that wickedness in high places which existed long before the war. They are now suffering for the political immorality of Bismarck, for the crimes of their militaristic system, for their whole autocratic and aristocratic and caste order of society, for their incredible vanity and still more incredible pride. For the Germany of 1914 there must in any event have come a day of reckoning—or there is no use in believing in the eternal verities, in believing that crimes against the rights and liberties of a whole people avenge themselves. So the Germans are paying anew for the "scrap of paper," for the brutal subjugation of Belgium, for the destruction of Northern France, for the shelling of women and children in lifeboats, for numberless crimes against humanity which gave to their enemies the excuse for wanton brutalities, for shameless hypocrisies, for the starving of nations, for sinking to the German level in many a council room. Yes, the Allies are avenged, and the world's morality. The Germans in this hour of agony and humiliation have had left only the will to make what they themselves call a magnificent gesture—the sinking of their fleet, a gesture which merely reveals anew to the world their utter moral bankruptcy.

Utter moral bankruptcy—that sums up Berlin today, and it has these five long years. Not that their worship of force, or their belief that might makes right and that the issue of progress or retrogression can be determined on the battlefield has set them particularly apart. Their depraved gods the Allies worship, too, if in lesser degree and with far greater skill in making black seem white. It is the utter inability of the Germans to understand the minds and desires and the moral reactions of the plain people of the world which has constituted their chief intellectual failure, next to the worship of the state which has led to their downfall. But it is not necessary again to dwell either upon their shortcomings or upon their present inability as a nation to gauge the situation, to make honest confession, and to start anew on a basis of honesty and righteousness and truth-telling to themselves and to the outside world. But the question now is whether Germany will survive at all, whether any Government can endure under these treaty conditions, Germany being half slave, half free. As to the future, prophecy is idle; much depends upon the spirit of the Allies. If it continues the same as at present, if the Allied administration of Germany is to be carried on with the ruthlessness of a Lloyd George, the brutalities of a Clemenceau, and the hypocrisies of a Wilson, the Germans have still far to go on the downward path toward chaos and anarchy. Toward this they are apparently headed now, if only because of their complete lack of leadership, the absence of any programme of regeneration and reconstruction, or of any moral purpose. Hunger, famine, and exhaustion have wreaked their will, as well as years of political immorality. The Government of Bauer is obviously the merest makeshift, set up to be execrated in German history because it signed the document no nation should ever have signed or been called on to sign. Because of the folly of the four old men in Paris who have created a wilderness and called it a peace, who have prated of justice and yet deliberately have drawn a document against which the humane and liberal and democratic forces of the world are everywhere crying out, the Germans may have both the treaty and Bolshevism or worse.

That this crime at Paris will have its logical consequences, there can be no question. It is bound to bring retribution in its train as certainly as was the rape of Belgium. There is a divine, immutable law in these matters; the fall of Orlando shows that it works as remorselessly as a glacier and as steadily. What individuals do now, is of little moment; what the great unleashed forces of humanity will do, is everything. The social upheaval will not stand still merely because Lloyd George, Clemenceau, and Wilson, having laid on, now say: "Hold, enough!" Block that movement to some degree they and their kind may and will; they may buy off or drug labor and the vast forces of democracy by one device or another. None the less the forces of liberty will move on; the existing capitalistic order has signed its own death warrant in Paris; it has shown that it can plunge the whole world into chaos and misery; and then has shown that it did not know how to extricate itself honorably and wisely from its own Armageddon. What *The Nation* said when the treaty appeared, it repeats now: The world is henceforth divided into two camps, radicals and reactionaries; the real, true revolution which is to free humanity has but begun. It ought to come without violence and force, but come it will, and it matters not for the moment that few can see clearly and that no one can say: "Behold the straight road out of the wilderness!" The Socialists believe that they can, but never were they so discredited by their own acts, their want of faith in themselves, their unreadiness to die for their beliefs. Yet never were we of such complete faith in the eventual triumph of human nature, in the ability of the human mind to work out a plan of salvation which shall bring the greatest happiness to the greatest number, as in this hour when humanity, by reason of the Peace of Paris, has touched the low-water mark of wrong-doing and degradation, when the future is clouded as never before.

The Failure of Moral Leadership

WHAT has confronted us at Paris and what confronts us at Washington is the failure of moral leadership. It ought not, we suppose, to shock us that there are dozens of our leaders, Senators and public men everywhere, who privately denounce the peace treaty on the ground of its hideous bad faith and immorality, yet dare not speak out against it, for this state of affairs merely illustrates the ordinary timidity of the congressional mind. The Opposition in Washington concerns itself openly only with the League covenant, but Democratic and Republican Senators alike do not hesitate to tell the newspaper men how absolutely they abhor the Wilson surrender at Paris and the character of the treaty. In private they freely admit their cowardice; yet they will not break with the machine, and they do not see how utterly they damn the whole system of which they are the product by their refusal to speak out.

The world is at its most terrible crisis. Perhaps the fate of civilization itself is at stake, yet our Opposition leaders play politics with the moral issue. They dare not voice the truth, refuse the treaty, and save the honor of the United States. Truth and high ideals abide firmly in the hearts of the American people. One has but to appeal to them in order to strike the spark from the anvil, but nowhere in Washington is there any one to rise and make a true and genuine and honest moral appeal to offset the flow of sweet-sounding, exquisitely phrased sentences with no moral firmness whatever behind them, which are soon to be heard again in the land, explaining that all is well, that a terrible

disaster and defeat are really a glorious victory.

There is no escaping the basic law of leadership; if its positive function is not utilized, it will exercise a negative function. President Wilson, claiming to follow instead of to lead the mass will, leads it nevertheless, but leads it downward. Sunk in our lethargy of democracy, waiting for a vote of opinion upon unknown issues, our mass expression becomes confused and dissipated, the issues themselves become lost in irrelevant superficialities, and instead of a deep moral integrity of purpose we manifest a shallow and vacillating inconsistency. The land appears to be caught in the snare of the most menacing delusion that could fasten itself upon the heels of human freedom. The less true its thought, the less clear its understanding, the more right and wise it believes itself to be.

Where is our positive leadership? Where is our healthy and honorable Americanism, our heritage of just dealing and right inclination? Where is the Republicanism of Abraham Lincoln, the Democracy of Thomas Jefferson? Where are the men to stand up for truth and honor and the safety of humanity? Not a solitary voice is raised among our leaders to sound the true note of the moral issue. The Opposition cowers with the Administration in the shadow of negative leadership—in fear of the phantom of war emotionalism with which it dares not grapple.

Through this failure of moral leadership it has been possible for America in six months' time to turn right-about-face on all her avowed principles in the war, and to be serenely unaware that she has turned. We were pledged to fight for the democratization of Germany. We were pledged to fight for self-determination and the rights of small nations. We were pledged to fight for a fair peace—a peace without economic discriminations or punitive indemnities. The honor of the nation, as well as the personal honor of President Wilson, was involved in these and many other pledges. We went out to fight for them. We made the victory possible. The enemy broke in revolution; the democratization of Germany had been accomplished. Again pledges were given, this time in the name not only of America, but also of all the Entente Allies. It was on the basis of these repeated pledges that the enemy entered into the armistice. Immediately additional armistice terms contrary to the whole spirit and letter of our pledges were presented to her. She accepted these terms, partly as a penance, and partly because she still had faith in the honor of her conquerors. And after six months, during which her people have been starved with callous cruelty almost beyond parallel or belief, a treaty denying every pledge that we had made, fulfilling every evil purpose against which we voluntarily had called our pledges into being, has been imposed upon her under threat of invasion. The fact of the democratization of Germany has been dismissed without a shadow of consideration. Self-determination and the rights of small nations have been gainsaid on every hand. Punitive indemnities of staggering proportions, impossible of fulfilment, have been demanded. Economic freedom has been utterly denied. The first and the last and all the intervening words of our pledges have been broken; the moral issue has been forsaken, the moral victory has been irretrievably lost. The result of our unmoral leadership at Paris, Mr. Wilson now tells the country, is a just and righteous peace. For the moment, the country cannot see and does not understand. Who is to awaken it from its evil dream?

But it is not only in foreign affairs that we need moral leadership. The country is filled with unhappiness and unrest due directly to the rise in the cost of living and the intolerance and ruthlessness of government since the war began. The country has once been drugged by words about "The New Freedom" and true democracy and the promised divorce of business from politics; it may be again. But if it comes to pass that the hypnotic powers of Mr. Wilson, to which *The Nation* succumbed in its turn, again succeed in substituting empty phrases for real leadership, then will our political estate merely grow worse. For the day of awakening is bound to come, the day when the masses will everywhere see that the United States has gone backward, not forward, under the leadership of Mr. Wilson, with its hopeless contradictions and never-ending insincerities; when they will realize that the League of Nations as drawn commits us to a policy of imperialistic interference in the affairs of all the world, and threatens to fill the future with constant warring in behalf of men and causes alien to our entire historic spirit and purposes.

We are paying the price for the falsities and hypocrisies which are the inevitable accompaniment of any war, but which, in the great struggle just ended, were raised to a pitch never before deemed possible. Out of the morass there is but one way—the road of truth and honest speaking, the proclaiming of the moral issue in reconstruction, and unswerving devotion to it. If there is one man in political America who is capable of grasping and voicing this issue, the future is his; the people are eager for it, perhaps the salvation of America itself depends upon it. Without it, we may have a hundred investigations of Bolshevism, and yet see the tide of unrest rise to engulfing heights. We need a spiritual revival.

Fourteen Questions to Mr. Wilson

MR. PRESIDENT, when you appeared before the Senate it was most gratifying to note that you did not come as a conquering hero, but in a rather subdued spirit and with far greater show of a desire to coöperate with the treaty-ratifying body than has been your wont. Your sudden readiness to meet with the newspaper men in Washington after two years of obstinate refusal and your offering of your services to the Senators were clear signs, we take it, that you realized that the way is not so easy for you as to permit a resumption of your old policy of isolation within the White House, your playing a lone hand and your giving orders to Congress as to what you wished done. We find, moreover, in the fact that your reading of your speech was not as effective as usual, ground for the encouraging belief that you realize at heart how you have failed to bring home the real charter of popular liberty which you promised the world, and for which it has longed with an ardor you have yourself beautifully portrayed. It was not a trumpet call to blow down the walls of the Republican Jericho that you gave forth; there was nothing in it to make your auditors believe that you had brought back "the right" which on March 5 last you declared to be "the only permanent thing in the world." More than that, as foreseen, you confined yourself to glittering generalities, passing over the bitter wrongs and cruelties of the treaty and making no better plea for its failure to live up to the Fourteen Points than that it "nowhere cut to the heart of any principle"—how near to the heart it goes, and in how many cases, you leave us in doubt. Again you ended on that high note of idealism that would be of such vast service to all the world if only you would live up to it in practice.

Today it becomes necessary for all who seek the truth about the situation to turn to you, the propounder of the doctrine of "open covenants of peace openly arrived at," and to insist that you now take not only the Senate but the entire country into your confidence. We are aware that you explained your complete abandonment in Paris of the policy of "open covenants of peace openly arrived at" on the ground that you did not mean that all discussions should be in the open, but only that *after* the drawing up of the treaty it should be fully published and subject to public discussion. We take you at your word once more and demand in the name of the fifty thousand readers of *The Nation* that you give to the American public specific answer to the following Fourteen Questions:

1. Will you or will you not give out the letters of Gen. Bliss, Secretary Lansing, and Mr. White, protesting again and again against the compromises made by you without their previous knowledge or coöperation and specifically the letter of Gen. Bliss, concurred in by the others, protesting against the Shantung surrender?

2. Was the Shantung concession the price paid by you for Japanese adherence to the League of Nations?

3. Did not your State Department, when you invited China to join the United States in severing diplomatic relations with Germany, either directly or through the American Minister at Peking or the Chinese Minister at Washington, assure the Chinese Government in your behalf that, if it came into the war, you would use all your powers to protect China's territorial rights in the Peace Treaty?

4. Subsequently, when China declared war against Germany-Austria did you or did you not again make such promises to China?

5. When you first urged China to come into the war, were you aware that the British, French, Russian, and Italian Governments had made secret agreements with Japan in February and March, 1917, to support Japan's demands for the cession of all rights in Shantung? When did you first learn of these secret agreements and when, thereafter, did you notify China of their existence? Or did you keep her in ignorance?

6. In yielding to those secret agreements when they were finally disclosed, did you or did you not sacrifice the diplomatic honesty and the honor of the United States?

7. Did you or did you not obtain oral promises in the Council of Three from the Japanese plenipotentiary with regard to the evacuation of Shantung within a given time? Are such assurances in the secret minutes of the Council of Three (or Four) or are they not?

8. What action did you take with reference to the impudent Japanese attempt to intimidate the Chinese delegation at Paris into permitting Japan to handle Chinese interests and, when this failed, to force the Peking Government to repudiate its own delegation at Paris?

9. Bearing in mind your self-determination principle, why did you refuse to receive the Egyptian delegation and the Korean delegation and decline to permit the Irish case to be presented to the Conference?

10. Why did you betray the Egyptians by recognizing, after all these years, the British protectorate over Egypt and then keep that recognition of yours secret until the very moment when the Egyptian delegates arrived in Paris?

11. Why did you refuse to protect national minorities in the League Covenant and propose treaties protecting such minorities only to the new states such as Poland and the enemy powers? Is there or is there not a gentlemen's agreement that self-determination within the Allied lands shall not be assisted or permitted by any Power?

12. Besides the Monroe Doctrine, what "territorial arrangements similar" to it are covered by the clause of the League protecting such arrangements? Is the burglarious Franco-British Accord of 1917, dividing Russia into spheres of action, thus protected? Or the Allied spheres of influence in China, or the British sphere of influence in Persia, or the secret treaty for the partition of Turkey?

13. What motives induced you to give your promise not to publish the treaty? Why, having assured Congress that you wished it to prosecute its inquiry into the leak most thoroughly did you fail to act when it appeared that copies were being handed around, one by Messrs. Davison and Lamont? Was it honorable to withhold the treaty from America when it was on sale abroad—even in Germany, and in English?

14. Finally, and most important of all, is it not true that when *all the British delegates in Paris*, Lloyd George included, asked you to help them modify what they considered the unduly harsh and cruel features of the treaty with Germany, you, voicing as you have so often asserted the aspirations of the common peoples and of humanity itself, declined to give your aid to these delegates, that being one reason why Lloyd George describes the treaty as "terribly severe"?

The Crime Against Russia

London, July 26.—The former Prime Minister, H. H. Asquith, speaking at Edgware today, said: "I regard with bewilderment and apprehension the part this country is playing in Russia. The country wants a clearer definition than has yet been given of what are our commitments, definite and prospective. I sincerely hope that the attempt to commit us further in Russia will be successfully resisted. The future government of Russia is a matter for the Russian people and for no one else."

PRECISELY, and the same is true of Hungary, as to which unfortunate country we learn this week that it is to be starved by Christian America and the Allies until it abandons the Government of Bela Kun. This with the consent and approval of Woodrow Wilson, who said to the Central Powers on December 4, 1917: "We owe it, however, to ourselves to say that we do not wish *in any way to impair* or to rearrange the Austro-Hungarian Empire. It is no affair of ours what they do with their own life, either industrially or politically. *We do not propose or desire to dictate to them in any way.*" Starving a people until they choose a different form of government is, of course, no affair of ours, and if Mr. Wilson were not morally bankrupt, if he were not unfaithful to his own idealism and to that of America, he would never consent to it.

As to Russia, what do we see? Silence and suppression of the truth as to what is going on behind the scenes; a twisting and ever-changing policy—for war one day, for peace the next. One month, an official announcement of an encircling policy as outlined by M. Pichon; the next, a peace offer to Lenin in the handwriting of Lloyd George's private secretary; the third, a decision to invade at once. A fourth sees the encouragement of the Finns to attack Petrograd, and the coldblooded sinking of Russian warships by British battleships, coincident with the withdrawal of the American troops from Archangel and the announcement by Lloyd George that no more English troops will be sent in. And then, last week, Mr. Wilson's explanation that we are in Siberia merely to aid the somnolent Mr. Stevens in rebuilding the Siberian railway and in protecting it so that Russia may have food—carefully suppressing the fact that this road is the great reliance of Kolchak. And on top of all, we recognize, or partially recognize, the impossible Kolchak!

Never, we believe, has there been, in any international entanglement in recent years, such contemptible fumbling, such tortuous diplomacy, such breathing war and peace at the same time. Why is it that there is such widespread disrespect for the four old men of Versailles? Well, the Russian policy alone would warrant it. Can anyone find fault with Chicherin and Lenin for speaking of the hypocrisy of the Allied and American policy toward Russia? Let him merely run over the files of the newspapers for the last six months and see how the Prinkipo proposal has alternated with acts of war—absolutely unconstitutional acts of war so far as America is concerned—the Bullitt proposal for peace, and Lloyd George's announcement that while no more British soldiers are to go to Russia, British tanks, uniforms, guns, cannon, and ammunition are going both to Denikin and Kolchak. Fifty times we have had the announcement that this policy was entirely successful and that the Bolsheviki were defeated; fifty times we have heard of Bolshevist victories. Today Kolchak, Denikin, and the Finns are all in hasty retreat, despite their Allied aid, while correspondents of *The Philadelphia Public Ledger* and *The London Times* declare that "the Bolshevists have got Russia"; that "the situation in Russia is exceedingly grave, almost hopeless, for the plans of the international financial interests seeking the downfall of the Bolshevists."

No wonder Mr. Asquith speaks out; no wonder British Labor plans to compel the Government to leave Russia. What will British Labor's feeling be on this subject now that it has learned that the Chancellor of the Exchequer, Austen Chamberlain, has increased his holdings in a Russian mining company by one thousand shares since intervention began; that Walter Long, Secretary of the Colonies, increased his five hundred shares in the Anglo-Russian Trust by three thousand, purchased seven weeks after the armistice? "Russia," Mr. Wilson declared, "will be the acid test of our democracy." It has been the acid test of *his* democracy. It has bitten into the metal of his declarations as to self-determination, and has proved it to be not pure metal but the basest alloy. Months pass without a clarion note from the President as to the pitiable, starving Russian people, starving by order of the Allies and America. Oh, yes, we are aware that it is not the fault of these outsiders, but that of the Bolsheviki. It is nothing of the kind; it is the fatuous policy of the Big Three which entrenches the Bolsheviki in power. They were not responsible for the breaking down of the railroads before the revolution, nor for Russia's economic collapse, but it is the fault of those who attempt foreign interference that it drives to Lenin's side Mensheviki and Social Revolutionists and many others.

To deprive Lenin and Trotzky of their right to call upon loyal Russians to defend the country from outside attack would be to deprive them of their strongest card. But, we hear it said, does not Prof. Henry C. Emery declare, in his most judicial and able article in *The Yale Review*, that it is the business of the world what happens in Russia, because it is class war that is on, and that Lenin must fight a world-wide warfare, if communism is to succeed anywhere? Granted, if you please, but when was any social upheaval ever checked by bayonets, and foreign bayonets at that? What is the best way to defeat the class war? Well, not by making British Labor and Continental Labor and the masses everywhere believe that Russia is being attacked in order to preserve capitalistic investments, but by building up happy and sound and properous commonwealths between Russia and the Atlantic Ocean, by ending starvation, by removing the causes of popular unrest, by disbanding armies, by reëstablishing the orderly processes of life throughout Europe, by removing as rapidly as possible all causes of social discontent. Violent Bolshevism of the Russian type can flourish, as Bavaria and Hungary have shown, only where there is hunger, exhaustion, despair, economic collapse. The millions upon millions of dollars that are going into Russia in the vain hope of defeating Russia in the field would be infinitely more effective if applied to the rehabilitation of the new and the old States that should be the western bulwarks against the advance of Bolshevism. Now let us have the truth, and above all else let us have a settled policy in America, let us have an end to the private war of Woodrow Wilson upon Russia, direct and indirect; let us have an end to the crime against Russia, let us follow the sound advice of Mr. Asquith and thereby once more be true to our American forefathers, and our highest ideals.

August 5, 1919

Senator Robert M. LaFollette
United States Senate
Washington, D.C.

My dear Senator:

I see it is stated in the press that you are going to speak against the Treaty. I hope with all my heart that you will speak not only against the Covenant, which is such a travesty on the League of Nations we have all been hoping for, but against the Treaty itself. The more I study it, the more I am convinced that it is the most iniquitous document ever drawn, that it dishonors America because it violates our solemn national pledge given to the Germans at the time of the armistice and because it reeks with bad faith, revengefulness and inhumanity. It is worse than the Treaty of Vienna. Evidently Mr. Wilson and I do not use and understand words in the same way, for when he says the Treaty constitutes a new order, my mind stands still and I doubt my sanity for, to me, it not only retains the old and vicious order of the world, but makes it worse and then puts the whole control of the situation in the hands of four or five statesmen -- and, incidentally, of the International Bankers. To my mind it seals the ruin of the modern capitalistic system and constitutes a veritable Pandora's Box out of which will come evils of which we have not as yet any conception.

As you are perhaps aware, I was in Germany for nearly four weeks in February and March, reporting on my return to Paris to our American commissioners (except Mr. Wilson), Mr. Lloyd George and numerous other officials. I went into Germany holding the current opinion in France, that the Germans were exaggerating their needs and sufferings for the purpose of influencing the peace negotiations, but I came away convinced that there had been no understatement. I was so horrified by conditions in Munich that I telegraphed to Mr. Hoover and Col.House that if food were not rushed into Bavaria " a Communist dictatorship would be established by the middle of April." No food reached Bavaria in time and a Communist dictatorship was actually established on April fifteenth, the exact middle of April. Col.House stated that he took my telegram into the meeting of the Economic Council which finally decided to lift the blockade.

I did not limit my observations to the hotels, but went to schools, market places, hospitals, public gatherings and stood in the long lines of gaunt, hungry and weak people waiting at the tobacco and other stores for supplies. I went into the Department of Food Supplies in Berlin and Munich and the Foreign Office in Dresden and talked with small salaried employees privately as to their conditions of life. I went to the soup kitchens in Munich and in Dresden and I brought away from all of these things a picture of suffering and misery and degredation that has haunted me -- I was so utterly unprepared for it. I cannot but feel that the continuance of the blockade during the armistice was one of the wickedest crimes in history. For that we Americans bear our share of the responsibility. If you had been with me in the hospitals and seen the children in the last stages of emaciation suffering from Rickets disease, tuberculosis of the bones and all the well-known ailments due to under-nourishment, you would have felt that this country and the Allies have much to answer for.

I am glad to tell you that when I got to Paris and talked with the leading American officials I found that they were all of my opinion, though, of course, being officials, they would not say so publicly, that our treatment of the Central Powers from the time of the armistice was utterly mistaken, that it endangered the safety of civilization and that it opened up Europe to bolshevism, besides wantonly starving women and children. Hundreds of thousands of people died in Germany, Austria, Hungary and Poland of starvation or diseases which they could not resist because of weakness on account of that infamous blockade. Our officials knew this and were utterly opposed to the policy which the French and English dictated, the English less so as time went on, but I met Mr. Hoover about the 26th of March in Paris on the very day that he had succeeded in getting the prohibition of the going out of the German fishing fleet lifted, and he told me that he had begun to agitate that on the 4th of December and to the end of March to obtain that little bit of generosity and decency. Of course, if this had been done by Prussians, we should know how to describe it. The infamy of the act is not altered by the fact that it was done by the French and the British and what could have been pettier and meaner, for the total product of the fishing fleet could only have saved the lives of a few thousand. I was mighty proud when I got back to Paris to find how well our minor officials (excepting Mr. Wilson whose cold heart was not interested in things like these so far as I could ascertain) had fought against this sort of inhumanity and brutality and how deeply they resented it, not, of course, because they loved the Germans, which they did not, but because they could see that this policy deprived the Allies of their moral superiority over the Germans and endangered the safety of France, Italy, Poland and Czecho-

Slovakia -- of our Allies. Of course, you are aware that in the Peace Treaty a large part of that fishing fleet is now taken away from Germany to take the place of ships sunk by the submarines and that 140,000 milch cows must immediately be taken away from the starving, suffering and innocent German children to be driven into France and Belgium where the need is not comparable with that in Germany. If it were, I should be in favor of succoring France and Belgium first.

Again, in the earnest hope that you will fight against the whole vile document, I am,

Yours faithfully,

An Appeal to America Not Yet Written by Woodrow Wilson

FELLOW-COUNTRYMEN! The past weeks have witnessed two outbreaks of such violence by one group of our citizenry against the other as profoundly to affect the conscience of all thinking Americans. I refer, of course, to the race riots in Washington, under the shadow of the Capitol, and in the city of Chicago. Coming at the very moment when the covenant of the League of Nations, which will constitute, protect, and advance the new order of the world, is being debated, these events are profoundly disconcerting, since they will immediately be seized upon in enemy countries and by hostile forces everywhere to cast doubt upon the sincerity of our professions. But if we were not in the act of reaching a decision of profoundest importance to generations yet unborn, we ought still to be deeply stirred by these terrible, these heart-rending crimes.

The evidence at hand points not only to a failure of the civil authorities to act promptly and so prevent loss of life; it goes to prove that in each case the white race was the aggressor. This makes the matter infinitely worse; it casts a stain upon everyone of the majority group in our land. It is the more censurable because our Negro troops are but just back from no little share in carrying our cause and our flag to victory. As they stood by the majority, so must and should the majority of our citizenry now stand by them with true Christianity. I speak the more feelingly since I, myself, am conscious of having neglected this vital subject; it is the first time during my Presidency that I have spoken out in regard to these relations of our component races. But the very fact that I have kept silent heretofore makes it incumbent upon me to speak out now when the clashing of races, if continued, will be fraught with gravest peril to our American institutions, and will make a bitter mockery of that appeal of our greatest President, "lest these dead shall have died in vain."

For we must not forget that these colored fellow-citizens of ours are what we have made them. They did not seek our shores, but for two centuries we profited by their exploited and unpaid labor, and when we set them free, we turned them adrift without a dollar, without recompense for lives of unending toil. The nation washed its hands of them; it left them ragged, unlettered, unguided, to bear responsibilities of citizenship soon to be severely limited, the prey of labor exploiters and unscrupulous employers. They never asked for reimbursement; they bore no grudge; a great and growingly prosperous section of our country, once ruined, has risen again by their toil. If they are uneducated, if they have troublesome social traits, if their labor is often uncertain, surely the fault lies with those of us who rule and hold every important political office in America. They are our wards and we cannot deny our trusteeship if we would. If they stumble and fall it is our fault as well as theirs. Why? Because the laws of this country—as I have written before—do not prevent the strong from crushing the weak. That is the reason; and because the strong whites have crushed and held down the weak blacks, the strong whites dominate the industry and the political and economic life of this country. *We must not pit power against weakness;* we must not permit any prejudice of caste or color or class to injure any group of citizens or make difficult their lot in life, or to deny to them one iota of any privilege which, under the laws of our country and of God, should be theirs. For, as I have said at another time, "this is the country which has lifted to the admiration of the world its ideals of absolutely free opportunity, where no man is supposed to be under any limitation except the limitation of his character and his mind; where there is supposed to be no distinction of class, *no distinction of blood,* no distinction of social status, but where men win or lose on their merits. I lay it very close to my conscience as a public man whether we can any longer stand at our doors and welcome all newcomers upon these terms." We truly cannot if we will not live in harmony, peace, and justice with ten millions of our countrymen. We cannot undertake the Americanization of those who come to us from abroad if we cannot Americanize ourselves. We should assume no new problems while our old ones are unsolved; we should attempt to supply happiness to no newcomer until we are satisfied that we can assure it for those already here. And as I have faith in America, so have I faith that we can work out this problem. Hence I shall call together at once in session at Washington the wisest of both races, that we may counsel together to find the way out and upward.

Yesterday, and ever since history began, men were related to one another as individuals, and it is impossible to escape this relationship if we would. We are still our brother's keeper and we must abide with him in affectionate goodwill since we cannot dwell apart. The same flag covers us all; the same love of liberty fills our hearts; the same blood of America pulses through our veins, sanctified but now upon the battlefields of France. I realize that at bottom economic questions as well as racial traits keep us asunder, for—may I not quote from myself again?—"the truth is that we are all caught in a great economic system which is heartless." "Why are we in the presence, why are we at the threshold of a revolution? Because we are profoundly disturbed by the influences we see reigning in the determination of our public life and our public policy. There was a time when America was blithe with self-confidence. She boasted that she, and she alone, knew the processes of popular government; but now she sees her skies overcast; she sees that there are at work forces which she did not dream of in her hopeful youth. Don't you know that some man with eloquent tongue, without conscience, who did not care for the nation, could put this whole country into a flame . . . crying, 'This is the way. Follow me!'—and lead in paths of destruction?" Shall we by a rule of bloodshed and violence, by injustice, by disfranchisement, by patent and shameless discrimination make ripe and ready for such a demagogue ten millions of our fellow-countrymen? I repeat, "We are not the friends of any class against any other class, but our duty is to make classes understand one another. Our part is to lift so high the incomparable standards of the common interest and the common justice that all men with vision, all men with hope, all men with the convictions of America in their hearts, will crowd to that standard, and the new day of achievement may come for the liberty which we love."

Some Astounding Diplomatic Revelations

WE publish in this issue of our International Relations Supplement a most interesting summary of material which the Russian Soviet Government has screened out of the sludge of the old Czarist Foreign Office in Petrograd. Like the secret treaties which were exhibited to the world by the same hands, it is of great assistance in straightening out our knowledge of the inside history manufactured by diplomats in the pre-war period. Russia wanted Constantinople; and it will be remembered that long before the ingenious plan of the "mandatory" had been concocted, the Czarist Government was to receive that prize with the full consent of the Allied Powers—on the usual highly moral pretext. The present document shows up the deal made with Italy over this matter in 1909, which bargains for a "mutually benevolent attitude" towards Italy's interests in Tripoli and towards Russia's interests in the Straits. The Straits were then the property of Turkey, a power friendly to Germany. The Tripoli war broke out in 1911; and we then have Isvolsky writing that Russia "must make sure in one form or another of a declaration from Italy that now that she is carrying into execution the claims on her side . . . she will equally in the future keep her word with us."

Isvolsky was Ambassador to France; and what he has to say about the confiscation of French public opinion through the press is simply priceless. "It is of the highest importance to see to it that we have a good press here . . . As an example of how useful it is to have money to offer the press . . . I know how Tittoni has worked up the leading French papers most thoroughly and with the most open hand. The result is now manifest to all." Here we have the diplomat's estimate of the press, expressed with the most naïve freedom and confidence. Isvolsky, too, was an Allied diplomat—he was no Bernstorff, nor was Tittoni a Dumba. They were brought up, presumably, in the most enlightened traditions of Allied diplomacy, or they could not have held their positions; and this—this candid and cynical proposal for the wholesale corruption of the press—is to us a touching evidence of the quality of these traditions. It affords ground for a profoundly interesting retrospect upon the part played by the American newspapers during the period of the war, prior to our entrance. An extremely clever political satire called "The Re-Conquest of America," was recently printed as a pamphlet and circulated widely. When all allowance is made for its obvious propagandist character, it nevertheless presents facts enough to indicate a distinct possibility of a dangerous English influence upon the American press.

In 1912 Isvolsky reports President Poincaré's assurance of French support in case a conflict with Austria involved the armed intervention of Germany. At the same time (September, 1912) the Russian Foreign Minister, Sazonov, visited England; confidentially informed Sir Edward Grey of the Russian-French naval agreement, whereby the French fleet would keep the Austrian fleet out of the Black Sea; and asked if England would do a like service by keeping the German fleet away from the Baltic coasts. "Without hesitation," Sazonov reports, "Grey replied that if the situation in question occurred, England would do everything to inflict the heaviest blow on German power." This, we repeat, was in September, 1912; and on June 11, 1914, *two months before the war broke out,* the following searching questions were put on the floor of the House of Commons:

> Mr. King asked whether any naval agreement has been recently entered into between Russia and Great Britain; and whether any negotiations, with a view to enable agreement, have recently taken place or are now pending between Russia and Great Britain.
>
> Sir William Byles asked the Secretary of State for Foreign Affairs whether he can make any statement with regard to an alleged new naval agreement between Great Britain and Russia; how far such agreement would affect our relations with Germany; and will he lay papers?
>
> Sir Edward Grey: "The hon. member for North Somerset asked a similar question last year with regard to the military forces, and the hon. member for North Salford asked a similar question also on the same day, as he has done again today. The Prime Minister then replied that if war rose between European Powers, there were no unpublished agreements which would restrict or hamper the freedom of the Government or of Parliament to decide whether or not Great Britain should participate in a war. That answer covers both the questions on the paper. It remains as true today as it was a year ago."

The Prime Minister was Mr. Asquith; and it is interesting to find Sir Edward Grey reported by Isvolsky in April, 1914, as saying that there were elements in the British Government which were "suspicious of relations with Russia," and mentioning Mr. Asquith as among them. But far more interesting is Sir Edward Grey's statement, according to Isvolsky, that there could only be a question of a naval convention between Russia and England, because the disposition of England's land forces was already arranged. This was in April, 1914; and on April 28, 1914,

> Mr. King asked the Secretary for Foreign Affairs whether he is aware that demands have been recently put forward for a further military understanding between the Powers of the Triple Entente with a view to concerted action on the Continent in case of certain eventualities; and whether the policy of this country still remains one of freedom from all obligations to engage in military operations on the Continent.
>
> The Secretary (Sir Edward Grey): "The answer to the first part of the question is in the negative, and as regards the latter part, the position now remains the same as stated by the Prime Minister in answer to a question in this House on the 24th March, 1913."

And on that occasion, March 24, 1913, when two members had asked whether England was under any obligation (and if so, what) to France to send an armed force in certain contingencies to operate in Europe, the Prime Minister, Mr. Asquith, replied:

> As has been repeatedly stated, this country is not under any obligation, not public and known to Parliament, which compels it to take part in any war.

One might go further, if space permitted, but it is unnecessary. The world is under obligations to the Soviet Government for dragging these filthy skeletons out of their closet, by no means because they are an edifying spectacle, but to enforce the lesson intimated by Carlyle, that the only way to reform any Foreign Office, whether in Berlin, London, Washington, or Petrograd, or wherever found, is to put a live coal under it. Gradually, we believe, but very surely, the peoples of the world will begin to inquire into the theory of the State and the nature of political government, in order to find out why the State cannot be served, under the principles of even elementary morality.

COPY

Aug. 15, 1919

My dear Lord Robert:

I am very happy to receive your kind letter of July 12th.

The argument that you make that the Peace League, if reconstituted, will reform the Treaty is the one that we hear most often here and yet we are not convinced by it. I know that Gen. Smuts would not have signed the Treaty if it had not been for his belief that any other course would have helped to starve to death a great many more women and children in the Central Powers because of the blockade. To me the whole Treaty is so bad and the placing of a foreign government over Germany in the form of the Reparation Commission is of such evil import to the future of the world that I am not willing to compromise on the basis that you suggest. I have not that faith in the powers that be who made the Treaty and who will control the League of Nations that is now so undemocratically constituted.

Nor can I agree with you in your belief that the only alternative for the world is the renewal of the old and frightful military burdens. There is another way out, and a very simple way out, and that is disarmament. If the wave of anti-militarism that is sweeping over Sweden, Norway and Denmark, so that it is almost unsafe, as my correspondents there report, for a Swedish officer to show himself in uniform, could sweep over the rest of Europe, it would be the greatest possible blessing. Disarmament would put at end at once to one nation's fear of another and the only reasons why the great nations will not do it is, first, the influence of colonies and over-sea po essions which are held down by force contrary to the will of the resident there like Egypt and India, and secondly the clamor of jingoes and munition makers.

I am not at all sure that it would be disastrous for America to withdraw from the whole mess, but I feel pretty clearly that it would be disastrous if an effort should be made to execute the Treaty as now drawn. What is happening as I now write in Hungary is, I fear, what is to be expected then. If the alternative is that American troops should be used in all these seething and turbulent countries in order to keep the peace and establish the kind of rule that the Big Four -- I think them a wicked Big Four -- drew up at Paris, why, then I for one must be counted out. This will seem to you sad nonsense, I know, but at least it is an honest and sincere opinion held here by growing multitudes.

I have not the slightest doubt that if the facts could be put before the American people as to the inhumanity of the Treaty, they would overwhelmingly oppose it. Meanwhile, the one hope that I have lies in the fine spirit and the desire to rectify the wrongs by men like yourself. If Mr. Wilson, cold and heartless as he is, would only give voice to a pledge of this kind, the situation might change here in his favor.

Most sincerely yours,

To
Lord Robert Cecil
London
England

P.S. Of course, the treaty will be ratified here with some amendments

More Revelations from Russia

WEEK by week, for the health of its soul, the world is called upon to hold its nose and inspect at close range the fetid and septic processes of diplomacy. The Russian Soviet Government continues to publish documents discovered in the Czarist Foreign Office, showing the nefarious connivances of the Allied Powers, up to the outbreak of the war. The Czarist Foreign Minister, Sazonov, visited England in the autumn of 1912 to promote the Russian game of grabbing Constantinople and the Straits, which were held by a country friendly to Germany. He mentioned the arrangements he had made with France about coöperation in the Mediterranean in case Germany saw fit to resist this buccaneering project, and asked whether England would do as much in the North Sea. Sir Edward Grey agreed "without the slightest hesitation," and furthermore communicated to Sazonov the terms of the understanding between France and Great Britain, by which, in event of a war with Germany, England undertook to assist France not only by sea, but by sending an expeditionary force to the Continent.

Sir Edward Grey, it will be remembered, in answer to repeated questions in the House of Commons, denied the existence of any such arrangement to the very last, as also did Mr. Asquith. His last denial was made about two months before the war began. Now, the first written evidence of this understanding appears in a correspondence which was in part read in the House of Commons on August 3, 1914, between Sir Edward and M. Cambon, dated in November, 1912; but Grey's communication to Sazonov antedates that, and therefore shows that it had been in force for some time. The fact is it had existed since about 1906, when Sir Edward took the first steps in the regular diplomatic technique by authorizing the "conversations" between the English and French military and naval experts. The correspondence between Grey and Cambon furnishes one of the finest specimens of the "gentlemen's agreement" that we have ever seen. It is smooth, ingenious, innocuous, reassuring, and may mean anything one wishes it to mean. One notes with interest that the one sentence in it which might perhaps have set the suspicions of Parliament aflame was never read to the House. It is given in full in the White Paper, possibly by oversight, and was published on August 6, 1914, after all the mischief was done.

King George was present at some of the conversations in 1912 between Sazonov and Grey, and Sazonov reports to the Czar that the King "spoke even more decisively than his Minister":

> With obvious excitement His Majesty referred to Germany's efforts to be equal to Great Britain in naval power, and exclaimed that in the event of a conflict the consequences must be disastrous not only to the German navy, but also for Germany's maritime trade, for "we shall sink every single German merchant ship we can get hold of." These last words reflect, apparently, not only the private sentiments of His Majesty, but *also the prevailing English attitude with regard to Germany.* (Italics ours.)

Let us see. Do we not remember some sort of official outcry from Great Britain against the inhumanity of sinking all English ships and some rather downright boggling at the inhumanity of the submarine campaign? It seems to us that we have heard something of the sort from propagandists in this country whose connection with the British Foreign Office was unacknowledged only by polite fiction. If Mr. George or Mr. Balfour had made this threat in a popular speech, one might put it down as the extravagance of an electioneering tub-thumping land-lubber who really did not know the significance of what he was saying. But the King of England is a sailor, a naval officer. If we remember correctly, before his brother's death changed his career, he had risen in his profession to the captaincy of a third-class cruiser. Moreover, he was speaking in the privacy of a diplomatic conversation where extravagance has no place. It surely is a most extraordinary thing that a sailor, a British naval officer, by profession aware of the serious implications of this threat, its weight of moral responsibility, should have made it under such circumstances. We should be happy to see this statement of M. Sazonov cleared up and proved libellous; and how fortunate for this purpose it is that M. Sazonov himself is available. He now represents the Omsk Government, or whatever is left of it, and was at the Peace Conference, hand in hand with the Allied representatives, who presumably still know where he may be had if wanted. We propose that he be confronted with this note and cross-examined on its content, say, by Sir John Simon and Professor Pokrovsky, or by Mr. James M. Beck and M. Chicherin. If the statement could only be established as a libel, not only against the King but against the English people, one could maintain all one's pride in the spotless purity of Allied intentions and go back undisturbed to one's comfortable belief in the unique and unprovoked responsibility of our late enemies; and of course, it is a great advantage to be able to do that.

It is interesting to observe that in April, 1914, there was no question of Belgian neutrality, of which so much was heard later, but Sir Edward Grey showed a clear disposition to "organize common operations of the English land and sea forces not only with France but also with Russia," which was precisely the commitment Russia wanted. Accordingly, Sazonov reported to the Czar the working details of the Russo-British naval arrangement. The British North Sea fleet should take as good care as possible of the German fleet, thus offsetting the superiority of the latter over the Russian fleet, and permitting a possible landing of the Russians in Pomerania. Further, since there was a shortage of transport, England was to send a sufficient number of merchant ships to Russian ports *before hostilities began.* England, according to the propagandists, was taken tremendously by surprise when Germany pounced upon Europe, but the foregoing does not seem to show it.

Quite interesting, too, is the warning sent by the French Government to Russia, after the Sarajevo incident, to do its mobilizing a little less openly. This warning was transmitted to Sazonov by Isvolsky, the busy Russian Ambassador at Paris. The French War Minister, according to Isvolsky, "expressing the same idea, said to Count Ignatiev that we should say that we were ready, in the interest of peace, temporarily to delay our mobilization-measures; which would not hinder us from going on with our military preparations and even strengthening them, while merely refraining from transporting troops in mass." As a candid exhibit of diplomatic morals prevailing between two particularly high-minded Allied Powers, we regard this as extremely hard to beat.

Why cannot honest men take service under a political

government and discharge it according to the principles of elementary honesty? When the public begins to press these questions, then it is on its way to a profitable reconstruction of society; and it is as raising these questions, therefore, and ranging them stark and uncompromising before us, that the documentary revelations of the Russian Soviet Government are chiefly valuable. The conclusion drawn by Pokrovsky is, we believe, inevitable: that responsibility for the inconceivable crime of 1914 "rests not with this imperialism or that, but with imperialism in general, the French, the British, the Russian, no less than the German and the Austrian."

The Treaty Defeated

THERE should be but one regret in connection with the defeat of the Peace Treaty, namely, that it was not rejected squarely upon the ground of its inhumanity, of its betrayal of solemn pledges given by the American Government during the war, and of its flouting of the great program for world reorganization formulated by Woodrow Wilson in the Fourteen Points. Instead, the defeat is largely due to a group of partisans, most of them narrow nationalists with no adequate vision of the true internationalism which the future holds in store for the world. Yet none the less do we rejoice that for the moment the country has been saved from the dishonor of acquiescing in a treaty which embodies so gross a breach of faith with the American dead in France and the American living everywhere who took at full value and held in honor the assertions of the President that we were in the war to safeguard democracy and advance the cause of human liberty.

As early as May 17 last, when the main provisions of the treaty were first made known, *The Nation* demanded that what it termed "The Madness at Versailles" should be defeated. The months which have passed since that time have witnessed a steady awakening of the public conscience. On the other hand, the issue has been befogged in a variety of ways, and the most appealing arguments have been advanced. The world, it was said, would collapse if the treaty were not ratified; we must swallow every one of the admitted iniquities of the treaty in order to set the wheels of industry in motion again; in the League (to be radically reformed, of course, as soon as organized) lay the one hope of the world. Arguments of that sort were best to be resisted, as the event has shown, by stout adherence to principle, and not by a tame yielding of principle at the demand of a present expediency. It was the old dilemma which reformers have so often faced, that, namely, of laying aside principle and conviction and assenting to evil lest a conjured vision of some terrible future prove a greater calamity.

We do not, of course, mean to imply that the change in popular sentiment of which we spoke has been due to a universal weighing of moral values, or that it is yet either comprehensive or complete. There has been far too much apathy, too great popular unfamiliarity with the treaty as a whole, a too easy acceptance of the specious argument that if America joined a league of nations its independence would in some way be jeopardized. We have more than once voiced our regret that the detailed prescriptions of the treaty, as distinct from the League of Nations covenant, were being too little discussed. What was everywhere to be noted, however, was a growing mass distrust, a growing conviction that something was wrong. More and more the plain people in whom Lincoln trusted have come to feel that somehow things went awry in Paris, as well they might when five reactionary chiefs of state undertook to legislate for a suffering world. If there has been no such change in public opinion during the past six months, why have we not witnessed a popular uprising against Mr. Lodge, to whom the press has attributed about every unworthy motive under the sun? Why is it that the elections, even in hide-bound Democratic districts, have shown a remarkable swing to the Republicans? Why is it that political observers admit that, were the Congressional elections to be held today, the Democrats would be defeated?

Yet the deepest gratification over the rejection of the treaty must be tempered with solemnity. Legally, the United States is still at war with Germany. A great war in which the United States bore a leading part is over so far as the principal and associated Powers which have ratified the treaty are concerned, but the United States is not a party to the settlement. A League of Nations of which this country is not a member may, perhaps, be set up. Undoubtedly, too, the action of the Senate will be interpreted in more than one European capital as a victory for Germany, as a lamentable evidence of grave dissension among the Allies, as a repudiation by the United States of the practice, if not the theory, of internationalism, and as an indication of the purpose of America to withdraw from the peace settlement and leave Europe to its fate. There could be only one greater misinterpretation of the Senate action, and that would be for the United States itself to accept such conclusions as sound. It was not because of tenderness to Germany, but because the terms imposed upon Germany were outrageous and impossible, that the treaty lay open to attack. It was not because the Allies could not agree upon a program, but because the Senate refused to allow the United States to become a party to a program which was bad, that ratification was refused. It was not because the American people are opposed to a league of nations, for they are, we believe, overwhelmingly in favor of such a league, but because they refused to be forced or cajoled into an agreement which violated some of their constitutional rights and in which the people had no voice, that the covenant provisions of the treaty have been spurned.

And the United States will not withdraw and leave Europe to its fate. It has indeed reasserted, in decisive tones, its historical opposition to entangling alliances, and it will not, we feel sure, allow its friendliness or its wealth to be used to pull European chestnuts out of the fire. But it must still stand by all its obligations to war-torn Europe and to suffering humanity everywhere, and it must not shirk. Wherever the schemes of reactionary politicians mean the oppression or destruction of any people great or small, there Europe must be assured that the weight of American opposition will be felt. The new states which the war has called into being, which look today with appealing pathos to the United States as the one great Power able and willing to insure them justice, must not look in vain. The huge tasks of economic or financial reconstruction which Europe faces—every day's delay in their prosecution is a menace to civilization itself—must continue to receive American sympathy and substantial help; and there must be no slackening of American benevolence for the poor, the hungry, or the distressed. What the Senate has done is to save the United States from participation in an entangling agreement under which it could have accomplished, in practice, no large or permanent good for the peoples of the world, and to leave it free to serve the world in humane, generous, and unselfish ways. The way is now open, as it has never been open before and as it never could have been open had the treaty been ratified, for the United States to show and the world to learn that "American isolation" means no abandonment of international coöperation, no avoidance of international obligations, and no engrossment in selfish or provincial aims. It is to this great task that the President and the Congress should now address themselves.

Our Chief Danger

"IN your rage for what you call law and order, you are in danger of going to such excesses as to become the most reactionary of countries"—these are the words of a distinguished English visitor who for some time past has been observing men and events in America. His amazement over the futile and arbitrary decision of Judge Anderson has been surpassed only by his feelings after a daily gleaning of the press. Fresh from the toleration of England, he reads of a socialist meeting broken up in Cincinnati by members of the American Legion who defy the Mayor when he rebukes them for their lawless acts. He learns of a police raid upon a "radical" headquarters after which the "premises where this raid was conducted were a wreck. Mirrors, electric light fixtures and a piano were in a state of demolition"—not by reason of acts of the radicals, but because of the deliberate and wanton mischief of those sworn to uphold law and order. Three men were treated by surgeons because of injuries inflicted by the police there and three others who were arrested were indignantly freed by a magistrate because the only charge against them was that one possessed a pocket-knife no bigger than the one the Magistrate himself carried with him.

That our police and prosecuting officials are so lawless, is what alarms this observer from abroad. Next to that comes the confusion of nomenclature which is going on. Thus every "radical" appears an outlaw; every communist is *ipso facto* one who seeks to destroy the government by force; the I. W. W. is merely to be regarded as an enemy of civilization and not as a symptom of a social disease; while any believer in the possibility that Lenin and Trotzky, despite their blood-letting, may have discovered something worth sober study and quiet investigation is held fit only to be deported at once, even if his ancestors came over on the Mayflower. The difficulty is that America has been profoundly ignorant of what has been the commonplace of European politics for decades. In Germany before the war it was only the Kaiser and the Junker who avoided all intercourse with Socialists. The latter were free to teach in the universities and schools and, in later years, to preach their doctrines publicly without governmental interference. What has been true of Germany has been true in even larger measure of France and Italy. But the United States still has only the vaguest conception of what socialism is; it does not differentiate between the types of socialism; it does not even understand the difference between socialists and communists and philosophical anarchists, between the mild and gentle philosopher of the Kropotkin type and the stupid and dangerous bomb-thrower. Unfortunately, the very men who seem to be the most ignorant are either those who are officially entrusted with enforcing our laws or those who, like the members of the American Legion, volunteer to control public opinion and enforce law and order. Thus Mr. Scott Nearing, whose pacifist teachings and abhorrence of violence make him a peculiarly useful person in talking to his fellow-socialists just at this time, is prevented from speaking at Grand Rapids by members of the Legion, whose former brethren-in-arms in Louisville have prevented Fritz Kreisler from giving a concert there because they do not wish any sympathy to be created for Germans or German art. In Reading, Pa., a serious conflict seems to have been averted only because the Socialists chose the better part and abandoned their meeting when menaced by a crowd of several thousand ex-soldiers.

Now the seriousness of this thing, quite aside from the lawlessness in which many of our officials are indulging, is this lumping all liberals and reformers as dangerous "radicals." All movements for genuine political progress may thereby be stopped with the inevitable result which takes place when one ties down a safety valve. But one cannot so much blame the local police officials who have had it drummed into their heads that it is the highest form of patriotism to ride their horses into processions of women and children or to break up the furniture and property of persons whose headquarters they raid, sometimes without warrants, when so many of their superiors have forgotten the fundamentals of American liberty and connive daily at violations of the Constitution and the Attorney General appeals to Congress for a law which is so loosely drawn as seriously to menace the right of public criticism. Well within his rights in asking Congress to define the crime of sedition and to strike at those who propose to accomplish changes by overt acts of violence, or by the threats of such violence, there is grave danger that unless this legislation is carefully revised it will go far beyond the mark, endanger law-abiding reform movements and drive underground where they flourish best the really dangerous movements against organized society which it is the duty of every government to watch and to guard against. It would be a misfortune, indeed, if the prevailing public hysteria, of which many of our public officials are the saddest victims, should make the situation worse rather than better, particularly as there is evidence that sufficient care is not being exercised to exclude from the country those who come here with the deliberate intention of using violence to upset the government.

None the less, if the situation in which the country finds itself today is an extremely dangerous one, it is because those who ought to keep the coolest heads, those entrusted with the carrying on of governmental functions, have become, we insist, among the most lawless. It is a time for everyone to keep cool. The Government of the United States is not going to be overthrown by force this week or next, not this year or next—never, we believe, unless our Mitchell Palmers, Archibald Stevensons, and our local police officials are permitted to establish upon American soil the kind of persecutions which horrified the world when the Czars were on their throne or our working people are led, like the miners, to believe that the Government is unjust to them and even deliberately hostile. Again it is no more just for the American Legion, a minority group, to impose its will upon the public as to what shall be said at meetings, than it would be for the I. W. W. to undertake to control all utterances in the public forum. From whomsoever such a proceeding may come it is un-American and wholly repugnant to the spirit of our institutions. It invites the very excesses against which all Americans protest who believe in evolution or revolution by peaceful methods. As we have so often pointed out, and shall continue to reiterate as long as *The Nation* appears, the only certain way to deal with the extreme advocates of change is primarily to remove those causes of social and political discontent which give the color of plausibility to their alarming agitation. In no other way is a modern state to be truly safeguarded.

Mr. J. Howard Whitehouse
Whitecliff Bay
Bembridge
Isle of Wight

January 19, 1920

My dear Whitehouse:

Your letter of the 14th of December has just arrived, more than a month on the road, and the Ruskin preceded it. I am deeply grateful to you for them both. Are you now the Warden of Bembridge School and are you living at the Isle of Wight? How delightful it sounds! I always thought the Isle one of the goodliest spots of the earth. How much to be envied you are if you are out of the hurly-burly of it all. With us, the fight goes on unceasingly amid the blackest reaction. You would not know the country. If we should just write the full truth about the situation here, it would be the clearest possible picture of the utter moral disaster that war is. They are sentencing men to fifteen years for passing a hand-bill urging a worker's protest against the intervention in Russia, and last week they gave six months to a man for sedition, whose sole offense was that he declared "Lenin to be the brainiest man in Europe", which is, of course, the truth as everybody admitted when I was in Paris and Berlin. The country is absolutely hysterical, if not mad, and all intelligent government has collapsed. But then if you are reading my <u>Nation</u> you are learning that.

As for House, the President has just thrown him over as he has all the rest of his friends who have dared to disagree

with him. I doubt if there ever was such a lonely figure as Wilson now is. Because House dared to differ with him and thinks the Treaty a disaster, he is not even able to obtain acknowledgment of letters he has written to the White House. This I know. When you think what services he rendered to the President, it seems the basest ingratitude. The President is still at that stage of recovery when he can only take two hours' outing in a roll-chair and whether he will get really well remains to be seen. Meanwhile we have the results of his autocratic government. The entire machine is at a standstill and the Attorney-General is ruling the country and trying to make himself the next President by his severity against all radicals and "Reds".

By the way, has not the time come for me to forward to you the papers which I have kept in my vault?

With kindest regards to you and your wife, if it is true that you have acquired one of late -- I hope it is,

Cordially yours,

Constructive Steps After the Treaty

TO *The Nation* the defeat of the Treaty of Versailles is a happy ending to the long and bitter struggle waged in the Senate. We rejoice that the good name of the United States is not to be marred by approval of a document conceived in iniquity and born of imperialistic sin; that the Senate of the United States has refused to approve a document which on its face convicted us of a breach of the national faith which was solemnly pledged when Mr. Wilson secured the armistice by the definite promise of peace upon the basis of the Fourteen Points. Other nations have seen no harm in forgetting their plighted word; fortunately the United States, chiefly through the courage and discernment of a dozen "irreconcilable" Senators, has been spared this disgrace. Yet we are under no illusion as to the motives which have led to this outcome. Only a handful of Senators have been influenced by principle or conscience or the country's honor. Contemptibly small politics have actuated both sides to the controversy; the Democrats have given an example of party servitude at the command of the White House which indeed affords a sad measure of the depths to which Mr. Wilson has lowered his party. As for Mr. Lodge, *The Nation* has no more love for him now than it has had at any time in the nearly forty years of his political career. A correct decision has been taken in the Senate as a result of mixed motives and impulses—among which a narrow nationalism has played a large part.

Nevertheless, the treaty has been beaten. The Senate has vindicated its constitutional right to its own independent opinion—despite the arrogant insistence of the President upon a course which would have entailed an unworthy compromise. But we have not been concerned with personalities in the treaty fight. The matter of chief interest today is the next step. With the treaty beaten and the state of war with Germany still continuing, what is the way out? The reply to this is the constructive policy which *The Nation* has advocated from the beginning. First, there should be an immediate declaration of peace with Germany by a resolution of Congress. If Mr. Wilson declines to approve the resolution, the burden of responsibility will be upon him. It is hardly thinkable that he would dare to veto it; but if he does, obviously he must find at once some *modus vivendi* which will permit the immediate resumption of business relations with the Central Powers, and the freest intercourse between those nations and the United States, unless all other nations are to deprive us of our proper share of trade with them. A continuance of the present anomalous situation, under which we are by a legal fiction at war when most of the world is at peace, is impossible for the year which must elapse before a new House and Senate—assuming a Wilsonian pro-treaty victory—can take their seats. In the two Knox resolutions already before the Senate there is material for a simple, straightforward declaration that the state of war is at an end. Senator France, too, has introduced a joint resolution providing not only for the reëstablishment of peace, but also for "the calling of an international conference to institute a Concert of Nations to advise concerning international coöperation as a substitute for the League of Nations, and for a national referendum." The resolution "authorizes and advises" the President to make an immediate and separate treaty of peace with Germany "without annexations or indemnities."

These are the first constructive steps that ought to be taken. The calling of an international conference to revise the Treaty of Versailles is the next. Everyone ought now to see that that treaty is going to pieces of its own weight. The Allies have already receded from their demands for the Kaiser and for the German war-criminals. The Supreme Council has awakened—too late, perhaps—to a realization of the fact that the amount of the indemnities to be paid by Germany must be definitely fixed, and that loans and raw material must be supplied to that country. More than that, largely through the publication of Mr. Keynes's book, it is now realized that the reparations sections of the treaty are so badly drawn that the experts themselves cannot come to an agreement as to what they mean. The revolutionary outbreaks in Germany, from both the Left and the Right, are the direct fruit of the treaty and of the foolish spirit of revenge of those who framed it, and at the same time are the clearest proof that the treaty can no more bring peace to Central Europe than it has brought it to Fiume or to Poland. The treaty must be revised at an early date, if Europe is not to collapse; while if communism triumphs in Germany, or that mentally, morally, and physically exhausted country disintegrates in civil war, many of the provisions of the treaty, such as the reduction of the German army and payments and reparations now due, will be obviously impossible of fulfilment. What the opponents of the treaty have been saying as to its destructive rather than constructive character is borne out by the news from beyond the Rhine. A new arrangement must be made for the sake of all concerned unless everything which was fought for is to be lost; and this time the basis of settlement must be the noble principles outlined by Mr. Wilson.

As for the League of Nations, with the defeat of the treaty the way now lies open for the organization, in due course, of a genuinely democratic league. We have been unmoved by the argument that the treaty should be ratified and its revision left to the League of Nations, because the conditions of revision are such as to give no guarantee that adequate revision could take place. We have opposed the League of Nations because it is a League controlled by a star chamber, composed largely of the very men who perpetrated the madness of Versailles. There is good reason for believing that, within a year or two, many of the men who have most bitterly fought the present League of Nations in the Senate will be working for the formation of a really democratic league, which will include Russia, Austria, Hungary, Mexico, and all the new nations. To work for such a democratic league is the final constructive recommendation which we have to offer. The rejection of the treaty by the Senate, and the refusal of the United States to enter the League at this time, put the United States in the strongest possible position to demand alterations in it as the condition of our future entry. The most prominent English Liberals and the most ardent English supporters of the treaty, like Sir Robert Cecil, have declared that without the United States the League is unworkable. So be it. Let the League be remodelled so as to give assurance that it is to become a democratic, peaceful world-organization, and not the device for the despotic and imperial control of human affairs by four nations which we are now witnessing, and the United States will join.

Trafficking With the Enemy in 1917

THE NATION publishes in its International Relations Section this week the Prince Sixtus documents, revealing the history of the secret negotiations carried on in 1917 between the Emperor of Austria and the President of France through the intermediary of a Bourbon prince, an officer in the Belgian army, who in the middle of the war traveled freely to and fro between Paris, London, and Vienna.

Prince Sixtus, and Prince Xavier, who seems to have accompanied his brother chiefly to give an air of family business to the travels, left the Belgian front in January, 1917, and met their mother and one of their sisters—Empress Zita of Austria was another sister—in Switzerland. Their mother informed them that the Emperor Charles desired to open secret peace negotiations with the Allies. The two princes returned to Paris, dined with the secretary-general of the French Foreign Office, and then returned to Switzerland, bearing an outline of Allied terms. There they met the personal envoy of the Austrian emperor, Count Erdoedy, who presented a memorandum prepared by Count Czernin, with addenda in the Emperor's handwriting. On their return to Paris, the French President received them at his home, thanked the princes for communicating with the enemy, and again outlined the Allied terms. This time the princes did not stop in Switzerland but slipped through to Vienna, meeting their brother-in-law, the Emperor, at his castle at Laxenburg. Again they returned to Paris; again they were received by the French President, and by the British Prime Minister, Lloyd George, as well. They made a second trip to Vienna, interviewed the Emperor once more, and returning, had long conversations with the French President and Prime Minister, and with Mr. Lloyd George, who took them to see King George. Then the princes dropped diplomacy and returned to the Belgian front.

The negotiations failed. Austria was ready to make a separate peace, supporting France's claims on the left bank of the Rhine, giving Albania to Serbia and the Trentino to Italy, but peace did not come for another year and a half, and another two million youth were shot down on the battlefields. They died, not, as they believed, to make a world safe for democracy or to defend their native soil, but because the old men who governed Europe on both sides of the trenches were cold and callous, without warm-blooded consciousness of the human significance of their hesitations and bargainings. The young Austrian Emperor and the Bourbon Prince, despite their primary interest in the maintenance of the monarchical principle, appear favorably in contrast to the timid and hesitant Count Czernin, the casual Lloyd George, the grasping Sonnino, Jules Cambon—whose "only fear" was that the people behind the lines would tire of the war and insist upon ending it—and that sinister old man, Alexander Ribot, who in the course of his five terms as Prime Minister and his eleven terms in various cabinet positions, has possibly done more to injure France than any Frenchman since Napoleon.

Poincaré and Ribot insisted upon the swollen Alsace-Lorraine of 1814 and the neutralization of the entire left bank of the Rhine. The Austrian Emperor was willing to support their claim then, and France, what with the Saar valley regime, has it now—much good that it has done her! The Italian claims were the real stumbling-block. Poincaré cunningly meditated that Italy had promised to declare war on April 26 and that she had not declared war until May 23, and that therefore France was not held by her bond to Italy. Ribot felt honor-bound to the letter of France's extravagant pledges to Italy and Rumania, no matter how many men might die meanwhile. They all offered parts of Germany which they had not won as compensation for the sacrifices asked of Austria. Lloyd George gloated that with America's aid the war could go on indefinitely. Sonnino wanted to appear before the Italian Parliament "with full hands," while Cadorna and the Italian King, fearful of revolution, were negotiating with the enemy unknown to their Prime Minister. Whenever they had no better excuse, they all blamed it on the people. Sonnino feared revolution if he did not annex the east coast of the Adriatic; Cadorna feared revolution if he fought on, and was content with the Trentino; Jules Cambon, later one of the five French delegates at the Peace Conference, agreed with Prince Sixtus that it was impolitic to dethrone Constantine of Greece because they would then lose the chance to repay themselves and their friends with slices of Greece—but, he said, public opinion demanded Constantine's head. As if the French people, every day receiving the little blue messages that meant a brother or a husband killed in battle, cared a fig about a street riot in the Piræus and a king in Athens! And when the Russian revolution came, these infinitely little men actually put their heads together to save the Czar —"France's oldest friend"—and dreaded the revision of their peace terms made necessary when Russia relinquished her claim to Constantinople.

What a dirty mess of sordid bargaining it all was! There was not even honor among thieves. Lloyd George faithfully promised not to tell his fellow ministers about the negotiations; Poincaré told only his prime ministers; none of them trusted the Italians enough to do more than hint that they had a channel for conversations, while it apparently did not even occur to them to impart the news to President Wilson. Meanwhile one of the Entente Powers was secretly dealing with Bulgaria; the Italians were promising to support Turkey at Constantinople; Lloyd George had an agent in Switzerland dealing with Count Mensdorff of Austria; Prince Lvov was sending envoys across the lines begging for peace; and, before summer came, Ribot had his own agent, Count Armand, in Switzerland. Meanwhile in all the Allied countries statesmen were professing that they would never shake hands with an enemy, and denouncing the "defeatists" and the socialists who wanted to meet fellow-socialists in neutral countries. "Communication with the enemy," "intelligence with the enemy," sent common men to jail. Poincaré and Lloyd George, behind the scenes, calmly discussed the advisability of a "horizontal alliance" with Austria.

The Sixtus documents are fragmentary in places, and they are only one chapter in the long story of dishonor. Slowly but surely the facts leak out, sabotaging the memory of wartime idealism as the diplomats sabotaged that idealism during the war. But memory is short. There is no evidence of a change of heart among diplomats, and the old men still plot death and starvation for the generations to come.

The Allies' New War

ON the Russian-Polish front Polish soldiers dressed in American uniforms are beating back into Russia the armies of the Bolsheviki. American aviators, in spite of "unfavorable weather," are dropping bombs on the Russians. Ukrainian soldiers under General Petlura are fighting side by side with Polish troops, exchanging their birthright of "the rich oil district of Eastern Galicia," now Polish territory, for the assistance of the Poles in freeing the remainder of their land from the Bolsheviki. A new war is on.

The French—for the sake of Ukrainian wheat—have from the start been supporting the movement of the Poles; and the British, who were talking peace to the Poles only a few weeks ago, are now reported in devious negotiations to secure the cooperation of Finnish, Hungarian, Rumanian, and Serbian troops. Meanwhile the Germans, for the sake of internal peace and Allied favor, are said to be offering their reactionary military organizations, such as the Erhardt marine brigade, for the establishment of peace and democracy in Russia. America, too, is not missing. Not only are our aviators acting as volunteers in the service of Allied imperialism, not only are our uniforms clothing Polish troops on Russian soil, but our money is to be devoted to the same high cause. Indeed, where else could the new European war be financed but in the United States? The British budget carried no more than sufficient provision for Great Britain's private wars in the East to which she is plainly committed. The French are solvent only by grace of an all-obscuring patriotic camouflage. The Poles are insolvent by common consent. It would appear that a new war might be a hazardous undertaking for the Allies, whose people are in no mood to bow under heavier burdens. But America, apparently, is again ready to step in and save Europe from the danger of peace. A Warsaw dispatch of May 4, tells us that "eleven billion paper marks are to be printed shortly by the Polish Government. . . . The issue will be made possible by the loan which is to be floated in both American and domestic markets in the course of the next few weeks." What security will be offered the supporters of the loan? The promises of an insolvent Polish Government? Poland has only one security to offer—the spoils of a victory not yet won, the tribute to be exacted from a still undefeated enemy.

If the British Government should succeed in turning this campaign into a world war, it might indeed be that "last war" of which we have talked or at which we have sneered. The world cannot stand perpetual devastation; Russia would indeed be forced into ruin, but Europe would go down into ruin with her. The chances are, however, that things will not go so far. The armies of Russia have retreated before, and every retreat has led the armies of their enemies into untenable positions, cut off from their lines of communication, out of reach of their supplies.

Even now, when things look darkest for Russia in the press of its enemies, certain important factors need to be considered. Russia is in practical control of the Caucasus. Georgia and Azerbaijan have refused to fight the Soviets; Baku and the oil lands are in the hands of the Bolsheviki; the Armenians appear to be making overtures in the direction of Moscow. The British navy is bombarding with little effect the towns of the Crimea. Russia has a government and a policy to hold it together and an army fighting to defend its own land. The Allies have, instead of a government, the Supreme Council, which with a sort of malicious senility creates and recognizes nations which do not exist, establishes boundaries on paper, and renders decisions regarding accomplished facts. Their policy is a mixture of insane vengeance and cold-blooded greed. Their armies are bands of mercenaries who would have to starve if they did not fight. As Walter Duranty, writing in the New York *Times* recently, observed: "Poland has a big army which she does not dare to demobilize as there is no work to give to ex-soldiers. Although the maintenance of this comparatively huge force is straining the country's feeble finances to the breaking point, General Pilsudski evidently considers it wiser to keep the army busy against the Reds than either to disband it or [let it] eat its head off in idleness." The troops might proceed to Moscow, says Mr. Duranty; "the chief objection to their doing so is that it is not quite clear what they would do when they got there . . . and that every Russian, whether anti-Bolshevist or not, would be likely to oppose a Polish invasion to the utmost." In the light of recent history it is to be hoped that General Pilsudski is not lying awake on his army cot thinking up occupations to provide for his troops in Moscow.

Some day a history of Allied policy toward Russia will be written. It can be compiled largely from the questions in the British House of Commons and the answers or evasions of the British Ministers. It is a history that will make Bolshevists smile cynically, but will make honest men of milder faiths sick at heart. Beginning with the adoption of a policy of intervention—to be carried out without interfering in any way with the internal affairs of Russia—continuing through a war of invasion and aggression against Russia carried on with no declaration of war on the part of any government, it has come to a period of diplomatic bad faith which has been more disheartening than the period of open warfare. First Prinkipo, then the Nansen mission, then negotiations with the Cooperatives, then the official decision to open trade with Soviet Russia, then the scheme for a League of Nations mission proposed while Allied dollars were driving Polish soldiers into Russia—one after another these plans, conceived in fear rather than justice, were killed by a frenzied hope in some new military venture. Each time liberals supposed that the Allies must see the idiocy if not the brutality of their tactics. Each time liberals were to learn that there was no folly too great for governments to commit in the hope of gain.

A dispatch from Washington in the New York *Call* of May 13 states that within the previous week a memorandum calling for a renewal of trade with Russia was presented to President Wilson. The memorandum was said to have been signed by Secretary Colby and all the heads of the State Department bureaus, including the head of the Foreign Trade Bureau and of the Russian Division. The President has so far failed to act upon the memorandum. How long is the United States to connive in the throttling of the Russian people? How long are the leading men of the country going to approve by their silence our part in the shady diplomacy of the Allied Governments?

The Menace of Another War

EUROPE hangs wearily and almost indifferent on the brink of another war. The callous statesmen who govern today do nothing to stop the threatened catastrophe. The outlook is gloomier than at any time since the failure of the Peace Conference sent the world's hopes crashing; but it is not without hope, and the hope lies in the Bolsheviki. Those astonishing statesmen who have refused to hold non-Russian territory, who have canceled the old Russian blood bonds held against China and Turkey, and who have made peace on more than generous terms with the little Baltic states, are today the single liberal force in European diplomacy.

The Bolsheviki replied to Mr. Lloyd George's crafty suggestion of a general peace conference at London by a lengthy note which said in effect: "Mind your own business and we'll mind ours." They pointed out that they had already made peace with Esthonia, Lithuania, and Georgia, and that they are negotiating peace with Latvia and Finland; and they recalled the anything but peaceful attitude of the Allies in warning the Esthonians, when Russo-Esthonian negotiations began, that if they made peace with the Bolsheviki it would be at their own risk. But times have changed, and so has the attitude of the Allies. The Red armies have driven the Poles back some two hundred and fifty miles—a greater distance than that which separates Paris and Cologne—and the British Government has developed a sudden interest in peacemaking. When the Poles invaded the Ukraine two months ago, Soviet Russia addressed a wireless message to the Governments of Great Britain, France, Italy, and the United States, announcing a desire for peace. The Polish legions were then advancing victoriously, and the note went unanswered. Today, the Russian armies are approaching the tentative eastern frontier of Poland drawn by the Supreme Council last autumn; Mr. Lloyd George cries out against the menace, and hastily suggests that everybody get together in London and talk things over. The Russians reply quite properly that they will be glad to treat with the Poles directly. They even say that they will give the Poles a better frontier than the Allies drew some months ago, and their acts in Esthonia and Lithuania give credence to their words. Their correct attitude makes more disgraceful the reported action of the Washington authorities in offering aid to the Poles.

It is little wonder that the Russians show small confidence in the good faith of the Allied peace proposal. The past and present actions of the British and the French give them every reason to suspect a trap. They have not forgotten that Lord Curzon induced them to cease operations against General Wrangel in South Russia pending peace negotiations, and that General Wrangel seized the occasion to open a new attack; nor are they unaware that five hundred British soldiers of various ranks were with General Wrangel's army. They are not ignorant of the three thousand Frenchmen, including nine generals, who are attached in various capacities to the Polish army; nor have they forgotten the British and French support given to Kolchak and Denikin and Judenich, nor the intervention at Archangel. Small wonder indeed that they refused to accept such Powers as disinterested mediators.

Indications are that the French Government will do everything in its power to sabotage the peace negotiations and prolong the war on Russia. Mr. Lloyd George, cannier and more cautious, works with both hands. With one hand he gestures to the Poles to open negotiations with the Russians; with the other he starts his war machinery into action in case peace fails. Military attaches are hurried from Berlin to Warsaw; military missions start from Paris; it is said that Foch may repeat his rumored visit of two months ago. Mr. Lloyd George knows well that British troops will not take kindly to another continental expedition, and reserves his promises to munitions and money; France, more generous—this France which cannot afford to pay the interest on its debt to America—is apparently ready to lavish munitions and men and money. We are not told upon what conditions this aid is promised; whether the opening of peace negotiations will put an end to the eastward current of war materials, or whether it is only the Russians who will be expected to cease military operations. If the Russians should, as it is reported they will, insist upon Polish disarmament as the first condition of peace, the Allied premiers fresh from Spa will find it hard to protest such a dose of their own medicine.

If this European crisis is safely passed, we shall have to thank the moderation of the Bolsheviki for that mercy, for there is nothing in present Allied policy to help the cause of peace. The Bolsheviki make stern but generous peace proposals and the Poles should accept them. For the Pilsudski-Grabski-Witos group it is indeed a Kaiser's choice. That aggregation of statesmen is tarred with the smirch of its imperialist pretenses. For it to abandon its territorial claims, as in any reasonable peace it must, would be to suffer a humiliation than which abdication could be no greater.

An even more serious question is the effect of the Bolshevik advance upon Germany. Colonel House believes that if Poland succumbs to Russian invasion, Germany too will turn bolshevist. He thinks that the Germans would hail the Russians as deliverers. It is doubtless true that the dictated peace terms have driven many conservative Germans in their despair and bitterness to such a pass; it is also true that large masses of radical German workingmen are heart and soul Bolsheviki. But the present German Government is of a different cast; it is dominated by men of the Stinnes type—millionaire captains of industry who believe that they can and will restore the old industrial Germany. The majority Social Democrats and the Center parties would stand with Stinnes against bolshevism; and if Soviet Russia drives its military frontier to the eastern boundaries of Germany, the reaction may be such as to force Germany to throw itself upon the Allies. Stranger things have happened. Red-hating has replaced Hun-hating in the circles that today dominate Allied policy, and if the Allies have to choose between Russians and Germans, they will doubtless choose the latter. Mr. Lloyd George, in the same speech in which he pictured the plight of Poland and the necessity of giving aid, spoke in the most cordial terms of Fehrenbach and Simons, Germany's new pilots. A German-Ally combination against Soviet Russia is not beyond history's capacity for irony. If French diplomacy succeeds in stiffening the Poles into refusal of the Soviet conditions, we may look for another Spa Conference concerned less with disarmament than with the price of military assistance.

Our Russian Policy

THE Wilson-Colby statement on Russian policy does nothing to promote the cause of world-peace and humanity. On the contrary, it serves to perpetuate strife on earth and ill-will among men. It helps to continue starvation of women and children. It may or may not materially affect the Russian government. For three years the Soviets have been engaged in beating off the combined military and economic pressure of the greater part of the world. The unctuous verbiage of the note to Baron Avezzana is therefore not likely to add materially to the burden of Lenin, who will probably smile, shrug his shoulders and dismiss it with some such word as "futile." But an American cannot dismiss such a statement of the policy of his own Government with the same nonchalance. It can affect and it does hurt America. It is another one of those revelations of ignorance on the part of our statesmen which make American diplomacy a laughing-stock, comparable only to the candid admissions of Messrs. Wilson and Lansing that they had never heard of the secret treaties until they went to Europe.

Entirely apart from the question of de facto recognition of a de facto state, the note is objectionable because it is an insult to France and England, which have recognized the independent Baltic states of Esthonia, Latvia, and Lithuania, and to the ten million people of those three countries, which have strugglingly built up democratic governments, which have indeed bought surplus supplies from our own War Department, been aided by our Red Cross, traded with American merchants, and communicated with the United States under their own postage stamps. Now Mr. Wilson suddenly tells them that he cannot recognize them as "separate nations independent of Russia" until he can secure the consent of Russia! All of these states have signed treaties of peace with Soviet Russia, and on terms very favorable to themselves, and live at peace with Soviet Russia as well as with France and England, which acted as godparents when they were first established; but Mr. Wilson, four thousand miles away, cannot recognize them "without the consent of Russia." This is an ostrich policy, a refusal to face facts, a policy of stubborn ignorance—and, more than that, it is out of harmony with Mr. Wilson's own previous policy. If he justifies his recognition of Poland because a recognized Russian Government, that of Kerensky, had already acknowledged Poland's independence, he cannot say the same for Finland, whose recognition he made conditional only upon the election of a constituent assembly. All three of these Baltic states long ago elected constituent assemblies.

Perhaps even more objectionable is Mr. Wilson's attempt to dictate to the Russians what form of government they may have. Lenin might well reply with a paraphrase of Mr. Wilson's own words:

> Upon numerous occasions the responsible spokesmen of the American Government have declared that it is their understanding that the very existence of the parliamentary form of government in America depends, and must continue to depend, upon the occurrence of revolutions in all soviet states, including, Russia, which will overthrow and destroy their governments and set up parliamentary rule in their stead. They have made it quite plain that they intend to use every means, including of course, diplomatic agencies, to promote such revolutionary movements in other countries. . . . We cannot recognize, hold official relations with, or give friendly reception to the agents of a government which is determined and bound to conspire against our institutions.

Lenin might reply to Wilson in such Wilsonian words, and his contentions would be borne out by Mr. Wilson's own note; but Lenin would not be silly enough to utter such bosh. He knows that such propaganda is merely a form of self-defense, and that Mr. Wilson, or his successors, will abandon it when peace comes and the ordinary processes of commercial exchange are under way. As a matter of fact, our government, prior to Mr. Wilson's regime, did not attempt to dictate to other nations the form of government which they must adopt, nor have other governments been accustomed to such intrusive habits. We have recognized governments where they existed and functioned, whether we liked their ways or not. We did not refuse to recognize the present king of Serbia, although his accession to the throne involved the midnight murder of the previous king, the queen, two of the queen's brothers, two members of the cabinet, and fifty other members of the court. And we were right, despite our horror at the murders. If the people of Serbia stood for Peter Karageorgevich, it was for us to do our business with the government which actually governed Serbia. And now when the Bolsheviki, despite all the months of newspaper rumors of imminent downfall, have governed Russia for nearly three years, overwhelmingly defeating an unexampled series of attacks upon them, it is for us to do business with them and to stop the moral posing which has already done us and Russia so much harm. Mr. Wilson's attitude is mere gesture; it is phraseology in a vacuum; his note is as unrealistic as if it had been issued from an Eskimo island.

One sentence in Mr. Wilson's statement might have a definite meaning outside the shadow-world of notes: he says that this Government will employ "all available means" to render Poland's political independence and territorial integrity effectual. What he understands by "all available means" is hard to say. Perhaps he means nothing at all; he has already lent money and sent supplies to the Polish army, and beyond that lies only the dispatch of troops. If Mr. Wilson should attempt to send American youth to fight for Poland after Poland's recent antics, he might learn something of the changed temper of the American people.

Yet none of the three great western Powers has acquitted itself in the Polish crisis with any marked grace or skill. Mr. Lloyd George's opportunism, devoid of principle though it be, serves England better than M. Millerand serves France or Mr. Wilson America. The French recognition of General Wrangel is consistent. The French Government has from the beginning done everything within its power to hinder any peace or understanding with the Soviet Government, and has aided any man or group of men who would fight it and acknowledge the old Russian debt to France. Recovery of the money which France lent to the Czar has avowedly been the controlling influence in French policy throughout. That the policy is blind, and hurts France, matters not. It may cost France men and money, but in all probability the Soviet Government will crush Wrangel as it has crushed Kolchak, Denikin, Judenich, and the Poles, aided as all of them have been by France or England.

The New War Drive

THE drive for a new war is on. Let no American who believes in peace or loves humanity underestimate the intention or the strength of the forces that have been loosed by the Wilson-Colby note to the Italian Ambassador, announcing the Administration's purpose not merely to harass but, if possible, to destroy the Russian Government. The note was precisely what a powerful element of sordid, selfish, and relentless interests in this country had been waiting for, and a pack of editors, special writers, and opinion-makers have already begun to bay noisily for American participation in a new international holocaust. We mentioned last week the assertion of a military critic that our war with Germany would be fruitless unless followed by another against Russia. Now comes Dr. Frank Crane, who ought to know better, and declares in regard to the Russian Government: "Sooner or later, unless it falls to pieces from its own rottenness, it must be faced and fought by the civilized nations. We can keep out of this row no more than we could keep out of the war with Germany."

Now it may be said that this is mere rhetoric; that the public is disillusioned in regard to European conditions and will not give, either of money or men, for another burnt offering on the altar of big business, special privilege, and world imperialism. But, after our experience in 1917-1918 with a censorship and a gigantic government-directed propaganda, nobody knows what can be done. For three years the seed has been planted through systematic suppression and misrepresentation of the facts in regard to the most interesting political experiment of modern times. The cartoonists have already distorted our late allies into hairy cave men and apes, and hundreds of editors are ready to prove them ten-fold more dangerous and inhuman than the Germans. The last was a holy war; the next would be a holy of holies.

Nor must it be forgotten that we are still in a state of war and Mr. Wilson can of his own volition revive the old machinery in so far as funds permit. "To the full extent of the constitutional power confided in the Executive every measure that can be legally taken will be adopted to render effectual the position of this country," said Secretary Colby to a Polish-American delegation. But Mr. Wilson did not let his "constitutional power" limit him unduly in his last war, and there is no reason to believe that he would in another. "The attitude of this Government can only be the attitude of its people," Mr. Colby continued, "and you, as American citizens, have the power to determine the trend and the weight of American public opinion." Perhaps so, now; but public opinion is easily superseded by government-made thought and national hysteria.

While there is still time, therefore, let every American **who loves his country and humanity make his opposition as plain to Mr. Wilson as British labor has made its attitude to Mr. Lloyd George, which action Mr. Christensen, the Farmer-Labor Party's candidate for President, has well described as "the foundation for a real World League of Labor by setting the glorious example of labor's power to veto war." Let us refuse to make or move a pound of war supplies or give a cent of money. Let us rather fill the jails from Portland, Maine, to Portland, Oregon, until their doors burst from overcrowding. For concurrence in Mr. Wilson's latest madness would not merely loose the dogs of war; it would unchain the jackals that would devour mankind.**

Japan wants three things in Siberia. It wants to control the Chinese Eastern Railway and as much as possible of the Trans-Siberian Railway. It wants to carve out "buffer states" which will enable it to exploit the body of Siberia while pretending that its soul is free. It wants to spill its excess population into a fertile and productive land. The first two aims, in common with all similar policies of other nations, are dangerous to the peace of the world and destructive of the integrity and independence of the Russian people of Siberia. The third is wholly justified. If they go unaccompanied by the threat of political control, there is no reason why the crowded masses of Japan should not find in the wide spaces of southern Siberia a suitable dwelling-place. Russia has shown no tendency to follow the American and Australian example of intolerance and exclusion. But Japan, seeking an outlet for its hard-pressed population, has no excuse for sending to Siberia the troops and guns and office-holders and carpet-baggers that make up the present invasion. The protests of the Department of State, animated not at all by the sufferings of the Siberians, may yet serve a useful purpose if they prevent the Japanese Government from following its emigrants to the mainland. Unfortunately, the Department of State has little chance of success. The Japanese Government knows what it wants in Siberia; and it will not be distracted by any Wilsonian admonitions against the absorption of a bit of Siberian territory here and a buffer state or two there.

The Japanese Government will, with complete assurance, pursue its Siberian policy until it is stopped; and if it is stopped it will be not by Woodrow Wilson but by the force that is at work at present upsetting the calculations of the map-makers of western Europe—the Soviet Government of Russia.

Mr. Lloyd George's policy, on the contrary, deals with Europe as a condition rather than as a theory. He does not like the Bolsheviki and says so; yet he admits that the Poles made an unjustified attack upon the Russians, and he does not attempt to duck the too obvious parallel between Soviet terms to Poland and Entente terms to Germany. He says in effect that England will not interfere unless the Russians attempt to enforce severer terms upon the Poles than the Entente did upon the Germans. And when he rose to speak in the House of Commons, he was probably already aware that the Soviet terms to Poland—rapid demobilization of the Polish army to 60,000 men, cessation of foreign military support, surrender of surplus munitions and arms, a commercial outlet to the Baltic, and distribution of Polish land to Polish soldiers—were very much more generous and humane terms than those which the Entente imposed upon Germany. For the benefit of his Tory majority in the House of Commons, of course, he had to do a certain amount of ranting against the Bolsheviki. We cannot praise Mr. Lloyd George's principles, for if he has any he has concealed or violated them as often as he has upheld them, but we are glad that there is one Entente statesman with sufficient political adaptability to face the fact that the Bolsheviki are the Russian government today, and must be dealt with.

"Pitiless Publicity" for Haiti

A FLOOD of statements, counter-statements and misstatements, admissions, confusions, and denials, regarding facts and policies in Haiti and Santo Domingo poured out of Washington last week. *The Nation* rejoices that the course of our Government in those republics will at last be forced to face the test of public knowledge and public opinion, and is proud that it led the way in exposing the facts. It was Senator Harding's repetition of charges first made in *The Nation* which unsealed the lips of Washington officials, but the long statements issued by Secretary of State Colby have been specific replies to charges which have been made exclusively in Mr. Herbert J. Seligmann's and Mr. James Weldon Johnson's articles in *The Nation.*

After all this outpouring from Washington, and the hasty defense and outcry against "radical criticism" by Administration newspapers, the case against the course of the United States in Haiti and Santo Domingo remains untouched. We intervened, *The Nation* believes, on quite inadequate grounds, although as to that opinions may honestly differ; having intervened, we relentlessly extended the scope of our authority in a brutal and unjustifiable manner, dissolving the Haitian Parliament at the points of American bayonets, forcing unwilling acceptance of an overbearing treaty, removing the entire Government of Santo Domingo and setting up an arbitrary Government by military fiat, killing thousands of opponents of our regime (three thousand in Haiti) as "bandits," establishing a strict censorship and so avoiding the test of public knowledge and opinion, and forcing upon the unhappy little republics financial agreements favoring certain American banks. Some of the worst abuses have been remedied, though the wounds remain; the *corvée,* or slave labor, which we revived in Haiti, has now been abolished; indiscriminate shooting and torture have been lessened; but the incompetent administrative methods of the Americans continue to be a luxury which the island cannot afford, the financial control lodged in American hands is still used, contrary to the treaty, to force measures in favor of the National City Bank of New York City, and the absolute domination of military rule to the exclusion of local civilian self-government persists in Santo Domingo. "Self-determination" and "rights of small nations" as used by American statesmen are still tragic jests in the Caribbean.

Secretary Colby and Secretary Daniels have both taken a hand in replying to *The Nation's* charges. On September 18 Secretary Daniels quoted Senator Harding's charge that "thousands of native Haitians have been killed by American marines." He called it an "unjust reflection upon the brave and patriotic members of the Marine Corps on duty in Haiti." But he did not and he cannot honestly deny that our marines have killed three thousand Haitians. On the same day Mr. Colby said:

> The American control in Haiti and Santo Domingo is not Administration control, but was undertaken at the invitation of those peoples and with public opinion of the United States and the better opinion of the two republics in favor of it. A solemn treaty was entered into between the two governments providing for the use of American naval forces to stamp down banditry there.

Mr. Colby is in error; American control of neither republic was undertaken at the invitation of the people. The attitude of Haiti is sufficiently shown in the pathetic proclamation issued by President Dartiguenave on September 4, 1915 (reprinted in *The Nation* for August 28, 1920), when American forces seized the Haitian customs-houses, two weeks before what Mr. Colby calls "a solemn treaty"—which Haiti, before that military occupation, had refused to accept—was forced upon Haiti. Military dictatorship and military censorship failed to give Dominicans in Santo Domingo so much as a chance to protest.

Long stories emanating from the State Department appeared in the newspapers on September 20. They informed us that Admiral H. S. Knapp had been sent to Haiti to investigate and adjust the difficulties between the National City Bank of New York City, controlling the National Bank of Haiti, and the Haitian Government and other commercial and financial interests, and that Major-General J. A. Lejeune had been in Haiti two weeks preparing a report on the American force of occupation for Secretary Daniels. Now General Lejeune, Commandant of the Marine Corps, naturally sees things through Marine Corps eyes; in a letter which *The Nation* printed in its issue of July 24 he virtually confirmed criticisms of our course in the nominally independent republic of Haiti and dismissed them with the sweeping remark that "as in all work in countries like Haiti mistakes are bound to be made." Admiral Knapp was in command of the American forces which seized the Government of the Republic of Santo Domingo in December, 1916; he signed the extraordinary series of "executive orders" transferring the various Dominican cabinet positions from Dominican citizens to officers of the United States Marine Corps, dissolving the Dominican Congress, and suppressing the institutions of popular government. In judging his fitness for his new task it is worth recalling "Executive Order No. 42 of the Military Government of Santo Domingo" issued March 17, 1917, and signed by this same H. S. Knapp, then "Captain, U.S.N., Commander, Cruiser Force, United States Atlantic Fleet, Commanding Forces in Occupation in Santo Domingo." It reads:

> The International Banking Corporation of New York City being about to succeed to the business of the bank conducted in Santo Domingo City by Mr. Santiago Michelena, which is the present appointed depositary of funds for the Dominican Government, it is hereby ordered and decreed:
>
> 1. That the branch in Santo Domingo of the International Banking Corporation of New York City is hereby appointed depositary of funds of the Dominican Republic on and after April 1, 1917.
>
> 2. The officer who, under the Military Government, is administering the affairs of the Department of Hacienda y Comercio of the Dominican Republic, is hereby authorized to execute any necessary contract in conjunction with the duly authorized representatives of the International Banking Corporation of New York City, in order to establish the respective rights, obligations, and duties of the contracting parties.
>
> 3. The transfer of the Dominican Republic funds from Mr. Santiago Michelena to the International Banking Corporation of New York City shall become effective April 1, 1917, previous to which date the contracts authorized under the second paragraph of this order shall be executed.

We copy the order verbatim from the official gazette of the Dominican Republic for March 21, 1917. In the issue for March 28 we find an "Agreement between the Military Government of the Dominican Republic, represented by Paymaster I. T. Hagner, U.S.N., the officer administering the affairs of the Department of Hacienda y Comercio, hereinafter called the Government, and the International Banking Corporation," whereby the Government, payment on whose debts had been suspended by one of Captain Knapp's Executive Orders, made the Government's debt to Mr. Michelena, *which the International Banking Corporation was about to take over*, a preferred debt over all other indebtedness, with interest at 9 per cent. We also find a "Contract" between the same parties, whereby the Government agrees to deposit all its revenues with the Corporation, receiving 2¾ per cent interest, less ¾ per cent to be paid to the Corporation as compensation for service as depositary.

The International Banking Corporation is affiliated with the National City Bank; Knapp is the man who is now selected by our State and Navy departments to investigate charges of improper favoritism to the National City Bank in Haiti!

September 21 brought another statement from the State Department. It was in part a justification of the original intervention in Haiti, repeating the high purposes announced at that time. Continuing, it mentioned that disorder in Haiti in 1915 "resulted in the landing of French troops in Port-au-Prince" even before American marines were landed, and said that further aggression was feared. French troops did land. Mr. Colby might, however, have gone further and mentioned the number of French troops landed: eight men were sent ashore to guard the Legation —not a serious menace to the Monroe Doctrine! The second part of the State Department's statement was in answer to Mr. Johnson's documented article in *The Nation* for September 11: Government Of, By, and For the National City Bank. This statement declared that:

> No assistance or support has been given the National City Bank in Haiti other than that which would be extended to any first-class American bank in any foreign country. Far from encouraging the National City Bank in obtaining monopolistic privileges, the Department has, in so far as it has had an opportunity to exert an influence, used it toward preventing the National City Bank from enjoying monopolistic privileges.

At the same time it was announced that the State Department approved the action of John McIlhenny, American Financial Adviser to Haiti, in withholding the salary of the President of Haiti and other cabinet officials, and stated that such action was taken to compel fulfilment of Haiti's treaty obligations.

What assistance or support the State Department stands ready to extend to any first-class American bank abroad, it is, of course, impossible for *The Nation* to say. *The Nation* did, however, charge, and it repeats the charge, which is supported by the protest of almost every important firm doing business in Haiti, with the exception of the National City Bank, that our State Department instructed Mr. McIlhenny to insist that the Haitian Government approve "a modification of the bank contract agreed upon by the [U. S.] Department of State and the National City Bank" and agree to a new charter for the National Bank of Haiti; that after the Haitian Government had reluctantly consented to sign, a new clause favoring the National City Bank was surreptitiously added to the agreement, unknown to the Haitian Government; that the Financial Adviser, to force the signature of the modified agreement, stopped payment of the salaries of the President of Haiti and of his cabinet ministers—not, as the State Department says, to force fulfilment of a treaty, but in violation of the treaty and to force acceptance of a clause giving to the National City Bank what the business men called "a sort of monopoly in the foreign money market." These charges, and the data substantiating them, are matters of record; *The Nation* printed official documents supporting them in its issue of September 11; they are not met and cannot be downed by vague generalities and implied denials.

Newspaper comment on the issues raised by Mr. Colby's various defenses has divided on sharp party lines. This is a pity; the issues have nothing to do with party politics. The New York *Times* is probably quite right in its cynical defense that a Republican Administration would have committed the same crimes. The crime remains; the Administration has suppressed free government in Haiti and Santo Domingo. A black stain must be removed from the American scutcheon, the American people must be made fully aware what is being done in their name, and the nation restored to a position where it can once more speak of freedom and liberty, of self-determination and small nations, without giving cause for cynical smiles in Europe and violent charges of hypocrisy throughout Latin America. Congress at its coming session must be prompt to investigate, and must tolerate no official white-washing.

The Defeat of Wilsonism

TO the fable of Phaethon must one turn for any analogy to the fate which has overtaken Woodrow Wilson—the one fell from the heavens after his wild ride in the chariot of the Sun-God; the other has fallen from the highest pinnacle of human hopes and aspirations which any modern has attained. Rejected now by millions of his countrymen and countrywomen, he is at once the most tragic and the most guilty figure on the globe. Less than two years ago he sailed for Paris bearing with him a charter of liberty for the race; upon him were centered the faith and all the hopes of the plain people of the whole world. Alas, no one could measure the disappointment and the heartbreak with which those who had knelt before him, actually and spiritually, witnessed the revelation that the new Moses was of such common clay as to abandon the tablets upon which he had himself inscribed another Messianic code for the government of tribes and nations, that he had stooped to scramble in the market-place of the victors. At once the hero fell from his pedestal; months ago Europe lost the last vestige of interest in Woodrow Wilson. Today we have the final touch in the crushing repudiation of the man and his works by his own people, and the tragedy becomes the grimmer, the more pitiful, when one considers the physical suffering of the man, for whom every humane heart can hold only pity. History may yet judge that there was a pathological reason for the disaster of Paris.

For the philosopher and moralist there is material in this overwhelming tragedy for themes without end in the centuries to come. Terrible as it is, it is also profoundly stimulating, for, paradoxically, it is both disheartening and full of encouragement to struggling humanity. If Woodrow Wilson fell as fell the angels, let us rejoice that his true measure was so quickly taken, that so correct a judgment has been passed upon him. There is no room here for lasting discouragement and no time for vain regrets. The unerring instinct of the plain American people has, in a situation of extraordinary complexity, administered a rebuke so stunning as to carry its warning for generations to those who espouse liberalism and then betray it; to that most dangerous of politicians, the pseudo-liberal, who stops at no compromise, who in the supreme hour when liberalism is put to the test takes on the manner and thought of the reactionary; to the politician who, voicing the loftiest of ideals, finds himself unable to give these ideals reality and substance when the final opportunity is at hand. That in order to administer this rebuke the American people felt itself compelled to the choice of the candidate of a group who mean still less well for the Republic is the dark side to the shield. *The Nation* would have had the people destroy both the old parties; but one at a time has been the popular decision in the absence of a real and vigorous liberal party and liberal leadership. There are times when the fire seems entirely preferable to the frying pan—if one does not dare to try for the hearth beyond. In this instance it was perhaps inevitable to set the unequivocal seal of disapproval upon the man who has betrayed liberalism in its own home; who was too proud to fight and then fought unnecessarily; who was for peace without victory and then, five months later, was for complete and crushing defeat of the enemy; who by faithlessness to the ideals he helped to set up has done inestimable harm by destroying men's faith in the attainment of the supreme objectives he outlined, and in the possibility of those ideals themselves. We are fortunate, indeed, that the verdict leaves no room for a Burleson or a Palmer to claim that their baseness has met with popular approval.

In place of moral instability and moral insincerity, reaction in all its stark nakedness is eminently preferable. The prime need is to doff sheep's clothing, to have men show clearly under which flag they fight. One can deal frankly with a Leonard Wood or a Harding because with them there is no danger of any illusions, or misunderstandings, or deceptions. One knows where they are to be found, however skilfully balanced their phrases, however apt their opportunism. At least they do not use the language of idealism to conceal their thoughts; they do not address their appeals to the stars when they are bent only upon things earthy, when they are frankly materialistic and frankly for the old order of special privilege and profit. The enemy will be in front and not in the rear ranks. Discouragement? Not for any real liberal. The horizon has cleared. Crass reaction we shall indubitably have to face, and repression and suppression as well. We shall see greater materialism, more control of the processes of government and of our social life by that invisible government which Woodrow Wilson entered office in 1912 to destroy and has left more firmly in the saddle than ever. But if the "New Freedom" is still in the offing, the louder the call to liberals to gird on their spiritual armor. The bigger and the clearer the fight, the better the struggle, the sooner will ideals be clarified and the lines be drawn.

As for Mr. Harding, nothing that he or his party or his campaign speeches have done has affected the result. His election is the gift of Mr. Wilson, and of no one else. The League of Nations debate has appealed only to the intellectuals, and so Mr. Harding's choice was fore-ordained months ago. He receives the greatest office in the world with the slightest record of achievement. Upon his lap has been placed this prize through no effort of his own, first by act of a small group of professional politicians at Chicago, and secondly, by the vote of the people given with no enthusiasm and often with the profoundest shame that such a choice should be laid before the American electorate. His negative campaign, his unimpressive personality, his inability to arouse popular interest in himself or his cause—all these bode ill for the success of his administration. For him we have few congratulations and much pity. The great economic forces which are shaping the destinies of the world are likely to have no mercy for him, since he neither understands them nor apprehends their existence. The champion of an outworn order, he can no more oppose the slow sweep of peaceable economic revolt than could King Canute the tide. Moreover, Mr. Harding has not been able to make it clear what position he will take toward the one great achievement of his party, which is the defeat of the Treaty. But of this we may be sure: He will labor in a fiercer light of publicity than has beaten upon any man of late years, and against the system that he represents will stand united the battalions of all the liberals and the progressives and the reformers and those supporters of the League of Nations who have really believed that it promises a better international order.

A Constructive World League Program

SPEAKING for the first time after his election as President, Senator Harding declared at Marion that the Versailles League of Nations is "now deceased" and reiterated his statement that when President he intends to "ask for nations associated together in justice, but it will be an association which surrenders nothing of American freedom." He has also reasserted his intention to invite, as soon as he returns to Marion, a group of prominent Americans to advise him as to the best plan. This is excellent policy provided that his visitors are not a narrow partisan body but represent all the points of view of those who will have none of the Versailles Treaty yet realize full well that some kind of an international association is urgently demanded. There could be no greater honor for the United States than to take the lead in building a really democratic peace league, free from all the defects of the present League —defects whose existence even its most ardent supporters admit—for no more important service could be rendered to a world in chaos.

As a contribution to the discussion already raging in the daily press as to the future world organization, *The Nation* submits its own constructive suggestions, hitherto made from time to time, for a policy to take the place of that advocated by President Wilson. Our program is as follows:

1. The immediate calling of the Third Hague Conference by President Harding as soon as he takes office.
2. The inclusion within the call to the Conference of all

nations, large and small, victors and vanquished alike.

3. The reference to the Conference of the task of codifying existing international law and of creating additional statutes, which should include:
   (a) The outlawing of war by the Conference, as demanded by Senator Harding during his campaign, by the abolition of war as a means of settling international disputes.
   (b) The creation of a genuine world court by empowering the Hague Court to pass upon all disputes relating to purely international matters, with power to summon all parties to a suit or controversy into court (obligatory jurisdiction).
   (c) The abolition of the doctrines of military necessity and retaliation.
   (d) Universal and immediate disarmament by all nations as the result of the above steps.
   (e) The remaking of the Treaty of Versailles and the treaties with the minor Central Powers so that absolute justice may be done.
   (f) The nationalization in each country (as promised by Lloyd George for England during the war) of every munition and weapon-making industry, including the building of warships of every kind.

The first duty of The Hague should be to *outlaw war* in accordance with the demand first made by Senator Knox during the anti-treaty fight in the Senate and by Senator Harding during the campaign. They are both absolutely right. The use of war as a means for the settlement of international disputes must be abolished, and this is the time to do it. Of all the defects which damned the Versailles League, the worst is the fact that it is based upon force and that it throughout contemplates the keeping up of armies and navies. As Senator Knox so well put it in his public statement of October 23:

> The proposed covenant, instead of abolishing war, actually sanctions, breeds, and commands it. Moreover, it absolutely requires that every future war shall be a potential world war and that we shall be an active participant in every such war. . . . Hold in mind that we are to give up the power to say when we shall have war, when peace, what shall our army number, how many vessels of war we shall have, how, when, and where, and under what conditions shall our army and navy be used. . . .

Senator Knox is a practical man who has been Secretary of State. He did not hesitate to demand "a true League of Nations under which controversies may be judicially determined and the curse of war outlawed and made an international crime." When a man of this type takes this position, the proposal to outlaw war cannot be set down as a mere dream of pacifist theorists or of unpractical idealists.

But Senator Knox has had other suggestions to make in line with the position of *The Nation.* These are that all annexations, exactions, or seizures, by force or duress, shall from now on be null and void. This great step forward is quite within the power of the Hague Conference, but beyond all this *The Nation* urges the establishment of a real world court. We have recently [September 25] pointed out how utterly faulty is the organization of the new world court to be established under the existing League of Nations. The Hague Tribunal, as at present constituted, similarly cannot function in a way to preserve the peace of the world. It should be reconstructed so that it may settle all disputes relating to purely international matters; it should sit as a judicial body with jurisdiction over all parties to a dispute upon the petition of any party to the dispute or of any nation which has entered into the agreement to make this Tribunal the real international court of the world as supreme in its field as our Supreme Court within our boundaries.

The point is, of course, that if war is outlawed such doctrines as those of military necessity, retaliation, and reprisal, now the excuse for many a wanton aggression and the starting-point of many an imperialistic land-grabbing venture, would be done away with. The Hague Conference would, therefore, have the vital duty of preparing the codification of the existing international law. But there is nothing more important for the Conference to do if it meets at The Hague than to demand immediate and universal disarmament. We have no doubt whatever that that would be one of the first planks in Senator Knox's platform and foremost among proposals which Mr. Harding may make. Unless disarmament comes soon, the financial ruin of Europe is inevitable. The assertion of French imperialists that the French army shall, League or no League, never be allowed hereafter to fall below a permanent peace strength of 700,000 men—a force larger by nearly 100,000 men than the Kaiser's army in 1913—shows what determined efforts must be made to do away with the whole business. Disarmament is, moreover, absolutely necessary to the welfare of the United States, for, according to official figures of the United States Government, 92.8 per cent of our enormous expenditure of $5,686,005,606 in the fiscal year ending June 30, 1920, or $5,279,621,263, went to payments for past and future wars—only 7.2 per cent for all the great creative expenditures of Government and the cost of the civilian machinery! No one can read these figures and not realize that disarmament is at once the most practical and constructive suggestion which can be made at this time. If President-elect Harding will but take the lead in these matters in accordance with his pledge, and deliberately call the nations in association to outlaw war, the Republican Party will have much to pride itself upon and the country still greater grounds for thankfulness for the "decease" of the Versailles League. If the United States takes the lead, the other nations must follow suit. There is daily proof that they will be glad to do so.

Free Trade and Peace

THE conference which framed the Treaty of Versailles has been compared, not without justice, with the predatory group that composed the Congress of Vienna in 1815. But with all its shortcomings the Vienna gathering took at least one step in advance of anything attempted by its modern imitator. Without having held before it fourteen points alleged to be idealistic or any moral principle whatever, it nevertheless took steps to remove from one part of the world certain economic barriers to trade. To the failure of the Big Four at Versailles to take similar action may be justly attributed much of the warfare that has followed the "war to end war," especially the war between imperialist Poland and its Russian, Ukrainian, and Lithuanian neighbors, and in a large measure the misery and chaos which reigns in what was once the Empire of Austria-

Hungary.

When the Vienna Congress sanctioned the renewed partition of Poland it added thereto a provision for absolute free trade between the politically separated sections. There were to be no custom houses between the Russian, Austrian, or Prussian parts of Poland. The use of rivers and canals within the boundaries of 1772 was made equally free to all inhabitants of the old kingdom. Thus Polish industry on all sides of international boundaries was equally free to obtain coal from the rich deposits in the southwest. The salt mines under Austrian domination could supply the wants of Russian and Prussian subjects. Iron ore mined in Russian territory could be transported free of duty to Prussia and Austria. Zinc produced under Prussian rule could be taken to Austria and Russia. Free trade in Poland had naturally the same results as interstate free trade in the United States. Industry flourished. There came a wonderful growth of cities and towns comparable only to similar growth in the United States. From a small town Lodz grew into a city of several hundred thousand inhabitants. Warsaw also increased in importance as a manufacturing center. There were metal factories and furniture factories, lime and cement works, and many other kinds of industries.

Although the Russian Government proved a cruel, tyrannical master in many respects, it was liberal to Poland in so far as encouragement to trade and manufactures was concerned. In 1859 the free trade area was extended from Russian Poland, or the "Kingdom of Poland" as it was then still called, throughout the whole region from the Prussian boundary to the Bering Sea. But Russia's protected interests objected to this. Lodz became at once so formidable a rival of Moscow that petitions went to the Czar complaining of the direful results of Polish competition. Whatever may be said of these complaints they were free at least from hypocritical pleas in behalf of the workingman. They did not charge the Poles with maintaining pauper labor. Not that Polish wages were actually high but rather the reverse. But low as Polish wages were they were higher than Russian wages; long as were the hours of Polish labor they were not so long as Russian hours. In Lodz the average working day was 11 hours, for which wages ranged from 30 to 50 cents. But in Moscow wages were less and the working day ranged from 14 to 16 hours. Judged by modern standards, of course, there was little that was wonderful in the better conditions in Poland. And these conditions had results impairing the value of free trade. With the growth of industrial centers came increase of rents to such an extent that it was, and may still be, a frequent thing for a dozen persons to live in one room. But that is another story. Just as better paid American labor today is able to meet poorly paid foreign labor on its own ground in successful competition, so the products of Polish labor met successfully the competition of more poorly paid Russian labor in purely Russian territory. This came to an end in 1869 when the shadowy "Kingdom of Poland" was abolished and become the Vistula provinces of the Russian Empire. Closer political union was then forced upon the Polish people but economic union was more restricted. Freedom of commerce was still allowed with the Ukraine but was cut off from the rest of the Empire. Finally in 1882 this remnant of freedom was also withdrawn. It does not appear that the protective system thus established had any of the results which the American Protective Tariff League holds must always follow.

Prussia and Austria did not wait so long as Russia to violate the trade provisions of the Vienna treaty. In 1861 a Polish representative in the Prussian Landtag introduced a resolution calling attention to disregard of treaty obligations demanding restoration of free trade. The plea met but good-natured contempt. What was this treaty but a "scrap of paper"? Again in 1879 the Polish delegation in the Imperial Reichstag demanded of Bismarck the commercial rights guaranteed their country at Vienna. Of course the attempt failed. Bismarck, with the political and economic ideals of a Taft, McKinley, or Penrose, could not be expected to do otherwise than refuse an appeal for free trade. Protectionism was allowed to have its way, breeding international friction, bickering, and hatred, and finally doing its share in bringing about the cataclysm of 1914. Whether the Polish and Russian representatives, who met to arrange terms of peace, have taken free trade into consideration has not been reported. Whether Poles and Lithuanians will take this matter up when they finally meet is also doubtful. But the incorporation of such a provision is essential to permanent peace. The history of Poland makes this fact so clear that it is hard to see how the delegates from that country can avoid taking the initiative in its reestablishment. Those to whom bolshevism is a bugbear will find in a policy of economic justice a reliable barrier against its spread, and free trade is an essential part of such a policy.

War, Waste, and Business

BIT by bit facts are emerging which show that our participation in the European War was attended with the same orgy of graft and incompetence that has been present in other conflicts. Many persons had hoped that the higher ideals professed would lead to a better morality in public service, and available information up to the close of the war seemed to bear this out. But that was due, it now appears, partly to the shortness of hostilities and partly to the fact that the social and legal code which ruled during the war made it impossible for anybody to utter a word of criticism without being branded by his associates as pro-German or prosecuted by the Government for sedition. The revelations of folly in aircraft construction provided the first considerable jar to our self-complacence. These have been followed by evidence of outrageous profiteering on the part of many of our most patriotic business enterprises; by charges that the War Department has held food and other supplies out of the domestic market so as not to lower prices to the disadvantage of business interests, and has scrapped or sold for a song a vast amount of material abroad; and now by testimony before a Congressional investigating committee which shows the United States Shipping Board's activities to have been redundant with incompetence, waste, and graft and its personnel to have embraced an extraordinary number of incompetents, scoundrels, and plain unvarnished thieves.

It is only fair to allow for a generous amount of ignorance and extravagance in connection with our shipping program. The job was at least second in importance, if not superior, to that of the War Department, but, whereas the army had a body of trained officers and an organization to begin with, the Shipping Board had to create out of thin air an industry which had become virtually extinct in

America—that of building and operating deepwater vessels. The need of new tonnage was vital; speed was a prime consideration. How to find or train technically the men to create and manage this new industry was a stupendous problem. But it is clear that the Shipping Board's activities have suffered not merely by haste and lack of knowledge but by the presence of scores of officers and other employees who have loafed in well-paid jobs, winked at graft in plain sight, or deliberately lined their pockets with plunder. And the worst of it is that this not only took place during the pressure of the war but has been going on ever since.

According to investigators for the Walsh Committee, heavy and inexcusable losses were sustained by contracts for shipyards so far inland that canals would have to be dredged in order to launch ships. One company was awarded a contract for ten vessels, but after six months the only visible construction was a tool house. The National Shipbuilding Company of Savannah established a yard a mile from the place where it had represented itself to have a going plant, and the Government had to supply money to dredge a marsh before operations could be started. The yard did not complete a ship. The case is now in the hands of the United States District Attorney, but it is declared that every effort is being made to shelve the prosecution. This same yard, which cost $285,000 and contained materials valued at $245,000, was recently sold for $39,000, although the Shipping Board had a standing offer of $65,000 for it without the materials. One thrifty contractor is cited who bought lifeboats from the salvage service of the Navy for $10 and sold them to the Shipping Board for $110. In the assignment of vessels for operation, well-established companies have found it impossible to get vessels, while inexperienced and irresponsible organizations known as "war babies" have obtained allocations. Among other companies successful in getting ships was one headed by a dealer in theatrical costumes. Gratuities and bribes have been common and political influence has been prominent. The financial affairs of the Shipping Board are in such condition that 4,000 employees, costing $8,000,000 annually, are still trying to straighten out the tangle. If we were not dulled to emotional appeals we should all hang our heads with shame at this exposure.

The Shipping Board scandals are an indictment of the methods of present-day American business. For the Shipping Board was above everything else the contribution to the war of our best business minds. It was organized and directed by Edward N. Hurley, Charles M. Schwab, and others of our most eminent captains of industry. American business has loved to regard itself as the most efficient in the world. It is true that in the direction of standardization and quantity production we are leaders, but extravagance and carelessness made it impossible for us adequately to compete in the international market—the acid test of industrial supremacy—until the European War gave us a unique and abnormal advantage. We are now facing a period of business deflation. If it is met honestly and intelligently, we shall benefit by it. If, instead, our business men try to save their faces and their jobs by reducing the wages of their workers and making organized labor a scapegoat, they will invite and deserve disaster. To begin at the bottom and work up is a good way in certain circumstances; but what our modern business system needs is an overhauling that will begin at the top and work down.

The Conscientious Objectors Set Free

NOW that H. G. Wells has given us newer and clearer outlines of history than we had before, we may even expect some day a complete and truthful account of American participation in the Great War. Here is a task for our generation of historians! Such a work would include volumes on "The Army in France" (not omitting a chapter on "Hard-Boiled" Smith); on "Graft and Waste in Washington," just now in the stage of original research; and above all on "The Destruction of Spiritual Values, or How Democracy Was Lost at Home." This volume will be long in preparation, for its story is not yet fully told. One chapter, however, has just been completed by Secretary Baker's announcement that all conscientious objectors have now been released.

Hisses and groans will meet the announcement. Their name will be legion. But in belatedly releasing the men who refused to kill for conscience' sake, Mr. Baker has been consistent. Well-intentioned throughout, unwilling to heed the baying of the journalistic wolf-pack or the clamor of the club-chair chauvinists, he meant well, but, like an illustrious predecessor, he meant well feebly. There have been many acid tests of American purpose in the war, but none more clearly such than our treatment of the handful of Americans who were not too proud but were too brave to fight, who unflinchingly faced and suffered hatred, ostracism, imprisonment, physical torture, and death for their faith. These four thousand, out of the four million called to arms, who resisted every form of pressure to make them fight, were possessed of a courage beyond the understanding of the mob. The coward would have backed down. The slacker would have done what indeed thousands of his brand, like the notorious Bergdolls, did—evaded registration or even more safely joined in the scramble for places in non-combatant services within the army itself. No, the true conscientious objectors to whom we refer, were not dodgers. They were above all things facers. And as time goes on and the already receding tide of hysteria and hate ebbs, there will come, along with the realization of the ghastly futility and madness of war, a clearer recognition of the pioneer courage and heroic martyrdom of these men. And while they suffered greatly, their sacrifice is not in vain.

To those familiar with war psychology, it is not surprising that the least belligerent, the least endangered, and the supposedly freest country involved should have traveled the furthest in the severity of its punishment of all forms of dissent. In other countries conscientious objectors were imprisoned, but their terms were short and obviously intended for restraint only during the period of hostilities. They were released soon after the armistice. But in free America not only was the imprisonment needlessly prolonged for over two years—longer than the terms given the few notorious enemy conspirators found guilty of plotting murder against our civilian population—but the incarceration was accompanied by unspeakable atrocities. A number died in prison, victims of beating and deliberate starvation. Others were tied up by the hands for days at a time, drenched in icy water, and compelled to remain in cells at freezing temperatures. A number of these died from pneumonia. Nor did the indignities cease with death. The wife of one religious objector, member of a sect professedly opposed to all forms of violence, coming to claim his body found it clad in the uniform which he had given his life to avoid donning. Instances of that kind were innumerable. The iron cage at Alcatraz, especially constructed for the torture of the conscientious objectors, an instrument recalling the medieval Iron Maiden, is the symbol of America's treatment of them and entitled as such to a place in our historical museum as a warning to coming generations. It is important that they should have this warning. The Civil Liberties Union which has done such splendid work in agitating for the mitigation of the suffering and the ultimate release of the objectors would be eminently fitted to assume this responsibility, and it is pleasing to record in this connection that a book on the subject by Mr. Norman Thomas is in preparation. It will belong in every public library, and in the event of other impending hostilities it should be chained to its shelf.

Other chapters in the history of our destruction of democracy at home are not yet complete. Other groups of men are still behind prison bars, victims of our ruthlessness. There are the soldiers, many of them boys, many of them volunteers, who, thrust from the unrestraint of American farm or city life into the rigid discipline of army and navy, were guilty of various infractions of discipline. Court-martialed for "disrespect" to a minor commissioned officer often totally unworthy to command, some are still serving the ferocious sentences imposed to convince the world that we were at war. Still others, equally unprepared for our sudden conversion to Prussianism, are similarly paying the penalty for some careless dissent from the orthodox view of the causes, purposes, or conduct of the war to make the world safe for democracy.

Another group are the I. W. W., about whom less truth is known by the American public than about the Solomon Islanders. Without a solitary act of violence proved against them, without a single change in the expression of their long-professed economic doctrines, these men still face the better part of a lifetime in jail. And there is Debs and a few others like him who would not be stampeded, who refused to hate, who obeyed the biblical injunction to "resist not evil," who like Martin Luther stood by their principles and "could do no other."

Well, the war has been over for two years and more. Who now dares assert that it was not the greatest failure in history? Who will deny that by it civilization is immeasurably set back? And who can assert that those who, before the shattering and revealing experiences of the last five years, saw clearly and so did move, were not at least as true patriots and humanitarians as the other millions and better prophets?

Christmas is at hand and the spirit of peace and goodwill is again supposed to radiate over the earth—at least over the Christian parts of the earth—so deeply devastated and now so sorely in need of healing. May we not hope that this spirit will express itself in a sweeping and complete amnesty to those in this country who are still in prison because they fought the good fight as they saw it, and kept the faith?

Preachers and the League

ANYONE returning to the United States after a long absence might be much impressed by the enthusiasm of clergymen and social uplifters for the League of Nations. Surely, he would argue, there is a genuine moral issue involved when such men and women declare themselves so vigorously for a League of Peace. Whether on further consideration he would share the enthusiasm which at first so impressed him is open to doubt; he certainly would not if his attention were called to a circumstance that has had too little attention. It is this: The clergymen and other moral leaders who have diligently exhorted their fellow countrymen on the subject of the League of Nations as the way to righteousness and peace have been for the most part silent on the obvious and indisputable moral issues of our time. They have said nothing about our ruthless imperialism in Haiti, nothing about the administration's private wars in Russia, its aid to Poland, its part in the blockade of Russia which still is costing the lives of unnumbered thousands of men and women and little children. They have been dumb before the sacking of Irish towns, pogroms in Belfast, and the death of hunger strikers; yet these things imperil the peace of the whole world. They have seen civil liberties ridden over rough shod by Secretaries Burleson and Palmer and they have held their peace. They have not denounced the continued imprisonment of conscientious objectors and political heretics. They have been silent in face of the institution of a Czaristic system of espionage and repression by Federal, State, and municipal officials. These facts are indisputable. They are matters of record. Why should our clergymen show so profound a concern for the League of Nations which at best is a debatable issue when they make no public or concerted efforts to right open and palpable wrongs?

One ventures to guess that the answer lies in the realm of psychology. Those who now valiantly support the League of Nations are the same who were the great protagonists of the war on moral grounds. In season and out of season they proclaimed a holy war to end war, to save the soul of America, make the world safe for democracy, and establish the rights of the weak and the oppressed. They, following the lead of that greatest preacher of them all, Woodrow Wilson, sought to make the World War, which was essentially a contest between rival imperialisms, a crusade greater than Peter the Hermit ever preached. Behold the result: Misery, hunger, unrest, hate, disillusionment. Never was nationalist, race, or class feeling higher. Armaments increase. New economic rivalries already divide the Allies. No sane man dreams that any one of the fundamental "moral" aims of the war has already been achieved. Literally the only vestige of justification for the protagonists of the holy war is the League of Nations. Few men are clear sighted enough or possess the moral courage requisite for the admission that all their hopes were vain and that we must take a new start to build a lasting peace. It is not merely the opinion of others that preachers and moral leaders have to fear, but the loss of their own self-confidence. To admit the falsity of their hopes or the failure of their methods would be a crushing blow to the inner

citadel of their being. The League of Nations *must* be the ark of their salvation else they are utterly shipwrecked in stormy seas. They believe because every instinct of their being demands that they believe—and without question.

One thing that makes this process easier for churchmen is that they are trained in accepting verbal solutions without too nice regard for realities. The whole process of theological readjustment which has enabled modern men to adapt themselves more or less comfortably to medieval creeds—valuable as in many ways it has been—has its obverse side. It makes for a clever casuistry rather than for downright mental integrity. It has trained men in the art of seeing how much one can say without saying too much. On the ethical side the fault of theological education is even more pronounced. Preachers are trained to speak phrases with regard to righteousness and justice which they do not interpret in concrete terms. No man can make these theological and ethical compromises in the pulpit without in time becoming himself far more expert in handling phrases than realities. He solves the old difficulty of putting new wine in old bottles by using not wine at all but only grape juice. And he himself doesn't know the difference.

But back of this faulty education lies something deeper. The main business of the liberal is to find an easy way to solve problems. He will do anything for peace except remove the economic causes of war. No one who studies the way economic interest, playing upon mob psychology, produces war, can believe in any cure for war that does not involve spiritual and economic revolution, the abolition of privilege, and the end of the whole psychology of domination. War is a cancer in the body politic. The League of Nations is a mere poultice for it. This fact your liberal finds it hard to face. For much is at stake. It is comfortable, safe, and morally edifying, for the preacher to support the League of Nations. But to denounce economic imperialism, to champion Haiti and Russia, to defend the prisoner of conscience, and the right of free speech—that's another matter. It is not very comfortable and in many cases far from safe. Of course, all this is not explicit in the minds of the excellent people who champion the League. Nevertheless, it remains true that the explanation of the concern of ministers, ecclesiastical bodies, and miscellaneous liberals for the League of Nations and their indifference to far more obvious moral issues can only be found in an analysis of the motives and interests which far more than reason sway the acts of men.

Disarm!

AT last sanity in things military and naval seems to be returning. After four years of preparedness mania and war orgy the country is awakening to the inescapable fact that the huge sums it is spending for wars past and future are bringing it to the very verge of bankruptcy. Those numerous American business men who have been about driven to despair in the effort to pay the fourth instalment of the income tax, on December 15, and the thousands who have been utterly unable to pay it, are reduced to these extremities chiefly because of the demands of the army and navy budgets. If all the reforms urged by President-elect Harding for the modernizing of the Government's business machinery were carried out, if efficiency by some magic were to be established over night in all the departments at Washington and every Government employee gave one dollar's worth of service for every dollar received, the net saving would be hardly noticeable in the budget which Secretary Houston calls for, of four billions. For the simple truth stands out that according to an official publication more than 92 per cent of the Government's expenditures for the fiscal year ending June 30 to July 1, 1920, went for pensions, the care of the disabled, the army and the navy.

So there is no worth-while cut possible save in the army and navy expenditures. But what does the Wilson administration advocate? Why, Secretary Daniels declares that it will be "a crime" if we do not go on building the greatest navy in the world provided we remain out of the League of Nations. If we enter it, the present fleet of 1,000 vessels must be kept up, he insists. On Wednesday of last week he denounced Senator Borah's proposal for a joint conference of Great Britain, the United States, and Japan to cut all warship building by fifty per cent. This the Secretary of the Navy declared to be little short of treason. On Thursday, however, he recalled the fact that in 1916 Congress passed the Hensley Resolution, appropriating the money necessary to send nine American delegates to an international conference to discuss the limitation of fleets. But the latest winner of the Nobel Peace Prize and his Cabinet have forgotten all about this; they have gone on threatening America with the burden of the greatest navy in the world as a club to drive the country into the League, while at the same time declaring that membership in that League will in no wise decrease our existing intolerable waste of treasure and of natural resources in coal and oil for a fleet which today constitutes the greatest menace to our friendly relations with Japan and Great Britain. Let no one deny this fact. The threat of the American fleet to England has been the theme of a violent daily discussion in the English press for the last ten days and also in Parliamentary circles. The British Cabinet, it is authoritatively stated, will plan its building program according to ours. At present it is building only six destroyers to our sixty-one.

Historically, England has for three decades past held that her fleet must equal the joint fleets of the two nearest rival Powers. As long as the present forces control her public life her policy of the greatest navy in the world will prevail despite the fact that England, too, is in a perilous financial position and that no one knows what kind of a workable budget Lloyd George will be able to produce in March next. A race between the United States and Great Britain as to which shall have the greatest navy on the globe can only have one outcome—war between the two countries, precisely as the naval rivalry between Germany and Great Britain would have led to war even if Austria had not attacked Serbia. Lord Fisher officially urged in peace time an attack upon the German fleet without warning and without a declaration of war. Some future Lord Fisher or some future American admiral will advocate a similar move on New York or London. As for Japan, Viscount Ishii's solemn statement at Geneva that it is useless to ask Japan to reduce her military or naval forces while the United States increases hers, tells the story. Almost daily the cables report the use the Japanese jingoes are making of the threat of our fleet to little Japan. There are, of course, other notes. Thus the friendly Osaka *Mainichi Shimbun* urges the abolition of the fleets of both countries and the application of President Monroe's Canadian policy by both nations, the United States and Japan.

Fortunately, the sound sober sense of America is beginning to manifest itself. Every thinking man knows that in keeping up a fleet we are preparing to fight Japan and Great Britain, for there are no other warships left in the world—France's navy need not be considered. Major-General Bliss sees that the first step must be taken by giving up our army. Senator Walsh wants us to confer on disarmament with the League of Nations. Senator Borah urges the practical step of an immediate conference between the three naval rivals for a vacation in warship building—we wish he had dared to come out for a complete scrapping of all fleets. In Congress, there is the growing determination to cut the army estimates to pieces. Congressman Mondell, the Republican leader, is naturally outraged that two years after the war to end war Congress is asked by Secretary Baker, an erstwhile charter member of the League to Limit Armaments, to grant to the War Department $615,000,000 *in excess of existing appropriations* for the coming fiscal year. Mr. Mondell not only proposes to reject this demand for more money; he intends to give Secretary Baker $200,000,000 less than he got for the current fiscal year. Mr. Baker's standing with Congress is not improved by the fact that he, as Mr. Mondell puts it, is so "contemptuous of Congress" that he "has been spending money not authorized by Congress"; that he is about to ask for a deficiency appropriation for 1920-1921, estimates as to which range from $60,000,000 to $90,000,000. Senator McCumber declares that by June 1 the Treasury's deficit will be not less than two billions of dollars and that there will be no money for a single new project. Appropriations, he warns, must be cut to the bone.

Even more important is the fact that the business men the country over, as well as its conscience, are being heard from in Washington. As economic reasons—according to President Wilson—brought on the war, so economic reasons are compelling us to retrace our steps toward the historic policy of an unarmed America. *The Nation* admits it would be better pleased if this return were due to conscience, to brotherly love, to religious scruples, to a realization that our grounding of arms would do infinitely more to make us friends in South America, in Japan, and England, or on the Continent than our entrance into a dozen peace leagues. We are nevertheless profoundly grateful and profoundly encouraged because, whatever the reason, sanity shows itself once more.

The Friendless Nations

"THIS period of our history would be a bad time for the United States to get into another war, for we have not a friend among the nations of the earth." Thus spoke the other day an elder American statesman, lately returned from Europe, where his name is as well known as in the United States. He was astounded at the bitterness of the criticism of America which he heard wherever he went. In England, in France, in Italy, so far from any feeling of gratitude for us, there was only dislike or anger to be found. For this he cited various reasons. In England our assertions that we won the war have rankled deep, and the rivalry in trade and in fleets, both naval and merchant, is doing much harm. Ireland is, of course, he added, a most serious menace to the friendship of the two countries. On the Continent he found a feeling that we have profited enormously by the war and have borne few of its pains. In France the vexation is not concealed; there the feeling is that we have not stood by our ally as we should have done. To newspaper readers some of these facts are commonplaces; but this man of international reputation could not get over the fact that our unselfish participation in a war for democracy, as he still believes it to have been, has left us entirely friendless—even in South America where our aggressions in the Caribbean and in the kindred Central-American republics have made every nation regard us with a suspicion, distrust, and dislike that a hundred itinerant Secretaries of State could not remove—least of all a Bainbridge Colby.

But what is true of the United States is true of England, while a section of the French press daily harps upon the new isolation of that shell-shocked and suffering republic. All the world believes that England has got away with far more of the swag of the war than it had any right to. Our own State Department accuses it of monopolizing the oil in its new mandatory territories. France insists that it got but little of the recompense it deserves for its martyrdom, Italy is furious because the Treaty of London has not been lived up to; and so it goes. No one is happy, no one is grateful to any one else. The Central Powers are, of course, still Ishmaelites; Czecho-Slovakia, Rumania, and Jugoslavia are so distrustful of Hungary that they have entered into a new alliance against her. At the League of Nations meeting in Geneva the outstanding fact was the line-up of the smaller nations against the great Powers which dominate the European world, a cleft which according to some press observers foreshadows the break-up of the League at its next gathering.

As for Russia, while England has now consented to trade with her, a notorious German general, Hoffmann, of unsavory Brest-Litovsk fame, joins with the French chauvinists in preaching a holy war against the Communists. Every item of news of the advance of communism inflames further the passions of those who see in the Bolshevists the enemies of civilization. In the East, Japan certainly belongs to the friendless nations. Returning travelers of importance report that her elder statesmen are well aware of it. America is against her and builds a fleet to menace her. China has dealt her industry a serious blow by its boycott of all things Japanese; Australia is drawing the yellow color line more sharply than ever. Hate, jealousy, bitterness, distrust, and anger are everywhere. No wonder the *Manchester Guardian* declares that the world is much worse off after the holy war to save humanity than it was before.

The situation is the more striking when one recalls the honeyed words with which the Allied delegations flattered our ears when they visited us soon after we entered the war. Then we swore brotherhood to England, to France, to Italy, for all eternity. Our blood was mixed with their blood on the sacred soil of Flanders, and ties had been forged which nothing could ever sunder. Lafayette, we were with you in reverence, kinship, and lasting good-will which no debt, no unpaid interest, and no failure to sign treaties could possibly affect. Well, we still pour out funds for France—not enough, it is true; we put our hands in our pockets for the diseased and dying children of Central Europe and Russia. But nobody loves us even for that, our Quakers excepted, those noble administrators of our mercy. And then there is China. China among all the nations still loves us, not for our alliance in the war to redeem the world, but for certain altruistic acts of ours in years past like the return of the Boxer indemnity and the insistence on the Open Door and fair play for the eldest nation.

Now the solemn truth is that this shocking loneliness and friendlessness of the nations which but yesterday believed themselves unselfish saviors of human society, are but another, if one of the most striking, of the moral damages of war, and particularly of such a war. What has happened should surprise no one who knows history. There have been holy wars before this, against Russia, against Napoleon, against the Moslem. But that did not mean that the brotherhood of joint warring endured. Indeed, the allies were always all too soon at swords' points again. The fact that France enabled us to win our freedom from Great Britain in the Revolution did not prevent us within seventeen years from entering a state of war with her which lasted for months, though without a declaration of hostilities. Let such another question as that of Venezuela arise and the United States would be swept by a wave of passion against England as it was when Grover Cleveland published the belligerent document which brought both nations to the verge of disaster.

No, lasting friendships are not forged on battlefields; of this the proof is again the bitterness of Canadian and Australian troops toward their British comrades. The nature of war itself forbids it; the ghastly crime of taking part in any such mass murder punishes direly those who participate. Was this truth ever clearer than today? Is it not true that materially the victors are almost as near disaster as the vanquished? Was it ever clearer that the moral damages of war far outweigh all possible gains; that there are no spiritual profits to offset the contents of that Pandora's box of hatred, deceit, lying, cruelty to innocents, and murder, which the first shot of every war lets loose? Plain it surely is now that when one would reclose that box one cannot at will recall the spirits of evil from their devilish work; many of them remain at large to plague all humanity.

The First Move for Real Peace

NOTHING could be in better taste and spirit than Secretary Hughes's note to the Germans in reply to that of the Foreign Minister, Dr. Simons. It generously recognizes the sincerity of the German desire to make reparations and to reopen negotiations with the Allies and it is even capable of the interpretation that our Government may itself open the way for a resumption of the negotiations so needlessly broken off in London. Naturally Mr. Hughes reaffirms the Allied belief in Germany's responsibility for the war, but the important thing is that the Secretary is dealing with our former foes in frank friendliness and with apparent faith in their word. That is both generous and manly and almost as if in response to the recent moving appeal of the head of the Reichstag, Dr. Fehrenbach, in the New York *Times*, for fair and sympathetic treatment of the new German democracy.

Even more important is the fact that the Harding Administration is at last beginning to move in foreign affairs. At this writing there is unanimity in the press reports as to what the attitude of this Government is to be when Congress assembles. We are to conclude promptly a separate peace with Germany; we are not to enter the existing League of Nations, or ratify in any way the monstrous peace of Versailles, but we are to insist upon our rights in the settlement. Most striking of all, it is said we are to move in the direction of the Knox proposals for a new and better world order—not at once, of course, but, perhaps, in due time. If this proves to be Mr. Harding's course he and the country are to be congratulated upon it. It means that there will be no split in the Republican Party on foreign issues; that the Knox-Borah wing has won. It means also that M. Viviani's mission to the United States has failed to affect the President and his advisers. The sole concession to that brilliant orator seems to be the proposal—which we trust will be promptly dropped—to make it the "declared policy" of this Government that it will regard any situation threatening the freedom and peace of Europe "as a menace to its own peace and freedom." While such a declaration cannot be binding upon future Administrations unless they wish it to be, it is emphatically a position which this Government should not take. If it were to be submitted to the American people today it would be overwhelmingly voted down.

If this proposed declaration stands, it will, moreover, be made the excuse of navalists and militarists for generations to come to keep in being the nucleus of an expeditionary force and the necessary transports. We sincerely hope that there will be a sober second thought upon this doctrine so entirely contrary to the whole spirit of our American foreign policy. On its face the proposed declaration is as vague as it is illogical. How great is to be the menace upon which we shall interfere in the wars of Europe? And how are we to judge just when any future struggle, if one arises, is so clearly a menace to our peace and freedom as to cause us to consult with "our chief co-belligerents for the defense of civilization"? This is plainly fustian, but dangerous fustian. We do not believe that it will satisfy the Foch school of French militarists. If it is to be adopted at all it should equally apply to any situation in which France or Great Britain might be the aggressors. It is within the memory of living men that Great Britain with France as her ally warred against Russia—also a war widely heralded as *the* war to end war—and, incredible as it now seems, one of the avowed purposes was to safeguard Germany's integrity from Russian attack. Seventy-five years are as nothing in the history of Europe. Who shall say what new and strange alignments may not take place over there within ten years?

But, waiving that, it is profoundly encouraging to have it stated with apparent authority that we are to get away from the hideous lie we are living—the pretended state of war with Germany—and that we are to end the debate as to whether we shall or shall not enter the League of Nations and ratify the Versailles iniquity in any degree. Against both of these proposals *The Nation* has fought from the day the Treaty was published. It naturally rejoices that the long fight actually seems won and that Mr. Harding is convinced that the American people voted against treaty and League last fall. But it trusts that the President and Mr. Hughes will not stop there. The proposed steps will vitally clear the political and international atmosphere; beyond that we shall still need, however, a sailing chart. These are not destructive measures now announced; wreckage must be cleared away before new construction can arise on the foundations. But once this is done the new structure must be built. For that Senator Knox has pointed the way. If he is allowed to frame the future policy we believe it will be substantially in accord with the program laid down by *The Nation* last fall for building a new world order upon the Hague Court, upon the idea of the outlawing of war, and the deciding of all questions between nations by judicial processes with no distinction as to justiciable and non-justiciable.

This, as we have said, is for the immediate future. For today it is reason for gratitude that some steps forward are to be taken and taken promptly. We sincerely trust that the opportunity will be given to Mr. Harding to mediate between France and England and Germany. The friendly offices of the United States should always be at the disposal of the Allies. Mr. Hughes is plainly convinced that the Germans mean to do the right thing. Dr. Simons has repeatedly stated that every decent-minded German wants to repair the destruction in France. He rightly complains that apparently for political reasons the French have not even discussed the repeated German offers of "labor, technical advice, and material assistance," although for two years past the cleaning up of the devastated districts and their reconstruction have languished. Here is a chance for Mr. Hughes to inquire as to the attitude of the French Government. He stated, too, in his memorandum that the American Government stands with the Allies in insisting upon Germany's making reparation "to the limit of her ability to pay." That is correct and just. But what is the limit of her ability? That is the whole issue today, and here again Mr. Hughes has his opportunity. Liberal opponents of the League and the treaty have never wished the United States to withdraw from all cooperation with Europe. They have protested against any acceptance of the League because, as Mr. Lansing put it, that meant merely an "alliance of the five great military powers" in a league "to be the prey of greed and intrigue." We must help Europe in every possible way—financially, morally, and economically—but with our hands and our policies unfettered by League or treaty.

Our Aggressive Foreign Policy

MR. HARDING himself may be infirm of purpose and without a constructive program, but there is no doubt of the determination of his Secretary of State and of his party to institute an aggressive foreign policy. This has so struck the Washington correspondent of the New York *Evening Post* that he is led to sound an alarm against the bellicose tendencies of the present Government. Is it preparing for war? he asks. Well, he should know, like everybody else, that nothing less than vigor was to be expected of Mr. Hughes and that the historic policy of the Republican Party is to show, or to use, the mailed fist when it comes to foreign affairs. The party is essentially imperialistic, and if it had not been it must be so now by reason of the big business forces that dominate it. If, on the other hand, it be rejoined that the Democratic Party has also been extremely imperialistic, notably in the Caribbean, we reply, Of course. Have we not been saying for a long time past that there is no essential difference between the two parties? Wilson Democrats are making much of the fact that at several points, notably Yap, and the cable question, the Republicans are paying Mr. Wilson the compliment of following in his footsteps albeit more vigorously, while the absence of any positive declaration thus far on our wrongdoing in Santo Domingo and Haiti is similarly suggestive. Well, what really thoughtful student of political affairs expected anything else?

It is true, however, that the Republicans are going to the mat with a good deal more vim and aggressiveness than distinguished the State Department in Mr. Wilson's time. Also, the saber is being rattled vigorously, probably for several purposes. It may be in order to impress the Japanese; it may be because of Mr. Harding's avowed belief that we cannot bring about universal disarmament until we have a lot to disarm and have impressed everybody with what a dangerous character we are. So it is announced that we are to concentrate the entire fleet in the Pacific; that we are to push forward the great naval base at Hawaii; that General Pershing is immediately to organize a skeleton war staff similar to that he headed in France, "to be instantly prepared for active military operations in time of war"—something hitherto supposed to have been the function of the General Staff. Also immediate and extensive development of the aeronautical services is to have the favorable attention of Congress, the dispatches report. Mr. Harding himself has added fuel to the flames. Not only is he especially interested in immediate strengthening of the Panama defenses, but in his inaugural address he gave considerable space to what would take place in our next war and threatened that everyone would have to take part in the conflict, without any exceptions, apparently, even for Quakers. Then he went out of his way to announce at the unveiling of the Bolivar statue that we should uphold the Monroe Doctrine to the extent of cheerfully fighting for it whenever necessary. No wonder that Washington correspondents are beginning to ask what it all means.

In our relations both with our Allies and with Germany Mr. Hughes's natural vigor of expression is making itself felt. We have told England in plain and unvarnished terms where she stands in the matter of her oil claims in Costa Rica, and we have about reached a deadlock with Japan over the question of Yap—the most miserable little island in mid-ocean that ever brought about an *impasse* between two great nations. It is currently reported that Mr. Hughes will shortly take up the matter of Shantung and serve notice on

Japan that she has got to fix the date for her withdrawal from that raped province and that she must do it quickly. Her conduct in Siberia, too, is to come under our review. The rest of our Allies have been clearly informed that though we are not a party to the Versailles treaty we propose to have every one of our rights under that treaty, not a jot nor a tittle less, and that there we shall take our vigorous stand. As for the Germans, we have twice lately rapped them over the knuckles, the second time in declining to arbitrate for them while also making the useful and wise suggestion that they and the Allies get together once more to negotiate the question of the indemnity. We have peremptorily served notice on Panama and Costa Rica that they will not be allowed to fight, no matter what they may wish to do, and we have laid down the law to Panama itself, again in no uncertain terms. If the Republicans go on this way they may certainly "point with pride" at their next national convention to the manner in which they have walked softly and wielded the Big Stick.

Whether they thus serve best the world, the poor, disorganized world, is another question. Certainly, he must be blind who does not perceive that our relations with Japan grow steadily worse. Not only have we challenged the whole system of mandates, which mean so much to Japan in connection with her part of the spoils of Versailles—and thereby also raised the question of the value of the secret treaties of 1917 under which our other Allies guaranteed certain spoils to Japan—but we are adding steadily to the unrest in that country in its relations to us. The organization last week of a group of Representatives and Senators of seven Western States under the leadership of a liberal gone wrong in this instance—Senator Johnson of California—to bring about complete exclusion of Japanese from America, will again react most unfavorably in the Island Kingdom, where it will be received as further proof of the dislike and hostility of the American people. Last week saw also the revival of the regularly recurring sensational stories as to the menacing program for naval construction upon which Japan is secretly working. Only the other day someone originated the story that Japan was obtaining a tremendous air fleet from England, and so it goes. If there is anything lacking in the old familiar game of setting one nation at another's throat, it is not visible in this instance. We are heading for trouble just as surely as were the British and the Germans when, about 1900, there began the press campaigns in both countries with the object of proving in each country that the other was menacing its trade and its future.

But it is this aggressive foreign policy that the American people voted for, whether consciously or unconsciously, last November. That it should give way to a spirit of friendship and conciliation without the rattling of the saber, in accordance with an enlightened, humane, and broadminded program to bring about reconciliation in the world, immediate disarmament, and a rational reconstruction along the lines of a true association of nations and the Hague Tribunal, goes without saying. But this can plainly come to pass only if public opinion promptly makes itself felt in Washington.

No War With England

X. Conclusion

To present cold facts without sentiment has been the object of this series. It is impossible, however, to conclude it without some warmth of expression, because it is impossible to consider an armed conflict between the United States and Great Britain without profound emotion. What has been set forth in the preceding articles shows only too clearly how dangerously contrary to one another the economic currents of the two countries are running—since this series began the split between the English and American oil producers in Mexico has steadily widened, while the Irish ulcer grows deeper and more virulent. We are aware, of course, of the widespread belief—recently voiced by the New York *Evening Post*—that war is so unthinkable as to make discussion of it utterly needless. They are not only superficial thinkers who write thus—they are grossly ignorant of our history of twenty-five years ago. Then it was the *Evening Post* which with *The Nation* fought unceasingly for justice to Great Britain when a single, totally unexpected message of President Cleveland literally brought the two countries to the very verge of war.

Had this country at that time tasted blood as it later did in Cuba and had not the English statesmen borne themselves with extraordinary forbearance and readily consented to arbitration there must have been a conflict. It is a historic fact that one day we were dreaming least of all of trouble with England over a Venezuelan boundary dispute and that the next day every jingo, imperialistic, and super-patriotic editor in America was howling for war. The *Evening Post* itself said at that time that Mr. Cleveland's message left "only to consider whether or not we will take up arms in behalf of Venezuela." What one President can do over night another can also. And it is a peculiar fact that unknown to the American public events are so shaping themselves in the race for oil that a Venezuelan boundary dispute may again furnish the spark for an international conflagration. Venezuela and Colombia face each other today virtually with daggers drawn over disputed oil lands, with England in the background as the supporter of Venezuela, while the progress of American oil prospectors in Colombia, coupled with our recent $25,000,000 payment to that country, foreshadows clearly the side on which the United States is likely to be.

But if we are, perhaps, in view of the World War's comradeship, in less danger of such a sudden outburst of temper, there remains the truth that our economic rivalries wax steadily and are being brought to a sharp and pressing issue at three points—the merchant marine, navy, and oil. Our great public, too widely disgusted with all politics, does not realize that the great competing industrial and financial interests are pulling the strings and jockeying for advantage at the very moment that their public speakers arise at banquets and denounce the Irish for disturbing the cordial relations between the two countries. Few Americans understand, for instance, the significance of the decision of the Lloyd George Government and its pliable Parliament to abandon the historic principle of free trade, under which England has waxed great, rich, and powerful, for a system of thinly disguised protection, under the excuse of protecting itself from "dumping." Here again England moves against the United States, not consciously, since this legislation is aimed at the Central Powers, but it will none the less have its effect. It is, moreover, an entering wedge, and the history of all protective legislation in all countries is that once the protected interests get a foothold they inevitably demand more and more. If these two great countries bar out each other's goods no one can question that there will be a still further increase in the political friction between them.

Now as to the remedies. Fortunately, there are a number of them. The most important lies in England's hands—a just solution of the Irish problem. It is unthinkable that England or any country can continue to govern a province seething with revolution and dissatisfaction. When that issue is settled the whole aspect of our relationship will change. Next, open diplomacy is what we sorely need. Our Department of State conducts negotiations and writes notes, and sometimes it tells us about them afterwards and sometimes it does not. The danger exists that we shall suddenly have sprung upon us a correspondence over Mexican or Mesopotamian or Venezuelan oil wells which will cause great popular excitement. That the personal contacts between citizens of the two countries should be increased is obvious. There should be a far greater interchange of students and professors, yes, of editors, and labor leaders, and business men. Loath as we are to suggest any new organization, we do pray for some alliance between the liberals of the *Manchester Guardian*-London *Nation* school with those of our own country and, indeed, of France, Germany, and other nations. In their cooperation—they are freest of any groups from prejudice or entangling economic alliances—lies hope because they realize best of all that the danger of war cannot be camouflaged by hands-across-the-sea or blood-is-thicker-than-water sentiments—every blessed editor of the New York *Sun* and *Tribune* forgot them on reading Mr. Cleveland's fiery outburst.

Beyond that lie the great economic issues of the time. With free trade everywhere, with balanced systems of production and distribution, with the workers and not the exploiters managing industry in largest degree, with the uncontrolled exporting of capital for overseas adventure—such as the forcing of the Six Power Loan on China against its will—at an end, with use rather than profit the chief aim in industry, the dangers of any war would vastly decrease. These remedies lie in the more distant future. They can only be brought about by vast economic changes. But they can be furthered, and the dangers of the existing business rivalries exposed, by pitiless publicity than which no more pressing duty rests upon the liberal press.

Finally, there is an immediate and drastic remedy so close at hand that it is impossible to conceive how President Harding can lose a single day in grasping it—disarmament on sea and land, and thereafter the establishment of a true and democratic league of nations. The abolition of our fleets alone would mean the banishing of fear of a sudden overnight clash in defiance of the excellent arbitration treaty which binds the two nations together. Then the limiting of our army to police-force size would send peace stock beyond par. How can any one hesitate? If England and the United States come to blows with the new "scientific" warfare, every sane man will despair of civilization.

Ireland on the Verge of Peace?

AT probably the most solemn moment in Irish history these lines are penned. Thanks to the mediation of General Smuts and doubtless to the urging of others of the British Premiers, Mr. Lloyd George has taken the honorable course, and Mr. de Valera with exalted spirit and courage has met him half way. Consequently there is an armistice in Ireland; the terrible warfare of brethren is halted, the shedding of precious blood stayed. That the hideous struggle may never be renewed must be the prayer of humane men and women everywhere. If only now these men in whose hands lies the fate of a race may have the wisdom the past has so sorely lacked!

There is but one issue now. Will Mr. de Valera accept anything short of complete independence? In his message to the American people seeking support, the President of the Irish Republic asks America's active aid to bring about "a solution of this problem on the only basis on which it can be solved—acknowledgment that Ireland should by natural right be free." That may mean that he will continue to demand complete independence and a recognition of the Republic, or that he will stand for the freedom of Canada and Australia and South Africa. The Premiers will undoubtedly urge this upon him; but he who knows best the temper of the South of Ireland, who has seen Irishmen by the hundred cheerfully going to their death for an Irish Republic, may find himself stopped by their memories from taking anything less. We hope that this will not be the case. To win, after all these centuries, dominion status, complete fiscal autonomy, and home rule in its entirety would surely be advance enough for the present day. Ireland, thus relieved of blighting and despoiling government by London and Dublin Castle, would arise and flourish like the green bay tree. It could continue, if it wished, to develop its language and its national spirit, to plan for future independence. The alternative means more bloodshed, more death, more ruin, and eventually complete destruction.

But, we hear voices say, why should the Irish take less than a loaf when they have plainly brought England to her senses? Well, they have achieved wonders. It was only the other day that Lloyd George and Greenwood were going to make of Ireland a wilderness rather than treat with the "murder gang." Now President de Valera finds himself in a position to turn any but the wisest of heads. By consenting to the armistice *England admits to all the world that she has been dealing not with a murder gang in Ireland but with a full-fledged revolution, as much warfare as the American Revolution of 1776.* By recognizing De Valera it admits that he is the *true and chosen representative and spokesman of the great bulk of his people.* It is true that the British Government addresses him as "Mr. de Valera," but so did they address as "Mr. Washington" another rebel, a certain General Washington, Commander-in-Chief, and after all that is a trifle. It is to his credit that Lloyd George had the good sense to admit defeat—Sir Philip Gibbs incidentally avers that it is the economic boycott of Ulster and the terrible losses inflicted on her merchants and manufacturers which has made the North ready to deal with Catholic Ireland. Plainly Mr. de Valera treats with both England and Ulster on equal footing. But, remarkable as all this is, President de Valera will know just how far Ireland wishes the self-determination of her fate to go today.

The Disarmament Conference and Its Possibilities

WITH the English protests against the sending of Lloyd George and Lord Curzon to represent Great Britain at the Washington disarmament conference we heartily sympathize, not because, like the London *Times* and Lord Northcliffe, we wish to attack Mr. Lloyd George's personal character, but because we believe with our London namesake that the less the coming conference smacks of Versailles and its personalities the better it will be for the conference and the world. For that reason we trust that neither M. Briand nor M. Viviani nor M. Tardieu will come over to speak for France. And on our side we sincerely hope that there will be no Elihu Root and no James Brown Scott and no Nicholas Murray Butler as part of our delegation. If this conference is to be dominated by the Europeans who helped to plunge the world into its misery and have proceeded to make the situation worse ever since there will be little hope that the meeting can achieve anything thoroughgoing. As for the Root type of mind, with all respect for its profound learning and its mastery of international law, what the hour calls for is younger men—men who at least dimly realize that the world stands at the threshold of a new order and are yet young enough to count upon witnessing the results of their handiwork.

Above all we trust that there will be no generals and no admirals assigned or appointed to the conference by any member of it. It was the German admirals and generals, who, as Joseph H. Choate testified, wrecked the Second Hague Conference. The best of these men in all countries are partisans unable to free themselves from professional prejudices and usually wedded to the idea that nothing can be done to cure the human being of his propensity to fight. Indeed, it is from these and from certain other vested interests that we may expect to have the question asked with increasing frequency as to what practical result the conference can accomplish.

Well, there are many practical things that can be done even if the conference balks at the chief task before it—the abolition of all naval forces save a few ships manned not for fighting purposes but for the police and rescue work of the seas, and the abolition of all armies. Take the submarine. Even naval officers have been urging that this weapon be banned for all time; and as for battleships the rapidly enlarging doubt as to whether they have any value in view of the development of aircraft—doubts stimulated by the American experiments now going on—ought to make it easy for the nations invited to agree upon the barring of all further battleship construction. It is this type of craft that has run up the costs of navies so enormously, the latest types costing between 40 and 50 millions of dollars apiece; moreover, those that are building will be years behind the times in their technical construction the day they are launched.

The danger will be, of course, that the various nations will endeavor to manipulate affairs so that they may be left each of them in the strongest naval position. Hence the only way to reduce them all to absolute equality is to abolish all the navies. We admit that the question of aircraft is more difficult because of the fact that commercial airplanes can speedily be made into death-dealing instruments. None the less, control of this branch of the military and naval service is by no means impossible. During the war Lloyd George solemnly promised the British miners that as soon as the struggle was over he would limit the making of all arms and ammunition and the building of all warships to state-owned arsenals and dockyards. The present advantage of this is that it would make very easy the control of one nation by the other nations, that is, it would not be possible for a country to conceal from its rivals what it might be doing in the making of arms and ammunition if it must carry on those activities in government arsenals which could neither be increased in number nor enlarged in size without the fact becoming public property. In Germany today the Allies are relying upon the extreme radicals and the Socialists to keep them informed as to just what the German Government is really doing in the way of carrying out the decrees of the Treaty of Versailles concerning disarmament. Fortunately there are and there will be in the United States, as well as in other countries, similar pacifist and radical forces which will tend to render any underhand work by any government impossible of concealment.

Again there is the matter of poison gas and the new so-called chemical warfare which the Allies denounced as a crime against humanity when Germany used it, but which we and they since have embraced with joy. This is the easiest kind of warfare for a disarmed nation to prepare for in short order, for there are many factories that can be utilized for this foul purpose with but slight changes. No one who has read Mr. Will Irwin's "The Next War" can fail to realize that if this sort of warfare is not immediately stopped it will endanger not merely whole nations—men, women, and children—but civilization itself if war on a great scale should occur again.

As for the armies, there are a number of measures that suggest themselves, such as the forbidding of conscription and the limitation of standing armies to a fixed percentage per one hundred thousand of population. Doubtless here England will present the most difficult problem since she insists upon holding great nations like Egypt and India in forcible subjection. But any one can conjure up obstacles; the encouraging thing is that necessity is the whip that drives. If the European nations do not disarm they can hardly escape bankruptcy. Curiously enough, and happily, too, it is, according to the Washington correspondent of the New York *Globe*, the fortunate situation of disarmed Germany which is also compelling the Allies to act; they see that Germany, freed from her crushing military taxes, will be able to get ahead in her economic reconstruction far more rapidly than the Allies. Indeed, Senator Borah has brought out the astonishing fact, which ought to be printed in large type on the front page of every American newspaper, that if we go on with our present armament burdens the people of the United States will have to disburse exactly as much for them during the next thirty years as will the Germans if they pay the 33 billions of dollars imposed by the Allies! Exactly the same burden placed upon Germany as penalty for her share in the war is, in other words, to be voluntarily assumed by the American taxpayers as their tribute to Mars. Was there ever greater folly? Every sane American ought to make it clear to the President that thoroughgoing and radical disarmament on sea and land is what this country wishes and proposes to obtain from the conference.

The Price of Peace

MR. HUGHES has set bounds to oversanguine expectations by reminding us that the coming Washington Conference is not a conference on disarmament, but on the limitation of armaments. He honestly attempts to avoid such tragic disillusionment as followed the Versailles Conference by stemming the extravagant hopes with which men greet these world assizes. The nations are not considering absolute disarmament; they will at most reduce burdens grown well-nigh intolerable. The conference will not achieve even this result without the pressure of public opinion which insists upon open sessions in order that it may secure the necessary information to guide its action. The assembled Lodges and Briands will be quite capable of using the conference to justify rather than to diminish great military establishments unless a resolute public insists upon its desire for constructive action. We are therefore sympathetic with every effort to mobilize the friends of peace behind the conference. But this can only be done intelligently if we face quite frankly the question, What can such a conference accomplish under the most favorable circumstances?

Certain definite things we may with reason hope. Limitation of armaments will: (1) save millions of dollars in taxes at a time when both retrenchment in expenditure and larger outlay for genuine public service are imperatively demanded from all governments; (2) reduce the size of the military caste which in proportion to its strength always and everywhere inculcates that false gospel of militarism which proved so disastrous in Prussia; (3) diminish the appeal to the jingo psychology which is inherent in mighty armadas and the glittering panoply of war; (4) reduce the temptation to business interests which directly or indirectly profit by armament-making to promote war scares in order to market their wares. This particular conference may also reach a *modus vivendi*—not a permanent settlement—in the Far East, giving liberal forces a chance to grow strong in all the countries concerned. (But this result is rendered less likely by the refusal of our Government to include Russia and the Far Eastern Republic in its invitation.) If in addition to whatever it may accomplish in the Far East there were even a remote possibility that the conference might accept the Pope's suggestion of repudiating military conscription, a really great forward step would be taken. This step seems wholly unlikely; nevertheless the conference, especially if its sessions are open, may serve by its discussions to strengthen the will to peace and enlighten those who seek it. These gains are worth achieving, but they do not make peace.

Why? First, because this limitation of armaments is to be based on the preservation of the *status quo* in international relations. To the intelligent Chinese there must be a grim humor in the spectacle of mighty nations indulging in spasms of virtue because they contemplate saving some of the money squandered on competitive armaments. These nations have not even contemplated putting an end to their imperialist program of exploitation; they merely seek a more economical method of carrying it out. Limitation of armaments, like the Versailles League of Nations, is essentially another attempt to substitute an imperialist trust for competitive imperialism. The psychology of imperialism is such that it is not likely to succeed. The old rivalries will remain. What the American "disarmament" (*sic*) advocate really says to England and Japan is: "Let us without altering the ratio of our military and naval power save some money. If we have to fight later, we will all have the same relative military strength." Does this sound cynical? It is virtually the position of so eminent a liberal as Mr. Frank Cobb, editor of the New York *World*, who, in an able article in the August issue of the *Atlantic Monthly* on the Economic Aspects of Disarmament, makes it evident that what he really seeks is not disarmament but cheaper armament. Elaborate military preparation, he argues, is demonstrably futile; victory goes to the nation economically best prepared; to mobilize one thousand chemists may be more important than to mobilize one million men. Aye, there's the rub! Even Mr. Joseph Choate, Jr., counsel to the dye interests, looks with equanimity on "disarmament" if preparation for chemical warfare goes on unchecked. To be sure the call for the conference invites discussion of the limitation of this new and most horrible form of warfare. But to hope for that if war itself is accepted as possible is crazy Utopianism. It is contrary to the logic and history of war. What the Hague Conference could not do to make warfare "humane," Washington will not.

War will never be conquered by so easy a device as limitation of armaments. Its menace will disappear only when men begin to reorganize society so as to remove the causes of war and meanwhile determine that whatever their differences, they will find other means to adjust them. If under the influence of some miraculous wave of enthusiasm every military Power turned its tanks into tractors and sank its ships in the deepest seas, *but kept the same economic and political organization and racial and national prejudices*, there would yet be a new war within a generation as disastrous as any Mr. Wells has foretold.

For the tap-root of modern imperialism, and hence of modern wars, is economic. Mr. H. N. Brailsford before the war gave the brief and classic statement of the case in his "War of Steel and Gold." The rivalries of great nations are at bottom the rivalries of their investors who, under our system of landlordism and of production for private profit rather than for use, have surplus capital on which they can get the largest return by investment in so-called backward lands. The situation Mr. Hsu Chung-Tze describes with regard to the export of American capital to China is a case in point. The rival investors did not deliberately will the tragedy of the Great War; they set in motion the forces which, given the prevailing nationalist psychology, inevitably led to war. And they have learned nothing from the issue of the conflict. Indeed, as Norman Angell has pointed out in his latest book, although the fruits of victory are dust and ashes yet there are more economic motives pushing toward war than before the Peace of Versailles. We have today a far larger degree of state capitalism under which nations as nations monopolize for their nationals natural resources, coal, iron, oil, and food, necessary for the life of their neighbors. In an earlier day, free trade made for peace. It has been defeated, not so much by old-fashioned protectionism, as by this new tendency to national monopolization. The Italians, in spite of many disappointments, still are urging almost as a matter of life and death a reasoned international control of raw materials. Every effort, Signor Tittoni told the Williamstown Institute, has failed because of the opposition "of a coalition of economic interests." Such a coalition is the appropriate fruit of our present economic system. Its end is war.

But though economic interests are at the bottom of our troubles, the peril of our present situation is possible only because of the intensity of modern racial and national feeling. The oil barons, for example, however unscrupulously they might grab for vast profits, could not, without the psychology of nationalism and the strange fetish of national honor, persuade even themselves, and certainly not their countrymen, to make war on a weak nation such as Mexico. The cheap patriotism which Lowes Dickinson regards as primarily a war phenomenon is in peace times systematically taught by capitalistically controlled agencies as a means to forestall industrial unrest. A people thus miseducated is only too ready for a fight. We cannot assume that "the people" if only they could get rid of the evil spell of governments would save us from war. It is true that the people would seldom vote for a war in a referendum; it is not true that they accept the psychology which makes peace possible. Most people have some one interest—freedom for this or that oppressed group, security against dangers, real or imagined—for which they care far more passionately and consistently than they do for peace.

Obviously in this situation the peace advocate who relies too much on the Washington Conference leans on a broken reed. Limitation of armaments, like arbitration treaties, world courts, a popular referendum before war, and other alleged panaceas, is worth something. But peace itself cannot be secured at so cheap a price. It requires a revolutionary change in our present politico-economic system and in its accompanying psychology. How can that be brought about? Partly, no doubt, by demonstrating, as Mr. Will Irwin has done so powerfully, the suicidal consequences of a new world war. Yet this alone is far less potent than many think. Mankind which was not scared into virtue by centuries of belief in an eternal hell will not be scared into peace by fear of destruction in a new war. Except Gandhi, no outstanding leader of an oppressed race or class has consistently developed non-violent resistance. Men of independent judgment will tell you that they accept Irwin's thesis, but that nevertheless the United States must be ready for a new war. Could pessimism go farther?

A second service to real peace is the demonstration of the fact that there are only losers in modern war. England, we say, won most in the last war; but save for a few miserable profiteers there is no Englishman who is not poorer for the struggle, no Englishman whose future safety is not more insecure because of the results of what he calls victory. It is logically true that the citizens of a nation which practiced intelligent non-resistance would probably be better off than the subjects of a mighty military power, yet this prudential consideration alone will not stem the tides of pride, fear, hate, and greed, which make for war.

There is a third service which our poets, our writers, and preachers could render. They could strip war both of its glory and its appeal to the ideal. "Thou shalt not make the next war holy," if accepted as a new commandment by the church, would help to avert another war. For soldiers, volunteer or conscript, would not fight for Yap, or the profits of oil barons and other investors. They fight for a menaced fatherland, for liberty, and for all the beautiful ideals which war betrays. Anatole France wisely pointed out that the worst wars are idealist wars. If you fight a man because he has what you want, some sort of settlement is possible; if you fight him because you consider yourself God's agent and him the devil's, there can be no ground for peace.

But beyond these services lies the primary necessity of ending the present chaos of jealous, shortsighted political and economic units competing ruthlessly for the essentials of life which they might enjoy abundantly if only they would cooperate honestly, intelligently, and on a world-wide scale. It is out of this chaos and the spirit which it nourishes that wars inevitably arise. But it is not Utopian to believe that there is in men despite their prejudices an instinct for fellowship which will make possible a peaceful cooperative society. Men have sacrificed incredibly for a vision of national unity and freedom; why may they not for a vision of world unity and freedom? The reorganization of society necessary to peace will involve sacrifice for certain individuals and groups; it will involve infinitely less sacrifice than new world war. It will not, as some Socialists have assumed, be the inevitable achievement of class war; it must be the creation of human intelligence and human will. And the final test of the Washington Conference may well be not the degree in which it lightens stupid and oppressive burdens of armament, but the measure in which it conceals or reveals the truth that peace is neither the product of a diffuse sentimentality, nor attainable by some simple formula, but the consequence of a way of life which hitherto men have rejected in their social, economic, and international relations.

The Moral Defenses of Imperialism

WE who believe that imperialism is the arch foe of world peace and that its primary motive is economic, need to remind ourselves that it has certain moral defenses without which it could not long endure. The white man never carries a burden which does not bring him profit or glory, but somehow he also persuades himself that as a laborer in the vineyard of the Lord he is worthy of his exorbitant hire. The horrible cruelties of the Spanish Conquest, the British slave traffic, and the chattel slavery of our own country were defended by a belief, by no means always hypocritical, that the victims ought to be thankful for the chance of salvation and civilization bestowed upon them by their masters. Emphatically the same thing is true of modern imperialism in its various forms. For the exploitation of a country like India, a class like our unskilled immigrant workers, a race like the Negroes, there is always the defense: these people are so much better off than if left to their own devices. And modern imperialism has often secured honorable agents. Many an English civil servant in out of the way corners of Asia, or American school teacher on Mindanao, or German doctor in East Africa, without personal selfishness, has served not merely government but sanitation, order, and "civilization" with a quite heroic quality. But such service has never altered the fundamental character of imperialism as a means of exploitation.

During the war imperialism, at least of the German brand, was out of fashion. But the pendulum has swung. Self-determination in Central Europe—that is self-determination as worked out at Versailles—in the opinion of competent observers has wrought economic devastation and substituted many petty tyrannies for the tyranny of the old Austrian Empire which so many brave men died to overthrow. Today, prominent liberals are far more concerned lest independence for Ireland, to say nothing of Egypt, should Balkanize the world than that Lincoln's principle that no man is good enough to govern another without his consent should be put in practice. In this popular defense of imperialism there are several discernible strands. The first is the aggressively benevolent idea of doing good to somebody. The eulogist of British rule in India, after a brief apology for Warren Hastings and a few of his successors, will eloquently insist that the British Raj restored order, established peace, built railroads, fought disease, abolished suttee, etc., etc. On Africa they are even more eloquent. Usually they expound a dubiously scientific doctrine of "superior" and "inferior" races or else they talk of more or less "advanced" peoples. So good a man as Sir Harry Johnston writes of the "Backward peoples" who have "mostly stopped in some rut" as compared with the "White man" who "has attained the powers and outlook of a demi-god." Obviously, the demi-god must rule, albeit, Sir Henry urges, he ought to rule decently and "without rudeness and racial arrogance."

Let us briefly examine the defense of imperialism in the classic case of India. It assumes, quite without proof, that the India of the eighteenth century could never have achieved internal unity or any measure of progress without British intervention. It underestimates Indian civilization and overestimates Anglo-Saxon. It forgets that if a monstrous custom constrained certain Hindu widows to immolate themselves on their husbands' funeral pyres, Anglo-Saxon Georgia, home of "the invisible empire," burns human beings at the stake to make holiday for the mobs. It has never adequately answered Lajpat Rai's argument, based on British records, that India before the coming of the British Raj was happier, more literate, less hungry and, above all, more self-respecting, than today. And the overwhelming condemnation of imperialism is the simple fact that India itself has weighed it in the balance and found it wanting. Gandhi goes too far, we believe, in his condemnation of Western civilization; his judgment is the judgment of a saint. The common people are not saints but neither are they such fools as to reject overwhelmingly the great gift of that white demi-god, the British Raj, unless it violated their inmost spirit.

Even in Africa, where undoubtedly the Negroes are in a primitive state it is false to believe that peonage to Europeans under civilization is wholly preferable to the native savagery. Mr. E. D. Morel declares that if the African system of land tenure existed in England "the English people would be a happier people," but over a large area the Western exploiter has rooted that system out. We are not arguing that the Western world has nothing to give or even that it has given nothing, but simply that a greater trust in the value of Western science, culture, religion, and organization, would have led to their propagation less by coercion and more by persuasion. The process might have been slower but it would be surer. It is not necessary to conquer a country to introduce sanitation, and it is impossible properly to develop native potentialities under the atrophying rule of the conqueror. What might have been done is suggested by a scathing Persian analysis of Lord Curzon's boast of English services to Persia. It recalls how much more valuable were the services of the American Colonel Morgan Shuster employed by the Persians as Treasurer-General than those of his successor imposed by the British. In virtually no country have the Morgan Shusters had a chance.

The second defense of imperialism is made in the name of economic realism. The world is economically interdependent; it cannot prosper as a congeries of small independent political units each of which imposes absurd economic restrictions. It cannot, in Sir Harry Johnston's opinion, allow semi-savages to drive their flocks "over plains and mountains that are little less than vast treasure vaults of valuable minerals and chemicals." Closely related to this argument is the belief that imperialism is a rough but approximately effective way to the world unity which ultimately is necessary to abolish war.

These arguments cannot be ignored. A prosperous world must be an economic unit. It is no ideal solution to say "Africa for the Africans" if that means permanent loss of indispensable minerals. But let the white imperialist press this point cautiously, lest he be asked by what right his race deprives colored races of access to millions of acres in Australia where a white man cannot live. Mankind has no choice today between learning to think and act in terms of world-wide cooperation or reverting to a primitive agricultural stage of development under which the earth cannot support its existing population. But it is precisely this desirable cooperation which imperialism can never obtain. Imperialism is not a road to, but a barrier against, internationalism. Imperialist intrigue today is reresponsible for no small share of the disastrous ultranationalism of Central Europe. Polish chauvinism is the foster child of French imperialism. Imperialism never contemplates any unity except one imposed by a class or race to its own advantage. The inevitable revolt against it drives men to excessive particularism and makes internationalism impossible. For centuries men have oscillated between imperialism and revolt. Once in the Middle Ages, it seemed as if Western Europe had almost attained a spiritual unity with group autonomy under the aegis of the church, but that hope passed. Today the true internationalist has no choice; he must turn from coercion to fellowship to achieve his desires, and only free men can practice fellowship. It will, for example, in the long run be easier to persuade a free Ireland to adopt a less dogmatic nationalism than to make her internationalist by force. For imperialism, let it never be forgotten, though it may have unselfish and even benevolent servants, is essentially and ruthlessly selfish—divisive, not unifying. It separates men into exploited and exploiters, and invites between the exploiters war for mastery. Even now the temptation assails America to develop its "sphere of influence" from the Rio Grande to the equator. Let her remember that every great empire from the days of Assyria until now has awakened that fury which has encompassed its doom. To substitute internationalism for imperialism is the essential condition of world peace. That process requires difficult economic and political and still more difficult psychological readjustment. It will be hastened when men begin to understand how weak are the moral defenses of imperialism.

War and Human Nature

THERE is a method of deducing the inevitability of war which makes superfluous any examination of the actual relations between men and hopeless any consideration of concrete proposals for preserving peace. The argument runs: You cannot change human nature; human nature is selfish. Therefore you cannot abolish war, poverty, or any of the fundamental social ills from which men suffer. "You cannot change human nature." How large is the orchestra which plays its variations upon that one theme! Great newspapers, army officers, captains of industry, gentlewomen in protected homes, clergymen of a church which professes to minister redeeming grace—all avow the same creed in justification of their skepticism as to any thoroughgoing plan for social amelioration. Now it is quite clear that this creed may be challenged along either or both of two lines: one may deny that human nature is so rigidly fixed as these pessimists allege, or one may affirm that even if human nature is in a large sense unchangeable, war and other social evils which had a definite beginning in human history may have a definite end. In other words there is no obvious axiomatic and inevitable connection between human nature or human selfishness and the long agony of the Great War. The connection may exist but it requires explanation; and it is precisely this explanation which is not supplied. Here, for instance, is our contemporary the *Christian Register* which having quoted from our editorial on the Price of Peace proceeds: "We think the tap-root of war is not chiefly economic, as that journal [*The Nation*] does, but a more human thing which includes economic advantage, namely, simple blind selfishness."

Such a generalization is anything but closely reasoned. Who by their "simple blind selfishness" caused the war? The men who fought, who endured every conceivable and inconceivable horror in the trenches and on the battlefields, the men whom the *Christian Register* was glorifying a little while ago as exemplars of the love which led a man to lay down his life for his friends? If indeed it was selfishness which led men to endure such agonies it was surely blind, but it was anything but simple. It requires explanation in terms of the psychological complexes and economic and political forms of organization which govern social relations. We have a right to demand of our pessimistic friends less slovenly thinking if they are to be our guides. And from some of them we have a right to demand proof of disinterestedness. Those who are most glib in asserting that the disproportionate division of the good things of life is due to human nature usually have the most good things to protect. The assumed universality of selfishness is too often, one fears, the defense against an uneasy conscience which demands by what right we are the complacent supporters or beneficiaries of a system whose fruit is war.

In raising these doubts as to the validity of the logical deduction of war from an immutable human nature we are not to be understood as denying that certain general characteristics of men have persisted since paleolithic times. Men nowadays are less hopeful of the easy perfectibility of mankind in the mass than were the romantic radicals of earlier days. The psychology of the individual and of the crowd has united with history in bringing back a sobering sense of our limitations. We are ready to deplore with the worthy bishop not so much our kinship with the tiger as with the ass. If reason be king at all in the affairs of men, his is no absolute monarchy. He sits on an uneasy throne which he must dispute with strange stupidities, mighty passions, devastating fears and hates. And yet here are men, lords over nature as are no others of the animal creation. Other living species have perished because they could not adapt themselves to their outward environment; no species has perished by its own internecine strife. Is it conceivable that such a fate is reserved for man? Is it thus that nature is to revenge herself on her conqueror?

No such melancholy conclusion is demanded by the facts. If in the course of history man has shown blind selfishness and strange stupidity he has also shown great powers of mutual aid and adaptability. Human nature has permitted enormous variations in men's way of living, in their moral standards, and in their degree of interdependence. Professor Sumner argued that every new invention created its appropriate *mores*. Ancient customs have yielded to the power of new ideas. In the long history of the race men have offered human sacrifices to their gods, degraded women to an inferior order of being, held human slaves, burned heretics, murdered each other in private quarrels to vindicate a thing they called honor. In dark forests, in gloomy temples, in the market-place and the forum brave men have cried out against all these things. And always they were told that to abolish human sacrifice, to treat woman as the equal of man, to free the slaves, to tolerate the heretic was against human nature. Nay, rather, it was against the unchangeable will of the high gods at whose behest these heroes suffered trials of mockings and scourgings and imprisonment, were stoned, torn asunder, tempted, slain with the sword. But they awakened a response in human nature mighty enough to overthrow the intrenched evil against which they launched their puny strength. Why should it seem incredible that men should refuse to that tawdry god, the political state, the human sacrifices they long ago denied to the lords of earth and sea and air? Why should chattel slavery have perished but the exploitation of the toiler and the landless men be immortal? It is all very well to remind us that human nature sets limits which the prophet and statesman cannot ignore. But what those limits are no man dares confidently assert. This we know. There are in human nature capacities for mutual aid on which we have scarcely begun to build and there is in the will of man a creative energy abundantly able to organize his social life so as to make war as absurdly unnecessary as it already is abhorrent to the human mind.

The Way to Disarm

THE way to disarm is to disarm. This is our reply to those of our readers who have asked us for a program and a platform for the coming Conference. It is, moreover, absolutely practical and, since the last war, no longer open to the charge of visionary sentimentality. *The Nation* long ago declared that the world must get rid of war or war will get rid of the world. A true description of this Conference would be that it meets not for the limitation of armament but in its essence to prevent the human race from committing suicide. For to this pass have we now come; the world is in ruins as a result of this last struggle; it is economically wrecked. In Central Europe it is by no means certain that civilization will survive; that five to six millions of human beings may yet die from starvation in Europe is the belief of hard-headed men who have lately surveyed the situation. Yet all of this was the result of a struggle which only began to draw in whole populations, had only begun to use the discoveries in the field of poison gas, chemical and aerial warfare which in the next struggle will blot out whole armies and cities. To commit suicide or not to commit suicide, that is the question before the Conference.

So our program goes far, far beyond a naval holiday, or limitation of armaments, or the forbidding of conscription, or the outlawing of submarine and poison gas, or making wars dependent upon referendums. We are for mustering out the navies to the last ship and disarming to the last man. These are our fourteen points of disarmament—all in one. If international disarmament does not come out of the Washington Conference we are for once in accord with William J. Bryan in demanding that the United States go ahead and disarm by itself. This country is powerful beyond any in its material resources; it is entirely self-contained and self-supporting; it cannot be starved out or subdued by any now existing Power. Its authority in the world is of the greatest. Let it but disarm and in time all the world must follow. The moral forces of every other country would compel their people to follow in our footsteps even if the disastrous state of their public finances and the increasing burden upon their productive powers did not drive them to such a step.

That preparedness means war and not peace is now the admission in England of so brilliant a military writer as General Maurice and in the United States virtually of President Hibben of Princeton and of Raymond Robins. It is only four years since these two Americans succumbed to the preparedness mania; they bore their share in the turning of the United States into an armed camp. Today they apparently have seen a new light. How can any reasoning man do else if he considers the outcome of the Great War itself? That that was a dead failure so far as its avowed objects were concerned every candid man must now admit. True, militarism was defeated in Berlin as it was in France in 1815 and 1870. But that it was stirred into new life in the countries of the Entente, and that it stalks in full regalia in one small nation after the other is beyond the need of proof. For the rest, the resort to arms has merely filled the world with such economic distress, bitterness, and hatred as to appal the most optimistic observers. It is still true that the way to cure war is no more by means of more war than the way to cure the drink habit is by increasing the amount of drink. President Hibben and Mr. Robins are now right; preparedness leads straight to more war. No single thing save one could so insure peace between the United States and Japan as the hauling up on land of the fleets of the two countries.

Save one thing. And that is a new way of life for the great nations of the earth. We admit freely that complete disarmament will not wholly insure peace as long as nations seek to impose their wills and wishes upon others as has Japan in Korea, Shantung, and Siberia, and the United States in Haiti, Santo Domingo, and Nicaragua. As long as two such nations violate the common decencies of international life, as long as a professedly Christian nation like ours will slay and torture a defenseless people who in no wise ever offended against us there can be no certainty that nations will be beyond attack from others as imperialistic as Japan or England or ourselves. What is needed is a complete moral revulsion against the whole miserable policy of dominating others by force and particularly a moral revulsion against the new prostitution of science to the business of murder by wholesale. The science that should be the very means to a better and richer life, a safer and happier one for the multitudes that toil—this is now to be the handmaid of war, capable of tearing down in a month the labor of centuries, for, we repeat, the will to war today is the will to suicide. For this we ask no one to take our word; let the curious study the speeches of General Fries, head of our Chemical Warfare Service, or the facts in Will Irwin's "The Next War"; let them recall the poignant regret of our poison gas officers that the unexpected ending of the war prevented them from trying out their new gas which would, they said, if released near a great city, kill some two or three hundred thousand persons. Was it not General Mitchell, assistant chief of our flying corps. who begged a month ago to be allowed to try a little poison gas and some aerial bombs on his striking fellow-Americans in West Virginia? Every practical test bears out the assertions of all the progressive officers of the army and navy that the day of the great battleship is over. That mankind will turn from now on to these new chemical means of destruction the power and range of which may be measured by the recent explosion in Oppau is the burden of every militarist's song—without regard to the fact that these terrible forces may some day master humanity and beyond question place power in the hands of a few miscreants to perpetrate indescribable horrors upon their inoffensive fellow men.

No, for once the ideal and the practical are the same. There is no road to the reduction of taxation and the restoration of business surer than that which leads through disarmament. Men will prate, of course, that war must ever be, that the passions of men can never be changed. So some doubtless spoke when the race began to eschew cannibalism and so we know they spoke when the duel was placed without the pale of law. Nor is it the passions of men that are to be feared today as much as the greed and cupidity, the blindness and cruelty and folly of diplomats and rulers. No people unwhipped by its imperialists hates another and no people but is capable of being moved by a new passion of fraternity, of brotherhood, of good-will, such as was preached in Galilee.

The Duty of Civil Disobedience

When an injunction issued in the public interest immediately results in spontaneous strikes where there was industrial peace, in restricting the production of coal at the approach of winter, and in threats by conservative labor leaders that they will choose jail rather than obedience, the plain citizen is warranted in suspecting bad laws and in being sure of a bad social philosophy. Judge Anderson's injunction against the United Mine Workers had all of these immediate consequences. The language of the judge was astonishingly confusing but the essential features of his decision were clear enough. The United Mine Workers have been trying to organize the West Virginia coal fields. This they have done not merely out of regard for their fellow-workers who now lack the benefits of organization, but also to protect themselves against the competition of coal fields whose lower labor standards tend to drag down wages and general conditions through the whole of the so-called "Central Field." This attempt at organization constitutes, in Judge Anderson's opinion, conspiracy between the union and the operators who have agreements with it to destroy competition, and as such a violation of the Sherman Anti-Trust Act. Hence he forbade the miners to spend more money in organizing the territory and forbade the operators to continue the check-off system, under which they deduct union fees from wages and turn them over to the union treasury, so long as such dues were used in the West Virginia field. This prohibition of the check-off has been suspended by the higher court, pending appeal. If the injunction is then sustained it will end agreements in the coal fields which were reached at the request of former Presidents of the United States. It will serve as an invitation to anti-union employers in every industry to ask injunctions against national unions which seek to organize their men, on the ground that free competition is destroyed thereby. But the very life of unions depends on such activities, and if the state can forbid them the workers are back in the helpless position of the early days of the industrial revolution.

And Judge Anderson's injunction is neither solitary nor unique. It merely illustrates the extreme lengths to which the coercive power of the state has gone. It can roughly be paralleled by judicial decisions and executive acts denying to workers the right to strike or to picket, as well as the ancient rights of free speech and assemblage. In support of the Railway Labor Board and to prevent a strike the Harding Administration was preparing to avail itself of every technicality, including war laws never intended for any such purpose, against the Brotherhoods. Attorney General Palmer used similar tactics in the coal strike of 1919. We have gone a very long way since Lincoln said: "I thank God we have a system of labor where there can be a strike and whatever the pressure there is a point where the workmen may stop."

Let no one take these words of ours as a light-hearted vindication of a right whose exercise involves the possibility of human suffering. It is a mark of the essential stupidity of our present system that strikes should ever be necessary; yet until we have learned to guide our tremendously complex and interdependent industrial system by principles of cooperation instead of subjecting it to the law of the jungle, the strike, and still more the labor organization whose weapon it is, affords the only defense for the workers against a despotic owning class which is becoming more and more closely identified with the Government. The function of the state as primarily to protect special privilege and private property has become so obvious as scarcely to require argument. When the Railway Labor Board, an agent of the state, was defied by the Pennsylvania Railroad, the Government showed no alarm. It was only when the workers threatened a strike that every department sprang to instant activity. The Sherman Anti-Trust Act long ago lost its terror for capital. It is today invoked to keep labor from effective organization.

This increasing regimentation of workers into an industrial army as part of a servile state is of course a natural complement to military conscription. When the state, organized primarily to protect property, claims the right to conscript men to kill or be killed in wars stirred up not by the natural antipathies of human beings but by the rivalries of predatory governments, it has already made itself a Moloch more terrible than any of the gods of antiquity. The Pope has referred to conscription as a blood-tax. It is worse; it is the negation of personality at the point of moral choice in the most desperate issues of life and death. While this sort of conscription and the espionage laws which accompany it are accepted complacently in civilized nations, it is idle to believe that lesser freedoms, such as the right to a decisive voice as to conditions under which one shall work, can be secured. That the states which exercise such coercive powers over the individual are nominally democratic, proves nothing. There is no tyrant more irrational or cruel than the crowd, and the manipulation of the crowd by those who enjoy special privilege has become a science.

How we shall escape from this tyranny and obtain the cooperation necessitated in an age of machine-production, is the supreme problem of our generation. It cannot be solved by men who live in an irrational awe of that artificial entity they call government. America owes all the best in her life to men who recognized "a higher law than the Constitution" and a power above government. Not Roger Tawney and the justices who promulgated the Dred Scott decision, but the great-hearted men and women who ran the underground railroad for the escape of fugitive slaves deserve the lasting gratitude of their country. What men once endured to abolish chattel slavery some men in the ranks of labor must do to end industrial peonage. The pioneers of labor's emancipation may have to practice the high duty of civil disobedience though they share the fate of Gene Debs and with him have to test in their own person the truth of Thoreau's great words:

> Under a government which imprisons any unjustly the true place for a just man is also a prison. . . . It is there that the fugitive slaves, and the Mexican prisoner on parole, and the Indian come to plead the wrongs of his race, should find them; on that separate but more free and honorable ground, where the state places those who are not with her but against her—the only house in a slave state in which a free man can abide with honor. If any think that their influence would be lost there, and their voices no longer afflict the ear of the state, that they would not be as an enemy within its walls, they do not know by how much truth is stronger than error, nor how much more eloquently and effectively he can combat injustice who has experienced a little in his own person.

The Franco-German Alliance

VOICES are raised once more urging that the United States and Great Britain guarantee, by a military alliance, the security of France. They tell us that if France is unreasonable in her demands for economic, political, and territorial guaranties, in her insistence upon the letter of her reparations bond, and in her wide-reaching political schemes in Eastern Europe, it is because she feels herself isolated and unsafe, and that the assurance of Anglo-American aid in time of need would soften her rancor and cut out the root of her imperialism.

We think such advocates poor friends to France and worse to Europe. We think their diagnosis of French psychology superficial, and their remedy likely only to aggravate the disease. For we believe that at heart the French phobia is, like the problem of the restoration of Europe, not military but economic. The boulevard press of Paris still prints occasional scare stories of secret German armament, but they are less and less frequent, and not at all believed in important circles. M. Briand recently had the courage, unprecedented in a post-war French Premier, to stand up in the French Chamber and tell his critics that such stories were nonsense and an insult to the intelligence of the Inter-Allied Commission of Control. The real French fear, which has made French ministers so implacable in the guard on the Rhine and about Upper Silesia and so eager for invasion of the Ruhr, is the fear of Germany's economic superiority. It is not a new fear. It antedates the war; and military alliance could only aggravate its embittering effect.

In 1870 France and Germany had approximately equal populations, and apparently equal industrial positions. Then came the Franco-Prussian War, and the German victory. In the forty years intervening between that war and the World War, French population remained stationary while German increased 70 per cent, and while French industry made slow if steady progress German industry passed through the astounding period of expansion which was paralleled only in America. The facts that Germany had begun to develop the use of steam power in her industry even before the Franco-Prussian War, and that her great *Aufschwung* occurred not in the period when France was paying the indemnity—and despite that holding her ground economically—but in the later eighties and the nineties, have never penetrated the French popular psychology. German prosperity followed German military victory. *Post hoc ergo propter hoc.* It was the Great Illusion: that victory was the cause of German prosperity. There is deep rooted in the French mind a tenacious conviction that Germany's economic advantage in the decades preceding the Great War was due to her victory in 1870; and the false corollary from a false premise was and is that a French victory should give France a similar economic advantage. Instead, the complex after-effects of the war and the peace, driving German exchange far below French, give German products the advantage in the foreign market, and keep the German factories working night and day while French factories are idle. Other factors—destruction in northern France (the importance of which is easily and often exaggerated), and the fact that French industry was largely luxury production, less needed in a period of international crisis—have contributed to the same effect. The frustrated French statesman becomes angry, as frustrated men do, and looks to political and military solutions, as is the wont of statesmen trained in the superficial school of traditional politics.

Hitherto France's allies—and liberals in general—have followed two courses. Most of the time they have sought to restrain France in her anger against Germany, acting as a sort of buffer between the two countries; yet they have supported France at the dramatic moments of her collisions with Germany. England has consistently played the role of mediator at relatively calm moments; but at critical junctures she has fallen in with France. The Silesian case is typical. It is universally believed in Berlin that the Lloyd George Government gave the Wirth Government definite assurance that if it would accept the Allied ultimatum regarding reparations last May, Britain would see that Upper Silesia went to Germany. Wirth accepted the ultimatum, and he has done his best to fulfil it, well-nigh ruining the German state finances in the process; but Upper Silesia was settled by a compromise which looks well enough on the map but which really gives the lead and the zinc, and almost all the undeveloped coal, to Poland. Britain's moderating influence availed little in the result; Germany lost the most precious part of Upper Silesia, and France remained as bitter and untaught as before.

Recently reparations policy has taken a new and significant turn. Abandoning the unsatisfactory method of Allied conference, which in effect amounted to British mediation between France and Germany, the French Minister of the Liberated Regions, M. Loucheur, undertook direct negotiations with the German Minister of Reconstruction, Walter Rathenau. The resultant agreements for the payment of reparations in kind, while attacked by many French industrials and by some intense German Nationalists, and protested by the British Government, give the first promise of real solution of the Franco-German problem since the armistice. We do not praise them unreservedly and in detail; but the method is right and is sure to be developed.

France cannot expect to emerge from the world calamity fortified or even upon an economic parity with Germany as before 1870, but she can work toward a natural continental commercial alliance, such as was slowly working itself out before the war. Therein lies her economic salvation. Anything which throws France into direct contact with Germany will help toward that end. Demands for payment in gold have forced Germany to issue paper marks and sell them until the mark has declined since the signing of the May ultimatum from one and two-thirds to one-third of a cent. That way lies disaster. Payment in kind becomes a problem internally soluble in Germany. Whatever tends toward French partnership in German industry, interesting France directly in German industrial health, tends toward European peace. Military alliances and political guaranties, diverting attention from the essential, can only hinder. The net effect of British mediation to date has been to embitter France against both Britain and Germany, and to keep her from understanding Germany. All unconsciously America has by its Hands-Off policy contributed in a very real sense to the peace of Europe. Signs are not wanting that the germ of Franco-German alliance has taken root—witness not only the Loucheur-Rathenau agreements but M. Briand's frank attacks upon M. Tardieu in the Chamber. That way lies peace.

The Great Beginning

By OSWALD GARRISON VILLARD

Washington, November 14

NOT in modern times has there been so clear-cut, so astounding, and so brilliant a feat in statecraft as marked Mr. Hughes's opening of the Conference on the Limitation of Armaments in Washington on November 12. It met in an atmosphere of doubt and pessimism; the feeling was that we were in for months of debate, discussion, intrigue behind closed doors, and silent but compelling pressure from the great imperialistic and financial forces in the world, with probably, at the end, as many of the English journalists openly prophesied, a complete fiasco. It was to be Versailles over again. America was particularly at fault because she had no clear-cut program to offer; so the talk was all about the Japanese British alliance, the fortifying of Guam, and the fate of China. And then—the Conference met, Mr. Hughes spoke, and in the twinkling of an eye the Washington world turned upside down. Or rather, to change the metaphor, Mr. Hughes cleared the decks by one superb gesture, brushed away all side issues, made the Conference and all the spectators realize that the great issue was *immediate* limitation of armaments, and presented so concrete and so far-reaching a proposal, in so straightforward, business-like, and impressive a way as to daze the delegates. The most experienced journalists present could not believe their ears.

Never was a secret so well kept. Not a single correspondent had a real inkling of Mr. Hughes's *coup*. No press association had had even a suggestion that so radical, far-reaching a proposal would be forthcoming the first day. So it came with all the force of a sudden and unexpected shock. Everybody believed that the first session would be entirely uneventful, the usual polite, palavering speeches of welcome and assurances of profound esteem, while keen and bright knives were kept up diplomatic sleeves, with an adjournment to the following week for a second meeting, at which committees would doubtless be appointed and the work leisurely begun. Not even when Mr. Hughes said, "The time has come, and this Conference has been called not for general resolutions or mutual advice, but for *action*," was there expectation of anything out of the ordinary. Mr. Hughes then at once put the ball into play. I could only think of a quarterback in the early football days starting a play before his opponents had really taken their places, in the hope of catching them napping.

Was there ever such a violation of all precedent in international conferring? Why, the Secretary of State was all but brusque in the way he tipped the Conference off that it was there not to eat and gossip and be merry, but to accomplish something quickly and go home. It was done in the manner in which our great financiers are supposed by the *Saturday Evening Post* to transact vast business in short order over glass-topped desks, and Mr. Hughes did it with a self-possession, a note of authority, a dignity of presence and presentation as if he had been doing that sort of thing every day in his life. It made one prouder than ever to be an American to see Mr. Hughes take control of that Conference, justify Mr. Balfour's praise of him as the man particularly fitted to be its presiding officer, and by the vigor and the character of his proposals make the United States not merely the dignified host of the gathering, but, in the best sense, its dominating, shaping force. Not, of course, on a platform far-reaching enough for *The Nation* and those who feel that this is the time to muster out the last private and last major-general and the last sailor and last rear-admiral, but so unexpectedly far-reaching when originating in hide-bound, conservative, imperialistic, official circles that pacifists and moderate preparedness advocates alike went out of the hall walking on air. One felt like flashing everywhere in the world one of those familiar wartime bulletins: "Our forces have clearly obtained a moral superiority over the enemy." Such is the inevitable result when statesmen cut loose from dry officialism and conventionality and take high and advanced ground; but it was all so unusual that some of the foreign correspondents and delegates are still wandering about, as I write, in a perfect daze, unable to take it all in.

Yet it was not Mr. Hughes alone who achieved all of the success of the day. Mr. Harding began the proceedings in just the right note, speaking with an earnestness and a warmth of manner and tone which convinced every one that his heart was in the Conference. Certainly no one could have delivered these words more impressively:

> Here in the United States we are but freshly turned from the burial of an unknown American soldier, when a nation sorrowed while paying him tribute. Whether it was spoken or not, a hundred millions of our people were summarizing the inexcusable cause, the incalculable cost, the unspeakable sacrifices, and the unutterable sorrows, and there was the ever-impelling question: How can humanity justify or God forgive? Human hate demands no such toll; ambition and greed must be denied it. If misunderstanding must take the blame, then let us banish it, and let understanding rule and make good-will regnant everywhere.

And every time that Mr. Harding touched on the subject of disarmament applause broke forth as it did later in redoubled measure when Mr. Hughes made his points—once I saw John J. Pershing the first on his feet to applaud a sentiment which if logically followed through would render his profession as supernumerary as the Beef-Eaters in the Tower of London.

Indeed, the audience played its part too. My mind went back steadily to the first session of that devastating Conference for Peace at Versailles. This Washington Conference is a thousand miles ahead of it! In Paris there were gathered the diplomats and generals who had done their share to plunge Europe into war and, having plunged it into hell, did not know how to extricate it until civilization faced complete disaster; then, being finally saved from themselves as well as from their enemies, knew not how to rebuild a world in ruins. I could clearly see again that room in the Quai d'Orsay in which nobody was allowed to sit unless a diplomat or a commissioner or a general—not even a humble representative of the *poilus* who died by the hundred thousand at the behest of these rulers of men who were themselves but puppets of international *haute finance;* no woman, of course, no spokesmen for millions of people to be given away to one Power or another, no representative of Russia or the beaten enemy. As onlookers only a group of newspapermen standing in an adjoining room and staring in upon a gathering dominated by formalism and imbued with hate and bitterness, without a single Christian thought or mood. Thank Heaven something of the freedom and freshness of America as well as the unconventionality of Mr. Hughes marks this Washington Conference. True, though the Unknown Soldier had been buried the day before, there were no privates of our army or navy permitted as spectators in the hall to represent the glorious dead or the living plain people who want to banish the uniform forever. But some representatives of the workers were there and many women, and the balconies were filled with people who lived and breathed, who responded to sentiment, who did not hesitate to charge the atmosphere with their own emotions, to applaud and to cheer, to let the conferees know where they stood, and that there were human hearts there and not merely the cold, austere automata of diplomacy.

Once more one blessed the House and Senate, for their members, crowded into one balcony, made it clear from the start that neither Mr. Harding, nor Mr. Hughes could go too far for them. The very men who have been voting billions for weapons with which to kill were cheering far-reaching proposals for disarmament with an enthusiasm to make one believe that they may go even further than Mr. Hughes when the next appropriation bills come in. More than that, when Mr. Hughes sought to adjourn the meeting, they took it out of his hands, insisting on the right to hear and applaud Briand and the leader of every other delegation. Therein, too, the morning was unlike any session of any similar conference. "Why, it was a regular political meeting. The delegates know now what a Democratic or Republican Convention looks like," said one English writer. But it was far more than that—it was the most powerful legislature in the world placing itself squarely behind the Executive in vociferous support of a splendid Yes, "a world-impressive proposal," as the New York *Herald* calls it. It was a demonstration without a trace of partisanship—a bit of "politics" that was quite content to have Mr. Hughes propose as an evidence of good faith to scrap more of our tonnage than anybody else's, throw away $332,000,000 spent upon ships now building.

Practical politics it unquestionably was—the best kind, and it will reap the reward which invariably follows upon a high-minded and wise and courageous act. As I heard it I found myself saying: "This probably saves the House next fall for the Republicans," but there was nothing in anything that Mr. Hughes said or did to suggest a political motive. Yet it is plain that his proposals constitute the highest form of political strategy, for if the attempt to limit arms fails Mr. Hughes and Mr. Harding can go before the country and say without fear of denial that they are not responsible; that they gave a lead which the others must have followed had they sincerely desired to relieve the world of part of the burdens that are crushing it.

Accept it at once, in principle, I believe they will. The Englishmen I have seen since, even the most jingo of them, say there is no other alternative. Angry and annoyed most of them are, for they are still thinking in terms of control in the Far East, of the old balance of power in Europe, of their "Britannia Rules the Waves." Curiously enough, they feel that we have been guilty of very bad manners, that we have lured them into our parlor as the spider did the fly, and then put them in a hole and done it publicly. The public avowal of Mr. Hughes's plan is what has stunned the French most. Apparently the English feel that there should have been only a mild cut. They say we could muster out every ship and soldier and still be safe, but that they live in the *Realpolitik* of Europe. "You have asked us to give up our controlling place upon the sea, but you leave the French army untouched, leave her free to dominate Europe, to impose her will upon the Rhine." To which my reply is: "Wait, wait. Mr. Hughes has only dealt the first hand. Limitation of land armaments comes third. No one knows what his plans are; but if he begins with such a stunning proposal at the outset, is he not likely to have something to say under Number Three when he reaches it?" At any rate, it is perfectly plain that when M. Briand speaks of Mr. Hughes's plan as "American diplomacy," he does so with the feeling that we are once more the bull in the old-fashioned diplomatic china shop. Here in this assemblage of distinguished foreigners it is once more clear what every returning traveler reports, that we Americans are coming everywhere to be dreaded as the most powerful, the richest, and the most dangerous of imperialistic nations. If we save the world from the burden of armaments we shall be no better beloved than the proverbial peace-maker.

For the moment that can be overlooked in the glory of Saturday's achievement. We have set up a standard for all sincere men to repair to and it will seem so reasonable and sensible, so generous and wise to the plain people everywhere and particularly in America that the diplomats must come to it. Let the public compel it even if there are those here to say that it will be a lynching or stampeding of our "guests" to exert great popular pressure. Let Mr. Harding and Mr. Hughes be buried under an avalanche of congratulations coupled with the demand that we go on with the policy in the matter of land armaments! Some wriggling we shall see. The British say that our proposal is unfair because it does not allow sufficiently for the age of ships and size of guns. To this the sufficient answer is that these are trifling items where the safety of the world is at stake; that if these details are to be wrangled over, then there is no real devotion to disarmament on the part of the dissenters; then they are here to maneuver once more for place and advantage in the good old outworn way without regard to the real interests of humanity or to the treasuries of the several countries now so heavily in our debt. The state of the British Exchequer and Lloyd George's fervent description of this Conference as the one "rainbow of hope" in the heavens will make for acceptance of our proposals. But there is a serious prospect that the English, and later the French, will come back with the demand that if they accept Mr. Hughes's plans we join in guaranties of one kind and another. The English frankly feel that we are selfish to ask them to do our wish and then to take no responsibility for the situation thus created. On both sides of the Atlantic we shall see fresh drives to put us into the League of Nations, which in its present form we must not enter, disarmament or no disarmament. At the cost of seeming ungrateful and unwilling to do our share later, we must give no guaranties of the kind we shall be asked to agree to and enter no entangling alliances. What ought to happen at the very next session of the Conference (Tuesday, November 15) should be the rising of Mr. Balfour to accept the proposal at least in principle on behalf of Mr. Lloyd George's Government, at which Mr. Briand ought to second the motion by officially declaring that the French Government will for ten years voluntarily abandon the building of all capital ships although France is not included in the Hughes plan. This should be easy for him to do because his Government has already abandoned battleship building and because, however great may be the German menace to France on land, that on sea is ended; there is no German navy left and none can be built on the sly. If France and England can do this Japan will follow suit; she would be ashamed not to.

How otherwise will Japan take it? Well, Americans ought to understand that Japanese politics turn largely on the rivalry of the Satsuma and Choshu clans, the former of which controls the navy and the latter the army. The Satsuma will only yield reluctantly under overwhelming pressure and so will Japanese big business which will be slow to accept the ending of all government work in the shipyards. The next few days will show several things: for instance, whether the Japanese Government will permit the publication in full in Japan of Mr. Hughes's speech without connotations and how soon. Then we shall see whether the merits of the case are to be obscured by the raising of some issue like the question of our fortifications or possible fortifications at Guam, at Corregidor, and in Hawaii. Somehow or other, however, it is impossible for me to believe that the Japanese will play in this Conference the stupid role of the Germans at the Hague.

In jubilating thus over what Mr. Hughes actually achieved by his sensational stroke, no one will, of course be misled into believing that the millennium is at hand. Those who oppose all weapons on spiritual, ethical, and Christian grounds, who care not a fig for balances of power and other militarist excuses, are enlisted in the fight to the end; they will not be rendered harmless by Mr. Hughes's proposal, heartening and electrifying as it is. The true and faithful advocates of disarmament who base their case on principle and were never misled by the preparedness mania of four years ago, or Mr. Wilson's foolish belief that war could be ended and the world redeemed by "force without stint," are in the position of those who expected only a few crumbs and suddenly find themselves offered a whole plateful of bountiful food. For everything that we shall receive we shall be grateful profoundly—but the fight will go on. It is splendid to have Mr. Borah's assurance that he is going to wipe out battleship and submarine. There will be no holiday for that, no rest by day or by night until the world is freed from all danger of that next war, which in the eyes even of the experts threatens the very existence of civilization. And this means the ending of chemical warfare, poison gas, and the airplane menace to humanity.

But those who know no compromise will stop cheerfully and happily to applaud Mr. Hughes and Mr. Harding for so brave, so tactically wise, so forward-looking a stand.

National Interests *vs.* Peace

PROMISING as has been the beginning of the Conference on Armaments, the sad fact remains that throughout the proceedings and the press discussions the note of narrow nationalism has been menacingly strong. Despite the world's crucifixion since 1914, the power of the old diplomatic phrases is still great. Delegates and foreign journalists arrived in Washington not to talk disarmament on its merits but prepared for an old-fashioned give-and-take, with more concern for trade routes, spheres of influ-

ence, and British "rights" in Hongkong than for reduction of the world's armament bill. It was because of this atmosphere that Mr. Hughes's concrete proposals came with such tremendous effect; delegates and journalists alike had wholly to recast their mental attitudes. The bewilderment of the correspondents was at once reflected in their dispatches. They complained of the provinciality of the Americans, who simply would not see that any serious naval disarmament would give the Japanese navy entire control of the eastern seas, menace India, and threaten French control of Indo-China. Sometimes it is worth while to be provincial!

The Allies, of course, approached this Conference, notably in regard to Far Eastern questions, with jealousy and suspicion and eager determination to get out of it as much as possible. And these very men, still talking about national honor and the right of national protection upon the high seas, are disregarding the national rights of China and instigating a propaganda for international control of that country because it has defaulted on some of its bonds. The loss of bond interest is, of course, one of the greatest stimulants to internationalism in our topsy-turvy imperialistic world. International action is just the thing when one's pocketbook is threatened, but as to approaching the problems on the Conference's agenda with the welfare of the world solely at heart, why that is a different matter.

The Chinese proposals similarly cleared the atmosphere because they laid down fundamental principles. The delegation might have come forward with requests for the cancelation of this concession, the return of that railroad, the release of that province. Instead it laid down a program which, if it is adopted, means wiping out a century of wrongdoing by the predatory Christian Powers and by Japan, and restoration of China as a respected entity with its breached nationality restored. The reaction to this program of the Powers who will sit in judgment upon China's fate in Washington will be the clearest possible test of the political and international morality of the judges.

When one reads M. Briand's insistence upon superior consideration for France and his assertion that her navy is too small and her army barely large enough, it is plain that the fundamental lessons of the struggle which so nearly ended in her defeat have not been learned by France. Yet the Conference itself is proof that we are moving in the right direction, even though Russians and Germans are absent. Already Mr. Hughes has suggested another naval conference and the Chinese have stipulated that there shall be "provision for future conferences to be held from time to time" to discuss Far Eastern questions. That points toward international government of the right kind—international consultation at regular intervals more or less in the open, at worst a great advance over the business of settling Far Eastern questions by secret *pourparlers* and such exchanges of notes as brought about the Lansing-Ishii agreement which we were long not even permitted to read.

Advocates of the League of Nations were certain that the meeting at Washington would compel us to join by sheer force of logic. But the first two weeks have passed with scarcely a reference to that feeble institution, and when one considers how this misbegotten child of Versailles has failed to take the lead toward disarming the world, but instead by its Vilna and its Silesian decisions has made rather for war than for peace, its condescending approval of Mr. Hughes's concrete plan is merely ludicrous. So far from helping the League, Mr. Hughes seems bent on demonstrating that another association of nations is possible. Throughout the treaty fight Mr. Wilson declared that there was no alternative between joining the League and having the greatest navy on earth and a nation in arms as well. Mr. Harding and Mr. Hughes have neatly punctured that folly. Just how much disarmament the controlling political and business forces behind the scenes at Washington will let us have is naturally not yet clear. Mr. Hughes's sweeping proposals may be blurred in a cloud of expert amendments, whittling the spirit out of his stand and leaving the deadly menaces of poison gas and submarines and the still more deadly menaces of economic and military rivalry untouched. The fact remains that through disarmament lies the path to that true cooperation of humanity whose final coming is as certain as that the world revolves. The oftener the nations meet in council the quicker will the pettiness of their narrow nationalism betray itself and fade away.

The Conference—The Second Phase

By OSWALD GARRISON VILLARD

Washington, November 21

THE Conference on the Limitation of Armaments entered upon its second phase with its second session on November 15. It was, I suppose, too much to expect that it should remain at that pitch of exaltation to which Mr. Hughes's proposal raised it. Yet there were great possibilities of other dramatic moments. By a hearty and unqualified acceptance of the Hughes program Mr. Balfour could have disputed the American leadership. Had Admiral Kato simply pronounced two sentences: "We approve Mr. Hughes's plan in principle. We accept it in its every detail," the audience would have gone wild with enthusiasm, Japanese stock would have been quoted at par, and England would have been relegated to third place. Those two sentences would have been conspicuous in every newspaper on earth. But diplomats are as dull and as lacking in ability to seize upon the dramatic side of a situation as they are timid. Mr. Kato's weasel words, like those of Mr. Balfour, spoiled the effectiveness of the acceptance in principle, and with the reference of both the great issues to committees the second and more secret phase of the Conference began.

But just how secret that is going to be remains to be seen. This is still a conference of surprises, and surprises so great that the most experienced press observers are admittedly well over their depth. The Chinese promptly astounded English and Japanese alike by laying down the exact program they desired, all the more astonishing because their delegation has been anything but united as to what was the proper course to take. So sweeping a position, based upon principle and carefully avoiding all detail, has again worried the Conference, and the uneasiness of the delegates is all the greater because it is universally taken for granted that it was the voice of China but the hand of Hughes. The anxiety of all our visitors as to what that dreadful man is going to do next is quite remarkable. For many of them this has become an uncomfortable guessing match.

Quite as sensational was the hoisting of a red flag of revolt by some of the Japanese correspondents on Thursday. Anyone who knows the Japanese press knows that it is more subservient to its government than that of any other country. Its writers have never approximated the position at home held by French, American, and British journalists in their countries. They have never been granted audiences by their public men, or recognized as being a Fourth Estate. Hence an action which would have been sensational if the work of any other press group, bears the aspect of revolution when taken by the Japanese. Running the risk, some of them at least, of losing their positions, of being accused of betraying their own leaders in the face of the "enemy," of deliberately embarrassing their delegates in the midst of negotiations, these twenty Japanese journalists went on record as opposing their Government and asking that it should recede from its position and accept the Hughes terms without reservations or any such alterations as those of Admiral Kato. What could be more gratifying than that? What more astounding? Glimmering has gone the old idea that Japanese journalists are merely spies and the creatures and tools of their Government; gone is the old idea that you can never find out what a Japanese really thinks. To Admiral Kato it must seem as if the heavens were tumbling. Who ever heard of men paid, not to talk but merely to report, taking a hand in the game as though they had some say in this gathering? Plainly this is the maddest and most unconventional of conferences.

What does so daring an act mean? Why plainly that there is a much more liberal sentiment at home, a much greater desire among the people of Japan for disarmament than had been suspected. I have talked with some of these Japanese newspapermen and find them not at all worried as to what will happen to their shipyards. They are not the least in sympathy with Mr. Balfour in his concern lest the charming art of making useless battleships at $35,000,000 per ship for the enrichment of some great industrialists be lost in the next ten years. They realize that their country has not stood well before the world and they are anxious to change that situation. They are not at all disturbed by the Chinese proposals and see no reason why their country should not go to work with them as a basis to develop a satisfactory settlement of the issues between the two countries. More than that, they are profoundly grateful that our daily press did not attack their country and its delegates severely after Admiral Kato made his blunder—as they call it—and they are still rejoicing that at the opening session there were louder cheers for the Japanese spokesman, Prince Tokugawa, than for Mr. Balfour. The warmth and friendliness of their reception here has had the inevitable result that such treatment produces—they are trying their best to reciprocate. But how Admiral Kato's position must have stung these proud-spirited men to make them call upon him and protest!

All of which is to the good. What if this Conference should really get out of hand? Here are the English demanding a modification of the submarine allowance in favor not of more but fewer ships. Here are the Chinese taking personally such a conciliatory attitude toward their Japanese oppressors as to make it difficult to recall how bitter was their bearing toward one another during the long trying months in Paris. No, the millennium is not at hand, dear reader; we are not even sure that here in Washington we shall get anything very tangible as yet. But it is necessary to record the fact that things are so unconventional and so contrary to what has been considered good form at previous gatherings of this kind as to give rise at least to faint wonderings whether after all some people are not taking seriously President Harding's fervent "It must not be again." It certainly begins to look as if the longer the Conference remains in session the more a radical sentiment might develop right here. Of course the French are yet to be heard from on the land disarmament question; there is a good deal of anxiety as to what Briand will do and say when he gets his chance to deliver the speech which is the main reason for his coming over. The French delegates are not happy here or well pleased with their treatment. Then it is quite possible that in the committees the detailed agreements may undo the fine principles laid down. Naval and military experts are usually the enemies of mankind and they are here today. But there is the Conference itself. It may decide to do some thinking and voting on its own account. It is not yet at all certain that the committee of admirals headed by Roosevelt the Younger will have its way. Indeed, we have yet to see what our own public sentiment will do if our experts insist upon declining the British submarine proposal on the absurd ground that we must have big ocean-going submarines in order that they may reach the Panama Canal safely—this from a Navy Department that was only the other day scored for not having one single ocean-going submarine ready for a long voyage, despite all the millions squandered upon them. The public ought to overwhelm Mr. Hughes with the demand that we lead the way in abolishing the whole sneaking, cowardly submarine fleet. This Conference is rightly the people's. Let them now give orders!

We need down here one great mordant humorist of Mark Twain stature to laugh out of court some of the pretensions now going about. Take the battleship situation. Grateful as we shall be if that folly is stopped for ten years, what earthly reason is there for keeping any battleships whatever? Why, no sound common-sense reason, of course. Take the question of the relation of the battleship to the airplane. Let us assume, if you please, that Sir Percy Scott and the other British and American officers who insist that the day of the battleship is gone forever are premature. Well, everybody admits that the air peril has become so great that new battleships must be built with special armor protection against bombing attack. The sinking of the old German battleship Ostfriesland off the Virginia Capes was accomplished by bombs that did not hit her but exploded in the water near her. But as we are going to scrap the newest and latest-planned ships first of all, we are plainly going to destroy those that are somewhat planned against aerial attack. Ergo, those that we shall keep afloat are the most vulnerable. Then why keep them afloat at all? If bombing machines continue to develop in the next two years as they have in the last two it will be folly to go to war with any battleships at all—perhaps it will even be sending men to sure death to let them go to war. Then why not scrap all the battleships? Because, the all-wise statesmen will tell you, the peoples of the various countries are not ready for anything more; that we must go slowly one step at a time and not get ahead of public opinion; that we must be "practical." So we really need some one to make people laugh at such timidity and cowardice, such inability to get away from preconceptions, conventionalities, and unrealities. We need a Mark Twain to make us, grateful for small favors as we are, ridicule this doing away with some battleships when the airplane and the dirigible and above all poison gas threaten the very existence of humanity.

Yet I for one feel that even if the committees repeat the history of Versailles over again we shall make great spiritual gains from the Conference here. I cannot sympathize with the radicals who scoff at the whole thing. A tremendous public education is going on, a vast public opinion is being created. The real sentiment of the American people is being allowed to make itself felt and to prove what *The Nation* has felt all along that the preparedness campaign was an artificial growth, stimulated by Wall Street money and paid propaganda and boosted by politicians for their own advantage. How the pacifists were denounced for saying that preparedness led to war not peace! Today everybody in Washington outside of army and navy circles takes this view and there are actually navy officers favoring disarmament. In fact one need only go to the Capitol to notice the tremendous effect that this Conference and the ensuing discussions are having on our politicians. They are hearing from the country by every mail, and the demand is not for limitation but for real disarmament. Even the chairmen of the military committees are reported to be much affected. That the army will go down to 100,000 in the next appropriation bill is a foregone conclusion no matter what the Conference does. And there will be a fight to muster out a good part of the navy's personnel as soon as the bill is presented. Again it is fashionable and not treasonable to hold in Washington the historic American view that this country's highest destiny is to be unarmed and unafraid!

What Is Lacking in Washington

MANY things are lacking at the Peace Conference—truth-telling, for instance, and the banishment of diplomatic insincerity. One longs to find in the dispatches the story of some delegate's rising to face the facts of the world as they are. The statesmen who sit around the green tables are precisely the type of men who pride themselves upon their practicality, upon seeing things as they exist, upon knowing just how far, to the inch, the public opinion (or big business) of their respective states will permit them to go. They are neither theorists, nor idealists; their feet "are on the ground." As Mr. Wilson was so fond of saying, they know what they want and how to obtain it. Real politics is their specialty. Were they not chosen to high office because of fitness for leadership?

Well, the simple fact is that these men in Washington are anything but practical. Perhaps this is due to their not being at heart really "sold"—to borrow an advertising phrase—on disarmament, perhaps to their overweening fear lest some one of them get ahead of the others. At any rate, the evidence is clear that on all sides are things that could be done to forward the momentous task in hand if only the men at those tables were not so very great, so very wise, and so very profound. Sometimes it is obvious that little children could lead them. What if some daring iconoclast should rise and utter a few commonplace but true phrases. We believe that panic would follow; that what, but for Mr. Hughes's enlightened and businesslike directness of plan and procedure, would be a mere structure of all but useless official formalism would forthwith collapse. One sighs, as one did in perusing the dispatches from Paris, for a few homespun, simple folk to discuss and settle the whole question as it is being talked over and voted on at Newton Four Corners, and in the general store at Sandy Gulch. It seemed as if official formalism did its worst at Paris; alas, it still survives as a mischief maker. What would happen, for instance, if some delegate, noting the demand for it in the powerful New York press, among the Englishmen, and in numerous other quarters, should rise to move the total abolition of the submarine? The fat would, indeed, be in the fire. The whole sacred agenda would tremble in the balance. The Conference would have to ask itself, Why the submarine? and there would be the gravest danger of the submarine being outlawed. Fortunately for the friends of the submarine, no delegate would think of so violating good taste and form; so the submarine is safe and England is allowed more submarines than she really wants.

The "great leaders" have brought with them advisers and councilors, aides-de-camp and scribes, secretaries and under-secretaries. But there is lacking a simple appreciation of the fact that those who should have been banned are the experts, naval and military. Had President Harding been wise he would have invited the Conference to Hot Springs, Virginia, thus taking it out of the atmosphere of officialdom, and have stated in his invitations that inasmuch as no American army or navy officer would be allowed within one hundred and fifty miles of the Conference under pain of court-martial our guests were asked to leave theirs behind—on the cowboy dance principle that "guns" simply must be left outside. From the moment the Hughes plan went to the experts trouble began: Experts must pick flaws else are they not experts and are thus not worth their salaries. And when it comes to consulting experts about plans which, if rightly interpreted, can only mean the beginning of the abolition of the profession to which they belong—well, it is expecting a good deal of human nature to ask that those experts do other than find reasons why any beginning of disarmament should be made as trifling as possible.

There are, however, far more vital things lacking at the Washington Conference than a failure to understand, a fact which Admiral Sims has just pointed out in his address before the Naval War College, namely, that the naval expert is the most ultra-conservative of all experts. Throughout the Conference thus far its artificiality has been disturbed by no single reference to the dangerous economic status of the world. We search in vain the columns of our dailies for a reference to the fact that the old world these statesmen typify is collapsing—is, as Mr. Wells has written, steadily going down into the abyss without as yet a single intelligent effort to stop its descent to Avernus. These men act as if in a sterilized vacuum, as if their proceedings bore no relation to the question of foreign exchange, to the condition of their mostly bankrupt treasuries, to the state of international trade, to the lack of free trade everywhere, to the growing numbers of workers and starving men in Europe, to the threat of a general European collapse in the spring. They talk, like M. Briand, the language of a dead past. Thus the realists are the most unreal; the men of affairs the most detached from the truly vital affairs of the hour; the practical men the most impractical since they shut eyes and ears to the toil and sorrow of the world. Believing that they are making the world over, they fail to see their perilous resemblance to him who fiddled while Rome burned.

Of course, it all goes back beyond that. Mr. Hughes truly remarked that there can be no real peace without the will to peace. But the will to peace must come from an appreciation of the spiritual values of the world; from a realization that war in its every aspect defiles the ark of the covenant of humanity, that it is a deadly sin against whatever is godlike in man. Peace requires a realization that, as the Great War finally proved, violence accomplishes nothing, and that, even now, the human race is paying a frightful price for its sin against all that is sacred. In the Washington Conference, if we judge aright, there is not one word spoken to show that the spiritual lessons of the war have been learned or even understood. The emphasis is all upon the need of cutting down expenses, lightening the burden. Undue sentiment—and certainly sentimentality—is, perhaps, out of place in such a gathering. But how one longs for a single orator to tell what these armament burdens mean to the poor, the lowly, the toiling; for a single speaker to voice the feelings of the poilus of all lands to whom war means death or unbearable suffering. Finally, the greatest lack of all is one clear note of brotherhood. To this Conference it is as though the Prince of Peace had never brought to men a message of good-will. Hence all that we shall get, little or great, from the Conference is merely on account. The will to peace cannot prevail while men will not see or refuse to use the talisman that even now lies within their grasp.

Briand's Failure

By OSWALD GARRISON VILLARD

Washington, November 28

A MASTERPIECE of falsehood and misrepresentation, an abject confession of fear of Germany, and a deliberate slap at the British—this was M. Briand's long-awaited declaration of the French reasons why their country cannot disarm. To hear him was, moreover, to listen to a fire-cracker where a bomb was expected. Aristide Briand can speak much better than he did at the third session of the Washington Conference—as I can testify of personal knowledge. He, moreover, weakened the force of his presentation by permitting himself to be stopped twice for the translation of what he had said. Again, he ended on a dull and quiet note, whereas he had a superb climax for the end of the second portion of his address. It was as if the consciousness of his bad cause fatally handicapped him. Certainly, so far as the Conference was concerned, if I may draw a simile from the football field, the French ran the wrong man with the ball. M. Briand being the captain insisted on taking it. But in this case Viviani was the man to have carried it. He would not have stopped for the translator and he would have poured forth such a torrent of eloquence that the galleries would have been electrified—even though he is only a glorious voice with no brains behind it. M. Briand received nine seconds of courteous applause when he sat down—that is all. It was not a triumph; not even a success with the thoughtful. And I am ready to wager my reputation that there was relief and rejoicing behind the masks of Root, Lodge, Hughes, and Underwood when Briand ended. Whether or not a long-heralded oration, like a watched pot, does not boil, any danger of a stampede of the Conference was averted. There was not even created the atmosphere of excitement which ought to have attended so significant an utterance.

One thing M. Briand unquestionably did—he widened the breach between England and France. Mr. Wells's vigorous characterization of it is mild and gentle as a summer zephyr compared with what the Britishers said of it privately, after they left the hall. One of the most brilliant women in the diplomatic corps here has asked me not to dwell upon this phase of it in my correspondence. But it is necessary to set forth the truth and, more than that, her own assurance that the breach is now about complete is another reason why the facts should be written—no harm can now be done by so doing. But to realize what M. Briand did to the British, one must note the fact that in his speech he *never once* referred to them or to their frightful sacrifices during the war, or to the "holy alliance" between them. On the contrary he dwelt upon the isolation of the French; he presented the case as if there were no other nations on earth save the French, Russians, and Germans. France, in his eyes, is the sole defender of morality and justice and liberty. It must have a huge army—his promises of reductions in size and of the term of service were as vague as Mr. Hughes's disarmament proposals were clear-cut and specific, and, apparently, simmer down to only 39,000 men—as if France alone would have to bear the whole brunt of another attack by "Huns" or Bolsheviks; as if France alone had saved the world when Lenin fought the Poles. As for Upper Silesia, nothing that he said cut the British more than his references to that imbroglio, where British and French troops all but came to blows.

When M. Briand sat down we were treated to an orgy of insincere flattery and lip-service. Probably not since Shakespeare gave us Marc Antony's oration over the body of Julius Caesar has there been a more brilliant example of that type of speech which praises while scarifying than that afforded by Mr. Balfour's reply. There is a *double entendre* in several paragraphs of that speech in which, after praising a mediocre address as one of the greatest of orations, a masterpiece, etc., he spoke of it as also a complete laying bare of the real inwardness of the French thought upon this subject—the heart of a nation. Mr. Balfour rose to bury M. Briand, not to praise him. He easily turned M. Briand's position by simply referring to the million British dead and two million disabled and wounded. France was not alone in defending liberty and justice, he said. If menacing imperialism should raise its head again England would once more be on hand to bear her share. Near the end he significantly remarked, after recalling that the English had fought for international liberty: ". . . if a similar necessity should again arise, if again the lust of domination, which has been the curse of Europe for so many generations should threaten the peace, the independence, the self-development of our neighbors and allies, how could it be . . . that we who had done so much for the great cause of international liberty should see that cause perish before our eyes rather than make further sacrifices in its defense?" Seeing that for many generations until quite recently it was the Napoleons of France and their predecessors who were possessed of that "lust of domination which has been the curse of Europe," and that the French are today trying to dominate all Europe by their military power, the deeper significance of Mr. Balfour's words is plain. Certain it is that many of the Englishmen felt that M. Briand had made a declaration of war against Great Britain. "The most infamous speech I ever listened to," said the dean of the English corps of correspondents to me when we met just after it.

Mr. Hughes, of course, in behalf of America spoke his share of meaningless platitudes. He was happy to assure M. Briand that France must not fear isolation—"there is no isolation for the defenders of liberty and justice." But fair words no more make defensive and offensive alliances than they butter parsnips. According to Mr. Hughes's phrases, the United States might go to the rescue of Germany some day if she should appear to be on the side of liberty and justice. What an atmosphere of cant and insincerity and hypocrisy! It was good to get out of the hall into clear and pure air again.

As for the mendacity of M. Briand's statements, five

minutes of cross-examination would have revealed it. If what he said is true, members of the Interallied Commission for the Disarmament of Germany ought to be court-martialed not only for dereliction of duty but for endless falsehoods. But they have not failed at their tasks. I take, for example, the following from the weekly *Manchester Guardian* of November 9 as to what M. Briand's own French General Nollet has achieved:

> General Nollet, president of the Commission for the Disarmament of Germany, interviewed recently in Paris by a number of political personalities, set the scaremongers at rest. He says that after eighteen months in Germany, visiting every hole and corner up and down the country where arms could be concealed, he is convinced that Germany today is really effectively disarmed. All her strong places and fortresses have been dismantled. The following war material has been either destroyed or handed over: 4,000 siege guns, 32,800 ordinary guns, 11,000 minenwerfer (trench mortars), 84,000 machine-guns, 4,200,000 small arms, 32,000,000 shells, 50,000 munition wagons, 55,000 military wagons, 11,000 field kitchens, 1,800 pontoons, and an immense quantity of miscellaneous articles. As far as the physical means of waging war is concerned, Germany is no longer a military power. General Nollet's declarations have had a great calming effect on French leaders' opinion, where at least it is beginning to be felt that the German revenge bogy is dead. This impression is all the greater as General Nollet, up till now, has always been pessimistic about German disarmament.

So far as the extract from Ludendorff's book which M. Briand read is concerned, as I heard him read it it sounded strangely familiar. It is not only the same sort of stuff that every professional militarist has been saying for a long time past; it can be paralleled in almost every sentiment by extracts from Theodore Roosevelt's "Strenuous Life." He, too, had this same belief that war is essential and necessary, and that without it the virile qualities of mankind will die. What M. Briand did not add is what everybody in Germany knows—that Ludendorff and his crowd, if they get into power, will face the same antagonism and hostility of the German workers which led to the ending of the attempted Kapp revolution in forty-eight hours.

Now, General Nollet is French and he is M. Briand's subordinate. One or the other is misstating; there is no alternative. It is M. Briand; he knows full well that quite aside from the question of armament Germany is deprived of her old allies and is economically crushed, with her laboring classes on the verge of starvation, her currency debased, her treasury practically bankrupt, the mark sinking out of sight, with food at prohibitive prices. Danger of a German attack there may be fifty years from now, if civilization has survived, but not sooner. And, of course, there would be no danger at all if France's attitude had been forgiving and generous to the Germans. She could not rise to such heights, and as for M. Briand, as my diplomatic friend said: "He *had* to make that speech or lose his job. And if he goes we shall get a worse one." But what an abject confession of French fear of Germany it is to so dread a beaten, wrecked, disorganized, and discredited foe!

Disarmament Is Not Enough

JAMES SIMPSON, partner with John G. Shedd in complete ownership of the great Chicago house of Marshall Field and Company, returns to America reporting that Europe is in a state of "financial and economic chaos" and that "unless something is done promptly to avert the disaster, which approaches with constantly increasing rapidity, it will spread from one country to another until we are all involved in the maelstrom." John F. Sinclair of Minneapolis bears much the same message. Frank A. Vanderlip, until two years ago president of the largest bank in New York City, returns more convinced than two years ago, when he wrote his gloomy "What Happened in Europe" and was forced out of office for it by then optimistic bank directors, that Europe is sliding downward and needs our help.

We have become hardened by many alarms; we have heard too much of imminent chaos and bolshevism in Europe. With our attention concentrated on politics, we have noted the slackening in the political revolutionary movement, and have neglected more fundamental economic currents. But the spectacular collapse of the German mark this autumn has made financiers gasp. Industry seemed to be booming in Germany; returning travelers were cheerfully reporting that Germany was hard at work and rapidly recovering. Then in three months the German mark dropped from about two cents to a third of a cent. Values were revolutionized overnight. The tumble of the mark meant that imported goods suddenly jumped to six times their former prices. Food and clothing began leaping skyward in price. Wages followed more slowly but as erratically. Some shops were emptied by purchasers mad to spend their marks before prices skyrocketed again, and others were simply looted. Germany, that had seemed the stable factor in Europe, became the least certain.

In the main the fall of the German mark was due to the necessity of printing millions of paper marks with which to purchase foreign gold to meet the reparations payments. But the sudden break was symptomatic of a deeper disease not confined to Germany alone. Europe is one body, and the terrible depreciation of currency is common to all Central and Eastern Europe. The value of the Russian ruble, once worth fifty cents, recently declined overnight from 1/1500 of a cent to 1/2000 of a cent. The Polish mark and the Austrian crown are at about 1/35 of a cent each; and the currencies of Hungary, the Baltic States, and Jugoslavia are also lower than that of Germany. Vienna has just had another outburst of anger against the comfortable hotels and shops for wealthy foreigners. Revolutionary leadership is less evident than a year ago; but conditions have become more revolutionary.

Already the collapse in Germany has shaken British financial experts into proposing a moratorium on German reparations payments, and the French Government appears ready to bargain for what she can get out of the wreckage. The first effect of that proposal was a spectacular recovery of the mark—only less disastrous in its chaotic effect upon production and exchange than the precedent collapse.

Inevitably when the whole question of German reparations is brought up for new discussion the question of allied debts follows it into the closets of statesmen. Political scruples in Washington cannot divorce the two problems. Few of the European countries can ever repay their debts to the United States. England probably can; there is a bare possibility that France might, though at bitter cost to herself and to us; Czecho-Slovakia, Italy, Rumania, and the rest almost certainly cannot. Talk of "refunding" is mere camouflage; it means postponement of the payment of interest, which in turn means increasing the debt still further and making it still more impossible to pay it. Congress and the American people may be fooled by calling cancelation "refunding" or "investment" for a time; but in the long run they will have to face the fact that for a large part of our wartime "loans" the only question is upon what terms they shall be canceled. If by forgiving our debtors we could buy an end of the grosser manifestations not only of British and French militarism but of their underlying imperialism we should have made the finest and most profitable bargain in history. Even as matters stand, it is obvious enough that the existence of these debts is one of Mr. Hughes's strongest arguments—though he refuses to mention it—in urging disarmament.

But disarmament is not enough. It can relieve somewhat the pressure upon governments, but something more is required for the salvation of Europe, something which has not yet even been discussed by statesmen. Since radical programs have very evidently not the kind of support to make them immediately effective, we must look to international action by business men and financiers as the immediate hope of saving Europe from the condition of the Balkans. If these gentlemen are still bound by a system which has been the cause of Europe's ruin and if they cannot plan its permanent cure, they may at least be capable of sufficiently far-sighted action to arrest her disease and give time for a growth of other forces which may bring salvation. Shall we be told that business ethics are bad? True, but so far as Europe is concerned, the vision of big business men is keener than that either of the politicians or the so-called middle class. Stinnes's genius fed Austria's factories with coal when long governmental palavers had left them idle. And Europe today seems to have left but two alternatives: to fall into a chaos which would euphemistically be called Bolshevism, out of which might after long misery grow a new society—and salvation by business men. In any such process America would have to share largely; but the American people are suspicious of Europe and of business men. They doubt the probity of big business, and their experience in making war and making peace has let them fall back on a plain refusal to risk more American money in efforts to help Europe muddle through. But that the people can be enlightened as to the economics and human realities of the situation the popularity of Mr. Wells's articles proves. Let America therefore take the lead in calling an international congress, not primarily of politicians but of business men. Let the more enlightened business leaders consult publicly with such Europeans as Ter Meulen, the distinguished Dutch proponent of an international currency, Hugo Stinnes, Walter Rathenau, M. Loucheur, Sir Philip Sassoon, and Mr. Keynes, and discuss their problems under the eyes of all America. The program they could evolve would be far from ideal, but it would be infinitely better than a policy of drift or the scheming of imperialistic diplomats. If they fail, then it will be plain that the fundamentals are wrong and more radical solutions inevitable. In any case international conference and action is the alternative to international ruin.

A Conference Cursed by Nationality

By OSWALD GARRISON VILLARD

Washington, December 4

"THE spirit of nationality rages like a pestilence; it is the curse of Europe," wrote Lord Hugh Cecil recently to the London *Times*. We have had a pestilence of nationality in the progress of the Washington Conference this week. Not that I would have *The Nation's* readers believe all that the headlines announce. This is one of the hardest gatherings imaginable to report. It began on an extremely high and exciting note which could not be held long, and with the best will in the world the men who are here to send out news every day find themselves hard put to it to fill the space assigned to them. "Shall we be pessimistic or optimistic today?" was the question, both naive and despairing, put to Secretary Hughes on Thursday by one of the fraternity whose earnestness and zeal for duty could not be questioned. There have been days when the news was neither optimistic nor pessimistic, when everybody was marking time, yet the spirit of nationality overshadowed everything. Nowhere an attempt to deal with an issue solely from the point of view of the interest of the world as a whole, or even of that of the masses here directly represented—only a nationally inspired desire to examine every proposal from the narrowly selfish point of view and to squeeze out of it all possible advantage by interpretation or bargaining. This is the reply to Mr. Harding's appeal for the nations here represented to do jointly what he said they could not do individually!

Japan has been individually striving to see just how much she could get by bargaining. Her acceptance of the Hughes battleship ratio has been a foregone conclusion. Should the Japanese bolt the opinion of the entire Allied world would be solidified against her. I am not overlooking that there is much meat in some of her contentions. Her delegates would be justified in seeking to get the United States to abandon its senseless fortifications in the Philippines and Hawaii and to announce publicly that it had no desire to fortify Guam. Those Pacific fortifications are aimed only at Japan and it would be a noble and stimulating act on our part, one worthy of Mr. Hughes's opening, to make this gesture. It is also quite within the right of Japan to seek to bargain as best she may for things she wants in China in return for her adhesion to the Hughes ratio. But does it really pay to come into such a Conference to bargain in that spirit? When I think how Japan could all but have dominated the Conference had she immediately accepted the Hughes proposal, how she could have put Great Britain in third place here, how she could have won paeans of praise from every honest section of the American press and a glorious amount of our good-will, it does seem to me that the Japanese have strained at a gnat to swallow a camel, that no amount of gain in Manchuria or profit in Shantung could compensate for the wonderful opportunity lost.

That there are liberal Japanese here who realize this and bemoan it despite the appeal made by their fellow Japanese to them to show an undivided front, I have already pointed out in this correspondence. But the curse of nationality is upon the heads of their delegates. They are thinking only of more lands to occupy, not of humanity; they are lusting for the iron and coal mines of China, forgetful or unknowing that vastly more worth while than all those mines are international good-will and the kindly opinion of mankind. By this time they should realize, too, that bargains of the Shantung kind in Paris net incalculably large dividends of ill-will and get Japan nowhere, for they settle nothing.

Some of my Chinese friends here are alarmingly distressed and excited at the prospect that the beginning of direct negotiations with Japan over Shantung means that some kind of a hateful bargain will be struck, perhaps before these lines reach their public. Well, if it is struck, it won't settle anything. The progress of events since Versailles proves that any such bargain will be as writ in water if the Chinese people decline to accept it, and continue to agitate. Where is there a remotely similar problem solved today? India, Egypt, Spanish Morocco, Tripoli? Nowhere; this is not the day for imposing one's will on anybody else or occupying other people's lands to impose one's will for the sake of access to minerals or oil. The movement for the independence of the Philippines isn't going to stop because Cameron Forbes and Leonard Wood have solemnly wagged their heads and revealed to the world the fact that their well made-up minds are still well made up and that therefore they think that the Filipinos are not quite ready to go it alone. In cases of this kind there is afoot a newly awakening race consciousness, or spirit of nationality if you please, which to my mind is of the profoundest significance and value. As the individual, the world over, is being taught that complete self-expression is the highest aim, so these struggling groups are likewise seeking to obtain their highest group self-expression. The only question is how, when nationality is achieved, it can be guided in the right paths to respect the rights of all others. The answer is certainly that we cannot expect it to follow them unless the great nations who so doubt the capacity for self-government of the struggling ones can themselves set a just and honorable example, can refrain from themselves exploiting Haiti, Santo Domingo, India, and Korea and Egypt and Tripoli and all the rest now enslaved.

I for one cannot be alarmed, even by the unpleasant phases of nationality we are witnessing here, as my British friends are by thoughts that if England has to give up India, Japan will take it. There are immutable forces at work here that so far transcend the daily give and take, the daily setting afloat of *ballons d'essai*, the daily intriguing for position that I find it hard to become interested in our hourly crop of rumors. Bargains we may see. There are indications that this next week while this issue of *The Nation* is being printed and distributed some of the largest issues may be settled in regular ten-cent-store style; but those bargains if they are not imbedded in ethics and founded upon right and justice will be as fleeting as the Treaty of Versailles, which Mr. Vanderlip has now finally come to characterize, in the manner of Gladstone, as the worst document ever struck off by a group of human beings at a given time. Perhaps I am all wrong about it, but I look upon this whole scene here in Washington as one of the dying flurries of the old system. These diplomats are so dull, so clumsy, and so small, so lacking in vision, so delightfully content with their achievements even when as Lilliputian as those of M. Briand, so totally unconscious that they are being driven along upon vast economic tides, by the pulsing of dynamic forces under the surface, that I cannot get angry, nor waste a second on pessimism, nor say, I told you so, nor prophesy an evil ending for the Conference.

It is so well to have this play in the open—the bargaining underneath is surprising and deceiving nobody—while the real game, such as this clear-cut photographing on millions of retinas of the extraordinary limitations of the Katos and Balfours, yes, even the Hugheses, is so great that it is all to the good to have it staged and the play go on. Even if this last week's dull scenes are followed by disappointment and tragedies, Mr. Harding may still be pleased that he has peopled the stage.

One poignant regret I have with me all the time. It is due to the absence of the only Government that has been truly enlightened in its foreign relations in the East in the last three years—I mean the Russian, of course—the Russia of Lenin, which voluntarily gave up its special rights and privileges in Persia and in China, drove the English out of Persia, and then voluntarily signed a treaty renouncing all the Czar's policy of force, pledging the Soviets' purpose "to see the Persian people independent, flourishing, and freely controlling the whole of its possessions," to bind which Lenin turned over free of charge to the Persians all the enormously costly Russian Government property in Persia. I cannot conceive of a diplomat or statesman here generous enough to present to another country a telegraph line free of charge as the Russian Government is today doing for Afghanistan. How it would clear the air here to have messengers from Lenin present—whatever one may think of his communism, or his bloody executions, or the modification of his principles, or the absence of democracy in his government—to put these little diplomats, so cursed with their nationality, to their trumps by dealing with the questions of armaments and the Far East like plain, common-sense men actuated by the ordinary moralities and a most extraordinary desire to do unto others as one would be done by. Plainly what is wrong here is the absence of a genuine Christian spirit.

The Conference Nears the Rocks

IT was with pride and complete satisfaction that Secretary Hughes announced to the waiting and eager Washington correspondents the compromise on his restriction program which the Japanese have so skilfully and determinedly forced. There was no doubt that to him and his associates it appears the greatest step since the armistice and one of the greatest ever taken toward peace and good-will among the nations. Yet among the waiting press-writers it created no such enthusiasm. The English correspondents notably were aghast that their country was to be compelled to expend about $125,000,000 to build two new ships solely in order that Japan's pride in her Mutzu might be gratified, and they could not help recalling that spokesmen for the Americans had repeatedly assured them since this Conference began that the way to stop building is to stop and the way to end a race fairly is to halt in your tracks. But whether it is because of Shantung, or Manchuria, or the Four-Power Treaty, or merely because of the superior skill and determination of the Japanese delegates, Japan has won a tremendous victory at the expense of our delegates who were at first determined that there should be no yielding of an inch, much less of a battleship. *We* were not going to fall into bargaining after the manner of Versailles!

But now Japan has obtained her battleship, so that she has two "post-Jutland" dreadnoughts to match our three while for the moment England has none. Next Japan has won her fight for the ending of the dangerous rivalry in Pacific fortifications and we are to be spared the folly and the cost of further fortifying the Philippines and of making a great naval base at Guam. If Admiral Kato is not thrice decorated for this, then the Regent does not know how to appreciate service to one's country. But far more than that is the discovery that the loosely drawn

Four-Power Treaty may easily be interpreted to include the main Japanese islands. True, this is vehemently denied by spokesmen for our Government. It is not, they say, their understanding of the meaning of the words of the treaty. Alas, when treaties are put to a test it is always the habit of statesmen to interpret them as they wish to and not necessarily as anyone may think the framers intended the documents to read. As for the press observers here, they are openly saying that the guaranty of aid which we refuse to give to France as protection against Germany only we are now giving to Japan as against all the world. They are not affected by the official declaration that the proposed treaty with France binds us to use force to protect her against Germany while the Four-Power Treaty is not specific as to what methods the four Powers shall use when they get together to decide what to do in the event of an attack, or the threat of an attack, by another Power. Even granting the position of our Government that this comparison is "beside the mark," there can be no question that, until the Four-Power Treaty is amended so as specifically not to bind the United States to the necessity of hostile measures, Japan is guaranteed American aid by the Four-Power Treaty in case of war with Russia or with a future reconstructed and armed China. Japan retains at worst most of the advantages of the Anglo-Japanese Alliance plus the support of France and the United States.

Perhaps another reason why there was no enthusiasm for the compromise in favor of Japan was the announcement that even this naval ratio agreement depends upon fixing a proper proportion for the naval strength of France and Italy. The press speedily found out and printed the amazing fact that France is actually asking for a battleship strength of 350,000 tons which would give her a "post-Jutland" super-dreadnought fleet of no less than ten modern ships to England's two. The English in Washington regard it as a direct slap at their country, a grave challenge and a most serious menace to their peace. It is bad enough, they say, that France should insist on her huge standing army; it is much worse that she should ask for a super-battleship squadron five times the size of Great Britain's. The fact that the demand is probably merely a basis for bargaining leaves it no less another great mistake in tactics. Whatever the bargain sought, it cannot offset the additional heat it brings to the already existing antagonism between the two great allies—proof of which is the fact that the official spokesman for England has let it be known that the English will walk out of the Conference rather than submit, and the news which leaked out that at the first session of the committee to discuss the French ratio Mr. Balfour made use of language so forceful and vigorous as to amaze. Mr. Balfour has been very long on compliments and flattery for the French orators ever since he got to Washington. It is plain now that a new style of speech has arrived.

As for the United States, if Mr. Hughes and his colleagues consent to any such plan they will have to admit that it whittles down their great saving in battleship tonnage by at least 175,000 tons. If they permit any such proposal to go through in addition to the large submarine tonnage asked by the French, they will thoroughly misrepresent the wishes and desires of the American people. The citizens of the United States will not even consider forgiving France any of her debts or the interest thereon if she is going to waste $600,000,000 on new capital ships—each new super-dreadnought costs in England today $56,000,000. With what face can France accept from England all the money that is so generously being poured into the "adopted" towns and cities in the devastated districts for reconstruction purposes if she can afford such funds for naval construction? She does not need to beg or to receive alms if she has such stupendous sums to waste on ships that will certainly be obsolete within a few years if the bombing plane and the submarine are developed any further. Adoption of the French naval program, so far from making for the peace of the world, would insure the same kind of naval hostilities between France and England that existed before the war between Germany and England. One has only to recall how, not long before the war, Lord Fisher, then First Lord of the Admiralty, asked the British Government's permission to sink the German fleet at anchor in Kiel harbor without even the preface of a declaration of war to sense what would be the attitude of British navalists toward any attempt to build up a great French fleet. It is no wonder that the cable reports that the news of the French demands for the best fleet in the world by 1935 "seemed so sensational that it was not credited when it first arrived in London." Certainly the British would have reason to consider that the new French fleet was aimed at them alone. For whom else could it be intended? The Italians, too, were outraged by the proposal. Her delegates are willing to go far toward real disarmament. What, they ask, does this French move mean? The making of a French lake out of the Mediterranean?

That the French demand will enormously increase the hostility to the Four-Power Treaty in Congress goes without saying, and so will Admiral Kato's diplomatic successes. That honest men can so differ as to what the "clear and plain language" of the covenant means shows the absolute necessity of subjecting it to microscopic examination. Indeed, if such shabby bargaining and squabbling goes on in Washington much longer the American people will turn away from the whole business with the same sickening disappointment with which they read of the final disaster at Paris. They will be more than ever "fed up" with foreign diplomats and their ways and will be more than ever likely to insist upon our letting Europe go hang while we go our own sweet way, which is wise enough so far as political entanglements are concerned, but may have disastrous results when the time comes for the United States to cooperate economically abroad—as some day soon she must if Europe is to be saved from complete economic collapse. Already Senators like Mr. Reed and Mr. Borah and Mr. La Follette who have come out against the treaty are feeling the turn of public opinion toward them.

The Conference faces the acid test. It is bad enough that its general atmosphere has become more and more like Versailles in the prevalence of fear, suspicion, jealousy, and bargaining. What is worse is that the public is beginning to question whether the delegates even came together honestly with earnest and humane purpose and with a real desire genuinely to decrease armaments. If the Conference breaks up, or if the French succeed in getting even five of the ten ships they ask, the disillusionment the world over will be of serious import, for it will make men in multitudes realize that there is no hope for the world as long as its present rulers continue to dominate and to misrepresent the desires of their people. Mr. Henry W. Nevinson is right in saying that even the Japanese compromise, quite aside from the French demands, "proves that the delegates, especially the Japanese, do not really contemplate peace, but work for reduced and more highly efficient instruments of war."

Meanwhile anxiety increases as to what this compromising Conference will do, or permit to be done, to China. Fortunately, at this writing the negotiations between China and Japan are progressing better than seemed possible two weeks ago. At least it now appears as if the Chinese might get the whole of Shantung back upon satisfactory terms. This again makes one regret that the Japanese manner of doing things so often makes against their interest. The opportunity which they lost at the beginning to achieve a moral leadership of the Conference second only to that of the Americans has already been pointed out in these columns. If they came with their minds made up to yield on Shantung it is a great pity from their own point of view that they did not announce it with a splendid gesture and the appearance of free and generous renunciation, and thus win the thorough good-will of everybody in Washington, especially the Chinese. It is obvious that Mr. K. K. Kawakami is correct when he says "Japan has lost a golden opportunity to assume leadership in the adjustment of Far Eastern affairs. However sympathetic to her we may be, we cannot but feel that Japanese statesmanship is sadly deficient in vision and foresightedness." It is his belief that Japan should have stated her program in unequivocal terms at the outset of the Conference. Instead, we have even seen the Japanese delegates asking for time to study the twenty-one Japanese points when the Chinese delegates brought them up, just as if they were something new about which they had to be informed! As it is, the fate of the Pacific Joint Conference hangs in a peculiar degree upon the outcome of the struggle between the Japanese and the Chinese; Manchuria may be the deciding point. A recognition of this fact is keeping many of the Senators from reaching a final decision as to their attitude toward the Four-Power Treaty. They want to know how the Conference is going to treat China because they believe that the Pacific islands treaty must be read in the light of what the Powers decide shall be done for the Chinese Republic. If that decision is imperialistic, if the agreement to be arrived at legalizes and sanctifies the Japanese position in China and notably in Manchuria, the belief will be that the spirit behind the Four-Power Treaty is much more imperialistic than now appears. At any rate, each day's delay in ratifying the treaty will make clearer than ever that the United States does not wish to guarantee Japan in any situation in China which it has achieved by force or compulsion.

Finally, the Richmond *News Leader* concludes an editorial on the Conference by the frank question: "Are we fooling ourselves about a limitation of armaments? Are the diplomats merely laying aside outworn weapons for new ones? Is the whole Conference a ghastly joke? God forbid!" The Conference cannot be merely a ghastly joke because of the enormous educational value it has had, because of the revelation of themselves and their methods which the diplomats have given before the onlooking world. But one of the saddest and most discouraging things about it all remains that with the English rightly demanding the total abolition of the submarine our American delegates are not only not helping but are throwing their influence against the proposal. It is easy to sneer and to say that England has everything to gain and nothing to lose by the outlawing of the submarine. That may be true if the world will persist in the madness of war, but the whole of a rational world has nothing to lose and everything to gain, not only by the disappearance of the submarine but the prohibition of bombing airplanes and poisonous gases which menace our whole civilization. American public opinion is overwhelmingly behind the proposal to do away with these foul instruments of warfare. The self-satisfied and happy Mr. Hughes cannot seem to find a moment to listen to the rising tide of public demand that the United States shall lead in abolishing them. It looks as if the Conference would be nothing more than the merest beginning of disarmament. Again the question arises: Is revolution the only hope?

Washington, Dec. 17 OSWALD GARRISON VILLARD

[Since this article was written has come the welcome news that Premier Briand has assured Ambassador Harvey in London that France will accept Mr. Hughes's suggested ratio of 1.70, as against 5 for the United States and Great Britain, 3 for Japan and 1.68 for Italy. But the dispatches are quite clear that this amiable retraction of the French demand is not born of love of peace. France apparently expects something from England—some advantage in negotiations on German reparations, or more probably consent to her demand for more submarines. The effect upon the Conference remains unfortunate.]

December 29, 1921.

Mr. John A. Hobson,
3 Gayton Crescent,
Hampstead, N.W. 3,
England.

My dear Hobson:

We were greatly interested in your letter of the 8th of December, for the Christmas wishes in which I thank you, in turn sending you and Mrs. Hobson my warmest New Year's wishes. Nothing would please me so much in 1922 as to be able to carry out the arrangement which I have suggested to you, but, alas, I am making no headway in that direction; the existing financial and economic conditions which are growing steadily worse in general, though some lines of business are being very profitably conducted, make increasingly difficult the financing of The Nation, so that I cannot see ahead clearly. I am, however, planning to go abroad on or about the first of April, heading directly for the Central Powers and Czecho-Slovakia. A short stay I must make in England on the way back if I can get my passport visaed by your authorities here, which is doubtful since I have just been refused a reception by Sir Auckland Geddes in Washington; although I am on the regular accredited list of correspondents at the Conference I have been ignored by the British officials. Having such very good friends as Nevinson, Wilson Harris, J. G. Hamilton, and others there, this has not affected me at all in the way of news-and-impression gathering. But if the attitude is persisted in and the Irish question is still unsettled, it may be that I shall have difficulty in getting to England.

The news that we are getting bears out well your letter with the growing indications of a general election and the apparent inability of Lloyd George to make any headway against the unyielding attitude of the French on reparations. It is reported that the Premiers will decide at Cannes to call a general economic conference, but what good that will do as long as they persist in their present attitudes toward Russia and Germany I cannot see. Of course, we are still very anxious about the Irish settlement, but cannot believe that the country will refuse it. I hope that our editorials on that subject and the position we have taken are commending themselves to you.

Nevinson has been rather too pessimistic, I think, about the Conference. While it has been anything but satisfactory to idealists and pacifists like myself it did make a brilliant start under Hughes's leadership, and if the English and Japanese had had half the same spirit which he showed a great deal could have been accomplished at the outset. Our Government's extraordinarily stupid position on the submarine question is inexplicable except on the ground of Hughes's worship of expert opinion. The country would acclaim the complete abolition of the submarine even though it would be of great benefit to England. Of course, we do not think that Balfour's plea for that has been unselfish, but, as I have said in The Nation, in this case the English Government's selfish wishes coincide with the wishes of humanity. I am more than ever impressed with the littleness of these diplomats and statesmen. They have been for all the world like children squabbling over the number of green, blue, and white marbles they had, and Japan's desire for her new and large Mutzu will cost your tax-payers a neat sum if your Government decides to go ahead and build two new ships. I wish England might take the lofty position of refusing to build any more naval ships even though the sacred ratio will be disturbed by doing so. Again, I am reminded of the old Arab fable of the traveler who found his way through a pass blocked by a huge obstruction. He found that he could neither crawl over it nor under it nor around it and, after trying everything for a long while, walked right through it. If these statesmen would only walk through their problems it would be extremely simple and easy to solve them, but their ways of mystery and secrecy and the conventional, red tape procedure with solemn platitudinous speech-making that they believe they have to go through -- all these things sicken one who looks on and realizes that civilization itself is at stake. Trying and cold-blooded and militaristic as many of our businessmen are, I have been wishing right along that the matter were in the hands of businessmen instead of the Balfours and the Briands and even the Hugheses.

Yet the successes are substantial. It is a good thing to stop building, to have discussed the submarine and to have started the habit of conferring on these questions. It was worth while to have the French come and reveal themselves to America as they have so completely done that I think the French myth is pretty well destroyed. Our country is being pretty rapidly disillusioned about the war; one finds very few people to say that we got anything out of it. The revelation of Japanese methods has been quite sinister, and that portion of the Conference may yet as I write break up in disaster.

We are tremendously depressed by the failure of our effort to bring about justice and freedom for Haiti and Santo Domingo. The Senate committee, whose appointment we brought about, has gone back on its repeated pledges to withdraw the troops. The atrocities are going to be glossed over and our occupation is to go on indefinitely. This means with Mr. Hughes's absolute approval, I am sure. His is a dreadful mind to deal with -- so set, so cocksure, so determined when once made up, that interference by the Almighty himself would not deter it or change it from a given course. The President's is an appealing personality -- big, good-natured, kindly, meaning to do the right thing, but oh! so poorly equipped for the task and the hour! However, we can only fight on. The joy is in the fight, and when we get an advance like the Irish settlement we can take heart and courage. The President has in my hearing several times refused to state whether we shall enter an economic conference or not, simply telling the correspondents that he would take this matter up when the present conference was over. But Hoover favors it very strongly. Francis Hirst, who is passing through, is eager to have him to preside over it. Many Americans have, however, taken Hoover's measure and are no longer enthusiastic for him. There are numerous reasons for this -- one is his attitude toward Russia, which is shifty and shifting. In a recent letter to me he made the amazing statement that, as he understood it, the whole foreign policy of our Government during the "liquidation of the armistice" had been directed to prevent Europe "from going Bolshevik or being overrun by their armies." Comment is unnecessary.

As I write, the news from Washington is extremely disappointing. Again the French! Well, it is much gained to have them and their policy understood in this country!

With my repeated wishes for your happiness in the new year.

Sincerely yours.

The Facts of Irish Freedom

WE confidently expect that the Dail will ratify the Anglo-Irish Treaty shortly after it reassembles on the third of January. If it should do otherwise we should still say that the Irish are the rightful arbiters of their own destiny and we should insist that it was neither just nor wise for the British to try to coerce them by violence into an agreement to which they cannot be persuaded by reason. But we do not expect this crisis to arise. The debate in the Dail expresses the natural opposition of a people who do not easily forget the long months and years during which "every Irish woman thanked God for the light of the morning." You cannot practice terrorism and then win an easy reconciliation. Every Irishman in his heart desires complete independence. Nevertheless the Dail will ratify because of the extraordinary capacity of its ablest leaders, both civil and military, to face facts. They may not like the shadow of the King's power that remains, but that shadow is not worth the price of war. Dr. Patrick McCartan put the matter bluntly but wisely when he said: "I am opposed to any king anywhere, but the republic of which Mr. De Valera was President is dead because it depended upon unity of the Irish people." Dr. McCartan's conviction that the Irish Free State had already won the acceptance of so many of the people as to make it impossible to take up the old fight is the more impressive because of his own long and utterly unselfish service to the cause. He knows not only the internal but the external situation. As the republic's first envoy to America and later as envoy to Russia, he spoke with authority when he declared that the Irish could not now go to any foreign Power and ask for recognition. These are inescapable facts, and however one may sympathize with the passionate sincerity of those who would make no compromise with Britain though it cost the life of every Irish man and woman it remains true that not in that spirit will the interests of Ireland be advanced or peace secured.

Opposition to the Anglo-Irish treaty is itself not united. It ranges from the impassioned no-compromise stand of Miss MacSwiney to the rather curious attitude of President De Valera, which Dr. McCartan plainly called a quibble. Apparently Mr. De Valera advocates not a life-and-death stand for the republic—he insists that he opposes this treaty because it does not make for peace—but some alternative of whose merits the public has not as yet had opportunity to judge. Mr. De Valera has never been a doctrinaire republican. He has always appreciated the need that Ireland live on peaceful terms with her powerful neighbor. While he was still in America he proposed a treaty with Britain rather like the arrangement the United States has with Cuba. Those who know the realities of American relations with Cuba might assure Mr. De Valera that Ireland's status under the proposed treaty will be infinitely preferable to Cuba's. Mr. De Valera's own reputation for statesmanship as well as courage has been so deservedly high that we can only wonder what is the explanation for his present position.

What gives an air of something like unreality to the opposition to the treaty is the failure of its critics to discuss Ulster. Alderman Cosgrave put the matter in a nutshell when he said that he preferred a dominion which would bring unity to the whole of Ireland to a republic for twenty-six counties. The Ulster issue is historically of British manufacture. Every consideration of reason demands that Ulster should be a part of Ireland, yet it is axiomatic that an independent Ireland could not coerce northeast Ulster—even if it so desired—without inviting not only civil war in Ireland but war with England and the loss of a very considerable part of the world's opinion which has supported the Irish in their own struggle for self-determination. Neither could an independent Ireland win the allegiance of Belfast as easily as can the Irish Free State. Ulster will not now feel that she is entirely without the Empire; she will have every economic reason to join with Ireland, and what is most important of all, the British will have everything to gain by seeing her throw in her lot with Ireland instead of remaining apart, an endless source of annoyance to every British Government. Even if there was no question of peace to obtain after so many centuries, the unity of Ireland is worth the little price of a rather cumbersome oath of allegiance and the presence of a Governor-General—whom the Irish people may if they choose keep in dignified and innocuous isolation.

A more serious objection to the treaty is voiced in Captain Monteith's letter published elsewhere in this issue. He argues that though the British army will be completely withdrawn the British navy will still control. He believes that the advantage will lie with battleships over garrisons. But an occasional battleship in Cork harbor can never terrorize Irish homes as constabulary and troops and Black and Tans have done. It cannot corrupt the Irish life or inspire Irish boys with false ideas of military glory to be won under the British flag in foreign lands. Nor will battleships in Cork harbor under the treaty do anything more than they would in a crisis if Ireland were nominally independent. Ireland cannot adequately arm against the British navy and Ireland ought not to enter upon so costly an attempt. The interest of her sister dominions, all of them free states, is a better guaranty against the tyranny of the British fleet than she could erect by herself.

Shall we be told that for Ireland to be a Free State associated with Britain is to make a covenant with imperialism? Rather is it true that Ireland and the Irish of the dominions can do more to check British imperialism than can Ireland as an independent state. Great Britain and the dominions constitute no true empire but a commonwealth of nations which, like the Union of our own States, is a real contribution to world unity. Assuredly the British Empire sins against freedom in its relation to India, Egypt, and other colonial possessions. But India's hope of freedom rests far more truly on the spirit and method of Gandhi than upon the chance of a new world war which Irish hostility to England might ultimately promote. Ireland within the association of British nations can, if she will, do a far finer thing for the freedom of India than Ireland whose protests threaten the peace of the world. There is no serious limitation on the Irish power to do all that a nation may to promote the happiness of her people and set an example to mankind. Under the treaty her future lies not with British politicians but with her own educators, cooperators, and labor unionists. Empires are breaking, political states grow tyrannous. The world needs Irish missionaries of freedom and cooperation as in the Dark Ages it needed Irish saints and scholars. Let Ireland now turn to the principles of George Russell's "National Being" with something of the enthusiasm which has made possible her national existence and she will bless mankind as at present she cannot do by an irreconcilable struggle for complete dissociation from the British states.

The Conference and Its Experts

By OSWALD GARRISON VILLARD

Washington, December 26

"PLEASE check your experts at Ellis Island and with the port health officer at San Francisco on arrival and call for them when you leave." This was *not* a postscript to President Harding's invitation to the nine Powers which are taking part in this Conference on the Limitation of Armaments but it should have been, for the experts have been doing their worst ever since they got here to bedevil the whole situation and to make as slight as possible the gains for humanity. "What would you?" said a distinguished Japanese to me. "The naval experts have been taught all their lives to measure the effectiveness of their own and the rival navies in tons. They have been balancing ton against ton and gun against gun until they have decided exactly what they think their particular nations must have in order to save themselves from destruction. Then they come over here and, of course, they have got to show us just how much they know and how skilful they are in working out each problem, and how important they are, and the statesmen are at first so filled with the idea that they must not disagree with these experts that they are very slow to upset them." This was by way of answering my protest that the Japanese experts' insistence upon the Mutzu had done Japan more harm in public opinion than a dozen Mutzus could compensate for in any save the narrowest of naval eyes.

But the Japanese experts are not the only ones that have done harm here. It is now well known that it is our naval experts who are persuading Mr. Hughes to defy the popular opinion in this country in favor of the abolition of the submarine. As to that opinion there can be no doubt. When the daily press of New York, with hardly an exception, joins the liberal and radical press in demanding the doing away with this sneaky weapon of war, it is pretty safe to say that the country is almost a unit against it. Some of the largest church and women's organizations are unqualifiedly on record to that effect here in Washington. But Mr. Hughes will not yield. He has so far headed off the British attempt to bring the issue before the whole Conference in open session—for fear, it is said, lest the galleries take violent sides with the English and stampede things a bit. I can see no other reason for this attitude in a delegation which speaks for the man who called this Conference in order to limit armaments than that the experts have persuaded Mr. Hughes that somebody else, presumably the English, have too much to gain by the wiping out of the submarine. Well, what if they are purely selfish? This wonderful opportunity, which may not recur, to abolish one of the weapons that threaten the peace of the world is probably to pass unused except that there is another compromise (compromise number 2478A since this Conference began) in sight by which Mr. Hughes will consent to lower the tonnage allotted by some thousands of tons—the English journalists here have never recovered from their amazement that Mr. Hughes at the outset offered them more tons of submarines than they needed or wished. "We thought," said they, "this was a conference to *limit* and not to increase any armament?"

The question is whether we are not asking too much of any professional man to request that he take part in the whittling down of his own trade with the belief openly expressed that these first steps will lead eventually to the abolition of the entire profession. When I read how the medical profession rages when anybody, be he scientist or chiropractor or somebody within the pale itself, tries to interfere with the well-oiled machinery I begin to feel that the navy people are behaving rather generously down here.

As it is we must expect to see the navy applauding the *Army and Navy Journal* for pointing out immediately after the publication of the Hughes proposals that the reduction in capital ships necessitated the immediate increase of the navy's personnel by *several thousand officers!* At the same time, while desirous of extending every consideration to men who feel as if they were being asked to commit a mild form of hara-kiri, it is only just to point out that navy men are proverbially slow to accept progress and new ideas, or to correlate their professional ideas to those of the world. No one should take my word for this. Fortunately, no less distinguished a man than Admiral Sims made this very topic the subject of his presidential address at the Navy War College at its opening last fall, and one need only take up the history of the development of such American inventions as the monitor, the submarine, the floating mine, and many another to find historical examples of what Admiral Sims plainly had in mind. Naval and military men were certainly the last to be chosen to act as advisers at this scene which was staged as the first step to free the world of all the theories and preconceptions they hold dearest.

It was bad enough to have this Conference in the hands of experts in statecraft and authorities in bureaucratic red-tape without asking in anybody else. What the situation now so badly needs is a liberal dose of business-like common sense, interpreted by men free from tradition and preconception, and ready to alter their plans for the better even if a proposal like the abolition of the submarine was not on the agenda when the curtain rose. I shudder to think what would happen if the thought should suddenly come to people here that there exists a simple way to end all the rivalries of naval experts, to satisfy the pride of all the countries big and small, to end the dread of France for Germany at sea or anybody else, and to put all the nations on an absolute equality. It is—hold your breath now!—the simple device of abolishing all navies. If you just did that you could forget all about ratios, for you would give everybody a square deal, the ratio for all would be 0-0-0-0-0-0-0 and each nation could employ Professor Einstein to work out a special theory of relativity. I guarantee he could prove to every one's satisfaction that each 0 really represented the potential naval power, past or future, of each country.

Alas, this simple remedy will not be tried here because it is so simple and because the experts have five hundred reasons to prove that the people would really not stand for it—the last refuge—or that it is all some pacifist tomfoolery not worthy of attention. If you should happen to remind them that an American President once did this and that we lived in peace for decades after he pulled all the ships of our navy up on the beach—but don't try it. The expert's dignity is not to be trifled with, even if you should suggest to him that the American patriot who did that in the days when we were poor and weak and forlorn was a chap by the name of—well, every schoolboy knows it, of course.

Outlawing War

THE failure of the Washington Conference to deal with chemical means of warfare or even to limit submarine building will cast a dark cloud over many fair hopes of peace. But that cloud will have a silver lining if by reason of this failure men's thoughts turn from the Utopian dream of limiting the destructiveness of war's weapons to the practical possibility of abolishing war. You may kill the man-eating tiger, you cannot pare his claws. You may end war, you cannot permanently persuade nations which contemplate the "necessity" of fighting to discard those weapons the use of which may give victory. These reflections gain point by reason of the timely appearance of a pamphlet, "The Outlawing of War," written by that able Chicago lawyer, Mr. Salmon O. Levinson, and issued by the American Committee for the Outlawry of War. The plan itself was originally drawn up by Mr. Levinson in collaboration with the late Senator Knox and in its essence was incorporated in a constructive program for peace published in *The Nation* for November 17, 1920. It provides for the codification of international law by a conference which will declare war a public crime and create an international court with affirmative jurisdiction to whose judgments nations will submit as the States of our Union now submit to the decisions of the Supreme Court. Armaments are to be drastically reduced and yearly reports thereon are to be verified by authorized committees. Far less satisfactory is the suggestion for the "substitution of a potential army through citizen soldiery on the Swiss model" in place of "professional soldiery." But the "Swiss model," as copied by great imperialistic Powers, would mean compulsory military training and service on a huge scale—a most inappropriate accompaniment to the outlawry of war!

Nevertheless, whatever may be true of details which are subject to modification the plan itself is simple, understandable, and entirely in the right direction. Professor John Dewey in his foreword suggests that any present scheme of a league of nations "is bound to make much of the sanction of physical force against recalcitrant nations. In that way it continues the old tradition of the lawfulness of war. What the world now needs is enlightenment and a concentration of moral forces." It is this which an international conference for the outlawry of war might easily provide. That such a conference of itself would obtain lasting peace we are less sure. The danger of future wars springs from three sources: (1) The revolt of exploited peoples from the domination of imperial Powers; (2) the revolt of exploited classes against an economic system which functions imperfectly and oppressively; and (3) strife between imperial Powers for mastery. It is this last danger—undoubtedly the most immediate, although not ultimately the most serious—with which alone Mr. Levinson's plan would deal. And even to guarantee the permanent outlawry of war between the great Powers, we believe will in the long run require a different economic organization and ethical viewpoint from those which prevail under our present imperial system, which in its very essence makes for the strife and spoliation the ultimate form of which is war. It is, however, reasonable to hope that the growth of a new attitude toward life would be enormously furthered by the focusing of public sentiment upon the madness as well as the iniquity of war. In short, this scheme for war's outlawry is a statesmanlike attempt to embody in recognized social usage something of that abhorrence of war which flaming spirits like Debs and Gandhi are preaching to men as the necessary condition of their salvation.

Mr. Harding and His Conference

By OSWALD GARRISON VILLARD

Washington, January 3

WHAT manner of man is President Harding, how is he wielding the powers of his tremendous office, and what do his slips in regard to the Conference for the Limitation of Armaments mean? These are the questions I encounter most when I leave Washington. They are not altogether easy to answer. But now that Mr. Harding has been for ten months President of the United States, it is possible to set forth certain facts about the man and his bearing in office. His relationship to the Conference helps to throw light both upon him and his mental processes.

Let it be said at once that no one could have opened the Conference in a more impressive or dignified way than did the President. He has a tall and striking figure; he dresses the part to perfection, and his walk and bearing are admirable. No one could have spoken more earnestly; if he was not quite as impressive as on the previous day at the exercises at the interment of the Unknown Soldier, that is because the setting and the occasion at Arlington naturally lent themselves more readily to the solemn and dignified, and the utterance of the President was naturally more charged with emotion. The foreigners were especially moved by the Arlington ceremony and not the least by the President's ending his address with the Lord's Prayer. Indeed, some of the English correspondents were disturbed as well as impressed. Did it mean that President Harding was putting himself at the head of what they described as "a Nonconformist movement" and injecting religion into politics? As they talked it over they became suspicious, despite my assurances that there was no especial significance in the President's extraordinarily dramatic recital of the Lord's Prayer, that there was some unfairness or trick in it. Did the President mean to meet the European diplomats panoplied in the armor of religious righteousness? That, their manner seemed to say, would be resorting to unfair practices—a sort of hitting below the belt! So divorced are religion and the higher international politics!

The President soon reassured these British correspondents by his complete and immediate withdrawal from the affairs of the Conference, and his business-like Baptist Secretary of State has injected no religious note into the Conference or committee meetings—at least so far as the outside world knows—to disturb anybody's equanimity. There has not been the slightest intrusion of the Golden Rule into any of the proceedings; it is as ignored as the commandments "Thou shalt not kill" and "Thou shalt not steal" are flouted. Moreover, I am inclined to believe that the President's now historic *faux pas* in connection with the Four-Power Treaty was really due to his detachment from the proceedings of the Conference and his failure to orient himself as to what his delegates were doing; the suggestion that it was a deliberate slap at Mr. Hughes is utterly ridiculous. It is impossible to believe that there was anything deliberate in his original interpretation. His lapses are due to certain clear causes. His great desire is to be on peaceful terms with everybody, which accounts for his entertaining William R. Hearst, whom no President for years has permitted to enter the White House. Hence, Mr. Harding would be the last to desire to give a public slap to the Secretary of State upon whom he has bestowed such complete freedom of action in dealing with American foreign affairs.

The keynote to Mr. Harding's character is, I think, his warmth and kindliness of heart. Therefore I am prepared to accept as true the New York *World's* report that he shed a tear or two in his interview with Mr. Debs. According to the *World's* reporter these two men "agreed that the world was in a troubled state, but the President said he believed the way to meet the difficulties was to adopt the tranquillity of Jesus Christ, to conciliate, mediate, to pursue the peaceful course." There we surely have the philosophy, political and social, of Warren G. Harding and the key to his mode of conduct. It and his unbounded optimism will be the sesame to explain many of his acts. I was present last summer when he told a group of journalists of the pardon he had extended to some four or five German-Americans of Covington, Kentucky, victims of our outrageous war madness and the brutality of some of our war sentences, men who were denounced by an utterly contemptible spy and informer. It was illuminating, indeed, to hear the President analyze this case, because he not only revealed his innate kindliness, his conscientious striving to do complete justice, the utter absence of bitterness or rancor in him, but also his clear understanding of the psychology of plain Americans. Undoubtedly he owes this in considerable measure to life in a small town; thus he was able to describe these Covington men to a former citizen of Marion who was present by likening them to an old man of the same type in Marion. Call this the fellow-feeling of Main Street for its own if you please. It was very human, very sincere, and touching.

One could not help letting one's mind go back to the brilliant personality which dominated the White House during the previous eight years. That highly trained and well-controlled intellect could feel profoundly the wrongs of groups of peoples, but very rarely the appeal of an individual case of wrong or injustice. It was difficult, indeed often impossible, to reach and touch Mr. Wilson's heart, to make him feel, for instance, what one of his black fellow-citizens suffered when he read of Mr. Wilson's segregating the black and white servants of the Government in the Departments at Washington. Had Mr. Wilson lived in Marion he would probably never have heard of any nice old German-American who ran a beer saloon in the Fourth Ward, and, if he had, he would not have understood the man or his aspirations. The point I want to make is that the tremendous change in the White House today is that there is a man in it with a heart full of sympathy for plain Americans, a heart which aches to do the right thing. If any reader of these lines wishes to get the exact point I am trying to make let him read the account in the New York *World* of Wednesday, December 28, 1921, of the interview between Mr. Debs and President Harding and then Mr. Wilson's un-Christian denunciation of Debs which Mr. Tumulty quotes on page 506 of his book with such satisfaction.

Frankly, as hearts go, it is infinitely better in this Republic to have the Harding heart in the White House than the Wilson heart. But a heart is not everything, though it may be vastly better than a cold, immovable mind. A brain is needed, too, and intelligence and understanding and knowledge in order to be a successful President. Mr. Harding's policy of seeking "to conciliate, to mediate, to pursue the peaceful course" may carry him far and yet leave his Administration a complete failure. In this crisis of the world's history it takes more than the President's good-will—and his belief, so widely advertised on the bill-boards, that we Americans of today are meeting our problems with the same courage and capacity as did the men of Lincoln's and Washington's time—to solve our and the world's problems. Now, how is the President on the intellectual side? Well, first it is to be noted that at the bi-weekly conferences with the newspaper men his personality has made an entirely favorable impression upon the rather critical foreign correspondents who have gathered to hear him answer questions. But it is his dignity, his high respect for his office, his kindly personality, his fellow-feeling for the journalists, of whom he was once one, and his evident desire to do the right thing, which has made them like him. His attitude on Russia, for instance, has heightened the pleasant impression. He sincerely wants to aid the starving Russian people and is not the least hindered in so doing by dislike of their present form of government. It is his aim to bring the United States and Russia together again in the old, warm friendship which existed before the Civil War and he is very certain that our benefactions in this direful emergency will make the Russians grateful debtors to us.

But when it comes to answering the questions put to him on economic and political problems the foreign correspondents and some of us Americans are struck not only by Mr. Harding's sometimes queer use of words but by the apparent absence of preparation and knowledge to enable him to reply definitely and decisively about the matters at issue. The lack of training and thought upon many political and economic questions is alarmingly evident. Of vagueness there is much, precisely as there was in his preelection speeches; there is the same tendency to generalize, to postpone the concrete, and to throw out suggestions for plans or proposals which are in no degree matured. As has already been stated in *The Nation*, the announcement that President Harding was going to spring upon us an association of nations to take the place of the League of Nations was the result of an off-hand question asked by a reporter. What the President meant was, I take it, that he believed that out of this Conference would come succeeding conferences and the getting together of nations from time to time, out of which in turn would eventually grow some form of association like an international court. But for a week the press was mightily stirred by the thought that the association of nations which Mr. Harding had so vaguely and indefinitely promised during his campaign speeches was really at hand. It scared the advocates of the League of Nations almost to death until it was discovered that there was nothing concrete behind it. It is now the belief that the rule requiring that questions be submitted to the President in writing was the result of this incident, but that this method of procedure does not prevent other hasty answers is clear.

Again, on one occasion the answers to four separate inquiries, three of which related to matters touched upon in his Message to Congress, were astonishingly alike. These matters were in hand; experts were working upon them; every consideration was being given to them; there would be definite plans before long, when, it was not possible to say; but when the proposals were forthcoming they would be found to be very fine indeed; a way out would certainly be discovered to satisfy everybody concerned. The result of all this indecision is that pressing issues are held up and problems are carried along by the Administration until the lapse of time itself, or some threatening development, compels action. Take the question of the economic conference. At first it was understood that we were to call it, and promptly. Then it was said that the matter would not be taken up by the Administration until the present Conference on the Limitation of Armaments was out of the way. Now it is announced that without waiting for the ending of the Washington Conference the President today looks to European nations to call a conference upon economic matters rather than that the initiative should come from the United States; that he takes the position that this country cannot alone cure the European situation and that the Continental Powers have many problems to solve before the United States can be of assistance—a statement which, if final, would condemn Europe to bankruptcy and disaster.

As for the Washington Conference itself, the President is profoundly optimistic about it. It is a howling success and as such it will be portrayed to the American people by Mr. Hughes and Mr. Harding when the curtain rings down upon a Conference which has risen to only about 10 per cent of its possibilities. It is the same with our general economic and financial situation. Perhaps Mr. Harding is being fed only on highly optimistic reports, but in any event we are assured for the one hundredth time that "everything is going to be all right soon," to use the slogan of one of the current plays. The trouble is that evidence of a grasp of the underlying principles is always wanting. It is necessary to call a ship subsidy by another name, the press is told, as if that would make it smell sweeter and take the curse off; but there is apparently no Executive realization that by whatever name it is called, giving subsidies is putting the Government into partnership with certain thereby privileged business men and guaranteeing them profits whether they conduct their business well or badly. The effort to help Cuba and other sugar-producing countries by admitting in bond for refining here some 500,000 tons of sugar which will thus not have to pay tariff duties is commendable, but is the merest palliative. The President seems to have no realization that what the situation calls for is the entire removal of the tariff, just as he has as yet given to the public no clear vision on the whole tariff situation. The effort to be agreeable is making itself felt in the desire to remodel the tariff so as to make it flexible and predicated upon the constantly changing rate of exchange.

So we are witnessing the very interesting experiment, by no means unlike the one we beheld in the first Administration of McKinley, of an effort to get along by compromising freely and keeping everybody good-humored. That in Mr. Harding's case this has a notable ethical or religious basis should not blind us to its dangers when it is unaccompanied by real knowledge of economic and international problems and firm clear-cut programmatic leadership. Never did the world need this leadership so much. Never did we have a clearer instance of what it can accomplish than was given us at the opening of the Conference by Mr. Hughes's proposal on the limitation of battleships. True, Mr. Hughes did not get all that he wanted, but he has obtained something substantial; he would have got a great deal more had he been similarly vigorous and outspoken in demanding the abolition of submarines and poison gas, standing with the British on that issue. A flippant colleague of mine here sums it all up thus: "The best I can say of Mr. Harding is that as captain of the team he ordered two men to walk, took a walk himself, and then stole second with two out."

Publicity and the Conference

By OSWALD GARRISON VILLARD

Washington, January 9

SENATOR BORAH, in his recent address before an audience of two thousand persons in this city, declared that the present Washington Conference was as secretive as the Versailles Conference. In this he is mistaken. This Washington gathering marks a tremendous improvement in the matter of giving out news. In the first place, Washington is smaller and for most of the correspondents there has been no language difficulty. In the next, the chairmen of delegations have been much more accessible, and, thirdly, there has been a much greater determination to see that the correspondents were informed. The Japanese, for instance, who at Paris were so inaccessible, have gone out of their way to meet the correspondents here, Baron Kato himself appearing on numerous occasions, with the aid of his interpreter. Finally, for several weeks past stenographic notes of speeches made in the committees have been freely placed at the disposal of the newspapers. This is certainly an innovation, yet I cannot see why, if these committee meetings are to be stenographically reported, correspondents should not be present to listen. We have had neither open diplomacy nor all the publicity that is possible. There ought to be more open sessions in such a conference and more public debate.

It is also a question whether there ought not to be an improvement upon the system of having a spokesman for each delegation who is not to be quoted. Mr. Hughes meets the correspondents every afternoon and answers such questions as he thinks he can properly reply to. Some of the questions asked him are foolish, some in questionable taste, and others would if answered require a reflection upon some other delegation. But Mr. Hughes can never be quoted; everything that he says appears as coming from "the spokesman of the American delegation," or as being the "opinion at the State Department." This camouflage deceives no one who understands the game and it has several times failed, as when it became known that President Harding held a different opinion as to whether the Four-Power Treaty covered the Japanese main islands from that voiced by Mr. Hughes. The press then broke right through the camouflage and told what Mr. Harding had said and what Mr. Hughes had said and no one was punished or rebuked for it. It is not an easy situation. Mr. Hughes has done his best to give news and has meant to be as frank and obliging as the system permits. But he has had to be silent many times and perhaps necessarily so on most days when delicate negotiations were going on behind closed doors.

By this I do not mean, of course, to defend secret diplomacy or anything approaching it. If there should be a succession of such conferences, every one of them should witness more and more publicity, more and more talking and negotiating in the open. There has been, naturally, much more going on behind the scenes here than has appeared in the dispatches. The negotiations between the Chinese and Japanese have had many ups and downs, yes, even sensational twists and turns, that have not seen the light of day. There will be an inside story of this Conference to be written by participants and press observers as there was after Versailles, and we may not know all that has taken place until some time has elapsed, just as we shall not learn whether anything at all has been accomplished until we know whether any of the series of treaties resulting from the Conference has been ratified by the Senate.

As for the correspondents themselves, they have been divided into two groups: the cynics, headed by Frank H. Simonds, with his inevitable French slant, and the optimists from some of the conventional journals and magazines who feel that the millennium has come much nearer. Between these extremes stand those who feel that the Conference has to date achieved about 15 or 20 per cent of what it could have accomplished had it been bent on genuine disarmament and determined to take long strides toward ending war. It will be time to judge how much the Conference has accomplished when it adjourns.

Mr. Balfour started in to receive the correspondents, and bore himself nobly until one occasion in the British Embassy, when he stood like a baited bull in the center of a circle of inquiring correspondents in the great ball-room. Everything went swimmingly until, when a pause came, a nasal American spoke up and said: *"Say, Lord* Balfour, tell us the population of the British Isles." Mr. Balfour, thus suddenly ennobled, scrutinized ceiling and floor very earnestly for some minutes and almost immediately thereafter other Britishers were found to meet the correspondents. The chief of these was Lord Riddell, about whom as much has been written as about any other figure at the Conference. He was careful to explain that he was not a government agent as he had been in Paris, but merely the representative of the British Newspaper Proprietors' Association loaned to the Conference in order to facilitate the getting out of news. Personally, he is very nearly an ideal man for the job as he is cynically humorous, witty, and affable, on good terms with everybody, extremely well informed as to the past and the present, while he knows just how to give out the news he is assiduous in collecting. To some it seemed as if he were merely a propagandist, but of this charge he is to be acquitted; at least he was no more so than any other spokesman for a country. It must not be overlooked, however, that he represents what is basest in journalistic life; his Sunday journal published in London, with an enormous circulation, deals in the news of the gutters. Not the least humorous incident of the Conference was the solemn mock defense of Lord Riddell's "ancient peerage" (awarded since Versailles) by one of his countrymen who insisted that, as beer had so often come into its own in the peerage, journalistic lubricity should not go without recognition. Lord Riddell himself did not hesitate to make fun of his own appearance in the pulpit of a Baltimore Episcopalian church of fashion in which he solemnly preached the sermon of a Sunday morning!

Mr. Hughes's conferences have also not been without their humor. There is one American correspondent who thinks that "M. Briand" means that the French Premier's first name begins with an "M." At least on every possible occasion he asks Mr. Hughes something about "M Bryand's" latest position. The correspondents so enjoy the joke that no one has explained to the questioner what the "M" really means. But the sensation of these meetings in the reception room of the Secretary of State was furnished by the veteran of all correspondents, the inimitably charming Henry W. Nevinson of the Manchester *Guardian.* When Mr. Hughes announced that France would consent to no limitation of submarines and auxiliary craft Mr. Nevinson asked if that left England free to build all such craft that she wished to. Mr. Hughes replied that it did. Whereupon Nevinson, looking more than ever like a figure direct from a canvas of Velasquez, drew himself up to his full British six feet and solemnly and loudly replied: "THEN SHE WILL!" Not even the Secretary of State could preserve his gravity, and Mr. Nevinson's private declaration of war upon France remains the hit of the Conference.

Asked the other day what man other than Secretary Hughes had made a great reputation at the Conference, my reply was: H. G. Wells. Certainly he overshadowed the English delegates, though there were many criticisms of his articles. Of course, he did not report the Conference; it was merely a background for his views. Even though it was evident that the interest of the series did not keep up until the end, his promulgating those views was one of the most worth-while things of the entire Conference. When its chief usefulness—its educational achievement—comes to be summed up Mr. Wells's contribution will prove to be very great. For at the outset he made people think; his gloomy views of the future of the world were of service in bringing our care-free and over-optimistic people to a better realization of the wreck which the world today is as the result of the war and one of the worst treaties ever drawn.

By contrast with his knowledge and skill few of the "trained seals," as the journalists by profession call the ex-statesmen, lady novelists, ex-diplomats, and literary "fellers" generally, who wrote up the Conference in its early days, shone in any degree. They faded away early to the great relief of the working fraternity. So disappeared soon the lights of French journalism who came with Briand, men like Pertinax and Lauzanne, writers of tendency with a far greater reputation abroad than at home. They did not begin to bulk with the Japanese, for instance, whose solid phalanx of fifty writers and correspondents contains some charming men and a considerable number of strong liberal tendencies. The Chinese group, though much smaller, has also attracted attention, perhaps in large measure because public sympathy is so with them in their fight for the freedom of their country. It would be difficult to find a more amusing speaker than K. P. Wang, associate editor of the *Shun Pao* of Shanghai; like others he burns with patriotic fervor for his ill-treated country.

As for the Americans, it cannot be denied that the contrast between them and the foreigners has not always been to our advantage. Our isolation in foreign affairs prior to the war did not lead to the development of a corps of political writers in this country as steeped in international relations and the significance of events political in other countries as are the French, the Dutch, the Italians, and the English. Even today the Washington corps is primarily concerned with matters domestic; not all went through the educative process of Versailles. Then, nearly all of our managing editors do not wish the development of men who write with a background of knowledge and experience in an editorial vein as does Frederick William Wile. If Pertinax took a job on an average American newspaper and tried to send in his views and opinions of events he would speedily be fired from the staff. Again, for most Americans the Far East is a closed book. Only the few men like Nathaniel Peffer who have lived there and speak the language of China or Japan really have the diplomatic history of the East of the last twenty-five years so completely at their fingers' ends as to understand at once that Mr. Root's five points for China, heralded by the ignorant as a new Magna Charta, are merely another of many avowals of virtue on the part of the Great Powers who have so persistently made a mockery of their professions soon after declaring them.

We shall doubtless have more American correspondents of the type of the representatives of the London *Times*, and of Mr. Maurice Low, of the *Morning Post* (who scored perhaps the biggest "beat"—on the Four-Power Treaty—of the Conference), Mr. H. Wilson Harris, of the London *Daily News*, and of Mr. J. G. Hamilton, of the *Daily*

Chronicle, in the years to come, but only if some one can persuade our managing editors that expert training and knowledge in international reporting have a cash value and that these must be expressed by a well-informed and interesting personality and not by a merely mechanical reporter.

Finally, if all the truth about the Conference has not reached the public some of the fault lies deep in the nature of our press as well as in the methods of international relationships and the spell of the past. It takes a long while to break away from old customs and traditions and the old terms of a long since outworn diplomacy. Thus, it was very difficult for the best of the Englishmen to free themselves from their life-long habit of thinking in terms of spheres of influence and all the other cant and hypocrisies which have grown up in connection with the race of the imperialistic nations for world domination—a race that has cost humanity seas of blood and wealth incredible and is in itself the greatest scourge of the globe.

M. Poincaré, Genoa, and the United States

M. POINCARÉ, convinced against his will, is of the same opinion still. Forced to accept the Genoa Conference in principle, he is endeavoring to make it futile. Let us meet to discuss the reconstruction of Europe, he says in effect, but let us agree in advance not to discuss any of the causes of Europe's economic distress. Let us send all our experts on finance and reparations to Genoa, and forbid them to talk about finance and reparations. Let us invite the Russians to discuss the reorganization of Russia with us, and bind them to unconditional recognition of the Czar's debts and unequivocal recognition of private property before they come. (One might have expected a Frenchman to be more reluctant to talk of unpaid debts.) To put it still another way, he says "I will go to Genoa and discuss anything with anybody, provided that they accept my point of view about everything beforehand."

The new French Prime Minister has discovered that conferences are a waste of time and produce only indefinite and vague results. He prefers the good old diplomatic method of discussion by note. Let each nation put its position clearly in writing, he says, and then let the other reply. That this slow and uncompromising method serves chiefly to stiffen each nation in its own nationalist point of view disturbs M. Poincaré not at all. It is a method admirably fitted for a Frenchman determined to stand guard over the rights of France though all the world perish. Mr. Lloyd George put the case against M. Poincaré brilliantly:

> You cannot have it out with a letter, you cannot reason with a diplomatic message. Come face to face, and I have profound conviction and faith in the ultimate reason of man. . . . [The only way is] insistent meeting, discussing, reasoning, and, let us say the word, conference. . . . If there had been a conference in 1914, in July, there would have been no catastrophe in August. . . . Each conference is a rung in the ladder that enables you to reach ultimate peace on earth.

As a matter of fact the Frenchman's unwillingness to go into open conference is the plainest kind of admission that he fears the weakness of his own case. M. Poincaré realizes that the world is against him, and that even the good old sentimental appeal to stand by France has lost its power. He was not so averse to conference in 1912 and 1914 when he went to Petrograd to confer with the Czar, Sazonov, and Isvolsky. With them he agreed and knowing he agreed he did not have his present fear of conference. M. Poincaré's record is very pertinent to the present situation. He made his debut in the first Dupuy Ministry twenty-nine years ago, and among his fellow-ministers as early as 1894 were Delcassé, the supreme jingo of recent French diplomacy, and Louis Barthou, Poincaré's present right-hand man, later famous as the author of the three-year military service law in France. He was in the reactionary Ribot Cabinet in 1895, and in the Sarrien Cabinet in 1906, with six future Prime Ministers—Barthou, Briand, Léon Bourgeois, Clemenceau, Doumergue, and Leygues—among his colleagues. His premiership in 1912 and the pre-war part of his presidency were distinguished by his intensely Russophile policy, by his intimate relations with M. Isvolsky in Paris, by his substitution of the belligerent Delcassé for the pacific Georges Louis as French Ambassador to Petrograd, by financial aid for Russian military railways, by a closer naval agreement, and by his promise to aid Russia in case of conflict with Austria. It should not be forgotten that M. Poincaré belongs to the old, old school of French chauvinism that dates back of Napoleon to Louis XIV and to the group of punctilious diplomats—the Berchtolds, Sazonovs, Jagows, Delcassés and their kin—who "did not want war but were ready for it," whose intense national egoism and utter lack of heart and vision did so much to make the Great War inevitable.

Such is the man who would hold up his hand and cry "Thou shalt not" to free discussion of the economic reconstruction of Europe. For the time being he is the spokesman of France; so long as he is at the helm it will be the task of the rest of the world to show France that acceptance of such a man only isolates her. Mr. Lloyd George's vigorous defense of the conference method was a reply to M. Poincaré; we hope that he will be as vigorous in defense of the proposed agenda and conditions of the Genoa Conference. At Genoa for the first time since the war all the nations of Europe were to have sat down together to face their common problems, not as victors and vanquished, but as partners in an emergent task of economic reconstruction. Inevitably that meant reconsideration of parts of the Treaty of Versailles and a new policy toward Soviet Russia—both of which M. Poincaré would rule out. If his policy prevails it dooms the Conference to failure in advance and America should not partake in it.

When this Genoa Conference was first announced, *The Nation* expressed its hope that the United States would take part in it. M. Poincaré's truculent conditions put the Conference in a new light. If they are accepted, American participation would be in effect indorsement of them. If, after holding aloof from Europe for months, we were to send an imposing delegation to a Genoa Conference held upon M. Poincaré's conditions Europe, unless we expressly disavowed them, would tend to believe that it was those conditions which had brought about our change of heart. We rejoice, therefore, that our State Department has delayed its reply. We hope that the publication of the report of the United States Section of the Inter-American High Commission, of which Mr. Hoover is chairman, was intended as an indirect expression of the Administration's views. That report finds rightly that American, even inter-American trade, cannot be restored until Europe's finances are put upon a sound basis. That, it declares, requires the readjustment of German reparation payments on a basis "calculated to be within the practical power of the German people to pay"; and a cessation of inflation of currency, involving reduction of the armed forces of certain of the continental Powers.

Therein is the germ of a constructive American policy—neither acceptance of European mistakes, nor proud aloofness, but active advice which implies readiness to help if the advice is heeded. Its implications, which the gentlemen who phrased the report may not have realized, are enormous. It implies just that policy of conference, compromise, and adaptation to economic necessities which Mr. Lloyd George is so eloquently advocating. It means counsel even with the hated Bolsheviks. Mr. Otto H. Kahn put the need of the hour well at a recent luncheon of the Foreign Policy Association when he said that the world had had enough of a policy of timidity and fear, that it needed to try out a policy of mercy and faith.

The Arms Conference: Its Balance Sheet

"WASHINGTON has been a success. Its inestimable value for us depends very little on the treaties and agreements which result from it. It will live in our memories as the occasion which definitely, and we believe finally, consolidates the friendship between the American and English people"—thus Mr. H. N. Brailsford cables from London to the Baltimore *Sun* and his words were anticipated by Mr. Henry W. Nevinson of the *Manchester Guardian*. If these two staunch liberals are right, if all danger of war with England has been allayed, then the Conference called by President Harding becomes indeed one of the most memorable in the history of mankind. To that view we are unfortunately not able to assent. It is our deliberate judgment that the Conference has accomplished great good if only because it has ended the naval rivalry between the United States, Japan, and Great Britain. Unfortunately, *The Nation's* memory reaches too far back in the past to permit it to ignore the fact that under what appears the calm surface of the relations between England and the United States are certain eddies and cross-currents which another Venezuelan message like that of President Cleveland might bring boiling to the surface.

But while we cannot be facilely optimistic, nor ready to take everything that has happened at its face value, we are only too happy, in assessing the achievements of the Conference for the Limitation of Armaments, to admit that there has been a definite limitation of naval armaments for which we would withhold no just word of praise from President Harding, or from Mr. Hughes, or from Senator Borah, whose pertinacity and wisdom compelled the Conference, or from the Conference itself. It may be that we have achieved only an inch of the ell of disarmament for which the whole world is aching; we may have taken only a first step, made the more easy because of doubts as to whether the battleship has any future value or not; but for every advance in the right direction at a time when the whole world seems bent on suicide we give thanks with full and grateful hearts. That may prove us gullible and foolish, easily imposed upon and ready to assume that good has been achieved where there has been only a cynical going through the motions; but such is our feeling and truth compels us to record it.

Not, of course, that any large part of that has been accomplished for which *The Nation* year in and year out appeals. This journal believes that there can be no safety for mankind until the sanctity of human life is acknowledged by states as well as by individuals, until the commandment "thou shalt not kill" becomes even for nations more than an empty creed. It is well aware that Washington has laid no ax to the roots of the tree of evil, that it has ignored all causes of the disease of war and dealt merely with one or two symptoms. Yet we would rather have had these symptoms treated and certain evils abated than to have had no effort made to combat the malady. We ourselves, as we have repeatedly said, are not interested in modifying or ameliorating war itself. It is an abomination beyond human defense or excuse, the sum of all evils, the total of all villanies. We stand with the London *Economist*, organ of that British finance which has so often been blood-stained in its economic imperialism, when it declares that "the friends of peace will be more profitably employed in endeavoring to remove the causes of war than in attempting to render it a humane and gentlemanly pursuit." We are not inclined, therefore, to count Mr. Root's resolutions forbidding submarines to attack merchant ships and outlawing poison gas as achievements of weight on the credit side of the Washington Conference's ledger. Yet in setting forth what the Conference has accomplished we shall endeavor not to be blinded by our own ardent desires so little realized.

So we believe that the limitation of battleship-building for ten years is a long step forward. It does end that naval rivalry which in *The Nation's* series of articles, No War With England, running from April 20 to June 22, 1921, we characterized as one of the gravest causes of friction between the United States and the British Empire. Nor is it to be waved aside as a mere scrapping of obsolete ships. For besides ending the race in battleship-building it has done much to stop the concomitant naval competition between Japan, England, and ourselves, which could have had only one conclusion. The future replacement battleships are to be of 35,000 tons only; that ends at once the building of larger and larger dry-docks and of greater navy-yard equipment and, probably, of bigger guns; puts an end to the talk of the necessity of larger locks at Panama to accommodate the sea-monsters of the future. More than that, a definite limit is set to the size and number of aircraft carriers—those monster vessels planned to release a hundred miles off the coast an evil brood of airplanes to bomb cities scores of miles within the enemy coast defenses. And with this there is set a definite number of submarines (they ought rather to have been wiped out) which the naval rivals may possess, the size of cruisers is limited to 10,000 tons, and the guns to 8 inches only—a size to disgust every naval officer who ever set foot on a battleship or studied Mahan.

Who can measure the psychological effect of all this? Will not the world gain immensely by ending one country's spying upon another, and by stopping the rivalry in sea-monsters carried on even in our illustrated dailies and weeklies? They will not be able to record the launching of a single dreadnought for years to come. It is a deadly blow at the glamor of the naval profession and it puts definite limits to the navy's apparently unlimited power of self-propaganda. For this we not only give thanks to Mr. Hughes who took the lead; we gratefully acknowledge the part played by Great Britain; *Punch* does not exaggerate when it depicts Britannia as laying the sword of naval supremacy upon the altar of disarmament. Who would two years ago have believed it possible that England would agree not only to a naval holiday, but also to the principle that our fleet should be as large as hers? The mere threat of Germany's equaling the British fleet made war inevitable; yet Mr. Brailsford reports that this sudden abandonment of the "age-long British claim" to complete naval supremacy has not even excited an outcry "from the fanatics of patriotism." Who shall deny that we have gained the inch? Or that this should be an inspiration to go further, now that the Irish Free State exists, to help remove other causes of friction and hostility and misunderstanding between the United States and Great Britain?

Similarly it is all to the good that the Anglo-Japanese Alliance seems ended—if a modified Four-Power Treaty is accepted; and the agreement to build no more fortifications on the Pacific together with the definite limitation of the Japanese navy has undoubtedly decreased the possibility of war between us and the Mikado's people. Some naval authorities privately aver that our promise not to fortify Guam or any other islands we may purchase or steal in the Pacific renders totally impossible the prosecution of war with the Japanese. We hope it is so; yet candor compels us to say that wars depend upon other things than these and that the Japanese and the United States are not nearer but further apart by reason of the Conference. Since it is the truth that makes us not only free but able best to deal with awkward problems, it is on the credit side of the Conference's ledger that we must place a clearer vision of the sinister and often cruelly oppressive character of Japanese imperialism in China and Siberia. It is well, too, that we have had the revelations of French fear, misrepresentation, and unabashed political imperialism, together with their refusal to cooperate in the main objects of the Conference, which darkened the picture at Washington and gravely intensified the growing feeling of bitterness and hostility between English and French. Unhappy as these revelations were, they alone would have made the Conference worth while, for their educational effect was of enormous value. Thoughtful America is now well out of the sentimental war-time idealization of the French. M. Briand and M. Viviani have enabled us to assay and to understand better the powerful political elements which, although we believe them unrepresentative of the French people themselves, yet succeed in retarding the economic recovery of Europe. It is rare that speeches carry so far and so precisely in the opposite direction in which they were intended as those of the French delegates. M. Sarraut's final *apologia* is at least proof that there has come to the remainder of the French delegation an appreciation of the fact that it is sometimes dangerous to play home politics at a gathering beyond the seas.

This clearer understanding of what the Japanese military rulers are at in Siberia and in China ought not to be a cause of additional suspicion and hatred, but rather a reason for further pity for the Japanese people who are so badly led. Not in decades does such an opportunity come to a nation to gain the confidence and friendship of another as Japan had to win America in Washington. True, the Japanese delegates return home with many apparent successes. The Four-Power Treaty is a feather in their cap; the cessation of their naval and fortifications race with us leaves them freer to devote themselves to their policy of aggressive imperialism in Asia; they have given up Shantung but kept a string to it; they have been left undisturbed in Siberia despite the publication of the Chita documents as to the essential truth of which there can be no doubt; their position in Manchuria and Korea is unshaken if not confirmed, and what they have conceded as to the future freedom of China can only be measured by their performance of their pledges in the years to come. But if they have obtained these successes, the delegates leave for Japan without luster or new honor. They fought the progress of the Conference at every point, with stubborn, meticulous, pettifogging resistance, yielding seldom and only under pressure. Their insistence on the retention of the Mutsu has probably condemned the British tax-payers to expend $90,000,000 unnecessarily. At all points they have shown themselves incapable of a generous gesture. Apparently as unable as the Germans to understand or to make use of the psychology of other peoples, the Japanese delegates have increased the longing for revolution and a new order in Japan so that there may come to the front other men and other morals under which no such violation of Japan's written word can take place as has occurred in Siberia. It was a grave fault of Mr. Hughes and Mr. Balfour—throughout the English have raised no finger to block Japanese aggression on the mainland—that the Conference was deaf to the pleadings of the Siberians. What restrained them might well have been in part their own uneasy consciences. Japan learned her imperialism, economic and political, from Western teachers. The Japanese have only to remind Americans of their exploitation of Negroes and immigrants at home, of their occupation of Haiti and Santo Domingo, and their refusal to recognize their neighbor Mexico whose government is more stable than the Chinese; they have only to speak to the English of India, of Egypt, and of concessions in China to make Anglo-American statesmen stumble in commending a virtue they do not practise.

But whatever the explanation the Pacific Question is not settled; and it will not be until Japan is checked, until Korea, Siberia, and Manchuria are freed again. It may be that a revived Russia will apply the remedy; for the present it is the duty of honest public opinion the world over to keep up the pressure upon Japan. Why has she yielded as much in Shantung? Because the opinion of the world was so unanimously against her as to make it possible for the Washington Conference to make of the Treaty of Versailles a scrap of paper so far as the Shantung clauses were concerned. That sacredly unalterable treaty which no French politician would permit to be touched where the money end of it is affected is breached and shattered by this new agreement.

China plainly has been only the step-child of the Conference—the Japanese effectually blocked revision of some of the concessions put upon her by force and fraud. But the laying before the world anew of China's plight is one of the great educational achievements of the gathering. And it is after all precisely in its educational worth that the real contribution of the Conference to world peace and disarmament is to be found. For a few weeks after Mr. Hughes's memorable opening the attention of the world was concentrated upon Washington and upon the question of a normal peaceful life for nations. The value of that cannot adequately be gauged; in a degree it can, however, be measured by the fact that it has greatly accelerated the movement for disarmament in this country where now few dare seriously to urge that universal military service and complete preparedness which it was the pose to advocate only a few years ago. Disarmament is the fashion once more. Disappointed as liberals must be that the Conference has achieved no more, that it has left land armaments wholly untouched, and that it has failed to scrap all naval armaments as it could so easily have done, let it be written down in truth that here in America it has helped to reverse the current of popular feeling, and this in shorter time than anybody had dared to hope. Abroad it has improved some international relationships and injured others; but it has proved that one of the greatest obstacles to a world in peace is the hardness of heart, the stubbornness, and the stupidity of men in high power who neither trust in themselves nor in humanity, nor believe in the teachings of the religions they pretend to serve and uphold.

Oswald Garrison Villard

M. Poincaré's Right and Left Hands

M. POINCARE has done what *The Nation* expected of him. He has sabotaged the Genoa Conference. One by one he takes up the questions that were to have been discussed there, and says, in the manner of a spoiled only child, that he will not discuss them. He won't play. He just refuses to discuss any contentious matter unless all the other nations accept his point of view beforehand.

Russia? Let Russia first unequivocally recognize private property and the Czar's debts, give "guaranties" that her word is good, and agree not to present counter-claims for the damage done by French invasions of Russia—then and then only will he meet the Russians. If there were nothing left to discuss he would discuss—short of that, No!

Germany? For nearly three years Europe has been sweating blood in the effort to get away from the impossible reparations provisions of the Treaty of Versailles. One after another French prime ministers have been forced by economic forces more powerful than political speeches to compromise, to whittle down those revenge-born clauses. Europe's recovery has been halted by their dead-weight. Finally, just before M. Briand fell, a moratorium seemed in sight; the Treaty of Versailles was giving way at a dozen points, and its revision seemed imminent. Revision of that unfortunate treaty was generally assumed to be the purpose of the Genoa Conference. In measured diplomatic terms, the correct phraseology of which conceals their essential hypocrisy and cruelty, M. Poincaré declares that France will not send a representative to Genoa unless assured that no attempt will be made to revise any of the terms of any of the treaties of peace. Finally he suggests that the Conference be postponed three months.

Postponement is of course inevitable. For a conference which meets without France and without the United States, or a conference which meets after agreement not to discuss any of the questions which most concern the future of Europe, is just one more conference and nothing more. The Genoa idea had significance because it was proposed that German and Russian representatives should for the first time meet on equal terms with the representatives of the Allied states to discuss together the problem of their common salvation. Genoa with the Genoa idea deleted would not be worth the trouble.

But postponement need not be disastrous. In three months M. Poincaré may learn much or he may even fall from office; and in three months the position of America may have changed. Strong influence was brought to bear to persuade the Harding Cabinet to participate at Genoa, and if American business conditions remain stagnant, as seems quite likely, the country will be far readier to participate at Genoa three months hence than it is today. The Washington treaties will probably be out of the road by that time, and the Government will feel readier for new responsibilities.

Nor will the reparations question remain stationary. The Cannes Conference did not disperse without taking any action. The reparations payments, arbitrarily fixed last May in a schedule providing for a total payment far less than that implied in the Treaty of Versailles, have again been set. This is a matter which, in the hurly-burly occasioned by M. Briand's retirement and M. Poincaré's advent, has gone almost unnoticed. But M. Poincaré has said that he feels bound by his predecessor's engagements at Cannes, and those engagements are of the first importance. We take from the London *Economist* the following summary:

> According to the decisions arrived at on May 5 last, Germany should have handed over to the Reparation Commission on January 15 the sum of 500 millions marks gold, less the value of the payments in kind, and on February 15 a second sum, in respect of the current quarter's yield of the 26 per cent tax on German exports, the amount of which was provisionally fixed at 275 millions marks gold. After deducting the payments that have been made in kind, these two payments were fixed respectively at 400 millions marks gold and 240 millions marks gold. On December 14, however, the German Government notified the Reparation Commission that it would be unable to hand over more than between 150 and 200 millions marks gold in satisfaction of both payments called for, and it intimated further that similar difficulties would be found in connection with the subsequent payments during 1922.
>
> The question was considered during the negotiations in Paris and in London and finally during the sitting of the Supreme Council at Cannes a decision was arrived at. On January 13 the Supreme Council notified the German delegates through Dr. Rathenau that a "temporary delay," the duration of which was not fixed, would be granted to Germany in regard to the January and February payments. It was stipulated, however, that during this temporary delay the German Government must hand over to the Reparation Commission every ten days the sum of 31 millions marks gold, the first of these payments becoming due on January 18. The German Government was further informed that it must within 15 days submit to the Reparation Commission proposals for the reform of its budget and its note circulation, together with a statement setting forth the program of payments it proposes to make during the coming year.

Germany's payments during January and February have thus already been reduced, M. Poincaré assenting, from 640 to 155 millions marks gold. Her payments for the entire year remain to be determined. Germany has made the ten-day payments prescribed at Cannes punctually; she has presented the proposals requested; and the Allied action upon those proposals is pending. Regarding them M. Poincaré has three courses open to him; he can discuss them by the intolerably long method of diplomatic notes, he can revert to the method of inter-Allied council which he has so contemptuously rejected, or he can leave the matter in the hands of the Reparation Commission. The last would seem, on the basis of M. Poincaré's past pronouncements, the most logical course for him to pursue; but it must lead very far from that rigid observance of treaty terms on which also he insists. For the Reparation Commission consists of financial experts, whose task is not so much to make political pronouncements that "Germany can and must pay" as to figure out possible schedules upon which Germany can work—which means, in the disastrous present, very small payments indeed. The prospect is that while M. Poincaré is sabotaging Genoa and proclaiming to the politicians that he will consent to no revision of the treaty, he will find a way to have the treaty revised despite himself.

The outlook for an early, open, frank discussion of the changing needs of Europe seems dim. But behind the façade the same forces are still at work. M. Poincaré will be forced to do what M. Briand was forced to do. Sooner or later there will be such a Genoa Conference as Mr. Lloyd George proposed. When it comes we hope the United States will be ready to play a wise and active part in it.

The Fate of Mid-Europe

IT is three years since Mr. Wilson, reading the Covenant of the new League of Nations to the assembled statesmen at Paris, announced that "the miasma of distrust, of intrigue, is cleared away. Men are looking eye to eye and saying 'We are brothers and have a common purpose. We did not realize it before but now we do realize it, and this is our covenant of friendship.'" Three years—but the things he announced then have not yet come true. The League excluded and still excludes Germany and Russia from membership. And the dead hand of the revengeful treaties which were born with the League has kept Europe from realizing that brotherhood in a common purpose which once seemed so near. Little nations were indeed set free, but in an hour of cruelly exaggerated nationalism. Each of the new little nations snarled at the others, established customs frontiers, and did its best to dam the currents of commerce that had linked it with the others.

So through these three years the people of Central Europe have had to wait for even that measure of relative peace which has been the lot of the victors. Austria has seen her unit of money decline in value from twenty cents to one thirty-fifth of a cent; Germany hers from twenty-four cents to half a cent, with all the upsets which that means. It is hard for comfortable Americans to realize the revolution in German and Austrian life caused by this catastrophic depreciation. The old German virtue of thrift has lost its stimulus. Money carefully invested has turned out to be money thrown away. Extravagance alone has stood the pragmatic test of these hectic times. The working-class has not improved its material condition in Germany and the middle classes have lost. The normal, healthy processes of trade and commerce have been hampered by uncertainty as to what Allied demands or hesitations might cause new crises—such as that in Vienna recently, when the police, understanding too well the spirit of the mob, stood by while hungry crowds ransacked the city's shops and robbed the rich men's hotels. Food may double its price overnight in those unhappy countries. And this because the politicians of the victor nations have not yet emerged from the hate-period into a frank acknowledgment of the necessity of economic collaboration.

That is why *The Nation* takes occasion, in this Mid-European Number, to call attention once more to the condition of Central Europe, where the new life stirring is ever hampered by the dead-weight of treaties which perpetuate the war-time hates. The lesser nations have indeed begun to show their elders the way. The little Baltic states first made peace with Russia in defiance of their mentors, England and France, and then began to move toward economic federation. The Great Powers, still reluctant to admit their mistakes, have followed to the extent of "de facto recognition." M. Poincaré reached the height of absurdity, indignantly denying that he had met any Soviet agent while admitting that he was negotiating with Moscow headquarters by wireless. Unurged by those who should have guided them, the "succession states"—Czecho-Slovakia, Rumania, and Jugoslavia—formed the Little Entente, and began negotiating commercial, customs, and arbitration treaties with each other; and finally the Czechs, by negotiating a series of treaties with their old enemy, Austria (printed on page 173 of this issue), have virtually taken that country into the Little Entente, thus paving the way toward eventual reestablishment of the economic unit of the old Austrian Empire.

The treaties are dead; such health as Europe has grows out of their death. So dead is the Treaty of St. Germain that the governments which drew the provisions for Austrian reparations have abandoned their claims and after long and cruel delay now plan to lend her money. The Bulgarians can pay no reparations. France and Italy have signed new peace treaties with a Turkish Government which openly rejects and defies the Treaty of Sèvres, and England soon will have to follow suit. Hungary has hardly pretended to execute the Treaty of the Trianon. Only Versailles still receives the faint honor of lip-worship. Even there, as Mr. Keynes remarks in his brilliant study, "A Revision of the Treaty," "the actions of those in power have been wiser than their words. It is only a slight exaggeration to say that no parts of the peace treaties have been carried out except those relating to frontiers and disarmament." Slowly and reluctantly the reparations provisions have been revised. Mr. Keynes's summary of the antics of Mr. Lloyd George and of the series of French prime ministers, attempting to cope at once with economic facts and with political conditions, is so witty a tale that future historians will find it hard to credit it. But behind its ludicrousness is the cruel story of the effect of these compromises and camouflages upon Central Europe. There the joke is less evident. Europe stumbles blindly and lamely along a path which she might tread firmly and hopefully had she statesmen with courage to speak stirringly of the need to revise the hateful treaties and to re-create Europe not in a spirit of vindictive revenge but in full consciousness of the economic necessity of cooperation and brotherhood. There are times when Mr. Lloyd George, for all his checkered past, comes near to being the man. His vision of a world conference in which Russia and Germany would sit side by side with the Western Powers, and discuss freely and without reserve whatever questions concern the restoration of Europe, was the vision which Europe and the world needs. May such a conference come before the misery and the breakdown of Central Europe creates new and ineradicable bitternesses!

Gandhi—The Way of Prophets and Saints

GANDHI has been arrested. The British Raj has answered the old question "What shall we do with our saints and prophets?" in the orthodox way of governments. Such is the end of a policy which has illustrated once more the futility of a belated and hesitant liberalism in time of crisis. That policy was an inept compound of concession and repression and its guiding principle was: Divide and govern. We credit both Mr. Montagu, until recently Secretary of State for India, and Lord Reading, the Viceroy, with liberal intentions. Their delay in the arrest of Gandhi even more than their support of the parliamentary institutions set up by the Reform Act was gall and wormwood to the old-time bureaucracy, but it did not satisfy India. They tried to strengthen their Government by importing the Prince of Wales, but to obtain a welcome for that amiable young man it proved necessary to arrest 5,209 persons in Calcutta alone. Repression became more and more the order of the day, and legal repression, as always, has been attended by extra-legal cruelty. But in vain were Indian leaders imprisoned; the ferment only increased. Finally as a last desperate measure came the Indian Government's note urging the adoption of uncompromising Moslem demands for the restoration of the Turkish Empire.

The immediate effect of the publication of the note was

the enforced resignation of Mr. Montagu, a political tempest in England, and the arrest of Gandhi in India as token of the definite adoption of the policy of the iron hand. For the present we are concerned neither with the justice and practicability of the Moslem demand which the Indian Government indorsed, nor with the plight of the British Empire, but with the Indian situation. The Viceroy's note which Mr. Montagu made public bears unanswerable testimony to the extent and power of the Nationalist movement. To disrupt it by buying off Moslem adherence to the national cause was the sole reason for the Government's unprecedented act. English opposition frustrated the payment of the bribe to the Moslems; it did not frustrate the arrest of the one man whose teaching has heretofore prevented violent revolt. When an alien government arrests a national hero who, its own apologists admit, is the most saintly figure in the modern world, no further proof is required that it rests its case on naked force.

Even so, the protagonists of imperialism, English and American, assure us that there was no other course open to the Government. However clouded England's title, she and she alone, it is asserted, protects India from external invasion and internal chaos and strife. She has brought justice and modern civilization to a country where they could not exist but for her strong arm. The argument is not convincing; it clearly overstates both the evil conditions prior to the British conquest and the blessings of British rule. It attributes material progress solely to alien rule rather than to the general march of science which has coincided with the period of British dominance. At best the imperialist case smacks too much of the argument of the burglar who would justify his continued occupation of another man's house by saying: "I keep order in the household and I keep other burglars out." The Indians are willing to take the risk of doing that for themselves. They believe they can end the economic drain of an alien rule which has multiplied famines, increased illiteracy, and reduced the people of a land which was once a synonym for wealth to the poorest on earth. They are weary of seeing their sons enlisted and their property taken to fight England's wars. They passionately affirm that in losing native government they have not even gained good government.

This Indian indictment with some changes lies not alone against Great Britain, but against Western civilization wherever it has been enforced on weaker peoples. Every imperial Power—and none more than our own—needs to consider its justice. One may admit a considerable service rendered by the rule of the British Raj and a real danger in its instantaneous collapse, and yet believe that it has earned the doom that lies before it. Indeed the question of the balance of good or evil in Western rule is almost academic in view of the plain fact of Eastern hatred of it. The exploited peoples of Asia and Africa are aroused; they are on the march; whether the force that challenges the West will be primarily national or racial, or a revival of Islam, the certainty of that challenge is plain. As well argue with the north wind as talk to Tripolitans or Egyptians or Indians of the blessings of hospitals and railroads when they feel that their pride is outraged by the conqueror. For some time—no man knows how long—the superior material equipment of the West will assure its victory. But if the future is to be one of stark conflict we face intolerable tragedy both for the imperial Powers and those who are rising against them. At best the future of the relations between the races is dark. The great hope is in such leadership as Gandhi offered—and this the British despised.

Consider the man. In the space of a few years he has done more for his people than any government in centuries. He has been the bearer of new hope and human dignity to the untouchables; he has been the weaver of bonds of unity between the Moslems and Hindus whom the British would keep asunder; he has fought the liquor traffic which was debasing his people, and the infamous opium monopoly by which, for its own profit, the British Government menaces not only India but all mankind. He has given to revolution non-violent instruments which promise the release of humanity from the seeming necessity of wars for freedom. He has sincerely preached love for the enemy. Not he but Lord Reading, by his refusal to abandon repression, prevented the proposed Round Table Conference which might have furthered the peaceful settlement of grievances. Even on the vexed question of the Caliphate we believe that Gandhi's voice might have been potent in persuading his Moslem friends to grant to non-Moslem communities the justice they seek for themselves. And it is this hope which the British Government has almost shattered—apparently with the consent of those British liberals who would approve the deportation or imprisonment of Gandhi while they praise his saintliness! Yet that hope is not dead while Gandhi's spirit is powerful in India. How long his people will follow the way he pointed out, we do not know; already there are signs of revolt. But this we know: If the Indian people, like the oppressed of other lands, finally take the way of the sword, the primary blame for the tragedy that will follow must rest not on those who have preached freedom and justice or even on those who seek them by violence, but on those who have made violence the very foundation of their continuing dominion over unwilling subjects.

"Less of Armament"

THE Conference on the Limitation of Armaments did not labor in vain. The Washington treaties have been ratified by the United States Senate, and Mr. Arthur Balfour has been made a Knight of the Garter by the two Georges. The reign of peace is about to begin. To make sure of it the British have put Mr. Gandhi in prison, the Japanese keep troops in Siberia and North Sakhalin, the United States maintains martial law in Haiti, and the French threaten to occupy the Ruhr and to change their ratio in the naval treaty from 1.75 to 2.5.

Rude voices intrude upon the rejoicing. The Senate is sure that the Four-Power Treaty is no alliance, but one of its authors, Senator Underwood, admits that should Russia attack Sakhalin she would find herself "involved" in serious difficulties with Great Britain, France, and the United States, as well as with Japan. And Baron Uchida, Japanese Minister of Foreign Affairs, is quoted as saying: "The Four-Power treaty was not intended to abrogate the Anglo-Japanese Alliance, but rather to widen and extend it." No foreigner, though, but Senator Wadsworth has dealt our faith its cruelest blow. After expressing his belief that explosive shells were in their permanent effects more horrible than gas he proceeds:

> In the future, if a country is fighting for its life, don't you think that this treaty [on chemical warfare] or any other treaty could prevent it from taking advantage of the chemical arm. . . . I don't think in a time like that this provision would be worth the paper that it is written on.

The one thing that might discredit Senator Wadsworth's prophecy no government in the world is doing. That one thing would be the absolute abolition of the chemical service in the armies. Instead, reports the New York *World:*

> A commission of British experts headed by Colonel M. L. Wilkinson is now in the United States investigating American

methods of producing noxious gases, with a view to incorporating into British practice any improvements. . . . Great Britain holds that the only adequate defense against poison gas in the hands of a possible enemy is preparedness. . . . American army officials said today that nothing would be kept secret from the British experts.

This last statement has, we believe, been denied by the War Department, which says that it is showing the British officers only what it would show the officers of any country; but the story stands as a proof of the good-fellowship among professional soldiers of different countries and not at all as evidence of good faith among governments in the abolition of poison gas.

These same soldiers are tremendously wrought up over the very moderate action of the House in reducing the army to 11,000 officers and 115,000 men. General Harbord says that "the country travels in a vicious circle of unpreparedness and post-war economy." Naval officers insist that with our reduced navy we should have a personnel of 128,000—an increase of 28,000 over our present strength! It makes one wonder whether they have heard of the Washington Conference or whether they, like miserable radical cynics, discredit its usefulness. Perhaps in their case a natural desire to preserve their own profession may warp their judgment. They might reflect on the frankness of a New York physician. A colleague at a medical meeting had attacked the so-called Cornell dollar clinic for pauperizing the people. This honest man declared that he was not worrying about pauperizing the people but the physicians! Might not an honest officer make a similar avowal that it is his profession rather than his country which is menaced by a reduction in armament?

We confess less fear than the soldiers of the iniquity of mankind and less trust in the ancient method of preparing for war in order to obtain its opposite—peace. Senator Borah, who initiated the congressional campaign for disarmament, has fittingly summarized the present situation:

> What has been realized is, however, very little when compared with what is still to be done. If this treaty [the naval agreement] can be regarded as a beginning we cannot praise it too much. If on the other hand it represents a completed work, then it must be declared to be a misfortune, for as we all know, the submarine, the airplane, and other instruments of warfare, the possibilities of which in the way of destruction cannot be overestimated, are not touched by this compact.

There you have it. The Washington treaties taken as a whole express a desire for peace. They lessen the tension of competitive navalism. But if the people are deceived by them into believing that agreement among empires is a satisfactory substitute for the abolition of imperialism and that a step toward limitation of armament is equivalent to the outlawry of war, then by reason of that deception our last state will be worse than our first.

American Imperialism in Samoa

THE NATION for March 15 included an article by Samuel S. Ripley and documentary material in the International Relations Section tending to show that the Navy Department was exercising the same high-handed and autocratic control in the Samoan Islands that this journal has exposed in connection with our treatment of various Caribbean republics. We present in this issue (p. 425) the Navy Department's defense, as embodied in a letter to Mr. Ripley's attorney, together with two agreements with Samoan chiefs upon which the United States bases its claim to sovereignty.

The United States obtained the right to establish a coaling station at Pago Pago by treaty with Samoa in 1878; a year later similar concessions were obtained by Great Britain and Germany. Political intrigue followed, of the sort all too familiar when "civilized" nations vie with one another for the control of a weaker country. Native wars were incited and in the course of a disturbance in 1899 several British and American sailors were killed. Thereupon Germany, Great Britain, and America undertook the partition of the Samoan group, the first two countries renouncing their rights and claims in Tutuila, Manua, and various smaller islands in favor of the United States. Ten years earlier, however, all three Powers had signed a convention with Samoa in which they recognized its independence. Hence, the United States could not receive any rights of sovereignty from Germany and Great Britain, the latter having none to give. We at once proceeded to administer "American Samoa," however, arranging for the trifling lack of any right to be there by two *ex post facto* agreements with native chiefs, the first concluded in 1900 and the second in 1904—neither of them acted upon by Congress.

The Experts Have It

THE House vote, 177 to 130, for an 86,000-man navy instead of the 67,000 recommended by the Appropriations subcommittee is regarded as a personal victory for President Harding. It is also a victory for militarism. It is a severe defeat for the American taxpayer, and for the principle of disarmament. Acceptance of the smaller figure would not have reduced the navy below the 5-5-3 ratio established at the recent conference; nor does the larger number alter that ratio in favor of American naval preponderance. "Pacifism" never figured in the extended debates in the House. Representative Patrick H. Kelley of Michigan, who skilfully led the fight for the smaller quota, and his chief supporters, many of whom as veteran members of the naval affairs committee are on intimate and friendly terms with many navy men, made unmistakably clear their determination not only to keep the American navy in the position assigned to it—which they were not obliged to do—but to give it the benefit of any doubt. And their defeat in the face of the array of facts they presented indicates that the naval experts still have the final word on matters not of technique but of policy.

The figure which the experts urge as indispensable to keep the nation safe has undergone various transmutations. First the General Board of the Navy insisted that 113,000 were essential. Then the Secretary of the Navy proclaimed 96,000 as the irreducible minimum. Finally the Commander-in-Chief of the Navy, also relying on the naval experts, declared that not less than 86,000 were needed. To these mobile claims the subcommittee opposed merciless facts. It declares for maintaining at full efficiency "an 18-battleship fleet with all the necessary destroyers, submarines, tenders, oilers, and tankers"; it then proceeded to add up the personnel carried on all these ships today—admittedly full complements—and all the existing jobs ashore. The total proved 2,000 short of the 67,000 proposed. Among the padded figures offered by various experts to explain the need for 86,000 men the Representatives discovered 100 men per ship equipped with spy-glasses to watch for submarines—in time of peace; 112 men per battleship to man anti-aircraft guns—a crew of fourteen for each of eight such weapons, while ten of the eighteen battleships have but two of these guns and the other eight but four. "After every essential place on shore was filled," the committee found, "when every man that is necessary for every navy-yard and training-school and hospital and everything else has been put in his place, they still had unassigned, performing no useful service to the government, 21,000 men." Against such facts the big navymen could reiterate only the broad assertion that one must leave the navy's needs to the experts. It was repeatedly brought out that not only do experts differ widely—as much as 400 men in their estimate of the number necessary to man a battleship—but that the same experts differ from themselves at different times.

A diversion in the form of a familiar bogy was created when one Congressman announced that men and not ships do the fighting and that "Japan has announced officially that the enlisted strength of her navy will be 68,252 or 1,000 more than the number proposed in the committee bill." Challenged as to the source of his information he referred with finality to the Bureau of Naval Intelligence. This cast a temporary spell over the House until the actual information was produced, to wit: "The Japanese Admiralty *is said* to be contemplating a reduction of 500 officers and 5,000 men. A proposed reduction of 5,000 men will be 68,252." By whom said is not revealed. But for many Congressmen anything from the Intelligence Bureau passes for unimpeachable wisdom. "Why have we an intelligence department if we cannot get reliable information?" asked one disillusioned Congressman after an omission of 19,500 marines from comparative tables was pointed out. Another replied "for fun." "For funds" would have been nearer the truth. The reason for an intelligence bureau in peace time is to keep up the biggest possible naval establishment by creating fictitious scares about the possibility of attacks from abroad.

Genoa: Dancing on a Volcano

By OSWALD GARRISON VILLARD

Genoa, May 2

"RUSSIA is hell, but Europe is a waste." Thus wrote the Russian writer Remisov in his tribute to Alexander Blok. Could Remisov have come to Genoa he would have found his words eminently justified. It is a desert of politics, unchristian politics, without ideals, without clear-cut aims, with the most vital issues before the world banned in advance; a mess of intrigue, carried on chiefly by little men, which may end in utter futility, which may record some slight successes. And meanwhile European humanity faces disaster! What Remisov meant has been explained to me by a German journalist who but recently came back from six months in Moscow, horrified by bolshevist Russia in which, he thinks, ten more millions will die of hunger, but still more horrified by the Europe which he now regards with utterly different eyes. Anti-Bolshevist as he is to his finger-tips he loathes this Genoa Conference still more. What is his one controlling thought? To get back to bolshevist Russia! It is hell, he says, but a hell that is vital, pulsing, out of whose horrible travail some good is yet to come for Russia and the world—if only they see it through. His fear is that the Russian delegation here will surrender to the money powers of Western Europe. Then, he says, there will go by the board the last bulwark against the crass, soul-destroying materialism of after-the-war Europe.

That is one of the great dramas being played here—this effort to buy off bolshevism through its terrible needs. Perhaps, this observer thinks, the Allies would make no effort at all to aid if they knew just how desperate the bolshevist situation is. Instead they are sermonizing, with much of that fearful Anglo-Saxon cant with which Mr. Hughes sermonizes about Mexico, when everybody knows that it is not real love of humanity which impels the Allies but French desire to get their money back and English thirst for Russian trade. Of course if there were the right spirit here the Allies would have said to the Russians "What, brothers, can we *do* for you?" The Russians would have told them and told them just what Russia could do in return. Instead the Allies have laid down their terms, cold-blooded bankers' terms, without the slightest vision of what may come, what *is* coming to crucified Russia.

There is another outcast nation here, permitted to sit below the salt but not to speak unless spoken to. Once again the fate of Europe hangs upon Germany, but simply and solely because if it goes down to its impending ruin Europe will go too, and first of all France, because of her terrible financial situation, for which she needs and deserves help and sympathy. To one like myself who has just revisited Germany after a three years' absence the imminence of the catastrophe is so obvious that one wonders how in the world men can meet in Genoa and talk of anything else. Financiers like Mr. Vanderlip who have the objective vision of the detached observer see it; so does every sound, unbiased economist. Every German official knows it; they are men crushed under a terrible burden; the tick of the clock on their walls is like the striking of the hours in a condemned man's cell. There are signs that Lloyd George realizes it; he says he does. He was appealing the other night to the fraternity of American and English journalists as if he were at last in earnest about undoing the crimes of Versailles of which he, Wilson, and Clemenceau were the joint authors. But how trust the man? As he spoke I could only see before me the Lloyd George of the "Hang the Kaiser" and "a ton for a ton" campaign of November-December, 1918. I could only remember how this man consented to the Boulogne program and thereby condemned Genoa to emasculation.

Meanwhile one sometimes asks why the skies do not fall upon those who frivol here. Nero was much more rational when Rome burned—presuming that he played well. Of course the crux is France. There are many Frenchmen who demand German money because they know that without it they face bankruptcy; these merit cooperation and aid. No sane German doubts France's needs or shirks his responsibility here. Alas, there are other Frenchmen, Poincaré at their head, who desire Germany's dismemberment and ruin. They will hail the day that she collapses. They applaud the Allied Commission in Berlin, which in sixty days sent one hundred demands, orders, threats, and instructions to the Wirth Government (including an order to change the color of the police uniforms in the city of Berlin at a cost of thirty million marks) because they know that this policy destroys the authority of the present German Government with its own people. They are actively behind the separatist movements in Bavaria and on the Rhine. They cannot pay interest on the American loans but they support monarchist and Communist movements alike within Germany. Today I read in cold type in *L'Ac-*

tion Française: "It is the destruction of Germany that we want."

Well, waiving humanity and Christianity and a few other trifles like that, one could perhaps understand the Poincaré policy if it had a foundation in self-interest. If Germany were in a water-tight compartment, and its extinction affected nobody else, one could imagine a certain type of human or inhuman watching its death struggles with sadistic glee, or with that utter callousness with which the German submarine crews left the survivors of torpedoed ships to row off by themselves into dark and wintry and overwhelming seas. But little Europe is not constituted that way; the fall of Germany inevitably means frightful effects for all her neighbors. A prominent Allied diplomat put it to me this way: "The world more than one hundred years ago got all through with the idea that it pays to destroy a people. It is a policy of suicide for France." Yet this all-overshadowing question the Conference cannot touch—though every non-official gathering comes to it at once. In this desert of Genoa we shall gather a pretty financial flower: the pious desire of the Conference that all the nations of the earth shall adopt the gold standard and the hope (destined to non-fulfilment) that our Federal Reserve Board join the central banks of Europe in creating additional reserves by depositing in certain centers (perhaps chiefly with us) the gold reserves of other nations. What the economic report is to be is not yet known. It too will give us a few harmless thoughts. It is impossible for anyone to get excited over the non-aggression pact, since it differs from the famous Article X of the League Covenant chiefly in the proposed number of its adherents. Will it keep France out of Germany? How can that be answered save by a forbidden discussion of the Versailles treaty? Thus we move around in circles.

Yet good may come out of this Conference—if Lloyd George is true to his new course, if it isolates France and makes clear to all the world, as the Prime Minister has threatened it shall, who is responsible for the failure and who endangers the very existence of civilization. Some indirect results have been achieved by the sitting down together of the Allies, the neutrals, the Central Powers, and Russia. That had to come some day; it should have happened three years ago. It has, of course, been accompanied by much writing up of the Russians and Germans as if they were wild jungle animals just brought into a compound. But that was inevitable at the first meeting; at the next meeting all will seem natural and normal. The tactlessness with which the German-Russian treaty was sprung on the Conference gave the opportunity for the pack to open up. But the baying ceased when it was discovered that Lloyd George as well as other British officials knew all along that this pact was on the way; when it appeared that the German-Russian treaty did not violate that of Versailles and was merely such as other nations had already signed with Russia. The furore is now over, and the victory remains with the Germans and Russians. Yet the question arises, in view of the economic conditions of both countries, whether it means more than that the dead past is now officially declared dead.

Next I count as a gain the cordial cooperation here of British and American journalists as well as the friendly relations with their German colleagues. Nothing could be finer than the way the British and Americans are pulling together, presenting a solid anti-jingo front—except only the Northcliffe press-men, many of whom do not share the views they are ordered to present. The results of joint experience in Washington and Paris are now being felt. Still more to the good is the crystallizing of opinion which is going on among all the press and non-official onlookers. This ought eventually to make itself felt even in distant America. But it is discouraging that of all our great financiers and business men only one, Frank A. Vanderlip, has seen the wisdom of coming here—how insular Wall Street still is! Fortunately we are well represented in the person of Mr. Vanderlip. I count his series of admirable, far-seeing articles on the economic situation here one of the really worth-while by-products of the Conference; *The Nation's* readers are, I hope, following them in the *World.*

No dispatches can even hint the beauty of the stage-setting. Genoa is a wonderful place for such a gathering, a city to dream about, and the Italian Government has proved a generous and thoughtful host. In this Conference, as at Washington, the Italians, notably Signor Schanzer, who found the way out of several difficult situations, have played an admirable part. All the Italian love of color and picturesqueness has come into play; the streets are brilliantly lighted and thronged by day and by night, and the wonderful palaces are so superb and impressive as to thrill anew even those who recollected them of old. Surely this charming birthplace of Columbus ought to have been the scene for the birth of a new world order.

What ought to have been done in Genoa is perfectly evident. It requires no seventh son of a seventh son to point it out. Primarily there is the German situation—more important and more pressing even than the Russian. Something must be done before May 31 to provide more money for France and yet leave Germany in peace, free to devote herself to work and to deal with her grave domestic problems. May 31 is the date set for impossible German payments, on which the French threaten further hostile action. The consensus of opinion here is that the only hope is in an international loan. The British lean to a one-year proposal and to the elaborate plan of Sir Robert Horne, which would reduce the total German liabilities to 45 billion gold marks of what may be called active liabilities. The Germans cannot, they say, pay even the interest on this 45 billions, but they and the French are, curiously enough, one in urging a four-year loan of four billion gold marks of which 2,500,000,000 would go to the Allies at once, 500 millions be held for interest payments, 500 millions for stabilizing the paper mark, and 500 millions for "clearing" German citizens who have had to pay damages at pre-war valuations, or for food. Of this loan Germany would raise a billion, one billion would, it is hoped, be placed in America, and the rest in France, Great Britain, and the neutral countries. This scheme, or some modification of it, must be accepted unless the gravest consequences are to follow on May 31. Since the issue has been avoided here, it now comes before the May 8 meeting of the committee of the Reparation Commission to which Mr. Morgan has just been added. The money cannot be raised in a month, but the policy can be fixed.

I have set forth above what should have been done for the Russian problem. Today we hear that the dominating Powers have no intention of offering money to Russia for the purchase of food! They do not yet know that famine and the terrible diseases which follow in its train are contagious. They are not moved by stories of little children wandering one hundred miles to American feeding stations nor of others dying by the hundred thousand. The incredible horrors of the Volga move no heart, not even that of the for-the-hour-repentant Lloyd George; here are only politics, petty, puerile politics, in a waste in which the puppets lack every element of greatness. Even common sense. Who can doubt that if common sense reigned here the Genoa Conference would within a week have adopted a customs union for Europe, thrown down the barriers which hamper trade and intercourse and travel, all those artificial obstacles with which the various countries, notably the new, are intensifying their own economic and currency ills? It is so obvious—as obvious as the need of land disarmament to help balance the budgets—that one listens incredulously, yet hears naught of such a proposal. The delegations do not recall that Germany's greatness dates from the Zollverein of the thirties, reinforced when, in 1870, the last barriers between the German states were thrown down. Why talk about non-aggression pacts when each nation is really waging a tariff war against its every neighbor?

Genoa, blind, sees nothing in this. Genoa is unstirred by the spectacle of 4,000,000 unemployed in Europe—nearly 10,000,000 workers in the whole world; a phenomenon unprecedented in human history. Yes, but the food is good here, the wines excellent, the opera entertaining, the dance places charming, the nearby Riviera towns well worth seeing. Did you notice how many hundreds of soldiers and carabinieri were on the streets? And isn't the life and color and vim of Genoa really quite too delightful?

The Republic of Brown Bros.

AMERICAN imperialism is no new birth. In some form it goes back to our earliest history; and almost precisely what has happened in Haiti and Santo Domingo in the past six years happened a dozen years ago in Nicaragua. Upon these three republics we have forced ruinous loans, making "free and sovereign" republics the creatures of New York banks, and in all three the armed forces of the United States have been used to put down the attempts of the people to free themselves, and to rivet fast American financial control. The men who do the dirty work have seldom known for whom they were working; they believed that they were performing an honest police duty.

The ordinary American citizen has not even been aware that we were conquering these countries, far less that we were doing so in the interest of small groups of bankers. The people can easily follow the movement of a regiment across the border into a neighboring country, but it knows little of the movements of the navy out of sight across the sea. It had no chance to advise about, to consent or not to consent to, our invasion of Haiti, of Santo Domingo, or of Nicaragua. Three successive administrations in Washington have given good evidence that they feared the verdict of the people as represented in Congress, for they made war without consulting that body. The Senate repeatedly refused to ratify the Knox-Castrillo convention regarding the financial subjection of Nicaragua, and the Bryan-Chamorro treaty was ratified in 1916 only because it disguised its real purpose behind the appearance of purchase of canal rights, and because it was shoved through at a time when all eyes were turned to Europe.

The case of Nicaragua, set forth by Mr. Turner in *The Nation* last week and this week in our International Relations Section, is particularly significant. We have been in Nicaragua long enough to see how the policy of financial imperialism works. Its beginnings there were more disguised than in Haiti and Santo Domingo. President Zelaya, whom we deposed in 1909, was in fact a bloody tyrant; law and order hardly existed; two Americans—members of a revolutionary army themselves—had been killed. All the common excuses for assuming the "white man's burden" were there. But, as usually happens, we imposed a greater burden upon the darker-skinned race than we assumed. We threw out one tyrant; we became tyrants as little considerate of Nicaragua's interest as the reprobate we expelled. For "we" came to mean not the American people as a whole, but a small group of bankers—Brown Bros. and Co., and J. and W. Seligman. The documents published in the International Relations Section this week show the State Department in Washington and the American Minister in Managua acting as private agents for these bankers, using American marines when necessary to impose their will.

The first stage was to set up a Mixed Claims Commission, consisting of two Americans and one Nicaraguan, to pass upon all outstanding claims. Nicaragua hesitated; she was made to accept the commission on a plan dictated by Washington, and, after she had accepted it, to modify it in accordance with Mr. Knox's second thoughts, legalizing a series of scandalous lottery and other concessions which had been canceled. A promise of a loan of $15,000,000 was dangled before her eyes; she was induced to name Brown Bros. to represent her in dealings with foreign bond-holders, whereupon they lent her one million dollars for one year (of which she got little), guaranteed upon the customs. When a new President had the country under control, and Brown Bros.' candidate had almost been driven out, we took a hand and set him up again. Naturally, the process cost money. Brown Bros. made more loans, all small and on short terms, secured upon the railroad, which they soon forced the Government to sell to them at about one-half the cost of construction, although it was giving a very fair return upon that cost.

Among the foreign claims taken over by the bankers was the Ethelburga claim contracted by Zelaya in 1909 at 75. Part of it had been used to fund earlier debts, part brought to Nicaragua and wasted; $1,800,000 had been retained by the Ethelburga Syndicate in its coffers until it should be used for railroad construction—although the Syndicate collected interest on it. This sum also Brown Bros. succeeded in taking over, and used it to pay back their own advances to Nicaragua. The railroad has not yet been built. The bankers forced Nicaragua to establish as a Connecticut corporation the National Bank of Nicaragua, with an authorized capital of $5,000,000, of which only $100,000 was paid up, and they forced Nicaragua to pay $40,000 annually to its American officials, whom the bankers appointed. They "lent" money but retained it in their own hands, using it to establish a gold standard which nearly ruined Nicaraguan business. They successively absorbed administration of the customs, railroad, national bank, and internal revenues, leaving the Nicaraguan Government an empty figurehead. In all this our State Department, our Minister in Nicaragua, our naval forces actively cooperated. We had a sample only the other day. On May 22 a revolution broke out against Brown Bros.' extremely unpopular President of Nicaragua. The revolutionaries seized a fort overlooking the capital. Immediately the commander of the detachment of marines (we have kept them in Nicaragua since 1912) informed the revolutionaries that he would use his artillery on them if they persisted.

The record is clear. The question is, how often shall it be repeated in other countries? New York bankers are now negotiating a loan to Peru, and Peru's customs houses have gone under American supervision as a preliminary step. What financial bondage is being imposed upon Guatemala with Mr. Hughes's aid will appear in a later article in these pages. There are, or were, twenty independent republics to the south of us. Five at least—Cuba, Panama, Haiti, Santo Domingo, and Nicaragua—have already been reduced to the status of colonies with at most a degree of rather fictitious self-government. Four more—Guatemala, Honduras, Costa Rica, and Peru—appear to be in process of reduction to the same status. Mr. Hughes is not treating even Mexico as a sovereign, independent state. How far is this to go? Where is it to end? Is the United States to create a great empire in this hemisphere—an empire over which Congress and the American people exercise no authority, an empire ruled by a group of Wall Street bankers at whose disposal the State and Navy Departments graciously place their resources? These are questions which the people, the plain people whose sons die of tropic fever or of a patriot's bullet, have a right and a duty to ask, and it is their right and duty also to insist upon public and specific answers.

Plain Speech About Ireland

LESS than a year ago Ireland was in the grip of the British terror. There was tragedy and suffering but there was life and hope. A united people opposed the Black and Tans—a people who gave evidence of courage, social idealism, and political capacity. Suddenly England proposed a truce and in the course of time a treaty was signed which gave the Irish the nearest approach to absolute freedom they had had for almost 800 years. Pending ratification the British turned over the government of Ireland outside of six Ulster counties to Irish revolutionists. There was general rejoicing.

Six months have passed. There are today three armed groups of Irishmen which between them overawe Ireland outside of Ulster: the Free State army, the Republican army, Rory O'Connor's independent Republican army, to say nothing of bandits disowned by all the armies. Banks have been looted, meetings violently suppressed, public and private buildings commandeered, newspaper offices wrecked. Irish blood has been shed in civil war and the fratricidal combat was arrested only by an agreement which deprived the people of a reasonable opportunity to hold a free election. Civil and religious war continues in Ulster.

It is more profitable to seek the explanation of these facts than to bewail them. First come the Ulster pogroms. It was imperative that Lloyd George should offset the natural suspicion as to his good faith by an earnest effort to persuade the Ulster Government, which he had created, to throw in its lot with the Ireland to which by every consideration of geography and history it belonged. Failing that, he was at least obligated to see that there was an end of the pogroms which Orange fanaticism—itself largely a product of British policy—had inflicted on the Catholic and nationalist population. Mr. Lloyd George did none of these things; his Cabinet helped to bring about a paper agreement between Sir James Craig and Michael Collins but it more than neutralized that effort by subsidizing the "Ulster specials" who made the pogroms. This was the negation of the peace Mr. George professed to seek. Orange pogroms invited reprisals and discredited the treaty.

But no believer in the greatness of the Irish people can accept the crimes of Orange fanatics and their British backers as a sufficient explanation for what happened in the rest of Ireland. Reprisals may be natural but they are stupid. To this day the Republicans who denounce the partition of Ireland and the horror of pogroms have proposed no better policy for winning Ulster, which Mr. De Valera himself admitted should not be coerced, than is afforded by the treaty provided that document is honestly carried out. Republican gunmen in Belfast have thus far only intensified the danger to their unarmed brethren, and a few outrages against Protestants in South Ireland, committed by criminals whom all factions denounced, have tended to obscure the guilt of the more numerous crimes of the Orangemen in Belfast. The Republican denial of the right of the people to pass on the treaty has had little direct relation to the Ulster problem. It has rested largely upon a metaphysical nationalism remote from the realities of everyday human well-being, which draws subtle distinctions between the "sovereignty of the people" and "the will of the people" as expressed at the polls. Mr. De Valera originally was no irreconcilable Republican; he himself had proposed an arrangement with England something like that which the United States set up with Cuba; he appointed negotiators knowing that the British would not accept absolute separation; he drew up a plan of "external association." If after the treaty was signed he decided to join the irreconcilable Republicans or to urge his alternative document it was his right and duty to argue his case before the people, to insist upon a fair election, and to accept its decision. Instead he became more and more the spokesman of a military dictatorship. He rebuked certain acts of violence, but his passion and power were thrown not against robbery and murder but against the men who had signed the treaty. Asked if the army were entitled to use force to prevent the election on the treaty and to suppress free speech he declared:

> The army, as the last defense of the nation, is entitled in the last resort to prevent elections such as those proposed, which may well be regarded as the device of an alien aggressor for obtaining, under threat of war, an appearance of popular sanction for his usurped authority. If Britain were to remove the threat of force and were to pledge herself to respect whatever decision the Irish people arrived at, and if the register were a valid one, then I would say, but not till then, that intervention by the army would be tyrannical and immoral.

In other words, an Irish army ought violently to intimidate Irish citizens in order that British threats may not intimidate them. This is the moral equivalent of the argument that the Germans had to invade Belgium in order to keep the French from doing it. Other Irish extremists go farther. They no longer talk about "the sacred rights of self-determination"; instead they say that "there is nothing sacred in majority rule," and they use that argument not to defend the civil liberties of a minority but to justify a military dictatorship in refusing to the people the right even freely to discuss a treaty which may involve the question of peace or war.

This tragic failure of Irish statesmanship is of concern to the whole world, for it menaces the friendly relations of great nations scarcely less than did the terrorism of the Black and Tans. Not military defeat compelled the British to seek terms, but English lack of heart for guerrilla warfare with a people seeking freedom, together with resentment at its cost and apprehension of its effect on Britain's relations with other nations. All that is changing fast. If violence continues, if the "agreed election"—despite the courageous independence of Irish labor and other groups—is as evasive of real issues as now seems likely, England may be rehabilitated in the opinion of mankind at Irish expense. The Irish extremists are playing with fire. Do they not see that their own arguments in favor of military dictatorship may be used to justify an intervention which Irish disorder invites? Do they not tremble lest neutral opinion might give even Britain a moral mandate to reestablish her power? Such a mandate would be wrong in principle and in practice but may be given. Surely a great people has not poured forth its treasure of loyalty, courage, and devotion only to create a nation disorganized by factional strife and dedicated to guerrilla warfare.

The foregoing editorial was already in type when news came of the great concentration of British troops in Ulster and their engagement with Irish Republican forces on the border. The effect of this precipitate and partisan action by the British Government—which has intervened not to put down murder in Ulster but "to protect" a province already adequately protected by its own forces—can only be still further to injure the hope of peace. The London *Daily News* has spoken words which are a credit to liberal sentiment in England in its vigorous condemnation of Mr. George for "faking a crisis for political purposes" and for his "deliberate attempt to engineer an invasion of Ireland through Ulster." Mr. Collins's protest against it is well grounded.

As we have appealed to the Irish not to sacrifice the realities of freedom to a military dictatorship of their own troops, so we appeal to the English people for the sake of the world's peace to permit no resumption of the old and discredited military imperialism which has made Ireland the island of sorrows for more than seven hundred years.

Austria—May, 1922

By OSWALD GARRISON VILLARD

Vienna, May 15

INTO the Hotel Bristol there walked the other afternoon on crutches the wreck of a woman to sell the guests autographed pictures of a wonderful actress, wonderful in her looks, her charm, and her histrionic ability. When I was last in Vienna Helene Odilon was probably the foremost actress in German-speaking Europe. Fortunes were lavished upon her, her salary was enormous, managers fell over themselves to get her to visit their theaters. Now fate has reduced her to absolute beggary. The queen of the stage is today hawking the pictures of her past as the flower-women pester one in the restaurants with their wares.

To many the fate of Helene Odilon seems the fate of Austria. In numerous ways the parallel is exact. Austria, too, is partly paralyzed; Austria, too, bespeaks public charity and needs it. For Austria, too, it is now a struggle to keep body and soul together. The gaiest and most gallant of cities, rejoicing in the pomp and circumstance of a court whose ceremonial exceeded that of any other in costly magnificence, with an aristocracy as light-living as any in the world, Vienna today appears somber beside the ghost of its own past, beside that Vienna which Kaiser Franz Josef gambled away when he allowed the mischief-makers of his Foreign Office to cajole or to lead him into the war with Serbia. Half her population today lives from hand to mouth, just being able to keep body and soul together. Many are slowly fading away from undernourishment. Nearly everybody dreads the morrow, dares not look into the future—certainly not the middle class, many of whom have lived so far only by selling their life-time acquirements. "Are Russian conditions coming?" is the query repeatedly put to foreigners suspected of having special knowledge. "Is there hope of help ere we perish?"—hard questions to answer when within a week the krone has dropped from 8,500 to 10,000 to the dollar and an official statement declares that the cost of living rose 25 per cent between April 15 and May 15; when the Allies move but slowly to give financial aid and will not admit the plain truth that the plight of Austria today is due far more to the Treaty of St. Germain than to the war. The crimes of the infamous treaties are bringing all Europe down; it is literally at the door of the old men who made them that here as in other countries life has for multitudes become merely a desperate struggle to exist, without rest, or peace, or joy, or pleasure, or color, or light, or hope, with dread ever clutching at their throats.

Not that Austria's situation is as hopeless as Helene Odilon's. The worst of it is that this decay of a state, this terrible suffering, is preventable. It could be speedily ended if all concerned were to buckle to the task with the will to victory over the existing economic evils. Indeed, there is much that is cheering about the situation. Beyond question the population looks and is a great deal better than it was two years ago. The noble work of the Friends Mission and of English and American generosity—unprecedented in the history of war—has saved thousands upon thousands of children as did the hospitality of neutral countries like Switzerland and Holland. Food there is now in plenty; it is no longer a wild, desperate struggle to get it, but the cost of it often puts it beyond reach. I hear it said that the working people have no reason to complain and it is true that some of them are doing very well—if they are not of the growing army of hard drinkers and if there are one or two wage-earners in the family besides the head. But a family I know of whose two heads bring in 210,000 crowns a month have a desperate struggle to live and educate their three children. When carfares cost 850 crowns a day—they will shortly be 1,200—when a pound of meat costs 1,200 to 1,500 crowns, when bread costs between 850 and 1,000 a loaf and may soon go to 1,200, when eggs are beyond reach, milk a luxury, and butter unheard of, when a piece of soap costs 850 crowns and is hardly usable then, and a collar cannot be bought for less than 1,200, then in such a family the matter of clothes becomes a catastrophe, even where the workers are skilled and draw much more than 210,000 a month.

Plainly it is not in the financial condition of the people that we must look for cheer, particularly in view of the unemployment. It is rather in their extraordinary patience and endurance, in the courage of their leaders, and in the undeveloped resources of even this fragment of a country which is all that the victors have left to Austria. This country has resources both in its people and its possessions. Even in its present state the skill of its workingmen has not suffered though their output has decreased per hour or per day. Austrians are an extraordinarily inventive people, as our Patent Office can testify. They have rare taste, as their shop windows bear witness—many Americans would rather shop here than in Paris. They are a people primarily interested in fine retail production; they are not naturally organizers or operators of industry on a great scale. But they are remarkably artistic and so we have it that, while multitudes suffer and wonder how they can keep body and soul together, in the fine arts there was never greater activity. Musicians, actors, sculptors, painters—wherever one turns the creative fever rages. The opera is superb and nearly pays its way. Even with the depreciated currency foreign artists are coming here to sing and play for a public which understands and appreciates. True, the opera audiences are largely composed of foreigners. Among the throng that stands every night at the opera are many who sat in the best seats before the war and among the Austrians present are many who were never able to go to the opera—these are familiar phenomena in all European countries. Of course, many who used to be the most regular attendants can no longer go. The old aristocracy has simply faded away. It can no longer be distinguished in the Ring; its once wonderful equipages have gone; it has in considerable degree retired to its country seats in mortal terror that it will find itself dispossessed from them. Yet somehow or other the commercially maintained theaters sustain themselves and all are hospitable to new talent and new ideas. I saw an exquisite performance given by Ellen Tels, the Russian dancer, and five of her extraordinarily gifted pupils, and the great audience seemed to me to be largely Viennese. That same evening there was opened in the National, formerly the Royal, Library an exhibition of books, documents, manuscripts, and other treasures, including two early Shakespeare folios, which this republican government had found in the library and proposes to make more generally available. The President of the Republic thought it worth his while to open this exhibit in person.

One finds it hard to believe, therefore, that a people so gifted and so devoted to the nobler aspirations of mankind can be in danger of perishing from the earth. But when one turns to the economic side of things it is hard not to surrender to the blackest kind of pessimism, which is particularly noticeable among the foreign newspaper writers in Vienna, especially those who have recently visited the Balkan states and Hungary. They frankly do not see any light ahead, not because they are without remedies to suggest or because there are no real remedies, but chiefly because there is nowhere in Europe that Christian and healing spirit of friendliness and good-will which seems essential to any restoration of Europe to sanity and order. The wickedness of Versailles has poisoned men's minds and souls everywhere; nationalism and militarism flourish, together with grim reaction, in more than one country. The old and new nations of Central Europe and of the Balkans dying of a common disease cannot come together for their common cause. A customs union of the Little Entente plus Austria, Hungary, Poland, Italy, and Germany is one of the first things that sound statesmanship would suggest. Yet it is today impossible. The attitude of the new countries, which in the last analysis owe their existence to American troops, is responsible. They are so jealous of their newly acquired sovereignties and their independence that they will not take any broad look at the situation; they fear that if they take one step toward real cooperation with Hungary and Austria they may lose some of their unrighteous gains at Versailles. At the Porto Rosa Conference some beginning was made toward the abolition of absolute tariff prohibitions among the new states and Hungary and Austria upon the initiative of Hungary; at Genoa even this little advance went by the board.

It astounded me, therefore, to find so much optimism among the heads of the Austrian Government. In the President, Dr. Michael Hainisch, in Chancellor Schober, in the president of the Parliament, Karl Seitz, and in others Austria has officials of which any country might well be proud. Their honesty, their integrity, their intelligence, their desire to serve are beyond question. Yet, after my talks with some of them I was amazed to find that to their minds the problem of Austria seemed so simple. What they are clamoring for is an Allied loan of twelve million pounds sterling—two pounds per head of population. With this granted they feel that the way to stabilization of the currency will be won, and the stabilization of the crown is, of course, the immediate requisite. One government expert with whom I talked is sanguine that with this loan the battle will be gained, because its granting, he says, will restore the shaken confidence of the Austrians in their Government and their future. At present there is a flight of capital out of the country which the Government cannot check. It does not go in large amounts in trunks over the border but it manifests itself in the constant buying of foreign currencies. Whenever anybody has anything to save he buys American dollars or English pounds. If confidence returns the people will begin to put their savings into Austrian securities and institutions and money will be forthcoming to develop Austrian enterprises.

I pointed out to him that the mere obtaining of such a loan would not of itself stabilize the budget and that to hold up the crown would call for the expenditure of a good deal of the twelve millions, just as a good bit of the two and a half millions already obtained by Austria has gone for that purpose. I asked again about the interest charges on the twelve millions, in itself a vast sum in the present depreciated currency, but this too could, he thought, be overcome and the budget gradually made to balance, for much of the twelve millions would go into constructive works, such as development of water power, the electrification of certain railroad lines, etc. The return of optimism he considered the crux of the whole problem.

Now courage and optimism are excellent things in a country's leaders, in fact they are necessary to success. But the Austrian Government has buoyed up the hopes of its people with promises based upon Allied assurances which often never came true, and the people are getting skeptical about new promises. They are losing heart. Every time that the cost of living rises, it sounds to multitudes like a death knell and they are not likely to stand it without protest indefinitely. They can see how it is that the vicious circle of higher taxes, higher wages, and higher costs operates, but what they ask for is some remedy. I am frank to confess that I think that they and the Allies have reason to feel that the Government could display more vigor in dealing with internal problems while waiting for the loan which they ought to have.

Experts admit that there are additional taxes which could be imposed upon luxuries and other articles, and that the machinery of collecting the taxes can be made more effective and productive. Then Sir William Goode, the English economic observer here, is correct in saying that as long as tariffs are imposed the Government ought to collect the existing customs duties at a rate equivalent to gold instead of as at present in the depreciated paper currency on a basis determined by an arbitrary multiple fixed from time to time. Difficult as it is, the problem of reducing the number of officials must be grappled with, not without sympathy and intelligence and the aid of special employment bureaus. Endless red-tape and inherited circumlocution and inefficiency must be done away with. Next, the Government ought not to let a day pass without devoting itself most earnestly to the development of agriculture. What is left of rural Austria produces only about two months' food for the nation.

But there are observers who believe that with scientific methods the productiveness of the land could be enormously increased. There is not a day to be lost. Again, much could be done by a vigorous government to attract more foreign travelers to Austria, which must in this matter take a leaf out of the book of Switzerland. It has wonderful natural attractions to lure people, quite apart from the charms of Vienna itself. Austria is in the position of a bankrupt who has got to use to the uttermost every asset he has to offer. That is the way a sound bankrupt, if one may use such a phrase, gets back to a solvent state. The present attitude of leaning back and placing all hopes upon drawing a rich Allied loan out of the lottery of fate smacks too much of the broken-down aristocrat seeking only to keep himself going in ease, and thinking only of paying interest, never of returning the capital. Whether the Allies give twelve or eight millions to Austria the fact remains that some day that loan has got to be repaid.

For that reason as for others the Austrian Government ought to be devoting itself to small economies. It ought to be doing away with such luxuries as the Spanish Riding School and its wonderful horses—a relic of the empire. It ought to utilize to the uttermost what it has taken over from the royal family—there are many minor works of art which could be disposed of for considerable sums in Berlin, London, Paris, and New York. Then, if it had the courage of Lenin, it would tackle the problem of the church. There are untold treasures in the churches, monasteries, and convents of Austria, which do nobody any good whatever. They are worth many times twelve million pounds, these hoarded jewels and precious metals. The possible income from them is supporting nobody; the church is not using them in any way. I know that this suggestion will be greeted with derision. Austria, a Catholic country, give up its church treasures? Lay profane hands upon the sacred private property of the church? Is it not bad enough that the wicked Bolshevists have been doing something of this kind? Well, perhaps it is a counsel of perfection. Yet I have a feeling that even well-intrenched Catholic dignitaries are amenable to reason. Certainly if I were one of them in Austria I should be thinking very seriously if there could be a better way of increasing the popularity of the church than by helping nation and people with the proceeds of unneeded and unused treasures, and I should be reflecting that there have been times in history when starving peoples have been known to help themselves both in palace and in cloister.

There is still another privileged class that the Austrian Government has not yet had the courage to tackle—the great land-owners. Their estates must be broken up. Scientific agriculture in the world will not be sufficient. There must be an early allotment of more farms to the workers; land not in use must be made to bear. There ought to be as intensive a garden-and-farm campaign to utilize every bit of ground as there was in America and in Germany during the war. Reduction of food prices and increase of the food supply are as necessary in this terrible peace as in war. The Government ought to be giving greater aid and attention to such admirable enterprises as the Austrian Land Settlements undertaken and carried on by the Friends Relief Mission. The city of Vienna has advanced credits of about 300,000,000 kronen, exclusive of mortgages to about the same amount, and has allotted, in conjunction with the state, about 800 acres for the cultivation of gardens and farming. On these settlements there are being built, with the further aid of foreign benefactions, admirable workers' cottages, a considerable part of the work on which is done by the workers themselves after working hours and on Saturday afternoons and Sundays. Here self-help and the best principles of the cooperative movement unite to contribute to the solution of the acute housing problem. On the small tracts of land behind their homes the settlers raise about all the vegetables they need, and each home has a small stable in which there are chickens, pigs, geese, goats, etc. Nothing that I saw in Vienna impressed me more than the possibilities in this movement. Yet the Government has still to throw itself into the movement with all the zeal the cause deserves. And of course an up-to-date Government in a tight fix and seriously desirous of serving its suffering people ought to be devoting itself to the whole great field of cooperative undertakings. Were I dictator of Austria I am inclined to think that my first act would be to appoint a Minister of Cooperation, with particular orders to combat the high cost of living by cooperative buying.

I am quite aware that Austrian readers of this list of constructive suggestions will shake their heads and say that this is all very well but that they live in a land where politics still rule. There you have it again. At every turn political considerations hamper the salvage work. They play politics in Austria as well as in America and elsewhere. I confess that I marvel how they can do so either in Austria or Germany. Where there is such terrible suffering, where whole classes are going down under one's eyes, I wish there could be applied some of the patriotic cries which we used to hear, so strident and raucous, during the war. There ought to be a solid front against death and starvation.

In Austria today the Schober Government lives by a coalition of Christian Socialists and *Grossdeutschen* which gives it a majority of only two or three votes. The Socialists are the formal opposition, and decline responsibility for the Government's acts, but they really exercise great power because they represent the masses of the cities and actually can and do bring about the fall of ministers. Alas, the Socialists have no more shown themselves equal to the emergencies and needs of the hour in Austria than elsewhere. Allowance must, of course, be made here as in Germany for the fact that the old Hapsburg and Hohenzollern systems killed all possibility of training democratic statesmen—who does not remember the shout that went up when Zimmermann became German Foreign Secretary, the first bourgeois ever to obtain that position? Austria has a long row to hoe and Germany, too, before its public men have been trained in self-government and parliamentary rule—if they can be when the Mother of Parliaments and our own Congress are in such deep decay. It is the day everywhere of small men in Parliament. It is a commonplace here that the leaders of the parties in the Austrian Parliament are much better than their parties. Under the Constitution of Austria today the President, Dr. Hainisch, has very little power. But it makes an American envious to see so highly educated, cosmopolitan, trained, and attractive a personality at the head of the state. It is not President Hainisch or Chancellor Schober that I criticise when I say that the Government is weak and should be more aggressive and vigorous in grappling with the situation; the responsibility rests far more with the utterly mediocre Parliament. But that is only another reason why those who lend money to Austria would be justified in coupling with the loan pledges that the Austrian Government devote itself to cleaning house, stop playing politics, and really set itself some of the tasks outlined above. Bad as the Treaty of St. Germain is, grave as have been the sins of the Allies, after all the salvation of Austria in the last resort must come from Austria itself and not through any loan from England or America.

Beyond that, however, it all comes back to the Treaty of Versailles and its companion piece in wrongdoing, the

Treaty of St. Germain. There will be no peace and no final economic salvation in Europe until these infamous documents are made scraps of paper. Never did *The Nation* do a better deed than in calling the former the "Madness of Versailles" the instant it appeared. Whatever trail one follows in studying these complicated European conditions one comes back to the fact that at the bottom of most of the evils lies that treaty and the spirit of bitterness and revenge in which it was written. With every day that passes without its revision the danger becomes greater that all Europe will perish from a peace which is more deadly than the war it sought to end.

Germany, 1922

IV. Some Hopeful Signs

By OSWALD GARRISON VILLARD

ON the 18th of June I saw the Hamburg and Nuremberg football teams compete in the Charlottenburg Stadium for the championship of Germany. For hours and hours they played in the longest game in the history of the sport, without being able to break the tie in the score, which came to pass fairly early in the game. There were at least 25,000 people present, and I confess that I had to rub my eyes when I saw that the teams had their organized "rooters" carrying flags and heard the organized cheers with which plays were greeted by the followers of the teams. Some of the spectators had come from distant cities to witness the match, which was, of course, the English game and not the American, and the newspapers made as much fuss over the struggle as ours do over the Yale-Harvard football games. All of which is a development of the new Germany. Wherever one goes in Germany one sees not only football games but crews on the rivers and other forms of outdoor activity. Now it is true that the beginnings of this go back into the last century, yet it is the universal testimony that there has been a tremendous increase in outdoor sport since the war. That I consider one of the hopeful signs of the times, for German youth got a good deal of its physical training in the old days in the army with its vicious overtraining, its bad moral atmosphere, and often worse barrack associations. Great pedestrians the Germans always were; the delightful custom of whole families going out for excursions and tramps remains, but the development of sport is of tremendous importance just now, furnishing as it does an outlet for the surplus energy of the young men and young women, inciting them to bodily development, teaching them cooperation and team-work, and above all diverting their minds from political and social conditions.

Athletics, too, have contributed their part to the freer and better relationship of boys and girls. It seems incredible to believe that even in the early nineties it was impossible for German boys and girls to go skating together without a chaperon; now they go off on tramps together all day long in the same normal and natural intercourse which marks the goings-on of our American boys and girls. That in itself spells a social revolution, precisely as does the attendance of young women at the universities. And this normal development is also furthered by the so-called *Jugendbewegung*, which is particularly carried on in the spirit of a new and a broader Germany. On Sundays and holidays one meets splendid groups of young men and young women, ranging down to small boys and girls, roaming through the country, often engaged in nature study. True, many of the university students are reactionary, chiefly young men who, like so many of our returned soldiers, served during the war and learned nothing from it, and there are associations formed by adherents of the old order in which the children are being marshaled into the narrowest nationalistic creeds —the sort of thing that our Daughters of the Revolution and other similar groups would heartily approve were the movement going on in this country. Fortunately, the liberalism of Germany is also at work in molding the spirit of the youth today and laying special stress upon moral and physical development through their associations. Some of the conventions run entirely by young boys and girls not yet of university age are, I am told, quite extraordinary in their interest in public affairs and their determination that the new Germany shall be nobler and better than the old. There is a strong anti-war tendency among them; indeed, the German pacifist movement is in a far healthier and more promising condition than the American.

Again, I was struck by the acceptance of the Republic as something that had come to stay by many men whose associations and traditions had led me to expect something else. Even when they were bitter critics of the Wirth Government and longed to bring about its overthrow I found that they did not question the present form of government. I was delighted, too, to see how many people of standing and influence have seen through the Hindenburg and Ludendorff humbug and have come to realize that the Kaiser was not in the least degree the superman they once thought he was. Side by side with much admirable analysis of the past of Germany and free admission of the stupidity which permitted the coming of the war and marked its conduct by the General Staff is the extraordinary resolution to work and build anew, upon which almost every writer who has visited Germany has commented. The determination to succeed and to retrieve the ground lost inevitably suggests a comparison with the similar spirit which built up Prussia at the close of the Napoleonic wars. If Germany is only given a fair chance she will be rebuilt in a surprisingly short time, her debts paid, and her people again placed in a position to contribute to the joint advancement of mankind. Adversity is a wonderful school if the lessons taught in it are applied and the spirit of the pupils is a good one. At present any wide intellectual revival lags because of the isolation of Germany and the other reasons I have already set forth in this series; but in the commercial field there is remarkable progress; industries are being rebuilt, plants are being modernized and brought up to date, and the necessary plans are laid to set about earning a large portion of the world's trade just as soon as economic and financial conditions again become normal.

It is unfortunate that the press of the country is not in a

condition to help as it should in this encouraging turning to work for work's sake. The nationalist papers are of course doing infinite harm, but the whole press of the country is in such financial straits that it cannot begin to carry on the purely cultural service, as opposed to political and news, that it ought to render. No less than one hundred and seventy German newspapers and periodicals gave up the ghost last winter, one of them, the *Laubaner Tageblatt*, at the age of one hundred and fifty years, the cause of death being largely the rise in the price of paper from 20 pfennigs to 12 marks 80 pfennigs. Again, the fact that only seven great German newspapers are making money means that deficits are being paid by individuals or groups and usually for selfish purposes. It is, of course, a bad sign that men of the type of Hugo Stinnes are buying up newspapers in every direction. Fortunately, that is offset in considerable measure by the appearance of a large number of publications representing new spiritual and political tendencies, just as in the United States we have small journals of protest against existing tendencies and conditions. It is a hopeful sign, too, that the profound German admiration of scholarship and of thorough research has survived the war.

Next to be counted among the hopeful signs is the growing solidarity of the German workingmen and their increasing influence upon the Government. It was not my good fortune to have time enough in Berlin to get into personal communication with the heads of the labor-union movement, but everything that I heard was encouraging. And it certainly marks a new epoch to find high officials turning to the unions as the great bulwark of German liberty and counting upon the general strike, which we here in America think such a terrible thing, as the reliable weapon which is going in the last resort to come to the rescue of democratic Germany and make the restoration of the monarchy impossible.

Most Americans are eager to know whether there is any prospect of the Kaiser or the Crown Prince coming back. As to that there can be a most definite answer: No. Both have lost their appeal to German imagination as well as to German common sense. If the empire should be restored it will either be a son of the Crown Prince who will mount the throne or the present Crown Prince of Bavaria. But I personally cannot believe that the trade unions will permit anything of the kind. If a throne is reestablished anywhere in Germany it will be for only a short time and the man who will sit upon it will have anything but a happy existence. The masses, I believe, are solidly convinced that it is a republic that they want and I do not think that the bulk of them can be misled even if economic conditions get very, very much worse than they are. It is certainly gratifying to find a former follower of the old regime, General von Deimling, a distinguished commander of armies in the war, declaring that the great hope for Germany today is the pulling together of all the German people in a true comradeship and that such a genuine comradeship "can only be built upon the foundation of a democratic republic." He especially appeals to the monarchists to recognize that "we now have a republic and we shall have that republic as far as any one can look into the future. The whole development of modern times moves in the direction of democracy." To this he added the warmest kind of a defense of the conduct of the Jews in the war, declaring that they had their full share of "front service, sacrifices of life, decorations and promotions. It is time that an end should be made to the attacks upon Jews in Germany, for the attacks destroy and do not build up." He added that he considered that what the German people had done since the armistice was wonderful; that it had so rapidly pulled itself out of the chaos of the debacle was marvelous.

General von Deimling is correct. To anyone revisiting Germany after three years' absence the change from the lawlessness of March, 1919, to the law and order of today is one of the best omens for the future of Germany. There is much complaining, of course. Many are down-hearted, yet on the whole one gets an extraordinarily moving impression of the power of human beings to fight on, to keep their nerve under most distressing conditions. One feels it more in Germany than in Austria; something of that same power of humans to forge ahead undaunted no matter what the difficulties must surely be an explanation of how the Russia of today lives. But it is not only the innate power of the human race for which one must feel respect in Germany. Despite all the contradictions and all the glaring contrasts and paradoxes, whether one likes Germans or not, one cannot come away save with a feeling of admiration for the way the people are buckling to their terrible tasks. The belief is unavoidable that here is an extraordinarily virile, resourceful, inventive, and able people that will yet survive the blunders of its rulers, and its own blunder in accepting such rulers, and will rise to greater spiritual and economic heights than ever in the past.

A Plea for Irish Peace

ONE who has recently traveled through County Kerry, Ireland, reports that fear keeps the country people off the roads and out of the fields and that in consequence of raids the county is actually suffering for lack of food and other necessities. Other counties are scarcely less badly off. The country is terrorized. Material losses are mounting ever higher. What is even more alarming to those who love Ireland is the news that a heavy emigration of young men is beginning for the first time since the hope of the New Ireland stirred Irish hearts.

The Free State Government holds the principal centers of population and has the support of the majority of the people, yet its military position is menaced by raids which do not spare the capital itself, and its moral status is seriously threatened by governmental incompetence. The Irish Parliament spends considerable time creating stern laws establishing military courts to judge, and an island prison camp in which to hold, Irish prisoners of war. President Cosgrave offers amnesty to such irregulars as will lay down their arms, underlining thus his threat of dire punishment to those who refuse to yield. Debates on the constitution are perfunctory—made so partly by the helplessness of the Free State Government against England, and partly by the failure of the Republicans to use the machinery of parliamentary action for a searching criticism and revision of Irish fundamental law. These shortcomings of the Free State Government are partially excused by the difficulties which beset it. No such excuse can explain the arrest of Robert Barton, who had been acting with official knowledge as a negotiator on behalf of the Republicans.

But if one is disappointed in the Free State Government, one looks in vain for any group which bids fair to do better. Irish labor gave promise of common sense and a constructive program which it has imperfectly fulfilled. It has not come forward as yet with any policy which may once more fuse the desires and affections of Irishmen. The Roman Catholic Church adds its thunders to the terrors of the state but fails to rise to the task of creating a spirit of unity and peace. There is no hope in the militant Republicans. The words will sound harsh to Irish-Americans who, inspired by a loyalty to leaders whom they had learned to love, like Mr. De Valera and Harry Boland and Liam Mellowes, by a justifiable suspicion of certain Irish-American politicians who oppose the republic, and above all by a devotion to the ideal of a republic which their American citizenship makes them hold dear, are partisans of the irregular soldiers out on the Irish hills. In this loyalty there is room for warm feeling and fine rhetoric. Alas, it does not serve Ireland's cause.

Once it might not unreasonably have been hoped by the Republican extremists that Ireland would rise behind them. But Ireland has not risen. In a country admirably adapted to guerrilla warfare a few hundred determined men may continue in banditry indefinitely; they cannot win or govern Ireland. What they do instead is to terrorize it. If it be glorious to die for one's country, how infamous to devastate it! There are those in this country pleading for help for the dependents of Republican prisoners and soldiers who have been terrorizing 3,000,000 Irish. The number of the terrorists is estimated at some 7,000. But is their lot worse than the lot of the millions of Irish people who, thanks to these terrorists, find their prosperity destroyed, their property subject to raids, and their lives menaced? The terrorizing Republicans are more likely to make Ireland a desert than a free nation. Every village they raid becomes a center of anti-republicanism if not of positive reactionism. For the first time in Irish history the tactics of Irishmen menace the Irish tradition in the hearts of the people. The trouble is that the extremists no longer go to the people with a positive ideal. Once they fought for the right of men to choose their way of life and obedience, but that ideal is meaningless in the mouths of men who would force it on their countrymen by bombs and the sword. Their chieftains, Mr. De Valera and General Lynch, have quarreled; but they go on fighting.

Ireland's continued failure is the failure of a great people to realize their own destiny; everywhere it strengthens the cause of those who believe in strong imperial government rather than democracy. Ireland must have peace and time to reintegrate her various policies. History will have plenty of lessons to draw from interesting speculations as to what might have happened if Lloyd George had acknowledged Ireland's independence as a matter of right and negotiated on that basis, or if Mr. De Valera had himself sat in the peace negotiations, or if he and his followers had submitted to a popular vote. But to talk of these things now or to discuss detailed terms of peace is folly. What Ireland needs now most of all is a truce to herald the new birth of an ideal, a baptism of self-forgetting love for the motherland which will stay the hands of those who would now destroy her under the tragic delusion that they by their strife are saving her from the wickedness of her other children.

Practically the great hindrance to peace seems to arise from mutual distrust. Yet certainly there are men of high integrity in Ireland. Such men as George Russell, poet, economist, and cooperator, Dr. Patrick McCartan, former envoy to the United States, Professor Eoin McNeil and his brother James, Bishop Fogarty, James and Stephen O'Mara, Thomas Johnson the labor leader, and James Douglas the Quaker patriot, are able, upright, and trustworthy men. General Mulcahy, commander of the Free State troops, has shown a more generous spirit than some of the politicians behind him. Cannot such men frame a policy? Can they not show their people the way out of the present wilderness? Might not the arms of both parties be surrendered to the people as represented in the Dail while men like these we have named act as a commission to guarantee good faith and to adjust such questions as might be referred by both parties to them? The commission as a guaranty of good faith ought also to stand behind an offer of a general amnesty to all who will lay down their arms, and it should obtain from the Free State Government a solemn pledge that an integrated and peaceful Ireland will be allowed to reconsider and revise the Constitution which is now in the process of adoption. Once Ireland can gain a breathing space, surely there are forces at work which will restore her health and in the process enlarge by peaceful means the boundaries of her freedom. Only Irishmen can save Ireland, but outsiders to whom Ireland was but lately the home of their hopes and the object of their endeavor have both a right and a duty to insist that blind force on neither side can save the Island of Sorrows from these last and saddest of her woes.

Mr. Weeks and the War Frauds

JOHN W. WEEKS, the Secretary of War, made a speech the other day in which he inveighed against "silly pacifists" and deplored America's shortcomings in the European conflict, particularly the failure to get airplanes, big guns, and high-explosive ammunition to the battle-front before the armistice. To guard against similar failure in the "next war" Mr. Weeks demanded a larger army and increased military appropriations.

Mr. Weeks's plea for greater militarism (he would use the pleasanter-sounding synonym, "preparedness") makes it unusually timely to inquire what he is doing to remedy the defects in his Department which the European War revealed as most important and the correction of which depends in no way upon a larger army or the other ways of spending the people's money that he advocates. For America did not fail in raising, training, and transporting troops. Her accomplishments in those directions were among the wonders of the war. Failure, where it occurred, was in equipping, supplying, and caring for her troops, and this was due not to lack of money or men but to deficient organization, method, and honesty in the war machine. What is Mr. Weeks doing to punish the perpetrators of our gigantic war frauds or to prevent their repetition in the "next war" to which he so cheerfully looks forward?

The public still knows little of the extent and character of the war and post-war swindles. It is somewhat familiar with the ship-building excesses and the airplane fiasco, but it regards the era of fraud as having ended four years ago, with the armistice, and as one of the inevitable and partly excusable aspects of war-making. The fact is that the post-war disposal of surplus army supplies has oozed corruption and dripped mire, continuing right down into the Harding Administration and Mr. Weeks's own tenure of office. Even more than Attorney General Daugherty (whose dodging of the issue is notorious) it is the business of Mr. Weeks to clean the muck out of his Department, to get rid of the blameworthy, and to clear the reputations of the honest and faithful. Instead we find him acquiescing in the policy of the War Department cabal that is trying to obscure the issue. Take Major W. O. Watts, formerly executive officer of the surplus-property division—he was discharged from the army because of his protests in connection with the scandalous leather sales before Mr. Weeks took office. After Mr. Weeks became Secretary of War members of the Graham investigating committee, both Republicans and Democrats, asked for the reinstatement of Major Watts. Mr. Weeks is said to have been favorably impressed, but before action could be taken contrary influences were brought to bear. In any event, Major Watts was not restored to the army. By contrast there is the case of Colonel L. E. Hanson. Two witnesses have testified that Colonel Hanson tried to thwart the cancelation (for fraud) of a contract for the sale of harness, but Mr. Weeks absolved the officer in a letter to the Attorney General as follows:

> I have the honor to inform you that I have had the matter investigated by an officer of the Inspector General's Department. The Inspector, after examining a number of witnesses, has come to the conclusion that the employees of the War Department who furnished information with reference to this matter to the Department of Justice were mistaken in what they think they heard and that they were precipitate and insubordinate in reporting the matter to your Department instead of to their official superiors.

Two members of the American Legion in Congress, Representatives Johnson of South Dakota and Woodruff of Michigan, have been foremost in demanding action on the war frauds by the Harding regime, and the *American Legion Weekly* has just completed a series of articles giving the most adequate and up-to-date account that we have seen of this extraordinary and disgraceful chapter in American history, of which the public knows so little and toward which it is consequently so apathetic. This account not only reviews scandals of the war period but it discloses the sale of surplus supplies after the armistice as enmeshed with secrecy, favoritism, and downright corruption. On the one hand there was a strong and generally successful attempt by business interests to prevent army supplies going direct to the public on terms which would materially relieve the consumer's burden or tend to break prices, then at their peak. On the other hand dummy and "shoestring" companies were organized, in which army officers and ex-officers were interested, to which supplies were almost given away. Favored concerns were allowed to put up less than the required deposit and were permitted to keep their supplies indefinitely in government warehouses at the public's expense. The competition of all but favored firms was eliminated by means of "negotiated" or "informal" bids.

Most amazing of all, perhaps, while with one hand the army was almost giving away supplies, with the other, says the *Weekly*, it was buying the same material for its running needs at market prices. In July, 1919, when consumers were paying twenty-five to forty cents a pound for sugar, the War Department discovered it had a "surplus" and turned over 46,000,000 pounds to the Sugar Equalization Board at 8¾ cents a pound. The latter, controlled by the trade, distributed the product to favored firms at cost, and some of the sugar was resold for as much as 29½ cents. Within a year the army's sugar supply gave out and it had to buy 35,500,000 pounds, mostly unrefined, at fourteen to fifteen cents. In January, 1919, it was decided to dispose of a large stock of a popular brand of cigarettes— retailing at twenty cents a pack—for 6 1/3 cents a package to welfare organizations like the Red Cross and Y. M. C. A. For some reason the makers of these cigarettes were favored as welfare organizations to the extent of about nine million packs. After paying a revenue tax of six cents a pack the net cost to the company was 12 1/3 cents. Early in 1920 the army returned to the same favored company and bought 2,515,350 packs of the same cigarettes at 14 1/3 cents. On April 21, 1921, during Mr. Weeks's own regime, a contract was made with a Philadelphia firm whereby a large stock of meats was sold at an average of 4.7 cents a pound. A War Department officer later estimated the stock as worth 21 cents. There was, besides, a provision by which previous buyers at less favorable terms might return their meats at cost to be turned over to the Philadelphia firm at the lower rate. Meats were so returned, and in some cases it is declared that they were sold back to the first purchasers, the two firms dividing the profit.

Mr. Weeks has a more important job than to scout "silly pacifists" or to propagandize for a larger army. An aroused public ought to compel him to get busy or walk the plank.

Anti-War Men Reelected

NO more significant fact stands out in the American election results than the return to public life of men who were driven from it because they refused to vote for war with Germany and stood upon their historic American right, almost unquestioned in any other war in which this country ever engaged, to dissent from its war policy. The outstanding case is that of former Congressman Clarence C. Dill of Washington, to which we called attention last week. He voted in the House against the declaration of war on April 5, 1917, as he had told his constituents he would do if war threatened, and for doing so he was, in the succeeding hysteria and passion, driven out of public life. When he declared his candidacy for United States Senator this year people scoffed. He won the nomination and then faced Senator Poindexter, so long a popular Progressive statesman that no one dreamed that he was beatable. During the campaign, Mr. Dill's anti-war record was cited against him. He gloried in it. He would say to the voters: "I promised you that I would do my best to keep this country out of war unless it was in danger of invasion. I kept faith with you, did I not? And I was punished for it. I am here today again for your votes, not regretting or withdrawing those sentiments." Curiously enough, this avowal was always followed by such applause that the opposition newspapers which had at first dwelt upon his "un-American conduct" found it convenient to forget about it. Mr. Dill now goes triumphantly to the Senate where he will be its youngest member as he is but thirty-eight years old.

Wisconsin has done more than return La Follette, who voted against the war and openly opposed it. Congressmen Cooper and Browne of that State, who were defeated, respectively, in 1918 and 1920, because of their attitude on the war were this year renominated and reelected. Congressman Berger did not have the chance to vote against the war, as he would like to have had, but he has been elected for the third time since the beginning of the war, and it is an interesting fact that the indictments against him in two United States courts in Wisconsin for his alleged violation of the espionage laws have been dismissed since his reelection. The Supreme Court long ago reversed the conviction secured in Judge Landis's prejudiced court.

In Ohio General Isaac R. Sherwood, the 87-year-old pacifist, who is also a veteran of the Civil War, has rewon his seat in Congress after having been ousted because he could not without protest see his country commit the blunder of entering a European war. In Montana, as we have also reported, the newly chosen Senator Burton K. Wheeler, who during the war was viciously charged with sympathy with sedition, found his record a help and not a hindrance. Congressman Evans of that State has been reelected on a platform calling for disarmament and a referendum before any declaration of war. His conscience troubles him, he says, because he is no longer sure that he voted right when he cast his ballot for war on that fatal April 5. Mrs. Winifred Mason Huck, of Illinois, is another newly elected member of Congress who favors a war referendum, as do La Follette and numerous others. As in England, the tide is turning with the electorate. And with the return to public life of men and women who will stand against war, there comes new hope of outlawing the most damnable and the foulest of human institutions.

How the League of Nations Is Used

THAT a determined drive is now on to put the United States into the League of Nations is perfectly obvious. Justice Clark, who resigned from the Supreme Court to take a leading part in this endeavor, begins his work with the new year, and a long list of sponsors comprising well-known men and women of both parties has been published as the opening gun. As mixed motives actuate these proponents of the League as impel the curious alliance of idealists and narrow nationalists who comprise the successful opposition. About this renewed struggle we shall have much to say in the months to come, and we hope before long to present to our readers a strong statement of the reasons of those who disagree with us from the pen of one of the ablest of them, in order that our readers may have both sides before them. We must say now, however, that the pro-Leaguers are wise in their effort to make theirs a nonpartisan movement, for even the ordinary politician should be able to see that for the Democratic Party to take up this issue again will mean merely renewed defeat. We are aware, of course, that Mr. Wilson hopes to lead the fight again; we are credibly informed that he demands the adoption of the treaty without the alteration of a letter or of a punctuation mark. That is, of course, to seek the utterly impossible. If the United States ever enters the League it will be, in our judgment, only after the present organization is largely made over and cut loose from that body of death, the Versailles Treaty.

Meanwhile we wish to call attention to the way the League is playing into the hands of the European imperialists. At Lausanne the other day, in congratulating Ismet Pasha on the entry of Turkey into the League of Nations, Lord Curzon uttered one of those cynically frank remarks indulged in now and then by diplomats which illuminate unexpectedly the smoothly whirring wheels that lie behind the outer mummery of imperialist diplomacy. "This makes many things easier," said Marquis Curzon. Press dispatches are not given to atmospheric color, but it may almost be assumed that he accompanied these words with a grim and sardonic smile. The significance of the statement points a neat little moral for America to contemplate. It helps us to see what the League of Nations is today, to understand its true function in the diplomatic machinery of Europe, and to observe how it works in the hands of the old-school diplomats who still speak for the nations of Europe.

For the inner meaning of Lord Curzon's plain remark it is necessary to go back to the time when the Lausanne Conference was discussing the subject of Mosul oil. The Turks had forced the issue by their intransigence, and the United States had suddenly come forward with one of her embarrassing demands which needed to be chewed over a little before it could be swallowed. With the American toe in the door, and Turkey pushing behind, the question of the Mosul oil fields had slipped in unheralded, as it were, and had at once begun to make itself vastly objectionable. The press of the world had begun to talk too plainly about the oil issue. The Conference too obviously was tackling in open session the real problem which confronted it—that is, the practical problem of economic grab. Who should get the Mosul oil fields? This, as every intelligent person knew, was the real question before the Lausanne Conference, as it was a chief cause of the Greco-Turkish War which made the Conference necessary. But for the Conference openly to discuss this question, and for the press openly to report the discussion, was too dangerous. It destroyed the moral illusion under cover of which imperialist diplomacy carries on.

Recourse was then had to an adroit moral flanking movement. The subject of Mosul oil was banished from the floor of the Conference. In its stead was brought forward into the glare of open discussion the question of the Greek minorities in Turkey. Here was a question of a humanitarian nature, to appeal to the sentiment of the world and to derive every ounce of value from the century-old tradition of Turkish violence and oppression. Before the Turks could even begin to stem the tide the word had gone out that Turkey proposed to expel beyond her new borders vast multitudes of her Christian population. The Christian nations were aroused; churches protested, and meetings passed resolutions. The feeble Turkish protest to this sentimental tidal wave, to the effect that they intended to do no such thing, went unheeded.

The time was now ripe for action. The flat alternative was laid before Turkey: Would she, or would she not, join the League of Nations and subject the safeguarding of her Christian minorities to the control of this body? For along with the moral agitation had gone the propaganda for the solution of the difficulty; and by this time it was fixed in the mind of the world that Turkish refusal to join the League of Nations would be tantamount to avowal of a policy of open violence toward her Christian minorities. If Turkey proposed to protect her Christian minorities, if she proposed to subscribe to common morality, she must join the League of Nations. Ambassador Child, holding a long conference with Ismet Pasha, spoke to him earnestly, as a friend. He pointed out the situation of Turkey with the moral sentiment of the world aroused against her, and how easy it would be for Turkey to accede to the Allied demand and win back the world's favor. He presumably said: "Why don't you join the League of Nations and stop all this clamor? Your opportunity is almost too easy. You would show the poorest political judgment, and make your position entirely hopeless, by refusing this opportunity." Whereupon Ismet Pasha promised Lord Curzon that Turkey would enter the League of Nations; and Lord Curzon remarked sardonically "This makes many things easier," the point being that England holds a mandate for Mesopotamia under the League of Nations, and that it is by virtue of this mandate that she is claiming for Mesopotamia the Mosul oil regions. Turkey, once a member of the League, will have put her head in the noose. She will have subscribed to the control of the League, and must abide by its judgments; to depart from this course would be again to raise the moral indignation of the world against her. But the League Council—controlled by Great Britain—will determine the boundaries of Mesopotamia. It will, it is fair to assume, declare the Mosul oil fields to be a part of Mesopotamia rather than of Turkey. England will get the oil. Turkey, a member of the League, will have practically no voice in the decision; while her membership in the deciding body will deprive her of the moral value of independent action. The lesson for America is simply that the League of Nations is still a very convenient noose in the hands of the imperialist garroters.

Germany's Moral Equivalent for War

OF all the ironies of history none is more tremendous than this: that in the early years of the twentieth century of the Christian era two great object-lessons in the power of passive resistance, preached by Jesus of Nazareth, should be given the world—one by a heathen Hindu, Mohandas Gandhi, the other by the militarists and nationalists of Germany. In all this conflict in the Ruhr nothing is of more permanent significance than the test of the pacifist method, and were it not so soul-stirring a test we should roar with mirth at this spectacle of the Hindenburgers practicing the pacifist's substitute for war.

Here are the Prussians themselves leading a united nation which, forced to forswear war, is yet determinedly resisting an invader. Pacifists have preached the possibilities of such a method for years; they have been met with the scornful reply that it was impossible, first, because no nation would ever try it, and second, because it would not work. Perhaps no nation ever would have tried it of its own free will; but the forced disarmament of Germany under the Treaty of Versailles left her no real alternative. There have been small local riots and outbreaks of anger; there has even been occasional bloodshed; but in the main the Germans have with remarkable consistency and discipline followed the pacifist technique. They have simply refused to carry out the orders of the invaders. Railway workers have stopped work when French soldiers assumed command of them, telegraph offices and telephone centrals have been cut off when French officers gave orders; miners have come to the surface when French engineers entered the pits; customs and bank officials have left their offices when Frenchmen gave them orders. Everywhere the French have been met by this paralyzing peaceful resistance.

It is too early to predict success for this method. In any case the economic loss will be terrific. Poincaré has made that impossible to avoid. And it is still possible that hunger or greed, powerful forces both, may induce large sections of the German workers, or important groups of German financiers, to break away, and to make a truce, profitable to themselves, with the invader. Passive resistance can be effective only when there is unity and a powerful national will. Thus far French methods seem to have effected just that national unity which caused many Germans to fear the test. Communists and capitalists both have been stirred out of their internationalism into the current of national resistance. Today in Germany no one would dare publicly take a contrary course. Foch's army is doing what Napoleon's army did a century ago; it is uniting Germany in a new patriotism. This patriotism has hate enough in its bosom and may some day express itself in a bloody war of revenge—there is no pacifist philosophy in its leaders—but for the present it is perforce limited to peaceful expression, and if the demonstration succeeds the pacifist philosophy may follow.

Significantly, too, no one is denouncing the Germans as cowards because they have not seized their pick-axes and tuning-forks and gone forth in a mood of romantic martial heroism to be shot down by French machine-guns. The newspapers that have most bitterly denounced pacifists as craven cowards in the past are today applauding this German method. The alternative, of course, is impossible. Suppose Germany had sent her Reichswehr into battle, suppose even that she had not been disarmed and had had an army worthy of the name, would she be any better off? It would only have meant the total destruction of factories that now are idle, the slaughter of thousands, or hundreds of thousands, or perhaps as in the Great War millions of her sons and France's. The decision would be no less problematical than today; but the cost would be infinitely greater. Nor even would the opportunity for heroism be greater; here in this firm stand of the German people against an invading army, without the firing of a gun or the throwing of a stone, is moral equivalent galore for every stirring act of heroism which war brings forth. Before the French are done, there may be men, women, and boys shot, thousands imprisoned, millions hungry. The religious sacrifice which has so often been praised as the unique expression of war time may be found here too. For the Germans in Belgium followed no sterner methods than the French are already carrying out in the Ruhr.

It requires discipline and devotion to carry a pacifist program through to victory. The Battle of the Marne did not mean that the German attack was crushed, and this first peaceful victory of the Germans may be no more decisive. The struggle may be long-drawn-out indeed. But the experiment has gone far enough to show the possibilities of the future. That there is an alternative to military resistance, and that it can succeed if a people is strong and united enough to will it, has been proved. And that lesson in itself, if it be rightly understood, may mark one of the decisive epochs of world history.

Let us not hesitate to apply this object-lesson. The pacifist is often asked, What would you have had France do in 1914? Suppose, he has answered—and until now the answer has sounded impossible—suppose France had refused to build an army 800,000 strong, but had said "I know my people; they are French to the core, and will never yield to an invader; we will not arm, and if the invader comes we will simply refuse to obey his orders"—would France, had she acted on that resolution, have suffered more or achieved less than she did? As it was, she lost a million and a quarter men killed, and another million maimed for life; her villages were ravaged, her industrial region crumbled, her whole people subjected to the long drain of a four-year war; and when it was over, her enemy was so exhausted that real reparations were impossible, and she herself so military-minded that she felt it necessary to keep half a million of her sons, and some hundreds of thousands of Africans, in permanent military camps, away from their homes where they might have been producing.

The answer to that question, after all, can only be hypothesis. But in the Ruhr just such an hypothesis is being tested out. Gandhi's experiment was necessarily limited because of the diversification of the peoples of India and their lack of national discipline. Ireland tried both military and peaceful methods at once. There in Germany is a people which, while still suffering from the shell-shock of war and revolution, has the habit of discipline. By the jest of fate the Prussians have been called upon to lead the first great national test of the power of pacific resistance. Could there be a more significant drama anywhere on the world's stage, or one more pregnant with significance for the future of the world?

The Next War

"THE next war"—it is easy to discuss it calmly in terms of Near Eastern intrigue and Western struggles for power, of French ambition, British suspicion, German revenge. In this issue of *The Nation* the next war is discussed in other terms. Through the collected facts of a man who is both an air pilot and a student of international law relating to the air we see the next war in terms of wholesale slaughter. We see battle lines blotted out, whole nations within the range of explosives of terrible power. We see populations standing helpless under a rain of deadly gases. In the past the imagination of H. G. Wells has made pictures of this sort of warfare seem plausible if slightly fantastic; the figures and expert observations of Mr. Royse—who knows the details of airplane construction, the mechanics of bombing, the latest inventions in destruction, and the air strength of the nations of the world—ring in our ears with the sound of unromantic truth. The next war may be fought for oil or steel or power or revenge, but it will be a war of blasted villages a thousand miles behind the front, of dead men and women and babies—a war of peoples, not merely of armies.

In his second article, to be printed next week, Mr. Royse seeks a way out of a world disaster such as this. Air armaments, he tells us, cannot be either limited or scrapped, unless the air itself is abandoned. Commercial aircraft can be almost instantly converted into war machines; today the great network of commercial air lines in Europe forms a reserve force ready to spring into active service at the first hint of war—France is ready now to fight the world in the air. Nor would the Powers agree to scrap a fighting machine which can be built up so rapidly and cheaply. A bombing plane with good aim can sink a dreadnought with hundreds of men—and the cost of the plane, as war machines go, is nothing. Battleships can harry coast lines and wage Gargantuan, clumsy fights at sea, but airplanes can terrorize whole countries and drive horror and demoralization into the heart of a people. It is little wonder that the Powers cling to their air forces through all "limitation" and that they subsidize at vast expense the ostensibly "commercial" companies running air lines across Europe.

Limitation is impossible; but Mr. Royse believes that international regulations regarding the use of aircraft offer a solution. He would make it internationally illegal to bomb from the air any civilian center, defended or undefended; make it illegal even to bomb supply depots or other military positions in towns or villages, since four out of five bombs dropped miss their mark and bring destruction to innocent people and defenseless property. Make this use of airplanes illegal, he says, and the horrors of the next war will at least be lessened. He admits that rules are disobeyed; but the outcry that was raised during the last war over rumors of dumdum bullets and shattered hospitals—even though the rumors may have been well founded—shows that such things can no longer occur as a mere matter of course without protest. If the bombing of towns behind the lines becomes something less than a commonplace of warfare, a regular routine, that much at least will have been gained.

Within the limits of a philosophy of desperation, this proposal may be the best that can be offered. Assuming the next war, it is well to attempt to limit the possibility of the extermination of peoples. But we cannot, quite so hopelessly, assume the next war. We are vividly aware of the chance of another general slaughter; we are all too conscious of the minor struggles which have filled all the years since the armistice; we see the open sores that cover the body of Europe, and the pressure of economic and political ambition that is driving the Western world toward collapse. But beyond these facts we see, too, the determination in the minds of millions of people that this collapse must be avoided. We must urge the outlawing of war if only to keep awake the conscience of the world and turn men's minds to the task of finding some way to peace. We *dare* not simply assume the inevitability of the next war and content ourselves with attempting to make it less deadly. Such an attitude would rather make it inevitable. We should take the appalling facts offered us by Mr. Royse and drive them into the consciousness of the world so that it may be aware of the fate in store for it. Then we should set to the heavy task of making the governments see with our eyes and abandon their reckless, desperate intrigues, and the economic philosophy behind them which means war in the future as it has meant war in the past.

Why Henry Ford Should Not Be President

By OSWALD GARRISON VILLARD

"IN my opinion he could realize his supreme ambition if he were to follow the example of a good shoemaker and stick to his last, that is, to the human and production problems in industry, and leave national, international, and racial problems alone." Thus Dr. Samuel S. Marquis upon the political ambitions of Henry Ford. No one could know Mr. Ford better than the man who has been for years his candid friend, his pastor, and his employee. For three years the head of the sociological department of the Ford Motor Company, Dr. Marquis has seen the inside of that amazing organization as have few others; and the results of his observation of Henry Ford the man, the manufacturer, and the employer he has set forth in a volume of collected magazine studies, "Henry Ford, an Interpretation," just published by Little, Brown and Company. It is a book of especial significance at this time, but it is remarkable in itself for its extraordinary detachment and its refreshing honesty, so rare in biographies of this type. Should Mr. Ford be nominated for the Presidency this book ought to be placed in the hands of every voter. For on almost every page are convincing reasons why he should not be sent to the White House.

"I know of no study more absorbing than the Ford psychology," writes Dr. Marquis. It is beyond question fascinating. No other man outside of political life has so challenged the admiration and the imagination of the American people, for no other man has risen as rapidly from poverty to the point where he either is or is about to be the richest man in the world. No other personality has been so much in the public eye and is yet so little understood—so rarely analyzed. "Tell us what manner of man is Henry Ford," is the demand most often flung at those who know him, or at the newspaper men who are supposed to hold a key or two to this complex, paradoxical personality—Dr. Marquis calls him a "puzzling mixture of opposing natures." "There rages in him," this Boswell says, "an endless conflict between ideals, emotions, and impulses as unlike as day and night—a conflict that at times makes one feel that two personalities are striving within him for mastery, with neither able to win a final decision over the other." What wonder that Ford "stuff" is the best kind of material for the padded pages of our Sunday newspapers? It is not only the puzzle of the man himself and his phenomenal rise; ever since the New York newspapers read the Ford Company's balance sheet for 1922, with its amazing entry of "cash in bank $151,000,000," they have been calling him the richest man on earth. That is enough to sell many a newspaper story, but even that is not all; his Presidential ambitions alone would entitle the most advertised man in the world to endless additional free advertising.

For those are serious ambitions and they are not to be disregarded because Mrs. Ford has stated to a reporter that "if Henry goes to the White House he goes without me." Dr. Marquis feels the menace of that candidacy throughout his study of the man, precisely as he reveals his belief in the unfitness of Henry Ford for the Presidency. Every detached observer who has studied the career of Henry Ford and knows the requirements of the greatest of offices at this juncture in the affairs of humanity must shudder at the thought of this man being in control of our national destinies. This is not because he is an uneducated man and has to sit with a dictionary on his lap when he tries to read Emerson. There are unschooled men who have natural aptitudes and good horse sense whom one would trust in any position. They have the inborn wisdom and patience of Lincoln; they have achieved an understanding of human nature; they have that divine sympathy which is the key to so many a human problem; and above all they are rooted in fixed principles. When such a man, be his name Jackson or Johnson or Lincoln, reaches high office we have the triumph of democracy; we have something to make every American a bit prouder, a bit taller, a bit straighter.

But Henry Ford is not one of these, despite his amazing successes. The milk of human kindness is not within him though he may be charitable and philanthropic. He is without the traits to offset the blanks in his scanty education. He is without a quality for which I can find no better word than the old-fashioned Yankee "gumption" which has helped so many a man over obstacles otherwise insuperable. He is without that patience which is wisdom and beyond price. He has no philosophy of the universe upon which to build. "He has," records Dr. Marquis, "the not uncommon conviction among mortals that he has a real message for the world, a real service to render mankind." He would like, so Mr. Ford himself has said, "to make the world a little better for having lived in it." Yet with that laudable ambition he has not learned to control and subordinate his self, or to think things through, or to order his mind. Dr. Marquis is quite clear on the latter point: "He [Ford] has in him the makings of a great man, the parts lying about in more or less disorder. If only Henry Ford were properly assembled! If only he would do in himself that which he has done in his factory!" There lies the reason for his intellectual failure and the eminent danger of putting him in any position in which his mental processes would be compelled to make far-reaching decisions outside the realm of automobiles and factories and multiple production. It is the reason why in my judgment it would be possible to stop at any one of the great factories that line the New Haven Railroad between New York and New Haven and pick out in each one some foreman earning $50 a week with no better education than Henry Ford who would be a far safer choice for the White House than the richest man in the world.

Inevitably my mind goes back to the day when Henry Ford announced his peace ship, not merely because I was with him and was the second man to be asked to go on the Oscar II and the first to decline (on the spot), but because that episode illustrates so clearly the weakness of the man's mental processes. I am quite of Dr. Marquis's opinion that the motive behind that venture "was a laudable one." Rightly handled it could have been made an amazing publicity "stunt" on behalf of that peace which all humanity desired, no one more so than the men in the trenches, which the governments of Europe were too rotten, too crooked, or too incompetent to make then or to make now. It was I who suggested that the slogan Mr. Ford hit upon for his venture, "We'll get the boys home by Christmas," be toned down or abandoned. "Why?" demanded Mr. Ford with instant suspicion. I pointed out that as the ship would not sail until December 4 and could not arrive in Holland before December 15, the time left before Christmas was too short even to communicate with the belligerents and get their replies before December 25, to say nothing of the impossibility of physically getting the millions back to their home in ten days after his arrival. My efforts produced no other change than the modification of the slogan to "We'll get the boys out of the trenches by Christmas," and that only when I suggested that a Christmas armistice might bring the men out on top of their trenches.

It was the mind of a suspicious child with which we had to deal; a mind without the necessary background of history and human experience to think its way through the first essentials of such a vast human problem. The instinct was sound; the necessary gumption lacking. So he and his guests went to sea in the Oscar II without his having even had the business sense to see for himself if those who had gotten him into the venture had any real assurances that their argosy would be welcomed by the neutral nations, to say nothing of the belligerents. One of the first questions the newspapermen asked him when he announced that he had "got the ship, boys," was what encouragement he had received from foreign governments to undertake the venture. He assured them that there were invitations, but, if the reports are true, not until there was almost a mutiny on the ship as she neared Norway did he trouble to read the letters—only to find that they were merely the most formal and polite expressions of good-will, such as would have been forthcoming for any move for peace. One dreads to think what a mind like this might do if intrusted with the handling of our foreign affairs.

To this a distinguished Republican Senator replied the other day that he would be willing to take a chance on that because Henry Ford would surround himself with able men. But this was precisely the argument advanced on behalf of Warren Harding when he was a candidate—and look what we got! More than that, there are certain traits in Henry Ford which were the worst traits developed by Woodrow Wilson during his sojourn in the White House. He plays a lone hand. Dr. Marquis even goes so far as to say that if Ford were President we should have a cheap administration because he would dispense with the Cabinet and a good many executives. Just as Mr. Wilson secluded himself more and more, so Henry Ford has said to an employee: "You know me too well; hereafter I am going to see to it that no man comes to know me as intimately as you do." Of Mr. Wilson the same words have been written which Dr. Marquis uses in describing Henry Ford: "The isolation of Henry Ford's mind is about as near perfect as it is possible to make it. For this reason the confidence born in him of success along one line never forsakes him when he enters other spheres of thought and action. Adverse criticism reaches him, of course, but it does not penetrate." Elsewhere this biographer speaks of Ford's "one-way mind"—ominous reminiscence of a "one-track mind" in the White House!

Again, both men have had a perfectly ruthless way of dealing with subordinates who have offended them. Dr. Marquis deplores and cannot defend the fact that Ford has quarreled with and discharged all the magnificent group of men who with him built his success. Every one of these men has been forced out of the company. Sometimes the quarrel was open and resulted in litigation; sometimes they were just dropped out. Sometimes subordinates have been thrown out under circumstances that reflect the utmost discredit upon Ford himself and reveal a side to his character that stamps him as at moments dangerously uncontrolled. Dr. Marquis observes that in many cases in which gross injustice was done to employees, Henry Ford, when cognizant of the facts, refused to lift a finger to right the wrong. One instance is worth going into at length—the summary discharge of a man whose task in the company "was a colossal one and greatly complicated by conditions which arose during the war." Dr. Marquis told Henry Ford that his treatment of this man was neither just nor humane, that it robbed him not only of his job, but of his reputation. Mr. Ford professing a desire to reinstate the official, Dr. Marquis went at his request to a certain executive to discuss the case with him. What followed we give in Dr. Marquis's own words:

> I told this executive that I thought he had acted most unfairly in the discharge of this man. "How do you know I did it?" he shot back. "Maybe you are barking up the wrong tree. How do you know the Chief did not do it?" I answered that I did not believe the Chief would be capable of doing such a thing. While we were in the midst of a heated discussion Mr. Ford came into the office. He listened to what we were saying for a few minutes and then turning to me said, "I did it. I discharged that man and what is more he is not coming back." This within an hour after he had said for the second time that he would be taken back. "What have you got to say now?" said the official. "I told you that you were barking up the wrong tree." "I have to say," I replied, "just what I have said before. The discharge was not merited, and the manner in which it was done was neither courteous nor fair." Mr. Ford then said, "Bring the man down to my office in the morning and we will go over the whole matter with him." I did as requested. Mr. Ford failed to keep the appointment. That was the end of the case.

It is not surprising that Dr. Marquis adds: "It is sufficiently painful and humiliating to be brought face to face with unemployment and all that follows—loss of income and of savings, accumulation of debts, eviction and hunger—without being kicked like a dog into it." Elsewhere he squarely places upon Mr. Ford's own shoulders the responsibility for this policy of "treat 'em rough" which seems to pervade the organization. More than eighty men in one department went home one evening without any intimation whatever that they were dismissed. "They came to work the next morning to find their desks and chairs taken from the room in which they worked. They were left to find out as best they could that they had been fired. The request to be permitted to tell men in a decent, gentlemanly manner that the company no longer required their services met with refusal." More than that, some employees came to work to find their desks *smashed with an ax*—a kind of sadistic vengeance which in no wise suggests the self-control and sense of justice which surely are requisite in any one who would guide the destinies of 115,000,000 of Americans. What if Henry Ford were President; if he became angry with some country whose methods he could perhaps not comprehend, would he not use our army and navy precisely as he turned to the ax to destroy his own property in the spirit of an angry child or of a defective? More than that, he is the victim of great gusts of passion as "sudden and terrible as those which break over the tropics." What havoc would not such storms create in the Executive Mansion?

To my mind labor has gone strangely wrong in its attitude toward Henry Ford. True he gives a $6 a day minimum wage but, as Dr. Marquis says, there was no excuse for a company in such a position not giving the original $5 a day. It is also true that he has a fine social philosophy as to the "down and out" and the ex-convict, that his theory of well-paid work as the salvation for most human shipwrecks is eminently sound. But these things do not offset the absolute despotism of the Ford management, its bitter opposition to all unionism, its refusal to introduce cooperation, and its working human beings at a terrific speed at such monotonous jobs as must inevitably affect the mental and physical health of those who labor for hours at one single, never-varying task. No, the American laboring men may be spellbound by the success of this mechanic who toiled with his hands, but they will err, indeed, if by their votes they place him in the position of ruling over the country's destinies.

Now, it would not be just, of course, to judge Mr. Ford solely upon the acts set forth above. Beyond question he is a genius in his own field, and his desire to create more work in the world for human beings is altogether to his credit. The fact that his companies continue to do well after the loss of all his earlier associates and executives shows that Mr. Ford is master of his business. His ability to get on without going to the banks for aid when he was apparently in distress several years ago is another achievement which reflects luster upon his industrial generalship. He is the only man I know who can do things that would ruin any other capitalist and still "get away with it." There seems to be no limit to his power of industrial achievement; the whole South yearns to have him take over the Muscle Shoals project, believing that with one wave of his fairy wand he will create new and unexampled prosperity for that section. For all the efforts of the older railway men to break the effect of Ford's success in running his railroad by attributing it entirely to the freight traffic which he is able to throw to it himself, there is no doubt that, coming to railroading with a fresh mind and freedom from red tape and the dry-as-dust methods of the older railway corporations, he has blazed the way and gotten new life and efficiency into what was a dead, or nearly dead, artery of traffic. His capture of the water power in St. Paul and Minneapolis, which ought to have been reserved for the public, is another instance of the ability of the man to affect the imaginations of his fellow-men. In anybody else this would have been denounced as a grab and a steal deserving of the utmost public condemnation.

Mr. Ford is beyond question philanthropic—he does give money away. There is a hospital upon which he has lavished millions, and he has doubtless done many private acts of generosity, though it seems to me he has by no means mastered either the art or the happiness of giving on a large scale. And here, too, his record is sullied. I am familiar with a case in which he publicly announced that he was going to give $10,000 to a certain cause, and then welshed because he did not like an interview given to the press by a single member of the group of men connected with the undertaking. For this trivial reason he refused to reimburse the organization for expenses incurred after his public promise. There is a Western college which makes a similar charge against him—again proof of his inability to control his feelings. In no such case is there evidence that Mr. Ford ever has moments of contrition and repentance. He, too, apparently feels that he can do no wrong; he, too, looks with suspicion and positive hatred upon anyone who dares to oppose him or to thwart him.

Nor has Mr. Ford ever expressed any regret at his own lack of educational opportunities. He has all the readiness, as the peace-ship venture showed, of the successful business man to consider himself fitted to deal with all sorts of questions without adequate preparation therefor. Imagine such a man passing upon a question like that of the Chester concession! The geographical ignorance of Lloyd George and Wilson at Paris has been the subject of many a jest and many an anecdote—Lloyd George could not at first distinguish between Silesia and Cilicia—but those men are towers of knowledge when compared with the master of the automobile industry. Ignorance of geography can, of course, be supplied, when those ignorant are willing to surround themselves by others having knowledge, and then to use that knowledge. But when it comes to the profound, deep-lying economic issues of the day, one cannot so safely or so easily suck the brains of others without at least running the risk of being deceived and imposed upon. Take Henry Ford's crusade against the Jews. I attribute it to nothing else than utter ignorance. He fell for the long-since exploded and overworked Protocols and every old slander—I have no doubt that if he does not believe in ritualistic murders it is only because he has not been plausibly told about them. So in the matter of finance, Henry Ford is utterly unsound. He would be guided by the fiat-money views of his friend Thomas Edison rather than by the opinion of the most liberal and detached students of finance and economics. But even there one cannot be certain. Dr. Marquis recurs several times to the "periodical convulsions" in the Ford company. Then, he says, "old policies are swept away. New policies are set up. Departments are turned inside out and upside down, or altogether done away with."

Yet there is no doubt that the movement for Henry Ford is very strong, and in the face of Dr. Marquis's testimony to his former employer's tremendous political ambition, it is impossible to take seriously the interviews which are beginning to appear setting forth that Ford is really not a candidate. Let anyone who is interested talk with the Ford agents; let him examine what is being done in certain States to nominate him in the Presidential primary; let him investigate the reports of the opening of Ford headquarters in various cities, and then let him read the announcement that if the public wants Henry Ford for President it will have to draft him. One can then draw one's own conclusions. Wherever he travels, East, West, North, or South, the observer will find the appeal of Ford to the imagination. The plain people are convinced that he is just one of them who has broken the bank, who played the luckiest card ever played by any mortal and carried off the largest sweepstakes from the green-baize table of fate. They believe that somehow or other in some miraculous way he will make over the government of the United States into that efficient up-to-date smooth-working organization it ought to be, and if he makes it over on the lines of his numerous properties nobody will object. They like him because, being rich, he still hates Wall Street and refuses to be drawn into it; that being enormously wealthy he refuses to go in for social ambitions and build a palace at Newport. They like him because his own private life is so exemplary, because he still holds to the wife of his youth, and adores his most promising and able son. They don't mind if he makes Fords and drives a Rolls-Royce, and that he lives in a big and particularly ugly house. They are tired, supremely tired, of politicians of the Harding type and others of the college-president type. They want a successful man of themselves to try his hand at the governmental game and bring them some relief. The farmers are crying out for him. He gave them the tractor; they would like to see him try to solve their other problems.

So that is why the best-informed political observers say that if Ford is nominated on the Democratic ticket he will sweep the country. That is why many of them think that even without the indorsement of either of the major parties he can run on a third ticket and be elected. If either contingency should come to pass the result would be disastrous to Henry Ford and to the country; it might readily bring about the complete collapse of our governmental machinery, which is steadily sagging to the breaking-point. It would be the triumph of the unfit; it would probably be the final attempt in American political life to fill the Presidency on the theory that any American, no matter what his education, his experience, his talent, or his knowledge, is equal to the job of solving the multitude of complex problems that sometimes make it questionable whether any man can be found with all the qualities essential to a successful President of the United States.

I have been observing political conditions in the United States and writing about them for the press for thirty years. It is my deliberate belief that during that time no candidate has been suggested so absolutely unfit for the White House as Henry Ford. Almost anything conceivable might happen to the Republic should he be elected.

The Crusaders for the League

"LEAGUE Drive Hits Capital; Foes Worried" says the headline over a Washington dispatch to the New York *Globe*. The correspondent reports these forces marshaled to put the United States into the League: the Federal Council of Churches of Christ in America, the World Alliance for International Friendship, the Church Peace Union, the World Peace Foundation, the preachers, the professors, the publicists. These people not only have enormous financial resources; they have the even greater power of moral passion. They are crusaders; they believe that they are marching with God, and they are appealing to the moral sentiment of America to join a league which will, they say, bring peace to Europe and the world.

But there is nothing more dangerous in all the world than sincere moral passion so convinced of its righteousness that it ceases to face the fact-data from which it draws its conclusions. What is this League? Has it made for peace? Can it make for peace? Would America's accession to it strengthen the forces of peace in Europe or the forces that now harry that miserable continent? Upon the answers to these questions depends the validity of the appeal of the Leaguers. They seldom stop to ask or answer them. They are, indeed, much the same group of earnest people who urged the United States into the Great War, also in the name of high moral principles, never stopping to analyze the aims of our Allies, never asking a statement of conditions of peace, firm in the conviction that if only we would go in our own nobility would somehow purify anything wrong in our associates and make everything right in the end. The treaty of peace brought no peace to Europe but the same good folk now tell us that it is all because of our desertion of Europe, that if only we would enter the League all would be well.

What has the League done for peace? It has "settled four major international disputes." These were:

1. The *Finnish-Swedish* dispute over the Aaland Islands—a trifle more important than the recent Panama-Costa Rica dispute.

2. The *Vilna* dispute, wherein the League attempted an honest settlement. But when Poland refused to bow to the League the League bowed to Poland, leaving as its "settlement" a new aching Alsace-Lorraine to trouble the peace of Europe in coming decades.

3. The *Upper Silesian* dispute. Let Mr. Lloyd George, an advocate of the League, describe the action of the League in the case of Upper Silesia:

> In Silesia two Powers of great authority in the League—France and Poland—were passionately engaged in securing a result adverse to Germany. The other party to the dispute had no friends and was, moreover, not a member of the League. Britain stood for fair play, but it was not a protagonist of the claims of Germany. Poland had a powerful advocate in the League, a country with a vital interest in securing a pro-Polish decision. In these circumstances the League ought to have exercised the most scrupulous care to avoid any shadow of doubt as to its freedom of all bias. Had it chosen distinguished jurists outside its own body to try the case as it did in the Aaland case, all would have been well. It preferred, however, to retain the matter in its own hands. Hence doubts and misgivings with which the judgment of the League has been received. . . .

4. The *Albanian-Serbian* dispute. Here the record shows that the League refused to take any action until after the Conference of Ambassadors had settled the major point at issue (unless advice to the conference to hasten its decision may be called "action"). When the ambassadors had settled the boundary-line and the British had lectured Serbia into withdrawal from Albania the League stepped in with a sort of commission of evacuation and claimed credit for the whole.

Meanwhile, according to a compilation made by Miss Frances Kellor, *since the Treaty of Versailles was signed eleven European states have resorted to arms to settle disputes with other Powers, and eight of these were members of the League. Three of the disputes were between members of the League—pledged by the Covenant never to resort to arms until after arbitration or inquiry by the League—and in four more the disputes were begun by members of it.*

The Covenant of the League, it will be recalled, provided

also that "any war or threat of war, whether immediately affecting any of the members of the League or not, is hereby declared a matter of concern to the whole League." Yet wars have come and gone, and the League has done nothing. It has done nothing in the Near East; it has done nothing in the Ruhr; it has been silent where a voice for peace has been most needed. Meanwhile its administration of the mandates has camouflaged such colonial crimes as the bombing of South African Hottentots by British airplanes, the conscription by France of black "wards of the League," and in the Saar Valley, within 200 miles of the League's headquarters, it has palliated what Mr. Asquith has called a "monstrous specimen of despotic legislation" without parallel in Czarist Russia. When the League dealt with the opium traffic it substituted for the Chinese proposal of restriction to "medical and scientific needs" the words "legitimate uses," thereby condemning India to further debasement in the interest of British government revenue.

There are good men working in the League and for the League, and the intentions of the American people are good. But that is not enough. When the Covenant of this League was first presented at Paris *The Nation* wrote that it was "the memorandum of a working arrangement having in view the organization and apportionment of the material results of victory . . . a permanent constitution for the cabinet conferences of the Great Powers which have been settling the affairs of the world since the armistice." There has been an earnest effort to make it something better, but the effort has not succeeded. The Covenant remains the same; the domination of the League by the Allied Powers is still secure; Germany and Russia are still outlaws. *The Nation* is not isolationist; we realize the interrelation of Europe and America. The League may reform itself and change its character, but the lesson of Paris and Versailles is fresh in our memories. It is our profound conviction that if the United States should join the League at any time in the near future the effect would be, not to bring peace and alleviation to Europe, but to strengthen, by our alliance with them, the disruptive forces that have been dragging Europe steadily downward since 1914. Let our pro-League friends drop for a moment their moral fervor, study the facts, not the theory, of this League, recollect Paris, and beware.

The Next Next War

WE live in days when men fear to face realities. Here are England and France, referring to each other as allies, maintaining an appearance of joint action in half of the world and negotiating for common ground in the rest, yet entering a race for the supremacy of the air in which no attempt is made to disguise the ghastly fact that they are bidding against each other, building great fleets of airplanes with which to fight each other in the next great war. We are not yet five years past the armistice that ended the war to end war, the war that was to teach us so many great lessons and set the world to rights, yet here are the two great Powers of Europe glowering at each other across the English Channel and beginning precisely the kind of armament race which, between England and Germany, prefaced the World War.

What else can Mr. Baldwin's statement in Parliament mean? "British air power must include a home-defense air force of sufficient strength adequately to *prepare us against attack by the strongest air force within striking distance of this country.*" Mr. Baldwin's announced intention to increase the home-defense air force from eighteen to fifty-two squadrons, almost tripling it, is a direct challenge to France. It is directed against no other Power. France recognizes that fact, and is replying in kind. We are back in the poisonous atmosphere that made the European war inevitable, and we are in imminent danger of repeating, even without the traditional lapse of a generation, that terrific experience.

It is not only in the air that England is preparing for the next great war. She is beginning work upon an enormous naval base at Singapore, which can be aimed only at Japan. It is to Japan what the fortification of the Kiel Canal was to England. Japan, perhaps in response, is flirting again with Soviet Russia. The play of the Powers in China all looks in the same direction. The British Government has demanded, according to report, the right to maintain its own guards along the Tientsin-Pukow Railroad. What that is likely to mean past history has made only too plain. Poor China, torn by internal dissension, striving to make in a few years the adjustment to modern industrialism and Western parliamentarian democracy which it has taken Westerners centuries to work out—if we have worked them out—lies like a carcass on the plains of Asia while the Western Powers and the financial powers within the nations wait like greedy vultures, held in check only by their mutual jealousy. It is the old, old story—the story of Morocco, of the Bagdad Railway, of the partition of Africa, and the end of the book is war.

Germany is disarmed; Austria is disarmed; Hungary and Bulgaria are partially disarmed; Russia has fewer soldiers than before the war—but Europe has more men under arms today than she had when the Great War found her an armed camp in 1914. She is still an armed camp. France, unable to pay interest on her own debts, unable even to pay the contractors for reconstruction in her own destroyed provinces, France, which pleads despairingly for more reparations, lends 400,000,000 francs to Poland and 100,000,000 francs to Rumania, and maintains a military mission in Czecho-Slovakia, and accordingly those young Powers, born of the war to end war, maintain armies greater than those of their imperial predecessors. We ourselves have a larger army than before the war, and are constantly being urged still further to increase it. According to President Harding himself—whose figures Secretary Weeks will hardly attempt to dispute—we spend 85 per cent of our national revenue on wars, past and future.

Nothing can be gained by sugary optimism. We must know where we stand. Nor will mere machinery help us. A world court, useful as it may be, will not get us very far without a new spirit in international relations. While France is in a mood to feel insulted and peevish when the Pope and the British Government indorse Mr. Hughes's suggestion for expert determination of what Germany can pay; while the representative of the United States can thump his fist upon the table at a Pan-American Conference and rule out the Monroe Doctrine from discussion by the American nations, declaring that it is a "unilateral" policy of the United States; while even the League of Nations, hailed by so many as a mechanical solvent of the world's ills, still bars Germany and Russia from the rightful position of full equality with the Entente Powers in the world's councils; while the Powers barter for oil rights in Turkey when talking of protection for Armenians, there is small ground for optimism.

Yet there are steps which may be taken, and it is in the power of the United States, fortunately removed from the immediacies of European hates, to take them. It may be impossible, for the present, to stop the economic and financial rivalries which are such fertile breeders of war, but there are indications that the financial powers are tending to become internationalized and to adjust their differences without intervention by governments, and meanwhile there are things that governments may do. We believe that Mr. Harding is sincere in his respect for the principle of judicial settlement of international disputes for which his speeches plead so fervently. Let him join hands with Senator Borah, with whom he finds himself in unexpected agreement, in the Senator's plea for submission of *all* disputes to a court. Suppose, instead of hemming and hawing about reservations designed to safeguard the isolationist policy of the United States, he should call a conference which would exceed in dramatic interest and in historical significance the Washington Conference with which he began his Administration, and that he should open it by saying to the representatives of the Powers assembled: "Gentlemen, there is no issue which cannot better be settled by a court than by a war. There is no national right or interest so sacred that it can stand above Right. I have consulted with the members of the Senate of the United States and I am able to say that the United States is prepared to submit every dispute which may arise between it and any other nation, great or small, to a world court. That, gentlemen, means that we are prepared to outlaw war, and that in turn opens the way to larger measures of disarmament than we have yet discussed, and to new hope for us all."

It sounds wild and chimerical? It is a possible step. And unless we conceive and take some such step, something which will catch the emotion of the world and give it one of those dramatic wrenches which sometimes do lift it out of its crusted ruts, we will bear our share in condemning the world to a repetition of the murderous cycle through which we have just passed, on an even more colossal scale.

Law—Not War

FROM Argentina to Australia, in Germany, France, Russia, England, Italy, Japan, and the United States hundreds of thousands of men and women commemorate, on July 28 and 29, the ghastly days in 1914 when war cut Europe in two, by the solemn resolution that there shall be "No More War." Some of the more thoughtful, in this country particularly, have made "Law—Not War" their slogan, and are directing their energy to machinery for the adjudication of international disputes.

The ninth anniversary of the Great War comes at a gloomy moment. The outlook for a Europe dedicated to peace has never been more clouded. The Ruhr is today a steaming cauldron of hate; France and England are glowering at each other's air fleets (H. N. Brailsford writes: "Our experience of naval competition with Germany has taught us whither the new competition in the air must lead"); the Balkans are no more peaceful than in pre-1914 days; the little nations of Central Europe maintain larger armies than did their imperial predecessors; France announces her intention to conscript a half-million-man army among those poor black peoples of Africa whom "civilization" was supposed to have pacified; China is falling a prey to military bandits and the Western nations are talking of endowing her with international armies as well; Russia turns from reconstruction, almost perforce, to "air weeks," and glorifies the Red Army.

All the more need, then, for pacifists and for thundering no-more-war demonstrations. There is need for realization of what war has meant and will mean. There is need for men with the voices of prophets who will cry out, as George Lansbury wrote to the absolute pacifists of the Fellowship of Reconciliation, the Women's Peace Society, and the Women's Peace Union: "We stand against all wars. We believe that killing is a blasphemy and a crime against God and man. I hope that America will stand with us in trying to rid the world forever of warfare and its monstrous inventions which, unless destroyed, will annihilate all civilized peoples." These people demand the immediate abolition of armies and navies, the instruments of war. They want total disarmament and they are not content to wait until another war has tested out the expert theory that one air battle, with modern explosives, can destroy a New York or a London.

We are with them heart and soul, although we have become a little uncertain of the permanent effect of pacific proclamations. We have too warm a memory of the ardent pacifists of 1916 who adapted their convictions without difficulty to "We are for peace, but—" in 1917. It is perhaps some such doubt which has led the National Council for the Prevention of War to abandon the old international slogan "No More War" for the "more constructive" slogan "Law—Not War." Whatever emphasizes the fundamental importance of referring to judicial decision every international controversy that threatens to grow into war, whatever stresses the fact that arbitration is always more honorable than war, points in the right direction.

The trouble with the new slogan is that it is not comprehensive enough. It does not have the appeal to the heart of that bitter cry of the European masses: No More War! It even suggests, to the unwary hearer—and most hearers are unwary—some relation to the futile plans to draw up laws to regulate war. And to many it narrows the issue to the question of the World Court at The Hague. That is a pity—for it drags all the petty disagreements of national politics and with them the tragic problem of the League into a discussion which requires rather clarification.

For the issues about which we ought to be debating are not: Should we join this court or that? Is the World Court too closely linked with the League? It is the irony of fate that the American people, which has for decades led Europe in preaching the substitution of law for war, should today be hemming and hawing about the form of this court when it might be pushing the world forward toward greater readiness to use any court. Senator Borah gave us the right lead when he insisted that we must preach the gospel of compulsory jurisdiction, proclaim our own readiness to submit all our differences to judicial settlement, and invite other

nations to show as much good faith. We have a great national tradition in which the names of Seward, Sumner, Root, and Bryan —yes, Bryan—bear an honorable part. If only our peace societies would all unite in proclaiming that law is always, *always* more honorable than war, and in urging Congress and the Administration to express that assurance, they might avoid the danger of contending for a shadow and contribute more certainly to the slow but ineluctable task of lifting a little of the gloom which, in these aftermath and prelude-days of war, is settling upon Europe.

The Only Hope

(*Special Radiogram to* The Nation)

By OSWALD GARRISON VILLARD

Geneva, September 30

UNDER the darkest skies Europe has seen since 1914 the fourth League Assembly comes to an end. The facts that the trouble between the Serbs and Italians is blowing over, that a Greco-Italian war has been averted, that the Ruhr resistance is at an end do not affect the intense depression among the Assembly delegates. "Over all of us," said one of the ablest and most influential Englishmen, speaking today, "hangs the shadow of the French army and the fact that their airplanes outnumber the British four or five to one. We have but substituted one militarism for another." And he agreed with one listener that the French today are more dangerous than was the old Germany because they are abler, more subtle, and less stupid.

There lies the stumbling-block to European progress and the greatest danger to the League itself. Throughout this session the French have tried to block every forward movement, have done their best to end the Temporary Mixed Commission on Disarmament, have opposed the effort to refer really important points to the World Court, have stood in the way of every hopeful suggestion.

Not over reparations only are the English and the French utterly opposed. Here they disagree at every turn. It is perfectly plain that the French do not wish the League to gain prestige though they are willing to use it for their own purposes. Since the Ruhr collapse all talk about French security, never in my opinion sincere, has stopped, and the French strength has been thrown into the effort to block disarmament.

When one recalls the historic opposition of these two nations and beholds the present situation one can only tremble for the future. England and France now lock horns at every point. Today wherever one looks the gravest dangers confront one. France is rejoicing over her great victory over the completely abased Germans, but all advices here foretell catastrophic events in Germany. Even French dispatches admit that Paris is anxiously watching, and is welcoming the Bavarian dictatorship and the state of siege there. The Communists are delighted over the German prospect. Most economists here do not believe that the French will have an easy task to reorganize and operate the Ruhr. They feel that Germany is too far gone to fail to collapse. This may be postponed. Watched-for revolutions rarely boil on time, but the fact is that the situation is so grave that the soberest men shake their heads in despair. *Nation* readers would be amazed if I could tell the names of those who have said to me that the situation is absolutely hopeless.

Fear of Mussolini is general. He is called a crazy man here—also a great man. No one can tell where he will erupt next, now that the Council of Ambassadors has given him the Greek liras so unreasonably. This is called downright robbery here; Englishmen are hanging their heads because the British Ambassador voted for this screaming injustice. Indeed, the way the League has been duped in this matter by the Council of Ambassadors is one of the hardest blows it has received. Mussolini can now claim that he has the complete approval of the Great Powers for his every act, including the Corfu murders. Liberals here utterly deplore the fact that two great nations have now upheld the principle that they can grab where they please and compel payments and submission. France and Italy, both members of the League, have thus deliberately violated the very spirit of the Covenant. The principle that force is supreme, charged to the Germans, is now triumphant again. It is a victory for the brute side of human nature. Then, too, France may have made the dangerous discovery that whole masses of industrial populations, whole peoples can be starved into slavery and submission—which is a terrible lesson to teach imperialists and big industrialists the world over.

Meanwhile, the League trembles in the balance. Five years after the war to safeguard democracy Europe rushes to economic disaster. One dictatorship follows another—Russia, Italy, Spain, Bavaria. Probably soon the whole of Germany will be subject to a dictator, but observers here feel that even so he could not hold himself in power long and that the Allies may be compelled to undertake the ruinous task of governing more portions of Germany than the Ruhr.

It is not time to despair yet. Information from a London source hitherto reliable reaches me that Mr. Baldwin is considering a new offer of startling importance, to buy off the French and get them out of the Ruhr and Germany altogether by assuming the position of guarantor of Germany at Poincaré's terms—fifty billion gold marks. If this should be accepted it would save Germany, give France her pieces of silver, and perhaps rescue Europe at a tremendous sacrifice to England. There is no other possibility in sight of immediate rescue, no other way quickly to restore England's lost prestige and rehabilitate her shattered influence since Mr. Baldwin assumed conduct of affairs. Even this solution would leave bitter rancor and festering hatreds, the inescapable legacy of the worst of wars, and would not remove the danger of future wars. It certainly would make inevitable a British-German alliance, as England would have intrusted her financial future to Germany's good faith. England would run a tremendous risk if the expected Communist rebellion should sweep Germany or, what is more likely, if an exhausting, bloody, planless civil war should ensue.

Over all broods the sinister spirit of French-Italian chauvinism, acting in the manner of pre-war diplomacy and greed and lust for power. No wonder people despair. Geneva feels intensely the failure of the Americans to aid spiritually and morally. They no longer expect our entrance to the League, but if no unexpected help such as the proposed British move just outlined comes, they feel that only America can save Europe from the bloody-handed, base-minded diplomats and the spineless prime ministers who are leading her to destruction. Liberals feel, like the editor of *The Nation*, that America has thrown away a glorious opportunity to lead the world, a leadership which was possible without war guaranties, without entering the League, and without entangling alliances.

What of the League?

By OSWALD GARRISON VILLARD

Geneva, October 1

WHAT of the League of Nations as its fourth Assembly comes to an end? Well, there can be no doubt that it ends with considerable gloom and little satisfaction with the results achieved. The gloom is not wholly due to the grave European situation which has overshadowed the entire meeting, nor to the incidents growing out of Mussolini's murderous acts in Corfu. "It is the poorest Assembly we have had," is the verdict of one of the permanent staff who will not admit much that is disadvantageous to the organization to which he is so devoted. It certainly has not sparkled; many of its sessions have been as dull as those of any American legislature, yet there has been great excitement within the ranks of the members and much indignation at the course of events. There have even been moments, as at last night's session, when there was mutiny in the air, mutiny on the part of the members of the Assembly against the acts and decisions of the Council. Yet there have been few moving utterances; only Nansen, Gilbert Murray, and Branting have really stirred the Assembly. It has not been, or has not been allowed to be, guilty of expressing any of the wrath and indignation it has felt at the procedure of Mussolini or the conduct of the Council of Ambassadors in calmly turning over to that brigand the fifty millions of liras which the Greeks put up as a guaranty of *bona fides*. Nor has the deep feeling held by many of the Assembly's members as to the events in the Ruhr been allowed to express itself except in the moving and downright speech of Gilbert Murray—always the scholar and honest gentleman.

For this Mussolini is in large part responsible. There would undoubtedly have been much said about the Ruhr situation had not the Italian dictator drawn his red herring across the trail just as it met and jeopardized the very life of the League itself by questioning its competence. Someone here has remarked that when you get a great group of men and women together in a foreign city like this they are only good for one big issue—they are not capable of more. That seems to be true of the psychology of this group, and so, to the delight of the French, the occupation of the Ruhr came up only once and the debate was choked off as soon as one or two lesser delegates had seconded Gilbert Murray's outburst—just as Nansen was declared out of order last night when he dared to express his opinion about the high-handed action of the Ambassadors. Perhaps the collapse of the Germans would have made any action as to the Ruhr impossible, but men like Professor Murray see very clearly that if the League is not to be allowed to have an opinion about acts as contrary to the principles of the League as that, the League will rapidly lose caste.

Indeed, if I were an advocate of the League as it is I should go away from here heartily discouraged, and that is, I think, the feeling of the liberal leaders who are honestly trying to make something out of this body in the interest of peace and humanity. They are whistling, some of them, like Robert Cecil, to keep up their courage; they are pretending that everything is going well, but in their heart of hearts they cannot be happy. In the first place, there is the quiet but never-ceasing effort of the French and Italians to sabotage the League. Next, it is now old enough to have growing pains and also to have developed some of the vices and weaknesses—such as log-rolling—of all legislatures. Then its activities are cleverly limited by its charter as if with malice aforethought—there was, for instance, no way in which it, since Greece was afraid to do so, could move to demand that Mussolini be made to pay for the human lives he so wantonly blotted out at Corfu. If, asked one of the protesting delegates at last night's session, the League cannot deal with acts of its members directly leading up to war, and the International Court cannot be trusted with strictly legal questions as to the League's competence, what is the function of either body?

When I first arrived here there was a general feeling that after all the League had gotten pretty well out of the Italian-Greek mess. The liberals acknowledged that the League had received a black eye abroad, but they felt that after the facts became known the League would regain its former position in public opinion. After all, they said, a war was averted and it would not have been had there been no League. They took the position that the Council of Ambassadors had accepted, with only one slight change, the proposals made by the League, and that if five private citizens had volunteered to settle the difficulty the League would have accepted such an offer provided the five were in a position to do the trick. The League, they said, is only an instrument to an end and if there is a better one why not use it?

The answer to that was, of course, that in the case of Mussolini they had used a worse one. As it was, this attitude of forced contentment was radically changed when the news came that the Ambassadors had calmly handed over the swag to Mussolini without even waiting for the guilt of anybody to be fixed. Rarely have I seen men so indignant. They not only felt outraged for the sake of the Greeks, they realized that they had been buncoed themselves and that the Ambassadors had accepted their terms merely in order to get around them. One of the Englishmen declared to me that Thursday was the blackest day in England's history since August 1, 1914. Gilbert Murray thanked God in the Assembly that the League had had nothing to do with that and uttered his profound regret that he could not say the same of the British Empire. The action of Lord Crewe broke the hearts of the high-minded Englishmen here. They would have been outraged enough had all the other ambassadors voted for this steal; they could not bear the thought that their own ambassador had by order of the Prime Minister joined in. This, following the rumors that Baldwin surrendered to Poincaré in Paris, seemed the last straw to men in Geneva who are up against sinister French and Italian opposition at every turn.

On top of that came the news that, finding it impossible to get the League's Council to agree to refer to the World Court the five questions arising out of the Italian challenge of the League's competence in the case of the Albanian murders, Lord Robert Cecil had agreed to the compromise the Italians asked and that these vital questions should go to a Special Commission of Jurists. The Council wrangled hour after hour over this and then Lord Robert announced it to the Assembly, not in sackcloth and ashes, but glorying in his shame. While he had felt, he said, that the matters ought to go to the World Court, still he was happy to record that there had been substantial agreement, the real object desired had been achieved, etc., etc. It was the worst kind of political trimming and compromising the old, old language of the expedient politician. Lord Robert has quite changed since he entered the British Cabinet—as was to be foreseen. It is said for him: "Of course, he is no longer free to act as he should like to now that he is in the Government!" You are quite expected to forget that last year when he was playing a different and finer role he was also representing a Government, that of South Africa. Fortunately, as already stated, he was not allowed to get off unscathed. One man after another got up to dissent. As it is, some of the smaller countries are still talking of drawing out. My judgment is that they will not now, but there is no denying the truth of a statement like that made by a Finnish delegate that the press in his country cannot understand why anybody should be allowed to remain one moment in doubt as to the competence of the League in so clear-cut a case. As Nansen put it, if he had been asked to create an absolutely perfect case for the League to act on he could not have produced a better one than Corfu.

Geneva is like Washington in that those at work in the League find it hard to realize the trend of public opinion outside of this locality. I am wondering tonight if Lord Robert has estimated the damage his compromise has done to the cause of the World Court in America. How can anybody get up to advocate the court in the United States and face the query why the League did not have faith enough in its own court to intrust to it such vital questions as its own competence but actually preferred instead to appoint a special court of political judges? For that is what these judges are going to be. Each member of the Council is to appoint one judge. Of course, each member of the Council will choose some one whose opinion he has ascertained in advance!

To illustrate the kind of slim behavior the honorable men in the League are up against, I may add that the Italians early insisted that they would not accede to the question of the League's competence being taken up unless the matter were separated from the Corfu affair. That was cheerfully accepted. Then, when the competence issue arose, the Italians promptly pointed out that a unanimous decision would be needed in the Council to settle the question of reference! Had the issues not been separated unanimous action would not have been required, if my information is correct. It is a constant struggle against the reactionary forces, with the smaller, and especially the Scandinavian, states playing a fine, brave role.

Meanwhile, it is only fair to acknowledge that the work done by the permanent secretariat and committees steadily increases in value. Those who carry it on say frankly that they need a great deal of time to build up their machinery, but they insist that it is far more effective than three or even two years ago and that it gets stronger with every year. But, as I have already pointed out, the one thing that is lacking in Europe is *time*. Already there is increasing pressure to cut the appropriations for the permanent forces and there is no doubt that the expense bears heavily upon certain nations, although it is pitifully small as contrasted with the price of one battleship.

The fate of the League as a machine for peace will not, however, be decided by the efficiency of its social or economic or legal bureaus but by political considerations. It is both the weakness and strength of the League that it is tied up with governments. It is its strength because in so far as the delegations represent the governments and speak for them their word is binding. Where the tie is loose, the home government sometimes fails to honor the obligations incurred by the delegation—as the French did on one occasion. One of the most thoughtful and influential and democratically minded men here told me that he absolutely opposed any plan to elect delegates through the parliaments or by direct popular vote because it would then be so easy for the home governments to ignore or even to thwart the actions taken here. So we must face the fact that the League is but a machine of the existing officialdoms in the various countries, that its source is the governments, and that it will only with great difficulty, if at all, rise above its source. All the governments are willing that it shall go on with its philanthropic work, regulate the traffic in obscene pictures and literature and the traffic in women, talk of improving conditions of labor—the chief cannon-fodder. But when it comes to interfering with the existing schemes of the chauvinistic governments of today, then the League must look out for itself. It may be that it will be killed by direct sabotage of the sort Mussolini, unwittingly perhaps, undertook; it may be that it will one day face an indignant withdrawal of the innocent smaller Powers who insist on taking the League seriously and dislike being buncoed; it may be that it will perish slowly by sinking into innocuous desuetude in both Assembly and Council. That it has done some excellent work no one can deny; that it might be welded into a great instrument for human righteousness is also true. But its survival as a really useful organization for justice as well as peace calls for the reform of certain governments which at present have not the slightest intention of being reformed but propose to carry on the world as if it were the same world that existed in 1914.

How to reform these governments which learn nothing and forget nothing and are now mere puppets in the hands of the great industrialists within their borders—that is the great problem of humanity. I asked one of the most distinguished and despairing members of the Assembly what he had to suggest. He has seen communism in Russia and is sure that that road leads only to ruin. Socialism has never had any attraction for him. He agreed to my statement of the problem—but when I asked him for his remedy he threw up his hands. The men here seem to know nothing of the possibilities of the cooperative commonwealth; they only faintly realize that political government has everywhere broken down, and they grope in the dark for a solution while fighting incessantly against the powers of darkness so conspicuous here. These are steadily sending Europe to its doom and will yet land her there if some miracle does not happen, such as a British buying-off of France in her relations with Germany or an awakening of America to the possibility of her using her good offices and influence—still tremendously potent in Europe—to bring certain countries to their senses before it is too late.

Mr. Villard is at present in Germany. The Nation *will publish in subsequent issues other articles from him on European subjects.*

The End of the German Empire

(*Special Radiogram to* The Nation)

By OSWALD GARRISON VILLARD

Essen, October 21

THE great German Empire founded by Bismarck is collapsing. It has all but ceased to exist. Not only is it flouted, ignored, and rebuffed by Poincaré, who is seeking to destroy its authority in a hundred ways. Not only is there a Stinnes *imperium in imperio* compelled to negotiate separately with the French as if Berlin were not concerned. Not only are Bavaria and Saxony almost at war with the Reich. The Palatinate, the Rhineland, and the Ruhr are now lost to Germany, perhaps for fifty years.

The French political policy, so absolutely contrary to the Versailles Treaty, has triumphed. The dismemberment of Germany is at hand, and the Balkanization of Europe as well. What we are seeing mortal eyes have never witnessed in our industrial age. Stark naked military power has triumphed as never before in peace. France cares little now what Berlin does, whether Bavaria secedes, or if England be angry. She has cut the heart out of Germany, seized the left bank of the Rhine (which Wilson prevented at Paris), and has done it by theft, chicanery, brute force, expatriation. Her representatives gloat over their triumph, ignorant or unaware of the lessons of history or of the absurdity of the idea that such a monstrous human wrong could go unpunished.

They make no concealment of their purpose. Their official press representative at Düsseldorf was brutally frank on Friday, saying that France will give the Ruhr workers the absolute choice of working for them or starving; that they will work as, when, and how the French want, for fifteen years to come. He declared that what the German people might think or feel was of no consequence. The French wanted their money, proposed to get it, and would continue to deport everybody whose conduct or bearing they did not like. Asked why the Palatinate and Rhineland were so much more harassed and subjugated than when I was here last year he said it suited his country to govern that way. As for the German railroads seized during passive resistance, he declared that they would never go back to the Germans—at least, he added, for sixty years, being governed meanwhile by an international commission. Germany, he said, would never be able to utilize them for mobilization again.

No honest American could have listened to his utterly cynical, cold-blooded presentation of a plan to dismember a nation and despotically enslave millions of its citizens, and still pretend that our intervention in the war had had any other result than to transfer militarism from Berlin to Paris, and in a more dangerous form—for where that of Berlin was stupid and inevitably self-destroying that of Paris is diabolically clever. I am not basing this on the word of one official. For his one frank avowal of policy there are a thousand facts visible here on every hand. It is an even more startling fact that the French can carry their policy of ruthless subjugation through unless an internal or financial upset causes her to desist. The Ruhr labor leaders say nothing can prevent the German laboring men being driven into absolute despair by the deliberate French policy of delaying the resumption of work and the approach of vast unemployment. The endless exactions, harassments, extortions, thefts of the conquering soldiery are in complete contrast to the British at Cologne. The truth is that the French are ruling as Napoleon did. They have learned nothing. They believe that you can reduce and humiliate these people as if they were Cochin-Chinese.

I am writing with no love whatever for the German Industrialists. It is true that their means are now exhausted. They did receive large sums from Berlin during the period of passive resistance, putting it chiefly into plant betterments to occupy the workers and prevent the loss of that money by the lightning-like fall of the mark. Trustworthy bankers say that unless the French reverse their policy there will be absolute collapse within two weeks. The French reply that this is all humbug, and point to the rise in the values of Ruhr shares. They quote Otto Wolff as saying before their staffs are dismissed the Industrialists will shake large sums out of their sleeves.

Meanwhile plants are daily shutting down; unemployment is menacing; shooting down hungry men and women is a daily occurrence. The local officials are at their wits' ends. Sometimes, as at Düsseldorf, they are allowed no police to uphold order. Sometimes they are aided by the French troops in cities where there are many French women and children. Sometimes there is deliberate incitement of the Separatists, the Communists, and the unemployed. There is no sign how far the French mean to carry their vindictive policy. It looks as if they meant both to rule and ruin, destroying what they cannot use, compelling the complete yielding of every German birthright of freedom and manhood. There has been the utmost delay in reinstating the railroad workers, half of whom will be discharged and their places filled by French workers now here, resulting inevitably in inefficiency and further delay in the resumption of work in the Ruhr. The postal men in Essen were summoned yesterday to go to work and then after much talk were told that everything was off and were sent home. All officials of whatever rank not born in the Rhineland or the Ruhr have been permanently dismissed, also all the higher officials, and their places have been filled by carpet-baggers from France. The French are blocking the resumption of huge plants by refusing to return great amounts of completed products which were seized, and by preventing export of coal, iron, and steel. Every possible obstacle has been thrown in the way of resumption. If what is being done here were done by Italians or Turks to Greeks or Armenians the heavens would ring with the protests of the world. This week is absolutely critical. The French must show their hands or a general collapse will follow. It is impossible to believe this was planned by Germans or that Germans have large sums of foreign currency. German labor leaders say this is not true. All groups are too badly scared. Even Krupp and the small companies are printing their own money. A cup of coffee at Düsseldorf costs a billion marks.

The terrible fact for the Germans is that the passive battle need not have been lost, at least not so soon. The people here were eager to go on indefinitely. The government lost the fight through inadequate preparation, by not planning for a two years' struggle, by throwing away resources, by waste and extravagance, careless and often corrupt management. Germans admit freely that that part of the passive battle was as big a disgrace as the other was honorable. The principle is unaffected by its defeat. What is happening is that between the upper millstone of incompetent political government at Berlin, beset by party squabbles playing politics, failing to put their own house in order and to convince the world of their honesty of purpose, and the lower millstone of French rapacity and utter ruthlessness the German people are being crushed and broken down until their only thought is how they can keep body and soul together with the dollar at twenty billions.

What form of government the French will give the stolen provinces is not clear. It is no longer necessary for them to promote a Rhenish republic, despite Aix. They expect the distracted, starving people voluntarily to ask their conquerors for anything that will enable them to live in peace without starvation and constant military despotism. Outright annexation will of course not be attempted.

We are witnessing hour by hour the fall of a great empire in a way to make inevitable a future war, filling Europe with hatred of an intensity never before dreamed. The French are unable to realize that their policies are certain to lead to their own ruin and to cause a coalition against her. Any temporary gain will be as nothing to the future ill-will of the whole world. No structure founded on such inhumanity, cruelty, and gross materialistic selfishness can endure any more than could Kaiserdom.

Did Passive Resistance Fail?

By OSWALD GARRISON VILLARD

Berlin, October 28

TODAY all Europe is in the control of an armed force. Might rules; the bayonet is king. Is it then true that the great weapon of passive resistance, in the spirit of Jesus, failed in the Ruhr, leaving its inhabitants more than ever the victims of a more brutal force than Europe has yet seen?

Well, the answer is that nothing that has happened in the slightest degree detracts from the power of the weapon of non-resistance and its availability in the future. The simple truth is that passive resistance in the Ruhr did not achieve its ultimate aim because, and *solely* because, the Berlin Government betrayed the cause of the German people by its mismanagement of the battle, the corruption which marked the financial side of the struggle, and the complete and absolute miscalculations on the part of the Cuno Government as to the duration of the contest and how it should be carried on.

It must be remembered that passive resistance began spontaneously in the Ruhr. When the French troops came in, the Ruhr workmen laid down their tools. Berlin had not thought of this plan of countering, but they seized upon it with joy and extended the movement not only throughout the Ruhr but through all the previously occupied territory. Naturally, being anything but pacifists, they did not bring to the struggle any loyalty to passive resistance on the ground of principle or religious belief. It was merely the one weapon to which they could turn. From the beginning Dr. Cuno was warned that he must prepare for a long struggle, perhaps for a year and a half of opposition, in order that when the spring elections of 1924 came on Poincaré would be compelled to admit that the Ruhr policy had failed to produce money for France or any supplies in considerable excess of the cost of the occupation. That would have afforded the best means of defeating Poincaré, who at this writing seems to be certain to get a new lease of power when the elections come. Dr. Cuno was, however, convinced from the beginning that it was only a matter of keeping up the resistance for two or three months, and he based his whole campaign upon this theory. No definite program for carrying on the struggle was, therefore, ever worked out. So far as I can ascertain there was not even any financial program resorted to in order to prepare for a long struggle; the sole reliance was the printing press with results anybody could foresee. Some effort was made to peg the mark at between 20,000 and 25,000 to the dollar, which succeeded for a time—long enough for some insiders, so many people believe, to enrich themselves thereby.

But there was no effort to plan for a new currency such as now (October 28) is just going into effect but which could as easily have been put into use ten months ago; there was no move to vote new taxes and otherwise to raise fresh revenues to support the battle; I cannot even find that the popular contributions to the Ruhr cause were adequately developed and encouraged by the Government. Far worse than that, tremendous corruption crept into the whole management of the finances, perhaps not so much in

Berlin as elsewhere. It was difficult—the money had to be got into the Ruhr by any possible method: the least suspicious-looking messengers had to be selected to carry the huge sums needed, for the French seized messengers and stole the money whenever they could get their hands on them. That naturally opened the door to waste and at times even to theft. But besides that, insiders did enrich themselves and enormous sums might just as well have been thrown out of the window. Again, the Germans were unable to sink party differences and rivalries even in this great struggle. The petty bickerings and strife went on in the Reichstag precisely as before. It did not become, therefore, the complete and overwhelming uprising of the nation that it should have been. It did cement the nation for a while in the first months of the fight; but after that the people, nervously worn down by nine years of constant excitement, suffering, and misery, failed to focus their attention upon the struggle for the reason that the leaders failed to furnish the necessary inspired, unselfish leadership without which no passive resistance can succeed. Germany needed a Gandhi, and there is no German Gandhi.

Even when the end came, when Dr. Cuno found that the mere printing of notes would not win the battle, there was the same old lack of frankness on the part of the Government toward its own people. He himself avoided the necessity of surrender by giving place to Stresemann, and Stresemann had to surrender so rapidly that infinite harm was done to the situation in the Ruhr by the failure to resume, or rather to surrender, gradually. It was just as in 1918; the German authorities put off their surrender too long and then were in feverish haste to get it over with. Dr. Cuno is an estimable man personally and no charge of personal gain is made against him. But, like so many other German statesmen, he was totally unable to gauge public sentiment abroad. From the very beginning he was convinced that speedy help would come from America and England. He even assured a private gathering of leading Hamburg business men in March or April that he had every reason to believe that aid would soon be forthcoming from the Anglo-Saxon countries. He suffered, too, from the fact that his finance minister, Hermes, was totally unfit for the position. He had been badly besmirched in a scandal in connection with profiteering in wines, but Dr. Cuno had to keep him because the Center parties demanded that as their price for supporting his Government. So the German people were betrayed again, and the weapon of passive resistance broke in the hands of men who used it as a tool.

No one who has not been in the occupied territories can understand the sacrifices the German people there made during the passive-resistance struggle. The minute it began the French increased the pressure upon them, especially in the districts which had been occupied since the armistice. The German population was terrorized and tortured in every conceivable way. Expulsions took place in every direction. From the little town of Gerolstein 2,000 of the 3,000 inhabitants have been driven out. At first those expelled were allowed to take their furniture; later expulsions were immediate, so that the families went out, leaving their furniture standing in the rooms, which were sometimes occupied by drunken and disorderly characters. Sometimes the quarters were occupied immediately by French officials. Try to imagine what it would mean to be living in the State of Connecticut and suddenly to find yourself cut off by a military barrier from all intercourse with New York and Massachusetts and Rhode Island, without telegrams, often without mail for days and often unable to get word from or to your relatives across the line, and always in terror of being ousted from your home and robbed of all your belongings at daybreak. Sometimes there were no newspapers for days; to get anywhere people walked six, eight, and ten hours to accomplish absolutely necessary business, and nobody ever rode on the trains run by the French. In one case a woman seventy-six years of age drove three days and nights without rest in a coal cart to go to a dying daughter. But if the daughter had happened to be beyond the Rhine she could probably not have gone to her.

It is to the infinite credit of the Germans directly affected that they stood all of this without complaint and with complete faith in the righteousness of their cause and the reliability of their weapon. They have not complained now, though their torture continues and they are beginning to understand how they were betrayed by their own Government. It is another evidence of the lack of a proper sort of nationalistic feeling in Germany, which is also demonstrated in the attack on Saxony and the disloyalty of Bavaria. More than that, the passive-resistance struggle was of course utilized by the great industrialists of Germany, who are its real rulers, for their own purposes. It was they who dictated the surrender, and a very hasty surrender, when it got too hot for them and they had begun to feel that if they did not get their plants into action again they would soon never be able to put back into service some of their most delicate and costly works. Dr. Cuno was their agent; his was "a business men's government"; while Stresemann and Stinnes are not friends the Stresemann Government is none the less one of reaction and under the circumstances is inevitably the creature of these conscienceless big-business men for whom, as for their brothers in business in other countries, there is but one motto: "Where iron is, there is the fatherland." There has never been any question in my mind that they would sell out to the French the minute they were compelled to or found it to their advantage to do so.

That in such a sordid struggle the great weapon of passive resistance should have been taken up by men most of whom were without true patriotism, or any ethical concept of what they were doing and what they were using, is a misfortune for humanity. That millions of oppressed Germans were led to make the necessary sacrifices to carry this struggle on for utterly different objects than those avowed is a crime against the German people. For it all Germany is now suffering and will have to suffer, the innocent and the guilty alike. It is another evidence of the way the German people are being crushed, exploited, and degraded between the upper and nether millstones of a horrible French militarism and the selfishness and falsity of their own changing governments and the real masters of those governments—the big industrialists.

From all of which I hope it will be clear to the *Nation* readers that passive resistance as such did *not* fail; that it carried on gloriously for eight months in the face of every possible obstacle; that it fell short of success against France because it was not honestly and efficiently supported at Berlin, and that there is nothing in this experience to prove that, given proper leadership and the adequate devotion on the part of all involved, this weapon of the spirit against force cannot again be used. Some day it may yet be, and with overwhelming success, against that naked brutal force which is today bringing civilization in Europe to its fall.

The Next War Draws Near

By OSWALD GARRISON VILLARD

London, November 16

"IF the Germans cut loose, our three divisions in the Ruhr are lost." Thus spoke a prominent French general in the Ruhr the other day to an Allied general, a former comrade in arms. By that remark the French general merely emphasized what is quite apparent to military observers—that the position of the French troops in the Ruhr is an extremely serious one if the Germans should finally be goaded into resorting to such arms as they have. The Westphalians are not like the inhabitants of the Palatinate and the Rhineland, who are in many respects the most easygoing and peacefully disposed of the Germans. The Westphalian is a rough, hard-working and hard-fighting being who has been for generations engaged in the most difficult of physical occupations. He has been extraordinarily patient and long-suffering under the harsh and brutal measures of the French; he held himself in check when, as he thinks, his comrades in the Krupp works were wantonly murdered by a frightened lieutenant and his file of men. But what worries foreign observers, and the French as well, is whether the day will not come when the Ruhr worker, seeing his wife and children dying of starvation before his eyes, will prefer to go against the French guns rather than endure such torture any longer.

This is no idle fear. It is not so very long ago that the leaders of the workingmen in a certain Ruhr town (there are very good reasons for withholding its name) went to the foremost industrialist and said to him: "Do you want these Frenchmen out of here? If so we'll throw them out by tomorrow morning. They are five thousand and we are fifty thousand." Naturally the industrialist was horrified. "Are you mad?" he asked. "Don't you realize that if you kill these French others will come here from Essen and Düsseldorf and destroy our city and everything in it?" He was able to dissuade them, and so have others elsewhere to whom the same suggestion has been made. But the question still remains whether these checks can be applied indefinitely; whether the hour will not come when there will be a resort to arms even if it means the end of everything. A year and a half ago two prominent German pacifists told me that if the French troops were not withdrawn from the Rhineland their countrymen would attack the invaders within five years with bare fists if they had no weapons. That was six months before the occupation of the Ruhr, whose horrors and vindictive cruelties they had not foreseen, nor the now impending starvation in the Ruhr.

The French are not blind to the danger. They show it in their obvious nervousness and the great displays of force they are constantly making. The French generals are plainly ill at ease when, as in Essen the other day, they ride through great crowds of ominously quiet and starving people. Especially do they show it in the cities like Mayence, where they have concentrated thousands of their women and children. They have compelled Mayence to build an entirely new quarter composed of magnificent apartment houses, each apartment in which has to be fitted up for the conquerors down to the last towel, the last piece of china, kitchen-ware, and bed-linen. In another section they have made the city build for them huge barracks, which is the clearest proof that they have no intention of ever vacating Mayence unless they are compelled to go. Now, on the night of the trial of young Thyssen when the verdict of guilty was pronounced by the French court-martial, there was an outpouring of the population of Mayence such as was not equaled in the enthusiasm of the first days of war. The French were powerless to control the crowd and wisely did not attempt to. The people vented their indignation at this travesty of justice by surging through the city for hours, singing patriotic songs. Had they been inflamed by incendiary speeches there would not have been a Frenchman alive the next morning, and every French apartment would have been ransacked as well. (This is not my opinion only but that of other judges.) If the reader of this article has followed the Separatist developments in the Rhineland, he must have been struck by the mildness of the manifestations in Mayence; this mildness is to be considered in connection with those huge apartment houses and the fact that 95 per cent of all the hotel rooms there have been commandeered by the French for the use of their officers and officials and the wives, children, aunts, and cousins these have brought with them. What would not a sudden uprising, even if quickly put down, mean to these non-combatants whose lives M. Poincaré is jeopardizing?

To return to the general situation, all the old military textbooks used to lay down the law that the last thing an army ought to do is to fight with a deep river at its back. Should hostilities begin again General Degoutte's troops would not be in quite the same fatal position as General Burnside's Army of the Potomac at Fredericksburg; he was able to withdraw his defeated army to the north bank only because General Lee failed to appreciate how easily he could drive the enemy into the water. The French in Essen are some distance from the Rhine, and there are nearly 200,000 other French troops across the river. But they are dependent for their supplies upon an intricate system of railways, which could be cut with the greatest ease by desperate men; to protect them, Allied military men tell me, it would be necessary to guard every culvert and every bridge. A prominent American diplomat declares that he has for months past awakened every morning wondering whether the Rhine bridges had not been blown up in the night. He has been prophesying for months past that there would be hostilities between November and April. If you ask him and the British officers I have talked with how in the world an unarmed and starving population can fight against an army perfectly equipped with tanks, endless machine-guns, and poison gas, they reply that desperate men will stop at nothing and that it will not do to think of the coming war in terms of the old. They agree, of course, that the Germans could not arm and equip and supply an army of the old type. If war comes, they say, it will take the form of a guerrilla warfare after the Irish model, with flying columns of about 250 men and one cannon, and much bombing from the air. The head of an important British military school has been quoted to me as saying that those are precisely the tactics for the Germans to adopt.

That these details are being discussed in cold blood; that British officers smile at the question, How soon will you be fighting on the side of the Germans? and show no signs of resenting it, is one of the most alarming portents of the times in Europe. For another war would settle nothing and could only add to the utter misery and destruction. If it comes, it means that those bloodthirsty Englishmen and Americans who regretted that the war ceased before the German Rhineland cities were laid waste will have their wish gratified. And if by any chance the Germans should win, there would be devastation in France such as has not been witnessed heretofore. Hate begets hate, oppression oppression, bitterness bitterness, revenge revenge. Whereas there was no hatred of France in Germany in 1919—as I can testify from my observations at that time, and I can bring hundreds of other witnesses, of every nationality, to confirm it—but only respect for the magnificent way the French had fought for their country, today all Germany seethes with hostility and the determination to conquer them some day or be wiped out. That this is the case is the completest proof of the folly of the French since the surrender, as it is proof that if they really want security they have gone about it just the wrong way. When I asked the French official at Düsseldorf whose duty it was to answer the questions of the foreign correspondents whether it was not regrettable that there should be such a growth of hostility to the French among the Germans he answered: "As to that we don't care at all."

But the soldiers do. They are taking note of it because it has a distinct bearing upon the next catastrophe and because they believe that if it comes to another struggle those who hate hardest and are most bitter will win, whatever the disparity in armaments. The Englishmen say that as long as they hold the Cologne bridgehead it will be almost impossible for the French to start off for Berlin from the Ruhr, and they think that it would take a long time and an enormous number of men to get to the German capital. Of course the deeper the French penetrate into Germany the more men they will need to guard their communications and the easier it will be to cut those lines. The English point out, too, that if the French should decide to extend their "sanctions" to the occupying of Berlin, they would immediately have to recall to the colors a large number of men, to demand so large a mobilization that there would be a revolt among the French people. Certainly the political Left would make a tremendous protest, and the Communist movement in France is growing much faster than people outside of that country realize—their daily paper in Paris has now a circulation of over 200,000. If Poincaré has to mobilize even a fraction of the reserves, some of the deluded French people will realize that the policy of vindictive brute force has failed. Where would the franc drop to then? Again, if the French should ever retreat from Germany, it would be like the retreat from Lexington and Concord—there would be a foe behind every wall and tree.

Could England keep out of a new conflict between Germany and France? Who can say? Her troops are in a most difficult position now in the Cologne area. They are surrounded by French and Belgians with whose policies they do not sympathize; whose policies are responsible for the rapidly increasing unemployment in the British zone which is giving the British officials such deep concern. One of the highest British officials in Cologne is not in the least hesitant as to where he stands: "My sympathies are with the extreme German nationalists." "I spits when I sees a Frenchman," said a British corporal who was just leaving Cologne after a long service abroad, including four years on the French front during the war. His regiment is, like himself, on the side of the Germans. What is more important is that Great Britain's trade interests all incline her to antagonism to the French. There are those who believe that a serious situation will arise in London if, as is threatened, the next French "sanctions" should mean a seizure of Hamburg. Then the lion would roar even if his mouthpiece is so weak a statesman as Baldwin, for that would have a direct bearing upon the question of unemployment in England, which is Baldwin's excuse for seeking a general election at this time. The Admiralty is being urged now to dispatch some cruisers to Hamburg so as to get ahead of a French move. It, if my information is correct, has its plans worked out as to what it will do if war with France comes. Its chief function will be to blockade the French ports, but not to occupy them, which will immediately raise the interesting military question whether ships can blockade harbors nowadays when the bombing air-machine has made such tremendous strides since the war as an offensive weapon.

A visiting European crowned head remarked in London the other day: "Everywhere I go these English tell me they don't *dare* to do this or that." But not all the English are afraid of France's power, for at about the same time a distinguished British soldier was declaring that the air defenses of London could be reestablished in forty-eight hours. "If we have to fight the French we shall dispose of them in five months with the aid of the Germans we shall arm," was his viewpoint. "If we had five shiploads of English airplanes we could begin to fight the French now," said a former German division commander in Berlin just four weeks ago; as it is we shall have to wait until after Christmas." I do not believe the stories that large numbers of men are being trained in Germany. Why should they be? Germany still has millions of war-trained soldiers—all she could possibly handle. There is no doubt, however, that there are groups of ex-officers meeting and planning for the next war and that cannot be stopped by any amount of Allied military control. The danger does not lie there but in the assumption of the government by men like Von Seeckt and Hindenburg, or the rising of the desperate people on the Rhine. I take no stock in the fixing of a nearby time to strike.

That was largely bluff, in my judgment. With Germany in its present chaos it is ridiculous to fix a time for anything. But I know and believe with all earnestness that what Poincaré is doing is bringing on the next war in Europe with giant strides, and that that war is inevitable unless the moral forces of the world are marshaled to stop what is happening in the occupied territories and to get the French out of all of Germany at once. It is for England and America to see that this catastrophe does not come to pass. They can stop it if they will. They will certainly be utterly lacking in true friendship and good-will to France if they do not unite to save her from the grave she is digging not only for herself but for all Europe. It is what A. G. Gardiner calls it in the London *Nation*, "the greatest crime in the history of Europe."

[*Mr. Villard's next article, Germany's Political Failures, will appear in* The Nation *for December 19.*]

Mr. Hughes Says: "Thumbs Down!"

"THUMBS down!" says Mr. Hughes in answer to Chicherin's proposal for the recognition of Russia. It is an old answer—so old, indeed, that it has become tiresome, and Mr. Hughes has felt it necessary to liven it up with a little jazz supplied by the Dime Novel Bureau of the Old Sleuth Division of the Department of Justice. The Secretary of State repeats the hoary old arguments against recognition: Russia's confiscation of American property, the repudiation of her debt, and her support of communist propaganda in the United States. Then seeing that his audience is going to sleep on his hands, he hastily calls on Mr. Daugherty for a saxophone sextette and some black-face artists to introduce an interlude of jazz. Mr. Daugherty kindly obliges, and the country is treated to a tale of alleged instructions recently sent by Zinoviev to the Workers Party of America, calling for the organization of "fighting units" and looking toward a day when it would be possible to "raise the red flag over the White House."

The whole tale sounds like fiction—far too naive to be believed of the Soviet Government in its present situation and mood. Senators Norris and Borah have challenged its authenticity with such insistence that Mr. Lodge has felt obliged to promise an investigation by the Foreign Relations Committee. The public will do well not to swallow the story until this inquiry shows on what base it rests. Mr. Hughes tacitly admits that he knows nothing of the truth of the tale himself, but says he has the assurance of the Department of Justice of its authenticity. If he had the assurance of the Department of Agriculture, of the Director of the Mint, or of the Coast and Geodetic Survey, the story might merit at least superficial credence, but in its post-war dealings with "red activities" the Department of Justice has such a record of fakes that it is entitled only to suspicion until it has produced convincing evidence.

Leaving aside for the present, therefore, Mr. Hughes's jazz interlude, what is there to the stipulations which he makes for recognition of Russia? The general demand that the Soviet Government shall not conduct propaganda in this country for the violent overthrow of our Government is reasonable, and not unacceptable to Russia. Yet there are certain difficulties here which need to be understood. Communist doctrine is aimed primarily at achieving a new industrial system. Nobody can predict how the workers of any particular country would carry it out, or how far, even if they were generally convinced of its justice. The assumption that widespread belief in communism here in America would be accompanied by a violent overturn of existing government is a conclusion unwarranted by history and resting largely on the fears of those who profess it. In any event, active propaganda for an industrial and political revolution in the United States does not now and probably never will come primarily from Russia. The convincing arguments against conditions in this country are not in manifestos from Moscow but in the facts which our own press, however unwillingly, is obliged to give us in regard to coal-mine monopoly, insufficient housing, profiteering merchants, greedy bankers, swindling business men, and corrupt politicians. This is propaganda dipped in fire.

And has Mr. Hughes forgotten that our own Government not merely propagandized for the overthrow of the Soviet Government but in common with the other Allies made actual war against it, although it never had the courage or the honesty to issue a declaration of hostilities? Has Mr. Hughes forgotten that "our boys" were sent to Archangel in the effort violently to overthrow the Bolshevik Government and to raise upon the Kremlin the flag of some scoundrelly adventurer who was willing to lick the boots of the Allies in return for their support?

Beside his fear of propaganda for the violent overthrow of the Government of which he is a nervous part, Mr. Hughes mentions two other stumbling blocks in the way of recognition of Russia: confiscation of American property and repudiation of the old debts. We are not aware that American property has been treated differently from that of anybody else. Confronted with complete ruin and industrial collapse in Russia, the Soviet leaders have been obliged to take many drastic steps, but they have played no favorites. Americans have been treated on a par with other foreigners or with natives. Besides, what right have we to talk of confiscation after our seizure of the chemical patents of private citizens in Germany, or after destroying the property of numerous foreigners as well as Americans by the prohibition amendment?

Russia's repudiation of the foreign debt contracted in pre-bolshevik days has been the strongest and most enduring excuse urged against her recognition both here and in Europe since the Soviet regime began. Is it not time to strip this argument of its humbug and hypocrisy? Russia's chief crime was her honesty. In a burst of open diplomacy the Soviet leaders declared that the Government *would* not pay the enormous obligations occasioned by the Czar or the war—a burden impossible to shoulder. France, Italy, and other debtors to the United States have been more canny: they have said they *could* not pay. But the result is the same. They have not paid, and in all probability they never will pay, either interest or principal.

The repudiation of debts by governments is a wholly familiar fact in history. It is often as necessary and as legitimate as for an individual—for whom we have provided a legal method through bankruptcy. Within even the present century Greece, Spain, Rumania, and Portugal have defaulted on large amounts of their public debt. A large number of our own States, not only in the South after the Civil War, but including Massachusetts, Pennsylvania, Michigan, and Minnesota, have been guilty of defaults. Every one of our European Allies in the World War has repudiated large amounts of public debt through the depreciation caused by going to a paper-currency basis. All Americans who bought French or Italian internal bonds during the early years of the war—as many living in those countries did—have had those obligations repudiated by 75 per cent through the fall of the exchange rate.

Mr. Hughes is harassed by fictitious fears and clings to outworn shibboleths. The Soviet Government can no longer be viewed as an accident or an experiment. Russia is the most hopeful country in Europe from the standpoint of the latter's industrial reconstruction and revival. Russia's fields can grow the grain of which her neighbors are in want. But first the barriers must be removed. We have our choice. We can recognize Russia and cooperate with her in reestablishing industry on a basis of self-help or we can ladle out charity to Europe by means of the soup kitchen.

The Great Bok Humbug

"BOK—Peace or Propaganda?"—this was the question we asked editorially in our issue of January 2. We were not to remain long in doubt. The award of the Bok prize has confirmed the fear that this might prove to be one of the most skilful advertising dodges since the days of Barnum, and one of the cleverest pieces of political propaganda in the history of the United States. Mr. Bok offered $100,000 for "the most practicable plan by which the United States may cooperate with other nations to achieve and to preserve world peace," and he intrusted the decision as to the "most practicable plan" to a jury of seven very distinguished and able men and women, whose integrity and disinterestedness are above question. It happens, however, that of the seven six were already committed to one plan, as members of the League of Nations Nonpartisan Association.

It is, then, hardly surprising that the jury awarded the prize to a plan which is simply a direct proposal to join that discredited and weakening League of Nations which the voters of this country so overwhelmingly repudiated when, in 1920, they elected Mr. Harding rather than Governor Cox. Every alternative proposal is coolly brushed aside. There is nothing new in the plan. It is the old, old story: Join the League. (Certain modest reservations, it is true, are suggested, but the trend of the argument minimizes them.) The anonymous author (can it be that he is that faithful advocate of the League, Professor Manley O. Hudson?) says that the League is in the field; therefore any other association of nations is impossible; ergo, we must accept the League. Disarmament, the outlawry of war, a democratized league—everything else is disregarded.

Fifty million Americans are to be asked to vote Yes or No on this proposal. It is beyond doubt better publicity than the League has ever yet received. But the propaganda goes even further than appears by this brief analysis. The plan itself is 2,000 words long; but on the ballots which will be used by the millions of the voters is a sugar-coated 133-word summary. With all respect to the jury, whose motives and whose sincerity we would not impugn, we must believe that they acted in a situation skilfully arranged for them and that they are not responsible for the disingenuous framing of the ballot. This summary places in the forefront the World Court proposal, although the author of the plan only incidentally mentions it. Probably nine-tenths of the fifty million who are to vote upon the plan will never read beyond the summary, and will conclude that joining the World Court is the salient feature of the author's plan.

The ballot misleads still further; it continues with these words: "Without becoming a member of the League of Nations as at present constituted the United States shall extend its present cooperation with the work of the League and participate in the work of the League as a body of mutual consent" under certain conditions. One would not think from this summary that the plan proposed membership in the League! Yet such is the fact. It points out that we could participate, without joining, in the humane and reconstructive agencies of the League; the conditions printed on the ballot, however, are those given in the text as conditions upon which the author thinks that the United States might join the League. It is difficult to avoid the impression that this is a deliberate attempt to induce an enormous body of Americans to vote in favor of the League without knowing it. For the present the World Court is featured; if the vote is favorable, it will be heralded as a victory for the Geneva League. It is a dishonest trick.

Even apart from the misleading character of the propaganda which surrounds the plan, there is little to recommend it. *The Nation* has long urged that the United States cooperate in those humane international activities which, begun long before the League was founded, are now grouped about it. By all means let us share in the tasks of suppressing the opium traffic, of ending the international white-slave trade, of promoting public health by international cooperation—but, good as these things are, it is ridiculous to exalt them above their measure. By all means let us help in any effort which really promotes the cause of judicial settlement of international disputes—but the record does not show that the League is advancing that cause. Most of the suggestions recommended in the plan for improving the League look in the right direction, but there is in them nothing to lift a miserable world out of its present war-ridden chaos. They provide for further development of international law, for opening the League to any self-governing state upon a two-thirds vote of the Assembly, for elimination of the provisions for the use of military and economic force, for safeguarding American hegemony in this hemisphere, and absolve us from League duties in enforcement of the Treaty of Versailles. These are sadly negative propositions.

Here is nothing to stir the pulses of the world, nothing new—merely a resuscitation of the tedious debate which has absorbed the Senate since May, 1919. Yet Mr. Bok calmly insists that the purpose of his award has been fulfilled: "to reflect in a practicable plan the *dominating* (italics ours) national sentiment as expressed by the large cross-section of the American public taking part in the award." Why, if he is so certain, take a vote at all?

It is a profound and bitter disappointment. There was a great idea in Mr. Bok's mind: to set the nation thinking about peace. It were a pity if he should merely revive the animosities of 1919. In those 22,165 plans there must have been something more inspiring, something more constructive and forward-looking. There is a world-need at this hour for a determined and complete outlawry of war, such as the late Senator Knox proposed and Senator Borah is advocating; there is a need for a new note. Simply to refuse burdens under the old Treaty of Versailles is not enough—that is not "cooperation." The old treaty must be scrapped and a new treaty written! Our hegemony in this hemisphere is no guaranty of world peace; and every international matter which called for courage and the will to grapple with offending members has left a stain upon the Geneva League. Possibly, when it admits all Powers upon equal terms—with Germany and Russia invited, as they ought to be, to sit upon its Council, and the hand of France and Britain removed from its throat—the League may develop into a conference which we might join; that is a matter for the future to decide. To join it today would be to put the seal of our indorsement upon a record of cowardice and failure. Is there not still a chance for some less predisposed committee to search those 22,165 plans for a program which looks forward, not back?

War Mongers

IF President Coolidge is sincere in his promise to carry forward the Harding policies, how can he square our naval missions in South America with the purposes of the Disarmament Conference? What use to join with the great

Powers of Europe in reducing naval armament and at the same time allow war mongers to visit the republics to the south of us to agitate for larger flotillas and other means of international destruction? Is the sight of war-ruined Europe so happy a spectacle that the people of the United States want to plunge another continent into the abyss?

We have commented several times on the míschievous effects of our naval mission to Brazil and the jealousy and ill-will that it is stirring up in Argentina. Our naval mission to Peru seems to be straining itself just as hard to get the republics of the West Coast to arm and fly at each other's throats. We are indebted to Dora Mayer de Zulen, a subscriber in Callao, Peru, for an account of how our official representatives have been constituting themselves drummers and touts for the munitions-makers. Rear Admiral Woodward, the head of our naval mission to Peru, chose Navy Day to place a wreath on the monument of Miguel Grau, who commanded the warship Huáscar in the Peruvian-Chilean War of 1879. *El Comercio* of Lima reports Admiral Woodward as saying upon this occasion:

> Last Tuesday I received a cablegram from the Navy Department of the government of my country, ordering me to celebrate this occasion by putting a wreath of flowers at the foot of the statue of the greatest of Peru's naval heroes, and I, with the greatest pleasure personally as well as in my character of head of the North American naval mission, render this small but sincere homage to the immortal memmory of Rear Admiral Miguel Grau.
>
> On this occasion let us take from the pages of history some of the bitter lessons which may be learned from the sad facts of 1879, when Peru—owing to its lack of preparedness for events—was obliged by its enemy to accept its peace conditions, simply because the Peruvian budget had provided but a small navy, incapable, therefore, of rivaling that of the enemy.
>
> The power of a nation and its naval power go parallel; a weak navy is but a preparation for defeat, for a defeat which means humiliation and disaster. National weakness has caused more wars than national strength.
>
> The efficiency of the navy and the army must not be thought of only when war is at the door. Years are needed to make these services ready for the call of the nation, and it is the statesman's duty to uphold preparedness to the extent of his possibilities and in a degree and in a way adapted to support the country's policy, for it is the statesman's exclusive responsibility to know how far the national interests require to be protected, and only he, and nobody else, is concerned with watching the growth of a military power adequate to probable emergencies. The navy is in the first instance the instrument of the statesman and secondly the weapon of the warrior.
>
> The loss of battles, either by sea or by land, may have happened in the debates of Parliament, or in the councils of government, or in the private offices of the navy and army departments, long before the battlefield.

Admiral Woodward detailed the peculiar lines of defense which topographical conditions obliged Peru to fol low and then concluded:

> With its present naval forces Peru has no dominion over the sea. The Peruvian Congress must sooner or later provide an adequate navy. Otherwise Peru will remain an artificial paradise exposed to unexpected panics, and what is worse, to a war at an inconvenient hour and to inevitable defeat. History is replete with examples of defeats in war owing to unpreparedness. Let us hope Peru will not add another chapter to the rest, which future generations would read with tears in their eyes. On the contrary, may Peru, while there is yet time, apply the lessons acquired at the naval battle of Angamos and write a new page for history on which will be inscribed in imperishable characters, for the observance of future generations, these words: *Prepare to the utmost for the execution of your national policy, for the defense of your country, and for the honor of your flag.*

It seems almost incredible that we should not merely allow, but apparently instruct, a naval officer to utter bumptious and war-breeding advice of this sort in Peru when at the same time President Coolidge is trying to adjust the historic quarrel over Tacna and Arica. This offering peace with the right hand and war with the left must produce an odd and far from favorable impression in South America.

The predecessor of Admiral Woodward at the head of the naval mission in Peru visited Bolivia, and there he exhibited an imposing film showing the splendors of our navy to a people which through defeat in a needless war was deprived of its coastland, and is continually seeking an outlet to the sea, at the cost either of Chile or of Peru.

If President Coolidge has any regard whatever for the peace policies of Mr. Harding, he will call these strutting bantams home and put them to work.

Our Own Peace Program

WE must confess that we were *not* among the 22,165 contestants for the Bok peace prize; we were too modest, and in addition had an underlying "hunch" that we were not sufficiently enamored of the League of Nations. But, now that the contest is over and an extra office boy is busily engaged in opening the rejected plans which come to us seeking a way to the public, a perusal of some of them has convinced us that perhaps after all it is our duty to recall to our readers the various steps which we have advocated as moving toward the elimination of war. We are the more encouraged to do so because a further pondering of the Bok peace-prize plan increases our belief that there is little in that plan which makes for peace. To our mind the objective is the

Outlawry of War.

War is today legalized and sanctioned; our whole structure of international law is built around it; most of its code deals with what can or cannot be done in time of war by belligerents or neutrals. To retain the system of war we have created a senseless, medieval distinction between disputes among nations by dividing them into justiciable and non-justiciable. The latter are supposed in some way so to affect the "honor" of nations that they can be ended only by blood-letting, even as in dueling days a man's life might be lost because some other fellow thumbed his nose at him and so tarnished his "honor." What is needed today is to make the resort to war *in any case* an international crime. This does away with non-justiciable disputes and also the right of self-defense when attacked. The attacker becomes a violator of law; the attacked is in no worse position than was Greece when Italy occupied Corfu; or China when invaded by Japan as in Shantung; or Haiti or Santo Domingo when we violated their respective sovereignties. The appeal then lies, clearly and definitely, to the conscience of the world and also to a

World Court with Compulsory Jurisdiction.

Should the true world court be that just established under the League of Nations or that of the Hague? It could be built on either; the important thing is that it shall have *universal compulsory jurisdiction* without which the existing courts are helpless to interfere in any dispute if one of the contestants declines that intervention.

Together with a genuine world court and the outlawry of war should come

COMPLETE DISARMAMENT.

No nation should be permitted to organize a force *on military lines.* Domestic law and order should be maintained by bodies organized and drilled as police and *not* as soldiers—a vital difference. The elimination of the professional military or naval man from the world, trained and paid as he is to plan, plot, and prepare wars and to dwell incessantly upon the next war and its danger and desirability, would be one of the longest steps toward world peace. Hand and hand with this should go the restriction of all manufacture of weapons to governments (as pledged for England by Lloyd George during the World War), so that no one should have the opportunity or the temptation to make private profits out of the sale or manufacture of war vessels or war materials. The desire for those profits has been the reason for many war-scares, and even wars.

The next step is, naturally, a

PARLIAMENT OF NATIONS

to which would be referred such questions (many of them now handled by the League of Nations) as the traffic in white slaves, opium, obscene literature, postal matters, international labor negotiations, maritime issues, etc., which were previously treated in special international conferences. This must be a parliament of *all* the nations of the world, not, like the League, an assembly dominated by the victorious Powers which the neutrals and the "pariah" nations are invited to join only when they are weak and "behave." Gradually by a normal and orderly growth such an annual or biennial convocation would come to deal with the equitable distribution of the world's supply of raw materials and similar questions of vital moment to the whole world which are now subject only to the laws of the jungle written and executed by the powerful countries of the globe. These now attain their will by theft, by conquest, by violence, by chicanery camouflaged as "peaceful penetration," "protecting nationals investing abroad," "spheres of influence," "mandates," "concessions to benefit the concessionnaire but also to uplift the natives," "aiding to self-government those not yet capable of self-government."

Are these

PRACTICAL STEPS?

Eminently so. The proposal for the outlawry of war has received the support of some of the most eminent jurists in the country, including Senator Borah, who has again introduced his bill committing the United States to this policy. The development of the World Court into one with compulsory jurisdiction was prevented by the League of Nations which eliminated the compulsory clauses. A campaign of education must be undertaken here. None of these proposals can be carried without careful planning and long-continued effort under sincere leadership. No scheme for eliminating war can be devised to be put into effect overnight. Any such proposal must encounter the greed of an acquisitive society ruled by private profit and the greed of nations intrenched in territory filched from others.

So far as the United States is concerned the acceptance of any such program means the turning over of a new leaf in its policy as to the Western Hemisphere, the abandonment of the present conception of the Monroe Doctrine under which we assume the morally indefensible position of telling the weaker nations to the south of us how they shall live and how they shall be governed, and of exploiting them financially precisely as England and France and Germany exploit, or exploited, their colonial territories. By forcing our will upon other nations we have produced in Haiti and Santo Domingo, and are in Mexico a contributory cause of, conditions which approximate a war status.

What is needed among all the nations is a genuine will to peace; in other words, a readiness to devote as much time, thought, and money to the elimination of war from the world as is now expended by the great nations in imposing their wills on others, in maintaining armaments, and in preparing for that next war which more and more experts, as well as the moralists and humanitarians, believe will involve the destruction of what is left of our existing civilization.

At Last a Pacifist Cabinet

RAMSAY MACDONALD'S Ministry has attracted the wide-spread attention a first Labor Cabinet deserves. To us, however, its pacifist character is as important as its Labor aspect. Both Mr. MacDonald and Mr. Philip Snowden, the new Chancellor of the Exchequer, proved themselves consistent pacifists in 1914 when they refused to countenance England's entry into the World War. During that struggle Mrs. Snowden held five hundred peace meetings at some of which her husband spoke; not until after the war was he molested. Then, although compelled to use crutches, he was thrown to the floor in a theater lobby and maltreated by some returned soldiers. Lloyd George and Sir Henry Campbell-Bannerman opposed the Boer War while their country was in it and became prime ministers afterward; but their opposition to their country's course was not based upon the principle that all wars are wrong but was due to dissent from the attack upon the Boers.

But the Prime Minister and the Chancellor of the Exchequer are not the only members of the new Government who refused to "go along" in 1914. Charles P. Trevelyan, the new President of the Board of Education, resigned from the Government in 1914 as a protest against the war policy. Margaret Bondfield, Under Secretary for Labor (she should have been in the Cabinet itself), opposed the war; Lord Parmoor, Arthur Ponsonby, and F. W. Jowett stood behind every peace movement from the time the war began, the latter two being founders of the Union of Democratic Control—an organization of protest against the undemocratic system of government, the secrecy, and the lying which put Europe into the war. Noel Buxton and Colonel Josiah Wedgwood took service during the war, the former on the civil side; both have been proud to call themselves pacifists since. On the other hand, Arthur Henderson, J. H. Thomas, and J. R. Clynes were the three Labor leaders in the War Ministry; yet no one can doubt that today their voices would be lifted in unison against any policy which would involve the use of force. Even the general who has taken over the Air Ministry, C. B. Thomson, the author of the striking article in last week's *Nation*, resigned from the army at the earliest opportunity in thorough disgust and allied himself with the Labor Party as the hope of the future. If Sidney Webb was not during the war attuned to its real significance and its uselessness save as a destructive force, he is surely of a different mood now. Viscount Haldane, perhaps the most unpopular man in England during the war because of his supposed partiality for the Germans, has recently declared that today he *is* pro-German. Indeed, it is one of the glories of this Cabinet that there is no one in it with any war hatred, no one unsympathetic with the present plight of the former foes or blind to the fact that the restoration of Russia and Germany is essential to the reconstruction of Europe. Finally, in Sir Sydney Olivier, the new Secretary of State for India, one of the wisest writers on the Negro problem in America and the British colonies, a former most successful governor of Jamaica, Mr. MacDonald has selected a man who should do much to improve the relations between England and India.

We are well aware that the Cabinet is, in some respects, a compromise; Mr. MacDonald has undoubtedly desired to draw from the Liberals some strong men of cabinet experience. That this maneuver has helped to wring from the London press the universal admission that it is a far stronger Cabinet than Mr. Baldwin's proves its immediate wisdom. Whether, in the long run, the great differences of opinion between a man like Lord Haldane and John Wheatley, the Minister of Health, who represents the radical Scottish Labor men, can be reconciled remains to be seen. The point we wish to make today is that this Ministry represents an extraordinary break with the past; no ministry in England or in any other country, so far as we are aware, has embodied such a spirit of pacificism, of humanitarianism, of internationalism, of freedom from all imperialistic and capitalistic influences. Whatever may be said of Mr. MacDonald's Ministry in the future, no one will be able to allege that it spoke the voice of privilege or that it sought to exalt England at the expense of other human beings.

Woodrow Wilson: A Supreme Tragedy

And so, once upon a time, there came out of the vineyards to speak brave words one as with a silver tongue. Young and old, rich and poor, stopped their work, gathering in the market-place, saying: "Behold, there is one who tells the truth. Do you not see that he is not of the Philistines? Let us listen and be guided of him." Whenever he spoke men echoed his words, so that more and more came to listen and to revere. When all the tribes of Israel went to war it came to pass that his words winged their way wherever men battled and women suffered; as men lay dying of their wounds they cried out to him to prevail in order that none others might perish like unto themselves. Widows with starving babes at their breasts called down blessings upon his name. Serfs and bond-slaves lifted up their voices before his image, saying: "Lo, He has come again." And when the day dawned when men fought no more, and he went abroad, humble folk kneeled down before him, crying: "Thou art the man!"

Yet one day, falling upon evil companions, his strength and wisdom went out from him and his voice was no longer as the trumpets before Jericho. Conceiving greatly he yielded greatly, doing wrong in the hope that some little good might come. Beholding, the people cried: "He is no longer the Messiah that he was. Do you not perceive how now he strikes hands with those who have misled us?" Soon were heard lamentations throughout the land. Men beat upon their breasts, declaring that woe was theirs, that darkness was now indeed upon all His people, and that there was no light upon the waters. Returning thence to his own tribe, men cast him aside, saying: "Thou hast no longer the voice of thy other days; we are betrayed and by thee shall we be led no more."

WOODROW WILSON came into the political life of America as if in response to prayer. It was given to him as to no other to step suddenly out of a cloistered life into high office. Then, as today, there was profound distrust of those conducting the government; startling revelations had laid bare both the corruption in big business and the control of the government by those in the seats of the commercial mighty. Neither the spurious liberalism nor the halfway, compromising reforms of Theodore Roosevelt, with his incessant knocking-down of men of straw, had satisfied the thoughtful or cut deeply into our political sores. To Mr. Wilson, as he once remarked in the office of *The Nation* during his governorship, what the country needed was "a modified Rooseveltism"; what he preached was not only that, but a far greater vision of reform, with a far keener and truer analysis of what was wrong. This he set forth with an extraordinary skill and eloquence which placed him in the front rank of American orators of his or of any time—by the beauty of his language, the wealth of his imagery, the aptness of his illustrations, and the cogency of his arguments.

His "modified Rooseveltism" seemed to the business masters of America far more dangerous than the doctrines of Roosevelt himself; they had known how to get around the latter when the pinch came. Wilson was of a different type. There was none of the swashbuckler and far more of the true crusader in him; his lips set in different and more dangerous lines; his eyes blazed with a different fire; here was all the stubbornness of the Scotch-Irishman with a Roundhead's absolute faith in the completeness of his wisdom and the infallibility of his judgment. Plainly he was not to be trifled with, and the way he went after the New Jersey corporations with his "seven-sisters" laws boded ill for big business everywhere. When the election of 1912 came Wall Street was ill at ease. Taft, its favorite, could not win; so the choice lay between the "wildness" of Roosevelt and Woodrow Wilson, who, as former president of one of the staidest and most conservative of universities, the very citadel of intrenched wealth, should have been safe and sane, yet was nothing of the kind. When big business men examined Mr. Wilson's speeches and his book, "The New Freedom," their hair bristled. Here was radicalism indeed. He declared that the government had been transferred from Washington to Wall Street, whither the President must go "hat in hand" for orders. He affirmed that the "strong have crushed the weak," and that therefore "the strong dominate the industry and the economic life of this country." "Our government" he asserted to be "under the control of heads of great allied corporations with special interests." Again and again he cried out: "We stand in the presence of a revolution . . . whereby America will insist upon recovering in practice those ideals which she has always professed, upon securing a government devoted to the general interests and not to special interests. We are upon the eve of a great reconstruction." Since "an invisible empire" had been "set above the forms of democracy" Mr. Wilson demanded an end to the "exploitation of the people by legal and political means," saying "the masters of the government of the United States are the combined capitalists and manufacturers of the United States."

This was treason, and when Mr. Wilson entered the White House the severance between it and Wall Street was complete. The members of J. P. Morgan & Co. were for the first time denied admission to the President's office. So far as Mr. Wilson could make it his was a government of the people and in its interests. To him men rallied in increasing numbers, even of the disappointed bands who had followed Colonel Roosevelt to defeat with a fervent personal idolatry and a religious enthusiasm unsurpassed in our history. Mr. Wilson's followers were actuated less by adoration of him than by admiration for his ideals; yet there were plenty to give him a personal devotion and loyalty such as men are capable of but once in their lives. This kept up even though a change rapidly came over the President. As Governor of New Jersey he had sat in an office where all might see him and approach; in the White House he became less and less accessible. What was probably an unconquerable shyness was coupled with much intellectual pride and relentless bitterness toward all who disagreed. No friendship could survive long when the other party to it criticized the President. It became more and more his habit to work alone. Thus it came about that when the Lusitania was sunk, the note that satisfied the country yet kept it calm was written in his closet without personal contact with any members of his Cabinet until it was read to them for their approval only—not for their criticism or advice. In this it resembled many another state paper.

Progress there was. The federal-reserve system came in time to take up the shock of the outbreak of the war; a system of rural credits was established; there was a real tariff revision downward; a beginning was made of a most hopeful series of arbitration treaties. The whole atmosphere of the government changed for the better. Then came the catastrophe of catastrophes, cutting squarely across the pathway to domestic reform, to end Mr. Wilson's "bloodless revolution." His first steps after the war clouds broke were all good; he commanded for the country a neutrality in thought and deed which he himself at first lived up to. His unusual executive talents were at their best. But the old spell was broken. Declining Mr. Bryan's God-given suggestion for an organization of the neutral countries headed by the United States, to compel respect for neutral rights and then to compel peace, Mr. Wilson gradually violated his own precepts for American neutrality. The powerful note to Great Britain in protest against the seizure of American ships on the high seas—the Solicitor of the State Department declaring publicly at this time that "there was not a canon of international law which England had not violated," a statement now admitted by Englishmen—lay upon Mr. Wilson's desk from May, 1915, until November, finally to be sent so emasculated that its author in the State Department could hardly have recognized it. As Mr. Tumulty finally confessed in his book, the scales were no longer held even. Yet when seeking reelection, Mr. Wilson eagerly benefited by the slogan "he kept us out of war," only to violate later this implicit pact with his people.

On January 22, 1917, Mr. Wilson rose to the highest point of his often extraordinary intuition and of his statesmanship. Then he gave utterance to words of profoundest wisdom, acclaimed at the time by almost the entire press of the country—these words that have been justified ten thousand times over by every event since the treaty of peace:

> *It must be a peace without victory. It is not pleasant to say this. . . . I am seeking only to face realities and to face them without soft concealment. Victory would mean peace forced upon the losers, a victor's terms imposed upon the vanquished. It would be accepted in humiliation, under duress, at an intolerable sacrifice, and would leave a sting, a resentment, a bitter memory upon which terms of peace would rest not permanently, but only as upon quicksand. Only a peace between equals can last.*

The crimes of Versailles, the collapsing treaty which has made that name infamous, attest the profound and perpetual truth of these words. There is no prophecy in history so justified by the event, so marvelous in its tragic fulfilment.

Three months later the breach of faith was complete. America entered the war. Wilson, the champion of democracy, struck it one of the deadliest blows received since the theory of democracy was conceived. That fatal day every reform for which Mr. Wilson had contended lay prostrate. For the first time he found himself congratulated by Henry Cabot Lodge, warmly indorsed and visited by Theodore Roosevelt, for whom there was in his heart the bitterest hate. He was acclaimed with joy by every munition-maker, every war profiteer, every agent of big business, all the evil forces against which he had fought for the "new freedom." To the partners of J. P. Morgan & Co. the White House doors now swung wide open. Positions of the highest responsibility were given to them; they were among his most trusted advisers at Paris. When the war ended the control of the government by big business and the war profiteers was complete—the gift of Woodrow Wilson himself.

What it was that won Mr. Wilson over to the war is not yet clear. It is the great unsolved mystery of his career. Whether it was due to the desire he cherished from 1914 on to be the arbiter and dominator of the peace, whether it was a yielding to the pressure of those who deemed the millions they had invested in Allied securities doomed unless the Allies won, whether an emotional desire to save the Allies from defeat, or sincere belief that no other way remained, is yet to be revealed. In any case Woodrow Wilson sinned against the very ark of the American covenant. Not a civic right of the American but was trampled upon with Mr. Wilson's knowledge and consent. The suppression of free thought and free speech, the terrorization of great masses of loyal Americans, the fettering of the press, the ruthless imprisonment of dissenters, the turning over of the destinies of the people to lawless officials and judges, the filling of the country with the bitterest diatribes of hate and Berserker rage—these Mr. Wilson neither checked nor reproved; they were "necessary acts of war time." He was unable to see that whenever and wherever liberalism links itself with war and war-madness it is liberalism which perishes. He could not perceive that he had struck down as with a dagger the causes he had held dearest. He could not, of course, for all his rare intuition, divine that he himself would be the most tragic victim of the anti-social, anti-democratic, anti-Christian forces which he had unleashed. It was the same Wall Street crowd, the same Henry Cabot Lodges and Theodore Roosevelts, who had applauded him in April, 1917, who were the first to turn and rend him when he had done what they had wished. This they did as soon as we were once more out of the hell of the war in which we Americans made so needless and useless a sacrifice. What honest American citizen who looks upon Europe today can deny that our hundred thousand dead might as well have perished against walls in the streets of New York for all they did to end war, safeguard democracy, or destroy that militarism which today rears its head more ominously than in 1914?

Yet the Fourteen Peace Points, whether they came, as alleged, from the pen of Walter Lippmann, or from Mr. Wilson's own, lifted the spirits of men; it seemed, if they could be achieved, that a new charter of liberty, a new world order would be mankind's. Mr. Wilson went to Europe exalted on high; he *was* the Messiah. And if only he could have met his supreme test he would rank today in the minds of men next after Jesus of Nazareth. The kneeling, praying masses before whom he passed, prayed and kneeled in vain. It was to Orlando, to Foch and Clemenceau, to Lloyd George, in whom the good and evil demons struggled hourly for control, that the victory went. Hate, revenge, and brutal force, the lust and avarice of the conquerors prevailed. It was indeed "a victor's terms imposed upon the vanquished," "accepted in humiliation, under duress, at an intolerable sacrifice," with the result that today the next great war looms upon the horizon. To Paris Mr. Wilson went unprepared, ignorant, by his own confession, of the secret treaties widely published in the United States ten months before his departure, which were the key to all the Allied acts from the day the war began. They were the explanation of the Allies' motives and the charter of the real aims so skilfully hidden behind altruistic assertions that the Allies were the anointed of God and their cause entirely unselfish and righteous. So Mr. Wilson was not on guard in Paris against aims as self-seeking and as godless as those of the enemies he had defeated in the war. Nor was he able to cope with what then confronted him. The evil habit of compromise, which came upon him in the White House, as on many another, making him accept doctrines which he had previously declared that he never, never would, beset him here. His personal weaknesses, like his compromises, fell upon him and disarmed him; his very taking counsel of himself became part of his undoing. But above all it was foreordained that the truth that good shall not come out of the evil of war should remain beyond challenge wherever men walk.

Upon these things will the historians of the future pass, each according to his bias and to his interpretation of state papers now sealed, documents now hidden, events yet to take place. Philosophers will always wrangle as to whether that man's offense is worse who deliberately destroys the rights and liberties of a people or the crime of him who exalts the spirits of men by a glorious vision of a new and inspired day, only to let the uplifted sink back, utterly disheartened and disillusioned, into the darkest slough of despond. As to the merits and demerits of Woodrow Wilson books will be written to the end of time. Those who worship him will continue to keep eyes and ears closed to facts they do not wish to hear; those whose very souls he outraged and betrayed will judge as through a glass darkly. But one fact no one can deny: Aspiring to the stars he crashed to earth, leaving behind him no emancipation of humanity, no assuaging of its wounds, only a world wracked, embittered, more full of hatreds, more ready to tear itself to pieces today than when he essayed the heavens. The moral of his fall is as immutable as the hills, as shining as the planets. If humanity will perceive and acknowledge it that will be Woodrow Wilson's priceless legacy to the world he tried to serve so greatly.

O. G. V.

Europe's Sea Power Bloc

DIPLOMACY, in post-war as in pre-war days, carries on under cover, and published treaties only record what the diplomats are ready to tell. The Franco-Czech alliance, printed in this week's International Relations Section of *The Nation*, registers little new in its explicit terms; its implications are more important than the phrasing of its clauses. After all, England had an even less explicit agreement with France and Russia in 1914; yet she felt morally bound to follow them into war. And her army was not, like the Czech army, "a child of the French army, with a French general at the top of its general staff, so that the unity of spirit and method assures common action in the face of a common danger"—as the *Petit Parisien* puts it.

Explicitly, France and Czecho-Slovakia agree to "discuss in common" what action they should take if their "security is threatened" (fine old wheel-horse phrases of diplomacy!) and to arbitrate their differences; and specifically, to prevent the restoration of the Hohenzollerns in Germany or of the Hapsburgs in Austria or Hungary, or the annexation of German Austria to the German Reich. It is, of course, no real business of France's or of Czecho-Slovakia's what form of government or what ruler the Germans, Austrians, or Hungarians may prefer; but the decisions here reaffirmed are decisions long ago made by the Conference of Ambassadors. The new factor, and the significant one, is that France and Czecho-Slovakia herewith serve warning that, like Italy in the Corfu dispute, they will act as they please, and not wait upon England or the League. They—no larger group—will decide what constitutes a threat of restoration or a menace to security, and will act, if they choose, as arbitrarily as France has acted in the Ruhr. It is only fair to add that when M. Poincaré urged a definite military alliance upon President Masaryk the Czech statesman refused it; it is also true, however, that without the form of words the alliance in germ exists, in the thousand French officers training the Czech army, and in the diplomatic dependence of the Czechs upon the French Foreign Office.

France already had an alliance with Poland; and Jugoslavia and Rumania were allied with Czecho-Slovakia. This treaty must have seemed to seal French hegemony in Central Europe. With Austria already a vassal of international finance and Hungary about to accept the same yoke French Mitteleuropa seemed achieved. Yet no sooner had this new alliance been signed than the rottenness in the edifice began to manifest itself. M. Benes, the able Czech foreign minister, who has steered his country's foreign policy since the armistice, went to the Belgrade Conference of the Little Entente, hoping to induce Jugoslavia and Poland to seal the structure with similar alliances, and to give the group a continental solidity by recognizing Russia and bringing her into the alliance. His plan fell flat; the other Powers disapproved his isolated action; Rumania, still at odds with Russia over Bessarabia, and indignant at the French protests against her oil-nationalization law and the consequent refusal of the French loan, stood sullenly aloof; England, rapidly followed by Italy, made peace with Russia while France wavered; and Jugoslavia suddenly, in the midst of the conference, announced agreement upon the Fiume question with Italy.

To face France's Continental Bloc a Sea-Power Bloc is arising; England and Italy are acting together; French domination at Tangier has driven Italy and Spain into each other's arms; Jugoslavia is turning to this group and away from the Little Entente; Turkey is settling her disputes with England more rapidly than those with France; and England has won the prestige of priority in recognizing Russia. France is left with Poland and Czecho-Slovakia (neither very friendly to the other) as allies, and with a disorganized Ruhr and an angry Rhineland on her hands, her hope of a Separatist movement dissolving in fearful massacres. The rapprochement of England, Italy, and Spain means, in time of crisis, a knife cutting France from her other great dream—her African Empire. French plans for a railroad across the Sahara are not mere romance; they should be read in connection with the introduction of conscription among the black peoples of Africa. French statesmen admittedly hope to more than compensate for their own low birth-rate by introducing Africa into Europe. But the Mediterranean lies between Africa and Europe, and England, Spain, and Italy dominate the Mediterranean.

All this, of course, is written in terms of the old diplomacy. Those are the terms in which Europe is thinking. There was a period, before the horror of the peace treaties was realized, when Europe was feeling its way toward a new diplomacy. Today again there is a new hope—in the presence of Ramsay MacDonald in the British Foreign Office. He sees clearly that barring a right-about-face Europe is headed for the abyss. The first necessity, of course, is to abandon the practice of alliances and oppositions, but no effective step has yet been taken toward that end. Until the League admits Soviet Russia and Germany on equal terms with France and England to its Council and Assembly it can only be an illusion and an impediment.

Set the War Truths Free!

SENATOR ROBERT L. OWEN has made a wise suggestion which is so wise that it will almost certainly be left unrealized. He has offered a resolution directing the Foreign Affairs Committee of the Senate to appoint a committee to study the question of the origin of the war. "More than 100,000,000 people in Central Europe now, five years after the cessation of hostilities, are still convinced," he says, "that their governments were not the only ones at fault in the days and months and years preceding the fatal first of August, 1914." And since these people know that the whole Treaty of Versailles rests upon the assumption of Germany's sole responsibility for the war, they attribute their present misery to a lie. Officially, our American Government still shares the assumption of 1914. Senator Owen, however, having studied the secret documents revealed since the armistice, has come to a very different conclusion; and he believes that any impartial commission would do likewise.

England's Labor Government is more likely to act on such a principle than the American Senate, or than Mr. Coolidge or Mr. Hughes. Indeed, Ramsay MacDonald could hardly render any greater service to the world than to appoint a committee consisting, say, of E. D. Morel, that brave prober of the dark corners of diplomacy; G. P. Gooch, the distinguished author of the "History of Modern Europe," and Professor Raymond Beazley, or some other equally fearless historian, and to instruct this committee to search the files of the British Foreign Office for material bearing upon the origin of the war. The German, Austrian, and Russian files have been searched by men far less friendly to their own pre-war governments, and the world, or at least that fraction of it which is willing to study facts and to revise prejudgments, knows what there lay hidden.

Only the French and the British archives remain secret. The same men rule in the French Foreign Office today as ruled there in the decade that brought on the Great War; Poincaré, the premier who cemented the Franco-Russian military and naval alliances in the days of the Czar, is at the helm again, busily building new alliances and signing military and economic "agreements," some public, some secret, just as in the days of 1912 and 1913. But in England there is new blood. Charles P. Trevelyan, who resigned from the British Cabinet in 1914 in disgust at the revelation of secret agreements made by Sir Edward Grey, has returned to office; Ramsay MacDonald and Philip Snowden, who throughout the war worked shoulder to shoulder with E. D. Morel in that Union for Democratic Control which has made so powerful a fight for open diplomacy in Great Britain, are in high office. They may not stay in power forever; it is an opportunity not to be lost.

England's archives, to be sure, are unlikely to contain such startling revelations as those dug out of the Russian file-cabinets. Senator Owen has rendered another public service by his study of the Russian documents, and by his public analysis of them in a speech before the Senate of the United States. This is a speech which should go far and wide, and be studied with care. There are points in which it goes beyond the considered judgment of the editors of *The Nation*. We think, for instance, that he passes too lightly over the stubborn determination of the Austrian military and diplomatic chiefs to humiliate Serbia, and treats too casually the attitude of Germany through most of July, 1914, when he sums up thus:

> The German militaristic rulers did not will the war, tried to avoid the war, and only went into war because of their conviction that the persistent mobilizations of Russia and France meant a determination on war and were secretly intended as a declaration of war by Russia and France against Germany. The records show that the Russian and French leaders were determined for war, and intended the mobilization as the beginning of a war which had for many years been deliberately prepared and worked out by the complete plans of campaign through annual military conferences.

Yet these conclusions, like those of Judge Bausman in his "Let France Explain," are the product of research and analysis, and are supported by documents of which most Americans are still ignorant. It cannot be denied that in the last days of July, when Europe was on the brink of war, the Kaiser and Bethmann-Hollweg did try frantically to put a check-rein on Austria; it is true that the Russian Foreign Minister telegraphed at a critical moment that "if there is a question of exercising a moderating influence in Petrograd we reject it in advance," and thereby deliberately destroyed a chance of peace; it is true that on July 30 the Russian Ambassador in Paris was able to telegraph to Petrograd that the French Minister of War had informed him enthusiastically "that the Government is firmly decided upon war"; it is true that the French and Russians had prepared every detail of their common military action and that the story of their being taken by surprise and caught "unprepared" was a legend; it is true that both the Russian and the French governments, and the British as well, deliberately falsified the texts of the rainbow books in which they professed to reveal to their peoples the negotiations which preceded the war.

Oil absorbs American attention for the present; and, probably the American diplomatic documents concerning oil—in Costa Rica, Colombia, Venezuela, Mesopotamia, and the Dutch East Indies—will, if Senator Dill forces Mr. Hughes to reveal them, be almost as significant reading as the pre-war papers. Nevertheless we still play a role in European affairs, and our attitude toward the European struggle is largely determined by the distorted views of Germany's sole responsibility for the war which are still so prevalent. If any commission could take action which would lead to a juster historical assessment of the causes of that catastrophe and force a deep revulsion of American feeling, it would perform an enormous service.

Our "Interests" in Latin America

THERE is plenty of idealism in America; there is abundant good-will toward our neighbors on the south; there are thousands of persons in the United States who have a genuine interest in the progress of the Latin American republics toward a better civilization. But there is little contact between such persons and the republics in question. The influences that have a vital and direct relation to Latin America are almost exclusively those of business and finance. Thus for practical purposes we have come to view Latin America, especially the Caribbean countries, not as collections of human beings with ambitions and aspirations like our own but as fields of exploitation easier and more profitable than any left at home. Looking at them with a purely business eye, we see these countries as places in which to lay out plantations near to cheap help and far from child-labor laws; in which to erect factories secure against labor unions and health regulations; in which to float loans at exorbitant interest on terms so inimical to the independence of the countries concerned that we would not dare to offer them to any State, county, or municipality at home. And so the United States, with all its idealism and its genuine good-will toward Latin America, has become, in fact, an all-powerful influence there against bettering the conditions of the workers, against social progress, against the very independence and democracy in government for which we contend so strongly in our own land.

Of this vision of Latin America as an oasis for business where labor organizations do not annoy, where laws may be defied or immunity obtained at moderate price from public officials, where social progress may be ignored, we get frequent glimpses. We note, for instance, a newspaper interview with F. J. Lisman of the New York brokerage house which recently floated a loan for Salvador, persuading Mr. Hughes to commit the Supreme Court and the Department of State to carrying out the terms of this speculation. Mr. Lisman, just returned from Salvador and Guatemala, sees that part of the world not as an aggregation of human beings but as an ever-developing plantation. Outside of bananas the principal product is coffee, while these countries will soon rank as substantial producers of cotton. "Labor is plentiful and wages low." Ah, yes, there is the kernel of the nut! And investors may rest assured that there will be alert American business men in Central America to see that labor continues to be plentiful and wages low.

The London *Economist*, in a recent issue, gives us a similar suggestion of Central America as a plantation run for the benefit of outsiders: "It is expected that the current Central American banana season will witness the handling of 38,000,000 stems of fruit, compared with 35,000,000 in 1923 and 34,000,000 in 1922. The widely extended cultivation of the trees undertaken by the United Fruit Company in Honduras is, however, threatened by political disturbances in that country." Political disturbances interfere with business. Hence, argue our business men, they should be prevented even if United States marines have to be called in to do it. Can it be possible, we wonder, that this business view of diplomacy has influenced Mr. Hughes in decreeing that there shall be no more revolutions in Central America and that only such governments as he likes shall exist?

But there are parts of Latin America which are viewed in terms of factories rather than plantations. In Peru the Cerro de Pasco Copper Corporation, an American company, built a couple of years ago a great reduction plant in the Oroya valley, one of the noted stock-raising regions of the country. This plant, we learn from a subscriber in Callao, Dora Mayer de Zulen, has become a political issue. Both the air and the water of the valley have been poisoned to a distance of many miles, with great losses to stock-raisers and agriculturists. A Deputy recently stated in Parliament that for the year 1922 alone stock owners lost 70,000 sheep, 6,000 oxen, 2,000 horses, and 7,000 llamas. As long ago as September 2 last a report adverse to the company was made by an engineer of the Department of Public Works, but it was suppressed and only became known through publication in *El Comercio* last January. The copper company has pursued a policy of indemnification rather than remedy, and has met attacks with promises and "stalling." Our correspondent writes that, Parliament having adjourned, nothing can be done before next summer at the earliest toward relief from the noxious plant maintained by this "great capitalistic kingdom incrusted in our hills."

It is well to think of these things when we hear that American warships, American money, and American men have been called upon to uphold our "rights" and "interests" in Latin America. The rights are not human rights. The interests are not even those of bona fide settlers; they are primarily those of absentee landlords who are trying to roll up profits abroad by the exercise of principles and methods which they find it difficult or impossible to practice any longer at home.

Our Preparations for War

FIVE years after the war to end war we are still going strong in our preparations for the next war which, if it comes, will doubtless be "sold" to the American people with the same disgusting hypocrisy as the last. The annual army appropriation bill has just passed the House carrying no less than $326,000,000 for the support of the military service in 1924-25. This is $16,000,000 less than the last appropriation bill carried, and of the total $37,250,000 is for river and harbor improvement. The army is kept for another year at the figure of 125,000 men and 12,000 officers, an effort to reduce the enlisted men to 100,000 failing by a vote of 189 to 33. Boys are hereafter to be permitted to enlist at the age of eighteen in the effort to keep this body of men recruited. No less than 68,071 of the 125,000 troops passed out of the army during the fiscal year 1922-23—a most expensive turnover; of these 12,168 showed their opinion of the kind of life they were leading by deserting at the risk of long prison sentences, while 6,864 more bought their way out of the army. Thus a total of 19,032 or 15 per cent failed utterly to appreciate the army in the terms of Secretary Weeks's description of it in his annual report: "Nowhere else can a young man be taught so well what it means to be a citizen as in the army under military instructors." The new bill supplies for a National Guard of 190,000 men (where 100,000 were deemed sufficient before the World War) and it provides training for a grand total of 500,000 men—regulars, reserves, National Guard, student and civilian attendants at training camps, etc. No less than $2,646,000 must be spent for new airplanes and equipment, $12,435,000 going to the air service for its routine expenses. As at present, we are to have a reserve of 80,000 officers any one of whom may be ordered to active duty—there were seventy-six such on duty last year out of the 76,923 carried on the rolls on June 30 last.

So far as the navy is concerned, some progress has been made in that the pending appropriation bill, which passed the House on March 21, carries appropriations, direct and indirect, of $294,442,867, or $104,000,000 less than was recommended by the budget-makers and $36,000,000 less than the sum voted last year. This represents the smallest appropriation for the navy since 1916, but it is none the less $137,000,000 more than was voted in that year. It is an interesting fact that Representative French, chairman of the Subcommittee on Appropriations, declares that the Conference for Limitation of Armaments saved the American people approximately $200,000,000, the cost of completing eleven battleships, and an annual expenditure in maintenance of from $200,000,000 to $250,000,000. The Navy Department is, however, urging the authorization of six 10,000-ton scout cruisers, four river gunboats, and an enlarged program for submarines. A bill to carry out the wishes of the Department has already been submitted to Congress, and if it is passed its cost must be added to the amount given above for the annual appropriation bill. The latter has been framed in accordance with the belief of the House Naval Committee that Congress wishes to maintain eighteen battleships in full commission, as well as 103 destroyers, and 84 submarines, together with many cruisers and auxiliary ships, all to be manned by an enlisted personnel of 86,000 men.

The best part of the bill is that, thanks to Representative Burns, a provision is attached requesting the President "to enter into negotiations with the governments of Great Britain, France, Italy, and Japan with a view to reaching an understanding or agreement relative to limiting construction of all types and sizes of subsurface and surface craft of 10,000 tons standard displacement or less, and of aircraft." That is the humane and sensible way of proceeding, but Mr. Coolidge has already let it be known that he disapproves any such proposal—he is on the side always of the big battalions. If appropriations are further to be cut public sentiment will have to bring it about, and it is high time that it expressed itself.

Still other measures looking toward the next war are pending before the House Committee on Military Affairs. These are proposals to grant to the President authority to "take the profit out of war." Mr. Bernard Baruch testifying on these measures expressed himself as favorable to anti-profiteering legislation. He would give the President power to mobilize money and industries as well as men whenever a "national emergency" arises. He believes that if the War Industries Board had been established at the outset of the war the rise in prices and the economic changes after the war would not have taken place. His proposal is essentially communistic. He would draft the entire population of both sexes, fix all prices for labor, regulate all distribution, and be absolutely despotic in his handling of the industries of the country; they would live or die or be abbreviated or expanded as the President willed. Of course, no such extraordinary power should ever be put into the hands of any man. The bills that should be passed now are entirely different ones. One should make impossible the declaring of war by the United States until a referendum of all the citizens of the country has expressed the people's mind on the issue. And the Congress should vote at once instructions to the President to move officially to bring about the outlawry of war the world over. These are matters upon which the mass of public sentiment is united; Congress would undoubtedly support the President in any such constructive steps.

General Dawes and the Politicians

IF the Dawes report had been made five years ago in peace-conference days, or four years ago in Spa-conference days, or three years ago in London-conference days, or even a year ago when the occupation of the Ruhr was new, it might have come as a fresh wind bringing relief to weary Europe. Today . . .

It begins right. The method of approach is right. The committee began, for the first time in history, to set the reparations question on its feet instead of on its head. Hitherto the Allies have begun with the question: How much do *we* need, or want? The answer was always more than the Germans could pay, and when the Germans said so the usual Allied answer was "Sign, and shut up." That pretty process occurred at Paris, at Spa, and at London, and every time economic facts gave the answer which the the Germans had not been permitted to make. In the course of years it dawned upon the Allies that the right way was to begin with the question: How much can Germany pay? The Dawes committee set out with that right principle in mind. But it began in Paris, where the ultimatum has become a governmental habit, and bit by bit the experts have compromised with the politicians. The report, apparently, is not a summary of what the distinguished business men and economists who wrote it thought Germany could and should (for economic reasons) be made to pay, but a compromise between that and what Poincaré, with his eye on the elections in May, was willing to accept.

Elections! There is the poison that has crept into what was to have been an economic report. Politics—partisan campaigns, reviving the moods and mistakes of these miserable post-war years—have done their dirty work, and will do it increasingly in the coming four weeks. It is so pitifully easy to inflame a people with preelection jingoism! A worse time could hardly have been chosen for the publication of the experts' report. The German elections are due on May 4; the French elections on May 11. The failure of the Ruhr invasion will be forgotten. Hasty and ill-digested excerpts from the report, hotly nationalistic pleas for its acceptance or rejection will sway the campaigns both in France and in Germany, and the result is as little likely to represent the sober second judgment of the electors as did Lloyd George's khaki election in 1918 or the bloc-national election of 1919 in France.

Unfortunately the Dawes report, if the preliminary summaries which have "leaked" into the press are to be trusted, gives all too much scope to the wild men in both countries. Mr. Arno Dosch-Fleurot, one of the most reliable and experienced European correspondents, reports to the New York *World* that the plan is for a five-year partial moratorium, in which Germany must meet the treaty charges (including the cost of the occupation) and make certain deliveries in kind, gradually adding cash payments until in 1929 (which the experts expect to be a "normal year") she will be asked to pay 2½ billion gold marks as reparations; this to continue thereafter and to be added to if an "index of prosperity" indicates the possibility of increase. To enable bankrupt Germany to meet the immediate payments a foreign loan of $200,000,000 is envisaged. A commissioner general, somewhat similar to the international dictator of Austria, is provided for, and associated with him are four chief commissioners who will also be foreigners. Subject to their general supervision is the gold bank, which is to have a monopoly of the issue of currency; one-quarter of its capital will go to the Reichsbank and three-quarters be put on the market, and its directorate will be one-half German and one-half foreign. A Bank Transfer Committee, of six foreigners, will supervise the purchase of foreign currency and the reparations payments. The railroads are to be transferred from the Government to a private holding corporation with nine German and nine foreign directors and be bonded for 11 billion gold marks. A transport tax involving another three-billion gold-mark bond issue (equivalent to 7½ per cent of the gross earnings of the railroads) is to provide another share of the reparation payments, and an industrial bond issue of 5 billion gold marks, which is considered roughly equivalent to the profit made by the industrialists during the period of currency depreciation, is to yield another share of the burden.

This involves a total of 5 billion dollars' worth of bonds sooner or later to be floated on the international market, apart from the $75,000,000 in capital stock of the gold bank and the immediate foreign loan of $200,000,000. These are figures almost as fantastic and incredible to the banker as to the layman. The interminable delays in the preparation of the Dawes report plainly indicate that the experts have not been agreed upon them, and the British Government has already given hints that it does not regard them as feasible. Yet already the jingoes are crying "Germany must be made to pay." In the idiotic words of the New York *Herald-Tribune:* "The Allied governments . . . have the means to compel German submission. If they stand together loyally to enforce the settlement Germany will surrender, as she did in May, 1921." What good did that surrender do? What good can any *surrender* do? Europe's need is not for surrenders, ultimatums, defiances, but for agreement; and no settlement or report can bring relief until it comes as an agreed basis for payment in proportion to an agreed capacity to pay. Germany will never pay until there is within Germany a substantial body of public sentiment which believes it worth while trying to pay; and no loan at all, much less the enormous loans here contemplated, can be floated in the international market without assurance of such a guaranty in German public opinion.

Apparently the Dawes report has been revised in consultation with French politicians of the ruling clique. It may well give the nationalist bloc a new lease of life, for it gives them a new golden hope to replace the Ruhr policy, once so radiant with easy money, now so discredited. The report might better have been revised in consultation with the liberal groups in both countries. Unless the summaries of it are misleading it is less likely to promote in Germany a willingness to pay than to foster the reactionary current which recently gave so tragic a self-revelation in the verdict of the Ludendorff-Hitler trial in Munich. Ludendorff, avowed commander-in-chief of the army of rebellion, was acquitted; Hitler, chief rebel, sentenced to five years in prison. Less than six years ago Ludendorff, clad in mufti, fled from revolutionary Germany to Denmark. Today he is again a national hero. That is the result of five years of ultimatums. Will the politicians ever let us have peace?

Blessed Are the Peacemakers

"Not a 'Whatever, Whenever, Wherever' card has been signed; no religious editor has tabulated 'conversions,' but judged by Christ's own evidences of discipleship—reviling, persecution, and hatred—the greatest revival in the history of American colleges has broken out at Northwestern University."—Bulletin of the Methodist Federation for Social Service.

THIRTY-EIGHT students at Northwestern University, some of them ex-service men, are taking Christianity seriously. They dared, as *The Nation* has recorded, to stand up and dedicate their lives to peace. They said that they would never take part in war again. As a result Northwestern has been stirred to the depths; Evanston has seen soldiers marching once more through its streets, Chicago's newspapers have used headlines big enough and black enough for a first-class murder or divorce. The Christian pacifists have been reviled, persecuted, threatened with expulsion and bodily violence; one student, victim of mistaken identity, has been kicked out of a classroom; the cowardice of mob hysteria has blared forth as if it were wartime—and hundreds of thousands of people have been set to thinking about pacifism.

The most ludicrous product of the profession of faith of the thirty-eight was a community mass meeting held, with the cooperation of the American Legion, in Padden Gymnasium at the university. This was to reinstil "patriotism" in the student body and to reinstate the university with the moneyed militarists. Part of the Chicago *Tribune's* account of this expression of a free American city, at an institution of "learning," under the aegis of a church dedicated to the Prince of Peace, follows:

> [It] was a rousing affair, reminiscent of the patriotic fervor of World War days. The "thirty-eight pale, anemic pinks," pledged never to fight for their country, were there, but silent and under enforced respectfulness. They heard themselves excoriated, ridiculed, and held up to public scorn, but only one had the temerity to ask permission to speak. He didn't get it. . . . Brigadier General Nathan William MacChesney . . . drew thunderous applause in his characterization of the thirty-eight as "spineless, pusillanimous pacifists" and his classification of Brent Dow Allinson [a war-time conscientious objector] with Benedict Arnold and Judas Iscariot. . . . "Though we believe in keeping open the doors of the university to all classes of students" [he said] "we want no one guilty of treason to his country." . . . Another speaker discussed throwing the pacifists "into the sewer with the other refuse." . . . Col. O. C. Smith, State commander of the Spanish-American War Veterans of Illinois, however, said the Padden gym meeting was too much of a whitewash for the university and not enough was done to purge the school of taint by pruning rotten branches. David Wollins, a pacifist who was expelled from Northwestern last Friday, came to the platform and introduced himself to Brigadier General MacChesney, saying he disagreed with the speaker. . . .

The *Tribune* added to its streamer-head on the front page, to its story, cartoon, editorial, and back-page pictures, a revelation of "How Dead Hand of Lenin Guides Youth of U. S. A.; Astounding Propaganda in Churches, Schools," and a persecution directory of all the pacifists they could locate at the school.

President Walter Dill Scott hastened to issue a careful statement of his and Northwestern's attitude. He claimed for both himself and the university a proud record of military service. He deprecated, however, handling the problem of the conscientious objector with "impulsive" methods. He reminded his audience that "it is an old problem and one that has presented difficulties in every land in which there are large numbers of Christians" (*sic!*). He did not recommend slicing off the heads of all these Christians as Diocletian's officer beheaded Maximilianus, although he recalled the case; he urged "converting" them by persuasion, as Alvin York was "converted"—he who came to shoot "an unbelievable number of Germans, and at one time took 132 of them prisoners in the Argonne Forest," 13.2 Germans for each of his fingers.

Perhaps the thirty-eight Christians and their sympathizers might not have brought about such a rain of modern savagery had they not happened to launch their views in the midst of a great campaign to raise an endowment fund for the university. Its publicity was more difficult to ignore than the resolution unanimously adopted more than a year ago by the [Methodist] Puget Sound Conference.

> Resolved, that we commend the attitude of the *Pacific*

Christian Advocate in its adverse criticism of the action of the trustees of Northwestern University in signally honoring the head of the United States Steel Corporation, than which no great organization in American industry has shown greater disregard for the Christian ideals repeatedly expressed in the social pronouncements of all of our churches. While we fully appreciate the personal and local elements involved, we feel that such action by one of our great schools tends to neutralize the positive Christian ideals to which we adhere.

The sensitiveness of such groups in the Methodist church affects the trustees at Northwestern, Methodist though it be, but little. They have managed to remain superbly oblivious of the memorial unanimously adopted on March 24 by 300 ministers of the New York East Conference asking the Methodist Church "to declare for an unalterable opposition on the part of our church to the entire war system, economic exploitation, and militarism. . . ." Will the Methodist church finally accept the sixth commandment which has been in their creed these 2,000 years? The "thirty-eight" have set an example.

1914—1924

TEN years ago this week Europe, rather casually, slipped into war.

It was a grim slip. Europe was appalled, but hardly surprised. She had been preparing for the war for two decades, and her statesmen had grown rather fatalistic about it. The Austrians preferred a European war to loss of their opportunity to crush troublesome Serbia; the Russians preferred it to a loss of prestige; for many Germans it was *der Tag*, and to many Frenchmen it meant the long-awaited *revanche*. No one dreamed of four and a half years of fighting, starvation, revolutions; of the absorption of distant continents; of a miserable post-war decade. After all, as we Americans learned so cheerfully three years later, it did make life interesting. Men lived dangerously, and they did not have time to think. The troublesome petty social conflicts of peace days were for the moment lost in the fires of war. An Oxford professor wrote a much-appreciated essay on The Peacefulness of Being at War.

We in America were very remote. It is difficult today to think back to those idyllic days when President Wilson was proclaiming the duty to be "neutral in fact as well as name," "impartial in thought as well as in action." Less than three years later those days already seemed distant of which Randolph Bourne wrote:

> To the American academic mind of 1914 defense of war was inconceivable. From Bernhardi it recoiled as from a blasphemy, little dreaming that two years later would find it creating its own cleanly reasons for imposing military service on the country and for talking of the rough, crude currents of health and regeneration that war would send through the American body politic. They would have thought anyone mad who talked of shipping American men by the hundreds of thousands—conscripts—to die on the fields of France.

We went into the war with a vim. Neutrality in thought or in action became a crime and we hunted down our pacifists to put them in jail. The mass of the people accepted the myth that they were fighting for an ideal, and when disillusionment came they lost faith in these ideals rather than in war as a method of realizing them.

For the Old World there was a brief glimmer of hope when the guns stopped firing. A new era seemed about to dawn. Russia had thrown off her czar, and all the Central Empires had put aside their kings. No officer dared show himself in uniform in the streets of Berlin. Militarism was for the moment utterly dead. Woman suffrage was suddenly granted in Russia, Germany, Austria, Hungary, Belgium. The French Chamber considered women's rights seriously for the first time in its history and a dozen countries passed eight-hour labor laws. The ranks of the labor unions swelled, and their power grew. Wilson, when he came to Europe, was hailed as a messiah, and everywhere men and women believed the old evils at an end.

Then Europe, too, was disabused. The German delegates at the Peace Conference were kept behind bars, like wild beasts; the secret treaties were incorporated, veiled only in pious phrases, in the peace treaty which President Wilson signed; the name "League of Nations" was given to a league of victors, which the well-behaved neutrals were invited to join (the Central Powers, Soviet Russia, and Mexico were left out); revolutions were drowned in blood in Bavaria and in Hungary (where the American relief agents joined hands with the counter-revolutionaries); and all the Western world, America included, continued the war on Soviet Russia, masking its capitalist hate of the workers' republic in a dreary succession of miserable lies. When Soviet Russia finally emerged triumphant from her war against the world she was so battle- and blockade-worn that she could no longer hope to serve as a beacon.

Gradually the darkness deepened. Italy plunged from chaos into bloody Fascism, and good men applauded it; Russia went through famine; France, refusing to face the emptiness of military victory, demanded of Germany more than Germany could possibly pay, and finally marched her soldiers into the Ruhr, while the mark lost its value and millions went hungry. Desperate Germans prayed for a return of the good old days of the monarchy.

Are we on the verge of a new dawn? Certain it is that for the moment a fresh wind is blowing across Europe. Ramsay MacDonald's Labor Government, slight as have been its concrete achievements, brought with it an atmosphere of decency and friendliness and of expectation of decency from others. The German elections were less of a reactionary landslide than had been expected; France ousted Poincaré and opened the way for new measures. The United States permitted its experts to aid in devising a plan for reparation payments which is today under hopeful discussion. Russia has, unaided by the West, stabilized her currency and resumed trade. Austria and Hungary have been put on a forced regime, under the auspices of the League, which has at least maintained life where there had been despair, and Germany has, for the time, stabilized her currency and made normal living once more possible. If we have abandoned bright dreams we seem at least to be drifting back to normalcy, where dreams may again become plausible.

Normalcy is an advance over the chaos of these later years, but the disposition to regard normalcy through rosy spectacles is a kind of shell-shock, a product of weariness. Normalcy is the pre-war state which produced the war and all our social conflicts, and with it goes that fatal fatalism which permitted the war to occur. Its motto is "What's the use?" The World War was not inevitable; it is easy today to trace a dozen links of causation which led straight to the cataclysm, but it is as easy to suppose a dozen slight changes in the course of history which might have avoided it. As Bertrand Russell pointed out in *The Nation* a year ago, it may reasonably be argued that Napoleon fell because he ate an unripe peach after the battle of Dresden; and if the Emperor of Austria, a very old man, had only eaten an unripe peach and died a decade earlier, or if the war had been postponed a few years until socialism in Germany and revolution in Russia had become stronger, the map and spirit of the world might be very different today. We do not need to accept war as an inevitable incident in normal living; we can change normalcy.

If the world accepts normalcy as an unmitigated boon and basks calmly in it, there is, indeed, little hope. The fact that it is not yet basking, despite well-intentioned efforts, is the real hope of the present hour.

Some of us hoped that the United States would take the lead in another great disarmament conference. Mr. Coolidge and Mr. Hughes, afraid of the political consequences, hesitated; and Geneva took the lead. The product of its effort is a compromise; it may include provisions impossible for the United States to accept. Yet if the text of this League protocol gives any serious hope of world peace the United States must agree to participate in the world disarmament conference, by whomever it may be called.

The New Peace in Europe

IN the first place, it is at least a negotiated peace and not a dictated one which has been concluded in London. In the second, the tone and spirit of the conference were different from those of any other since the war. In the third, there was a determination to reach a successful conclusion, and as a result of all this we have the beginning of a real peace. A step forward has been taken which ought to be a milestone in the return to sanity and good-will in Europe, a beginning of the end of bitterness and hatred, a first genuine move toward readjusting relations in Europe. When it is recalled that only last fall Europe seemed drifting rapidly into a new war—the present Lord Thomson, the Secretary of State for Air in Mr. MacDonald's Cabinet, wrote in *The Nation* last January: "The French Government should be made to understand that, in the last resort, force can be met with force"—it is evident that a far-reaching change has come over Europe. French, Germans, and English have met on an equal footing, negotiated in a friendly and fair way, without threats or saber-rattling, have come to respect and value each other in the process, and have shaken hands at the conclusion of the negotiations. If this is not a cause for world-wide jubilation we do not know what could be.

At the same time we are under no illusions as to the settlement. It has been a series of compromises in which Germans and French have been controlled by fear of their respective parliaments. We do not doubt that M. Herriot instead of evacuating two towns on August 18 would gladly, so far as he personally is concerned, have ordered all the troops out of the Ruhr. Fear of Poincaré and the Nationalist forces in the Chamber compelled him to insist upon a year for the evacuation of the Ruhr and the righting of that hideous wrong to an innocent and ill-treated labor population with which, as an individual, M. Herriot without any doubt has the profoundest sympathy. Treaties and agreements that are built upon such compromises are usually as if erected upon shifting sands. Nor are we certain that the agreement itself is possible of execution by the Germans. When so profound a student of European affairs as Mr. Maynard Keynes declares that the compromise is unworkable, we very much fear that the Germans may have committed themselves to a program beyond their power in their compelling desire for some kind of basis for progress and the financial and commercial upbuilding of their country, with the inevitable result that they may before long again be accused of Punic faith. That is in a measure guarded against by the system of arbitration proposed in the case of a default; but the mischief is done as soon as it is spread abroad by the hostile press that the Germans have welshed again. We share the opinion of the Union of Democratic Control in England that the principle underlying the whole reparations problem is morally wrong and politically unwise, and we find it difficult to see how payments can be made by Germany on the scale demanded of her without unsettling economic conditions in Europe. And yet we do not see what else could have been done by all concerned save to accept the Dawes plan and try it out.

To us, however, the most sinister aspect of this settlement is the increased power over Europe it gives to American finance. We are well aware that the conduct of the individual financiers in London has been helpful, straightforward, and above board. It has happened that in insisting upon the terms for the marketing of their bonds they have fought the battle of common sense and justice. These American bankers are themselves largely pawns in the game. By force of circumstances we are being maneuvered into a position where Europe and England are becoming literally vassals of our money market, and that is anything but a fortunate situation for the world. The danger of it can only be offset by enlightenment, friendly good-will, and the absence of economic and military imperialism in the Government at Washington.

To Ramsay MacDonald, in our judgment, belongs the chief credit for what has happened. We are well aware that Mr. Coolidge and Ambassador Kellogg are throwing bouquets at each other and that there is much ado in the press about the wonderful role played by the Americans during the negotiations. We would not withhold from Caesar one iota of the praise that is due him; to Owen D. Young, General Dawes, Col. Logan, Ambassadors Houghton and Kellogg, and all the other Americans, we record our unstinted praise and our admiration. But the day when the change came over Europe was the one on which Ramsay MacDonald, the pacifist and internationalist, took office. From that hour the new spirit has arisen; from that hour the menace of war, so apparent in England in November, 1923, began to disappear. We hear from some quarters much criticism of Mr. MacDonald because he, a minority Prime Minister, has not achieved greater domestic reforms. We have no hesitation in recording our opinion that the treaty with Russia and the settlement of the reparations problem, incomplete and temporary as they are, are none the less achievements to make it possible to say that the British Premier has justified his ministry one hundred times over. It will stand forth for these things alone as a great and noble-spirited Government of England.

The Way to Disarm

A NEW wave of optimism is sweeping over Europe. It finds its expression in the serious attempts to work out a program of disarmament at Geneva. Never, since the Hague conferences—unless in the restricted discussions at Washington—has the problem of disarmament so won the limelight of the world's attention. Pacifists and theorists have argued about it; statesmen and politicians have shrugged their shoulders and remarked "Yes, it would be ideal, but . . ." Today at last the prime ministers are awakening to the realization that unless they can solve the problem of this ideal all their other achievements will be wiped out.

It is a great forward step that the League is inviting all the nations of the world—Germany, Soviet Russia, and the United States included—to a disarmament conference next June. Unless all the great nations which are potential military Powers participate in such a conference it will be foredoomed to sterility. If the correspondents rightly predict that the French Government will offer no opposition to the proposal to admit Germany to the League and give her a permanent seat on the Council, there is still more cause for rejoicing. Nothing, however, so imperils progress as a too facile optimism. It is not enough that the minds of men in high position are at last puzzling over the if's and how's of disarmament. At Geneva last week two fundamentally opposed theories of disarmament and security clashed, and there is danger that the discussion may simply accentuate the contrast between these two views and render progress more difficult.

Ramsay MacDonald faced the issue squarely in his opening address. The Cecil-Requin Treaty of Mutual Assistance, which the British Government rejected, had made provisions for mutual assistance in case of war the basis of the move for disarmament. "We believe," said Mr. MacDonald,

> that a military alliance in an agreement for security is like a grain of mustard seed, small to begin with; that is the essential seed of the agreement, and that seed with the years will grow until at last the tree that has been produced from it will overshadow the heavens, and we shall be back exactly in the military position in which we found ourselves in 1914. . . . The danger of supreme importance which is facing us now is that national security should be regarded merely as a military problem based on the predominance of force.

Mr. MacDonald therefore urged that the nations begin by agreements for general arbitration rather than by attempts to win security by military means. "The essential condition of security and peace," he said, "is justice, which must be allowed to speak. That is arbitration." And he proposed, in substance, an agreement for obligatory arbitration.

In his reply, generous-spirited as it was, M. Herriot made clear the fundamental flaw in French policy. It relies on force. It refuses to admit that there is any safety without predominant force.

> You cannot have justice without some force behind it. . . . We must make what is mighty just, and what is just mighty, if we are to give the peoples what they desire, if we are to save them from a repetition of their sufferings. We must realize that we have to provide for their security. . . . Arbitration, security, and disarmament are inseparable.

Those were warm-hearted words, very different from the utterances of a Poincaré. But behind them lurks the same old fallacy of reliance upon physical force. Translated into concrete terms, as they were by the French delegation at Geneva, those words meant a military alliance to preserve the *status quo*. That may not be what M. Herriot intended by them, but it is the interpretation given by the French Foreign Office and by the Paris press. It is the meaning followed in the discussions at Geneva by the representatives of the Little Entente, including that astute prop of French continental policy, Mr. Benes, the Czech Foreign Minister. Lord Parmoor so understood them when he sagely replied that in the last century some 700 arbitral decisions had been made but that in none of these arbitrations had any adequate force or "sanction" been provided. Yet he could find no single case in which the award or decision of arbitration had not been accepted.

If the French insist upon military or naval sanctions as part of the program for disarmament they will arouse that fear of the League as a super-state which has caused so much antagonism not only in the United States but elsewhere. The British Government hastily disavowed Lord Parmoor when he rashly suggested that the British navy might be used as part of an international law-enforcement force. Security is a shy and evasive thing; it resides in the minds and hearts of men, not in alliances and armaments. That is the lesson which nations must learn. Military security for one nation must always imply a threat to another. The way to disarm is to disarm; the way to peace is through arbitration; the only permanent security rests in mutual confidence.

"Ain't Goin' to Study War No More"?

THE League of Nations has at last buckled down seriously to its primary task. The Assembly of the League, in which the little nations as well as the great take part, has done what the Council, dominated by the Great Powers of the war-time Entente, had failed to do: It has forced a world move toward disarmament. It has taken action worthy of that oft-forgotten preamble to the League Covenant: "The High Contracting Parties, in order to promote international cooperation and to achieve international peace and security *by the acceptance of obligations not to resort to war* . . . agree to this Covenant of the League of Nations."

Representatives of forty-seven nations submitted the protocol elaborated in the commissions of the League. Aristide Briand, six times premier of France, pledged the ratification of France, declaring that:

> The protocol framed by the League of Nations constitutes the most formidable obstacle to war ever devised by the human mind. If it is voted you, its framers and sponsors, will have the right to say you have installed peace in the world.

Since the Hague conferences no such serious effort toward peace has been made by the nations of the world, and the Geneva protocol is a glorious advance over the Hague conventions. It ought to be, with the World War intervening. And yet, with the fresh memory of that "war to end war" and of the peace that came so near to ending peace, the world must push beyond oratorical enthusism and analyze every fervent hope. It will not do to break the heart of the world again.

What is this "most formidable obstacle to war ever framed"? It is, first of all, not a treaty for disarmament; that is left to a conference to be called next June, if meanwhile three of the four Great Powers (Great Britain, France, Italy, Japan) permanently represented on the League Council and at least ten other Powers ratify the protocol. It is intended to be a treaty of security, making disarmament possible. The method of attaining that security is a compromise between the point of view represented at Geneva by Ramsay MacDonald and that represented by the French spokesmen. The Geneva protocol, while it begins with an agreement for compulsory arbitration, ends with a series of sanctions to be applied against a state which breaks the agreement. There lies the danger. The protocol is not merely a covenant to outlaw war; it is a covenant to outlaw any nation that resorts to war, and even, perhaps, an agreement to make war jointly against any such nation.

Agreement upon compulsory arbitration is a giant step forward along the path to world peace. It is a development of an historic policy of the Government of the United States. We accepted arbitration in days when the idea of international arbitration was young; we led in the struggle to establish effective international courts at the two Hague conferences; Elihu Root was chairman of the commission which drew up the first draft of the present World Court, providing for universal jurisdiction, for arbitration of all international disputes. That provision was rejected by the Council of the League, although it is the very cornerstone of any possible peace. That the League has now returned to it proves that even among diplomats progress is possible.

But this agreement among the members of the League not to have recourse to war against each other (except in case of resistance to immediate acts of aggression) must be studied with its context. It suffers, first of all, from the fundamental defect of the League—its own exclusions. Provision can be made for inclusion of Powers which, like the United States, remain outside of the League of their own free will; but what of Powers, like Germany and Soviet Russia, which have been deliberately excluded? The protocol provides an opportunity for them to sign, but "on the dotted line." No peace-pact can appeal to them unless they have a share in framing it.

A second difficulty has been over-advertised on its less important side. The Japanese delegation demanded that the protocol include some provision for discussion of disputes which the World Court might declare to be matters of purely domestic concern; and the final draft includes a provision permitting discussion of such questions before the Council of the League. The Japanese presumably had in mind the possibility of raising the question of immigration before an international forum, and that, in the present state of American opinion, would not be tolerated. The suggestion of such a possibility in connection with the League can only prejudice American opinion against the whole program—even against any arbitration agreement. Yet sooner or later American opinion will have to awaken from its provincialism. The world is not a series of hermetically sealed chambers. If Brazil, in a captious mood, were to refuse to send us coffee or rubber; or if European countries should dare make laws restricting the privileges of American business men, we should cease talking of "purely domestic affairs." Indeed, Mr. Hughes has shouted from the housetops his conviction that Mexican and Russian laws are as much his business and Mr. Doheny's as they are Trotzky's or Calles's.

To experienced European minds, indeed, the loophole allowed must seem, if anything, too small. The Italians would like to discuss the question of international allocation of raw materials. Even more pressing is the question of European boundaries. The protocol would seem to rivet upon Europe the chains cast in 1919. French statesmen are already glowingly proclaiming that it eternalizes the boundaries fixed by the treaties. Those boundaries may be an improvement upon the prewar frontiers; but some among them cannot be maintained forever. Jugoslavia holds a section of Macedonia which is predominantly Bulgarian in population; Italy holds the purely German South Tyrol; and Poland has an extended eastern frontier which even Polish statesmen admit in private must be revised. How shall opportunity be provided to correct those unrighteous frontiers?

If a Power refuses arbitration, or refuses to accept the decision, and makes war, it is defined as the aggressor and in that case a whole series of sanctions are set on foot against it. What these are the cabled summaries do not make clear. Even the New York *Times*, usually so invaluable for its complete texts of important documents, printed only a muddled summary of the protocol. Yet the question of these sanctions, demanded by the French, is all-important. If, as some dispatches hint, they militarize the heart of the peace pact, another great hope will go a-glimmering.

The Preparedness Maniac Again

THE preparedness maniac is again abroad in the land. He has learned nothing from the World War. Logic has departed from him if it ever rested within his mind. He still places his entire faith in force and in a preparedness which never protected anybody and never will. When he is of the army or navy type he fills the air with alarums if he believes that a single battleship gun has not just the elevation that somebody else's has. He lives in a perpetual state of fear and of panic. He sees enemies at every turn, and if the course of history removes three or four possible rivals on the sea he concentrates his attention upon the remaining one or two. Publicly he will assert that blood is thicker than water, that we are bound to our allies by sacred ties sanctified in the shedding of our unforgettable blood; privately he puts spies on English battleships, and plays endless war games, with England as the enemy, in which the entire American battle fleet is always sunk and only 58 per cent of the British. Thereupon he imparts this dreadful information to our jingo editors, to naval and military experts who make their living by writing and lecturing on our unpreparedness. The dailies begin to howl, berate, denounce, to prophesy the end of the American Government, and then do their best to hasten the catastrophe by giving currency to every rumor, suspicion, charge of falsehood and sneaky underhandedness which will serve to embroil this nation with one of our two possible naval rivals, Japan and Great Britain.

This is no exaggeration, but an exact statement of what has been and is going on. The propaganda has, indeed, gone so far and given such evidence of an organized undertaking that President Coolidge found it necessary to speak strongly against it in his annual message. Within two weeks he has again let it be known that he takes no stock in this hysteria; that he is more than ever set against any international armament race and any sensational congressional overhaulings for the purpose of starting fresh jingo fires—and he appears still opposed to the elevation of the battleship guns. If he still permits the tactless and dangerous naval maneuvers off Hawaii and the coming cruise to Australia—where the anti-Japanese politicians may be counted on for calculated indiscretions—his Secretary of the Navy has ordered two captains before a court of inquiry to ascertain how confidential information in their possession found its way to the most belligerent of the civilian "experts" and through him to the newspapers. That is a commendable move. If naval officers, however sincere and able and however honestly alarmed for the welfare of their country, are behind this campaign we ought to know it.

The worst offender is, as usual, Bradley A. Fiske, a retired admiral whose stock in trade is appearing before men's and women's clubs to prove that preparedness alone will save; that preparedness is necessary to protect our women, and that, as the bulk of our women are tinged with pacifism (we quote from a recent bit of his rubbish), they must be taught that men are for war and preparedness only in order to protect their women in their virtue and the enjoyment of the luxuries of civilization. Some millions of farmers' wives and factory employees who have never seen those "luxuries" may think what they like of that. Finally, in the face of the record of our American manhood in the World War, he declares that the fiber of our manhood is gone because we are not adequately preparing.

Now, with these demagogues abroad in the land, it is time once more to set down a few unimpeachable facts as to this question of military preparedness. *Preparedness never kept any nation out of war.* While usually portrayed as an insurance for peace, it is a preparation for war, and it inevitably leads to war. The United States during its history as a nation has had five foreign wars, each one of its own seeking—that of 1812 with England, the brief hostilities with France, the Mexican War, the Spanish War (and the Philippine), and the World War. The state of our military and naval defense had nothing to do with our getting into a single one of these; we were put into each by executive and congressional acts. Our foremost historian, James Ford Rhodes, has just proved how unnecessary it was for President McKinley to put us into the Spanish War; General Grant in his memoirs called the Mexican War, in which he served, "one of the most unjust ever waged by a stronger against a weaker nation." Had we been as prepared as Europe in 1914 these wars would still have occurred, for they were brought on deliberately for ulterior purposes. As for the World War, President Alderman of the University of Virginia in his recent official eulogy of President Wilson before Congress has done history the service of repeatedly saying "President Wilson put us into the war because. . . ." That is the simple truth. Not Congress, not the people, but a single man put us into the war and he would have done so had we had ten times as much or ten times as little armament.

Preparedness never saved any European nation from war. Napoleon III thought he had a big enough force to beat Germany in 1870. The conversion of Germany into a military machine did not prevent her being dragged into war in 1914 by her ally, Austria. Russia was ready in 1914 to put larger legions into the field than any other country in the world; did they keep her out of the war? England voluntarily went in, without regard for the state of her preparedness. As for France, it is the happy custom of our militarists to point to her as the victim of unpreparedness. Her own General Buat, the late chief of staff, has declared that the French army was the equal of the German and surpassed it in some services.

Preparedness is never more than relative. No general and no admiral in human history has had men or ships enough. If you give them what they ask for safety against one nation, they ask for more to guard against two nations combined. The little nations can never hope for adequate preparedness against the great. They should follow the program of Denmark and disarm totally—they would be safer if they did. Advocates of preparedness insist that if the little countries of Europe—Switzerland, Holland, Norway, Denmark, and Sweden—give up troops their manhood will perish. But there are no hardier, manlier lands than the Scandinavian, although for years they have had relatively small armies. There is no argument of the preparedness war-mongers that is not similarly vulnerable—as vulnerable as it is destructive, archaic, anarchistic, and anti-Christian.

Tariffs Versus Free Trade in Europe

BEFORE us lies a memorial signed by 104 of the leading economists, scientists, and business men of Germany, which declares that the time has come for a new commercial policy in that unhappy country. The memorial declares that a number of the signatory scholars approved the economic acts and principles of their country before the war but that they are all now agreed that her changed condition requires a new policy, and that even a reversion to the pre-war tariffs would work grave harm to agriculture, now in anything but a happy condition. They voice their opposition to *all* tariffs save those which might mean a liberalizing of some phases of international commerce, and they warn the public that any artificial increase of the cost of living in Germany just now would be especially dangerous. It is clear to these students and practical men alike that if their nation is to be stabilized, both as to manufacturing and agriculture, the trend must be away from tariffs and not toward them, and that otherwise Germany cannot conquer world markets as she must if she is to pay her debts.

This is one of the most hopeful and rational notes that have come out of Germany since the war ended. Whether the 104 can swing the Reichstag to their view that Germany needs not more but less tariffs is a matter for demonstration. As it is their names command great respect and connote much influence. When other countries are putting on tariffs against Germany—even England to the tune of 26 per cent—it will be all but miraculous if her politicians can be brought to see that economic safety and progress lie not in the direction of engaging in tariff reprisals but in turning directly toward free trade. Before Germany lies the most difficult economic problem which has confronted any modern nation—to keep her industries going and her people content, with a living wage and adequate conditions for health and a modicum of happiness, and at the same time to pay off debts the like of which no nation has heretofore had to face. To achieve this calls for economic statesmanship of the highest order. Fortunate indeed will be that country if its leaders lower tariffs to the disappearing point.

We are the more impressed by this remarkable proposal of a "brand-new commercial policy" in Germany because of the announcement that under Prime Minister Baldwin the free-trade flag will be still further lowered in Great Britain. Although the election was fought on an entirely different issue we have already had an outline of the fiscal policy to be followed by the new Ministry, showing clearly that the party which was defeated on the protection issue not fourteen months ago will throw its weight in that direction despite the lack of a popular mandate. Mr. Baldwin has gone so far as to say that a bill will be introduced this year "entitling any industry which can prove itself substantial and efficient to general protection against unfair competition due to depreciated currency, longer hours of labor, or lower wages." This would open the door wide, if only because it will be to the political interest of the Conservatives to find as many lame industries as possible. Especially does the term "depreciated currency" bode evil both for those who are to judge when, where, and how long a depreciated currency has worked injury to a British industry and to the taxpayers. A currency may sink suddenly, and (as Germany and Austria have both shown) it may recover quickly, or a new and sound one may be introduced. The problem is obviously one of enormous difficulty. Mr. Baldwin is not deterred by it. Replying to a question from Mr. Lloyd George, he stated that if one country was found to be injuring a British industry a general tariff would be levied against all countries and not merely against the one doing the underselling. Here we have the protection doctrine revealed in all its stark, selfish nakedness.

Mr. Baldwin next suggests the ancient heresy of taxes upon food. In view of the history of the corn laws and the triumphant fight of Bright and Cobden against food taxes it would seem that no person would ever suggest such a thing in England again. Mr. Baldwin now sets forth that there can never be a complete system of preference until the home country consents to have taxes "on food of normal, general, and daily consumption." This, he admitted, was not yet within the realm of practical politics, but he did not hesitate to bring it up for discussion. He declared, too, that his entire proposals were not meant as a wedge for the introduction of the protective principle, but, as the London *Chronicle* points out, if Mr. Baldwin is allowed to carry on his policy for three or four years England will be definitely transferred from the free-trade to the protectionist category.

As a matter of fact England is already protectionist, and the further the whole plan of imperial preference is carried the more surely will be the drift to straight-out protection of the American kind. Mr. Baldwin proposes to spend five million dollars a year subsidizing importers who bring in meat, apples, etc., in excess of guaranteed quantities. That is nothing more or less than putting a food tax on the British consumer even though it comes from the general treasury. Since then Mr. Baldwin has had another thought: he now proposes to exclude *all* foreign foodstuffs except such limited quantities as may be imported, upon special licenses, after the colonial quotas have been filled. Even that does not tell the whole story. Charges are being made in this country that the customs receipts in Great Britain and Ireland in the year 1922 stood at $13.98 per capita as against the $3.12 which protectionists assert is what was raised in America in the same year.

This backward step in England is one of the most discouraging signs of the times. Since the war we have been drifting into a condition in which each state erects as high a customs barrier about its boundaries as it possibly can. Thus France, England, and Belgium bring about conditions in Germany which subject the German population to mere wage slavery, and then put on tariffs against the cheap goods produced by these people when they are reduced to the direst struggle for existence. With these tariff barriers, and the tariff rivalries they signify, come hatreds, competition, and ill-will all over Europe; they work against peace as effectively as the various peace agencies make toward peace. Free trade and peace go hand in hand; protection in its sordid selfishness spells economic and later physical wars. Between them the world must choose.

The Politics on the Rhine

THE dead hand of politics lies heavily once more upon the European situation. Again its affairs are being conducted not with a brave desire to improve conditions in the speediest possible way, but primarily with regard to each statesman's home political conditions. Thus, as we stated last week, the explanation of the Allied refusal to evacuate Cologne has at bottom nothing to do with the question of whether Germany is or is not disarming in accordance with the Versailles Treaty. Were the British to move out, the French troops remaining in the Ruhr would be surrounded by Germans on three sides, and so great is French fear of even an unarmed Germany that Premier Herriot would in that case in all probability be forced out of office and a reactionary of the Poincaré type be put in his place. Hence the orders to the Interallied Control Commission to find Germany guilty of violations of the Treaty of Versailles. That was not difficult. Article 429 reads: "If the conditions of the treaty are faithfully carried out by Germany"—then Cologne will be evacuated in five years. The Allies being the judges—no impartial body was set up to pass upon the facts—the slightest infraction could be seized upon as an excuse to decline to evacuate, and this is just what has happened. To aid Herriot the lie has been created that Germany has been guilty of bad faith.

We have no doubt whatever that this has been done with the prior knowledge of the German officials, and we, therefore, are but little moved by the bitter protestations of Dr. Stresemann. His speech to the foreign correspondents on December 30 was eloquent and unanswerable. On the face of things he has a perfect case and the German people are justified in the wave of anger and disgust which has swept over their country. The bitter injustice of the Allied procedure must rankle in every heart which is still capable of feeling—yet we have no doubt that Dr. Stresemann had his tongue in his cheek and that the German Government, for all the demands of editors as friendly to the Allies as Theodor Wolff of the Berlin *Tageblatt* and Georg Bernhard of the *Vossische Zeitung* that Germany take vigorous counter-measures of an economic nature, will, in the last analysis, do naught. The reason for our belief is that practically the same thing happened when the Dawes Plan was adopted in London. The Germans then insisted upon the immediate evacuation of the Ruhr and made a tremendous uproar to the effect that they would not sign unless the French and Belgians left the Ruhr at once. They were privately told that if they insisted upon this Herriot would fall and they would have to deal with Poincaré or some one of his type. So they agreed, but kept up their uproar as to the outrageous terms imposed upon them—for home consumption. It appears in the dispatches that the British are now working for a compromise—the New York *Herald Tribune* says joint evacuation of the Ruhr and the Cologne district in April or in May. This means that the *sub rosa* agreement with Herriot in London to give him a year to evacuate the Ruhr will be lived up to and the flank of the French Ruhr army "protected" by the British until the end of the year.

But, we hear the question asked, isn't it true that there have been German attempts to deceive the Allies in the matter of disarmament? Undoubtedly. There are foolish or criminal nationalist organizations in Germany, with a mentality corresponding to that of our National Security League or American Defense Society. We have no doubt that some of those organizations have concealed weapons and have drilled their members and planned a day of revenge. But these things are as trifles. It appears to be true that the Control Commission found fourteen old guns concealed at the Königsbrück drill-ground, and some old military equipment at Ruhleben and elsewhere, as well as 45,000 steel bars "suitable for making rifles" at Karlsruhe, and 25,000 molds for rifle barrels at the Krupp works. What ridiculous discoveries when one considers the equipment needed for a new war! Germany must have, roughly, put ten millions of men into the field during the war. She could not fight another with fewer men. As far back as 1922 General Nollet, head of the Interallied Control Commission, reported that it had supervised the destruction of 33,000 cannon, 87,000 rapid-fire guns, 4,500,000 rifles, and that Germany was entirely disarmed as to air forces and equipment. The British Under Secretary for War on May 7, 1923, declared in the House of Commons that Germany had carried out the delivery of arms and ammunition in an entirely satisfactory manner. Only on five points was there in 1922 and 1923 a difference of opinion between the Allies and the Germans: (1) The organization of the police; (2) the making over of factories used for war materials; (3) the delivery of certain unauthorized material; (4) the handing over of certain documents relating to German armaments at the time of the armistice; and (5) the alteration of certain military laws. True, Poincaré on March 5, 1924, hinted that there were still other points upon which he desired additional assurances, but most of the things now trumped up were not specified before. The hollowness of some of the new Allied contentions is illustrated by their objection that the officer commanding the Reichswehr is unprovided for and "therefore unallowable." As a matter of fact the law under which the Reichswehr and the commander exist "was altered at the *express desire of General Nollet* and was approved by him in its present form"—General von Cramon, head of the German Disarmament Commission, testifies to this out of his own knowledge.

Of course, every military man knows that Germany *is* disarmed. It has no Zeppelins and no military airplanes. It has no tanks, and in all Germany there are probably not as many motor-cars of every variety—trucks, pleasure cars, cags, etc.,—as are to be found in a city like Buffalo. Yet military men believe that the next war will see only motorized vehicles. How could Germany build an adequate number overnight? It could not in months create the necessary gas equipment or gas masks. It has no fleet, and every fort on the Rhine has been wrecked. It has not a single siege gun or gun carriage. It has no general staff and no reserve of medical supplies or equipment. When we look at the swollen militarism of France, its huge forces of tanks, airplanes, and heavy artillery, its gas service and its great standing army, we are more than ever convinced of the absurdity of the Allied contention that the Germans are really such a menace as to call for the retention of Cologne.

No, it is politics, and rather base politics, at the bottom of it all—base even though the motive is to keep in power the somewhat liberal Government of Herriot. For whatever may be said in behalf of this new Franco-British intrigue, it is a cowardly thing once more to besmirch a disarmed and helpless people and to pretend that they are guilty of something of which as a people and a government they are innocent. That the German politicians are "sitting in" does not alter the character of the intrigue, the result of which will be to inflame once more the hearts of all Germans and keep alive the idea of revenge which may yet reduce France, England, and Germany to ashes.

Arms and the Armers

WITH joy we record that Mr. Coolidge has initiated conversations looking toward a further reduction of armaments and that a favorable response has been received from Great Britain. Like Mr. Harding, Mr. Coolidge waited, after various gestures, until Congress expressed its desire that such a conference take place, but that does not detract from the importance of his act nor the credit which he will earn if the conference meets and achieves something. Equally commendable is his bold statement to a group of women advocating preparedness that we "can and should set an example of moderation in armament."

Already, of course, voices of pessimism are in the air. France, it is reported, is "cold" and will not accept the invitation. The conference will lead only to limitation of the competition in small cruisers or "possibly" in air armaments. Well, that "possibly" covers such a tremendous possibility of good for all mankind that the slightest chance of accomplishing it ought to be accepted and be made the most of. Undoubtedly there will be opposition both here and abroad. Those of our naval officers who have so disloyally held out against the destruction of the battleships called for in the Washington treaties are sure to be heard from again. It may be taken for granted that they will not be silent spectators at the further reduction of their field of activity; especially as they must know that if there is another sharp limitation of the navy Congress will not fail to muster out a number of superfluous officers.

As for foreign opposition, well, let us take France. The same newspaper that brings word that official Paris is entirely cold toward the proposed conference brings the news that that country has a half promise of getting another one-hundred-million-dollar loan from the United States, provided she balances her budget. These two things should be directly connected—if we are going to give any more money to that country. We should frankly say to her: "If you are not interested in cutting down your tremendous financial burden to the extent of halving the naval budget which will do you no good whatever, then we are not interested in aiding you to bolster up the franc." The very fact that the debt discussions are so much to the fore makes the calling of a conference now of especial timeliness; they must be linked.

We hope public sentiment will at once rally behind the President. We would appeal to all our readers to let the President hear the real sentiment of the country in this matter, that he may thus be strengthened against any intrigues which may be set on foot in Washington itself to render futile the efforts now under way. There is a special reason why we feel that the project ought to appeal now not only to our readers but to the general public, and that is the exhibition which has been going on in Washington for the last few weeks as to the expertness of our so-called experts, both military and naval, and the fresh demonstration that if we are to put our national safety in the hands of the professional warriors we are building not even on sand. We are constantly being told by some of our daily newspapers that we must accept without question the views of Admiral Jones or Admiral Smith because they are admirals. Yet what do we see? The most bitter divergencies of opinion, recriminations, charges, denials, and counter-charges, which simply reveal the fact that the military and naval services are precisely where they have always been—groping in the dark, with practically no scientific basis whatever for their pretensions to establish military and naval policies.

We do not propose to enter here into the controversy as to whether there should or should not be a unified air service at Washington. When we are so eager to have all air armaments abolished we can only say a plague o' both your houses. But the fact remains that not only are the various services at odds as to whether there should be union, but they cannot agree among themselves as to the exact value of any given experiments or what can or cannot be accomplished by the new bombing machine. That there is an aggressive minority which believes that the future of warfare lies in the air we can well understand. Every reform in the navy, where there is one, has to be forced through by such a minority, precisely as Admiral Sims first made a reputation for himself by attacking gunnery conditions and bringing about a change in the methods of target practice. If General Mitchell is censured by the Government for his outspoken advocacy of the airplane, that would be but in keeping with tradition in both army and navy; incidentally it is worth noticing that Lord Thomson, the accomplished Air Minister in the Ramsay MacDonald Government, stands with General Mitchell both as to the necessity of a unified service and in his high estimate of the powers of the airplane. Rear Admiral Shoemaker has denied that after the battleship bombing tests of 1923 he changed a statement to be issued officially in the name of General Pershing, saying: "It's true, every bit of it, but, my God, we can't let this get out or it would ruin the navy;" but he might well have said it, or someone for him, for the history of naval development is punctuated by just such remarks. After the Civil War two of the great inventions of that struggle, the submarine and the monitor, were entirely discarded, the latter because it was not considered a comfortable sea-going ship. For generations our naval men have been followers and not leaders—did they not demand in 1915-16 larger submarines merely on the ground that Germany was reported in the press to have larger boats than we? Even today the submarine remains the foster child of the navy—two have been wrecked recently, and it is charged that we have very few others that are seaworthy or up to date.

But why go on? We simply wish to point out again that he who puts his faith in professional fighting men is nothing less than a simpleton. Even President Harding stated to the Washington Conference that he had abandoned his old idea that armaments protected. Certainly, the total failure of all the calculations and prophecies of the military and naval men made in advance of the World War show how unreliable these so-called experts are. And they are the worst kind of experts because they are nurtured in fear, trained to fear, and taught that they wax great only by spreading fear and prophecies of subjugation. Any detached, scientific approach to their problem is thus, *ipso facto*, barred. Finally theirs is an unmoral profession certain ere long to be abolished. Why should we longer allow the world to be dominated by men who have a personal stake in keeping alive the spirit of wholesale murder?

Disarm Now, Mr. Coolidge

AN EVENT of extraordinary historical interest has just taken place in England—the abandonment of a policy and a tradition adhered to for at least three and a half centuries. Ever since the defeat of the Armada England has considered her "wooden walls" on sea, or their successors, the first line of her defense. Through them Britannia ruled the waves; upon them she staked her safety. It was always the navy first and the army, like Marryat's little boat, "a long way behind." And now it is officially admitted in Parliament that henceforth it is the air forces of Great Britain and not her battleships which constitute the first line of defense. At the very moment that General Mitchell is being disciplined in this country for advocating a unified air force Great Britain has established unity of command among its air forces. Explaining an extra appropriation of $10,000,000 for air defense, Sir Samuel Hoare, the Air Minister, declared that air fighting had brought about a revolution

> far greater than the revolution produced by the invention of gunpowder in the later Middle Ages; and for a country like ours which, up to a few years ago, depended for its defense almost entirely on the sea and its navy, this revolution means more than to any country in the world. . . . The central and undeniable fact is that an air force today . . . can make life well-nigh unendurable for popular living, mainly in the large cities.

No less than $101,500,000 were appropriated to make possible Sir Samuel's first steps toward trebling the present air fleet in order to make it superior to that of France.

So the historic competition in armaments between those two Channel neighbors is on again, precisely as if the blood of their lost millions had not intermingled in the World War. More than that, France is building up her navy at a greater speed than any other nation. Thus, she is today adding no less than 125 cruisers, destroyers, and submarines to her fleet, while England is building only 16 and her latest appropriations do not provide for any new construction whatever. The *Manchester Guardian* points out that the five chief signatory Powers to the Washington treaty are today constructing 289 cruisers, destroyers, and submarines—more than were under way prior to that conference. The *Guardian* also shows that naval architects everywhere are seeking to get around the treaty while keeping within its technical requirements. Take the cruisers, for instance, of which Japan is building eleven, the United States nine, Great Britain eight, France nine, and Italy five. Before the Washington Conference, a light cruiser could fire a broadside of 600 pounds, whereas the newest cruisers fire one of 2,226 pounds; they are no longer classed as light cruisers, and though their tonnage has been limited to 10,000 these ships are four times as formidable as those of 1921, and faster and better protected. In the field of the airplane carrier there has been a similar development.

Plainly, then, the hour is ripe for President Coolidge to move definitely toward the promised disarmament conference. We have repeatedly praised his refusal to be stampeded into armament competition by our generals and admirals—he has undoubtedly learned by this time that if they could they would have every American man and woman under arms or under military control. But he does not stop our loose-tongued militarists from spreading hatred and fear. Doubtless he is unaware of the testimony given by Major General Lejeune, commanding our Marine Corps, who not long ago boldly declared to the Naval Committee of the House that the General Staff is systematically working out plans for seizing all the islands in the Pacific on the route to Japan in the event of war. Writing on this question of Japan's naval policies the London *Nation* finds in Japan's fleet or building policy no suggestion that that country is contemplating an aggressive overseas campaign. On the contrary, her retention of her old-fashioned coast-defense ships, her refusal to build large submarines, destroyers, or 10,000-ton cruisers of wide steaming radius seems proof positive that Japan is preparing only for a defensive campaign. But while the London *Nation* acquits Japan of any design to carry on an overseas war, it dwells upon General Lejeune's testimony and the British threat of the Singapore base as examples of the very thing which, if kept up long enough, will inevitably frighten Japan and compel her to other plans and policies.

With Congress off his hands, Mr. Coolidge could now well afford to devote himself to working out with Mr. Kellogg and Senator Borah a plan for immediate action. Nor should he allow himself to be dismayed by the practical abandonment of the Geneva Protocol. That protocol would need many alterations before it could become a genuine covenant for peace. What Mr. Coolidge is aiming at is, first, further disarmament on sea—perhaps also in the air; then, an inquiry as to whether disarmament on land is feasible. The British Government has officially voiced its friendliness to the proposal. There are signs that it will be welcomed in Japan. If French politicians do not react favorably to the proposal Mr. Coolidge holds in his hands the means to interest them. At least it might be possible to inquire into the relationship of the building of 125 light vessels for the French navy, which played so undistinguished a part in the World War, with the steadfast refusal of the French Government to say what it will or will not do in the matter of even the interest on its huge debt to us. Why should the world be asked to wait any longer? Fifty-six years ago John Bright, that great peace-loving Englishman, made a suggestion to which no sane answer has yet been returned:

> I do not know whether it is a dream or a vision, or the foresight of a future reality that sometimes passes across my mind—I like to dwell upon it—but I frequently think the time may come when the maritime nations of Europe—this renowned country of which we are citizens, France, Prussia, resuscitated Spain, Italy, and the United States of America—may see that vast fleets are no use; that they are merely menaces offered from one country to another; and that they may come to this wise conclusion—that they will combine at their joint expense, and under some joint management, to supply the sea with a sufficient sailing and armed police which may be necessary to keep the peace on all parts of the watery surface of the globe, and that those great instruments of war and oppression shall no longer be upheld. This, of course, by many will be thought to be a dream or a vision, not the foresight of what they call a statesman.

America—The World's Banker and Policeman

WE have become the greatest money-lending nation in the world. More American money is invested abroad today than British, and vastly more than French or German or Italian. Wherever men seek capital—in China, in the East Indies, in South America, in the ruined countries of Europe—they turn to our American Wall Street for help. And Wall Street, lending them the money, sets the terms upon which they shall be permitted to develop and rebuild themselves. Oh, it is a great thing to be an American these days. Our money is the soundest and we lend more of it than any other country in the world; we finance and "stabilize" the earth. We have eleven billion dollars invested outside our country, the Department of Commerce boasts; each year the world pays us its tribute—nearly a billion dollars of interest. No empire in history has ever been so rich or so powerful; what we say "goes."

And we boast—forgetting the Indian wars—that we have achieved this preeminence without resorting to the old brutalities of war. We have not sought to conquer territory; we have simply made the most of our opportunities for trade. Nature has favored us somewhat, to be sure. We have only 6 per cent of the population of the world, and 7 per cent of its area; but from our little 7 per cent of the surface of the earth we produce 20 per cent of its gold, 25 per cent of its wheat, 40 per cent of its iron and steel, 52 per cent of its coal, 60 per cent of its copper and cotton, 66 per cent of its petroleum, and 85 per cent of its automobiles. Yet we have not contented ourselves with our home resources; we have reached out through all the world to safeguard ourselves against the exhaustion of our home resources—and to find lands where labor is cheaper. The Guggenheims have put millions into development of the copper mines of Chile; the United Fruit Company controls virtually the entire trade of whole republics in Central America; the sugar companies grouped under the National City Bank have made Cuba one of the richest provinces in the world; our oil companies, aided by Mr. Hughes, have forced Britain to relinquish her monopoly in Mesopotamia and Persia, and have their explorers seeking traces of oil in all the continents of the earth; and now our great banking houses are reaching into the hearts of the old empires, and buying into the continental combines which used to share in the exploitation of the backward countries.

This accretion of our power is so recent that we are barely awakening to it. Before the war we were busy developing our own territory. That struggle marked a revolution in our economic history. Our eyes turned outward. We had been occupied with our own resources, opening up the West, expanding our home empire. We had begun with a few petty investments in Latin America in the opening years of the century; our first considerable foreign loan was to Japan during the Russo-Japanese War. But the total was trifling. Even after recovery from the panic of 1907 we sent little money beyond our borders. In the three years 1911, 1912, and 1913 the total amount of foreign corporate loans floated in the American market was only $180,000,000. But in 1920 the total was $464,000,000; in 1921 $600,000,000; in 1922 $900,000,000; and we are now investing abroad at the rate of more than a billion dollars a year. In the last six years we have accomplished in foreign investments what it took England a century to achieve. We have even invaded her dominions; more than three times as much American capital as British is today invested in Canadian manufactures.

In the years before the war our money had to compete with money from other countries. A Latin American republic, seeking a loan, could turn to Paris or Brussels, Rome or Berlin, London or New York. Competitive conditions were such that one group of bankers was not likely to be assured a monopoly, or granted terms which gave it control of a country's government. We did, to be sure, take over Nicaragua in 1912; but it was during the war, in 1915 and 1916, that we sent our troops into Santo Domingo and Haiti and imposed on those countries the onerous loans and conditions which make them today mere provinces of Wall Street. Since the war we have not been quite so crude; but our bankers, encouraged by the State Department, have secured an increasing area of control without the use of armed forces. Our troops have, it is true, been landed from time to time in Honduras and Guatemala; but the Lisman loan obtained American control of Salvador without use of troops, and the Equitable syndicate persuaded Bolivia to turn over its entire fiscal system to a commission of three, two to be named by the bankers, without official intervention by Washington.

The course of events in these little Latin American countries is significant because it indicates the course which, unless the American people awaken to conscious control of their foreign policy, we are likely to follow in other countries. Our people do not realize to what extent the Government is using their money to assist private business interests in developing foreign trade; and when they learn of it they are sometimes blindly filled with patriotic pride rather than with alarm born of a higher patriotism. We are becoming, in the interest of Wall Street, the policemen of the world. We police Cuba, Panama, Haiti, Santo Domingo, and Honduras with our armed forces; our business interests have obtained virtual control of Guatemala, Salvador, Costa Rica, Colombia, Bolivia, and to a lesser degree Peru; the story of interference by American business in Mexico is too well known to require repetition; and now, we—using the word "we" in the confused sense usual in Washington, identifying private business interests with the people—"we" are spreading into Asia and Europe.

Too little emphasis was laid last winter upon Section 2 of the Naval Appropriation Bill, upon which Secretary Hughes of the State Department insisted with exceptional passion. This section authorized the construction of six river gunboats, to cost, *exclusive of armament*, not to exceed $700,000 each.

> These river gunboats [said Senate Report No. 664] are for the protection of American citizens and American interests on the Chinese rivers. . . . The number of shallow-draft, high-speed gunboats now available is entirely inadequate to provide protection to the growing American interests in this part of the world, and the State Department considers the earliest possible construction of additional vessels of this type to be imperative for the proper protection of American citizens, especially in the present disturbed condition of China. Mr. Hughes stated . . . "Our chief commercial and missionary interests are centered in the Yangtze River, which drains the whole of central China. Because of the existence of this river, with its branches, it is possible to extend a very considerable degree of naval protection to our interests in that valley. . . ."

Five million dollars for gunboats to patrol the interior of China! More millions for our marines in the Caribbean! Where is it leading us? Where will it stop? It would seem ridiculous today to foresee some future Secretary of State asking Congress to appropriate money for shallow-draft American gunboats to patrol the Danube and the Rhine. But looking at our history of the past decade, that would be the logical development. First, the money is invested; then the State Department intervenes; finally the marines follow. It is the historic course of empire. The money-lenders of the world become its policemen. We are already the world's greatest money-lenders; how long will it take us to become its greatest policemen?

Preparing the War with Japan

THE Hawaiian maneuvers have, as we have already pointed out, proved precisely what everybody knew they were to prove—that the fleet is totally inadequate to its task and that the islands are dreadfully underfortified and undermanned. We defy anybody to suggest any defense and attack maneuver by our forces which would not end with precisely the same "lessons." So a new raid on the Treasury is being planned. The chief of staff has left Honolulu for Washington to report in detail on the weaknesses "clearly demonstrated during the war game." The Hawaiian division "must" be increased from 7,000 to 20,000 men. The War Department will take this opportunity to ask Congress to enlarge the army from 118,000 to 150,000 men so as to increase the force in Hawaii. Congressman Butler of Pennsylvania, chairman of the House Naval Committee, has already announced that he will offer legislation designed to make Hawaii "the strongest military outpost in the world," a Gibraltar of the Pacific, and the House Naval Committee, headed by Chairman Butler and duly coached by a number of naval officers, will junket to Hawaii on June 4, sailing on an army transport by way of the Panama Canal. They will, of course, approve Mr. Butler's plans. Navy and War Departments rejoice to think that despite the economical Calvin Coolidge legislation calling for vast sums will be proposed to strengthen our hold on Hawaii when Congress assembles. We are witnessing the beginning of a hue and cry which will undoubtedly make its mark upon the appropriation bill next winter.

Now there are in this matter several facts of which every sane legislator ought to take cognizance. In the first place, the proposal further to fortify Hawaii is a direct violation of the spirit if not the letter of the Four Power Treaty. In that document it was solemnly agreed that the contracting parties should not further fortify their Pacific possessions. It is true, of course, that Hawaii was excepted on the theory that it is a part of our continental possessions. But the effect of pouring more millions into Hawaii against a possible naval attack is obviously contrary to the whole purpose of that treaty and of the Washington Conference—to put an end to competitive armaments by land and sea, and especially to prevent the additional fortification of outlying possessions. More than that, it will be directly aimed at Japan. From the beginning of the maneuvers the pretense has been made that these exercises were aimed at no one in particular. That is the merest poppycock. The whole plan was to simulate an attack by Japan and Japan alone. Every naval and military officer knows that, and so does Japan. There are only two other navies in the world beside those of Japan and the United States, those of France and England. France is an impossible enemy in the Pacific; England could not and would not attack us there if she went to war with us, not even if she had big bases at Singapore and Hongkong.

Since it is aimed at Japan Congress should next inquire whether in the event of war the Japanese strategists would be so eager to commit national hara-kiri as to attack Hawaii and so kindly test for us the adequacy of our defenses. Japanese authorities talk freely about their plans if they are attacked by the United States, as they are beginning to think they will be, and declare that, not being insane, they have no thought of sending their inferior fleet 4,000 miles from home to attack in its own waters the larger fleet of a Power having unlimited resources in men and money. They plan to do precisely what the Germans did in the face of a superior British fleet, to stay at home under their coast defenses and ask the other fellow to attack—and Britain did not dare to do so, although only a few miles away as contrasted with the 5,000 miles between San Francisco and Tokio. Doubtless we shall be told that this is typical Oriental duplicity meant to mislead, but Congress could discover, if it wished to, that we have plenty of naval authorities who believe that the Hawaiian Islands, even if fortified to the limit, will be only a strategical hindrance and weakness in war time; there are plenty of officers, we are told, who think the 5,000-mile attack on Japan so unprecedented in its strategical and tactical difficulties because of the enormous distances as to border on the impossible.

Undoubtedly the maneuvers just ended have brought the war with Japan a step nearer, and the arming of Hawaii will further help to produce it. Discussion and talk and preparation inevitably breed war, and so does rivalry in navies and fortifications. The World War proved that if it proved anything. Germany and England would have been at each other's throats eventually even without the pistol shot that fired the powder-train. If we are correctly informed, the patriotic propaganda is ready with which to "sell" the war with Japan to our people. The slogans are not to be "a war to safeguard democracy" or "the war to end war," but the "white civilization above the yellow" and "Do you want your wife in a yellow man's arms?"

Peace or "Prosperity"?

MR. COOLIDGE'S address to the graduating class at Annapolis is welcomed by many as an important declaration of peace. We do not wish to detract from any influence it may have in that direction. We think Mr. Coolidge is wholly sincere in a desire for no more war, and his speech at Annapolis, coupled with his announced desire to reduce the army appropriations, is not merely lip service in the cause. The trouble is that, although genuinely eager for national peace, Mr. Coolidge understands too meagerly the economic and political conditions upon which it must rest to be a great influence in advancing it. We find thoroughly admirable, for instance, the statement:

> I am not unfamiliar with the claim that if only we had a sufficient military establishment no one would ever molest us. I know of no nation in history that has ever been able to attain that position. I see no reason to expect that we could be the exception.

But when in the same address Mr. Coolidge says that "the true spirit of American institutions requires that each citizen should be potentially a soldier," we wonder if Mr. Coolidge isn't one of those who love peace so much that they are willing "to fight for it." We suspect that his philosophy of peace is nourished on the same sort of sentimentalism that thrust America into the World War.

We used just now the phrase "national peace." Advisedly. Mr. Coolidge is undoubtedly devoted to national peace. We question, though, if he has got as far as international peace—if he understands on what it is conditioned or would be willing to pay the price. Probably his idea of peace, like that of many other honest but uncomprehending Americans, is a world free of war in which the United States, nevertheless, has a dominant and superior place. It is a world in which American "prosperity" is still maintained with all that that means of exploitation of one class by another, of one nation by another, of one race by another, of one school of thought by another. We fear that between peace and "prosperity" (his kind) Mr. Coolidge will practically always choose the latter. We doubt if he cares enough for—or knows enough about—international peace through liberty, equality, and fraternity to set himself against, say, our financial imperialism in Latin America or our industrial feudalism here at home. Perhaps the fact that our business-controlled press is generally so laudatory of Mr. Coolidge's address at Annapolis is sufficient proof that it contains nothing alarming in the direction of international peace.

From the practical standpoint the best thing Mr. Coolidge said was his condemnation of those in the Navy itself who are trying to set Japan and America at war:

> The officers of the navy are given the fullest latitude in expressing their views before their fellow citizens, subject, of course, to the requirements of not betraying those confidential affairs which would be detrimental to the service. It seems to me perfectly proper for any one upon any suitable occasion to advocate the maintenance of a navy in keeping with the greatness and dignity of our country.
>
> But as one who is responsible not only for our national defense but likewise our friendly relations with other peoples and our title to the good opinion of the world, I feel that the occasion will very seldom arise, and I know it does not now exist, when those connected with our navy are justified, either directly or by inference, in asserting that other specified Powers are arming against us, and, by arousing national suspicion and hatred, attempting to cause us to arm against them.
>
> The suggestion that any other people are harboring a hostile intent toward us is a very serious charge to make. We would not relish having our honorable motives and peaceful intentions questioned; others cannot relish having any of us question theirs.
>
> We should not forget that in the world over the general attitude and one of the strongest attributes of all peoples is a desire to do right.

This is straight talk. The President does not mention Japan in so many words, nor name personally those talky-talkers like the retired rear admirals Fiske and Rodgers; but there is no doubt about his meaning. Retired rear admirals have been a nuisance and a danger in America for some years. By trading on past performances and their navy connection, they have obtained a hearing for views that would not be taken seriously as coming from someone else. Sensible Americans may know that the shells these ancient mariners toss into the air are duds, but seen from across the Pacific they are as dangerous as any others.

Mr. Coolidge's speech at Annapolis may not be an important milestone toward international peace, but if it stops some pestilential naval oratory it will at least lessen immediate danger of conflict.

Germany's Peace Offensive

GERMANY'S answer to the French security notes is another step toward peace. A long vista of negotiations opens ahead, but Europe is on the right road. And vastly more important than the phrases of the diplomatic notes is the fact that the French troops are out of the Ruhr. That mischievous invasion of German territory plunged Europe anew into a haze of war talk. Drums beat, troops marched, men talked angrily. Hate boiled on both sides of the Rhine. France was still so bitter that Herriot, a year ago, dared go no further than to give a secret pledge that the French troops would come out in August, 1925. Germany, naturally, has not yet recovered from the ill temper stirred by Poincaré's act of war, with all its ruinous aftermath.

Now the troops are out at last. France is back within the military frontiers set by the Treaty of Versailles. Stresemann's note, and his subsequent speeches, clearly imply his expectation that in return for Germany's agreement to a security pact France will go further and consent to evacuation of the Cologne sector. The treaty, it will be recalled, provided that the Cologne sector would be evacuated after five years, if Germany had fulfilled her obligations under the treaty, the Coblenz sector after ten years, and the Mainz sector after fifteen years. Cologne was due for evacuation in January, and there is only the scantest of technical excuses for the delay. England and France punctually notified Germany that because of her defaults they could not proceed with the withdrawal as scheduled, but it took them three months to agree as to what the defaults were. Let us hope that the day of such chicanery is past. Germany is making the modifications in her military system which the Allies suggested, and complaints on that score seem to have ceased. The irritating presence of the French troops in the Ruhr is no more; if the Allies will only proceed to liberate Cologne, too, at once, they will go far to give the fulfilment policy in Germany the support which it needs.

France has been taught to put her faith in force. She has acquired a habit of looking eastward at her larger neighbor, and of shuddering—and believing that only an army on guard can preserve her. Possibly the amicable tone of the present discussions will help to cure her of that unreasonable state of mind. The urgent need of her troops in Morocco may also be of assistance. Sooner or later she will have to rely for security upon the pledged word of other nations—including Germany—and upon the rightness of her own actions. Ten years hence, fifteen years hence—some time—the whole Rhineland will have to be evacuated; and if she taxes herself eternally to maintain, with a population two-thirds of Germany's, an army five times as large, she can only lose in the economic competition which lies at the root of national power.

Germany has offered France a pledge never to make war; to accept the Western frontier as binding and to resort to arbitration in case of disputes concerning the Eastern frontier. France replied, insisting that Germany first join the League of Nations, and reiterating, in somewhat ambiguous terms, her right to resort to force if Germany failed in her treaty obligations. Germany's reply is, as M. Briand said, a reasonable basis for further negotiations. She is willing to join the League, but only upon assurance that she will not be obliged to violate her neutrality by aiding in a war or by transshipping foreign troops across her territory. Forced by treaty to reduce her army to 100,000 men, she feels she has the right to ask that she be freed from military obligations. Furthermore, she naturally declines the suggestion that France—ally of both Poland and Czecho-Slovakia—become a "guarantor" of Germany's treaties with those nations. Some of the most controversial points the note leaves untouched.

And that may be just as well. The fundamental need is for a peace atmosphere. Too much debate can spoil the air. It is something to be grateful for that Germany and France today find it possible to write polite notes without thumbing their noses at each other. There is, of course, a certain unreality in this long-range hallooing by means of studiously worded notes. How long will it be before their representatives can sit down together, face to face, and actually work out an agreement? Perhaps, when the two nations acquire the habit of friendly conversation France will throw off that strange obsession which has led her to demand that every "peace pact" be sealed by military guaranties. When the nations begin at last to talk peace in terms of peace, instead of thinking of it in terms of threats and penalties, Europe will really have emerged from her dismal war psychosis.

Outlawing War by the World Court

A POLL of the Senate is said to show a small majority in favor of our entry into the World Court on the basis of a compromise between Senator Pepper's plan and the so-called Harding-Hughes-Coolidge reservations. Nevertheless any small majority in favor of the Court will have hard going against the powerful opposition of the chairman of the Committee on Foreign Relations. It is not merely Senator Borah's strategic position, but his intellectual ability and moral passion which make it so important to win his advocacy of any plan for international justice. He has stated that he will support our entry into the World Court only if it can be coupled with the outlawry of war and the codification of international law.

Hence the peculiar significance of the proposal recently advanced by a mixed group of men and women, some known for advocacy of the League and the World Court and some for opposition to the League and advocacy of the outlawry of war. This program contemplates immediate entry into the Court on the basis of the Harding-Hughes-Coolidge reservations plus an agreement that our adherence is limited to a five-year period unless within that period a general treaty embodying the principles of the outlawry of war has been negotiated and adopted.

This proposal has been criticized as impracticable on several grounds: (1) Europe will not now accept the principles of the outlawry of war as an institution; (2) the United States which might like the idea of the outlawry of war will not accept the affirmative jurisdiction of the Court over all justiciable questions, which is essential to the outlawry of war in practice; (3) the practical difficulties of a codification of law will prove insuperable at least within a five-year period.

We can only tell by trying. The German offer of a security pact provided that the nations signing should outlaw war between themselves; and the effort of the Geneva protocol to define and outlaw aggressive war was a step toward outlawing war. As for the codification of international law, draft conventions for the Pan American Union have already been prepared for consideration and the League itself has at last made a beginning. The real difficulty, we fear, may be America's refusal to accept compulsory jurisdiction over all non-domestic quarrels. And without this we cannot see any great gain in joining the Court at all.

Of course enormous problems remain: the underlying problem of the economic causes both of war and imperialism; the problem of keeping law fluid so it will not freeze into unchanging form, perpetuating existing injustices; and the details of procedure. But at least in America all these problems will be easier to face if the spirit of constructive adjustment of differences which brought together men hitherto so opposed in tactics as former Justice Clarke of the League of Nations Nonpartisan Association and S. O. Levinson, author of the plan to outlaw war, can be made to prevail. It may be long before lovers of peace will reach complete agreement on method or philosophy but every bit of united action they can honestly take together will confound the cynics, the militarists, the worshipers of selfishness and force, whose preparation for new wars imperils all hope for the future.

Twin Military Evils

PRECISELY as was to have been expected, the Secretary of the Navy, the Acting Secretary of War, the leading generals and admirals who have testified before the Air Inquiry Board appointed by President Coolidge have expressed complete satisfaction with the present organization of their forces and have declared that nothing whatever was wrong beyond the fact that Congress was not giving them enough money. Thus it is more than ever apparent that if there are to be any changes they can only be brought about by outside pressure. Both the army and navy are plainly going to "pass the buck" to Congress, their favorite occupation, and to insist that if only more millions were given to them everything would be well. Their personnel and equipment are, they say, superb—the Air Board was actually told that America led the world in flying, although every sane student of the problem knows otherwise. And the complacency of Secretary Wilbur hardly seems shattered when now, on top of airplane, dirigible, and submarine disasters, we learn that he falsified the record, that Commander Lansdowne *was* opposed to the Shenandoah's last trip, and that the acting chief of naval operations, R. H. Jackson, on August 12 last overruled his recommendation in the following remarkable letter:

> Your recommendation to make the flight the second week in September has not been approved. By starting on September 2 the Shenandoah would fly over State fairs as follows: Columbus, Sept. 3; Des Moines, Sept. 4; Minneapolis, Sept. 4; Milwaukee, Sept. 5; Detroit, Sept. 5. This includes all the State fairs except that at Indianapolis.

This proves beyond question the charge of politics made by Mrs. Lansdowne in her first outburst of grief, which she subsequently modified under official pressure. What has naval flying to do with State fairs?

Politics and conservatism—these are twin evils of the military and naval services, and they have been so in Great Britain and the United States from the beginning of military history. Let us take some historic facts about the navy. Was the Monitor actually a government vessel when she steamed to Hampton Roads? She was not. Despite the fact that it was known in Washington that the Confederates were armor-plating ships, the Monitor had to be forced upon the Navy Department and had actually not been definitely accepted when she stopped the victorious career of the Merrimack. Throughout the war the heaviest fighting thereafter was done by the Monitor, but when the war was over the Navy Department discarded this remarkable invention chiefly because of the lack of modern ventilating equipment and the fact that there was little deck space available in a sea way and none on which to parade the marine guard. When the war was over it sold to foreign countries its most modern monitors, forgot all about the Confederate invention of the submarine, did not bother further with torpedoes or mines, and let twenty-five years go by before really beginning to experiment with any of these instruments. Yet in the World War the Allies were compelled to build monitors. We invented the submarine sixty years ago and the modern submarine, too, but this boat was taken up and developed in England and Germany far in advance of any action by us. In 1915 the head of the submarine division of the Navy Department appeared before the House Naval Committee and demanded larger submarines on the ground that the Germans had them. On cross-examination it appeared that the only knowledge of these submarines in the possession of the Navy Department was the testimony of an American boy who had served briefly on one. We invented the airplane, but in its uses we have been far outstripped by the European Powers.

As for the inevitable demand for larger appropriations, that is of course the invariable outcome of every maneuver and every inquiry and every other happening affecting either army or navy. Yet there is hardly a business organization in the world as loosely or as uneconomically managed as is the army. Here are two concrete examples. Since the removal of the troops who were the custodians of the Yellowstone National Park the present admirable civilian management has saved hundreds of thousands of dollars in expenses besides giving far greater efficiency. Take the case of Colonel Mitchell. He gave his final provocative statement to the press and announced that he knew it would lead to his court martial. There was no mystery about it; he openly said that he was going to give the interview and then gave it. The War Department could not be satisfied with that. It could not send him a wire; it could not even ask the general commanding at San Antonio, nor the lieutenant colonel and assistant inspector general on duty there to inquire of Colonel Mitchell whether he was correctly quoted. It had to send a colonel and an assistant inspector general all the way from Washington to San Antonio and return to find out officially what every man knew—at a cost of hundreds of dollars for railway fares and subsistence! There you have the evil at its worst, and that is why the presumption of being in the right is always on the side of men who finally kick over the traces and insist upon "starting something."

Russia—Guest or Ghost?

CHICHERIN sleeps in Berlin while the British, French, and German delegates discuss security at Locarno, but his shadow stalks wherever his Western neighbors meet. Wild rumors of Russian attempts to sabotage the proposed agreement fill the columns of the newspapers, and an uneasy sense of insecurity dominates the gentlemen who have come together to establish Europe's security. "What will Russia do? What is Chicherin up to?" are questions on every lip.

And why not? The Allies, after six long years of futile palavers, have at last come to the obvious, commonsense conclusion that in planning the security of Europe they must take Germany into consideration. Guaranties must be mutual; Germany must be protected as well as France; she must be treated as an equal and given the same promises as are exacted of her. Those kindergarten lessons are proclaimed today in every French newspaper, where only a year ago the Poincarist mood of ultimatum and compulsion still ruled. The Prime Minister of France has publicly proclaimed that "Franco-German reconciliation is like the keystone of European civilization," and no man denies him. But although Germany is at last admitted to the inner councils Russia is still left out, and the arguments which apply to Germany apply equally well to Russia.

It is Western Europe's fault if the uninvited Mr. Chicherin fills the security conference with alarm. He frankly regards the proposed security pact as a British plot directed against Soviet Russia; and the English have made no effort to unconvince him. It is, he says, a mutual security alliance among the enemies of Soviet Russia, and he suspects secret understandings regarding possible military action against the incubus in the East. Perhaps he is all wrong; possibly there is a substantial germ of truth behind his suspicions. In any case, left in isolation, it is natural that he should endeavor, both in Warsaw and in Berlin, to make his own agreements for the safety of his country. Stresemann has just negotiated a commercial treaty with him—through which some of the American capital recently lent to Germany will find its way into the forbidden land of Russia—and Poland appears to have listened to Chicherin with a new friendliness.

That, too, is natural—and well. A year ago France was insisting upon the right to send troops across Germany in order to defend Poland and Czecho-Slovakia. Germany naturally refused this invitation to become a sort of second-hand battlefield. France has not yet withdrawn her demand, but the new amicability of her prime minister indicates that she has lost interest in her old military program. So Poland feels deserted and joins eagerly in conversations with her Eastern neighbor—a simple act of common sense, however disturbing to the dovecotes of Allied diplomacy.

Germany, meanwhile, basks in a new sunshine. Courted by Russia, she can afford to be coy with France. The Locarno conference is largely of her making; its program is essentially her program; the Allies have refused her demand that the question of war guilt be reopened courteously enough, on the plea of avoidance that a security conference is not the proper occasion. The vistas seem magnificent.

But those who have followed the negotiations of past years, who recall the reiterated reports of brilliant progress, will smile a little sadly at the new communiqués. For until Russia is a guest, not a ghost, at these conferences they cannot move much further than their predecessors.

Russia in Wall Street

RUSSIA not merely is coming back; she has come back. Americans, fatigued by years of theoretical discussions of soviet methods, have paid too little attention to the remarkable advances which Russia has been making. American business men, however, are not asleep. For poverty-stricken Russia is importing American goods, despite the difficulties caused by lack of governmental recognition, at an amazing rate. In 1924 she imported more American goods than pre-war Czarist Russia did. In August, 1925, she took more American goods than she had done in the entire year of 1923. And she did it with the aid of credits advanced by canny American bankers who saw in Russia perspectives of increasing American business.

There are still papers like the New York *Times* which editorially pooh-pooh the reports of their own correspondents in Soviet Russia. These editors have acquired a habit of which they cannot rid themselves, but the bankers who recently met to hear the reports of one of their number just returned from Russia are more interested in present-day facts than in their prejudices of yesteryear. And one may suspect that ex-Governor Goodrich, once of Mr. Hoover's American Relief Administration, has not been spending months in Russia solely in the interest of his Indiana farm. Governor Goodrich has been in the past one of Mr. Hoover's most faithful correspondents, and there is no reason to believe that their relation has changed. Correspondents in Russia report that he is struck by the agricultural revival in Russia, and believes that the Soviet crop estimates, however favorable, probably underestimate the success of the crop; he is also impressed by the "orderly and relatively efficient work in the factories."

In the first half of 1925 Russian trade with the United States amounted, according to the Department of Commerce, to nearly sixty million dollars. Only six millions of this were imports from Russia into the United States; the rest were goods exported from America to Russia. But this disproportion is hardly greater than in pre-war days, when Russia shipped us about eight million dollars' worth of goods each year, and imported more than forty million dollars' worth. The significant fact is that Russia is back in the market, despite all the handicaps which a hostile world has imposed upon her. Her cotton-goods industry operated last year at 92 per cent of the 1913 output; her metal industry at 90 per cent; coal at 79 per cent; oil at 85. The car loadings were four-fifths of the 1913 figure, despite the amputations of her territory on the Western front; and she actually produced four times as much electric power as in that pre-war year. Lenin's dream of an electrified Russia is becoming more than a dream.

Another aspect of Russian industry is also worth considering. The cotton-goods industry produced last year (1924-25) more than five times as much goods as in 1921-22, with less than twice the number of workers and less than three times the number of spindles; and the goods were marketed at prices 50 per cent lower. Russia's labor is not merely returning to work; it is working more efficiently.

Russia's foreign trace of course implies an increased confidence among non-Russian business men. While the business world as a whole has maintained its suspicions of the terrible Bolsheviki here and there experimenters have entered on the pioneer path of friendly and normal trade relations. Nor is it outside speculators and concession-hunters who are blazing the trail. The New York correspondents of the Soviet State Bank are today the Guaranty Trust Co., the Equitable Trust Co., the Irving Bank-Columbia Trust Co., and similar firms. The Chase National Bank and the Equitable have dealt in large figures with the Amtorg Trading Corporation and the All-Russian Textile Syndicate, through which the Soviet Government makes its largest purchases in the United States.

But after all, compared with the possibilities of Russian trade, this return to the level of 1913 is but a drop in the bucket. Large credits will be impossible until official recognition gives a new and evident stability to the situation. The Russian Government cannot yet maintain deposits in American banks, and has to form American corporations to do its business here. The largest American credits which Russia is receiving come indirectly, through British and German agents. As M. Gurievich, of the Supreme Council of National Economy, put it the other day:

> German firms, for instance the Krupps, have come here, received large orders on credit terms we can accept, and then, with the order in their pockets, borrowed money from American banks in order to swing the contracts. They pay American banks 4 or 5 per cent, and charge us 9 per cent. They use American money to get a firm foothold in the Russian field.

That, of course, cannot long persist. A business administration such as we have in Washington, will not eternally bury its head in the sands heaped up by Mr. Hughes's prejudices. The Government which excludes Saklatavala gladly grants visas today to Russian Communists who come with orders for cotton and machinery in their hands, and the time may come when Big Business will force the Government to recognize the Bolsheviks.

The Great Advance Toward Peace

BEYOND all question what has happened at Locarno is the most hopeful event since that worst of days, August 1, 1914. For the first time since the era of Charlemagne France and Germany have pledged themselves not to attack one another, have outlawed war against each other. The German Government has forever renounced all claim to Alsace-Lorraine, and has accepted the existing French boundaries as the definite delimitation of Germany's westward expansion. For that the world may sing te deums. Locarno not only punctuates the bloodiest and most disgraceful chapter in human history, it opens up a whole realm of possible new developments. If Germany and France can outlaw war with the cooperation of England, Italy, and Belgium, why not the whole civilized world? Who now will dare say that France and all the other Allies cannot disarm and at last turn to the reconstruction of Europe? Who can say, with Aristide Briand himself pledging that the alliance of the Allies is finished and that the very name is to disappear from the language of diplomacy, that Europe cannot at last in dead earnest put an end to the hatreds and bitternesses of the war and begin its spiritual disarmament and reconciliation?

It is idle, of course, to deny that what happened at Locarno should have taken place at Versailles; that the seven long years since the armistice with their spirit of revenge, the desire to humiliate and abase the former enemy, the readiness to starve to death women and children and to inflict such immeasurable suffering as that in the Ruhr and the other occupied territories constitute a shameful and utterly unnecessary chapter in the history of every conniving nation. We are not of those who would close the book of memory upon those direful years for we believe that the events from 1914 onward must be kept before oncoming generations in order that the world may be warned against repeating such incredible folly and again intrusting its destinies to such faithless leaders as Sir Edward Grey, Asquith, Lloyd George, Poincaré, Viviani, Bethmann-Hollweg, the two Kaisers and their guilty crew. But while we cannot forget these years, we are of those who pray that the new chapter will genuinely mean a new era for all humanity. If the statesmanship is there, Locarno may be but a beginning and not an end, the beginning of an epoch.

Locarno's great achievement is an atmosphere rather than a text. There are always loopholes in any text. A Poincaré might interpret Article VI of the treaty of mutual guaranty, for instance, to suit his own purposes. "The provisions of the present treaty do not affect the rights and obligations of the high contracting parties under the Treaty of Versailles," it reads. Poincaré held that treaty to permit his invasion of the Ruhr; if that is not changed of what lasting values are then new pacts? There are suggestions that the new arrangement may be used to isolate Russia still further and to present a solid European front not only against the United States but against the rising demands of Africa, India, and Asia for deliverance from the yoke of white imperialism. That the reactionary and chauvinistic press of France, England, and Italy has been the first to acclaim these new treaties of peace is not encouraging. A recrudescence of Kaiserism in Berlin, of Poincaréism in France, and of the secret alliances and deceitful trickery of Greyism in England may, indeed, upset those alliances. But if our rejoicing is tempered by these considerations, we still cannot but give thanks for the immediate relief that the new concord has brought, its restoration of Germany to full fellowship among the nations, and, best of all, the triumph of generosity and good will and sanity in France.

What now will be the role of the League of Nations? There is a prospect that it may cease to be the creature of England and France, that with the entrance of Germany into the Council there will be vigorously presented to Council and Assembly a different viewpoint from that of the war victors. There is, therefore, a prospect of stirring exchanges of opinions, and even of facing issues, like disarmament, which the League has burked. The fact that Germany has received the promise of a seat in the Council and admission to the League itself, not by action by either Assembly or Council, but from the four leading members of the League, speaks volumes for the lack of democracy of that organization and reveals patently enough how certain the chief allies are that the League will do as it is told. Once in, Germany will, we take it for granted, raise the disarmament issue and compel a decision as to whether her fellow-members shall be allowed to keep up great standing armies or navies while she herself remains disarmed. In that she should have the moral support of President Coolidge and his Administration. Our own hope is that the new shift will compel the League to vigorous action along certain lines in which it has been content to let the years roll by without accomplishing anything.

Next to disarmament the most pressing need of Europe is for a tariff union. Nothing could accomplish so much for the spiritual disarmament for which we have just appealed and for the economic restoration of Europe than the establishment of a customs union. Here again is a great opportunity for Germany. Surrounded by high tariffs on all sides, she is yet expected to produce enough money to meet the demands of the Dawes Plan. It was the German customs union of 1834 that resulted in the tremendous development of the German states years before the Empire was reconstituted at Versailles in 1871. Who can doubt that the breaking down of tariff barriers now would mean the accomplishment of what still seem economic impossibilities? For the new and small states that have been created since the war the levelling of the tariff barriers with which they are surrounded could only mean their flourishing like the proverbial green bay tree. Austria, Hungary, Czecho-Slovakia, Lithuania, Latvia, Esthonia, Poland—there is not one of these but would benefit incalculably by a free exchange of goods. No other measure would do so much to break down the nationalistic obsession out of which grew the war; no other act could so effectively develop the interchange of thought and the friendly intercourse of the nations. Washington seems to take it for granted that there will be a general European economic conference before long. Here is the opportunity for the advocates of free trade.

Meanwhile the Locarno treaties stand, if for nothing else, as complete justification of those who, like *The Nation*, have preached, in season and out, the reunion of the enemies of the past upon the simple basis of mutual good will and the determination to build a new, a sane, and a just Europe.

The Revolt Against Military Training

The object of all military training is to win battles.

The inherent desire to fight and kill must be carefully watched for and encouraged by the instructor.

The principles of sportsmanship and consideration for your opponent have no place in the practical application of this work.

WITH such maxims as these, taken from the prescribed "Manual of Military Training," did the opponents of compulsory training at the College of the City of New York launch their remarkably skilful and energetic campaign against it. The college publication, the *Campus*, took the lead. The whole college was aroused. Although an optimistic dean expressed the opinion that not more than half of the regularly enrolled students would vote on the question of a petition to the trustees for the abolition of compulsory military training, before the end of the second day of balloting over 2,000 out of 3,200 had voted, and the final vote was 2,092 to 345. We are informed that this is the largest total vote which any referendum among the students of the College of the City of New York has ever called out. The interest in the question was obviously intense and the result of the referendum is decisive and immensely encouraging.

What the trustees will do with this petition is another matter. Sidney Mezes, the president, is already on record in favor of continuing compulsory military training. Mr. Mezes will be remembered as the man who marshaled the American experts on peace in behalf of his brother-in-law, Colonel House, when we were preparing to make a peace appropriate to victory in a war to end war. According to one newspaper report he believes that this training in killing is good "both for the health and the patriotism of the students." It must disappoint even his optimism to find that his students have so little appreciation of what is good for them.

As a matter of fact, none of the conventional justifications for compulsory military training in our colleges is intellectually creditable. Military training is by no means the best form of physical exercise. Military discipline demonstrably has not produced that type of self-discipline upon which the best citizenship depends. It is only for propaganda purposes that army officers speak of military instruction as a training for citizenship. When they are candid they admit that its real object is "to win battles." Least of all does the kind of teaching given to our Reserve Officers Training Corps tend to produce the friendly spirit which is essential to international peace. Thus an Iowa student writes: "While I was in military classes I was having nurtured in me distrust of other nations." He went on to quote his officers as having said: "We are getting the dirty end of the stick on the 5-5-3 ratio. Other nations are not disarmed like the United States. Look out for Japan."

Universities and colleges which owe allegiance to the world-wide republic of letters and science are the last places where this sort of teaching should be given—where an element so alien to academic freedom as the typical military mind should be given such large powers over students. It is therefore intensely disappointing to those who look to our institutions of higher learning for intellectual and social leadership to find the average college president the eulogist of a system of compulsory military training which in so far as it is effective is necessarily destructive of the highest ideals of his profession. The tendency of many of our colleges and State universities to make military training compulsory for their students, without any necessity whatsoever in law, is in itself a kind of disloyalty to the deeply rooted American aversion to compulsory military training and service. Whatever the law says, it is compulsory military training and service when a boy anxious for an education can secure it only at the price of at least two years' required work in military courses.

If the attitude of many college and university authorities is disappointing, the increasing spirit of revolt in student bodies is correspondingly heartening. Students of the University of Wisconsin took the lead in the campaign which forced the State legislature to abolish the compulsory feature of military training in that great university. Students in Pomona College persuaded the board of trustees to end compulsory military training in that institution. Last spring students in Howard University and the University of Minnesota made notable protests against compulsory military training. An effective agitation is beginning at Ohio State University and we know not how many others. The University of Missouri, like the College of the City of New York, recently arranged for a student referendum under supervision of the Student Council on the question of compulsory military training. But before the vote was taken the regents unanimously indorsed compulsion and at the request of the president the vote was called off. Influential groups of students, however, are so determined that they are already talking of following the example of the Wisconsin students and carrying the fight to the State legislature. In examples like these—and they are increasing fast—is new ground for confidence in the spirit of youth, new ground for hope that America may be restored to leadership in the pursuit of world peace.

Militarizing America's Youth

WHAT happened in the Great War, fought ostensibly to end war, to turn American college campuses into parade grounds? What facts in the present situation lead us to trust for the preservation of peace to the military training of high-school boys? It is time that we Americans should face these questions squarely and ask ourselves where we are going.

The War Department thinks it knows. It is using military training in high schools, colleges, and summer camps as the nearest thing it can get to universal military training and service. In General Pershing's language it is popularizing "by all available methods" the "preparation for military service." These methods include compulsion in some 197 secondary schools and colleges wherever complaisant trustees can be found to enforce it. They include all sorts of rewards and blandishments from cash to glory where compulsion as yet is not or cannot be applied. They include also plain misrepresentation. Thus American fathers and mothers are assured by the preface of the Junior Reserve Officers' Training Corps Manual: "The purpose of this book is not to make soldiers out of your boys but to develop them physically, morally, and mentally into the best type of citizens, capable of defending our flag should anything arise." The army officers are officially instructed: "Always remember that men are the material being trained and molded for the work of battle. . . . They are being trained to be soldiers." And the students are told: "Success in battle, whether attack or defense, is the aim of all military training."

Such are some of the facts that have been brought out in the recent revolt of the students in colleges as far apart as the University of Washington and the College of the City of New York against compulsory military training. These revolts are encouraging; they have nowhere been crushed by temporary defeat, but only in Pomona and the University of Wisconsin have the students won. And in the high schools there has been no shadow of revolt. In short, the problem is for the nation; not alone for the students.

So much is made clear by the timely appearance and wide circulation of Winthrop D. Lane's pamphlet on "Military Training in Schools and Colleges," with a foreword signed by more than fifty influential Americans including four United States Senators. Mr. Lane's quiet, carefully documented statement of fact ought to undermine the foundations of the elaborate structure of militarism which is rising with dangerous rapidity.

We have been told, even by liberals, that it is folly to speak of the R. O. T. C. in our colleges as contributing to the "structure of militarism." It promotes little enthusiasm for drill and less for war. The officers in charge are of high caliber. The Daily *Princetonian* in commending the fight of the College of the City of New York against compulsion spoke in the highest praise of the quality of leadership in the elective training course at Princeton. Now all these things may be true without proving that military training is innocuous. Military drill has never in any land made the average man *like* war; it has made him *accept* it. And that is what counts. The man who has taken military science even under compulsion as part of the price of his education, still more the man who has taken it for money or honor, has given hostages to the future. He is part of a system which in an emergency he cannot desert without some feeling of disloyalty. That is what the officers in charge know and that is the result they seek. Moreover, too many of them not merely teach a general acceptance of war and the warrior's interpretation of history; they point to specific possible enemies—usually Japan—and thereby directly menace peace. We happen to know a corps commander in charge of R. O. T. C. work in an important area. He is an officer and a gentleman who has risen by hard work. He confided to some of his friends that if only the Great War had lasted a little longer he would have been a brigadier general. By personal preference he desires peace, not war. But he simply cannot imagine a world without war. He honestly loves the army. He is infinitely credulous concerning all the "menaces," red and yellow, domestic and foreign, which bring such fearsome thrills to the National Security League.

Such is militarism whether in Prussia, France, or America. Let it continue to march hand in hand with American economic imperialism and this our country will become by reason of its very might the worst obstacle to the peace of the world. And in this process of militarization, as Mr. Lane points out, the universities may find that by giving over to the War Department such large areas of academic life to control they are introducing an element possibly more dangerous to academic freedom than ecclesiasticism or big business.

Now this situation which has stolen upon the people more or less unawares is by no means irremediable. That is proved by the fight in the colleges and by the weight of some of the signatures indorsing Mr. Lane's pamphlet. The most obvious objectives are (1) the entire abolition of military training in secondary schools where by the universal agreement of psychologists and educators it does not belong; and (2) the abolition of compulsion in the colleges. The former is in the hands of boards of education; the latter of boards of trustees and regents. It would be a great gain if both these ends could be obtained.

But the real remedy for the militarizing of our most ambitious youth goes deeper. It is not enough that students should not be compelled to take military training; they should not be bribed or cajoled into it. It is high time for Congress to amend the law and stop the appropriations which subvert our institutions of learning from their proper function of education for peace. Tribes and nations since history began have sought safety by sacrificing the bright years of youth, its hopes and dreams, to war or preparation for war. And their sacrifices have been in vain. It is for our colleges to discover a better and nobler way of happiness and safety. To ask them, of all places, to become temples of a militarist cult, dedicated to the god of battles—this is to ask of them a betrayal of their very souls. For they exist to woo the young man to love of science and art, beauty and truth. These are not purely national; they are not born of war; they are stifled by the discipline of the martinet. They spring from the peaceful intercourse of peoples and the commerce of great minds; they grow strong only in the free air of fearless inquiry. In their increase is our hope. It is a hope not found in any military manual.

War Claims and National Honor

AGAIN has Senator Borah scored heavily. The plan recently announced by the Administration providing for the return of the sequestrated alien property and the payment of American claims is the direct result of the movement, initiated by Senator Borah and his supporters, for the disposition of one of the most deplorable legacies of the war. Secretary Mellon's belated acceptance of the doctrine he now announces that "As a matter of broad national policy it is believed the United States should recognize the property rights of private individuals even though we were at war with their country, and not use this private property of nationals to pay claims against their nation," is a tribute to the soundness of view and judgment of those who, like *The Nation*, have given expression ever since 1918 to this self-evident truth.

It will be recalled that the most solemn promises were made in 1917 that the sequestrated property would be returned at the end of the war. The overwhelming victory, however, impaired the national morality and, having the power to be as lawless as it chose, the Administration simply changed its mind. The Knox-Porter resolution contained a provision to the effect that we might "retain" the sequestrated property until Germany made "suitable provision for the satisfaction of" the claims of American citizens.

The present Administration plan provides for the return of the property in kind amounting to some $150,000,000; for the $150,000,000 of seized cash the owners are required "voluntarily" to accept $50,000,000 in bonds and $100,000,000 in cash. The owners of the ships seized in American harbors at the outbreak of war and of radios and patents used by the United States are to receive "fair and reasonable compensation," not to exceed $100,000,000 in bonds, an ambiguity presently to be discussed. The claims of American citizens against Germany, estimated, including interest to 1926, at $180,000,000, will be paid by $80,000,000 in cash and $100,000,000 in bonds. To make up the $80,000,000, $31,000,000 of undistributed interest, accumulated on alien property funds down to March 4, 1923, will be used, together with the $50,000,000 of alien property cash for which the owners must "voluntarily" agree to take bonds.

The $250,000,000 worth of bonds provided for in the plan, and distributed as mentioned above, are to be issued by a trustee or trust company and to run for twenty-five years at 5 per cent interest, guaranteed by the United States. Principal and interest are to be payable in marks or dollars, at the option of the United States. They are to be served in first instance by the receipts coming to the United States from the Dawes Plan, under the head both of Rhine army costs and claims, as allocated under the Paris agreement of January, 1925. For the Rhine army costs priority payments are to be made to the United States amounting to $13,000,000 per year, of which one year's instalment has already been paid. Under the head of claims we are to receive 2¼ per cent of the German payments, not exceeding $10,000,000 per year, with no priority.

The crux of the solution lies in the acquiescence of the Administration to devoting Rhine army costs to the payment of claims of American citizens. This was proper for two reasons: first, because those costs would have had to be borne by the United States in any event, and secondly, because the naivete of the Wilson and Harding administrations permitted the Allies to embezzle these funds, about $250,000,000, after Germany had paid the amount to the Reparation Commission for our account. When Washington woke up to the facts and demanded our quota, Poincaré calmly informed the Department of State that the money had been spent and that we were privileged to ask Germany for it a second time. We lamely took the advice; hence the Wadsworth agreement of 1923, providing for the reimbursement of the United States from *future* German payments, which, in turn, gave way to the Paris agreement of 1925 under the Dawes Plan. For the claims proper, the Allies at Paris in 1925 generously let us have 2¼ per cent of the German payments, which it was known was quite insufficient. Again the ineptitude of the Administration brought about a diplomatic defeat. The British and French governments to the last hoped to force us into a policy of confiscation, and none more than they will regret that we have manifested a partial respect for the principle of immunity of private property, the gross violation of which by those nations is likely to cost them heavily in the future. The effort to escape the charge of confiscation by alleging that Germany is obligated to compensate its expropriated nationals only adds the immorality of hypocrisy to the offense of theft.

It was, therefore, only proper that the United States Government, which was responsible for the short-changing received at the hands of the Allies, should itself bear the risks of the Dawes Plan and should not penalize for its own shortcomings the owners of the sequestrated property or, indeed, the American claimants against Germany. Hence the provision for guaranteed bonds to be served out of the Dawes Plan payments. The American claims of $180,000,000 include $2,500,000 for Lusitania victims, about $15,000,000 for requisitions, about $25,000,000 for private debts and estate claims based practically on the depreciation of the mark, and about $60,000,000 for marine insurance companies.

The Mellon plan of settlement warrants certain comments. The $31,000,000 of undistributed interest belong not only to Germans but to American citizens and others whose property was seized and later returned, yet who were victims of the unjust rule that the Government does not pay interest on its obligations unless the law especially so provides. While it would be extremely difficult to allocate the sum, it would probably not be impossible. Again, it is extraordinary that provision should be made for "fair and reasonable compensation" to German shipowners, owners of radio stations and patents expropriated by the Government, yet that the liability should be limited to a specific total sum, $100,000,000. It is known that these assets were worth immeasurably more; $100,000,000 is therefore neither "fair" nor "reasonable." If the United States is liable, it is liable for the real value of the expropriated property and not for an arbitrary, fictitious value set in advance by the taker alone.

Again, it is understood that as a condition of receiving so much of their property back the German owners had to waive all claims for the devastation wrought upon it by the overzealous and destructive policies of A. Mitchell Palmer and Francis P. Garvan, Alien Property Custodians. This demand is unworthy of the United States and amounts to a partial confiscation. Senator Borah should not let it pass.

But on the whole the plan of settlement is to be welcomed, although it contains defects which should be corrected in Congress. It may cost the United States little. Whatever it costs it will be a cheap price to pay for rescuing us from a horrible mistake of policy and for restoring in some measure the national tradition and international law.

Budgets, Taxes, and Waste

PRESIDENT COOLIDGE and Secretary Mellon are very proud of the tax reductions they have already accomplished and are now about to carry further with the aid of Congress. The President ascribes them in considerable degree to the budget system. "Without it," he says, "all the claim of economy would be a mere pretense." He cites the reduction of the departmental estimates for ordinary purposes—from $4,068,000,000 in 1922 to $3,156,000,000 for 1927—as the best possible proof of the value of the budget and of the Controller General. That the control of the budget has accomplished much good and that its establishment has been a long step toward scientific control of our national finances no one will, we think, deny. But while the machinery of budget-making may be all that is desired, the question must still be raised, as with every other governmental device, whether those who are operating it are doing so wisely and to the public interest. Neither a reduction of taxes nor of the budget is necessarily a good thing. It depends where the savings are made.

Take the example of Belgium. American financiers have just compelled a cut of $350,000,000 in the budget of that country as the price of advancing funds to stabilize the Belgian currency. Is the cut made in the cost of the useless army which could successfully defend Belgium against no adjacent Power, save possibly Holland? Not at all. The outcry in Belgium against the United States which has arisen since the facts became known and have been officially admitted by M. Vandervelde is reported to be in large measure due to the cutting of the appropriations for important social and cultural purposes. Belgium naturally resists any outside interference with her budget. She has a right to feel keenly, after all her experiences and hardships since 1914, that if some of the most important social services of the country are to be sacrificed to such an extent this particular budget-saving becomes not a blessing but an evil, the responsibility for which must be shared both by the Belgian Cabinet and the American financiers. Similarly it is of the utmost importance to find out in our own case whether the cuts are made in the right place and whether the taxes to be remitted are the proper ones.

A perusal of the President's budget messages and of Secretary Mellon's statements leaves us still unconvinced on more than one point. Thus the saving in taxes is to be only $336,000,000, less than 10 per cent of the amount to be raised in the coming fiscal year. Now, to maintain that the lopping off of $336,000,000 is necessary, as the President suggests, on the theory that undue taxation is confiscation of private property, seems to us absurd. So does the hoary old Mellon contention that if our high taxation is not reduced there will not be sufficient money available for new financing or for new business enterprises. The ridiculousness of that view is evident if we but consider the daily export of American capital to Europe and the willingness of the lenders to export a good deal more if Mr. Mellon were not using his control of private loans to compel debt adjustments—as he himself admits—and if we consider the almost incredible sums now being put into building enterprises. Thus, during the month of November, building and engineering contracts awarded in the thirty-six Eastern States amounted to $464,683,100, the highest recorded figure for any November and 23 per cent greater than the figure for November of last year. In New York and northern New Jersey alone the amount so invested rose to $160,629,500.

In the light of these figures anyone who maintains that it was necessary to cut $336,000,000 from the tax levy to keep business from being hamstrung through lack of capital is seeking to throw dust in people's eyes. The cut may be defended on other grounds—that too large surpluses make for waste and extravagance or that the individual burden of the small taxpayer is thereby reduced. But it cannot be truthfully alleged, as both Mr. Coolidge and Mr. Mellon have said, that it is necessary to make these cuts in order to keep business going and earning enough surplus so that new enterprises may be founded and old ones expanded. Let anyone read the list of extra dividends declared in the last few days in Wall Street and he will be convinced.

It must be noted, too, that this cut in taxes is made with little reference to the budget figures. The President has asked for appropriations for total expenditures for the fiscal year 1926-27 of $3,494,222,308.44. If that budget should be adhered to it would mean a cutting of government expenditures by $124,452,691. As a matter of fact, the budget for 1925-1926 called for only $3,267,551,000, but extraordinary or unforeseen expenditures will, it is now estimated, compel the government to disburse $3,618,675,000 by July first next —a little difference of $351,124,000 between the guess and the fulfilment. Contrasting, therefore, the original estimate for 1925-1926 and the proposed budget for 1926-1927 of this great administration of economy, it appears that so far from being a reduction the new budget is actually an increase over the old of $226,671,308.40.

Doubtless the public will continue to believe that Mr. Coolidge is economizing. As a matter of fact, if he really wishes to economize, he could not only keep this year's budget at last year's figures but he could reduce it still further. After solemnly assuring the American Legion that no army or navy protects a country from attack, and in the face of the coming disarmament conference, he has allotted an additional $20,000,000 to the navy while cutting the army by $4,124,000. The Veterans' Bureau is to receive $53,000,000 more and the pension roll goes up $8,000,000. These are necessary expenditures and merely the forerunners of still vaster ones to come. Others are waste.

The thoroughly uncivilized character of the budget, as well as the cost of wars, past and future, appears from the figures accompanying the budget compiled by the Budget Bureau itself. From this it appears that the general functions of government receive only 3.35 cents out of every dollar spent by the government, whereas 16.32 cents go to the national defense and 16.55 cents go to military pensions, retirement pay, and other expenditures growing out of past wars. Only 5.60 cents is spent upon public works and 7.40 cents on other civil functions. For our costly mercantile fleet we spend 1.88, for public debt retirement from ordinary receipts we spend 14.76, and for the interest on our public debts 22.75 cents. The government thus admits that out of every dollar 70.38 cents goes to wars past and present.

Is the World Court an Agency for Peace?

ONCE more we are asked to state our position on the World Court as an instrument of peace and as a step toward that community of nations which has been mankind's goal for centuries. Those who question us admit that the Court has its defects, but they advance the same arguments used when anyone points out the faults in the organization of the League of Nations. These are: "Well, come in and join and we'll improve it"; "Our own form of government was a failure at first and had to develop gradually into a real success"; "The Court, like the League, is young—give it the opportunity to grow"; "Like all reformers you refuse to join the Court because it does not exactly suit you instead of being practical and taking a three-quarter loaf when you can get it."

To these queries and comments we reply once more that we are opposed to the United States joining the Court except with a reservation that no force shall be used in carrying out any decrees affecting the United States, and with other safeguards. It is a sham and a pretense to offer the Court in its present form to the American people as an instrument of peace. Not only do multitudes so regard it but they also have been given the idea that everybody will run to submit his grievance to it and that the Court can compel attendance in some miraculous way even if offending nations are not members of the League or the Court itself. It has carefully been kept from the public that the Court's jurisdiction is extremely limited, so much so that, aside from the matter of advisory opinions, which may be requested by the Council of the League of Nations, it cannot take cognizance, even by consent of the parties involved, of those political and economic questions which today chiefly cause war. If force is to be used to carry out its decrees, it will by that much contribute to the continuance of war in the world. It will legalize wars sanctioned and provided for in the name of peace precisely as the Covenant of the League of Nations today provides and plans for war. Both contemplate keeping alive standing armies and the professional soldiery whose talk does so much to make peoples and governments plot, plan, and provide for war. Why should we in an era when the people of the world are thirsting for peace deliberately set up new institutions that make for force? If there is one lesson from the World War it is the utter failure of force. In China it has failed and in India; wherever one turns. It settles nothing; at best it merely postpones issues. Then why should reasonable people go into organizations which talk about sanctions, by which they mean not public opinion but the law of tooth and claw, of the bomb and of poison gas? What intelligent people are trying to do is to *outlaw war.* That is what counts and not the setting up of new international bodies or courts that *legalize* war and deliberately contemplate the creating of war in given contingencies.

Of course, we are well aware that at this point we shall be asked whether any court can get on without a force *in esse* or *in posse* ready to carry out its decrees. We are fortunately in a position to quote some extremely practical statesman who have intrenched themselves on exactly the same ground in this matter of force. There was the late Senator P. C. Knox, for instance, a big-business man, a former Secretary of State, and a former Attorney General. He was absolutely opposed to the use of force to support the decrees of a world court. No one will charge Charles E. Hughes with being a pacifist or an impractical editor. Yet he has stated that "when nations agree to submit a dispute to a tribunal and to abide by the decision, its observance is a point of international honor of the highest sort. You can really have no better sanction that this." He also pointed out that "all contrivances for maintaining peace by economic pressure, as well as by military force . . . are likely to fail when they are most needed because national interests are diverse and unanimity of action under stress of crises . . . is well nigh impossible." Mr. Hughes is a modern. Oliver Ellsworth once stood before the Connecticut Convention to declare that the States must choose between a coercion of law and a coercion of arms, and to assert that the latter would lead inevitably to a war of States. James Madison stated that "the more he reflected on the use of force, the more he doubted the practicability, the justice, the efficacy of it." A union of States, containing such an ingredient, seemed to him to provide for its own destruction. The use of force against a State would look like a declaration of war. John Marshall also had his doubts about the use of force. As long as force is provided for the World Court, or the United States cannot safeguard itself against the use of force in matters to which it is a party, or in the outcome of which it has an interest, we shall have to stand with Senator Borah in thinking of the Court as an instrument of war and not one of peace.

There are other points which we might dwell upon, such as the question of advisory opinions through which the League can exercise political control over any country, even one which is not a member, as witness the treatment of Turkey in the Mosul case. Some advocates of the League are frank to say privately that that is what they want, just as they say privately that they believe that our entering the Court will get us into the League and that is why they are for it, while at the same time trying to prove publicly that the Court has no relationship whatever with the League. But we do not care to go into these points at this juncture. What is controlling with us is this question of force.

We would once more make our position plain: *The Nation* is in favor of a World Court with obligatory jurisdiction in legal questions, but depending only upon its moral authority for the bringing of disputants into court and for the enforcement of its decrees. We desire a court absolutely separated from the League of Nations, controlled as it is by a group of three or four powerful countries. We believe in a court which shall not be called upon to give advisory opinions to the League or its Council and will be unable to do so if asked, but shall be willing to give advisory opinions to individual nations in their individual capacity and not as members of the League. We desire no sanctions for such a court save public opinion; we are opposed to the use of any political or military machinery to enforce any decree, and we submit that the success of arbitration since 1787 affords no room for doubt, despite four or five rejections of arbitral decisions, that the authority of the kind of court we have described would be sufficient to make the nations of the world accept its decrees. If any nation did not, it would face world-wide odium and reproach, but even such a refusal could be only a temporary backset to a court rightly organized and avowedly conducted with entire faith in the public opinion of the world.

Our Naval and Army Waste

ON one day, February 16, the two houses of Congress voted appropriations of no less than $660,925,940 for national defense. Of this vast amount $339,300,000 was in the army bill, which was passed by the House without a record vote. In the Senate the navy bill, containing $321,495,940, slipped through easily. On the same day it was announced that the House Naval Committee had agreed to a five-year naval aviation program, costing $100,000,000, to be expended at the rate of $20,000,000 a year. With this sum we are to build two dirigibles, each three times the size of the ill-fated Shenandoah; a metal-clad dirigible; and one thousand new airplanes—all of this despite the fact that no progress whatsoever has been made in remedying the conditions in the army and navy brought out by General Mitchell and other reliable witnesses. We are going ahead trusting the expenditure of this vast sum to the same people who have shown their incompetence, with the inevitable result that we shall have extremely little to produce for the expenditures and shall probably see the three dirigibles go out of business as rapidly as did the Shenandoah.

Since 1885 the United States has spent no less than eight billions of dollars upon its navy alone. For the fiscal year 1923 the appropriations were $322,532,908; for 1926 they fell to $317,000,000, and for 1927 they have again gone up $4,500,000. The Senate restored to the bill two items, aggregating $9,000,000, for new airplanes and aircraft equipment, and for continuing the Lakehurst air station, which had been struck out by the House. In the navy, therefore, the Coolidge policy of economy will have resulted in decreased appropriations of $1,500,000 over 1923. If to this is annually added the $20,000,000 recommended by the House Naval Committee we shall be spending about $19,000,000 a year more on our navy.

Not the least discouraging feature is that so vast an appropriation as that of the army bill can be jammed through the House without adequate discussion or analysis. We are particularly disappointed that the Progressive group in the House did not at least offer an amendment putting a definite limit on the number of reserve officers and forbidding the use of regular army officers or men in the high schools of the country. The fact is that there are now approximately 90,000 reserve officers who have been commissioned since the war. If the War Department continues its policy of commissioning them without limit there will soon be more reserve officers than there are soldiers and officers in the entire regular army. Since these reserve officers are not paid and have to purchase their own equipment Congress has not interfered. The result is that the General Staff is building up in these officers another military machine which is already exerting pressure on Congress for larger and larger appropriations. Congressmen and Senators who dare to speak out against our drifting into old-fashioned German militarism find themselves assailed by letters from reserve officers throughout their States. The effort of the War Department to muzzle those reserve officers who happen to have liberal opinions was brought out in the case of Captain Paxton Hibben. Press dispatches stated after the first mobilization day that it was the intention of the War Department to place one reserve officer in every community as a center of militaristic and nationalistic propaganda hidden under the name of patriotism. Where is this Prussianization to stop?

But this is not the only subject into which both House and Senate ought to delve before passing such an appropriation bill. The army itself is scandalously over-officered, while its regiments are depleted and many of its companies are nothing less than a corporal's guard, partly because of the effort to keep in existence so many regimental organizations and because of the evil of detached duties. The entire service is discouraged by the present management, and some of the best officers, like two of the world fliers, are quitting the service. More would go if they could find opportunities outside. Yet we have a huge list of generals and colonels and we are actually able to detach no fewer than 768 officers for teaching at colleges and schools. Most of the training given by these officers is absolutely worthless from the strictly military point of view. It is their military propaganda which the War Department values. Since the ablest gymnastic instructors in the country are agreed on the worthlessness of two drills a week from the physical point of view, Congress ought to abolish the whole thing. But Congress does just what the War Department asks, and this in the face of the fact that the majority's President, Mr. Calvin Coolidge, in his speech before the American Legion on October 6, declared that "no nation ever had an army large enough to guarantee it against attack in time of peace or to insure its victory in time of war," and asserted that everyone knew that the old military systems and "reliance on force have failed." Yet we go ahead squandering half billions on force. And the practice goes on because nobody or no group in Congress is determined to call a halt or study this question of defense intelligently.

The League Unveiled

AGAIN has the League of Nations revealed its inability to grapple with an important issue; this time so spectacularly that even its ardent champions are abashed. When the League kept silent in the face of the Ruhr outrage, defaulted on the opium issue, ran away from the Mosul question, and abdicated its functions when Mussolini murdered defenseless orphans in Corfu, we heard apologies and excuses without end. The League was young; give it a chance. By turning over the Corfu incident to the Council of Ambassadors the League's Council showed, we were told, great skill in avoiding an issue which might have disrupted the organization, an issue the ambassadors could handle as well. Thus ran the excuses. Now even the New York *Times* admits that it is "vain to deny" that the Geneva fiasco is a blow "to the prestige of the League." We are even spared the familiar poppycock that if the United States had been in the League this would not have happened. True, the *Times* comforts itself with the thought that all will be well in September when the Council will be reformed and Germany triumphantly admitted, and it gleefully declares that at least this proves that the League is not a superstate since the vote of one minor Power upset the program.

Out of that hope and that assertion the advocates of the League may get what comfort they can. The fact remains that the spectacle at Geneva was as humiliating as it was disgusting—and alarming. For here was deliberate trickery; here was evidence that Europe has learned nothing whatever from the alleged war to end war; here was the breaking of faith by England and France and Italy because, having made secret agreements at Locarno, they found themselves unable to deliver the goods or did not wish to when the time came. No sensible person can believe that Brazil out of mere incarnate deviltry of its own, out of wanton selfishness, put the League on the rocks. Had that been the case the welkin would have rung with denunciations of Brazil, and rightly so. Instead, there is hardly a word of castigation—merely a hasty creating of a committee to suggest some way of reconstituting the Council when the September meeting takes place. Brazil's action was actually welcome for the delay it created. Even the most anti-German correspondents admit that Germany acted correctly. The truth is that there was a deliberate effort to recreate the old, deadly European balance of power and that the chief Allies, after publicly declaring their purpose to put Germany into the League, found themselves unable to do so because of private commitments by their envoys, one of whom, Austen Chamberlain, was at once disavowed by public opinion at home. Again, we have the confession of the correctness of the opposition's constantly voiced contention that, as long as the Council is organized as it is, it is useless to expect the League radically to reform itself or be the instrument of anything but the will of France, or England, or the Franco-Balkan group of states. Finally, as Gilbert Murray has written to the London *Times*, the League abdicated. There was no public meeting of the Council and no meeting whatsoever of the Assembly. As he puts it: "The League ceased to function while particular groups of Powers met and struggled and bargained in secret."

We have not the least desire to say we told you so. We are too aghast at the sordid spectacle of the same old kind of diplomacy which led Europe to disaster; at the vision of nationalism run wild which all the European correspondents of the great dailies have presented to us. For the nationalism the League is doubtless not to blame. Yet it is the very state of mind which the League was supposed to exorcise. What the correspondents have cabled has been more than confirmed by the unprecedentedly frank statements published from the White House as to the reports given to the President by Ambassador Houghton and Minister Gibson, who were specially summoned from Europe to discuss the situation. They are reported to have set forth that the League "is no longer a world league, but a European council which is in process of splitting into two camps and destined to lapse into impotency." It is further declared that the Powers neither wish to disarm nor to have the United States in their councils, and that each faction "is seeking to use this country as a catspaw to pull its own particular chestnuts out of the fire." As for disarmament, the report avers that the proposals are but "gestures to forestall the demands of Germany that the agreement embodied in the Treaty of Versailles for general disarmament be undertaken as soon as Germany is in the League." These diplomats are even indirectly quoted as saying that the present governments of Europe "are thinking only of national prestige and imperialist ambition, and of setting up combinations and alliances which will be able to face any other combination or alliance which an opposing group of nations may propose." Is there anything in this to encourage Americans to enter the League?

But, we hear it said, are you not then abandoning all hope for Europe; are you not presenting merely a picture of a Europe once more armed to the teeth and headed for destruction; are you not yielding the ground to every militarist in the United States? We cannot deny that this news from Europe will hearten every American militarist. Senator Reed even goes so far as to declare that if the American people understood it they would be drilling in every county in the land—a ridiculous absurdity. But we are not discouraged by all this because the situation has not fundamentally changed. *The Nation* has said from the day the Treaty of Versailles was published that there could be no peace in Europe until that infamous document was done away with, and it has opposed both the League and the World Court for the adequate reason that both of them kept alive the spirit of militarism and of making war which is at the bottom of all the mess in Europe. We have never faltered in our belief that the world was divided into two camps the day that the treaty was signed, and that until a new social spirit comes there will be little hope for a rapid advancement of mankind, however great the encouragement of a Locarno. We are now inclined to think that the revelation of what the League is, the unveiling of its inwardness which we are just beholding, will do more good than harm if it ends the agitation for our entrance into the League and compels us to face the facts to decide whither we are heading, and to work out a foreign policy which shall not be based on force or be the excuse for army and navy, but shall be founded upon the historic American doctrine of keeping out of entangling alliances and political commitments. Let us keep to ourselves politically.

The Nakedness of Colonel House

By OSWALD GARRISON VILLARD

"THE Intimate Papers of Colonel House,"* by the Colonel and his editor, Professor Charles Seymour of Yale, do more than tear the mask from the face of the most amazing character and the most interesting lesser personality of the Wilson Administrations. They strip him to the buff. No more extraordinary self-revelation can be found in the memoirs of statesmen and public men, and it is the more remarkable because of the unconsciousness of the revealing. What could have induced Colonel House thus to show his hand and to step out of the character of the man of silence and mystery which he played upon a world stage is not clear, unless it was that he felt the necessity of replying to the letters of Walter Page. To him the Colonel *has* replied, and in doing so he has demolished with a few rounds of grape the elaborate structure of glorification lately set up about the former Ambassador to Great Britain. But in so doing he has bared himself, retaining not even a fig-leaf, and the picture is not one to enchant in so far as his political activities are concerned. True this Texas comet, which suddenly shone in the diplomatic heavens and made its rapid and brilliant way through that celestial sphere, cast a bright light while it traveled on its way. It did illumine the heavens; it did focus upon itself the attention of all astronomers and observers. But when it faded out it left the heavens exactly as they had been and thereby only accentuated the remoteness and the dulness of the professional statesman-stars across whose orbits the comet had flashed.

Beyond doubt here is an engaging personality. Shrewdness, the ability to draw others out, a tremendous power of sympathy and quick understanding, of eager friendliness, of apparent unselfishness, of profound interest in world problems—all of these combined, in addition to his personal attractiveness, to fit Colonel House for the role of king-maker and of king-director. As to this we have the testimony of Viscount Grey, who yielded on sight to the Colonel's charms. "It was not necessary to spend much time in putting our case to him. He had a way of saying 'I know it' in a tone and manner which carried conviction both of his sympathy with an understanding of what was said to him. . . . I found combined in him in a rare degree the qualities of wisdom and sympathy. In the stress of war it was at once a relief, a delight, and an advantage to be able to talk with him freely. His criticism or comment was valuable, his suggestions were fertile, and these were all conveyed with a sympathy that made it pleasant to listen to them." H. N. Brailsford adds this to the picture: "House had a way of impressing his personality with some unconscious magic on those with whom he talked. He seemed curiously modest. He talked very simply. One felt . . . his courtesy and sincerity." But this work has not proved him to have been entirely sincere or disinterested. It makes it clear that if he waved aside high public office, such as the Secretaryship of State, it was because he wished to be President or nothing—"nothing less than that would satisfy me . . ." he himself says. He obtained precisely what he wanted, namely, the position of the power behind the throne, and it flattered his vanity and caressed his ego far more than would have been the case had he accepted the Secretaryship of State and been held accountable by the country and the press for his official acts.

Public men, office-seekers, press men—whose editorials and dispatches he constantly dictated—came to him for aid, for news, for a thousand different things. He was errand boy, court chamberlain, buffer extraordinary, minister plenipotentiary, chief justice, writer of presidential notes, opinions, and speeches, chief of the secret service, the perfect counselor, and finally the self-appointed arbiter of the world's destiny. There is nothing like it in the political history of the United States, and nothing like it in the history of the modern world. Foreign diplomats took their orders from him—Spring-Rice came to House's heel when called like a well-trained setter (see Vol. I, p. 326). On one occasion, writes the Colonel to Wilson, "Spring-Rice wished to know if he was doing anything wrong or everything to please the State Depart-

* Houghton Mifflin Company. 2 vols. $10.

ment. It was rather a staggering question, and I had to tell him that some of his methods might be improved upon. *He promised to do better*" (italics mine). Even when so big a man as Franklin K. Lane wished to find out if he was doing well as a Cabinet official and pleasing the President he went not to the President but asked Colonel House. There can be no doubt that no other private citizen ever wielded greater power; and it, of course, could only have been wielded by a big and able man. This he did by the consent of the President, conscious and unconscious. It is safe to say that such an arrangement would have been tolerated by no other personality than that of Wilson, whose shyness, aloofness, and embarrassment in meeting people, as well as his laziness and procrastination, made him only too happy to have in Colonel House a friend who kept away hundreds of bores, saved the executive offices from conducting much correspondence that otherwise would have poured in upon it, and relieved him of endless labor.

There is no denying that in these volumes Colonel House and his editor, Professor Seymour, reveal constantly a very great satisfaction with the achievements of Edward M. House. To them it is not only an all but impeccable record but the most magnificent credited to any man among all the leaders of all the nations which were drawn into the war. Others might err—even President Wilson could blunder—but it is not often that Homer is allowed to nod. They are right in taking satisfaction in it, and the hidebound partisans of Woodrow Wilson are equally justified in gnashing their teeth over this record. They cannot deny that Colonel House helped to force Bryan upon the President, made up the Cabinet, and furnished ideas for it. It was the Colonel who, we now learn, originated all or a good part of that magnificent program of social and economic reform which made the first two years of Wilson's regime so brilliant in achievement. They cannot deny that when it came to foreign affairs House took the lead, that he conceived policy after policy, and that Mr. Wilson accepted them and constantly wrote to him asking him for advice and aid as to how he should reply to a letter or a note or what policy he should institute or follow. Here is proof that House composed some of Wilson's most important speeches.

Besides the Cabinet officers, Colonel House chose the ambassadors—a sorry job he made of it, too—and actually notified them of their appointments and told them how they were to behave. The most amazing thing about it all is the way the Cabinet officers and the diplomats submitted to this government by an irresponsible individual. The Secretaries of State were apparently willing that they should be ignored and the public business conducted by Colonel House on secret instructions of which they were ignorant. Cabinet officers reported to him; they frequently could not communicate with the President or see him for weeks at a time—Lane alone was allowed to discuss with Wilson the Lusitania note before it was written, and that only over the telephone. The more the President lost faith in some of his Cabinet and his diplomats, and he lost that faith quickly in several cases, the more he was willing that Colonel House should take them off his hands. How Walter Page with any self-respect could have retained his position as Ambassador to Great Britain is beyond explanation; he must have been supremely dense not to have suspected that House was in London because the President, who often did not answer his letters, had no further use for him, and not to have insisted upon his resignation when he found that he could not take part with Colonel House in urging mediation upon the Allies.

Now, with all respect to both House and Wilson, the role assumed by Colonel House was one that could only result in disaster, as it finally did in the irrevocable break between the two men. This was due apparently to the feeling of the President that his Cardinal Wolsey had been faithless to his god in the White House, just as once before the relations between Colonel House and the President were summarily broken off—something not recorded in the volumes before us. Moreover, the position that House assumed compelled, I am inclined to think, insincerity and double-dealing, and more so as time went on. He became more and more Machiavellian. Thus, he claimed to be a pacifist—Professor Seymour even dares to say that this man who approved the slaughter of men, women, and children at Vera Cruz, the lawless invasion of Mexico by Pershing, and the murder of nearly three thousand Haitians under President Wilson's orders, "was himself, perhaps, the most sincere pacifist in America. . . ." (Vol. I, p. 21.) Well, if deceiving the pacifists who came to him in good faith and belief in his sincerity makes House a sincere pacifist, he is entitled to the credit. His real attitude he reveals when he boasts (Vol. II, p. 96) that he stirred up a controversy between a group of them "*as usual* . . . which delights me."

Again, at the very time that he was making the pacifists believe that he was one of them he was working with General Wood in the interest of preparedness and plotting how he could bring the President over to all of General Wood's plans for armament. Similarly he was for ruthlessness in dealing with any disturbing elements in the country. He wanted Congress to give the President more power for the immediate deportation of "hyphenates," he consulted with chiefs of police as to how drastically disturbing elements should be handled if it came to disorder. "I urged Baker to use a firm hand in the event trouble should manifest itself in any way. I thought it was mistaken mercy to temporize with troubles of this sort"—in which attitude he again unanimously agreed with his friend the Kaiser and once more showed himself the "sincere pacifist." Subsequently he always appeared to sympathize with those who came to him protesting against the infringement of American rights and liberties after the outbreak of the war, and particularly against the maltreatment of conscientious objectors, and to regret those official excesses. It is impossible now to believe that he was not in thorough accord with what actually took place—to the nation's dishonor.

His job compelled him to be all things to all men, compelled him to toady, compelled him to play one group against another, the Germans against the English, the French against the British. It compelled him more and more to devious ways which he herein sets forth in complete nudity, as, for instance, when he proposed to the British Cabinet a plan to get the United States into the war on the side of the Allies through a set of terms phrased in such a way that the Germans would fall into a trap. If the Germans refused to bite, he, Edward M. House, an unofficial citizen of Texas, promised the British Government that the United States would enter the war on the side of the Allies!*

Here we have the most startling revelation of all. This official-unofficial intriguer had grown so great in his self-

* "It is in my mind that, after conferring with your government, I should proceed to Berlin and tell them that it was the President's purpose to intervene and stop this destructive war, provided the weight of the United States thrown on the side that accepted our proposal could do it. I would not let Berlin know, of course, of any understanding had with the Allies, but would rather lead them to think that our proposal would be rejected by the Allies. This might induce Berlin to accept the proposal but, if it did not do so, it would, nevertheless, be the purpose to intervene." (House to Grey, October 17, 1915, Vol. II, pp. 90-91.)

esteem and his power by 1916 that he did not hesitate to gamble with the lives of American citizens as if they were his peons. He cites Gerard's indignation with the Kaiser for speaking of the German, Russian, and English people as if they "were so many pawns upon a chessboard," but on his lone authority House brushes aside the Congress of the United States and repeatedly notifies Sir Edward Grey that in certain contingencies the United States will join forces with the Allies. As Professor Seymour puts it (Vol. II, p. 179): "House promised that if the Germans refused to accept the terms he had outlined, the United States would enter the war. This tentative understanding, of course, was to be dependent upon the approval of the allies of Great Britain." Nothing said about the approval of the White House, although Mr. Wilson was at that time entirely opposed to our entering the war—House felt sure the President would obey him! Nothing said about the Congress, the war-making power in the United States. Nothing said about the American people, who might have been expected to have some say as to whether their sons should be swept into the war. So it went right along. House promised from the beginning that the United States would enter the League of Nations, forgetting to his cost the existence of the United States Senate. Yes, even as far back as 1913, before the war, he had the effrontery to offer the Kaiser, whom he was so soon thereafter to call a bloodthirsty wretch, an alliance with the United States. "I spoke of the community of interests between England, Germany, and the United States, and thought if they stood together the peace of the world could be maintained." On January 11, 1916, he records that he told Balfour and Grey that Wilson would throw over our historic policy of no entangling alliances with Europe and would enter into an agreement with the European nations in matters such as navalism, militarism, etc.—George Washington supplanted by Edward M. House. On February 7, 1916, he records: "I again told them [Briand and Cambon] that the lower the fortunes of the Allies ebbed, the closer the United States would stand by them."

Curiously, while he was doing this he was bewailing the fact that the destinies of the people of Europe were being settled by their leaders without their knowing anything about it. Thus he wrote on June 23, 1916: "It is not the people who speak, but their masters, and some day, I pray, the voice of the people may have direct expression in international affairs as they are beginning to have it in national affairs." This from the man who, without official authority, was, with Woodrow Wilson, the master of the fate of the American people—who were, for all House's pious wish for democracy in international affairs, permitted by him and by Mr. Wilson to know nothing about what was going on behind the scenes. Professor Seymour recalls with satisfaction that the purpose of House's most important trip to Europe offering mediation never reached the press of the United States.

The history of statecraft surely contains no record of anything approximating the naivete and the innocence and the self-conceit with which House tackled the European problem. Never having had anything to do with foreign affairs in any capacity theretofore, he assured the Kaiser on June 1, 1914, that the President and he "thought perhaps an American might be able to better compose the difficulties here and bring about an understanding with a view to peace than any European, because of their distrust and dislike for one another." *"I had undertaken the work,"* he continued, *"and that was my reason for coming to Germany,* as I wanted to see him first"—a kindly consideration that must have gratified His Majesty. House of Texas was in the field to compose differences and dislikes rooted in a thousand years of peace and war! But that is merely one sample. What could surpass his writing to Woodrow Wilson on June 17, 1914, that the French "statesmen dream no longer of revenge and the recovery of Alsace-Lorraine. The people do, but those who govern and know hope only that France may continue as now"? At the very moment that House penned these lines, Poincaré was plotting a world war and, a month later, left for Russia to complete those negotiations for the attack upon Germany which came to naught only because Serbia struck first. He was so ignorant of the actual causes of the war as to do England the gross injustice of saying she went into war "primarily . . . because Germany insisted upon having a dominant army and a dominant (*sic*) navy" (June 29, 1916). It is no wonder that the Germans smiled behind Colonel House's back when he first came to Berlin in 1913, and said: "Er ist zu einfach"—he is too simple.

And simple he was all the way through. He would suggest his mediation scheme to the French ministers and the fact that they listened earnestly to him and said "how interesting" convinced him that he had impressed them with his cause. Despite his natural sagacity and power the British Cabinet strung him along for months so that he could write the most encouraging letters to Mr. Wilson, and then it all came to naught. Naturally, he blames the British Cabinet ministers, even his friend Grey a bit, and bewails their inability to seize upon the golden opportunity: "Colonel House was naturally and bitterly disappointed," writes his Boswell. Often he was delightfully fooled by the British ministers, as on February 14, 1916, when he had a long talk with Lloyd George, Balfour, Grey, and Asquith: "We all," he says, "cheerfully divided up Turkey both in Asia and Europe." But as Professor Seymour points out in a footnote his hosts did not take the trouble to tell House about the secret treaties which these same four gentlemen had already signed partitioning the Turkish empire as part of their unselfish war for liberty and the rights of small nations and the self-determination of peoples. Finally, what could surpass in incredible, overpowering egotism House's writing to the President on February 1?, 1916: "In my opinion hell will break loose in Europe this spring and summer as never before; *and I see no way to stop it for the moment. . . .*"?

Yet curiously enough, while being fooled by individual ministers, House at times showed that he did understand the motives and the character of the governments with which he sought to cope. The Germans he sized up admirably; he took their measure well and gauged their weaknesses, strength, stupidities; their political follies; their self-suicide. On May 17, 1916, he wrote to Wilson: "The more I see of the dealing of governments among themselves the more I am impressed with the utter selfishness of their outlook. Gratitude is a thing unknown, and all we have done for the Allies will be forgotten overnight if we antagonize them now"—incidentally a delightful admission that the United States *had* been helping the Allies during the very time when President Wilson had officially called upon his countrymen to be neutral in thought and deed! On April 30, 1916, he was even franker: "What the Allies want *is to dip their hands into our treasure chest.* While the war has become a war of democracy against autocracy, not one of the democracies entered it to fight for democracy. . . ." Again, writing on May 24, 1916, he said: "It is evident that unless the United States is willing to sacrifice hundreds of thousands of lives and billions of treasure we are not to be on good terms with the

Allies. . . ." House was always properly and righteously expressing his abhorrence of German militarism, as when he wrote to Grey that Germany must be taught its futility. But when it came to the pinch he was equally ready to suggest that we do precisely the same thing that the Germans had. Thus he regrets constantly that we did not arm to the teeth the minute the war began so that we could have compelled England and Germany to yield to us, and he does not see that that was precisely the Kaiser's philosophy of using might to do what he thought was right. In the event of the failure of his mediation he for a time believed we ought to arm on sea and on land to the limit and then retreat into our shell and sit waiting for anything to turn up that might. In other words, he was as bankrupt of rational remedies as any of the European statesmen that he criticizes. He wanted his League of Nations only, apparently, if we could enter the war in such a manner that we could dictate the peace.

And how he wobbled as to whether we should or should not enter the war! Immediately after the sinking of the Lusitania he declared: "America has come to the parting of the ways, when she must determine whether she stands for civilized or uncivilized warfare. We can no longer remain neutral spectators." On August 22, 1915, House urged the President to send Bernstorff home at once, although he believed that it meant war, but Mr. Wilson refused to be convinced. Every now and then the President did refuse to follow the dictates of his mentor and Colonel House confesses that he overplayed his hand on occasion. By January 6, 1916, House told Sir Edward Grey that he was advising the President against actually breaking with Germany and thus recorded his opinion: "I thought it far better for the democracy of the world to unite upon some plan that would enable the United States to intervene, than for us to drift into the war by breaking diplomatic relations with the Central Powers. . . . I confess having advised the President against an actual break with Germany at this time"—an entire change of front. By July 16 of that year he had swung around once more and it is written that he felt that ultimate cooperation with the Allies in the war was "inevitable."

But when it came to the Presidential election of 1916 Colonel House was all for trumpeting the fact abroad that Mr. Wilson had kept the country out of the war and for concealing the fact still further that he [House] had done his best at times to put the country into it and still believed it inevitable. Politician that he was, he knew well that the mass of the plain people were utterly opposed to our going to war, and so he cynically recommended to the President that he play up to that sentiment—even Professor Seymour finds it necessary in a footnote to gloss over this inconsistency. "The keeping the country out of war, and the great measures you have enacted into law, should be our battle-cry," wrote House to Wilson July 5, 1916. Assiduously the cry of "he kept us out of war" was spread all over the country, and it undoubtedly won the election for Wilson, because the multitudes of mothers who voted for him did so because of the implied promise in that slogan that Wilson would continue to keep the country out of war. Let anyone who questions this reread the keynote speech of Governor Glynn of New York at the St. Louis convention which renominated Wilson. That speech of Governor Glynn's was read and edited by House and Wilson before it was delivered—"The President and I will aid him [Glynn]," wrote House, "in preparing the keynote speech. I agreed to take charge of it, and after the speech is finished I am to send it to the President for criticism." Yet Professor Seymour thinks it would have been "rather Quixotic" for House to fail to take advantage of this peace-desiring American mood, although he "had himself advocated a plan" which, if accepted, "would have brought us into the war." This is what happens to the morals of certain types of idealists when they get into politics and have power placed in their irresponsible hands.

Thus runs this chronicle of egotistic futility to the very end. House could see clearly the weaknesses of the Allied statesmen, as when he wrote: "My observation is that incompetent statesmanship and selfishness is at the bottom of it all. It is not so much a breaking down of civilization as a lack of wisdom in those that govern; and history, I believe, will bring an awful indictment against those who were shortsighted and selfish enough to let such a tragedy happen." And yet he had no other vision than to drag America into the mess, and when he and his chief reached Paris (his views as to Paris we shall doubtless get in a later volume) they were checkmated, overwhelmed, routed by the very shortsighted, incompetent, selfish statesmen whom he so denounced and by their own lack of wisdom and force. Lowes Dickinson has written of these statesmen: "What little puppets, knocking away, with Lilliputian hammers, the last stays that restrain the launch of that great death-ship, War." When it came to docking that ship and putting it out of commission again, House's little hammer was not as efficient as that of the other Lilliputians. He could see clearly that if the Germans won "the war lords will reign supreme and democratic government will be imperiled throughout the world." But he could not see that the abandonment of his and his chief's soundest position that there should be "peace without victory," "no victors and no vanquished," insured the similar imperilment of democracies by the complete victory of the United States and the Allies, so that today democracy is dead in Italy, Russia, Greece, Hungary, and Spain, and totters in as many more. House had a conception of compelling peace, but he wanted to do it alone with Mr. Wilson, and he declined the safe way urged by Secretary Bryan (whom he called a mischief maker), namely, the rallying of all the neutral nations to demand the cessation of the war, a practical and entirely wise proposal urged again and again, but in vain, upon House and Wilson by the smaller neutrals. So the Colonel's triumphs turned to ashes. The unbiased historian must declare him as discredited as any of the other war lords if measured by his achievements and the results of his policies. Colonel House will not be judged by the record of this book alone. The Wilsonians will have the next inning and there are many letters omitted from these volumes which will then see the light of day. They will be certain to bring into sharper relief his self-contentment, his frequent errors, and the extent of his frailties.

On all counts the record must not be allowed to stop here. Nemesis, the Nemesis of stark Greek tragedy, awaited the Colonel at Paris. Nothing came of his plan for dictating the peace, beyond the League of Nations, which may not survive the year. The friendship which was the most valuable thing in the world to him came to an abrupt end and this time was not restored. Colonel House was never again allowed to see the President he helped to make and so largely inspired. That President went into the war against his better judgment. He knew that "it would mean that a majority of the people in this hemisphere would go war mad, quit thinking, and devote their energies to destruction. . . ." "Once lead this people into war and they'll forget there ever was such a thing as tolerance." He knew that a peace dictated by the victors would rest upon quicksand, for he said so January 22, 1917.

By this his own record there rests upon the Colonel's head a large share of the blood guilt for those 70,000 American soldiers who were done to death in France in considerable degree because of House's unofficial administration of our foreign affairs—as uselessly done to death as if they had been shot down on the prairies of Nebraska in cold blood by their own fellow-citizens, so far as the realization of the Fourteen Peace Points or any of the American ideals in entering the war is concerned. For the condition of Europe today is infinitely worse than in June 1, 1914, when Colonel House turned up in Potsdam, calmly assured the Kaiser that only an American could solve Europe's troubles and end her rivalries, and added: "Kaiser, I am here."

April 21, 1926

My dear Stanwood:

Of course we believe that we can be sure of the results of our preachments along certain lines. For one thing, we are the only people holding to the spirit and the tenets of the founders of the country in our fight for personal liberty, and against the military system which, as President Coolidge said to the Legion, protects and safeguards nobody. We are absolutely certain that a continuance of the present system and conditions can only result in an explosion similar to that in Russia and marked by even greater excesses and bloodshed.

Do you not see from the very fact that not over 50% of the people go to the polls that you and yours have destroyed the faith of Americans in their government and their institutions? It is not we who keep men from the polls; we liberals go ourselves and do everything we can to get our friends to go. You and your kind have so destroyed the interest of the people in their country and their government that they are utterly disgusted and do not care a tinker's dam what happens.

At one point I take the sharpest issue with you--I *want* to break down reverence for the State whenever it sets up to control the conscience and the personal liberty of individuals, if only because the State has of late, in all countries (see Memoirs of Col. House for proof) degenerated into control of the destinies of the people by two or three irres-

----2

ponsible men drunk with power and all too often deliberately crooked, like Mussolini. There are many things above the State and superior to it, and one of these is Christianity. Where the teachings of Jesus and allegiance to the State conflict, you will invariably find me putting Jesus above the State. Reverence for the State?--Lord, what has the State been and what is it today in the United States, but big business personified? What was it in Germany? What was it in Russia? What is it in Italy and Spain? Why *should* we reverence it? It is meant to be the servant of peoples, and it has become their master and beyond their control, slaughtering millions as it will.

Sincerely yours,

Mr. S. Stanwood Menken,
52 William Street
New York City.

Our Faltering Faith in Democracy

WHY is it that the faith in democracy of so many Americans falters? It is only eight years since we were risking our all to make the world safe for democracy. Now, wherever one goes, one hears doubts. Every catch-word, every high-sounding phrase of war days has disappeared. On either hand are frank envy of the Italian and Spanish dictatorships, disgust with the shortcomings of parliamentarism and the ardent wish that Congress could be prorogued for years or altogether abolished, and a total loss of faith in the wisdom of the multitude. Every altruistic appeal for pure democracy falls on deaf ears; political progress languishes because so many have, for the hour, lost interest in matters political.

The intense hatred against the Soviets is based not on their being run as an undemocratic oligarchy but because they oppose the institution of private property. A distinguished and titled foreigner who has just returned to Europe is telling people over there of his surprise in finding Mussolini the most popular man in the homes of the wealthy he visited here. Business everywhere worships Mussolini because he frankly says that he "wipes his feet on liberty," that "the old liberal democracy is dead," and because he is the apostle of efficiency and of doing things.

Now, the interesting thing is that this obvious loss of the old American faith for which our men are supposed to have died in France is coincident with a greater effort to teach patriotism and to compel loyalty to the ideals of America than we have ever before witnessed. Our school-children are compelled daily to salute the flag, to chant an oath of loyalty, to swear fealty to the Constitution, to write essays about it, to believe that it is the summation of human achievement in politics. They are marshaled into patriotism on Washington's Birthday and Lincoln's Birthday, the Fourth of July, Flag Day, Navy Day, and some on Defense Day. When they get to college they have patriotism inculcated into them in the Reserve Officers' Training Corps by excellent imitations of the Kaiser's goose-stepping lieutenants.

We have all but stopped immigration, and a hundred different agencies are at work Americanizing the foreign-born who are here. And while we Americanize them the prosperous and pedigreed Americans, the old stock itself, more and more lose faith in the fundamentals which the Americanizers are teaching. We regiment and we machine-make the products of our public schools and teach them, in so far as they think at all, to think alike and to believe absolutely in the existing social, political, and economic order; and then we find the descendants of the earliest settlers joining Elbert Gary in praying for a Mussolini in the White House and in showing utter indifference to our daily violations of some of the oldest American traditions and of the Constitution itself.

Well, the explanations are numerous. In the very effort of idolizing the founders, the warriors and statesmen of the past, we forget to inculcate the *spirit* of our institutions. We tell the children that they must worship Washington and Jefferson and Hamilton and Lincoln and Grant, and never tell them why. Abstract liberty is not put upon a pedestal; democracy is not taught as *democracy*. Every effort is made to induce the oncoming generation to accept their elders' appraisal of our country, and never to rouse their curiosity to ascertain what is behind our institutions, lest they discover that there is something wrong with them or in some way imbibe an admiration for another kind of government. And yet, per contra, there are none so afraid for our government as the fiercest of our Americanizers and our standardizers. Let one poor Bolshevist knock at our doors and they see the end of the American republic. They would prevent, if they could, the slightest discussion of communism lest somebody like it better than our own forms of administration. Hence, they insist upon everybody's believing with them and forget to make it clear why they should believe and what the basis for each belief is. They have developed a form of ancestor worship which can brook no protest and no apostasy.

But while they worship the ancestors, they themselves forget, if they ever knew, what those ancestors severally stood for. So they are filled with horror when a Rupert Hughes says that George Washington was like every other prosperous gentleman of his time, a good sport who liked his dance, his song, his wine, and dared to be interested in women. The leaders of the movement to purchase Monticello have appealed for public support because they believe it to be a patriotic act to exalt Thomas Jefferson now that the republic is menaced by bolshevism, completely forgetting, if they ever knew, that Thomas Jefferson preached physical revolution against the government every twenty-five years and otherwise uttered sentiments which would place one in jail were one to call oneself a Socialist or Bolshevist and utter them publicly in some of our cities today. Finally, we have a country sunk in materialism which is perfectly willing to go through patriotic forms and to let it go at that, provided that no tradition and no politician and no Congressman and no President interfere with the gentle art of making money in the largest possible quantities in the least possible time.

The fact is that the more we regiment the less patriotic we really are likely to be, the more we shall pull away from the spiritual thing which is America. That can with great difficulty be put into words, because it is a conglomeration of a great many things, such as tolerance and good-will and justice and fair play, honest dealing with one's fellow-men, true liberty, true equality, and genuine fraternity. Patriotism is not a thing that can be bought nor can it be forced into people without its nature undergoing a chemical change in the process. When it is so forced in, it becomes as much of a drudgery as compulsory drill or enforced churchgoing. True patriotism is something that sprouts almost of its own accord. It is nurtured by gratitude, not by favors received at the hands of a privilege-bestowing government—by equality of opportunity and equality of justice. Given these things in America and the democratic faith is saved. Yet it is those who bask most in the government's sunshine, those who are protected and advantaged at the expense of their countrymen, who insist on patriotism by prescription, like so many allopathic pills. They are the ones who cheered loudest for the war to safeguard democracy and now, admitting, as they do, that it had nothing whatever to do with democracy, wonder, perhaps, that democracy has so few friends among themselves.

Wanted: An American Program for Disarmament

THE approaching meeting of the Preparatory Commission of the International Conference on Disarmament, to which President Coolidge, with the approval of Congress, is sending an American delegation, offers a new opportunity to America and to American friends of international peace. It will be recalled that at the time of the Washington Disarmament Conference, in 1921, the impressive demonstration of many different groups of American citizens impelled Secretary of State Hughes to make far more progressive proposals to the meeting than he otherwise would have made; they were largely responsible for whatever measure of success that gathering on naval armaments achieved.

It is frequently said by spokesmen purporting to reflect the mind of the Administration that the United States is not interested in the question of land armaments and has nothing to contribute to the subject of their reduction. Both statements are palpably untrue. The American people are vitally interested in land disarmament, because the existence of large conscript armies in the world is a serious contributing cause of fear, and fear destroys that confidence without which international disarmament and peace are difficult to obtain. It is sufficient to recall two recent American initiatives to be convinced that there are significant American ideas and practical proposals to be made to any disarmament conference that really wants to disarm. The first of these is the germ idea of the resolution twice introduced in the Senate by Senater Shipstead of Minnesota, calling upon the President to negotiate treaties with every military Power, under the terms of which compulsory military training and service would he reciprocally prohibited and abolished within the territorial jurisdiction of each state. This is the same idea which is being agitated by the youth movements of Great Britain and Switzerland, the latter looking to the League of Nations to initiate such an international treaty for the suppression of conscription as it has already initiated for the suppression of slavery and the slave trade in the mandated territories and in Angola.

Another American idea is one in which the Carnegie Foundation is interested; it is a proposed revision of international law, specifically a codification of Pan-American international law, according to which several new definitions and doctrines of right and of non-violent coercion are advanced. Perhaps the most important of these is that which declares henceforth to be illegal the acquisition of all territory by the exercise of force and violence, this proposed reform to be established by the voluntary acceptance and proclamation of all the American republics. The suggested codification would also narrowly limit the permissible use of the blockade and other forms of "sanctions" and subject the whole process of coercion of a delinquent or an offending state to American international control through development of conciliatory, judicial, and arbitral processes in the Pan-American Union.

A third American idea of great significance—the economic embargo, originally applied by Thomas Jefferson—is one which, when fully developed to meet modern conditions and applied internationally, may prove to be the master-key to the puzzling problem of sanctions in a world in which public opinion is more or less free and active and, when sane, is the only guaranty of security. Considered from the point of view of the rights and duties of neutrals, America has a right and a duty to propose and proclaim what might be called a policy of the Closed Door—a voluntary recognition of the duty of a neutral nation to close its markets against sale of munitions and contraband of war to an aggressor state, the fact of aggression or offense or violation of obligation to be determined by a respected and impartial international judicial body, possibly the World Court, but not by any political sanhedrim such as the Council of the League. When aggression is defined as refusal to submit an international controversy to arbitration or to international inquiry and conciliation, such a revision of the doctrine of neutral rights and duties would place the moral and economic power of the neutral world on the side of defense, arbitration, and inquiry, instead of on the side of aggression, naval power, and violence, where it now is.

The doctrine of neutrality is an American doctrine. It began when George Washington and his Cabinet, disregarding the pledges of military assistance contained in our treaty with France of 1778, proclaimed a new policy in 1793, suited to the exigencies of the young nation and of inestimable worth to the subsequent history of all nations. It lies in the power of the United States to bring this doctrine up to date, to revise and apply it in a way that will make impossible a repetition of the dangerous conflict that arose between the United States and Great Britain in 1916, concerning neutral rights upon the seas.

Big Brother or Big Bully

WHAT are we up to in Nicaragua now? With the withdrawal of our marines from that republic last year, and the resumption of control by Nicaragua of its bank and railways, there appeared to be hope that the long period of interference on the part of the United States had ended. Vain expectation! When we are not interfering for the selfish advantage of big business, we seem destined to be meddling for what defenders of such a policy would doubtless call "Nicaragua's own good." We are playing either the big bully or the big brother. And a policy that permits us to play the big brother allows us also to play the big bully.

It will be recalled that the present President of Nicaragua, General Chamorro, obtained office last year by forcing out his predecessor. General Chamorro belongs to a party and a family that have long been serviceable to the commercial interest of the United States, but we have refused to recognize him because of the treaty signed in 1923 with Central American republics in which it was mutually agreed that recognition would be refused to governments set up by force. Commenting on this action in our issue of June 23 we observed that the Department of State was deserving of credit for logically standing by its announced policy in an instance where it worked against our interests. But we added: "Whether the policy itself is a sound one is another matter. *The Nation* believes that the old practice of international law, by which any established government is recognized regardless of origin, is wiser and less provocative of meddling in other people's affairs."

Recent news from Nicaragua seems designed expressly to bear out the last sentence. Advices received by Nicaraguans in this country, if accurate, indicate that our chargé d'affaires at Managua has been conducting what amounts to a deliberate and organized attempt to drive General Chamorro out of office. A telegram from President Chamorro himself, dated June 10, says, when translated:

> The American chargé d'affaires, Mr. Dennis, came today to see me and notified me that he was going to undertake a campaign to enlighten the Nicaraguan people about the necessity of forcing me to retire from power, and that in case I did not retire voluntarily the United States would compel me by force, because it was going to accomplish its purpose whether I was willing or not. . . . He has already had the first handbill distributed.

Another telegram says that on June 15 Mr. Dennis called a meeting at the legation of various members of the Conservative Party (that of General Chamorro) to discuss the situation and had previously made public a statement in which he said that "my Government cherishes the hope that the Nicaraguan people by a return to a constitutional form of government will make it possible for the United States Government to extend recognition to such a government and to enter into formal diplomatic relations therewith."

All this, it must be obvious, is an entirely different thing from merely refusing to recognize an existing regime because it was set up by force. It is a practical invitation to the friends of General Chamorro to desert him as they would a sinking ship—and to his opponents to overthrow him by any means at their command. When one recalls that President Cleveland sent a British ambassador packing because he indicated a preference in a pending presidential election, one realizes the extent of the breach of diplomatic etiquette and practice of which we are guilty in Nicaragua.

But the Department of State and the sponsors of the treaty of 1923 will reply that the intrigue is for "Nicaragua's own good." We don't doubt for a minute that in their opinion it is. And that's precisely the point we would make against a treaty that prevents the recognition in Central America of a government that is set up by force. Our own republic could not have been recognized in 1776 under such a rule. To decide if a country has what Mr. Dennis piously calls "a constitutional form of government" involves a judgment upon its domestic affairs which cannot well be neutral. It is none of our business to play either the big brother or the big bully in Latin America or elsewhere. We are rapidly becoming the world's worst meddler both at home and abroad. And we won't get back to legitimate international practices until we cancel the Central American treaty of 1923.

Why Not a Peace Department?

OUR federal, State, and city governments spend many million dollars every year to prevent fire, crime, and disease. Everybody accepts this preventive policy as sound common sense. Now comes Kirby Page, effective peace pamphleteer, with the question: Why not apply this notion of governmental prevention to war? Why should government be captured by the militarists? Why not a Peace Department alongside the War Department?

Propaganda has become one of the chief functions of our government departments. Mellon preaches against large taxes; Kellogg preaches on the dangers of Soviet recognition; Hoover preaches on standardization; all the generals preach on preparedness; the White House spokesman preaches on "economy." This national homiletical chorus is nearly always special pleading of the rankest sort. It shouts investing-class economic creeds and old-party nostrums. Done in the name of community welfare, it is no more entitled to the public frank than, let us say, the preaching of Aimee Semple McPherson. If we must continue to pay for the preaching of generals to make us more military we might as well pay some one to make us more pacific. Why not have a Peace Department to preach peace at us?

Mr. Page has put down in businesslike figures a plan for spending $100,000,000 a year (less than the annual pay roll alone of another army or navy) for a national Peace Department. His results are rather astonishing. For one-third of the cost of the battleship Colorado we could have a Federal Department of Peace with a cabinet secretary, assistants, clerks, and stenographers; ten regional secretaries at $6,000 salaries; forty foreign offices with five foreign secretaries each and liberal allowances for running expenses. For thirteen million more there would be peace publications galore, an *International Peace Review* with a circulation of a million, twelve million peace pamphlets, five million dollars' worth of posters, twenty peace films a year, and peace libraries distributing a million books a year. Add five million for an International University; then forty million for 10,000 American students abroad and 10,000 foreign students coming to America at $2,000 a year each. Take a million for an annual Peace Day, a few millions more for exchange professors and "Citizens' International Friendship Camps," and there are still five of the hundred millions left for disaster relief funds and international health service.

Every item of this Peace Department program offers a peace counterpart to some military institution which is considered necessary. An International University is to stand over against West Point and Annapolis; world friendship cruises would be designed to offset the flourishing of our navy in the Pacific; peace monuments would compete with our war-memorial atrocities. Our military leaders have been acting on the assumption that if they talk military ideas long enough and lustily enough the new generation will succumb to the volume and repetition. They are quite right; so is Mr. Page. Official propaganda may be the best thing with which to kill official propaganda.

When Mr. Page's Peace Department is established we would like to be assigned the task of spending the five million a year on posters. We recall those posters in front of our federal buildings which picture trim young gentlemen writing letters under palm trees, the caption being, "Where Will You Spend the Winter? Join the Marines and See the World." Our posters would be more realistic. We would have pictures of marines cleaning up a native village in Haiti with rifle fire or breaking a strike of Chinese students in Shanghai, and perhaps a marine peeling potatoes. Underneath there would be statistics of the proportion of marines who never reenlist. Then if some unemployed youngster joined the marines he would know what he was getting into.

America's Crop of Hate

By OSWALD GARRISON VILLARD

London, July 24

LET no one be deceived by the reported demonstrations against American tourists in Paris. They are sporadic and local, and not yet serious—probably provoked in many cases by over-stimulated and bad-mannered Americans. But no observer can truthfully report that the situation, either in England or France, is satisfactory for those Americans who ardently desire that their country shall not only live in amity with the leading European nations but shall have their good-will and regard as well.

Here in England there is an increased dislike of us—particularly among the privileged Tory classes, but also among many plain people who come in contact with the rowdy American tourists who appear whenever one of the great liners discharges its cargo at Southampton or Plymouth. That this feeling against America is growing is admitted by people who are working earnestly for the maintenance of friendly relations between the two countries. They hope that it is a passing phase. They speak of its being part of a summer "stunt" of some of the sensational newspapers. Americans who live here say that there is a recrudescence of this debt propaganda every summer when the American tourist season is at its height. It is idle, of course, to say that the whole thing is due to the debt settlement, but, on the other hand, it cannot be denied that the recent English settlement with France, and Mr. Mellon's most unfortunate letter on the subject, with its unsupportable statements, has fanned the flames, leading not only to Churchill's and Snowden's speeches in Parliament but to the effective Foreign Office answer published yesterday morning. That the British Government should feel it necessary thus to reply to a statement by an American official, not officially addressed to it, is in itself an indication of the gravity of the issue.

The debt settlement bulks large. Ill-mannered tourists, rich Americans who buy up precious old English pictures and show places, and even take down houses to move them bodily to America; the old critical attitude of the two nations toward each other—these all contribute to the ill-will; but the simple truth is that America is reaping the whirlwind which she sowed when she entered the war, and not only in England but all through Europe. A shrewd observer remarked the other day that the best friends America had in Europe today were the Germans, which, he added, "is not saying much." It was of course idle to expect that all those noble sentiments uttered during the war about eternal chains of friendship binding us to our Allies, and the imperishable memory of the blood of our youth poured out on the same battlefields, should last. They were often founded on absolute misconceptions and on war lies. In an emotional state bordering on insanity we endowed our Allies with nobilities which they did not possess. The coming of peace made inevitable a let-down. We all got back to earth, and discovered that we were human and frail and still had our own faults instead of being so many archangels going to the rescue of liberty. The bad peace, the frightful economic sufferings, the new jealousies, and the crushing weight of the debt have all added to the disillusionment. Each nation declares that it won the war; but nothing infuriates all the others so much as to have the United States, through its leading men, insist that we did so. Every time a Senator or a Congressman or a Cabinet official or a general says that, he rubs salt in the wounds.

No military alliance for war purposes ever breeds a lasting friendship. The Crimean War was heralded as meaning union of France and England, in brotherly good-will for ever, but as soon as it was over England and France began to arm against each other just as they had in all the previous centuries. The French alliance with us in the Revolution did not prevent our coming to blows with them in a little war before the end of the century. That fact the orators forgot to mention in 1917-1918. The more the Great War recedes into the past the more will all our sins in it return to plague us, and by us I mean every participant, on whichever side. The more the American people study the war, the more they will find it was not what they thought it was, either in purpose or execution. The more the squabble over debts continues, the darker will be the glasses through which Americans will view their former Allies, and the more the European nations will call Uncle Sam Uncle Shylock.

All this is bad enough for the future peace of the world, but it becomes worse if we realize that our debt policy plus our tariff policy and our position as money-lenders to the world are gradually forming a European alliance against America. The European nations are frightened by our tremendous financial power; they cannot borrow money elsewhere, but they are trying to find means to defend themselves against our pressure to make them pay their debts, and our refusal, by means of our high tariff, to let them pay with goods. Take a country like Belgium. It is placing itself in the hands of the American money-lenders because it must, not because it wants to. And Wall Street finds itself compelled to lend money to Belgium or refuse aid to a stricken nation which it alone can save from bankruptcy. I am told that M. Caillaux, when he came on his flying visit to London, said that France and England were both controlled by great groups of financiers, the only distinction being that the industrialists ruled one country and the big financiers the other. But above and behind the industrial-financial groups in both countries stands the American money-power which, by force of circumstances, is beginning to dominate the world—within a year it may be writing that Dawes Plan for France which Mr. Snowden, the ex-Chancellor of the Exchequer, has just declared inevitable. I acquit the American money-power of deliberately planning to achieve a dominating position in Europe. It too is, I believe, merely reaping its share of the whirlwind. Unfortunately I cannot credit its members with enough brains to see that this was just another of the inevitable results of America's entrance into the war. It would be amazing, perhaps, if we should live to see a European Customs Union against America, but it is not impossible.

Well, what can America do under the circumstances? Indubitably, *The Nation's* policy of urging the cancelation of the debts that we shall never be able to collect and accepting funding arrangements based on capacity to pay is the correct one. I am not, of course, optimistic enough to believe that we should receive many, if any, thanks from those whom we released from indebtedness. We have so bungled the whole matter, especially in our manner of making the settlements, that almost irreparable harm has been done, but there is time yet for a *beau geste*, especially if that means the removal of a festering sore.

Why not, I hear someone say, enter the League? It is not necessary to rehearse here all the arguments against that move, but it is worth while recording one's belief again that the entry of America into the League of Nations would not mean a revival of the comradeships of the war, or anything approaching them. From the very beginning, we should have to decide whether we would be pro-British or pro-French in the League, for the rivalry between those two Powers is the story of the League. We should then have to decide further whether we would be pro-Pole or pro-German or pro-Italian or pro-Spanish or pro-Rumanian and Slovakian. Europe is a continent seething with hatreds and jealousy. It is impossible to be here and believe that the situation is not just as bad as it was two and a half years ago. Many think it worse, if only because of the rise of Mussolini. Why, in Heaven's name, should any American wish to tie us up intimately to such a situation? The monstrous conceit which makes some people think that we could, by joining the League, compose these differences by our influence and example is only equaled by the gullibility of those who still think that the war accomplished something for the safeguarding of democracy and liberty and the ending of war.

Professor Sam, Militarist

IN South America Uncle Sam is rapidly becoming a professor of military expansion. While our representatives at Geneva discuss disarmament our admirals in Brazil and Peru have for several years been teaching these South American nations to build larger and better navies for new wars. The project began in November, 1922, when sixteen commissioned and nineteen petty officers were dispatched by the United States Government as a naval mission to Brazil. Some naval missions are brief dress parades; this mission is no dress parade and it is not brief. It has already spent almost four years in Brazil teaching the Brazilians naval tactics and helping to expand the Brazilian navy. Recently the State Department announced that Brazil had renewed the contract for our naval mission for another four years from November, 1926. Unless someone interferes Professor Sam will stay in Brazil until 1930.

Peru is also one of our military clients. An American naval mission has been in Peru more than two years helping to reorganize the Peruvian navy, and there is no indication of an early withdrawal. Peru, it may be noted, is building part of her new navy in America; two Peruvian submarines were recently launched at New London.

Does our Government appreciate the danger to *us* from this military intervention in South America? If under our tutelage Brazil gets so strong and rambunctious that she makes war on Argentina and Peru fights Chile, we are likely to see an attempt at intervention by the League of Nations. Peru and Chile belong fully to the League and Argentina has never actually resigned. League intervention would be called for upon a declaration of war and, if any of the countries involved had begun the war in violation of the covenant, they would be subject to blockade. Our own commerce would be interfered with; what would happen to the Monroe Doctrine nobody knows. There are some who would want us to hurl Europe out of America by force. Do we want that sort of a melee? If not, why do we help one American nation that is a member of the League to arm against other American nations that are members of the League?

Another question should be faced by our Government. When we teach South American nations to fight, how do we know that they will fight *with* us in a war? Why shouldn't they fight *against* us? Take, for example, a war with Japan. The South American nations are restive under our financial domination. Japan has not attempted to rule them. An alliance with Japan is quite as natural as an alliance with the United States.

What right have American officers on the payroll of American taxpayers to spend their time teaching other nations to fight? Offhand, we would say that they have no right at all except in the case of allies during a war. When a few Russian officers appear as military instructors in Canton, China, the press of the Western world denounces Russia for attempting to use the Chinese for selfish (Russian) ends. Are we doing in South America what Russia is charged with doing in China? Probably the intentions of Congress were legitimate enough when the special act of 1920 was passed authorizing the President to accept the invitations of South American republics "whenever in his discretion the public interests require, to detail officers of the United States naval service to assist the governments of the republics of South America in naval matters." The act is innocent enough on the surface; it was renewed last May with even more sweeping provisions, allowing us to lend army and marine as well as naval officers. The Congressmen who voted for it no doubt considered the act a means of strengthening the friendship between Latin America and the United States, a military bulwark for the Monroe Doctrine. So it might have been if *all* the South American nations had invited help. But to date only two have asked for assistance, Brazil and Peru.

The effect of extending military aid of any kind to *some* of the South American republics is unfortunate. Brazil's greatest potential enemy is Argentina; we are helping Brazil but not her rival. Peru's nemesis is Chile; we are certainly not helping Chile. To all appearances we are helping Brazil to get ready for a war against Argentina and Peru to get ready for a war against Chile. If Brazil and Peru are not preparing to fight their South American neighbors, what are they getting ready for?

It is a peculiarly tactless thing of our Government to keep a naval mission in Peru at the present moment. Chile is seething with bitterness against the United States because our representatives seemed to favor Peru and condemn Chile in the Tacna-Arica dispute. Probably Chile deserved the condemnation but her sensitiveness cannot be ignored; if we presume to act as judge it is hardly a wise thing at the same time to play the role of a military auxiliary of Chile's avowed enemy to the north. The Peruvian militarists who want the people to believe that Tacna-Arica is worth dying for do not need the support of an American naval mission.

Who is paying the costs of our South American naval missions? The law authorizing these missions provides that the naval officers lent to foreign Powers shall receive "*in addition to* the compensation and emoluments allowed them by such [South American] governments, the pay and allowance of their rank in the United States naval service." (Italics ours.) A fat bonus for lucky officers! The foreign governments pay the expenses of our naval missions but we continue to pay the salaries, and the act of 1920 makes no provision for reimbursing the United States Government for these salary costs. If the thirty-five commissioned and petty officers of the mission to Brazil received the lowest pay given to the lowest commissioned officer after ten years service in the navy, our salary bill for the eight years in Brazil would be more than $700,000.

The question of costs, however, is trivial compared to the major question: Are we allowing our admirals to Balkanize South America? Apparently we are. We are encouraging armament rather than disarmament in a continent which may easily destroy itself in a competitive armament race. We are callously drifting into military arrangements which destroy our claim of impartiality; we may awake some morning to find that we have helped to divide South America into military blocs. The next session of Congress can do much for permanent peace in South America by terminating Uncle Sam's engagement as a military instructor in Brazil and Peru.

Germany Enters the League

EIGHT years after the Armistice Germany has at last gone through the formal ceremony of readoption into the family of nations. She has been admitted to permanent membership in the Council of the League of Nations, along with Great Britain, France, Italy, and Japan. By that act she, who was forced by browbeating ultimatums to sign the false Peace of Versailles and the subsequent series of impossible agreements, is recognized as an equal by the Great Powers of the world. Europe and the League grow in moral stature as a result.

Diplomacy had to turn somersaults and diplomats to pen miracles of compromise clauses in order to achieve this result, and the details of the process of admission were still unsettled when this issue of *The Nation* went to press. Apparently the total membership of the Council is to be increased from eleven to fourteen. Five seats will be permanently assigned to the "Great Powers"; the other nine members will be elected in batches of three, for three-year terms; three—and only three—of the nine may, by a two-thirds vote of the Assembly, be declared eligible for reelection. The scheme was to provide reeligibility as a sop for Brazil, Spain, and Poland, the three hold-up nations which in March dissolved the pleasant haze of the "Locarno spirit" by demanding permanent seats or nothing. Brazil, however, sulkily retired from the League after the March fiasco, and Spain in early September withdrew her delegates from Geneva following the failure of her spectacular attempt to blackmail France and England into giving her a free hand in Tangier in return for good behavior in the League. (What effect Spain's even more recent dabbling in military revolution will have on her international fortunes remains to be seen.) These two may, as a result of their diplomatic pettishness, lose even their semi-permanent seats.

Austen Chamberlain, British Foreign Minister, and Aristide Briand, French Foreign Minister, although largely responsible for the failures of March, deserve high praise—along with Lord Robert Cecil, who "found the formula"—for standing firm through the midsummer and rescuing the tossing craft of the League. Had Germany not been admitted on fair terms in this recent attempt the League might as well have dissolved. These two men, representing the greatest Powers of the old world, had it in their hands to crush the League or keep it. In the end, they kept it. They risked the secession of three nations, two of them closely allied to their own countries, but they kept the League. Yet in so doing, they revealed again the fragile nature of this over-praised and over-feared world-state. The fateful decisions were not made in the council-halls of Geneva, but in the tete-a-tetes of the foreign ministers of France and England. The revelation is significant; it should not be forgotten.

There were hints, before the League sessions, of a Mediterranean block, which was to threaten Franco-British hegemony. But Mussolini, while he can bluster safely at home, lacks allies abroad, and his imperial ambitions have no lure for Spain. The much-heralded Italian-Spanish treaty was forgotten the moment Spain suggested that Tangier, where Italy has a shadowy claim, be made exclusively Spanish. Will Germany, as a permanent member of the League Council, provide the balance-wheel which Europe needs and offset Franco-British hegemony? That, too, remains to be seen, and one of the most interesting tests will come in the work of the Mandates Commission.

In European affairs the League has functioned with a measure of success. It abdicated in Vilna, twirled its thumbs in the Sarre, and stultified itself at Corfu, but in a dozen minor disputes it has provided a machinery of reconciliation, and it has been a serviceable clearing-house of miscellaneous information. Its conception, however, was more grandiose. It was to be the carrier of the world's conscience. It was to provide machinery by which the backward people of the earth—in particular, the inhabitants of the former German and Turkish colonies—could be led gently into the sweetness and light of modern civilization. Now, there were a few small nations which took that ideal seriously. And the Permanent Mandates Commission of the League has, in fact, provided a sounding-board for colonial protestants—patriots, we called them in 1776—which did not previously exist. But the rules of the game made the sounding-board feeble. Protests could be received from anybody, but they must be transmitted to the mandataries, the objects of the protest, for comment before report was made; the protestants could not be heard in person; and as a result, the protest was always smothered.

In the midst of the hullabaloo about Spain and Poland and Brazil and Germany the Permanent Mandates Commission came forward with a modest request. It did not get much space in the papers, but, in view of the fact that the French, as agents of the League's good-will, have been massacring Syrian men, women, and children for months, it deserved it. The Permanent Mandates Commission asked that it be permitted to hear witnesses in person. Austen Chamberlain frowned at it through his monocle, and said "No." Aristide Briand smiled and said "No." Belgium and South Africa, which also administer former German colonies as mandataries, also said "No." Japan discreetly did not speak. But therein was revealed the essential, fundamental canker in the League's soul. It was born as an ideal perverted to serve Versailles imperialism and it has never recovered from that stigma. The little nations of Europe have valiantly striven to convert it toward the ideal, the admission of Germany marks an appreciable step in that direction; but the canker remains.

What the League does about its Mandates Commission, then, will indicate the direction of its evolution. Will it turn backward and make of itself a comfortable machine by which the Great Powers of Western Europe regulate Europe and their imperial world? Or will the pressure of the war-time neutrals, which have been the real heroes of every session of the League, make of this mandate system a real improvement over the ancient brutalities of colonial administration?

In two other respects the League marks its own provincialism. It is an organ of the Western World, and the representation accorded Asia is trifling. China, which includes a quarter of the human race, was not accorded the courtesy, in the scramble for seats, that was granted Poland. And, most important of all, the League still, and of its own will, excludes Soviet Russia.

The Great Free-Trade Manifesto

OUR readers who recall that *The Nation* has been advocating free trade ever since its foundation in 1865 as the most constructive and most pacific measure this country could possibly adopt will understand our elation over the bankers' manifesto in favor of free trade, published throughout the world on October 19. We have reprinted it elsewhere in this issue for purposes of record because we believe it to be a shining milestone of human progress. Here are many of the foremost bankers in the world who have come together to admit the truth of what liberals have been saying again and again since the wicked peace, that the greatest need of the world is the leveling of all tariff barriers. So much a matter of common sense has it been that we could not see how any one could question it. Were the new European states created merely to stem the flow of goods? Were the hatreds of after-the-war to be measured by the height of the tariff walls?

Well, at least the leading financiers have come to see that vastly more important for the restoration of Europe and for its relations to the United States is the sweeping away of these Chinese walls of protection. They have come to it not as idealists or theorists but as practical, hard-headed business men. It has taken war's aftermath to make them appreciate what they should have learned long ago from the history of the United States and from the amazing rise of Germany after the Zollverein of 1832-1835, when it abolished all the tariff and customs walls between the several German states. It was this that created modern Germany and led directly to the proclamation of the empire at Versailles in 1871. If it is right and wise for the small states of Europe to put up barriers against one another today Germany should hasten to restore the tariffs between her several parts. No one would dream of advocating it.

Now these financiers are alarmed because "at no period have impediments to trading been more perilously multiplied without a true appreciation of the economic consequences involved." They point out that the breakup of the old political units alone dealt a heavy blow to international trade. Old markets disappeared and new racial animosities divided communities long since united in trade. Licenses, tariffs, prohibitions of all kinds were imposed, with the result that prosperity rapidly declined. The change of flags in itself would not have meant so much. Thus, the transfer of Silesian mines from Germany to Poland would have made little difference if there had not been erected immediately a tariff wall to make it more difficult for Germans to buy Polish coal. The bankers are right when they say that "too many states, in pursuit of false ideas of national interest, have imperiled their own welfare and lost sight of the common interests of the world, by basing their commercial relations on the economic folly which treats all trading as a form of war."

On the contrary, trade ought to be one of the greatest bonds to tie nations together, to mingle their interests so that it should be impossible for war to arise. Always believers in free trade on economic grounds, we have of late years been more than ever impressed by its necessity to pacify the nations that were lately in the war and prevent any further trade rivalries of the purely nationalistic kind which too often insure war. Richard Cobden was, of course, a leader in suggesting the relation of free trade to peace. "It has often struck me," he wrote, "that it would be well to engraft our free-trade agitation upon the peace movement." Again, writing on September 14, 1859, he said that he saw in free trade the only hope "for any permanent improvements in the political relations of France and England. I utterly despair of finding peace and harmony in the efforts of governments and diplomatists. The people of the two nations must be brought into mutual dependence by the supply of each other's wants. There is no other way of counteracting the antagonism of language and race. It is God's own method of producing an *entente cordiale*, and no other plan is worth a farthing." If these words were just and true then, they are still more applicable to the war-wrecked nations of Europe today.

Now, if we in this country were really desirous of helping Europe there would be universal acclaim of the sound position taken by the bankers. Instead, the protectionist dailies, Mr. Mellon, and the President have fallen over one another in their eagerness to have the American people understand that that is all very well for Europe, but has nothing to do with the United States. We must and shall, they say, uphold that hoary old fraud, that breeder of socialism, that widener of class differences, that mother of trusts—our protective system. And they take this position at the very moment when our differences with Europe over the war debts are so much to the front, when everybody knows that since our debtors can pay us only in goods we can help them to pay—if we insist upon those debts—only by lowering or abolishing our tariffs. It is a fair measure of the parochial quality of Mr. Coolidge's mind that he takes this attitude and arranges for Mr. Mellon to reassure at the earliest possible moment the protected manufacturers of America. It does not surprise us, however. For fifty years the Republican Party has battened on the graft of the protective tariff. It has filled its coffers with campaign contributions sometimes wrung from the protected, sometimes freely offered in order that the donors might dictate the schedules of the next tariff bill.

But if America lags we may rest assured that the campaign now started by the bankers will go on in increasing measure. It is one of those issues that cannot be settled until it is settled aright, and the continuing disorganization of Europe through tariffs makes it absolutely certain that the fight will go on with increasing vigor. Without free trade Europe must languish. The recent free-trade congress in Denmark and the first Pan-European conference held under the leadership of Count Coudenhove-Kalergi in Vienna at the beginning of October are signs of the times, for Pan-Europe and free trade are nearly synonymous. As for the American bankers, headed by Mr. J. P. Morgan, who have signed this momentous document, we congratulate them upon their courage and vision. They will be heartily abused for their share in it, we are well aware. But, as we have frequently pointed out, the battle is on between the American financiers who have invested great sums abroad and the protected manufacturers. The harder they fight the nearer the day when justice shall be done and the American people be led to adopt the only sound international economic policy.

Germany Revisited

By OSWALD GARRISON VILLARD

Baden-Baden, September 28

"THE one bright spot in Europe," I heard Germany called in London amid a general chorus of pessimism and gloom—the one bright spot economically and financially. And so I found it after visiting some ten cities and spending a number of weeks within its confines. Not that Germany presents to the visitor any startling picture of happiness and prosperity. Far from it. If the cities are outwardly repaired and no longer sadly down at the heel, there is still enormous suffering behind the newly stuccoed fronts of the great apartment houses. Indeed, if you should talk with the average German he would tell you of hardships, disappointments, losses, and almost intolerable suffering, in considerable part due to the necessary process of sanitation and of reorganization. To get the measure of progress, therefore, one must compare the Germany of today with that which I saw in 1923; one must not look at individual trees but at the health of the forest as a whole. If one does that, then the conclusion is irresistible that Germany has gained enormously in three years and that, if nothing untoward happens, this conquered country will in a few years surpass in prosperity and economic health her chief rivals of the World War—if indeed she has not already done so.

Primarily, the greatest change is in the mental attitude of the people themselves. Three years ago they were still smarting under their overwhelming defeat and the stigma put upon them by the Allied nations of being mad dogs deliberately bent upon wrecking the world that they might dominate it for their own selfish purposes. Today they have put nearly all of that behind them—save only the extreme Nationalists and the survivors of the old military caste. They are spiritually disarmed. They have said *Schluss* to the war episode and they can now talk about it with amazing detachment and objectiveness. They can see far more clearly the errors they, or rather their rulers, made. The lapse of years, of course, makes it easier for them to review the past without bitterness, with clearer perceptions of all the factors involved, with a real understanding of the way they and all the other nations were betrayed by their rulers. This is remarkable to an American who knows how long it took to win over the defeated Confederacy to an acceptance of the results of its appeal to arms.

Three years ago there was still a lot of whining and complaining in Germany. Today, even those who say to you frankly that they do not see how Germany can meet the crushing burdens of the 1927 and 1928 Dawes payments discuss the situation without complaint. It has become a purely financial problem, and many of them see that the compulsion to work and to economize and to live simply which the Dawes plan exercises is really a boon; that it is compelling a discipline of enormous value in holding a beaten and stricken people together. One hears, I repeat, of innumerable cases of dreadful suffering, especially among what is left of the middle class. Appeals for aid in genuine cases of utter despair and absolute poverty pile up. For here is a country in which old age has become something terrible, since all savings have been wiped out, every before-the-war life-insurance policy is valueless, all endowment funds for hospitals, homes for the aged, schools, universities, and the rest have been wiped out; every provision for age has vanished. Thousands upon thousands of people who felt their futures safe have nothing whatever to look forward to. The more favorably situated can just make both ends meet, but they cannot spend an extra three marks for a concert ticket; as for the journeys they so loved, they are now prisoners the year around in the places where they happen to be. On top of all this the so-called "rationalization" of industry, the wiping out of myriads of unnecessary businesses, together with the great combinations that are being formed is constantly throwing multitudes into bankruptcy or depriving them of their places. It is easy to understand the reparation official in Berlin who declared that he could not continue to hold his position if he allowed his mind to dwell upon the cases of individual hardship which came before him.

There is still alarming unemployment, now gradually decreasing, as Parker Gilbert, that extraordinary American official in charge of reparations, has prophesied that it would, but still so ominous as to make Germany ask herself, like England, if there are not several millions too many of her citizens in the world. This unemployment does not, of course, include only those who appear at the registry offices. There are multitudes of others, not of the manual-labor class, who can find no work to do, or are breaking their hearts in positions wholly unsuited to them. Among those who have jobs the pay is often preposterous. I know of a chief engineer in a going Berlin engineering concern who gets less than $100 a month, while ordinary servants can be had for from $6 a month up. This particular chief engineer is only one of many who daily watch every barometer of trade with trembling hearts because they know that if their work fails them they cannot hope to find other jobs. Everywhere businesses stagnate or fail for lack of capital. Finally, there is the grave lack of housing, so serious that to cities like Heidelberg no one is allowed to move unless by an exchange of apartments under which some Heidelberger moves to the city from which the new person comes. The municipalities rigidly reserve the right to quarter strangers upon any householder or apartment-dweller who in their opinion has too much space. In Baden-Baden the owner of one large estate has had nine families quartered upon her property.

All of this would be enough to render hopeless almost any people. Yet the improvement in morale and courage in Germany is everywhere noticeable. There is more cheerfulness and vastly more resignation; there is much more evidence of wealth and prosperity. There are, of course, many who have wealth—those who coined money during the war or were able to hold on to large estates or had money abroad, chiefly bankers and manufacturers. The dailies that were so near disaster in 1920-1923 now have the look of success and progress. Their circulations are increasing; their advertising is excellent. They are far more hopeful in their tone, especially those devoted to the republic.

The entrance of Germany into the League of Nations,

the steady cleaning up of the economic situation after the inflation folly, the extraordinarily rapid reconquest of the seas by German shipping, the increased activity of the shipyards, the prosperity of the railroads, which carried 33.6 per cent more passengers in 1925 than in 1913, the host of new inventions, the great combinations in trades forced by the Dawes plan, and now the international iron and steel cartel—all of these give the press opportunities in plenty to cheer up their readers. They do not, of course, dwell upon the seriousness of the evils that will follow in the train of these enormous combinations of capital and of the coming in of huge sums of foreign capital through which great mines and large industrial companies are passing directly over to American or other ownership—America has already invested $900,000,000 in Germany since the war. The superstate of German industrialism grows by leaps and bounds and promises work for more and more. In connection with unemployment it must not be forgotten that great numbers of *rentiers* and retired persons are now working who never worked before; that the war brought masses of women into industrial life and 600,000 men who formerly were absorbed by the army and navy must now be provided for in private enterprises.

Work, work; it is the gospel of work which is saving Germany, as well as civic discipline and the determination to rebuild the fatherland and restore it to the pinnacle it once occupied. Still it remains a marvel, this sudden liquidation of the war mentally, this acceptance of the inevitable. Let no one think that it has been achieved without cost. The price Germany has had to pay for her Kaiser and his criminal mismanagement of her foreign affairs is apparent on every hand. The aspect of the people one sees bears eloquent testimony to this. There used to be handsome men, especially in uniform, and handsome women in Germany. Now one sees them not at all. The crowds appear coarsened; never a beautiful people, they seem positively ugly, and as if to show their desire to be nothing else innumerable men shave their heads so that they are as bald as eggs. The women wear costumes far out of style; if they ever displayed taste in dress it has disappeared. The aesthetic side of life has for the present gone by the board.

Sport has taken a tremendous hold. There is a nationwide movement to substitute gymnastics for the old military drill and a determination to follow the Greek example, but for the present the cult of beauty is dead. Dire national need and suffering for twelve long years have made it impossible, have destroyed refinements, the things that charm and grace, by taking away the means and leisure necessary to them. Music still flourishes and art too; the theater fights its way on. But for the present—and for years to come—it is the struggle for material existence which controls with individuals and with the various administrative units. The latter are building canals and railroads and are electrifying the country at a tremendous rate; the impelling motive is quite as much to give work to men who would otherwise be receiving unemployment pay as to increase the economic and industrial power of the country. Incidentally the republic is strengthened thereby.

The German Republic? It has gained greatly in three years. In 1923 one could meet many people who still felt a good deal of sympathy for the Kaiser. He had blundered, yes, but he had meant well. Today one still finds monarchists, notably in Bavaria, where some people continue to believe that, despite the federal constitution, Rupprecht will be proclaimed king. But nowhere does one hear any longer regret for the Kaiser or the slightest suggestion that he or one of his sons might some day rule again over Germany. I have heard Rupprecht praised as a good sort, and the Grand Duke of Baden is still popular, but repeatedly working people have said to me that two millions of Germans but not a single member of the imperial family fell in battle. The stigma of coward attaches to the Kaiser more than ever. Even those who think him in some respects misjudged, or say he was mentally unbalanced, declare he should have died at the head of his troops. I doubt if Emil Ludwig's brilliant study of the Kaiser, as utterly destructive of him and his pretences as any anti-German foreigner could possibly ask, could have had three years ago the success it has just achieved. In the more severely critical discussions of the old regime one finds everywhere the clearest proof of the ground lost by the monarchists and won by the republic. To this Ludendorff has contributed not a little by showing himself a weakling in his beer-cellar revolt in Munich and a man utterly destitute of political sagacity, one might almost say of common sense. He has destroyed his own great reputation while Hindenburg has kept his and, barring one very bad error, has set an admirable example of a national executive who can keep his mouth shut. Ludendorff's divorce and remarriage, and the revelation that in the critical days after the war he was busy shipping some of his fortune out of the country in direct violation of law, have all helped to deprive him of popular respect. With him the old order suffers.

Time, of course, aids the republic and so does the order within its boundaries. There is no longer any torture like the Ruhr invasion to upset the people; the French are behaving better, and there is the promise that all the occupied territories will soon be free, that Eupen and Malmedy will be repurchased and the Saar freed from the menace of a change of nationality. The adoption of the Locarno treaties; the admission of Germany to the League and its Council; the amazing prospect of a real Franco-German peace—even if it is only a prospect—and the alliance between German, French, Belgian, and Luxemburg steel and iron magnates have all heightened the prestige of the republic. Every month that passes strengthens it. Every year new voters take their places who have known nothing else since their period of maturity. In Germany, too, nothing succeeds like success. If Stresemann—whose great development as a statesman must be admitted even by those who dislike his personality and his manners—achieves the concord with France, with the aid of Hindenburg's quiet and steadying influence, it is hard to see what grounds the Nationalists and monarchists and extreme conservatives will have for their opposition, especially if economic conditions continue slowly to improve.

The great industrialists themselves are holding out olive branches to organized labor. One of their chief spokesmen has publicly urged the entrance into the government of labor—a remarkable change of heart which bodes great things for the future of German industry, as does also the extraordinary discovery of a means of obtaining all of Germany's oil and lubricants from coal and coal derivatives which would, some bankers believe, in five years render Germany free from dependence upon America, Rumania, or Russia for oil and gasoline now costing her hundreds of thousands of dollars annually. One no longer hears grumblings that things weren't so terrible under the monarchy. The Communists are steadily losing ground and influence. The bitterness of party strife is, perhaps, less intense. Fortunately the long list of political assassinations seems at an end. If the Reichstag still suffers from a surplus of parties and the politicians are mostly selfish and lacking in vision, if the ministry is still without a strong, harmonious, and homogeneous majority—why, the republic still lives and has for all time demonstrated its right to live by its Locarno treaties and the possibility of that real brotherhood of France and Germany which nature intended.

There are dark sides, of course, besides the dreadful individual suffering and the hundreds of thousands of existences utterly warped or ruined by the war. The purely political situation is none too good. There are many reforms needed. There is endless reconstruction still to be done. The sense of gross injustice to Germany in the matter of the war guilt has not wholly disappeared and will not until the sole-guilt charge is disposed of, until many others besides Briand testify to German gallantry in war, and recall that war spells atrocities on all sides. The working classes are bearing a frightful burden and must not be further depressed if they are to retain decent living conditions. If bad times should come, there will again be grave trouble.

There is no millennium in sight in Germany. Her fundamental governmental problems are still to be solved. She is erecting under foreign duress an industrial Juggernaut which may prove to be more threatening to popular government than is the case anywhere else. My point is simply that for the hour Germany is facing to the front, is bearing almost intolerable burdens stoically, and is progressing steadily. She is paying a terrific price for the past but she is accepting that as something as inevitable and as scarcely more worth discussing than the rising of the sun. If she can continue in this spirit, if her admirable self-control and readiness to work should last, if the public order continues and the narrow partisanship of politicians sinks into a genuine desire to place country above party, if there are no baleful outside influences like the collapse of the franc, and if nature is normally favorable, there seems no reason why in fifteen years her economic and financial soundness should not be beyond question. The Germans are winning by the arts of peace what they lost in war. They seem to be demonstrating anew how sweet as well as bitter may be the uses of adversity.

What Cost Mussolini?

By OSWALD GARRISON VILLARD

Paris, September 27

SAID an important American diplomat the other day: "I am little interested in what returning Americans tell me about the great improvement in outward conditions in Italy—that the trains are running on time, that the country has been cleaned up, that people are working, that there are law and order. Any tyrant can accomplish that. What I should like to know is what price Italy will pay for Mussolini about twenty-five or thirty years from now." The truth is, of course, that one can pay far too high a price for outward efficiency and order. Yesterday I met a tourist just in from Rome who is enthusiastic in his praise of the new Italian regime. He recited with the greatest satisfaction that the friend with whom he is traveling was fined twenty lire on a train near Milan because an official came through the car and found that the American had his shoes on the seat opposite. "And the streets! You should see how clean they are and how dirty they used to be!" So it goes on every hand here in Paris. American worshipers of efficiency, of the god of getting things done, as well as our captains of finance and industry, make the air resound with paeans of praise for the man who "has put everybody to work and saved Italy from Bolshevism." It never occurs to them to ask the price that is paid for these things.

These adulators of Mussolini never look below the surface. Is it true that Mussolini saved Italy from Bolshevism? There are many to dispute it. It is a slogan, a trade-mark, a catchword, and so it is eagerly snapped up. Ask people for particulars and they tell you of the attempt of the automobile workers and others to control their factories in Turin, and speak of the bomb explosion in the Diana Theater in Milan. Do they inquire whether everybody is really at work in Italy, and if so, how many days a year and at what rates of pay? No, indeed. The mere statement suffices. Does it ever occur to them to ask how many men are in prison as a result of Fascist activities, with or without charges being filed against them? Do they stop to inquire into Mussolini's personal record? Of course they don't do any of these things. If they did they would find that it is only six years since Mussolini was openly preaching anarchy and the destruction of all government; on the 6th of April, 1920, twelve months and eighteen days after the founding of Fascism, he wrote in his own paper, *Il Popolo d'Italia:* "Down with the state in all its forms and incarnations. . . . To us there remains only the consoling religion of anarchy." Probably 10,000 persons are in jail for having offended Fascism in one way or another, among them an Englishman who got eight months for saying in a restaurart, among other things, that he was tired of seeing Mussolini's "mug" on every wall. Do they ever stop to inquire, these enthusiastic Americans, as to the sources of their news about what Mussolini is doing and saying? Are they aware that the strictest kind of censorship exists in Italy, and that any man who criticizes the Dictator can be sent to jail for thirty months? Are they aware that Mussolini's speech or utterance, before being printed, has usually been revised and edited by the official press bureau?

If they have heard that the entire opposition press has been suppressed in Italy, they have forgotten it. They do not trouble to ascertain that no Italian daily dares to print an account of such a thing as the recent alleged attempt* upon the life of Mussolini until the story has been written precisely as Mussolini desires it to be told. They assume that Italy is content and happy because they hear no protests against what is going on, and they are not aware that he who criticizes the Dictator can immediately be sent to jail for months—jailed immediately with no possibility of rescue by a habeas corpus proceeding, or any other. In their laudation of Mussolini's law and order they remain in ignorance of the fact that the whole Italian judicial system smacks of the Middle Ages and is utilized by the Dictator to crush anyone who opposes his will. If they read of Italians of the highest standing, like Professor Salvemini, being deprived of their citizenship and all their property merely because of daring to criticize the despot, these Americans are not interested—no more than are our great financiers who rise at public luncheons and "bow down before the solemn and majestic and lonely figure of Mussolini." They do not look into the actual conditions of Italian finance and inquire, among many other things,

* This refers to the fifth attempt of September 11.

why it is that the Government is having millions advanced to itself by the treasury with the distinct statement that, by virtue of a royal decree of June last, it shall not account for these millions. Finally, these Americans never take the time to inquire why it is that the Vatican is openly turning its guns upon Fascism, or to ascertain just what is the condition of the agricultural workers under the Mussolini regime. The indisputable facts as to the murder of Matteotti they do not care to know, or they pass the incident over as a trifling peccadillo of friends of the great and lonely and majestic figure.

The diplomat I quoted is right. The interesting thing is not what Mussolini may achieve in the six months or six years that may yet be his, but what is the price for this horrible strangling of liberty, this destruction of every vestige of democratic government, this brutal enslaving of a people for the exaltation of a megalomaniac who, in his speeches at least, is full brother to the ex-Kaiser. All Europe today is anxious as to what he may do tomorrow in international relations. He nearly wrecked the League of Nations three years ago by his assault on Corfu. His attacks upon Germany in regard to the agitation over the Tyrol and upon France for granting the right of political asylum to Italian refugees are samples of the way he keeps the chancelleries of Europe in turmoil. No one knows where he will break out next, or how. He is as adept in rattling the saber in its scabbard as was the Kaiser. Fascist leaders talk recklessly of war with Turkey or even with France. The danger is that in order to save himself he may resort to arms like other pinchbeck Napoleons. Meanwhile, he is the *enfant terrible* of Europe and all Europe is paying for him in increased nervous tension and uncertainty lest it pay also a fearful price in blood. Why has France placed three more divisions on the Italian boundary?

Whenever Mussolini falls, Italy will have to pay the piper. It will be lucky if it does not find its finances completely wrecked and its future heavily mortgaged. It will have laboriously to reconstruct the whole financial and economic structure of the state and the institutions of democracy which Mussolini has pulled down. It will have to revive the faith of the people in the processes of democracy. It will have to end government by fiat, government by passion, government by prejudice, government by corruption, government by brute force. It will find a people disappointed, disillusioned, and with much less courage for undertaking the remodeling of the state. At least the thousands of imprisoned political victims of the great and lonely and majestic figure will be released. The miseries and sufferings caused by the tyrant can never be undone or compensated for. But there can be a return to normal and civilized government even though it be less efficient on the surface. The alternative of such a people living for generations under the domination of a dictator and his successors is simply unthinkable. The world has its cycles of reaction, but it has also its cycles of revolution and evolution.

For Americans Mussolini is serving an extraordinarily useful purpose. You can measure a man's devotion to the democratic ideal and his belief in America's principles of government by the attitude that he takes toward Mussolini. If with some knowledge of what is actually happening in Italy an American still prefers the Mussolini type of government, he is plainly disloyal to our American political principles. Curiously enough, the adorers of Mussolini include primarily those who shouted loudest for war in order to make the world safe for democracy. They are the ones who cry most loudly against the dictatorship of the Bolsheviks in Russia at the moment they laud to the skies the dictatorship of a handful of Fascists. If the Bolsheviks should prove as successful outwardly as Mussolini, we may yet have our captains of industry and our casual tourists singing the praise of the men who may then have brought "order out of chaos" in Russia. Incidentally these American adorers of Mussolini have no time to waste on such happenings as the indictment of two of the Harding Cabinet for corruption in office. Why should they? Many of them subscribed to the eight-hundred-thousand-dollar memorial to the man who gave America the crookedest Cabinet in the history of the American Presidency. And they see nothing inharmonious in their ostentatious worship of the American Constitution and form of government and their loud-mouthed admiration for the majestic figure in Rome. They support public-school contests in oratory upon the subject of our Constitution and the advantages of our Congress over all others, while they whoop for joy when they hear that Mussolini has driven another nail into the coffin of Italian representative government. Let us hope that when the inevitable crash comes in Italy they will recognize the folly of their present position in supporting what a Fascist friend of mine, with unintentional humor, calls the "superdemocracy of Mussolini."

Storm Signals in Mexico

NO, not Mexican signals, but United States signals, and for the fourth time in 1926. Secretary Kellogg has broken loose again. He has, first, inspired a vicious press attack on Mexico apropos of Nicaragua, so that for several days our highly reliable dailies were filled with assertions that from Mexico, that hotbed of Bolshevism, a most dangerous communistic and anti-American propaganda was going all through Central and South America. This he followed up by similarly inspired suggestions that if Mexico persisted in her course in regard to her constitution and land laws there was every prospect that there would be a rupture of diplomatic relations. Simultaneously with this appeared the stories of various minor revolts and of impending revolts in Mexico to which we have already referred. Never was there a clearer case of government-inspired propaganda, and, to our regret, we must record that the Associated Press lent itself to this outrage by carrying the sensational anti-Mexican matter without citing the source. Hitherto it has been Associated Press policy, according to our understanding, to state the origin of a story in order that no charge of being used for propaganda purposes might lie against it.

We regard these developments as serious despite the fact that this is the fourth flurry in this year and that the English oil companies in Mexico have announced their acceptance of those provisions of the Mexican petroleum laws which have so excited our State Department under Messrs. Hughes and Kellogg. Our anxiety is due to the fact that the foreign policy of the United States is in the hands of two exceptionally weak men, Mr. Kellogg and Mr. Coolidge, the latter of whom has, if Washington dispatches are to be trusted, about made up his mind to attempt to break the third-term tradition by becoming a candidate for the Presidency in 1928. Weak men are more to be feared in our foreign affairs than strong men—witness the readiness of William McKinley to plunge this country into war

with Spain purely for partisan reasons, to which fact the historian James Ford Rhodes is the latest witness. We are well aware of the high-sounding words used by President Coolidge in regard to our foreign affairs, to which the New York *World* calls attention in this connection. He said to Congress that for a hundred years we had been pledged "to the peaceful settlement of controversies between nations; by example and by treaty we have advocated arbitration." He also told Congress in his last message that "the policy of our foreign relations, casting aside any suggestion of force, rests solely on the foundation of peace, good-will, and good works." But coming from Mr. Coolidge these sentiments are nothing but the ordinary politician-bunk. They mean nothing. They afford not the slightest guaranty that our policy toward Mexico and Nicaragua will be decent or humane, for Mr. Coolidge is the tool of big business and what big business wants he will do. If our capitalists who have investments in Mexico do not desire to be reasonable and sensible, like their British brethren, we shall undoubtedly have a rupture of diplomatic relations and a policy based upon force—perhaps even a nice little war.

We therefore urge all who have the interest of both countries at heart to rouse themselves once more to make it known in Washington that they do not propose to have the United States play the bully and put itself in the position of attempting to dictate to Mexico what her laws and her constitution shall be—a policy we should never dare to assume toward any country of our own size. Right now is the time to make those protests felt in Washington, not after the breaking off of relations. This time those who deliberately seek strife with Mexico are reinforced by many thousands of our countrymen of the Catholic faith who, not without some reason, feel themselves outraged by the policy of the Mexican Government toward the Catholic faith. President Coolidge wisely refused to make this religious issue the basis of a remonstrance to the Mexican Government—a fact we are glad to record to his credit even though we cannot help suspecting that he was more afraid of the Catholic issue than inspired by a desire to keep his hands off a purely domestic Mexican issue. But multitudes of Catholics will stand behind Congressman John J. Boylan of New York in his announced determination to compel the Foreign Affairs Committee of the House to act upon his resolution for the severance of diplomatic relations with Mexico. Fortunately Senator Borah has spoken out well and refuses to be stampeded in this direction.

Again must we call attention to the deliberate propaganda to get us into war with Mexico. The worst offenders are the owners of the Chicago *Tribune* and *Liberty*, men who in their callous disregard of justice and right-dealing are constantly urging upon the United States the forcible annexation of Mexico upon the purely materialistic ground that the Mexicans are not exploiting their natural resources and that therefore we should. *Liberty* has just been caught printing a picture which purported to portray "Catholics Withdrawing Deposits from the Bank of Mexico in Protest Against the Seizure of Church Property," whereas it was a picture taken and published eleven months before the attempted boycott, in fact before the troubles with the Catholics began, and represented persons depositing instead of withdrawing funds. It is thus that feeling is aroused against Mexico, and always these inciters to strife assume that the United States is inevitably and invariably right, and that we have the power, the right, and the duty to supervise her conduct of her own affairs and even of her foreign relations.

The assertion that Mexico is bolshevik and is spreading bolshevist propaganda is the merest nonsense. Under President Calles, as we have repeatedly pointed out, there is being carried on a progressive, social policy in the interest of the Mexican masses, which the United States in some respects ought rather to be imitating than criticizing. Least of all should there be criticism of her oil laws at the moment when Fall, Sinclair, and Doheny are on trial for alienating part of the birthright of the American people. If certain Mexicans choose to supply arms to revolutionists in Nicaragua, they are merely imitating what United States citizens have been doing in most of the republics to the south of us for the last hundred years. Blustering against Mexico and the threats against her can have only one effect—the rousing of all the Central and South American republics against us.

What Does the War Lord Mean?

DWIGHT F. DAVIS, Secretary of War, has raised more questions than he has answered in his letter to John Nevin Sayre, Vice-Chairman of the Committee on Militarism in Education. Mr. Sayre wrote to the Secretary saying that on a recent speaking trip in opposition to compulsory military training in the colleges he encountered definite interference from Lieutenant Colonel George Chase Lewis, stationed in Oklahoma City with the Ninety-sixth Division of Infantry. Mr. Sayre had promised to address students of the University of Oklahoma at Norman on December 9. Previous to his coming Colonel Lewis wrote to President Bizzell, saying that Mr. Sayre was advocating a Bolshevist program and concluding: "I trust you will be able to curtail pernicious activities at Norman." A group of students which had tried to arrange a meeting for Mr. Sayre under the auspices of the Young Men's Christian Association of the university were unable to obtain its facilities and so Mr. Sayre spoke in the Presbyterian church, off the campus. Colonel Lewis came to the meeting and denounced Mr. Sayre.

> I should like to know [wrote Mr. Sayre to Secretary Davis] whether you consider it a proper function of an army officer to attempt to shut off free speech for peace in universities, Y. M. C. A.'s, and even churches. . . . Finally, may I ask if the War Department does not take energetic measures to restrain Lieutenant Colonel Lewis and others in activities similar to the case mentioned, will I not be justified in charging that the War Department is responsible for the campaign of defamation of character and attempt to repress free speech for peace, in which its subordinates are engaged?

In reply to Mr. Sayre Secretary Davis wrote:

> It is contrary to the policy of the War Department to make adverse criticism of any individual or organization and no army officer has the right to speak for the War Department contrary to its established policy.
>
> On the other hand, it appears that Colonel Lewis was expressing his individual views as a citizen and that he did not even inferentially imply that he was expressing the views of the War Department.
>
> It is manifestly beyond the power of the War Department and, if possible, it would be obviously opposed to the principle of freedom of speech for the War Department to attempt to control all expressions of opinion that officers of the army may make as private citizens.
>
> I can assure you that the War Department has never attempted, directly or indirectly, to repress free speech on any subject whatsoever, either by those who favor or those who oppose its policies.

If Colonel Lewis was expressing merely "individual views as a citizen," how did he come to sign himself "Lt.

AMERICAN LEGION
OFFICIALS ENDORSE
POISON GAS
AS HUMANE
WAR WEAPON

Drawn by Harry S. Bressler

Col. U. S. Infantry, Oklahoma City"? And has Mr. Davis never heard of the case of Captain Paxton Hibben of the Officers' Reserve Corps? How did it happen that Captain Hibben, who was not in the active service of the War Department at all at the time and was earning his livelihood as a civilian, was haled before a court of inquiry for advocating the recognition of Russia by the United States?

Mr. Davis may genuinely wish the War Department to be for free speech; we hope so. But the war machine which he only temporarily and partially controls acts otherwise. Its autocratic spirit and tradition is one of the outstanding perils to America.

War or Peace?

PRESIDENT COOLIDGE, in his message to Congress justifying his private war in Nicaragua, uses all the assorted excuses which he, his Spokesman, and Mr. Kellogg have used on previous occasions. For the first time, however, he has assembled them, and they must make impressive reading for Latin Americans and Europeans.

Recall, first, what Mr. Coolidge is seeking to excuse. We have landed marines in the capital of the Sacasa Government of Nicaragua, ordered the Sacasa army to disarm or get out, censored its communications, blockaded its ports, ordered business firms in its territory not to pay customs duties or internal taxes to its agents. On the other hand, we have landed troops in the rival capital to protect the rival President, and announced that we will give him every facility to buy munitions in the United States and elsewhere. A score of American warships now watch the Nicaraguan coast; thousands of marines stand on guard; American fliers in American airplanes, in the service of the Nicaraguan Government, patrol the Nicaraguan air. At last Mr. Coolidge admits that it is intervention, and offers his complete assortment of excuses.

First, he insists that his favorite President is the constitutional President. His own account of Don Adolfo Diaz's election is enough to deny his argument. Don Adolfo was elected by a rump and illegal Congress, after Emiliano Chamorro had driven the constitutional government, in which Sacasa was Vice-President, out by force of arms.

Second, Mr. Coolidge suggests that it is his duty to aid Diaz because some Mexicans have aided Sacasa. After the interference of which the United States had already been guilty in Nicaragua; in view of the long record of would-be Mexican revolutions fitted out and equipped in the United States, Mr. Coolidge's moral indignation at Mexican friendship for Nicaraguan revolutionaries is ridiculous. Mexico has the same right to ship arms as we.

Next, Mr. Coolidge says that American investments in Nicaragua need protection. Can he name one estate that has been endangered? Does he intend to enunciate the doctrine that American marines must be landed anywhere in the world where revolution, civil war, or rioting suggests the possibility that maybe, some time, somewhere, somehow, American property may be endangered?

Mr. Coolidge's fourth excuse is the canal. There is no Nicaraguan canal as yet, but ten years ago we bought a right to build a canal. Mr. Coolidge does not say that it has been threatened; it has not been threatened. What has it to do with our intervention?

Fifth, Mr. Coolidge fears that if the revolution continues the Nicaraguan currency will be inflated, thereby menacing American business interests. The logic of his argument would imply that the United States must intervene wherever in the world the stability of a currency is threatened. Soldiers and marines will be busy indeed!

And after this the man has the audacity to conclude: "I am sure that it is not the desire of the United States to intervene in the internal affairs of Nicaragua or of any other Central American republic"! What is his message but the most ferocious doctrine of universal intervention which any statesman has ever propounded? What but a principle of universal war? And what is his intervention but an indirect threat to induce Mexico to yield to the oil magnates?

This is doing us infinite harm wherever men can read from the Rio Grande to Cape Horn. Mr. Coolidge and Mr. Kellogg may achieve a distinction which they never meant to acquire—they may become the real founders of a complete Pan-American union of offense and defense against the United States. Already the faint hope of settling Tacna and Arica has faded. The whole world is appalled at our bullying self-righteousness. What may not happen if we continue? Had anyone predicted three years ago that the unorganized masses of China would within three years be sweeping the foreigners into the sea and hauling down the British flag from places where it had flown for sixty-five years he would have been written down a madman. From an American friend in Guatemala we hear that "the prestige of the United States in Central America has never been so low since Roosevelt stole Panama." The worm will turn; when the South American republics realize, as this is teaching them to realize, that they must unite against the Colossus of the North, they, like the Chinese, may realize what a weapon lies in their hands in the economic boycott. Already Mr. Coolidge has done enormous harm to American business in the Southern Hemisphere.

If any spark of decency remains in the Administration it will accept President Calles's offer to arbitrate the difficulties with Mexico, and withdraw the marines from Nicaragua.

No, Mr. Coolidge—No!

SO it is not Nicaragua after all, nor even Mexico, but Moscow that Mr. Coolidge and Mr. Kellogg have been gunning for! Once more the American people are asked to believe that the Bolshevists are after us and that we are saving our homes, our firesides, our women, by establishing a front in Nicaragua and letting the "Bolshevist Government" of Mexico know that we shall dominate in Central America and that anyone who gets in our way will be crushed and broken. There it is in its stark nakedness, this new policy to which his followers are giving the name of "the Coolidge doctrine"!

In all our experience American statesmanship has never touched such a low level. Mr. Kellogg's Bolshevist outburst is an insult to the intelligence of every sane American. His quotation of Chicherin's desire to use Mexico as a base for Communist anti-American activity, with his suppression of President Calles's ringing reply telling the Russians to keep their hands off, is proof of a deliberate duplicity which alone ought to compel his retirement from office. No wonder that the Cleveland *Plain Dealer* calls his effort a "dud," that many Republican newspapers say that neither he nor the President made out a case. The truth is that in this emergency the lives of thousands of Americans, the honor of the United States, and the peace of a continent are in the hands of the two most incompetent politicians this country has ever intrusted with its highest offices. Every step the Administration has taken has proved the absence of a clear-cut policy. It has blundered, blundered from one position to another, advanced one excuse after the other. It began by saying that it was merely protecting American property in Nicaragua and then moved on and on until the Bolshevist bogy was trotted out. It is impossible, after reading the documents, to believe that either the President or his Secretary of State really know or understand the case. What is happening is that they are being led into one position after another by the machinations of subordinates hidden away in minor positions.

Let no one be misled by the apparent improvement in the situation as this issue of *The Nation* goes to press. *There can be no safety in the situation as long as our marines are in Nicaragua and as long as we have a Secretary of State filled with fury and hatred toward Mexico.* True, the fine and outspoken position of such papers as the Springfield *Republican*, the Baltimore *Sun*, the New York *World*, the St. Louis *Post-Dispatch*, and many others is cause for great satisfaction, and so is the outpouring of private protests directed to the White House. Many preachers like Henry Sloane Coffin, S. Parkes Cadman, and Harry Emerson Fosdick have spoken admirably. The Methodists and the Masons are making their great influence felt. The united Southern press is whipping the recreant Democratic Senators into line against the Coolidge policy. Many Catholics are dissenting from the anti-Mexican crusade of the Knights of Columbus. But although the forces for peace have gone into action quicker than ever before, the need for them to continue in action is tremendous. The Administration is quite willing that the impression shall go abroad that things are quieting down. But the danger remains. A few shots in Nicaragua, a mob outburst in Mexico against Americans in official or unofficial life, and the fat may be in the fire. If there are attacks upon American property in Tampico—and renegades can easily be hired for that—the fleet and its guns will appear at once. If a pistol-shot in Bosnia could plunge a world into war what may not a shot in Nicaragua or Mexico do?

No, there must be no relaxing of the efforts of every humane and decent American to bring pressure to bear on Washington and let the President know that neither now nor hereafter will this country stand for a policy of force and that the public desires a new Secretary of State, not one who, for physical reasons alone, is unfit for the position he seeks to fill. Above all else Congress should be called in extra session—the new Congress will be far less in favor of the "Coolidge doctrine" than is the present one. It is openly stated in those misguided business and religious circles which seek a conflict with Mexico that action will come as soon as Congress is out of the way. True, there can be no formal declaration of war until Congress votes it, but any Administration can make war, as Woodrow Wilson, to his shame, twice made war in Mexico and once in Haiti—something that profoundly embarrasses the Democrats in the present crisis.

Already the most insidious argument to combat in Congress is the one which says: "Well, we made a mistake in going in but now we are in we must stay in; our prestige demands it"—with the variation that if we should retreat now our actions would be regarded as a sign of weakness by the Latin Americans who "understand no argument except that of force," as one news agency puts it. That is just the way reckless or incompetent statesmen take to insure to themselves support for acts which cannot stand the light of reason. Once the almost inevitable incident occurs, it is "Stand by the flag and the President"—last week a Representative stated that he was for the American President as against the Mexican whatever the former's stand or acts might be. Passion, a misguided patriotism, unreasoning national prejudices—these come into play at once. Already we have the atrocity story. On January 14 the New York *Times* printed on its first page the account of a Mexican boy's tongue being cut out, and the killing of five boys under twenty. Next will come the cutting off of children's hands and women's breasts, and then the crucifixions on barn doors.

Against these things only a steadfast and lasting opposition on the part of every peace-loving person can prevail. The program is simple: The marines must come out of Nicaragua; any dispute with Mexico must be arbitrated. Since Calles has offered to arbitrate even a domestic law, the United States, for so many years the chief advocate of international arbitration, must accept or write itself down a complete hypocrite. The imperialists, the advocates of war are unceasingly at work. Those who believe in international morality and decency must likewise be unceasing in serving notice upon President Coolidge that the American people do not propose to be betrayed into bloodshed in Nicaragua or Mexico, that they still believe in the right of small nations to self-determination, and that they scorn the doctrine that war-might gives us the right to say how people shall live or think or act in any weaker country.

The Monroe Doctrine and the Coolidge Doctrine

THE powerful uprising of popular feeling against the threat of war with Mexico has, for the present at least, compelled the Administration to modify its tone, and arbitration of the outstanding differences seems likely. The marines, however, remain in Nicaragua; and public relief at the removal of the imminent threat of war seems to have obscured the fact that we are continuing to commit the crime of military interference with that small republic.

Despite the contradictory excuses offered by the Administration, certain facts stand uncontested. No American or other foreign property had been injured by the revolutionaries when we landed our marines; no American or other foreign lives had been lost. There was no threat of foreign intervention; at most the British and Italian representatives at Managua asked the American marines to give the property of their nationals the same special protection which was contemplated for Americans. There had been, we repeat, no damage to foreign lives or property; only that threat of damage which any revolution must cause. How does this relate to the Monroe Doctrine whose name the Presidential Spokesman uses so recklessly?

James Monroe was a cautious soul, fearful of political entanglements in either hemisphere. It was only when there seemed a real possibility that Bourbon France would form an offensive alliance with Spain to recover the old Spanish colonies, then young republics, in South and Central America, that President Monroe took action. And the momentous words in which he enunciated a century ago what has come to be known as the Monroe Doctrine sound strangely mild today when a score of battleships patrol the coast of Nicaragua and United States marines guard the capital.

> The American continents [said Mr. Monroe], by the free and independent condition which they have assumed and maintain, are henceforth not to be considered as subjects for future colonization by any European Powers. . . . We should consider any attempt on their part to extend their system to any portion of this hemisphere as dangerous to our peace and safety.

Yet Mr. Coolidge explains that the Monroe Doctrine required us to intervene in Nicaragua. Piffle! Mr. Coolidge does not know what the Monroe Doctrine is.

The Monroe Doctrine, to be sure, has undergone certain sea changes in the course of a century; but never before has it been stretched so far from its original shape. President Polk, in the forties, suggested that the doctrine might require the United States to occupy territory of the Southern republics to prevent the introduction of the European system; President Grant, in the eighties, announced that the doctrine did not permit transfer of American territory from one European nation to another—but neither he nor Polk carried his new principles into practice. Mr. Blaine, as Secretary of State in the eighties, sought to extend the doctrine to the assertion of the exclusive right of the United States to umpire in all disputes between other American Powers, or between those Powers and Europe—a right which, one need hardly add, is admitted neither in Europe nor in Latin America, although it has become increasingly a habit. (The fiasco of Mr. Coolidge's "mediation" between Peru and Chile may put an end even to the habit.)

Theodore Roosevelt made the most striking additions to the Monroe Doctrine—but though he made the phrases "dollar diplomacy" and "big stick" current he never went so far as Calvin Coolidge. While he suggested that we might have to act as an international policeman in flagrant cases of wrongdoing by a Latin nation, he also said:

> If a republic to the south of us commits a tort against a foreign nation, then the Monroe Doctrine does not force us to interfere to prevent punishment of the tort, save to see that the punishment does not assume the form of territorial occupation in any shape.

And Roosevelt declared that

> It has long been the established policy of the United States not to use its armed forces for the collection of ordinary contract debts due to its citizens by other governments. We have not considered the use of force for such a purpose consistent with that respect for the independent sovereignty of other members of the family of nations, which is the most important principle of international law and the chief protection of weak nations against the oppression of the strong. It seems to us that the practice is injurious in its general effect upon the welfare of weak and disordered states, whose development ought to be encouraged in the interests of civilization; that it offers frequent temptation to bullying and oppression and to unnecessary and unjustifiable warfare.

Two short decades later, we have moved so far that a President of the United States justifies the use of military force not merely to enforce payment of contract debts but to ward off a threat of possible danger to property, and even suggests that we must use our troops to prevent a possible inflation of the currency!

A billion and a quarter dollars, the Department of Commerce says, is the rough total of American investments in foreign capital securities in 1926. Never in history has one nation poured forth so much money in a single year. Nor is this all: when Belgium, Italy, Hungary, Bulgaria, Honduras, Costa Rica, or Salvador, the Hugo Stinnes Corporation, the Swedish International Match Company, the Trinidad Oil Fields, the Chile Copper Company, or the South Porto Rico Sugar Company floats a loan in New York—as all of these, and many others, did in the last quarter of 1926—the fact is publicly noted; but when an American oil or copper company invests more money in its own estates in Chile or Mexico no public record is made. We are aware how loans from government to government have embittered our relations with Europe; most of us admit that without the loans from banks to Central American governments our increasing tendency to dictate in the Caribbean would at least have been more restrained. Whither are we bound?

The Coolidge message excusing intervention in Nicaragua made no distinctions of size and geography. Americans have just lent $1,500,000 to the Housing and Realty and Improvement Company of Germany and $2,500,000 to the German Protestant Church welfare institutions. Logically the Coolidge doctrine would justify us in landing marines, in case of another German civil war, to defend the houses and hospitals in which Americans have invested their cash. It sounds ridiculous, but it is no more absurd today than Mr. Coolidge's present doctrine would have seemed in the days of President Monroe.

Kellogg Must Go

MR. COOLIDGE, having made a worthy appeal for another conference to reduce armaments, finds himself turned down by both France and Italy. Apparently he and his inept Secretary of State failed to follow the usual procedure of sounding out in advance the several governments through our ambassadors and so laid themselves open to this contretemps. In addition it has been explained for them that their letter of invitation was "misunderstood"—as if it were not the first duty of a statesman in a matter of this kind to make his meaning clear and straightforward. The result is primarily the humiliating reply from France, whose Foreign Minister, M. Briand, apparently took a vicious pleasure in reminding the United States that it was not a member of the League of Nations and protested solemnly that his country could not join in a special conference to limit navies when the League was at work on a general disarmament program. If this answer seems in part a disingenuous and deliberate French effort to shelve anew the question of disarmament—some of the arguments advanced could have been equally well used in connection with the Washington Conference—Mr. Kellogg invited it by insufficient forethought and preparation. He even gave the impression that he was deliberately striking at the League. This is what is called great statesmanship by our noble President and his Secretary of State.

This blundering is only characteristic of the Coolidge-Kellogg diplomacy in every other field. In China the plan for the neutralization of Shanghai was turned down by all three of the Chinese groups. It was absurd on the face of it to ask the Nationalists calmly to agree to abandon a chief aim, control of one of their own large cities. Here, too, Mr. Kellogg got hold of an excellent idea and jumped to use it without adequate understanding. Both his gestures to China have failed utterly. He has now no independent American program, but is apparently merely playing second fiddle to the British. The English Government is at least frank about its militaristic policy, which is so properly characterized by Bertrand Russell elsewhere in this issue of *The Nation*. It is rushing thousands of troops and many warships; we are shipping in marines little by little and preparing more and more for hostilities in such a way that the individual movements of troops and ships attract less attention. But there is every indication now that if the Cantonese arrive before Shanghai and the big guns go off we shall be foremost in the "policing." Anything may happen when there is no clear-cut principle or policy behind our actions, when we merely drift, failing to notify the world just what we are up to. Putting forth promises to do what the Chinese wish "if, but, and when" gets the United States nowhere and will eventually win for us the same hatred which now accrues to the British and threatens them with the complete ruin of their trade and position in the East.

If we look to the south of us there is the same amazing record of blunders. As for Mexico, we are marking time; we are apparently in a deadlock which will last until Congress is safely out of the way, when the President and Secretary Kellogg will, we very much fear, begin drastic action against the Republic of Mexico. Secretary Wilbur's harping on the bolshevist menace in his speech at the New York Republican Club indicates that that fake issue is still to be kept before the public. We do not believe that the outpouring of public protests has as yet been sufficient to deter the Administration from its program to "discipline" Mexico and any other country to the south of us which does not do our will. To Nicaragua, where the Sacasa forces, which Washington opposed, are sweeping the country, we are rushing additional thousands of marines to deprive the constitutional party of the victory which it has clearly won—all of this under pretense that we are protecting American property. In Panama Mr. Kellogg's offensive and defensive treaty which we were to have put over so easily has been rejected by the legislature. In Tacna and Arica we have scored a monumental failure because of the blundering in Washington. In the matter of the World Court, Mr. Coolidge was passionately for it and forced it through the Senate; now he takes his defeat on that issue lying down. He will not even state whether he will do anything about it or whether he intends to leave matters as they are.

As for the debt settlements, our Administration has achieved no action from France on the agreement with that country. It may have been good policy to make those settlements with Italy and Belgium at a few cents on the dollar, but the net result is that the American public has been deceived and Europe merely irritated. As for Russia, we are still pursuing the ostrich policy of pretending not to know that that great country is there, while we tremble at the slightest word of any bolshevist leader or group which points at us. And what is the net result of it all? Why, we are uniting all Latin America against us as a nation of sinister and hypocritical imperialists and are destroying American business and business opportunities from here to Cape Horn. In Europe they think us a blood-sucking miser, and are slowly being driven into union against us. In Asia, as we have said, we are becoming a mere tool of Great Britain in the estimation of a great people who felt that they had a right to the sympathy, cooperation, and moral support of a nation which also once threw off a foreign yoke. We have no friends left anywhere.

Now, if the Government could show some actual achievements, some record of having accomplished something, to offset its blunders, that would be another matter. We cannot discover that it has achieved a single genuine success of moment. And yet the business men of the country and even a part of the press which has not yet altogether abdicated the critical faculty, still pretends that Mr. Coolidge is a great President, that he is wise, sagacious, farsighted, and the best friend of business that we have ever had in the White House—he who is destroying our prestige and influence in the market of South America. If public opinion were alive and awake today as it was before the war the Coolidge Administration would stand condemned throughout the country. Only the absence of an intelligent opposition in Washington—the Progressive leaders are too few to be effective—prevents the complete exposure and condemnation of Mr. Coolidge and Mr. Kellogg. That only makes it the more desirable that those Americans who believe in old-fashioned honor, integrity, and decency should be insistent in their demands for a new Secretary of State. No matter who succeeds him the time has come to say that Kellogg must go.

Basing a War on Rumors

TRADITIONAL Coolidge cautiousness has been tossed overboard by the President in his haste to execute his latest hostile move against Central America. Hereafter he will first ship his marines and airplanes (equipped principally for bombing purposes) to Nicaragua and elsewhere, and then inquire into his reasons for doing so. The guilt of the accused party will be subjected to examination after the accused party is dead. How can any other interpretation be placed on the President's explanation, given orally to the press on February 18, that in sending 1,600 additional marines and six DeHaviland bombers to Corinto he was acting upon information which to him "looks like a reliable report." If this policy is generally followed by the Coolidge-Kellogg regime in the future, marines will be sent on wild expeditions all over the world, not to protect American lives and property but to run down the innumerable reports of dubious reliability which steadily pour into the ears of important Washington functionaries.

Eight hundred additional marines landed at Corinto, Nicaragua, on February 20; the transport Henderson left Newport, Rhode Island, on the same day with 565 marines, planning to pick up 1,500 more at Philadelphia and Norfolk, for Caribbean service. The railroad is to be guarded, the chief cities of Nicaragua occupied, by marines and bluejackets. When the new orders are carried out 5,750 armed men will be stationed on Nicaraguan soil under the American flag or aboard the United States naval vessels now lying off the coasts of the Central American republic. This military force, of a size to satisfy the ambitions of the most outspoken imperialists, will provide eight protectors for each of the 700 American citizens who, according to the most authentic records available, have established their residence in Nicaragua! The Washington correspondents have expressed the guess that these armed men will be used either to "neutralize" the entire country—a euphemism for turning it over to Diaz—or to establish a military protectorate identical with that in Haiti.

Two hundred marines and six airplanes left San Diego for Corinto on February 16. Lesser naval officials explained that while the planes were ostensibly intended for observation purposes, they were in fact equipped with stores of 25-pound bombs, presumably to be dropped for "moral effect." On February 17, however, Rear Admiral Latimer, in command of the special United States service squadron in Nicaraguan waters, expressed surprise at the Navy Department's action in sending him reinforcements. He had not asked for the additional marines, he declared, adding that "there is really no need for them, as there already is a sufficient number of marines and bluejackets in Nicaragua to fulfil requirements."

The joke obviously was on the admiral. He is on the scene of action, but obviously the "apparently reliable" information which reached Washington, and made necessary the tripling of his force, had not reached him. On the same day Secretary Wilbur, probably with his mind on naughty Nicaraguan bolshevists and their contemplated seduction of little American children, announced that not only were 200 marines and six airplanes being rushed to Corinto but that the additional force of 1,400 marines was even then being made ready for a trip to Nicaragua. When his attention was called to Admiral Latimer's statement that reinforcements were unnecessary, Mr. Wilbur smiled sweetly as though to say: "Well, that's a good one on Latimer." Then he added that if the admiral were unable to find work for the extra leathernecks, he was at liberty to send them back.

The White House Spokesman, coming to bat for a moribund State Department, got into action on February 18. He frankly assured the assembled Washington correspondents that this Government did not intend to permit other foreigners to send rifles and bullets into Nicaragua; that privilege, he implied, was reserved for Uncle Sam. Nothing was said, of course, as to what right the United States had to take such action. The Spokesman maintained a profound silence as to the right, vigorously maintained by the United States during the World War, of citizens of a neutral country to sell munitions wherever they pleased —a right which would seem to belong to Mexico as well as to the United States in the absence of a declaration of war.

What the Spokesman—who was, we may reveal, Calvin himself—said, according to the short-hand notes of a skeptical correspondent, was:

> It is difficult to get any information upon which you can rely absolutely, but in case of peril of this kind it is assumed that *anything that looks like a reliable report should be acted upon*, and [we should] be prepared to meet that serious effect that could accrue from such a situation.

It looks as if the marines were going to be busy.

The Military Menaces the World

MR. H. G. WELLS did an excellent service by his smashing discussion of the military situation of the world in the New York *Times* of March 6. The question Are Armies Needed Any Longer? he answers emphatically in the negative. The war of the future, he declares, "is from first to last a job for technicians and artisans. There is no more use for drilled troops in it than there is for the Greek phalanx." The professional military classes, he points out, will everywhere try by treaty to put off the use of the latest chemical methods in order to save themselves from extinction. But the fact to him is clear that "the evolution of war is abolishing the soldier altogether." "All these handsome individuals running about or galloping about in tabs and buttons and gold lace are of no earthly use at all. . . . The soldier in uniform is as out of date today as the man in armor was in 1600." Hence Mr. Wells is grateful to the United States Senate for killing the treaty to end the use of poison gas. He wants the new warfare developed to the fullest extent. He even welcomes the use of deadly bacilli—anything to make war as horrible and as deadly as possible—and he ridicules those who, like *The Nation*, are trying to stop chemical warfare.

Now as to this, Mr. Wells may be right and we wrong. It depends in some measure on whether you believe in setting afloat, in order to end war, forces which may conceivably wipe out whole populations. The question is whether, after such a struggle, there will be enough left of the world for anybody to care whether war goes on or not. But with his contention that the modern soldier is an utter anachronism we are in entire accord, as we are with his assertion that the desire to retain their profession makes the "professionally belligerent class, officers, their womenkind, and every sort of person who upon occasion wears uniform and a sword, and is entitled to a salute," favor war. The officers often believe that they do not favor it. They sententiously remark that they are the ones who cannot favor war, since it is they who pay the price. But the possibility of war they insist upon; for otherwise they would be kept out of jobs. Hence their bitterness against all pacifists who are bent on eliminating the fighters as well as war. Hence their growing fury because some churches begin to attack war seriously—it was an American Major General who denounced the American churches a couple of months ago in New York because, he said, the churches were becoming pacifist! As Mr. Wells shows, our military believe that they must defend us against the people next door, and the military next door believe that our forces are only waiting to spring upon them. Military men everywhere insist that national honor is in their keeping, and their "dread" of war was well illustrated by a recent dispatch in the militaristic New York *Herald Tribune*, which reported the army and navy men in Washington as being furious at the inaction of the Government in the Mexican crisis—they wanted to show Mr. Coolidge how to deal with Mexico.

Every thesis Mr. Wells lays down he could prove to the hilt in this country. Many competent witnesses declare that Englishmen do not want war today; that the bands may still play for an expedition to China or some other remote clime, but that England is through for the present with any really first-class war. They may be right; we hope so; but certainly here in America we are more belligerent than ever before, and, as Mr. Coolidge boasted recently, we have 610,000 men under arms annually—nearly as many as the German standing army of 1914—as a result of the war to end war. We now have nearly 100,000 reserve officers, and at least 22,000 active army and navy officers who are propagandizing for war and military training and have adopted the Prussian military ideals for which we once excoriated the Kaiser and his group. An active lieutenant colonel has just been speaking throughout Illinois by order of the War Department, seeking to create an opinion against the Congress—whose creature the army should be—and to develop sentiment in favor of larger war appropriations. Press dispatches have reported the War Department as determined to put a reserve officer in every hamlet and town to create nationalistic and "patriotic," i. e., militaristic, feeling. The army and navy propagandists are everywhere aided by big business men.

Of this there has been a most interesting example in Detroit, where there has been a struggle between the pro-war business men and the churches which would astound Mr. Wells. There the Board of Commerce has compelled the weak-kneed and cowardly Y. M. C. A. to adopt a resolution approving of "the National Defense Act, as amended in 1920, which provides for the voluntary organization of Reserve Officers' Training Corps camps"—a resolution received by the board with "delight and satisfaction." Why was the board so concerned? Not because of any imminent danger of foreign invasion; not because the big business men have the slightest knowledge whether the summer training camps have any military value or not. Their concern was revealed at a meeting between some of the board and a few protesting ministers. According to the Detroit *Free Press*, "those favoring the Defense Act said that adequate preparation was the *bulwark against revolution*." There you have it. The United States army from 1866 to 1898 numbered only 25,000. Was big business interested? Not at all. But the situation has changed now. The World War gave a Socialist or Communist government to nearly every country in Europe. It released new ideas which terrify the American business men. Hence they back the training camps and the R. O. T. C., not for the military training given but for "the ideals of citizenship" inculcated there by the military preceptors. General Pershing hardly speaks of military instruction in his appeals for the camps; he calls them a great school of citizenship. Well he may. Blind obedience to the present order is what the business backers of the camps want. No liberal-minded or anti-war person would be allowed to speak at them, nor would anybody be permitted to quote President Coolidge's saying of October 6, 1925, that "we know, and everyone knows, that these old [military] systems, antagonisms, and reliance on force have failed," and that "no nation ever had an army large enough to guarantee it against attack in time of peace or insure it victory in time of war." If General Pershing thinks at all he knows that Mr. Wells is just about correct when he declares that "it is the country which has the courage to scrap its army most completely which may come nearest to winning in the next great war," and that the military training at the camps is worthless.

The British-American Alliance

THE Cantonese have taken the native city of Shanghai, and the Guaranty Trust Co., together with J. and W. Seligman & Co., have made a one-year million-dollar loan to the little Diaz "Government" in Nicaragua. As we write, fifteen hundred American marines in full war regalia, tin hats included, are policing the tumultuous streets of far-off Shanghai, and 5,000 more are on duty maintaining "neutral zones" in Nicaragua. Relations between the United States and Mexico are strained, and Mr. Kellogg is solemnly debating with himself and his cronies the advisability of lifting the arms embargo and inviting another revolution as a means of imposing our oleaginous will upon the Calles Government.

Shanghai is a long way from Mexico City or Managua, but a spark of sympathy binds the remote cities. Bolshevism? No, it is not Bolshevism which is making the whole world kin, but a common sense of the oppression of Anglo-American imperialism. As Senator Borah said in his New Haven speech: "Communism and Russian influence have no more to do with either the origin or execution of [Mexico's] policies than they have to do with the policies of our own government." Nor is there Bolshevism, in any special Russian sense, in China. There is, of course, a determination to break the ancient bonds which have fettered China's youth to a dead past, and a special passion to do away with those shackles which foreign nations have imposed upon China. But to assume that a few Russian agents with a few thousand dollars could turn the course of history is puerile. The Bolsheviks have undoubtedly sought to stir up revolution in a dozen different countries, but they have never yet made a revolution which would not have occurred without them. In Germany, Bulgaria, Poland, Esthonia they have failed. In China the revolution is still a rising tide, and the Russians have won prestige because instead of seeking to dam the rising tide of Nationalism they have swum with the current. Some of us regret that America did not have the vision to act as aid and abettor to a movement so like the struggle which gave our own country birth as a nation.

But there is a kinship between what is happening in China and what is happening in Nicaragua and Mexico, and it will be a pity if our statesmen and business men do not read the lesson. China has reached a riper stage in the history of empire. Time was—and not so long ago—when foreign nations could do in China what America is doing in Nicaragua today. They intervened, they lent money, they carved out spheres of influence, and took over the customs. We are but repeating the ancient story of imperialism. Encouraged by the State Department, a group of New York bankers are providing the funds to aid one party in Nicaragua to defeat the other. Diaz has been beaten in battle after battle. By his own admission he was unable to hold his post without aid from the American Government. He was without prestige and without funds; now our bankers give him the money with which to win prestige. Presumably the bankers' money will pay the DuPonts and the Remingtons and the others who will supply Diaz with guns and gunpowder. And when the shooting is over, what then? Diaz will still be incompetent; we shall have to help him hold power. The Marine Corps publicity department, which floods the country with stories of our beneficent rule in Haiti, will flood the country with feature picture-stories of our success in Nicaragua. A decade ago similar stories of the virtues of foreign "aid" to China still flooded the press of the entire Western world. Then—something happened in China. It will happen in the Caribbean, too. These people seem to us incompetent today—able only to eat bananas and write poetry. We will teach them, as we have taught the Chinese, how to organize, how to equip armies, how to fight. And in time they will turn our lessons against us.

It is natural that the British should be eager to help us embark upon the course of empire. Their great empire, stretched across the Seven Seas, is in process of disintegration. What is happening in China is the greatest blow which British prestige has suffered since the American Revolution. It shakes India; it imperils Hongkong, Singapore, Aden, Egypt, the Sudan and the Suez, Cyprus, Malta, Gibraltar—that entire chain of foreign fortresses over which the British imperial flag flies. If one colored people can throw the British out of its territory, cannot another? Perhaps, after all, there is nothing supernatural about the people of that little island off the West coast of Europe. But if the great young empire of the Western Hemisphere, rich America, the new marvel, the traditional friend of democracy and of oppressed peoples, can be brought to act like Britain and with Britain, a new prestige comes to the relief of the British Empire. No wonder, indeed, if the British are willing to send a warship to Nicaragua to help bolster up the Coolidge-Kellogg policy of aping British imperialism; no wonder if the British in China ask that we stand shoulder to shoulder to them in defense of white prestige.

Of course, the program is not set forth in such crass terms. The American people, dulled as they are today, would not permit so gross a betrayal of their ideals. So we are presented with the camouflaged scarecrow of world-wide Bolshevism. Wherever a people dares demand its freedom from foreign interference, that is Bolshevism. Wherever the universality of white empire is threatened, the threat is Bolshevism. Of course, we are all against Bolshevism. Thus the British-American alliance is cemented.

There is, as yet, no formal treaty of alliance. There are, probably, no documents recording the intimate collaboration. But the habit of cooperation with Great Britain has grown mightily since the days of the Washington Conference, when Britain, at our behest, denounced the British-Japanese alliance, assuredly not without expecting from America a *quid pro quo*. Joint action is not, necessarily, a bad habit; more than once in recent years British-American cooperation has been a force for sanity in European affairs (although today England is, unfortunately, acting as aide to Mussolini). Both nations want above all that peace without which profitable, orderly trade seems difficult. But collaboration, when it takes the form of aggressive imperialism, may be dangerous. America does not need to set herself against the new tides of national and race liberation. We do not believe that she wants to lead in that direction. Under the cloak of anti-Bolshevism, she is being pushed.

1917-1927

TEN years ago the American people reversed its national tradition against entangling alliances and participation in the political struggles of Europe in order, as it fondly believed, to make the world safe for democracy, safeguard the rights of small nations and the principle of self-determination, and establish the reign of law by waging a war to end all war. Had our entrance into the war been excused upon the ground that as guardians of the rights of neutrals we could not permit international law to be violated, it would have been necessary to defend these rights against the equally grievous and ultimately more serious violation of neutral rights by the British Orders in Council. Sagacious minds in 1917, familiar with the development of European struggles for political and economic supremacy, were loath to permit the United States to throw itself into the cauldron merely to aid one party to a traditional European war. They were unconvinced that the grounds of intervention alleged were sustainable by the evidence involved in the issue, or achievable by war.

In November, 1916, the American people had fairly well recorded its insistence on non-intervention. President Wilson in December, 1916, had declared that the struggle involved no moral issues and ought, therefore, to be brought to a sensible close. Unfortunately, by his condonation of Allied violations of the rights of neutrals he had so weakened the force of his proposals for peace that Mr. Lloyd George felt no need for heeding them and demanded a knock-out. Lloyd George ultimately got it with our help, and future generations of Europeans, and of Americans as well, must pay the penalty for the mistake.

From January to April, 1917, a press campaign, the like of which has never been witnessed in the United States, wrought the East into a state of mind where the Wilsonian formula of the moral issues seemed to be accepted by a considerable number of our people. A show of unity was achieved; but it was always a show only. Actually, the country was divided, and while opposition was suppressed in the way that governments can suppress it, the opposition was silenced rather than convinced. The mob spirit, an artificial exultation, ruled supreme, and that is good neither for leaders nor for led.

If the causes and justifications for our intervention were based on facts, some evidence of their truth ought now, after ten years, to be apparent. At least, we have now, in the calmness of reflection, an opportunity to take stock and to determine whether the policy of intervention was wise or not. What do we see? By abandoning the rights of neutrals we threw international law into chaos; the refusal of our State Department to press our neutrality claims against Great Britain was a further blow at international law. The theory of the League of Nations, that neutrality is an undesirable and improper status, is likely to find support in the fact that neutral rights have been put at the mercy of any powerful belligerent. Another most effective blow on behalf of anarchy was given by the Treaty of Versailles, in which the trustees of civilization began a raid on some of the most fundamental principles of international law because they saw in it a momentary gain. We refer, primarily, to the confiscation of private property under Article 297, a precedent which may be dangerously extended. This example, destroying what little progress international law had made, has thrown us back toward the days of anarchic barbarism.

The disarmament of Germany was to have been the first step in general disarmament. Who can read the news of the Geneva "Disarmament Conference" with any belief that the Allied Powers, masters of Europe's fate, have any serious intention of disarming? They have made such a mess of European political and economic conditions that even with the best intentions the problem is one of enormous difficulty. In the course of our quixotic intervention, we contracted a national war debt of twenty-five billions, and have apparently incurred, in addition, the enmity of our European debtors, notwithstanding the cancelation of billions, for continuing to suppose that their signatures were genuine.

In our own administration of the war policy we debauched the national traditions. We are now among the most distinguished confiscators of private property of which history has any record, notwithstanding President Coolidge's unctuous remark that we have "scrupulously observed" the principle of international law that private property is immune from violation or confiscation. Someone should call the President's attention to the Chemical Foundation case before he makes further charges against Mexico. Public and private morality seem to have gone into eclipse; after the emotional debauch of war days we are no longer capable of rousing ourselves to end real evils at home. We smile at corruption in high places; we are content to see the government become the tool of those who least need its aid; we sneer at every effort at reform as an outbreak of "bolshevism." We, who preached so nobly about "the rights of small nations" ten years ago, pay no attention to them in our own back yard but play the strutting bully ourselves.

And Europe? Well, look at it. Is there any sign there that the last war is over, that the next is not on its way? Have the trustees of civilization made an arrangement under which Europe can live in peace? We doubt it. At the moment, we see the most dangerous diplomatic struggles in Italy, Jugoslavia, France, England, Poland, Russia. Have they promoted democracy or the will to peace? The predictions and promises of 1917 are sad reading today. The United States might have led in liquidating the war had our leaders seen and understood it in the light of past history. Instead they greeted it as a "different" war, a holy crusade, prolonged it to its bitter conclusion, and made inevitable a treaty of peace as sadistic as any treaty that has disgraced the pages of recorded history. Our President and our people were betrayed by that treaty, but, unhappily, not many have yet realized the fact. It dashed every hope of a regenerated world, and not even the League of Nations can make much impression on the forces which it set in motion. It is not unfair to say that American intervention in the war made possible the Treaty of Versailles and its horrible consequences. The lapse of ten years can hardly give a thrill of satisfaction to those who brought us into the war, who commemorate it with pride while handing its bleak heritage of burdens and hates to the generations coming after.

Ten Years After

By OSWALD GARRISON VILLARD

TEN years only since 1917. Yet a lifetime of dramatic events to which there is no end has been crowded into them. Is not Shanghai just proclaimed by its conquerors as a base for that world revolt which *The Nation* declared inevitable when the infamous treaty of peace was published in May, 1919? Shanghai is, indeed, as long a way from Paris as 1927 is from 1917; it is merely another proof that if you go to war you cannot tell where the war will end any more than you can prophesy the date of its conclusion. Its ramifications are endless; its reverberations carry to the ends of the earth. Because of it men may die in furthermost isles; you begin war in Cuba and you complete it among Malays on the other side of the globe. Only one thing is certain: Wherever war, there liberty shrivels, lies insensate—dies. You may glorify the struggle as you will, and supply it, if you please, with aims as lofty as you can possibly portray by pen or voice; you may attribute to yourself and your allies the purest motives, the noblest objectives, the most humanitarian desires. You will inevitably fail to achieve those ends, and your beautifully cadenced words will turn to ashes because it is ordained by the way of the world that goodness and virtue, the safeguarding of human rights and what is called civilization can never be achieved by letting loose hell upon earth.

Why We Went to War

We shall fight for the things which we have always carried nearest our hearts, for democracy, for the right of those who submit to authority to have a voice in their own governments, for the rights and liberties of small nations, for a universal dominion of right by such a concert of free peoples as shall bring peace and safety to all nations and make the world itself at last free.—From Wilson's War Address to Congress, April 2, 1917.

So after ten years the picture is clearly drawn for everyone who cares to see, whose eyes are not wilfully blind. Woodrow Wilson himself declared that the "full price of peace" would be "full, impartial justice—justice done at every point and to every nation . . ." What a mockery, what a still-born judgment! To what deliberate violations of this sacred pledge did he not sign his name and put his country's honor in trust at Paris! Each passing year has made plainer that democracy was never so unsafe, that the rights of small nations were never so jeopardized—those small nations to whom Mr. Wilson pledged the victory, and "the privilege of men everywhere to choose their way of life and of obedience." His own nation still subjugates Haiti, to the conquest of which he personally sent our troops to take a toll of 3,500 Haitians officially reported dead; it still overruns Nicaragua with marines, and threatens Mexico because its people demand the "privilege of men everywhere to choose their way of life and of obedience." To Russians we deny this same privilege because we hate the form their revolution has taken, and think infinitely more of our individual properties than of their human rights.

In Europe the crass and cruel injustices of the peace treaty still cry to high Heaven for redress. In the Tyrol as in other states they curse the name of Wilson, the author of their misery. There is evidence that today the Germans are more popular in France than the Americans; that the acclaim which greeted our plunge into the war has turned to envy, bitterness, and open revolt at what they call their bond-slavery to our Treasury. Everywhere in Europe the tide of hatred against America rises. Before he died Woodrow Wilson himself said: "I would like to see Germany clean up France"—adding, "I would like to meet Jusserand and tell him that to his face"; the French invasion of the Ruhr was for him the last straw, the climax of "French bad faith, ingratitude, and avarice," the final pricking of his self-blown bubble that the peace would spell "justice done at every point to every nation." Yet he died still blind to the fact that he chose the worst method in the world to achieve his purposes; the method that made success impossible.

With the menace of a new war in the Balkans hanging over Europe, on this tenth anniversary of our joining the war to end war; with more, and more dangerous, treaties of offense and defense in effect than ever before; with probably as many men under arms in time of peace as bore them in July, 1914; with all Europe headed straight toward an economic alliance against their "saviors" of 1917, only a man with superb indifference to truth and the realities can assert that the Americans who fell in France did not die in vain; that the world is better off for the blood-bath from which it emerged in 1918 with all its evil passions unleashed. To scan extracts from Mr. Wilson's utterances made when war began is to read the proof of the total failure of the United States to achieve a single one of its major objectives. True, the Hohenzollern fell, but the system of which they were but a revolting product remains. The virus of it has entered our own American veins. Moreover, most of our Allies in the war to banish war are today busily engaged in placing every obstacle in the way of disarmament. In eleven European countries despots wipe their feet upon the prostrate bodies of Liberty and Democracy, though none but Mussolini dares to avow it and to boast of profaning the twin goddesses in behalf of whom Woodrow Wilson summoned this country to war.

Force—force without stint—Wilson called for and used, and two million Americans made the great parade across the Atlantic. True, we kept faith with the war-makers' promises that we sought and would take no recompense for ourselves—no land, no booty, no indemnity. But the parade lies nine years to the rear of us and the world is unchanged; the great objectives unachieved. Hate, bitterness, tariff hostilities, the lust for power, for more places in the sun, for more colonies, for the domination of this sea and that littoral—these are our daily grist of news. The ideals of 1917, the hopes, the ambitions, the pictures painted by the smoothest of orators—where are they now? Based on lies, buttressed by endless hypocrisies, fortified by tales of crimes that were never committed, championed by ignorance of what it was all about and of the historical background and implications, the victory was gained only to be utterly lost.

Ever since it has seemed as if America *had* lost its soul. There are voices heard in every direction, nothing clear and nothing definite; no leadership, no guidance, no appeal to our nobler selves. We lost the war and we are drunk by a prosperity which has made us so indifferent that, the gates being left unguarded, the domestic enemy has entered and taken every salient and every trench. What has the country gained at home? Where are the causes that Woodrow Wilson and Theodore Roosevelt championed in 1912 and until we went into the war? Has the nation found spiritual peace and content? Does it face the future united, unafraid, resolute to progress, to continue the development of a sound democracy devoted to justice, jealous of the rights of each and every one? Read the platform and speeches of Woodrow Wilson when he first sought the Presidency and you read of things as remote as the days of Lincoln. There lie promises unfulfilled, a program shattered; a new way of life unchampioned today, yes forgotten. The crassest of materialism reigns in Washington by grace of Woodrow Wilson's plunge into the war, and where materialism is there sits corruption. The Denbys, the Falls, the Daughertys, the Dohenys, now all condemned by one court or another, are some of the responses to the appeals for war, to the setting free of the passions that war spells. These are some of the most striking results of the effort to achieve righteousness at home and abroad by unparalleled blood-letting.

Who speaks now of the referendum, recall, and initiative, of the popular control of our natural resources? Who demands that the people shall master their government? Who denounces monopoly? How few excoriate, as did Mr. Wilson, the situation under which, to use his words, "a comparatively small number of men control the waterpowers" and the railroads; yes, "control prices" and "the larger credits of the country." "There is hardly a part of the United States where men are not aware," Mr. Wilson declared unchallenged, "that secret private purposes and interests have been running the government." Today—1927? Why, we have thrown wide open the doors and invited in these same few dominating men and their followers and turned over the government to them—and the man who opened those doors was Woodrow Wilson himself. It is now a government by, for, and of Big Business, with its completely subservient employee in the White House.

"His master's voice has spoken," said Woodrow Wilson on reading President Coolidge's message to Congress in December, 1921. It did not breathe, he declared, one single human hope; but he still could not see that he himself had foreordained the election of Calvin Coolidge on that fateful April morning in 1917 when he threw every liberal cause overboard in favor of force without stint, in favor of our intercession in an Old World quarrel as hoary as the ages. History would have told him that, if he had listened to it, and human experience could have proved to him that no war but brings in its train the triumph of conservatism, of reaction, with corruption unending. So it has been with us. The business world we were to have rendered untrammeled, with special regard for the little man, is more than ever trammeled by greed and privilege; the industry we must humanize is still not humanized. The plain people for all their movies and motors and radios are neither "cheered nor inspirited" with prospects of social justice and due reward. The mockery of the courts, the failure of justice, the lawlessness of constituted authorities—these still face us and were abated not a whit by all the high-sounding phrases by which we were lured to wholesale murder just ten years ago.

Of course the contrary is today being written. We are told that the country was united by the war as never before. Yes, united by conscription, united by the terror of an inquisition, united by the padlock and the jail, united by the mob! What specious falsifying of history! Woodrow Wilson himself said in 1915 to the newly naturalized citizens he was so soon to persecute and prosecute: "Humanity can be welded together only by love, by sympathy, by justice, not by jealousy and hatred." Well might he have added: "And not by vilification, not by discrimination, not by the compulsion of consciences, not by the dashing under foot of the inviolable rights of peoples and mankind, not by the murder of millions." The scars of these ten years cut deep; they are not expunged; they are not forgotten; they were not given new cuticle by the Armistice nor by the Treaty of Versailles. Everywhere sections pull against each other, bloc works against bloc, and the bulk of the men who fought in France are today the least liberal, the most immune from all the ideas of social justice and human rights which Wilson preached—until April 6, 1917.

Politically the country lies dead. Between the parties there are no issues, no fundamental differences. It now appears as if the question in 1928 would be: Shall we have a Protestant or a Catholic, a Wet or a Dry? The choice will be between two men who have not as yet glimpsed the possibilities of the leadership this, our America, might exercise beyond all the seas. The one in power mocks our democracy and our humanity in Nicaragua, in Mexico, in China. Bullets, bullets, bullets—these are his threats, these his remedies—ten years after we were told that justice alone was thereafter to rule the world and that strong nations should not be "free to wrong weak nations and make them subject to their purpose and their intent." Ten years after the utter futility of force was proved to all mankind!

Woodrow Wilson's Wisest Words

They imply, first of all, that it must be a peace without victory. . . . Only a peace between equals can last. Only a peace the very principle of which is equality and a common participation in a common benefit. The right state of mind, the right feeling between nations, is as necessary for a lasting peace as is the just settlement of vexed questions of territory or of racial and national allegiance. . . . I am proposing, as it were, that the nations should with one accord adopt the doctrine of President Monroe as the doctrine of the world: that no nation should seek to extend its polity over any other nation or people, but that every people should be left free to determine its own polity, its own way of development, unhindered, unthreatened, unafraid, the little along with the great and powerful.
—From Woodrow Wilson's Address to the Senate, January 22, 1917.

Looking Toward Peace

WHEN Aristide Briand, the French Foreign Minister, said last spring that France would be glad to agree with the United States to settle mutual disputes by arbitration and to renounce recourse to war, surprisingly little attention was paid to the suggestion at first, but it has recently crystallized in two definite proposals. The American Foundation, established by Edward W. Bok, has given to the press the draft of a general treaty for the settlement of all international disputes through conciliation, through arbitration by the Permanent Court of Arbitration at the Hague, or otherwise, or through judicial settlement by the Permanent Court of International Justice (World Court). Almost simultaneously, James T. Shotwell of the Carnegie Endowment has made public the draft of an arbitration treaty that could be entered into between the United States and France or any other nation. Mr. Shotwell was assisted in drafting this treaty by Professor J. P. Chamberlain of Columbia University. The proposal has the indorsement of Nicholas Murray Butler, president of Columbia University.

While drawn in response to Premier Briand's suggestion, the Shotwell treaty is not limited to France. It is hoped that it may serve also for agreements with Great Britain, Japan, Germany, Italy, and other countries. Its appearance at this hour is especially timely because the Bryan arbitration treaties—with France, Great Britain, and Japan—all expire next year and new agreements are desirable if the movement toward international peace is to continue. The draft treaty of Messrs. Shotwell and Chamberlain is for the most part a combination of the principles and machinery of the Bryan treaties and of those negotiated at Locarno in 1925 between representatives of France, Germany, Belgium, Great Britain, Italy, Poland, and Czecho-Slovakia.

The first article of the proposed treaty renounces war as a means of settling disputes although with some qualifications. The stipulation shall not apply, says Article 2, in the case of "the exercise of the right of legitimate defense, that is to say, resistance to a violation of the undertaking contained in the previous article, provided that the attacked party shall at once offer to submit the dispute to peaceful settlement or to comply with an arbitral or judicial decision." The Monroe Doctrine is also preserved by excepting from the operation of Article 1 "action by the United States of America in pursuance of its traditional policy with reference to the American continents, provided that the United States will use its best endeavors to secure the submission to arbitration or conciliation of a dispute between an American and a non-American Power."

The proposal of the American Foundation is the more comprehensive, as it is a general treaty and includes international disputes of all sorts, even those which are supposed to involve "national honor." It is suggested that the House and Senate, by joint resolution, request the President to call an international conference for adopting the treaty. But the very comprehensiveness of the plan probably militates against its early success. Moreover, the advocates of the plan feel that the entrance of the United States to the World Court is a prerequisite to its adoption. The Shotwell treaty is less ambitious but more immediately realizable. It could be used as the basis of an agreement between the United States and any one other country without reference to our membership in the World Court.

Those Balkans

EUROPE has been suffering a series of mild earthquake shocks, and wondering whether they marked a process of settling down or indicated a new era of activity on the part of the row of political volcanoes along her Eastern frontiers. The Anglo-Russian break sent a war shudder across the Continent; there followed another of Mussolini's saber-rattling speeches, then a new Albanian crisis and a Rumanian coup d'etat; and now the Soviet Ambassador to Poland has been assassinated.

Poland and Russia have speedily made up their minds to peace. Poland is loading the diplomatic couriers with apologies, regrets, and explanations; and Russia, despite Litvinov's note, seems to be turning her wrath against England. England, the Soviet leaders say, is really responsible for the current convention that ordinary laws do not apply to Russians. The defiance of law in the British-inspired raid on the Soviet Legation grounds in Peking and the British raid on the Soviet offices in London seems to have led Russian monarchists to believe that they could even go so far as to murder Russian officials with impunity. There may be something in the theory; but it verges on the realm of diplomatic psychoanalysis, which is unsteady ground. And, if the reports be true, it is unfortunate that the Russians' nerves have been frayed to the extent of indulging in more political executions. All Europe needs a return to normal. Britain's anti-Bolshevik spree nullified the good effect of Russian participation in the Geneva conferences; and Russia's own excesses may still further deepen the gulf which separates her from the rest of Europe.

However, it is in the Southeast of Europe, in that perennial hatching-ground of wars, the Balkans, that the smoke conceals real fire. One never knows just how seriously to take the words of a paranoiac like Mussolini; they may mean nothing more than a small boy's excess of good spirits. But even if he does not mean his own words seriously, some of his nervous neighbors may take them so. He has just shouted:

> We must, at a given moment, be able to mobilize five million men, thoroughly armed; we must strengthen our navy; and our air fleet, in which I believe more and more, must be on such a large scale and so powerful that the noise of its motors will surpass every other noise and its wings will obscure the sun from our land. Then, when, between 1935 and 1940, we shall reach the vital moment of European history, we shall be able to make our voice heard and to see at last that our rights are acknowledged.

Since Mussolini's idea of Italian rights occasionally seems to involve restoration of the entire Roman Empire, such speeches are disturbing. A few days after this oration Mussolini was able to continue the Italian conquest of Albania. The Albanians arrested an interpreter attached to the Serbian Legation in their capital, Tirana; the Serbs, seeing behind this arrest the hand of Italy, demanded his release; Albania refused; the Serbs broke off diplomatic relations. Since the negotiation of the Treaty of Tirana (see the International Relations Section of *The Nation* for January 12) Albania is no longer an independent nation; Italy is her guardian, and shares in any dispute she enters; and Sir Austen Chamberlain's refusal, at the time of the last Italo-Serb dispute, to permit this treaty to be brought before the League, has given it an unusual sanctity. The net result of the recent outburst is that Italy has tightened her grip on the eastern shore of the Mediterranean.

There are signs, however, that England is tiring of Mussolini. He is an uncertain friend and an exigent ally. No one in Europe knows just what Sir Austen Chamberlain and M. Briand said to each other when they were closeted together in London in May, but their meeting was too elaborately staged, simultaneously with King George's elaborate welcome to the French President, to be a mere formality. And one cannot be friends, in Europe today, with both Italy and France. A week after these meetings the Rumanian overturn occurred, and the Government which had been selling itself to Italy was replaced by one with closer ties to France.

Balkan politics are too involved for any American to understand them or for any two Europeans to agree about them, but certain trends seem to be defining themselves. Hungary and Italy, both in the hands of irresponsible autocrats greedy for more territory, are drifting into a natural alliance. Rumania, hitherto Italy's staunch ally, cannot be friends with Hungary's friends, and is returning to its old allegiance to the Little Entente, more or less under French inspiration. Italy is seeking everywhere for allies which may help it to dominate Southeastern Europe, and is ready to growl and shake a sword and even run the risk of war at any time that Mussolini sees any chance to gain a point or win prestige or limelight as a result of it. Italy has sought to destroy the growing Serb-Bulgar friendship, to hem in Jugoslavia and Austria by an alliance with the Hungarian despots, to win a new field for exploitation in Rumania, and to expand its boundaries in North Africa at the expense of France. The Fascists regard French Savoy and French Tunis, as well as an indefinite area in the Balkans, as part of Italia irredenta. With England's support, they have just succeeded in one forward move. There is no telling where Mussolini may break loose next.

The British Menace

THE bloodhounds are loose again. With Sir Austen Chamberlain, British Foreign Minister, cracking the whip, the dogs of intolerance are baying all around the world. Ernest Marshall, London correspondent of the New York *Times*, deserves the blue ribbon.

> The Moscow murderers [he writes] have put themselves beyond the pale. They have shown themselves to be the mad dogs of the world, whose extermination [*sic*] is a necessity for the well-being of the rest of the community.

Other correspondents and statesmen and near-statesmen yelp in the same chorus. We seem, for the moment, to be back in the howling days when every German was a baby-killing Hun, or in that post-war Silver Age when the *Times* announced the death of Lenin and a new Russian massacre at breakfast every morning.

The Russians have had their own outburst of terrorism. Their nerves apparently frayed by the attacks upon them in Peking, London, and Warsaw, and by Sir Austen's attempt to unite Europe in a new crusade against them, they have gone back to the time-honored Russian system of political execution. Of course the Riga and London and Warsaw stories of wholesale executions are propaganda lies; but the facts admitted in Moscow are bad enough. Twenty Russians accused of various counter-revolutionary machinations —many of them of spying for the British officials in Russia —have paid the death penalty in Moscow and Leningrad, and there have been other executions in Odessa and elsewhere. Soviet Russia, after almost ten years' existence, ought to be beyond such Oriental methods.

But it would be amusing if it were not tragic to see the British Tories holding up their hands in horror, and their international propaganda army marching forth on a holy crusade of protest. It is not so long since British Tories cheered General Reginald Dyer, who gave the order that murdered 300 Hindus in the market-place of Amritsar; these same pious gentlemen cheered for joy when Chiang Kai-shek, without even the formality of a trial, butchered 300 Chinese Communists; they make every excuse for the obscene brutalities of Mussolini's Italian terrorism.

The effort to rouse the world to a new anti-Russian frenzy is, of course, just another chapter in the history of the British Empire. The Chinese Revolution has already damaged British prestige throughout the East; the thought of its possible effect upon India makes any imperialist shudder. And, since Britain dare not strike directly at the Chinese, for fear of rousing even greater disturbances, she strikes at the Russians, who have dared to sympathize with and aid the Chinese movement of national liberation. Hence the sensationally staged Arcos raid, the break in Anglo-Russian relations, Sir Austen's desperate effort at Geneva to convert the League into a new Holy Alliance, this time directed against revolutionary Russia as a century ago the monarchs united against revolutionary France.

Like the Russians whom they denounce for it—like all governments indeed—the holier-than-thou men of Britain lie and spy. In the House of Commons on May 30 Commander Kenworthy asked the Foreign Secretary whether any of the anti-Russian documents printed by the British Government were seized in the Peking raids. Sir Austen answered "No, sir." Mr. Kenworthy asked, then, how documents which passed between Moscow and Peking were obtained? Sir Austen declined to reply. "Are we to understand," Kenworthy persisted, "that that part of the Trade Agreement which referred to mutual abstention from propaganda and interference has been broken by His Majesty's Government?" Such an idea, Sir Austen said, was "absolutely contrary to the facts"; but Kenworthy asked: "If that is the case, how is it possible for communications passing between Russia and another foreign country to get into the hands of the right honorable gentleman without such interference?" "That is the question," came Sir Austen's weasel answer, "which I have respectfully declined to answer—and I again decline, on the grounds of public interest"—a virtual confession of guilt.

Such is the man—and the government—who denounces the Russians! Fortunately, this man's effort to persuade all Europe to join him in formal expression of moral indignation at Russian propaganda has met difficulties. France and Germany resisted it; Poland feared, naturally, that it would aggravate her strained relations with Russia. When British pressure was at its tensest M. Briand became opportunely ill. No one, so far as is reported, suggested a joint denunciation of Britain's anti-Russian propaganda. Yet the British have already killed the spirit of Locarno; even Mussolini has hardly done more to revive the war spirit in Europe than the die-hards of Tory England.

The Naval Proposals at Geneva

THE tripartite naval conference which began its sessions at Geneva on June 20 took a leaf out of the book of the Washington Conference and opened its program with definite proposals on the part of the American and British delegates. The United States offered to extend the 5-5-3 battleship ratio adopted at the Washington Conference for the United States, Great Britain, and Japan to cruisers, destroyers, and submarines, and to limit the cruiser tonnage to 250,000 or 300,000 for the United States and Great Britain and to 150,000 or 180,000 tons for Japan with 10,000 tons as the maximum per ship. For destroyers the offer is: 200,000 to 250,000 tons for America and England, and 120,000 to 150,000 for Japan. For submarines, the proposal is: 50,000 to 90,000 for the Anglo-Saxon countries, and 36,000 to 54,000 for Japan. Promptly W. C. Bridgeman, First Lord of the Admiralty, the spokesman for Great Britain, proposed that the future size of battleships be reduced from the present limit of 35,000 tons to 30,000 tons, the life of the battleships be increased from 20 to 26 years, and that the rights of the three Powers under the replacement tables agreed upon at Washington be waived. He also proposed limiting the size of all future cruisers to 7,500 tons and their armament to six-inch guns after an agreement is reached on the number of 10,000-ton cruisers which the Powers will build under the Washington agreement. The Japanese delegation made a straightforward proposal to this effect: "None of the conferring Powers shall, for such period of time as may be agreed upon, adopt new building programs or acquire ships for the purpose of increasing its naval strength," which is good as far as it goes, but merely prevents increased competition.

These seem to us good but timid proposals, so far from revolutionary that it would seem as if they should be accepted with only a few days of discussion. The American proposals contemplate the extension of the principle of the absolute parity of America and Great Britain on the sea, and the limitation of Japan to three-fifths of their respective fleets, so that there can be no question of any armament competition between these three Powers hereafter. Mr. Bridgeman's program goes further, in that it opens up the question of the Washington agreement and proposes its modification as noted above. That will undoubtedly be deplored; it is probably not wise to take up the Washington agreement in any way lest there be a reexamination, perhaps for the worse, of the rules there laid down. It is the more questionable because the other naval Powers which signed at Washington are not represented at Geneva, except that France and Italy have "observers" or "informers." There should be no excuse given to France or to Italy for disregarding the conclusions of the Washington Conference as Mussolini is already threatening to do. Again, Mr. Bridgeman's proposal of six-inch guns only for cruisers and their limitation of cruisers to 7,500 tons is bound to cause considerable outcry. Indeed, the mere suggestion of this limitation has already called forth from navy maniacs of the William H. Gardiner type emphatic protests and assertions that this is merely a clever trick on the part of Great Britain. Since she has the greatest fleet of merchantmen of 7,500 tons or more, and merchantmen cannot be armed with guns heavier than the six-inch, it is argued that she has everything to gain and nothing to lose by the decrease in cruiser size and by the use of six-inch guns. There will also be a protest against the proposal that the United States should scrap more tonnage than Great Britain and Japan. Secretary Wilbur has just assured the graduating class at the Pennsylvania Military College in advance of the publication of his superior's Geneva plans that there will be no further scrapping of American ships in consequence of an international agreement. Mr. Butler, chairman of the House Naval Committee, approved this disloyal sentiment.

For ourselves, we confess to disappointment that a program just outlined by Commander Kenworthy, himself a naval officer of distinction and a member of the British Parliament, was not offered by his countrymen at Geneva. He would stop the building of all kinds of battleships and proposes the reduction of the 10,000-ton limit for cruisers to 6,000 tons. Under the Treaty of Versailles no German cruiser may exceed this size—a fact which we fear has played some part in the decision of Mr. Bridgeman, or rather of the British Government, to suggest 7,500 tons for cruisers. We regret, too, that the United States did not lead off with a demand for the total abolition of all submarines instead of merely favoring it if all the nations agreed to it. We cannot believe that, if Japan, Great Britain, and the United States were to announce their willingness to do away with this vessel of war, an international agreement to that effect could not be obtained from all the other maritime Powers. An English expert, Arthur H. Pollen, writing in the American *Foreign Affairs* for July, declares that the submarine is useless and especially so against its main enemy, the battle fleet; hence he asks the two Anglo-Saxon countries to renounce both the submarine and torpedo.

We regret the absence of these more vigorous proposals at Geneva especially because English public sentiment has shown itself to be remarkably ready for far-reaching action to reduce her present naval burden, the Japanese delegates to Geneva seem to be in a better spirit even than they showed at Washington, and we believe our own countrymen to be ready for radical changes. None the less, on the principle that even a quarter of a loaf is better than no bread, we shall be thankful even if the American proposals alone are adopted. Many of our American radicals and liberals felt that the Washington Conference was a fraud and accomplished nothing but limiting the numbers of obsolete battleships. We have never shared that viewpoint and can cite the remarkable decrease in the familiar campaigns to stir up naval rivalry and fear between the United States and Japan as proof that the Washington Conference did bestow far-reaching benefits upon the world. Since then the navy maniacs have spent their time in portraying England to us as the enemy and in making such charges of trickery and deceit against out former ally as Mr. Gardiner has just voiced again. Along that road lies war, not disarmament or peace. We trust that public sentiment in America which seeks the limitation or the abolition of armaments will at once make itself felt and ask of our delegates and of President Coolidge who directs them that we go beyond our proposals and abolish the battleship, the submarine, the torpedo, and even the naval airplanes. The churches must now be heard if they desire worthwhile results at Geneva.

Lindbergh and the Army and Navy

By OSWALD GARRISON VILLARD

COLONEL WILLIAM MITCHELL is anathema to many people. To them he is a "kicker"; a chronic fault-finder; a "publicity grabber"; a man who "went back on his own crowd"; who "bit the hand that fed him." Just now he has denounced the navy's attempt to take Lindbergh into its camp and has therefore again earned the abuse inevitably showered upon one who seeks to reform an organization not quietly from within but through outspoken public criticism. He has just been described by the Assistant Secretary of the Navy, Theodore D. Robinson, as "a man who, on the face of it, doesn't know what he's talking about, and, if he did, couldn't tell the truth about it, anyway"—a retort not unexpectedly hot when one reads it in connection with Colonel Mitchell's assertion that "it is the saying now 'Join the navy and see the world, but join the naval aviation and see the next world.'" His real offense, however, is that he calls attention to the deliberate efforts of the navy—and he might have said the army, too—to annex all possible glory for Lindbergh's flight.

Colonel Mitchell points out, in a letter to the Washington *Post*, that the dominating navy crowd has tried to conceal the fact that as far back as 1921 the airplane maneuvers showed that battleships were useless because of the development of aviation. He declares that "the naval propagandists still hedged behind the cry that airplanes could not fly across the seas," and that "they were successful in preventing service pilots from doing it." When, however, the civilian Lindbergh flew across the sea the navy knew that his flight would be a tremendously powerful lever for the aviation group in Washington, "because the use of the airplane, an economical instrument, would cut down appropriations for battleships, save money for the taxpayers, and sea-power would become secondary to air-power." They had, of course, done nothing whatever to forward Lindbergh's flight or anybody else's, precisely as they did nothing to aid Commander Byrd, a retired naval officer, in his flight to the North Pole; precisely as they had sent the gallant and unfortunate Commander Rodgers on the Hawaiian flight without giving him adequate gasoline to carry him through, and then made such faulty arrangements that although Commander Rodgers stayed afloat for nine days the navy could not find him until he drifted ashore. Colonel Mitchell even charges the service with having brought about this brave officer's death through letting him fly when he was not fit to do so, and directly asserts that the deaths of sixteen naval fliers in and about Hampton Roads within thirty-five days are due to the incompetence and inefficiency of the men directing naval-aviation affairs.

As to this, Colonel Mitchell may or may not be correct—he sometimes mars his case by exaggerated statements. He is, however, absolutely right in pointing out that the navy sought at once to claim Lindbergh for its own. Lindbergh's return on the cruiser was ordered by the President, against the young man's wish. As he neared the Capes navy and army aviation squadrons were ordered out to greet him. The military crowd was not idle. They had him promoted to colonel in the Army Reserve; then General M. M. Patrick, head of the army aviation, announced that a specially picked aviator would fly over the Memphis and drop a new colonel's uniform, and Major General C. C. Hammond of the Militia Bureau officially wirelessed him to wear it at the ceremonies in the Capitol. Every effort was then made to give a military character to the reception celebration. Army, navy, marine corps, and National Guard units were, according to press reports, in line for this boy, who had no connection with military affairs except a captaincy in the aviation of the Missouri National Guard—almost an honorary title. Then Lindbergh was compelled by the committee to perform that singular rite now expected of every distinguished visitor to Washington, namely, to lay a wreath on the tomb of the Unknown Soldier, though what the Unknown Soldier had to do with transatlantic flight is hard to see. At the tomb there was mounted a military guard of honor to salute the Minnesota boy aviator; he was conducted to the spot by a brigadier general in full uniform, with all his medals. He was then rushed out to the Walter Reed General Military Hospital and agonized by the sight of some of the horribly mutilated victims of the war—precisely as if he were an English or French field-marshal, just back from the war, and not a young post-office aviator. When the scene of action was transferred to New York, the entire National Guard of the city, some 10,000 men, was paraded in honor of this civilian aviator. The crowds were not demonstrative when the troops passed; they were not there to see a martial display, but to greet a plain American youth, who had the good taste and good sense not once to wear the brand-new colonel's uniform, but stuck to his blue serge suit. More than that, the army recruiting posters have everywhere declared of Lindbergh, "the army helped to train him"—a partial but misleading truth.

There is intrinsic evidence that much pressure was brought upon Lindbergh to emphasize the military and to voice preparedness propaganda. He did not say a word of use to the militarists until his speech of June 15, at a luncheon in New York, when he declared that aviation preparedness would help to prevent war, and that the men who could best be transformed into military pilots were civilian fliers with long experience—a mild enough statement. Not once has he referred to himself as colonel; up to this writing, he has not even acknowledged his promotion to that rank. In no speech did he refer to the military turnouts for him; military strutting is obviously as far removed from his makeup as it could well be. According to his pictures, he has refrained from wearing any of his medals, by day or by night. But that has not prevented Admiral Burrage from announcing that he will make a determined effort to have Lindbergh transferred from the Missouri National Guard and army reserve to the navy, so that the navy may have the benefit of his counsel and advice, which, of course, it did not seek before his flight, and which, if it were of the Colonel Mitchell variety, would lead to his being immediately damned by the military and naval cliques in Washington, which dominate those services. As a matter of fact, while Lindbergh said that the air corps would never take the place of the navy, he described the sinking of a battleship and dwelt upon the cheapness of the operation, even if half the attacking fliers were killed, saying that a battleship could be sunk by aviators for one-fifth or one-tenth of its cost. He made it clear that he did not believe that anti-aircraft guns could protect a ship, which is exactly Colonel Mitchell's position.

Thus far the exploitation has gone. The real significance of the whole thing lies in the fact that this military and naval propaganda is unceasingly at work. *The Nation* has just commented on the fact that some of the motion-picture magnates have been made commissioned reserve officers, and that the War Department has not contradicted the assertion that in return the motion pictures are to be used more than heretofore to aid military propaganda. At the summer training-camps for civilians, and those of the Reserve Officers' Training Corps the straight-out military doctrines we used to call Prussian are being taught. The Scabbard and Blade, an R.O.T.C. organization, publishes regularly attacks upon some of the most prominent people in the country, such as Senator Borah, ex-Governor Sweet of Colorado, Senator La Follette, Mrs. Carrie Chapman Catt, Francis B. Sayre, son-in-law of Woodrow Wilson; John Dewey, Zona Gale, and many others, and is charging them with being Communists and dangerous citizens—unrebuked by the War Department. The alliance of the War Department with the big-business organizations is open and above-board, and is justified on the ground that in the next war to end war all industry must pass into the hands of the government—communism with a vengeance!

The American public is singularly unaware, and singularly indifferent, to this determined militaristic propaganda, which often takes the form of attacking anyone who dares to speak the truth, of breaking up meetings, interrupting speakers, etc. If the Lindbergh episode and Colonel Mitchell's comment on it have helped to open the eyes of some persons to what is going on, it will not be the least of Lindbergh's great services to his country.

The Scandal at Geneva

THE Disarmament Conference at Geneva is degenerating into a sorry spectacle. The assembled admirals and generals, and the few civilians scattered among them, show no desire to give the world a hearty shove along the path of peace; they have no slightest thought of really disarming; they are haggling and bargaining like a lot of Grand Street peddlers, each seeking to work out a "ratio" which will give his country some advantage in some class of warships.

Britain is deaf to suggestions of reducing the number of light cruisers—a class in which she far outranks the United States and Japan; the United States is eager for limitations which strike Britain, but regards proposals to reduce the big ships beyond the scales of the Washington Conference as violations of "sacred treaty rights." Mr. Hugh Gibson, chairman of our delegation, was even quoted as mouthing this jingo sentiment: "The United States will insist upon equality with Britain in all categories of ships unless forced into a situation where she might regard equality as insufficient"! In that bullyragging spirit peace is not made. That is the spirit which has aroused dislike of America in Europe; if continued it will make the conference the starting-point of a new international naval rivalry.

The treasury men know that the new naval race is pinching as much as the inter-Allied debts. Winston Churchill openly struggled against the British Admiralty when preparing his budget two years ago, but he was beaten, and Britain accepted the fifteen-cruiser program which is today one of the horrid specters of Geneva. It was the admirals, not the civilians, at Washington in 1921 who deliberately left the loophole for cruisers which is causing such ill feeling today. Mr. Churchill, who has been a jingo in his day but is a realist as Chancellor of the Exchequer, declared two months ago:

> There are only three great Powers able to keep a battle fleet in existence. An agreement between these three great naval Powers to abate the rate of their construction, or to limit the size of their ships, or some other agreement of that kind—in that lies the greatest hope of contraction in naval expenditure.

And of peace. Those three Powers are meeting at Geneva today—and they are throwing away their opportunity, gambling with the hopes of the world. Will the civilian governments who appointed these reckless admirals recall them or give them vigorous instructions before it is too late, or will they let the conference end in agreement upon meaningless nothings, pointing the way to new rivalries and opening new vistas of war?

Possibly it is just as well that the officers and technical experts should thus early display their uselessness as leaders of a conference for the reduction of armaments. They do not want to disarm; at most they want to balance arms. They shudder at the thought of scrapping any of their lovely naval toys in the interest of economy and peace. They want to keep all they have, but to prevent the other fellow from building more. It would seem incongruous, of course, to introduce women, or labor leaders, or ministers of the gospel into such a conference. But if governments wanted to disarm, they would send such messengers; and the technical experts, the generals and admirals, instead of dictating policy would be the servants of policy. If the governments had even been sincere in their protestations of economy, they would have included in their delegations representatives of the suffering treasuries.

From Geneva to Honolulu

WHILE the Geneva Disarmament Conference is spouting hot lava and suspicion, a less noisy but far more genuine disarmament conference is meeting at Honolulu. The Institute of Pacific Relations is drawing together for the second time a group of unofficial delegates of most of the great Pacific countries. We say "most" advisedly, because this Honolulu conference follows the tradition by omitting from its sessions representatives of Soviet Russia. It was, for Europe, a great thing when Frenchmen and Germans learned to drink beer together and meet as friends, but Europe will not settle down until the same atmosphere of friendly confidence extends to sessions with Russians. It is a great stride forward for Americans and Japanese to light each other's cigarettes while discussing California's immigration laws, and for Englishmen and Chinese to consider over their teacups the future of Shanghai; but there are dangerous reserves to any meeting which first excludes and then elaborately ignores its exclusion of representatives of any great country. And Russia is, indisputably and sometimes menacingly, one of the great Pacific Powers.

When statesmen admit that they disagree, the fact somehow contrives to seem disastrous. Every European diplomatic pow-wow since the war, however violent its private disagreements, has concluded with a solemn assertion of complete agreement. This Honolulu session is franker. It meets avowedly to discuss the points of friction between East and West, "with the hope that an honest attempt to state these differences may lead to a way to reconcile them." It certainly has the courage of its hopes. As a preliminary to its sessions, data have been assembled upon some of the most prickly problems. Professor Eliot Mears of Leland Stanford University has collated American laws affecting Orientals. The Australians have made similar studies; the Japanese have tabulated their laws dealing with foreigners.

At least something is gained by the discovery that none of the countries facing the Pacific cares to give aliens the same privileges which it allows its own citizens. Sir Frederick Whyte, first president of the Indian Legislative Assembly, who heads the British delegation, has prepared a monograph on "China and the Foreign Powers" which reveals the painfully honest effort of a born proconsul of empire to understand the raucous language of young Asia.

One must not expect immediate effects from such a conference. No treaties will emerge from it; no battleships will be scrapped as a result of it and no colonies will be relinquished. But it may go far to establish the habit of joint discussion of international problems which is, after all, more important than courts or treaties or battleships. And the habit of joint discussion, shallowly rooted even in Europe, is a growingly important matter in the Pacific. Far as we have progressed since the days of the Boxer expeditions and indemnities we are still in the ultimatum-stage of manners when it comes to China. No foreign Power has been willing to accept the Chinese suggestions of a joint investigation of responsibility for the Nanking affair. The foreigners have assembled the testimony of their own nationals, and have thought that enough.

As Benton MacKaye says elsewhere in this issue of *The Nation*, there was a time when we had a planet but not a world. There were several worlds. Today the Panama and Suez canals, the Trans-Siberian railway, the ocean-bridging airplanes are knitting the world's civilizations into one fabric. China and India, with half the earth's man-power, are no longer to be remote, romantic countries, nor can we afford to treat them as pariahs. They buy our mineral oil and weave our silk and grow the beans that yield other oils for our industries. Their civil wars climb onto the front pages of our newspapers; perforce we begin to distinguish between Chang and Chiang. America, more or less unconsciously, is accepting their new importance. The Pacific Coast thinks New York provincial because it pays so much more attention to its Lindberghs, Chamberlins, and Byrds than to the Pacific-flying Maitlands, Hegenbergers, and Smiths. San Francisco-to-Hongkong interests it more than New York-to-Paris—and it is thinking in more contemporaneous terms than are we of the Atlantic Coast. It is not without significance that the first five Presidents of the Nineteenth Century had all seen European service; and that from Andrew Jackson's day to Roosevelt's only one President had seen Europe before he entered the White House. We began as an Atlantic colony of Europe, dependent upon Europe for ideas, for literature, for industrial resources. Then we turned our back upon the Eastern ocean and molded an inland nation. Today that nation faces two seas. Already one President of the United States has seen service in Asia before taking the country's helm; others are sure to follow. We will no longer be dominated in our outlook by the traditions of a single ocean; we are, as a nation, a bridge between two civilizations. In our day a Londoner can reach Shanghai more rapidly by passing through the United States than by following the ancient route through the Mediterranean and the Indian Ocean. Such facts mold history.

But East is East, we have been saying, and West is West, and never the twain shall meet. Poet never composed a more dangerous lie. The twain do meet. They meet in the public schools of California, in the treaty ports like Shanghai—and, fortunately, in the Institute of Pacific Relations at Honolulu. They meet, and they modify each other. One of the preliminary studies for the Honolulu meetings was a rather tragic investigation of the second-generation Oriental in America. Boys and girls, put through the mill of the American public-school system, become, psychologically, completely Americanized. They refuse to speak their parents' tongues; they lose all understanding of the land of their origin—but retain the physical stigmata which bar them from most channels of advance in this race-conscious country. One homesick son of Los Angeles who had visited the cherry-blossom country of his fathers, wrote in ecstacy when he returned to familiar sights: "It takes a Hearst paper to make me feel at home." Ridiculous as these extremes sound, they are evidence of the fundamental human kinship. There is no barrier to understanding and sympathy in brain and blood cells. We can meet, we can talk together, we can understand. The college presidents and professors, the ministers, labor leaders, and social workers from both sides of the Pacific who are meeting today in ing against mutual suspicions which are potentially far more dangerous to the human race than those which have flared so vividly at Geneva.

Nicaragua's New Bondage

THEY are now engaged in proving that the 300 Nicaraguans whom American marines and bombing planes murdered on July 17 were "bandits." That is the immemorial habit of imperialist usurpers—the British called the Boers bandits and the Irish republicans mere gunmen; the French called the heroic Riffians bandits and doubtless the ancient Egyptians applied similar names to the armies they defeated. It does not alter the fact that American marines ought not to be doing police duty in Nicaragua, and that Latin American hearts from Cape Horn to the Rio Grande beat in sympathy with any Latin who fights the Yankee invasion of a Latin country.

If, however, the authorities in Washington are sincerely interested in tracing down large-scale oppression, we suggest that they turn their attention to a document signed more or less at their own suggestion on March 31 last—between Dr. Zavala, financial agent for the American-aided Diaz regime in Nicaragua, and representatives of the Guaranty Trust Company and of J. and W. Seligman and Company of New York. It compares favorably, to be sure, with the usurious loans recently made in Los Angeles by leaders of the Better American Federation and the best local banking circles; but as government financing we have never seen anything to equal it.

This extraordinary contract, to begin with, opens a 6 per cent credit of $1,000,000 for a period of one year, which may under certain conditions be extended for another six months. Of course no one would ask a bank to lend the money that belongs to its depositors without securing good collateral. In this case one may feel sure that no depositor will complain—the bankers have taken all Nicaragua has—serape, sombrero, sandals, and shirts. Two months before the negotiation of this loan the Nicaraguan Congress had voted certain emergency taxes—an export tax on all coffee up to 65 cents per 100 pounds; a 50 per cent increase in customs duties on tobacco, wines, and liquors; a 12½ increase in other import duties. All these were mortgaged to the bankers as collateral for this credit.

But this was not all. As further collateral the bankers put a mortgage on 50 per cent of the surplus of the national treasury revenues. (Fifty per cent had similarly been mortgaged to New York bankers in 1917.) And, since Mr. Diaz, even with American marines to do his police work for him, is unlikely to have a surplus, the bankers went further still. They put a mortgage on all the capital stock of the National Bank of Nicaragua, an American corporation with a paid-in capital of $300,000 and a worth of twice that, and on all its dividends. They went still further. They added a mortgage on the entire capital stock of the Pacific Railways of Nicaragua, which, efficiently managed by the J. G. White Corporation, associated with the Seligmans, is worth more than the total amount of the credit extended by the bankers!

According to the former Nicaraguan Consul General in New York City, the bankers were not satisfied with this. The deposits of the bank and the railroad in Canadian and other banks, said to total more than $400,000, were transferred to New York City, for the benefit of the credit-givers. (One wonders whether the money which the bankers lent to Nicaragua was actually the Nicaraguan money which they had transferred from other coffers to their own.) And then they capped the climax. They included in the contract an agreement which substantially said that they would not only mortgage half Nicaragua for their million-dollar loan but would furthermore spend the money for Nicaragua. They explained frankly that the money would be used primarily to equip, arm, and maintain the Diaz soldiers (thus, some one may have hoped, eventually making it unnecessary for American marines to uphold that tottering regime). Money for other purposes will be released only upon approval by a special committee of three, two of whom are Americans! One of these Americans is the American manager of the National Bank of Nicaragua; the other is the American High Commissioner. Now the office of High Commissioner was instituted, we understand, in connection with the financial plan of 1920—drawn up by the Nicaraguan Government with another consortium of New York bankers. As then, the Secretary of State of the United States appoints the High Commissioner, who, nevertheless, (possibly in order to avoid difficulties with the law) is not considered an official of the Department of State. The Department of State insists upon this fine-drawn distinction between appointee and official; but in any case, the net result is that the bankers use a government appointee as their agent and representative in Nicaragua.

The contract is long, and contains more serfdom for Nicaragua. Among other things it provides that for five years the two New York banking houses have an option on all new Nicaraguan financing.

Here, we submit, is an interesting case study for any government official seriously interested in the problem of oppression in Nicaragua. It would be an excellent thing, indeed, if the Department of State would give this matter its serious attention, and inform the public upon the result of its cogitations. For this kind of oppression concerns the American people as a whole far more profoundly than the effort of a barefooted army to support itself on a jungle countryside where an American planter happens to have a small property. It was, we take it, to this loan that Mr. Hoover referred when, last spring, he made the unwelcome remark about loans for unproductive purposes which Mr. Kellogg so bitterly resented. Such loans, which, made with State Department approval, involve the utilization by bankers of State Department designees, involve us in a constant risk of bloody intervention. Suppose Nicaragua should seek to finance herself from other banks, violating its agreement with the New York bankers; suppose it should seek to spend some of its amply secured credit in ways of which the High Commissioner, named by the State Department, did not approve—what then? More work for the marines!

Bankers have often complained that they are unjustly accused of shaping State Department policy. Sometimes, they say, the State Department begs them to make loans to help its previously determined policies. By an incredible series of blunders the State Department is now committed to maintaining Adolfo Diaz in office as its puppet president of Nicaragua. Surely no sane business man would want to risk money on so feeble a character as Don Adolfo. Is the State Department of the United States itself primarily responsible for this shoddy pawnbroking?

To Disarm, Disarm

WRITING in the London *Nation* on the eve of the Geneva Disarmament Conference, Commander Kenworthy, M. P., himself a distinguished naval officer, expressed the fervent hope that whatever else the British Government might do it would not send high naval officers to carry on the negotiations. But that is just what Mr. Baldwin did. He chose the civilian First Lord of the Admiralty, surrounded him by admirals and captains, and added for good measure Robert Cecil who, knowing better, can always be counted on to compromise with wrong. Mr. Coolidge did the same thing. He picked as the only civilian delegate, Hugh Gibson, a delightful personality, a promising but still second-rate diplomat, and then added a lot of naval officers the chief of whom, Admiral Hilary P. Jones, is of the type of mind which thinks it absolute treason to criticize any action of the Navy Department or of the United States Government. The Japanese were craftier; nevertheless their delegation comprises almost the same mixture of diplomats and naval officers.

So what has happened at Geneva is merely what was to be expected—the navy men have dominated and we have seen a disarmament conference on the verge of disruption or of becoming a conference for the increase instead of decrease of fleets. Experts these naval men are called and as such widely regarded. Yet they have actually expected sensible people to believe that they can plot and plan exact ratios of battleships, cruisers, submarines, and all the rest—as if they could foresee proportions and situations ten or twenty years hence. They, of course, did not foresee in the last war that they would need a fleet of mine-layers and have to build monitors and endless patrol boats; nor did any naval officer, least of all in Berlin, suspect the power and range of the submarine, or the uselessness of battleships, or the necessity for aircraft-carriers. No one has ever been able to prophecy what a war by sea or land will bring forth; it cannot be done. But if it could be, the very last persons who should be called into a naval disarmament conference are the navy men. One might just as well ask medical men to take part in an assembly to decide how much work should be taken away from them and handed over to the osteopaths. It is demanding too much of human nature. These officers have been trained to consider themselves essential to the life of a nation; they are convinced of the absurdity that nations only exist if they have "adequate" armaments (which "adequate" no naval or military officer has yet defined since wars began) and, therefore, they are bound to resent, consciously or subconsciously, the demand that they help to do away with their profession. So would a fundamentalist minister feel if he were invited to take part in a conference to reduce his kind by one half.

So Mr. Coolidge—whatever may yet come out of Geneva—blundered frightfully in not picking a strong body of civilians committed to disarmament and told to achieve it or to come home on their shields. The practical men and women of this world are not always the experts by any means, least of all experts who have a direct personal stake in their own findings. Mr. Coolidge had the example of Mr. Hughes at the Washington Conference before him and a proposal was worked out for Geneva, but it lacked either as powerful a personality or as dramatic a setting, and in Washington civilians dominated. It ought to be plain now that the way to obtain disarmament is not to ask it of men who make their living out of the war business, but of men and women—yes, women—who really believe in peace so much that they will gladly take risks and if necessary suffer for their beliefs. Dyed-in-the-wool peace-lovers and not fighting men are the ones to achieve peace, as long as our practical business men and so-called statesmen refuse to see that war impoverishes everybody taking part and actually threatens the existence of civilization itself.

The way to disarm is to disarm. A truly Christian, peace-loving nation would do so without regard to the policies of others. The United States did so from 1820 to 1860 and had no fleet worthy of the name from 1870 to 1898. Nobody ever attacked us, nobody ever exploited us, yet several nations could have helped themselves to all our Atlantic seaports had they so desired. They respected us far more then than now when we have joined the imperialistic, big-armament game. Yet we actually have, among the many other childish moves at Geneva, a revival of President Wilson's stupid and wicked threat that if the others do not do as we wish we shall build the greatest fleet in the world and show them how vast our resources are. Well, fortunately, there is Congress to be reckoned with, and Senator Borah has already let it be known that so far as his influence goes we shall do nothing of the sort. In that direction lies that same naval madness which brought Germany and England into conflict. If on the other hand President Coolidge really desires to give proof to the world of our pacific intentions as a nation, he will decrease armaments of his own accord without fear of the nations to whom we swore eternal fealty ten years ago and against whom we ought never to be plotting and arming. There are no naval rivals other than Japan, France, and England.

The Disgrace at Geneva

IN one of his most self-satisfied moods President Woodrow Wilson, who was then leading the country to preparedness and into the war, declared that the trouble with the pacifists was that they did not know how to get what they wanted, whereas he and his school knew exactly what they wanted and just how they were going to get it. To that boast fate returned the answer in our loss of all our war objectives, save one, and the disaster of Versailles. He died broken and defeated. We recall this incident now because the collapse of the Geneva naval disarmament illustrates again how little the men who believe that national safety lies only in the sword know where they are going and how they are going to get peace. They boast that they are the practical men and the pacifists mere theorists. There were no pacifists at Geneva, just practical statesmen and practical naval men, and they have not only not disarmed, they have fanned anew the embers of international hostility and ill-will. The situation appears worse than when they met; they have even jeopardized a renewal of the battleship agreement when it expires in 1930. If the conference breaks up it will be with ill-will on our side; on the side of the English the charge is made that one of our admirals from the first primed the American correspondents with attacks upon the British. The New York *World* reports from Washington that there is no concealing the fact that official circles blame the Washington battleship lobby for part of the failure. In England Austen Chamberlain has officially stated that the British position was entirely misrepresented over here.

It would seem as if this fiasco—and it will be a fiasco even if some compromise is patched up—of the one independent and bold excursion into international affairs by President Coolidge ought finally to open the eyes of some of his adorers to the grave danger of having a pitifully weak and inept man in the Presidency. From the beginning his conduct of our foreign affairs has been futile to a degree. He insured the disaster at Geneva by the composition of the delegation he sent there. Having aroused Latin-America against us to a pitch of enmity never before known, he now makes us the laughing stock of Europe and has seriously endangered the relations of the two great English-speaking nations. We recognize the joint guilt of the jingo Conservative Government of England. But talk about good intentions and inefficiency! What could be worse? With as able an ambassador as Mr. Houghton in London, Mr. Coolidge could certainly have discovered in advance the exact prospects of success for such a conference.

All of which brings us back to Ambassador Houghton's admirable plea at the Harvard commencement for a hundred-year peace pact between ourselves and the three leading nations of Europe. If there could be a Locarno between England, France, Belgium, and Germany why not one between the United States, England, and France, to say nothing of Germany? What has become of our hundred per cent patriot warriors of ten years ago? They were then for arresting any one who dared to criticize our British ally. Now they are with the admirals for a new armament rivalry with that same beloved ally! As we write the Navy Department announces the award of contracts for five more cruisers. They can only be used in a real war against France, England, or Japan—our allies of 1917-18, those who helped us to make the world so safe for democracy!

Personal and Private

August 22, 1927.

My dear Houghton:

I think you will be tremendously interested in the enclosed remarkable article by Prof. Albert H. Putney of the National University Law School as to the executive assumption of the war making power. This is so intimately bound up with the problem that you touched upon in your Harvard address that I am sure you will be glad to see it if you haven't already done so. This summary proves what I have maintained for some time past, that the war making power has entirely gone out of the hands of Congress and in that way the Constitution has been nullified. Wilson's action in denouncing the "twelve willful men" was a deadly blow at the independence and autonomy of Congress. I think you will agree with me that the power the President wields over the daily press could at any time so arouse public opinion that it will be impossible for Congress to exercise its proper discretion as to declaring war. When it comes to that issue I emphatically believe that there should be secret balloting in Congress!

Cordially yours,

Hon. Alanson B. Houghton,
The American Embassy,
London, England.

Something New in the World

TEN years ago something new was born into the world —something fresh and live, infectious and creative. The world into which it was born did not like it. At first it did not even take it seriously. It seemed to be just the temporary rioting of a few wild soapboxers, annoying because it interrupted the business of winning the war. Today the world is engaged in rectifying the mistakes of a war won too thoroughly, while Soviet Russia, still hated and feared by the West, is enthusiastically celebrating its tenth birthday.

Russia's March Revolution ousted the Czar and substituted a regime which, seeking to undo the worst abuses of autocracy, clung to the old forms of legality, promised the peasants new land legislation, and sought to reorganize Russia to continue fighting the war. The West accepted even that mild regime doubtfully, conditioning its approval upon the new Russia's success in killing Germans. Kerensky's Government pleased neither its Allies nor its own people, and in November Soviet Russia was born to the twin battle-cries of Land and Peace. The Bolsheviks made no effort to keep the peasants from driving out the feudal landowners and appropriating the soil of Russia to themselves, but rather encouraged them to take at once what legislation might have brought them after many years. It shouted peace from the house-tops; it urged the conscripts to go home and till their new-won fields; and it sought with pathetic earnestness to persuade the world to make peace upon the basis of "no annexations and no indemnities." The Powers, desiring both annexations and indemnities, were ready to let millions of human beings bleed to death rather than admit a peace without victory.

When Trotzky, without an army behind him, stood on his soapbox at Brest-Litovsk and orated over General von Hoffmann's head, calling upon the German masses to join Russia in revolution, the Kaiser's ministers saw only a chance to win a battle, and made the ephemeral peace of Brest-Litovsk. The Allies were no wiser. The first point upon which Germany, England, and France joined hands was common opposition to Lenin's Government.

The Allies begged the Germans to keep their troops in the Baltic provinces until they could themselves organize anti-Bolshevik crusades. British, French, Japanese, and American troops were landed upon Russian soil long after the Armistice; every anti-Bolshevik freebooter found the Allies ready to finance and equip him; and while the people's armies of young Russia crushed one after another of these terrific counter-attacks the war-worn country was racked and torn and brought to the depths of distress. Surely no government in history ever attempted to build upon more ruinous foundations. Yet this group of men whose lives had been passed in prison and exile, who had had no training in government and administration, who sought to apply in their country principles untested and uncharted, did succeed in building a stable government out of that chaos—and a stable government founded primarily on an honest desire for the happiness of the people.

The West is disillusioned today, weary after the emotional debauch of a war which almost drove democracy out of our world. But Soviet Russia has become a land of hope, a country where millions of men and women feel a new intensity in the dull business of living. It must be judged, in part at least, in the light of what it followed. It rose on the ruins of a country soaked in the bloody tyrannies of Czarism and sunk in the hopelessness of medieval feudalism. Roger Baldwin elsewhere in this issue gives, we believe, a fair picture of the new freedoms of Russia. The old bourgeoisie is still harried and persecuted as labor was until a decade ago. But women have a freedom exceeding even that of America and Scandinavia; children have a primary consideration unknown elsewhere; and the whole machinery of the state is directed toward raising the standards of living of the millions. No government in history has set out so deliberately, and so successfully, to annihilate illiteracy, to build up mass health, to set its people economically free. There is no divergence of testimony regarding the devotion of the Communist commissars. They sacrifice themselves to their ideal as ruthlessly as they do others. They live on a salary of 250 rubles a month and if they are caught in peculation they suffer more rigidly than mere laymen. The usual perquisites of rulership are not theirs. Comparing this regime with the callous class contrasts of Czarism, or even with the aimless profiteering of the present-day West, one feels the breath of a new life.

Russia is far from her goal of socialism, or communism. As Louis Fischer suggests elsewhere, the effort to build the economic life of a nation upon the principle of planned common welfare is an experiment still. The valid criticism of Russia's method would be that it does not work; and only today, after the harsh years of counter-revolution, blockade, and famine, is that question receiving a fair test. The second decade—if England does not first produce another war—will tell.

In its first decade Soviet Russia has had most influence upon the world in the field of foreign relations. It hoped in its early days that the fire of its own revolution would spread—and the cruel ashes of that hope still scar Europe. Yet it was a natural hope; the Western governments were sponsoring rebellions in Russia, and the Bolsheviks only followed the Western lead when, through the Third International, they sought to organize revolt behind those hostile governments' backs. It is not only the fear of the Third International, however, which has set the West against Russia. The Soviets early began publishing the archives of the Czar's diplomacy, and the crass light they shed upon the hypocrisy of Allied pretensions was bitterly resented. They sapped the war myths, and made a joke of the slogans which sent millions to futile death. M. Chicherin, Russia's able Foreign Minister, has again and again punctured the armor of his opponents and revealed behind their puffed-out fronts the inspiration of oil, of steel, of military power.

But Soviet Russia's cruelest sin against the imperialist West has been committed in Asia. First, by giving a new freedom to most of its subject nationalities, and second, by treaties with the independent nations of the East, it set an example to the white empires of Asia which they have no inclination to follow. It abjured the special privileges to which America and the other Powers still cling in China; it canceled Czarist concessions in Persia; it helped the Emir of Afghanistan.

Peace or War?

PEACE and war—the press is full of news relating thereto. The Disarmament Conference of the League of Nations is meeting at Geneva with the Russians in attendance. The British press is still stirred by the cut in the Admiralty's building program and the extraordinary public manifestations of a desire that England shall disarm and keep out of dangerous foreign entanglements. "Disarmament," Ernest Marshall cables to the New York *Times*, "has been easily first among the week's topics. Speeches innumerable have been made about it both in and out of Parliament." The politicians, he says, "realize that a generation which is still scarred by the wounds of war wants peace preserved and believes that the old Roman doctrine that being prepared for war is the best way of avoiding it was exploded in 1914." Mr. Marshall also reports that, in addition to Field Marshal Sir William Robertson's recent unqualified denunciation of war and his demand for disarmament, another distinguished general who fought with honor in the World War is standing for Parliament as an advocate of universal disarmament. As for Lord Robert Cecil, he has not only resigned from the Cabinet on the disarmament issue, he is constantly speaking on the question. Indeed, he has just stated in *John Bull* that war is "international madness"; that the world must "disarm or perish"; that delay is most dangerous, and that "every month we delay, the old vested interests, material and moral, strengthen their hold." This weekly declares in a special issue devoted to disarmament and peace, that a million British men ought to refuse to fight under any circumstances.

Yet Europe is shivering with alarm over the Polish threat to Lithuania, with its possibility of another war between Poland and Russia, the unsettled conditions in Rumania, and the continuing menace to peace which is Mussolini—a menace little diminished by the new offensive and defensive alliance between Italy and Albania. Russia herself is kept in a constant state of unrest because of her fear of an attack headed by the British. So the daily dispatches from abroad speak of "half a dozen" places in the Near East where hostilities may flare up at any moment. Lord Robert Cecil has thus the best of arguments for declaring that there is no time to lose, and Lloyd George has joined Foch in declaring that a new world war will be here within ten years if things continue as now. So apparent has been the menace to peace that a War Danger Conference has just been meeting in London and was addressed, among others, by General von Schoenaich, a former German army officer now an ardent pacifist, and, in the form of a communication, by Henri de Jouvenal, lately one of the French delegates to the League of Nations. Speaking to this conference, Francesco Nitti, the former Premier of Italy, declared that never had the nations "armed themselves in so mad a fashion as since the existence of the League of Nations." He, too, deems war inevitable if Mussolini remains ten years at the helm of Italy. That dictator's plan of making a great Italian empire Nitti characterizes as the creation of the "vanity of a madman." At this same conference America was denounced by Englishmen "as undoubtedly the most ruthless and aggressively imperialistic nation at present," and as "the source of the greatest danger of future wars." "They cry peace, peace, but there is no peace."

And in this emergency where stands the United States? Well, President Coolidge has signalized the opening of the Disarmament Conference by saying that "there is no short cut to peace any more than to any other form of salvation." The Borah proposal to outlaw war is something to approach with fear and trembling, he is quoted as saying, the chief obstacle to the plan being in his mind that provision in the federal Constitution which gives Congress the sole power to make war. Next, blowing hot after this cold draft, Mr. Coolidge is quoted as comforting himself with the thought that a treaty providing for the outlawry of war, "while it would amount to a declaration of policy [*sic*], might be helpful in promoting the sentiments of peace." Here we have the characteristic attitude of the statesman in office toward any new proposal for exorcising war. He fears; he trembles; he vacillates; he wonders if public sentiment will back him up; he hopes that it will help to strengthen the spirit for peace, but he sees constitutional or other difficulties in the way; finally he issues a statement as confused as the one above. To take his courage in both hands and to insist that the obstacles shall be overcome and the definite advance toward peace made—that is beyond him.

Naturally Senator Borah challenges the President's position, with all the weight of his standing as a high constitutional authority, and declares that the reverse of what the President says is true; that there is nothing in the Constitution to prevent the United States from entering into contracts with other nations to outlaw war. If the President were right it would then be his duty, in our judgment, to work for a constitutional amendment to legitimize the proposal which is one of the great steps toward peace that the world can take promptly. We do not claim for it that it will end all war. We do maintain that it is one of the steps to remove the evil which Lord Robert Cecil is correct in saying must be banished or it will destroy the world.

We are aware, of course, that President Coolidge sincerely desires to achieve something notable for peace before he leaves office for good. Trustworthy information which comes to us from high sources makes it plain that he is talking and thinking a good deal about it. The danger lies in his timidity and in that ineptitude which made him ruin the tripartite naval conference at Geneva by failing to ascertain diplomatically in advance of its meeting what could be accomplished, and by selecting a second-rank diplomat and a belligerent naval officer to represent the United States. So, while he feels himself compelled to throw cold water upon Senator Borah's plan for the outlawry of war, he makes no mention of Ambassador Houghton's far-reaching and vitally important proposal to take the war-making power out of the hands of the "little groups of men" who constitute cabinets and governments and to put it into the hands of the people themselves by ordaining a referendum on war. Here is another constructive plan which, as we have already pointed out, is a great contribution to the discussion. That Europe is so filled with talk of disarmament and war prevention is the most hopeful sign that the calamity may be averted. But why should not America sound the note of courage and of leadership instead of one of doubt and vacillation?

Russia Leads the World

THE way to disarm is to disarm. This was Mr. Litvinov's bold challenge to the governments of the world assembled in the Disarmament Conference at Geneva. He dared them to wipe out armies and navies and air forces; to destroy all weapons, fortresses, military supplies, and all means of chemical warfare; to end forever all military training, and military ministries and general staffs; to prohibit military propaganda and military education. In other words, he proposed a clean sweep of the whole damnable, murderous business of teaching and preparing human beings to kill each other. He dared the nations to prove that they were really sincere when they called upon each other to disarm, and not merely bent upon the hocus-pocus of striking off one class of ships here or reducing an army by 15 or 20 per cent there. He dared them to abide by the commandment: "Thou shalt not kill," and to prove themselves Christians. To the Allies his demand was that they prove the sincerity of their pretentions that the last conflict was "the war to end war." [The full text of his proposal appears in this week's International Relations Section.]

Thus he took the ultimate position, and he has encountered exactly the fate which inevitably comes to a radical who desires to go to the root of things, to cut to the bone. He has been ridiculed, abused, denounced, and cartooned as bringing a Trojan horse to Geneva. The half-hearted sponsors of peace, the compromisers of the daily press who admit that war is hellish and then but a dozen buts so that there shall be no far-reaching reform, the embattled militarists and their followers who find themselves facing the possibility that they may lose their jobs, the defenders of war as an end and a glory in itself—all have joined to deride this preposterous suggestion. Litvinov, they say, is obviously insincere; does not the Soviet regime exist only because it uses military force against its enemies? He is again insincere in thus challenging the nations because he knows that what he suggests is a counsel of perfection, an impractical, visionary proposal which no one would or could accept—he would be the first to have his withers wrung if it were accepted. It was a skilful dialectician's trick to put the other nations in the wrong. It was a superbly clever piece of propaganda to put Russia into the forefront at Geneva and it was at the same moment an incredibly stupid act, because it immediately united against her once more all the nations around the Council. It was an idle gesture and, having made it, Litvinov might now be expected to get down to business and join in the task of lopping off a battleship here and a regiment there.

Thus run the comments—and so they would run if in any other field of action the Russians or anyone else should produce a plan which really meant something, which really struck seriously at vested interests. That this is what the armies and navies have become was stated clearly by Lord Robert Cecil—we quoted him last week as saying that "every month we delay, the old vested interests, material and moral, strengthen their hold." Of course they do. Each month the great economic interests encourage the upbuilding of armaments and carry on the trade rivalries that lead directly to war. They are the great propagandists against disarmament; they fan the flames of nationalism even while they organize international trusts and consortiums; they demand large standing armies in order to maintain the social and economic status quo; they want to be armed against any domestic uprising. They want armies to protect themselves—as if arms would help against the Russian economic doctrines. If Russia disarmed by herself, a large part of our press would still be picturing the Soviets as planning some night to murder our women and children in their beds. Why not? The press is largely in the hands of the masters of capital whom Woodrow Wilson termed the "masters of America." Why should it not have greeted Litvinov's proposals precisely as it did?

Exactly the same would its reaction have been if Jesus Christ himself had appeared at Geneva to read this radical peace proposal to the conference. He, too, would have been portrayed as a designing long-haired Jew, or at best as a wild-eyed fanatic, dangerous to the world because he preached the impossible. Do not all who demand the ideal make far more difficult the paths of the "practical" statesmen who, with their feet on the ground, seek to approach each goal by one "rational" step after another, not, as the cant runs, "going too far and too fast for public opinion"? Well, for ourselves, we care little for these critical comments, and we care at this hour very little for the motives of M. Litvinov. It may all have been a clever trick. It *was* a clever maneuver, but we deem it a very great service to humanity. It is always dangerous to let loose a new idea in the world, and there are millions of people, many of them bearing upon their bodies the scars of the last conflict, who will never forget that one great government has made this proposal of complete and absolute abolition of the obscene institution of war. They will continue to ask themselves why this ideal is not attainable. They will find no other answers to their question but the stubbornness of those vested interests, the army and navy and the munition-makers, and the other profiteers by war, and the masses of compromisers and casuists who year in and year out throw cold water upon any proposal which would advance the interests of the masses of mankind.

Litvinov has shot one of those arrows into the air that fall no man knows where. The Disarmament Conference can never meet again without having the ultimate goal plainly in view. They may trim and compromise and shilly-shally all they please, but whether they like it or not the final objective will be there before them and they cannot gainsay it. It is, of course, too much to hope that in this Christian America there will be an articulate body of opinion to support so radical a demand. From all sides we hear that the whispering campaign against the Russians gains ground day by day. In women's clubs, meetings of the Daughters of the American Revolution, and elsewhere there is, we learn, an almost sadistic dwelling upon the horrors of Bolshevik rule. Before us lies a screed from a citizen of Washington, D. C., declaring that England, France, and Germany have all been won over by the Soviets to a secret agreement to destroy the United States! To such as these the Litvinov move will be but the voice of Jacob.

For ourselves we welcome with all our hearts the Russian proposals. It is our deliberate judgment that if persisted in they will give to the Soviets the moral leadership of the world.

Abolish the Submarine

ONCE more a submarine disaster has shocked the entire world. If there is anything more horrible than the fate of gallant men slowly asphyxiated in a steel coffin, although able for a time to communicate with their fellows, we do not know what it is. To our lay minds the rescue operations were a disgrace to the navy as to whose boasted efficiency we have long been skeptical—how can a navy be efficient that is headed by men like Daniels, Denby, and Wilbur? We shall, of course, await an inquiry by Congress before forming our final judgment, but why a rescue fleet should connect one airline to the sunken submarine and then have to go back to Boston for a second when that snapped; why the mother-ship should have been at anchor in a nearby harbor without steam up; why a patrol-boat should have been going at 18 knots in restricted waters; and why the navy has persistently refused to attach lifting rings to submarines and acquire the right kind of a floating derrick after the fate of the S-51, are beyond us. The navy will have to answer satisfactorily these and many other questions if the tombstones of the dead on the S-4 are not to be inscribed: "Murdered by the incompetence and red tape of the navy to which they belonged."

Well, we can only reiterate the demand for the abolition of all submarines which we have voiced so often. Strongly urged at the Washington Conference for the Limitation of Armaments, the proposal to do away with this weapon of war was there blocked by the French, who next to the English had suffered more from the German submarine than anybody else. It was widely hinted that they preferred not to give up the submarine in order, curiously enough, to have a new and most dangerous means of attacking their late allies, the British. British suggestions that the English were in favor of doing away with under-water boats were met with the scornful remark that of course the English had everything to gain by abolishing the greatest menace to their carrying trade in time of war. The Americans were not ready to force the issue; they were content to rest upon their oars, believing that they had achieved a great deal by checking the production of battleships. So the submarine stayed—to be a menace to its crew in every navy of which it is a part.

Now the facts which made the submarine such a despicable weapon of war in the hands of the Germans are unaltered by the years that have elapsed since the armistice. Naval men everywhere admit that it cannot be handled so as to avoid the danger of sinking women and children as well as men passengers on liners, not even when the commanders have the best of intentions. For to identify a ship running without lights at night, sometimes in high seas, is an extremely difficult task for the commander of a little ship, itself bobbing about on the waves and in danger of being sunk by a single shot. It is no wonder that hospital ships were sunk by accident and that other mistakes occurred which lent color to those charges of submarine atrocities which Admiral Sims declares to have been practically non-existent. Even when a passenger ship is captured in broad daylight on a smooth sea, the submarine obviously cannot perform the functions of a cruiser and remove the passengers to safety. It was formerly alleged that the naval use of the submarine would lead to its commercial development, but the fact is, of course, that no one cares the least bit about the possibility of a commercial submarine, or wastes five minutes of time in discussing it. It is as a weapon of war alone that the submarine has any use.

As such it should be barred by a concert of nations. Certainly there can be no question of ratios or preponderance of strength in submarines if that form of vessel is barred. This would simply put all navies on an equality. This, obviously, is a matter that the League of Nations ought to take up, and, if it is not able to move, either the United States or Great Britain should take the lead. No one can rightly charge us with desiring an unfair advantage if we seek to outlaw a weapon which had best never been invented. It is one of the subjects which should have been taken up at the unfortunate tripartite naval conference in Geneva. Mr. Coolidge seems to think now that because that failed we must build up an enormous fleet. On the contrary, the failure of that undertaking should be the clearest incentive to attack the evil of naval armaments from another angle. It can be done by direct communications from Washington to the other governments. Enlightened statesmanship in any of the great countries could make the move and save the world the horror of these recurring tragedies.

When Is a War Not a War?

WHY, obviously, our government declares, in Nicaragua. In the very week when our Secretary of State has published his correspondence with France urging an agreement to "renounce" war between the two historic republics, we are sending the major general commanding the Marine Corps, with one thousand more marines and perhaps half a dozen warships, to Nicaragua. They will not, of course, engage in "war." They are sent merely as police to put down an uprising of "bandits." It is no war, although, seven days after the attack upon the American column which resulted in five Americans being killed and twenty-three wounded, the seriously injured could be removed from the scene of the attack at Quilali only by most daring work on the part of Marine Corps aviators. During that week the American public was informed that the country around Quilali had been cleared of the "bandits," yet the dispatches report that at each halt of the airplane to pick up a wounded man "Sandino snipers peppered at the plane with rifles from the surrounding hills," and a fighting bomber circled around Quilali dropping bombs on the hilltops so as to keep down the fire of the enemy. There are obviously "bandits" and "bandits"—the French in Syria who have been killing thirty thousand of the best Syrians also use the word to describè their enemies—but it is a new thing for an American government to be compelled to remove its wounded through the fire of "bandits" and under the cover of a bombing machine, and to admit that the losses have been proportionately as high as in our hardest battles in France.

The truth is, of course, that this is war, nothing more and nothing less, and the government might as well admit it. One does not send a thousand marines to reinforce a force of two to three thousand more if the adversaries are merely bandits. As it happens, there is official report that those who attacked the Americans at Quilali were well armed and equipped, and freshly uniformed. It is even reported that they are being trained by two American captives, which, incidentally, is the first word that we have received that there have been American prisoners in the "bandits'" hands. If further proof that this is a war were needed it would seem to come in the attempt of the marines to blacken the character of General Sandino. The intelligence bureau of that corps declares that Sandino is "a brave man but with a shady record, having served with Pancho Villa in Mexico"—a lie, as Mr. de la Selva points out on another page—and having been convicted "of a violent crime in Masaya." The Marine Corps further reports that this "bandit" carries "many flags, all with a red and black background with skull and cross-bones worked into the red and black." It fails, of course, to add that red and black are the colors of the Nicaraguan labor movement. Doubtless more atrocity stories and bolshevik bogies will follow.

The truth is that we are witnessing deliberate warfare—another case where the American Executive has usurped the power of the Congress to make war, precisely as did Wilson twice in Mexico and also in Haiti and in Santo Domingo. Everybody in Latin America knows that Sandino is not a bandit, but that he is a patriot fighting a madman's fight against overwhelming odds. It may be possible to fool the American people as to what has happened in Nicaragua; it may be possible to get the support of the bulk of the daily press of this country on the morally indefensible ground that having got into this mess we must see the thing through, but nobody will be fooled in Latin America. Undoubtedly the effort will be made to prove that the new uniforms and the arms and ammunition are coming from Mexico, and to portray this as fresh evidence of Mexican hostility to the United States. It is, of course, nothing of the kind. We have no right or power in law or morals to forbid the Mexicans to sell arms and ammunition in any direction that they please. We who have financed and made money out of a hundred revolutions in Central and South America cannot reserve to ourselves the right to a monopoly of this sorry business.

So, just as we are appealing to France to end the possibility of war, and endeavoring to define what is aggressive warfare and an aggressor nation, we are carrying on a peculiarly offensive aggressive war against a little neighboring country. The time-honored excuses that we have to defend American property, that if we did not restore order some European nation would do so, are being worked again. But worst of all is the plea that because we have blundered and lost American lives we must refuse to retrace our mistaken steps. Fortunately, there is an awakening public conscience on this matter. We have had a moving protest from one father whose son was slain; and a call has been issued for a conference on the bloodshed in Nicaragua, to be attended by such persons as Stephen P. Duggan, William Allen White, Everett Colby, Mrs. Franklin D. Roosevelt, Raymond B. Fosdick, and George Foster Peabody. It is a time for mass meetings of protest all over the country, and we hope that they will be forthcoming. Above all we welcome the continued frank speaking in Congress of Senators Norris, Wheeler, Nye, and Heflin and of Representatives Huddleston and Bloom. Even Senator Edwards of New Jersey, who can hardly be called an habitual idealist, has been moved to protest.

It is time, indeed, for Congress to assert its rights as the war-making branch of the government. If there is any clause in the Constitution which is a dead letter it is that reserving to Congress the right to declare war. The failure in that document to define what war is constitutes an essential weakness. As a matter of fact, the Executive can and constantly does invade foreign territory with the armed forces of the United States without authority, and that fact is the reason for the growing Latin-American dread of us. Any President, as things stand today, can maneuver the country to the brink of war and then demand that Congress support him, assert that those who oppose war are unpatriotic and wilful men, summon to his side the press of the country, and appeal to the public to stand by the President and the flag. Every hoary device of the professional patriot to make people rally around the flag and to defend the national honor and prestige, however disgraceful the means by which we got into the fix, will then be used. Nicaragua today marks a disgraceful failure of American statesmanship. The real patriot will say so and will not for a single instant countenance the suggestion that rather than admit our blunder we should continue to fight an illegal and unwarranted war.

What They Die For

THE marines are pouring into Nicaragua; in the end, we suppose, they will occupy the villages, send columns into the mountains, and round up the recalcitrant patriots—as Pershing's men, and Wood's, and "Hell-roaring Jake" Smith's troops did in the Philippines a quarter century ago. Flames of decency still burn in the United States, as the stirring letter from Sergeant Hemphill's father, quoted by our Unofficial Spokesman, shows; but the heart of America, blunted and corrupted in the struggle against Philippine freedom, still further dulled by the hypocrisies of the World War, seems to beat to other rhythms. Yet the war in Nicaragua is about the meanest, least justifiable enterprise in which this nation has yet engaged.

Everyone seems to agree that we have "blundered." Few seem to think that the way to repair a blunder is to shift gears and head in the other direction. And few seem to realize that anything is happening in Nicaragua except battles with Sandino. Behind the battle-line, however, American control is being riveted upon the little country in a fashion which no election can repair; its resources have been used to fight America's battles, and now they are being pledged for years to come to New York bankers.

There is open talk of a new loan to Nicaragua, on terms which even the puppet Diaz resents. It will be recalled that the marines kept President Diaz in office when he had lost all control over his own country. We did not come to his aid free. We compelled him to buy peace. Colonel Stimson's "peace plan," forced on Nicaragua last spring, was one of the most sordid maneuvers in the history of imperialism. Stimson went to the Opposition leaders, and told them that if they continued to fight the whole force of the United States would be employed against them, but that, if they would surrender their arms, they would be paid in gold dollars for their guns and ammunition. Craven Moncada, the Liberal leader who is now defending American policy, accepted the bribe. The "bandit" Sandino patriotically refused it, and faced death to defy the dollars and bullets of the Yankee colossus. But Diaz had no money to pay Moncada to surrender; and our Government did not foot the bill. Indeed, it persuaded the Guaranty Trust Company to lend the money to Diaz. And the terms of that loan were a scandal, even in Wall Street.

For a one-year loan of $1,000,000, Diaz was forced to put a mortgage on the capital stock and dividends of the National Bank of Nicaragua (a corporation with a paid-in capital of $300,000 and worth twice that) and on the entire capital stock of the Pacific Railways of Nicaragua (worth more than the total amount of the loan); to pledge the export tax on coffee, the new customs duties on tobacco, wines, and liquors, and the increased tolls on other commodities; to give the bankers a five-year option on new Nicaraguan loans; and to transfer to New York, for the benefit of the credit-givers, the bank's and railroad's deposits (said to be above $400,000). The contract also provided that the money would be used primarily to buy (American) munitions and, apparently, to bribe Moncada—and would be expended under the direction of a special committee of three, two of the three being Americans, one named by the State Department, the other by the bankers.

That loan expires on March 31—although it includes a provision by which it may be extended for another six months. Negotiations are now under way for another loan to replace it, and also to cover the enormous expenses incurred by Diaz in maintaining himself in power against the wishes of his countrymen. Diaz signed that loan contract willingly enough, but apparently the terms proposed for the new loan are worse still—they stump even Diaz, who is reported to be about to resign in disgust. A letter received by a certain large business house in New York from another business house in Nicaragua asserts that the difficulties of the business situation there are not due to war depression but to the fact that the Diaz Government

> is negotiating a loan with certain New York bankers to obtain money to pay the war debts and damages, and the Government does not want to accept clauses of the contract which the bankers demand and, therefore, to force the Government to come to terms, the bank has stopped all operations with the exception of collecting. This, of course, as they control the custom-house revenues and the Banco Nacional de Nicaragua, establishes a short and vicious circle. Currency is getting scarcer every day, and in the end it will all go to the Banco Nacional, for the customs duties are the most exorbitant ever heard of.

The business man adds his prediction that the legislature will have to accept the bankers' terms. Meanwhile the State Department, supporting the bankers, is demanding that the legislature also revise the Nicaraguan Constitution to permit United States marines to supervise the elections. A pretty business indeed for the United States of America to be supporting! A fine cause to die for!

Mr. Coolidge at Havana

URIAH HEEP spoke at the opening session of the Pan-American Congress at Havana and never did that oily person mix to a greater degree sanctimonious preaching of the Golden Rule, shameless hypocrisy, and platitudinous humbuggery. With all the meaningless words squeezed out of it, Mr. Coolidge's speech boils down to nothing. There is not an original thought in it, not a new policy, not a constructive suggestion—merely that assumption of American supremacy in all undertakings and ideals which invariably infuriates all of Europe. No man with any sense of humor could have made such a speech. He has only himself to blame if everywhere in South and Central America people conceive of him as speaking with his tongue in his cheek, as the personification of Yankee boastfulness and vanity. He talked exactly the same kind of bunk which he would have offered to a convention of Rotarians or of the American Legion.

What could he have thought that his audience was? He lauded the Cubans for their intellectual qualities which, he declares, "have won for them a permanent place in science, art, and literature." The other nations represented have also reached high points of cultural development. Yet he expected them to swallow things like this at the very time when Haiti is ruled by our marines and at the moment our aviators in Nicaragua reported that they had killed forty Nicaraguans—sex and age not stated:

> We have kept the peace so largely among our republics because democracies are peace-loving. They are founded on the desire to promote the general welfare of the people, which is seldom accomplished by warfare. In addition to this we have adopted a spirit of *accommodation, good-will, confidence, and mutual helpfulness*. We have been slow to anger and plenteous in mercy. [Italics ours.] . . . We must join together in assuring conditions under which our republics will have the freedom and the responsibility of working out their own destiny in their own way. . . . We shall have to realize that the highest law is consideration, cooperation, friendship, and charity. Without the application of these there can be no peace and no progress, no liberty. . . .

The men who heard this canting stuff have memories. They recall not only Haiti, Nicaragua, Santo Domingo, and recent Mexican history; they remember also the Mexican War with its theft of Mexico and Arizona—that war which Ulysses S. Grant, Mr. Coolidge's predecessor, called not an act of consideration and good-will but the most despicable and indefensible of wars. They remember when Mr. Coolidge spoke of Cuba's possessing her own sovereignty, and being free and independent and peaceful, that it was the United States which forced Cuba into the World War merely in order to gain possession of a few German ships; that American garrisons are encamped on her soil on territory ceded to the United States under compulsion—and that Cuba lives under their threat; that Cuba's independence is gravely limited by us through the Platt Amendment.

No, Mr. Coolidge's smooth words at Havana will butter no parsnips. Say what you will about Latin-Americans, their weaknesses and their vanities, one cannot accuse them of being fools or dolts. They know the value of ceremonial politeness and of palavering as well as Mr. Coolidge. The Havana Conference is open. It should demand that the United States square its deeds with Mr. Coolidge's words.

Our Mad Dogs of War

THE mad dogs of American life, endangering not only the peace of this country, but Anglo-Saxon friendship and cooperation—yes, the peace of the world—this is what our raving admirals are becoming. We refer especially to Rear Admirals Hughes and Plunkett—the latter plainly aspires to be the von Tirpitz of the American navy. Speaking before the House Naval Affairs Committee, Admiral Hughes, who is admittedly the author of the three-billion dollar navy-increase program, for which Secretary Wilbur is the window-dresser and the stuffed front, declared that the building program was aimed at the English navy. Addressing the Republican Club in New York on January 21, Rear Admiral Plunkett called for an unsurpassed fleet, advancing every one of the hoary old arguments about preparedness which the war so utterly discredited and Calvin Coolidge himself says are untrue, and in answer to a question of a reporter of the *Herald Tribune* stated that his prediction of an early war related to Great Britain. This the Admiral subsequently denied, saying that he had meant only to predict war with "our trade rivals" and that he hoped that we could avoid that if we were fully prepared. What a spectacle! What an outrage against decency! What a deliberate effort to embroil two countries which but a few years ago pledged eternal amity and good-will!

Of course Admiral Plunkett meant England. There is no other fleet against which we could possibly be arming, for the preparedness which he advocates bids fair to give us an armada bigger than those of Italy, France, and Japan combined. If these men have their way we shall be in for a full-fledged race of armaments with Great Britain to which there can be only one outcome. It is the most menacing situation which we have yet confronted in Anglo-American relations. England has not done one thing since our men were dying together on the battlefields of France to merit any such acts of baseness as this deliberate invoking of hostilities with the original mother-country.

That Calvin Coolidge permits this thing to go on without rebuke is utterly disheartening. It is fresh proof of what we have repeatedly pointed out, that he is a President who does not govern in the sense of controlling his subordinates. It is known that the navy has been disloyal to him as it was to Harding so far as the Washington Disarmament Conference is concerned. He himself has expressly said that preparedness never protected any nation from war nor guaranteed success in any war. Again and again he has stated, notably in his last annual message, that he is determined that the United States shall not engage in any naval-armament rivalry. Yet he allows his admirals and Secretary Wilbur to make absolutely hypocritical these assertions of his that we are not going to pour out our wealth for battleships and cruisers to vie with England and Japan. In the face of such statements as those of Hughes and Plunkett and recent ones of Secretary Wilbur silence on the part of the Chief Executive is cowardly. More than that, it will be taken abroad to mean that he connives with these admirals. It will reinforce the charges, now current against us all over the world, that our acts and our words are wholly antagonistic to one another. It is his duty to speak out ringingly and emphatically, instead of which he leaves the task to Senator Borah.

Mr. Borah, we are sure, has rendered no better service than by his clear-cut denunciation of both those admirals. "I regard," he said, "such declarations as mischievous to a degree." "Sheer madness," he correctly calls their propaganda, and he continues:

> A few days ago an admiral in the English navy put out a similar statement. If anything could possibly bring on war between two great nations it is these enlarged naval programs in connection with declarations from the navies of the respective countries that war is inevitable. This was the insane policy which obtained between Germany and Great Britain from 1900 to 1914 and was one of the great contributing causes to the World War.

Even if they believe this sort of stuff, Senator Borah says they ought not to be allowed to talk it, and we think that he is right. The position of the naval and army officer is different from that of other citizens in the matter of free speech. He gives his opinions into the keeping of his commanding officer when he puts on the uniform. The press listens to him because he is a general or an admiral, and when he speaks people suppose that he represents the opinion of his superiors. The President of the United States has the right to demand of army and navy officers that on these matters of international affairs they should be silent, if only because they cannot be non-partisan. Admiral H. P. Jones was reported by the press as rejoicing that the Disarmament Conference, to which he was a delegate for the purpose of having it succeed, was a failure—a case of most complete disloyalty to his Commander-in-Chief. Such as he cannot be unbiased, because their profession is at stake; if disarmament succeeds they and their ilk will disappear, or be on the retired list as relics of a butcher's trade happily done away with by the advance of civilization.

We repeat, these are the mad dogs of American life, and as long as they are afflicted with this form of rabies they should at the very least be adequately rebuked by their government, that the whole world may know they do not speak for it. We send men to prison every day for stealing from three dollars up. How small is the injury such men do to society compared to the potentialities of evil which may come out of the words of a Plunkett or a Hughes—which evil inevitably will come if they are allowed to go on talking. Senator Borah is right; we are getting into the same position to England as was Germany in relation to Great Britain, and the result will be the same. There are a large number of societies and organizations in this country, like the English-Speaking Union, founded to preserve the peace and advance the friendship of the two Anglo-Saxon countries. If they do not exert themselves now they ought to go out of business, for we are heading straight into war with England—a foreign correspondent recently absent from Washington for six months informed us a month ago that he was appalled on his return at the talk of war with England which filled Washington. Mr. Coolidge is incredibly ignorant if he is not aware of this, or of what it will lead to if it is not stopped. If he does not speak out now he is betraying his country and degrading himself.

The World Talks Peace

PEOPLE are talking peace. Statesmen, churchmen, educators, editors join in a swelling chorus. "War with the United States is unthinkable," says Sir Austen Chamberlain, British Foreign Minister, apparently in reply to Admiral Plunkett's damnable New York speech. Whereupon the British House of Commons cheered. M. Briand, Foreign Minister of France, is ready to outlaw war, and Paul Claudel, the French Ambassador to the United States, boldly declared when signing the Franco-American arbitration treaty, that "'Outlawry of war' is one of those well-coined words which not only have a striking meaning but a working power, one of those words which have a great future because they are cautioned by a glorious past." The German Government has drawn up for a Prague conference its suggestions of methods looking to the abolition of war. Our own Government has declared its readiness to outlaw the submarine and dispatches from London indicate that the British Government favors the suggestion.

The big-navy plan for a moment obscured the peace talk in this country, but the jingo program is not going through without a fight. The Rev. S. Parkes Cadman, president of the Federal Council of Churches; the Rev. William P. Merrill, president of the Church Peace Union; and George W. Wickersham, Attorney General in President Taft's Cabinet, have signed a circular telegram urging the churches to help in rousing the country against the big naval program which, as they say, "seriously jeopardizes" the whole world movement for peace. The National Council of the Episcopal Church calls the pending naval bill a "menace," and Methodists, Congregationalists, Quakers, and others have spoken as bravely. An Emergency Committee on the Big Navy Bill has been formed in Boston, and its letterhead bears the names of the cream of New England. In the South the Richmond *News-Leader* says the bill is "nothing less than an invitation to war." Senator Borah from the West calls it "sheer madness." The voice of peace has not been drowned out; the House Committee will probably rewrite Secretary Wilbur's swollen navy bill.

The Washington Government is plainly awake to the necessity of taking some action looking toward peace. Its submarine suggestion looked in that direction, and the elaborate publicity with which it surrounded the signing of the pitiful little arbitration pact with France indicates that it feels the pulse of the country, and knows that its big-navy program will do it no good unless it takes counteracting steps toward peace. Now, it was well to renew the Root and Bryan arbitration treaties, but the country knows that they have not been strengthened. The new treaty establishes no safeguards of peace which were not in existence before the World War swept down upon an overarmed world.

Article I of the treaty signed with France on February 6 agrees that all disputes, "of whatever nature," shall, if diplomacy and arbitration fail, be submitted for investigation and report to a commission of conciliation. That is the old Bryan treaty, signed with many nations in 1914, and it was and is a good provision. Succeeding articles provide for arbitration, as was done by the Root treaty of 1908, with this difference: that whereas the Root treaty excepted from arbitration questions which "affect the vital interests, the independence, or the honor of the two contracting parties," or which "concern the interests of third parties," the new treaty excepts any question which "is within the domestic jurisdiction of the high contracting parties; involves the interests of third parties; depends upon or involves the maintenance of the traditional attitude of the United States concerning American questions, described as the Monroe Doctrine; depends upon or involves the observance of the obligations of France in accordance with the Covenant of the League of Nations." That is more specific than the language of the 1908 treaty, but if anything it is even more exclusive. "It seems to me," a French Senator said, "that every possible subject of conflict has been carefully omitted."

Unlike the Root treaty, which had to be renewed every five years, the new document has no time limit. Furthermore, a preamble has been added, reciting that France and the United States are

> Determined to prevent so far as in their power lies any interruption in the peaceful relations that have happily existed between the two nations for more than a century;
>
> Desirous of reaffirming their adherence to the policy of submitting to impartial decision all justiciable controversies that may arise between them;
>
> Eager by their example not only to demonstrate their condemnation of war as an instrument of national policy in their mutual relations, but also to hasten the time when the perfection of international arrangements for the pacific settlement of international disputes shall have eliminated forever the possibility of war among any of the Powers of the world.

Those are fine words to put in any treaty. But, unfortunately, they must be looked at in the context of their history. M. Briand wanted to negotiate a treaty definitely and totally outlawing war. Our State Department refused. The words were deported to the preamble, because a preamble, unlike the articles of a treaty, is not legally binding.

Secretary Kellogg's plans and ideas throughout these arbitration negotiations have been uncertain and conflicting. There are intimations that he is at present engaged in the effort, first, to negotiate similar arbitration treaties with the other nations of Europe, and second, to work out some system by which the Great Powers of the world may take joint steps to prevent any war arising anywhere. We do not know the details of this plan, and we may do Secretary Kellogg an injustice, but it smacks to us of the Holy Alliance. We suspect concerts of the Great Powers, and fear that such a system might work rather to prevent small national movements toward freedom than to block the really dangerous belligerence of the big nations.

Yet this talk of peace, small as may be some of the points upon which it is focussed, helps. The first step toward peace is to talk peace, want peace, will peace. More important than the text of any treaty is the spirit in which it is drafted. That is why the attitude of our State Department seems to us a positive menace. That is why the outburst of protest against the navy bill and the widespread uneasiness about our Nicaraguan adventure seem to us genuinely encouraging.

War in Nicaragua

IF the American people had that sense of humor upon which they so pride themselves, the nation would have rocked with laughter when the Senate Committee on Foreign Relations announced that the Marine Corps would have to stay in Nicaragua in order to insure a "fair" election! The Senate had just refused to seat Frank L. Smith, elected by the people of Illinois, and William S. Vare, elected by the people of Pennsylvania, because of gross misuse of money in their campaigns; the Supreme Court had just branded a Secretary of the Navy and a Secretary of the Interior who had been Mr. Coolidge's honored Cabinet associates as guilty of collusion and corruption; the former chairman of our ruling party, also a former Cabinet member, had just admitted that he had lied about his campaign expenditures, and he and his associates are at this moment being exposed in deliberate and deceitful circumvention of the law. The State of Indiana has been struggling to get rid of its corrupt Ku Klux Klan officials. And at such a moment the venerable Senators, led by Senator Borah, stand up and with straight faces announce that the marines must stay in Nicaragua to teach the benighted Latins all about honest voting. That ought to be enough to make even Calvin Coolidge relax into a hearty guffaw.

Of course the marines are not engaged in preaching democracy to the peons on the coffee plantations. Instead, they are up in the sparsely populated hill-country, killing Sandinistas. As the incomparable Will Rogers puts it, they "are doing all they can to see that there are fewer votes to supervise and Sandino is doing all he can to see that there are fewer marines to supervise." Statistics presented to the Senate Committee on Foreign Relations by naval officials tell another part of the story. Up to February 1 the United States had sent 4,609 marines to Nicaragua. Sandino believes he has killed five hundred Americans; the Navy Department admits that 21 have been killed, 45 wounded, and 1,410 returned to the United States as "casuals"—some suffering from tropical fever. The United States has—or had—six De Haviland bombing planes, two amphibians, six observation planes, six Vought corsairs, three Fokker transports, and six Curtiss Falcon planes in Nicaragua; at least three of these have been forced to the ground, and ten others have been hit by Sandino marksmen. No one knows how many Nicaraguans we have succeeded in shipping into the great democracy of the dead.

This is not an election; it is war. The Constitution declares that only Congress has the power to declare war, but the State Department and the marines are as contemptuous of the United States Constitution as of the Nicaraguan. The Navy Department and the Treasury admit that this is war. The Comptroller General ruled on September 15, 1927, that officers without dependents were not entitled to rental allowances "since they were serving in the field in the face of an enemy," which, according to the *Army and Navy Register*, means that the United States is in a state of war with Nicaragua. More recently the Comptroller General has stated that the Secretary of the Navy has recognized the situation in his citations for the award of the navy cross, stating that "in the case of individual officers on duty in Nicaragua there have been actions, battles, and an enemy."

These, to be sure, are technicalities; to the parents of the boys killed in action the meaning of this war goes deeper than any bureaucrat's ruling. We quoted some weeks ago the comment of John S. Hemphill, father of a Missouri boy killed in action; Emil Pump, of Council Bluffs, Iowa, whose son John was killed in Nicaragua, made similar comment to the Des Moines *Tribune:*

> It's only a rich man's war [he said]. And not a single one of us will be hurt or benefited no matter how the fight turns out. Coolidge just pulled a fast one on Congress and, as a result, they have sacrificed my boy and others to protect the big bankers' interests. But I hope they will send John back home here now. The rich men will not want him dead, but we do.

Emil Pump came closer to the truth than Senator Borah. The marines did not go into Nicaragua to reform the electoral system; they went there because American investors had preceded them and because the criminally stupid young men in the State Department recognized an impotent down-and-out as President of Nicaragua and called upon the marines to make good their folly. Half the country, including Senator Borah and the New York *World*, now seems to think that because we made that ghastly mistake we must stand by it, no matter how many lives it costs. There are even Senators who, forgetting their scorn for treaties negotiated by a mere Woodrow Wilson, plead that the marines must stay until a Henry Stimson's agreement for a marine-controlled "fair" election is fulfilled.

We will never get out until we divest ourselves of that murderous sense of superiority which deludes men like Senator Borah into believing that we have a moral obligation to kill Nicaraguan patriots who object to marine control of their elections. Consider the hypocrisy of it! In order to maintain the military control which General McCoy believes essential to an "honest," Yankee-controlled election, we have demanded that the Nicaraguan Congress tear up as a scrap of paper the electoral provisions of their national constitution. In the name of marine-enforced democracy we have attacked constitutionalism, declaring that the United States would, "by means which it does not feel called upon to outline in advance," see that its will was done. Suppose, under such circumstances, a President is finally elected. The very fact that he has been elected under Yankee auspices dooms him to unpopularity from the start. He will be as unable to retain his seat without Marine Corps aid as was the unfortunate Diaz. What then? Will not the young men in the State Department still feel that their prestige and the nation's are at stake and that the marines must keep their President in power?

The way to get out is to get out. Sooner or later—and for the honor of the country we wish it might be sooner—the United States, more and more unpopular, will have to appeal to the other Powers of Latin America to help us out of this mess, as they helped us out of the Mexican mess in 1916. That would go far to meet Sandino's suggestion made to Carleton Beals. It would be common sense. It would head toward peace. Our present course does not.

Rejecting Peace

THE eager enthusiasm with which the Powers at Geneva rejected the Russian proposal for complete disarmament does them no credit. They were assembled in a "Preparatory Commission on Disarmament," called together under the auspices of the League of Nations, and the Soviet Government did them the honor to suggest serious action in disarmament. It appalled them; Mr. Litvinov's own statement explains why:

> There has been more than enough discussion of disarmament [he said]. I venture to furnish the members of this commission with a few data from which it will be seen that in addition to the general Assemblies of the League of Nations and the Council meetings, thirty-eight sessions of which occupied themselves with the question of disarmament, not fewer than fourteen different commissions have devoted more than 120 sessions—not sittings, mark you, but sessions—to this same question, on which 111 resolutions have been passed by the general Assemblies and Council alone.
>
> Turning to the results of this vast quantity of work, the documentation of which has taken reams of paper, we are forced to the conclusion that not a single real step has been taken toward realization of disarmament. . . . The Soviet Government declares that it is ready to abolish all military forces in accordance with its draft convention as soon as a similar decision is passed and simultaneously carried out by other states. The Soviet Government asks the other governments represented here if they are also ready.

Count von Bernstorff for Germany, and Tewfik Pasha for Turkey, replied that they were ready to discuss sympathetically the Soviet proposals for complete and immediate disarmament. The Western Powers, led by England, replied with sneers and jibes. The very idea of complete and immediate disarmament was repulsive to them. They had not sent delegates to Geneva, it plainly appeared, with any intention of disarming, or of moving toward disarmament; they desired merely to use the word "disarmament" sufficiently often and sufficiently loud to placate the peace sentiment at home.

Lord Cushendun's speech ridiculing the Soviet position was a disgrace to Great Britain. He carried into the session of the Disarmament Commission the grim campaign which Britain is waging upon Russia on a dozen fronts. The attention paid to the Amir of Afghanistan in London—the parades of tanks, the air maneuvers, the submarine excursions—are part of the same campaign; a silent war is being fought in China; and the British are resentful because they permitted the Russians to steal a march on them and to suggest to the League the inclusion of Turkey in the present Disarmament Conference.

Lord Cushendun did not so much discuss the Soviet proposals for disarmament as denounce the Soviet Government; and in so doing he falsified history. If there is any point upon which the Soviet scutcheon is clean it is on this very matter of foreign wars. Its first years were clouded by a war waged against it by the Allies because it dared make peace with Germany and propose peace for all the world. France and Britain, the United States and Japan, sent their soldiers and munitions into its territory without declaration of war. Lord Cushendun called the Soviet interest in disarmament "sudden." But as far back as the Conference of Genoa, in 1922, the Russians suggested a discussion of disarmament—in vain. It was not Russia's fault that she was not represented at the Washington Conference on the Limitation of Armaments, and Lord Cushendun grievously misstated the fact when he credited the League with any share in the achievements of that meeting. He objected because Soviet statesmen and the Soviet press have denounced the League, but so have the American press and American statesmen; and Mr. Litvinov's history of the League negotiations upon disarmament shows that participation in these sessions is no evidence of interest in the subject. For that matter, Viscount Cecil resigned from Lord Cushendun's own Government in protest against its attitude on the question of armament.

Our own American representative joined in cold-shouldering the Russian proposals. He thought them so divergent from the committee's draft that they were not even worth further study. But there is no evidence that he or anyone else at this Disarmament Conference—except the Russians and the disarmed Germans—had any interest in any program of disarmament, least of all in such a sweeping program as the Russian. The conference adjourned futilely and foolishly, having done nothing except to advertise Western hypocrisy.

What *The Nation* said four months ago it repeats: "The way to disarm is to disarm. . . . We welcome with all our hearts the Russian proposals. It is our deliberate judgment that if persisted in they will give to the Soviets the moral leadership of the world." They have been persisted in; and the action of the Western Powers has strengthened Russia's moral position.

Japan's War in China

JAPAN'S military party has won, and the Japanese are back in control of China's sacred province of Shantung. A state of virtual war has existed for a week about the capital, Tsinanfu, and as a result 3,000 Chinese and 50 Japanese are dead, and the Japanese hold the city. They have also taken over the entire Shantung Railway, built by the Germans and Japanized during the World War, but returned to China in 1922. Thirty thousand Japanese troops are already in Shantung, 14,000 of them at Tsinanfu, 245 miles inland.

The Japanese general, clearly, acted as military men often do—brusquely and imperiously, overriding the civilian consul-general and issuing short-term ultimatums. Who fired first in the fatal melee no one seems to know. But the essential point is that Chinese resentment of the presence of Japanese forces in the heart of China expressed itself in open rifle fire. That fact has tremendous significance. Never, since Boxer days, have the Chinese been so bold. The story of the passionate boycott after the Treaty of Versailles confirmed Japanese control of this same province of Shantung is still fresh in Japanese and Chinese memory. Men threw their Japanese hats into bonfires. Mobs invaded stores which dared sell Japanese goods. Japanese ships were not allowed to land their cargoes. A student deliberately broke his finger to sign an anti-Japanese protest in blood. But in 1918 no Chinese troops would have stood for five minutes against Japanese.

Some Japanese circles realize the danger. To any one who knows the ease with which, in the past, the Japanese government has controlled the press and inflamed the population, it is amazing that certain Tokio dailies are still protesting against the unrestrained course of the soldiers in Shantung. Evidently there are powerful commercial groups in Japan which foresee and fear the inevitable loss of trade. It is even possible that the military men have defied civilian orders—it would not be the first time in Japanese history if they did. And if, after such an outbreak, calm civilian opinion should get the better of the jingoes and force a peaceful settlement, that event in itself would be epoch-making in the East. It would mean that the feudal regime in Japan was really dead, and that the new bourgeoisie had come into its own. It would open new vistas of democratic development for all Asia.

Those vistas, however, are not yet open. The present fact is that the Japanese are mopping up in Shantung. General Fukuda at Tsinanfu has forced all Chinese troops to withdraw at least twenty *li* from the city; other Japanese commanders are seizing and disarming Nationalist troops wherever they meet them. Chiang Kai-shek's drive upon North China has been checked, and Japan has taken back what she restored in 1922.

In 1897, in the days of the "Battle for Concessions," two German missionaries were killed in Shantung, the "sacred province" of China, where Confucius was born. Germany saw her chance, and took it. She seized the port of Tsingtao and forced China to grant a ninety-nine year lease for it, as well as other preferential rights, in Shantung. When Japan entered the World War in August, 1914, she immediately set out to eject the Germans from Shantung, at the same time announcing that she intended to restore the leased territory to China. Possession, however, seemed to change her mind. The Twenty-one Demands of 1915 included an express transfer to Japan of all German rights, and even of privileges not enjoyed by the Germans. China, on entering the war, declared all her conventions with Germany abrogated, and at the Peace Conference took the position that this abrogation left no German rights to be transferred to Japan. But Japan was in possession; and secret treaties bound England and France to support her.

Anti-Japanese feeling ran high in those days. In the end Chinese economic pressure—plus the attitude of Britain and America—led Japan, after the Washington Conference, to withdraw her troops and return to China political control of Shantung. She retained, however, the German mines and property rights which she had seized, and she handed over the railroad only after prolonged negotiations. If Japan complains today that China is two years in arrears on the interest due on the railway notes, it is pertinent to recall that at Washington the Chinese representatives offered to float an internal loan and pay for the railway at once. Japan refused; she wanted, she said, to retain an interest in the railway for some years. The Chinese have a right to suspicion.

Presumably Japan is not playing for Shantung alone. Through her ownership of the South Manchuria Railway she virtually controls the three provinces of Manchuria. Chang Tso-lin, chief of the Peking, or Northern, Government, is also war-lord of Manchuria, and has played ball with the Japanese for many years. When, in December, 1925, a revolt threatened to overthrow Chang, it was Japanese intervention—although they denied it at the time—which decided the issue in his favor, and he later publicly thanked the Japanese for their aid. Again last summer Japan's sudden thrust of troops across Shantung protected the retreating Northerners and broke the force of the Nationalist attack.

To say that Japan's shipment of 14,000 troops 250 miles inland is mere "protection of foreign lives and property" is absurd. The Japanese have been attentive observers of recent events in China, and they must have known how such an act would affect the Chinese. They have no treaty rights in Tsinanfu. There is no "leased territory" there. But the Japanese commander arbitrarily outlined a zone into which he forbade Chinese troops to penetrate, and proceeded to fortify it. England cannot protest, because of the precedent of her own illegal course at Shanghai; and indignant Americans must admit that there is a certain parallel between this policy and our own in Nicaragua.

Nicaragua, however, has half a million people, and China four hundred millions. Ethically, we are not on a very different footing from the Japanese; but the possible consequences to the peace of the world are roughly proportionate to the population. Apparently both Japanese and Chinese are hesitating, appalled by their own foolhardiness. But the tide of battle is rolling on toward Tientsin, another great center of foreign population, defended by foreign troops; and in China today North and South, gun in hand, unite in resenting these cancers in the body of China.

What Is News in Haiti?

WE of *The Nation* think what is going on under the American flag in Haiti important. The destiny of American democracy depends in large part upon the manner in which we meet such imperial problems. When the United States forces a constitution and treaty upon a tiny republic at the point of the pistol, takes over the treasury and cuts off the salaries of recalcitrant officials, refuses to make payments in accordance with decisions of the Haitian Supreme Court, and, finally, annoyed at the court's independence, insists upon a new constitution giving the Executive, and, through the Executive, the United States marines, more power over the judiciary—when such things happen, they seem to us to constitute news in the sense of being interesting and significant happenings.

But they have not seemed to be news to the managing editors of the newspapers of the country or to the press associations. Little news has been put on the wires from Haiti, and that little has not been played up prominently. The assumption has been that Haiti did not interest newspaper readers; and perhaps the assumption was correct. At any rate, it seems to us, the question has never had a fair trial, unless in the New York *Times*. The *Times* sent one of its ablest correspondents, Clarence K. Streit, to Haiti at the time of the Lindbergh flight, and kept him there long enough to acquire the knowledge for several of the best articles on Haiti which have appeared in any American periodical. But most of the newspapers have not had correspondents in Haiti, and the news they have comes from a biased source. The Associated Press and the United Press correspondents in Haiti are both officers in the Marine Corps!

Two weeks ago *The Nation* printed an article by L. J.

deBekker, News Are Scarce in Haiti, complaining of the news sent from Haiti and urging a Senatorial inquiry into conditions in that unhappy country. The *Editor and Publisher* has replied in a violent attack upon *The Nation* and Mr. deBekker. The *Editor and Publisher* has a right to attack that article. We have frequently criticized the newspapers for inaccuracy, and our own article was inaccurate. More than anyone else we regret that fact. But we think that the *Editor and Publisher* should have gone further in its investigation. The facts are not precisely as Mr. deBekker stated them. They are worse.

Mr. deBekker stated that the Associated Press was represented in Haiti by Captain Craige, U. S. M. C., former Marine Corps publicity man, and the United Press by H. P. Davis, author of "Black Democracy." He mixed his men, or his press associations. Captain Craige is the United Press correspondent; Mr. Davis was for many years representative of the Associated Press. Lately, as the *Editor and Publisher* points out, he has been replaced by Frank Evans. The *Editor and Publisher*, however, fails to add that Mr. Evans is an officer of the United States Marine Corps, chief of the Haitian gendarmerie, and, like Captain Craige, a former publicity man for that service!

It is, of course, difficult for a press association to find an unbiased correspondent in an out-of-the-way corner like Port au Prince; but does any editor in America think that the Haitians can possibly get anything like a fair break on the news when both of the chief correspondents in their country are officers of the occupying army, subject to discipline from their official superiors?

There has been news about Lindbergh and Will Beebe and archaeologists in Haiti, but almost no political news, and what there is is now subject to occasional censorship by President Borno. (Incidentally, Mr. Davis, the former Associated Press correspondent, assures us that his dispatches were never censored, either by Borno or by General Russell.) Mr. deBekker said that "no newspaper in America has been informed that Haiti has a new Court of Cassation [supreme court]," despite the importance of the story. The *Editor and Publisher* replies that both news associations sent out stories on the subject, the Associated Press on October 25, January 10, and March 31. That may be; but we have searched the files of five New York newspapers on the corresponding dates and not found a line on Haiti. Mr. deBekker should, of course, have inquired of the press services before making so sweeping a statement; but he knew that the press-clippings services had brought him no copies of the reports which the associations say they sent out. The fact is that Mr. Streit's stories in the *Times*, written after his return from Haiti and after the amendments had been put through, are the only adequate account we have seen in any American newspaper.

The *Editor and Publisher* has been a zealous fighter for an independent press. It wants, we are sure, unbiased news as much as we. But its editorial on Mr. deBekker's article was a partisan defense of the press associations and gave a distorted picture of the treatment of Haiti news by the press associations and the Marine Corps.

Those "Peace Pacts"

THE Kellogg peace pacts have been signed at Paris by the United States, France, Germany, Great Britain, Italy, Japan, Belgium, Poland, Czecho-Slovakia, and the British dominions; and other nations will be permitted to ratify them at a later date. Upon the earnest insistence of Germany, it is reported, even Russia's signature will be accepted. Talking motion pictures have recorded every moment of the solemn ratification of this new "charter of peace"; and the world has been informed *in extenso* that war has been outlawed and a great forward step toward peace been made.

There is no doubt that these treaties are the product of a world-wide demand that the statesmen move to outlaw war. They have never been popular in the chancelleries; and it has been the people's voice for peace which has insisted that they be drafted and signed. But in the drafting, perhaps, something of the original ideal has been lost. Edwin M. Borchard, professor of international law at Yale and one of America's leading international jurists, analyzed the pact at the Williamstown Institute (his address is reprinted in our International Relations Section this week) and concluded that "It constitutes no renunciation or outlawry of war, but in fact and in law . . . the most solemn sanction of specific wars that has ever been given to the world. . . . No such broad claim of the right to make war has ever before been recognized." No one refuted Mr. Borchard's analysis of the technical legal effect of the treaties and their accompanying notes. Those who disagreed with him asserted, first, that the notes were not to be taken as seriously as the treaty itself—a strange quibble for those of us who would take the pledges of nations seriously; and, second, that whatever the legalistic meaning of the documents their psychological effect was to commit the world against war.

We believe in reading treaties before signing them. Mr. Borchard's analysis deserves the most careful attention. The United States Senate will shortly be faced with a most cruel dilemma. It will be called upon to ratify, or refuse to ratify, a treaty initiated and sponsored by our own Administration about which the hopes of the world for peace have clustered. A Belgian at Williamstown warned his hearers that Europe could not stand the shock of a rejection of the treaties by our Senate; it "would be water dropped on the mill of the Bolshevists." But if disillusioned men cry out again that their statesmen have deceived them, whose will be the fault—those who point out the illusions dangled before the peoples or those who cynically prepared the pretty mirage?

The world has been led to believe that these treaties point the way toward peace. Despite the subtleties of the reservations and interpretations of their phrasing, they can still be made a force for peace. If the statesmen who preached peace at the birth of these pacts carry on with the logical consequence of their own words, and begin a real disarming, the world will be reassured. The test of the pudding is in the eating; if the statesmen believe in their pact the obstacles to disarmament are slight.

Unfortunately, there is more talk of an Anglo-French naval agreement than of disarmament, and there are more men under arms in Western Europe today than in 1913.

Fighting Against Disarmament

DISARMAMENT is still a rosy mist on the far horizon. The peoples may demand action, but the governments tread warily at the mere mention of the dangerous word. Neither Washington nor London nor Paris has the slightest desire for any radical step toward disarmament, and the hullabaloo about the Franco-British agreement is, in fact, a series of maneuvers designed to throw the burden of the failure upon the other fellow. Each government wants to build more ships of certain kinds, and resents efforts to limit such action; and all the governments are willing to welcome open-armed any step toward reducing other navies if only it will not disturb their own.

Yet it seems to us that the American Department of State has a special right to protest against the secret Franco-British understanding. There is no reason to mince words; it was a secret agreement designed to checkmate American plans at the next international conference to limit armaments. The French have consistently refused to limit submarines or to compare their conscript army with the small volunteer armies of the Anglo-Saxon countries; the British have refused to accept limitation of small cruisers carrying six-inch guns and had refused to accept the French position on submarines and on land forces. The two Powers met (secretly) and agreed (secretly) to support each other's positions and to accept limitation only of the large cruisers so dear to Washington's heart. They say that this was intended to facilitate the cause of disarmament, but they can hardly expect to be believed. While the British press has in general accepted the government thesis that a vast armada is necessary to protect Britain's trade routes, not a single British newspaper, so far as we are aware, has defended this compromise with France, or the manner of its negotiation.

The American reply was sharp. The Franco-British "proposal," it should be recalled, had not been communicated to the United States until after a storm of protest in the press on both sides of the Atlantic had produced a counter-storm of contradictory explanations in the British and French parliaments and semi-official press. Washington rejected the proposal outright. It called it "even more unacceptable than the proposals put forward by the British delegation at the [Geneva] conference, not only because it puts the United States at a decided disadvantage but also because it discards altogether the principle of limitation as applied to important combatant types of vessels."

The United States, the note said in a passage which deserves emphasis, would be glad to agree to abolish submarines altogether; but it would not except from limitation small craft carrying as destructive torpedoes as the large craft which would be necessary for defense of our long coast-line. The Franco-British proposal, it said, "would actually tend to defeat the primary objective of any disarmament conference for the reduction or the limitation of armament in that it would not eliminate competition in naval armament and would not effect economy. . . . [It] would inevitably lead to a recrudescence of naval competition disastrous to national economy."

That is a vigorous tone for a peaceful diplomatic communication. It was, we believe, justified by the circumstances. And it would be supremely justified if it should lead to some new step toward a Franco-British-American agreement intended, not as was this discredited proposal, to block disarmament, but to check naval competition and to limit the growing rivalry in various classes of fighting ships. The Washington note reverted to a suggestion made by M. Paul-Boncour of France at the first session of the preparatory conference on disarmament held under the auspices of the League of Nations; possibly steps can be taken along that line.

The most disquieting aspect of this whole series of negotiations is its revelation of the complete absence of any really impulsive drive for peace. The foreign offices, having signed the carefully guarded Kellogg pact and advertised it as a far greater step toward peace than it was, are continuing to plan for war. The Paris correspondent of the New York *Times* cables that "It seems months and, indeed, years since August 27, when the Kellogg pact outlawing war was signed at the Quai d'Orsay. For since then no one has ever heard of the pact except to hear it sneered at. . . . It certainly seems as dead as the dodo."

We now know that while France and England were arranging with the United States the details of the historic scene in the Salle d'Horloge, when all the nations met to outlaw war, they were secretly scheming to outmaneuver Washington and prevent effective limitation of land or sea forces. (Washington's note replied only to the Franco-British naval agreement; but it is now admitted that France and Britain also reached certain conclusions hostile to any attempt to abolish conscription or reduce land forces!) Britain was simultaneously organizing a mock air raid on London to advertise to the Londoners the need of spending more money on military airplanes. France was preparing to refuse to evacuate the Rhineland unless Germany should agree to accept a system of refined blackmail by which she would pay extra for fulfilment of her treaty rights.

It is not a pretty picture. And, despite the sun that shines alike upon the golden beeches of Europe and the flaming maples of America, this is not, in any political sense, a pretty world. The discouraging nationalisms of pre-war days persist, and, while the names of the foreign secretaries sometimes change, the old crew of officials schooled in pre-war and war diplomacy still rule the chancelleries. A genuine spirit of peace is not in them. And the will for peace of the masses will have to become more articulate and intelligently directed before it can be finally effective. If Germany is disarmed, and Russia ready for disarmament, France still adores Poincaré; England thinks that peace means a world wherein Britannia rules the lands as well as the seas; and here in America we seem to be about to elect as President a man who talks in terms of prestige-diplomacy and thinks that a nation must be feared to be respected.

Fiasco as it is, this latest revelation of the shallowness of British-American friendship, of the weakness of the drive for disarmament, is not a backward step. Progress cannot be based upon illusion. The extravagant hopes that clustered about the Kellogg pact have been shattered. Very good. We know better where we are. We understand better the magnitude of the task that still lies before us.

The Real Issues of the Campaign

THEY are forgotten—the real issues of the campaign. They have been thrust aside, pushed into the background by issues created by the personality and the faith of one of the candidates. It is Rum, Romanism, and Tammany Hall (in place of Rebellion) of which we hear. It is an alarming, as well as a highly discouraging, phenomenon. We sympathize entirely with Nicholas Murray Butler's admirable letter to Michael Williams, editor of the *Commonweal,* upon the religious hate and bigotry brought out by this campaign. President Butler said in part:

> Men and women who continue to call themselves Christian, at their head great companies of those who for some inscrutable reason feel they have been divinely appointed to preach the gospel of Christ, are betraying that Lord and Master as truly as did Judas and denying Him as truly as did Peter. Men and women who with calm effrontery continue to call themselves followers of Thomas Jefferson and believers in his political doctrines are daily contradicting by voice, by pen, and by deed the most fundamental of all the principles which that great philosopher taught. . . .
>
> To what a pass has the nation come when millions of those who have passed through the common schools, and many of them also through institutions of higher education, are still the willing weapons of a religious hate and a malice that are as immoral as they are un-Christian and anti-American!

The bringing up of these issues has put into the background the fundamental principles upon which the campaign ought to be fought. There is only one candidate who has been steadily pounding upon the economic questions which the public ought to be discussing, upon the question of the control of the government of this country by organized wealth. He, it is needless to say, is Norman Thomas. One may agree with the Socialist platform or one may not, but the fact is that it alone continues the fight which was also waged in varying degrees and on different platforms by Theodore Roosevelt and Woodrow Wilson in 1912. It matters, of course, profoundly if we are going to slip back into an age of bigotry and religious hate and passion. We thoroughly respect those who find this the paramount consideration in the campaign. But at bottom remains the question which will not be denied: Shall the people rule in America, or shall the corporations and their tools, the bosses? This question is eternal until it is answered aright. If it is thrust into the background now, it merely means a delay in facing it, for faced it must be.

In an artificially stimulated and maintained prosperity we are declining to grapple with fundamental economic conditions. The condition of the woolen and cotton industries, the serious unemployment, are glossed over by Mr. Hoover and his associates, or they are misrepresented, as Secretary Davis has misstated the question of unemployment. The coal industry is, if anything, in greater chaos, and there is no leadership from within or without. In the field of water-power the country faces an issue of stupendous import. Shall the last of our great natural resources be utilized for private profit, or shall they be reserved, developed, and if necessary managed, directed, and operated by governmental authority?

In the railroad field no one knows where he stands—certainly not the railroads. The merger program sponsored by the recent Congressional act has been the subject of endless hearings and debates. It has progressed not one step. The oil industry cries out itself for a dictator who shall limit production, stop the frightful waste, the wild competition, the over-supply in a business which a couple of years ago was reported to be so near extinction as to menace the continuance of the automobile. Everybody admits that the prosperity of the farmers is the very essence of a sound economic life, and yet neither of the leading candidates has advanced a really constructive suggestion.

But leaving these basic economic problems, there are great human issues about which almost nobody speaks—greater economic security for the worker, to be obtained through old-age pensions, insurance against sickness, accident, and unemployment; and in still other ways. Year after year has passed since Secretary Hoover called his Conference on Unemployment in 1921, but we are wholly without provision to meet another emergency. Our lawmakers can draft laws to make Wall Street safe for the most gigantic speculation in modern times, but no one can draw a bill to provide machinery to function when millions are out of employment. No one is planning, outside of the Socialist Party, for greater industrial democracy and greater economic justice. It is only now, nearly at the end of the Presidential campaign, that the leading candidates have begun to discuss at length the protective tariff—that great source of corruption, that great machinery for the creation of economic injustice, that great creator of privilege.

Then there are the vast issues of war and peace, with all their ramifications. The invasion of foreign countries by American troops, our relationship to the other nations of the earth, the foreign debt to us—can anyone say with a straight face that these vital questions, which may mean life or death to hundreds of thousands of American boys, have been adequately discussed in this campaign? Certainly not by the two major parties. Governor Smith has kept almost as far from the Caribbean as from the Negro problem in the South, and neither he nor Mr. Hoover has had one word to say about the disenfranchisement of millions of our fellow-citizens. Mr. Hoover is concerned with our outward safety. Like the Czar of Russia and Kaiser Wilhelm he has put his faith in military and naval defense, and then has subscribed to the crassest possible policy of isolation and of national selfishness.

A thousand wrongs in American life cry out to high heaven for redress, but we are told to consider how rich and how happy we are, and how we can add to that happiness and prosperity at the expense of other peoples. And even this prospect is overshadowed by the steam and smoke engendered by the fires of religious hate, bigotry, and prejudice. Those are right who declare that the battle for personal liberty, for freedom of conscience and thought, must be fought anew in every generation. It will be fought out, and so will the struggle as to whether the United States is to be the property of a favored few or of the great masses of the American people whose labor and whose toil create the wealth that we have.

RUSSIA
from a Car Window

by

OSWALD GARRISON VILLARD

Reprinted from
THE NATION

I.
The Observer's Problem

I. Moscow

MOSCOW at last! The first impressions are utterly disappointing. The city is shabby, down at the heel, badly paved, it vividly suggests Berlin immediately after the war when every stucco building was faded, dirty, peeling, cracking. Gradually, however, the visitor begins to feel the charm of which foreign residents speak. When he returns to it the third time he finds himself moved and impressed. The Oriental in its architecture stirs him; the Kremlin's skyline appears as one of the most impressive and beautiful sights in the world; the Red Square, with that amazing Cathedral of Saint Basil, has a power and an originality not to be denied. Everywhere churches and separate buildings begin to stand out. Then one realizes that the worst pavements are a heritage from the Czar, that this is a capital in the remaking—that there have been far more important things to do than to lay pavements. For everywhere buildings are coming down and new ones going up; on the outskirts arise those great apartment houses for workmen which make it clear that, whatever else may be said of the Moscow of the Bolsheviks, it will never be stained with the infamy of those old-law tenements in New York, with their 250,000 windowless rooms which no authority has yet been able to wrench from the grasp of the private-profit-making landlords.

It would take the canvas and the genius of a Tolstoy or a Dostoevski adequately to portray all of this wonderful activity. It has, I repeat, in many of its aspects nothing to do with communism. As it is, the number of new plants and new industrial enterprises is overwhelming. At Leningrad the Soviets are far along toward the completion of the greatest lumber port on earth—four ports in one—with all the work of handling done, a minimum by human labor and a maximum by electricity. It already exports 1,000,000 tons of lumber annually. The Dnieper power plant is to be the largest in the world. They are building a merchant fleet of six hundred steamers. The railroads are being modernized with amazing success and greatly developed; they are operating 50,000 cars daily as against 20,000 three years ago. Everywhere we went there was feverish activity; everywhere the claim that where industry had not far surpassed pre-war activity it was close to it. It is impossible for a layman to understand how so much could have been done in so short a time; how such a vast machine, whatever its defects, could be built so rapidly and work so well; and how the stupendous sums necessary for it are obtained. It is a gallant, far-sighted, magnificent effort to rebuild an ancient commonwealth and to bring relief and happiness and well-being to one hundred and fifty million souls.

III. The Spirit of the Government

I. The Great Fear

"WHAT of the Government of the Soviets? Is it sincere? Has it abandoned its anti-foreign propaganda? What is its attitude toward the payment of its debts? Is it planning to conquer the world?" These are but a few of the many questions hurled at the visitor to Russia. They cannot easily be answered. I am prepared to say, however, that I believe that the Soviets genuinely desire to be a peaceful government; that they are planning their armaments for defense and not for offense, and that the strongest wish the government has is to be let alone. Like many other Russians, the Commissar for War, Mr. Voroshiloff, has in various speeches declared that Russia will soon have to be fighting for its life against the capitalist nations, and has been talking the same militaristic buncombe voiced by every war minister and militarist the world over. Much of this sort of thing is done deliberately in Russia in order to keep the government before the people in its role of defender of their rights and of the ark of the Communist covenant. But there can be no doubt that there is genuine fear of another attack upon the Soviets by the capitalist nations. Can anyone blame them?

Put yourself in their place. Supposing certain foreign countries claiming superior virtue and greater social, economic, and political vision had planted armies on American soil, encouraged civil war, supplied arms and ammunition to one side, and killed and wounded many thousands of Americans. Would any American be blamed eight years later for believing that those same nations might repeat the same wicked acts, especially if they admitted no change of heart or regret? As this is written the dead bodies of the pathetic American soldiers who were killed in the Archangel district are being returned to the United States. They had no personal quarrel with the Soviets or their subjects; they were the pawns of Woodrow Wilson in his illegal and unconstitutional war on Russia. Most Americans have completely forgotten that we sent two armies into Russia, without a declaration of war, to fight and kill. The Russians have not. In a workers' club in Nizhni Novgorod, where some of us made a totally unexpected visit one evening, we found a teacher showing an illuminated map of Russia to a group of boys and girls. For our special benefit he turned on the lights which showed where the American troops invaded Archangel and Siberia. The Russians are surely sincere in saying that they wish no more such outrageous and murderous attacks, as those which occurred in Arch Angel.

This is not a defense of the Soviets' policy of keeping their people in a state of alarum. To me it seems as if they ought to muzzle their war minister. Such speeches are as hateful to me in Russia as when they come at home from talking generals of our own army, or from officials of the National Security League and the American Defense Society. Mr. Voroshiloff simply plays into the hands of the cynical and hypocritical statesmen at Geneva who, while pretending to wish to disarm, refused to discuss the Russian proposal for complete and genuine disarmament offered by Litvinov—the only decent proposal forthcoming from anybody. Such speeches as M. Voroshiloff's may achieve the desired results at home; they cost too dearly abroad.

Far wiser and finer was the attitude of the Soviet Government after the seizure of the Chinese Eastern Railway by the Chinese last July. Their refusal to go to war was, of course, sneered at. They were pacific, the foreign press declared, because they could not afford to be anything else; their Communist system, their great work for industrialization, would collapse if they went to war. Undoubtedly there was much truth in this. Yet I am convinced that other motives also controlled. The Russian army, under a descendant of Field Marshal Blücher, could have taken Harbin easily and readily defeated any army the Chinese could have thrown against it; foreign experts declare that the Red Army is a good one. By such action the Russians could have added considerable stretches to the communized territory of the world, have achieved a great deal of prestige and possibly some indemnities, and thrown all Chinese out of a large part of the Chinese Eastern Railway. It had excuses enough according to pre-World War standards. Had its honor not been impugned? Had its citizens not been thrown into Chinese jails by the hundreds?

II. A Bolshevik Statesman

At the height of this crisis I was one of the American journalists who interviewed Commissar J. E. Rudzutak, the Soviet Minister of Transportation, one of the three foremost personalities in the government, who is also first vice-chairman of the Council of People's Commissars. This impressive man, who looks like an efficient German schoolmaster, answered freely and fully every question put to him. There would be no war with China. There could be no thought of that. Yes, the seizure of the railroad would cost the Soviet heavily—25,000,000 rubles a year. But to go to war for *that*? How many millions would it cost a day to fight a war with China? Not once did any of the familiar shibboleths come from his lips, no buncombe about national honor, no resort to Theodore Roosevelt's pet phrase that there are worse things than war, no assertion that the glory of the Russian people would be upheld in blood, not one word to inflame the populace or to arouse further the wrongdoers in China. Instead came a quiet, firm insistence that whatever other nations might have had in mind, when Russia signed its name to the Kellogg Pact it meant what it said. It would not go to war. All this without "side," without passion, without the manners of the self-conscious Western statesman bent on impressing his audience. Others in this group of American journalists besides myself wrote this down as a genuinely thrilling interview; we had seen and reported too many statesmen of the other kind not to be moved by the contrast. Incidentally, M. Henri Barbusse, the distinguished Frenchman, has just published a collection of seventy documents of the Russian Government issued between 1917 and 1929 bearing upon peace and disarmament. I think he is correct when he writes that "despite the innumerable international obstacles put in the way of the Soviet Union by its imperialist foes and opponents, it has never relinquished its aspirations toward peace, never lost an opportunity of demonstrating them, and never refused to take the initiative in advancing the affairs of peace."*

We took up in this same interview with M. Rudzutak the question of Russia's relation to the United States and asked why he was not satisfied with the existing trade relations.

* I do believe that the facts stated here are essentially altered by the subsequent happenings.—O.G.V.

Normality, he replied, is not to be established by accidental contacts. He explained that any large amount of business with the United States would require long-term credits which involve complicated legal questions. The operation would be a matter of years and this fact alone called in turn for diplomatic relations. Russia, he said, was ready to discuss the question of the payment to the United States of the many millions advanced to Kerensky's government by the United States, but when it came to the repayment of the Czarist debts his answer was emphatically no. His people, he said, did not feel that it was a proper debt since it was used in part for the support of the police, the gendarmes, and the troops which held the Russian people in subjection. He added that he spoke with some feeling in this matter because he himself had been sent to prison for ten years and he was sure that some of that money helped to keep him in jail. The war, he went on, started without consent of the peoples, cost 10,000,000 lives and untold suffering, and the money that made it possible should not be repaid. It was not a question of the amount, he stated, but of principle. When I asked him if in any settlement of the American claims the Soviets would submit bills for the damage done by the American troops in Russia, he replied "most assuredly"—which means that Uncle Sam will have to pay a very large bill, indeed.

As for the much-mooted subject of propaganda against the governments of foreign nations, he declared that no government with which the Soviets now have relations has been able to prove any hostile propaganda whatsoever. The Soviets, he went on, even limit their diplomatic representatives in their personal freedom in political matters, and had just recalled a minor official in the Turkish Embassy for his activity in connection with the Turkish Communist Party.

He insisted that the Soviets would use, and are using, no influence to change any governments anywhere, but he added: "In this respect we can complain of some foreign governments which urge us to change our form of government." He suggested that there were organizations in America that were very much interested in propaganda to overthrow the present government of Russia.

He declared that his government was ready to send a mission to the United States to discuss all outstanding issues. It has repeatedly offered to do this, but there has been no satisfactory reply from the United States. M. Rudzutak then stated his belief that there was organized propaganda at work in other countries to prevent the United States and Russia from coming together. As for the Third International, he declared that the Soviets are no more responsible for it than the United States for the K.K.K., or Italy for the activities of the Catholic church.

III. The Compelling Motives

Obviously what the present controllers of the government are striving for is to make Russia self-contained and self-sufficient. To an outsider it would seem as if, from their point of view, it would be wiser and safer for them not to have close business relations with the greatest capitalist nations, that it would be better for them to lift themselves by their bootstraps, rather than to enter into those elaborate financial arrangements which so easily lead to quarrels, misunderstandings, and then diplomatic entanglements. The answer has already been given in the first of these articles: The Soviet leaders have a slender margin of time. Hence their ardent desire to bury the hatchet even at the risk of another such sudden and damaging rupture of relations as took place with England. Hence their willingness to enter into close diplomatic relations with the United States and England, the two nations most suspicious of them and hostile to them.

These motives will, I believe, induce the Soviets to desist from foreign propaganda if once they get relations established with the United States. They have left far behind them the days when they believed a world revolution at hand. They ought to have learned from their experience in England and Germany the utter folly of the attempt to propagandize abroad. They did do a lot of damage in Germany for a time. Then they had to stop their activities. In England they admittedly spent millions some years ago, but when the ballots were counted in the election of May, 1929, out of a total of about twenty-two millions less than 50,000 were cast for Communists—I have seen the figure put as low as 39,000. Obviously, the Soviets wasted every ruble they spent in Great Britain. Stalin, Rudzutak, and their associate directors of the Russian state ought to be wise enough now to see that the only sound propaganda is to make a complete success of their government and of their economic system, and to prove that it is a better way of life for mankind. If they do that there will certainly be no need whatsoever to agitate abroad, especially if by that time they should be willing to share their power with larger groups, abandon their bloody repression, and move in the direction of complete freedom.

Meanwhile Russia arms. There is no doubt that it is carrying its military training of youth into the schools and the clubs where children congregate. The Russians are doing precisely what the American General Staff would like to do, inculcating nationalistic and militaristic ideas in every child no matter what the age. Our supporters of universal service would also like to pump into every child under our flag the doctrine that the proudest distinction open to it is service in the army, and that the severest sentence which can be passed upon a criminal is to deprive him of his right to serve with the colors. If we gave our militarists free rein there would be no difference whatsoever in their policies and the extent of their propaganda and those of the Bolsheviks. Both desire to adopt precisely the pre-World War tactics and philosophy of the Germans. Arguing with some teachers in Nizhni Novgorod about their instructing boys and girls in the use of the rifle, we encountered a passionate defense of it on the familiar ground that all the capitalist nations were certain to attack Russia. When I pointed out that their language was identical with that of the militarists in all capitalist nations, our new-found Russian friends appeared as hurt as they were puzzled. "But we are *right*," they replied; "we are never going to attack. We are going to be the ones attacked." No amount of arguing could make them see that a persistence in this attitude of theirs is bound to lead to repercussions abroad and to deliver other peoples more and more into the arms of their militarists; that such a policy is certain to produce a conflict.

IV. The People Not Militaristic

Other Americans who were in Russia when our delegation was there reported that they ran across many who declared that the Soviets would not fight China, but said: "Wait until 1932 and then let the Chinese attack us." I encountered nothing of this. I cannot feel that the people are anything like as badly humbugged by their militarists as were the Germans in January, 1914. The Russians are still too near the horrible mass-murders of the World War and of their civil war. Nor do I see anything sinister in the fact that in their industrialization program the greatest at-

tention is being given to their heavy industries. This would have to be the case if the country were absolutely pacific and without a single soldier. For what the Russians need most today is steel and iron for new buildings and innumerable rails, railroad cars, automobiles, trucks, tractors, plows, harvesters, and all the implements of modern agriculture and transportation. While we were not taken to any of the factories in which guns and munitions are made, we found that the impression is widespread that although hundreds of thousands of men and women are being given some military training, there are no very large stores of military equipment on hand and that much of the artillery is antiquated. We heard very little of the development of the chemical industry; yet this, in the eyes of many, perhaps most, soldiers, is the vital arm in the war of the future. That industry may, of course, be important in Russia and quite concealed. But it seems as if the Soviet leaders must recognize that all the attention they devote to purely military affairs retards by so much the fulfilment of their five-year program and thereby threatens their success in their race against time.

What a wonderful lesson for the world it would be if these leaders were but willing to lay aside their arms, confident that the workers of the world would never permit their governments to attack the Soviets if they remained unarmed and obviously friendly to all and without military ambitions! Unfortunately, even idealists like these, when in office, turn to the familiar technique of repression at home and to the sword for defense abroad. The pacifist Wilson of 1914 became in two short years the militarist Wilson demanding, as at St. Louis, "incomparably the greatest navy in the world." The liberal democrat Wilson became in three years the complete autocrat, imprisoning as many as possible of those who, like Debs, dared to oppose his course, and determined to brush aside all who dissented from his demand for "force without stint." The spirit of the Bolsheviks who dominate Russia is much the same.

It is, of course, a bitter disappointment that Communists whose desire it is to exalt the masses and to free them from the tyrannies and unfairnesses of capitalist society should adopt the same methods as those whom they reprobate. But surely there is no need for those of us who are onlookers to be pharisaical and hypocritical about it. It is no worse for a Stalin to do these things and teach reliance upon gas bombs, airplanes, and heavy artillery than for a Mussolini, or a Churchill, or a Hoover, or a de Rivera. They are all parts of a mad world and preachers of a mad philosophy which during four insane years brought humanity to the very edge of the abyss.

V. Cultural Freedom at Home

It is pleasanter to turn from Russia's attitude toward foreign countries to certain phases of its domestic policies. It has, for example, granted full cultural freedom to the Ukraine, to Georgia, to the Tartar Republic, to the German Volga Republic, and to other separate government units, and has just now set up a new republic quite near the Afghan border, in response to popular demand. However much one may regret the increase in the number of languages when the whole world ought to be moving toward a single medium of communication, the Soviets have shown great wisdom in reversing the policy of the Czars and granting linguistic freedom to all groups which desire it. For example, the Czars long sought to suppress the Ukrainian language—until 1905 there was no Ukrainian press; the Soviets have made it the first language in the Ukraine just as they have permitted the Germans of the Volga Republic

to speak their mother tongue while the Tartars and all the rest of the varying groups rejoice in similar freedom. In the schools of all these linguistically different republics Russian must also be taught—every Russian child must learn two languages; indeed, the pure Russians are now to learn English in their schools, German having just been ousted from the second position—an extremely important decision.

The effect of this policy in the Ukraine has been extraordinary—for one thing an amazingly rapid creation of a Ukrainian daily press and literature. At Kharkov we of the American-Russian Chamber of Commerce delegation were shown a large collection of standard works of all the world—even "Uncle Tom's Cabin" and an anthology of recent American poetry—all brought out since the conferring of linguistic autonomy. In the first nine months of the fiscal year 1928-1929 there were printed 12,200,000 copies of books in Ukrainian, and 7,200,000 periodicals and pamphlets were sold or distributed, for the sum of 15,000,000 rubles—this in a country which is still 20 per cent illiterate but hopes to wipe out all illiteracy by 1932. There are today 232 Ukrainian dailies and the several racial minorities within the Ukraine, such as Germans, Poles, Moldavians, Greeks, and Bulgarians, have their own press.

To turn to Georgia, where the Soviet regime was established with great harshness and the driving or blotting out of a whole section of the population, the present head of the Soviets in Tiflis listed for us the following benefits which Bolshevik rule has conferred upon the Republic:

1. It has abolished feudal land ownership and established peasant ownership.

2. Peasants and workers have been relieved from all payments to feudal landlords, pay no rents, and but small taxes.

3. Church and state have been separated.
4. Universal education has been affirmed in principle.
5. An oppressed colony of the Czar has become a free state.
6. In place of autocratic Russians appointed by the Czar, native Georgians conduct the government.
7. All local government officials are elected by the people instead of being chosen in Moscow.
8. Free development of native Georgian culture, art, and language has taken the place of compulsory Russification.
9. Friendly interracial cooperation has been encouraged between Armenians, Georgians, and Azerbaijans instead of their being played off one against the other.

"Georgia," he said, "is far better off under the Soviets." There can be little doubt that this is true.

If this generous treatment of national minorities now in control of some Soviet states is the height of wisdom, it is in marked contrast with the attitude of Moscow toward those beyond the Russian borders whose philosophies are so different from their own. Somehow or other I believe that if Lenin had lived the spirit of the government would be different. It would not fear so much, or inculcate fear of other nations so widely for its own ends. The Soviets should at least realize that fear responds to fear, hate to hate, and hostility to hostility. Naturally, the Soviet leaders say that as soon as they are secure and communism safely established they will cease to take life to safeguard them against the failure of their sacred experiment and will bestow greater freedom upon their people. One wonders. Dr. Arthur Feiler, a distinguished editor of the *Frankfurter Zeitung*, recently asked a high Russian official how soon he thought the time would come when he and his associates would turn back authority to the people. The frank reply was: "Never." One need

not take this too seriously, but it is true that this is the inevitable tendency of men in autocratic control of nations.

VI. Recognition by The United States

As for our own relations with Russia, I am more than ever convinced that we should recognize the Soviets at once and resume diplomatic relations with them, and I should attach no terms beyond an agreement for a conference to settle the question of war debts and the bill to be presented by Russia for our inexcusable military attacks upon the Russian people. In Moscow, among the men I met privately without any official Russian's knowledge, was one who had many reasons to be bitter against the Soviets. He had a long list of friends who had been exiled or imprisoned; he may himself be in Siberia by now. But he begged me to continue to urge the recognition of Russia by the United States. "Nothing," he said, "could do more to help us than that. The sooner international relations are normal, the sooner will the force of the world's public opinion be felt here, the sooner will the Soviets reach the point where they will desist from repression and give up the punishment of those who differ from them." The man who said this had lived years in America; for all the wrongs he sees about him, he is convinced that the Communist experiment is priceless and that it should not be allowed to go down because of the blunders of the leaders. Colonel Hugh L. Cooper, the great American engineer I have already cited, declared to us: "If it were in my power I'd give those fellows (the Soviet leaders) every opportunity to try out communism to the nth degree. I'd do anything to help keep them in power until they work out the changes now necessary in Russian life." This is wisdom and common sense.

Can War Make Peace?

A READER sends us one of M. E. Tracy's recent editorials in the Scripps-Howard newspapers and asks us for our comment. The article, which was written before Bolivia and Paraguay agreed to submit their differences to a commission set up by the Pan-American arbitration conference contains this statement:

> What the Pan-American conference should do is issue orders instead of making appeals. It should warn both Bolivia and Paraguay that their dispute over the Gran Chaco is properly subject to arbitration, that the two governments have solemnly sworn to let it be settled that way [Mr. Tracy refers to the Gondra arbitration agreement], that war represents a breach of faith, that the Western World will not stand for it, and that if either or both governments persist measures will be taken to compel respect not only for their treaty obligations but for the duty they owe to keep the peace.
>
> There are plenty of means by which the Pan-American conference could enforce its will. It could arrange for a general embargo on exports and imports affecting both countries. It could do the same with reference to foreign loans, trade, and financial transactions. It could take the Gran Chaco away from both Bolivia and Paraguay and put it under a mandate form of government.

Our correspondent says that the argument seems sound to him. "Yet I feel, from several years reading of *The Nation,* that you disagree, and I should like to know why." Our correspondent has not read our columns in vain. We do disagree, and we are glad in a brief way to indicate why. It is well to point out at the outset that the Pan-American arbitration conference has no authority to commit the governments behind it to the drastic action which Mr. Tracy proposes. But supposing that they all agreed to support such action, we believe it would be almost the worst thing that could happen to the cause of peace in the Western Hemisphere. Mr. Tracy, it is true, does not say directly that he would make war upon Bolivia and Paraguay in order to compel them not to make war upon each other, but his proposal to put the disputed territory under a mandate government implies that, while to enforce an economic embargo might mean armed conflict with the leading commercial nations of Europe. Indeed Mr. Tracy goes on to envisage a sea of gore and rather to exult in the vision:

> Before we get through with the job we are not only going to write a code but back it up in the same old fashioned way that all codes have been written and backed up.
>
> We are not going to reduce war without battle any more than we have reduced murder without killing.
>
> For the first few centuries, at least, any practical war prevention program may involve as much strife and bloodshed as would have occurred without it. The difference is that we would be struggling for an object that all humanity could visualize as worth while, instead of wasting life and property in futile attempts to grow great at each other's expense.

This is a frank restatement of the doctrine of war to end war—that chimera which dogs the peace movement at every turn. It is the doctrine which led to four years of unparalleled destruction and anguish in Europe only a decade ago, especially to our participation in it. Can anybody at this time point out one way in which the cause of peace or civilization was served by that carnage? The swashbuckling of the Kaiser was ended only to be superseded by that of Mussolini. And though few of our people recognize it, the hard fact is that the Europe of today fears the imperialism of the United States as much as the Europe of 1914 feared the imperialism of Germany. *The Nation* has a profound distrust of force as an instrument with which to make peace. We are aware that nations use—probably will long have to use—a certain amount of force within their borders to uphold their laws, but we do not believe that this requires the taking of human life except in rare instances. We do not believe with Mr. Tracy that capital punishment prevents murder; on the contrary, the whole history of crime suggests that the severest punishments have failed as deterrents and have lessened the respect for human life in the community. Mr. Tracy's conception of a holy war "that all humanity could visualize as worth while" is sheer sentimentality. That is what every nation has always drummed itself into believing in regard to any sordid adventure it has engaged in.

Some day, perhaps, we shall have a world government. Even sooner, probably, we shall have a unified government for the Western Hemisphere. But in the present stage of human development *The Nation* is fearful of any union of nations which relies upon a common army to enforce its wishes either within or without its limits. That is one of our chief fears in connection with the League of Nations. Theoretically, a world government with an army to carry out its orders would be splendid. Practically, with politics and government what they are today, such an arrangement would almost certainly lead to the smothering of minority action or progress. Had the League of Nations had the power ten years ago, for instance, it would almost certainly have crushed the experiment in Russia.

Our world is still one in which force plays a large part. No one now alive will ever see it otherwise, but the use of force is nevertheless diminishing both in extent and degree. The hope of civilization lies in accentuating that movement. Such things as police power, punishment for crime, the right of revolution, and civil war raise knotty questions for every believer in peace. It is very hard to work out a complete and logical philosophy to cover all these questions, but it is not difficult to reject a piece of such unnecessary and obvious meddling as that suggested by Mr. Tracy. Intervention in the affairs of a nation is always to be deplored, but if inevitable international action is to be preferred to interference by a single government. In its Latin-American policy the United States has unfortunately ignored this truth so far. But international action is certainly never justified unless international interests are vitally and continuously affected, which nobody would maintain in regard to the practically unknown region of the Gran Chaco.

Finally, events themselves have showed the needlessness of Mr. Tracy's war-making proposals, for since he set them forth a little patience and tact have led both Bolivia and Paraguay to accept peaceful arbitration.

January 24, 1929

Dear Mr. Nevins:

I am deeply gratified by your letter of January 23rd. I am very so ry indeed if I have misunderstood your attitude. Of course I was not aware that you wrote those editorials in the World; I had supposed they came from Lippmann's hand. I still feel, however, that I merited mention in the list of editorial writers because after all I gave an enormous amount of time and energy to the editorial page and several times acted as editor-in-chief over long periods of months.

No, I regret nothing I have ever written about Woodrow Wilson or the League of Nations. On the contrary I am sharpening my pen for a biography of Wilson and - confidentially to you - I should like to call it "The World's Greatest Criminal." That really represents my feeling about him. As for the League, I am happy to record its progress and give it full credit for every good thing it does. But I cannot close my eyes to its very great defects and the fact that it is still deeply involved in that body of death, the Treaty of Versailles.

I am very sorry if you or anybody else in the World has thought our treatment of it unkindly. We all value it beyond anything in journalism in New York and our anxiety about its future represents merely the warmth of our attachment to We cannot see it losing advertising and standing still in circulation and constantly jettisoning the principles of Joseph

Pulitzer without a protest, especially when the Post-Dispatch stands up so straight and is such a splendid newspaper. By the way, if you wish to hear about what's wrong with the World, talk some time with some of the Post-Dispatch people as to what they think of the World's treatment of big news stories. The World can be saved if it will only begin to print the news. You cannot, however, expect me, a dyed-in-the-wool free trader, to do else than weep when I see the World following Al Smith in his tariff absurdities. Cobb would never have fallen for that sort of thing.

With renewed and most hearty thanks for the friendly tone of your letter, and the assurance of my readiness to consider the incident closed and the matter forgotten, I am,

Sincerely yours,

Mr. Allan Nevins,
Department of History,
Columbia University,
New York.

OGV

RG

P.S. Please do not soften what you say about the Nation in your revised edition; leave it just as you had it. And as for my connection with the Post, merely add my name to the list of editorial writers, and I shall be quite content

Teeth for the Kellogg Treaty

OUR feeling that Congress does not take the Kellogg Treaty seriously is reinforced by its attitude toward the proposals of Senator Capper and Representative Porter to give the agreement teeth through use of the embargo. Certainly both of these resolutions contain dynamite. While designed to accomplish excellent objects, their application might entail consequences which should be thoroughly explored and considered before any action is taken. Senator Capper recognized this by announcing that he did not expect to ask for action in regard to his resolution either at the present or at the extra session of Congress; his idea was to obtain public discussion of the plan between now and the regular session of the next Congress. His proposal, as also that of Representative Porter, deserves the careful and serious attention of all Americans.

For this reason it is dispiriting to see most of the members of Congress, and other public officials, running away from the Capper and Porter proposals as fast as their legs will carry them. The Capper proposal, when first published, received a great deal of attention in the press, including much favorable comment. But hardly a dozen men in Congress have cared to talk about it publicly and most of them have made brief and guarded comments which contributed nothing to the discussion. The general desire seems to be to envelop the proposal in obliterating silence as soon as possible. Similar treatment has been accorded to the Porter resolution, which was made public only a day after Senator Capper's suggestion. Mr. Porter announced that his resolution had the support of Secretary Kellogg and that the latter would come before the Committee on Foreign Relations to say so, but when the head of the State Department appeared his approval was vague and indefinite, and his entire conversation showed that he did not understand and was not interested in the subject.

The gist of the Capper plan was printed in our last issue. It would empower the President to forbid the exportation of "arms, munitions, implements of war, or other articles for use in war" to any country which the Chief Executive judged had violated the Kellogg Treaty. The Porter resolution would extend an existing law, passed in 1912, by which the President may place an embargo upon the exportation of war munitions to an *American* country, or to one where we exercise extraterritorial rights, in case of conflict. Mr. Porter would make this apply to *any* country in which the President determines that "conditions of domestic violence or of international conflict exist or are threatened." In other words, the President could throw his might not only against a nation which went to war in the face of a promise to arbitrate, but he would have similar power in case of domestic revolution, or merely in event of a threat of one or the other of those situations.

As we said last week, the Capper resolution is a logical extension of the Kellogg Treaty; it is designed to put teeth in it by means of economic pressure. Those who take the Kellogg Treaty seriously ought to favor peaceable means for giving it authority, although, as we pointed out last week, the power to declare a nation to be a violator of the Kellogg Treaty should not logically be vested in our President alone. A violation of the treaty is an offense against all its signers and is a question to be established by a common decision rather than the individual determination of any one nation. Other commentators on the subject have stressed this point, as well as the difficulty of deciding if a nation has violated its treaty obligations. "How shall we know," asks the New York *Evening Post,* "which is the nation that 'violates' the Kellogg peace pact? And what shall we do if that formally labeled 'violator' appears to us to be fighting a righteous war and one that supports our own national interests?" The Detroit *Free Press* sees a still further objection: "The sanctionless nature of the treaty was what commended it to a large element in this country that has steadfastly refused to enter the Covenant of the League of Nations. . . . A punitive armament embargo would hamstring the anti-war pact by alienating the sympathy that it attracts because of its purely moral obligation."

Except for the objection to giving to our President alone the power to determine that some other nation is a violator of the Kellogg Pact, the Capper resolution seems to us to be safer and more logical than the proposal of Representative Porter. The Capper resolution confines action to actual war and to the signers of the Kellogg Treaty. The Porter plan would give our President a roving commission as a knight-errant of peace which, beautiful in theory, might in practice result in some vicious meddling. There would be scant prospect that the President would take action against the larger nations, but he might easily be induced to intervene in the quarrels of smaller ones and would naturally be under pressure to use his power against "radical" governments. The latter danger would be still greater in the case of revolutionary movements within any one country. We have already seen this in Latin America, as witness recent history in Nicaragua. In reciting the history of the present embargo law—applying to American countries, or those where we exercise extraterritorial rights—Mr. Porter said that it had been invoked three times, in each instance against Mexico. But Mr. Porter forgot the exceedingly instructive story of the embargo as used recently by President Coolidge in Nicaragua. At the time when the Liberal forces, in support of the constitutional claims of Sacasa to the Presidency, began their campaign against the self-elected President, Diaz, there was an embargo against shipment of arms from the United States to Nicaragua. It had been laid, perhaps properly, to prevent sporadic revolutionary activity. The embargo should either have been continued as it stood, or lifted entirely. But Diaz was our puppet, and early in 1927 we clamped down the embargo tighter than ever against the Liberals but lifted it for Diaz. A little later our Government itself sold him arms. This was not calculated to bring peace but solely to serve what Washington regarded as our national interests. In fact our policy kept the Diaz Government alive at a moment when otherwise it would have been quickly deposed and brought about a long and bloody period of civil strife, not even yet ended.

War Lies

ONCE more the war atrocity. A dispatch from London reports that Sir Berkeley Moynihan, an army surgeon, has said in a recent speech: "We heard in 1916 that the Germans were going to use the plague as a weapon and we actually recovered plague bacilli from bombs dropped over the Fifth Army. The plague is spread by a parasite of the fleas on rats. So we encouraged cats, owls were protected, and gamekeepers were encouraged to keep down rats and so prevent the spread of the plague." In other words, the rats ate the bacilli from the fragments of the bombs dropped over the Fifth Army; the owls and cats that lived in the trenches—and were always spared by the German shells and machine gun-fire—ate the rats and were carefully petted and encouraged by the gamekeepers, who, as everybody is aware, were attached to every battalion to keep it supplied with nice, fresh, hot, and tasty game just before it went over the top!

What could be more ridiculous than this revival of the atrocity charge? Every intelligent person knows that if in 1916 there had been the slightest evidence that the Germans were using a plague bacillus it would not have remained Sir Berkeley Moynihan's private property for one day, much less thirteen years. For in 1916 the Allies were putting forth every possible atrocity story to win neutral sympathy and American support. We were fed every day with the stories of the Belgian children whose hands were cut off, the Canadian soldier who was crucified to a barn door, the nurse whose breasts were cut off, the German habit of distilling glycerine and fat from their dead in order to obtain lubricants; and all the rest. Had any story so good as that of plague bacilli been available, it would have been spread all over the world by the most efficient factory of lies developed during the war in any country—each and every nation had one, including our own—which happened to be the English.

We should not be dignifying this yarn of Sir Berkeley were it not that it appears just after the publication of a notable book by Arthur Ponsonby, M.P., entitled "Falsehood in War."* It is a brief work, but its pages contain devastating proof not only of the fact that "when war is declared truth is the first casualty," but that it is the first casualty by reason of deliberate intention, often on the part of those high in authority. In every case Mr. Ponsonby does not ask the public to take his word for it, but gives official proof, or evidence of a kind that cannot be questioned. Thus we have this statement by Colonel Repington in his "Diary of the World War," vol. II, p. 447:

> I was told by Cardinal Gasquet that the Pope promised to make a great protest to the world if a single case could be proved of the violation of Belgian nuns, or cutting off of children's hands. An inquiry was instituted and many cases examined with the help of the Belgian Cardinal Mercier. Not one case could be proved.

Similar evidence is given by the former French Minister of Finance, M. Klotz, who was censor for the French press at the outbreak of the war. That, however, has not kept a Liverpool poet from publishing recently a patriotic poem in which occurs the following verse:

> They stemmed the first mad onrush
> Of the cultured German Hun,
> Who'd outraged every female Belgian
> And maimed every mother's son.

Again, everybody heard of the Louvain altar-piece wantonly thrown into the flames of the burning library by a German officer. At the Peace Conference compensation was demanded for this, yet the altar-piece was actually rescued by a German officer and is in the possession of the City of Louvain today. Similarly there was no crucified Canadian, and the British officer who invented the pitiful story of the cruelly treated baby of Courbeck Loo has confessed that he invented the baby and then killed it when he received five thousand offers to adopt it. But Mr. Ponsonby does not stop with telling the story of fake atrocities and faked photographs. He deals with the doctoring of official papers, especially with the lies told in all countries to create news. He gives moreover the facts as to the deliberate falsification by Sir Edward Grey in the House of Commons in 1911, when he deceived not only his country but most of the members of the Cabinet of which he was a member by his assertion that England had no binding agreement with France in regard to Belgium. Never was a statesman so clearly convicted of mendacity. Yet as late as 1921 he was reiterating his statement, perhaps in order to make himself believe it. Mr. Ponsonby has done an admirable piece of work, which ought to be read thoughtfully by every intelligent person. For when the next war breaks out statesmen will lie again; again deliberately set out to deceive and to cheat the people in order to make them hate and fight.

* E. P. Dutton and Company. $2.

April 17, 1929

Dear Mr. Baker:

I now have your letter of March 25th. I am sure you are right that Wilson's statement to me beginning, "I am a Democrat" was written while he was still President, and it was part of my campaign to bring it to the notice of the public in the Evening Post. It must have been in '10 or '11. Do you think it is of sufficient importance to send someone to search the files of the Evening Post for those years? I can only guess that it was written in the spring.

Replying to your inquiry, I am still a Wilson Democrat on all domestic issues. I have since realized, however, that my use of that phrase has led to some misunderstanding of my position and so I am glad of the opportunity to amplify it to you. I hold Mr. Wilson responsible for the present reactionary situation and for the way in which special privilege is intrenched in this country as never before. Speaking before the recent Institute of Statesmanship at Rollins College, Florida, I challenged the audience to deny that we are in a worse plight than we were when the Lusitania disaster made it impossible for Mr. Wilson to go on with his domestic program. I hold him entirely responsible for the existing situation because of the criminal blunder he made in putting us into an European war out of which we have won nothing, save the ill-will of most of the world. Never were lives more uselessly sacrificed than those that we wasted in France. It would have been better if they had been murdered in cold blood on Broadway.

You know, of course, that democracy was not made safe for the world by our intervention in the war, and it has never been less safe than today, since the democratic movement got under way in England. And as for the war to end war, when was there ever a greater humbug perpetrated on a great people? It may interest you to know that the Board of Aldermen of the city of Montreal congratulated Queen Victoria at the outbreak of the Crimean War on her noble policy in entering the "war to end war", and to drive the Slavic Hun out of Europe!

I am intending, as soon as I retire as editor of the Nation in 1933, to devote myself to a book on Wilson which will give to you and his special friends great pain. It will be as strong an indictment of what I consider his treason to democracy, and his own ideals in entering the war as I can possibly make. And I shall give special attention to the way in which he changed his mind on about every possible question. As I look back upon those days prior to 1915, with the old enthusiasm Wilson had it in his power then to make over America, to take it back to the paths of Grover Cleveland; the most glorious of opportunities was sacrificed because of his desire to dominate the peace terms.

The only thing that can be done about it now - to answer your question - is to begin building a new party from the bottom up - a slow and tedious task - until a new leader is found, or social and economic changes take place. This task is one that must be essayed unless we are to be permanently enchained by those whom Wilson called the real masters of America, its Big Business men.

Sincerely yours,

Mr. Ray Stannard Baker,
Amherst, Mass.

OGV

RG

An Advance Toward Disarmament

TWICE in one week was Geneva electrified by declarations made in behalf of the United States by Hugh S. Gibson at the meeting of the Preparatory Disarmament Commission. Unfortunately the second declaration was as reactionary as the first was progressive. On April 22 Mr. Gibson broke the deadlock on naval reductions by suggesting that a common unit for measuring ship strength be sought, on the basis of which the United States would be willing to accept the French proposal of 1927 for limitations based both on total tonnage and by categories. This was a substantial concession from the United States *in behalf of disarmament*. But four days later Mr. Gibson made another concession. He dropped in behalf of the United States—and thus compelled other countries to follow suit—the previous insistence that reserves be counted as part of a nation's army strength. This is as definitely a concession *in behalf of armament* as the earlier action was against it. For it permits the iniquitous institution of universal military service for young men and allows France, Italy, and other continental nations to maintain their reserve forces at whatever strength they please apart from any limits which may be set for standing armies. We feel that this concession betrays the whole principle of army reduction and—unless modified—the usefulness of the Preparatory Disarmament Commission will be confined hereafter to naval limitation. In the latter direction, however, Mr. Gibson's earlier proposal is full of hope.

Not, of course, that we look to complete disarmament as a result of this proposal. As our readers are aware, our belief is that the way to disarm is to disarm, and we see no sense in the richest and most powerful country in the world, with its titanic resources and impregnable shores, haggling with other nations over precise ratios or equalities. No two navies could ever be made equal—not if they built ship for ship jointly; any high officer's single blunder can wreck an armada. But as long as our government has not the courage and wisdom to go ahead on its own and again set to the world the shining example of fearless disarmament which marked its national life for the first century of its existence when it was weak and struggling, we are happy to acclaim any move which points in the right direction. We cannot but admire, too, the tactics which suggested the new move just at this hour. Whether consciously or not, Washington seized the psychological moment. In the middle of its electoral battle for life the Baldwin Government in England was bound to acclaim the new proposal; by some suspicious minds it is already regarded as a Hoover effort to save Mr. Baldwin and Mr. Chamberlain, whose mishandling of the tripartite naval conference possibly did more to bring their Government into disrepute in England than any other of their sins of omission and commission. We do not believe that Mr. Hoover has been as subtle or as Machiavellian as that, but we do acclaim the choice of this hour to compel Great Britain to meet the new move in terms of cordial friendliness. That is a gain for the whole world.

Just what is the new move? At Geneva in 1927 the deadlock occurred because Great Britain and the United States could not agree on the number of cruisers. The United States wanted more big cruisers with eight-inch guns, and Great Britain more small cruisers. "We believe," said Mr. Gibson then, "that the maximum size of each category should be prescribed, also the maximum caliber of guns, because we are convinced that we cannot go wrong if we deal with tangible and visible characteristics rather than complicate the problem by dealing with characteristics that are not openly visible to all the world that cares to see." No total tonnage for these respective categories could be hit upon which satisfied both these countries. The French suggested in vain that an effort be made to combine what is known as the global plan with the category plan, so that if each nation were awarded a total tonnage in a given class of ships, one category might be increased by borrowing tonnage from another category, the total amount, however, not to be altered. Thus, if the United States were awarded, let us say, 200,000 tons in submarines and felt that it wanted more destroyer tonnage and less submarine, it could borrow 50,000 tons from the submarine class. Similarly, England might build more cruisers by borrowing tonnage from the destroyers, but since the maximum could not be exceeded, too great a tonnage could not be built up in any one category. Since the Americans flatly refused this French compromise in 1927 it was certainly a great step forward for Mr. Gibson to say: "My government is disposed to accept the French proposal as a basis of discussion." That is the crux of the whole matter. He reopened a deadlocked situation by this admission of an American change of front.

More than that, Mr. Gibson reinforced this simple proposal with words which are very suggestive of a new spirit in the White House or the Department of State. He said in effect: "Let us substitute reduction for limitation as our basic idea; limitation may mean either more or less of armaments, but reduction can mean only less." Again he declared that "methods are of secondary importance," and that "any approach . . . on purely technical grounds is bound to be inconclusive." If by the latter sentence he meant to imply that the day is over of the pettifogging and opinionated naval technicians who have wrangled over little technical details, and contributed so largely to the defeat of the will to peace of the plain people of the naval Powers, this again is a very great step forward.

Finally another hopeful thing is the recognition on the part of Mr. Gibson and the others at Geneva that the Kellogg Peace Pact does put upon all who signed it some responsibility for attacking the problem of navies in its spirit. Mr. Gibson put it squarely when he said that the new approach must be from the point of view of the Kellogg Pact, and that if the problem was tackled from that angle "a common-sense agreement" ought to be forthcoming. Of course, the Labor Party in England has acclaimed the new move. So will Russian and so will German opinion, and so will the people of France. It remains to be seen how far the politicians at Geneva will permit this new spirit to make itself felt.

Mr. Hoover Moves Toward Peace

HIGHLY encouraging are President Hoover's Memorial Day speech, Secretary Stimson's clear statement as to the burden upon all Americans of the naval program, and the press reports that the President is determined to move at once for genuine disarmament—he forfeited his Sunday holiday (June 2) in order to work on the problem. We could not deny, if we would, that there were in his Arlington address some of those weasel words with which every American statesman finds it necessary to embellish his sentiments whenever he ventures timidly toward peace. In the presence of so many veterans, Mr. Hoover found it necessary to repeat the old falsehoods that our armaments are merely for defense; that we must have a "just preparedness for the protection of our peoples," as if we had not lived more than a century of our national life in happiness and safety with no preparedness at all.

But we have no desire today to dwell upon the weaknesses and compromises of Mr. Hoover's speech. We are far too grateful for the numerous evidences that he is awake to his greatest opportunity to serve his country to cavil at any part of its expression. We are especially gratified by the statement of Secretary Stimson, commenting upon the Budget Director's certification that we Americans are obligated now—though building no battleships—to pay $1,170,800,000 for new naval vessels, among them the fifteen new cruisers which were voted last winter and are now rendered obsolete by the epoch-making new cruisers which Germany is to build. When before did a Secretary of State comment upon the wastefulness of our naval building program? And when did any Cabinet officer discuss this subject with special reference to the fact that if we go ahead with our program "other nations will be impelled to follow suit," and therefore "the burden of unproductive expenditures which will be imposed upon the economic world during the next fifteen years can be to a certain extent realized"?

Remarkable as this is, even more striking is Mr. Hoover's dwelling upon the point which we have sought to stress ever since the Kellogg peace pact was signed:

> Despite the declarations of the Kellogg pact, every important country has since the signing of that agreement been engaged in strengthening its naval arm. We are still borne on the tide of competitive building. . . . Fear and suspicion will never slacken unless we can halt competitive construction of arms. They will never disappear until we can turn this tide toward actual reduction.

No one else in official life has gone so far as to point out that our sincerity and that of every other nation which has signed the Kellogg pact is to be tested by our readiness to give concrete proof of disarmament; that we mean what we say; that our nation's signature is something better than a dicer's oath. With the Labor Party at the helm in England the hour is more auspicious than ever before. So we are sure that every American who believes in peace and abhors war will set himself to upholding the President's hand. We trust that the White House will be deluged with telegrams of congratulation and praise from all over the country.

The Liquidation of the War

POLITICALLY speaking, the World War ended with the Treaty of Versailles ten years ago; financially considered, the liquidation of the conflict has only now been definitely adjusted. Perhaps it is too much to say that the financial obligations of the war have even now been arranged, but at least the only important issues outstanding are the settlement of the French debt to the United States and an agreement between Germany and Belgium in regard to payment for the debasement of the Belgian currency during the war. Fortunately both these issues seem destined to be settled shortly in consequence of the agreement on the fundamental question of German reparations to the Allies.

We should be thankful and encouraged that this great problem of reparations has been settled in as little as ten years, for post-war hates and reprisals have died slowly. When one considers the fiery threats and demands which Raymond Poincaré and most of France were making for several years after the war, it is a tribute to the commonsense of the French and their normal love of peace that their delegates have finally accepted the terms just worked out in Paris. Likewise, when one reflects on the misery and bitterness of the Germans after the occupation of the Ruhr and the collapse of their currency, it is nothing less than a marvel that they have maintained their equilibrium and are now undertaking to underwrite peace in Europe by assuming a gigantic share of the war bill. Of course, ratification of the Paris agreement by the parliaments of the various nations concerned is still necessary, but successful opposition is unlikely. The German Government was wise in sending to Paris as its chief negotiator Herr Schacht, for the head of the Reichsbank belongs to the conservative wing of German politics, and his acceptance of the Young plan has presumably spiked the guns of factions which might otherwise have made trouble. In France the immediate political situation has greatly favored a conciliatory attitude throughout the negotiations and seems to assure acceptance of the terms. France is faced with the payment of an uncomfortable bill on August 1—$400,000,000 due to the United States for army supplies bought after the end of hostilities. But if the Mellon-Bérenger funding plan is accepted by France, the immediate debt will be merged with the larger amounts borrowed during the war and payments on the total will be made over a period of years. Premier Poincaré has been wanting to get the Mellon-Bérenger plan through Parliament, but his only practical hope of doing so lay in first obtaining a definite settlement of German reparations.

So far as the settlement itself goes, as we remarked last week, nobody is wise enough to say whether Germany is assessed too much or too little. Neither can anybody determine at this time whether she can make the proposed payments. The high recuperative power which she has shown in the last ten years suggests an affirmative answer, but the question of the transfer of payments may become an obstacle even if Germany is otherwise capable of carrying out the plan agreed upon. Anyhow the annuities under the new arrangement are less than under the Dawes plan and are limited to a fixed—though long—period of years. The Dawes plan called for annuities of $600,000,000, with uncertainty as to when they were to end. The Young plan calls for annuities averaging $492,000,000 for thirty-seven years, and then for annuities averaging $408,000,000 to the fifty-ninth year, when all payments cease. Obviously, there is an immediate advantage for Germany in the Young plan, and there is every reason to believe that the present arrangement will be modified in her favor before the end of the period now set. About two-thirds of the sum called for under the Young plan is destined for the United States in payment of the Allied debts, and all payments after the thirty-seventh year are calculated for that purpose. As we said last week, we do not believe that future generations of our people will want to exact such tribute.

With the adoption of the new program, all the machinery of the Dawes plan will go by the board; also the Reparation Commission will cease to exist. The Transfer Commission will be superseded by the new Bank for International Payments, and the excellent Agent General for Reparations, S. Parker Gilbert, will be out of a job. We have no doubt, though, that a high post in the Bank of International Payments awaits him if he wants it.

Americans may well be proud of what their fellow-citizens, acting unofficially, have done in the present settlement—especially of the efforts of Owen D. Young, who as chairman of the conference saved it time and again from disaster. On the other hand, Americans have no reason at all to be proud of the role of their government. Official Washington has clung to the ridiculous fiction that there can be no connection between German reparations and Allied debts to us. Fortunately our unofficial delegates in Paris held to no such absurd doctrine, and the Young plan recognizes the complete interrelation of the two problems. All signs suggest that official Washington will have to begin to talk sense soon, however. Under the present funding schemes Great Britain is the only country which is undertaking to pay back anything like its actual debt to the United States. The MacDonald Government will undoubtedly demand a reopening of the debt accord in order that Great Britain may be placed more nearly on an equality with other debtors. In the course of a comparatively short time we think the United States will realize that from both an ethical and a business standpoint our attempt to squeeze every possible drop of blood out of Europe is a mistake. In the face of the generous proposal of the Allies to evacuate the Rhineland, the United States ought to do something, too, in the cause of world peace. The financial costs of the World War have finally been distributed as between Germany and the Allies. No better work for peace could be done by the United States than by scaling down to the most nominal sums its claims against Europe.

In reply to the question "Who won the World War?" somebody once answered "Who won the San Francisco earthquake?" The agreement at Paris recognizes that modern war is everybody's loss and nobody's gain. The sooner and more equally those losses are accepted by all—America included—the better.

Peace Pact and Disarmament

THE Briand-Kellogg pact is formally in effect, and the peoples and governments of the world now face the stern task of building the peace. The pact, despite the strictures of its critics, means, or may mean, a first step in that great work; despite the plaudits of its friends, it of course means no more than a first step. Friends of peace may congratulate themselves that that step is taken, and Americans may take justifiable pride in the recent action of our President and Secretary of State in connection with this international engagement.

During the weeks of midsummer madness just past certain forces in China and Russia were working the peoples up to that stage of insane fury where war becomes a reality. It was our own Secretary of State who at the right moment reminded the two governments, theretofore apparently growing more and more belligerent, of their obligations under the pact. Since that time the exchanges between Nanking and Moscow have become more moderate, and the present outlook is for a settlement of the real differences between the two governments on a basis of reason and common-sense, not of hatred and bloodshed. We do not say that the pact prevented war, for we do not believe that it did. We do say that the pact gave Secretary Stimson a good opening, which he utilized skilfully, and that to such an extent the treaty made it easier for the governments of China and Russia to take the way of reason. We rejoice that it was an American secretary of state who in a crisis first successfully invoked the pact, and that its moral authority is in so far enhanced.

Distinctly more important, probably, in the long run, and no less creditable to Mr. Hoover's Administration, are the exchanges now going on between Washington and London in respect to the reduction of armaments. The events of the past month are full of encouragement to the friends of peace, and we should be less than fair if we failed to express our hearty appreciation of the steps Mr. Hoover has taken thus far, and our hope that he will not hesitate or falter in the good work so well begun; for of course the big fight is all ahead.

Mr. Dawes's first speech served notice on the world, and particularly on the generals and admirals, that so far as the Administration was concerned, our government was actually ready to reduce its armaments. All the silly talk about yardsticks and parity and like nonsense does not alter the significance of one basic fact: the responsible heads of the British and the American government are ready to sit down together as intelligent and friendly human beings and talk over plans of cutting navies and taxes, instead of leaving it to professional fighting men and their civilian allies to scare us all into believing that it can't be done. Prime Minister MacDonald, in discussing parity, points out that the governments have agreed to a certain elasticity in meeting their peace-time needs, and that technical considerations will not be allowed to interfere with the main purpose. This is to say that parity is poppycock, and that the governments have agreed on reduction as the important thing—which it is.

And now comes Mr. Hoover, the very day before the peace pact goes into formal effect, saying flatly:

> The American people should understand that current expenditures on strictly military activities of the army and navy constitute the largest military budget of any nation in the world today, and at a time when there is less real danger of extensive disturbance to peace than at any time in more than half a century. The hope of tax reduction lies in large degree in our ability to economize on the military and naval expenditure and still maintain adequate defense. Our whole situation is certainly modified by the Kellogg pact.

This statement the President follows up with actual figures of such expenditures for four of the leading powers, showing us outlays on the army and navy above a hundred millions more during the past year and two hundred millions more in the present year than our nearest competitor, Great Britain, and more than three times as much as Japan. Further, he points out that the $685,000,000 of last year will rise to $803,000,000 three years hence if our plans be not changed. These are not the words of those advocates of "adequate" defense who forever demand more guns and ships and planes and poison.

Nor is this all. Mr. Hoover announces the appointment of a commission (unfortunately from the general staff) to study reduction of army costs; and then, plainly by agreement with Mr. MacDonald, who makes a corresponding announcement in London, he gives notice of delay in laying down the keels of three of the five cruisers in this year's building program, the other two being under contract in private yards, where the work can less readily be stopped—a fact worthy of remark in considering the forces back of naval building. Small wonder that that doughty naval expert and Briton-baiter, Representative Britten, gives forth an agonized wail that the President is violating the intent of Congress, and that the misguided president of the American Legion utters a shout of alarm. It is only the first faint rumbling of the storm that will come; for the President actually proposes to cut down army and navy expenditures, on the ground that the pact really means something. That is the way to make it mean something, and we honor the President for his action.

We are not so silly as to imagine that Mr. Hoover has turned pacifist, but we do say that, within the limits of his ideas and his position, his moves up to this point have been admirable. Thus far, with the MacDonald Government collaborating in England, his task has been comparatively easy; now comes the real fight and the real test of the President, who does not love a fight. But the army and navy and all their war-making allies in Congress and out of it will unquestionably gather their forces and fight for their life. Their forces are immensely powerful. No indirect methods, no simple, quiet conferences with a few leaders will do the work that must be done. We believe that Mr. Hoover can find irresistible popular support for the moderate measure of armament reduction at present contemplated if he will use the power of his position to make the issue clear. Will he lead the American people to take this short step from fear toward friendliness? It is a great task for any man.

Much Ado About Disarmament

WE were much interested, as were many others, in the report last spring that Ramsay MacDonald proposed to visit the United States to discuss the naval armament situation with Mr. Hoover. Mr. MacDonald has an interesting personality and a winning manner, and his position as Prime Minister of Great Britain is obviously one of importance. If he could sit down with Mr. Hoover and talk the matter over, it seemed natural to suppose that some of the larger difficulties in the way of an Anglo-American agreement about armament reduction might be ironed out, and the way smoothed for a presentation of the subject to Congress and Parliament. The suggestion, indeed, was more than interesting; it was intriguing, and the newspapers of both countries played it up valiantly.

No sooner had the proposal been launched, however, than it began to be buffeted by head winds and bad weather. The first public intimation that Mr. MacDonald might take a few weeks off and cross the Atlantic was made, if we remember rightly, on June 10 at London, and was favorably received. Six days later Ambassador Dawes, who had just arrived in England, saw Mr. MacDonald in Scotland, and the next day Mr. MacDonald told the correspondents that the visit depended upon the diplomatic situation, "but I should think I probably would go." By June 26 things looked a bit doubtful, the diplomatic condition, it appeared, being an agreement between Great Britain and the United States about a naval conference. By July 1 the sky was further overcast: Mr. MacDonald would come if he were invited, but he had not decided when—probably not until October. Press dispatches of July 18 agreed that the visit would probably be postponed, but on the 24th Mr. MacDonald again was coming in October.

Meantime Ambassador Dawes had been busy discussing the armament question at London and had described the Hoover "yardstick," happily in general terms only, to the Pilgrim Society; a bill empowering the President to make secret purchases of war materials in certain cases had been prepared by the Secretary of War; a railway shipment of fourteen-inch guns had arrived safely in California; and Mr. Hoover had halted plans for the construction of three cruisers and demanded that army costs be cut down. Within a week after these latter incidents Mr. Hoover was backing water on the army cut, the British Admiralty was joining in the London parleys, pay increases for the American army to as much as 105 per cent in some cases were being demanded, and Washington announced that parity had been accepted as the basis of an Anglo-American agreement and that the navy was going ahead with the plans of the three cruisers whose construction had been held up.

All this, while rather confusing to the man in the street, seemed to make Mr. MacDonald's visit only the more urgent. The question of the visit dropped out of the news until August 21, when it was again reported from Washington that Mr. MacDonald would not come unless a basis for a naval conference had been found. Something went wrong, or else something happened between twilight and dawn, for the next day the same Washington announced that Mr. MacDonald and his daughter were coming about the middle of October. London, cautious about denials, understood that the coming would not be in October's first week. On August 25 Mr. MacDonald was coming late in September; on the 28th his arrival had been placed between October 1 and 10; on August 30 the Baltimore *Sun* announced that he would arrive on October 4 and sail on his return on the 12th. Twenty-four hours later Mr. MacDonald was quoted as saying that his coming "must depend upon the agreement"; on September 2 London was doubting that there would be any visit at all, while on September 3, the day on which Mr. MacDonald made the optimistic speech at Geneva which Secretary of State Stimson promptly dashed with tepid water, White House officials were reported as saying that "nothing was known" there about the visit "beyond what had appeared in the newspapers."

The country is still waiting for Mr. MacDonald, and we still hope that he may find it possible to come. The reason for all the backing and filling, however, is clear enough. Mr. MacDonald has long been enthusiastic about armament reduction, and as soon as the May election made him Premier he set out to do something about it at once, forthwith, without delay. Then public opinion, and the Admiralty, and the naval experts, and Australia, and the Singapore base, and the naval plans of Italy and France, and the Palestine disorders, and reparations all got in his way and the great reformation slowed down. Mr. Hoover, who has not yet learned that politics is not quite like railway building or dam construction, also wanted naval armaments reduced now and limited hereafter, and set up Mr. Dawes to explain all about the virtues of the yardstick; but the Dawes speech, when critically examined, turned out to offer only the old hokum about cooperation between statesmen and experts—two aggregations that have not yet been able to agree upon anything either among themselves or with one another. On August 14 we were told, on what was claimed to be authority, that the yardstick had been abandoned and a ship-for-ship arrangement substituted. Now, as far as the drippings of news from secret conversations indicate anything, the two countries are back where they were at the beginning, and where they have been ever since Mr. Coolidge's three-Power conference broke down in August, 1927, namely, at the issue of parity. As nobody has any but a vague notion of what parity means, and even Mr. Hoover's engineering-mindedness is unable to show how it might be attained, the outlook for an agreement that will let Mr. MacDonald take ship seems remote.

It is time that the farce were ended. Three years of more or less continuous discussion of armament reduction have produced thus far nothing of importance except talk—and a steady increase of armaments almost everywhere, with the United States well toward the van. What the country wants is action, not politics, debate, and expert hairsplitting. If Mr. MacDonald still thinks that by meeting Mr. Hoover he can get something practical done, we hope his visit will be made. If he is not sure of being able to do that, it were better that he should not come.

Disarmament Difficulties

THE French naval memorandum, made public on the day after Christmas, served at once to emphasize the difficulties facing the London Naval Conference and to indicate its possible usefulness. The note serves notice that the French navy is going to be based on the needs of the French empire as understood in France—an uncompromising suggestion of the difficulties of the conference—and declares that "the conference will fail to achieve its object to the full unless it makes it lead to a general agreement in Geneva as to the methods for the limitation of naval armaments."

The accomplishment at London of anything worth while depends on a rare combination of idealism and hard-headed realism. Probably no man in public life combines those qualities in higher degree than Ramsay MacDonald, and it is good that the conference is to have the advantage of his leadership. Yet no one should be betrayed into false hopes on that account. At the time of Mr. MacDonald's visit to our shores last summer, his earnestness and eloquence led many enthusiastic observers to feel that the day of peace on earth was very near. At that very moment, however, more hard-headed critics pointed out that aside from psychological results the immediate practical outcome of the MacDonald-Hoover conferences, as far as the public was informed, had been precisely nothing. Since that time a somewhat bewildered American public has learned that despite President Hoover's statement plans of the Navy Department for cruiser building have not been held up by a single day. Mr. MacDonald did make a gesture toward delaying naval construction; yet if we are not mistaken all inquiries addressed to the present British Government concerning actual naval work have been answered to the satisfaction of alarmed patriots who feared an undue weakening of the navy. In both countries there has been a gap between talk and action that is painful to contemplate. Yet we are not inclined to charge either of the chief leaders concerned with hypocrisy. The hard realities of the situation have proved too much for the idealism that found expression in public utterance. Appeals to popular sentiment have run afoul of contracts and political commitments. Ramsay MacDonald's pacifism is genuine enough, but when it comes to actual naval cuts the Admiralty holds the trumps, and the blessed state of parity is to be achieved, it appears, by our building up to Britain instead of Britain's building down to us. If results are to be achieved at London then, it must be by a clear understanding that words, however eloquent, are no substitute for deeds.

From this point of view the elimination of the Paris peace pact from the London discussion may be by no means an unmitigated loss. President Hoover and Prime Minister MacDonald based their disarmament pronouncements on the idea of the peace pact. The French Government says of the pact: "It is undoubtedly a real step toward the preservation of peace, but it cannot be looked upon as sufficient in its present state to guarantee the security of nations." The note goes on somewhat cruelly: "It was this consideration, no doubt, that prevented the British Government from contemplating a substantial reduction in their naval armament and the American Government from giving up the prompt execution of their latest naval program."

It is time to stop talking nonsense about basing naval limitation on the peace pact. If the pact means anything, it means that the nations accepting it are not going to fight. But navies are made to fight. As long as you maintain navies then you are proceeding on the assumption that the pact, for practical purposes, is meaningless; and the idea of basing naval limitations as opposed to abolition on the pact is logically nonsense. Neither Mr. Hoover nor Mr. MacDonald last summer had the slightest idea of scrapping his country's navy, nor will a single delegate come to London with such an idea even remotely in mind. How then could a resulting treaty possibly be based on the pact? To attempt any such logical feat is simply to darken counsel by words without knowledge. And the frank elimination of the Paris document, while it may dash unjustifiably high hopes, may also serve to keep men's eyes on the practical realities and possibilities of the situation. The conference in fact is going to make little practical difference in the actual business of naval construction unless the governments concerned experience a change of heart of which there is no evidence. The French note is clear and frank on this point. It says flatly that the French navy is going to be based not on sentiment embodied in the peace pact but on "national needs," taking into account France's geographical position and colonial empire. Such an attitude deals openly with existing political realities in terms of force and supposed national interests. Such an attitude makes striking naval reduction well nigh impossible. Yet such an attitude seems in fact to be taken, as far as we can see, by all the Powers concerned, though none of the others has stated it quite so plainly. We should approach the conference, accordingly, with no illusions.

Because of these difficulties, shall we simply wash our hands of the conference? By no means. The world is as it is; if we expect little, we may be grateful for not much. If definite plans of limitation, carefully worked out, can be put forward, some slight measure of relief from competitive expenditure may be achieved, as happened at Washington. Further, a fillip may be given to the lagging work of the League's Disarmament Commission, through which France insists, perhaps rightly, any approach to a general move toward armament reduction must come. Finally, the conference, happily, is going to contain some men, at least, who really believe that reason can take the place of force as the ultimate international arbiter. Let their hands be strengthened by the support of the world's peace forces, and this conference may take on the character of a cooperative attempt at solving common problems. If it does, it will be worth while, no matter how small its concrete achievements. For the attainment of peace is a matter both of public sentiment and of the right organization of international relations. The peoples, eager for peace, will back their government representatives, we are confident, in every move they may make in the direction of armament reduction.

Liquidating the War

PRECISELY what the members of the reparations conference at The Hague agreed to when, on January 20, they signed the protocol approving the Young Plan cannot be fully known until the texts of the twenty-odd documents are published. A curious indefiniteness has hung over the reported proceedings of the conference from the first. Dr. Hjalmar Schacht, president of the Reichsbank, for example, stirred up a great political row in Germany by insisting that the report of the Young committee which he signed was not identical with the Young Plan which Germany was asked to accept, and even threatened to debar the Reichsbank from subscribing to the capital stock of the Bank for International Settlements; but no American correspondent, as far as we have noticed, took the trouble to point out wherein, if at all, his contention was well founded. More curious still, the bank plan, the most novel feature of the Young scheme and a matter of the greatest international importance, has hardly figured in the dispatches to the American press at all.

The main outlines of the great settlement, on the other hand, are clear. Two important modifications have been made in the reparations part of the Young proposals. The schedules of German annuities have been altered by deducting the amounts which Germany will pay directly to the United States under the treaty recently concluded, and sanctions may be imposed upon Germany for default in its payments if the World Court finds that the default has been intentional. Preliminary arrangements are also reported to have been made for the mobilization of a part of the annuities in a $300,000,000 loan, and for the allocation of the loan among the world's financial markets. The United States, it has been intimated, will be looked to for a subscription of about one-fourth of the amount, but the loan itself probably cannot be floated before May. The vexatious question of the non-German reparations, with Hungary stubbornly opposing the claims of the Little Entente states, has been settled in principle only, the actual working out of the details of a complicated compromise being left to a small commission sitting at Paris.

The most important administrative feature of the agreement is, of course, the approval of the Bank for International Settlements, the statute of the bank as drafted by a commission at Baden-Baden having, apparently, been accepted without material change. It will be recalled that the bank, as originally planned by the Young committee, was to enjoy, in addition to most of the usual banking privileges, vast powers of participation in trade and industrial development wherever the directors chose to operate. The volume of adverse criticism which this proposal of a gigantic super-bank evoked evidently impressed the Baden-Baden commission, for in drafting the statute they threw all these general provisions overboard and confined the bank strictly to the banking field as an agency for handling reparation payments. The bank, which is to be located at Basle, will have a capital of 500,000,000 Swiss francs (about $96,500,000), one-fourth of which must be paid in; it will be entitled to a commission of one-tenth of one per cent on the payments which it handles; and it will have the use of non-interest-bearing deposits of 125,000,000 marks contributed one-half by Germany and one-half by Germany's creditors. A writer in the *Frankfurter Zeitung* estimates that the bank should be able to earn 14 per cent on its paid-in capital, but a substantial part of its net profits will eventually go to reduce the amount of the German annuities.

Legally, what was done at The Hague does not put the new scheme fully into effect; first, because the protocol must be ratified by the various governments concerned and, second, because the bank cannot be organized until Switzerland has removed a constitutional obstacle to the grant of a charter for more than fifteen years. The German payments, however, will now be made under the new schedules. To the extent that the Hague settlement puts an end to a controversy which has embittered European politics for ten years, reduces Germany's burden, provides for the commercialization of the German annuities and their administration through a specially organized bank, and removes all justification for the further maintenance of French troops in Germany, there will be profound satisfaction over what has been achieved. The uncertain element in the transaction is the bank, an institution managed by directors most of whom will be chosen with an eye to politics, subject to political pressure if its course is not satisfactory either to Germany or to any of the creditor governments, and so contrived, through its provision for American representation in its directorate, as to keep up, indirectly at least, America's connection with a reparations issue with which the American Government has repeatedly declared it would have nothing to do.

A Crisis at London

UNLESS something radical is done, and done quickly, to straighten out the extraordinary situation at London, the London conference is likely to go down in history as one of the most disastrous attempts at international cooperation in which the United States has ever engaged. Two problems in particular, both of grave seriousness, confront the American delegation. The first is to insure the attainment of one of the two main purposes for which the conference was called, namely, the actual reduction of existing naval armaments. The second is to avoid entangling the United States in a European security pact. For the existence of both of these problems in their present acute form the Hoover Administration and its delegation at London are so far responsible that the failure of the conference, if that calamity should happen, would be properly chargeable to the United States more than to any other Power.

The statement issued by the French delegation on February 11, calling for 724,479 English tons of naval craft by the end of 1936, with 240,000 tons of that amount to be built during the period, contained nothing new except the figures. Weeks before the American delegation, surrounded by an imposing array of experts and helpers and attended by a squad of uniformed marines, departed from New York the French government, in an elaborate memorandum to the British government, had traversed comprehensively the business of the conference and outlined in detail the position of France regarding its naval needs.

Instead of showing that it had grasped this situation and was prepared to meet it, the American delegation has strewn its course with some amazing blunders, in all of which, apparently, it had the approbation of Washington. When Mr. MacDonald, the question of battleships having been thrown to the fore, proposed to consider at once the abolition of that type of vessel, Mr. Stimson turned him down; the conference had been called to deal with cruisers, and there must be no interference with that grand design. A single preliminary skirmish over the abolition of submarines caused Mr. Stimson to throw up his hands, and the fight was lost before it had fairly begun. An exhibition of bungling that was a disgrace to American diplomacy concealed the fact, until an alert press forced it out, that the United States, champion of armament reduction, was actually proposing to build another battleship at a cost of from $35,000,000 to $50,000,000. The publication of the French statement of February 11, followed by the overthrow of the Tardieu Government, completed the moral rout of the embattled Americans, this time with the British close at their heels. It was matter of common knowledge that M. Tardieu's tenure was precarious, as it was that no succeeding ministry would be likely to modify greatly the French demands, and that any modification that might be conceded would still leave the way open to largely increased building; but the Stimson aggregation could only betake itself to gloom and leave the correspondents to cable that reduction was no longer even a pleasing hope.

The second problem is equally grave. France is willing to trade tonnage for a security pact, with the covert understanding that the United States shall be one of the guarantors. It is the old game of maneuvering the United States into burning its fingers with European quarrels, yet the American delegation is actually reported as not wholly unfavorable to the suggestion. Senator Robinson, to be sure, has spoken out in reiteration of the time-honored American policy of keeping America free, but it was immediately noted that he did not wholly close the door; while Mr. Hoover, fresh from his fishing exploits in Southern waters, allows himself to be represented as deterred from entertaining the proposal, not because he himself will have none of it, but from fear of the irreconcilables in the Senate. In other words, where the reply of the American delegation should have been a prompt and emphatic "No," there is real danger that the delegation, with the tacit acquiescence of Mr. Hoover, may allow the United States to become entangled in the net which France has spread for it, and that America, in addition to losing the naval reduction which it hoped for, may emerge from the conference with its hands tied. If that is the outcome, it will mean that the danger of war will be greater after the conference than it was before.

It is time that the country waked up to the significance of what is going on at London and Washington. An unprepared and inept delegation at the Ritz is losing its grip on the realities of the armament situation, and a political trimmer at the White House is aiding the decline. The American people want naval armaments reduced and limited, but they also want to see American independence scrupulously preserved. They are not yet ready to barter statesmanship at London for a dreary program of backing, filling, and drift, nor statesmanship at Washington for a record catch of sailfish on a Presidential junket.

Headless Washington

By OSWALD GARRISON VILLARD

Washington, February 20

THAT is what Washington is—utterly headless. The breakdown of leadership is really appalling. I doubt whether it has ever before been as bad, for the problems of government steadily grow more involved, more difficult, and more numerous, and call more and more for vision, ability, and consistent statesmanship if they are to be solved. One has the feeling that everybody in Washington is floundering in a situation which he cannot control. One wonders whether the whole system is not cracking. When one beholds three important investigations going on simultaneously; when one watches the Senators trying frantically to keep up with their work on committees of inquiry in addition to their regular committee and Senatorial work; when one visualizes the multitude of problems which are half solved, or are waiting solution at every turn, such as Muscle Shoals, Boulder Dam, the Mississippi flood prevention, the inland waterways situation, to say nothing of the railroads, prohibition, the tariff, and all the rest, one is compelled to ask oneself whether the business of government has not become too complex and too difficult for the machinery we set up in 1789.

The chief failure is, of course, in the White House itself. Not that anybody should have expected anything else. Mr. Hoover has never shown moral courage, nor the capacity for leadership, since his Belgian days. As Secretary of Commerce the whole philosophy of his job was to collate figures, to progress in the coordination of industry by means of trade understandings and agreements—which may yet be held in court to violate our laws—and then to smooth the way for big business in every legitimate manner. Why should one have expected a complete change in the moral make-up of the man or in his political theory when he reached the White House? The entire legislative situation here in Washington today is due to Hoover's inability to refuse to promise the extra session to Senator Borah when Herbert Hoover, still a candidate, was striving for the goal of his ambition. He did not dare say no to the Senator from Idaho for fear that he would lose the farmers' vote. The extra session has come and gone, we are at the end of the third month of the regular session, and there isn't the slightest prospect whatever that the farmers will get any of the tariff aid which, together with the creation of the Federal Farm Board, was the object of the special session.

You cannot lead a nation that way, not even if you have the Republican leaders to breakfast every day in the week, and especially not if you have the kind of leaders to handle whom Mr. Hoover has to ask to his table. Watson, Tilson, Longworth, Snell, Wesley Jones, McNary, Wood, Andy Mellon—not a real idea, much less a principle, in a carload of such as these. But how in turn can they be blamed? After the White House breakfast on February 17, there was the usual press talk that the President was now "going to take a hand"; that he would "warn Congress sternly," especially the Senate, that something would happen if they did not move. It was suggested that he was on the point of going over the heads of the legislators to appeal to the country. All of this sort of thing until a day later the Washington *Star* appeared with the reassuring but hardly unexpected headline that Mr. Hoover had decided not to interfere with Congress. It was a wise decision, for the truth is that when he asked at his own breakfast table whether he could do anything to hasten the Senate he was bluntly informed that if he tried to do anything it would be disastrous. To such a pass has come the "leader of his party." It remained for a Democrat, Congressman Garner of Texas, to speak the truth in meeting. Declaring that "the titular Republican leader in the White House is either lacking in courage or capacity to lead," Mr. Garner added that there is not a Republican leader in the Senate or House "who has the faintest idea of what the President wants, and, worse still, they haven't the slightest idea that he wants anything particularly constructive or progressive." The apparent failure of the London conference makes it clear that the President has blundered there in letting the delegation go abroad without a clear-cut policy determined in advance and a readiness to achieve some disarmament come what might. And Mr. Hoover sorely needed a success in foreign affairs to conceal his nakedness at home!

Now the astonishing thing about it is that many of the problems which confront the government are those in which Mr. Hoover was supposed to have shown peculiar fitness and capacity. They are economic problems, business problems, often engineering problems; for the political issues are being steadily shoved aside for business and economic ones. If the President has convictions and yet gives no clear-cut, convincing note, he is without courage. Never did a man need more to study the career of Grover Cleveland. In his second term that President aroused a storm of hostility. He, too, was charged with being the servant of big business, but at least no one could doubt where he stood or what he wanted. It is simply impossible to think of Mr. Hoover's doing what Mr. Cleveland did when he wanted reelection—plumping for a tariff for revenue only when all his advisers told him that if he came out for that his defeat would be certain. To this he replied: "Very well, gentlemen, then we shall be defeated." If Mr. Hoover ever does anything to electrify the country in some such way, the Washington corps of journalists will surely lose a number of its members from heart failure. At present he sits in the White House and sulks, calling the Senators every kind of name, yet unable to make a stepping-stone of his dead self and stir the country by taking a militant position and assuming the leadership not merely of his party, but of the whole country.

Still another reason why he cannot do this is that he, like the rest of Washington, is without a definite program, either political or economic. Here he is no worse and no better than the men in Congress—not even the Progressive group, which remains the one hopeful portent in the entire situation. Most people in Washington do not know that we are on our way somewhere, socially and economically. Few of them can visualize the whole forest, they are busy at best in repairing an occasional tree, filling a hole here, running a rod through a trunk there. As for having any sailing chart for their political progress, they do not know that such a thing exists. They cannot realize that we are in the midst of a tremendous economic revolution. They cannot put together the innumerable items of economic news that stare out at us from each daily paper—that the railroads are being consolidated; that there are only thirty tire companies left out of three hundred; that the great Vacuum and Standard Oil companies have come together; that mergers are expected in the automobile field and a dozen others; that at every turn there are combinations and consolidations; that but for the fear of our anti-trust laws we should be seeing in this country precisely what has just happened in Germany —the bringing together of every iron and steel plant in the country, so that the industry is being governed as a whole by a steering committee for the purpose of modernizing the weak, financing the struggling, dividing the domestic field among the plants best fitted for each line, and preparing for exports with which to conquer the European markets. Instead, we have in Washington the headless and planless effort to stop a combination here, to control another there, to beat the devil around the bush by the inter-trade agreements to which I have already referred. And constantly the Senate has to give its time and strength to muckraking various official bodies, or overhauling official activities to prevent the perversion of government by the deliberate turning over to private business of certain governmental functions, or their complete warping by the servants of big business whom Mr. Coolidge and Mr. Hoover have appointed to positions in which they are supposed to be the watch-dogs of the government. This sort of inquiry is sneered at by the press; it infuriates big business, and the public becomes cynical about it. But if anything should stop it, that would be nothing short of disaster. It is quite true, as one news bureau has said, that the Progressives feel that if they do not keep on their job there will not be a single natural resource of any kind, capable of being turned over to private exploiters, which will not be turned over by Mr. Hoover if he is allowed to have his way during the next three or seven years. It was only this week that Senator Couzens, who is presiding over the hearings of the Senate Interstate Commerce Committee, declared, after hearing certain charges as to what has been happening in the Federal Power Commission, that "conditions in the commission have become so intolerable that it presents one of the rottenest exhibitions of government I have ever heard of."

Speaking of programs, and the lack of them, what could be more pitiful than the attitude of the Progressives and the Democrats on the tariff? Here is a God-given issue at hand. The Democrats in Congress, having also no leadership of any kind, and having been betrayed on the tariff issue by their party convention and their party candidate of 1928, are naturally unable to agree on any policy or to take any definite general position. They are also engaged in getting their feet into the trough as rapidly as possible. The most disgusting example of this practice has been afforded by Senator Copeland of New York. Did he, for example, vote against the Aluminum Trust, which robs every housewife in America for the benefit of poor, starving Andrew Mellon and his family? He did not. He said he had been told that the workers in some aluminum factories in the State of New York would lose their jobs if we did not help Andrew out. He could see only the votes of his constituents, nothing else. He has forgotten, if he ever knew, that the historic Democratic policy has been a tariff for revenue only, and he is certainly not of the opinion that the interests of the entire country are superior to those of a handful of workers. He goes round the country making speeches against graft, and then votes freely for the "honest graft" of protection, whenever he thinks that any factory owner or worker in New York State may be helped by his vote. He is in no wise different from nearly all the others in his party. Certainly none of the so-called Democratic leaders have any real thought that there is a principle at stake here.

Neither have the Progressives. They have stood together much better than was expected; for once Senator Borah has really shown leadership. Remarkable as it seems, he has regularly attended group meetings of the Democrats and Progressives; for once he has shown symptoms of the fighting leadership that he might have exercised years ago, if his ability and brilliance had been matched with equal courage. He might well have been the most influential figure in political life today. The Progressives have fought hard against many tariff increases. They hit the Aluminum Trust a staggering blow; they have so far kept the Senatorial tools of the sugar barons from still further mulcting the American people. They have cooperated far better with the Democrats, and the Democrats with them, than had been deemed possible. Yet they, too, vote now and then because of some State interest, for things which they ought to oppose, just as Senator Norris actually voted for a sugar bounty for the Nebraska beet-sugar growers. What could they not accomplish if they realized that there was a principle at stake in all this? They are greatly stirred up because the farmers are going to be buncoed again and are not going to be brought within the charmed circle of the protection grafters. They are doing their best to see that Mr. Hoover and his party live up to their promise of agricultural tariff relief, but in doing so they cannot lay claim to holding any moral position. They are debarred from attacking the whole system because they seek favors for their several States.

It has been rightly said that without vision the people perish. Doesn't that apply to government as well? How long will it be before the so-called leaders here can see that the days of tinkering, and of stopping leaks, and of patching, and of taking one timid step in this direction, and another in the other direction, are rapidly nearing their end? The time is surely at hand when there must be a nation-wide protest against the whole business of compromising and of special privilege and favoritism, which in one form or another is corrupting the government, weakening its machinery, and making impossible any grappling with our general economic problem on the basis of genuine and far-reaching economic reform. Leadership here? There isn't any. Few of the observers even realize what it is all about and where it is taking us—least of all, apparently, the man in the White House. Naturally, he is the most conspicuous target; he ought to be. There is criticism on the part of the regulars, even those who do not like Mr. Hoover, that certain groups are out to "get him." Why not? There could be no greater service rendered to the country today than to make it clear just how bankrupt the White House is, and whither its conduct of affairs is taking us.

Parity the Enemy

IT is now plain that the naval conference in London is near the rocks, and this is true despite Ramsay MacDonald's radio appeal of March 9 to the American people to shun the pessimists. Nothing but good luck can save it from becoming a genuine disaster to all the world and the most lamentable breakdown of statesmanship since August, 1914. For this the American delegation will not be able to escape a large share of the blame. It has been extraordinarily weak. It has lacked courage. It has blundered damnably. It has forgotten the words and promises of its own members, notably those of Messrs. Stimson and Gibson. It plainly went to London without a clear-cut policy or a program, and it has obviously been inspired by nothing from the White House. Mr. Stimson has merely muddied the waters by his statement of March 5 intended, he said, to refute the "impression that the work of the American delegation at this conference is likely to result in an increase instead of a reduction in the tonnage of the navies of the world." The most superficial examination showed that Mr. Stimson had submitted no figures to prove that his promised net reduction of 200,000 American tons was in sight, "and an even larger reduction on the part of the British fleet"; that his figure was "contingent upon some reductions being made in the fleets of other Powers." Next, Mr. Stimson resurrected obsolete cruisers (including Sampson's flagship at Santiago thirty-two years ago), submarines, and destroyers to make even this promise possible. Finally, it appeared that Mr. Stimson got some of his reduction by counting in ships authorized but not yet begun! Whatever else may be said of this statement it smacks of despair and self-delusion.

Aside from the fallibility of the delegation itself, what is it that has wrecked our undertaking in London? We answer this question by quoting from a dispatch in the New York *Times* from its correspondent, Edwin L. James. Reporting in it the sullen reaction of our delegation to the cablegram of criticism from 1,200 American protestants, Mr. James, whose language is obviously directly inspired, concludes his dispatch thus:

> America can have parity at the cost of sacrificing her reduction principle at this conference and paying a billion dollars. She can have reduction at a cost of sacrificing her principle of parity and saving a billion dollars. But to obtain parity and reduction both at this conference is beyond the abilities of Secretary Stimson and his colleagues. It is also beyond the abilities of the 1,200 signers of Mr. Fosdick's cablegram.

The New York *World,* which has ignominiously hauled down its flag by saying that "we cannot hope to reduce existing fleets or reduce the fleets we are building," but that "we can still hope to reduce the fleets we would have to build if the conference fails," similarly admits that parity is the controlling influence. Thus, it says that "the only conceivable basis of agreement between two Powers of such magnitude is equality" and that "any other basis of inferiority and superiority would be the source of perpetual irritation." "Parity," it declares, "is valuable. It costs a price. The price is naval construction up to a standard fixed by Great Britain. . . ." Writing from London in the *New Republic,* William T. Stone, of the Foreign Policy Association, declares that our delegation is "more concerned . . . with precise mathematical parity than with possible ways of achieving reduction."

Here then is the chief enemy—this new, un-American, recently unheard-of doctrine that we must have parity with Great Britain. We have existed as a nation for 154 years, and no one ever pretended to assert until the last few years that we needed parity with the mother country. We were for generations completely unarmed, notably from 1830 to 1860 and from 1870 to 1900, and never did Great Britain seek to take advantage of it, not even under the terrific incitement of Grover Cleveland's Venezuelan message. But now all is altered. Not at *a* price as the *World* says, but at a terrible price we are to have parity—at the cost of building still larger fleets, of reducing not at all; at the cost of an armament race with Great Britain; at the cost of being feared and therefore hated by all the other Powers; at the cost of a billion and then of untold additional millions of dollars; at the cost of some of our finest American ideals.

And parity, what is it? A chimera. The *World* rejoices that by "an act of high statesmanship and profound common sense" we have eliminated the question of relative naval bases, the merchant marine, trade routes, inland versus continental strategy, financial resources, and industrial resources. What remains? Mere numerical parity. Just as though any two nations could be on a par even with exactly duplicate fleets when the vital question is the brains of the respective commanders, the drill and efficiency of the crews, their marksmanship, their will to win—all the personal factors—and even these, as the battle of Jutland showed, may be offset by weather conditions. Parity is a myth, guaranteeing no victory, but only insuring war.

Will Americans yield to this folly? We cannot believe it. Who has authorized the *World,* or our delegation in London, or President Hoover, or the Congress, or anyone else to say that the United States must have parity? Who has had the authority to say for the American people that, having grown great and rich and powerful, a "world Power," we must, therefore, assume a crushing naval burden which we declined to consider when we were weak and young and totally undefended? Who has given the *World* the right to assume that if the conference fails we shall have to build vast new fleets to our own impoverishment? Has anybody asked the American people for its views? Not Mr. Hoover. He would be careful not to seek to ascertain definitely whether the people of this country, opposed to its business leaders and its politicians, wish to embark on this policy. We do not believe for an instant that the aroused conscience of America or its moral forces will submit to any such interpretation of America's future. There will be no yielding without a tremendous struggle, without proper characterization of those who would fasten upon our industry military and naval burdens which, as Mr. Hoover admits, are already greater than those borne by any other nation on earth. On this line there are Americans ready to fight, not only all summer, but as long as they live.

Conscription

ON April 1 the House of Representatives resolved itself into Committee of the Whole to consider the conscription of men and money in war time. This is merely another milestone in the ten-year-old argument that has been occupying the Committee on Military Affairs and the American Legion and plaguing those members of the citizenry who oppose conscription by whatever name it is called. The resolution in question the other day was one introduced by Representative Snell providing for the creation of a commission to "study and consider the feasibility of equalizing the burdens and to minimize the profits of war, together with a study of policies to be pursued in event of war, so as to empower the President immediately to mobilize all the resources of the country." With several minor amendments and one very important one, the resolution passed.

Proponents of the measure divided themselves into two camps: those who said the resolution would eliminate that naughty and unpopular fellow, the war-profiteer, and those who said it was perfectly meaningless and harmless and therefore they proposed to vote for it. Those who opposed it pointed out that whereas the alleged purpose of the measure was to provide some means for placing the burdens of war upon capital as well as labor, actually it did nothing of the kind. The Constitution of the United States provides that the government may not confiscate property without just compensation. Therefore the idea of conscripting capital in war time—without, of course, compensation—is clearly unconstitutional. The burden of conscription would, accordingly, fall upon labor, and capital would be left to its own devices. At this point in the discussion Representative Huddleston of Alabama introduced his important amendment to the bill, which was passed by only 123 votes to 120. The amendment provided that the commission "shall not consider and shall not report upon the conscription of labor."

Debate on the resolution provided some very elegant Congressional oratory. Gentlemen who frankly looked forward to the next war and wished to prepare for it gave place to gentlemen who remembered that there was in existence a Kellogg pact to outlaw war; gentlemen who talked vaguely about conscripting capital were reminded not only that capital cannot, by the Constitution, be conscripted, but that capital has a way of protecting itself in emergencies of this sort, mainly at the expense of labor. On the whole the discussion was highly illuminating. It disclosed that there were men in the House willing to consider favorably the idea, as Mr. Huddleston said, of permitting the government to seize "upon a workingman whether a farmer or a mechanic or whatever he may be" and put him to work for a private industry at a soldier's pay so that the owner of the industry might make a profit out of his labor. But others vigorously opposed so thoroughly un-American a procedure. It is evident that a body of opposition to a conscription law exists and will be heard. The resolution, as amended to exclude labor, is meaningless. But let no one suppose that therefore the idea of universal conscription of men, if not actually of money, is dead and need not be guarded against. Loose talk about prohibiting war profits must not be allowed to confuse the issue. Conscription is still a menace.

Another War Truth

AN extraordinary and vitally important historical admission has just been made by David Lloyd George as to the manner in which England entered the war in 1914. It was made in the course of a debate on April 7 in which Prime Minister MacDonald reaffirmed his readiness to consult with the leaders of the Opposition concerning any particular phase of the negotiations of the Naval Disarmament Conference in order that Mr. Baldwin and Mr. Lloyd George should be posted as to exactly what was taking place. Mr. Lloyd George heartily praised this attitude of the Prime Minister and went on to say that it was very important that "we should know what we are being committed to because these commitments are matters of peace and war." He continued as follows (italics ours):

> There has been a good deal of discussion as to whether or not we were committed in 1914. If we were, we were committed to *something which was very vague,* but where it was a question of honor, *whether there was a real commitment or not,* we gave the benefit of the doubt to the others. We don't want those conditions to arise again. We don't want any commitment by which the French will assume we have incurred certain obligations which we did not intend to incur.

We have in these words high confirmation from one of England's war premiers of the worst charges made by the critics of Sir Edward Grey and the Asquith Government as to their plunging England into the hell of the World War at a cost of a million British lives. It was known at the time that the commitments to France had been concealed not only from the British people and their Parliament, but also from a majority of the Cabinet. They had even been jesuitically denied. Only a small inner group knew. But when the fatal hour came Sir Edward Grey and the Prime Minister assured the country that the agreements with France were solemn and binding, admitting of no question and no indecision. The honor of England, they stated, was absolutely involved. Now we have Lloyd George's word for it that, in that same historic Parliament, it was all "very vague," that there was doubt as to whether there was a "question of honor"; but "whether there was a real commitment or not" the statesmen then in charge were willing not only to sentence to death a huge number of their countrymen, but to jeopardize the very existence of Great Britain herself.

This confirms us in our belief that the men who so light-heartedly plunged England into the war should rank among the great criminals of our time. Even before the war began, England's economic and financial position was being seriously challenged by Germany and the United States. It is at this hour not established that she will ever regain the status she held on August 1, 1914. We know that some of her industries have not rewon their former health, and that there has hardly been a time since the armistice that there have not been from 800,000 to 1,500,000 persons out of employment. That the Empire has passed its prime and that it is actually disintegrating is the opinion not merely of foreign observers, but of numerous Englishmen whose judgments are worth having. And this disintegration was enormously accelerated because there was some "very vague" commitment between an inside ring in the British Cabinet and the French government, and their respective military staffs; because, as Lloyd George says, England gave the "benefit of the doubt" to France in 1914; because Edward Grey and one or two others insisted that the sacred honor of England called for the most frightful blood-letting in history!

If Lloyd George now has had a change of heart on this as on so many other matters, that is surely to the good. It is a step forward in government, too, that Ramsay MacDonald is willing to consult with the Opposition, and to let Parliament as well know just what commitments his Government proposes to undertake. But that, of course, is not enough when it comes to a matter of war and peace. There we must continue to take our stand with Alanson B. Houghton, lately our Ambassador to Great Britain. Having been a diplomat and a highly successful one, he insists that no small group of men in high office is wise enough to be intrusted with the power to make war; that no government should have the right to begin hostilities without having a plebiscite of the masses, who are the ones who pay the price when war comes. Sir Edward Grey sat safely at home and never risked his skin after condemning a million of his fellow-citizens to death—a whole generation whose absence goes far to explain why it is that England in industry and commerce seems to lack at this moment its historic aggressiveness and efficiency. The oncoming generations in Europe certainly have the right to demand that they shall not be condemned to death because somebody had a "very vague" commitment with somebody else, and was at the same time able to say whether or not the country should go to war.

Billions to "Reduce"

NOTHING in the imagination of a Dean Swift could be more cynically ironic than the outburst of big-navy propaganda that has followed immediately upon the heels of the London conference. Before the treaty is ratified we have a few striking coincidences. The fleet steams into New York. One hundred and thirty-one airplanes fly over the city in battle formation. The New York *Times* reports:

> "What couldn't they do to us if they dumped some bombs and gas?" a policeman wearing World War service stripes said as he gazed upward from Times Square.
>
> "Such a fleet could wipe out the city in minutes," Lieutenant Commander A. E. Montgomery, who led the parade in a big Hornet-powered Martin bomber, said in answer to the same question later in the day.

The next day front-page reports tell how the 131 planes "destroyed" all of New England, "bombing" Providence, New London, Lowell, and Boston. Nothing is added to these reports. The sky-gazers and newspaper readers, however, are no doubt expected to use their imaginations. Their minds may then be rich soil in which to plant the conclusion: "We must have a very large fleet in order to make it impossible for any other fleet to launch airplanes against our cities." Granting, however, that such a fleet of planes really could wipe out our great cities in minutes, and that no adequate defense could be made, the only logical conclusion is that another war would be too horrible to contemplate, and that if it occurred the size of our navy would make little difference.

These naval airplane demonstrations occurred on the same day that Chairman Britten of the House Naval Committee introduced his bill to authorize, prior to July 1, 1936, the construction of 240,200 tons of new naval vessels. The purpose, of course, is "to give the United States parity with Great Britain." Mr. Britten estimates that the new construction will call for an outlay of $498,000,000 by 1940, which, added to requirements for authorizations already made, will make a total of $937,000,000 to be expended within the next decade. Even so, Mr. Britten is not quite sure that "the expenditure of a billion dollars in the next eight years will properly provide for the national defense in an emergency." Senator Reed of Pennsylvania, returning from the naval conference, is also quoted in an interview as favoring a seven-year building program entailing an average annual naval expenditure of $100,000,000 a year. Senator Robinson takes a similar stand. Chairman Britten is very sad. He wants to build because it is his opinion that the American delegates were "out-traded" at London. But Senator Reed wants to build ships for exactly the opposite reason. "In substance," he is quoted as saying, "we have a chance to build up our fleet, while Great Britain and Japan more or less stand still."

If there is any possibility of heading off this orgy of spending and building, which must result in more international distrust and hence more spending and building, it can be realized only by vigorous outspokenness on the part of those who still believe that the naval limitation treaty, unsatisfactory as it is, is at least not a naval enlargement treaty. We recommend to all our readers the course of Mr. Herbert Fordham, who writes to Representative Robert L. Bacon:

> Thank you for your letter inclosing a copy of an address on boy scouts. While it is gratifying to learn that you favor boys and boy scouts, it might be more helpful to learn that you favor certain ends which some of us intend to achieve:

There follows a list of six of these, of which numbers five and six are:

> 5. We intend not to "reduce" our navy by spending from half a billion to a billion dollars in building ships that we do not need and do not desire.
>
> 6. We intend not to be maneuvered into a war with Great Britain by attempting "parity." To build up our navy to the size of the British navy can have no meaning except preparation for war with Great Britain. Without war against Great Britain we have no need for "parity." With war against Great Britain we need not parity but superiority.
>
> Are you with us?

Apostles of Passive Resistance

THE scene at Peshawar described in an article in the present issue—the spectacle not only of revolutionary leaders voluntarily giving themselves up to the authorities, but of unarmed men deliberately baring their breasts to British rifles and calmly allowing themselves to be shot—all this seems almost incredible to the Western mind.

But it should not be forgotten that the doctrines of non-cooperation and non-violence, though they are at present taken far more in earnest and held against greater provocation in India than they have been anywhere else in the modern world, are not exclusively Indian doctrines. Within the last century the idea of passive resistance has been held by several great predecessors of Gandhi. Gandhi himself, as was pointed out in an article in our issue of May 21, has frequently confessed his debt to Tolstoy. Tolstoy, in turn, acknowledged his debt to William Lloyd Garrison:

> The principle of non-resistance to evil by violence, which consists in the substitution of persuasion for brute force, can only be accepted voluntarily. . . . Garrison was the first to proclaim this principle as a rule for the organization of the life of men. . . . Therefore Garrison will forever remain one of the greatest reformers and promoters of true human progress.

The doctrine of non-violence, in short, though it has remained for India to give it by far the most remarkable application in our time, owes a great debt to American thinkers. We find the doctrine clearly enunciated not only by Garrison, but by Emerson; and it was acted upon by Thoreau.

> The country [remarked Emerson in 1844] is frequently affording solitary examples of resistance to the government, solitary nullifiers, who throw themselves on their reserved rights . . . who embarrass the courts of law by non-jury, and the commander-in-chief of the militia by non-resistance.

In Thoreau we find the American archetype of such figures. He was opposed to a government that was supporting slavery and prosecuting a war of aggrandizement against Mexico. "I quietly declare war with the state," he said, "after my fashion." When he refused to pay his poll tax, he was put in jail. But he declared:

> If the alternative is to keep all just men in prison or give up war and slavery, the state will not hesitate which to choose. If a thousand men were not to pay their tax bills this year, that would not be a violent and bloody measure, as it would be to pay them and enable the state to commit violence and shed innocent blood. This is, in fact, the definition of a peaceable revolution, if any such is possible. If the tax-gatherer, or any other public officer, asks me, as one has done, "But what shall I do?" my answer is, "If you really wish to do anything, resign your office." When the subject has refused allegiance, and the officer has resigned his office, then the revolution is accomplished.

If the followers of Gandhi adhere steadfastly to this plan, their ultimate success is far from hopeless. As they love liberty, let them not break faith.

The Right to Revolution

WILL the right to revolt survive? The Declaration of Independence, as most Americans have forgotten, expressly declared that ". . . whenever any Form of Government becomes destructive of these ends [the right to life, liberty, the pursuit of happiness, and government by consent of the governed] it is the Right of the People to alter or abolish it, and to institute new Government . . ." All over the world the right to rebellion has been and is recognized by everybody save those actually in control of governments. It has been accepted as a matter of course and all successful revolutionists have been acclaimed as heroes and servants of humanity, whereas the unsuccessful have been consigned to the firing squad and contumely. But recent events have caused many to wonder whether the new technique of despots, and the increasingly centralized power of all governments, is not in a fair way to rob the people of their historic right to throw off any government which seems to them intolerable.

That modern inventions have played into the hands of governments nobody will deny. The growing destructiveness of these inventions in the field of warfare tends to strengthen those in power. The bombing ability of airplanes, the use of gas and of tanks augment tremendously the odds in favor of the in's and against the out's. Even more so do the modern press and the modern methods of communication—motor cars, telephone, radio, wireless. When all portions of a country can be explored either by reporters or the spies of authority flying from boundary to boundary in a few hours the possibility of concealing revolutionary preparations becomes slight indeed. The patriots at Concord and Lexington could not have hidden many supplies had British airplanes constantly watched them from overhead. When Washington started his march to Yorktown he crossed the Hudson at Dobbs Ferry, not twenty-five miles from British headquarters. Yet his troops were well through New Jersey before definite knowledge of this movement roused the British in New York City to action. Concealment of troop movements when war has begun can still be achieved, but our Southern and Western States, if they should decide to revolt against the Union, could not do in the way of preparation what the incipient Confederacy did so easily in 1860-61.

If we look abroad the point we are seeking to make becomes even plainer. No serious person believes, today, that there is any likelihood of organized revolt against Mussolini. Some day his whole regime may collapse in a violent convulsion akin to chaos, but the future surely holds in store no new Garibaldi to campaign with a thousand or a hundred thousand. In Russia, too, it appears as if the present dictators could be overthrown only by some great disaster or by complete economic collapse. Vast spaces there are enough in Russia; as far as distance and lack of communications are concerned it might be possible to stage an old-fashioned revolt; but there is surely no opportunity to acquire in advance all the food supplies and the military equipment necessary.

But what of India? That country is today the most interesting on the globe, for the reason that a very old yet new technique of revolution is now being used there which may prove that the Indians, at least, still possess that right of rebellion which our forefathers prized above all else. If non-resistance to physical acts on the part of the overlords, coupled with absolute disobedience, can break down a government that rules without the consent of the governed, the greatest lesson in its history will have been taught the world. Despots will certainly tremble everywhere if they find that airplanes, tear gas, police staves, rifles, and machine-guns are of no avail against a people which welcomes prison and courts death and suffering in preference to the continuance of a regime it detests. You cannot massacre a whole people; not even soldiers can continue for very long to shoot down unresisting men who bare their bosoms to the fatal lead. Certainly England today holds her Indian Empire by the most tenuous of strings; the only question is whether there is sufficient determination and solidarity to go on with the protests and the sacrifice.

Moreover, it is not only the active non-resistance of the Indians—to write an apparent contradiction—which counts. Little by little the English are being forced into an ignoble and an impossible situation. They are insisting upon holding a country which they won by a victory over a third nation; they know that the country is overwhelmingly against them; they are bewildered because the people they dominate refuse to take them at their valuation. They cannot understand that one little man whom they have placed behind bars exercises an authority far beyond their own and has achieved the love of millions they cannot win; they cannot understand why force no longer avails, or the wholesale arrests with which they have filled their jails. They have proscribed the National Congress as an illegal organization; some of their myrmidons have banned the Gandhi cap which even the children are wearing. Nothing avails. There is here a clash not only of civilizations, of national points of view, but of a greater philosophy with a lesser—that of Christ who refused to lift one finger to save himself; who put all his faith in the things of the spirit and the refusal to do evil that good might come therefrom.

Perhaps what is demanded here can only be achieved by a nation like that of the Indians with their mysticism, their spirituality, their faith, their peculiar beliefs, their history. Perhaps; but our faith in the eventual all-conquering nature of Gandhi's weapons is complete. How pitiful it is that Ramsay MacDonald and his Government cannot see it! How disturbing it must be to all members of the Labor Party who are at the same time followers of conscience and lovers of humanity when they read of the police beating unresisting persons until foreign correspondents can look on no longer; when they read that their agents are using all the weapons of imperialistic authority! What a pity they cannot recall what their great statesman Richard Cobden once said: "Can we play the game of fraud, violence, and injustice in Asia without finding our national conscience seared at home?"

Treaty and Peace Lovers

THE letter from Roger Baldwin, which we print in our correspondence columns this week, makes a definite challenge to peace-lovers and moves us to restate our own position on the pending naval limitation treaty. Mr. Baldwin cannot understand why uncompromising devotees of peace do not come out against the treaty, disregarding the fact that they will then find themselves allied with jingo Senators and admirals. He also asks whether this treaty fight will not reveal "the bankruptcy of the middle-class liberals, of the radical pacifists." We hardly think so, but needless to say we respect highly the position of those who see eye to eye with Mr. Baldwin. Our readers have been too often made aware of our willingness to take the uncompromising, idealistic position at any cost, as in the matter of India, for example, to make it necessary for us to assure them that fear of standing with the belligerent admirals and Senators had nothing to do with our stand.

Our position has been this: We have held that the London conference was a miserable failure; that if it should result in our building up to parity, or increasing our navy in any degree, we should consider it a disaster; it would make the word limitation a ghastly joke. We have seen from the time the treaty was written only one possible worth-while outcome of it, and that is the end of all talk of naval rivalry between the United States and Great Britain; precisely as the Washington conference, which seemed to so many liberals nothing but a deception and a snare, put a definite end to the talk of war between Japan and the United States, stopped the admirals from asserting that we were in grave danger in the Pacific, and led our sensational Sunday editors to drop their portrayal of the coming Japanese-American hostilities from the list of their available scare stories. If the ratification of the treaty with Great Britain has a similar effect in stopping the mouths of our war inciters, in and out of uniform, we are for it.

That does not mean that we shall agree for one moment to building up our fleet to parity with Great Britain. We have already stated in clearest terms that this does not need to happen and we have urged (in *The Nation* for April 30) all our readers to do their utmost to prevent the voting of a single additional ship. One of the greatest fights ever waged will be on in Congress after the ratification between those who are opposed to further warships and those super-patriots and manufacturers of ships and guns who will at once be in the breach demanding that we build up to parity. There should be no quarter in this struggle. But we would remind Mr. Baldwin that this fight will be quite as inevitable if the treaty is defeated as if it is ratified. With an intellectual density and moral obtuseness we ourselves cannot remotely fathom, Mr. Hoover has joined his immediate predecessor in declaring that if there is no limitation then there will be a race in armaments between this country and Great Britain. Why there should be this finality of decision we cannot understand. Mr. Hoover and his delegates to London have constantly talked about what the American people want, and how large a navy they will demand in this or that contingency. They have no right to assert that they know. The American people have never been asked to express their views about this whole navy business. No referendum has ever been taken; the politicians and armament-makers have seen to that and will fight to the death any proposal to make legal such a popular vote. We deny the inevitability of any such armament race, but if the treaty is defeated the issue will be joined, the race will be on.

We and those who feel as we do have no zeal whatever for the treaty; we are almost entirely indifferent. We shall be but little more interested if it is defeated than if it is ratified. It is the struggle which is bound to follow after the vote upon it which we wish to stress. We can only say in behalf of the treaty that fighters for peace will be in a little bit better position if it is approved than if it is defeated. We cannot rise to heights of indignation against it. If we could the caliber of the Senators, with one or two exceptions, who are opposing the ratification would fire us to the boiling-point. Our natural inclination is to take after them, whatever they espouse, as a pack of hounds takes up the trail of the fox. The more they talk the greater the discredit they will cast upon this whole naval business. It is really incredible that men like Mr. Stimson and some of his associates should dare to pretend that this treaty bears in the slightest degree any mark of genuine constructive statesmanship. We notice with interest that Dwight Morrow has never opened his lips about it since he returned from London, not even during his recent Senatorial campaign in New Jersey.

Our Attitude Toward Russia

By OSWALD GARRISON VILLARD

WHAT should be the American attitude toward Russia? Because of the renewed anti-Russian campaign, the amazing and humiliating performances of the Fish committee of the House of Representatives, the embargo upon pulp wood, and the demand of Matthew Woll and his followers that by 1932 all trade with Russia be proscribed, the subject has been in recent weeks the foremost one before the country. It is therefore worth examining dispassionately and at length both as to principles and as to policy, all the more so since I find here and there liberals and idealists who are sincerely worried as to what is the right attitude. They ask whether in the name of humanity and liberty the United States should not make effective its disapproval of both the Russian and the Italian dictatorships to aid in bringing them down in a collapse which would enable the masses of both countries to erect more democratic governments.

To this the answer must be no, so far as any censorship of other governments by our government is concerned. Until the Administration of Woodrow Wilson it had been the usual policy of the United States to recognize every de facto government without inquiry as to whether the hands of its masters were free from blood, how they attained power, or what treatment they were according to their subjects. I recall only one case in Europe, that of the Serbian regicides, in which recognition was withheld by any of the great Powers.

The reasons for this answer are obvious. If each country is going to sit in judgment on the manners, morals, and past record of every other, the world will be in for endless trouble and bloodletting. Practically no country, certainly not the United States, can come into court with clean enough hands to be able honestly to put on the judicial ermine. Finally, in numerous countries—the United States, for instance—any given administration is a political one which cannot be trusted to be unaffected by purely political considerations, such as the voice of organized labor, or of organized big business. The relations between nations are easily disturbed, and when disturbed are pacified only at tremendous costs—often in human lives. It is plain, then, that so far as possible they should be kept out of the hands of political officials, especially of such underlings as our present Assistant Secretary of the Treasury, men not directly charged with responsibility for foreign affairs. That gentleman has backed and filled in such an extraordinary way in the present controversy and has displayed so much personal bias as to make it clear that he is without the judicial quality needed in so complex and and serious a situation.

That public sentiment in the United States has not always been content in the past with a policy of recognition as a matter of course, without reference to conditions in the recognized country, is true. During the Czar's regime, after the revelations of George Kennan concerning the horrors of exile in Siberia and of the prisons in eastern Russia, and later after the frightful pogroms in which so many Jewish men, women, and children were butchered in cold blood, strong representations were made to Washington to sever relations with such a country. There was a time, too, when sympathizers with the dire plight of the Armenians sought to have the United States break off relations with the "Terrible Turk." But not until Woodrow Wilson began playing cat and mouse with Mexico in connection with the Huerta regime, if I remember rightly, did we officially begin to use the procedure of recognition as a means of approval or disapproval—or, as in the case of Mexico, as a weapon actually to overthrow the status quo. Actually we have refused to recognize Russia because we disapprove of her economic system, because of her refusal to pay us moneys she owes us, because of our dislike and distrust of her rulers. It is her manners as well as her words which have been used as the excuse for refusal to recognize what is certainly a well-established and going concern.

But there is indubitably a respectable section of the American people who think that we ought to make Russia feel the lash of our hostile public opinion; that it would serve the reds right to break off all trade with them. I know of one who has lived for years in Russia and seen such horrors in the prison camps there that he would gladly join Mr. Woll, though he would be quick to admit that the horrors in our own prisons as proved by the Columbus, Ohio, prison fire and the recent jail uprisings would justify strong foreign protests. These protestants against Russia would have us forbid any American to enter the land of the Soviets and would sever all trade connections. They are morally outraged when *The Nation* and other journals speak of the $700,000,000 of American trade with Russia during the past few years as a reason for not breaking off relations. They say that that is a big-business argument unworthy of idealists; that even if it should throw millions of Americans out of employment we must break off all relations so that the Russian people may realize the low position in the world to which their present rulers have brought them. We must not compromise with evil.

To this the answer has already been given: we are not called upon nor are we morally in a position to intervene in Russia's internal life or to pass judgment upon the acts of her rulers. One has only to think of the feeling which would be aroused in Great Britain if we should sever relations with her because of her terrible misgovernment of India —a record established by the testimony of many high-minded English men and women and admitted by Ramsay MacDonald himself in his pre-office demand for India's complete independence. One can imagine the rage in the American press if France or Italy should propose to cut off diplomatic and trade relations with us because of our lynchings—the blackest stain on any nation in the world—and because of our cruelty to the Negroes. I must admit, however, that when Italy did close her legation in Washington for a period of years because of the refusal of the United States and the State of Louisiana to make any reparation for the shocking mob murder of a number of Italian citizens, there was then little protest. Any radical action by the United States against the Soviets would be readily explained to the Russian people as a purely capitalistic move against communism under the hypocritical guise of a moral protest. The result would be that the business which Russia now sends to the United States would go instead to France, Italy, England, and Germany.

It may be a regrettable state of affairs that we cannot bring moral force to bear on a government that seems to us to be clearly in the wrong. But can we be sure that our judgments as to what is right or wrong in other governments are right? That the information we base our decisions upon is correct? Here is Matthew Woll quoted as asserting that he can exclude all Russian goods under Section 307 of the new tariff law because every worker in Russia is an indentured slave to the brutal and cruel oligarchy which enforces its will upon him. I have no desire whatever to minimize the evil side of the Communist rule in Russia, or to excuse in the slightest degree the horrible injustices and wrongs which are daily perpetrated, but Mr. Woll's statement is an absurdity. The *New Freeman* has just recalled that highly significant story of the visit of some British miners to a Russian mine and their resulting criticisms. The Russian workers answered that their visitors ignored one thing. The British miners were curious. "Our mines *belong to us,*" the Soviet workers answered. There are vast multitudes in Russia who are conscientiously and enthusiastically with the Soviet rulers. It is as near the truth to say of them that they are slaves at forced labor as to assert the same of American labor, which dances to the tune of the capitalist piper, upon whom depends how near to or how far from the line of bare subsistence the worker and his family are compelled to live.

The only safe way to influence other countries which seem to us to be following false gods is by public opinion expressed in the usual way, and not through governmental action. Thus, there are many Americans like myself who feel that the Italian dictatorship is just as odious and just as hostile to our American institutions as the Russian; that the Italian Fascist activities in the United States are far more dangerous and insidious than any Russian Communist activities "in our midst." But we are utterly opposed to the breaking off of diplomatic ties or the cessation of business with Mussolini's subjects. Mussolini and Stalin can no more be overthrown from the outside than can Herbert Hoover be driven out of the White House by foreign pressure.

It is possible that constant foreign criticism may finally influence the policies of both Russia and Italy; indeed, I thought that the recent soft-pedaling of the anti-religious campaign in Russia was plainly due to aroused public opinion in other countries. It is to be hoped that similarly, in time, the rising tide of world-wide resentment against American imperialism in the Caribbean and our cruel, callous, and selfish tariff policy may finally pierce the crust of American self-satisfaction, self-contentment, and conceit.

Meanwhile what should the American policy toward Russia be? First, recognition of the Bolshevist government. It is absurd to do business running into the hundreds of millions with Russia—it will soon be far greater than it is now—and then to deprive our traders of the protection which goes with diplomatic relations. To pretend we are not doing business with the Soviets when we are is certainly unworthy of any decent government.

Secondly, we should court the exchange of visitors from and to Russia in order that Russians may then see for themselves where our institutions are superior to theirs and vice versa; we are without fears that our own securely established institutions will collapse because of the propaganda of such foreign visitors. We should, however, make it perfectly clear to the Russians that in inviting them as guests to this country we expect them to behave as guests and that we shall hold them to that standard. We should point out to them that at home they savagely exile or execute without fair trial anybody whom they suspect of seeking to overthrow their institutions and economic system; that they obviously are without any right to enter our country to interfere with our institutions. This does not mean that Russians should be debarred from making addresses over here or from interpreting their beliefs to us.

Thirdly, we should seek in every way to make the Russians feel that we regard them as members of the human family on equal terms with all others and to include them in every international action. The more we show our confidence in them the better will they react, the quicker will they get over their obsession that we are seeking to combine with other capitalist nations to destroy them. This is of enormous importance because, as long as this situation exists, there exists the threat of war; with it removed I believe that the Russians will prove to be the most pacific of peoples, readier to disarm than any other Continental nation.

Fourthly, as to the so-called menace of "dumping," we have laws upon the statute books aimed to prevent this very procedure (not that I approve of them; the only sound remedy for such an abuse of international trade lies elsewhere). As for the coal and lumber which they are sending to us, they constitute so far only a fraction of 1 per cent of our domestic consumption, and the same is true of the pulp wood that we are now importing. It is not less trade with Russia which we need but more, and as free as it can be made. Especially is this true today when our export trade is in such a parlous condition and Congress and the Administration together seem determined to smash all they can of it. Here, too, the tying of Russia into international trade on the largest possible scale will not only make for peace in the world, but will also tend emphatically to modify the aggressive attitude of these new zealots for communism and to help them to understand and respect the motives and the ideals of other people.

Let us do away with our craven fears of the Communist menace. As I have so often said, if the Bolsheviks can prove that theirs is the best way of life for all mankind, the whole world will accept their doctrines. If they fail to prove this they will probably retrace their steps in a capitalist direction. I suppose it is too much to expect that those like Matthew Woll and Congressman Fish who are so terrified by the Russian menace may see something good in Russia. As a matter of fact, besides the bloody and bad side there is a great deal of fine idealism, and a genuine desire to uplift humanity and to modernize Russia under the Soviets. It behooves us not to ignore this. We are certainly the last people in the world to cast stones indiscriminately, for the sad fact is that of all peoples we are the most feared, disliked, and hated.

Is It Another War?

NO intelligent person has a right to feel surprised at the prediction made the other day by an English speaker at the Williamstown Institute of Politics that another big war is to be looked for between 1935 and 1940. Ever since the Allies forced upon Germany and the other defeated Powers the hateful peace terms of 1919, it has been clear to everybody who cared to see that unless the wrongs then inflicted were redressed and the forces of vengeance which the treaties let loose and magnified were destroyed, it was only a question of time when the world would again be at war. Professor C. Delisle Burns may or may not be right in indicating a date; the precise date does not matter. The important thing is to realize that another war is preparing, and that nothing short of herculean effort by the friends of peace can prevent its arrival.

What, in substance, are the conditions that are breeding war? The essence of the political situation in Europe today is the existence, as the direct result of the peace treaties, of territorial and political arrangements which can be maintained only by force. The most obvious evidences of this fact are the offensive and defensive alliances which France has industriously built up with the new states of Eastern Europe, and the Little Entente which certain of those states have formed among themselves. Only by standing together can France and the succession states hope to retain the political control over Germany and Austria which they wrested from the Peace Conference. How unnatural is their position and how great their fear that they may lose it appear clearly enough in the extreme irritation occasioned in France by the recent intimation by Italy and Germany that the peace treaties must be revised, and the heated resentment of France and Poland over some indiscreet remarks of a German minister, Herr Treviranus.

Hence the extraordinary spectacle of loud or fervent professions of peace balanced by systematic preparations for war. In spite of the League of Nations, in spite of Locarno and the Paris anti-war pact, the nations that fought Germany in 1914-18, or that profited by the defeat of Germany and Austria in those years, are getting ready to fight again. Armies and navies, air forces, land and seacoast defenses, chemical warfare, the organization of industry for the production of war materials, the formulation of plans of campaign—all these familiar incidents of "preparedness" are being more sedulously attended to today than at any time since the World War armies were demobilized, especially in the United States. It is idle to protest that this intense activity and huge financial outlay are designed only to meet the needs of national or international police or the aggression of some nation that may lose its head and run amuck. What is going on is deliberate preparation for war, and for a war whose justification will be found in the necessity of maintaining by force a treaty arrangement which could not otherwise last a year.

What, if anything, can be done to fend off the catastrophe? There is little to be hoped for in declarations of good intentions. No more solemn renunciation of war has been or can be made than that contained in the Kellogg-Briand anti-war pact, yet that pact is being openly flouted by every important nation that subscribed to it. Nothing is to be gained by affecting to see a dawning millennium in the conclusion of treaties whose underlying purpose, once they are scrutinized, is only to make an unholy peace more secure. Of all the agencies ever set up for the cultivation of international good-will the League of Nations has proved itself one of the feeblest, and the World Court can only sanctify what the Paris negotiators decreed.

The possibility of averting another war lies in other directions. Much may be done by unsparing exposure of the forces, especially the political forces, that are working for war. A generation ago the ambitions of imperial Germany were the greatest single menace to world peace. Today that role is played by France and its allies, and by Italy with its plans for combating France in Eastern Europe. There must be unyielding resistance to every legislative or executive action that looks toward an increase of armaments or industrial organization for war. There must be insistence, wherever and whenever a plea for justice can be heard, that the peace treaties shall, as soon as possible, be revised. Not all the wrongs of the peace can now be righted, but many of them can, and until they are the world will try in vain to build a stable peace on injustice or to make vengeance and plunder, if they are well stuck to, comport with international fellowship. It will be no light task to accomplish any of these things; nothing but concerted effort can make an effective impression upon any of them; but unless they are accomplished we cannot hope to escape another war.

The League Shuns Disarmament

THE Assembly of the League of Nations is again at work. A year has elapsed since it last met. What has it accomplished during the twelve-month on the most important of all issues before the world—disarmament and peace? The answer is—nothing, save that it has sponsored the publication of some figures as to the increasing armaments of the militaristic nations, which figures constitute its own grave indictment. For it has been charged with certain responsibilities under the Treaty of Versailles which created it. In this, its organic act, the chief Powers that sponsored it pledged themselves to disarmament. Eleven years have elapsed. There has been no decrease, but steady increase in expenditures for war. The Geneva report is that no less than $3,750,000,000 was what fifty-three nations, Christian and otherwise, spent in 1929 in preparation for the next war. The officials were reported to be "optimistic" because this disarmament bill was only $100,000,000 larger than a similar bill for 1928! They maintained that optimism in the face of the fact that the world launched 50 per cent more cruisers in 1929 than in the last years before the World War and that it has today three times as many under construction as in 1913. Indeed, during the past year the only action which can be construed as pointing in the direction of limitation of armaments came as the result of action by a non-member—the United States. The League's Disarmament Commission meets, talks, studies, adjourns. It is explained that it is "clearing the ground," "exploring the bases for land disarmament"—"a grave and difficult task."

But the fact remains that it rejected with contumely the only clear-cut and sincere proposal to disarm and to disarm at once ever made to it—the Russian plan that was brought to it by M. Litvinov.

The growing danger of war is the complete answer to the excuse that the problem is difficult. Granted that it is, there is no time to lose. It is idle to waste years exploring the bases for scientific disarmament when every preparation for the approaching catastrophe is under way; when the situation between Italy and France is so delicate that the French do not dare even to permit the Minister of War or the foreign military attachés to witness their High Savoy maneuvers near the Italian border lest dangerous military importance be attributed to them. They have not had to be so secretive about some of their other maneuvers. At Lyons, for instance, they have this summer staged a night air attack upon the city under the direct supervision of the General Staff. As far as possible the exact war conditions were simulated. Thus, the populace being notified by sirens that the "enemy fliers" were at hand, took refuge in their cellars and in the specially prepared bomb-proofs, while the city was plunged into complete darkness. The fire department was called out to extinguish pretended blazes, the Red Cross representatives in gas masks took care of "poisoned" and "wounded" citizens, and the "enemy fliers" constantly threw down upon the city articles intended to represent gas or other bombs. The anti-aircraft cannon fired steadily until two o'clock in the morning—in short, nothing was left undone to represent war-time conditions.

With what result? The commanding general, Serrigny, in his official comment upon the maneuvers declared that the anti-aircraft defense had not sufficed to save the city from any massed attack from the air. In recording these facts General Berthold von Deimling, the former German corps commander, declares in the *Berliner Tageblatt* that in every similar instance, notably in recent "attacks" upon Milan, London, and Paris, the result was the same—a complete fiasco on the part of the defense. As for air counter-attacks, General von Deimling declares that there can be no hope of success for the counter-attackers unless there is sufficient advance notice of the attack and the direction from which it is to be expected to enable the defensive blow to be struck at exactly the right time and place before the enemy's objective has been attained. He points out in this connection that the development of the bomber has gone on so fast that it can not only carry the enormous load to be dumped, but can now actually defend itself against attack. General von Deimling thus comes to the same opinion as General von Seeckt, who has just resigned as commander of the German army, that about the only way of counter-attacking is to strike the enemy on his own territory before he can cross the frontier. The future war in the eyes of these experts becomes then nothing but a mad rush by all parties to the conflict to be the first to get their airplanes over the frontiers and to destroy immediately all enemy chemical, automobile, and airplane factories, all flying fields, and important towns.

General von Deimling cannot refrain from asking, in view of this prospect that all important cities that can be attacked will be immediately bombed, gassed, and set on fire, how any military department or general can pretend hereafter that any amount of preparedness will protect any of these strategic points from utter destruction. He is right. The old argument that safety can be secured by a given preparation has been utterly finished. A million infantry scattered along the seaboard, and a full arsenal of anti-aircraft cannon besides, will offer no guaranty whatsoever that Birmingham and Manchester and Edinburgh will not be bombed within twenty-four hours after the declaration of war. "Is it not suicidal mania," he asks, "for the European states with their sensitive industries to destroy their economic life and their culture by poison, by fire, and by shells?"

From his own people the General demands in the coming election a choice of representatives in the Reichstag to form a government absolutely opposed to the ideal of armaments and war. He believes, however, that it is only by the rousing of the masses of the various peoples that safety will finally be attained. He does not mention the League of Nations. We repeat that upon its handling of this question depends beyond all else its success and its usefulness to the human race. It must demand prompt action by the leading Powers; it must make them prove that they were sincere when they signed the disarmament clause of the Treaty of Versailles, when they went to Locarno, and when they signed the Kellogg Pact. If they will not act they brand themselves not only with insincerity and hypocrisy, but with complete responsibility, even now, for the next conflict.

Soldiers Old, Soldiers New

By OSWALD GARRISON VILLARD

I

Coblenz, October 6

IMAGINE a great plateau high above a city on the Rhine, framed on two sides by tall autumn-tinged trees and offering on the left beautiful views to the hills on the banks of the river; elsewhere charming prospects to far-distant hills which at the horizon, under a dark, lowering sky, appear to be mountains. Picture to yourself next in the right angle made by the trees in the background four small, well-separated grandstands with a high speakers' tower in front of the first. Then look from the grandstands and people over the plain before you upon a sea of men in uniform, 167,000 strong—so the loud speakers insist—and you have a vision of the eleventh annual field day of the Stahlhelm, the militaristic American Legion of Germany.

It is indeed a sea of humanity—I use this overworked, worn-out phrase deliberately because the field-gray of the uniforms and the unending ranks of men do suggest waves of the ocean. But the waves of the ocean are restless; this mass of gray humanity stands for hours and hours in a wet field without food or drink, yet without restlessness, with perfect discipline. At no time is there a marked volume of sound from them; not even when the command "at rest" comes after long standing at attention with knapsacks on backs. And these are by no means youths; the bulk of the "Steel Helmets" are men who fought for four years—to be a *Front-Stahlhelmer* one must have been six months on a firing line. Here and there are officers fairly covered with decorations; the number of iron crosses one sees is incalculable. Many of the men have traveled two nights and a day without sleep; 1,700 motor buses have helped to bring them from all parts of Germany. They have been quartered from Leipzig to Bingen-on-the-Rhine. Every *Gau,* or district, has brought more men than it notified headquarters it expected to furnish. Hence a delay of two and a quarter hours in the beginning of the ceremonies while steamers make additional trips to nearby towns to bring patient men to join the still more patient waiting throngs, whose composure is in no wise affected by two sharp drenching showers.

Men in gray, men in gray, still they come. At last the end. Then a salute of eleven guns, and the leaders arrive with much ceremony to take their places on the speakers' stand. They receive no greeting cheer. These are soldiers, not idle spectators, before them. Even then the speeches do not begin. From the right flank comes a procession of no less than 1,200 flags, flags of all the branches and districts and sections and states, chiefly the German battle-flag, since the Stahlhelm is forbidden to use the old black, white, and red of the empire and will not carry the white, red, and gold of the republic. In the stiff wind the flags flutter gloriously, the varied colors more vivid than if the sun were shining. Franz Seldte, the commander and founder, gives the order *"Das Ganze—kehrt"* and the whole mass faces the flags as they pass around the rear of the assemblage. For forty minutes the soldiers stand rigidly at attention; for forty minutes a band pounds out one single marching air; for forty minutes Seldte and his second in command, ex-Lieutenant Colonel Duesterberg, stand at the salute. Not until this theatrical spectacle is over can the exercise begin with praise of the dead of the war by a clergyman, introduced by a superb hymn played by massed bands.

Yes, there are clergymen still to be found here to lend themselves to this pagan worship of Mars. This one, like our Mannings at home, is on intimate terms with God, whom he has apparently forgiven for granting victory to the Allies and permitting them to occupy German territory for twelve long years. At least he is as certain today as his brethren were at the outbreak of the war that the Germans are a chosen people; that God has great things still in store for them if they will but unite in the spirit of the Stahlhelm. More than that, he is certain that the two million Germans who fell did not die in vain. That he iterates and reiterates. Somehow out of their suffering, out of the waste of their lives, Germany is to be made over, according to the prescription of physician Seldte. This prescription, after another moving national hymn sung by all, Herr Seldte proceeds to give once more. It is no firebrand speech; his utterances, like Hitler's, are taming down. With his demand for a revision of the Versailles treaty, for the withdrawal of the monstrous lie that Germany was solely guilty of beginning the World War, every liberal can agree. Sinister, however, is the slogan he again voices: "Victory rests upon sacrifices and *arms.*" For the Hitler victory at the polls Seldte takes the credit, for it was the Stahlhelm, he says, which led in the work of freeing Germany from internal and external enemies. He reads—to "bravos"—the resolutions just passed by the board of directors and sees no inconsistency in urging complete political unity for all Germans while demanding also the complete abandonment of the "fruitless Marxism of the Prussian dictatorship"—Duesterberg had put it more clearly the day before, saying that "that nation which first removes the poison of Marxism from its veins by a nationalism embracing all classes will win the war." Germany has only to follow the Stahlhelm and unite itself, and then "the Germans alone, in spite of everything, will be the true victors in the first [!] World War." Neither of these self-appointed leaders knows exactly how the twelve or more million Germans who voted for the Communists and Socialists are to be weaned from Marxism—save perhaps by knocking them on their heads. But still they cry: "Away with all petty quarrelings of brothers"—and still they are certain that they are on the high road to achieving all the purposes of the Stahlhelm. And while they put their faith in sacrifice and arms, they declare in the next breath that they know that Germany can carry on no war today and that they are for achieving their ends by legal means. Of course, we also hear the familiar words of the American Legion: "We, having known war, want peace."

Franz Seldte has finished. In unison the bands play and the crowd sings—the Deutschland song. Next the dedication of the flags of the newly organized districts—this flag business plays an enormous part in the life of the Stahlhelm. And then as Seldte and Duesterberg march past the front lines of the troops, like kings and field marshals of old, the crowd of spectators melts away—among them three genuine Italian Fascists, numerous brown-shirted fascist followers of Hitler, the vicious anti-Semite Hakenkreuzler, and the correspondent of the Paris *Matin,* with plenty of material to stir the anger and blood of Poincaré, the French nationalists, the Camelots du Roi. Is there, indeed, not a magnificent army *in posse* here? My neighbor, who wears its uniform, told me so last evening at supper. Large enough, he thinks, to beat France. . . . But if the crowd hurries off, the soldiers stay. Not until eleven hours after their arrival does the tail end of the procession, twenty-seven kilometers in length, leave the field.

A great day for the Stahlhelm—its greatest, so they say around me. Many more present than in Berlin, far more than in Munich, and every man paid for his transportation out of his own pocket. One hundred and sixty-seven thousand men, not even one-tenth of the German war dead. These fields beyond the living could hold all the wickedly butchered. But they would crowd the green-and-brown-carpeted hillside even to the very edge with its somber trees. If these ghosts stand there, what are they saying of this return to the worship of the god that cost them their lives and plunged all Europe into desolation?

It is pleasanter to go down to the city and stand in front of the castle by the reviewing stand. By four in the afternoon the hosts appear; not until nine does the last *Gau* come into sight. The impressiveness of that review cannot be denied. These men, after this exhausting day without food and the sleepless nights, are amazingly vigorous, their bearing erect, their strength unchallenged. Clean-shaven, even the Bavarians (what has become of the German beard?), with only a very few Falstaffian paunches and strikingly few spectacles. These older men have kept themselves in marvelous physical trim since the war. Indeed, it is the veterans who do the historic goose-step best as they pass in front of the leaders and who win the "bravos" of the experts around me. The younger men, the new crop of Stahlhelmers, are green enough in their marching and often pale-faced.

Here comes a group of miners from Essen clad in medieval guild uniforms to break the monotony of the field-gray. Whenever laboring men appear—and there are many, for the Stahlhelm is bent upon making inroads into the unions—the crowd applauds and cries out the Stahlhelm fascist salute, *Front-Heil* (success, or fortune, at the front). The younger men chant it like a college boy's slogan; as they go down the narrow street into the town they answer the *Front-Heil* of sympathetic townspeople with the fascist arm salute. Alongside the reviewing stand, among the onlookers, is no less a person than the Crown Prince himself, with two of his brothers, watching the honors go to Seldte and Duesterberg. Night before last he took the salute at the grand tattoo which marked the ending of the torchlight parade. They say he was cheered; pictures of him sold well in the crowd. Yet it would be idle to claim that he made a stir; the local newspapers hardly mentioned his appearance. As for the crowds, even for Sunday, they were not great. The Stahlhelm sympathizers were there, but not the workers and the mass of middle-class people, and of these is Germany.

A million men the Stahlhelm claims. There are still sixty million Germans. Seldte's work is but begun; it has begun enough to injure Germany by stirring the chauvinists abroad to bitterness and rage. It has earned the right, both by its numbers and by the enthusiasm of its members, to be taken seriously. It is, finally, the direct product of Versailles, of the foolish and stupid policy of the Allies, notably the French, of the twelve years of occupation by foreign troops, of the demand for impossible reparations payments, and of the steadfast refusal of the war victors to disarm and to keep their solemn pledges given in the Treaty of Versailles. When the Stahlhelm demands a return to the Wilson program of the Fourteen Points, it takes a sound and entirely justifiable position. To the Allies' violation of their armistice pledges is above all else due the extraordinary, the impressive, the entirely saddening, and, probably, the menacing spectacle I have just described.

II

Soldiers new in Germany have been on trial in Leipzig on charges of high treason before the Supreme Court of the Reich. The verdict, dismissal for the two active officers and a year and a half in a fortress for the three accused, less the time already served, was cabled two days ago. What has interested me has been less whether they were really guilty of treason than what manner of men these new Reichswehr officers are. They told their story plainly in court. If there is bitter disappointment in democratic circles here, it can be understood. For they and the Allies intended that this should be a democratic army. The old cadet corps, in one of which Hindenburg was educated, were abolished, and service in the ranks was made the only avenue to commissioned rank. The old hateful caste distinction between officers and men was successfully done away with, for from the September maneuvers here come excellent reports of the camaraderie of officers and men. Instead of sitting far apart in the rest periods, the correspondents report that the men gathered around their officers as the center of their life. That neither discipline nor efficiency has suffered is similarly the testimony of observers; indeed, only the highest praise is given to the troops, and the men are reported to have responded to the terrific demands upon them in a remarkable way.

All the more striking, therefore, is the evidence brought out at Leipzig, not only by the prisoners at the bar but by numerous witnesses, that the new Reichswehr is deeply affected by the nationalist movement; that numerous officers have begun to dabble in politics, to take sides between the Left and the Right parties, and to show the same tendencies toward megalomania and militaristic exaltation of their profession which was so objectionable in a large portion of the officer caste in the old army and navy. The two active officers, Lieutenants Ludin and Scheringer, are certified by their superiors to have been most excellent officers. One is the son of a professor, the other of a retired general. What was their grievance? The army was not being conducted "nationally enough," said Lieutenant Ludin. More should have been done to protect the officers. From what? Why, "in the newspapers, theaters, and literature, the army and the officers are being constantly attacked. The government has done nothing against this." "Do you think that the government can close the theaters if there are isolated instances of attacks upon the army or its officers?" asked the presiding judge. "Yes, indeed," Lieutenant Ludin replied, "that the government could have done." Obviously, he and his fellows were but a step from the point of view that led officers to run any civilian through who "insulted the uniform."

A little later, Lieutenant Ludin denounced the government, saying: "We can have no confidence in the government of this republic which continually thinks like pacifists and does not protect the interests of the army." A final grievance of Lieutenant Scheringer was that their commander in Ulm had once ordered them not to appear in the streets in uniform at a time of Communist demonstrations and much excitement. Other military witnesses declared that the government was "pulling the ethical ground out from under them by its conduct." When asked whether they would shoot their fellow-citizens by order, some of the witnesses said that they would shoot either Communists or Nationalists if they were ordered to do so, but it was evident that it would be far easier for them to give the order to fire on the Communists than on those who "think nationally." "That is the most difficult question you could put to us," said one officer. Another declared that there was a great difference between loyalty to the constitution of the republic and to the country itself. One could be loyal to the constitution and still be opposed to an administration which did not think nationalistically enough. Lieutenant Scheringer openly stated, by the way, that he thought the Reichswehr should never shoot at the National-Socialists.

The Leipzig court had a difficult task before it. The prisoners were obviously very young, mentally underdeveloped, and politically entirely uneducated. Their testimony suggested commonplace freshmen rather than officers of twenty-five or twenty-six who had risen from the ranks. If the court found them guilty, it knew that they would be treated as martyrs by the Hitlerites. If the court dismissed them as *dumme Jungen* (stupid boys) it would appear to them and their associates that they had the right to go ahead to organize the Reichswehr politically as a branch of Hitler's "Nazis," and it would encourage such Socialists as may happen to be in the service to recruit for their party. In other words, it would be giving permission to the Reichswehr to destroy itself by internal political conflicts or to become, perhaps, the instrument of a single party—even though that party should be, as Hitler's is today, a minority party. To that, however "nationally" it thinks, the great bulk of the German people do not belong and, I believe, will not belong unless driven to it by suffering, want, economic and spiritual misery and exhaustion, and the criminal folly and stupidity the Allies and America have shown in dealing with Germany from the day of its surrender to the present hour.

Berlin W.10, October 31, 1930.
Herkuleshaus, Herkulesbruecke

The Right Honorable J.Ramsay MacDonald,
Prime Minister,
Downing Street,
Whitehall,
London.

My dear Prime Minister :-

The candour and frankness of your letter can only cement and honor our friendship. Nonetheless, I must regret that I wrote you, for the very heat of your words shows that I did precisely what I had not meant to do - burdened you and roused you when you need all your precious strength for more worth while things than confuting an obscure, itinerant editor.

I cannot now venture either to answer your letter in detail or to seek a controversy. That again would be an imposition and an arrogance. I have no doubt that, if I held your exalted office even for a day and felt the weight of its dreadful responsibility, I might look upon such problems as India in another light. To judge by ninety five per cent of the men I have known well who have taken high office, I should soon be reproaching old editorial friends for maintaining the positions I once assumed prior to taking office and asking them why they should expect me to lead by bold iteration of opinions once held before public opinion was "led and brought into line ". I might then even apply to the attitude of a given editor the word "cowardly" and thus enable him to add a new adjective to the many hundred epithets accumulated by him in the course of a life time of journalism ! All of which merely means that the chasm which separates a responsible official from an unofficial scribe remains unbridged.

I am sorry, indeed, if we of The Nation have given currency to any unfounded or ignorant statements and should be grateful to any secretary of yours who would, hereafter, send us corrections. As to Lord Irwin, I referred, of course, to his original statement of November 1929, subsequently weakened by himself and others. May I point out that others beside myself are deluded? Within two weeks I have seen a report of a lecture of our mutual friend S.K. Ratcliffe, in which after severely criticizing Ghandi, he also severely blamed your Government for its failure to live up to Lord Irwin's promise. I do not see how you can find it possible to deny that the Indians, particularly the moderates, have since then repeatedly demanded that either the House of Commons or the Viceroy make some further pronouncement of the attitude of the Round Table Conference concerning Dominion status in order to clear the air of the vagueness purposely created by other responsible party leaders after Irwin's first clear promise of Dominion status. The whole world knows that no such further pronouncement has been made; that most of the Indian leaders have lost faith in the British Government's words in consequence, and that even those who were willing to accept Dominion status last May, have now joined the ranks of the extremists and are demanding complete independence as a consequence. You speak of public opinion as not being prepared. I know of no better way to prepare it than to state the ultimate aim in the India situation and then to defend it and to be prepared to stand or fall by the result.

I have no doubt that many of the atrocity stories are exaggerated for partisan purposes, but I can bring you entirely trustworthy American witnesses, one extremely pro-English, who witnessed and reported shocking things and who were themselves the victims of the strict censorship which, despite official denials, has been enforced in India. Before I sailed, the great United Press put into my hands concrete evidence of this censorship in the form of mutilated dispatches.

Into a defense of Ghandi I cannot enter here, but you will pardon my amazement at the bitterness of your denunciation. I well know the difficulties of the situation. I realize as well, perhaps, as any outsider can what the consequences of a sudden withdrawal of English authority and officialdom would be. Yet I feel that there is nothing so important in the whole world as the triumph of the principle of non-resistance, which you characterize as 'sentimental non-resistance'. With the civilized world perishing in the sight of our eyes because it will not give up the absolutely futil and unchristian resort to force, to me the fact that so deeply religious a man as yourself reacts so violently and antagonistically to this practical application of the fundamental teaching of Jesus

Christ is utterly discouraging. I deny that there has been any appreciable violence or bloodshed on the part of Ghandi's followers; that has been on the other side. But I do not deny that, if the present situation in India continues without a clear-cut definite promise of Dominion status, with the date attached, bloodshed will inevitably come, not because of Ghandi, but because of the unwillingness of those who do not profess his doctrines to remain content with the situation - a situation which has just sent Nehru to jail again for two years and keeps Ghandi in jail without trial under a John Company statute of 1829.

I admit frankly that never in my life time has there been a problem in which the ideals of democracy and self-determination have been put to such a severe practical test as this. I am sorry that I cannot compromise and, as Wendell Phillips once said, that "I must entrench myself upon principle and leave the working out of details to Almighty God". Doubtless, you will reply that the responsibility of your office forbids you the luxury of dealing in any such sentimental nonsense. But I must continue to cast in my lot with the sentimental nonsense of my grandfather, Mr.Garrison, from whom, through Tolstoi, Ghandi received his idea of sentimental non-resistance. I must do this even at the risk of seeming to you, whose character I so highly esteem and whose friendship I so value, to be merely pleasing myself with saying "Lord,Lord" and forgetting "that that pleasant little exercise may not only be futile but be mischievous", of continuing to persist "in an easy-oozy way of facing life in a half dreamy and rather cowardly way."

Good heavens, my dear friend, you took the idealist way in 1914 and know how hard it was and what men called you. Can you really think that I have chosen the easier way ? The simplest thing in the world for an editor would be to dismiss the whole thing, as so many of my colleagues have done, by simply saying:" MacDonald knows best. Ghandi is a thousand years ahead of his time. Let him have his way and he will reduce India to collapse and anarchy. The world must put down impractical visionaries and fanatics like this ".

Again accept my gratitude for your outspoken candour and remember, please, that however misguided I may be I remain,

Your very sincere friend

The Way to Disarm

IT is time that the curtain was rung down on the disarmament farce that is being played at Geneva. Not only are the debates in the Preparatory Commission getting nowhere, but it is obvious that the talking delegates have no real heart in the business and that their governments have no intention of reducing armaments in any manner or to any degree that would make the reduction worth while. Such hope as once obtained of achieving disarmament through a world-wide international agreement has dwindled to a shadow, and for the Geneva discussions to go on is a pure waste of time for all the parties concerned and a serious injury to the cause which the conference was expected to promote.

The subject of the great disarmament play was set by the framers of the Covenant of the League of Nations, and the performances have been going on intermittently for more than ten years. Article 8 of the Covenant recognized that "the maintenance of peace requires the reduction of national armaments to the lowest point consistent with national safety and the enforcement by common action of international obligations," and bound the Council, "taking account of the geographical situation and circumstances of each state," to formulate "plans for such reduction for the consideration and action of the several governments." By the same article the members of the League further undertook "to interchange full and frank information as to the scale of their armaments, their military, naval, and air programs, and the condition of such of their industries as are adaptable to warlike purposes." The opening paragraph of Part V of the Treaty of Versailles, setting forth the restrictions imposed upon the armaments of Germany, declares that Germany undertakes to observe the restrictions "in order to render possible the initiation of a general limitation of the armaments of all nations."

The League began its task by creating, in 1920, a commission of military and naval experts, only to learn shortly that the experts could not agree. It then tried a commission of experts and politicians, which sat until 1924 and accomplished exactly nothing. In 1924 it promulgated the Geneva protocol with its "sanctions" for any nation that ventured war without the blessing of the League, but the protocol went to the lumber room, where it belonged. Then, in 1925, came the Preparatory Commission, charged with the duty of preparing a program for a general disarmament conference. The commission hitched along until March, 1928, drew up a draft convention which satisfied nobody, and saw agreement vanish into thin air. The Kellogg-Briand pact, with its renunciation of war "as an instrument of national policy," offered a ray of hope and the commission met again, to be sidetracked for the London naval conference with its delusive program of parity, and chilled by the realization that none of the nations which had accepted the peace pact was abating materially its preparations for war.

Now, after a recess of more than a year and a half, the Preparatory Commission is again preparing, with the United States undertaking to boss the job. Anyone who can discover progress in the daily reports from Geneva has indeed a discerning mind. Bundles of old straw are being threshed over again and some new bundles have been added to the pile. Italy and France are at odds over naval parity, my lord Cecil is shocked when the arming of British merchant vessels is mentioned, France has not yet accumulated sufficient security to permit it to do anything and stands aghast at the suggestion of making public the exact state of its armaments, the allies of France have no minds of their own but keep their eyes fixed on the Quai d'Orsay, while Germany and Russia make the delegates shiver by declaring, the former that it expects the disarmament requirements of the Versailles treaty to be carried out, the latter that it is not interested in pretense but wants something genuine and thoroughgoing. The honors of evasion and dissent seem pretty evenly divided between Great Britain, France, and the United States, but the gaudiest decoration thus far has been won by the United States, which, after graciously accepting a variety of proposals that made no great difference to it, flatly refused to approve a budgetary restriction on expenditures for armaments. What with backing and filling, mutual suspicion, and repeated undoing of what had apparently been agreed upon, the outlook for agreement has become as insubstantial as a dream and as gloomy as a London fog.

There is no reasonable hope of bringing order out of this chaos. The only way to disarm is to disarm, and the United States has a greater obligation than any other Power to lead the way. If the United States wishes to redeem its reputation for sincerity, let it cut loose from the Geneva conference, call a halt in its own program of naval building, and reduce its present monumental outlay for preparedness. Its own hands would then be clean and other nations would have a great obstacle taken from their paths.

On the German Front

By OSWALD GARRISON VILLARD

Berlin, December 17

"ALL QUIET ON THE WESTERN FRONT"—but not in Berlin. Nobody had ever heard of Erich Maria Remarque until his book appeared and sold to the extent of one million copies in Germany alone. Now the German government, plus one Dr. Goebbels, National Socialist, has added enormously to his fame by forbidding the movie version of the book—and thereby has antagonized every liberal and every liberal element in Germany. Indeed, so disheartening is the action of Brüning and Herr Curtius that there are those who fear that the date of the beginning of the collapse of the German democracy will be December 11, 1930, and that the fate of this Republic will always be linked with the banning of a single film.

For, say what you please, the forbidding of "All Quiet on the Western Front" has been a surrender to the mob. It is notice that if organizations or parties do not like a certain play or production they need only demonstrate sufficiently to have their will. I am well aware of the government's defense, for I listened for three-quarters of an hour to a very high official trying to convince the foreign-press correspondents of the justice of his position. He was very glib—almost eloquent. He showed at once the complete ease and self-possession of the trained lawyer and he pleaded his case with near-eloquence and obvious sincerity. Yet I do not believe that he convinced a single listener or that any foreigner left the room with his opinion that the government has yielded to the Hitler gang being changed one iota. Indeed, privately I am told by officials that that is really the case; that the Prussian police could have insisted successfully that the performance go on in Berlin, but that in Hamburg, Hanover, Leipzig, and many other cities this would have been impossible.

It certainly cannot be denied that the outpouring of men at the Nollendorf Platz Theater was as menacing as it was impressive. Americans must not forget that Germany today is a series of armed camps. There are nearly a million uniformed and well-organized men in the Stahlhelm, the militaristic veterans' organization; there are about three and one-half millions in the Reichsbanner, the republican organization of war veterans and young men who consider themselves the special guard of the Republic. There are at least 500,000 brown-shirted Hitlerite Hakenkreuzler, 300,000 in the secret Communist "Red Front" organizations, and fully 700,000 in the loyal "Young German Order" and similar associations. Not a day goes by but some of the men in these organizations are killed or wounded, not a day on which some of their meetings are not broken up by force. Force is the order of the day. For example, the Reichsbanner, with whose aims all republican readers of *The Nation* would surely sympathize, has openly declared within the last week that from now on it is going to take the aggressive. Thus, in Magdeburg, where Hitler is scheduled to speak soon, its leaders have served notice that they will do a little interfering with free speech and free assembly themselves. They have served notice on the "Nazis" that Hitler will be permitted to speak only if 300 seats in his meeting are given to the Reichsbanner and if one of its speakers shall have the right to orate for one hour in reply to Hitler! The head of the police has called the leaders on both sides into consultation and it is now expected that he will forbid both the Hitler meeting and the one planned by the Reichsbanner for the same evening, on the ground that they both menace the public order.* So far has the anxiety of the Berlin police gone that all outdoor public assemblies, all demonstrations, all marching in column formation has been forbidden. Not even the unemployed are permitted to march to the city hall to protest against their plight.

Germany is seething politically—there can be no question of that. Two nights ago there were four simultaneous Reichsbanner meetings to protest against the banning of the Remarque film. The one that I attended was crowded to the doors, with a fine orderly crowd of working people and small shopkeepers; a prince of ancient lineage sat upon the stage in the Reichsbanner uniform. Long before eight o'clock the police barred entrance into both halls because they were dangerously crowded. The Hitler meetings are jammed similarly and would be, I think, even if there were no orders issued to the faithful to attend. On the streets outside of these meetings, even in the center of the city with large numbers of police in readiness, there are frequently dangerous affrays. Tomorrow night the former executive officer of the cruiser Emden, Kapitän-Leutnant von Mücke, one of the most gallant figures of the World War, is going to start to denounce Hitler, his associates, and all his works, of which he, von Mücke, was formerly a distinguished part—concerning which he now proposes to turn state's evidence. No more lurid posters were ever displayed than those announcing this meeting, for they declare that von Mücke will "tear off the mask" and reveal that many of Hitler's immediate supporters are "thieves, liars, falsifiers, and men guilty of crimes against morality." It is generally expected that this will be a battle royal—I profoundly regret that a previous engagement in Munich will prevent my attending this delightful party.

* The Hitler meeting was duly forbidden.—EDITOR THE NATION.

Meanwhile, all of this is very hard upon the nerves of the government and of the "Schupos" or police. Night after night in every city these men have to do extra and hazardous duty—a police colonel was murdered in Hamburg two weeks ago. They are nice-looking men, spotlessly uniformed and extremely well equipped. I watched them handling the huge and really menacing Hitler demonstrations—undoubtedly staged as a test of the efficiency of the Berlin Hitler shock troops—and admired their self-restraint. When it comes, however, to sailing into a mob with their hard-rubber clubs, they are accused of brutality and lack of discrimination; but one of the highest officials in the land declared to me that the police have orders to be savage when the order to disperse a crowd comes and that no other policy will make possible the maintenance of order or keep the Republic safe.

The Republic does rest today upon the force of the police and it is admitted that the Minister of the Interior, Herr Severing, has them well in hand and that they are zealously loyal. Whenever a higher police officer shows the slightest sign of friendliness to the "Nazis," he is rigidly dealt with. None the less, the Communists complain that the "Schupos" refuse them aid when they are attacked or raided by the Hitlerites, while the latter also violently denounce Herr Severing and his "police-hounds." The "Schupos" are certainly not the least bit weak in dealing with the Communists, who appear today much less aggressive than the other groups. I have also been to some of their meetings only to be shocked by the signs of want, fatigue, and hunger, the poor clothes, the utterly pallid faces, the plain evidences of a desperate struggle for life, with much resultant premature aging.

Yes, Berlin seethes. The Germans, unlike our own people, talk and think in political terms—largely driven to it by the all-prevailing anxiety, the fear as to the future, the terrible unemployment; by the hope that somewhere they will hear a word of cheer and encouragement. "Hugenberg is our only hope," writes to me the wife of a distinguished university professor. There are multitudes who find in Hitler, or Goebbels, his aggressive Berlin lieutenant, or Otto Braun, or Severing their only hope. For Germany *is* discouraged, downhearted, dispirited this Christmas. There is a good fighting spirit still in many quarters, but the prevailing unemployment alone is enough to discourage a people, for it is not only among the unskilled or the skilled factory laborers. Suicides of destitute men of education and talent who have no hope of a job are frequent; in every class of life the emergency exists. I heard yesterday of a young diplomat dropped merely for reasons of economy. Although much influence has been exercised in his behalf, he is without work. Nobody knows what to do with the multitudes who are graduating from the universities as doctors and lawyers. The

Berlin chamber of lawyers (which corresponds roughly to our bar associations) came very near passing a resolution forbidding the admission to practice of any more lawyers!

All the more reason why the government must not yield to any such threats as those which caused the banning of "All Quiet on the Western Front." The official defender to whom I listened gave us, of course, to understand that there was no yielding; that he had seen the film—he himself spent four years at the front—and that it was so one-sided and failed so completely to bring out the heroic side of war and of the German soldier in war that it was quite impossible. It was, however, all his own reaction to the film; what he liked and disliked. Not a word did he say about the deep underlying principles involved; nothing about the freedom of the stage and of opinion. He was sorry, of course, that it had been necessary to overrule the *Oberprüfungsstelle,* the competent body of censors which originally passed the movie.

He was particularly anxious that the government's point of view should be spread abroad, and that it should be made clear that the government's action had been started before the Hitler disorders began; as to them he snapped his fingers. It is carefully explained also that the federal government has no control over the *Oberprüfungsstelle* and cannot act until after it does; but the government could easily have prevailed upon the producers not to show the film at all, even if it had to offer some compensation. There are but few signs here, unfortunately, that Germans in authority have a better understanding than heretofore of foreign mentalities. Apparently this official did not realize that this film had already been shown in the United States, England, France, and elsewhere in the world, and that no sane person, except supersensitive German Hitlerites or militarists, or persons with wrecked nerves, could possibly see in this picture anything derogatory to the German soldier or the German nation whether at peace or at war. It was a magnificent opportunity which the government lost, not only not to yield to the demagogues but to increase respect for itself at home and abroad and to let people see for themselves how false were the assertions of Goebbels and the whole Hitler crew. But the thing has been done; the government is completely compromised. The Social Democrats, the backbone of the government's support in the Reichstag, are rising in protest, and Goebbels has made good his boast of two days before the banning, that "Hitler is at the gates of Berlin."

Meanwhile, Brüning has come comfortably through the Reichstag's second session with increased majorities, thanks in considerable degree to the agreement not to debate upon the Polish situation and other aspects of foreign affairs. As to both the latter, there must be a day of reckoning, and it is now confidently believed that Curtius will go and that there will be a new minister of foreign affairs by the middle of February—probably Brüning himself. The feeling of outrage toward Poland steadily increases. Even the Reichsbanner leaders are beginning to demand the release of the Polish corridor, and the government naturally seeks to cut the ground from under the feet of the "Nazis" by becoming more vigorous in defense of oppressed German minorities. It remains a government of compromises, fighting against time in the forlorn hope that in the spring there will be greater industrial employment—as if that could come in any great degree without a general improvement all over the world. The politicians who are pessimists still look for a collapse in the spring; some say frankly they don't care what happens: "Europe is lost anyway."

Somehow, I cannot share their feeling. Europe has, it is true, never been in as bad a way since the war as it is now because of the war-creating, hate-creating Treaty of Versailles, because of the reparations and debts, the high-tariff walls, the world-wide industrial chaos and depression. But to anyone who saw Germany as I did during the civil war of February and March, 1919, during the invasion of the Ruhr and the inflation period, it is not easy to prophesy any general collapse either of Germany or all Europe. They suffer and work and get by somehow. But he would be a fool indeed who denied that wherever one scans the horizon the outlook is of the darkest.

Can Germany Pay?

By OSWALD GARRISON VILLARD

St. Moritz, January 2

CAN Germany pay the reparations demanded of her and her debt to the United States? Of course, Germany can. A pound of flesh can always be had if there is no convenient law or trick to prevent, or the debtor does not perish. If the Allies and the United States insist, Germany can be made to pay in the course of generations, even if its government takes advantage of the moratorium provided under the Young Plan—as it probably will. But the question which the nations involved should put to themselves today is not Can Germany pay? but Should Germany pay? Can they afford to let Germany pay them at the cost of further introducing into the currents of world trade an unnatural factor which beyond doubt has had its share in causing and prolonging the present world-wide industrial crisis? Can they permit Germany to pay them at a cost of still lower standards of living, of enlarging the risk of German economic collapse, of inviting revolution and chaos, of arousing a bitterer spirit of resentment and a hatred of those who are helping to force Germany into its present straits?

Yes, Germany can pay, and you will find foreign observers in Berlin, official and unofficial, who will undertake to prove it to you in marks and pfennigs. They scoff at the idea that it cannot, and declare that "if Germany gets away with this it will get away with anything." First of all they point to the totally unnecessary naval expenditures, including the latest appropriation for beginning a second "pocket battleship." The ships now built or building could not protect Germany at all and are therefore merely a concession to national pride and to the nationalistic desire to keep in existence a nucleus of ships and men for a future large navy. Then there are the military expenditures. They can well be cut—they have been steadily increased—especially if the Reichswehr be regarded, as it should be, merely as a national police force and not as an army for foreign wars—which it cannot be without tanks, heavy cannon, a huge fleet of airplanes, and poison gases. So far I am entirely with the critics. Here much money could be saved; but only the German pacifists and a few enlightened economists and editors are for it. Suggest such a thing—as I repeatedly have done—to the ordinary German and he recoils in horror. To him it means throwing Germany open to Polish invasion; even the fleet is eloquently defended upon that ground of the Polish menace.

But other cuts in German federal expenditure? They are neither as easily suggested nor as practical—in many cases they are open to grave question. The critics dwell upon the fact that the city of Berlin has just opened a marvelous new museum costing millions, which was ten years in building; that Berlin and many other municipalities have established since the war new parks, new municipal bathing places, great stadia for athletics, like the one at Frankfort-on-the-Main, and all sorts of recreation grounds, besides putting up model municipal apartment houses to accommodate at least four million people. Cynical foreigners cite the fact that the federal, state, and municipal theaters in Germany are run today at an annual deficit so huge that journalists are asked not to print it and it has not appeared in the German press. It runs into many, many millions of marks, quite a percentage of the annual cash tribute to the Allies. Belgian and French observers note these things and say: "That money is rightfully ours."

They are on much safer ground when they declare that if Germany increased its inheritance taxes to, say, the English level, it would largely increase its revenues and help to wipe out the remaining inequalities in wealth—there are still two thousand admitted millionaires in Germany. These advocates of exacting the pound of flesh also call attention to the fact that despite the bad times the dividends of 142 German companies recently studied by a Berlin banking house have decreased only from 6.57 per cent in 1929 to 6.26 per cent in 1930. This is to them proof that German industry is neither overtaxed nor overburdened. So is the fact that the Rheinmetall-Gesellschaft, with its gross income reduced from 56,000,000 to 45,000,000 marks, has none the less increased its charges for depreciation from 2,430,000 to 4,080,000 marks, and is still able to report a net of 1,920,000 marks as against 1,810,000 marks in the previous year. The directors of the Gutehoffnungshütte have just increased its dividend rate from 7 to 10 per cent. One single family, the Hamels, owners of two-thirds of the stock, received no less than 6,000,000 marks as against a beggarly 4,200,000 marks the year before—but one does not hear of any bonuses or exceptionally high wages for the workers of the concern.

Next the critics have seized upon a remarkable article by the Minister of Finance, Hermann Dietrich, which recently appeared in the *Berliner Tageblatt,* entitled The Transfer Mechanism—an article hastily disavowed two days after publication. It seems that Herr Dietrich had promised an article to the *Tageblatt,* which received this one with his name attached and promptly printed it. Immediately it was explained that Herr Dietrich had not written it, that it was a memorandum prepared for him by some subordinate which the Finance Minister had not even seen. It was further declared that this memorandum presented only a one-sided view of the reparations payments. But the mischief had been done. The article was eagerly seized upon as showing that the necessary transfers under the Young Plan can all be made without disturbing trade; that there are automatic compensations and international financial readjustments which will easily take care of any situation that may arise. "There, you see," the cry went up, "the Reich's Finance Minister admits that the Young payments can readily be made without disturbance at home or abroad." To which the answer is that in the article itself it is stated that the mechanism described in it "must not be overloaded," and that if there should be a complete withdrawal of foreign credits the economic life of Germany would at once be "entirely paralyzed"; there would be a complete collapse of the whole internal banking and credit system and of the public finances. Elsewhere in this article there is reference to the immediately depressing effect upon the financial and economic situation of any home political development which might create anxiety or distrust abroad.

That there is room for further reforms than those embodied in the Brüning sanitation measures, just agreed to by the Reichstag after their proclamation by the President, is perfectly true. For example, the German government is by no means always efficient in the conduct of some of its multitudinous businesses. Thus, the Deutsche Werke in Kiel, a government concern, has just incurred a loss of 10,000,000 marks through faulty construction of two large ships built on order for a Norwegian shipping company. Arbitrators have decided that the ships must be taken back and that the German government must pay 6,000,000 marks to the Norwegians. The total loss will go to 10,000,000. One hears the same complaint among big business men here as in the United States—that when the government begins competing with private industry the losses and waste are great and the injury done to private enterprises serious. A writer in the *Tageblatt* declares that in certain of these government concerns the losses will run to many millions; that the government has tried making motor cars, windows, sashes, doors, and machinery of all sorts, always with losses and always hastily changing from one thing to another. Here again, critics say, a lot could be saved toward reparations.

The German League for Human Rights has still another and a most admirable suggestion for improving the condition of German finances—not, of course, because it wishes the reparations payments to continue, but because it wishes to aid in the solution of the terrible economic crisis. It urges the immediate lowering of all the German protective tariffs. One of the many grave derelictions to be laid at the doors of the Social Democrats is that they have connived at and aided in the development of the existing tariffs, which raise the cost of living to every German and, precisely as in the United States, take the form of special privilege for certain classes. In a notable address before the league on November 21, Dr. R. R. Kuczynski, well known in the United States as a statistical expert and a lecturer at the Robert Brookings Graduate School in Washington, D. C., pointed out some facts in regard to the working of the agricultural tariffs. He showed that the great agrarian interests, notably in East Prussia (which has really governed Germany for as long as our protected manufacturers have run our government), have received large government subventions and tax exemptions in addition to the high tariffs they demanded. These favors have annually cost the city consumers "several billions of marks." But the farming industry declares today that despite all this it is worse off than ever, that all these measures have helped not at all. Yet a ton of rye which could be bought last summer outside of Germany for 60 marks cost 180 marks in Germany—a gift by the government, through its tariff, of no less than *120 marks per ton* to each and every grower of rye. Similarly the coal syndicate charges 16.89 marks per ton at home and is now seeking to market coal abroad at 10 to 12.50 marks per ton. These are but two of many examples.

But granted the overwhelming benefits which abolition of tariffs would confer upon Germany, our question remains: Should Germany, even if aided by changes in fiscal policy and by more economical administration, still be compelled to pay the reparations?

My answer is, No. This is not because of a desire to see Germany wriggle out of obligations solemnly entered into; from the beginning I have felt that Germany ought to pay a reasonable and just amount for the actual destruction in France and Belgium. After studying the German situation at first hand for the last four months, my reasons for now believing more than ever in the desirability of canceling the reparations and debts are these:

1. While, as stated above, reparations are not a major cause of the present economic depression they are contributory, and they place Germany in the predicament of having to meet the world-wide crisis with this extra burden of approximately $500,000,000 a year in payments to the conquerors.

2. There is a limit beyond which no people can, in humanity, be depressed in their standard of living, and the bulk of the German people have reached that limit, with 3,750,000 registered unemployed and an additional multitude in the classes which do not resort to the public registry offices to seek the dole. Today no fewer than 16,600,000 Germans have an *annual income of less than 600 marks, or $150.*

3. If the German people are still further depressed economically there will inevitably come fiercer internal political conflicts, more and more rioting for food, and the strengthening of all the reactionary elements, especially the National Socialists, with probably a dictatorship to follow. It is all very well to tell a people to give up their museums, their parks, their theaters. But these are safety valves; they give the people something to live by, some intellectual stimulus, something to keep them from despairing. The cities must offer more to their inhabitants if only to offset the horrible depression caused by the unemployment, the bareness, and the hardships, the almost hopeless situation which every young German faces when he enters upon his business or professional career.

4. A disorganized Germany means a disorganized Europe, and a disorganized Europe means an economically maladjusted and depressed world, including the United States. So serious is the existing crisis that only shortsightedness amounting to criminal folly will counsel any policy which even remotely threatens the collapse of Germany.

5. The psychological effect of the canceling of reparations and debts upon the mentality of all Europe would be incalculable. In Germany it would go far to insure political stability, even if the direct economic results proved—as they would—not to be so great as the average German expects. It would stimulate trade, reassure capital, and stop its flight to Switzerland, Sweden, and Holland. It would give a breath of life to an all but perishing people which has just come through the sorriest Christmas since the war.

6. In good-will alone, wiping out the reparations would pay all the creditor nations in dollars and cents, and most particularly the United States. How many billions is the world losing annually by the present economic depression? Any sacrifices toward stopping the present fearful loss and the waste of the unemployed millions of workers will be money well expended.

As long as the reparations burdens continue, so long will Germany regard the rest of the world with the bitterness of one who feels himself gravely discriminated against. The German people are not unaware that since their representatives signed the Young Plan the changed financial situation, because of the depreciation of gold, is compelling them to pay actually some 12 per cent more than they agreed to. It must not be forgotten that there has arisen a new generation in Germany which has no memory of the war, or only the vaguest; that these young men and women feel it to be a crime that they should be compelled to pay for the sins of a government dead twelve years, for a war in the making and waging of which they had no part whatever. The American public must not overlook the fact that it is precisely from this section of the German population that the National Socialists are drawing large numbers of recruits.

The enthusiasm of German youth for Hitler and his motley following is in considerable measure due to the fact that vague as their program is—it is as full of platitudes and glittering generalities as most of the speeches of Theodore Roosevelt and William J. Bryan—it is at least a program. And it conjures up a picture of a freed Germany, again mistress of its own house. German boys and girls are today craving leadership as perhaps never before. If they are to be driven permanently into the camp of the Hitlerites, it will be an ominous thing for Europe and the world for several generations to come—if Europe survives. It will inevitably mean the awakening of that fierce aggressive nationalistic spirit which French politicians say they gravely fear, and are doing all they can to produce—a spirit not existent in Germany immediately after the war and one far from controlling there today.

Germany wants peace. I called a couple of weeks ago upon a high financial authority in Berlin—one who still holds high office and wields great power. I wanted to talk finance with him, but he only wanted to talk *peace* with me. "Why can we not have peace in Europe? Why will not America now insist upon disarmament, a final settlement of the war issues, and of all the financial questions? As long as these things continue there will be and can be no peace in Europe, no security, no happiness. We are drifting steadily toward a new war and a catastrophe. Yet we Germans are absolutely desirous of peace—as we have just shown again in Geneva with no success and little support."

I repeat: Against this drift to chaos and misery every possible brake should be applied, and none could be so potent psychologically as the settlement of the reparations problem. It is the capitalist system which is on trial, which is at stake. If the capitalist governments continue to rule Europe as incredibly badly as they have done and are now doing, and Russia succeeds in her communist experiment, Moscow will not only be knocking at the gates of Berlin in a dozen years, as Professor Calvin Hoover wrote in the October issue of *Harper's Magazine,* it will be leveling every gate in Europe. Talk of the menace of Russian dumping! Why, that is but a speck upon the horizon compared with the state of bitterness, of fear, of anxiety, of armament rivalry, and of trade warfare through protective tariffs, yes, the state of international anarchy which constitutes today what men call Europe.

The German statesman was right. Why does not

America act? Why does not Mr. Hoover vision that before him lies today a most glorious opportunity to reestablish America in the position of moral leader of the world which it for a time held? Mr. Hoover! *Mr. Hoover!* Fate surely dealt the world a tragic blow when it placed him in the White House in this hour of extremest danger.

Wanted: Another World Conference

By OSWALD GARRISON VILLARD

London, February 18

EUROPEAN conference has followed upon European conference. And so many of them have ended in total failure or a flimsy pretense of success that people everywhere are cynical or disgusted, declaring that "they always end in talk." Fortunately there are exceptions to the record—first of all, the notable success of the late Indian conference, which achieved the apparently impossible, thanks to the courage, skill, and persistency of Ramsay MacDonald. But if there were no favorable precedents whatever, it would still seem to me that another conference ought to be called at the earliest possible moment.

What kind of conference? A conference among the heads of a small group of nations—Italy, the United States, Great Britain, France, Germany, and Belgium—for the purpose of examining immediately the actual situation in Europe and taking some steps to end the present world-wide economic crisis. Here again I hear dissent: Has there not just been an economic conference at Geneva, which gave to the press of the world an excellent statement of economic conditions, signed by twenty-seven nations? The answer is that this is not the time for statements, whether they are signed by twenty-seven nations or by all the nations on earth. What the hour calls for is *action,* and action before it is too late. As I have pointed out before in this correspondence, there is no time to be lost. This is, of course, not simply my own humble opinion. It is the deliberate judgment of the leading economists with whom I have talked in Germany and Austria this winter, and it is the opinion of a number of people whom I have seen here in England. And it must be a conference of heads of governments because it must be a gathering of men who can act, or can give reasonable assurances that their governments will be bound by whatever decisions are arrived at. That this makes the participation of the United States practically impossible is plain. Probably nothing on earth would induce Mr. Hoover to follow Mr. Wilson's precedent and cross the seas to attend such a meeting, even if he were to become aware of the gravity of the world situation, as he gives no sign of being today. He would undoubtedly have to send a substitute—woe betide should it be Mr. Stimson or Mr. Mellon—and whoever it might be would be handicapped by having to ascertain not only the opinions of Mr. Hoover, but perhaps even the wishes of the Senate. None the less, a conference is needed and needed badly, with or without the United States. Upon this point all thoughtful men here not in office agree.

The primary reason is, of course, that the present economic crisis is a world crisis. There are those here, like Maynard Keynes, who think that it may last as long as the economic depression which followed the Napoleonic wars. The world was an infinitely smaller entity then. It is a commonplace that the World War made us realize for the first time the world's present economic unity and the absolute dependence of one nation upon another. The crisis is driving this truth home with irresistible force: it seems impossible for America to return to its previous prosperity without Europe's complete restoration to economic health, while, conversely, everybody here feels that there can be no hope of overcoming the crisis on this side of the Atlantic until recovery is assured in America. Why should there not be a conference to deal with this unprecedentedly dangerous situation?

The minute one raises the question in official circles the obstacles are presented. What, it is asked, can Europe do if America will not move, since America holds the key to the whole situation—the golden key? What practical thing could such a conference achieve? Well, perhaps an agreement to reduce the tariffs which everywhere in Europe and in America hinder the progress of the world's trade as beaver dams block the flow of mountain streams. But the French are unyielding on the question of tariffs. What is the use? The answer is that the first advantage to be gained would be a psychological one. The entire business world of Europe would breathe anew if it learned that governmental heads were conferring upon emergency measures. In Germany especially, the summoning of Chancellor Brüning to such a conference would have immediate and far-reaching reactions. It would come at a happy moment, on top of his parliamentary successes and the relatively favorable action taken at Geneva upon Germany's anti-Polish protests. It would refute the arguments of the Hitlerites that the Chancellor is without influence in international affairs, and that nothing whatever is being done by him to improve Germany's international situation. To all this the doubters reply that if such a conference met and returned empty-handed the result would be far more discouraging than if it had never been called together. They overlook the fact that a free interchange of opinion between the heads of governments could not be other than valuable, even though the foreign ministers of the same countries met less than two weeks ago in Geneva.

Next comes the question of precedents—precedents are the joy of an office-holder when he cannot conjure up any other obstacle. It is explained that such a conference must have Briand in it to be successful, and you could not have Briand if other countries were represented by their prime ministers or chancellors. Nobody seems to want the attendance of Mussolini. I have already referred to the hampering American precedent. The others at least could be brushed aside. It is easy to prophesy that they will be brushed aside if the crisis becomes serious enough. But this question of America is more difficult. Onlookers here have been struck by the many signs of a changing public opinion in America. Bush, Hurley, Owen Young, Nicholas Murray Butler, Outerbridge, Warburg, Speyer, Wiggin—the list of those asking a reexamination of our relations to Europe is growing every day. Europeans are properly impressed by it. Naturally, they do not always understand that the bankers cited are under suspicion, first, because they are international and Wall Street bankers, and, secondly, because some of them have made loans to Germany and it is therefore felt that their advice is not unbiased—a consideration which cannot apply to Bush, Butler, or Outerbridge. But if responsible opinion is changing in the United States, the process is too slow to be really helpful. There is no time to wait, not even for a year, at the end of which time Mr. Hoover will be facing the question of his renomination and reelection. If the crisis in America continues to be as severe as it is now, or the recovery is extremely slow, the politicians will surely be much more ready to understand that they cannot hope for a return to normal times until America has helped to put Europe on its feet. Even then there will be the difficulty of forgiving debts when there is a large Treasury deficit, with the danger of an increase of income taxes clearly in the offing.

None the less, if things continue as they are in Europe, the day will come when Mr. Hoover, the politicians, the press, and the public will have squarely to face anew the question of reparations and debts, which Mr. Hoover, in his unhappy speech to the American Legion in Boston only last fall, declared to be an accomplished fact which no proper American would seek further to discuss or to reopen. The reason for this is that if things continue as they are, Germany will ask for her moratorium, to which she is entitled under the Young Plan, and the French and English will find themselves in an immediate quandary as to how they can continue to pay America when Germany ceases to pay them. If there is one thing which is keeping Philip Snowden awake at night it is surely the dread lest he suddenly hear that he must include in his extraordinarily difficult budget the amount of money for the United States which now automatically flows from Berlin to Washington by way of London. It would seem an impossible task to obtain this additional amount—£38,000,000—from the British taxpayer.

But what will the American government do if, after Germany defaults, the British and French refuse to go on with their payments? Mr. Hoover will certainly then discover that reparations and debts are after all not a finished fact, and that it will be quite in order for a loyal and patriotic American to discuss these questions, and even to take part in a conference which would not only consider them, but would see if something could be done about moving the mass of gold accumulated in the United States and France, and would deal with the question, among others, of leveling all tariffs. Let no one underestimate the seriousness of the situation which will arise if England and France also ask for a moratorium in their debt payments. That it will cause anger and bad blood in America there can be no doubt. To the average American who does not know what the real situation over here is, it will doubtless seem like wilful defaulting on a debt of honor—a poor reward, indeed, for the financial rescue of the Allies when they were bankrupt in 1917. All the more reason for the proposed conference, if it can do anything whatever to head off any such outburst of feeling in America, or at least prepare the public for what may prove to be the inevitable, and make it clear that *every consideration of self-interest* should make the American taxpayer eager to get rid of debts owed to him which are largely contributing to the terrible losses being inflicted in America by the present crisis, with its dreadful unemployment, poverty, suffering, and complete dislocation of our social and economic life.

Here in London the financial world is again opposed to the Labor Chancellor of the Exchequer. A number of Germans in key positions have told me of their being strongly urged by British financiers to help in bringing about a moratorium by Germany. The London "City" wants the Germans to start the ball rolling by refusing further payments. The British financiers are united in their belief that this question of reparations and debts is at the bottom of the world crisis. They do not by any means believe that this is the only thing that is wrong with the financial world. Like the German financiers and statesmen with whom I have talked, they understand that there are numerous other causes at work. But they do firmly believe in the enormous psychological effect of a joint cancelation of debts, as well as the economic advantages. They are quite clear in their own minds that even the passage of German money through London to New York has its deleterious effect, and they want the whole problem tackled, and tackled quickly. I believe that they would unanimously stand behind the British Prime Minister if he should decide to call the conference herein suggested. More than that, important English organizations like the Quakers and the League of Nations Union are interesting themselves in this question. A committee of the Friends has been for some time past writing to the United States to let it be known among the Quakers there that the present situation is not to be trifled with, and that America should take the lead.

For one, I should not be afraid that any such conference as is here suggested could meet and adjourn without really accomplishing anything. It would be well worth while even if it merely discussed the question of the unhappy burden put upon Germany by the rise in the price of gold, which increases her debts between 10 and 30 per cent because of the dropping out, in the Young Plan, of the gold clause contained in the Dawes Plan. Should this injustice be done away with, Chancellor Brüning's position would be enormously strengthened. Such a conference would naturally first discuss economic questions, but it could not get very far in the consideration of these matters without touching upon the issues of war and peace in Europe. Europe cannot have that feeling of security necessary to a sound economic life until certain dangerous political symptoms are done away with. It is not surprising that European statesmen are as reluctant to tackle these problems as most American politicians are slow to study with open mind the question of the debt settlements. But here, too, the simple fact is that Europe cannot go on under these conditions and survive. It is not surprising that a Frenchman, Count Vladimir d'Ormesson, has just declared, in making his suggestion that half of Germany's debts be remitted, that the next two years will "decide the fate of Europe." It is a daily occurrence to meet men who see an entirely communized Europe within ten years if something is not done.

If this is so, then, obviously, everything ought to be tried, to prevent a catastrophe. Is it really true that Europe would be worse off if such a conference were called and came away without any concrete achievement? I do not think so. It should not meet with a definite program to be accomplished, but if, after meeting, its members went away unable to achieve anything in the face of the threat of oncoming disaster, then we should at any rate have gained the knowledge that European governments are once more bankrupt in statesmanship, that the men who now hold office are incompetent to govern in this emergency, and that the capitalist system is deservedly nearing its end.

The Naval Agreement

NOBODY except naval experts and a few government officials is likely to pay much attention to the statistical parts of the British memorandum in which the terms of the Franco-Italian naval agreement are set out. Figures of tonnage or gun caliber are of slight significance to the average man or woman, and even the experts do not always agree about what the figures mean. What most people will want to know is whether the agreement really puts an end to competitive naval building by France and Italy; whether, if it does, it also disposes of the disputed issue of parity between the navies of those two Powers, and whether it paves the way to the general reduction and limitation of armaments of all kinds which an international conference is scheduled to undertake in February, 1932.

The first of these questions may, with some qualification, be answered in the affirmative. It will be recalled that the refusal of France and Italy to accept the tonnage limitations of the London naval treaty because of their dispute about parity resulted in the inclusion in the treaty of a safeguarding provision which permitted either of the three signatory Powers—the United States, Great Britain, and Japan—to increase its tonnage in case the Powers that did not sign increased theirs. The elaborate programs of competitive building which France and Italy have prosecuted made it reasonably certain that Great Britain, at least, would feel compelled to resort to this so-called escalator clause, and it is this danger that the accord recently concluded appears to have averted. France and Italy will continue to build, but the building will be according to a scale and not competitive. The scale, it must be admitted, is liberal, and the British Admiralty is reported as thinking that the tonnage balance will still dip unduly against Great Britain, but we have the government's word for it that the escalator clause will not be invoked.

The parity issue, on the other hand, has been only postponed, to come up again at the latest in 1936 when the London treaty will regularly be reconsidered, but quite probably in 1932 when the whole subject of disarmament is before the international conference. France, meantime, will enjoy the superiority of 150,000 tons more or less upon which it has insisted, the principal difference being that the distribution of tonnage among the various categories of vessels will be somewhat more to Italy's advantage. France can thus claim that it has surrendered nothing important, and Italy can profess satisfaction in the prospect of a fleet better adapted to its special needs, notwithstanding the continued inferiority in global tonnage. The fundamental issue, however, remains almost exactly where it was when Mr. Henderson and Mr. Alexander began their negotiations at Paris and Rome.

Has the outlook for the disarmament conference, then, been improved? In one important respect it has. If, when the conference met, France and Italy had been engaged in a competitive struggle, the former to maintain its naval superiority and the latter to achieve parity, the chances of agreement upon any plan of general naval reduction or limitation would have been appreciably dimmed, while if the navies proved unmanageable the land and air armaments could hardly have been dealt with at all. There is encouragement in the willingness of France and Italy to accept the British good offices and temporarily drop a controversy which was setting all Europe by the ears and affecting public opinion in the United States and Japan. The general subject can now be discussed without at the same time watching the progress of a race. The concession is by no means entirely satisfactory, and it does not, in and of itself, contribute in the slightest degree to the solution of the parity problem, but it nevertheless has the advantage of not complicating the matter by setting it in terms of out-and-out competition building.

The hope that Italy and France, having been helped to an accord at one point, may find a way of harmonizing their differences at another is probably the chief reason for the added interest that is being shown in the preparations for the conference next year. There is certainly need of all the cheerfulness that can be mustered. What with armies, navies, air forces, chemical warfare, budgetary control, parity, offensive and defensive alliances, and all the other issues that war involves, the conference may well turn out to be the most important international meeting since the peace conference at Paris, for the task before it is nothing less than a sweeping reorganization of world policy in one of the most important aspects of international relations.

The New Drive Against Russia

By OSWALD GARRISON VILLARD

Berlin, February 27

NOT a day passes but there is fresh evidence of a new drive against Russia. Indeed, it is impossible to pick up a copy of the London *Times* without finding from one to three items dealing with the menace of the Soviets. Thus we learn that no less than two leagues have been formed, with the usual complement of titled gentlemen, admirals, and generals, to protect the English public and English industry from the contamination of slave-made goods. It is declared that practically all Russian labor is enslaved by Stalin, and therefore everything that comes out of Russia should be boycotted. The action of the United States government in shutting out timber and pulpwood from northern Russia unless the importer can prove that it was not produced by convict labor and the complete boycott proclaimed by Canada are heartily acclaimed in London and elsewhere. The intense British anti-Russians wish and demand that the MacDonald Government take the same course. They rejoiced to learn that the recent visit of Mr. Bennett, the Prime Minister of Canada, to Washington was exclusively concerned with the question of joint action of Canada and the United States against Russian imports.

This campaign against Russian exports comes at a welcome moment. The excitement over the anti-religious attitude of the Soviets which reached such great heights about a year ago is dying down. None the less, the Christian Protest Movement formed in England in December, 1929, under the chairmanship of Prebendary Gough, Vicar of Brompton, has just reported that during its first year it held some 270 meetings in London and elsewhere, and that it has cooperated with similar protest movements in twelve Continental countries. It declares that its effort has been to keep its campaign entirely within religious lines. Nevertheless, if resentment can be aroused against Russia on the trade side, it will not hurt this other movement; on the contrary, it will help to keep it alive. The Catholic Women's League of England is not so careful to separate politics from religion, for it has sent a resolution to the British Secretary of State for Foreign Affairs, Mr. Henderson, to the effect that the League, representing the organized body of Catholic women of England, "in view of the pitiless cruelty of the present rulers of Soviet Russia toward the workers employed in their timber industry, as revealed by the sworn statements of escaped nationals now resident in England, . . . calls upon His Majesty's government to denounce these inhuman practices and to use every resource available to procure an alleviation of sufferings unjustly inflicted on helpless victims."

In the recent by-election in Fareham this vital question of Russian slave labor naturally came to the front, since Fareham is a glove-making center. The successful Conservative candidate reported that his audiences were "increasingly interested" in the dumping of timber, gloves, and other goods produced by slaves and forced laborers in Russia. It is, of course, too good an issue for Winston Churchill to neglect, and in his long speech of February 19 in Parliament he not only declared that the Five-Year Plan in Russia "would succeed in so far as it made for the economic ill-usage of other people," although it would fail to help the economic welfare of the Russians, but he asserted the "impossibility of standing against exportation by a state irrespective of profit and cost of production" to be a clear reason why England should turn from free trade to protection. Even more significant was his statement that "the government ought to take counsel with every friendly Power" to "try to concert joint action against the uneconomic exportations which were in increasing measure to be apprehended from Russia." Despite his break with Baldwin on the Indian question, there is no doubt that Churchill here voiced the prevailing sentiment in the Conservative Party. When it comes into power again it may be relied upon to take the lead against Russia.

The French are already at work. Not only are the conservative and reactionary forces in France taking exactly the same position; two important officials are touring Central Europe with a view to seeing how far the various countries, such as Czecho-Slovakia, Jugoslavia, and others, will go toward an international action against Russia along economic lines. There is plenty of evidence elsewhere that there is a systematic effort on foot to bring about an international economic boycott. One of the vice-presidents of the International Chamber of Commerce has been circulating widely a rather lengthy document urging business men to get behind such a boycott. I need not rehearse here to the readers of *The Nation* what has been suggested in Congress this winter, but I look within a year for the organization of American anti-Russian societies like those in England, and I expect soon to hear the cry raised that no more American engineers or workers be allowed to go to Moscow to aid in building up the system which is so hostile to the capitalist world. We shall hear more and more of Russian dumping as time passes. Louis Fischer dealt admirably with that subject in *The Nation* of December 17. I cannot add to what he has said or do else than stress the humor of the situation. Whereas until recently all the wiseacres of the capitalist world in politics and industry were certain that Russia could be ignored because the Five-Year Plan would fail and communism, as Mr. Hoover has so often assured us, was totally unworkable, they have now all suddenly discovered that the Five-Year Plan is to be such a howling success as to menace the very existence of capitalist society. Needless to say, these gentlemen would be just as excited about the Russian menace if the convict-labor issue had never arisen at all. Incidentally, they are quite oblivious of the fact, especially in the United States, that if times get worse in Germany and that country is to continue to pay reparations, it will have to dump harder to get any income from abroad, and that that dumping will be far more serious than the comparatively little which Russia is undertaking to do.

Please do not underestimate the seriousness of this move for a united economic boycott of Russia. It would unquestionably block effectively the development of Russia all along the line. That country would undoubtedly be able to carry on, precisely as it found itself able to get ahead slowly without the aid of foreign capital after its efforts to borrow abroad were effectively scotched. But it would take years to industrialize Russia, and the cost would be infinite.

There are, of course, certain obstacles to be overcome before there will be a united circle of impassable walls erected against Russia—an economic circle this time rather than the cordon of bayonets which was drawn around her, with the approval of the Allies and of America, at the time of the making of the Treaty of Versailles. Communists with whom I have talked here share the belief prevalent in Russia that any economic boycott will be a prelude to a united military attack upon the Soviets. The suggestion is absurd today. With Germany in the hole in which it is industrially, agriculturally, and financially, a war is utterly out of the question. You not only could not enlist Englishmen for such an armed attack upon Russia, but I have pretty good evidence that the present British government does not intend to allow itself to be led into an economic boycott or to the voicing of protests of the kind that the Catholic women have just asked for, despite its intense feeling of opposition to the Bolshevists. The industry of Europe, moreover, is collapsing, and more than one state will refuse to give up its Russian business which it needs so badly this year. In Germany the labor leaders will oppose a boycott if only because they are being driven to believe that for a long time to come about 3,000,000 Germans will be normally idle.

It is an interesting fact that six of the most prominent German big-business men left for Russia yesterday at the invitation of the Soviet Government to study conditions in Russia and see what plums can be picked up there to keep German factories at work. There is plenty of other evidence that in the existing emergency Germany is more and more turning to Russia and is looking with jealous eyes upon the huge contracts given out in Moscow to American engineering firms and engineers.

On the other hand, I find many sincere and honest people of Socialist leanings who are not ill-disposed toward Russia but who think Germany has troubles enough without being bothered by Russian propaganda. They are perfectly willing that Russia shall do within her own borders whatever she sees fit, but they are growing very uneasy about the influence that Russia may have over Germany's fate in the years to come. For example, I have just talked with a prominent business man who feels that his whole future and that of his family and his country are jeopardized by the Russian industrial menace. He is much less worried by the dumping today than by his fear of what Russia will be doing to the world ten or fifteen years from now, and he feels that there is justification for any and every economic action against Russia. He admits, however, that so far as he knows it has not yet been possible to bring about an agreement on any one policy to be pursued. But he says that sentiment is crystallizing to the effect that no special favors should be shown to the Russians in the way of special or long-term credits. The drift is to treat Russia in this respect precisely like any other country. None the less, the nearer we come to the end of the Five-Year Plan, now compressed to four years, the greater will be the alarm in Europe.

In Berlin one has many chances to get first-hand reports from Russia, for Americans are coming in and out all the time and passing through Berlin, and so are Englishmen and Germans. The situation as portrayed by these travelers, some of whom have lived in Russia for many years, can be summed up as follows: There is no doubt that the plan is going through and that it will be acclaimed by the Russian government as a triumphant success, no matter in what degree it succeeds. It is, of course, unthinkable that Stalin and his associates will admit failure, and as the preparation of figures of their "achievement" is in their hands they can do what they like with them. Since they have repeatedly changed the plan since its inception, it remains to be seen what they will decide to have been their real objective. What will happen after the program is "finished" is an entirely different question. The American engineers with whom I have talked, who are now working in Russia, believe that the experience of the Stalingrad tractor factory is typical of what will take place. It was well and quickly built by Americans, but the Russians to whom it was turned over could do nothing with it, so that a hurried call had to be sent for some thirty-five American mechanics and engineers to come and run it. It is reported that they have not yet been able to get the production up to maximum. A German manufacturer who is supplying Russia with a large amount of machinery was being condoled with by a friend on the ground that he would lose his present prosperity in two years more, when the Five-Year Plan would be complete. The German laughed and said, "Don't worry. The Russians are wearing out and using up my machines within two or three years after their installation." These instances could be multiplied indefinitely. The hasty summoning of American railroad men to take hold of the railroads is further proof of the point I am making. A German who has lived ten years in Russia showed a group of persons within a week what purported to be official figures recording that there had been 13,000 accidents, large and small, on the railroads within twelve months. An engineer who handles enormous quantities of raw material in Russia spoke of the unending delays and difficulties he had with his shipments. He was, by the way, quite certain that if the Soviet leaders had allowed themselves ten years to do the job they are trying to put through in four years, they would have made a tremendous success of it at much less expense and without having put their people to the torture of undernourishment and general misery in the meantime.

There is no variance in the descriptions of the suffering of the people. As to food supplies, there can be no question that the situation has grown much worse since the summer of 1929 when I made my visit there. Bread alone seems to be adequately supplied. The allowance of milk for a child in Moscow is twenty-four glasses a month. A letter has just been received from an American woman who returned to Moscow in January after a vacation in Europe. She writes that she can hardly stand residence in Moscow, so tremendous are the appeals to her sympathy and to her indignation. The requests for help are unending.

If this is the correct picture it certainly does not portray a triumphant Russia so successful at home as to have money, time, and energy left for propaganda abroad on a large scale. As every intelligent person knows, the Russian government is not dumping because it wants to or because of any malign plan to wreck European capitalism. They are ruthlessly depriving their people of what we should consider absolute necessities of life in an attempt to obtain foreign moneys. It is quite possible that in two years more they will be dumping much less in the effort to make good their promises to their own people to supply them by that time with adequate clothing, shoes, furniture, bedding, and food. This possibility will not weigh with those who are engineering the new drive against Russia. Nor will the fact that any obstacle put in the way of the free movement of trade from one country to another is certain to come back as a boomerang upon those who created it. Witness the effect of the reparations payments upon the American people; witness our enhanced tariffs which are checking our imports and exports and decreasing the purchasing power of Europe in the markets of the United States.

The Church Pacifist

OUT of 19,372 Protestant clergymen replying to a questionnaire sent out by the *World Tomorrow,* no fewer than 12,076, or 62 per cent, believe that the churches of America should now go on record as refusing to sanction or support any future war; while 10,427, or 54 per cent, are personally prepared to state that it is their present purpose not to sanction any future war or participate as armed combatants. These are surprising figures. Eighty per cent of the clergymen favor substantial reductions in armament even if the United States is obliged to take the initiative and make a proportionately greater reduction than other nations are yet willing to do, while 62 per cent believe that the policy of armed intervention in other lands by our government to protect the lives and property of American citizens should be abandoned and protective efforts confined to pacific means (critics of the Administration's present Nicaraguan policy please copy); only 43 per cent regard distinctions between "defensive" and "aggressive" war as sufficiently valid to justify their participation in a future war of "defense"; only 45 per cent could conscientiously serve as chaplains on active duty in war time; and only 13 per cent favor military training in schools and colleges, while 66 per cent favor immediate entry of the United States into the League of Nations.

The questionnaire, signed by ten prominent clergymen, was sent out to all the ministers of more than a dozen leading denominations, constituting 53,000 clergymen (including 3,000 theological students) out of the total of more than 100,000 in the United States. Unfortunately, because of limitations of time and expense, the inquiry was not extended to the Jews, Roman Catholics, Lutherans, Southern Baptists, and Southern Methodists, so it is impossible to make comparisons among some of the largest and most important religious bodies in the country. It is probably true, as Kirby Page suggests, that the opponents of war replied in larger proportion than did the friends of the military system, and the published returns offer some confirmation of that idea. It is probably true also that the pulpit is more pacifistic than the pew, and certainly everyone is much more in favor of peace at a time like this than at a period when Mars has displaced other deities as the object of state worship. Nevertheless, we find it impressive that more than half of the clergymen replying, constituting a fifth of all the ministers canvassed and a tenth of the total number of clergymen in the country, have declared their purpose, for whatever their declaration may be worth, to take no part in any future war. The friends of peace without undue elation may well thank God and redouble their efforts.

An examination of the returns by denominations yields interesting results. Taking the most searching question, that on personal participation in any war, the denominations stand in the following order, beginning with the most pacifistic: Evangelical Synod, Methodist Episcopal, Reformed, Disciples, Unitarians and Universalists, Congregationalists, Baptists, Presbyterians, United Brethren, Episcopalians. On the other six test questions (omitting that on the League), the Evangelical church stands consistently in first, second, or third place, except on the question of unilateral disarmament, where it suddenly drops to ninth place. May German antecedents and sympathy with a disarmed Germany in an armed world be in any degree responsible? The Methodist Episcopal communion, whose great numbers give it large influence in the total returns, runs along pretty consistently in second, third, or fourth place, followed in order by the Reformed and Disciples churches. At the other extreme are the conservative Episcopalians, who stand consistently in tenth place on every one of the seven test questions, with the Presbyterians eighth or ninth on all of them; the United Brethren doing generally a little better; the Baptists standing seventh or worse on every question; and the Congregationalists sixth, but with a strange individualistic aberration to second place on the question of armament reduction; and the Unitarians and Universalists fifth. We do not undertake to explain these differences on religious grounds, but leave to the students of such questions the interesting correlation of these results with the economic and social status of the various religious bodies concerned. Broadly speaking, in the church as outside it, wealth, social position, and in some measure intellectual sophistication are accompanied by a favorable view of the war system.

We have left the League of Nations question for separate examination. One might guess, perhaps, that the more pacifistic the group, the more strongly it would favor the immediate entry of the United States into the League. The opposite comes nearer being true, though the returns are not conclusive. The Evangelical clergymen stand first in their opposition to entering the League, while the Episcopalians, at the foot of the list in all that makes for peace, are surpassed only by the Unitarians and Universalists in their eagerness to get into the world organization, and are followed by the Congregationalists. The Methodists, however, desert their pacifist colleagues on this question, standing next to the Congregationalists, with the Presbyterians in sixth place. Putting the thing in the light most favorable to the League, it appears doubtful whether the pacifists in the churches believe that American adhesion to the League would really make for peace.

It would be foolish to attach too great importance to the results of this questionnaire, or to undertake to draw from it too fine-spun conclusions. No one can tell today how far the present pacifists in the pulpit or out of it would stand the test of war; and no one knows how far a pacifist clergyman, even if he were willing to go to the last extreme at such a time, would be able to carry his congregation with him. The church historically has been closely tied up with the war system, and those bonds are not broken today, however many the individual clergymen in actual or threatened revolt. None the less, making all necessary allowances, we welcome this showing as an encouraging sign that there is at work within the churches a powerful leaven, and that those great organizations are not likely to be swung over without powerful protest to the support of our next military adventure. Let the watchmen on the towers of Zion, then, cry aloud and spare not.

Europe's Darkest Hour

By OSWALD GARRISON VILLARD

EIGHT months in Europe—ranging from London to Constantinople and studying conditions at first hand. What is the final upshot? What are one's ultimate opinions? What does one make of it all?

Primarily, the gravity of the situation and the dangers which overhang Europe stand out in my mind: the economic and financial chaos on every hand, the bad psychological state of one country after the other. And then the dread specter of militarism and war that looms over all. Everywhere it appears as if the present economic system were tottering to its fall. To one of the foremost German statesmen I summarized my impressions by saying that there was agreement among those with whom I talked in Germany that if Europe continued to be governed as it is there would not be a capitalist government left in ten years. To which the statesman replied that the figure was entirely too high; that it would be nothing like ten years if things went on as they did. He himself is, moreover, terrified by the tension on the Polish-German border; he had just returned from there and was astounded by the state of nerves and the absorbing fear of his countrymen. What would happen if an officer commanding a Polish or German patrol should lose his head and permit some minor aggression? He did not know; he lived in dread of it.

Fear, hate, hunger, poverty, the deadly lack of work, the loss of hope—one meets them on every hand. They dog one's footsteps in the streets of Istanbul, the byways of London, in every lane of every German town. Turn where you will they are there. You cannot escape them among the bare hills of Sicily, on the plains of Rumania, on the mountain slopes of Bulgaria, wherever farmers produce and cannot sell. "How is Budapest?" you ask of friends when you arrive there. "Dead, dead," is the answer. "And no hope anywhere." Yet everybody knows there are ways out—if only statesmanship could lend itself to the task; if only old hatreds, old nationalist ambitions, old, long-since-outworn rivalries and jealousies did not prevent. Let no man look upon this scene and declare that there is a bright side to war, or that war accomplishes any moral reform, or frees men's minds, or safeguards democracy, or creates a new order of life. The truth is that you cannot wander about Europe and believe that the World War is over; it will not be in its consequences in our lifetime.

Next to the danger of economic collapse the specter of war and the preparations for war remain, I repeat, most vivid with me. Soldiers everywhere. The late General Tasker H. Bliss, when acting as one of our peace commissioners in Paris, said to me: "Don't let anybody fool you about the causes of this war. It came just because there were too many fellows running around Europe with rifles in their hands." There are a million more fellows running around Europe with rifles in their hands than there were when the murder at Sarajevo started the disaster. Why should anyone think that Europe is safer with all this additional preparation for war than it was then? President Hoover is right to insist that disarmament is absolutely necessary for the financial sanitation of Europe. Far more than that, it is absolutely necessary for the moral sanitation of Europe. I have come back more than ever in favor of the canceling of war debts and the stopping of reparations, but I certainly do not wish to see America take a step in this direction without exacting the most definite pledges for radical disarmament on sea and on land.

Everywhere nations are helping to impoverish themselves by keeping fellows, often ragged and dirty, with rifles in their hands. There is Angora, the new capital of Turkey, placed high up in a desolate region purely for military safety by that able dictator and despotic ruler of his country, Kemal Pasha. It is hardly safe to drive in any direction out of Angora because of the military zones you constantly run into. Sometimes you may enter under restrictions; into other zones it is a deadly offense to set foot at all. But Kemal only remembers that under the peace treaty Constantinople can be neither fortified nor defended; that he defeated the Greeks in the war after the World War when they were within twenty miles of Angora. And so he arms, arms, arms. The suffering of his people is very great; Constantinople, the goose that laid the Turkish financial egg, is steadily decreasing in numbers and waning in power, but Kemal arms and arms and drills and drills and thus robs his people of much money they sorely need.

Please let no man think that I am unduly impressed by this. Hubert Griffith, the English journalist, has just published a "travel notebook" of a journey over much the same ground that I have covered. He is not a pacifist, but he surely has the right to talk as a pacifist, for from his seventeenth to his twenty-first year he was a private, a staff officer, and in the flying corps. And this is what this ex-soldier writes:

> What have I seen tragic? . . . The last thing, and the continuous thing that includes all other things, is armies. I have seen armies, I am sick of armies. One cannot get away from them. I saw an army in Poland—at my first cafe in Warsaw I thought I was at a military musical comedy; Hungary has an army, Jugoslavia has an army—and policemen wearing bayonets and revolvers; Turkey has an army—not only armies proportionate to the country's population, but large armies, and armies that swarm up and down the streets with swords and medals and spurs and uniforms. . . . A present peace-time army is the idlest, most mischievous, and most dangerous thing in creation, and to dress it up in a Hollywood dream of gold braid and scarlet or blue cloth is a senseless provocation of mob mentality.
>
> How many wars can a man even now only in middle age recall in his lifetime—the World War, the Balkan War, the Russo-Japanese War, the Boer War, the Sudan campaign, Somaliland. . . . Has the river of blood ever for more than a few years together ceased flowing? The only method that has never been tried is the method of there being no armies. . . . My quarrel with half the nations of Eastern Europe has been that one cannot go into a cafe without tumbling over someone or other's sword. One officer at least resigns his commission.

Thus Mr. Griffith in an impassioned plea for the United States of Europe. He held no brief, when he made his trip, for anybody or anything. He had no orders from his newspaper as to what he should write; he owed no allegiance to any political party or creed, and yet as he took his way over this same track he found his whole soul crying out against the monstrous doctrine that because wars have been they must be again, that the United States of Europe is a chimerical dream. His conscience revolted against these preparations for the next war that struck him in the face at every turn, and spelled not the avoidance of war, but invitations to the final disaster of Europe.

So this is what Europe looks like today, dressed up in its uniforms, in its old uniforms of hate, oppression, and slaughter, those uniforms meant to hide the most grinding poverty, suffering, and despair. Not in Germany, of course, nor in Austria or Hungary, for these are disarmed. Yet so strange is humanity that in those countries the demand grows steadily that they, too, shall be armed, shall dissipate their resources, shall have the right to waste man power, to pile up debts upon debts, to be as stupid and as foolish as all their neighbors. Mr. Griffith is right, there are ways of escape from all this chaos. I have stressed in my letters from Europe during the last eight months the various problems to be grappled with, the tariffs which throttle one country after another, armaments, the psychology of fear and of hate, the heaping up of gold in Paris and in Washington, the folly of reparations and of the war-debt payments. These and others are the breastworks to be taken. They can be conquered only by international action and cooperation. Let no man be in any doubt about that point. The present crisis is the worst in history because it is world-wide. It is the simple truth that no one nation can hope to work out of it except by some fortuitous happening. Why are the nations not working together, through their rulers? Why are the latter not meeting like the executives of a great endangered bank, if only to get to know one another, if only to exchange views, to plan for united action and a united front? One of the best-known diplomats in London declared not long ago that he had never been able to see why the rulers were not meeting for just this purpose. It is an international problem, he said, not a national one, and can be solved only by men with authority sitting in almost continuous session.

The beginning has been made. The British Prime Minister has invited the German Chancellor to come to Chequers to talk. Not until June, unfortunately, and M. Briand will not be there. Perhaps by that time the latter will have fallen, or will be so very securely settled in the presidency of France as to have lost already his influence in the European scene. And this brings us to the chief obstacle to a better world—France. If Europe goes down in the next five years the responsibility and guilt of France will be greater than those of any other country. Rotten with gold, still the victims of a psychology of fear, constantly whipped up by conscienceless politicians, the French seem bent upon throwing themselves in front of every movement that makes for the peace of Europe, excepting always Briand's adoption of the plan for a United States of Europe. But even here M. Briand has his limitations and his country its blind eye. They are outraged at the proposal for a German and Austrian Zollverein, although that is the most statesman-like move since the peace of Locarno, and Germany's renunciation of any possible reconquest of Alsace-Lorraine and a long step toward a united Europe. I do not deny that there is in France much genuine fear of Germany. It is groundless, and the French state of mind could be cleared up on this question if there were only French leaders honest and unselfish enough to undertake it. Instead, the politicians and dishonest journalists play upon it as the politicians in our South so long played up and whipped up prejudice against the Negroes for their selfish ends. Today, one feels like writing, France is the enemy of mankind. For it arms and arms and arms. It makes no determined effort for immediate economic cooperation; and M. Briand plots for a customs union against Germany and Austria.

All this instead of another step which could be taken at once—a genuine rapprochement between Germany and France. Either side could move in this direction. Because of political ineptitude, or because of a fear of rebuff, or for some other reason, Germany has not made the advances that it could, though there is a strong group in and out of the German press which knows that that is the quickest way and the soundest way to lay the specter of hostility. In France the will to a complete union in friendship is sadly lacking. Yet the very first move on the French side to proceed in the spirit of Locarno would be acclaimed in Germany. Instead, they are lining the German frontier with the most up-to-date defenses. Yet the more they defend and arm and prepare, the greater appears the funk in which they live. Their vast superiority in airplanes, poison gas, tanks, and heavy guns, all of them absolutely denied to the Germans, apparently means nothing to them. They are credited with having 5,000 military airplanes. With these they could destroy every city on the Rhine with all their men, women, and children in forty-eight hours. Against them the Germans have nothing but relatively few commercial airplanes. That by itself would seem to be military superiority enough for the French. But they apparently cannot be reasoned with as long as their politicians and their journalists capitalize their fears. Exceptions there are enough. There are many men and women in France with good-will toward Germany and every other nation. All last winter Frenchmen and Frenchwomen of distinction were accepting invitations to Berlin and other German cities and making welcome addresses upon the subject of German-French fellowship, but officialdom prevents these voices from becoming the voices of the nation.

I thought it highly significant that when Frederic R. Coudert of New York recently returned to Paris after some time in Germany he gave to an American newspaper in Paris an interview which constituted a vigorous criticism of the French attitude in European affairs, quite along the lines that I have written. He declared that Germany was disarmed and pacific, and suffering the greatest distress, and that French policy was all wrong. I cite this because nobody has been a more distinguished friend of France in the United States than this New York lawyer who is himself of pure French descent. The truth is that the French are now as self-satisfied and as smug as were the Germans before the war; their praise of their own culture sounds highly Teutonic. More than that, they feel, even at the moment when they proclaim their fear of Germany, that they are in a highly favorable position since they have most of the gold in Europe and the largest army on the Continent, while they are developing their colonies as vast military reserves.

The only hope in France is that the coming elections will produce a violent swing to the left; that the pinch of the industrial crisis, which is becoming acute, may make them realize that after all they are of the economic fellowship of Europe, and that they cannot rise superior to that for anything more than a short period; that if Germany goes down and Austria and Hungary starve, France will inevitably follow suit; that if bolshevism conquers in Germany, their own doors will not be unassailable. Time should bring reason with it. Unfortunately there is little time to wait, to lose. That was what leading German statesmen said when I told them that public opinion in America was changing on debts and reparations, but very slowly. "We cannot wait so long," was what they said. Quite true. Europe cannot wait. It must move. The roads to safety, peace, and happiness I have named are open. Will they be taken?

Upon the answer to this question depends the fate of more than one nation. Meanwhile, if I were a Bolshevist, the last thing I should do would be to propagandize, to seek to convert others, or to stir up unrest and rebellion within any other country. I should just sit still. For the rulers of Europe are deciding, and not the men in the Kremlin in Moscow, whether Europe shall go Bolshevist or not.

An Army of Four Million Men

THE head of the army, General Douglas MacArthur, Chief of Staff, appeared on May 13 before the War Policies Commission and revealed the War Department's plan for drafting the man power and material resources of the nation on the outbreak of war. It calls for the immediate mobilization of 4,000,000 men, and for the seizure of all federal, State, county, and municipal buildings to house and shelter troops in place of the huge cantonments of the last war. Purchases of the 4,000 essential items (there are 700,000 on the War Department's shopping list) are to be allocated *in advance*—now—and not to be regulated by competitive bidding, but the contract is to be so drawn as to limit profiteering and "to deal effectively with the over-acquisitive [!] contractor." None the less, there is to be set up "an agency to determine prices for general government buying," so that "the government will not necessarily upset economic and industrial conditions." "Price-control efforts," we further learn, "will be directed gradually, and in general recognition of their necessity and reasonableness."

In other words, the whole pretense that there will be conscription of wealth as well as of men is frankly abandoned. We are again to tear the conscripted man, willing or unwilling, from his home and deprive him as ruthlessly as we please of his right to life, but we are again to treat our great capitalists with courtesy and all consideration. So much for the American Legion's demand since 1922 that "dollars as well as men be drafted" in the event of war. General MacArthur thus not only scorned the Legion, but he went out of his way to oppose Bernard M. Baruch's plan for "price-freezing" at the outset of war, under which prices would be stabilized by federal law at a level existing on a designated "normal date." There is nothing in General MacArthur's suggestions which really offers sound opposition to the profiteering that disgraced our last war. Who would run his "agency to determine prices for general government buying"? The army? Who will be in the army then? The day after war is declared the leading industrialists will be in it. For at previous hearings it has been openly admitted that the War Department has already commissioned no less than 14,000 industrialists throughout the country as "contact men." This is fully half, if not more than half, of the entire number of reserve officers in the German army at the outbreak of the war in 1914. Is there the slightest prospect that these men will not dominate any general purchasing agency? Or that they will even be satisfied with the opinion of the present National Commander of the American Legion that a return of 7 per cent on property during the next war will be "about right"?

As for the rest of the plan, never, so far as we are aware, even in Germany in the palmiest days of its militarism, did any generals advocate the immediate military seizure of all public buildings to house troops. It is quite characteristic of the extreme militarist mind that it brushes aside all consideration of the civil government when war begins—it was this contempt of the Ludendorffs and Tirpitzes for the German civil authority and their defiance of it which as much as anything else brought about the German disaster. What would become of all our federal, State, county, and municipal governments if the military should occupy their buildings on the outbreak of war and throw them into the street? And how in heaven's name could one drill and equip four millions of men in the corridors of our federal courts or post offices or customs houses? If for no other reason, the whole MacArthur plan ought to be thrown out because of this very stupidity.

But the militarists' self-revelation does not stop there. General MacArthur and the War Department have now placed themselves squarely in the position occupied by the worst of the European militarists of 1914—they would refuse exemption from military service to anybody. No Quakers, no clergymen, no men who have given their lives to pacifism, nobody is to be exempted; all are to be dragooned into the ranks to kill or be killed. The conscience of the individual is now entirely to be violated by the Moloch of the state. What punishments our militarists will now decree for those who next dare to keep their souls stainless does not appear—death, we suppose, as was the original proposal of the officers of the Judge Advocate General's department in 1917.

As for the problems of the mobilization of civilian labor, there General MacArthur walks as lightly as he does in treating of capital. "Conscription of labor would be so resented by the workers affected that they would not lend their best efforts to the production of needed supplies." How cowardly! How unworthy of a true patriotic militarist! If conscripted men in the ranks are to have their wishes disregarded, if they are to be compelled to serve by use of torture, the rifle-butt, the solitary cell, as in 1917-19, why regard the wishes of the munition-maker? Let force be applied to him as well. Let him, too, be spread-eagled to cell doors, manacled and chained, hurled into lightless dungeons. Why permit the all-conquering state to be defied by threats of factory slacking, of unpatriotic "soldiering on the job"?

As to demobilization, General MacArthur urges a commission to deal with that problem from the start so as to be ready when the war ends. Ready for what? Victory or defeat? Ready when? Who can say? The General is careful to declare that "this plan does not envisage any particular enemy." No, indeed. How could it? There is not a country in the world today that would contemplate suicide by attacking the United States. There is not one which will ever have reason to war upon us unless we war upon it—not a single one of our foreign wars was other than of our own seeking. As for the waste of war, the General is not interested. So far as reported, he makes no provision for adequate pay or for the bonuses, insurance, or pensions that invariably cost more than the war itself.

And what hypocrites General MacArthur makes of his Commander-in-Chief, the President of the United States, and of each and every one of us! For we are the ones who declare that we won the war to end war; that we originated, signed, and ratified the pact to outlaw war, and pledged our holy word, our sacred honor, to abide by the Kellogg Pact and never again to war.

Red Menace and Yellow Journalism

By OSWALD GARRISON VILLARD

IT is always the open season for attacks upon Russia. It would be hard, however, to find a more striking attempt to stir up ill-will against Russia and to coin money out of that effort than is now being indulged in by the New York *Evening Post,* once the high-minded, ethically conducted, and respected newspaper of Horace White and Edwin L. Godkin. What makes this particular instance so flagrant is the deliberate sensationalizing, which frequently nearly crosses the line of misrepresentation, in the headlines written by the editors over the articles by H. R. Knickerbocker on Russia and Russian trade.

Mr. Knickerbocker is the Berlin correspondent of the *Evening Post.* Last fall he went to Russia and after traveling there for six weeks did a series of articles—not, the Russians think, without some bias, but none the less a straightforward and honest piece of reporting—for which he was awarded the Pulitzer prize for 1930. But even this series was exploited by the headline writers in the office of his newspaper in a way that must have made Mr. Knickerbocker redden with shame. The very title put upon the book into which these articles were made, "The Red Trade Menace," showed a bias which Mr. Knickerbocker certainly did not have when he went to Russia or when I talked with him on his return to Berlin. He is not the kind of journalist who takes orders to color his stuff. Where his articles were anti-Soviet, they were so written because he felt that way. If he erred at points, it was owing to faultiness of vision and background, and not because he deviated from the standards of ethical reporting because somebody else told him to do so. What he was bent on was portraying Russia in the fall of 1930. He was not there to play up the Russian trade menace.

And how were those articles treated by the *Post*? The first article carried the caption "Soviet, on Iron Rations, Wars for Trade Primacy, *Post* Survey Reveals." The next day the headline reader learned: "Famished Moscow Short All Food Except Bread." Once more: "Reds Use Forced Labor in Forest, *Post* Finds." The reader, however, found that while the kulaks, in uncertain numbers, were compelled to work in the lumber camps, the writer could discover practically no convict labor, and so far from finding that all Soviet labor was forced labor, he discovered a labor turnover in all industries so extreme as to cause severe financial losses. Some days later the reader even learned that of the forced laborers "178,000 Men Quit Torturous Soviet Coal Pits in Year," which looked pretty bad till he read below that conditions in the mines were so difficult that the men preferred to go and work elsewhere, so that the Soviets had to depend on the enthusiasm of their shock brigades of young Communists to get out the coal they wanted. Rarely has an honest reporter, trying hard to present a true picture of what he saw, been worse served by headline writers. If Mr. Knickerbocker was not outraged, he was entitled to be.

The success of this series, which is said in newspaper circles to have added 20,000 readers to the *Evening Post* during their continuance, emboldened the paper to try it again. This time Mr. Knickerbocker traveled about Europe. When his copy began to appear, the headline writers repeated with this result: "Red Trade Raids Europe, Survey by *Post* Reveals. H. R. Knickerbocker Finds Soviet Goods Flooding Twelve Nations. U. S. Markets Are Heavily Affected. Continent Feels Menace, Wonders if Economic Cordon Can Be Set Up." The reliability of this introduction may be gleaned from the fact that Soviet exports constitute *2 per cent* of world trade, and as this 2 per cent is distributed over the entire world, it is obvious that it must take very little to flood a nation. But let us return to the headlines. Here are some more: "Italy Backs Soviet Trade and Bars European Bloc. Two Dictatorships Stand United Against Economic Cordon." "Soviet Oil Floods Italy, Supplies Fascist Fleet. Great Plant at Savona Undersells America 20 Per Cent. France Sees Peril if War Develops. Italian State Corporation Distributes Products. Monopoly for Reds Looms." "Soviet Cuts Grain Price to Outstrip U. S. in Italy. Regularly Shades Grain Rate to Keep Below Competitors. Passes U. S. This Year in Anthracite Sales." Precisely as in the earlier series, the headlines are deliberately calculated to excite alarm in the mind of the reader, and to cause hostility. We are accustomed to gross misunderstanding and misrepresentation of our capitalist society in Communist writing and especially in the Moscow dailies, but it may be doubted whether we shall find there any statements better calculated to arouse fear and hatred than the treatment of Mr. Knickerbocker's facts by his editors.

Now as to some of the facts. In Italy, for example, the reader will discover that 16 per cent of the wheat imported is drawn from Russia, whereas, as Mr. Knickerbocker himself points out, before the war as high as 60 per cent sometimes came from the Czar's dominions—plainly a dreadful case of "flooding." As for the ruinous flooding of Italy with Russian coal, Mr. Knickerbocker reports that in 1930 Soviet anthracite constituted about 2½ per cent of Italy's imports of 12,000,000 tons, and that the Italians expressed themselves ready to take all the anthracite they could get from these wicked Russians. Why? Because it was cheap and of good quality. There you have the abominable conduct of the Soviets clearly revealed. As a matter of fact, Russia exports in large amounts, just as capitalist countries do, precisely those goods for which she has natural advantages or other special facilities—lumber, oil, furs, wheat, textile piece goods, and flax, to mention them in order of importance during 1930. She imports industrial equipment, tractors, cotton, iron and steel manufactures, and other products for which other countries at this time have relative advantages.

As for unfair competition, Mr. Knickerbocker finds that "Soviet prices are, as a rule, just low enough—but always low enough—to get the business, and not, if the Soviets can help it, any lower." Heaven help us, but we had thought that that was exactly the way that everybody got foreign business! These Soviet trade practices are precisely those of any big American industrial concern under similar circumstances. Indeed, under the compulsion of the reparations and debts payments, the Germans are doing precisely that same thing. For example, the Belgians and Poles and other neighbors of Germany were able last year to buy a ton of German rye for seventy marks less than any German consumer himself paid within the boundaries of the German

Reich. It would be just as fair to attribute deliberate political motives to the German exporters as it is to attribute them to the Russian. But the whole slant given to Mr. Knickerbocker's articles is that this is all part of a deliberate effort to break down the capitalist governments of Europe. That the leaders of the Soviets would be glad to see the capitalist governments fall everybody knows, because they have said so from the outset of their experiment. But what every honest student of Russian conditions also knows is that they are compelled to send out everything that they can possibly deprive the Russian people of in order to get foreign currency, or credits, with which to buy machinery from England, Germany, and the United States, and all the rest of the materials that they need to industrialize Russia.

If they were such devilish schemers as the *Evening Post* headlines are calculated to portray them, would they, as Mr. Knickerbocker says, reduce their prices only just low enough to capture other markets, or would they not be selling at half- or quarter-price? Mr. Knickerbocker adduces no facts to suggest, and does not himself suggest, anything other than the ordinary commercial motives behind Russian-Italian trade, or anything but the usual commercial practices on the part of Russia in trying to sell its goods in Italy. If the story concerned any other country on earth except Russia, indeed, it would be looked on merely as a striking example of hustling for trade, of trade recovery and development, but not as a "menace" to anyone except rival producers in other countries now forced to face a vigorous new competition. Naturally, the appearance of any new competitor gives serious concern to business men, but it should never be occasion for terror, or for wild charges of dumping and unfair competition. Moreover, the simple fact remains that even when nations like Germany, Russia, France, and Great Britain dump goods in another country, they are paid for what they deliver by the goods of the country to which they deliver. A cash transaction practically never takes place. It is, of course, hard luck for the *Evening Post* that its yellow headlines came in a week which saw the warm and friendly reception of the Soviet statesmen at Geneva and London on terms of full equality.

Why then all the sensational headlines and advertising? First and foremost this atmosphere is created to sell papers. Let us breed hatred and fear and thoroughly confuse readers, if only thereby the circulation figures can be swelled in a year when every newsstand notices the shrinkage of its sales. Secondly, it may be an attempt deliberately to create hostility toward Russia for ulterior political purposes. No greater disservice could be done to the United States than to create a feeling of unreasoning terror about what the Russians are doing and going to do, if only because we need their trade badly in this crisis. There is, finally, still such a thing as responsibility of the press. We are entitled to expect of it not only enterprise in the learning of facts about the experiment carried on by the Soviet Government, but a decent sincerity and sobriety, not to say honesty, in the presentation and weighing of those facts.

We Need Russia

GIVEN free play, the economic forces now at work in both Russia and the United States will in all likelihood bring these two countries closer together. Diverted or handicapped by a hostile public opinion—the goal of men like Ralph Easley, Secretary of Labor Doak, Matthew Woll, and Hamilton Fish, of organizations like the National Civic Federation, and of newspapers like the New York *Evening Post*—the same economic forces will without doubt widen the present cleavage between Russia and America. By constantly arousing American public sentiment with their hysterical speeches, sensational statements, and scare headlines, these men and organizations are building up hatred and bitterness, creating anti-Russian feeling of a most dangerous kind. That way lies neither political nor economic peace. In such an inflamed atmosphere one could not look for reasonable understanding between the countries; one could only hope that no small accident or incident would turn this hatred of Russia into an open demand for war. Unfortunately, it appears almost certain that the propaganda drive of the Russophobes, instead of decreasing, will increase in scope and intensity as Russia's economic strength becomes more apparent and our own system continues to lumber along from mistake to mistake.

We do not question the sincerity of these persons who are forever agitating against the Soviet Union. They unquestionably feel that Moscow presents a real threat to our institutions and our much-vaunted individualism, and there can be little doubt that many of them have felt the pressure of Russian commercial and industrial competition. But we cannot agree that Moscow will at any time in the foreseeable future upset our institutions, though it is probable that if communism succeeds, its influence may in the course of years serve to modify them. Nor can we agree that the erection of an economic *cordon sanitaire* about the Soviet Union will either convert Russia to capitalism or solve the problem involved in Russia's trade relations with America and the rest of the world.

In point of fact, we need Russia exactly as Russia needs us. Even by the most careful planning and with the most generous of outside help, the Soviet Union cannot hope to complete its industrialization program for many years to come. Able and dependable economists who have studied the problem put the number of these years at no less than twenty-five, though most of them agree that perhaps it will take a period longer than fifty years to put Russian industry on a plane nearly equal to our own. During this period the Russians will need to import goods of many kinds, but particularly agricultural and heavy industrial machinery; they will have to import capital in various other forms, much as we imported capital from Europe in the century and a half of our own industrial development. Russia will also need financial aid in the shape of credit, and credit can only be sent to it in the form of goods or services. Where is Moscow to buy these goods? It will want to buy some, if not a large proportion, of them in the United States, but we must be ready to offer it moderately reasonable terms lest we lose its trade to Europe. Russia has already shown a marked preference for American products. We have created an industrial machine that Russia wishes to copy, and we have developed agricultural machinery for use over a terrain very similar to that of the grain-growing areas of the Soviet Union. Hence we possess the technical knowledge and the experience necessary for the production of the kind of machinery which the Russians consider peculiarly suited to their needs, while this knowledge and experience are largely lacking among European manufacturers.

Nevertheless, Russia has in recent months unmistakably revealed that she prefers to deal with Europe when she is denied fair treatment at our hands. Were this policy to be continued over a period of years, we should stand to lose not only our fair share of the growing Russian trade, but also a large part of our present trade with Western Europe, for if these European countries are to sell to Russia they must buy from Russia in increasing measure. In 1929 we sold goods worth $2,300,000,000 to Europe, which was almost half of our total exports. We have now to choose between the blind philosophy of the Easleys and the Wolls, which is having the effect of driving this lucrative trade toward Russia, and a more reasonable and intelligent attitude, which would in large part conserve this trade and at the same time open the expanding Russian market to us.

Now, Mr. Hoover, Disarm!

JUST what caused President Hoover to change his mind so suddenly as to Germany, reparations, and debts, we, being without the confidence of the White House, know not. But when the realization came to him at last that Europe was, as *The Nation,* and higher and better authorities than ourselves, had for weeks been maintaining, on the verge of a terrific catastrophe, President Hoover lost not a minute in acting and acting spontaneously and well. Late, of course, he was. It is yet to be shown how far a year's postponement of European payments will set the millions of unemployed in Europe and America to work, how far it will block the headlong plunge of the European Powers toward bankruptcy, anarchy, and chaos. But nothing has happened since our last issue appeared to make us question that a marvelous step toward the rehabilitation of Europe is now assured. More than that, we believe—tell it not in Gath, which is Paris—that the Young Plan payments will never be renewed in full, that the plan itself is definitely breached and must be made over, and that another advance has been made toward the rewriting of the Treaty, that is the Madness, of Versailles.

These things lie in the future. As soon as the decks are cleared—and we have no fears as to any serious obduracy on the part of France—the next immediate objective is the Disarmament Conference at Geneva, in 1932. There lies the next rampart to be taken by storm, for within it is one of the six or seven major causes of Europe's falling to its present low estate. The swollen armaments of Europe have contributed not one whit to its safety or peace. On the contrary, they are one of the potent reasons why Fear stalks abroad in all the lands overseas touched by the World War. And hand in hand with Fear run Suspicion and Hate, its handmaidens. Each government watches what the next is doing. Each government demands more ships and gases, men and guns, tanks and planes; yes, so do even the happily disarmed nations. If this state of dread and unrest and incredible waste is not concluded, there can be but one end to it all—another holocaust with dire results.

If any man would deny this contention, let us point out to him what the actual figures are: Belgium's debt payments to the United States were but 2.01 per cent of its budget for 1930-31, while for armaments it is expending 10.3 per cent. France paid only $44,350,000 to the United States in 1930-31, while its military and naval expenditures reached the enormous sum of $432,000,000—2.24 per cent as against 21.9 per cent. Even in Great Britain, sorely harassed as it is, only 4.2 per cent of its budget came to us, while military and naval expenditures took 14 per cent. In Italy the comparison is even more striking. Its payments to the United States are only six-tenths of 1 per cent of its entire budget, while *more than one-quarter,* 25.4 per cent, goes to preparations for mass murder. So in Rumania, so in Poland. Only in Germany is the proportion reversed; its military and naval expenditures—still much too high—constitute 11.6 per cent of the total, whereas for reparations and external war charges Germany is assessed no less than 22.04 per cent of its outgo. If the mere forgiving of these smaller sums for one year can thrill the whole world, set every market to throbbing, and specially cause to rejoice the nations of Europe, what would not be accomplished if the insane waste of money for armaments were even cut in half?

Fortunately, Mr. Hoover has come more than ever to see the tremendous opportunity to end this waste of treasure, this criminal diversion of valuable capital. He has not always seen clearly in this matter, nor striven toward the goal as effectively as possible. We are not forgetting his repeated appeals to the nations to disarm, but we must recall, too, the wretched tactics and strategy on our part in the all but abortive Naval Disarmament Conference in London. Headed in the right direction, Mr. Hoover has not picked the right men to represent us, nor known how to give them a program. He has not correctly portrayed in his public addresses the military situation and policies of the United States. He has repeatedly stated that we could not reduce our land armaments because we had already gone so far in that direction. Even in his address to the International Chamber of Commerce in Washington on May 4 last, he said: "The United States has a less direct interest in land-armament reduction than any of the large nations because our forces have already been demobilized and reduced more than all others." Obviously he forgot Germany and Austria and Hungary and Bulgaria—the beaten Powers now disarmed. He did real injustice to England, which alone has decreased its expenditures for army and navy, reduced its officers, and cut and slashed year by year until its Navy League is frantic, as Mr. MacDonald declared in his remarkable speech on June 29. He forgot his own Presidential message of December 3, 1929, in which he said: "After 1914 the [our] various army contingents necessarily expanded until the end of the Great War and then proceeded to the low point in 1924 when expansion again began. In 1914 the officers and men in our regular forces, both army and navy, were about 164,000; in 1924 there were about 256,000, and in 1929 there were about 250,000." In his next sentence he admitted that "our citizens' army, however, including the National Guard and other forms of reserves, increases these totals up to about 299,000 in 1914, about 672,000 in 1924, and about 728,000 in 1929." There has been no change since 1929 except in the direction of further increase—the War Department continues to commission reserve officers, and it is understood that there are now close to 110,000, although we did not have five such officers when we won the war to end war. How could Mr. Hoover forget facts like these—that our forces had been increased from 299,000 to 728,000 and more—and dare to say to the visiting members of the International Chamber of Commerce that our land armament has been "reduced more than all others"?

But if this is a sorry example of loose Presidential thinking, three recent happenings have given us hope that here, too, Mr. Hoover has seen a great light. In the first place, the President has announced that on his present trip to Europe Mr. Stimson will discuss the question of disarmament with the heads of other governments. Next, Mr. Stimson's publishing on June 15, voluntarily, a complete statement of our effective military and naval forces (without reserves) is additional proof that the government is ready to lay its cards on the table even now. Finally, and most important, there is the Administration's recession on the matter of budgetary limitation of arms. No less than thirty-eight national organizations had appealed in June to Mr. Hoover to accept the principle. But at every conference hitherto the United States has opposed the plan of reducing armaments by limiting military and naval expenditure. Thus Ambassador Gibson has made the point that monetary fluctuations and differences in the various countries prevent this method of limitation from being "a true measure of armaments or a fair basis for limitation of armaments." The United States Government has also been opposed because acceptance would involve some form of international supervision by the League of Nations, and the United States did not wish to put itself in that position. Hence, the sudden change of position of Washington gives ground for hope that this time the United States will enter the Disarmament Conference with a fixed policy and, what is more important, a spirit of determination to achieve concrete results, instead of taking the attitude at the outset that it could not consider this or compromise on that, and that so far as its land forces were concerned it had nothing to yield, although its total military and naval expenditure, as Mr. Hoover himself has pointed out, is "in excess of those of the most highly militarized nations of the world," and the "programs now authorized will carry it to still larger figures in future years."

The way to disarm is to disarm. There is no prouder chapter in the history of the United States than the fact that during the first 111 years of our national history our regular army never rose above the figure of 25,000 men, and our fleet was negligible save during the Civil War; during this long period we never had a foreign war that was not of our own seeking. If Mr. Hoover were the ardent peace lover, the sincere and earnest Quaker, that he claims to be, he would have insisted from the moment of his taking office that there should not only be no further increases on land and at sea, but that our military and naval forces should be steadily reduced as conclusive proof to the other nations of the world of our sincerity in urging disarmament. If the other nations of the world have not believed in our sincerity in urging them to disarm, we have only ourselves to blame. Mr. Hoover should now enter the Disarmament Conference determined to disarm, and let it be known that the United States is ready to lead the way.

We have still another constructive suggestion to make. There are two men on the other side of the ocean, Prime Minister MacDonald and his Foreign Secretary, Mr. Henderson, who have their hearts set upon a great success at Geneva in February of next year. We urge upon Mr. Hoover that through Mr. Stimson or directly he come into touch with these two gentlemen, and agree with them upon a radical program of reduction as to material, ships, troops, and expenditures, to be presented jointly in the name of the two great Anglo-Saxon countries at the very opening of the conference. There could be no better or more effective strategy than thus to take the offensive, and none that would as certainly bring about a long step toward the freeing of the world from the criminal waste of armaments that protect nobody and are merely guaranties of the continuance of war.

Impatience for Peace

ALL that words can do for peace was done on July 11 at the great demonstration meeting in Albert Hall, London, when 8,000 persons inside the hall and many times that number outside heard Ramsay MacDonald, Stanley Baldwin, and David Lloyd George tell them, in language that there could be no mistaking, what the Government of England meant to do to stop war. The Prime Minister's speech came first. He spoke not only of the united enthusiasm for peace that exists in England but of the folly of preparation for war: "History is one unbroken story of armed peoples attacking armed peoples." Unfortunately, he added, "the sentiment of peace is universal. The practice of peace is circumscribed." The coming Geneva conference on disarmament *must* bring results.

Mr. Lloyd George was equally pertinent. We have talked peace and prepared for war, he said. We have had disarmament conferences, a Locarno agreement, a pact to renounce war—"proposed by a country whose armaments were much more powerful than they were before the war and whose armaments have increased since they signed the pact to renounce war." And since then all the nations which attended those conferences, which signed that agreement and that pact have become more militaristic than ever. "They have kept Germany to her promise but they have broken their own." "The world is going on steadily, horribly, stupidly marching toward war, that catastrophe, singing the songs of peace and preparing for war."

These are not merely words, they are facts. In France, in the United States, in Germany, in Japan, even among England's navophiles it is evident that the lesson of the last war has not been learned. We have thought that an overpowering sentiment against war would have to spring up from the people of every great nation. Governments make war, we have said time and again; peoples must make peace. It may be that, owing in part to the present condition of the world's finances, this state of affairs is changing. Governments may begin to realize what a powerful instrument they are controlling, that the safety of mankind rests on their refusal to unleash these engines of destruction, to arouse the war spirit, to give the jingoes in any country free rein to print their lies and their half-truths in order that an enemy may be created and a war begun. The speeches of these three men indicated something of the kind, as did the remarks of the chairman, Field Marshal Sir William Robertson, fifty years a soldier, when he said: "I believe the majority of the people in the world now think war hurts everybody and helps nobody—except the profiteers—and settles nothing."

No sounder truths about war and peace could have been spoken. What remains? Patience, said Mr. Mac-

Donald, patience and persistence and faith. Impatience, said Maude Royden, the only woman speaker, impatience from the common run of people, so that the negotiators for peace would be compelled to get results. Words for peace are very well. But what we must have in addition is a burning, an unconquerable, an undeviating hatred of war, any war for whatever reason. When war becomes unthinkable, then, and then only, is peace assured.

France Against the World

By OSWALD GARRISON VILLARD

WHAT is the actual situation of the world today? Europe is on the verge of financial collapse because Germany hangs in the balance. To save the Reich, Mr. Hoover proposed and carried through the moratorium of one year, the best psychological effects of which were spoiled bv a two weeks' delay due to French haggling over tne proposal. Germany was further aided by the announcement, after the seven-power conference, that certain short-term credits would be frozen, but every effort to get the American banks together to advance a credit of $500,000,000 failed—beyond question because of French opposition. Meanwhile, though there is conflicting evidence of what took place when the heads of the French Government met Chancellor Brüning and Foreign Minister Curtius in Paris, the fact remains that the French, who were in the best position to help Germany, have not done so. The rumors still persist, despite denials in the name of Premier Laval, that the French are refusing to aid unless Germany makes political concessions which will violate its independence and will cause the fall of any German Ministry which agrees to them. The next few weeks will tell whether the Germans can save themselves, or whether it will be a question of further help in order to save Europe and the capitalist system, and to prevent an unparalleled disaster in the United States.

Meanwhile, it is obvious to every man of affairs, wherever he may be, that the Young Plan is dead and can never be revived; that if Mr. Hoover made any mistake in connection with his moratorium proposal it was in not asking for a two-year debt vacation instead of one, since in less than a year from now the whole question of reparations and debts will come up again at the worst possible time—in the middle of an American Presidential campaign. More than that, the Versailles treaty is equally finished; it is so dead that it cries to high heaven for decent interment with the customary rites. But the French will agree to neither one of these accomplished facts. They refuse to admit that anything has happened to the Young Plan beyond a temporary postponement. If, as Briand has *twice* said, they consider the Austro-German customs union a cause for war, what will his Government not say to the man who declares the Versailles treaty is on the scrap heap? The whole hegemony of France hinges on that treaty; its whole system of satellite nations, so elaborately built up by force and subvention, by skilful playing of the financial cards among people in distress and in need, will collapse. The present vicious arrangement of Europe with which France is entirely content (save that its militarists still desire the left bank of the Rhine) will come in for a new deal—the Polish Corridor, Upper Silesia, and all the rest. Not Alsace-Lorraine, of course. There Germany is on record as having formally and permanently abandoned all claims—in my recent stay of six months in Germany I never heard from any source the suggestion that Alsace-Lorraine might be, or ought to be, recovered.

France will stand against any further help for Germany—unless paid the price of political subservience. Against any reconsideration of the Young Plan—unless it is given a price—France will set itself with all its strength. Against any revision of the Versailles treaty France will throw all its power. More than that, France stands out today in all the world as the one country which opposes thoroughgoing disarmament—except on *its* terms. It wants every step taken to be from the point of view of what it thinks it needs and what it fears. No, not what *it* fears. I do not believe that of the French people. I should have said "what the politicians now holding office fear, or pretend to fear." I notice that every time Briand makes an intensely pacifist speech his hearers wildly applaud him. I notice that the press associations all report that the reception of the Germans by the crowds in Paris was remarkably friendly and generous despite some cat-calls. I notice that there is no real public opinion in France; that the masses have no way of making themselves heard. The provincial press is negligible. The Parisian press is about the worst in the world. Where it is not deliberately corrupt, it is under the influence of the financiers, or is entirely controlled by the Government. The American newspapers, which solemnly reprint the views of the French editors whenever any important thing happens, do a great injustice in not telling the American public that most of these journals represent crooked financiers, or crooked politicians, or crooked editors, or editors who take their orders—if not their pay—from the Government. Let nobody think that such as these represent the mass of the thrifty, home-loving, law-abiding, peace-desiring people of France. Nothing of the kind. It is no more possible to deduce from a *Temps* or a *Matin* article what Bretagne thinks of a world proposal than it is possible to gauge the feeling of the people of Kansas and Oregon by the editorial solemnities of the New York *Times* or *Herald Tribune*.

But there the situation is. ***Every move now being made to rescue Europe encounters French opposition. Every hope of a favorable outcome of the disarmament conference,*** which is to set the world free from the slavery of armaments that hideously waste national resources and spell *war* not peace, ***is menaced today by the French.*** There is the plain truth. We had a Tammany boss in New York once who, when the facts were revealed as to the rottenness and corruption in Manhattan, sat back defiantly, his black cigar in his mouth, his thumbs in the armholes of his waistcoat, and asked the citizenry: "What are you going to do about it?" Today, that is the question France is posing to the rest of the world. In the words of the jingo rhyme they say: "We have the ships, we have the men, we have the money, too." They have the largest fleet of fighting airplanes in the world.

They have enough formidable submarines to keep England on the anxious seat. They have the largest and most effective army. They have huge gold reserves—so great that, like our own, they menace the stability of world finance. They owe no money to England, but England owes money to them. Their country is restored. Despite huge armament expenditures their annual deficits are not alarming. They claim officially that they have only 35,000 unemployed when Germany has over 4,000,000, and we at least 6,000,000, and England 2,000,000. The effects of the world crisis are only felt in France here and there—in the bankruptcy of their leading steamship lines, in the severe falling off in the number of tourists, especially American, in incidental strikes and distress in certain trades like the woolen industry. Superficially they are "sitting pretty." The economic tornado has not hit them full force.

They are "sitting pretty." What are *you,* and we, going to do about it? The consensus of public opinion about France's dog-in-the-manger policy and its danger to the whole world was never more united—it is as united as public opinion in 1914 was everywhere in regard to the German violation of Belgian neutrality. Today public opinion outside of France is so wholly opposed to the French that it would be a shock to the good people of that republic if they realized it. Everywhere the belief is that France blocks the road to a genuine peace in Europe.

What are you going to do about it? When there was all that hullabaloo about the "Beast of Berlin," when our leading clergy and moralists were raving that Germany was the mad dog of Europe, the remedy suggested was to get America to apply, in Woodrow Wilson's words, "force—force without stint" and to complete the circle imprisoning the mad dog. That application of force was a miserable fizzle. It won no victory, it achieved no peace. It left us the horrible legacies of Versailles; it left us the conditions which have led to the present economic catastrophe of the world. It left us this very problem of France, for it transferred the seat of military power in Europe from Berlin to Paris without in the least changing its character, and once more we are faced with the problem of what to do with a country which is today outraging and defying the public opinion of the rest of the world.

What can we do? First, we can organize public opinion behind the governments which, like those of the United States and Great Britain, are determined that Europe shall not collapse and that the disarmament conference shall succeed. Mr. Hoover, Ramsay MacDonald, and Arthur Henderson have done splendidly in calling for disarmament. In both countries public opinion is rapidly being mobilized in their support. Wherever our public is approached, whether by individual speakers or peace caravans or in any other way, the public response is complete. Every one of our innumerable societies dealing with peace and international affairs is working as never before. So in England. Petitions in their most conservative universities have produced a unanimity of support for a cut of 25 per cent in armaments never before seen, never before possible. The press and public, and especially the women, are determined that the biased naval experts and the admirals shall not spoil this conference.

Second, there must be increasing outside public pressure brought to bear upon France—despite the difficulty of getting news through to the French people. Here the international bankers could help a lot—if they would dare to stand up against the Bank of France. They may yet be compelled to do what they now think impossible if Germany collapses financially and economically. Third, there should be pursued by the other governments a steady policy leading to the isolation of France, especially with regard to the disarmament conference. *The Nation* has already made the constructive suggestion that Great Britain and the United States should agree in advance upon a radical program such as the abolition of all poison gas, submarines, aircraft, and battleships, the limitation of all remaining ships (cruisers and the rest) to 10,000 tons, and of all guns to light field-artillery size, and a cut of at least 50 per cent in expenditures, this program to be urged and advocated at the very outset of the conference by at least a dozen Powers under Anglo-Saxon lead, exactly as Charles E. Hughes electrified the Washington arms conference in 1922 by offering a specific program the minute it met. This program, whenever decided upon, should be communicated *at once* to the French with all possible courtesy and good-will, with all possible urging that France, too, adopt it before the conference meets.

It is impossible to believe that such a move would not call forth the enthusiastic adherence of the vast bulk of the conference—it includes all the nations, even Russia—and it is also impossible to believe that if such a program were accepted by all save France and its satellites, France could hold out and definitely set its face against world opinion. Proof of that is to be found in its final acceptance of the Hoover moratorium. It will in any event haggle, bargain, growl, delay, and talk about its special dangers and problems. But it cannot wholly defy Europe, America, and Asia without facing world-wide excoriation and isolation. Like every other country it needs good-will; it must have it to progress financially and economically. More than that, if the rest of the world is ready to disarm radically, could any French Government defend itself to its own parsimonious citizens if it refused them a glorious opportunity to lift some of the tax burdens from their backs?

If France should then still refuse to disarm? Then (fourthly) let the other nations go on with their outlawing of battleship, submarine, and airplane. The generals and admirals will rave at such a suggestion and declare that it would make every other nation vassal to France. Nothing of the kind. No country would be allowed by its own citizens to use outlawed weapons upon peoples who would refuse to fight back in kind.

But, fifth, if the latter proposal sounds too idealistic, there are ways of organizing against France, and to these it may be necessary to turn. There is the League of Nations, for one thing. It is impossible to believe that it would rest supine under such circumstances, for, if it did so, it would admit the correctness of the frequent charge made against it that it is under the control, or controlling influence, of the French. The vital stake the League has in the disarmament conference may be realized if one remembers that upon its success probably depends the question whether Germany and the other disarmed countries will or will not remain in the League. As for the other signatories to the Treaty of Versailles, their honor and their words are in the balance. They pledged disarmament in that treaty. France may wish to have it known that her signature at Versailles has no greater value than a dicer's oath; the others do not and will not. The same is true of the signatories to the Kellogg Pact. Did they mean what they said when they signed that document, or did they not? If France insists on maintaining armaments which overawe the rest of Europe, the other great Powers have still another reason for making it clear to France that they can no longer stand for any such policy, especially as it is, economically speaking, a rule or ruin policy. The world has a right to demand of France that it shall keep its word and conduct its relationships with other peoples upon the principle that it has forsworn war forever; not that, having taken a solemn oath to abstain from war, it shall go on conducting its international affairs as if it had never heard of the Kellogg Pact. Certainly it would not do a whit differently, if it had never signed the pact, than it is doing now. Why did the French sign the pact and praise it to the skies if it meant nothing to them and only encouraged them to continue to take counsel of their fears, to continue to arm and to hold a pistol at the heads of all the Powers in demanding the special terms and concessions which are deemed necessary for French safety—as if no agreement to abolish war existed?

President Nicholas Murray Butler of Columbia has just urged that Congress pass at once the Capper resolution introduced two years ago, making it possible for the President to use non-forcible sanctions or disciplinary measures against any adhering nation which violates the Kellogg Pact. This resolution would permit both an economic boycott and the placing of an embargo upon shipments to any violator who goes to war. All of this has to do with the future. One cannot, however, but feel that something like a moral embargo must ere long come to pass if France should menace the whole future of the world and deliberately block the way to that disarmament which is one of the most vital steps toward recovery. Certainly something like this must have been in the mind of Noel Baker, parliamentary secretary to Foreign Secretary Henderson, when he told the Socialist Workmen's International at Vienna on July 28: "We shall proclaim every government which opposes disarmament a deadly enemy of mankind"—a remarkable statement from so responsible an official. As already quoted in *The Nation*, J. L. Garvin, the veteran editor of the *Sunday Observer*, declares that America and England will have to take separate action against French policy within three months. It is impossible to believe that in this most dire crisis in the world's history one nation will be permitted, through the incredible obstinacy, shortsightedness, and self-will of politicians temporarily in power, to block the rehabilitation of the world.

Disarmament Both Hot and Cold

JUST when Mr. Hoover has been so ardent in publicly stating that there must be disarmament, and linking his every action for the rescuing of Europe with disarmament, comes the disheartening announcement of Secretary Adams, with, it is stated in the dispatches, the consent of President Hoover, that the navy adopted a "new policy" for a fleet that "in every important respect will conform to the provisions of the London Treaty for the Limitation of Naval Armaments." In other words, we are to build up to the British strength just when the times are bad and Mr. Hoover has been berating every bureau chief for not having cut rigidly his estimates for the next fiscal year; and so we are to have two new aircraft carriers, six fleet-submarines, one flying-deck 10,000-ton cruiser, one London-treaty six-inch gun cruiser of about 10,000 tons, one destroyer, one destroyer-leader, and complete airplane equipment for the aircraft carrier Ranger now under construction, the whole to cost $129,385,000. It is officially announced that the purpose of the Administration is "to create, maintain, and operate a navy second to none and in conformity to treaty provisions," that the program will be approved by the bureau of the budget and the President, and will give employment to thousands of men, a large part going in wages "to skilled mechanics and other workers in the shipbuilding and ordnance trades."

The last argument for this expenditure is similar to that made by Ramsay MacDonald when excusing the building of cruisers by the first British Labor Government. It cannot be justified on that ground. The real reason is, we suppose, the stupid old one that the President thinks we must have something more to "bargain with" when we enter the disarmament conference next February. It is that incredibly mad military and naval mind at work again of which Professor Ross of the University of Wisconsin speaks in the article printed elsewhere in this issue of *The Nation*. The plan, of course, will have no such effect as is intended. In the first place, it is too obvious, too transparent, and too openly stated. In the second place, it will stir up all the admirals, the Navy League, and the professional imperialists in Great Britain. In the third place, wherever it is read under the sun, it will cast doubt upon the sincerity of the disarmament position of Herbert Hoover. It will be said of us abroad that we are no more sincere in our advocacy of genuine disarmament than are the French. At home it ought to be clear that money spent upon any such program in this time of acute national distress, when the President himself has said that we must rigidly reduce our expenditures, would be nothing less than a criminal waste of public funds. Fortunately, it is yet to be authorized by Congress, and we hope that Congress will take the bit in its teeth under pressure from public opinion and will refuse to be misled by the specious argument that this throwing away of money upon armaments that will be worth nothing five or ten years from now should be sanctioned in order to give employment.

We confess that Mr. Hoover's policy in this matter leaves us gasping. Perhaps it is to be explained by the charge made in the new "Mirrors of Washington" that Mr. Hoover is greatly influenced by the last person who is with him. How can he again make an appeal to an international body, as he did in his address to the International Chamber of Commerce last May, in behalf of disarmament? If Mr. Hoover were a true statesman and a true Quaker, he would now be saying to Europe: "Gentlemen, we ask you to disarm. If you do not, we are going ahead on our own. We are not afraid. For more than one hundred years of its existence when it was poor, weak, struggling, torn by internal dissension which finally led to a bloody civil war, and when it was creating homes for its people in the once trackless wilderness, this country had no fleet, and its army never exceeded 25,000 men save in war times. It was undisturbed, and never attacked, although its thousands of miles of coasts were for generations absolutely defenseless, and could have been taken at any time by the French, British, or Russian navies. It is now going back to its historic American policy with all the more courage and cheerfulness because it demonstrated during the World War that it had the most magnificent resources in men, materials, and wealth of any country in the world. It considers itself unassailable today. It proposes to devote its wealth in this emergency to reconstructing its economy and to keeping alive and content the millions of unemployed and starving men, women, and children within its borders. It will leave to others the un-Christian policy of squandering its national wealth on plans to kill, which can have only one outcome if persisted in—the destruction of the present economic system, and the establishment of a totally different one." If Mr. Hoover could say this the whole country, yes, the whole world, would rise and acclaim him.

The President, Congress, and the Navy

IT is gratifying, indeed, to record the President's insistence upon cuts in the navy budget and to read that he really became indignant at the undercover opposition to his economy plans by high officers of the navy. This is no new phenomenon. Even under Mr. Coolidge there was rank disloyalty to his half-hearted disarmament moves—disloyalty which went unrebuked. It would be interesting indeed, if it should be possible to reveal the precise relations between high naval officers and the Navy League, which is now weeping bitter tears over the straits to which the navy has already "been reduced." Nothing could give us a better standing on the naval side of the Geneva disarmament conference than the ability to say that we had substantially cut our budget before going to Geneva, had reduced the number of active ships and cut the enlisted personnel by thousands.

We welcome, too, the gage of battle which has been flung to President Hoover by Senator Frederick Hale of Maine and Congressman Britten of Illinois, respectively chairmen of the House and Senate Naval Committees. By all means let us have a show-down. Senator Hale, one of the smallest politicians in our public life, sees himself fighting the battle of an endangered Congress. The Constitution has empowered the Congress alone, he says, to decide what the national defense needs, and he proposes to protect the Constitution and the rights of Congress from the vicious assaults of President Hoover—provided, however, that at the critical moment the navy and the General Board inform him that it is really necessary to go through with the program of building up to the limit permitted by the London treaty for naval limitations. Ought not someone to defend the Congress from this unconstitutional prerogative of the admirals of dictating what the national defense shall be? As for Congressman Britten, who, as our readers are aware, recently induced the Navy Department to order the North Atlantic fleet, contrary to its wishes, to Montauk Point for a rest period, when he has a financial stake in the real-estate speculation there, we are perfectly willing to pit against him Chairman Will R. Wood of the Appropriations Committee, who has recently no less than three times publicly declared that it is time to cut military and naval appropriations to the bone, since there is no necessity whatsoever for the swollen armaments we now have. By all means let us have a show-down—preferably on the floor of the House and Senate. These army and navy appropriations bills are enormously important. For years they have slipped through without any adequate debate, although they have not only national but international ramifications. Nothing could be better than a first-class public give-and-take between those who still believe in the exploded theory of force and in useless weapons like the outmoded battleships, and those who wish to free the world from the curse of armaments.

As a matter of fact, Mr. Hoover could go a good deal farther and faster than he is going. The budgets of West Point and Annapolis could and should be cut; there are too many cadets for the needs of either service and both institutions are heavily overstaffed in comparison with civilian colleges. Mr. Hoover does not propose to reduce the strength of the navy below 75,700. Why do we need so large a force? There is only one fleet which rivals our own, and the country which possesses it trembles on the verge of bankruptcy and is even more eager for disarmament than are we. If ever a war with England was unthinkable, it is today in view of Great Britain's inability to raise funds to protect its own currency; its dire economic distress; its grave social unrest. Who else menaces us? Not Japan certainly; not Russia, which has no fleet; not Italy or France. We are maintaining our sixteen battleships merely because we have got into the habit of it; because our armament profiteers, Navy League, and naval officers, with their vested interest in maintaining a fleet, are constantly propagandizing for it and are trying to persuade the nation that we must continue to waste not only $750,000,000 a year on army and navy upkeep in this industrial crisis, but actually spend $750,000,000 more to build our fleet up to the limits permitted by the London agreement.

But while we think Mr. Hoover could cut much more vigorously than he has, we repeat that we are heartily grateful for the fight he is making. The whole spirit of the Administration fills us with hope that it at last means business. Here, for example, are excerpts from the remarkable speech made by William R. Castle, Jr., Undersecretary of State, before the Advertising Club of Boston:

> It is safe enough to say that the seeds of the depression were sown in the World War. . . . The billions wasted in munitions brought no return whatsoever.
>
> It is said that the world spends annually three billion dollars on armaments, and yet it is clear that the individual nations would be just as safe if the volume of this construction were proportionately cut one-half or three-quarters. Every nation needs an army for internal police purposes but beyond this every soldier is a potential offensive force.
>
> We fought, or said we fought, a war to end war. We have made anti-war treaties that cover the globe, but as long as we pour money into competitive armaments we admit that war is always imminent. We make a travesty of our high-sounding treaties.

This is true statesmanship. This sounds a true call to the nation. This is the kind of courage and truth-telling that we have a right to expect from men in high office who seek to lead. We hope that every reader of *The Nation* will send his individual thanks to Mr. Castle. Meanwhile, even the United States Chamber of Commerce has seen the light and demands that "every possible step be taken for international disarmament."

There could be no better augury for the role which our

country is to play at Geneva than this voice from the State Department. As we have said before, that conference may prove to be a milestone in the history of humanity; it may easily decide the fate of Europe. If it fails, the consequences will be so disastrous to the political and economic life of the whole world and the stability of all the capitalist nations that no one can look upon the possibility of failure without tremendous misgiving. We believe that if the Hoover delegation to Geneva shows the courage and frankness of Mr. Castle, it will win a great victory.

President and Navy

PRESIDENT HOOVER has struck back with unaccustomed vigor at the crowd of "little" big-navy men who have been attacking his economy program. "In order that the country may know the untruth and distortions of fact" concerning the strength of our naval forces which have lately been circulated by the Navy League, Mr. Hoover has announced the appointment of a committee, "including members of the Navy League, to whom agencies of the government will demonstrate these untruths and distortions of fact." Bravo, Mr. Hoover. We shall welcome any investigation that will successfully expose the malicious propaganda of these persons who are bent on making the United States more militaristic at a time when the whole world is crying for peace and disarmament. Public exposure and condemnation of the big-navy crowd will help not only to show that the Administration is sincere in its efforts to reduce armaments, but also to suppress, at least for the time being, a serious menace to the peace of the world.

We do not want to minimize the importance of Mr. Hoover's action, but we do wish he had had foresight and courage enough to place himself in a stronger position. He weakened himself considerably by his Navy Day tribute, in which he indulged in extravagant praise of the navy's tradition and personnel. This sounded suspiciously like a shamefaced apology for his efforts toward economy. It suggested that he was going into the disarmament matter against his personal wishes. Again, in his challenge to the Navy League and its chairman, William Howard Gardiner, he descended to a level of acrimony unbecoming a high government official. Even if we remember the Navy League's allegation that he was "abysmally ignorant" of naval problems, Mr. Hoover's strong rebuke of Chairman Gardiner, and his demand that the latter be prepared to apologize publicly, smacked of personal spleen. They might have been worthy of a Tammany mayor, but certainly not of a President of the United States.

Of course, this does not mean that the big-navy people, including particularly Mr. Gardiner, can on any grounds be excused for their blustering and bullying. The Navy League's assertion that the Hoover program would make for "bigger and bloodier wars" is not only sheer nonsense but positively vicious. Chairman Gardiner's sneering reply to the Hoover statement, in which he expressed surprise "at the President's suggestion that he himself will appoint a committee to investigate a matter touching administrative policy, in view of the fact that Congress is the investigating branch of the government," was that of the gutter politician. Charles Francis Adams, Secretary of the Navy, also showed where he stood when he inferentially supported the Navy League by attacking the World Peace Foundation. He charged the Peace Foundation with disseminating misleading information, although its information was based upon official reports. This was but one of a number of big-navy gestures that have come from Mr. Adams. It is impossible to see how Mr. Hoover can continue to put up with such apparently deliberate sabotaging of his naval policy by one of his Cabinet officers. Secretary Adams should be required to resign at once.

The United States and Manchuria

IN all the welter of the conflicting news from Manchuria nothing stands out clearly save that more than ever the world's peace machinery is at stake and that the time has come for the United States to show its hand and lay its cards upon the table. We have heard and read the evidence on both sides from the most competent authorities. We are entirely convinced that no matter what the Chinese provocation, there is no defense for the Japanese aggression, and that, if there is not a united and determined front by the League and the United States, the Japanese will sooner or later annex Manchuria as they have Korea. What we need most to throw light on the situation is for our State Department to let us know what it has actually been doing and why it is that in at least a section of the Japanese press the belief prevails that the United States has been supporting Japan rather than the League. Our Administration owes it to itself to make its own attitude clear to every American citizen, unless a hideous injustice is to be perpetrated in Manchuria, the seeds of future war sown, the League of Nations humiliated and defied, and both the Nine-Power Treaty and the Kellogg pact definitely breached.

Since the capture of Mukden on the night of September 18 the American people have been kept in the dark as to the exact position of their government in the Manchurian controversy. The State Department has acted with hesitation and with secrecy. The American consul at Geneva did, of course, participate in the deliberations of the League of Nations Council a month ago; it is also true that Ambassador Dawes has been sent to Paris to be near the Council during its present discussion of the Manchurian question; and it is equally true that the State Department has professed a desire to see this question peacefully settled. But it has sent numerous communications to Tokio the contents of which have not been made public, and it has acted very slowly in supporting the various measures the League has taken to bring about a settlement.

It is not particularly important now to point out that Washington could have invoked either the Kellogg pact or the Nine-Power Treaty immediately after the first outburst in Manchuria. Perhaps the State Department had excellent reasons for hesitating at that juncture. But why, after publicly promising to support the League's program so far as it consistently could do so, the department should have waited several days before joining with the League when it invoked the Kellogg pact on October 17 has never been satisfactorily explained. Certainly there would have been no inconsistency in hastening to support a treaty to which the United States was not only a party, but of which it was the chief sponsor. Again, the State Department hesitated after the League Council voted on October 24 to request the Japanese to withdraw their troops into the railway zone before November 16. Several days were allowed to elapse before any communication touching on this point was sent to Tokio from Washington. And even here the strictest secrecy was observed. No one outside the State Department and the Tokio Foreign Office knows what the United States has said to Japan in connection with the League's demand that Japan withdraw its troops. The American press and public are simply told that the department is following a policy of "responsible silence," and that the people must "take the department on trust for a while." It was just such "responsible silence"—a phrase which would doubtless have appealed to Isvolski, Poincaré, Baron Holstein, and the British Foreign Office had it been invented in time—that helped to bring on the World War. How can the American people, viewing today the disastrous results of an era of secret diplomacy in Europe, take "on trust" the utterances of their government when it insists on following precisely the same perilous course?

The net consequence of this secret diplomacy has been to raise a suspicion in Geneva that the United States is sabotaging the League's efforts, and to encourage Tokio into believing that the United States has covertly been supporting the Japanese position in Manchuria. The Osaka *Mainichi,* the Tokio *Nichi-Nichi,* the *Japan Times,* and other influential newspapers have openly interpreted the American policy as one of partiality for the Japanese. In an editorial dated October 19 the *Japan Times* said: "Official circles Monday intimated that the present attitude of the United States toward the Manchurian incident, which has been misunderstood to some extent in Japan, especially after the recent participation of an American observer in the League Council, has now come to be appreciated considerably by the Japanese government *as it has been made clear that the United States government is very favorably inclined toward Japan."*

The State Department has sought to excuse its secrecy on the ground that publication of the various notes that have passed between Washington and Tokio would embarrass the "peace party" of Japan in its attempts to curb the militarists in Manchuria. Such an excuse might be understood if there really were a "peace party" in existence in Japan today. But the liberal opponents of the militarists, far from seeking to curb them, have been united behind them ever since September 18. The Osaka *Mainichi* and the Tokio *Nichi-Nichi,* the two great liberal newspapers, have long opposed the often unrestrained activities of the military clans. On November 15, however, Hikoichi Motoyama, owner of these papers, revealed in an article published by the New York *Times* that this excuse of the State Department for its secrecy is now without warrant. Mr. Motoyama said: "It is not always that we Japanese people agree with our government, but in the main issues regarding the Manchurian question *the whole nation is in perfect accord, regardless of political parties or philosophical schools. We stand united behind our government."*

If it is not true that the United States has been covertly supporting Japan in the present emergency, the State Department will have nothing to lose and much to gain by dropping all secrecy and coming out into the open with its Manchurian policy. But if it continues its present course, it cannot complain if the suspicion remains that it is misleading not only the League of Nations but also the American people, who are not unfriendly to Japan but who want to see justice done. Secret diplomacy has never in history been shown to be a firm or lasting foundation for international justice.

Japan's "Victory"

ON the face of the Manchurian situation Japan appears to have won a smashing victory. It has consolidated its gains, advancing far beyond its previous lines, and, with supreme insolence, has ordered the Russians not to send troops into the zone of Russian influence—in other words, not to do what Japan itself has done. Now, after having imposed its military will upon Manchuria and Russia, its representatives announce that they are ready for an after-the-fact investigating committee to be appointed by the League of Nations and to be headed by one of the most bellicose American generals. Meanwhile, Japan will be creating subservient local governments in the captured cities and will insist that all of this is merely to protect its interest in the South Manchuria Railway, which its spokesmen disclose to be as vital to Japan's defense of its homeland as the Panama Canal is to the United States.

To all of this we can only repeat that it seems to us as cold-blooded a bit of militaristic aggression as is recorded anywhere, and that, while we favor an impartial fact-finding inquiry by the League, we trust that no stone will be left unturned to get the Japanese back to their former positions, and later out of Manchuria altogether. We see no reason whatever why the Japanese crime of conquering and subjugating Korea should be reenacted at this hour in Manchuria. We are well aware of the Japanese justifications for this action: treaty violations by the Chinese, injustice to and even murder of Japanese nationals, the breakdown of local and provincial governments. They are familiar enough in every such military intervention, wherever it takes place and under whatever flag, whether in Manchuria, or Tripoli, or Nicaragua, or Haiti. There is always bad government, always insults and injury, and then the inevitable bloodshed and taking over of more or less of the weaker country's sovereignty and rights.

We can well understand why there are anger and surprise and resentment in Japan that this "civilized" procedure is being denounced by the rest of the world. The Japanese public knows, of course, that almost none of the great nations now seeking to limit its activities, and stop its aggressions in Manchuria, are taking a seat in court with clean hands. They have been guilty, too. But what the Japanese must realize is that the existence of the League itself and the signing of the Nine-Power Treaty and the Kellogg pact were meant to put a stop to this very thing, to usher in a new order of society. The integrity of China was specifically guaranteed in the former treaty. For the United States and the League to sit calmly by and witness the rendering of these treaties null and void was unthinkable. Nobody has any right whatever to criticize the League and the United States for acting. The only sound basis for criticism is that they did not act quickly or vigorously enough, that our own State Department has wobbled and blustered, and unfortunately succeeded in giving the false impression that it favored Japan when really the opposite was the case.

In other words, the Japanese are thinking in terms of a bygone era, and this remains true enough though the Japanese people are entirely united behind their government. They must, however, be prepared to pay the price of their mistake. In the first place, China has a deadly weapon to use and has already begun to use it—the boycott. The newly arrived Minister from Siam to the United States, who was until recently Minister in Tokio, reports that the boycotting of Japanese goods by China and Russia, together with the grave depression already felt in Japan, has created a serious problem in the latter country: "Japan, I was in a position to observe . . . could little afford such a boycott." From Canton and other Chinese cities comes a report that "the business of Japanese firms has almost ceased," and that the pickets are beginning to seize Japanese goods that remain unsold after two months' warning that no further sales would be tolerated after a given date. This is as it should be. We cannot see why any Chinese should refrain from joining such a non-resistance movement. We hope that they will refuse to deal with Japanese on any terms, to the extent of rendering the residence of Japanese in China impossible.

But we are not content to stop there. We still feel that the prestige of the League and of the United States demands the development of the severest pressure, and the application of sanctions whether a fact-finding commission is appointed or not. That commission can only establish details as to who was the aggressor, what the sequence of events, and what the Japanese have actually done. The fact of the aggression is perfectly clear; the obvious danger remains of a complete Japanese control of Manchuria by the elimination of anti-Japanese elements in high places in Manchuria and the erection of a government which will recognize Japan's rights and interests to the extent that it wishes them recognized. The more that outside pressure is brought to bear either through the Chinese boycott or the action of the Powers, the greater the chance that Japanese civilians will be able to assert a greater authority over their militarist adventurers who have outraged Manchuria, and succeeded in getting the approval of their government and their deluded fellow-citizens. How much that strengthening of civilian control is needed appears from the rumors that the position of Baron Shidehara, the present Foreign Minister, who has been responsible hitherto for the moderate attitude shown toward China by Japan, has been so shaken that he may shortly retire. This would be a genuine misfortune.

But most important of all is, of course, the necessity of upholding the treaty and establishing the power of the League as a reliable agency to prevent war. If Japan succeeds in holding what it has seized in Manchuria, the prestige of the League will be at a low ebb. Should it be followed by disaster at the coming disarmament conference, the League will be so damaged as to raise grave question of its future usefulness. If Japan takes over Manchuria after what has been nothing else than war, and the sanctity of the Kellogg pact is not upheld, that document must be regarded as having been fatally breached in its first test. If Japan can defy the Nine-Power Treaty, then the United States might just as well denounce it as of no further value. What the Japanese people do not realize is that their word and their sacred honor are at stake.

Congress, Debts, and Bankers
An Appeal to Reason

By OSWALD GARRISON VILLARD

THE House of Representatives having voted by 317 to 100 for the bill to authorize the moratorium to our foreign governmental creditors promised by President Hoover last summer, the Senate is also engaged in passing it. That is right and proper. It settles the question whether Congress will or will not approve the President's action. Unfortunately, the bill contains a proviso flatly rejecting the idea of the cancelation or reduction of Europe's debts to the United States.

This is sheer folly. For one thing, no one can foresee what the European situation will be three months or a year or two years from now. For another, the gravity of the European situation which led President Hoover to proclaim the moratorium is unchanged. As these words are written, dispatches from Washington announce that President Hoover has just communicated to a number of the House leaders at breakfast "a very black picture of conditions in Central Europe." The truth is that Germany is still on the verge of collapse, and the economic fate of England is as closely allied with that of the Reich as it was during the events of July and August last. As things stand, Germany will not be able to resume reparations payments at the end of the moratorium—it must never be forgotten that she has made payments heretofore solely with money borrowed abroad—and England, for one, will not be able to continue to pay debts to us if the money she received from Berlin and Paris fails to arrive. As long as debts and reparations stand in the way, it will not be possible to rehabilitate the shattered nerves and restore to balance the psychology of Europe. Until this question is settled, the normal processes of trade cannot recur. As long as debts and reparations continue on the books of the nations, they will form a barrier to the recovery of our own country over which no tide of returning prosperity can easily flow. As long, moreover, as the Congress demands that debts must be paid, and continues to maintain high tariffs so that our debtors can pay us only, or chiefly, in gold, there will continue to be a heaping up of that metal in the vaults of the United States Treasury. There it will further upset the equilibrium of trade, and make difficult the return of the world to the gold standard—twenty-three nations are now not operating on that standard. As long as the Congress continues our tariffs at the height at which they are, it will make increasingly difficult the payment of the debts if they can be paid at all.

It is therefore folly, I repeat, for Congress to tie its hands now, or to lay down any rigid rules for the Administration to follow. That it is extraordinarily difficult in these hard times for Congress to contemplate the renunciation of debts which were incurred by the debtors in good faith at a time when the getting of money meant victory or an immediately negotiated peace, is perfectly true, as is the fact that we have already made substantial reductions, so substantial that in the case of Italy the debt payment to the United States is only 0.6 per cent of the annual budgetary expenditures. But this is a topsy-turvy world, and it is a fact that the payment of reparations money has been doing injury to our business life, by unsettling trade in the debtor nations and introducing into it an economic factor not created by the normal processes of give and take in international barter. It is not to be denied that Nicholas Murray Butler had considerable truth on his side when he said that the receipt of these moneys is actually helping to drive prosperity out of the homes of American workingmen and women. And of what avail are payments to the United States when those reimbursements are achieved only by our lending money to Germany with which, after passing through another set of hands, the payments are made to us?

But, I hear it said, the Allies are perfectly able to pay if they will stop wasting money on armaments, and in other directions. We have seen a Machiavellian campaign in the *Saturday Evening Post,* given tremendous circulation through the notorious Chemical Foundation, to prove that Germany has been deliberately wasting her money on unnecessary municipal and other expenditures for which she borrowed large sums from abroad for the express purpose of so involving the United States and other lenders of money with her domestic economy as to be able to enlist the international bankers in her campaign to get rid of her reparations obligations. I would not deny that there is capacity to pay in Germany and the Allied nations. As to the former, I wrote that from Germany last winter (*The Nation,* January 28, 1931). But the question was then and is now whether the United States should compel the payment of these debts at the cost of a steadily decreasing scale of living, at the cost of misery and suffering which in turn make for the general instability and unhappiness of Europe, factors which in themselves work against the restoration of normal trade conditions. It is undeniable that the countries that owe us money could readily pay us if they would only stop some of the insensate waste of money on armaments. I have always favored our country's insisting upon a substantial reduction in armaments as a prerequisite of the cancelation of the debt of any country, though it would hardly be decent for the United States to demand that without some action on its side, when our own governmental appropriations for army and navy run up to $775,000,000, when influential members of Congress are demanding the building up of our fleet to treaty limits.

But these are details, important as they may seem. The vital fact is that *the whole world stands on the brink of the gravest economic disaster in all history.* Beside that everything sinks into relative insignificance. The menace of that collapse is so great that the debts seem of relatively slight importance. If Europe crashes, we of the United States shall lose so much money as to make the debts seem a bagatelle. We shall lose it by the collapse of foreign trade, the inability of foreigners to travel in this country, their inability to pay private debts, in a dozen different direct and indirect ways. That is the real choice which is offered to the Congress. When in the face of that it undertakes to bind the hands of the Executive, it should remember that with Europe prostrate the United States cannot possibly recover by itself, Herbert Hoover to the contrary notwithstanding. That superficial gentleman has injured his own case for a liberal international settlement by telling the Congress that we could pretty nearly recover no matter what happened in Europe—a marked contrast to his own assertion that the reason we are suffering from the depression is the unfavorable effect upon us of the European economic misadventures. We do not mean to suggest that the President should have the right to settle these matters by himself; but he should be free to negotiate, to keep in touch with the heads of other countries, and to make recommendations for immediate action in case of emergency. The Congressional vote may be taken as barring him from that.

Instead, however, of a clear realization of the gravity of the European situation, and the unalterable fact that we are involved in it and cannot hope to escape from it unless we are willing to make substantial sacrifices, the whole issue is being confused by this question of capacity to pay of the individual countries, by bringing up the false charges of an international conspiracy to rob us of what is rightfully ours, and by the assertion of Senator Reed that the issue is whether the "private claims of some American citizens should be given priority over the intergovernmental claims which are the claims of all American citizens. . . ." The latter sentiment finds expression in the violent and outrageous utterances of Representative McFadden, who has not only accused President Hoover of selling his country out to German interests, but has laid at the door of certain bankers in the United States, notably so admirable, wise, and patriotic a citizen and banker as Paul M. Warburg, the responsibility for suborning the President and engineering the campaign to get rid of governmental debts so that those bankers who have loaned a lot of money to Germany may be rescued at the expense of all their fellow-citizens.

Fortunately, such violent absurdities defeat themselves. I am more concerned with what seems the disposition on the part of certain of the Progressive Senators, who are and have been righteously alert to the unfavorable influences of international bankers upon our relations to other countries, to swallow the doctrine that the whole situation of the world has been brought to pass by these international bankers and by the Germans, so that the latter and our Allies might escape just responsibility for their debts. It is with them that I should like to reason. I should like to point out to them that in this case the wishes of the international bankers coincide with what is for the very best interests of all the peoples concerned. I should like to remind them that the liberal journals in this country, both daily and weekly, have been pointing out for at least ten years the impossibility of collecting these payments from Europe. These journals are not the mouthpieces of the international bankers. More than that, it is time to point out to them that the leaders of the Labor Party in England have been for years certain that payments could not go on, that there must be a complete remission of debts and reparations; surely no one will charge the Labor Party with having been a tool of the international bankers—did it not break with MacDonald in the last election because, for one reason, it refused to accept banking dictation? Again, if the Progressives in the House and the Senate could travel abroad they would find that wherever men thought their thoughts, and talked their talk about the rights of the plain people against the modern control of economic and political life by great capitalistic influences, those men would be foremost in asserting that there must be a cancelation of the debts and reparations which, day by day, create bitternesses, hostility, and hatreds, and add to the moral and mental unsettlement of the world.

There lies before me a pamphlet entitled "The Crisis," by Ernest Bevin and G. D. H. Cole, two of the foremost and more radical leaders of the Labor Party. No one could possibly accuse them of being willing to pull the chestnuts out of the fire for the international bankers—since the recent election Mr. Cole has come out with a demand that Great Britain immediately socialize its entire banking system. What do they say in their pamphlet? "Complete cancelation of war debts and reparations is the first obvious step toward the recovery of world equilibrium." Elsewhere they speak of "this farce of war debts and reparations." And they declare that "it is plain to any rational person that Germany and other debtor countries are burdened with international obligations which they can never possibly meet." It is no exaggeration to say that these are the views of the democratic forces in all the countries involved.

The only question is whether the United States will be big enough and broad enough to make what is on its face an unquestioned sacrifice. It is a widespread belief among men of the highest economic standing that the United States would actually profit in dollars and cents by cancelation. It would not be difficult to demonstrate the soundness of their view statistically. Our national income in 1929 was estimated to be approximately $90,000,000,000. The latest statistics published by the Federal Reserve Bank of New York show that industry and trade are running at more than 25 per cent below the level of normal years. These statistics indicate on their face a loss of not less than $22,000,000,000 in our annual national income. Compared with this, our receipts from the war debts are only $240,000,000—barely more than 1 per cent of this loss through demoralization in world trade. But even supposing that the sacrifice should be great, the simple truth is that the world cannot be set on its feet again unless every country is ready to make some sacrifice. By setting the example the United States would be in a position to demand that others do likewise. It should also heartily join in the proposal of Ramsay MacDonald for an international economic conference, yet if that economic conference should come to pass, the first question that would come up would be the question of the cancelation of war debts and reparations, as well as the reduction of tariffs, and the question of raising and stabilizing the world level of wholesale prices. Indeed, there is no possible way of approach to the world's problem which would not involve cancelation. The handwriting is on the wall. Signs of the collapse of the existing order are on every hand. There is very little time left. If the Congress takes the position that there cannot now or at any future time be a revaluation of these debts, a scaling down and ultimate cancelation of them, then it will bring the impending disaster in Europe and America within sight, and will insure losses all over the world that will make reparations and debts seem the merest trifles.

War in India

WAR is on in India. The harassed and despairing world is now to be the scene of another bitter and, we fear, bloody struggle which can have only one outcome—the end of British control in India. With Mahatma Gandhi in jail, Nehru sentenced to two years of hard labor, and more drastic measures of repression daily being applied, the British government is trying in 1932 to rule by force and violence an unwilling people. The issues are substantially the same as in the previous clashes; but this time Gandhi enters upon his campaign morally strengthened. No one now can say, as many said during the last crusade of civil disobedience, that the Indian leader has shown unwillingness to discuss controversial matters, for he sat through weary weeks at the Second Round Table Conference, steadily more convinced that British promises of autonomy were meaningless and would not be carried out except under conditions so guarded as to nullify them. The final break came over the refusal of the Viceroy, the Earl of Willingdon, to discuss with Gandhi the stern enactments recently instituted in Bengal, the United Provinces, and on the northwestern frontier. These measures, ostensibly set in action to prevent assassination or lesser crimes of violence, were so extreme that every vestige of freedom could be denied to Indians and every kind of Nationalist assertion ruthlessly put down.

It is clear as crystal that after the demise of the Labor Government, which left an unenviable record on India, the National Government intended to resort, if "necessary," to the sternest expedients in order to quell the expected uprising following the fiasco at London. Gandhi points out, with justice, that the pact he consummated with Lord Irwin, the previous Viceroy, tacitly permitted the continuance of civil disobedience and the boycott during negotiations. But no such mood is now discernible among the British leaders, even that erstwhile champion of Indian self-government, Prime Minister MacDonald. The absolute outlawry of the Indian National Congress, the barring of Nationalist literature and messages from the mails and wires, the confiscation of property and contributions to the cause of *swaraj* are threatened and doubtless will soon be in actual operation. Well may Gandhi predict a reign of terror. During the civil disobedience of a year ago the innumerable annoyances by the Indian crusaders brought ferocious floggings, torture, even at times the actual caging of demonstrators.

It seems to us that Gandhi, whose inconsistencies have been more than a few, has maintained throughout the present conflict a straight and unassailable position. During his first public address on arriving in London he said: "The Congress wants *freedom*"—and his voice underscored the word. Continuing, he declared: "The Congress has chosen as the method of winning this freedom, *truth* and *non-violence*. If the dumb millions are to win freedom, it can be secured by these means and none other." His frequent hesitations, his kindliness to the English when in England, his patient willingness to wait as long as any hope of a genuine settlement remained were not recessions but were all in keeping with his way of life. There is a damning contrast between this frail but mighty rebel and the Empire that he challenges. The official pomposity of a Willingdon fades into insignificance beside the nobility of the man who, smiling into the faces of those sent to carry him away to prison, declares in transparent sincerity: "We are prepared to sacrifice all. We shall forget families and friends, we shall sacrifice our property, we shall bear the utmost privation and greatest oppression, including *lathi* and machine-gun. But we shall bear no hatred toward the British." In this spirit and by this sign will India conquer.

If I Were Dictator*

By OSWALD GARRISON VILLARD

IF I were dictator? Well, I am sure that what I have to say will disappoint many readers who look for far more radical and violent changes than I have to suggest. I am conscious that the immediate remedies that offer themselves to me will seem lacking both in originality and in thoroughness, perhaps because I have not lost faith in democracy or the workability of our institutions, provided that these are adjusted to modern economic, social, and political conditions. The fault, in my judgment, has been less with the economic and political system under which we have lived than with the men that we have chosen to work it. But the evolution of capitalism has given ever-increasing opportunities for the selfishness and greed of the average human being in industry and politics, and these traits are bringing down the structure. We in America have learned the bitter lesson that uncontrolled individualism, whether rugged or otherwise, leads but to despair.

If I were dictator I should begin in the field of international relations, since it is in that field that we are today most menaced by conditions which not only threaten the peace of the world, but make an early recovery from the economic chaos impossible. I should first of all muster out the fleet, laying it up as did Thomas Jefferson when President, and reduce the regular army to the police force of 25,000 men which it was at the outbreak of the war with Spain. I should retire every single one of the talking generals and admirals and send them all to Guam with the direction that they put that island into a state of 100 per cent preparedness and play at war maneuvers to their heart's content. Resuming the historic American attitude of being unarmed and unafraid, I should say to the rest of the world: "See how genuinely pacific we are. We have done away with the arts of war, have ceased to teach our soldiers how best to disembowel their fellow-men or how to kill innocent women and children by the use of aerial bombs and poison gas, which are not selective in dealing death and destruction. We are ready to take the risks of peace. We have faith not only in our own moral strength; we know that in modern war there are neither victors nor vanquished, but that all suffer alike, and that less than ever can one be assured that the heaviest battalions and the best generals will be on the side of right."

If I were dictator I should abolish every tariff because I know that the rapid rise of the three great industrial nations of modern times has been due chiefly to the fact that within their respective empires it has been free trade that has made them powerful and prosperous. Particularly I should say that this is true of the United States; that if tariffs are the blessings they are said to be, then we should surround every one of the forty-eight States of the Union with those magic walls which are supposed to raise the standard of living and bestow prosperity upon all inside their circle. I should put an end to the abomination that we must protect all trade within purely arbitrary geographic lines. I should first of all abolish the sugar tariff against Cuba, an island almost within sight of our shores, whose sugar would come into our country free and untaxed if the American flag floated over Morro Castle in Havana; instead of which, merely because Cuba is outside of our national lines, we raise the price of sugar to every man, woman, and child, and destroy the value of great American investments in that island. Also we help to reduce the working masses in that country to misery and despair, and help to render them the helpless and hapless victims of a ruthless dictator—merely in order to insure profits for some of our citizens who unnecessarily entered the sugar business at home.

If I were dictator I should serve notice upon Japan that if she did not withdraw within her former lines in Manchuria I should invoke an international boycott to compel her to do so, and, to demonstrate that I meant what I said in all sincerity, I should withdraw every last American soldier from Haiti, Nicaragua, Cuba, Samoa, and the Philippines. I should free the latter before their inhabitants had time to petition me for this action and so live up to our plighted national word. Then I should offer to China every possible help in the way of financial aid and expert advice and service to enable that harassed country to constitute a strong and honest central government. I should immediately recognize the Russia of the Soviets with every gesture of friendship and good-will to the Russian people. I should not be afraid of communism because I should set out really to constitute an honest and efficient government for the United States, one responding to the will of the American people as expressed through the initiative and referendum, and I am bold enough to believe that if I could have my way, our own system of government as reconstituted would not only challenge comparison with the Soviet program, but would seem infinitely more desirable so long as the Soviet Government is a bloody-handed class dictatorship.

To accomplish this I should do everything in my power to bring about economic equality, and equality before the law. As I do not believe in prisons as they now are constituted, I should relegate to prison farms every single American official—and their number runs into thousands upon thousands—who violates the law, believes himself superior to it, and connives at the abuse of personal liberties by men in the garb of police officers or in that of civil authority. For I believe that the chief explanation of our being the most lawless civilized nation is to be found in the fact that we have more lawless officials sworn to uphold the law than any other nation on earth.

I should remove from the statute books by one stroke of the pen every law regulating the private morals of individual citizens. I should declare that, however men and women behaved in their relations with one another, it was their own affair, save where the public peace was disturbed. I should, however, continue and increase the control of the sale of narcotics, and my government would be as rigid as that of the Soviets in preventing the exploitation of the bodies of women for the gain of individuals. Censors of literature, art, or the theater would be my special game. I have long wondered where would be the proper place in which to exile the censors and snoopers, and then it came to

* The last of a series of articles on this subject.—EDITOR THE NATION.

me—the Virgin Islands! I should seek to find a method of dispensing liquors and wines in a way rigidly to control the drink habit, so that men should not profit by catering to that appetite of their fellow-men which undeniably has done more than any other one thing to fill our jails, our hospitals, and our asylums. I should appeal to my subjects to join me in treating alcohol from the same standpoint as that from which we treat the abuse of drugs, believing that unlimited use of alcohol is almost as much a danger to the race as is unlimited use of opium.

I should at once tackle the disgraceful statistics which reveal to all the world that the death-rate in childbirth is higher in the United States than anywhere else. I should follow the policy advocated by Governor Alfred E. Smith of New York when he asked the legislature to see to it that every community in his State received adequate medical and nursing care, and I should make it possible for the poor to have not only adequate medical care, but the dental service of which they are today deprived because it is beyond their means. And, of course, I should make free for all the necessary information as to birth control. I should free our schools from the domination of all the politicians and all the priests. I should introduce self-government not only among the scholars, but among the teachers, and I should not only guarantee absolute freedom of teaching but see to it that every new or old ism was carefully explored within the classrooms of school and college. One of my first steps would be to make impossible the control of our colleges by boards of trustees comprising wealthy men devoted chiefly to the old order of society and to the prevention of the teaching of new doctrines and new theories of economic and political life. I should read to each board of university trustees the famous words of Patrick Henry: "Give me liberty, or give me death," and then give them their choice. I should ask them not to come to me to explain that there are "certain things" that must not be laid before the "immature minds of undergraduates," and that there must be some limits to liberty and free speech lest they degenerate into license. If anyone sneaked through into my audience chamber and began to address me with the words: "I believe in liberty and freedom, but there are limits," I should immediately sentence him to twenty-five years on my most northern Alaskan prison farm, in company with all those benighted citizens who might appeal to me to continue intercollegiate athletic contests under present conditions. William Green and Matthew Woll of the American Federation of Labor I should designate as Governor and Deputy Governor of the Aleutian Islands. For Mr. Hoover and his Cabinet, and other talkers of economic nonsense, I should reserve the Island of Yap with the requirement that morning and evening they should meet together to inform one another that prosperity is just around the corner, and that every day in every way things are getting better and better.

Then I should give my attention to the revision of our own government, to vital alterations in our Constitution, a noble document, admirably constructed for the use of thirteen struggling States along the Atlantic seaboard when they did not know their own hinterland, when not one citizen had yet crossed the continent overland. I should change the Constitution so that the state should take over and operate, either directly or through some government corporation like the Mississippi Waterways Corporation, the railroads, the pipe-lines, the telephone and telegraph, the radio, the mines, the oil wells, water power, and all other natural resources, thus making enormous savings, closing avenues to the making of excessive fortunes, and destroying the foothold of many masters of privilege. By income taxes and inheritance taxes I should make impossible the transmission from one generation to another of swollen fortunes. I should enormously lighten the burden of taxation by having the profits of public utilities go into the pockets not of stockholders, but of the communities which operate them, or into a general treasury. In other words, I should endeavor to create social control of institutions as a source of funds for a progressive social policy. I should further reduce the expenses of government by saving almost entirely the $750,000,000 now devoted to the annual upkeep of the army and navy. I should seek in every way to redeem my country from the stigma placed upon its common sense by the present Secretary of the Treasury, Mr. Mellon, when he twice declared in his annual reports that 85 cents out of every dollar raised by taxation now goes to wars past and future.

With the money so saved and earned and raised, I should rebuild our cities so that every slum would disappear. I should frankly and boldly imitate the Russian government in that I should stress above all else the welfare, the prosperity, and the happiness of the plain people of Abraham Lincoln. Instead of making this a government by and for the well-to-do and rich, I should make it a government primarily concerned with the welfare of the toiling masses, and I should let the rich go hang. The ablest men that I could find I should set to the problem of the farmer, gradually and voluntarily bringing about the creation of great co-operative farms, and working out the problem of large industrial agricultural enterprises versus individual farming. I should find some way of eliminating the middleman so that the farmer living within forty miles of our greatest cities would no longer get between three and five cents a quart for the milk that sells at around fifteen on the streets of the metropolis.

Turning to the States, I should so devise their constitutions as to abolish the bicameral legislatures along the lines of a plan suggested by Senator Norris, creating a single chamber of some twenty-four members, more in the nature of a governor's council, to be elected without benefit of party. I should take every office now bestowable by a politician and put it under rigid civil-service rules. So with our municipalities, I should eliminate politics and make the office of mayor a scientific job to be held by professional mayors freed from all political control, precisely as is the case today in Germany, instituting local referendums that the people might vote upon policies. Judges I should put to work, real work, and I should make them simplify the processes of law so that they would be humanized and speeded up, as is the case in England; and, as is the case in Russia, I should abolish the death penalty, and go farther than Russia by abolishing it for political offenses as well. Divorce would be, as now in Spain and in Russia, by mutual consent, and as in both those countries, there would no longer be any distinction, legal or social, between children born in or out of wedlock.

As for the immediate emergency, I should at once introduce the five-day week, and remove from industry all children under the age of eighteen. I should institute a scientific system of unemployment insurance, and make the system of old-age pensions recently adopted in New York State nationwide. To take care of the existing unemployment, I should immediately sell a bond issue running into the billions and utilize the proceeds for great public works, and especially for the rebuilding of our cities so that no city dweller should remain in dark and unsanitary quarters. Planning? Of course. Not only for caring for the unemployed today but for a general overhauling of the economic system in the belief that it is not overproduction but underdistribution which is troubling us and especially to prevent the recurrence of depressions like these. Naturally this would entail first of all planning to end the enormous waste of the competitive system in such an industry, for example, as that of the makers of rubber tires or of the producers of oil. But the most important means of ending the existing economic crisis would be those measures for the regulation of international trade, including means of putting an end to the hurtful heaping up of gold in this country, which I have already outlined, the abolition of tariffs, the forgiving of debts and reparations, complete disarmament, and the ending of the rule of fear and suspicion and hatred among peoples—at least so far as our example could bring this to pass.

By this time, I am sure, more than half the people of this Republic would have risen against me; the generosity of my dictatorship would be too much for them to stand. But one last thing I should strive to do before I was led off to the guillotine. I should close two-thirds of the churches of the country, allowing only those to remain open that were absolutely dedicated to peace at any price, whose ministers agreed that they would go to prison—our present type of prison abomination if you please—for life before one word of approval of mass killing should cross their lips. They would have to promise, moreover, to preach but one sermon a year dedicated to abstract theological doctrine. The rest of their time they would have to give over to social endeavor, to true spiritual leadership, according to the teachings of Jesus of Nazareth, preaching sermons directly connected with the problems of society and the practical welfare of those about them. Finally, just to show that I was human and therefore extremely inconsistent, I should once more turn censor myself and abolish lip-sticks, high-heeled shoes, silk hats, all remaining Ford cars of the original model, the Navy League, the Civic Federation, and the Protective Tariff League, not to mention *Ballyhoo, College Humor,* the tabloids, and the *Saturday Evening Post.* I should send Henry Ford himself, with his humbug reputation as a model employer of labor, to join the heads of the American Federation of Labor in the Aleutian Islands.

If these things that I have outlined seem inadequate to some, too radical to others, as well as inconsistent, please remember that I have none the less stressed liberty in all the relations between human beings, and that I have had no other object in view than social, economic, and political equality. In other words, I have suggested nothing which does not seem to me in keeping with the true spirit of American institutions, with democracy and the desire for life, liberty, and the pursuit of happiness. Sometime, soon it is to be hoped, we must come to some such recasting of our governments—city, State, and national; if we do not, then we may be sure that a totally new system, whether that be communism or something else, will have to be devised to insure equality of opportunity and of life, to curb and restrict greed and appetite for wealth, and to end all the special privileges which have been established under our modern industrial system and our government—as it has been perverted from the control of the masses into the hands of the dominating few.

Youth Votes for Peace

HOW stands the legend of undergraduate indifference to current issues, in the light of the vote taken by the Intercollegiate Disarmament Council in seventy colleges on questions regarding war and peace? A high percentage of the students cast ballots—84 per cent of the entire student body at Amherst, 78 per cent at Yale, and 70 per cent at Mt. Holyoke. That the returns are representative is indicated by the participation of large and small institutions, of various types, in widely separated sections of the country. Among the colleges were, for example, Dartmouth, Wellesley, Virginia Polytechnic Institute, Rollins, Kansas, and Southern Methodist.

In the long vista of warrantable gloom, this is indeed a cause of cheer. For not only have 92 per cent of the 24,345 students voting declared, in general terms, for reduction of armament; no fewer than 63 per cent have urged independent disarmament by the United States without waiting for other countries. On this issue, at least, when an opportunity is offered for the expression of opinion, our college students are not only thinking, but thinking boldly. One out of every seven who replied even went so far as to propose 100 per cent independent disarmament. And if skeptics incline to view these results as due to sentimental idealism, growing out of remoteness from contact with public affairs, let them ponder the vote on military training—a matter of intimate concern in many colleges where it is compulsory, and a question of moment for every young man who faces the possibility that training for war may prove to be an actual rehearsal of what is to come. Here, again, the balloting is consistently anti-war, 81 per cent opposing compulsory drill and 38 per cent—in our judgment, a remarkably high proportion—desiring the abolition of military training altogether in all colleges.

What effect this veritable cry for peace will have on the faculties of our colleges and universities remains to be seen. Official boards, trustees, and presidents, though usually in favor of peace, often have a way of disregarding the wishes of their students when these depart from tradition or run counter to the ambition of vested military interests to use youth for their own purposes. But we are hopeful that this poll may stimulate teachers, especially, to keep on courageously with their task of freeing their institutions from the clutches of war ideology.

While student interest is still keen, however, there are certain further queries we should like to pose. Is disarmament enough? Are the undergraduates who have clearly registered their unwillingness to follow the drums along the avenue of preparedness for war equally ready to enlist, definitely and unequivocally, in the world-wide campaign of war resisters already organized among the young men and women of twenty-two countries? Will they soon be counted among the active workers in the War Resisters' League, the Fellowship of Reconciliation, or similar expanding agencies eager to enrol young persons in the crusade to drive war off our planet? Are they sharing in the struggle to create a social order which will make peace possible? In the long run the answers to such questions will determine the effectiveness of these awakened undergraduates.

Unless We Cancel the Debts

IT has now become apparent that the probabilities are immensely against any enlightened action on war debts or reparations either from France or from America. The crushing burden on Germany, of course, cannot and will not be paid. Every unbiased observer and every recent expert committee reports this either guardedly or bluntly, and the present German crisis makes it entirely obvious. French statesmen continue to act as if they had never read the reports or heard of the crisis. As for Congress, it has gone out of its way to say quite plainly that it is opposed not only to any cancelation of the war debts, but to any reduction of them, or even any further moratorium. It has flatly refused to revive the War Debt Commission, for fear such a commission would discover that the debts had to be scaled down. In brief, it has refused to do what any intelligent banker, no matter how lacking in altruism, does—it has refused to investigate its debtors' capacity to pay. It has preferred a wilful blindness. Mr. Hoover, in his turn, has rid himself of the problem by retreating behind the absurd fiction that reparations are purely the concern of Europe.

Under such circumstances, it seems futile to continue to point out how insane our policy is. It is more profitable, perhaps, to ask ourselves what is now most likely to happen. The present moratorium on German reparations expires on July 15. The next debt payments from the Allies to ourselves are not due until December 15. It is possible, therefore, that under the pressure of events France will consent to extend the German moratorium for five months. Germany will continue to insist on a final settlement by July, but no matter what further collapse occurs in Germany, this request will probably be ignored. Farther than this slight extension of the moratorium France is extremely unlikely to go. How can the French Government be expected to consent to any reduction of the reparations worth talking about when it has had the most emphatic notice from Congress that under no circumstances will we in turn consent to deduct a penny from the war debt? What, then, will France do before the extended moratorium period expires? Doubtless it will join with England and the other Allies in requesting a further extension of the moratorium from us. If this request is made before election day, Mr. Hoover will of course refuse even to submit it to Congress. If it is made after election day, Mr. Hoover will probably submit it, but Congress will in any case reject it. The Allies will then notify us that they are taking advantage of the clause in their war-debt contracts permitting them to suspend payments for two years.

The next move will probably be Germany's. Whatever German Government is in power will demand complete cancelation of all reparations. It is possible that France will then extend the moratorium on the unconditional payments, but it is much more likely that it will refuse even that. Germany will then repudiate the reparations. This will leave several courses open to France. It may proceed to apply "sanctions" and move troops into Germany; but it may hesitate to do this through inability to see just what the troops would do when they got there. If the French seized mines, they would have to operate the mines; if they seized railroads and factories, they would have to operate them also. And this could not be done in a partial way; it would have to be done completely. The French could not operate an automobile factory, for example, unless they operated the railroad bringing raw materials to the factory and shipping out the finished product, as well as the contributing steel works, glass works, leather companies, tire companies, and so on—at least to the extent that such semi-finished materials could not be profitably imported from France or elsewhere. But obviously not a fraction of the excess skilled French labor could be found to carry on such work. It has been suggested that French industrialists might take control of German industry. But even if we assume that they could secure ownership, either of bonds or stocks, the problem of reparations would hardly be changed. True, it would cease to be a problem of taxation, but it would continue to be a problem of transfer; and if the payments existed on any scale comparable with those under the present reparations, the system would be just as certain to break down.

It is possible that much of this may become apparent to French statesmanship before any action against Germany is taken; but whether it does or not, it will become apparent very shortly after action is taken. France's next step, therefore, will be to combine with the other Allies to request an international conference for the drastic scaling down both of debts and reparations. This Congress will reject. France, England, Italy, and the rest will then notify us that they are unable to make further debt payments. Senators Borah and Johnson will make scorching statements condemning Europe for its repudiation of a sacred contract, and the American press will swell the denunciatory chorus. European statesmen and press will reply to Uncle Shylock in kind. Stocks and bonds will probably undergo another collapse; the economic crisis will become worse everywhere. Mutual bitterness and recrimination will continue for years; America and the Allies will throw up still further discriminatory tariffs against one another, and help still further to ruin one another's foreign trade. Statesmen on both sides of the water will continue to feel righteous indignation and thorough self-satisfaction.

Such is the future we have to look forward to if we base our view on a cold weighing of the probabilities. Events may not occur in the order named; but the final result can hardly fail to be the same. There is, of course, one chance in ten that a miracle will happen, and that Congress and the Administration will forgive the debts purely out of intelligent selfishness. In that case, of course, we shall not get our money either, but we shall at least have the world's good-will, and in such an atmosphere confidence and trade would rise like a submerged raft from which a great rock has been rolled off. There is a huge psychological difference, which we have not yet remotely begun to appreciate, between what follows when a creditor forgives a debt and what follows when a debtor repudiates it. It remains to be seen whether that difference can be understood before it is altogether too late.

Who Wants to Disarm?

AT Geneva are gathered the representatives of virtually all the nations of the world. They have come together for the avowed purpose of working out a program for reducing national armaments. It is clear that the peoples of all countries want actual, sincere disarmament. It is not so clear that their representatives in Geneva have any such desire. True, they say that they want to reduce armaments, and they know that their people want this done, but no delegation except that of Soviet Russia has yet offered a concrete suggestion that would help bring this about. The hypocritical proposals of France we have already discussed. France has been denounced ever since the war as a militaristic country. The French now wish to get out from under this censure, not by reducing armaments, but by sharing with the rest of the world the responsibility for maintaining a huge war machine. The British, taking issue with the French on the question of a League of Nations army, have nothing practical to offer in its place. Sir John Simon, the British Foreign Secretary, wants to discuss the entire question on the basis of the draft convention which several preliminary conferences labored over and never got completed. He would support "the establishment of a permanent disarmament commission," abolish gas and chemical warfare, and "press for the abolition of submarines." The Soviet delegation has reiterated its plea for complete abolition of all arms and armies, but if any other delegation is planning to support this proposal, the fact has not yet been made public.

Germany, of course, is in no position to lay down the law to the other Powers, to say that this or that plan will lead to actual disarmament. But the Germans have public law and, if there is such a thing, international morality on their side. The Allied and Associated Powers at Versailles twice promised Germany, once in a note to the German delegation and later in the League Covenant, that its own involuntary disarmament would be followed by a reduction of the military forces of other countries. Chancellor Brüning has now called upon the world to redeem this pledge. He told the Geneva conference that Germany wants "a general disarmament which would be put into effect for all nations according to the same principles and which would create an equal measure of security for all peoples." But beyond this generality the German Chancellor has had nothing specific to offer.

Ambassador Gibson, acting chairman of the American delegation, presented what was, next to the French proposal, the most definite and detailed program the disarmament conference has yet heard. The American program has nine points. It supports the British thesis that we already have sufficient peace machinery and that this machinery should now be made secure by reducing armaments. It denies the contention of André Tardieu and the French that world peace must first "be organized." But examined closely, what is there of real value in the American program? Nothing whatever. The first point suggests the willingness of the American delegation to discuss disarmament. The second expresses the hope that France and Italy will forget their differences and accept the London naval treaty. The third recommends indefinite further cuts in naval forces, if France and Italy can come to an agreement. The fourth, fifth, sixth, and eighth points would abolish submarines, protect civilians from aerial bombardments, abolish gas and bacteriological warfare, and place special restrictions on tanks and heavy mobile guns. The seventh, referring to something called "the computation of the number of armed forces on the basis of the effectives necessary for the maintenance of internal order plus some suitable contingent for defense," is unintelligible. The ninth point merely presents another excuse for postponing acceptance of budgetary limitation of armaments.

Where in this whole detailed program is there to be found the slightest hope of real disarmament? Naturally, great naval Powers like the United States and England want to abolish submarines, which are the only defense small countries have against the big fleets of their more fortunate neighbors. And how are civilians to be protected from aerial bombardments? Unhappily, Mr. Gibson does not say. Nor does he mention the fact that the United States has already signed two treaties looking toward the abolition of gas and chemical warfare, neither of which has been ratified by the Senate, though both have been before that body for from seven to ten years. In short, the American program, as the New York *World-Telegram* has pointed out, is "only another plan to make war pretty, which can't be done."

Starting with nothing, the Geneva conference will now proceed to discuss this nothing for several months. What it will wind up with cannot be foretold. Why has not some delegation besides the Soviet group, which will not be taken seriously, mustered up courage enough to come forward with a plan to slash all armaments 25 per cent, or 50 per cent, or to abolish them entirely? The question remains, Do the people gathered at Geneva today really want disarmament?

No War with Japan

IT seems necessary to remind Washington once more that the American people do not want war with Japan. The college professors, amateur diplomats, and munitions-makers who are advocating an economic boycott, or are spreading rumors of secret war preparations, do not speak for the majority of the people. Thus far, to be sure, the government has proceeded with tact and caution in dealing with the Shanghai crisis, and there is every reason to believe that the Administration is sincerely anxious to avoid complications in the Far East that might involve us in armed conflict. But there is no guaranty that this discreet and careful attitude can or will be maintained, and many forces are at work that might quickly compel the United States into a position where war would be unavoidable. One of these factors, and perhaps the most dangerous, is the growing demand for a boycott of Japan, a hostile measure in itself and one likely to lead to war. An unknown factor, but one laden with dynamite, has to do with Japanese aims in China.

We cannot be certain as to the real Japanese objectives on the Asiatic mainland. Japan has for years been bent on keeping China divided and weak, knowing that a united and strong China would probably threaten its national existence. The Chinese revolutionists of two decades ago were aided and comforted by the Japanese militarists, their leaders even finding refuge at various times in the home of Tsuyoshi Inukai, head of the conservative Seiyukai Party, and now Prime Minister of Japan. The infamous Twenty-one Demands and the seizure of Shantung in 1915 were clearly intended to divide China and reduce it to a state of perpetual vassalage. Throughout the civil war from 1922 to 1928 the Japanese were active behind the scenes—though occasionally they came boldly out into the open—in endeavoring to check any tendency toward Chinese unity. More than once they sent troops into Shantung, Manchuria, and other sections to embarrass the victorious Nationalist armies whenever the latter appeared about to bring the whole of China under Nationalist rule.

There is other evidence at hand to suggest that the Japanese are interested in something more in China than the mineral resources of Manchuria. For example, what was the real meaning of the proposal to "internationalize" the five principal commercial cities of China which the Foreign Office in Tokio advanced some weeks ago? This was surely no hopeless shot in the dark, no mere trial balloon. The Japanese mind does not work that way. The Japanese knew that the proposal was certain to be rejected by Washington and London. What, then, was its purpose? Opinion is growing that it was intended to provide an excuse in advance to cover Japanese aggression elsewhere in China. When, let us say, the Japanese are "provoked" into intervening in other sections, they can readily say that they foresaw the necessity for such intervention and had, indeed, warned the Powers to join with them in preventing incidents that would make intervention unavoidable. And we already know how easily provocative acts can occur. We have seen more than enough of this in the last few months at Mukden, Tientsin, Shanghai, Nanking, Swatow, and in other cities. That the Japanese are prepared for hostile action extending far beyond the Shanghai area is all too evident. Every important Chinese port has more than its normal complement of Japanese war vessels. In Shanghai harbor are concentrated forty of these men-of-war, and in the fight against the Chinese army near Shanghai are three entire divisions of Japanese troops, with more on the way. In other sections of China Japanese military units are gathered awaiting action, the largest concentration, numbering more than 11,000 soldiers, being in the Tientsin area, which from a strategic standpoint controls the province of Shantung and most of North China.

Their pride stung to the quick by the unexpected resistance of the Chinese in the Shanghai sector, the Japanese are now planning to send a large army into China. How far they intend to go in "punishing" the Chinese for their determined defense of the homeland is open to question. Nevertheless, there is already talk of a "national" government being set up in Tokio for the "period of the emergency." This can only mean that the Japanese are planning war on a grand scale, for a national government, which would amount to an open dictatorship, could have no other purpose. Again there is little doubt that the militarists are interpreting the results of the February 20 elections—in which they and their ultra-conservative colleagues won a sweeping victory—as giving them fullest authority to go ahead with whatever plans they may have. A war involving the whole of China is bound to affect the interests of other Powers. Modern wars have a way of dragging supposedly neutral and disinterested nations into conflict. If the Japanese really mean to take over and "neutralize" the important commercial centers of China, they will thereby clash with the American principle of the "Open Door." It is hardly to be supposed that Washington would sit idly by while the Japanese were thus treading upon this sacred principle.

But perhaps greater danger lies closer to home. There are, for example, the many rumors to the effect that the government arsenals, navy yards, and munitions depots are secretly but feverishly preparing our war machine for any eventuality. There are the diplomatic and military "experts," who, having convinced themselves that war with Japan is inevitable, are now urging that we jump into the present conflict and have it over with. Finally, the demand for an economic boycott is spreading. From that quarter comes the most serious threat of all. The boycott is a hostile weapon; it constitutes the use of force against a presumably friendly Power. Such an application of force would be a measure of war. To be effective it would have to be supported by a war psychology, and this can only be whipped up by means of an officially conducted propaganda campaign. The boycott is too explosive a device to be trifled with. Even a private boycott, one not supported by the government, might readily stir up dangerous, uncontrollable hatred of the Japanese. Then it would be too late to remember that it was intended only to force Japan to make peace with China.

War by Boycott

THE agitation here for an economic boycott of Japan has been temporarily scotched by Senator Borah's firm opposition and by the apparent attitude of the British and French governments, but there can be little doubt that it will make its appearance again as soon as the meeting of the Assembly of the League of Nations is under way. It is only natural, of course, that those opposed to Japan's brazen and barbarous attack on China should wish to see the League and the Powers take every possible step to bring that attack to a halt; but before they approve such a weapon as the economic boycott they ought gravely to consider its probable consequences.

That a successful economic boycott would be close to ruinous for Japan there can be little doubt; few of the great Powers are so dependent as she is on foreign trade. But economic ruin means unemployment, famine, and starvation; it includes the civilian population, women and children, as well as the military, and it affects most precisely those who are already weakest. The economic boycott is not a peace weapon, but one of the deadliest of war weapons, and there is not the slightest doubt that the Japanese would consider it as such. Moreover, like other weapons of warfare, it hurts the nations that use it as well as the nation against which it is used. And it does not hurt them equally, but merely in proportion to their previous trade with the boycotted nation.

In the present instance the lion's share of the burden of such a boycott would fall upon the United States. Our trade with Japan is incomparably larger than that of any other nation; it is three times as great as that of China, which ranks second. As there is no equality in the burden of a boycott as among nations, neither is there any as among industries. Raw silk, for example, comprises two-fifths of Japan's total exports; the United States takes practically all of it; of our imports from Japan four-fifths, in value, consist of raw silk. Our exports to Japan show the same lack of balance. Fully one-half of them are in our raw cotton, of which Japan takes 40 per cent; the remainder consists mainly of lumber, iron and steel, machinery, petroleum, and automobiles. The outside burden of an economic boycott against Japan, therefore, would not only fall chiefly on the United States, but within the United States itself it would fall chiefly on two industries—cotton growing and silk-fabric manufacture, gravely increasing the distress in the South and the unemployment in the North. Obviously no one with elementary notions of justice would hold that the moral conscience of the world should be satisfied chiefly at the expense of American cotton growers and American silk workers. Japan could only be expected to strike back, and she would strike back chiefly at the United States, because we should have become her chief economic enemy.

The reasons for opposing an economic boycott in the present instance are obviously reasons for opposing the economic boycott in principle. Not only would there be no equality of trade loss among the participating nations in the present instance; there would never be such an equality of trade loss. Always some of the nations employing the boycott would suffer more than others through the sheer moral accident of having heavier trade with the nation against which the boycott was directed. It should be clear that if the economic boycott ever became established as a recognized weapon by League members and "neutrals" for disciplining nations, there could only follow an exacerbation of the present perilous tendency toward economic nationalism, isolationism, and "self-containment." Individual nations would prepare themselves against such a step by raising their tariff barriers still higher. A tariff is nothing more nor less than a partial economic boycott; like an outright boycott, it is essentially a weapon of war. It does not consist in a refusal to sell goods, but in a virtual refusal to buy them, which, by removing means of payment, soon makes it impossible to sell them either. The League and the Powers, including ourselves, should bend every effort to make peace in the Far East, but we must make peace with the methods of peace, and not with the methods of war.

The "Clerks" and War

IN a recent issue of the Parisian review *Europe,* M. Jean Guehenno addresses an open letter to that distinguished but none too effectual body which is known as the Permanent Committee on Intellectual Cooperation of the League of Nations. He assumes that its orators mean what they say in their eloquent speeches concerning the function of the intellectuals in promoting the harmony of the world, and he assumes still further that they are as disappointed as the rest of us to discover that they can think of no projects likely to be more generally useful than M. Bela Bartok's request for an international library of phonograph records, or Mr. John Masefield's proposal to endow a traveling company of declaiming poets. To assist them, he tells an anecdote so pointed and makes a suggestion so concrete that we are determined to pass both of them on to our readers in the hope that other learned bodies may also profit.

It seems that when Ernest Renan began to advance in years he was struck by the fear that senility might lead him to retract the propositions which he had always defended. He might even, he realized, be converted by some too skilful priest and leave behind him one of those deathbed retractions of which the church is so proud. And so he took a wise precaution. He set down in black and white an advance retraction of any retraction he might subsequently make, and he requested that the future should consider as his true thoughts those which he had uttered while still possessing the full force and the full liberty of his spirit.

But, says M. Guehenno, these cooperating intellectuals have even more reason than Renan to fear a self-betrayal. However boldly intellectuals may speak now, however international-minded they may be, there is every reason to assume that should any crisis arise they would recant as their equals recanted before, and that all the beautiful internationalism of M. Valéry and Mr. Masefield would be forgotten in the ardent patriotism of each. Pacific sentiments flourish only when they are not of the slightest use, and there is always time between the "strained relations" and the "declaration of war" to discover abundant excuse for bellicose pronouncements all the more effective for the very reason that they come from persons notoriously pacifistic before. But if the members of the League's committee are sincere, let them follow Renan. Let them sign now a statement expressing their present opinions, and let them issue a warning in advance against any concessions which either hysteria or social pressure may later cause them to make. Meanwhile, admirably enough, M. Guehenno, their spokesman, says:

> Do you not know, gentlemen, that without you, without us, war is not possible? All our speeches, all our articles, all our songs are necessary before the poor bread-eaters of the world can be led to the trenches and the grave. Only we can lie well enough to make their death seem beautiful. Fifteen years ago we were engaged in this strange task. We became disgusted enough to swear never to participate in it again. It was a politician who said, "As long as I am here, there will be no war." Have you the same courage? Dare you to say that, no matter how long the war lasts, you will not be there?

Recognize Russia

THAT Congressman Rainey of Illinois, a Democratic leader of the House of Representatives, has joined Senators Borah, Johnson of California, and Robinson of Arkansas in urging the immediate recognition of Russia is highly significant of the changing opinion in our official life. "Our failure to recognize Russia," said Mr. Rainey, "is an economic crime." He pointed out that whereas in 1898 there were eighty-four American ships plying steadily between the United States and the Black Sea ports, what little cargo now goes to Russia is carried by tramp steamers. He declared that there was no forced labor whatever in Russia. "Russia," he added, "is the greatest market in the world, but we won't admit that it exists. We sit back and let our factories stop running and our people stay idle. That is foolish." Quite right, but it is by no means as foolish as some of the other situations that arise out of our attitude. The coming World's Fair in Chicago has invited the participation of the Russian Government, which is eager to take part but cannot do so because the government in Washington declares that the red Soviet flag may not be hoisted over any Russian building in Chicago or anywhere else! This is also the reason that there is to be no Russian building in New York's Radio City. Yet we pride ourselves upon our shrewdness and our common sense!

If the opposition to recognition of Russia were in accord with our historic traditions and our usual course of action, and were based on principle, that would be one thing. It is, however, largely due to the belief that if communism succeeds in Russia it will spread to America, and therefore we must not do anything that would in any wise contribute to that success. It is fear, craven fear, which controls, with the question of payment for the American plants seized by the Bolsheviks and the debt owed to the United States as side issues. Yet that fear was never more ridiculous than today, for if communism is spreading rapidly in the United States, as some people fear, that is due not to Russian propaganda but to the breakdown of our own economic machinery, and to the rising tide of indignation among 12,000,000 unemployed who through no fault of their own are facing destitution and are compelled to beg for charity. It is not the Kremlin which is endangering capitalist civilization in America, but the absence of any leadership at home, and the failure to recognize some of the fundamental causes for the chaos in which we live. Nothing is sillier than to think that we could bring about the downfall of the Russian Government by cutting off all intercourse with the Soviets and forbidding any American to enter that country, as some of our hundred-per-cent patriots would like to have us do. If Russia does not find the cooperation here which it desires, it will be able to buy what it needs elsewhere in the world. There is doubt that the Conservative Government in England will continue to do business with Russia, but Germany, France, Italy, and all the rest of the world are most eager to sell goods to the Soviets. Everybody who has dealt with Moscow declares that the Russian Government could not be more honorable in its dealings, or prompter in its payments. It has disbursed billions of dollars to foreign countries, but there is not yet a recorded case where a payment has not been made on the day set.

As for the property taken away from Americans, the Russians have repeatedly declared their willingness to discuss indemnities to such American concerns as the International Harvester Company. It has, moreover, repeatedly offered to take up the question of the Czarist and Kerensky debts, subject to certain reservations. The United States has already written off as a total loss a large percentage of the loans made to our Allies during the war. It might just as well write off these Russian loans, and perhaps if it does Russia will not present the large bills which it has a right to send us for the murder of Russian citizens by American troops in the Archangel region without a declaration of war, and for the similar unconstitutional and unwarranted appearance upon Russian soil of the American army of General W. S. Graves. These, we insist, are details which could be worked out in a few days should the government in Washington desire to remove all the obstacles to recognition.

The Administration cannot now remain unaffected by the fact that so conservative a Democrat as Senator Robinson of Arkansas declares that he advocates Russian recognition "as one feature in the policy of promoting amicable international relations and stimulating our foreign commerce." Senator Johnson's position is even more startling. His first point is that "there are billions of dollars' worth of future orders in Russia for American workers to fill and in these times it is simply economic idiocy, by our policies, to exclude Americans from trade and commerce which could so readily be obtained." Far more important is his second contention that the United States ought to recognize Russia as a move to head off another world war. Speaking of the tension existing on the Manchurian border between Russia and Japan because of the latter's aggression, he says that "a spark may set off the powder barrel at any time. Japan seems to think that Russia's downfall would be acclaimed the world over. Some gesture on the part of the United States, therefore, could well be made to rid her of any such idea." We surely have progressed some distance when a United States Senator from the Pacific Coast is willing to have it known that in the event of a conflict between Japan and Russia the moral weight of the United States will be on the side of the wicked Bolsheviks.

Now is the time, if there ever was a time, to recognize Soviet Russia. Every sane consideration demands it even without regard to the existing depression. How a government faced with such wholesale suffering as there is in America today can refuse to act is beyond us. To *The Nation* the subject is of such tremendous importance that we have gladly dedicated this issue to the subject. It *is* one of the greatest opportunities before America. The Secretary of State may persist in his refusal to move, or Mr. Hoover may. Either faces the possibility, if not the probability, that deaths by starvation of American citizens may yet directly be laid at his door, if he refuses to give to American industry the chance to enter into immediate contracts with Russia for billions of dollars' worth of supplies. O.G.V.

Europe in Extremis

OMINOUS for the whole world is the dismissal of the Brüning Government, coming as it does on the eve of the Lausanne Conference and presaging not economic betterment in Germany but greater political and social confusion. It happens, if we may judge by recent public utterances, just when the realism of France was beginning to make itself felt in the right direction of a common-sense and generous settlement. Now President Hindenburg has messed things badly, when every effort should have been made to permit Chancellor Brüning to carry on at least until the Lausanne meeting was over. At this writing no one knows whether his successor is to be a general or a dictator, or a combination government with Hitler in the Cabinet. In any event, the situation in Germany can only get worse, and with it that of Europe. No one will charge the London *Economist*, or Sir Walter Layton, its editor, with being sensationalist. But here is what the paper says in the current issue, as cabled from London:

> International commerce is perishing with catastrophic rapidity. . . . Let us not mince words; with every factor in the existing situation making for a shift toward economic collapse, the prospects for next winter, both socially and politically, are terrifying unless by resolute action on the part of international statesmen the influences now at work can be reversed. The conference at Lausanne offers the last opportunity.

Edouard Herriot, who is likely to be the next French Premier, has just published an article in which he professes disquietude both at the German military budget and the Hitler "anti-Polish agitation." Add to this French fears over the present change in the German government, and all of the new French attitude of compromise may be lost.

Observers who had been closely following recent developments in Germany had been warned to expect the fall of Brüning. Yet the news that he and his Cabinet had resigned came as somewhat of a surprise. It had been hoped to the end that he would once more ride out the storm. For twenty-six months, through one of the worst periods in Germany's history, he had surmounted every difficulty despite the fact that he had had to work with an extremely slender majority in the Reichstag, and one that was none too friendly to his policies. Even the rising tide of Hitlerism had not caused him to depart from his calm and certain ways. The fact that the change was made at this time gives color to the reports that Brüning's fall was the result of intrigue and reactionary conspiracy. We know that the Junkers of East Prussia were fighting him tooth and nail because of his plan to settle unemployed workers upon their estates. We know, too, that a military clique headed by General Kurt von Schleicher, Secretary of State in the Ministry of Defense, had been seeking increased political power. It was this clique that forced the resignation of General Groener as Minister of Defense after Groener had brought about the suppression of Hitler's Brown Shirt army. The generals frankly looked upon Hitler's armed forces as a necessary and vital branch of the Reichswehr. But it is not clear whether Hindenburg was really moved by the maneuvers and whisperings of the generals and other participants in the rumored anti-Brüning cabal, or whether the President lost confidence in his Chancellor for other and more substantial reasons. If it is true that Brüning was retired as the result of intrigue, then it must be said that Germany has learned little since 1914, for it was just such intrigue carried on by Baron Holstein and others which contributed so largely to the diplomatic debacle that forced the World War upon Europe.

Chancellor Brüning had in his twenty-six months in office greatly increased his personal prestige and hence the prestige of Germany. With a newcomer in the Chancellorship, and that person very likely an extreme nationalist, not only will Germany suffer, but this increase in nationalism will react upon the whole of Europe. There have of late been many indications of growing unrest, particularly in Southern and Eastern Europe. There is disaffection in the Jugoslavian army, and a minor reign of terror has taken place in that country. Premier Jorga of Rumania is in difficulty because of the financial situation and also because the leaders of the once-defunct Bratianu-Liberal Party are growing restive. Fascism has recently made sweeping gains in Austria. Czecho-Slovakia, which is at last really beginning to feel the effects of the economic depression, is also now for the first time since Masaryk became President showing signs of an extreme nationalist trend. In Poland there has been no let-up in the persecution of the national minorities and the radicals. Now with the reaction about to triumph in Germany it is more than possible that the uncertainty and unrest which have engulfed these neighbors will increase to a point threatening the political and economic stability of the entire world.

The German Republic Totters

THAT the German Republic is in jeopardy must be obvious to everybody. The sudden return of Paul von Hindenburg to his war-time mentality has resulted in the establishment of a reactionary regime composed of aristocrats, big business men, and militarists—the worst possible combination—which menaces at every point the maintenance of republican institutions. More than that, the proclamation of new elections for the Reichstag on July 31 will result in the taking over of the government by the Hitler forces unless all signs fail. They will have no difficulty in getting on with those in charge of the present reactionary rule, who are now trying to obtain control of Prussia by having the Reich take over its government. Whether this will precipitate a conflict with the trade unions and the Communists time will show. The heads of the state governments have already protested. The *Vorwärts* has been quick to declare that the final struggle is at hand between the reactionary forces and those who believe in the revolution of 1918. At any rate, until this question is settled there must be great anxiety and an intensified internal conflict which bodes ill for the peace of Germany and the economic rehabilitation of the world. From every point of view there is nothing more important today than the question whether the German Republic will live or yield to a dictatorship.

Why is it that the Republic is so threatened fourteen years after its founding? Some say this is another failure of democracy. Others insist that the Germans are merely throwing off a blind set up to make the world think that their character had changed, and that they are now returning to their old role and revealing the same inherent imperialistic tendencies which were heralded to the world as so dangerous to it in the war years. Does it mean that the bulk of the German people, nurtured under the monarchy, naturally favor autocratic government with centralized control? Or is the sudden collapse of the government into the hands of the old gang due to economic conditions rather than to political desires or to inbred tendencies? To our minds this event is the natural outcome of the Treaty of Versailles and the treatment given to the Germans ever since their defeat in 1918. It has been repeatedly pointed out in these columns that if the United States and the Allies had deliberately planned their course to make the existence of the German Republic as difficult as possible, they could hardly have done otherwise than they did. At home, on the other hand, the new German state has had to face the anti-republican elements, while year after year the industrial and economic situation of the Reich got worse and worse, so that today, as Chancellor Brüning has just testified, one-half of the workshops of Germany are closed and 6,000,000 German workers are without means of livelihood. Any form of government which had to face these facts after fourteen years would find it hard indeed to hold its own.

We do not believe that this is a failure of democracy, or that it means that Germany is inherently monarchistic or imperialistic, although there are, of course, many devoted monarchists and militarists. Certainly the workers are overwhelmingly pro-Republic and utterly opposed to any form of dictatorship, whether from the left or the right. What has happened is that the bulk of the German people must now pay for the failure of the Socialist governments of the past to rise to their opportunities immediately after the war—their failure to reorganize, their failure to make the revolution as thoroughgoing as it should have been. This, coupled with the economic distress, has so exhausted the popular forces that the reactionaries, thanks to Von Hindenburg, had only to sit still and let the plums drop into their laps. It was the workingmen of Germany, and not the middle classes, who defeated the Kapp Putsch in 1920. The question now to be answered is whether the trade unions, worn down by suffering and unemployment, by lack of adequate food and adequate earnings, have still left within them the power and unity to repel this attempt to overthrow the Republic.

Looking back, it is plain that the revolution did not go far enough in 1918. It was not radical enough. Not a day should have been lost in breaking up the great estates, in smashing the power of the great East Prussian agrarians who for so long have been the real rulers of Germany, as the big business men of America have so long ruled this country. Precisely as was the case in England when the British Labor Party came into power, the German Socialists were weak in not immediately proceeding to socialize certain of the leading industries, thereby breaking the strangle-hold of the great industrialists. When the Reich collapsed, the German leaders appointed committees to report which branches of industry could be considered ready for socialization. The committees reported on coal, potash, and electrical production, and drafted a general socialization law. A second commission, appointed in 1920, reported a weak dilution of the original plan, and with this ended all efforts toward direct programmatic socialization. Thus the opportunity was lost to take control of key industries.

Finally, it remains to point out that the government was repeatedly weak in dealing with such menacing manifestations as the "private armies"—the Steel Helmets, the

Hitler shock troops, and similar bodies, although it did some years ago dissolve the Communist "Red Front" organization. Certainly no government ever paid a higher price for an error of judgment than has the German Government for its failure to expel Hitler after he raised the banner of revolt in Munich with General Ludendorff, and was caught red-handed. It is an open question, also, whether the government has not been weak in permitting the members of the Hohenzollern family to remain on German soil. But even in judging the government for these shortcomings one must never lose sight of what has been going on in Germany during these crucial years: the economic distress; the sense of infinite wrong done to Germany by the Treaty of Versailles; the false accusation of sole responsibility for the war; the Ruhr invasion; the frightful loss of wealth due both to the war and to the inflation, and many other factors. All these incidents, plus the weakness of the government, the failure to carry the revolution through with vigor, and the survival of many militarists and monarchists, are today the reasons why the German Republic totters.

"Take Away the Army"

CAMILLE ROMBAUT, a French war resister, has been sentenced to four months' imprisonment for refusal to perform military service. His trial at the ancient fortress of Lille was spectacular and received publicity throughout Europe, the hundreds of protests evidencing the recent growth in the war-resistance movement. M. Rombaut had a circle of influential friends; his defender was a well-known professor from the famous law college at Lyons; and Rombaut himself peculiarly symbolized the change that has taken place in many minds since the war. During the conflict, as a boy of fourteen, he bravely destroyed the telephone and telegraph lines which served the German headquarters in the very town from which, eighteen years later, he has been shipped off to jail.

That the revulsion against war and militarism is at last beginning to penetrate the French populace is apparent and is causing some concern to the militarists. Georges Soyeux and Fernand Plaquevent some months ago notified the authorities of their unwillingness to serve, and as yet neither has been arrested. M. Plaquevent wrote to the Minister of War: "I took part in the massacre of 1914-18. I never hated the Germans. The war deeply influenced my ideas. . . . Now I stand by the words of Victor Hugo, 'Take away the army . . . and you end war.' I have therefore decided to work for the abolition of war and the removal of its causes." Alfred Nahon, Paul Personne, and Charles Launay have followed with a similar forthright refusal to serve, despite all consequences. Interestingly enough, when Albert Einstein and Lord Ponsonby, the latter acting as chairman of the War Resisters' International, last May issued an appeal to men of military age to resist conscription, and several thousand new members joined the organization, France supplied more than any other country. Noting the trend, a French deputy, Georges Richard, is planning to introduce a bill recognizing the right of conscience. A similar measure failed of passage in the Belgian senate last year only by a vote of eighty-nine to sixty-one, and its adherents are rapidly multiplying in the present parliament.

In many regions of the world where the movement was formerly weak or non-existent, gains are being made. New groups have been established in several cities of Latin America. In Spain, where a strong pacific mood is discernible under the new republic, three groups have been organized in as many cities, while the Provincial Federation of Trade Unions in Almeria, the most southeasterly province, has unanimously adopted the complete pacifist program of the War Resisters' International. In Finland a new alternative service law has been put through as a sop to growing pacifist opinion. More than 7,000 young Swedes recently notified their government that they would never serve in the army. In reactionary Bulgaria the clergy of the Congregational and Methodist churches have come out for uncompromising war resistance. And the war resisters behind the bars in most countries of the Continent—twenty-four in Holland and seventeen in Belgium, for example—are serving as centers for a rising agitation that may in time reach those in high places who perpetually talk peace and unceasingly prepare for war.

An Open Letter to Oswald G. Villard

DEAR MR. VILLARD: In your issue of May 11, 1932, you wrote an interesting and important letter to Governor Roosevelt. This letter ends with some fourteen pertinent questions to which you asked an answer, yes or no. You do a public service in trying to compel candidates to face real issues.

Of course neither you nor I nor anyone else has a right to ask of Franklin Roosevelt any more than that he shall declare where he stands as a Democrat. We all know that he is not a Socialist or a radical of any sort. There is, however, about your open letter something more than a faint suspicion that perhaps you and *The Nation* would be comparatively well satisfied if Governor Roosevelt were to declare himself on the liberal side of your fourteen questions. It is this suspicion that prompts me to ask you in turn to declare yourself categorically on some deeper questions than you have raised for the Governor to answer.

All that you have said about Governor Roosevelt's equipment and opportunities, I can say of you and more. It is because of the place that you personally hold in American life and the immensely useful role filled by *The Nation* that it seems to me worth while to ask you to declare yourself once again and very explicitly on the fundamental problems of our times. These questions go much deeper than a half-hearted approach to government operation of the railroads and possibly of the power industry. The importance of any answers to these specific questions which you ask on power and the control of industry is considerably affected by the answer to a preliminary and more fundamental question. Are you seeking to patch up for a while longer the capitalist system or are you seeking to change in orderly fashion that system to the end that we may establish a cooperative commonwealth? It is this basic inquiry which prompts my specific questions:

1. Do you believe that the capitalist nationalist social order is doomed? Yes or no?

2. Do you believe that the effective management of the machine age in its present development, as well as the realization of any worth-while ideals of plenty, peace, or freedom, requires social ownership of those things necessary for the common life and their management for use rather than for profit? Yes or no?

3. Assuming that you share in some degree the present enthusiasm for economic planning, do you believe that such planning can be plastered on the essential and chaotic planlessness of our profit system? Yes or no?

4. Do you believe that capitalism can remain capitalism and yet get rid of unemployment and abolish cyclical depression? If so, how?

5. Do you believe that the world can stagger out of the depths of this depression without consciously lightening its present load of fantastic debts piled up during the war and post-war years? If so, how?

6. Do you believe that our present capitalism or the fascist form of capitalism to which we may be drifting can reasonably be expected to preserve the peace of the world if the struggle for material advantage, prestige, and power implicit in it continue to characterize all social relations, foreign and domestic? Yes or no?

7. Assuming that you acknowledge the fantastic and cruel insanity of our present system and the essential reasonableness of socialism—I use the word in a most inclusive sense—do you think it is possible to plan for a relatively orderly and peaceful transition? If so, by what means?

8. Do you believe that the process of transition requires as its basis and inspiration the assertion of a new and revolutionary philosophy of loyalty to a cooperative society, in a classless world in which the solidarity of workers with hands and brain will cross national and racial lines? Yes or no?

9. Do you believe that an orderly transition period requires careful plans consciously directed to the rapid socialization of land, natural resources, banking, and the principal means of production, their functional administration, and their control under a general planning board? Yes or no?

10. Do you believe that taxation of land values and of incomes and inheritances should be used not merely to provide the revenue but also to bring about an actual transfer of ownership and control? Yes or no?

11. Do you believe that it is essential to build up organizations of the workers with hand and brain in consumers' cooperatives, in labor unions, and in a political party which will express the needs and ideals of the workers? Yes or no?

12. If you believe in such organization, is it not more reasonable to accept the Socialist Party and to work to make it stronger rather than to wait vainly for the emergence of some non-existent mass movement, progressive rather than Socialist in nature, and more appropriate to an earlier stage of capitalism than to this hour of crisis? Yes or no?

NORMAN THOMAS

Mr. Thomas's questions are frequently not clear, lack adequate definition, and nearly all smack of the oratorical, thus making it extremely difficult to give him categorical answers. None the less I reply as follows:

1. Yes, if it continues as it has since 1914.

2. In ignorance of what "those things necessary for the common life" are, or what constitute "worth-while ideals of plenty" I answer no, while favoring the socialization of utilities, pipe-lines, the public ownership of natural resources, and the control and direction of such broken-down industries as coal and iron.

3. Yes. But in using the phrase "planning . . . plastered on . . . planelessness," Mr. Thomas puts the question in a biased form.

4. Yes, by unemployment insurance and planning, and by government control of key industries as above.

5. No.

6. No.

7. Yes, by the same kind of evolution by which we are now proceeding, with greater speed than most people realize, toward increasing socialization, frequently proposed and carried through by the conservatives themselves.

8. Yes. "My country is the world, my countrymen all mankind."

9. Yes. I believe that the transition period requires orderly planning, but I am not certain that nearly so much socialization will be required as this question assumes, and I specifically except the land.

10. Within limitations, yes; again excepting the land.

11. Yes, but I am opposed to any party which shall be restricted to being a purely one-class party, on whichever side that might be organized.

12. No.

OSWALD GARRISON VILLARD

The Militarists Take Prussia

CHANCELLOR von Papen did not hesitate long in seizing power in Prussia. Whether he did so with the connivance of Adolf Hitler and the fascists matters little. The republicans of Germany are now confronted with an accomplished fact. The Republic itself survives—but only on paper. More than two-thirds of its people and territory are now under a military dictatorship. The shell of the Weimar Constitution remains, of course, but apparently only to serve the purposes of the militarists. They are emphatically declaring that they acted wholly in accordance with the rules laid down in that document. But precisely the same position was taken by Luttwitz, Ehrhardt, and the other reactionary leaders during the Kapp *Putsch* in March, 1920. They captured the central government by a surprise march on Berlin, established what they called a "Government of Labor," and then sought to justify their coup d'etat by declaring that they were merely seeking "to restore the essence and spirit of the Weimar Constitution, which had been shamefully mishandled by the legitimate government." Now the very same groups have seized power, using the very same excuses; but this time the militarists, junkers, industrialists, and other extreme nationalists appear likely to succeed. But it would be the success of machine-gun rule, not of honest government.

In 1920 the reaction was defeated by the discipline of the organized workers. The Berlin Government had been forewarned, but sought to ignore the warnings. It was not prepared to offer resistance when the reactionary troops came through the Brandenburger Tor and marched up Wilhelmstrasse to take over the government offices. The Cabinet fled to Dresden. But the working class was ready to fight and die for the Republic, which was then less than two years old. The leaders of the trades unions and Social Democratic Party promptly published a manifesto calling upon their members to strike. "Everything is at stake," the appeal read. "No business must be run so long as Ludendorff's military dictatorship prevails. Therefore cease work. Strike! Cut off the resources of this reactionary clique. Fight with all means for the maintenance of the Republic. Let there be a general strike all along the line. Proletarians, unite! Down with the counter-revolution!" So successful was the general strike that the industry and business of the entire country was tied up within a few hours, and five days later the militarists and nationalists admitted defeat.

That was twelve years ago. Despite the hardships of the war, the German labor movement, for years the best-disciplined and best-organized in Europe, remained the only stable force in the country. Since then the strength of the labor movement has been eaten away by inflation, continued unemployment, the economic disintegration of recent years, and the wavering policies of its own leaders. Today as never before the workers of Germany are beaten, without hope. A working class cannot subsist on starvation rations for years and expect to retain enough strength and spirit to combat an offensive such as that launched against the German workers and lower middle class by Hindenburg, Von Schleicher, and Von Papen. Therefore, if we except the editorial outcry of the *Rote Fahne,* the Communist organ, there has been no demand whatever for a general strike to crush the latest attempt to set up a military dictatorship. The workers are taking their whipping lying down. For this reason, and for this reason alone, is the dictatorship likely to remain in power for some time to come.

However, there is still real danger that the new regime may precipitate bloodshed, perhaps civil war. We do not yet know what part Hitler has played in the maneuverings of Von Schleicher and Von Papen. If the militarists come to terms with the fascists, these two groups together can probably dominate Germany without fear of serious or important opposition from the Socialists and Communists. In that event we may see a coalition government in which Hitler and his lieutenants would be given some portfolios, but with the actual power remaining in the hands of the Reichswehr generals. Such a government, though resting in the final analysis upon the bayonets of the army, would have the unquestionably valuable support of the increasingly popular fascist movement. On the other hand, if Hitler should win a majority in the Reichstag elections of July 31 and decide thereupon that he wants all or nothing, there may be trouble ahead. It is hardly to be supposed that the militarists would have taken such energetic measures in Prussia had they any idea that they would soon have to yield their newly-gained authority to Hitler.

Having captured Prussia, will the militarists now move against the other German states? And if they do, what will be the result thereof? A dictatorship for the whole of Germany, or a dissolution of the federation created by Bismarck in 1871? It is worth noting that Von Papen is moving with great caution in his relations with the other states. He must be aware of the deep-seated antagonisms that divide Munich, Stuttgart, and Karlsruhe from Berlin. He must know that there is strong sentiment, particularly in Bavaria, for separation from Prussia. He has his hands full in governing the latter state, and more than full in trying to solve the German economic puzzle. It is likely that he will not seek to make his task altogether impossible by proceeding against the other states, especially when he does not know to what lengths they are prepared to go in resisting an extension of the dictatorship to their territories.

But the sight of a military regime in Prussia is terrible enough. Whatever may be the outcome of this dread-inspiring development, is it not fresh proof of the utter folly of believing that good may come out of the crime of war? Even Mr. Wilson, we believe, were he alive, would have to admit that, with the old guard again in charge in Berlin only fourteen years after the armistice, with democracy collapsing everywhere in favor of dictatorship, with armaments greatly grown since 1914 and the League of Nations weak and ineffective, and with our own country deep in economic disaster, it would be impossible today to claim a single solid gain as a result of our determination to enter the World War in order to make over the world by wholesale murder in favor of the Fourteen Points and the establishment of permanent peace.

Progress at Geneva

IN many respects we sympathize with the criticisms directed by Germany, Russia, and Italy against the Geneva arms conference, which took a six-months' adjournment on July 23. These governments pointed out that the conference had taken no step toward the reduction of armies and navies, and that it had failed to abolish "aggressive weapons," grant Germany juridical equality with France, or solve the Franco-Italian naval problem. As we said last week the outcome is on the whole a bitter disappointment. Nevertheless, the very fact that the conference has been able to accomplish something demonstrates that its efforts have not been wholly in vain. It should not be forgotten that these disarmament negotiations have taken place during one of the most critical periods in world history. Every country, gripped by the depression, has vainly attempted to protect itself by nationalistic measures whose only effect has been to create international animosity and to intensify the depression. Moreover, in the Orient a "war" has been fought between Japan and China, while in Latin America there have been renewed threats of war between Bolivia and Paraguay. In Europe new apprehensions have been aroused by the establishment of a Junker dictatorship in Germany and the high-handed overthrow of Social Democratic rule in Prussia.

Under such circumstances, it would have been easy for the arms conference to have adjourned in open bitterness and complete disagreement. Fortunately this result has been avoided. It is true that the conference has not concluded a general disarmament treaty; but it has adopted a number of important provisions which may be embodied in such a treaty when the conference reassembles next January. Thus, the governments have agreed to the abolition of all bombardment from the air—an extremely important provision, especially from the standpoint of civilian populations. They have sanctioned the French proposal for the internationalization of civil aviation, as the one effective means of preventing civilian craft from being converted to military use upon the outbreak of war. They have decided to limit the size of land artillery and tanks and to prohibit all forms of chemical, bacteriological, and incendiary warfare—all of which is good as far as it goes, but, if adopted, only makes war a little less horrible. Finally, they have agreed to establish a permanent disarmament commission to supervise the execution of the disarmament treaty, when finally completed, and to act as an organ of conciliation when any government believes that its security is threatened by the armaments of a neighboring power. During the next few months committees also are to study the best means of securing a reduction in the present size of armies and navies, of securing the limitation and reduction of military expenditure, and of controlling the private manufacture of arms. Although this list of accomplishments does not secure any immediate relief from the burden of armaments, the Geneva conference, we repeat, has succeeded in keeping alive the goal of disarmament in a period when it might easily have been abandoned, and in taking certain steps toward insuring that the goal eventually will be realized.

During the next six months the United States will have an opportunity to take three steps which in our judgment will greatly facilitate the work of the arms conference when it reconvenes. In the first place, the American Government should reexamine its naval and military policy to see whether it really conforms to the doctrine laid down by President Hoover that in view of the anti-war pact armaments must be used only for defense. It is clear to us that there is no danger threatening the "defenses" of the United States which justify building up to the parity levels of the London naval treaty. It is also clear to us that the simplest and most far-reaching means of securing naval reduction lies in abolishing the battleship. If England and Japan consent to such abolition, no one can argue that the United States should retain the battleship for "defensive" purposes. Likewise, the Hoover disarmament proposal of June 22 should be amended so as to discard the provision increasing the American army to 200,000 men. Congress should also radically amend the National Defense Act of 1920 under which the American army today consists of a skeletonized force, manned by an excessive number of officers, the purpose of which is to throw six field armies of 4,000,000 drafted men into Europe immediately upon the outbreak of war. The assumption that the American army is to be employed primarily in fighting battles in Europe is utterly inconsistent with the principles of the anti-war pact. The American army should be transformed into a genuine defense force, thus saving millions of dollars to the taxpayer and proving our sincerity.

Secondly, the United States should assist in strengthening the procedure for the pacific settlement of disputes. Until an adequate means of peacefully composing international difficulties is established, it is unlikely that the world will achieve a large measure of disarmament. *The Nation* does not believe that the United States should become involved in any system of international sanctions; but it does believe that it should work for the development of international organization, based upon pacifist principles. We hope therefore that President Hoover will send a strong delegation to the September Assembly of the League, to consider what joint action, short of the application of sanctions, should be taken upon the report of the Lytton commission concerning the Sino-Japanese dispute.

Finally, we again enthusiastically support Senator Borah in urging the American Government immediately to convene an international conference to attack world economic problems, including the cancelation of all war debts. A year ago no French cabinet would consider wiping out the Young plan because of fear of being immediately overthrown. Last month, however, M. Herriot, realizing the disastrous consequences of failing to settle the war-debt question, consented to the virtual abolition of reparations. The very audacity of the move changed the attitude of the whole world toward France and greatly strengthened M. Herriot's political position at home. Opposed as it is to a Republican victory this November, *The Nation* is frank to admit that Mr. Hoover's prospects for reelection would be greatly increased if he followed M. Herriot's example and made a bold effort at solving the international economic problems. Will Mr. Hoover have the courage and the imagination to act?

Mr. Stimson on Peace

SECRETARY Stimson's admirable address on the present status of the Kellogg Peace Pact, before the Council of Foreign Relations in New York on August 7, has very naturally echoed around the world, for it is a remarkable statement of what the United States Government thinks has been accomplished thus far by the Pact of Paris. It has especially stirred the authorities in Japan, and well may they be aroused if Mr. Stimson's words are taken at their face value. For he has made it clear once more that the American Government has not the slightest intention of recognizing the validity or legality of a single act of Japan's in Manchuria. Indeed, Mr. Stimson recalled that on March 11 last forty-nine out of fifty nations, constituting the Assembly of the League of Nations, with Japan alone dissenting, indorsed the action of the United States. No one could have been more careful than was Mr. Stimson in his every reference to Japan. But it is the facts and, let us hope, a guilty conscience, which make Japan wince whenever this matter comes up.

For the rest, Mr. Stimson's speech was extraordinarily well reasoned in its analysis of what has thus far been accomplished by the new attitude of the world toward war. It was not in the least a partisan or a campaign utterance, but merely a careful lawyer's analysis of the gains achieved. It is impossible to have heard it or to read it without being convinced that the Secretary desires to bring this new policy to complete fruition at the earliest possible time. And though the nations affected have not yet given the highest proof of their approval of the treaty by wholesale disarmament, it is none the less a momentous happening when an American Secretary of State solemnly reiterates his belief that war is not only outmoded, but impossible at the present state of the world's history as a means of settling international disputes. The Kellogg Pact, he stated again and again, "rests upon the sanction of public opinion, which can be made one of the most potent sanctions of the world."

Mr. Stimson pointed out that the old conception of

international law was based upon the idea that each war was a private fight from which every neutral was barred. Now, instead of a war being nobody's business, it is everybody's business. A neutral nation not only has the *right* to speak out if it chooses but even has a *duty* to do so in order to preserve peace, lest even a tiny blaze again become a world-wide conflagration. Again, Mr. Stimson asserted that as long as the signatories of the pact support the American policy which the Hoover Administration "has endeavored to establish during the past three years of arousing a united and living spirit of public opinion as a sanction of the pact . . . consultations will take place as an incident to the unification of that opinion." We unqualifiedly agree with Mr. Stimson that if this policy is carried on by the nations in the spirit in which he spoke, the world will have taken a tremendous step toward peace. At the same time we must point out that as long as there are a million more men under arms than in 1914, and disarmament conferences lead rather toward increase of armaments than genuine disarmament, Mr. Stimson lays himself open to the charge that he is describing rather an ideal state than an existing one.

Japan's Challenge

JAPAN has challenged the new Stimson peace doctrine. Through Foreign Minister Uchida, Japan has given notice that it intends to approve the new territorial arrangement in Manchuria, that is to say, it intends to recognize the "independent" government of Manchukuo. Everyone knows that this supposedly independent state is the creature of Japanese militarism; all neutral observers are agreed that Manchukuo would automatically pass out of existence with the withdrawal of Japanese military support. Even ignoring the precedent Japan established in Korea, it is hardly enough for Count Uchida to say that Japan is not "seeking to annex Manchuria or otherwise satisfy her thirst for land." The fact remains that in violation of the Washington treaties and the Kellogg Pact the Japanese have by force of arms set up a puppet government in a section of Asia which the United States, Great Britain, and other Powers have long considered an integral part of China. It was just such a partition of China that the Washington treaties were designed to prevent. Secretary Stimson has three times declared that the United States will never recognize any territorial or other arrangement arrived at in violation of these treaties or the Kellogg Pact. The test of this policy will come when Japan formally acknowledges the existence of an independent Manchurian government, which it has itself created.

Obviously a challenge of this nature must be met, if the peace treaties are to survive. But it cannot be met by resort to war, for that would defeat the very purpose of the Stimson doctrine. It can only be met by the pressure of world opinion united against treaty violators. The United States has put forward a practical and just method of dealing with this situation, but some of the great European Powers, notably England and France, remain ominously silent. True, their delegates in the League Assembly did join with the representatives from forty-eight other nations in approving a resolution indorsing the Stimson doctrine, but neither Downing Street nor the Quai d'Orsay has to date publicly declared that it would support the State Department in refusing to give international sanction to Japanese gains in Manchuria. Nor has either suggested any other way of dealing with this violation. There is reason to believe that the continued silence of France and England has really encouraged Japan to take a determined stand against the Stimson doctrine.

It is now reported that "because of anxiety in high quarters over what is regarded as growing tension in Japanese-American relations," Vice-Admiral Kichisaburo Nomura will be sent to the United States on a "good-will mission." We shall welcome Admiral Nomura. He will learn much here that ought to help his government rid itself of its false notions concerning the American attitude toward the Manchurian question. He will learn, to begin with, that there is no "growing tension in Japanese-American relations" except that which arises from America's insistence upon faithful observance of the peace treaties. Japan can correct that upon its own initiative. If Tokio does so, it will promote genuine good-will between the two countries. And that is all the State Department desires.

Threatening the Peace of Europe

GERMANY has finally requested that it be permitted to enlarge its military establishment. It wants that equality in armaments which the victorious Powers promised at the peace conference, but it is no longer pleased to wait until the other nations have established equality by reducing their armaments to the level of the German forces; instead the Von Papen-Von Schleicher regime is insisting that equality can only be attained by building up the German military machine. On June 16, 1919, the victors at the peace conference declared:

> The Allied and Associated Powers wish to make it clear that their requirements in regard to German armaments were not made solely with the object of rendering it impossible for Germany to resume her policy of military aggression. They are also the first steps toward that general reduction and limitation of armaments which they seek to bring about as one of the most fruitful preventives of war, and which it will be one of the first duties of the League of Nations to promote.

Thirteen years is a long time to wait for a promise of this vital nature to be fulfilled, especially when those years are filled with anxieties and uncertainties. Yet Stresemann or Brüning, even in the face of the probable failure of the disarmament conference at Geneva, might have remained patient a while longer. But General von Schleicher, the militarist who has learned nothing since 1914, is made of different stuff. In the stricter sense, though we do not sympathize with it, his impatience is justified. How derelict the League has been in performing this one of its "first duties" is all too tragically apparent. At every turn, disarmament has been sabotaged by the Powers controlling the League, particularly by France. If the change in German policy now means the end of the world disarmament effort, as seems probable, these Powers must bear their full share of the blame. Moreover, if they now concede equality to Germany on the basis General von Schleicher has demanded, if they now retrace those "first steps" taken at the peace conference which were to lead to general disarmament, they will in effect be admitting that they never really intended to disarm, that they were simply using this pledge as a means of disguising their subjugation of Germany, and that they were finally giving in only because their hypocritical gesture at Versailles had been exposed.

But it appears highly unlikely that this concession will be made, not alone because the Powers do not care to expose their own hypocrisy, but for other and no less selfish reasons. The chief stumbling block, as in the past, will be France and its allies. French hegemony in Europe is based upon French military supremacy and nothing else. Geographically and economically, Poland and the countries of the Little Entente are closer to Berlin than to Paris. The greater part of their trade is with Germany, Austria, and Hungary rather than with France, which, indeed, enjoys less than 10 per cent of the total of the foreign commerce of its allies. Thus it can be seen that only the military predominance of France, plus a common desire to prevent any revision of the peace treaties, is holding this system of alliances together. By the same means France has been enabled to dictate to the rest of the Continent in the matter of reparations, treaty revision, the Austro-German *Anschluss,* and international finances. Therefore, if Germany should gain military equality, which because of its larger population and longer frontiers would really mean military supremacy, the positions of Paris and Berlin would be reversed. The latter would then be in a position to dictate. It should be clear that France and its allies will not readily allow Germany to regain its military supremacy.

In his radio speech of July 26, however, General von Schleicher pointedly suggested that if equality in armaments is not granted, Germany will be compelled to enlarge its military forces upon its own initiative. What will France do then? How will it meet such a deliberate challenge to the Versailles Treaty and the status quo of Europe? Upon the answer depends the peace of Europe. In 1924 French troops marched into the Ruhr when Germany balked at paying the reparations demanded by the peace agreement. It is not probable that France will attempt the same thing again. In the first place, French public opinion has undergone a radical change in the last few years. Secondly, the invasion of the Ruhr in 1924 found Germany exhausted, spiritually as well as financially; the invasion at worst could only have led to an internal collapse in Germany, and not to armed resistance; but today Germany's fighting spirit has been revived, perhaps out of sheer desperation, but nevertheless to a point which makes it almost certain that the militarists and Hitlerites would meet force with force. In our judgment France would think twice before attempting to inflict any penalty of that sort on Germany. Still, there is the warning which Robert Dell sounded in *The Nation* of September 7, and a careful reading of the French press shows that this warning must be taken seriously. Mr. Dell wrote:

> The French general staff and the French nationalist politicians are not in the least afraid of Germany. They intend to make sure that German armaments shall never catch up with the French, and what they long for is an excuse for walking into Germany and finishing the war which, in their opinion, as M. Poincaré said not long ago, is not finished yet. General von Schleicher has given them a hope that they may sooner or later be provided with the necessary excuse, and also an opportunity of scaring the French people out of the desire for disarmament so emphatically expressed last May.

It is high time the statesmen of Europe awakened to this grave situation. There is no hope of reasoning with the stupid militarists in Berlin, nor yet with the nationalists of France. But other public leaders, such as Ramsay MacDonald in England and Edouard Herriot and Léon Blum in France, who have large followings in their own countries, must bestir themselves. In the last analysis it is upon them and their people that rests what small hope is left of actually bringing about disarmament in Europe. The chances that these men can accomplish anything are slim indeed, but if they fail, what is to prevent Europe from plunging into another mad armaments race and perhaps an early war?

The Answer to Germany

PRESIDENT HOOVER'S statement on September 20 urging Germany to continue its participation in the work of the Geneva arms conference was a statesmanlike appeal, which may assist in breaking the Franco-German deadlock. Apparently this statement was issued to contradict Paris dispatches to the effect that Ambassador Edge and Senator Reed had given assurances to Premier Herriot that the United States supported the French position in regard to the German plea for equality. It would be manifestly improper for any American representatives to give assurances which would be interpreted in Paris as establishing a Franco-American entente against Germany. From this standpoint President Hoover was justified in saying that the United States was not a party to the Treaty of Versailles and that the German arms problem was "solely a European question." Nevertheless, in pleading with Germany to remain at the arms conference and in emphasizing the desire of the United States to reduce armaments "of the world, step by step," the President threw his full support behind the position that the only sound means of meeting the German plea for equality was for the rest of the world to disarm. In opposing the rearmament of Germany, while in effect admitting that the German plea for equality is well founded, the French, British, and American governments have committed themselves more strongly than ever before to concrete reduction when the Geneva conference reconvenes. We hope that the Papen-Schleicher Government will be intelligent enough to realize that it has thus won a victory, and that it will take part in the meetings of the conference bureau.

There are a number of signs that the present French government, in contrast to its predecessors, is willing to accept an immediate measure of armament reduction. The new spirit which appears to be dominating French foreign policy was indicated last July at Lausanne when the Herriot Government virtually agreed to wipe out all reparations. There is considerable evidence, moreover, that France will abandon its alleged entente with Japan and join the United States in taking a strong stand against the recognition of Manchukuo. In his Marne-anniversary speech of September 11 Premier Herriot praised Secretary Stimson's recent address upon the anti-war pact, and declared that France had received the Hoover arms proposal of last June "with the most sincere respect and that it had studied and was studying this proposal in order to associate itself in an effective manner with such a remarkable initiative." Of equal significance the nationalist Paris *Temps* is publishing a series of editorials stressing the necessity of reorganizing the military establishment of France partly on the ground that the present financial burden of this establishment is "insupportable."

In view of this new attitude, the outlook at Geneva would seem considerably better than in the past, provided Germany—and Soviet Russia—will only be patient for a few months longer. Whether or not Germany returns to Geneva, the Allied Powers and the United States should proceed to find a formula for reduction. The simplest way to start is to agree to abolish the weapons which have been denied by the peace treaties to Germany and the Central Powers. The Allied Powers and the United States should undertake to abolish all battleships above 10,000 tons, submarines, military aviation, tanks, long-range artillery, and poison gas. By such a step they would at once place themselves upon the same status as Germany in the matter of "aggressive weapons," and would also make possible enormous savings.

Secondly, the Powers at Geneva must agree to some reduction, perhaps 20 per cent, in the number of their effectives. The Germans, however, cannot reasonably ask the French at once to reduce their army to 100,000 men—the present German level—because of the fact that the greater number of French soldiers are conscripts and hence individually inferior to the German professional type. This problem of finding a system of measuring the comparative value of a professional and a conscript soldier should not, however, prevent the French from agreeing to a 20 per cent reduction in their effectives, provided one other problem is solved. This problem arises out of the existence of huge, vociferous "private armies" in Germany, such as the Steel Helmets, the veterans' organization, and the Hitler storm troops. French public opinion is unanimous in declaring that these "private armies" should be taken into account in measuring the actual military strength of the Reich. For many years, moreover, the French press has charged that the Germans are concealing huge armaments and munition dumps, in violation of the peace treaties. Although many of these charges sound utterly fantastic, they continue to be reiterated, thus poisoning Franco-German relations as much as any other single issue.

Fundamentally, the dissolution of the German "private armies" depends upon the growth of pacifist sentiment in Germany, which in turn depends upon economic improvement and a rapprochement with France. Nevertheless, we believe that France is justified in raising the question of "secret armaments" and of "private armies" if it will carry this principle to a logical conclusion. Obviously no agreement abolishing aggressive weapons will be effective if private firms in any country remain free to manufacture such arms; obviously no agreement reducing the size of regular armies will be effective if governments remain free to organize subsidiary military forces. For this reason an armament treaty must place all private munition manufacture under severe control, as well as limit such bodies as the Fascist militia, the British territorial army, the National Guard of the United States, and, most important of all, the trained reserves of countries continuing conscription. We believe France should be supported in its position on the German private armies only if France is willing to permit the international regulation of its trained reserves. Previous French governments have adamantly refused to allow these reserves to be restricted by any reduction agreement. The test whether the French government today is dominated by a new international spirit will depend upon whether it is willing to reconsider this position. If so, the prospect of satisfactorily settling the Franco-German military problem, upon which the fate of the Geneva conference depends, will brighten considerably.

THE POT AND THE KETTLE

Roosevelt and Hoover Militarists Both

FOR the man or woman who believes that peace is the supreme necessity for the world in this crisis of its history, who believes that another war will end our modern civilization, who realizes that great armaments do not make for peace but lead only to conflict, there can be no choice in this election except to vote for Norman Thomas. Between the other two candidates there is no difference whatever. Both learned nothing from the World War; both are wedded to the old order; both fail to realize what Viscount Cecil pointed out in the New York *Herald Tribune* of October 9—that force is bankrupt, and that it can accomplish nothing in the way of restoring the world to the paths of sanity and peace. Mr. Hoover, a sham Quaker, believes in going on peace missions to other countries on battleships. He is for what he terms an adequate armament for defense, although he well knows that the French, with a fine army, one in some respects better-equipped than the German army (according to General Buat, former Chief of Staff), were not able to safeguard their country alone, although the entire nation was in arms; nor could the Germans prevent their country from going down to defeat. He is for a large navy—this professing Quaker. It is a miracle that under him we have not yet yielded to the demand of the big-navy people that we build our American fleet up to the limits permitted by the so-called Disarmament Treaty of London. He wishes himself thought of as a great humanitarian, as the rescuer of the Belgians, and as the man who fed the starving Russian and German children. But he is still willing to expose his people and the rest of the world to the supreme disaster of another war. He has not even been able to put through any measure of real naval disarmament, and of course he has not the courage, nor the vision, nor the spirituality, nor the religion, nor the ideality to counsel his fellow-countrymen to disarm without waiting for the disarming of others. He does not wish us to return to the historic American policy which marked the first century of our national life—of being without an army or a navy, and without fear.

I cannot for the life of me see that there is the slightest difference between his point of view and that of Franklin D. Roosevelt. Mr. Roosevelt has been a naval enthusiast from childhood up. His collection of prints of naval battles and historic warships is, or was, one of the best extant. He was as happy as his distinguished fifth cousin, Theodore Roosevelt, when he became Assistant Secretary of the Navy. He was liked by the naval officers because he talked their language, believed with them, sympathized with their demands, besides being a good executive and a charming person. In this campaign he has declined to be drawn out by any questioning as to how he will stand on matters connected with the peace of the world, such as disarmament and the recognition of Russia. In his speech at Los Angeles, however, he did touch upon the navy, to recall that when Assistant Secretary of the Navy he was instrumental in having the Pacific fleet visit Southern California, so "that the national government recognized from the naval point of view the existence of Southern California." The Governor then went on to say the following words:

> And I don't need to tell you as a former Assistant Secretary of the Navy that I thoroughly understood the great value of an adequate navy toward commerce, not only in times of war, but in times of peace.

In the days leading up to the war, and at the beginning of the war, Franklin Roosevelt was among the earliest to call for a fleet second only to that of England, addressing Bible classes, patriotic societies, and the National Civic Federation in behalf of his program. In Washington, before the House and Senate Committees on Naval Affairs, he demanded that the government adopt "a great building program" and declared that "not one dollar, not one ship, not one man" could be deducted from the building program he urged. He was ready for a competition of armaments with Germany or England, certain that he could outdo them. When in October, 1916, during the Presidential campaign, Charles Evans Hughes suggested that the navy should pay less attention to its building program and more to its target practice, Mr. Roosevelt heatedly replied that Mr. Hughes had "insulted" every officer and man in the navy. Of course he uses the familiar language of the militarist: "We should all work against war, but if it should come we should be better prepared than we were before. . . . I am not militaristic by any means." And then he contradicted himself by saying, "I do not believe in a large standing army, as you know, nor in a large navy," just after having said that he wanted us to be *better* prepared for the next war than we had been for the last.

Again, we must not forget that Mr. Roosevelt favored our intervention in Mexico and believed that we should tell Mexico where it "got off." He connived in and welcomed the pulling down of the Haitian Republic. He has twice denied to *The Nation* that he made the remark attributed to him in the press when on a speaking tour in the State of Washington—that he had written the Haitian constitution and forced it down the throats of the Haitians. But he does not deny that he was entirely satisfied with what was done in Haiti and particularly with the act of Smedley Butler in dispersing the Haitian legislature with a pistol in his hand and a battalion of marines at his back. If he gets in, and the opportunity arises, he will not only be for a bigger navy than we have had, in my judgment, but he will be thoroughly imperialistic if there is any trouble in the Caribbean.

I repeat, the one candidate who has a thoroughly practical and a truly humanitarian attitude toward war and the weapons of war is Norman Thomas. We know where he would stand if some day he should be elected President, because during the last war he let everyone know his conscientious objection to war in its every form—at no small cost to himself.

OSWALD GARRISON VILLARD

THE GERMAN PHŒNIX

THE STORY OF THE REPUBLIC

OSWALD GARRISON VILLARD

Editor of THE NATION

HARRISON SMITH & ROBERT HAAS

NEW YORK · 1933

To

Friedrich Hilgard, Henry Villard and
Carl Schurz

Three Traitors of 1848

FOREWORD

THIS book is an effort to appraise the actual achievements of the German Republic, to record its many substantial accomplishments, to picture the events which led up to the great change of 1932, and the situation at the close of that year. That the Republic, for the moment, is but a shadow of what it was intended to be is undeniable. Yet it is difficult to believe that Germany with its traditions and its heritage will long remain at the mercy either of dictators or demagogues. The circumstance, however, that the Republic is, temporarily, in its twilight has made it seem the more desirable to record the efforts of its founders to establish a true democracy upon the ruins of the Empire and the extraordinary progress since 1918 toward a socialized State. Many of the changes, much of the new orientation, cannot be lost no matter what the form of the new governmental control. That the presentation is from a liberal viewpoint, with especial sympathy for the workers, is obvious.

So there came 1918, and Saxony, Prussia and Bavaria, and the empire in Berlin had collapsed; the proudest and most powerful structure in all Europe lay in ashes, and the soldiers came marching home to moral and spiritual ruins more appalling than all the destruction in France. Here was what was left of an intellectually humbled, and stunned, and dazed people. Never was pride so abased and self-confidence deeper in the mire. Those who had had such faith in their Kultur, their Germanic *Manneskraft,* their unequaled intellectual achievements, their extraordinary industrial successes had failed just where they expected to win—at the top. Fathers and mothers besought the returning hosts, and the hosts their brothers and sisters, to tell them what had happened. How *could* it have happened? What did it mean? What was there left? Whither could Germany turn now? What was still to come? Was the world at an end? How could God so have veiled his face to his chosen people? Was there any hope? Completely dazed they saw the old order, which had seemed the mightiest fortress on earth, collapse—collapse and disappear, leaving nothing to swear by, nothing to hold on to, nothing to believe in, nothing to comfort, nothing to encourage, nothing to give the slightest hope in the years to come. Complete bed-rock substantiality had become overnight nothing but insubstantiality; in place of the tangible was the intangible. Not a value remained unchanged. Not the most devoted Republicans could trust their eyes when the immovable monarchies crumbled into the dust like the mummied bodies of the old Kaisers in Speyer the instant they were exposed to the air.

"The Wittelsbachers," said Kurt Eisner, a Munich journalist, frequenter of quiet cafés, and then the tragic brief President of Bavaria, "ruled us seven hundred years. I drove them out in seven hours with seven men." Men who witnessed such disintegration as this held their heads in their hands and besought people to tell them if they were awake or asleep, sane or mad; if what they beheld was true or not. Men in field-gray, who dirtied their boots once more in these ashes of the old Germany, trembled for the moment, too. Was it the Day of Judgment? What had Germany done to receive the utter fury of the gods? Had they not merely defended their homes, their hearths, their firesides . . . ?

Still the troops came marching home, more and more; some among them who so proudly and perfectly had swept through Brussels in unending human waves of gray, irresistible then, a revelation of a world of power raised to the highest degree. Now the world gazed upon them again and wondered how they would return to peace and those ruins of all that had been. It remembered that in the wreck of France in 1871 it was amazed that the Commune had been no worse. But here was the greatest mass of beaten, outraged, and embittered soldiery the world had ever seen. What would happen? As they marched in, many regiments cast off their officers as they crossed the home frontiers, quickly forming Workmen's and Soldiers' Councils, when the officers themselves did not abandon their organizations. They beheld their old State governments sinking, disappearing as they advanced. Somehow, stunned and suffering as they were, these men took it for granted that their kings were to go. Had they not disappeared in France in 1871 and in Russia the year before? Well might these defeated hosts have asked themselves how they should take revenge. Who should be their victims? Should they, as a Pretorian Guard, take over the fatherland? So they marched on, these men in their worn and torn field-gray into the chaos that was Germany, to find women and children starving, an unyielding enemy refusing to relax the food blockade until the peace was made, until, as it happened, 300,000 people, women and children died of starvation and malnutrition and the diseases incident thereto.

And then as the world watched agape, it appeared that these scarred soldiers took no revenge, murdered no one, planned no Pretorian Guard and, all save the few who went to the Spartacists, melted back into the ranks of the people, discarding their uniforms as soon as they could find jobs and civilian clothes. The miracle had happened. The beaten troops abandoned war and revenge. They fused themselves into the ashes. . . . By December the millions of defeated soldiers "had disappeared from the earth."

Yet law and order all but vanished. The people thought and fought only for each day, fought like animals for food, for what passed for food. Vast throngs from the cities overflowed the land to beg, borrow, buy, and steal from the farmers some means of keeping body and soul together, when the official ration of a few crumbs did not even cover the palm of one's hand.* How money was obtained, whence it came, what authority produced it, nobody stopped to inquire if there was only enough to provide sustenance. The best hotels in Berlin served viands that foreigners could hardly swallow; the Germans who could afford them wolfed them down as if entirely delicious. If only the arteries of communication could be kept open, the supplies for the cities! Gas and electricity

* Such a ration was shown to the writer in Dresden in February, 1919.

ceased, the trolleys stopped. In Berlin there were days when no provisions moved; many were days in reaching destinations ordinarily a few hours away; as late as February, 1919, communication with South Germany seemed for the visitor practically impossible. Train coaches were dirty, disordered, disreputable; through their broken windows the crowds climbed and fought and struggled and pushed, with or without tickets, frantic after long hours of waiting during which no one could give a single item of accurate information. If only the cities held together, the houses did not actually fall into the streets, and the streets open to swallow those whose horror of each hour was surpassed only by dread of the morrow! This was peace; this was defeat; this revolution; this the death of the old, the birth of the new which was to make over Germany and the world.

Then as the days passed, machine guns were heard in the streets; rifles cracked incessantly. The Spartacists, that is, the Communists, were at work. "Free corps" appeared, at first sanctioned and begged for by the Government, and later a dangerous menace; associations led by old officers, as ruthless and murderous as the original Ku Klux Klan, vainly bent on restoring the lost German World; finally there came to life an irregular but governmental security force to restore order. Even in March, 1919, cannon roared in the streets of Berlin watched by curious crowds wholly unafraid; barbed-wire entanglements in the streets and guards in full campaign outfits suggested the war front. Still the cracking fabric of the State held; still there was some determined effort to hold it together—by the Majority Socialists. It was they, these formerly despised, hated, and often imprisoned men, who now controlled what was left of the German Reich, and prevented a final disintegration while capitalism was *hors de combat.*

Perhaps it was the German love of peace and order that was responsible for all this; perhaps the sound German respect for the rights of individuals; perhaps the Reich and its component parts fell into the hands of the Social-Democratic leaders too easily, without their firing a shot, or taking a life. Perhaps the capitalist ex-lords scuttled too quickly to their holes and lay too low in the early days of the Republic to make the new rulers realize the potentiality for future evil that was in them. The leaders themselves were often lacking in vision, and the fact remains that the Revolution was neither drastic nor thorough enough. There was not even a purging of the governmental departments such as is going on at the present hour with the tables turned. It must not, however, be forgotten that no official responsibility had ever previously come to the Social Democrats, as a party of the nation, until suddenly they had to take over the entire government. In this crisis the Germans indubitably paid the price for their old governmental system and policies whose aim, especially under Bismarck, was to keep the people in leading strings, dependent upon their government, to hold well in check democratic movements and institutions, to prevent the rise of able and dangerous liberal leaders, to repress the growing Socialist menace by laws aimed directly at them and their organizations. In view of this historic background is it surprising that the infant Republic was without men of commanding stature to attend its birth? There was no Washington, no Jefferson, no Mazzini, and no Lenin. There were simply honest, plodding burghers who had had experience in local governments, or in the Reichstag as part of the opposition, or had had no experience at all.

Thus in various ways the Germans were not wholly ready for the democracy which in considerable degree Mr. Wilson and the Allies forced upon them. The Social Democrats, Ebert among them, as late as October, 1918, not only failed to demand a Republic, but as stated, actually accepted a plan for a constitutional monarchy to be headed by the eldest son of the Crown Prince. It must be pointed out here, however, that if no nation could, or should, assume the burdens and accept the penalties of a republican form of government until it is in every way ideally prepared for them, the world would to-day still be in the grip of absolute monarchies. The way to become a republic is to turn the monarchists out and govern oneself the best one can—badly if necessary, but still to govern oneself haltingly, stumblingly, perhaps, as did the United States during the years from 1781 to 1789. The French are in the habit of pointing fingers of scorn at German governmental ineptness, and of protesting at the apparent collapse of the Republic into the hands of some of the old rulers of Germany. They are conveniently forgetting when they do this not only the reëstablishment of the kingdom under Louis Philippe, and of the empire under the second Napoleon, but also the monarchistic Cabinets which for more than twenty years ruled and at times endangered their republic. Why should one not expect the Germans to go through their period of weakness and reaction after such examples as these?

This lack of solidarity, this inability of the Germans to subordinate any partisan motive in a grave emergency, indubitably arises from their remarkable individualism, their innate tendency to split up into endless groups of varying opinion. This is a too common failing among the intellectuals of all lands, and is precisely one of the chief difficulties in the way of organizing in the United States a new and independent and progressively liberal political party. But it is especially a German characteristic upon which Bismarck commented more than once, which he often cleverly exploited to further his own ends. Even when the Germans do not actually come to blows, they often find it extremely difficult to reach working agreements and honorable compromises without calling each other names. On the other hand it must be admitted that in their labor unions and many of their militant organizations, like the *Stahlhelm,* they have shown remarkable *esprit de corps,* ability to hold together, and to cling to their associates.

The 1918 to 1924 rulers of Germany were compelled to present the best front they could to the Allies, and that was perhaps one reason why the leaders failed to turn promptly and aggressively upon the elements at home which have about dug the grave of the Republic. Again, their attention was distracted from domestic issues and problems by the extraordinarily difficult task of dealing with the Allied Commissions which occupied Berlin and took over some of the functions of the government as, for example, the reorganization of the army. At the same time the new republican government had to carry on the task of paying the economic and financial penalties for the loss

of the war and collecting the enormous quantities of material which it actually delivered, for which so little credit has been given it. Again, these tremendous reparations payments "in kind" put such a burden upon the government that it was compelled to seek the coöperation of the men who had built up German industry, but were at heart hostile to the continuance of a Socialist Republic.

It is possible that Anglo-Saxons with a greater tradition of self-government behind them, due to the fact that they had been allowed to exercise it to a greater degree in local affairs, and had not been suppressed for generations by a vigorous, reactionary government, would have done better in a similar emergency, especially because of their greater self-reliance and quicker adjustability. This must, however, remain pure speculation. One may admit readily enough that the Germans are not naturally talented in the art of political government, any more than they are gifted in dealing with other mentalities and other nationalities and races. But in the last analysis the period of the birth of the Republic and its early life was one to test the souls of men and of supermen. One cannot, therefore, withhold admiration from the original leaders of the Republic, while admitting their mistakes and compromises and regretting that they were not drastic enough in their house cleaning to insure the duration of the edifice they raised so quickly under such incredibly difficult conditions. Few men have ever launched and governed a new State under such profoundly trying circumstances, with as complete uncertainty as to what the future held in store for their defeated country.

So to-day we see little left of the Republic of 1918 but a shell. The spirit of the first democratic government is gone. The mass of the people are disillusioned, dissatisfied with the Republic because of the steady deterioration of life due to the long-drawn-out economic, social, and political misery, which has its roots in the war and the Treaty of Versailles. Millions and millions of the unthinking have sighed for the good times of the Kaiser and the Empire without realizing that if the latter had survived to this day in Germany it would have been facing the same direful economic problems and evils. At least thirteen million others have been disaffected by a conscienceless demagogue, without stability, sound principles, democracy or statesmanship; with his teachings of bitterness, international hatred, class hatred, narrow nationalism, and his false pretense that his is the party of radical socialization really devoted to the welfare of the masses. Take the recent Von Papen Government, with its noblemen and Junker. It was a cabinet without youth, without even younger men, all of whose members, with the sole exception of the Minister of Finance, had played some sort of a rôle in the days of the Kaiser. It was a cold-blooded, hard-boiled government of men who have had much experience in ruling, either on their estates, or in industrial and financial life, well capable of governing for the benefit of themselves and the business and vested interests which they represent. Truly conservative, they are the type to be found in every country—the type that is certain that it rules by the divine right of those who succeed and possess largely under the modern capitalistic system, and it is the same type of Cabinet which has now taken office under Von Schleicher. Nothing democratic there!

V

THE "MILITARY MENACE"

Let any people who really believe the French ballyhoo over the alleged German military menace attend the annual maneuvers of the *Reichswehr,* the German army of to-day. Unlike conditions under the Kaiser, these fall field-drills are open to all who wish to observe. Foreign military attachés—except the French and Polish—are invited, and find it hard not to spend a good deal of their time laughing. For they are likely, as they ride over the countryside, to find what seems to be a fighting tank in some lane only to discover that it is a road-tank, built up with camouflaged pasteboard to represent a fighting machine, but without guns, for these were forbidden at Versailles. At any moment they may run across a soldier who bears upon his chest a sign indicating that he is the 300th or what not company, or regiment, of infantry. If the observers discover infantry covered by what seems to be heavy guns emitting puffs of smoke they can ascertain at once that these forbidden arms are only "Quakers"—wooden imitations of the real thing. In the absence of heavy artillery one sees signs attached to light guns indicating that they are to be considered as perhaps twice their actual caliber. There are no airplanes and no facsimiles thereof; but one can see dozens of "Hanomags"—the German equivalent of the Baby Austins—also decked up with paper turrets to indicate that they are to be considered the latest most up-to-date caterpillar, cross-country tanks! If there ever was play soldiering this is it.

Indubitably the German army is man for man the finest in the world. It has the pick of the vast army of the unemployed and recruits must agree to serve twelve long years in order to prevent the passing through the ranks of many men, whereas France, Italy, and others of the Allies stick to short-term universal military service. Every German soldier is chosen for his intelligence; every one is trained to be a future officer. There being no cadet schools, entrance to the commissioned grades is only after at least four years' service in the ranks. Again, in order to prevent a large number of men being drilled and then sent back to civil life as an unorganized reserve, only five per cent of the force can be discharged in a year for all causes—such as punishment, disability, illness, family misfortunes, and expiration of enlistment. So the German army of to-day strives to give to each soldier the maximum of training in as many branches of the modern army as possible, and every effort is made to bring out whatever qualities of leadership he may have within him. Moreover the old officer caste has disappeared; soldiers and officers rejoice in a comradeship never before known in Germany. But when that is said and done what could 100,000 such men do to create the millions of trained men a modern army requires? The little German army would be overwhelmed in twenty-four hours by advancing French hosts; it could not hold off the Poles long enough to enable the organization of a group of armies—Berlin is no further from the Polish border than New York from Albany—even if there were available all the necessary supplies, such as rifles, heavy guns, hand-grenades, revolvers, uniforms, the incredibly large supplies of shells needed to keep an army

going for a single day; poison gas, hospitals, nurses, doctors, intelligence officers, motorcycle men, telephones, radios, tanks, and all the rest.

An American need only recall the prodigious efforts made by his own country in 1917-18 in order to train 3,000,000 men for service in France to realize what such an undertaking would mean. It would obviously be impossible even to begin such a task with armed forces pouring over into Germany, and 5,000 French airplanes crossing her borders. And still the insincere French politicians —worthy of no better name—fortified as they are by their alliances with Poland, Rumania, Czecho-Slovakia, and Jugo-Slavia, pretend that there is such a thing as a German menace! Therefore, from the United States and England they demand security pacts although they have the largest and best equipped army in the world, the greatest air force, ever-increasing Negro reserves in Africa, and have lined their frontier all the way from Belgium to Switzerland with most formidable forts, concrete trenches, and machine-gun nests. Moreover, the French demand that these security treaties shall be absolutely binding and automatic and shall compel those signing them to send their youth to death for France in the next war, whether the French be right or wrong, their fighting justified or unjustified.

All of this French fear, whether real or pretended, is, of course, a tremendous recognition by them of the superior military ability of the Germans, especially as the *Reichswehr* is restricted to 94,900 privates and non-commissioned officers, and 3,798 officers. The United States army had on January 1, 1932, 12,000 officers to about 125,000 men, and also approximately 130,000 reserve officers where Germany has none. Germany, alone in Europe, has no militia and no organized reserves behind its army. In all its remaining forts there are only 22 guns of large caliber, and these are at Königsberg on the Polish-Lithuanian frontiers. The army, which is organized by the law of March 23, 1921, into seven divisions of infantry and three of cavalry, has not only no heavy artillery, but no siege guns, and is permitted to have only 288 pieces of light artillery, 1,134 light machine guns, 792 heavy ones, and 252 mine throwers—not enough to equip a brigade. The Reich cannot itself manufacture arms, and the manufacture by private companies is limited.* Until January 31, 1927, all manufacturing was carefully supervised by the Allies. All of the forts on the French boundary have been destroyed; on the other frontiers there are only thirteen fortresses all told, of which but one, Königsberg, as stated, has heavy guns, and this fort cannot be modernized.

As for the *Reichswehr* officers, the Reich has probably done all that it can to keep them out of politics. Under date of October 8, 1930, after the trial of three lieutenants at Leipzig because of their being affected by the Nationalist movement, General Wilhelm Groener, the then Minister of Defense, issued a general order to the effect that a *Reichswehr* officer has only to obey; he is not permitted to question his orders, or to voice opinions about the politics of his country, or the management of the *Reichswehr*. If he is dissatisfied or impregnated with any political doctrines he is in duty bound to resign; that is, he will do so if he has "any sense of honor" and "courage to tell the truth." In this attitude, General Groener took the only permissible course, the only one followed in every other country, unless conditions in Russia are different. It is not, however, to be assumed that all the officers at once resigned who were not heart and soul with Dr. Bruening's

* The Reich holds a majority control of the stock of the chief munitions-making plant, the *Rheinmetall* company.

conduct of the Republic. Had that been the case promotions would have been very rapid, indeed. Many of the officers are praying for the complete success of the Hitler movement, hoping thereby to see the *Reichswehr* become as large and as powerful as the army of the Kaiser—no military man has yet been found in any country who did not think the army or navy to which he belonged should be enlarged.

There is to-day no way of telling just how loyal to the Republic the *Reichswehr* is. It is generally accepted that as long as President von Hindenburg lives there will be nothing to fear from it, however devoted some of its officers may be to the Nationalist cause. When, however, the Field Marshal dies, or retires as President, the question whether the *Reichswehr* will be true to its oath to preserve the Republic may present itself at once. It goes without saying that the *Reichswehr* can be relied upon against any Communist *Putsch;* although there are rumors from time to time of efforts being made to "bore from within," there is little to indicate that the efforts are succeeding. Curiously enough, one of the three Nazi officers convicted at Leipzig and sentenced to imprisonment in a fortress, Lieutenant Scheringer, suddenly turned Communist while in durance vile, and fourteen other officers joined him and were at once forced out of the army. No similar case has thus far been reported. Far more ominous is the steady increase of officers belonging to noble families who are finding their way into the commissioned ranks, perhaps in response to an appeal said to have been made by a former commander, General von Seeckt, to the nobility, to "send us your sons."

To restore the old army even if Germany should "throw off its chains" and arm as it pleases, is impossible.

VI

HITLER AND HIS CAUSE

LET it be said at once that Adolf Hitler is as much the creation of the wicked Treaty of Versailles as is the economic crisis in which the world now flounders. Given Germany in the straits that it is, and a dictator or demagogue was certain to emerge. It is not Hitler who has created the mentality which turns to him in this hour of deadly economic peril, nor has he produced the tension in which men are ready to grasp at any straw of salvation. It is not he who has created the recrudescence of narrow nationalism (though he has contributed to it) which is sweeping over Germany, for that is, first, but a part of the nationalist wave which is inundating the world as one of the worst heritages of the World War and the peace, and, second, the inevitable result of years of misery, suffering, and as it seems to multitudes, of slavery to their conquerors. Any one who preached the doctrine of Germany for the Nordic Germans, of a Germany self-contained, independent of the rest of the world, freed from impossible reparations and going its own way to happiness, prosperity, and power would have a hearing and a tremendous following at this time. When every living German craves nothing so much as peace, quiet, the right to work, to be free from international control and espionage, to be able to hold up his head in the world, naturally masses turn

to the man whose words are the suavest, who promises the earliest release from misery and paints with reckless brush, in most vivid colors, the paradise into which he alone is ready to lead the hosts of the anointed. Hitler found the setting for his rôle ready to hand. His is a honeyed voice bidding men follow him out of the Slough of Despond. It is eagerly listened to.

His case is unique in the history of demagoguery since he was not a citizen of the country in which he stirred the hearts of millions to mutiny and rage years after he was caught red-handed in treason to that State. Tolerated for some years after his abortive effort in November, 1923, in the Buergerbraeu, the largest beer hall in Munich, when, with General Von Ludendorff and a handful of his National Socialists he proclaimed a revolution, he rose with extraordinary speed to extraordinary power. That *Putsch* was so abortive as to be merely ridiculous. It ruined the brave General von Ludendorff, for this hero of the World War lay down on the floor the minute the bullets began to fly. Hitler, too, seemed hopelessly extinguished. He fled abjectly, to be caught after taking refuge in the attic of a country house. Sentenced to five years in prison, he served less than one. Right there the German Government erred gravely. It should have put him, on his discharge, into an automobile, shoved him back into the Austria whence he came, and politely told him to acquire Austrian nationality and stay there. It thought, like most observers, that this cheap adventurer was finished, that he was too ridiculous and too notorious to be worth bothering about. It remembered, too, that he had served efficiently in the ranks of a German regiment during the war, in which he was both wounded and gassed. So it let him stay on, only to have him reappear in 1928 a far abler man who had learned a lesson, who thereupon waxed stronger so rapidly that within two years the magic of his voice built up a following of six million and increased his representatives in the Reichstag in the election of 1930 from 14 to 107, and to 230 in the election of 1932. It was in that year that he threatened the very existence of the government, declaring that he and not the Chancellor was the true spokesman of Germany. With complete arrogance he declared that when he became the head of the government he would then "give the German people the form of organization and government which suits our purposes and will give us the power to conquer Communism and the pest of Marxism. The present State, with its present Constitution, is not in a position to do this."

At heart he remained the Hitler of the Munich *Putsch* while pretending that he was really devoted to legalistic methods. He missed several chances to take over the authority of the State by force, notably in the fall of 1930, and the spring of 1932; but his irresoluteness of purpose comes out clearly in his appearing in the October-November, 1932, campaign as a defender of parliamentary rule, and the critic of the Von Papen Government on the ground that its demand at Geneva that Germany be allowed to re-arm might again bring war to Germany. This from a man who has repeatedly declared that sooner or later Germany will have to fight both Russia and France! "Our people," he once assured an audience of university students, "must place itself in opposition to the other peoples with all the power that it has, for not the best economic policy nor excellent goods carry a people on, but only the greatest vitality which it can throw into the scales. *The sword has always decided in the end.*" * But the greatest of his blunders he made on September 13, 1932, when he called upon the President and demanded that he be given a 75 per cent participation in the Von Papen Government. Here was a genuine test of his statesmanship, but he not only failed to win over Von

* See *Völkischer Beobachter*, December 9, 1930.

Hindenburg who, it is said, hates to remain in the same room with him, but met with a most humiliating refusal of his every condition or demand. In this connection the *Stahlhelm* has charged, without refutation, that Hitler asked the venerable President to grant him three days of complete freedom for his shock troops to do what they wished—Von Hindenburg to guarantee that neither the legal authorities nor the police nor the army would in any way interfere with what his soldiers undertook to do during that period. Acceptance of this impudent demand would have meant that Germany would have been bathed in blood for three days, that the ensuing pogroms would have made the massacre of Saint Bartholomew's Night seem a kindergarten performance.

The more one studies Hitler's turnings and twistings the greater is the astonishment that this man could be taken seriously at all. Thus, he aligned himself first with the Hugenberg Nationalist Forces, then with the Von Papen clique, and then made overtures to the Catholics, while his legislative representatives have not hesitated to vote on occasions with their sworn enemies, the Communists. Hitler is bitterly anti-Communist, but his platform contains out-and-out Communist policies. Thus, he is for the nationalization of the banks despite the fact that for years his means came largely from the big-business and Junker class. He is against "slavery to interest" (*Zinsknechtschaft*) and in order to do away with the necessity of paying interest, he proposes unlimited quantities of currency without basing it on gold—that is, he desires inflation pure and simple. He, like the Bolsheviks, insists that there must be no more living off unearned income without work. Every one must labor "in a productive way, either by mental or physical effort." All large enterprises must become profit-sharing, and the State is completely

to control foreign trade. All existing trusts and monopolies are to be nationalized—practically all corporations; all businesses now nationalized or conducted by the government will so continue. Department stores are to be taken over by the municipalities and space in them let to small store-keepers, who are to have the first opportunity to fill municipal, communal, State, and national purchasing needs. Ground rents are to be abolished, and the large land owners are to be expropriated, their estates being divided among workers and peasants. It is hardly necessary to add that Hitler—even at this late date—demands the punishment of all Germans who profiteered during the war, and the confiscation of their ill-gotten gains. He believes, too, that the first duty of the State is to see that all citizens have a chance to live and support themselves. He is all for a "prosperous middle class;" for raising the standards of health and protecting mother and child; for a new school system to fit leaders for his scheme of society; for the abolition of child labor and better protection of the aged.

Hitler is sworn to stop the "malicious spreading of lies in politics and through the press," the press to be conducted only by simon-pure German Nordics. It will be a crime for a Jew to become a journalist. All newspapers "working against the commonwealth" are to be forbidden, and strong legal measures will be taken, if he wins the power, to stop all forms of drama, art, and literature which "have a demoralizing effect upon those who behold them." In other words, he is committed to a strong fascist censorship, something that was anticipated in considerable degree by Chancellor Von Papen. As to the right to one's religious creed, why, yes, that is to be permitted as long as that creed "is not dangerous to the State's existence" and does not "offend against the moral feeling of the

Germanic race." Who is to judge? Why, Herr Hitler, of course, the all-knowing, and his leaders. The party itself "stands for positive Christianity without linking itself to any special faith," but it is convinced that the convalescence of the nation can only take place if the commonwealth is put above all individual interests and beliefs. As to the monarchy, Hitler on occasion has spoken thus: "The National Socialist movement has nothing whatever to do with monarchies. The vital problem now facing the German nation is not whether the King of Prussia will again become German Kaiser, but whether Bolshevism will destroy the German people, their culture, and their economic system." * But it must be added that since the disastrous Presidential election there has been an increased interest on the part of the Nazis in the restoration of the monarchy which is coincident with a sudden activity in the movement of the sons of the Kaiser, including the Crown Prince. It is all a mélange of Communism, Socialism and Nationalism—the product of callow minds, and but little studied and understood, least of all by Hitler.†

One of his adulating biographers frankly admits that he knew at first nothing about economics, but thanks to his "geniality" (!) (*Genialität*) and his ability to distinguish between motivating causes and "phenomena," he has been able "to recognize the principles which guarantee the safety, the development, and the prosperity of the economic life of the people"—in which case he is certainly far ahead of the economists and statesmen of the United

*Interview in New York *Times*, December 20, 1931.

† "The answer is that few Nazis, even among the leaders, have thought the (economic) subject through." Harold Callender, New York *Times*, Sunday Supplement, January 3, 1932.

States, France, England, Italy, and all the other countries.* Unfortunately for Prof. Stark, the author of this adoration, there is not a field in which Hitler is so far to seek as precisely in this one of economics, national, and international. But then Hitler prides himself on being anything but international—he is even opposed to getting financial help from abroad. Thus he wrote on December 7, 1931: "I say all promiscuous borrowing must stop. I am confident that the world will soon feel vastly different about Germany when it is proved that the sole aim is to reconquer and create confidence in our entire business dealings." His objective is a strong, self-contained Germany, free from the sapping of its vitality by international Jews and money lenders, raising all the capital it needs at home, paying no tribute, withdrawing from the world of international business, being entirely self-sufficient (the doctrine of "*Autarkie*"), and consuming all her own products except what will be needed for export to buy from Russia and other neighbors on the east such foodstuffs as Germany itself cannot produce. Thus the world may go hang! The wicked Bolsheviks have done this. Why not the great, the ennobled Germans, purified by the leadership of this dream hero, Hitler?

Perhaps it was this economic nationalism which won for Hitler for several years the generous financial support of big-business. There could certainly have been no greater anachronism than the German captains of industry supporting a party which plans to nationalize the banks and to break up the great estates and advocates other proposals which, if advanced by any large party in the United States, would throw our Wall Street magnates into spasms of fear, and lead our patriotic societies to demand the erec-

* Prof. Doktor Johannes Stark, Adolf Hitler's Ziele und Persönlichkeit. Deutscher Volksverlag, München, 1930.

tion of guillotines on every avenue. To the outsider it seems that somebody has been fooled in Germany. If, during these years of their support, Hitler had an understanding with his moneyed backers that he would be safe, sane, and reasonable when he took over the government, then it was his great army of followers that was being fooled. It is true that Dr. Gottfried Feder, long Hitler's theoretician and teacher of economics, has declared right along that there are two groups of capitalists, those engaged in productive industry and those who are traders and money lenders, and that for his part he is not willing to apply nationalization to the heavy industries founded or conducted by the Krupps, Thyssens, Abbes, Mannesmans, Kirdorfs, and Siemenses, and others, all of whom, curiously enough, appear to have contributed to the Hitler treasury.*

It is a fact, as a Reichstag inquiry brought out, that the Federation of the Iron Masters of the Ruhr, and the Württemberg machine industry invested large amounts in Hitler's cause. But the great Bavarian magnates were ahead of them.† The famous house of Maffei, Herr Hornschuh, a rich manufacturer of Kulmbach, Privy Councilor Aust, head of the Bavarian Federation of Industries, and his son-in-law, Herr Kuhlo, are among the first who "staked" Hitler, preferring his brand of Bolshevism to the brand of Socialism professed by the present government and to the menace of Communist Germany. Other industrialists helped some of the Munich newspapers to see

* This recalls vividly Theodore Roosevelt's differentiation during his Administration between the good and bad industrialists of America,—those for him and those opposed.

† For these and many other interesting facts as to the use of money in European politics, see "Das Geld in der Politik" (Money in Politics) by "Morus." Berlin, 1930, Fischer Verlag.

Nazi light by giving them financial aid. Only a bank here and there appears to have backed the Nazis. But naturally Hitler has stood well with the munitions makers; even the famous *Skodawerke,* formerly Austrian, but now Czecho-Slovakian, felt that a Hitler victory would be best for their balance sheets, and contributed accordingly. Of course that great swindler, Ivar Kreuger, thought well of Hitler, and some of the largest concerns in Berlin, like the Borsig Works, and the great Siemens plants, gladly permitted Nazi recruiting agents to enter their premises in order to offset Socialist and Communist propaganda among their workers. Indeed, the great bulk of the younger industrials was to be found in his camp, which may be taken as the measure of their own wisdom and vision unless they have ulterior motives. Gifts from abroad Herr Hitler is always ready to accept, provided that they do not come from Jewish hands. Why not? After all, the heads of great financial and business enterprises whereever situated speak the same language and think the same thoughts—with rare exceptions. It does seem, however, as if this peerless leader was taking some chances of having "dirty Jewish money" pass through his hands when he accepted a contribution of 330,000 francs from an anonymous Swiss friend. Or was he just a profiteer in hiding?

Curiously enough, the United States must bear the odium or the credit, whichever the reader prefers, of having suggested to some German industrialists the advantages of close alliances between politics and large scale business. Thus, the so-called Duisberg system, originated by Karl Duisberg, the former chairman of the board of the great *I. G. Farben* Company, came from that gentleman's discovery of the very great influence American business has upon our political life. Speaking in November, 1926, to an economic association formed to bring the industrialists together in an offensive and defensive alliance, Herr Duisberg said:

In treating important economic problems a new approach must be made, and America has taught us how

it should be made. America's political life is dominated by organizations representing economic interests. The organizations discuss the outstanding issues and adopt new policies. In Germany these questions are decided in the Reichstag. We must mend our ways and make our influence felt on the political parties. . . . In order to carry out the ideas of our association money is needed. America knows this and our friends must learn to emulate this example.

But this is not the only instance of American inspiration for Nazi and allied developments. Hitler borrowed much of his material as to the Jews from the rehash of old lies and superstitions in a book, written for Henry Ford by some employee, which the auto manufacturer himself later repudiated. Again, much of Hitler's exhortations, especially to youth, are amusingly like Theodore Roosevelt's commendations of the Ten Commandments and the Strenuous Life. Thus Hitler is hot for sports and complete physical training for all classes; he is bitterly down on present-day "slothfulness" and "flabbiness," and, of course, he, too, believes that, in the last analysis, war is the supreme goal and the supreme, ennobling satisfaction in life. Precisely like Roosevelt, Hitler stands for all "the old forgotten virtues of our forefathers, their frugality, inner discipline and honesty which are the cornerstone of any State and commonwealth." As if from Roosevelt's crusading Bull Moose speeches of 1912 come these words from Hitler: "On to victory, like knights without fear or blame, we shall charge through hell, death and damnation. . . . We shall have to hack our way through a purgatory of lies, slanders, terrorism and persecution, but we shall win through." From America, Hitler also declares, he learned his policy of strict exclusion of all immigration, except that which is entirely satisfactory to him. Finally, it must be noted that it is to an American, Madison Grant, that Hitler in large part gives the credit for his adoption of the creed that the Nordic Germans alone are fit to rule, and for his promises that the State he proposes to set up shall do everything to cultivate that racial stock and to destroy or declass all others in order to achieve the ideal German race.

How far this mania has gone with him and his followers appears clearly from reports of the Congress of National Socialists, Pharmacists and Physicians, held at Leipzig in December, 1931, at which the Nordic race was modestly described—as German *Kultur* used to be glorified until it was let down by defeat in the war, the Revolution, the "stab-in-the-back" and the "great betrayal"—as "the finest flower on the tree of humanity," * and where the elaborate Nazi plan for its purification was evolved. Yes, for its purification, for it appears that though it is still the finest flower on the tree of humanity it has been sadly infiltrated by poorer stock. Hence these Nazi gentlemen of drugs and medicine are one in the belief that the race must be further bred "according to the criteria of race hygiene and eugenics." Special bureaus dealing with racial questions were to be established and charged with supervising the marriages of all loyal Nazis.† Miscegenation, not only of whites with blacks, but between superior and inferior Nordics was to be strictly forbidden (our Southern States please take notice). First-class Nordics could thus easily enter the bonds of matrimony; second-grade Germans would possibly be permitted to do so, and, if so, for a

* See the New York *Times*, December 8, 1931.

† A beginning has already been made; a member of the Hitler shock troops about to marry is obligated to report the race, ancestry, etc., of his fiancée to headquarters in order to obtain permission to wed.

limited time only; but the third-rate Germans (to think of the Nazis admitting that there are such!) would be gradually eliminated through compulsory sterilization. This happy and simple process of emasculation—doubtless at birth when the "patient" could not object—is a favorite medicine of the Hitlerites, it is such an easy and pleasant way of getting rid of the fellow you don't like. Besides taking care of any undue increase of population in place of birth control (let the women still have their childbirth pains to keep them contented), you can narrow the circle steadily until you have eliminated everybody but Nazis and captains of industry. Even then, however, the German Nordics may need more room. "If," said a certain Dr. Stemmler at the Leipzig meeting, "the 'genuine' Germans so restored to their pristine purity should find their dwelling place too narrow for life's needs, there would be nothing left for them but to conquer more room, sword in hand"—let us hope with better results for themselves and the world than in 1914-18.

It is, of course, clear to all anthropologists that it will be extremely difficult to define pure Nordics by more serious tests than blue eyes and flaxen hair. What, for example, is to become of the Bavarians with whom Hitler has made his home for twenty years? They are not of a Nordic type, but belong to the so-called Alpine family. We presume that Herr Hitler would permit them to continue to intermarry—in the second grade. But those millions of Germans to the northeast and east of Berlin who are deeply infiltrated by Slavic blood? We suppose that there will be no hesitation as to them. All Slavic blood surely has within it the virus of Bolshevism and is beyond doubt the most menacing, with the exception of the Jewish blood. Plainly here, too, only emasculation will do. Unfortunately, there will be doubtless as many difficult cases just on the line to puzzle the future miscegenation courts, or purity boards, to be established by Herr Hitler, as in the American South, where every year hundreds, if not thousands, of very white Negroes "cross over" and become white men or women without detection.

All of this Nordic stuff makes amusing reading. But as a whole there is nothing amusing about this Hitler movement. It holds within it not only the portent of most dreadful tragedy, but has also placed under the harrow of grave anxiety and fear a considerable section of the German people. The worst part of his program is his anti-Semitism. Until it was forbidden by the government, the Hitler press daily published the filthiest attacks upon the Jews, even printing pictures of sexual perversions and of rape which were laid at their doors, as if no Gentile degenerate had ever existed. In many cities the Hitlerites organized an advertising campaign to boycott all Jewish business. The slogan "Do Not Patronize Jewish Lawyers and Doctors" has appeared in innumerable places. Many more than a hundred breaches of the peace are attributable to this foul campaign of incredible mendacity, perversity, and hate in the small towns of Germany. "Thousands of lives have been ruined by it." Even on the *Kurfürstendamm* in Berlin the Hitlerites staged in broad daylight what was nothing less than a pogrom, and involved the smashing of numerous stores; the perpetrators were arrested and tried—and escaped with ridiculously low sentences, if they were convicted. Why has Hitler marked the Jews for vengeance? Because, he says, the Jews alone are responsible for the World War, for Germany's loss of it, and for every single phase of the present economic misery of the world. Had there been no Jews in the world none of these things would have happened. Peace and prosperity would have

reigned everywhere. Hence Hitler decrees that they must pay the price of these colossal "crimes."

If he takes power the German Jews will suffer the immediate loss of their citizenship and be deprived of every single one of their civic rights. They will live as aliens in their native land. They will be taxed without representation, and have no part in their government. As for those Jews, now resident in Germany, who since 1914 have sought refuge within its boundaries, they are to be shoved back to wherever they came from. For all that Hitler cares they shall go back stripped as naked as when they entered the world. He is not in the slightest degree interested as to what fate may await them at the hands of the Bolsheviks, the Poles, the Czecho-Slovaks, and all the others to whom they may be returned at the point of the bayonet. They may be useful, able, earnest, law-abiding citizens, not engaged in money-making pursuits—that will make no difference. Their birth and their race alone will count. Already both the German and the foreign-born Jews have had a taste of what will happen to them if Hitler wins, for followers of his have been in control of Thuringia and Braunschweig, and other States and there Jewish rights have been ignored, Jewish officials driven from the public service, Jewish citizens "cheated, boycotted and plagued in every conceivable manner." * Far worse than that, the Jewish males are to be emasculated, if Hitler has his way, and all are to be killed of whom it can be proved that they had anything to do with the Revolution, or the "stab-in-the-back" myth. Hitler himself has been guilty of making such threats not only against the Jews, but the Gentile Revolutionists of 1918. It was at the trial of the three lieutenants at Leipzig in September, 1930, that he declared

* See Hitler and the Jew, by Otto Wolfgang Brodnitz. *Opinion*, New York, December 7, 1931.

that when he came into power "heads would roll in the sand"—this at the moment when he was protesting that he would find his way to power only by legal and pacific means, and would never, never dream of a *Putsch* or a march on Berlin. True, the bloodiest and most shocking utterances are not Hitler's but those of his lieutenants. Upon them Hitler puts no muzzle. He himself is openly for hanging the bulk of the Ministers of the recent government, and therefore he does not object when his lieutenants say that the road to Berlin must be lined by the heads of Jews and Socialists—some even go so far as to declare that they will hang all Socialists and Communists, a little matter of disposing of some thirteen millions of Germans. That the Hitlerites themselves are National Socialists and favor some Communistic theories, is not to prevent the extirpation of all Socialists who are not of the Hitler brand.

It is easy to say that these are the ravings of mad men, and that once they assumed the responsibilities of governing Germany they would become realists and see the utter folly if not the wickedness of bathing Germany in blood. It might be pointed out, too, that, even if there were no bloodshed, the proposal to expatriate all foreign-born Jews and to declass all the German-born, and to drive them out of the marts of trade and finance would throw the industrial and professional life of Germany into disorder.

Hitler has not, however, merely inflamed the passions of the youth of Germany; he has confused their minds by his tortuous course on foreign affairs. It is known that an emissary of his to Paris allowed the French to understand that he would not bite very hard if he should come into office, that he would not be particularly anti-French, or very belligerent, or repudiate such debts and reparations as may be remaining when he takes office. Indeed, he has publicly stated that the world must not expect anything sensational from him if he takes power. And then in the next moment he declared not only that national safety lies only in the sword, but that eventually, if justice is not done to Germany, it must again make war on France and of course on Russia, too, because of its Bolshevism! He preaches the doctrine of economic insularity and political aloofness on the part of Germany. He makes light of the League of Nations, and the next moment turns around and abuses the Allies because Germany has not been allowed to become a full-fledged member of the family of nations. In January, 1932, he felt that the overthrow of the Bruening régime would constitute the greatest "external political success for Germany." He then went on to say: "Such an overthrow—legally to be sure—constitutes the sole possibility of transforming Germany from a helpless passive object into a valuable and active member among the European nations. Only when Germany can offer something will she be given something; only when friendship with Germany means an advantage to the rest of the world shall we have any practical working basis."

Hitler is at his best when he vents his bitterness and hate, especially his hatred of those who made the Revolution. This "crime of the Revolution" as he calls it made him, he says, weep for the first time after he had seen his mother lowered into her grave. "What followed," he writes, "was terrible days and worse nights—I knew that all was lost, only fools could bring themselves to hope anything of the magnanimity of the enemy or of liars and criminals [at home]. Hate grew within me these nights, hate for those who committed this deed. I, however, determined to become a politician." Politician he became, and not a statesman, surrounded by small and cheap politicians, some of them of dubious character. That he was able to continue his career as a politician after the great blunder of his Munich *Putsch* is proof enough that there is something much more in the man than merely a voice; that there is within him a power to be taken seriously. His is plainly the type of mind that has come to the front in numerous other countries—the mind of the compromiser, the mind of the superficial commentator upon world affairs, the mind of a man who has no difficulty in shifting his position as often as may be necessary and of reversing those positions whenever in his opinion it is desirable to do so. To this he adds the reputation, not unknown elsewhere, of being a politician who is extremely careless of the truth in his dealing with his fellows, who does not keep his promises and is untrustworthy in the inner leadership of his party as well as in his policies.*

* Cf., for example, the speech of Kapitänleutnant Hellmuth von Mücke, the chief hero of the German cruiser *Emden,* in Berlin on December 18, 1930, explaining why he could no longer continue to work with Hitler or remain in his party.

How could Von Hindenburg even for a moment consider sharing the government of Germany with such a man? There have been many explanations. One is the constant argument that if he were taken into high office the responsibilities incurred thereby would sober him as it has so often sobered the wildest radical and rendered him quite conservative. This school of thought believes that to compel a Hitler to face realities, such terrible realities as now stare the German nation in the face, and to apply the touchstone of daily service to the nation to his "bookish theoretic," would be the best means of bringing him down to earth and making him realize, for example, what would happen to all that is left of Germany if he should seek to carry out his anti-Jewish policy and to send the foreign-born Jews across the border and drive the German-born entirely out of the day-by-day business, economic, and professional life of the nation. It is a fortunate thing for Germany, indeed, that this proposal has so far not prevailed. A compromise government made up of such diverse groups as Hitler and his immediate associates and the Nationalists who have now seized the government, would merely lead to friction and controversy and bickerings which would sooner or later destroy any coalition government, unless the other side were to give Hitler free hand to carry out certain portions of his program. The man who has said that within his own party: "My will is law for the party and with the possible exception of Russia and Italy there is no political organization anywhere which is so completely answerable to its leader," is hardly the man to work long in harmony with others. He was, from that point of view, correct in demanding of Von Hindenburg a seventy-five per cent share in the Cabinet—which meant that his policies would prevail.

Should Hitler win control of the government the loss

to Germany would be incalculable, not only in the bitterness which would ensue and the setting of race against race and class against class, but also in the denial of equality and in the regimenting of men's minds and filling them with outworn shibboleths which the world must discard or perish. It would mean the loss of great cultural and national values. It would mean the complete wrecking of what is left of the Republic; that is, the defeat of the highest democratic aspirations of a great people. It would mean the substitution of another and a more dangerous and ruthless autocrat in the place of the Kaiser—a dictator whose mere accession to power might destroy the last of Germany's financial credit abroad, and also the remaining hope of great masses that their long period of trial by fire is nearing its end. An enemy of Germany should pray for Hitler's taking control of the country. Every friend of Germany must pray that his power will steadily decrease; that his ability to charm the multitudes will wane; that the recession of his forces, now begun, will rapidly continue and that he himself will speedily disappear from the German scene. It is a good omen that, as these lines are written, two of his lieutenants, Gottfried Feder and Gregor Strasser, have broken with him and left the party's management.

Issues and Men

AFTER fourteen and one-half years of service as Editor of *The Nation* I have relinquished that post to become Contributing Editor and turned over the complete control of the paper to three of my associates—Freda Kirchwey, Henry Hazlitt, and Joseph Wood Krutch—and Ernest Gruening, formerly a member of the staff. This does not mean a complete separation, if only because I shall remain as owner and publisher. But I have felt that the time had come for me to free myself of the burdens of active editorship so that I might have more time for speaking, especially over the radio, for writing books, and for engaging in other literary work which has necessarily been limited heretofore. I cannot deny, however, that the break, though primarily a shift in functions, involves a sentimental wrench. My grandfather, William Lloyd Garrison, was a contributor to the first volume of *The Nation,* and my father, Henry Villard, to the third issue, in July, 1865—just after his return from the front after four years of active service in the Civil War as a war correspondent. My uncle, Wendell Phillips Garrison, one of the two founders of the paper, was literary editor and editor during almost his entire active life. Finally, my son, Henry H. Villard, contributed an article to *The Nation* in the issue of November 2, 1932. Five other members of the family have written for it. In the light of this record, it will be clear how much *The Nation* means to me, and how impossible it would be for me to stop writing for it.

Under the title, Issues and Men, Oswald Garrison Villard, The Nation's *Contributing Editor, will write a weekly page of comment on personalities and public affairs.*

Now that I can look at the problem of the liberal journal in a more detached way, I should like to take this opportunity to urge the vital necessity of maintaining it at all costs. It is apparent to anyone with a mind and a conscience how desperate is the present national emergency. But perhaps only those who are giving their lives to the problem of economics and government can realize how essential it is that there shall be free and outspoken journals of opinion such as *The Nation,* the *New Republic,* the *Survey,* the *World Tomorrow,* and the few other publications, both daily and weekly, which can fairly be classed in the group of progressive-minded and economically free journals.

The pressure upon the daily press to conform, and not to attack evil, or espouse new causes, or advocate drastic remedies, grows greater with the depression. Loss of advertising cannot be wholly offset by economies or reductions in the cost of production, or by the laying-off of employees. Hence those newspapers that are weak or timid or deliberately allied with the great business forces which have too long dominated our political life are more careful than ever not to go counter to the prevailing currents of opinion. They have plenty of excuses: they do not wish to "rock the boat"; they assure you that if officials are corrupt or lawless, if the police are brutal and ruthless in dealing with those who dare to exercise their right of public assembly and protest, it is kinder to "treat 'em rough" than to have riots or bloodshed. It is better, they say, to breach the Constitution, to perpetrate much injustice, than to risk disturbance of the public order. Privately they admit that the old order is in a bad way, but publicly they insist that all is well or will be very soon. They do not print all the facts about what is happening the country over—the misery, the suffering, the hunger, the deaths by starvation; to do so, they say, would be to depress the American morale and create the wrong psychology. They are one with President Hoover, whose falsification in 1929 and 1930 of the facts of the depression is not only defended but praised as having been necessary to keep up the country's courage. Surely that is an insulting derogation of American stamina, American bravery in the face of odds, American ability to fight in the last ditch with back to the wall!

In other words, the bulk of the daily press fights blindly and often stupidly for the old system. It has no new program, no plan for reconstruction or reorganization; it merely holds on, hoping that somehow or other prosperity will return so that there may be business at the old stand in the good old way. Surely, we need a free and outspoken press as never before to demand that this chaos and misery shall never come to pass again; to insist that there are ways out to a normal and decent world; to refuse to listen to the suggestion that we must go back to the cycles of great apparent prosperity alternating with horrible depressions, that we must again be a country governed by and for the rich, with materialism our god, the narrowest nationalism our nation's goal, and the heaping up of riches our be-all and end-all.

Of course I know that the liberal journals of opinion also have their weaknesses; that they often err in their judgments, and at times in their methods. They have the defects of their qualities. All of them face recurring deficits, and all but one are greatly handicapped by their lack of funds. We of *The Nation* have rarely produced an issue that came within 50 per cent of our ideal of what it ought to be. We are compelled by the logic of our positions, and by the mass of error and injustice which we must attack, to seem captious, overcritical, unduly fault-finding, never satisfied, never content to allow to frail human nature its due proportion of inherent weaknesses. It is charged that we are never ready to see anything but pure black and pure white, overlooking all intervening shades. Well, many of the criticisms of us may be true, but still I maintain that the liberal press is indispensable and serves a profoundly valuable purpose—yes, an absolutely necessary one—if the country is not to go on the rocks of blind conservatism, base intolerance, and criminal refusal to face conditions as they are.

And so I bespeak your support for *The Nation,* and for the editors who have so generously volunteered to take the burden and responsibility from my shoulders.

Oswald Garrison Villard

Issues and Men

The Army and Navy Forever

WHY is it that the army and navy appropriations have become so sacrosanct in Washington? It is true that there have been some pay cuts in both the army and the navy, but the vast total of the outlay for army and navy remains untouched. It is as if a curtain of inviolability had been thrown around them, or as if there were evidences that the country was in danger. The Navy League representatives, of course, have been to Franklin Roosevelt to show him how rapidly we are dropping to third —or is it fifth?—place, while the Chief of Staff has solemnly informed the country that in the matter of land armaments we stand in seventeenth place. Some of the vital services of the government, such as education, are being sharply curtailed. Why is it that there is such hesitation about reducing the army or navy? The Appropriations Committee of the House of Representatives has reduced the new army bill by only $60,000,000. Nominally the cut is $110,000,000, but $50,000,000 of this amount is accounted for by non-recurring emergency construction which is ending in the present fiscal year. The military side of the War Department's work is actually cut only $31,584,000. Even this reduction was at once attacked, particularly the bill's suspension for a year of the citizens' military training camps, which have thus far been attended by 377,000 young Americans eager to learn how to kill other human beings and to be supported while doing so. But the bill does not even move to reduce the number of officers in the regular army from 12,000 to 10,000, as last year's bill did, and it does not specify that as vacancies in the lowest grade of the corps of officers occur, there shall be no fresh appointments. Yet the army is dreadfully over-officered compared to the number of men it actually has in the ranks. It has many more colonels than can possibly command regiments, far more generals than ever before in our history, and the retired list is stuffed with many of the temporary officers of the World War.

Now is this necessary? Let us leave aside the fact that for more than one hundred years of our national existence we never had a regular army larger than 25,000 men and officers, and that during most of that time we had one of only 10,000. Let us not dwell upon the facts that we were solemnly assured that we had won the war to end war, and that we have signed the Pact of Paris forever outlawing war as an instrument of national policy. Let us look at the world as it is. What nation could possibly go to war with the United States today? Not Germany certainly, nor Russia, which is obviously willing to let Japan go as far as it likes in Manchuria rather than endanger the very existence of the Communist system by getting into a war. And surely not France. The wildest jingo never suggests that we shall go to war with France. Nor does anybody suggest that Mussolini's fleet is a menace to the United States. England? Well, there is certainly no danger of that in view of the critical condition of Britain's industry, the prostration of most of its basic industries, and the financial debacle of last year which made it abandon the gold standard—to say nothing of the historic friendship between the two countries and the pledges of eternal friendship we gave when we joined the Allies in 1917. There remains, then, only Japan, which would seem to have its hands full in Manchuria—Japan, whose adventures in China have made that nation so unpopular with the rest of the world that it could hardly expect anything but a united front against itself in the event of hostilities with a Western Power. But, we hear it said, is it not true that there exists an alliance between England and Japan, tacit, it is true, but none the less binding? Would not these two countries be glad to join forces against us?

Well, the answer is that 60 per cent of Japan's trade is with the United States and this would cease on a declaration of war; that the yen has steadily lost ground for the last two years; that nothing would so jeopardize the Japanese adventure in Manchuria and Jehol; and that it would be impossible for Japan to find the money necessary to finance a war with the United States. The first result for England of alliance with Japan would be the loss of India, which would certainly take the opportunity to throw off British control. The simple truth is that there is not a nation in financial condition to undertake a struggle with the United States, and certainly not one whose military officers and financial and economic experts could hold out the slightest hope of gaining anything whatever from war with the United States, whether that war should be successful or unsuccessful. Have we not learned the great lesson of the World War and its aftermath—that the victors are punished as much as the vanquished? But still the Congress acts as if we must not reduce the army by an officer or a man; as if we must not lay violent hands upon our obsolete battleships. And the militarists and navalists are crying out that if there are any reductions in the armed forces, the legions of the unemployed will only be increased. To this the answer is that the discharges could be gradual, and that if necessary it would be better and cheaper for the United States to give these men a bare living sustenance in civil life than to maintain them in barracks. Certainly if unnecessary pensions were cut off, there would be no difficulty in giving these discharged men a dole until such time as they were absorbed by the farm or by industry. As a matter of fact, there was more than one general in Washington last winter who admitted privately that the army would be much more efficient if it had several thousand fewer officers. Whether they were right or not there is today no sound reason why the army and navy appropriations should not be cut by several hundred millions of dollars, as a long step toward that disarmament for which even Senator Jim Watson of Indiana is apparently ready, now that he has introduced a bill for the United States to offer to the rest of the world a 50 per cent reduction in all armaments for a period of ten years.

Oswald Garrison Villard

Do We Need a Dictator?

EMPHATICALLY not! Nothing in the existing situation, grave, critical, and menacing as it is, warrants the overthrow of our system of government or the concentration in the hands of the incoming President of powers which are not already his under the Constitution. Congressional government has not broken down. The time has not come to abandon our faith in our democratic institutions, or to proclaim to the world that they cannot stand the stress and strain of the present economic crisis. There is no inherent virtue or wisdom in a dictator not to be found in a President. The mere appointment of a dictator, or a dictatorship of three or five, will not in itself solve any of the innumerable problems before us. Similarly it should be clear that the so-called obstructionist tactics of the Congress are not wholly responsible for the failure of the country to recover from the slump or to see before it a clear road to the restoration of our lost prosperity and economic well-being.

What we are suffering from is far less the weaknesses of the Congress than the total absence of clear-cut, wise, and constructive leadership in the White House. After all, the Executive is there to lead, not only because he is the head of his party, but because he is also the head of the nation. The truth is that we have had no White House guidance of a progressive kind, none to challenge the imagination or to sketch out far-reaching policies, since the first two years of Mr. Wilson's Administration. We have had from Mr. Hoover the weakest kind of effort to provide a program for the country and its parliament. He misconceived the crisis from the beginning, misrepresented it to the public, announced that it was rapidly passing by and was nothing to be worried about. When he was forced to admit the gravity of the situation he was unable to make any worth-while recommendations. It is not possible to know at this date whether Mr. Roosevelt will be able to prove to the country that he has sufficient knowledge and wisdom to guide us in this emergency. But if he has not that wisdom now, how on earth will it help to give him additional power? Such a grant will not open his eyes to economic truths that he does not already see; it will not give him greater resoluteness of character or endow him with stronger leadership.

The truth is that we are again chasing after a mere slogan in our old familiar American way. Last year everybody was calling for the balancing of the budget. Wall Street, Mr. Hoover, and the conventional editors were all crying for it. Secretary Mills assured us that if the budget was not balanced, disaster lay immediately ahead. *The Nation* was scorned because it declared that the budget could not be balanced and that it would not ruin us if it were not. But a bill was passed, Mr. Hoover and Mr. Mills declared that the budget *was* balanced, and the banker and newspaper packs promptly went baying off in another direction. Next came the demand for economy; that was to be the cure-all. Innumerable wiseacres at solemn dinner tables demanded a national cabinet—merely because England had one, although they did not know whether the result in England was favorable or unfavorable. And now it is dictatorship—with Walter Lippmann well in front calling it "the paramount issue," "the right direction." He is certain that the only thing to do is to give to the President "the widest powers over the administration of the government and over expenditures which it is possible to grant him under the Constitution"—just as if the President did not already possess all the powers which the Constitution allows him. No latent Presidential powers are hidden away in the Constitution to be conferred upon the President by some vote of the Congress.

Mr. Lippmann is also certain that we must choke off "unlimited debate and obstruction" in both houses of Congress and he wants to restore to the Executive certain rights and powers which have been "usurped" by Congress because of Congressional yielding to petty local influences. Is there anything in the situation which could not be squarely met by an Executive of courage, independence, and force, ready, as were Woodrow Wilson and Grover Cleveland in their time, to go over the head of Congress and appeal to the public if Congress should prove recalcitrant? Indeed, Congress is waiting for just this sort of leadership. Moreover, when Congress meets again there will be an overwhelming majority of Democrats in both houses—not one-quarter of the Senate will be composed of Old Guard Republicans. Doubtless unduly large majorities are unwieldy, but in this emergency the party leaders will be only too happy to follow Mr. Roosevelt's requests, if he proves that he knows his own mind, has a program, and is determined to put it through—even to the extent of withholding patronage until he achieves it. But if he fails to do this, hamstringing the Congress and laying the foundations for a complete dictatorship will not help us.

But even if this should aid us temporarily, it would be better to suffer the delays which may come from a stupid and frightened Congress than to open the way for a dictator. Let us not have even the nose of that camel thrust into the tent of American government, let alone his head. One needs only to look at the latest dictator in Europe, Adolf Hitler, to see how quickly the liberties and rights of individuals may be menaced by a demagogue certain that his country's parliament also is of no further use, that his ideas are the cure-alls for his country's ills. Of course there should be reasonable, voluntary limitation of debate in the Senate in this emergency, but criticism is not always merely a means of delay. Far from it. Nothing in Mr. Roosevelt's record warrants the belief that everything he recommends will be completely wise.

Few journalists ever wrote more damning things about a public man than Walter Lippmann was writing only a year ago about this same Franklin D. Roosevelt to whom he now wishes to give tremendous power. If the President-elect sounds the keynote and takes the aggressive in well-reasoned suggestions, Congress will follow him willingly or will be compelled to by public opinion. But the Senate is the only debating forum left in America. As such, it is of inestimable value to our institutions, to our liberties, to the possibility of our progress along wise and sane lines. Muzzling it is no more desirable than to end all public criticism in the press and elsewhere. But if we muzzle Congress, muzzles for the rest of us will come as a matter of course, particularly if the emergency should become more critical.

Issues and Men

Congress Votes for a Bill

ABSIT omen! Not since the declaration of war against Germany has the Congress of the United States done anything as amazing as it did on Thursday, March 9, when it voted to make Franklin D. Roosevelt, in financial matters, dictator of the Republic. In some respects this action was even more astounding than the fatal vote of April 2, 1917, to which most of our troubles of today are due, for then at least Congress understood what the immediate issue was. On March 9 the House of Representatives, probably for the first time in its long history, voted for a bill which only one member had seen and held in his hand. The others listened while the clerk read the text. The eight or nine men who rose to speak about the bill spoke briefly, but not briefly enough. The cry of "Vote, vote," went up as soon as some of them concluded. Then, without further ado, the Representatives unanimously approved the bill.

Now, if the bill had been such a simple one that everybody knew just what it meant, such action might have been understood. Suppose it had read:

> WHEREAS, The Congress of the United States has been trying for three and one-half years to legislate prosperity back to the United States, and whereas, it is now scared to death at the imminence of financial and economic disaster and does not care what happens as long as something happens, be it
>
> *Resolved,* First, that the Congress hereby passes the buck to the new President in the belief that his wisdom will be greater and the actions he may take will be wiser than theirs; second, that it hereby abdicates its constitutional functions and responsibilities and turns over the safety and financial security of the Republic to Franklin D. Roosevelt, and may God have mercy on his soul.

If the bill had read thus, it would at least have described accurately the frame of mind of Congress and the action proposed. As it was, no Congressman could have understood in full the contents of the real bill, or its ramifications and implications. All they wanted was to get it off their hands. They were as hysterical as their predecessors of 1917. Then the Congress voted in fear of an aroused and deceived public opinion and of the wrath of President Wilson—many in both houses voted against their consciences and their sound sober sense. Had they not just heard the President denouncing the "twelve wilful men" who had opposed his bill for arming our merchant ships? Were those men not thrown by him to the ravening wolves of the daily press, the hysterical patriots, the financiers who were interested only in saving the vast sums they had lent to the Allies?

As I sat in the Senate throughout Thursday's debate I could not but recall the scene of sixteen years ago. Then, too, men voted aye because they thought there was nothing else to do; the next day the country rose exultant in its belief that war was going to be banished from the world, that democracy was to be made safe everywhere, that the millennium to be achieved by mass murder was at hand. We are witnessing the elation following this setting up of Franklin Roosevelt as financial dictator. Will history still further repeat itself?

In the Senate the scene was as tense and dramatic as such a historic occasion ought to be. Ex-Senators and Representatives stood around the walls of the chamber, which appeared strangely unfamiliar because of the few desks on the Republican side of the house and the great majority on the Democratic side. The galleries were jammed and long queues sought entrance. Senator after Senator rose to his feet to declare that he did not believe in the bill or in making the President dictator, but that he would vote for it because of the national emergency. Senator Connally of Texas declared that never in his life had he expected to vote either in war or in peace to confer such powers upon the Executive as he was now going to do. Senator Vandenberg of Michigan made the most forceful and unanswerable speech against it—and then voted for it. Huey Long really astounded even conservatives, and men as prejudiced against him as I am, by his courage and directness and the ability of his attack, but none the less he voted for the bill.

Indeed, as I looked at the faces of the men on the floor I was struck not only by their deep concern, but by their obvious agreement with the opponents of the bill. There was no doubt that many were wrestling hard with their consciences. All that Carter Glass could say for the measure was that it was the best of those that had been offered to his committee. He could not, or would not, answer Huey Long's charge that this bill would put thousands of State banks out of business. Robert M. La Follette, Jr., repeated history in that, like his father in 1917, he spoke and voted against the bill—a worthy son of a great father. Unfortunately, he, too, felt the pressure of time and spoke too quickly to be as effective as usual. Here are the seven who voted against the bill: Borah, Carey, Dale, La Follette, Nye, Costigan, and Shipstead, with Senator Norbeck paired against it. Borah did not speak. Dale of Vermont is himself a bank president. They may be right or they may be wrong, but they were sincere, honest, and brave, and they saved a little of the reputation of Congress as a calm reasoning body.

All through the debate the Senators were told that there was not a moment to lose, that the bill must be in the hands of the President within a few hours, so that four or five thousand banks could be notified at once that they had the President's permission to reopen on Friday morning. But the banks were not reopened on Friday morning or Saturday morning, and comparatively few on Monday morning. No harm would have been done if the debate had gone on through Friday, and probably much good. The danger is now not that Congress will fail to give the President what he wants, but that it will act too quickly for the best results, and for the safeguarding of our liberties.

Oswald Garrison Villard

Issues and Men

An Open Letter to Colonel House

SIR: Have you read the news from Germany? If so you are most assuredly entitled to pity. You must be lying awake nights horrified by the fact that German militarists, against whom you and Woodrow Wilson called the United States to war in 1917, are again intrenched in Berlin and that they have celebrated their accession to power by permitting nation-wide prosecutions and persecutions, and by throwing into jail thousands of people—all guiltless of any overt acts. For it was you and Woodrow Wilson who, believing that militarism could be overcome by militarism and war cured by more war, hailed the German defeat in 1918 as meaning the freeing of the German people from the fetters placed upon them by their abhorrent war caste under the Kaiser's rule.

Then you and Woodrow Wilson congratulated the American people upon their success in making the world safe for democracy, and on winning the war to end war. Today you read that a dictator rules Germany who demands the restoration of universal military service and complete arms equality with the other nations, and the revival of the old military order; who is pledged to tear up the Treaty of Versailles. You read that associated with him in the government are Field Marshal von Hindenburg and Lieutenant-Colonel von Papen, who, as German military attaché, was rightly sent from this country in disgrace in 1916. Further, if you read the dailies—I should not blame you if you never took another one in your hands—you have learned that within fifteen years after our victory in the war to end war there are a million more men under arms in Europe than there were on August 1, 1914, when the World War began. And that Lloyd George, your former associate, has just appealed to the National Council of Evangelical Churches urging "a world conference of all Christian churches to cry a halt to war before it is too late," because "all nations are marching toward the battlefield with the dove of peace embroidered on their banners."

Never, I venture to assert, has the progress of events so completely unmasked the hollowness and folly of a given policy or piece of statesmanship as have these last fifteen years the complete futility of your and Mr. Wilson's theory that if the United States threw itself into the World War it would be able to dominate the formulating of a peace to make over the world. That was the doctrine of Norman Angell and Herbert Croly and Walter Lippmann, to which you listened so eagerly, which you later adopted. Today, what do we see? The United States has failed to gain a *single one of the major objectives* for which it went into the war. Democracy the world over is menaced or destroyed or in ill repute—even in some circles here in the United States. Militarism destroyed? Today we ourselves have larger and costlier military and naval establishments than ever before in peace time. Largely as a result of our participation in the war we are plunged into an economic distress unsurpassed in our history, with 14,000,000 of our people unemployed. The very soldiers forced into our army and the killing business by the universal draft favored by you and Mr. Wilson have in part revenged themselves by menacing the financial stability of the country. We are not even to have returned to us the billions upon billions of American money we poured into the coffers of our Allies, chiefly because their repayment so gravely injures us and our trade. Today the world groans under tariff burdens unequaled in history, which have effectively throttled the trade of the world. Do you by chance recall that one of your Fourteen Peace Points called for the "removal, so far as possible, of all economic barriers and the establishment of an equality of trade conditions among all the nations consenting to the peace"? I hope you do not; otherwise it must add to your mental torture as you look back on the past. Can you deny that the world's tariffs are higher than ever before and are steadily going up?

If you are following what is happening in China you will have noticed that war on a large scale is on again; that Japan is drawing out from that association of nations which the remaining admirers of Mr. Wilson claim to have been the superlative achievement of his career. That League faces more than one acid test. Perhaps you have forgotten that the fourth of your peace points specified that "national armaments will be reduced to the lowest point consistent with domestic safety"? And that positive assurance was given to Germany that in return for her forcible disarmament the Allies and America would disarm promptly? Today the League is powerless to bring about disarmament and, despite the last-hour efforts of Ramsay MacDonald and Benito Mussolini, seems incapable of taking this vital step toward the safeguarding of our civilization. As for the German collapse, I earnestly hope for your peace of mind that you have not noticed that it is the unanimous testimony of the most competent foreign observers, as, for example, Edgar Mowrer in his book entitled "Germany Turns the Clock Back," that the disaster to the German Republic and the rise of the Hitler despotism are due in largest measure to the treaty of peace of which Wilson and you were in considerable degree, according to your own statements, the architects. At least, heaven be thanked, it was never ratified by the Senate of the United States! Look at Italy, look at Hungary, look at Poland. Can you maintain that their situation is better than it was when the war began? On the contrary, it is infinitely worse. They live under the heel of terror. Will you not maintain that the Austrian people have a right to their "own way of life"? But that, Colonel House, was what we guaranteed to do when we went into the war—safeguard little nations everywhere. What a humiliation it must all be to you if you ponder upon these things, as your mind wanders back to those cemeteries of the American dead in France, to whom this country gave its solemn pledge that there should be no further war, that the nations, like the oceans, should be safe and free, and that autocracy should be banished from this earth!

And that reminds me. Have you by any chance recently reread President Wilson's speech to the American Federation of Labor delivered in Buffalo, November 12, 1917, when we were well along in the war? He said:

> What I am opposed to is not the feeling of the pacifists, but their stupidity. My heart is with them, but my mind has a contempt for them. I want peace, *but I know how to get it* and they do not.

Now, frankly, Colonel House—I am asking you this question while the guns roar in China and in the two undeclared wars in South America—did Mr. Wilson really know how to get peace? Can you wonder that pacifists everywhere have today only contempt for your and Mr. Wilson's intellectual processes and your stupidity? In the next paragraph in that speech Mr. Wilson declared:

> You will notice that I sent a friend of mine, Colonel House, to Europe, who is as great a lover of peace as any man in the world; but I didn't send him on a peace mission yet. I sent him to take part in a conference as to how the war was to be won, and he knows, as I know, that that is the way to get peace, if you want it for more than a few minutes.

Years, Colonel House, we all know are but minutes in the lives of nations. But, honestly, did you and Mr. Wilson get us peace for more than a few minutes? Economically speaking, you did not get us peace for a single moment. I can bring you into touch with dozens of leading men on both sides of the ocean who will say to you as frankly as they have to me that as a matter of fact you and Mr. Wilson did not bring about peace at all, that the war has steadily gone on ever since that time. And now, with the mental and physical successors of what you were pleased to call the "Potsdam gang" in complete control in Germany, ready to strike hands with the Italian tyrant, is it any wonder that the British Cabinet is reported by one of the most reliable correspondents in London to be holding itself in readiness for emergency meetings at any hour of the day or night? Are you still as sure as you were in 1917 that you knew better than the pacifists? Do you remember that it is stated on page 80 of volume two of the "Intimate Papers of Colonel House" that you believed in 1915 that it was possible for the United States "to carry along," but you were convinced that "in the process the moral credit of the United States with the world would disappear and at the end of the war we should find ourselves without friends"? Well, Colonel, won't you tell us what moral credit the United States has left today in the world? What friends has it left? Will you undertake to deny that we are the best-hated nation on earth?

I suppose it is too much to expect that even this fact will cause you to question the superhuman wisdom which you and Mr. Wilson displayed in those crucial years. But I do want here to make acknowledgment of one of the most extraordinary prophecies of all times. Woodrow Wilson in his speech of January 22, 1917, said:

> It must be a peace without victory. It is not pleasant to say this. . . . I am seeking only to face realities and to face them without soft concealment. Victory would mean *peace forced upon the losers, a victor's terms imposed upon the vanquished*. It would be accepted in humiliation, under duress, at an intolerable sacrifice, and would leave a sting, a resentment, a bitter memory upon which terms of peace would rest not permanently, *but only upon quicksand*. Only a peace between equals can last.

Do you remember what you wrote in your diary at the time? Here it is: "He [Wilson] read the address which he had prepared in accordance with our understanding last week. It is a noble document and one which I think will live." You were right. It will live. It will live because it was the absolute truth and history has completely justified it. But it will also live as a monument to the folly and blindness of the two men who, having stumbled upon this truth, forgot it, abandoned the sound policy that it called for, and demanded, in Mr. Wilson's words, "force, force without stint."

Well, we used force without stint. We took part in drafting a peace which was imposed upon the vanquished. The results you see before you wherever you turn—a world in a quicksand, in chaos, a world with the spirit of war and war preparation more in evidence than ever before. Our armament bill, plus that of the nations of Europe, is now about five billion dollars a year, according to Herbert Hoover, at the moment when we and they are in economic ruin and, according to the International Labor Office, are maintaining fully 30,000,000 workless people. You see a world with great masses of people dominated by tyrants, some who found in the Treaty of Versailles their greatest aid in overcoming opposition and who openly say that they will no longer be bound by its provisions; a world so confused, so bewildered, so oppressed, that the most optimistic are now ready to admit that civilization is in jeopardy. I know well the plea that is put up in your behalf and that of Mr. Wilson. You meant well; you both tried your best at Paris; you were overcome by the brutal and vengeful statesmen with whom you found yourselves at the peace table; it is really wonderful that you were able to modify the treaty as much as you did. Accepting this as true—which I emphatically do not—for the sake of argument, please recall that these wicked statesmen were the very men whom you both recommended to the American people as entirely trustworthy, high-minded, unselfish, for whose cause, so you assured our drafted youths, it was right and just and noble and patriotic for them to die. You knew the treaty was bad, but you advised Wilson to sign it, and he signed it—as he should have, since some of the worst clauses in it were of his own creation.

"We are now about to accept gauge of battle with this natural foe to liberty and shall, if necessary, spend the whole force of the nation to check and nullify its pretensions and power"—thus spoke Woodrow Wilson of the German government on April 2, 1917, to Congress. The brutal and unscrupulous group of men which has just reinslaved the German people is worse by far than the government of the Kaiser, because it has declared openly that liberty is not essential to the individual citizen, and that freedom is not requisite in the modern state. It has made a mockery of German *Kultur* and German reverence for learning, conscience, and the liberty of the individual and the state. Yet it is not sixteen years, Colonel House, since you and your chief called upon the American people to make the world safe for democracy by joining in the mass murders in Europe. What agonies of regret, what tortures of conscience must be yours!

Oswald Garrison Villard

Issues and Men

The Folly of Adolf Hitler

THE folly of Adolf Hitler lies in the fact that he knows neither the history of his own country nor that of the world, and that he has not fathomed the true aspirations of men. There is in him a good deal of Dr. Coué; he believes that if you chant often enough "Germany, Awake," Germany will "awake" to accept his doctrines. The post-bellum Germany has been anything but asleep; there was a fine republican structure erected upon the ruins of 1918 and in the process of being enlarged, strengthened, and adequately furnished—only now to be destroyed. But waiving that, his speeches abound in phrases which indicate his belief that greatness can be achieved by wishing yourself great and thinking yourself great and declaring that you are a great and a united people. Here is a typical passage from his speech at the opening and closing of the Reichstag on March 23:

> The contemplativeness of cosmopolitanism is rapidly disappearing. Heroism is to ring passionately as the shaper and leader of political destiny. It is art's task to express this spirit of the times. Blood and race will again become the source of artistic inspiration. It is the task of the government to see to it that, just as in the period of restricted political power, the inward vital forces and values of the nation shall receive the most powerful stimulus.

The idea is the old one that if you can mouth sententious words like these often enough you will attain great things and achieve epoch-making results. As much of a philosophy as he has, he frankly admits that he has gained in considerable degree from America. From Madison Grant has come his doctrine of pure Aryanism; from Henry Ford's book on the Jews, much of the material for his crusade against them; from our Republican and Democratic politicians, the technique of extracting huge campaign funds from the great industrialists; and from our immigration laws, his plan to shut off Germany so that new elements from outside may not enter. Beyond that he has brought together all the remnants of the philosophy of the imperialist and dominating capitalist classes—where it has not been destroyed by true democratic movements or popular uprisings. He does not know that until the World War the whole trend of events was away from these outworn philosophies, or that, despite the rise of dictatorships, they are more than ever discredited. The ultra-conservatives who dominated the governments of Europe, either directly or in the background through their control of finance, industry, and natural resources, could not keep the world out of the disaster of 1914, could not stop that disaster after it began until the United States came in, and have not been able to keep the world out of the economic chaos in which it finds itself. The leaders of the great business men the world over are utterly discredited, but Hitler in his folly undertakes to rebuild Germany with the aid, advice, and consent of the Hugenberg group of bankers and industrialists and reactionaries, while his own platform is the most extraordinary melange of opposing and contradictory doctrines ever brought together in modern times. Thus he declares that communism must be rooted out and all Communists ruthlessly extirpated. Yet his own platform contains numerous Socialist and Communist planks. Thus he has declared at one time or another for the government's taking over all the import and export trade of the nation—a terrific task. He is for nationalization of the banks, for the return of the railways to government control, and for state ownership of all cartels and trusts. Yet in the speech from which I have quoted he declared that his government "would seek to promote private initiative with the fullest recognition of the rights of private property."

When it comes to the question of his history Hitler has evidently never read the career of Bismarck. Had he done so he would have found that in 1878 Bismarck felt just as bitterly against the Socialists as he himself does today, and in October, 1878, had an act passed which declared illegal all associations, books, and newspapers directed toward the alteration of the state and society of that day, and gave the government the power to supervise or to expel all the Socialist leaders, and even to proclaim a state of siege and suspend individual liberties in whole districts. The Socialist agitation was driven under ground and this statute remained on the law books until 1890. But all this while the Socialist movement grew apace. Adolf Hitler might also have studied to advantage the history of Russia—but why go on? I admit, of course, that a dictator today has a thousand times more power than had Bismarck, the Chancellor, in 1878 and 1885. Nations may be held in servitude for long years, but unless the dictator can make good by vastly improving the status not only of the dissenting portion of the populace, but of his own followers, his fall is inevitable.

Hitler's greatest folly of all was permitting his shock troops to get out of hand as soon as he triumphed. That was intentional, of course; it must never be forgotten that last summer he asked Hindenburg for a three-day suspension of all laws so that his Nazis might wreak their vengeance on their enemies. He did not ask Hindenburg's permission this time, but just went ahead. In his Reichstag speech he said: "We need contact with the outside world and our foreign markets furnish a livelihood for millions of our fellow-citizens," and then he and Germany "awake" again to find that his lawlessness and the unconstitutional arrest of thousands of people have deprived him of the sympathy of the best friends of Germany in Great Britain and the United States and France. Incidentally, it has cost the German nation, besides the respect and good-will of the world, millions of dollars' worth of orders that were canceled as soon as the Hitler news came to these shores. Precisely in such incredible stupidity as this lies the best hope that Germany will be able somehow or other to purge itself of Hitler and Hitlerism.

Oswald Garrison Villard

Issues and Men

The President and a Big Navy

As I write there are strong indications that President Roosevelt will yield to the demand for building the navy up by some thirty new ships. It is reported that the appropriation for them will be hidden in the proposed public-works bill and thus slip through without opposition, whereas if there were a separate bill there would be every opportunity for blocking it, or at least for numerous protests. The public-works bill will, it is expected, be jammed through by the force of the same vote-but-don't-read-it-or-argue psychology which has resulted in driving through Congress the legislation thus far asked by the President—I had almost said passed by the President, for that is what it comes down to.

It will be a misfortune, indeed, for the country as a whole if another $230,000,000 should be wasted in this way. It is true that these thirty ships are not to include any battleships or battle cruisers, but the fact remains that in our hour of greatest distress we shall be lavishing money upon a purely unproductive undertaking. It would be far wiser, if it is necessary to support the men who would work on these warships, to give them a handsome dole and let it go at that. But this is not what is desired by the munitions manufacturers and shipbuilders—I do not for a moment believe that Congressman Vinson was correct when he stated that 85 per cent of the money expended would go for wages. Once you build one of these ships it becomes a permanent liability until it is scrapped. It means increased annual appropriations for its upkeep, its personnel, and its movements. It means, unless the ship is to be kept "in ordinary," that a considerable crew will have to be kept on board to maintain her. The more ships, the greater will be the demand upon Congress for more sailors. The more ships built, the greater the demand by the shipbuilders for still more vessels to keep the yards busy, until it seems that the private shipbuilding yards do not exist to build for the navy as needed, but that the navy exists for the pleasure of the shipbuilders. Only last week the leading aviation generals, including the outspoken former General William Mitchell, testified again that no ships except submarines and scouting vessels were of any value; that the new bombing planes would do away with large vessels—at least that was General Mitchell's contention. But that does not stop the navy propaganda of the Hearsts, Brittens, and Vinsons.

As for the President, he has been deeply interested in the navy ever since boyhood, and he pretty well soaked up the big-navy propaganda when Assistant Secretary of the Navy. His collection of prints of naval battles was for a long time considered one of the finest in the United States. He saw nothing wrong in the overseas aggressions of the Wilson Administration of which he was part. I refer especially to Haiti, Mexico, Santo Domingo, and Nicaragua. Hence the big-navy people feel that he is definitely on their side. I wish he might take warning from what happened to Ramsay MacDonald when he yielded to the big-navy propagandists in his first government and built three cruisers, on the ground that he could not allow the shipbuilding industry to die out. That not only stamped Mr. MacDonald as inconsistent so far as his pacifist views were concerned, but it immediately laid him open to tremendous pressure. If three ships, why not five? Why not ten? Three ships would not go very far toward keeping the shipping industry alive, and did he not realize that this or that category of ships was seriously underbuilt? Your big-navy maniac is never satisfied.

The wasting of this $230,000,000 now would offset many of Mr. Roosevelt's savings in other directions. It might possibly be excusable if we were actually in danger of war—that is, if any sane human being still believes that anything is to be gained by war, and that you can be sure of victory under any circumstances. Well, the navy is keeping up the talk and many newspapers are helping the propaganda along: that we are in grave danger of war with Japan; that Japan has beaten us in capital ships; that Japan is voiding the London pact by building a Manchukuoan navy which will really be a reinforcement of its own, and so on and on. To this we reply that we are a long way from a war with Japan; that the next war means suicide for our entire capitalist civilization—what is left of it; and that this President Roosevelt knows, or ought to know, as well as the rest of us. And of course these thirty new ships will not insure our victory if we are attacked. President Coolidge put it just right to the American Legion on one occasion when he said that no country ever had an army or navy large enough to keep it out of war, or to insure victory to itself after it had got into war. But most important of all, armaments do not make for peace; they only increase tension and make for war. And how can we set ourselves up as critics of Hitler as he proceeds to arm Germany up to the pre-war standard if we go on piling up our own armaments? Certainly, if we engage in a naval race with England, or with England and Japan, there will be only one outcome—another terrible conflict.

No, Mr. President, don't mar your highly intelligent record by pouring $230,000,000 down a rat-hole. The resources of the country are not unlimited. We can pour out billions and half-billions and quarter-billions for some time, but in due course there will be an end to it. We are hearing a lot about the necessity of restricting public-works appropriations to self-liquidating projects, and there is a good deal to be said for it. Warships are neither self-liquidating nor productive of more wealth or employment, nor are they constructive uses of capital. In from ten to twenty years there will be nothing to show for them. A single new invention may make them out of date almost as soon as they are launched. Finally, when we are preaching disarmament to the rest of the world, let us set the example ourselves, and let us again, as through the first hundred years of our history, be unarmed and unafraid.

Oswald Garrison Villard

Issues and Men

The Damage to America in London

"A CATASTROPHE amounting to a world tragedy"—this is what Franklin D. Roosevelt said the failure of the London Economic Conference would be. Ramsay MacDonald said: "The fate of generations may well depend upon the courage, sincerity, and width of view which we are to show during the next few weeks . . . We must not fail." And Cordell Hull declared: "If, which God forbid, any nation should obstruct and wreck this great conference with the shortsighted notion that some of its favored interests might temporarily profit while thus indefinitely delaying aid for the distressed in every country, that nation will merit the execration of mankind." Even the King declared in his opening address that he could not believe that human beings were unable to solve the problems before them. But the failure is there patent to all men. This effort to find solutions for the capitalist world's misery has failed so completely that Moscow must be overcome with amusement. The peoples who read the declarations that I have cited above are justified now in expecting the prophesied disasters to begin.

The responsibility for this rests primarily upon the United States. It is now perfectly plain that the alleged preparation for the conference in the preliminary conversations in Washington amounted to precisely nothing. There was none of the preliminary spade work essential to the success of a conference unless, as at the Washington Conference for the Limitation of Armaments, one nation is ready to offer a concrete proposal for immediate action. In my judgment the fate of the conference was sealed when Cordell Hull not only muffed the opportunity offered to him by MacDonald to open the conference for business, but failed to produce concrete American proposals when he finally uttered the commonplace generalities that made up the bulk of his speech. If America had nothing definite to offer, who could have? I shall never understand why Franklin Roosevelt sent a delegation to London without a program, a policy, or definite instructions, a delegation headed by a low-tariff man whose associates were high-tariff men, apparently trusting to luck that they could do something and then changing his mind as to what he wanted them to do.

This has resulted in the final blow to American prestige in Europe. This is the real catastrophe for us, this and the fact that numerous superficial Americans are now saying, "Well we are glad we have fallen out with those damned, word-breaking welchers. We don't want to play with them and we don't care what they think of us—not in the least." Well, let me explain how rational and naturally pro-American Europeans, and especially Englishmen, feel about us. They are completely bewildered by our constant changes of front, reversals of opinion, and failure to live up to our agreements. They say: "With the best will in the world, dear Americans, we don't know how to do business with you. There was Norman Davis. He made a speech which was everywhere hailed as epoch-making. It seemed to us a complete reversal of your isolationist policy and a promise to stand with us in examining the question of guilt if another war should come and to throw your strength against the aggressor. No sooner was the ink dry upon our exclamations of joy than other interpretations of the speech were given which whittled it down to a point where it seemed to mean nothing. Then Mr. Roosevelt demanded that the World Economic Conference agree upon 'a fixed measure of exchange values . . . and we believe that these must be gold.' Soon after the conference met to carry out his behest he denounced it in vituperative language for seeking to do the very thing he asked of it! Then let us remind you that you took part in the making of the Treaty of Versailles; that you failed to ratify it and failed to enter the League of Nations which your own President created. How can we negotiate with you on any subject and feel that you mean what you say?"

I can only answer this by hanging my head. Of course, I explain that I didn't want the Treaty of Versailles ratified, and that I believe in Congressional control of the executive's acts, feeling that that alone has saved us from many a blunder and from having absolute dictators in the White House in foreign affairs. But this doesn't answer my European friends.

As for our American isolationists who rejoice that we made fools of ourselves and acted abroad like flighty, unreliable boors, I can only admit that their school is probably in the saddle now; that when Congress meets again we shall find ourselves in the midst of a terrific demand that we let Europe go to hell in its own stupid way, and much boasting that we can get on without the rest of the world. To which I reply, as I have many times before, that we *can* go it alone and bid the world go hang, but that if we do so we can never hope to recover even the normal prosperity of ante-World War days. Curious how some minds work! The other day I dined with a former American diplomat who, despite the failure in London, was surer than ever that we were on our way to an Anglo-American entente. He warmly defended our plan to build up the navy on the ground that sooner or later the united American and British fleets will impose peace upon the world. I pointed out to him that our announcement of this plan had already produced dispatches from Japan announcing great alarm there and a determined demand by their naval jingoes for a bigger program, and that the present distrust and loss of faith in us in England were being exploited by the big navy men there, and have put back prospects of an Anglo-American entente for many years.

All of which brings up the question anew whether capitalist society can possibly save itself from utter chaos. For the first time I have come back from Europe—my seventh trip since the war—to admit a sense of almost complete hopelessness. If some trick of nature itself does not get us out of our economic mess, how can our leaders possibly rescue us? Certainly the London Conference dealt a deadly blow to the world's progress and international cooperation.

Oswald Garrison Villard

Issues and Men

Sir Edward Grey

IT is never an easy thing to write of a deceased statesman. If you praise him, your eulogy is discounted, for plainly you do not wish to speak aught but good of a dead man. If you criticize him, then it is quite obvious that you are lacking in the essential decencies; you do not know that it is the worst possible taste to speak ill of a man who has hardly reached his grave. So you are expected not to tell the truth—even if the air is full of falsehoods about him. You are not to confute those lies when they are made, but are to wait until some more fitting time, presumably when his body has moldered in its grave and nobody cares any longer.

I am moved to these reflections by some of the comments on the death of Viscount Grey. Here is the New York *Evening Post* saying that in 1914 "Lord Grey stood to us as the symbol of the righteousness of the Allies and the unrighteousness of the Germans"; "he stood for the character and integrity of England against the atrocious Teutonic manhandling of the truth." Colonel E. M. House announces that "Lord Grey was one of the noblest figures I have ever known in public life. . . . His spoken word was as good as his written word. . . . With his death the world loses a statesman of the first rank, and one with an unsullied name." When I read such words as these it is not possible for me to stay my pen. For truth has greater rights than those of friendship, and I, for one, cannot but recall certain facts which cannot be spoken or written away—least of all by Colonel House.

What are they? First, that Sir Edward Grey, as he was known in 1914, was, more than anyone else, responsible for England's entering the war; and, second, that having made a binding verbal agreement with France to fight for it under certain contingencies and having repeatedly denied publicly that any such agreement existed, he demanded of the British people that they make the horrible sacrifice of their sons because of the commitments which rendered any other course incompatible "with the honor of the nation." As David Lloyd George, then Prime Minister of Great Britain, put it in the House of Commons on August 7, 1918, shortly before the Armistice:

> MR. LLOYD GEORGE: We had a compact with France that if she were wantonly attacked, the United Kingdom would go to her support.
>
> MR. HOGGE: We did not know that!
>
> MR. LLOYD GEORGE: If France were wantonly attacked.
>
> AN HONORABLE MEMBER: That is news.
>
> MR. LLOYD GEORGE: There was no compact as to what force we should bring into the arena. . . . Whatever arrangements we come to, I think history will show that we have more than kept the faith.

Mr. Hogge was wrong. He could and should have known that Mr. Lloyd George was right, for on August 6, 1914, at the very beginning of the war, Lord Lansdowne, speaking in the House of Lords, said that England must go to war for two reasons: "treaty obligations, and those other obligations which are not less sacred because they are not embodied in signed and sealed documents." He then continued:

> Under the one category fall our treaty obligations to Belgium. . . . To the other category belong our obligations to France—obligations of honor which have grown up in consequence of the close intimacy by which the two nations have been united during the last few years.

If further evidence is needed there is any amount of it. Marshal Joffre testified before a Paris commission on July 5, 1919:

> The intervention of England in the war had been anticipated. A military convention existed with England which could not be divulged as it bore a secret character.

In the French Chamber, on September 3, 1919, M. Franklin-Bouillon referred to the protection of the Anglo-French understanding of 1912, "which assured us of the support of six divisions." Lord Haldane, in his book "Before the War," stated that as far back as 1906 the military problem before him as Minister of War was "how to mobilize and concentrate at a place of assembly to be opposite the Belgian frontier" a British expeditionary force of 160,000 men. In the official records of the war, published in Great Britain, is to be found a memorandum of Sir Eyre Crowe to Lord Grey, dated July 31, 1914. He argued that it was quite correct to say that there was no written agreement binding England to France, but that the very existence of the Entente forged a *moral bond* compelling England to side with France and Russia: "This honorable expectation has been raised. We cannot repudiate it without exposing our good name to grave criticism." Lord Loreburn, in his book "How the War Came," says not only that there was an obligation, but that "the concealment from the Cabinet was protracted and must have been deliberate"—by the honorable Sir Edward Grey. There is the then Prime Minister, Asquith himself. Speaking on August 3, 1914, in the House of Commons, he said "that Great Britain was fighting to fulfil a solemn international obligation." If it be argued that he referred to the Belgian obligation, let us quote Austen Chamberlain in the House of Commons, February 8, 1922:

> We found ourselves on a certain Monday listening to a speech by Lord Grey at this box which brought us face to face with war and upon which followed our declaration. That was the first public notification to the country, or to anyone by the government of the day, of the position of the British Government and of the obligations which it had assumed.

This was not a pacifist who spoke, nor an anti-government and anti-war man, but Austen Chamberlain, the pro-war Conservative himself.

Now where did Sir Edward Grey stand during this time, this great lover of truth whose spoken word was as good as his written? On November 27, 1911, speaking in the House of Commons, he said:

> First of all let me try to put an end to some of the suspicions in regard to secrecy . . . We have laid before the

House the Secret Articles of the Agreement with France of 1904, and there are no other secret engagements. . . . For ourselves we have not made a single secret article of any kind since we came into office.

As Lord Arthur Ponsonby, to whose "Falsehood in War-Time" I am indebted for the preceding quotations, put it: "The whole of this is a careful and deliberate evasion of the real point." But assuming that Sir Edward Grey told the truth on that date, and that the commitment to France took place in 1912, the fact is that Sir Edward Grey continued his denials of any such alliance before the war, during the war, and after the war. For instance, on March 10, 1913, Lord Hugh Cecil said in the House of Commons:

> There is a very general belief that this country is under an obligation, not a treaty obligation, but an obligation owing to an assurance given by the Ministry in the course of diplomatic negotiations, to send a very large force out of this country to operate in Europe.

To this Mr. Asquith replied: "I ought to say that it is not true." But the unrest in the House of Commons would not down. On March 24, 1913, just two weeks later, Sir William Byles and Joseph King asked the Prime Minister what obligation there was "to France to send an armed force in certain contingencies to operate in Europe," and Joseph King asked "whether in 1905, 1908, or 1911 this country spontaneously offered to France the assistance of a British army to be landed on the continent to support France in the event of European hostilities." Again there came the official denial. When war came, however, Sir Edward Grey was of the first to declare that the honor of the nation was involved.

It then appeared that these agreements had not even been made known by him as Foreign Minister, or by Mr. Asquith as Prime Minister, to the entire Cabinet. Only a small group of ministers inside the Cabinet was permitted to know the truth. Even on August 3, 1914, Grey insisted "that we have no secret engagements which we should spring upon the House and tell the House that, because we had entered upon the engagement, there was an obligation of honor upon the country." In his book he defended the answers to the King-Byles questions by stating that they were absolutely true. "Parliament," he said, "has unqualified right to know of any agreements or arrangements that bind the country to action, or restrain its freedom. But it cannot be told of military and naval measures to meet possible contingencies." Compare this casuistry with Lloyd George's statement as late as April 7, 1930, when he praised Prime Minister MacDonald for his readiness to consult with the leaders of the Opposition concerning every phase of the negotiations of the Naval Disarmament Conference, and said: "We should know what we are being committed to because these commitments are matters of peace and war." Referring to 1914, he then said:

> If we were committed, we were committed to something which was very vague, but where it was a question of honor, whether there was a real commitment or not, we gave the benefit of the doubt to the others. We don't want those conditions to arise again. We don't want any commitment by which the French will assume we have incurred certain obligations which we did not intend to incur.

Needless to say, Viscount Grey, as he then was, never challenged these words of Lloyd George.

In the generations to come, if there is any reason left in the world after that World War to which England was committed so frivolously and so needlessly, people will everywhere wonder at a state of things by which the fate of a nation could be disposed of by a few high officials acting in complete secrecy. More than that, they will wonder that a Foreign Minister of Great Britain could be a man so little interested in the rest of the world that when the foreign affairs of the United Kingdom and its colonies and dominions were intrusted to him he had never but once set foot outside of Great Britain. Then he went over as a "tripper" to France for a Saturday and Sunday!

During the war nobody was more earnest in his propaganda to bring the United States into the conflict. No wonder Colonel House praises him. Together they had committed the United States to coming into the war in certain contingencies long before Mr. Wilson's campaign for reelection on the plank, "He kept us out of war." Not even Colonel House denies this now. One thing Viscount Grey wrote in a preface to "America and Freedom," an English edition of President Wilson's statements on the war, is worth quoting today:

> If the result of this war is to destroy in Germany the popularity of war—for before 1914 the prospect of war was popular, at any rate in books that were widely read there without resentment, if not with approval . . . then the world may have a peace and security that it has never yet known. . . . We want to be sure that when this war is over Germany will not begin to prepare and plan for the next war.

Lord Grey lived long enough to see Germany fall into the hands of a far more dangerous autocrat than the Kaiser ever dreamed of being. He lived to see Hitler and his associates pronounce war the greatest objective a country could possibly have, to see them expel or imprison all pacifists and the leading workers for the League of Nations, and begin the task of drilling and arming the youth of Germany from the age of ten years up, as they were never drilled by the militarists of the Kaiser.

In other words, he lived to behold, and Colonel House with him, the complete futility of all the bloody sacrifices of 1914-18 and the worse than futility of the so-called treaty of peace. If such men had real consciences—but let us not touch upon that. Perhaps their incredible belief in their own rectitude and infallibility and wisdom, and their admiration for one another's nobility and truthfulness, is a divine dispensation—so far as they are concerned. But the fact remains that between the nobility of the Kaiser, and the nobility of Lloyd George and Asquith, and the nobility of Sir Edward Grey and Colonel House and Woodrow Wilson and the Czar of Russia and a few others, liberty has perished in Germany, Russia, Italy, and Poland; and General Johnson assures us (last week in Chicago) that "the dictatorship in force in Russia, Germany, and Italy is repugnant to Americans, but we may have to resort to these methods if the NRA fails."

The next time international war comes, I'm in favor of having a few liars and dishonorable people in charge of several governments!

Oswald Garrison Villard

Issues and Men

Litvinov and Recognition

"MAXIM LITVINOV lacks Chicherin's formal diplomatic background and training; but he possesses a naturally keen mind, quick to seize a point in negotiation and slow to relinquish it." Thus writes William Henry Chamberlin in his book "Soviet Russia" of the man who has just landed in America to negotiate with Franklin Roosevelt for the recognition of the Soviet Government. He is a Jew, and he took part in the revolution with Lenin. He is, Mr. Chamberlin adds, "a portly, paterfamilias type of man, who, with his lively English wife, usually presides at the entertainments which the Foreign Commissariat gives in the ornate 'Sugar King's palace' directly facing the Kremlin. . . ." He is an effective speaker, or was when I heard him at the World Economic Conference in London last summer. He has sarcasm and wit, and he has used that sarcasm repeatedly with telling effect in the negotiations of the Disarmament Commission at Geneva.

There, in London, and elsewhere Litvinov has shone because he was able to make concrete and sincere proposals for disarmament and for economic rehabilitation. Had the Allies really meant business in the matter of disarmament, they must have seized upon the radical proposals made by Litvinov for general disarmament; had they done so, Hitler would not be in the strategic position he now occupies. In London Litvinov's offer of a billion dollars' worth of business from Russia to prime the various capitalistic machines, provided that proper terms were granted, was the only substantial contribution made at that abortive conference. If he succeeds on his present mission, the United States will get the bulk of that business, provided that the necessary arrangements are made for the credits for which Russia must ask. He was the only man who came back from the London conference with some real bacon, for he took the opportunity while the conference was wasting time to go over to Paris and carry on some important negotiations with the French government to improve mutual trade relations. He also negotiated non-aggression treaties with a string of border states from Afghanistan to Esthonia, induced Great Britain to abandon its embargo on Russian imports in return for the release of the two convicted British engineers, and borrowed $4,000,000 from the United States with which to buy American cotton. As *The Nation* said at the time: "He is the 'Boy Who Made Good' of the conference." More than that, he laid the foundations for the subsequent non-aggression treaty with Poland which is one of the wonders of the world.

The thing that has amazed me about the public reception of the President's announcement of his readiness to negotiate with Russia for resumption of relations is that there has been no terrific outburst of protest from the Daughters of the Revolution, the Sons of the Revolution, Ham Fish, or Ralph M. Easley. I thought that they would be holding mass-meetings at Carnegie Hall and making the heavens ring with denunciations of the proposal to take the bloody hands of the Russian Communists, the would-be destroyers of the sacred Christian religion and, what is worse, of the still more sacred right of private property. But there hasn't been a peep from them. The truth is that these people are in a hole because they belong professionally to the "stand-by-the-President-and-the-government" crowd. They are always for upholding the authority in Washington and ready to hang dissenters every day of the week. Now, if they oppose Russian recognition, they will be in the position of assailing the President in this grave crisis in our history. They will be "rocking the boat," something that no respectable S. A. R. or D. A. R. or stock-gambling bank president ever does.

Of course I do not mean to imply that the ever-vigilant Ralph Easley is asleep. Dear, no. That high-minded and liberal-spirited person has just sent out to the newspapers on behalf of a society with a short name—"The American Section of the International Committee to Combat the World Menace of Communism"—a pamphlet called "Communism in Germany" which, as its subtitle tells us, contains "the truth about the Communist conspiracy on the eve of the national revolution." In other words, this is a pro-Hitler pamphlet, by one Adolf Ehrt, intended to justify the Nazi revolution on the ground that it alone saved Germany from going Bolshevik. If this action does not entitle Mr. Easley to the historic German decoration of the Red Eagle, Third Class—if the Hitlerites have revived the medal which once hung so proudly on the breast of Nicholas Murray Butler—I do not know what could. And his associates on this committee? Why, they too are among our most progressive and public-spirited citizens, all old, dear friends: our modest, but not forgotten, Archibald E. Stevenson of the New York Committee to Investigate Seditious Activities; Harry A. Jung of the American Vigilant Intelligence Federation; Elon Huntington Hooker, chairman of the American Defense Society; and then our favorite New York Congressman, Ham Fish, Jr. These men will some day be heading us into the fascist camp and will justify their attempt to wreck the American republic on the ground that they had to do it to save us from these horrible Litvinovs and Stalins. Heaven bless their souls, they will never learn that the real dangers to America are the Albert Wiggins, the Charlie Mitchells, and their ilk, plus the Samuel Insulls and more of that stripe, to say nothing of the tariff barons and other ruthless exploiters of the American people.

Well, the world goes on and Litvinov is here to negotiate with the President, to the special chagrin of Ralph Easley's new ally, Adolf Hitler. To my mind there can be only one just criticism of Franklin Roosevelt in this connection, and that is that he did not recognize Russia on March 10, last. How amusing it would be if this new Russian business turned out to be just what was needed to prime and start up the great American industrial engine!

Oswald Garrison Villard

Issues and Men

The Nazi Child-Mind

COULD anything be more typical of a certain type of German mind than Hitler's "triumph" in the election just held? You suppress all opposition parties, you lock up in concentration camps your chief political opponents, you control the entire press, the radio, and the stage, you threaten anybody who dares oppose you, you send Brown Shirts to make sure that everybody votes for the only men you have permitted to be nominated for public office, and then when you have thus dragooned the voters into giving you a 92 per cent vote you turn to the rest of the world and say: "See how the entire nation stands behind me!" Only a German could be capable of this—only a German like Hitler who has never been abroad and, with his chief associates, has no knowledge or understanding of other peoples and their psychology. It is a childish performance which ranks with that incredible stupidity of 1917, when Herr Zimmermann of the Berlin Foreign Office sent a telegram to Mexico offering to give back to it the States of Arizona and New Mexico if it would enter the war on Germany's side. It was the result of the same mental processes as those which led Von Papen to assure Ludendorff and Hindenburg that the United States could not raise an army or send it to France in time to be of any use to the Allies and to forget all about the immediate financial aid which the United States could give within a week after joining forces. It is the same type of mind that subjects its prisoners to horrible cruelties in the prison camps, murders at least 2,000 unresisting persons, and then really believes that this can be kept from the rest of the world as easily as it has been kept from the German people as a result of the government's taking over and dominating the press. It is the same type of mind which not only swallows all the age-old, long-disproved lies about the Jews, but accepts the absurd pretense of Nordic and German superiority and racial purity and really believes in the myths which it thus makes its own.

It is precisely this immaturity of mind which makes it so hard to deal in the international field with a Hitler or a Göring. I do not doubt that the great mass of Germans who voted to support Hitler's withdrawal from the League of Nations and his demand that Germany be allowed to rearm were entirely and voluntarily with him. There was no need in their case to let it be known that if people did not vote promptly they would first be warned and then escorted to the polls. An equally unanimous vote on these questions could have been obtained by Dr. Brüning or any one of his predecessors. Of course every sane German has asked that Germany be restored to a position of equality with the nations which conquered it. It was never necessary to take a plebiscite on that. But if it had been, there would have been no need to destroy all the political parties in Germany save one in order to take it. If Hitler really thinks that his dragooned election told the rest of the world something it did not know, he is much less clever than has been supposed. Personally, I am surprised that the vote for him was not 100 per cent instead of a mere 92. Oh, yes, I know that he acquiesced in advance to a small minority in opposition so that he might contend that it really was a free election in which those who were opposed to him had the right to register their disapproval. But that can deceive no one. As it is, the only significant thing about the election is that the Catholic church did dare to advise its followers to oppose Hitler and that immediately after the election the former Chancellor Wilhelm Marx and other prominent Catholics were arrested on the same old charges of corruption which Hitler has brought against many and proved in only a few cases—why prove them when the mere bringing of charges sufficiently discredits your adversaries?

But while there is this astounding immaturity of mind, so unable to assay world opinion and to judge the effect upon it of any given action, it is idle to deny that in Hitler's case it is coupled with great shrewdness in dealing with his fellow-countrymen and unbridled mendacity and misrepresentation. Machiavelli has been outdone; the Hitler technique surpasses his. Some day when Germany has worked out of its present insanity, there will be a marvelous opportunity for someone to write a book about the lie and its use under Hitler. Never has there been a national movement so entirely built upon falsehoods and never have there been people so eager to swallow them as the exhausted and ill-treated Germans. The whole movement began with the lies that Germany was not defeated in the war but was ruined by Jews, pacifists, and Socialists who stabbed the army in the back at home, and that the Germans were in no wise guilty of bringing on the war, which like the peace of Versailles was the work of the international Jews. Here again you have the childlike mentality. These things go over because the Germans, always victims of an inferiority complex and always stirred because the rest of the world will not accept them at their own valuation as the greatest of all nations, are ready to believe anyone who plays up to their national prejudices and tells them what they wish to hear about their terrible maltreatment. If Hitlerism were not such a menace to the whole world, one would almost wish that the Germans might never awake out of their present dream.

One thing one must say for Hitler—he is the master-showman of the age. Mussolini has done quite a little in that line but Hitler has outdone him. I have just heard from two anti-Hitlerites, who were at Nürnberg for the great Hitler display, of the marvelous staging of the whole great scene, the tremendous sense of solidarity in the vast throng of Brown Shirts, the glorious singing, the dramatization of the whole ceremony of the laying of the wreath by Hitler upon the grave of the unknown soldier. They admitted that they were more deeply stirred and moved by this performance than by anything else they had ever seen. Hitler has outdone Barnum as he has proved that many more than one sucker are born every minute. Circuses Hitler has provided in full measure. Now the question is, How about the bread? Even a child-mind in a land of myths requires something substantial to exist. Despite his promises, Hitler has not appreciably reduced the number of unemployed, and the peasants of Germany are just as concerned with the low prices of their agricultural products as are our own farmers. From Bavaria comes news of growing dissatisfaction and unrest. That cannot be serious at present. It will be a long time before it is sufficient to exercise a modifying—or intensifying—effect upon Hitler. Meanwhile let the pressure go on! It must not be diminished by an iota.

Oswald Garrison Villard

Issues and Men

The United States and the Next War

MY prolific friend and former colleague on the New York *Evening Post,* Frank H. Simonds, has just published a startling book on the European situation in the light of Hitler, entitled "America Faces the Next War" (Harper and Brothers). Like myself Mr. Simonds has frequently been called a pessimist because he has been guilty of looking darkly upon the European situation, and like myself he has a number of fulfilled prophecies to his credit. His present book will not lead anyone to dub him an optimist. He is frankly of the opinion that there is going to be a "next war" in Europe. "Men may still assert," he writes, "that a new war in Europe has not yet become inevitable. With an even greater show of warrant they may argue that it is not today imminent, but what no man can longer deny with reason after the German election of November 12 is that war is a present possibility, and that, in 1934 as in 1914, European peace will be at the mercy of an incident." Mr. Simonds is entirely correct. You cannot sit down and say that war will come next spring, or next summer, or a year hence. Wars do not come that way, and this holds true even if there were some lucky guesses which fixed the coming of the war in 1914 pretty accurately. Wars are much more apt to come by such incidents as the blowing up of the Maine or the pistol shot at Sarajevo. And I am afraid that I must also associate myself with his belief that another war in Europe is on the cards. Before Hitler's potential army became a reality, there were 1,000,000 more men under arms in Europe than there were in 1914. We knew then that those swollen armaments must inevitably lead to war, and now we have not only larger armaments but the iniquitous Versailles treaty, against which Mr. Simonds has repeatedly spoken out admirably, to make altogether likely another world catastrophe. In addition, Germany is, to use Mr. Simonds's words, "in the hands of insane nationalists and mad racists, and those of its citizens who are still of sound mind are interned as dangerous to society."

But the most important part of Mr. Simonds's book is the last chapter, United States, Neutral or Belligerent. He is emphatic in his belief that if Europe is plainly marching toward a new war, "American statesmanship is just as unmistakably following a course which must presently make American participation in that conflict inevitable." His reasons for this belief are that in foreign affairs the New Deal is "only the old Wilsonism in a fresh disguise," with the single difference that Mr. Wilson wanted to end a European struggle and Mr. Roosevelt is trying to prevent one. He points out Mr. Wilson's two breaks with historic American policy: first, his expansion of American policy to include the question of peace for Europe, and, second, his taking the conduct of foreign relations out of the hands of the Secretary of State and putting it in those of his unofficial agent, Colonel House. Now, Mr. Simonds thinks, President Roosevelt by his participation in the League Disarmament Conference also includes European peace in the direct scope of American foreign policy, and is using Norman H. Davis in the same capacity in which Mr. Wilson used Colonel House. Frankly, I think this analogy forced. Mr. Roosevelt expanded but little our already existing participation in the Disarmament Conference; he let Mr. Davis talk instead of keeping silent, although present, at the proceedings. Nor can I feel that Mr. Davis's activities are quite as unofficial as were Colonel House's. Of course there should be no ambassador abroad not under the control of the State Department and authorized by Congress.

There the fact is, that Europe is heading for war and that American policy is not clearly defined. I have already stated in these pages my feeling that admirable as Mr. Roosevelt's record has been in many domestic fields, it has been a failure in international affairs, with the exception of Russian recognition. I feel that the danger to the United States is enhanced by the President's drifting in foreign matters, and by his inability to get time to think properly about our international complications, more than by any determination of his to be mixed up in the European situation. It must be admitted, however, that the result will be the same—whether we drift into another war or deliberately maneuver ourselves into it. Next, Mr. Simonds feels that all the American equivocation and ambiguity of recent years could have been avoided if our government had faced two facts: first, that all discussions of European armaments must be political, and, second, that America cannot achieve anything in this field without being willing to make definite commitments as to its own part in any future struggle. Mr. Davis did this last summer, when he promised that in the event of the Allies being attacked, the United States would alter its traditional policy on neutral rights to the advantage of those attacked. Finally, Mr. Simonds thinks that the spirit of Europe in 1933 is indistinguishable from that of 1914 in its irreconcilable nationalisms.

Lewis Gannett, of the New York *Herald Tribune,* has characterized Mr. Simonds as "one of the most exciting and excitable, provocative, informed, and prejudiced, brilliant and abusive writers on international affairs in America today." That is a very apt description of him, but it should not prevent anybody from reading this book and seeking the author's views on the situation which he outlines, but for which, however, he does not specify a remedy. Certainly there is nothing that demands more solemn thought on the part of the American people and the Administration than this problem. We have already challenged England by entering upon a new armament race, and England has answered that challenge, and so will Japan. All the more, therefore, we ought to outline publicly and promptly our policy in regard to Europe. We should say above all else that under no circumstances will the United States ever be brought into another European struggle; that its institutions are still rocking from the shock of the war into which Mr. Wilson put us so lightly; and that America must face the next war by keeping out of it at all costs.

Oswald Garrison Villard

Issues and Men

The President's Disarmament Opportunity

THE President has won deserved applause for his return to the question of peace and disarmament in his address at the Woodrow Wilson dinner of December 28. He then made the daring and wise proposal that the nations insure peace by pledging themselves to abolish offensive armaments and never to cross the boundaries of their neighbor states. If this program were followed, the whole aspect of the world would change. It would certainly be a test of the sincerity of the tiresome assertions by statesmen everywhere that they seek only the defense of their countries. If you listen to them, you can only wonder how it is that any wars ever take place. On the other hand, the military men employed by these gentlemen are always saying that the truest defense is a quick and overwhelming offense—a theory that Theodore Roosevelt was always harping upon. If President Roosevelt should ask the nations of the world to meet in convention and reinforce the Kellogg-Briand Pact by pledging themselves to his two latest proposals, we should certainly be able to find out whether the countries that are so certain—like our own—that they never, never are aggressors in international strife are genuine in their professions or not.

Now when the President made that speech he was perfectly aware that the Disarmament Conference at Geneva has had before it the major aspects of the proposal to discard offensive weapons which he mentioned. For in Geneva the effort has been to outlaw all bombing planes, poisonous gases, heavy artillery, and tanks. Plainly Geneva offers the opportunity to achieve one of the President's objectives. But, it may be said, the Geneva conference is dead, Germany has withdrawn from it, so why waste any more time upon it? The answer is that the Disarmament Conference is not dead, and that the withdrawal of Germany, largely due to internal political considerations, may as a matter of fact make it easier to negotiate with that country than if its delegates were at Geneva working in the open and closely watched by the excited public sentiment at home which Hitler has created and which, some people think, is now beginning to be a little worrisome and out of hand. Certainly there is every evidence that negotiations are still going on. The press reports direct communication between France and Germany. Whether the next step is achieved by direct negotiations or through the conference, the simple fact is that something has got to be done about the German demands and the general question of disarmament unless Europe is to drift aimlessly while Germany proceeds to arm in defiance of the Allies and the Treaty of Versailles. It may be an impasse at the moment, but the way out has got to be found unless everybody is to sit down and resign himself to the coming of the next war.

Here lies the President's great opportunity. Now would be the psychological moment for him to come to the front with a definite proposal for the solution of the Franco-German problem of the moment and with definite concrete suggestions concerning what the United States is willing to do. I am well aware that the Disarmament Conference is dealing with land armaments, but I would have the President bring in naval armaments as well without waiting for the next naval conference, now scheduled for 1935. I would have him take a leaf out of Secretary Hughes's book and electrify Geneva, as Mr. Hughes electrified the Washington Conference for the Limitation of Armaments by the practicality of his proposals. I would have him announce that he was recommending to Congress immediately the decrease by one-third of the United States army and the mustering out of 50 per cent of our reserve officers as evidence of our good faith, and that he was willing to stop the building of new ships and to accept the Hoover proposal for decreasing existing naval forces by one-third upon a similar agreement to act by England, Japan, France, and Italy, provided, furthermore, that France and Germany accepted a compromise proposal offered by the President to end the existing deadlock between those two countries.

It would be an enormous advantage if the initiative came from the United States, for that would save the face of the French and make it much less possible for Hitler to convince his people that the result was brought about by his aggressive stand against the Allies and his withdrawal from the Disarmament Conference, by which he frightened the French into a compromise arrangement concerning German rearmament. As for the exact form of the proposal, that would not be difficult to arrive at. I believe that the President and Norman Davis could very quickly work it out. My reason for this is that the Germans and French have twice been on the *very verge of agreement,* once just before the Tardieu Government fell and spoiled things, and again when the Germans withdrew from the conference. If they were so near to a satisfactory working plan then, they could hardly decline to accept one now, unless Hitler is determined to bring upon his country the hostility of all other nations.

While no one else is in such a strategic position to do this as the United States, it should be our policy first to ask Great Britain to join with us in this offer to Germany and France. But if for one reason or another England refused, we could and should go it alone. I believe that this offers a certain way, perhaps the only immediate way, out of the deadlock. Such a move, even if it were only partially successful as far as disarmament is concerned, would give a marvelous uplift to all Europe. Indeed, it would change its whole psychology, which is now rapidly drifting toward a state of mind which makes everybody speculate how soon another conflict will come. It would be a vital contribution toward economic recovery, for it would restore confidence in a sane future, and without confidence there can be no progress toward a genuine rehabilitation of Europe and our own country.

Oswald Garrison Villard

Issues and Men

Masters of the World

THE *Atlantic Monthly's* publication of the suppressed and lost William Bayard Hale interview with the Kaiser in 1908 is another evidence of the excellent journalism of its editor, Ellery Sedgwick. But the interview itself reveals little that is new. A mass of indiscretions which the German Foreign Office was well justified in suppressing at any cost, it confirms what is generally known of the Kaiser's looseness of tongue and affirms especially the picture drawn of him by Prince von Bülow in his "Memoirs." There is, however, one passage in it—the concluding one—which will be read with profound satisfaction in Germany:

> "The future," the voice rang out, "the future belongs to the White Race, never fear!" His shoulders squared, his eye flashed, I could see the eagle above his head. "It belongs to the Anglo-Teuton, the man who came from northern Europe—where you to whom America belongs came from—the home of the German. It does not belong, the future, to the Yellow, nor to the Black, nor to the Olive-colored. It belongs to the Fair-skinned Man, and it belongs to Christianity and to Protestantism. We are the only people who can save it. There is no power in any other civilization or any other religion that can save humanity; and the future—belongs—to—us!"

There you have the Nordic doctrine as it was in 1908; it did not keep the Nordics, plus many Latins, from tearing each other to pieces for four years and giving those dreadful colored races a clear and shining example of the innate superiority and Christianity of the Fair-skinned Man.

The Kaiser's Nordicism has been improved upon by Hitler, who has more and more restricted the term Nordic to Germans or those of the "pure" Germanic stock, with the United States excluded because it is a mongrel nation. Hitler's attempted excision of the Jew from German life is to be followed by the elimination of the Slavic influence, not an easy task when one recalls those millions of Germans east and northeast of Berlin who are deeply infiltrated with Slavic blood. But the determination is there. Nor has the German belief in the superiority of German Kultur and in the superior mental processes, ability, and innate righteousness of the German people been really shattered by the disasters of the World War. The Jews, Communists, and pacifists were responsible, according to Hitler, for bringing these Nordic supermen to the dust. But not Jews, or Communists, or pacifists put Germany into the war and alienated the entire world. The Kaiser and his Nordic generals did that.

Curiously enough, the most outspoken challenge to the assertions of the Kaiser and of Hitler that the Germans hold the future of the world comes from the other great fascist camp. It must make Hitler writhe to read such words as those which Mussolini uttered on April 21: "No people in any part of the world present such a spectacle as the Italian people; disciplined, informed, tenacious in their efforts, they have reached the horizon of their greatness." How unworthy and ridiculous this is! There is hardly a drop of Nordic-Germanic blood in Italy—even if there are blue-eyed and blond Italians. How can Mussolini dare to assert, not only what we have just quoted, but that the sixty-year program of internal and external expansion he has just outlined will give Italy the "primacy of the world"? There's the challenge for you, Herr Adolf! Of course Brother Hitler will reply that Nordics don't have to wait sixty years; that they have already arrived. Has not Dr. Joseph Goebbels, the Hitler Minister of Propaganda, in speaking of the Nazis' "historical mission," recently said: "I am convinced that what we are doing today is pioneering work for the whole civilized world. . . . What we do today will in ten years be a model for the whole world?" Hear that, Mussolini!

The truth is that not these nations alone believe that they are God's anointed. I have already quoted from Lord Beaverbrook's incomparable speech at Putney, England, in which he said: "Why did God raise up the British Empire? Why did God raise up the Israelites? Why has God maintained the British Empire during the tempests and trials of centuries? Why has God made us the greatest, finest, and most powerful people in the world?" (Loud applause.) Similar national egoists are to be found everywhere. Are not Americans without number certain that we are God's chosen people? The French, despised Latins as they are, have no doubt of the superiority of their culture, their literature, their language, their art, and their ideals. And on the other side of the globe the yellow Japanese (who, the Kaiser said in this new-old interview, were "devils, that's the simple fact"; whose headship of Asia "would be the worst calamity that could threaten the world") believe that they are by divine right the rulers of Asia, chosen as sacred instruments to teach the nasty-smelling Western pale-skins their place.

Fortunately, humanity may take heart in recalling that similar manias have had their day in the world and have passed out. In the current *American Mercury* S. Miles Bouton quotes Adam Müller, the romanticist, as writing this in 1809: "The great federation of European Powers shall come some day, and will fly the German colors, for all that is great, fundamental, and eternal in every European institution is German." The day of Müller has long since gone and no European federation, unless it is enslaved, will fly the German flag. Mr. Bouton concludes his article thus:

> The Nazi leaders declare that their Third Reich will endure "forever." If history has any meaning, and if all human experience is not a lie, they are mistaken by a good many millennia. The end will come sooner than horrified civilization, deceived by the "election" of November 12 and unaware of the hidden currents in Germany, as yet dares to hope. The only thing uncertain is whether the end will come through revolution or through war. If it be war, that will also be the end of Germany.

Oswald Garrison Villard

Issues and Men

Dr. Fosdick Renounces War

IN "penitent reparation" to the Unknown Soldier, the Reverend Dr. Harry Emerson Fosdick, undoubtedly the most influential clergyman in New York City, has gone the whole way in his denunciation of war. He has declared that he will "never again, directly or indirectly, sanction another war." He added, "I'll see you in prison first." Remembering what he did in France during the World War, he used these words:

> I renounce war because of what it does to our men. I've seen it. I renounce it because of what it forces us to do to the enemy. I renounce and will not sanction it because of its consequences and the undying hatred it nourishes. I renounce it and never again will I be in another war.
>
> I stimulated raiding parties to their murderous tasks. Do you see why I want to make it personal? I lied to the Unknown Soldier about a possible good consequence of the war. There are times I don't want to believe in immortality—the times I want to think that the Unknown Soldier never can realize how fruitless was his effort. The support I gave to war is a deep condemnation upon my soul. . . .
>
> The noblest qualities of human life, which could make earth a heaven, make it, in war, a hell. Men cannot have Christ and war at the same time. I renounce war.

It is true that Dr. Fosdick has talked in this vein for some time. His Christmas sermon went far indeed, but not as far as this. At New Haven, too, he spoke recently to the same effect, but now he has burned his bridges behind him. He has taken the irrevocable step. Others might voice such sentiments and recant in war time. Dr. Fosdick cannot and will not. To do so after this would be moral suicide.

This is a cause for genuine rejoicing. And so is the fact that five former army chaplains declared at the same conference at which Dr. Fosdick spoke, in the Broadway Tabernacle in New York, that they would not again serve in that capacity. They, too, are tired of urging men to kill other human beings, and then getting up in their pulpits and demanding allegiance to the Commandment "Thou Shalt Not Kill." We have the fact also, just brought out by the questionnaire of the *World Tomorrow*, that nearly 14,000 out of 20,000 clergymen have gone on record as saying that the church should not sanction or support any future war. The simple truth is that if war continues unchecked, the Christian church as we know it will go out of business. Lloyd George was for once right when he declared that if the churches of the United States and Great Britain permitted another war to come, they should padlock their doors for all time. There are some compromises that the modern church cannot survive.

Only a few weeks ago we had the student strike against war. Though it was pooh-poohed by the press, which played up certain amusing incidents at Harvard and elsewhere, it was a most promising beginning of a nation-wide agitation, and if its organizers profit by this year's experiences, it should be still more striking next year. Only one college president, Henry MacCracken of Vassar, was so wise and farsighted as to put himself at the head of a body of his students and march through the streets of the adjacent city, but perhaps others will follow his example another year. Only the other day I met a mother whose son brings home from Yale many of his classmates. She told me that they were eager to sit up until one or two o'clock every night discussing the situation of the world and their own poor prospects in it. I asked if they were radically minded, and she said that they were not, but that there was one thing they seemed to be absolutely united on—they would not permit themselves to be drafted into war, and they were working on plans for avoiding any such draft.

So we have had no little snarling in these last weeks from some of the few clergymen who still believe that the Prince of Peace can best be served by wholesale murder, and from military officers, who are naturally furious. The latter can never criticize their opponents without abuse, misrepresentation, and attribution of bad motives. What has become of the chivalry of the warrior of which we used to hear so much? Here, for example, is a Major A. P. Simmonds of the United States Army, retired, who declares that anti-war propagandists are "either too yellow to fight, or want to grab off something." This was in an address to the Government Club in New York City. Colonel H. P. Hobbs, Chief of Staff of the First Division, declared that the recent peace parades in various schools and colleges were "un-American"! It is un-American to preach against war and march against war, although this colonel and many others were called out in the last war in order to end war! Was it un-American and unpatriotic of Mr. Wilson to hold that up to us as the objective of the struggle?

Of course the reactionary clergymen feel themselves more than ever called upon to defend their position. Dr. Henry Darlington, that wise shepherd of the Church of the Heavenly Rest, who so warmly applauded the lynching in California last winter until he found that his congregation would not stand for it, and then decided that he had spoken too hastily, has discovered that "religion and patriotism go hand in hand, while atheism invariably accompanies radicalism and bolshevism. It is true, also, that pacifism has a passion for treason."

The anger of the militarists is perfectly understandable. They know that our people are quite aware that our going to war was a useless crime against America, that we got nothing out of it but misery, and that it nearly ruined the Republic we love. It must gall them to read that of the class of 1924, of Yale University, now ten years out of college, and therefore between thirty-one and thirty-four years of age, 43 per cent have just voted that they will not take up arms to defend the United States even if it is attacked. How magnificently encouraging this is!

Oswald Garrison Villard

Issues and Men

The Shamelessness of Newton D. Baker

WHEN the World War broke out I organized almost at once a "League to Limit Armaments." It started with a bang. About the first acceptance I got was from Newton D. Baker. The membership was distinguished, for the horror felt at the first terrible news had not yet been displaced by angry and bitter and deluded partisanship for one side or the other. People then placed the blame upon the huge armaments of all the European nations.

That scene in a private dining-room of the Railroad Club in New York came back to me the other day when I read in the newspapers that almost my first member of the short-lived league had appeared before the House Military Affairs Committee to demand the immediate increase of the United States Army by 2,063 officers and no less than 47,000 men. But he wasn't satisfied with that. He told the committee that "he could not imagine an army less than five times the present size of ours having the slightest effect on the military policy of any other nation. It is a waste of public money to have an army that is anything less than adequate." He then went on to admit that at the end of the war to end war he had urged Congress to establish at once an army of 500,000 men as the necessary force, but that Congress had been "wiser and luckier than I" in not granting his request of that time. That did not prevent him, however, from assuring Congress on May 28, 1934, that 14,063 officers and 179,063 men were the exact number of men we need in our army now to preserve our country intact. Not 170,000 nor 180,000 but exactly 179,063. All your militarists know exactly how many ships and men will save us.

Then this great statesman and ex-member of the League to Limit Armaments reminisced. He who had made such eloquent speeches as he drafted young Americans to their death in 1917, with the solemn promise to them and their parents that if they would only go out and die this war would end war and make the world safe for democracy, now recalled that at the end of the war "it was reasonable to suppose that another would break out. We had the Thirty Years' War as an example. The most able historians thought that the Armistice marked the end of an episode, and that a fresh grouping of nations would again attempt war." So there you have it. Just when Woodrow Wilson was congratulating the country that we had ended war and were about to make over the world, when we were burying the Unknown Soldier with such pomp and ceremony because he had laid down his life to do away with armaments, Newton Baker, in consultation with "the most able historians," was convinced that all that he and the chief he still reveres had said to the American people about the purposes of the war was just so much bunk and hokum.

But the recent works of Newton Baker do not end with his testimony before the House committee. Two weeks later he delivered the commencement address at West Point, just before handing the commissions to the largest class that ever graduated. Did he devote that speech to a demand for the reform of one of the costliest, worst-run, and most inefficient educational institutions in the world? He did not. He went back to the past again. He said:

> Democracy is the most perfect form of government ever devised by men, and the most difficult. We can have it only as long as we are worthy of it. One country after another in Europe has bundled up all the authority of government and taken it away from the people and handed it to some despotic form of dictatorship or dictatorial oligarchy. It is not because they undervalue democracy but because democracy is possible only to highly educated people.

So here we have the final and lasting truth. Here we have the exact reason why the Germans, admittedly the most highly educated people in the world, have abandoned democracy. Here we have the exact reason why the Americans, with their shamefully high percentage of illiteracy, have made as much of a success of democracy as they have. When Newton Baker talked drivel of this kind, perhaps he thought that he must talk down to the intellectual level of West Point. If not, he has certainly undergone a sea change in his mental processes. I am aware that many people will ask: "Can't you let a man honestly and sincerely change his mind on a matter as grave as that of armaments?" But the trouble is that Newton Baker has changed his mind all along the line. From having been an ardent disciple of Tom Johnson in his efforts to free the people from corporation domination, he has become the lawyer and chief counselor of the Van Sweringens, one of whom is under indictment for some of his activities in connection with the brothers' financial overlordship of Cleveland. The man who was a reform mayor of Cleveland, ready to starve for his ideals, is now one of the leaders of the party machine and a rich man, as the result of having thrown overboard those youthful ideals.

But nothing seems to be so shameful as his admission that the slogans which he and Woodrow Wilson used to put us into the war were pure bunk intended to deceive. He does not even pretend that they were honestly mistaken or misled. He admits that he knew it wasn't going to be a war to end war when he was giving his allegiance to that doctrine. I heard him make his eloquent speech at the Madison Square Garden convention in which he told how it had wrung his heart to the depths to tear American boys away from their parents and send them to their deaths. He did it so well that men all around me wept. Why did he not tell us then that the war slogans were bunk? If he lives long enough and fascism comes to America, I will bet one hundred to one that he will come out for it and assure us that while democracy "is the most perfect government ever devised by men," we can have it no longer because, in his judgment, we are not worthy of it.

Oswald Garrison Villard

Issues and Men

The Strange German Character

THE blood-bath in Germany by means of which Hitler has "purged his party" of its alleged mutineers—as to whose guilt no evidence has as yet been allowed to reach the outer world—cannot fail to do the German people harm wherever the news of it is read. For, as *The Nation* has said, those horrible reports cannot be laid at the doors of Jewish libelers or foreign enemies; fifty deaths are now officially admitted, which means that the actual number must be very much larger. This standing up and shooting after three-minute trials of leaders who the day before were among the elect of the Hitlerites, or the outright murder of others like General von Schleicher and his wife, we might expect in a Balkan state or in a South American revolution, but never in a country which boasts of its high *Kultur* and its civilization. These horrors will only start up afresh, and seem to justify the wartime-atrocity propaganda stories of the Allies. They will stamp Hitler for all time as a bloody tyrant who lost his head and slaughtered left and right without any thought of what this would do to Germany's standing before the world. They will raise up dozens of enemies for him in the Storm Troop ranks for every leader that he kills. Murder on this scale inevitably begets more murder.

Yet so odd is the German character that I have no doubt that we shall have thousands of prominent Germans applauding Hindenburg's telegrams of approval to Goering and Hitler and having no difficulty whatever in rationalizing acts which they would be the first to denounce as evidence of purest barbarism had they occurred in any other country than their own. I expect also that in Germany and among myriads of German-Americans there will be plenty who will swallow the statement of that silly ass, Dr. Hanfstängl, that Hitler by his murders saved not only Germany but all the world. His reasoning is, I suppose, that if Hitler had fallen Germany would have been lost and without Germany the world could not survive. This again reflects the amazing processes of the German mind. Hanfstängl probably thinks that the fiction that Hitler by his accession to power saved Europe as well as Germany from communism was widely believed here and there and that this theme of Germany's noble saving of the world by killing mutineers without counting the cost will also render service in whitewashing men who are, if the truth be told, among the worst and bloodiest criminals in the world.

Only last week I received a letter from an old friend in Germany, the wife of a distinguished university professor in a Hanoverian city, repeating the old story that "if the National Socialists had not won, bolshevism would not only have conquered Germany but all of Europe perhaps with the exception of Italy." "So," she added, "the National Socialist success was our sole salvation from complete bolshevist barbarism." Undoubtedly the writer believes this absurdity; there is a certain childishness and gullibility in the German character which makes their minds more susceptible to mass psychology than even the American mentality—as Hitler has demonstrated so clearly. I have no doubt my correspondent will similarly agree with Hanfstängl that Hitler has again saved the world by slaughtering those fifty good and true, pure-blooded, and blond Aryans, without a drop of Jewish blood in their veins, of whom she and all National Socialists were so proud until recently. Until, in fact, Hitler a fortnight ago decided to butcher them—as the noble fifty had previously imprisoned, tortured, and butchered in those happy days of March and April, 1933, when they were free to wreak their vengeance upon any and all pacifists, Socialists, Communists, and all other individuals whom they disliked. Salvation from bolshevist barbarism? Good heavens, how can one differentiate morally between the slaughtering of the bolshevists, between Mussolini's atrocious blood-letting in the early days of his regime, and these foul crimes of Hitler? There may have been more in Russia than anywhere else but that does not mitigate the guilt of Hitler and Goering a single iota. I shall write my correspondent that barbarism already rules in the Third Reich and that it will be amazing, indeed, should the threatened economic disaster come on top of the Hitler murders, if we do not yet see the establishment of a communist government in Germany, and not in the far distant future either.

Yet I have no doubt that in the face of all this barbarity, the odd German character will manifest itself anew by more of the unending bitter complaints that we have had ever since 1914, that the world does not understand Germany, that it is unjust to it, that it is so credulous as always to believe the worst of Germany. There will continue to be the same bewildered protests that the Germans are not accepted by the rest of the world at their own rating as the greatest and most cultured race in all the world, who, as Hitler has said, are a people divinely appointed to lead the human race to greater heights than have ever been achieved before. They will resent bitterly the world's irresistible outcry because the assassins of General von Schleicher "accidentally killed" his wife when they killed him. Ludwig Lewisohn put it rightly some months ago when he wrote in a magazine article that the Germans were suffering from a hopeless inferiority complex; that their greatest cross is that they cannot win the good-will of the rest of the world and the recognition of their complete superiority to everybody else.

Oh, the pity of it! The pity that a people of such great qualities, such lovable traits when taken individually, that such kindly and well-meaning millions so gifted in all fields of science, industry, and invention, are impelled by some terrible daemon to put themselves always in the wrong, to ruffle the feelings and outrage the sensibilities of the rest of the world they seek so eagerly to win to a recognition of their own innate kindliness and desire for righteousness!

Oswald Garrison Villard

Issues and Men

Hitler's "Me und Gott"

IT is impossible to read Hitler's defense of his atrocious murders without taking heart. I am aware, of course, that he has strengthened himself at home for the moment by his horrible acts. When a dictator slaughters like that he stuns his country and, for the moment, paralyzes opposition. I have read of the cheers and approval with which his statement was greeted in the Reichstag and in the press, and how the latter is falsely misrepresenting to the German people the burning indignation of the public opinion of the world. Nonetheless, knowing the Germans as I do, I cannot but feel that this orgy of blood-letting marks the beginning of the end of Hitler. It may take a long time to rid the country of him; but, as Wendell Phillips once said apropos of slavery, "so, when the tempest uproots a pine on your hills, it looks green for months—a year or two. Still it is timber, not a tree." Hitler remains as dictator, but no longer the defiant head of a people which he insisted was united to the last man. A tyrant who begins to kill traitors must more than ever be on the look-out for their friends, their sympathizers, their relatives, their avengers.

Again, there must be some reason left in Germany, and just as Verdun opened the eyes of millions of the Kaiser's subjects, who had still been living in the intoxication of the "absolutely united Germany" of the first war years, to the hopelessness and folly of the German cause, so Hitler's speech—to say nothing of the cause of it—must give sight to many hitherto blind. For if there is any logic left among his adherents, if they are able at all to analyze in cold blood Hitler's speech, the following facts established by the tyrant himself—not by any critic or enemy—stand out clearly:

I. As the Kaiser identified himself with God, so Hitler declares: "In this hour I was responsible for the fate of the nation, thereby the supreme court of the German people during these twenty-four hours consisted of myself." Me und Gott!

II. Hitler admits that he knew in May of the traitorous plans of his chief of staff, Captain Roehm, and that he let him *from then on* continue to weave his plot instead of immediately dismissing—or killing—him and thus preventing his corruption of other Storm Troop leaders and persuading them to their deaths.

III. Hitler admits that he had known since May that Roehm "and the circle devoted to him broke all the laws of decency and simplicity, but it was even worse that his poison began to spread in ever enlarging circles." But Hitler allowed the poison to spread for two months longer, precisely as he had always known that in making Roehm, the open pervert, chief of staff he put into one of the highest offices a man whose homosexual love letters had been *published and satirized* freely in the German press as far back as 1932. He also admits that Heines, Hayn, Heydebreck, and Ernst were all of this type—yet he made them leaders and exemplars to the Storm Troops, upheld and glorified them *until they turned against him.*

IV. Hitler admits that in his Storm Troops there was (a) licentiousness, (b) corruption, (c) dissipated living—in his own words "bad conduct, drunken excesses, and interference with decent, peaceable folk—and (d) favoritism, which worked great injury, "the oldest and most faithful Storm Troopers were pushed more and more into the background." Yet the Storm Troopers were absolutely the creation and creatures of Adolf Hitler, who, by his own admission, took no steps to end the demoralization of his private army of which he says he was aware months and months ago—which speaks volumes for his worth as an executive and a leader.

V. Hitler admits the execution of "three special guard members who had made themselves guilty of disgraceful maltreatment of prisoners taken into protective custody"; similar entirely substantiated charges of torture and murder of prisoners have been known to Hitler but denied by him from the very beginning.

VI. Hitler admits that he caught no one red-handed; that not one single overt act had been committed before he struck, and he glories in the fact that his victims were shot on the shortest possible notice, or, as in the case of Von Schleicher and his wife, without notice at all.

VII. Hitler passes over the deaths of the Catholic leaders murdered by him without the slightest reference to them or attempt to connect them with the alleged plot.

VIII. Hitler admits the gravity of the economic situation which in his earliest speeches he was going to cure at once and he has to fall back upon the absurd theory that Germany can be saved from disaster by the skill and inventiveness of her chemists and scientists who are to provide substitutes for cotton, wool, rubber, manganese, aluminum, the precious metals, and all the other raw materials upon which Germany depends.

But finally, and most important of all, is the fact that, like all dictators in history, Hitler after a year and a half of power has so completely identified himself with the state as to make any move against him personally a crime against the state. The Roehm revolt, if such there was, was not aimed at the German people or at the German state; Hitler declares that they wished to get rid of him and that they wished to make the Hitler revolution really the radical, National Socialist one Hitler fooled millions into believing that it was to be. All sane Germans cannot fail to see this, nor to realize that, having got rid of the Kaiser, they have placed over them a man who has now made himself the supreme authority beyond and above all law and courts and has arrogated to himself power of life and death over any one whom he may accuse of conspiracy against him. I cannot yet believe that in the long run the German people will stand for anything of the kind.

Oswald Garrison Villard

Issues and Men

The War Anniversary

I HAVE read carefully various articles on the twentieth anniversary of the beginning of this world's nearly successful attempt to commit suicide, and am heartened by the absence of braggadocio and by the frankness with which the loss of the war is now admitted. For example, writing in the New York *Herald Tribune,* Leland Stowe sums up the net results of our attempt to end war by more war and to safeguard democracy by mass murder as follows:

> Twenty years after the outbreak of the war "to make the world safe for democracy" 354,000,000 out of Europe's 550,000,000 people are living under dictatorships in twelve European countries, and democracy is banished from four-fifths of Continental Europe. Twenty years after August 1, 1914, Europe's political and social foundations are beset by the most serious disintegration yet recorded in the peace times of the twentieth century. Today, more than ever, Europe soberly realizes that the peace treaties have brought anything but peace.

Sir Philip Gibbs has this to say—he has done valiant service for the truth since he first announced that "Now It Can Be Told":

> Looking round the world today one sees no assurance of peace. The nations are arming again. Men who remember the last war seem to be preparing for the next. *Nothing was learned, nothing was settled, by that monstrous struggle.* The ruin of it still exists. The economic downfall of civilization is due to that and to nothing else, because of the heritage that was left in men's minds and the destruction of intelligence.

Then we have Senator Borah's frank speech of July 4:

> We went into a foreign war, a war having its roots in wholly foreign policies. We left our dead on foreign soil. Those policies of those countries remain the same. Europe is no nearer peace than before. We have our dead and crippled, our maimed and insane, our wrenched and twisted institutions, while Europe retains her bitterness, her dissension, her old balance of power. . . . The Versailles treaty was a result of the war we helped to fight—one mad round of war and vindictiveness and dictatorship and repudiation seems to be the most pronounced result of our entrance into European affairs.

But vastly more thrilling to me than this was the recent confession of a friend who was a high official in the Wilson Administration. With some trepidation I asked him if his conscience did not trouble him when he lay awake nights because of his vote to put us into the war, he having just said that "all our financial and economic troubles are due to our having gone into the war." Without a moment's hesitation he answered me with two words, "It does." Naturally I recalled to him how some of us had labored with the Administration in 1917 not to make the ghastly mistake of committing us to a European war with which we had really nothing to do, and how we were derided and accused of being pro-German for doing so. Those were tense days in Washington! Those who wanted to put us into the war were like bloodhounds after their prey. They were brutally intolerant and ready to smash anyone who opposed.

I was struck, too, by the absence of paeans to Woodrow Wilson in the articles I read. There are still plenty of his admirers; few now fail to admit the loss of the war and of its objectives but many still look upon him as a great leader whose defeat at Paris is not to be laid at his door but to be attributed to the malevolence of Henry Cabot Lodge and to Orlando, Lloyd George, and Clemenceau. How can one fail to indict Wilson's judgment when one reads Mr. Stowe's summary, when one witnesses the complete breakdown of the Disarmament Conference, the virtual collapse of the London Naval Agreement, the increased armaments everywhere? In his admirable little volume just published by Macmillan entitled "Europe Between Wars," Hamilton Fish Armstrong quotes General Tasker H. Bliss—a real statesman in uniform—as replying thus when Newton Baker, of the War Department, at a critical moment in the war asked him his view of its duration: "By the analogy of other great wars, I should say thirty or forty years. There may be a pause—an armed truce—while both sides lick their wounds and collect their forces. . . . But then the war will go on until one side or the other is obliterated as a fighting force, or until civilization ends in a chaotic breakdown." Is not this remarkable prophecy dreadfully ominous today?

The defenders of Wilson will now rise to ask how I or anyone else could possibly have expected him to read in the stars all that was to happen. "He had to judge the things as they were," is the usual phrase. Yes, but his speech of January 22, 1917, conclusively showed that he then read the stars correctly. For he declared that there must be "no victors and no vanquished," because if there were victors, there would be a dictated peace which would not last. That was a much more remarkable prophecy than the vision of General Bliss. What caused him to change his mind is the great mystery of Woodrow Wilson. I have asked a number of his intimates, but they can throw no light on the subject.

But these are backward looks. Today we face the disasters the war produced. We read of General Göring's plan to overrun and conquer all of Europe by means of aerochemistry and airplanes. Ernst Henri declares that "the new vast German aeroplane industry which has arisen in a few months in the middle of Europe . . . can turn out 2,000 machines every four weeks." These will carry 5,000 kilos of new gas which no gas mask can ward off, and also great loads of plague bacilli, cholera vibrions, pneumococci, and influenza germs, "which are being cultivated by special Brown staffs." When one reads things like this, even though they may be exaggerated, the mind stands still. Twenty years after 1914 the world plans its complete destruction!

Oswald Garrison Villard

Issues and Men

The Boycott of Germany

FROM a distinguished American of long European experience come these words: "The net result of the silly boycott of German goods has enabled Schacht with some justice to postpone payment of interest on our debt there, and in addition has cost us scores of millions of dollars per year in American trade with Germany." There is considerable truth in these words. Schacht, who is now the complete financial and economic dictator of Germany, has just put it this way: "If German goods are being barred or boycotted, the foreign bond-holder and the foreign exporter are the losers. When we are boycotted commercially and defamed politically it is not Germany that suffers but the Australian wool grower, the American cotton planter, the yarn spinner in Lancashire, the Scottish herring fisher, and the Spanish orange grower." Again, this is partially sound, because it is perfectly true that we cannot sell American goods to Germany unless we are willing to take German goods in return. But Germany does suffer and Schacht knows it. I have never failed to admit that a boycott is a two-edged sword, and that, if carried far enough, it may create a dangerous situation which might even conceivably lead to hostilities. None the less, the fact is that the boycott of Germany has grown out of a world-wide belief that Germany has gone temporarily insane, and that some measure must be taken to let its people know that the moral indignation of the world is deeply aroused and is finding a way of making itself felt commercially.

It would of course be a great deal better if the boycott could be restricted to the spiritual field: if public opinion could be so aroused as to make things extremely uncomfortable for Germans traveling abroad; if there could be a complete shunning of Germany by foreigners. That would be one way of bringing home to the German people the feelings of the rest of the world. This is difficult because Hitler and Goebbels completely control the German press. They do not allow the publication of any facts relating to the boycott or its extensive character. It was months before Hitler would mention it. Then he said only that the boycott in the United States and Great Britain "was dying out"—one of the *Führer's* innumerable lies. But so serious has been the development of the boycott that Schacht himself sees it can no longer be ignored or pooh-poohed or attributed merely to the international Jewry. In the desperate economic straits in which Germany finds itself, it has become necessary—or expedient—for Schacht to let the outside world know how concerned he is over the boycott.

If this costs the United States, England, and other countries millions of dollars, I cannot see that that is necessarily the decisive factor. On the contrary, it seems rather creditable that nations and individuals are willing to undergo a loss rather than do business with those who have reduced Germany to its present low estate. In the United States we are accused of being a country that puts dollars above ethics, and everything else. If large numbers of our business men, our importers, and our dry-goods stores are unwilling to handle German goods, does it not show that we have some idealism and moral indignation left, and that in the commercial boycott we are beginning to forge a new weapon in international relations? That goes far deeper than the question of whether we are cutting off our nose to spite our face in imposing the German boycott. I am sorry for the loss of business, especially during this depression, but the policy of international protest seems to me far more important. Moreover, if we could only end the senseless deadlock with Russia, we should speedily get enough business from that country to offset our voluntary loss of sales to Germany.

As long as the Hitler Government remains, it is a menace to the peace and welfare of the world, to democratic institutions, to liberty and humanity everywhere. Why have we not the right, therefore, to utilize any peaceful weapon we may have to bring about its downfall, or, if that is not possible, at least to let multitudes of Germans know how outraged some people—almost all of them formerly warm friends and supporters of Germany—are by what is taking place in that country today? Hitler's control of the press cannot possibly conceal the facts from the bulk of the German business world. They know what is going on even if the prostituted German press cannot talk about it.

I have never believed in Schacht, even when he properly pleaded that Germany be freed from the economic fetters of the Treaty of Versailles. It is my belief that if a Communist government were to arrive in Berlin and were to ask him to continue to head the Reichsbank, he would serve it as loyally as he is serving Hitler, and as he formerly served the republic until he was supplanted in the Reichsbank by Dr. Luther. It is almost amusing now to find him coming out into the open and saying that he has not the slightest thought of living up to the recent special agreements for payment to England, France, and other countries. In a special interview printed on August 26 he said of these arrangements: "They just simply won't work. . . . They are unreasonable and unfeasible." Then why did Germany sign these agreements? To sign them and then immediately to repudiate them is to make his nation's word no better than a dicer's oath. The *Times* has recently recalled Schacht's utterances in his book "The Stabilization of the Mark" and in a speech delivered in New York in October, 1930, in which he declared that whoever invested any money in Germany after the war in any form "will not be disappointed, because Germany will pay the debt. And I include the . . . Young loan . . . because it does not matter what the reasons for that loan were . . . it matters only who has invested his money in that loan." And now he deliberately says there will be no payment of Dawes or Young bond coupons, and that, as for the principal, there will be an indefinite moratorium.

Oswald Garrison Villard

Issues and Men

The International Traffic in Arms

WHEN it comes to internationalism, pure and unadulterated, commend me to your big business men. You can always count on them to stand up in a merchants' association meeting or that of a chamber of commerce and denounce those misguided persons who believe that in international organization lies the chief hope of saving our present civilization. The internationalist of this type your business man classifies with Communists and everything else unpleasant. But, good heavens, when it comes to *practicing* internationalism you can't beat the banker, the manufacturer, the exporter, and the importer. They don't know any national lines when it comes to doing business, and they are absolutely opposed to giving any consideration whatever to international good-will or sound international policies if these conflict with their getting the almighty dollar. They don't care a straw to whom they sell airplanes, submarines, poison gas, rifles, munitions, battleships, or anything else. They are after the business and they propose to get it.

Senator Bone described the situation very accurately when he let out to the reporters who are covering the arms inquiry in Washington what some of the manufacturers were saying privately to the members of the committee. Senator Bone declared that these "merchants of death" admitted *in camera* to the committee that they knew this armament race we are engaged in was going to bankrupt the world, but that if they did not sell munitions somebody else would, so what was all the fuss and bother about? You cannot, of course, make a man like President Carse of the Electric Boat Company see that there is something immoral in licensing submarines to Germany contrary to the Treaty of Versailles. You cannot make the gentlemen of the aircraft companies, who are selling airplane engines to Germany by the hundreds, feel that there is something wrong in rearming a country with which we fought only a few years ago and whose subsequent disarmament we helped to decree.

I know the defense put up by these airplane gentlemen—that the airplane engines were for commercial aircraft. But there isn't anything selective about such an engine. If it can pull an airplane through the air from Berlin to London in two hours and a half with a load of passengers, it doesn't refuse when asked to repeat the trick with a load of soldiers and bombs. Of course it is not beyond the bounds of possibility that these same engines may some day be directed by men engaged in hurling bombs upon American soldiers. This seems utterly impossible now, but so did our going into the World War seem beyond the range of reason. Here again I suppose the answer will be that if we Americans don't give the Germans the airplanes they want somebody else will. Nor must it be thought that only Americans behave this way. We are all tarred by the same brush, especially England, which has apparently forgotten that the noble army that it sent to the Dardanelles was torn to pieces by British-made shells fired from British guns supplied by the British armament trust. Of course British gun-makers would explain that they never dreamed that there would be war between England and Turkey, but that is surely no alibi. I have not the slightest doubt that the British armament makers will be perfectly willing to supply Adolf Hitler with all the armaments that he can use and pay for without stopping to consider whether those armaments will not some day in the future be used against the flower of Great Britain. And not merely the flower of its youth. Bombs are no more selective than airplane engines. If English-made bombs are dropped on England in the next war they will fall on English women and children as well as on English men.

It is refreshing, therefore, to have Secretary Hull declare that his department is absolutely opposed to the export of arms or munitions to Germany. He was able to prove that he had taken this position as far back as August 5, 1933, and that he had notified an aircraft company on September 11, 1933, that "this government would view the export of military planes from this country to Germany with grave disapproval." But let us go farther than that. Let us forbid the export of arms in every direction, and then let us go ahead and declare a national monopoly of the business of making weapons of death. It would help us enormously in meeting the problem of the gangster, who has no more difficulty in buying sub-caliber machine-guns from the company that makes the Thompson weapons than has Holland or Germany or any other country. During the war Lloyd George solemnly promised a delegation of coal miners that if, thanks to the Almighty, England won the war, he would immediately proceed to nationalize the manufacture of all deadly weapons. I suppose that people will say that this is chimerical, that the nation must have private manufacturing establishments capable of making arms, which on the outbreak of war may be immediately set to producing ing shells, hand-grenades, mines, and all the rest. Others will argue that if the government takes over this industry it will immediately create great factories and insist upon these arsenals working steadily and piling up more and more munitions, with the local politicians helping in order to get more jobs for their respective voters.

Beyond doubt these are arguments worth considering. But surely something must be done about the present internationalism of the munitions makers and their stirring up of war scares and armament rivalries. This is nothing but a form of anarchy. Are we going to sit down and admit that we are doomed to that anarchy and that reasonable human beings can work out no other way of life? If so, the world is not only going bankrupt, as the munitions makers admitted to Senator Bone, but the nations are going to kill each other off.

Oswald Garrison Villard

Issues and Men

The Peace Cause Moves On

DESPITE all the discouragements, the movement for peace goes on. Who can doubt it who follows the activities of our chief church organizations? Year by year some of them become more militant, more determined in their opposition to all war. What lover of peace can read the pastoral letter just published by the House of Bishops of the Protestant Episcopal Church without joyous amazement? Here is what they say about the abominable armament business:

> The passions that are stimulated by greed and unholy ambitions have found fresh expression, and are fostered and promoted by the infamous practices of the manufacturers of munitions and armaments, whose soulless enterprise knows neither friend nor foe in the prosecution of its nefarious ways. For greed of gain and wickedness of design the industry has no parallel in modern times. It foments strife, fans the flame of hatred, embroils nations in bitter rivalries, and uses the ill-gotten wealth at its command to inspire fear and to provoke war. It is a major factor in creating unrest and generating suspicion among peoples.

If that does not sound exactly as if it had come from the columns of *The Nation,* what could? It is what we have been saying for years. But let us read further in this pastoral letter:

> War is outlawed and solemn peace pacts affirm it. . . . As Christians we can have no part in any program which is designed to violate these principles enunciated by the Prince of Peace. War is murder on a colossal scale.

That is precisely what some of us were saying all during the World War at no little risk, and it is of course directly contrary to what Bishop Manning and that eminent Episcopal rector, Dr. Darlington of New York, have been teaching right along. But the bishops do not stop there. Many of them upheld the World War. They have seen the light, and here is what they now say:

> The testimony of the Great War shows the wicked folly of such a struggle, and its aftermath has shattered the world's hope and issued in confusions and disorder, the magnitude of which we are yet incapable of measuring.

Dr. Darlington, who is chaplain of New York's crack cavalry regiment, should be interested in this assertion of the bishops:

> The Christian Church cannot and will not deny loyalty and fealty to its Lord by being partner in any scheme, national or international, that contemplates the wholesale destruction of human life. *It refuses to respond to that form of cheap patriotism which has as its slogan: "In times of peace prepare for war."* It regards as wicked the waste of the nation's wealth in the building of vast armaments and the maintenance of greatly augmented forces on land and sea. [Washington papers please copy, and Franklin D. Roosevelt please read.]

A few weeks ago the Presbyterian Synod of the State of New York met at Buffalo and indorsed the recommendations of its committee on social service. After citing the stand of the Presbyterian General Assembly in supporting all conscientious objectors to war and demanding that they be excused in educational institutions from all "military instruction without loss in academic standing or official censure of any kind," and after expressing its opposition to military training in schools and colleges, the committee urged the Synod through its pastors to influence parents "to refrain from sending their children to schools where military training is required." This savors of a boycott, and it is strengthened by the fact that the Synod approved opposition to the appropriation by the State Legislature of any funds for the drill hall at Cornell, where there is compulsory military training. When one remembers that the bulk of the members of the Synod were encouraging preparedness in 1915 and 1916 and then shouting for the war and proclaiming it to be God's will, it is plain that we have come far in a short time. The Synod does not propose to be caught napping the next time. It therefore indorsed the recommendation of the committee that the churches should now make clear to all their members the economic price to us of neutrality if war should break out anywhere in the world, and educate them to be willing to pay the price of relinquishing our trade as a neutral rather than to be drawn into "the madness of war." As the committee said, "The economic price of neutrality is as nothing beside the spiritual and human price of war." The Synod also instructed the committee to follow the Senate investigation into the manufacture of war munitions and to make suggestions hereafter as to the advisability of investing church funds in corporations which have a major interest in war material.

There are other reasons for hope in this matter of peace. If the Japanese seem bound to make trouble over naval armaments, the impending settlement of Japanese and Russian friction in Manchuria by the sale of the Chinese Eastern Railroad removes that danger of war which alarmed our highest officials at the turn of the year. There are still sore spots galore in Europe, over all of which hangs the menace of Hitler. But speaking as rector of St. Andrew's University in Scotland the other day, General Smuts, who foresaw at Paris the wickedness of the Treaty of Versailles and denounced it when it was finished, declared to the students that, despite the failure of disarmament and the "vogue of silly drilling, strutting about in uniforms and shirts of various colors," he did not find a real war temper anywhere or the material conditions necessary for a modern war. He was much more alarmed by the new tyrannies in Europe than by the danger of another great war. Encouraging all this is; still it calls for redoubled activity against the militaristic forces of evil now so strongly intrenched in the United States as well as abroad.

Oswald Garrison Villard

Issues and Men

Must We Fight Japan?

THE title given to a new book by Nathaniel Peffer is "Must We Fight in Asia?" He answers his own question in the affirmative. There is no help for it; it is manifest destiny. We are reaching out for new fields for trade, and we have had our eye on the Pacific ever since 1849, when we began to lay covetous eyes upon the Philippine Islands, and ever since President Millard Fillmore explained to Congress that the reason for our being the first to recognize the independence of the Hawaiian Islands was that "they lie in the course of the great trade which must at no distant day be carried on between the western coast of North America and eastern Asia. . . . "

America, Mr. Peffer says, "is in the Far East irrevocably," if only because it has committed itself to "a perilous position in the most turbulent quarter of the globe," because of its attitude on Manchoukuo. Therefore he comes to the decision that "sooner or later America must yield, Japan must yield, or they must go to war. America accepts the fact that Manchuria has become Manchoukuo, a Japanese colony; or Japan rescinds Manchoukuo's independence and returns the territory to China—or America and Japan fight." He asserts that if we go to war with Japan, after a long struggle we shall come out of it in possession of Manchoukuo, as the Spanish War left us in possession of the Philippines, and thereafter we shall be an Asiatic power. He calls upon America to prepare for the inevitable.

Mr. Peffer admits that we have only slight trade interests in the Pacific, our mercantile investments in Asia being only $200,000,000, a sum we should spend within two weeks after the declaration of war. He admits also that Americans don't want to fight in Asia, but says that is of no importance because indifference or hostility to the war could easily be overcome by government propaganda. "No people," he writes, "can resist the compulsions of propaganda created and disseminated by a government or compact ruling group which knows what it wants and has command of the channels of opinion." So the outcome seems to him plain and inevitable. I do not deny either the gravity of the situation or the truth of what he says as to the power of a President—who is not even the whole government—to put us into war. McKinley put us into the needless Spanish War, *after* Spain had surrendered on every important point, by concealing the surrender from Congress and the people. The President has usurped the power of Congress to declare war, and by his appeals to public opinion, to a blind patriotism, and to loyalty to the flag can swing the country as he wishes.

So Mr. Roosevelt, single-handed, can put us into war with Japan if he so desires. Already he is moving in that direction. The building of a huge army air base in the Hawaiian Islands—aimed only at Japan, of course; the holding of fleet maneuvers, the largest ever undertaken in time of peace, off the Aleutian Islands; the announcement that we are to increase our fortifications in the Pacific—all these must have an immediate and powerful effect upon the Japanese. These facts, plus our refusal to let them arm to an equality with us, plus the increase of our navy to 110,000 officers and men, plus our building up to treaty limits, are all the material the Japanese jingoes and militarists need to frighten and arouse their own people: "Don't you see how the United States is planning war upon us?" If this policy continues, war with Japan will come.

But must it be? Must war come? There is no "must" about it. It need never be. The American people do not want it; they have burned their fingers too badly too recently. They have learned that victors gain nothing by their victory. They can stop the drift into war if they will. There is no such thing as a manifest destiny driving us to seek enlarged markets in China, for we are deliberately cutting off our world markets everywhere—we have just thrown away marked trade advantages in South America, and actually handed them over to Japan through our political arrogance, our invasions of foreign soil, our high tariffs, our refusal to consider Latin American needs and business conditions. We could win infinitely greater markets by simply lowering our tariffs and deliberately setting ourselves to regain and enlarge the markets we had prior to the recent economic disaster. The chief difficulty is simply that the American people no longer have any control of the war-making power. I have complete faith in their pacifist intentions, but they cannot voice their desires in the matter; they lack the referendum and the initiative, urged by both Theodore Roosevelt and Woodrow Wilson. Of course the militarists say that we can't have a referendum when the enemy is landing on our shores, but as every one of our foreign wars has been of our own seeking, and was a long time in coming on, we could in each case have obtained the views of the people. It is idle to say that a nation which created the draft machine of 1917 overnight cannot create the necessary machinery for a vote on war in no time at all. The only trouble is that we don't do it.

Yet I have tested many audiences in the last two years in many parts of the country on this proposal, and have invariably received enthusiastic applause. Isn't it time to start such a movement? Of course meanwhile we can use the time-honored methods of making our opinion against war with Japan felt. We can use our common sense in discussing the matter, and we can let the White House and the Navy Department know how we feel about it. These establishments, like our Members of Congress, are extremely sensitive to public opinion. A friend of mine wrote a vigorous protest to the Navy Department and got an early reply. Twenty thousand letters of protest would make the whole department sit up and take notice. If we do nothing at all, we, too, shall contribute to the drift into war with Japan.

Oswald Garrison Villard

April 22, 1935

My dear Mr. Secretary:

I wish to associate myself with Nicholas Murray Butler's letter to you of April 15, and the many similar letters which you must have received, in regard to the fleet manoeuvres in the Pacific, and the military manoeuvres along the Canadian boundary. We are rapidly sinking to the level of Hitler and Mussolini in our bowing down before the god of war. That a Christian nation such as we pretend to be, in such an hour of crisis, is actually planning to spend $1,125,000,000--that is the figure at this writing--upon military and naval expenditures in the coming fiscal year, when according to official figures more than 20,000,000 Americans are on the bread line and in receipt of doles, is one of the most humiliating and discouraging happenings of recent years. How can it be reconciled with the President's statement to Congress in his Annual Message, that there was not the slightest danger of our having trouble with any nation?

I hope you will do me the favor to peruse the enclosures clipped from the New York Times. They speak for themselves. Why can we not set ourselves determinedly to working out the program of these 217 Americans in Japan? I earnestly hope, too, that you will do everything in your power to end any further manifestations of this kind, if it is too late to stop the manoeuvres this Spring.

I am more moved to write this letter because of my high approval of all that you have done, and are doing, for the cause of peace, both personally and as Secretary of State. But I surely do not need to tell you in what high regard I hold you.

Yours very sincerely,

Hon. Cordell Hull,
Secretary of State
Washington, D.C.

Issues and Men

Government by Gangsters

WHAT has just occurred in Germany bears out anew the London *Times's* comment after Hitler's bloody purge of June 30, 1934, that for the first time in history a great government was being run by gangsters and with gangster methods. Adequately to picture what is happening in Berlin one must visualize, if one can, Al Capone and a Dillinger in charge of the city of Chicago and running it as they saw fit. This is no exaggeration. There is vastly more blood upon the head of Adolph Hitler than on all the gunmen in the United States put together—he murdered fully 1,254 in the "purge" of last year alone. Now he has ordered the renewal of the attacks upon the Jews, the Catholics, and the Stahlhelm, and may be counted on to carry on the war against the Protestant clergy.

Whom has Hitler just placed in charge of the Berlin police? A man of high character, sworn to uphold the law, to keep order, to protect all classes in the community? Not at all. He has installed a notorious Jew-baiter, Count Wolf von Helldorf, who was himself in 1930 sentenced to six months' in jail for instigating anti-Jewish riots and taking a leading part in them. If this is the proper course of action, then Mayor LaGuardia is entitled to go to the Tombs to pick his next chief of police. This is serving notice upon all the Brown Shirts and police in Berlin that they will be protected however much they may maltreat or torture the Jews, men or women—for defending a woman from Brown Shirts an American naval cadet has found himself in jail. Naturally the Nazis have turned around and declared that the responsibility for all this rests upon the Jews—that their "provocative attitude" gave rise to this righteous outburst of mob violence against them. Men and women living in terror of their lives for the last two and one-half years deliberately invited mob indignities and violence! That is what the rest of the world is asked to believe.

If that is characteristic of a certain German mentality, so is the wholesale admission by Hitler that Germany is not united under him, by his again declaring war upon the Catholics and the Stahlhelm. The Concordat with the Vatican, so praised as proof of Hitler's and Göring's statesmanship, has all but gone by the board, the Vatican making protest after protest against its violation, and Hitler in turn demanding that the clergy subordinate itself to his state and to his orders under penalty of immediate arrest. As for the Stahlhelm, that association of officers who served in the war, how many times have we not been told that it had been *"gleichgeschaltet,"* that, especially in view of Hitler's rearming Germany, it was entirely in sympathy with the Nazis? Again and again we have had Hitler's assurance that the solidarity of Germany behind him was beyond question, and that all but a handful of malcontents were on his side. Now we know that that is far from the truth, and the fact is confirmed by a statement of Dr. Robert Ley, the Nazi dictator of labor, on July 22. There is "still a long road ahead," he said, before the last German "regardless of whether he be Protestant or Catholic" has been converted to Nazism, "only through which the German people can become eternal."

The way to bring that about of course is to beat up and imprison anyone who does not agree with you. That is the method that has notoriously succeeded during the world's history in converting people to one's beliefs. But of course the appointment of Count von Helldorf, and of Hans Kerrl, as Under Secretary of Church Affairs in the Reich Ministry of the Interior, is proof positive that the Nazi party itself is not unanimous. These men represent the radical wing and as such their appointment must be unpalatable to the more conservative side, and to those officials like Dr. Schacht, who know that every new outburst of intolerance and violence injures the German nation in every country outside of its borders. Finally, it is quite characteristic of Hitler that while these things are happening and all Germany, according to the dispatches before me, is in a state of tension and fear of another bloody purge, he himself has ducked and disappeared. He is reported on a yachting cruise in Norway, the significance of which will doubtless become clearer in the course of the next few days.

Profoundly grieved as I am at the renewed attacks upon the Jews, I rejoice heartily over these latest developments. They must open the eyes of those Americans who have just returned from Germany to tell us that all was harmony and union there; they must convince any open-minded person that the dictator has not yet had his way with all the German people; and they have certainly refreshed the memory of millions as to the gangster character of the Hitler government. Americans are thus reminded once more that because a dictator can make trains run on time, clean the streets, drive the beggars into hiding, and supply bread and circuses, it does not mean that there is either genuinely good government or happiness among the people. There is every evidence that in Germany as in Italy there is a steady sinking of the standard of living. The newspapers report the closing of one German factory after another. Is it surprising, therefore, that it has been decided to whip up the party loyalty by attacks upon the Jews and the Catholics? That is the oldest trick of the dictator. "When things are going badly with you, start something," runs the rule. Give your followers something to attack. If there is an enemy to concentrate upon at home, so much the better. If there is none, why there is always an Abyssinia available, there is always the sacred honor of the country to be avenged. Hitler's course is no different from the conventional one of the dictator. But when he attacks the Stahlhelm he plays with fire; it is closely allied with the Reichswehr and that organization, which can break Hitler overnight if it chooses, is well aware of what is going on.

Oswald Garrison Villard

Issues and Men

Terrifyingly Uncharted Paths

WHATEVER the outcome at Geneva—and as I write the issues are still trembling in the balance and Mussolini has not yet spoken—it is obvious that there lie before the nations in the League terrifyingly uncharted paths. The President himself admitted this when he skilfully fenced with the reporters who asked him what action he and the heads of other nations could take in the way of sanctions if Mussolini went ahead on his abominable course. He could only reply that the State Department was studying the situation. So are all the other foreign offices and so are the responsible leaders—wondering what in the world they can do to isolate the conflict, and to bring pressure to bear on Italy without thereby involving the whole world in another conflagration which it is in no condition to stand. The very word sanctions is so new in the vocabulary of man in its sense of international punishment that it illustrates in itself the staggering novelty of the situation which confronts us. The word was not, of course, coined at Versailles, but its use in this sense of punishment was never general until it was embodied in the peace-treaty covenant, and until it was utilized by the French when they undertook that indefensible invasion of the Ruhr which brought about inflation and gave Hitler his excuse and opportunity.

Perhaps I am wrong as to England. There was something so amazingly straightforward, so frank and open in Sir Samuel Hoare's speech to the Assembly that it is possible that the British Cabinet has already logically weighed the results of opposing Mussolini and made up its mind on what it was prepared to suggest if sanctions should become inevitable. Meanwhile, however, there is obviously no consensus of opinion about what can be undertaken, only speculation as to whether isolation can be attempted without provoking immediate hostilities. What economic pressure can be applied? If Italy is to be boycotted, what articles shall be declared contraband? Can an iron ring be drawn around Italy? And are those nations which depend so much upon their trade with her to subject themselves to immeasurable inconveniences for the sake of the general welfare?

To answer such questions, overpowering in their number and importance, the League ought to have months, if not years, in which to plan and to prepare. Perhaps it is just as well, however, that these questions must be met without delay. Planning in advance might send us on the rocks upon which have foundered so many international conferences, the rocks of rivalries, bureaucratic timidities, staunch devotion to precedents that could not apply here, interminable arguing and discussion.

How great is the risk of all this is so obvious as to forbid comment. One of the most dangerous phases is certainly the alarming British naval maneuvers in the Mediterranean, which are likely to invite reprisals in a sudden offensive on Italy's side; yet I cannot quite see the logic of the British Labor Party position, which is opposed (if the London dispatches are correct) to applying any sanctions to Italy. Surely if Mussolini goes ahead, it means the end of all the peace machinery created since the World War. True, this machinery has failed us before when the situation was not so desperate. But how can anyone deny that if some measure short of war cannot be devised to hold in check a crazy nation we are at the mercy of the creators of war? Of course I am well aware that boycotts and sanctions are acts of war and that they may well lead to war, but grave risks must plainly be taken in this situation. If Italy should attack Ethiopia it is hard to see how it would be more possible to isolate the war than it was to isolate the Austrian attack on Serbia. We shall have war, probably a long and bloody war, if Italy is allowed to go ahead, and no man can guess what effect it may have on the relations of the black and white races throughout the world. Is it or is it not worth while to set sail upon uncharted seas in the hope of uniting world opinion and power against Italy, in the hope of forcing her to end the struggle before long?

I hope that no one will write in and say, "So you have given up your pacifism!" Nothing of the kind. There has been no change in my belief that war is never justifiable, but the hour has come when the voice of reason seems unable to control, when we are being pushed over the abyss by the deeds of a madman. Without changing my belief that war is the sum of all evil, that it can never be anything else than a disaster, and never yet has produced good results, I feel that the nations involved are more than justified if they attempt now, even at the risk of war, to find a substitute for it in the economic boycott, in measures short of war, provided they go into the undertaking with the determination that they will refuse to be drawn into actual hostilities even in the face of overt attack. If a nation cannot conquer war, the time has come not only to inquire, as my friend Joseph Wood Krutch did recently, whether Europe is a success but also whether our civilization is a success. It is the most desperate and challenging of adventures which confronts the League. Must it not be entered upon?

In the background of it all lurks a far more sinister and dangerous figure than Mussolini himself, Adolf Hitler. He will be the chief beneficiary if Mussolini defies the League, gets away with it, and destroys Abyssinia to make it his own. It is more than possible that Hitler will burst out of his country within the next few years at the head of the most daring, best-equipped, and best-disciplined army that the world has ever seen if the example is not put before him of another dictator held in check by the moral opinion and the economic—not military—forces of the rest of the nations.

Oswald Garrison Villard

Issues and Men

"If This Be Treason"

I AM not a dramatic critic and am, of course, leaving to Joseph Wood Krutch technical criticism of the new play "If This Be Treason," written by John Haynes Holmes and Reginald Lawrence, and produced by the Theater Guild at the Music Box Theater in New York City. But I cannot deny myself the opportunity of expressing my admiration for the excellence of the acting and the courage of the play and of calling attention to its extraordinary timeliness. There were moments when it stirred me as I have rarely been stirred at the theater. If the movement was not always as smooth as it might be; if there was, to me, considerable artificiality at points, the play still stands out in my mind as remarkably moving and as an honest, straightforward effort to portray dramatically the greatest problem which confronts the world. And this at the very moment when there is being fought out at Geneva the issue whether one nation shall or shall not be allowed deliberately to rob and despoil another nation and to murder its citizens by wholesale for the piratical purpose of adding to the attacker's land and riches.

It is easy to understand the indignation which "If This Be Treason" will arouse in many super-patriotic bosoms. If the Admiral commanding the Brooklyn Navy Yard, who so glibly urged in the Hearst papers not long ago our joining hands with the Germany of Hitler and with other countries to make war upon Russia, were to enter this theater he would have to be tied at the end of the first act. He would certainly call upon the heavens to fall and crush those who dare to portray a President of the United States as refusing to go to war with Japan after that country had attacked Manila and killed or wounded a thousand American sailors and marines. Others will seek to ridicule the whole thing and to declare that it is all preposterous. Its critics cannot, however, charge that the authors have failed to present the pro-war argument, for several of the characters in the play voice it in the fairest and most forceful manner. It is only the "unpatriotic" character of the play upon which they can dwell, the "impossibility" of the denouement, and the general lack of what they call reasonableness and sanity.

Yet the central thesis of the play is exactly that which we see being worked out in Geneva—that conferences between the heads of nations to make peace should be held before hostilities begin instead of afterward, when the multitudes have been slain, robbed of their lives, tortured to their last hours, without ever having been asked whether they were willing to make the sacrifice. If I remember rightly, in backing up the British government the other day President De Valera of the Irish Republic made exactly this same argument. The time to make peace is certainly when the battalions are marching, when the troop ships are on the tide with their holds jammed with death-dealing instruments. Mr. Holmes and Mr. Lawrence put their hero to the supreme test by having him sworn in as President just as Japan strikes, when the outgoing President has apparently enmeshed the country in the conflict, and Congress, stampeded by the warlike elements, is ready to declare war upon Japan. Whether the solution, the revolt of peoples against governments, is within the range of human possibility is the moot point. But however the people may decide the question for themselves, there was never a greater necessity for laying this problem before the American public than today, in view of the overwhelming vote in Congress for the neutrality legislation which the President first opposed and then grudgingly accepted. I am bold enough to believe that this play will meet with a popular response wherever it is shown, and I wish it could be put on in every city in the land. If the country had any sense of what is important and vital and true, all sorts of medals and honors would be showered upon the authors, and upon the actors, who add so much to the sincerity of the performance.

There are two aspects of the American war situation which have been strongly accented in this play. The first is the horrible ease with which men in high position forget the personal side of war when the crisis nears. They seem wholly to divest themselves of the ordinary emotions of humanity when the bands begin to play, and salve their consciences by prating the conventional arguments about national honor and the insults to the flag. When Woodrow Wilson addressed a great Red Cross meeting in Washington soon after the outbreak of war, there was a smile upon his face as he said to his audience that we had only just begun to fight, and had only just begun to receive the lists of dead and wounded. His mind was closed to any effort to realize the enormity of the suffering which he had inflicted upon individuals, upon families, by putting the country into war—after having told me and others that no matter what happened he never, never would do it. Somehow or other, pity, compassion, and mercy seemed to go out of this man and out of the souls of so many others in high office when war was declared. Hence, though one may doubt whether we could ever have such a brave and humane President as Mr. Holmes and Mr. Lawrence portray, one knows that the possibility of choosing such a President ought to be held up constantly to the American people.

Secondly, I come back to my old thesis that war has now become such a monstrous thing, so diabolical in all its aspects, and so certain, as we all now know, to ruin victors and vanquished alike, that no one man, no small group of men, no Congress should have the right to declare war. The Congress of the United States has lost the war-making power guaranteed to it by the Constitution; it has been usurped by the Executive. All the more reason that the Executive should be compelled to disgorge that power and that we should establish the rule that no war may be declared save by a referendum vote of the American people.

Oswald Garrison Villard

Issues and Men

Lansing Self-Revealed

SECRETARY LANSING'S worst enemy could wish for nothing better than the publication of the "War Memoirs of Robert Lansing" (Bobbs-Merrill). It has done irretrievable injury to his character and his record as Secretary of State by revealing the duplicity diplomats always permit themselves and his avowed insincerity in pretending to be neutral on taking office. At the very beginning of this book there is printed the memorandum in which Lansing set forth his views on entering the Cabinet. It shows that he had not the slightest intention of holding the scales even and that he was completely infected by the idea that "the German government is utterly hostile to all nations with democratic institutions because those who compose it see in democracy a menace to absolutism and the defeat of the German ambition for world domination." If that was entirely untrue then, it is in part true now, and may become entirely so as a result of our participation in the war and of the Treaty of Versailles. What a pity that Lansing and Woodrow Wilson did not survive until this hour to see the results of their intervention—to see the world on the verge of another war, this time with a genuine absolutist, within seventeen years of the close of their war to end war!

Throughout this volume--which, curiously enough, bears the name of no editor or sponsor—we have the picture of Lansing pretending to hold the scales even, when he was really determined that the country should go into the war just as soon as the public was ready for it, that is, was sufficiently deluded by our officials and aroused by German atrocities and criminal stupidity. This was his objective, and he admits it with no sense of shame. He sets forth with complete cold-bloodedness that he deliberately stalled in taking the British to task for their conduct toward the United States, which, as he once said to me and as his Solicitor of the State Department, Cone Johnson, openly stated, "violated every canon of international law." He here confesses regarding this strife with the British: "I did all that I could to prolong the dispute by preparing, or having prepared, long and detailed replies, and introducing technical and controversial matters in the hope that before the interchange came to an end something would happen to . . . make the American people perceive that German absolutism was a menace to their liberty. . . . Everything was submerged in verbosity. It was done with deliberate purpose." What deceit and double-dealing! Nowhere is there the slightest evidence that he knew anything about the war aims of the Allies, or their conscious duplicity, or the secret treaties, or anything of the realities of the situation. Worse than that, there is not one line to show that he ever considered what the effect of war might be upon the United States and his fellow-citizens. Like Woodrow Wilson, he never was able to visualize what war might mean in death and suffering to a part of the youth of America and to their parents.

It is true that he once drafted a stiff note to Great Britain, in May, 1915, which he does not refer to in this book; Mr. Wilson retained it on his desk and sent it out in an emasculated form in October. Lansing gave me this information at the time and authorized me to publish it. I scored a great beat in the New York *Evening Post,* and that evening Mr. Lansing denied to all the other Washington correspondents and Secretary Bryan that he was in any way responsible for my publication or knew anything about it. Similarly he used the New York *World* to publish the Albert papers, stolen—with complete morality, of course—by government agents, and the Associated Press to publish the infamous Zimmermann note, because it did not suit him to tell the truth about how it was obtained. I have always maintained that the President could have put us into the war against Great Britain by merely reciting the facts of its conduct. He could certainly have kept us out of war by using those facts to balance the injury done to us by the Germans. The only difference was that the Germans took American lives, and the English did not. Lansing admits this very clearly, for he says positively that we should have gone to war with Great Britain if it had not been for German stupidity.

Lansing did not, it now appears, believe in the American people. They were to be told as little as possible and then only what their rulers wished. They were to be "educated" to believe what he wished them to believe so that we should go to war with Germany. If anybody tried to educate them the other way, that was bad propaganda. He was horrified by the unethical acts of the Germans, and unmoved by the starvation of the German people by the Allied blockade. He really believed that there was such a thing as "civilized warfare," and that the British were carrying on such a war.

What makes me feel especially bad about it is that when Bryan resigned, I, among others, was asked by the President to suggest his successor. Since the President would not consider my first choice, I, who was trying my best to keep the United States out of the war, suggested, God help me now, Robert Lansing. There is an excuse, however; to me he represented his attitude in such a way that I had no reason to believe that he did not sincerely desire to avoid war. The action of the Congress in insisting upon neutrality at the present time shows that we have learned a lot, and that some Americans in official life are determined not to have the wool pulled over their eyes again. In this connection I must add that in a letter of September 6, 1915, not published in this book, Secretary Lansing argued that we should go to war in order to preserve prosperity and get back the moneys loaned abroad! It was the exact viewpoint of the firm of Morgan. There were American traitors in 1915!

Oswald Garrison Villard

October 21, 1935

Dear Miss Pratt:

Miss Grossel has asked me to give you a statement of my views on neutrality. I do not quite go as far as Raymond Buell, but I believe in putting teeth in the present neutrality legislation by extending it to loans and credits, and I believe firmly that Congress should keep this matter in its own hands and not give the President freedom to act. I admit that this may work hardship at times. I confess that sentimentally I would like to see the President permit the export of arms to Ethiopia, but in the long run I am sure that this country will be far safer if we stick to keeping the power in the hands of the Congress. In the main I find myself strongly in sympathy with Henry L. Stimson's letter to the New York Times, notably in his demand that the cupidity of our exporters should not be permitted to embroil us in another war. The point I particularly wish to stress in my talks is that we may have to pay a heavy price for neutrality, that in any event we shall always pay some price, but that any price we may pay for that is vastly cheaper than war.

Cordially yours,

Miss Pratt,
The Foreign Policy Association
New York City

Issues and Men

The War and the Pacifists

BITTERLY discouraging as the needless and useless bloodshed in Abyssinia is, I still cannot feel that anybody who knows that it is wrong to take human life need be too downcast by this fresh outbreak of war. On the contrary, there are many encouraging signs that we in America are now far removed from the gullibility and the ignorance and the stupidity that made it possible for the propagandists and the bankers to put us into war in 1917. In the first place, Mussolini's crime is so crass and so obvious that no one is being misled by any talk of Italy's needing "her place in the sun"—how sadly reminiscent that is of the German propaganda in 1914!—and the necessity of civilizing a barbarous people. That doesn't go down in 1935. Pirandello and other defenders of the noble Mussolini may plead with Americans to side with the Italians all they please, not ¼ of 1 per cent of the American populace will do so, excluding persons of Italian birth or ancestry, and a lot of these are too sensible to be swayed merely by their former national allegiance. Abroad the overwhelming determination of the British people that there shall be collective control of berserker nations is one of the most heartening things in the whole picture. Yet they do not want war, those eleven millions who voted in Lord Robert Cecil's referendum of last spring, and they will keep their country out of war if they possibly can. They are the answer to Frank Simonds's recent letter to *The Nation,* which takes the point of view that there is nothing in this whole situation except the determination of the imperialist powers to hold on to what they have and the desire of those powers that are without colonial possessions to obtain them. Public opinion is aroused in England because it knows that if this business of war cannot be stopped it is going to be the end of everything. If Mussolini cannot be checked now, Hitler cannot be when he decides to set the world on fire.

My "hopeless and incurable optimism," as some of my critics and friends describe it, is further reinforced by what is happening in the United States. During the war-time mania of 1917-19 I never dreamed that I should live to see the time when public opinion in the United States would be practically united in recognizing that we were lied and deceived into going to war, and that it was a great disaster out of which we got nothing; and when Congress would actually proceed to put a stop to those processes by which Wilson, House, Lansing, and J. P. Morgan and Company brought us into the war. Only yesterday I read a book review in the New York *Times* in which one of the staff writers was practically allowed to say that the House of Morgan's helping to get the United States into the war and its helping the Allies to win "were 'achievements' in a sense, but in the light of subsequent history they were not achievements of the sort to win this nation's unmitigated gratitude." Robert L. Duffus, who wrote that, would hardly have been allowed to utter such a treasonable sentence in the *Times* even five years ago. I do not lay so much stress upon the President's declaration that the United States will not be drawn into a war, because, after all, he is at bottom a politician, and he would yield to the bankers and to public clamor and take the advice of a muddle-headed and incompetent old gentleman like Colonel House as readily as did Wilson. But the spirit of Congress fills me with amazement and joy. Here is an interview with Senator Frederick Van Nuys of Indiana, serving notice on Roosevelt that Congress next year will make the neutrality laws, which it passed contrary to the President's wishes, as "ironclad as legislation can make them so that under no conditions could any President . . . bring war upon the United States without Congress playing a part." He also declared that the embargo act will be made more stringent at the next session of Congress, by which I hope he means that next January Congress will make it absolutely impossible for American bankers and industrialists to do again what they did in 1918, aided by the shortsighted man in the White House and his Cabinet, with the admirable exception of William Jennings Bryan. It is not only that this spirit is abroad in the land that is so heartening, but that it is a *militant* spirit—so militant that it will not allow the President or any successor to have discretion in this matter.

I have just listened to the radio speech of a reserve army officer. Of course he talked the professional bunk about adequate preparedness, when neither he nor any other living man can say what constitutes military preparedness, since no one can tell if we are going into the war business what enemies we shall have, how many, or in what quarters of the globe. But the astounding thing to me was that he told his great audience that everybody understood now that we had been put into the war in 1917 because "English propaganda was more effective than German propaganda." Why, a lot of us nearly went to jail in 1917 and 1918 for saying that very thing. More than that, this speaker went on to call upon his audience to believe not one single word of the war stories from either side and to close their minds to atrocity propaganda. Then I must not forget to recall to my readers that extraordinarily useful and truthful book of Walter Millis's, "Road to War." No one can read that volume and not be convinced. It is an absolute justification of the pacifist position. A few years ago it would not have seemed possible that such a book could be written and widely circulated.

Finally, we have the President's orders forbidding the export of munitions and warning Americans that if they travel on the ships of belligerent nations in war time they do so at their own risk. What a marvelous advance! A similar proclamation in 1915—the one that William J. Bryan begged for, and for which he was derided and vilified —would have kept this country out of the World War. Disheartened? No, indeed; how could anybody be?

Oswald Garrison Villard

Issues and Men

Mr. Lamont Defends the Morgans

THOMAS W. LAMONT has criticized in a letter to the New York *Times* a review by Robert L. Duffus of Harold Nicolson's life of Dwight Morrow. Mr. Duffus dared to disagree with Mr. Nicolson's portrayal of the House of Morgan as a highly benevolent institution actuated solely by love of humanity and rendering inestimably valuable services to the Allies—and therefore, incidentally, to the United States. Mr. Duffus wrote of "the manner in which our financiers actually made us an ally of the Allies while we were still officially neutral," and also used these words: "Let it be admitted that in helping to draw the country into the European war he [Dwight Morrow] had a part in decivilizing the world." Mr. Lamont ventures "to inquire what Mr. Duffus thinks our firm or Mr. Morrow did to get the United States into the World War."

Mr. Lamont then proceeds to assert (1) that he and his partners in favoring the Allies were but a part of a "heavily preponderant majority that hoped the Allies would win"; (2) that he and his partners did not carry on "propaganda in favor of our going to war," or seek "to influence Washington in favor of war"; (3) that the vast sum (more than $30,000,000) which the Morgans made out of selling supplies to the Allies and floating their bond issues before the United States went into the war did not determine "the pro-Ally sentiments of Morrow or Morgan or any of us"—"we were pro-Ally by inheritance, by instinct, by opinion"; (4) that no one "can believe that the Allies' demand for American supplies was created by our firm"; (5) that there is current a new and false version of the causes of our going into the war to the effect that "it was American business men rather than Germany that got us into the war," and that "it will not do good but harm to encourage the acceptance of this myth."

First of all let me point out that Mr. Lamont has knocked down men of straw he himself set up. No one has charged the Morgan firm with indulging in propaganda. They did not have to do so. That was done for them by their employers, the British government, with precisely the same complete disregard for truth that characterized the Germans, and with vastly more cleverness and ability. No one has charged the Morgan firm with having influenced Woodrow Wilson to go into the war, for Mr. Lamont knows, as I know, that under Wilson, until we got into the war, the White House was closed to the House of Morgan—for the first and only time. No one has charged that the Allies' demand for supplies was created by the Morgans; no sane man would think of doing so. They are only charged with taking a modest 1 per cent of the blood money. And of this modest 1 per cent Mr. Lamont is proud. No one has charged that preponderant American opinion was not on the side of the Allies. It *was*. But this does not mean that the preponderant sentiment *was in favor of our going into the war* to aid the Allies and to make safe for our democracy the Allied bonds floated by the House of Morgan. That was something entirely different. Indubitably the men and women Mr. Lamont and his associates met socially and in a business way were for our entering the war. Why not? But the country as a whole voted Mr. Wilson back into the White House because "he kept us out of war," a phrase written into Ollie James's keynote address at the St. Louis convention and, as we now know, read and approved in advance by Colonel House and Mr. Wilson, who well knew the pacifist temper of the people. Not a single one of these charges answered by Mr. Lamont was made by Mr. Duffus, or even referred to by him in his review.

I agree that "it will not do good but harm" to encourage the acceptance of the "myth" that American business men helped to get us into the war—which is the only charge Mr. Duffus made—that is, harm to the bankers. But the question is not of harm or benefit to the Morgans or anyone else; the question is simply, What is the truth? I have no doubt that Mr. Lamont, for whom since our college days I have had a warm personal regard, believes that he and his associates were not influenced by the huge sums that they were making by their association with the Allies. I cannot believe it, because I do not think that there are any persons in existence who would not be consciously or unconsciously affected by such an association. I know I should have been. That they would have been pro-Ally if they had never made a cent out of the war I gladly recognize. So was I, and so was any man who valued ethics and justice on the day the Germans swept into Belgium. But all this cannot veil the fact that the huge vested interest in the war created by British purchases engineered by the Morgans went far toward pushing us into the war, and would have helped to do so had the Germans refrained from their wicked submarine warfare. Mr. Lansing's letters prove this as Mr. Lamont should know. He insisted to Mr. Wilson that we must go into the war lest our vast Allied-created prosperity be checked and an economic crash ensue.

The gentlemen of the House of Morgan live in an exalted and rarefied atmosphere to which few of us can aspire. Perhaps that is why they often seem so detached from the realities and facts of American life. One would think that they would at least recognize that the neutrality resolution passed by Congress, which Senator Van Nuys and others say will be strengthened just as soon as Congress meets again by forbidding credits and loans to belligerents, is a vote to make it impossible for the Morgans or any other bankers to repeat their procedure in any future war. They are not to have the opportunity to decide, however justly, which side they think Americans should favor and then ally themselves with it. They will be compelled to be neutral—Mr. Lamont has written, "We were not neutral for a single moment"—to be loyal and not disloyal to their government's neutrality.

Oswald Garrison Villard

Issues and Men

Neutrality and the House of Morgan

Those were the days when American citizens were urged to remain neutral in action, in word, and even in thought, but our firm had never for one moment been neutral; we didn't know how to be. From the very start we did everything we could to contribute to the cause of the Allies. Mr. J. P. Morgan himself never attempted to be neutral in feeling. He spoke his mind with shy frankness both in and out of season.

IN these words Thomas Lamont has described the attitude of himself and his partners toward the World War. They are quoted again in Nicolson's new life of Dwight Morrow, and Mr. Lamont has confirmed them in a recent letter to the New York *Times*. The firm is very proud of its attitude at that time. Very well; let us examine it. At the outbreak of the war the President of the United States called upon every American citizen, in the interest of keeping this country at peace and out of the European disaster, to be "neutral in thought and deed." Most patriotic citizens endeavored to live up to that Presidential counsel. Many besides the members of the Morgan firm did not. Like the Morgans they were on the side of England by tradition, inheritance, taste, and business and other associations. Mr. Morgan owned a great deal of property there, and his banking house in London was, and is, a most influential British institution. On the other side, most of the German-Americans were as divided in their loyalty then as they are today when they worship at the barbaric shrine of Hitler. As a result, the German-Americans were excoriated by press and public. The Anglo-Americans, being, most of them, rich, privileged, and powerful, or of the intellectual elite, were rarely rebuked by anyone, yet the disloyalty to the policies of our government was precisely the same in both cases.

Now what Mr. Wilson meant was not that American citizens should not make up their minds about where they thought justice and right were, but that they should neither so plan nor so act as to involve the United States in any way in the European struggle. Mr. Wilson himself was naturally pro-Ally, yet for a long time he maintained the position which he asked the country to assume. One reason for his anger at Walter Page was that that gentleman entirely forgot that he was American Ambassador to Great Britain and went to Lord Grey and others for counsel on how he should stand toward his own government. The Morgans went ahead entangling themselves and the companies they were interested in more and more inextricably with the cause of the Allies. Not only did they make enormous sums by acting as agents for the British government, but many of the corporations in which they held stock also profited largely by the war contracts. As Mr. Lamont has said, they did not cause the Allies to place contracts here; it was the war that did that. They were merely fortunate in being selected to "run the pie counter, and when you are at the pie counter you cannot help eating pie," to borrow the apt phrase of one very closely allied to a member of the Morgan firm. Mr. Morgan's very connection with his London house made his New York firm the logical agent in America for the British government. They leapt to it with a greater enthusiasm because, as Mr. Lamont says, they did not want to be neutral. They did not at first ask whether this would bring the United States into the war or not. Later on when things were going very badly with the Allies and it looked more than doubtful that the British bonds floated in this country would be worth the paper they were printed on, they were perfectly willing that millions of young Americans should be shipped abroad to the shambles which so nearly finished the world and accomplished nothing—not even the destruction of German militarism.

The excuse made by many pro-Ally Americans was that there was a higher law; that conscience and moral indignation overruled both patriotism and loyalty to the policy of their government. The world was on fire; they must take sides. It was Evil against Good; who could hesitate? It was the same argument that we heard so often in prohibition days; people declared they would not obey a law which revolted their consciences. In many cases, as I pointed out at the time, people, deliberately or unwittingly, confused their consciences with their appetites. The same is true of the purveyors of supplies to the British government. They thought they could differentiate between their consciences and their financial interests. The result was that we got into the war much more rapidly and surely than would have been the case if the bankers had been prohibited from doing business with either belligerent.

All of this brings up the question whether these men can or cannot be considered loyal and patriotic Americans who put their own country's interest above that of any other country or group of countries. Of course the first answer will be that they were serving humanity, and that humanity is superior to the welfare of any one nation. Unfortunately for this argument, time, the remorseless, has passed judgment. We know that humanity was not served, and if the members of the House of Morgan had had vision at the time they would have known that you cannot advance the welfare of the world by wholesale slaughter; that you cannot cure war by war, or do else than debase all mankind in the futile effort to shoot goodness and virtue and your point of view into those whom you consider erring human beings. The Morgans were rich and powerful, and what is known as society and big business sided with them. We got into the war and we "won it," so it is said. The common people of America don't think so, but they are an ignorant crowd. They are even determined today, as I pointed out last week, to prevent any other Wall Street advocates of the higher altruism from ever again making colossal fortunes out of the blood, misery, and suffering of multitudes.

Oswald Garrison Villard

Issues and Men

Honor to William J. Bryan

MY conscience is troubling me a good deal these days in regard to William Jennings Bryan. Not that I was one of those who vehemently denounced his resignation from the Cabinet of Woodrow Wilson or his earnest efforts to keep Americans from traveling in the war zone. My criticisms were based upon other things. They trouble me now because as I look back on those war years I can see how eternally right he was in his main contentions, and I am sorry that I helped to create feeling against him by attacking him on other lines. So I feel like getting up a great mass-meeting in Carnegie Hall in New York to do honor to his memory. There should be no difficulty in getting distinguished speakers because the correctness of his attitude and policy has now been so clearly demonstrated that Congress has voted his neutrality policy and the President has put it into effect.

It is easy to recall the names that were applied to Mr. Bryan's action when he demanded that Americans should give up their right to travel in the submarine-infested war zone. It was craven cowardice; it was supine submission to the devilish Hun, and gave consent to the German campaign of atrocities against shipping. But today the President by proclamation, acting under the orders of Congress, has notified American citizens that they must not travel at sea on belligerent ships in the expectation that the American flag will protect them if they do so. They go at their own risk. How is that for a wholesale justification of Mr. Bryan? Even more striking is ex-Secretary Stimson's coming out in favor of the extension of the embargo on munitions and implements of war to cover all those essential articles and raw materials which are included in the ban of the League of Nations, in order that Italy should not buy here what it cannot get elsewhere—oil sales to Italy increased in volume roughly 600 per cent in August and September last, and large amounts of cotton and other materials for Italy are steadily being shipped from the port of New Orleans. I think that I should ask ex-Secretary Stimson to be chairman of my Carnegie Hall meeting.

Then I should have a sinners' seat on the platform which I should grace with a number of prominent newspaper editors. There would be a special bench for the editors of the New York *Times,* and as they filed in I should hand them typewritten copies of this passage from Secretary Bryan's resignation: "But even if the government could not legally prevent citizens from traveling on belligerent ships, it could, and in my judgment should, earnestly advise American citizens not to risk themselves or the peace of their country, and I have no doubt that these warnings would be heeded. President Taft advised Americans to leave Mexico when insurrection broke out there. . . . I think the same course should be followed in warning Americans to keep off vessels subject to attack." To this I should append this extract from a *Times* editorial on Bryan's resignation:

> It was inevitable that the people of his own country would condemn him for insisting upon a policy of abandoning their rights, a policy of supine acquiescence in wrong, in deeds of outrage and murder, in crimes that have sent some of them to their deaths and threatened the peace and security of all of them.

Then there would be special seats for the editors of the now extinct New York *Globe,* who wrote that "instead of promoting a peaceful settlement Mr. Bryan practically throws his influence in the other balance." The Seattle *Post Intelligencer* should also have delegates present to be reminded of their description of Mr. Bryan as "a pacifist temporarily bereft of reason and lost to sense of patriotic duty; a misplaced figurehead." The editors of the Memphis *Commercial Appeal* would sit nearby recalling their words: "Mr. Bryan's views, turned into a national policy, would mean national suicide." And there would also be a seat reserved for my predecessor as editor of *The Nation,* who had this to say about the Secretary's resignation:

> All that we wish to point out now is that Bryan's statement bears on its face such proofs of mental confusion, such an inability to follow a course of reasoning, and such gross inconsistency with what Mr. Bryan has himself said and written as to show that the State Department was no place for him. It is not needful to dwell on the inherent absurdity of Mr. Bryan's position.

But Mr. Bryan is not the only one whom I would commemorate in Carnegie Hall. Two recent happenings have attracted my attention. The Oregon State Federation of Labor at its recent meeting passed a resolution going on record "in tribute to the high courage and character of the late beloved Harry K. Lane, and [urging] that all organizations and newspapers which eighteen years ago impugned the motives and integrity of Senators Lane, Robert M. La Follette, Sr., George W. Norris, and other Senators who voted against our government's entrance into the war take steps to note on their records the events which have justified the Senators' stand." The resolution added that "the passage of time, the rise of dictators in Europe, the duplicity and machinations of munitions makers, the crumbling of world peace once more, all have served to vindicate the heroic stand of Senator Lane." Senator Lane, alas, cannot be with us; he died of a broken heart in the middle of the storm of unjust and scurrilous abuse that raged around him. The other event is the unveiling of a memorial to Senator William J. Stone on October 11, with a dedicatory speech by the worthy son of Champ Clark, Senator Bennett Champ Clark. Senator Stone, too, was one of the "wilful men" who dared to be true to his conscience, his oath of office, and his country. I would call the roll of honor of these "wilful men," wilful in their unsurpassed courage, their wisdom, their true patriotism.

Oswald Garrison Villard

Issues and Men

Elucidation and Correction

IN the mass of comment received by me upon my recent articles in *The Nation* in regard to Robert Lansing and the activities of the firm of Morgan in war time, I am disturbed to find myself charged with "malice" and "vindictiveness." I have only lately been accused of being too friendly to the Morgans, but this is less important than the charge of being unjust to them, of not presenting their side of the case correctly and adequately, and of writing "excitedly" and "immoderately." So, at the risk of overtaxing the patience of my public, which has had an uncontemplated series of articles from me on this subject, I shall write one more statement of my position in order to make clear some points that seem to have caused misunderstandings, and to correct statements in which I have been betrayed into injustice.

That I have written with heat on this subject of the war and how we got into it, I cannot and would not deny. I am tempted to reply in the words of my grandfather when he was criticized for writing immoderately about slavery under the United States flag: "On this subject I do not wish to think, or speak, or write with moderation." But, as he sought, not always successfully, to do what he called "exact justice" to his adversaries, so I wish to do complete justice to all concerned in this historical discussion of what happened from 1914 to 1917, which has suddenly been started anew by the appearance of Robert Lansing's book, by the publication of Harold Nicolson's life of Dwight Morrow, and by Mr. Lamont's recent letters to the New York *Times*. If I have fallen into the common error of reformers in unfairly criticizing *men* rather than the *system* of which they are the products and the example, then I must openly and squarely plead guilty and express my regrets.

As to my cherishing malice or vindictiveness against the members of J. P. Morgan and Company, that is absurd. Let me restate my feeling about them: My high personal regard for Mr. Lamont dates back, as I recently wrote, to our college years. I respected and admired Dwight Morrow, and in my review of Nicolson's life of him I wrote that he had no reason to be ashamed of what he did as a member of the firm of Morgan. Mr. Leffingwell gave service highly valuable to his government when he served in the Treasury Department before entering the firm, and he stands high in the opinion of all those who know him. I have respected Mr. Morgan because of his modesty, his refusal to spread himself and his philanthropies over the front pages of our newspapers, and his civic attitude in general. I defended him against the attacks made upon him in connection with his income-tax returns, which attacks I still believe to have been 80 per cent hypocritical, and the other 20 per cent ignorant. Here again it was the system, and not the men, which was at fault. But the fact that these men have much civic responsibility, and mean to serve their country, must not bar any independent editor from voicing his protest when they consciously or unconsciously, voluntarily or because of the system, lead in directions that seem to him to bode ill for the social safety and the peace of the United States.

When I wrote of these men and Lansing as being "traitors" in 1915, I of course did not mean that they were traitors to their country in the ordinary sense, but that they dissented from the policy of neutrality proclaimed by the President. I know that they did not deviate from the old-fashioned policy of "strict" neutrality as laid down by the State Department itself. I meant, and I said, that for reasons that they deemed just, ample, and sufficient, they threw themselves on the side of England and refused to be neutral in spirit as the President had urged us all to be. When we got into the war, there were no more loyal and efficient Americans. Mr. Wilson's valuation of Mr. Lamont's services at that time is clearly demonstrated by his making the latter a chief economic adviser at Paris, whose advice he, unfortunately for all concerned, frequently failed to take. Again, I have pointed out that the British government could not have obtained better or cleaner or more competent men to handle their cause here; when I said that they profited indirectly as well as by their direct charges, I meant that they, like all the rest of us who owned bonds and stocks, profited by the tremendous boom all along the line. As Mr. Lamont has pointed out in his book on H. P. Davison, and I am glad to recall here, the firm was careful as a general thing not to assign contracts to bidders in whose organizations the firm or its individual members were interested. Of the hundreds of firms dealt with they were interested in only eleven and to an extent not to exceed 3 per cent in any one of them, and in these cases they reported the facts promptly to the British government. It is also true that the United States government was well aware of the operations of the firm. But this governmental inconsistency does not vitiate the fact that from the beginning the firm threw neutrality to the winds.

I am assured by critics whose judgments I may trust that I was wrong in saying that the Morgans shared Lansing's belief that our going into the war would preserve our prosperity; I am assured that some of them did not wish us to go into the war at all. I gladly accept these statements and sincerely express my regret for a contrary belief and consequent criticism. My difficulty was, perhaps, that I could not recall that during those critical months prior to our going into the war in 1917 those of us who were working tooth and nail to keep us out of it ever got any aid or encouragement from any one of them by public statements or in other ways. Nor can I recall from them a warning about what it would mean to American fathers and mothers if we should go into that struggle. How glorious it would have been if they had voiced these feelings publicly at that time! But that does not abate my satisfaction at learning now the truth. It gives me ground for the sincere hope that they will join those of us who are trying to make impossible the recurrence of events which so gravely divided the American people and led us into a struggle the sole outcome of which, plus the treaty of peace, has been the creating of a far worse Germany than that with which we set out to do battle in 1917.

But when this is said and done, my attitude toward the fundamentals of the war-time situation remains unchanged. I still feel that nothing should be left undone to prevent any recurrence of the conditions under which the Morgan firm assumed the agency in this country for the government of one of the belligerents and proceeded to place contracts for billions of dollars' worth of supplies for the Allies. I repeat my belief that not the best of men can remain unaffected in their judgments as to national policy by such a relationship; that the horde of contractors who profited by the creating of shot and shell and guns were given an incentive, consciously or unconsciously held, to put us into the war on the side of the Allies in order that, as Robert Lansing argued, our great war-created prosperity should continue. I believe —and I am encouraged in this belief by the reactions of not less than 125 audiences I have addressed on this and cognate subjects during the last two years—that the country wants a real neutrality in the next war which will keep us out of it, which means the prevention of any Americans profiting by such a struggle or taking sides in it in a business way. I still think that the merchandising of war materials is a horrible business, to be outlawed and taken over by the government at the first moment possible. Indeed, I dare not describe my feelings about that industry lest my pen and my passion against it again run away with me. But I can say it is a business that no true follower of the Nazarene can consistently touch or in the slightest degree profit by. If this is fanaticism, make the most of it!

Oswald Garrison Villard

Issues and Men

The Great British Referendum

IT is a curious fact that it was a peace vote which more than anything else drove the National Government in England into the aggressive and dangerous stand it has taken against Mussolini and into assuming the leadership of the League of Nations. I am well aware that many people still believe that the only possible explanation is British self-interest, the fear that if Mussolini conquers Ethiopia he will go farther and strive to make the Mediterranean an Italian instead of a British lake—how well founded that anxiety is was shown in an article in *The Nation* of October 16. But whatever the contributing causes, I remain of the opinion that the votes of nearly 12,000,000 English men and women polled by the British League of Nations Association last spring, under the leadership of Lord Robert Cecil, was the most potent force in the vitalizing of the English government on this issue and in its sudden determination to make the League of Nations justify itself and stop the unprovoked war against Ethiopia. Its upholding that stand in the recent election campaign resulted in its winning a larger majority than had been expected. It seems to me plain that Lord Robert Cecil—if he deserves the credit for the referendum—may well be called the savior of the League. For everybody agrees that if the League had remained inactive in the face of this Italian iniquity, it would have become merely a subject of contempt and ridicule.

Instead, the League has won millions of adherents all over the globe. Here in America there are innumerable people who for the first time are ready to join it—of course with certain reservations to prevent our being liable for a part in League-ordered wars. If the League really puts its pacific boycott through, preserves every foot of Ethiopia, humbles Italy without firing a shot, and thereby demonstrates a new technique in stopping wars and preserving, in Wilson's words, "the rights of small nations everywhere," it will have achieved the greatest step forward toward the abolition of war yet taken. It is impossible to deny the truth of what Winston Churchill has just said—that "such a system of pains and penalties was never proclaimed against a single state in the whole history of the world. We are in the presence of a memorable event." Even if it should turn out that England's sole motive in resurrecting the League was to safeguard itself against Mussolini and Hitler, that would not detract from the credit due to the British government if the intervention proves a success.

It is worth while, in view of what has happened, to reprint the referendum figures. Here they are: total votes cast, 11,627,000. Now when this vote was proposed and while it was being taken, the government sneered at it and the Tories and diehards said it would prove nothing. It was supposed that it would peter out for lack of funds. However, the money was found, and as the votes rolled in, the Liberal and Conservative politicians sat up and took notice. They could not deny that 11,627,000 votes out of a population of 44,000,000 was a genuine cross-section of the British public. It was too large for the Baldwins and Churchills to ignore, and so overwhelmingly one-sided as to make it impossible for anybody to deny that it was an unanswerable popular mandate. Winston Churchill himself has been one of the greatest critics and antagonists of the League. Today he marvels and approves without reservation. It is as if the ghost of Henry Cabot Lodge had appeared to acclaim the event and to beg the Senate to vote us into the League.

Whether or not this pacific boycott leads to actual hostilities, whether or not the Ethiopian war, as Raymond G. Swing and many others think, proves to be a "little war" carefully prepared in advance to save Mussolini's face, to be ended by a cession of Ethiopian territory to Italy, nothing can dim that British referendum. It answers those who say that you cannot have a people voting on questions of war and peace. It sets a precedent of which every country should take note, and especially the United States. There were some who begged that alleged great democrat (with a small *d*) Woodrow Wilson to take a vote of the country in April, 1917, to ascertain what was the will of the American people. Mr. Wilson wrung his hands. It could not be done because it never had been done. There was no machinery for it in the Constitution. A few weeks later General Hugh Johnson and General Crowder set up overnight the draft boards for registering millions of young men—which proved conclusively that it would have been no task at all to take a national vote on the war. Now the British have shown the way. No American statesman can henceforth seek to hide behind the Wilsonian excuses. Lord Robert Cecil has demonstrated that it can be done by private subscription in short order, by a machinery created on the spur of the moment and run chiefly by unpaid workers. This polling of about one-quarter of a great people has had results which have stirred the entire world.

I hope it is true that some of our peace organizations are planning a similar vote in the United States. The wonder is that our League of Nations Association has not already launched it. Perhaps they are waiting for the Presidential elections to come and go. I hope not. It is so vital and so thrilling a moment and President Roosevelt is so big-navy mad that there would seem to be no time to lose before letting the Administration and our army and navy lobbies, our fighting admirals and generals, know just where the country stands. Of course everything will depend upon the questions selected for submission. I for one cannot but believe that, whether the vote is for our entry into the League or not, it will be emphatically and overwhelmingly for our keeping out of war at all costs and using all our influence in behalf of those who are striving to make the League what its founders wished it to become—the destroyer of war.

Oswald Garrison Villard

Issues and Men

A Kept Merchant Marine

DETERMINED efforts are under way to put a ship-subsidy bill through Congress as soon as that body meets. Secretary Roper has become an ardent advocate of it, apparently in ignorance that what he urges spells a complete break with the historic policy of the Democratic Party. Since the Republicans have long been committed to a government-paid merchant marine there will be plenty of Republican votes for this measure. Many Congressmen and Senators who are now outraged because the New Deal has "destroyed" the character and sturdy self-reliance of the American farmer by paying him for obeying its orders will not be able to see anything wrong in fixing the profits of American shipowners and making them up out of the general taxation of the people. They will turn their backs upon the recommendation of Senator Black's Committee on Mail and Ship Subsidies, which is that, if subsidies are needed, the only way of escaping graft and corruption is by government ownership and operation. They will not spend a moment in studying the relation of our tariffs to our high shipbuilding costs. They will be concerned only with creating a new privileged class, with showing the American flag on "all the seas," and with having a shipping reserve for war time.

Yet if there ever was a field in which there should be no legislation without a most careful and far-reaching survey of the whole situation, this is it. We cannot legislate for ourselves without any regard for our rivals on the seas, however much we may wish to do so. For the action of other nations is bound to affect us, and every time we take a stand or pass a law the governments of several other countries will probably immediately seek to offset our action by legislation or decree. Most of the advocates of subsidies feel that we ought to fight for "our share" of the carrying trade but do not realize that other countries are bent on fighting for their share. This brings us at once to the questions: How much ocean trade will there be if and when normal economic conditions return? Can there be no other way of sharing it than by a fierce rate-war competition, with every government paying the losses of its nationals out of its general funds?

It is so obvious that this will lead nowhere that Secretary Roper himself admits that it will be desirable to have an international conference to obtain an agreement on the rates and relative sizes of the subsidies to be paid by each nation. To my mind this is just as impossible as the proposal to pay to each American shipbuilder the differential between what the ship costs him and what it would cost abroad. That sounds very simple and easy, but when you examine it, it at once appears wholly impracticable. Take the phrase "would cost abroad," for example. Where? In England, or Japan, or Germany, or Italy? In the cheapest shipyard in England or a more expensive one? In a shipyard not subsidized by its government or in a subsidized one? And how is the exact cost of the ship abroad to be ascertained? Presumably by an agent of the Department of Commerce. But will a foreign shipyard give its cost sheets to any American official who comes along? That seems incredible. Moreover, conditions on the ocean and in economic life are changing so rapidly that the entire cost situation might have changed by the time the American official succeeded in getting the necessary facts, if he were allowed to do so. Of course if our government would be satisfied with a general figure—that the whole ship cost $3,500,000, let us say, to build in England—this argument of mine would not hold so far as detailed costs are concerned. But costs of construction vary so much in Norwegian, Dutch, German, French, Italian, and English shipyards that I cannot see how they could be used as a satisfactory measuring stick for subsidies to American shipbuilders who demand government aid.

It is, however, gratifying to note that there is at least a thought of international action. During the World War the Allied Trade Council in London allocated shipping all over the world, to neutrals and belligerents alike. If a world trade council were to be set up now, it could perhaps devise some method of allocating world trade to the various shipping nations that would do away with the whole vexed subsidy question and bring some order into the chaos of the ocean. That chaos, by the way, might be increased in a remarkable degree if Russia should decide to expand considerably its merchant fleet. This fleet can undercut any other for the reason that it is government owned and operated throughout, and that its crews, like so many other Russian workers, seem to be actuated by a passionate devotion to their government's economic ideals. Russia is threatened today by Germany on one side and Japan on the other. Would it not have the right to demand a very large merchant marine for use when the next war comes? What if Russia should insist that all the supplies that it buys abroad should be brought to Russia only in Russian bottoms? After all, the amount of trade in the world is limited, or at least it will be until the world becomes sane again, levels its tariff barriers, and sees that the road to true prosperity everywhere is through the development of international trade. It all reveals another field in which international cooperation is direfully needed. Without it there is no hope of anything but cutthroat and wasteful competition, resulting in heavy losses to be paid for by those taxpayers who may be induced to do so by appeals to their national pride.

Here we also have a picture of what narrow nationalism means. It spells national destruction or national folly in its every phase. Yet the patriots in Washington who will cheerfully vote the new subsidies will do so without thought of where this whole policy will lead us. At least they should insist that if any subsidies are granted they should be limited as to time and should be terminated if, after a fair trial, it appears that we cannot soon have a self-supporting and an honestly and efficiently run merchant marine.

Oswald Garrison Villard

Issues and Men

A World Public Opinion Exists

WHATEVER the final outcome of the disaster into which Laval and Hoare plunged the League of Nations, it has had one great result. It has proved anew that in those countries which are not throttled by dictatorships public opinion can rule; that when the facts in a given situation are available, there is also a world opinion capable of overthrowing ministries and reversing national and international policies. Hoare was compelled to resign not merely by the indignation of the British public, shocked beyond measure by the League's betrayal by the English and French governments, but by the universal outburst of anger and criticism in the United States, in the Scandinavian countries, and in the British dominions. This was admitted at the very beginning of the debate in the House of Lords when Lord Davies declared that the Hoare-Laval surrender to Mussolini had "outrageously shocked" the peoples across the Atlantic and that the government had "stemmed the rising tide of cooperation with the League of Nations."

So Sir Samuel Hoare was jettisoned to save the newly constituted British Cabinet, and at this writing it is not yet clear whether the Laval Cabinet will ride out the storm. But enough has happened to make it beyond dispute that there is a profoundly concerned world opinion, more aroused to the danger of war than at any time since 1919, and in many quarters determined to save the League and make it the great instrument for peace that it was intended to be. That such an international uprising would not have come to pass if the proposed robbery of Ethiopia had been a slight one is probably true. From that point of view the very blackness of the British-French perfidy was a godsend. Nobody could quibble about it. Nobody could say that this was not a black but a "gray" case. Nobody could defend the offer to Mussolini of more of Ethiopia than he had asked for. And no sane or honest person will defend it today on the grounds Hoare urged—that it was the only thing to do because England alone was furnishing military and naval forces and the threat of war was alarming. Real statesmen would have foreseen this danger.

But there the fact is. The League has been saved not by the statesmen who pretended to uphold it, and imposed sanctions in accordance with its Covenant, but by the plain people everywhere and the press where it is free. In England the 11,600,000 who voted in the referendum of the League of Nations Union to stand by the League made their power felt. Everywhere liberals and labor organizations responded to the gravity of the situation, and the proposal was killed even before it was submitted to the League by Eden and Laval. It was not necessary for the Council to vote it down, nor was the admirable Ethiopian protest needed to inter, without benefit of clergy, the whole nefarious scheme. That Great Britain and France stand somewhat rehabilitated today is not due to the politicians. They who are so quick to prate about the honor of the country were the ones to betray it. If some of it is left untarnished, that is due again to the aroused opinion of the masses who, we are so often told, cannot be allowed to vote on questions of war and peace because these are too delicate and too involved for the masses to understand. Well, they understood this issue. They were quite able to recognize as black a piece of treachery as could possibly have come to pass.

Of course, the people have been tricked before. Indeed, many of the critics of the League and the cynics in the press declared from the start that "a little war had been arranged" and that it would be stopped and Ethiopia dismembered before any great harm had been done. But these writers reckoned without their host. They overlooked the fact that we have come a long way from pre-war days, that whatever else the League has done it has helped to educate the people everywhere to an understanding of international problems, and that in the United States, too, there are far more people thinking intelligently about foreign affairs than ever before. Here is a vast reservoir of power for honest and intelligent statesmen to draw upon, to turn to for aid and support. Here Baldwin and Hoare would have found, and can still find, their best protection against the threats of war of the irresponsible dictator of Italy. Here is the clearest proof that if they had appealed to all the world for support in their original course they would have been triumphantly upheld. Mussolini, for all his ability to delude his pitiful subjects, could never have held out against the response which these statesmen would have had. But no, your Baldwins and Lavals cannot work in the open, cannot follow a straightforward manly way, cannot take the world into their confidence. They must meet in secret, take counsel of their fears, while lacking the brains even to suspect to what utter humiliation their course is leading them.

Well, let some more statesmen blunder like Baldwin and Laval, and we shall not only have the smaller nations taking the management of the League out of the hands of England and France and making it a really sincere and democratic body, but we may even live to see the peoples taking a stand against all the militaristic and nationalistic policies which are making world recovery impossible. Today let us fall back upon the great achievement abroad and give praise to whom it is due. There is nothing in what has happened to make Hitler or any other dictator rejoice—far from it. As for Mussolini, he must recognize that the campaign against him has now passed out of the hands of perfidious and malleable governments. Baldwin and Laval may have forgotten that Mussolini said to the French Ambassador last summer: "If you brought me Abyssinia on a silver tray, I would not accept it, for I am resolved to take it by force." Others have not. They know that if he is to be encouraged to take Abyssinia, other dictators will follow suit, and the world will be well on the road to chaos and destruction.

Oswald Garrison Villard

Issues and Men

Roosevelt Betrays Neutrality

THE President has done nothing more incomprehensible than to abandon his own neutrality measures and to substitute therefor the bill which at this writing has been passed by the House and is now pending in the Senate. This extends the existing law until May 1, 1937, and adds to it a provision placing a ban on loans and credits and also one to clarify or define the status of the South American states. The very point in the Administration bill which the State Department especially desired, namely, the granting to the President of the power to place embargoes on certain materials if in his judgment it was wise to do so, has been deliberately jettisoned. The result could not be more unfortunate unless we were to abandon entirely the effort to keep the United States out of the next war. Italy is reported to be greatly cheered because of the collapse of our leadership in this matter, and the corresponding discouragement in London and Paris will be enhanced by the news of the latest Italian victories in Ethiopia.

But the international aspects of our policy are dealt with in another column. I wish to take this opportunity, after a visit to Washington, to put on record my belief that the reason for the lamentable legislative situation is not what is being put forth by friends of the Administration in and out of office. It is not true that the bulk of the Senators have yielded to pressure brought by the cotton, oil, steel, and shipping groups. That representatives of these industries have been in Washington in large numbers is correct. But the simple fact is that it was the Administration that hauled down the flag. If it is an open secret that Senator Pittman never cared for the bill which he sponsored and that Senator Robinson could hardly be called enthusiastic about it, they would none the less have brought it on to the floor of the Senate, as it would have been brought out in the House, had the President declared it a "must measure" and said that he could not afford, and they could not afford, to go before the people next fall without showing increased safeguards along the lines suggested by the State Department itself. Why was it that Secretary Hull and his assistants spent the greater part of a month testifying before the responsible committees of Congress in support of this bill? Just to waste time? Certainly not.

But the reply always is that Senator Johnson threatened a filibuster and that so many Senators had yielded to the industrial lobbies that there was nothing else to do. This observers without number absolutely deny, notably the twenty-one Senators who came together on February 14 resolved to make a last-ditch fight for the Administration's neutrality measure, which they had generously accepted even though many of them preferred the Nye-Clark bill. If it is the lobbies which have won this fight, why would not a brave champion of peace in the White House come right straight out and say so? Failing that, would not a real fighter have insisted on a poll in the House and Senate and then pointed to the men who voted against the Administration measure as the ones who had put their political welfare, or their fear of the "interests," above their duty to the whole country? But no, it was the Administration itself that told the key men in both houses to abandon the real bill and substitute this compromise, the purpose of which is to throw the whole issue over until after the election.

What makes this surrender the more censurable is that the mass of people in this country have given overwhelming testimony to their desire for a neutrality law with teeth in it. Admiral Sims asserted before the Economic Club in New York City recently that in all his experience he had never seen audiences so determined upon the country's being kept out of war and upon having a real neutrality measure as on his recent speaking trip in the South and Southwest. He declared that he could not speak on any subject without having to talk about neutrality before the evening was over. I had exactly the same experience on a long speaking trip last fall, and Congressman Maury Maverick also told the Economic Club that after speaking in twenty-four states during the recess of Congress he could uphold Admiral Sims's statement at every point. It is a first-class political blunder for the White House, and it will not be concealed by putting the blame on certain industries—and on the peace movement.

Yes, on the peace movement. Amazing as it seems, the responsibility for this débâcle is shared in the eyes of the Administration by the peace organizations and the big-business lobbies! A government official assured me that the peace organizations were responsible because they had not organized all the states and roused public opinion to such an extent that the outpourings of protest would have offset the lobbies on the other side. I have heard many charges brought against the peace movement, but I give a prize to this one. It is one of the strangest and most unmerited yet. That official showed that he was unaware of the fact that some of the organizations had done the very thing he wished. Why had not a certain society moved? he inquired. He insisted that he had not heard from it, but when he spoke a letter from him acknowledging receipt of its expression of opinion was on file in the society's office.

Well, if this sort of weakness continues; if everything is to be sacrificed to playing politics between now and the election, and to the President's desire to get Congress out of the legislative trenches and on its way home by the first of May, we may see the Roosevelt stock drop still lower. One hears in Washington astounding tales of the slump in Roosevelt sentiment in various states. They may or may not be true, but the fact is undeniable that it is the President himself who is jeopardizing his chances for reelection. No one else, not the Republicans, not the Al Smiths, not the Liberty League, but just the man in the White House—and this despite the rising tide of prosperity.

Oswald Garrison Villard

Issues and Men

BY OSWALD GARRISON VILLARD

UNDER the heading The Fallacy of Conquest, Nathaniel Peffer recently contributed an admirable article to *Harper's Magazine*. Dealing with the stupidity of those who believe that a nation can add to its wealth by subjugating native peoples or robbing them of part of their territory, it brings the discussion up to date by taking up directly the case of Italy, Germany, and Japan. Especially valuable is his demolition of the current humbug that we must deal gently with these nations because they must have their "place in the sun," because they are without sufficient colonies, or because their overflowing populations cannot be adequately maintained on the territory they have. Mr. Peffer confirms what some of us have been saying right along—that colonies do not today relieve congested populations. England, the largest colonial power, would gladly export two million workers if it could. The dominions have put up immigration bars against the mother country, and the tropical colonies take only Englishmen of the ruling class. British labor cannot compete with tropical labor.

The biggest humbug of all is the demand of Germany for the return of its colonies, which Hitler recently made a prerequisite for limitation of air armaments in his talks with the British Ambassador at Berlin. Ever since the war, whenever I have visited Germany, I have been assailed by people who asked me why my demand for justice for the Germans did not include the return of their colonies. My first answer was my opposition to any country's governing subject races. My second objection was to the harsh militaristic character of Germany's colonial administration. My third was that Germany did not get anything out of her colonies and that they were not population outlets.

This always brings a roar of dissent, but I have never found that one of my interrogators knew how many Germans were living in German colonies before the World War. The guesses ranged up to 500,000. Actually, as Mr. Peffer points out, there were only 24,000 Germans in the colonies, 22,000 of them in the 900,000 square miles of their African territory. Mr. Peffer also shows conclusively that possession of colonies no longer guarantees enjoyment of the economic perquisites thereof, for trade no longer follows the flag—Japan, as he points out, is getting the trade of England in India, the Malay Peninsula, and elsewhere. Again, he rightly stresses that "possession of a colony grants prior right but not monopoly. . . . Great Britain controls the rubber of Malaya, but it had to come to terms with American manufacturers." He does concede that expansion to secure access to raw materials "still has a certain validity. . . . Possession of a colony does give prior rights to such natural resources and at least yields a profit from their exploitation." But that is all the profit that the whole colonial business gives to conquerors and exploiters; "it does not solve the fundamental economic problems of a country." Even that profit can quickly disappear if there is charged against the colony the cost of administering and policing it and its share of the cost and maintenance of the cruisers and battleships needed to "protect" it in war time.

In the case of Italy and Ethiopia the situation is clear. There are no great supplies of raw materials in Ethiopia. There are indications of diamonds and gold, but not sufficient to warrant any serious exploration in search of them. There is no coal, no genuine sign of oil. Even if there were raw materials, the cost of getting them out would be prohibitive. The current jest that if there had been wealth in Ethiopia, England would have stolen it years ago is altogether justified. As to the boast of an Italian general on taking Adowa that there would be a million Italians settled there within ten years, that is absolutely absurd; there are only 4,283 Europeans in Eritrea, which has been Italian territory for fifty years. Japan stole Formosa, Korea, half of Sakhalin, and all southern Manchuria, but its overflowing population will not go to those territories, and despite all our alarmists they have gone to the Philippines in far smaller numbers than the Chinese, though there has been no bar to their entrance. People accustomed to one kind of climate are not eager to go to a different one, and farmers who would emigrate need capital, which farmers today do not have.

There is a bait for dictators in the man-power of colonies. Is not that one of the major objectives of Mussolini in Abyssinia? France would cling to its colonies for that reason even if they all put it deeply in the red. Press reports say that there are more French colonial troops garrisoned in France than ever before. The French armies would probably have collapsed early in 1917, or sooner, if it had not been for the colored troops and the Indo-Chinese work battalions. Today, with its falling man-power, France needs those colored troops more than ever, and I have seen apparently reliable statements that the government is steadily building up black reserves in Africa. Mussolini, as everyone knows, dreams of other than African conquests. What a help it would be if he could throw, in addition to his Askaris, let us say 300,000 well-trained Ethiopians on to a European battlefield! They could no more protest than can the French colonial troops, or could the hapless Indian troops in 1914 when England threw them into the holocaust that concerned them not at all. As long as war continues I fear we shall have the imperialist powers clinging to their colonies in order to squeeze out every black soldier that they can.

Issues and Men

BY OSWALD GARRISON VILLARD

OUR extraordinary lurch into enormous armament expenses goes on apace, and every day brings additional proposals for military or naval increases. Now comes the news of a proposed five-year program calling for 4,000 army planes at a cost of $70,000,000. A bill to this effect has been offered by Chairman McSwain of the House Military Affairs Committee. Mr. McSwain's contention is that though the Morrow board fixed the ratio between the navy and army forces at ten to eighteen, the naval aircraft authorized or built total 2,190, while the army authorization still remains at 1,800, when it should be 4,000. The new Chief of Staff, General Malih Craig, has made the usual appeal for increased armaments; in a speech over the radio he declares that he is not in favor of an overwhelming force but only of an army of reasonable size with effective reserves.

The amount of money appropriated continues to stagger the public. The War Department's military expenditures have increased from $108,382,063 in 1913 to approximately $375,000,000—the total of the strictly military expenditures in the pending record-breaking army bill of $543,000,000. The navy bill, if it stays at the limit fixed in the new budget, will bring the total for army and navy to approximately $950,000,000, to which will be added sums set aside by the WPA and PWA not yet expended which may carry the total as high as $1,200,000,000, or much more than the entire cost of the United States government in 1916. The President is also asking in an especial bill that the naval reserves be increased by no less than 110,000 men; thus we shall have an additional fixed charge for the maintenance of these reserves as soon as they are established. Last year the Congress authorized the construction of six new air bases to cost $12,000,000, but that money has not yet been appropriated. The navy has just asked for an additional 221,000 tons of auxiliary ships merely to carry ammunition and supplies, and so it goes. When is it to end?

It is obvious from this that we are engaged in an armament race with the rest of the world. Russia has taken the lead with the largest standing army in the world, 1,300,000 men, costing, with the Russian navy, the huge sum of $7,000,000,000 a year. To this is added the announcement that they are going to build their navy up to rival the Japanese.

No one knows what the Germans are spending on armaments or how rapidly their plans are going forward, although even conservative observers calculate that by 1939 they will be "ready." Ready, that is, to plunge the world into another period of slaughter. Stanley Baldwin gives as one of the reasons for the great new British arms program the fact that certain ships now building for the German navy will be completed in two years instead of five. Hoover, when he was President, bewailed the fact that the world was spending $5,000,000,000 a year for armaments while many countries were on the verge of bankruptcy. I do not know whether he included the Russian figures in this estimate or not, but if he did, the world's army and navy expenditures have gone up at least seven or eight billions a year more because of the German rearmament, our own great increase in expenditures, and the enormous Russian outlay. It would not be surprising if the world were spending today twelve or thirteen billions a year for increasing armaments. Yet Calvin Coolidge spoke the truth when he said that no amount of armament ever kept a country out of war or insured it victory when it got into war.

It is plain that we are rapidly reaching the ideal of all militarists, when the world will be entirely in arms. But will the world be a better and safer place with all the nations armed to the teeth? Wouldn't they be just as well off relatively if none of them armed at all? If it is true, as so many people insist, that armaments lead to war, of course these great equipments and huge armies will sooner or later lead to a terrific explosion. Stanley Baldwin declared only three years ago that if a new armament race began, a number of nations would be bankrupted. Somehow it seems to me perfectly idiotic that human beings should continue to place their faith in weapons and armed men instead of trying to find some other way of settling their international disputes.

So far as we are concerned, it would not be out of place for the American public to ask its government, first, against whom we are arming; secondly, whether we are getting a dollar's worth of defense for every dollar invested, since high army and navy officers declare that this is not the case; thirdly, whether we have a defense program which is meant for defense and not for offense; whether there is any coordination whatsoever between army and navy—which army and navy officers also deny; whether if we are truly on the defensive and have no idea of aggression, as the President has repeatedly said, the last time at the grave of the Unknown Soldier on last Armistice Day, we need 35,000-ton battleships, and so on. One of the highest officers in the navy assured me only a week or ten days ago that it would be impossible for the American and Japanese fleets to wage war against each other. If this is true, ought we not to make a great change in our whole policy? As it is, it is contended that we are ladling out money with little or no reference to any sound policy, just as the President has been pouring out money for public works without a far-reaching program.

Issues and Men

BY OSWALD GARRISON VILLARD

AT LAST we have a clearing-house and coordinator for the many peace organizations of the country. The National Peace Conference, which is holding its first meeting in Washington in the week of April 21, represents some thirty-five national anti-war societies or associations which are especially interested in improving international relations before the world is finally wrecked by war and the armament madness. The purpose of the conference is to avoid duplication of effort, to bring about a united peace front as far as that is possible, to develop a unity of program, and above all to make the peace movement more realistic and much harder hitting than ever before. This conference has been in an experimental stage for some three years. Now, as a result of impetus given to it at a meeting called by Nicholas Murray Butler, it is well on the way to accomplishing its purpose. It is emphatically not another peace organization. It is the *agency* of the bodies which comprise its membership, each of which has two representatives in the conference. It makes suggestions and offers programs. It informs its member societies what the different organizations are doing so that they may cooperate if they desire. It will probably publish soon a bulletin of information. It will, of course, sponsor mass-meetings, and it is already carrying on a radio campaign. It will voice its opinions and issue the usual press releases and engage in the usual open and above-board peace propaganda—activities which have already caused that noble, honorable, and high-minded American William Randolph Hearst to go into spasms.

The conference has appointed a number of committees and doubtless will appoint more. It is getting in touch with sympathetic persons who are distinguished in the fields of international law and international relations in order to have the benefit of their advice. It is especially interested in matters of national defense, and recently published the protest of more than 700 prominent men and women against the mad rush in Congress to militarize the country by voting billion-dollar appropriations for army and navy. To list the organizations which have thus far joined would take most of my remaining space, but it is worth while to point out that conservative and radical peace organizations are at last under the same banner, the Carnegie Endowment for International Peace, for example, together with the Fellowship of Reconciliation and the Women's International League for Peace and Freedom, the National Council for the Prevention of War, the League of Nations Association, the World Peace Foundation, the National Council of the Y. M. C. A., and many others equally well known. Frankly, nothing has given me greater hope for the peace movement except the extraordinary turning to it of youth in the universities and colleges of the land—the National Student Federation is naturally a member of the Peace Conference.

Indeed, the more I travel around the country the more I am impressed by the great strength of the peace sentiment. The insistence upon new neutrality legislation, the determination that this country shall not take part in the next European war, the clear understanding on the part of the people that our going into the last war was an unmitigated calamity—all these things convince me that if this sentiment could only be organized it would exert a tremendous influence and bring Washington to book—especially that astute politician in the White House who has been so rapidly militarizing the country without in the least taking the country into his confidence about it. It was especially gratifying to read that a strong delegation from the People's Mandate Against War has followed the Peace Conference's lead and has demanded of the Democrats in Congress that they return to the platform of 1932 in this matter of large military expenditures; it has also asked the Republican leaders who are crying out so vociferously for economy and a balanced budget why they have not demanded economy in the matter of armaments.

All this merely reinforces the point that the time had more than come for a coordination of the peace forces. And it is not merely the money side of it of which I am thinking. I am far more concerned with our building up the professional military and naval group than with the billions we are squandering. Dorothy Bromley in the *World-Telegram* has just reported a conversation with a naval officer in Washington who told her that this country ought to have a dictator, that Mussolini was the greatest living man, and that the final word on all American foreign affairs should be in the hands of the military branches of the government! There is loyalty to the Republic for you. Nor is this an exceptional opinion. Anybody who knows how military opinion is running in Washington can tell of other officers who talk in this way. Secretary Ickes has said that the spearhead of fascism in this country is appearing in the effort to muzzle and control college and school teachers. I think a much more dangerous spearhead is to be found in Washington in military and naval circles.

Finally I must not fail to add that the National Peace Conference has been extremely fortunate in getting Dr. Walter W. Van Kirk as director. Long associated with the Federal Council of Churches and an admirable interpreter of religious news over the radio, he has established the national office of the conference at 8 West Fortieth Street, New York, where full information as to the work may be obtained. It deserves to grow into the most important and influential body of all those seeking to preserve our peace, our institutions, and our very civilization.

Issues and Men

BY OSWALD GARRISON VILLARD

THERE are two phases of the Spanish struggle that I wish specially to call attention to. One is the fact that the present round of fighting is only a round, no matter who wins it. The battle will go on until the Spanish workers and peasants have come into their own. If the present régime collapses, which may prove to be the case before these lines go into type, we shall undoubtedly see a terrific reaction with the usual concomitants of bloodshed, wholesale executions, concentration camps, and the like, and the establishment of a military dictatorship. The other is this fresh proof of the danger which comes to any republic from the existence of a large standing army.

Apparently the Spanish government has not had the strength either to put an end to sporadic lawlessness, notably against the Catholic church, or to take drastic measures with the army. When the king was driven out in 1931 thousands of officers were put upon the retired list or dismissed outright, but they have remained in Spain as foci of discontent and of hostility to those in power, and they are doubtless in entire sympathy with the uprising that began in the colonies and crossed over into Spain. It is beyond doubt a terrible situation, with all sorts of dire possibilities, such as the breaking up of the country into several parts. But the fact remains that this revolutionary outburst comes not from communists or other left-wing radicals, or from the land-hungry peasants, or the organized workers, but from the military men sworn to uphold the existing government.

The unrest which has marked these post-war years in Spain is the more striking because Spain was the only western European country to keep out of the World War, during which it prospered greatly. Much of that prosperity, if not all, has now been dissipated, in great measure because of the internal upheavals, but also because of those African colonies which, like Cuba and the Philippines in their day as Spanish possessions, have been such a drain upon the country's finances and manhood. The second article I wrote for *The Nation,* back in 1894, was a description of my visit to Melilla into which the Spanish army had then been driven by Moroccans. I was only ashore a short time, but what I saw of the conditions in the camps prepared me for the incapacity of the Spanish army to put down the insurrection in Cuba in the years 1896 to 1898. I have never forgotten the horrible insanitary conditions, the quality of the food served out to the troops, and the under-sized and pitiful Spanish boys who composed the rank and file and were being sacrificed in a war about the purposes of which they knew nothing. After the World War I met the German aunt of the King of Spain, a former Bavarian princess, who was then visiting with her daughter, the Princess Pilar, in Munich. I asked her about conditions in Spain and expected a rosy response. Her face fell. "I was so happy," said she, "that we kept out of the World War and even gained in prosperity by doing so, but now we are slaughtering our youth again in Africa. I wish I could understand these things, but I cannot. My nephew, the King, tells me that we must fight again in Africa because of our national honor, that we must hold those colonies come what may. I cannot understand it. I cannot understand," she repeated, "why this 'national honor' should make us butcher our youth in Africa and throw away all the money and the advantages that we gained from not going into the World War." Unfortunately it was the nephew who controlled and not this humane and kindly woman, and thousands of Spanish boys perished thereafter as well as thousands of Moroccans.

Certainly the colonies have revenged themselves once more upon the Spanish government. Perhaps the present rulers if they had had time would have decreased the army on African soil and sought to rule in accordance with the socialist spirit of good will and friendliness rather than by force of arms. If this administration in Spain goes down it will be simply due to the enmity among army officers for a new deal which was to have brought some hope and some economic satisfaction to the millions of underpaid and undernourished Spanish peasants and workers who have toiled for many generations for absentee landlords living in the greatest possible luxury in Madrid, or Seville, or abroad.

We have no definite statistics as to how far the redistribution of land has gone during the last twelve months. The very fact that it was under way undoubtedly goaded the reactionaries and the privileged classes to make a final stand against the expropriation of the great estates. If it is correct that the peasants are rising to help the rebellion it must be due to their ignorance of where their hope lies; they are surely forging new chains for themselves. I am afraid it is true that when popular revolutions take place it is absolutely essential to make them thorough. I do not mean by this that republicans and socialists and liberals should resort to violence, to mass murder and the concentration camps, but I do not see why they cannot use their power to grapple effectively with the reactionary elements to the extent of removing every last one from positions of importance, and if necessary using the right to exile. The trouble with the 1931 revolution, like that of 1918 in Germany, was that it stopped half way and did not carry out radical social and economic reforms. The present leftist-Republican Cabinet has only had five months in which to move, but one can do a great deal in five months if one will take a leaf out of the book of dictators and house-clean just as vigorously as they, only humanely.

Issues and Men

BY OSWALD GARRISON VILLARD

THE Supreme Court's upholding of the joint resolution of 1934, which authorized the President to proclaim embargos of arms and munitions, tremendously heartens all who believe that the existing neutrality legislation which will expire shortly should be reenacted and that everything possible should be done to reinforce it. If there is one thing that the American people want above all else it is to be kept out of the next war, and they are willing to make any sacrifice to that end. That the President and Secretary Hull realize this is plain from Mr. Roosevelt's peace speeches at Chautauqua and in South America and from Mr. Hull's earnest and moving address at Buenos Aires. Everyone who like myself constantly travels up and down this country knows that, as the late Admiral William S. Sims testified last winter, there are few audiences which do not voluntarily bring up the question of war and peace.

Despite this there is a distinct rift in the government and another in the peace forces on the question of neutrality. The State Department sticks to its position that legislation should not be mandatory for the President but should give him the power to interpret any war situation and apply an embargo according to his judgment. The President himself desired this when the fight for neutrality legislation began, but he subsequently modified his position and accepted provisions to which he was at first reported to be opposed. In the peace movement Raymond Leslie Buell, of the Foreign Policy Association, is against rigid mandatory legislation because, so he says in a recent bulletin, the neutrality proposal made by Secretary Hull in his draft convention at Buenos Aires "would penalize the victim of aggression to the same extent as the state violating its obligations." He fears that if the proposal is carried at Buenos Aires, the Latin American states will "drift away" from the League of Nations.

But the proposal that Washington shall have the right to decide as between the aggressor and the aggrieved seems to me to insure our taking part in future wars. It means setting ourselves up as judges in a war with which we may have no concern. It means that we shall aid those whom, at the hysterical moment of the explosion, we believe to be aggrieved. Who can be sure under such circumstances? It took years for the historians to bring out the relative responsibility and guilt of the nations which took the world to war in 1914 and to establish that Germany was by no means the sole criminal. President Roosevelt has on several occasions said that the aggressor nation is the one whose troops first cross another's boundaries. Do we really know today whether or not French troops crossed into Alsace-Lorraine before the Germans entered Belgium? We certainly did not in the fall of 1914. Not only is the role of deciding which is the aggressor in a conflict extraordinarily difficult; it would obviously be extremely dangerous if the aggressor should hold us accountable for aid to the nation we considered aggrieved.

The American people, I believe, want no risks of this kind taken. They want cast-iron, automatic, mandatory laws—I do not undertake to say now how extreme—that will say, "A plague o' both your houses, we are going our own way." They will not be moved by the argument that the wrong may triumph. They are thoroughly convinced that right and justice were not born of our participation in the World War, and that they were deceived into entering it by lying propaganda, the entanglement of our big business men with the English war machine, and the false Wilson slogans. They have no desire to usurp again the seat of the Almighty and pass judgments to be backed up by war. They will not be moved this winter by frantic arguments that this policy will wreck the League of Nations, for they wish to have nothing to do with the League. They will not be swayed by assertions that this would be an ignoble and selfish course and perhaps lead to the downfall of civilization. They will reply: "We had enough of all that bunk from Woodrow Wilson with his war to safeguard democracy and end war. We propose to be purely for ourselves this time."

That mandatory neutrality legislation will take us on uncharted seas is perfectly true. We shall be reversing our historic neutrality policy, and we shall have no precedents. But there are many untried departures in international relations, and anybody's guess as to how any policy will work out is little better than anybody else's. The American people are ready for the risks involved in mandatory legislation, and it is theirs to decide. They are, many of them, aware that the power to make war has slipped away from Congress, where it was placed by the Constitution, and now rests squarely in the hands of the President, as President Roosevelt admitted when he declared at Chautauqua that no neutrality legislation would keep us out of war if a President and Secretary of State wished to put us in. Can the people be blamed if they are opposed to granting the President more power to get us into war? He has usurped that power from Congress as it is.

I most earnestly appeal to every reader of these words and every lover of peace to make his wishes felt in Washington by the time-honored method of addressing his Senators and Congressman and President. There is no more pressing or patriotic duty than this.

Issues and Men

BY OSWALD GARRISON VILLARD

Walter Lippmann's Prize Piece

I WAS much tempted during the last campaign to offer a prize of $1,000 to be awarded to the daily newspaper columnist who wrote the silliest article prior to the election, my plan being to ask the editors of the Baltimore *Suns,* the St. Louis *Post-Dispatch,* and the *New Republic* to act as judges. But I did not happen to have the $1,000 available, and the plan came to naught. I used to think, as the weeks wore on, that Mark Sullivan would be an easy winner if only because of his original and startling discovery, in the middle of the campaign, that there were two new ideologies menacing democracy at work in the world, namely, the creeds of the Communists and the fascists. But each time that I thought he had nailed down the hypothetical prize along would come an article by Walter Lippmann so overpowering as to put Mark into the background.

One of these Lippmann triumphs has been recalled to me by a recent article of his in the *Herald Tribune* entitled Effective Neutrality. The mid-campaign effort was a gem of purest ray serene. The whole of the first column dealt with the next war in Europe. We were told that European military men felt that it would be short, must be short, that every effort would be made to avoid trench warfare and to end the war quickly by destroying the enemy's capital from the air. We then learned how vulnerable the European nations are because of their relative nearness to one another and the concentration of their financial and commercial power and all their government bureaus in their capitals. The thesis was laid down that England, France, and Germany would have to surrender if their capitals were destroyed. As far as that the article read just like a military essay, and then with the turn of the column the real objective appeared. This military stuff was only a prelude to an argument against Franklin Roosevelt's reelection. I did not get it at first, my brains being old and dull, but after a while it hit me.

Here is the argument, as Lippmann put it: A vote for Roosevelt would be a vote for a man whose whole idea was to increase the power of the federal government and to concentrate that power in Washington. Of course he could not do it in four years. But if he were reelected, the tendency would be confirmed and approved, and in the course of time we should be just as dangerously vulnerable to airplane attack as Berlin or London or Rome or Paris, with all our governmental activities in one basket. It might, of course, be several decades before this situation could come to pass, but still the thing must be scotched in November, 1936, once and for all. Therefore all good citizens and true, all who wished to preserve our institutions from destruction from the air, must vote for Landon. Q.E.D. The fact that General Hugh Johnson, a trained soldier, declared the next day in his column that Lippmann's entire original premise was false, and that the countries he named could fight on if their capitals were destroyed, did not really mar this masterpiece. If there ever was a prize-winner, this was it.

Now we have another gem from the same pen. In his Effective Neutrality Lippmann brushes aside the legislative proposals both of those who favor complete mandatory laws and of those who desire permissive legislation. With a stroke of genius he ends the whole debate. We need do only one thing to be safe and that is to "found our neutrality on a program of military preparedness," for that "kills two birds with one stone." It "makes our neutrality effective, that is to say, likely to be respected," and "it relieves the depression, which would inevitably produce the social discontent in which war fevers are generated." Those who remember 1914-17 will recall how great were social discontent and the depression when our factories all over the country were working day and night for the English and French war machines and employment was at its maximum. The next pearl of wisdom is that by immediately going on a war footing we should provide "useful and patriotic work for those who would otherwise be the leaders and the rank and file of a war party." "This," he says, "is no small help in the preservation of peace," for it was not the Allies, nor the J. P. Morgans and the du Ponts who were the war-mongers, but Theodore Roosevelt and Leonard Wood.

This, Walter Lippmann says, is "the only prudent and effective way to remain neutral, at peace with ourselves, and reasonably sane." Well, let us hope that no Hugh Johnson will take hold of this argument, for such a man might point out that war parties are not the creation of months but spring up overnight, that nothing could strengthen a war party more than mobilization, that mobilization inevitably brings not calmness but hysteria, and that with three million men being trained the demand of future Theodore Roosevelts and Leonard Woods to go somewhere and do something with our champing military strength would acquire dangerous if not fatal force. It is impossible to think of any other plan which would more certainly involve us in war. Lippmann himself admits a doubt, for he claims only that mobilization would make our neutrality *"likely"* to be respected.

In case anyone should ask why I proposed to limit my competition to the dailies and did not include those who write weekly columns, I hasten to explain that I wished to save the judges from the possible embarrassment of having to give me back my own money.

Issues and Men

BY OSWALD GARRISON VILLARD

Germany and Ethics

WHATEVER else may be said about the European dictatorships, they are compelling us to test anew our standard of values in ethics as well as our political beliefs. They are, for example, presenting us at every turn with the age-old question as to whether the end can ever justify the means. Hardly a day goes by that I do not meet somebody just returned from either Germany or Italy who tells me how marvelously happy and prosperous the people are. "You may say what you please about Hitler," is what they say, "but Germany never looked so well. The people are polite. They go out of their way to be nice to foreigners. There seems to be no discontent whatever. Of course the dictator does many things of which I disapprove, but you must be fair and give him credit for the good things he has accomplished. It's not all bad."

I find it hard to reply politely. I am tempted to imitate Dorothy Thompson, who usually says: "I will not debate with anybody the exact merits of a bloody-handed murderer." I, too, am not interested in an effort to evaluate the exact ethical worth of a man who had no less than 1,254 men and women and youths killed in one night and then stood up in the Reichstag, swore that there were only seventy-seven murdered, and assumed in emphatic language the complete responsibility for their deaths. "I assumed the supreme power." I cannot be enthusiastic over the good manners of the Germans toward foreign visitors, for I think of the 25,000 men and women still confined in concentration camps and often horribly tortured and maltreated. I deny emphatically that the man responsible for these and many other crimes against humanity can in the slightest degree atone for those crimes by building a magnificent stadium and superb roads, or by freeing his people from the yoke of the unjust Treaty of Versailles.

Any dictator can build good roads. Any dictator can send 3,000,000 Christmas baskets of food to the destitute and needy with his picture and the words: "Your Leader is thinking of you." Any dictator can enforce outward order and militarize his people. I do not have to go to Germany to know that superficially things look well; that the streets are clean and free of beggars; that there is universal politeness; and that by means of the huge army, the compulsory work camps, the great rearmament orders to heavy industry, and the concentration camps, the number of unemployed has been reduced by the dictator from 6,000,000 to 1,000,000. Nor do I have to go to Germany to know that side by side with this "progress" and the great change in the psychology of the youth of Germany, the whole intellectual life of Germany has been destroyed; that three years have been cut out of the primary educational system and one year out of the university course; that academic freedom is no more; that the press is denatured and dead; that there has been created an atmosphere of fear and domination and of disregard of the most precious human rights in which no creative spirit or instinct can survive.

These things alone seem to me so infinitely worth while and necessary to the spiritual development of a people that I cannot feel that the material achievements of Hitler and Mussolini weigh many grains beside them. Their material advances are in the first place not the sole prerogatives of dictatorships. In the second place, the achievements of both the Italian and German dictatorships have been purchased by a distinct lowering of standards of living; and, finally, we do not yet know whether they will not crash financially. Certainly the regimentation of the whole people in order that what there is in the way of butter and other fats may be evenly distributed does not warrant the belief as yet that even on the material side the dictatorship is a howling success. "Guns instead of butter," is General Göring's slogan. Well, I believe, like Anthony Eden, that for the health, safety, and sanity of peoples the world over and for their future happiness and security butter is preferable to guns.

No outward order or material accomplishment can offset the ethical and spiritual degradation of a people. No roads or other public works and no beautifully drilled armies and navies can possibly counterbalance the misleading of a great people by the doctrine of force, by the teaching that war is the supreme good, by the dissemination of utterly false and unscientific racial theories, and by the assumption that there is wisdom enough in any dictator to guide the intellectual development of many millions of people. Of course the economic welfare of the people must be a government's primary concern; without that there can be no other advance. But the question is simply whether material prosperity is to be vouchsafed to a lot of disciplined slaves or to free men living in that atmosphere of individual liberty and experimentation and self-expression which history has invariably proved to be the sole condition under which humanity progresses.

How any loyal American—loyal not to the flag, the mere symbol of our nation, but to its fundamental principles—can indorse the regimes of the dictators is beyond me. Yet I meet these disloyalists at every turn, with their panegyrics on the great progress of Italy and Germany. Again I deny that the outward material progress achieved by Hitler in any way offsets or compensates for the misery, the injustice, the blood upon which it is built.

Issues and Men

BY OSWALD GARRISON VILLARD

THE European dance of death goes merrily on. In the past few weeks the press has reported the following developments in the armament race: The French Parliament has voted, 405 to 186, in favor of the government's vast new national-defense program, the Communists all voting aye. The outlay is to be 19,000,000,000 francs in the regular estimates and another 19,000,000,000 to be spread over the next four years, thus "heavily mortgaging the future," as the dispatches report. Of course, both the Defense Minister and the Air Minister reported that there was no cause for alarm. Yet the new appropriations were voted although the French Republic has no money to pay its international debts and cannot balance its budget.

From France's Polish ally comes this report: During the next four years Poland will spend one billion zlotys for defensive purposes, one-half of which will come from a recent French loan. Another bill, just introduced in the Parliament, calls for the expenditure of 264,000,000 zlotys for "general economic purposes," which sum, it is admitted, is in large part to be spent on defensive projects.

Berlin, next to Moscow, is setting the pace, and the news comes from there that Hitler's military expenditures for the year 1936-37 will reach the staggering figure of 12,600,000,000 marks. At the end of this first four-and-one-half-year period Hitler, so the London *Banker* estimates, will have spent no less than 31,100,000,000 marks upon armaments. This does not mean immediate economic disaster for the Reich, but it does mean that the scale of living of the masses is steadily sinking and that Germany is isolating itself economically. All of which, Hitler says, is necessary in order to revive the old Germanic virtues in his subjects and restore Germany to a position of equality in the family of nations—and in the race toward destruction.

From Moscow comes the almost incredible figure of an annual expenditure of $12,000,000,000 to make Russia safe from capitalist attack. Gone are all the old ideas of internationalism, of the solidarity of the workers of the world. Nothing more is heard of any refusal to slaughter the dupes of the capitalist countries. The whole national emphasis is as much on national defense as on anything else. France officially says that the Soviet air fleet is better than its own, and Stalin's standing army is admitted to be larger than that of any other country.

England still hopes to escape a capital levy to provide means for its new armament, on which, the government has announced, $7,500,000,000 will be spent in the next five years. Three new battleships will be laid down this year, and there will be a large increase of the air force.

And here's a dispatch saying that the French have decided to extend their "Maginot" line of fortifications to cover the Swiss and Belgian frontiers, although no one knows whether they will really avail in the next war. It is widely believed that the Germans are not in the least perturbed by the line and expect to jump over it with a huge airplane force and to go through it with tanks of high speed, or to pass the fortifications at night with small infiltrating squads which will then unite and attack the line from the rear.

If bankruptcy and/or war do not result from this mad race, then all precedents will fail. Meanwhile the costs, staggering as they are, are not the worst feature of this mad militarism. Everywhere the armies are becoming so powerful as literally to control the fate of nations. In Russia, if the Red Army decides to unhorse Stalin, he will go. Hitler will rule just as long as he holds the loyalty of his army. The horrible tragedy of Spain shows what can happen when the army turns traitor to the legally constituted government. In Japan the army seems about to have its way with country and people. Nearer home, the dictators in the Caribbean are intrenching themselves by making their armies more efficient. But they can be ousted on the day their troops decide that they want some other "leader" to rule them. So we have the astounding anomaly that the armies which were built up to safeguard countries from external attack have become the chief danger to the states they were to preserve. If it be objected that this has always been the case, I reply that the danger was slight when armies were small professional forces and not "nations in arms." Now that the whole life of nations is being made to center more and more about the military, and that those who control the military are controlling more and more the entire industrial machinery, it will be hardly surprising if soldiers arrogate to themselves the right to interfere in purely civilian affairs and to prescribe in peace time as well as in war time what form of government their countries shall have. Naturally they nowhere favor democracy. Democracy and militarism cannot mix—not even under the Stars and Stripes.

I wish the editors of *The Nation* would reprint from our daily press of 1914-17 some of the Wilsonian phrases against Prussian militarism and some of the editorial denunciations of the wickedness of that military spirit and its menace to the unhappy state that harbored it. I urge this not to show how mistaken the Wilsonians were but just to make people realize that if militarism was dangerous in 1914, it is much more so today; and that the new military technique is menacing democracy everywhere.

March 26, 1937

Dear Holmes:

Many, many thanks for your nice letter. I knew that you were on the right side and that cheered me not a little. I *do* feel a profound sense of depression. To put it more accurately, I feel that I have been left high and dry by a backwash, and I wonder if you and I, and other steadfast liberals, are not merely back numbers left stranded because of the alarming clash between radical and fascist forces. I find myself more and more moved to live quietly in the country and to dodge work of a philanthropic character that I would have welcomed ten years ago. Of course with me this has something to do with my having passed my 65th birthday. But I was surprised to hear from The Nation this morning that they are getting many letters criticizing me as a reactionary and canceling subscriptions. New times, new morals once more.

To me the attitudes taken by The Nation this winter are simply heart-breaking. Lerner's jesuitical article on on the Moscow trials, his coming out for armaments and for keeping the country ready to help out the democracies if they should be attacked by the despots, these, and many other things, are hard to bear. But, who knows, the tide may turn. The utterly disheartening thing is the lurch into militarism everywhere. The people are really behind this mad expenditure for army and navy in Washington which cannot be defended on any practical ground whatever, even from the point of view of the militarist.

where we were in 1917, a handful of us holding out. Hitler has absolutely swept these men into line for war. They have forgotten every lesson of the World War, just as have the members of the American Legion. And now the infamous Hill-Sheppard Bill has been favorably reported in both Houses. It is certain that democracy will be dead the minute we go to war. I told them that last night and they could not deny it, but it made no difference. We are to bluff Hitler and Mussolini into being peaceful by marshalling superior battalions against them and then they won't start anything! What is the use of history or experience? They learn nothing and forget everything.

Faithfully yours,

Mr. John Haynes Holmes,
26 Sidney Place
Brooklyn, New York.

April 15, 1937

My dear Holmes:

Many thanks for your note and the copy of your letter to the Editors of The Nation. I am sure that printing Broun's article was the right thing to do. If it has not been printed he would have denounced us as suppressing his freedom of speech and probably would have resigned with a splash. As it is, the article is going to do both Mr. Wertheim and me good, I feel, because it is going to bring in others precisely the reaction that you have felt.

I both wanted your presence and rejoiced that you were not there at Ben Huebsch's last night, when Harold Laski talked informally about the British Labour Party. Their complete collapse on war he admitted in reply to questions from me. Neither the party nor the trade unions any longer talk about stopping all war by refusing to make deliveries of munitions or to let ships sail with them. This is due to the fact, he said, that they are now convinced that the democracies can be saved from fascism only by having Russia, France and England ready to go to war within the framework of the League. That represents the point of view of his fraction of the group, but the bulk of the party is ready to go to war at any time--only George Lansbury holds out.

More discouraging than that was the fact that of that group of old liberalsfighters, like Morris Ernst, Art Hays and about 25 others, only Ben Huebsch stood with me in opposition to all war. Max Lerner, as his recent editorials in The Nation have shown, is opposed to any disarmament here and to rigid neutrality; we must save the democracies, he insists. Dear friend, we are back just

I was glad to see that the Times has awakened to the fact that these armament expenditures are jeopardizing the world's recovery. If that idea gets around among business men it will help a lot.

I have agreed to testify in Washington against the Court proposal, but I believe I shall be torn to pieces by the pro-Roosevelt people on the committee. I am no good on the witness stand.

Thank you again, dear friend, for your generous words, and believe me, as always,

Faithfully yours,

Mr. John Haynes Holmes,
26 Sidney Place
Brooklyn, New York.

Issues and Men

BY OSWALD GARRISON VILLARD

The War—Twenty Years After

THESE lines are being formulated on the twentieth anniversary of America's entrance into the World War. In 1917 I was a member of the board of directors of the Associated Press. I sat alone in one of its offices as they brought me the "flash" that Woodrow Wilson had appeared before Congress to demand the declaration of war; of all those Associated Press directors I was the only one to oppose this national action. As I read that dispatch and knew that the end of the fight to keep the United States out of the war had come, I confess I could hardly keep back the tears. It seemed to me as if I were witnessing the death of the American Republic. I knew it was the end of Woodrow Wilson as a liberal leader and of his "New Freedom"—we had to wait twenty years for the New Deal, its successor. I knew that it meant the retarding, if not the destruction, of every liberal and progressive movement and the triumph of black reaction. I was not wrong, for the prosecution of the war was promptly turned over to the very big-business men whom Wilson had inveighed against as the "masters of America" who had stolen the government.

Just one week later, on April 13, 1917, in the midst of the first hysteria of the war, I wrote to my good friend, Joseph P. Tumulty, secretary to President Wilson. Here are some extracts from my letter:

> You have had my sincerest sympathy during these trying days, and I am glad to learn from your message through Dave Lawrence that you have not altogether forgotten me in this crisis. I know how you must have been suffering mentally and morally, and I can, I am sure, wholly enter into the feelings that must have been yours. To see your beloved chief congratulated by Henry Cabot Lodge, warmly indorsed and called upon by Theodore Roosevelt, and acclaimed with joy by every munitions maker, every agent of big business, and all the evil forces combined, against whom he has fought for American democracy until recently—all this, I know, must have caused you profound concern and unhappiness.
>
> As for the conscription proposal, of course you were good enough to prepare me for that. Do you remember our ride with Dave down to Mr. Burleson's office, when you assured me that the President would never, never sign such a bill? And do you remember my saying that you two [the President and Tumulty] were the "weakest links in the chain"? Remembering certain similar incidents in the past, I came back from Washington feeling convinced that the President would be won over to universal service before very long; and my reputation as a prophet has been enhanced.
>
> Believe me I am ready for any concentration camp, or conscription camp, or prison, but I am *not* at war and no one can put me into war—not the President of the United States with all his power. My loyalty to American traditions and ideals renders that impossible.
>
> We shall see what we shall see, but what I should like to know now is, what shall we newspapermen say who loyally supported the President's speech of January 22, in which he said: "It must be a peace without victory. . . . Victory would mean peace forced upon the loser, a victor's terms imposed upon the vanquished. It would be accepted in humiliation, under duress, at an intolerable sacrifice, and would leave a sting, a resentment, a bitter memory upon which terms of peace would rest not permanently but only as upon quicksand"?

Well, the years have brought their compensations. This prophecy of Wilson's which I have just quoted has been triumphantly upheld; his war speeches, with all their fustian, false sentiment, vindictiveness, and, often, falsehood, have perished or are vanishing. I never dreamed that I should live to see an Institute of Public Opinion take a poll in which 70 per cent registered their deliberate opinion that our entry into war was a horrible mistake. Never did I think that I should live to see the twentieth anniversary of the war marked by the most widespread acclaim and recognition of the six Senators and fifty Representatives who stood by their convictions and voted against the war resolution. Senator Norris, the dispatches report, "has never been so sought after for interviews as in the last day or two." Yet I remember how John Sharp Williams, Senator from Mississippi, denounced Norris in the Senate as a disgrace to the United States, "a pro-German, a pro-Goth, a pro-Vandal." Williams is dead and forgotten. In his extraordinary record of achievement, in the majesty of his patriotism, in the glory of his consistent fidelity to conscience, George Norris stands out today as the greatest figure in our Congress. And here is Congressman W. A. Ashbrook, of Ohio, who voted for the war and is still Congressman, admitting what I wrote at the time, that if "the members of the war Congress had voted their honest convictions . . . that great blunder of twenty years ago would not have been made." He does not hesitate to express humiliation and shame that he voted for it.

I am sorry that Woodrow Wilson is not alive, and Robert Lansing, and some of the others who put us into that war. This is not vindictiveness, but only the wish that they might have lived to be convinced of the utter folly, now so completely demonstrated by Adolf Hitler, of their theory that you could shoot democracy into the Germans and militarism out of them. And *are* the foundations of our Republic as safe and sound as when we entered the war? Is the future secure? I seem to recall some words about "All they that take up the sword . . ."

Issues and Men

BY OSWALD GARRISON VILLARD

Another Word on Neutrality

BEFORE these lines reach their readers it may well be that the conference committees of House and Senate will have agreed upon a report on the neutrality bill and that this measure will have been signed by the President. But that does not mean that the fight will be over; already it is planned to put the "cash-and-carry" provision, which is likely to be struck out of the Senate bill, into a new measure. So I wish to take this opportunity to point out what seem to me fallacies in the editorial position of *The Nation* on this subject, and particularly in Vera Micheles Dean's article, in the February 6 issue, entitled A Challenge to Pacifists.

The chief point at issue is the question whether the United States should or should not pass a law which would cut it off from delivering supplies to the democracies in Europe if they should be attacked by the dictatorships. "Any policy," stated a *Nation* editorial, "which would arbitrarily cut off all American trade with belligerents in the event of war would react directly to the advantage of Hitler and to the disadvantage of England, France, and the other democratic states which are normally dependent on American supplies." Mrs. Dean went farther: "Pacifists and radicals who prefer the continuance of democratic methods of government to the ruthless techniques of fascism must be prepared to defend their choice. Democracy must not be left unarmed."

Well, I am prepared to accept the challenge. First let me point out that if this policy is to control, the United States will find itself again just where it was in 1914 to 1917. I am one of those who believe that of the several causes of our going to war a tremendously important one was the tying up of our great industrial plants and munitions factories to the Allied military machine, with a resultant rain of gold from the Allies. The same thing would happen again. We should again be told that we were making the world safe for democracy, and if the democracies had their backs to the wall, the argument might be even more effectively used than in 1914-17. And the outcome would be the same. We should be precipitated into the struggle, and the result, even if we did not send a soldier abroad, would be disastrous. If we do get into the next war, it will mean the disappearance of our democracy. The laws now on the statute books and those pending in Congress today guarantee that; neither the editors of *The Nation* nor Mrs. Dean can deny it.

My next point is: How do they know that we ought to be on the side of the democracies, that the cause of the democracies will be any juster than that of the Allies in 1914-17? Of course their war methods will not be any different. There is nothing to choose between a democracy and an autocracy when they go to war. One murders just as inhumanly as the other. Democracies deprive the individual of the right to decide his own fate, abolish all personal liberties, and lock up or shoot dissenters just as readily as the dictatorships. Morally there was not one thing to choose between the Allies and the Central Powers in the last war. The excuse for England was Belgium, but we know very well now that the compelling reason was the desire of the controlling class in democratic England to smash the German navy and eliminate a dangerous economic competitor. Even Woodrow Wilson admitted that the origins of the war were purely commercial. Now I don't want to see the United States expending American money and, what is vastly more important, American lives, to insure the safety of British democracy of the Baldwin kind, or even the Ramsay MacDonald kind. I don't want to uphold a nation which holds down the natives of India and uses its airplanes to this very hour to bomb any subjugated native people who wish to govern themselves, however badly. The democracy of France looks more hopeful today, thanks to Blum and the People's Front. But even if it were the best democracy ever known I should do everything in my power to prevent the United States from being drawn into another war on the excuse that we must save that democracy. The way to save democracy for us is to keep it intact in the United States, prevent our democracy from turning into a war-time dictatorship, conserve its resources for the benefit not only of our own people but of all peoples after hostilities have ceased. I want the United States to remain a great reservoir of means and strength, especially moral strength, available to put the world on its feet after the next holy war.

Save the democracies? What editor, what Mrs. Dean can know whether the democracies may not be the aggressors for their own selfish ends? Have they forgotten the Crimean War waged by democratic England, the subjugation of Egypt in 1881, the wickedness of the Boer War? I can conceive of a situation arising where my moral judgment would put me on the side of the dictators—I mean as to the ethical merits of the struggle—just as I know that the misconduct of the Allies produced Hitler. Finally, deny that it is the duty of the United States to sit in judgment, like Jehovah, and then sacrifice its sons for the side that it thinks right on the basis of such little or such biased information as is available in the hysteria and excitement leading up to a war and after the war censorships are clamped down. I know the charges of selfishness and all the rest that are brought against this attitude, but as a pacifist I accept Mrs. Dean's challenge and say I'll never countenance any war, or our selling supplies to one side or the other.

Issues and Men

BY OSWALD GARRISON VILLARD

WHATEVER else may be said about the temper of the American people, there can be no doubt that they are today united in their opposition to being drawn into another war. Even if a European conflagration should take place, I should be quite optimistic about our staying out of it. I have not forgotten the effectiveness of the British propaganda in 1914-17, or the results of our business and financial entanglements with the Allies. But I am heartened by signs on every side that the lessons of the World War are not forgotten. The American Legion at its New York meeting, for example, took a strong stand against further experiments in making the world safe for democracy. One may not agree with its recommendations for safeguarding the country, but one must feel grateful that it stood so unequivocally for peace.

Even the Secretary of War, whose Assistant Secretary, Mr. Johnson, constantly demands a greatly increased regular army and rates us as less effective from a military standpoint than Sweden, told the Legion of his satisfaction that it made no "fantastic recommendations for a huge standing army or for an unbalanced expansion of one arm to the detriment of other branches." He also warned the veterans not to take sides in hostilities abroad and urged them to follow Washington leadership in "problems in which the preservation of our own peace and neutrality is of final importance." He wound up by calling upon them "to recognize and scotch any propaganda which might lead to our involvement in a foreign war. Preserve for yourselves and posterity that priceless boon of liberty that can be secured only through a lasting peace." This is in delightful contrast with the spread-eagle speeches which we have had from high officials in the past, and beyond question it is a politician's recognition of the mood of the country today. The Administration certainly knows what the people are thinking on this issue. The Seattle *Post-Intelligencer* has been taking a poll on whether the United States should withdraw both its citizens and its troops from China, and the vote has been overwhelmingly in favor of getting out. At one stage of the voting the proportion was as high as thirty-seven to one. Similar polls in California have shown similar results, which is the more remarkable in view of the closeness of the tie between California and the Orient. It is safe to say that the White House mail reflects a like trend.

Another reason for believing that there is little danger of our being drawn into a future war is the strength and vigor of the peace movement. I have already called attention to the fact that the National Peace Conference now represents approximately forty peace organizations, many of them with millions of members. It is the first cooperative front ever formed by the peace movement in this country. That does not mean that it always presents a solid front. The constituent organizations have the right to their own interpretation of events, and if they disagree with the decisions of the conference they take their own stand. Thus, there is a strong division of opinion as to whether the United States should or should not put the Neutrality Act into effect, but there is no division whatsoever in the determination to keep the country out of war. These organizations are not going to be fooled again by foreign propaganda. Indeed, whereas there was colossal public ignorance of European affairs in 1914-17, there is today, notably in the universities, a very large body of persons who are thoroughly conversant with what is going on abroad. In 1914 there were almost no editorial writers outside the cities of the Atlantic seaboard and Chicago who understood foreign conditions. Today there are many all over the country, and the press is maintaining abroad a remarkable corps of well-informed correspondents.

More than that, the peace movement has long since got beyond the stage of deprecating war on purely sentimental grounds. On September 19 the National Peace Conference began a nation-wide campaign for economic disarmament with an international broadcast. The first speaker was the Secretary of State. He was followed by representatives of the leading nations, including Anthony Eden, a spokesman for Premier Chautemps of France, Prime Minister King of Canada, and the President of Colombia. This campaign will continue through the winter. It has the approval of the Administration and is being warmly supported by the League of Nations Association of Canada. It is bound to do much in educating the American people to the necessity of lower tariffs and the advisability of giving the less favored nations free access to raw materials. The National Peace Conference declares that the American people must understand that between 1914 and 1918 their position changed from that of a debtor to that of a creditor power. It will take up the question of the possible liquidation of war debts and will urge the United States to cooperate with the other nations of the world, directly and through the peace machinery, in establishing international economic and social justice. It takes as its motto these words of Secretary Hull: "Many nations are caught today in a stifling net of mutual distrust, of political hostility, of an exhausting and suicidal race for military power, of continuing economic warfare. A demobilization of all these armaments—moral, political, military, and economic—is necessary for durable peace."

Issues and Men

BY OSWALD GARRISON VILLARD

I CONSIDER Franklin Roosevelt's speech in Chicago on foreign affairs the most important and perhaps the most pertinent speech that he has made since he became President. At last he has spoken out on the intolerable conditions in the world and called things by their right names. I regret only that he did not use the words Japan and Italy. He might just as well have done so, for everybody knows what he meant. But I am not willing to quarrel with him about that. Some weeks ago I took the liberty of telegraphing to him that he now had the opportunity, by speaking out on foreign affairs and characterizing things properly, to reassume the moral leadership of the world which Woodrow Wilson abandoned when he surrendered to the "peacemakers" at Paris. If the speech that he has now delivered is followed up with prompt and vigorous efforts to get other countries to join with him; if he will cooperate with the League of Nations, a committee of which has just urged that the signatories to the Nine-Power Pact be called together to consider Japan's breach of that treaty, at least to the extent of consulting openly about what can be done to restore law and order in international relations, this Chicago speech may prove to be one of the great turning-points in the history of international relations. Even if he goes no farther, he has rendered a tremendous service to the world. His words will be acclaimed by liberals and peace-lovers wherever they are read, and will arouse corresponding anger among the dictators and war-makers, in the brigand nations which today jeopardize not only the peace of the whole world but the actual stability of civilization.

I have said "if the speech is followed up" it will be of enormous importance. I find many skeptics. They say that F. D. R. never follows through; they recall his speech to the Woodrow Wilson Foundation soon after his inauguration, in which he made the sound suggestion that countries should pledge themselves not to send their troops over their own borders and not to manufacture the implements of aggressive and offensive warfare. He never followed this up, and they ask what reason we have to expect anything different now. My reply is that the situation is entirely changed. The world is in the worst jam in which it has ever been, with, as the President said, the whole structure of international law, comity, and honesty between nations collapsing into chaos. It is simply impossible not to move now.

I am well aware of the dangers; there is the risk that we shall embark upon another holy crusade, this time to save civilization in China, and that we shall play up the atrocity stories and rouse a spirit of hate here in America out of which will grow the desire for war. That must be guarded against as the President has done so far by stressing the fact that the United States does not propose to be drawn into any war. That will have to be reiterated every time we take any action. The greatest risk in my judgment is simply whether President Roosevelt himself will stand fast. He put the case with exact truth and complete clearness in his Chautauqua speech in August, 1936, in which he said that he knew very well that no matter what neutrality acts or other legislation might be passed, in the event of a dangerous situation leading to war everything would depend upon the men who happened to be in the White House and the State Department at the moment. A Cabinet officer told me in Washington not long ago that he was convinced that there had never been a President in Washington as devoted to peace as Franklin Roosevelt. Well, Woodrow Wilson was also devoted to peace and yet yielded to pressure. We can never be sure what men will do under given circumstances. But this I know full well: if something is not done to remedy this situation we shall plunge into chaos as the President has said, and we may plunge into war. Let us take a firm moral stand now against the aggressor nations and let us adopt measures without delay to check Japan—measures which shall stop far short of war.

What would I do if I were in the White House? First I would address a letter to all the leading democratic nations asking them to join the United States in a reiteration of the President's position, stressing not so much the bombing of cities in China and the brutal murder of defenseless men, women, and children as the violation of treaties, because there we have a direct concern, being a signatory with Japan to the Nine-Power Treaty, the Four-Power Pact, and the Kellogg Pact, and historically committed to upholding the integrity of China. After publishing such a document, I should call a conference of those nations signing it to decide upon further measures by which the whole force of an outraged world opinion could be directed against Japan, and to discuss the question of recalling from Japan the ambassadors and ministers of those nations. To the meeting of the signatories of the Nine-Power Treaty, I should send Secretary Hull himself and give him a free hand to lead in formulating opinion in that group against Japan. Pending developments, I should continue to voice the moral indignation of every decent person in the United States against what Japan is doing in China, so that the government of Japan would never for one moment be without a realization of the indignation of the United States. The question of an economic boycott I should leave for the present to individuals. Finally, I should enforce the Neutrality Act.

Issues and Men

BY OSWALD GARRISON VILLARD

AGAIN the political kaleidoscope is making strange bedfellows. The New York *Herald Tribune* and six of our most earnest and sincere peace societies are one in believing that President Roosevelt's Chicago speech has set us directly upon the path to war. As I am an official of one of those societies and differ with its conception of the situation, and as I have received requests for a clarification of my position, I shall restate the situation as it appears to me.

Naturally, if I thought the President's course would put us into war I should oppose it instead of having urged it in advance. And if I felt that moral leadership of the world in protest against the brigand states was incompatible with complete American neutrality in the wars in Spain and China I should be opposed. I am still completely isolationist so far as using any force whatsoever or taking part in joint armed action against Japan or any other nation is concerned. I still desire the immediate enforcement of the Neutrality Act. The President in his Chicago speech stressed the desire of the American people to stay at peace and declared that we had no intention of going to war. To this the reply is made that he frequently changes his mind, that Wilson also repeatedly asserted that the country was not going to enter the war and yet was forced into it, and that when you begin interfering in the affairs of other nations you may easily find yourself at war. The Emergency Peace Campaign feels this so strongly that it has issued a little circular drawing a parallel between what has been done so far and the events of 1916 and 1917 which started us along the road to war.

To this my reply is that we are taking a big chance in trusting to the President—to any President—but that we are obliged to. I again call attention to Mr. Roosevelt's statement at Chautauqua that no matter what neutrality laws we might pass, peace would depend upon the men who, when danger came, were President and Secretary of State. The power of the President to put us into war is beyond question; Wilson exercised that power six times, twice against Mexico and against Nicaragua, Haiti, San Domingo, and Germany. A certain amount of risk is unavoidable; even if we absolutely isolated ourselves, and kept silent about the lack of morals and the inhumanity of the brigand nations, we should still be in danger in a war-mad world. But it has been the historic attitude of the United States to express its opinion against international wrongdoing and to voice its sympathy with the victims of aggression. Our government championed the Jews in Russia at the time of the Kishinev massacres, and President Cleveland defended the cause of Venezuela against Great Britain—not wisely but with good motives. It has been perfectly obvious for a long time past that the world was waiting for someone to say the things that the President is saying. The reception of those words in the democratic countries abroad proves that. It is undeniable that everything depends upon the next step; I said last week that *if* the President's Chicago speech were wisely followed up it might be a turning-point in world affairs. That meant, of course, that if it were not wisely followed up or if it were not followed up at all, we should have to take a different view of the situation.

Is there not a great difference between our situation today and that of 1917? Twenty years ago we were deeply involved in the war then raging; our whole industry had become a part of the Allied military machine; we had made loans of great amounts to the Allies. Men high in the government, like Robert Lansing, as we now know, were urging that we go into the war to continue the war-time prosperity by which we were profiting. For three years we had swallowed propaganda we now know to have been deliberately deceitful. Today the situation is entirely different. We have our business commitments in both China and Japan, but what they are calling for is not war but peace. If war continues, those interests will be irretrievably damaged. We are not supplying vast quantities of military supplies to the two belligerents in Asia. Moreover, the public is disillusioned; it has not forgotten our experience in making the world safe for democracy, and our politicians in Washington are entirely aware of the pacific temper of the people. I submit that we are in a totally different and far safer position now than in 1917.

Would the enforcement of the Neutrality Act interfere with our leadership in a spiritual union and perhaps even a boycott against Japan? I cannot see that it would. What the President has done is to state an attitude and not a program. What this attitude will do for the world in the long run we can only know as the policy gradually unfolds, but at least, thanks to him and fifty-two nations in the League, Japan has not gone unwhipped of justice. It has been branded before all the world as a transgressor, and that is a great deal. The cynics will say it is nothing; they have no faith in spiritual and moral values. They will insist that the President is not saving Japanese and Chinese lives. Not yet, perhaps, but one cannot tell. Personally I hope that there will be further steps to send Japan to Coventry and to prove that the nations can bring to book one of their number without committing the supreme folly and the supreme crime of resorting to useless mass murder.

Issues and Men

BY OSWALD GARRISON VILLARD

"WHAT is the use of the Brussels conference? All its members will do is to talk and talk and get nowhere, just like the Non-Intervention Committee in regard to Spain. At best they will pass a few resolutions and then adjourn. Unless you are willing to back up your opinion by acts, it is all perfectly futile." This is the sort of thing I hear on all sides. I deny its correctness, for I have not lost faith in the power of moral indignation to limit and control international wrongdoing if it is properly directed and adequately expressed. But whether I am right or wrong I do not see how any intelligent man can deny that it would have been a genuine misfortune if the world's sense of outrage at what Japan is doing in China had not been voiced by someone in high authority. Only Franklin Roosevelt could have done it, and he did it admirably. It shook up the dictators, startled their kept newspapers, and worried them so that they are today saying that the United States will do nothing at Brussels except "proffer good advice." The German press expresses earnest hopes that there will be a "retreat from Chicago" and that the "Wall Street crash" and something they call "the revolt against Roosevelt" will keep the United States from urging a strong line of action. Their hopes betray their fears. The more the President directs a verbal barrage against the dictators the more uncomfortable those rascals will be.

As for the conference itself, my guess is that it will first of all try to get the Japanese to join it, and if it fails in that, will urge them to state just what their objectives in China are. It is impossible to look farther ahead at this moment. This is a case where the policy will have to be developed step by step. I admit that it is extremely unfortunate that the United States is not to be represented at the conference by a man of force and ideas. Mr. Davis has a pleasant personality and easy Southern manners which make him an agreeable companion and doubtless of use when it comes to toning down acrid discussions, smoothing ruffled feathers, and generally playing an ameliorating role in such a gathering. But he has never yet displayed vigorous leadership or advanced constructive suggestions. I can think of at least twenty-five men who would do better; indeed, I feel that this conference is so vitally important that Mr. Hull himself or ex-Secretary Stimson should have represented the United States.

Let us suppose that the Japanese refuse mediation but allow the world to know on what terms they will make peace. If their terms are such as have been telegraphed from China—at least three Japanese-controlled states similar to Manchoukuo, and a prohibition of China's having an army, navy, or air fleet—we may be certain of a world-wide outburst of further indignation at Japan. How little its statesmen have learned! One would think, after the failure of the Allied and American efforts to disarm Germany, that no sane man would advocate a similar folly elsewhere in the world, but there the proposal is. It can be stopped by a united front at Brussels, if only because its denunciation by eight powers would make it impossible for China to accept. China must not be allowed to yield. What will come after that no man can forecast. Whether there will be governmental boycotts or spontaneous boycotts among the several peoples such as are now being engineered no one can guess. Then will come the danger of actions which may lead to war. But the fact that we cannot see all the way is no reason why we should not essay the road at least as far as the first turn.

The world's situation can be put in a few words: We know that force heals and corrects nothing; that war leaves only worse evils in its train than those it sought to eradicate. We know that the victors in a war pay as high a price as the vanquished. We have the word of conservative leaders like Hoover, Coolidge, and Stanley Baldwin that armaments do not insure freedom from wars but lead to them, and that the cost threatens bankruptcy to all the nations in the armament race. We know that the world is arming as never before. In addition, we are all aware of the existence of three brigand nations whose pledges no man can trust. That is the situation. What shall we do about it?

Those cynics who believe only in force or who think that international disaster is inevitable are for placing all their faith in more weapons and more wars. Those persons everywhere who feel it incumbent upon them to try to free the world from this dreadful circle in which it is caught of ever more armaments and ever more wars and ever greater suspicion and hostility believe that every avenue short of war must be tried. Brussels is one way—the rallying of what is left of the moral opinion of mankind against at least one aggressor state. If it fails we shall be no worse off. And even in failure, I believe, there will be some gain. Lose faith in the weapons of the spirit? Not I. Having seen the utter failure of mass murder to right wrong or advance the human race one iota, I am more than ever a believer in passive resistance, in spiritual revolt, in the castigation of offenders by the most immoderate language and by non-intercourse. I know and hear of no better way. On what side do you wish to fight, friends? With those who worship might and barbarism or those who stand with the angels and have an abiding faith in human nature and a better world?

Issues and Men

BY OSWALD GARRISON VILLARD

What Is a Liberal?

TWO readers of this page have written to ask me to define liberalism. I told them that they were setting me the hardest possible task. I felt, of course, as complimented as the ragged colored man who was asked to change a ten-dollar bill. But my old inferiority complex stepped in to warn me off. "You will only fail," it whispered to me. Curious how confidential and insinuating our inferiority complexes become! And how they crowd everything else out of the picture. We all of us used to be pestered by a demon called Lack of Self-Confidence, by another known as Indifference, by still another, Laziness, with Cowardice bulking large in the rear. But we pay no attention to them now. We contemptuously ignore them or kick them out of the way. If our conscience troubles us, if we have twinges of remorse, if somebody says, "No matter what your excuses, you know you should have done that," we hastily hide behind our I. C. It covers not only a multitude of sins; if we try hard we can make it cover all our sins.

Speaking of liberals, I wonder if you have all noticed that the embattled democracies abroad are acting today just like the tired post-war liberals and radicals we used to hear so much about? The latter were wont to explain to us when we went to them asking for aid on one or all of the numerous liberal fronts, that they really were emotionally exhausted—sucked dry. They had put all they had in them into opposition to the war or the peace of injustice, or into succoring Belgians, Russians, German babies, Kentucky miners, Tom Mooney. They *had* to insist upon being allowed to lie fallow for a while until they found new wellsprings of compassion, refilled their exhausted reservoirs of hot indignation, found fresh fuel for their reformatory motors. This had a reasonable ring to it; we dissenters did live a decade in those two war years. But the fact is that those reservoirs of indignation never again were filled, those motors which once drove on to unselfish deeds never again possessed the necessary coordinated cylinders hitting at once. Well, so it is with the endangered democracies abroad. They are tired. Their emotional capacity is exhausted. They simply cannot become aroused over anything. Ethiopia leaves them cold. Those poor murdered blacks burned and butchered by bombs from the air and the land—what liberal democratic nation could really get excited about them? Were they not half-naked savages, 70 per cent of them disease-ridden, syphilitic, capable of most horrible cruelties toward their own slaves? Why get excited about *them?*

Before I define a liberal, let me speak of Spain. When one beholds the horrible suffering there, the wanton butchery by rank outsiders of men, women, and children, the utter, the damnable ruin of a historic people guilty only of seeking to leap from feudalism into modern social liberty at one bound, one wishes there were a just and omnipotent God in heaven to behold what has come over those tired democracies. They cannot move. They cannot rouse themselves. They cannot damn as one man the foreign authors of that misery. And now China. Look way over there? Nothing much worse than Spain. And those are yellow men. They do not suffer as we do. They have not our sensibilities, or our fear of death. Death to them is normal. It comes to millions of them at a time from hunger, from the swollen waters, from the locusts, or because the gods withhold the rain. Oh, no. These democracies must not rouse themselves, must not burn with unabatable wrath at wholesale torture and unbelievable wrong, dictated only by the desire of madmen to rob others of what is theirs. They might themselves be drawn in. And we? Well, our American liberals say that in behalf of these democracies we must go to war and sacrifice our youth abroad!

Now as to what a liberal is—excuse me, one minute more. Have you noticed that those democracies for which we are to fight are ruled, so Norman Angell writes in the current *Forum,* by "drift, inertia, indecision, short-sightedness, division of council, disunity, the refusal to make material sacrifice"? That their enemies, who openly demand the complete destruction of democracy everywhere, are actuated by "immense energy, courage, boldness, a readiness to take great risks and undergo infinite suffering, an amazing capacity for sacrifice"—all on behalf of "gross aggression and conquest, the destruction of freedom, of the right of self-government and democracy, the very enthronement of ruthless cruelty and oppression"? Doesn't that sound familiar? We used to use just such phrases to rouse the tired liberal for the sake of the victims of injustice everywhere.

Somehow or other there seems to be a limit to the capacity of the human mind and the human soul to suffer for others. We read of the horrible massacres in Shanghai and put the story down with no more than a sigh. The first time we see the torn and mangled bodies of women and children in the movies we go home to a restless and troubled night. The next time we are struck by the fact that the horrors are not quite as terrible as in the first film. The fourth or fifth time we are affected hardly more than by the pictures of a wrecked airplane.

Oh, yes, about that liberal. Hang it all, the page is done and there isn't any room to tell you what I really think a liberal is. But I shall get around to it, just bear with me. I shall define that liberal from A to Z and pin him lifelike to a card like a butterfly in a museum—what's left of him. So good-day to you!

Issues and Men

BY OSWALD GARRISON VILLARD

IN AN unusual editorial called America's Aloofness, divided into three parts, the New York *Times* on November 30 railed against the "isolationists and pacifists in Congress and their vociferous supporters in the country" who are "chiefly responsible" for the loss of leadership in world affairs by the United States and the impotence of the Nine-Power Conference in Brussels. These wicked pacifists and isolationists believe, it seems, "that we can stay out of any world conflict," and they oppose any strong peace measures by this government "even though to abstain from such might mean the loss of freedom to those who regard it as highly as they themselves, and an impairment of liberty to men and women in this very hemisphere." In recent years, the *Times* declares, these miscreant Americans have seized upon every occasion when our government was "seeking to express its scruples of conscience against treaty-breaking and aggression, to proclaim that in no circumstances would this people do anything effective to restore moral standards among nations." The *Times* asserts that as far back as when Japan seized Manchoukuo these pacifists and isolationists gave notice that it was the fixed future policy of the United States to keep out of war "however clear the threat to our own institutions."

The editorial then attacks the Neutrality Act, which, it seems, serves notice to the world that the United States is only out to save its own skin and will stand by and see the world remade on fascist lines without interference and "without understanding that this would mean anything dangerous to us at all." But in the third section the *Times* is frightened by its own boldness and says that "this is not a preachment for war measures. The people of the United States are set against military expeditions, and rightly so." And then it goes on to list some effective peace measures short of war, like a trade treaty between England and America, public and private cooperation between the two countries, and understandings on trade, money, and credit which "will serve as certain weapons against treaty-breakers." If our government will only publicize the fact that we will stand sympathetically with the great democracies in measures short of war, "without resort to the substance of sanctions or war," all will be well. "Treaty-breakers and dictators will then take prudent council among themselves."

To me this is one of the most inconsistent and ill-informed editorials I have ever read, but the *Times* announced the next day that it had met with great acclaim in Washington. Now as one who is pretty close to the peace movement in this country I want to ask the *Times* what all the shooting is about. The bulk of the peace movement as I know it is entirely for measures short of war *which will not lead to war,* and it will heartily welcome the accession of Mr. Finley and Mr. Sulzberger of the *Times* to its ranks. The only split in the peace movement is over the question of what measures short of war may be utilized without actually precipitating hostilities. If the *Times* could throw some light on that it would give us a worth-while editorial. Most of the peace movement, I know, is ready for measures of non-intercourse with outlaw countries, such as the *Times* suggests; the dissenters are only those who feel that this might lead to war. It is true that the peace movement is absolutely opposed to any hard-and-fast alliance with Great Britain, but I know no pacifist who is not willing to have this country tell the world again and again and again that morally and spiritually it stands with the democracies abroad, and that it will aid them in their fight against fascism if they are sincere about it—which the recent course of the British government renders highly doubtful—provided always that we, as the *Times* demands, are not drawn into war.

The *Times* flatters the pacifists and isolationists enormously when it tells them that they and not President Roosevelt and the Congress are formulating the foreign policy of America. But here I want to impart a piece of news to the *Times* which is quite fit for that newspaper to print. It is that the American people are overwhelmingly opposed to any measures leading to war; in my long experience as a journalist I have never seen public opinion so united on any other question as on this. The politicians in Washington know it, and if they strengthen the neutrality law at the coming session of Congress it will be for that reason and not because of any influence of the pacifists and isolationists. The *Times* might even ask the Postmaster General, who certainly has "both ears to the ground," why he recently made a speech at Portland, Oregon, giving the most positive assurances that this Administration would take no step whatever to put us into war. Honestly, John Finley, didn't that have a much greater effect on the fascist nations than any of the pronunciamientos of our peace societies that you so deplore?

A sad thing about all this, as the *Times* will soon find out, is that its editorial will not satisfy its English and French friends. They will be content with nothing less than a promise that if necessary we will go to war for them, as we were persuaded to do in 1917. London and Paris will wail when they read that, so far as war and overseas expeditions are concerned, the *Times* has gone over to the pacifists.

Issues and Men

BY OSWALD GARRISON VILLARD

Can We War on Japan?

TO THIS question the answer is emphatically "No." The army and navy know this and most of the State Department officials, too. The President knows it, for as far back as July 1, 1923, he wrote an article for *Asia* in which he said that, of his own knowledge as Assistant Secretary of the Navy, many officers of both services admitted that in the event of war the Philippines could not be held, although at that time the Japanese fleet was less than half of our paper strength—"the line of communication was too dangerously long." The opinion at that time was that the war would have to be decided not by military measures but by "economic issues." This was the belief, he said, at a time when "offensive operations over long sea distances were less difficult than now." If, he wrote, Japan thought in 1914 that it could attack us through Mexico or direct invasion of the Pacific coast, "it is safe to say that her strategists have now tacitly abandoned such ideas." Speaking of the situation in 1923, he repeated that after the first year or two of hostilities economic causes would become the determining factor. He added:

> Tableau: Japan and the United States, four or five thousand miles apart, making faces at one another across a no-man's-water as broad as the Pacific. Some genius then might arise to ask what it was all about and what the use was of the atrophy of national life and development. . . . If, then, it were realized by the people of this country and of Japan that a war would be a futile gesture attended by no sufficiently compensating results, each nation might be in a fair way to change its apprehensive habit of mind.

This article *Asia* deemed so important that it printed it for a second time in March, 1934.

I have yet to meet army or navy officers who believe that the situation has materially changed since Franklin Roosevelt wrote thus about it. I heard the late Admiral Sims declare that we could not wage war on Japan nor Japan upon us; that if our fleet reached Japan it could only fire a few rounds at the coast and then return to its home base. He was positive in his statement that our fleet could not maintain itself off Japan if it got there, and that the enemy, if he knew his business, would not give battle but stay safely in port until our ships had sailed away. The crux of the whole thing is the absence of a great naval base capable of provisioning, refueling, and repairing the fleet—Manila is too far away, and so is Hongkong if that should be loaned to us. Several high officers of the army express the same view, saying privately that a conquest of Japan is impossible, that we cannot hold the Philippines and could not reconquer them if the Japanese took them. They agree with Franklin Roosevelt that it would take two years to get the war under way, and they scoff at the suggestion that Japan could land and maintain troops upon our soil.

General Johnson Hagood avers that we never on a single day landed enough supplies in France to maintain our army while it was in that country; if this is perhaps an exaggeration, it cannot be very far from the truth. Yet in 1917-18 we had a fleet of more than 3,000 ships carrying our men and supplies across the sea, and they were not seriously molested by the enemy's submarines. No sane man who visualizes the fact that our Pacific coast is more than twice as far from Japan as our Atlantic coast is from France, and realizes how limited are the Japanese supplies of oil and gasoline and how small is the Japanese merchant fleet, can contend that we are in danger of invasion by the Japanese. Moreover, to move an army across seas today would require one-third more ships than in 1917 because of the increased size and number of the cannon, tanks, motor vehicles of every description, shells, and airplanes necessary for a modern expeditionary force. The Japanese have shown extraordinary organizing ability and amazed military men by the way they have provisioned and supplied with ammunition their many columns in China. But the job of landing in America would be beyond their genius or that of any other country.

But we are told that we must not say this; that it is wrong for the peace societies to talk about a war referendum, about our being unwilling ever to go to war, not because the President and the Cabinet want to go to war but because they want to keep up the bluff that they may have to do so—the kind of stuff that Alf Landon telegraphed to the President. The peace lovers are accused of dividing the nation when it ought to be presenting a united front. We are supposed to keep quiet and not say what we think and what the American people want, namely, no war in the Pacific under any consideration. How absurd to demand this policy of us! It immediately makes the Administration as much a dictator of our minds as Hitler is of the German mind or Mussolini of the Italian. Moreover, the representatives of those countries know perfectly well how our people feel. You can't choke off debate in Congress. The Japs can find out how the American people are thinking without any difficulty. They know what Franklin Roosevelt wrote in *Asia* in 1923, and they know that there have been no changes in relative armaments or in new types of war vessels to make any important change in the situation in 1937.

Issues and Men

BY OSWALD GARRISON VILLARD

THE news that President Roosevelt is going to ask Congress for more money for the navy, somewhere between $560,000,000 and a billion, in addition to the regular appropriations for army and navy, which have now risen to the astounding total of $1,250,000,000 a year, is disheartening but not surprising. I was so sure that he would plunge us into militarism and navalism if elected that I refused to vote for him in 1932 and 1936. I have no doubt that Congress will grant the money and that the business world will approve of it despite all the howls about balancing the budget. We are in a state of hysteria because of the Japanese developments, and most people say that they are for any amount of armament if that will only keep us out of war. But as Calvin Coolidge said to the American Legion, no amount of armaments ever kept any country out of war; Stanley Baldwin, now Earl Baldwin, said a few years later that if Europe rearmed it would not mean peace but war.

The new Roosevelt program is being represented to the country in the newspaper dispatches as "rearmament." That is, of course, an absolute falsehood. We have never been armed as this program now proposes to arm us. Next it is represented as a good thing because it will put a lot of men to work building battleships and cruisers, and so prime the pump once more for the heavy industries. That is also dubious. The chief beneficiaries of battleship and cruiser building will be the six shipyards that have a monopoly, whose bids on the last two battleships advertised were so high that the government decided to build them in two of its own yards. When done, the battleships will represent pure economic waste. At best their life will be twenty years; there are plenty of army and navy officers who believe, as did the late General William Mitchell, that the day of the battleship was over long ago. As for priming the pump, even the New York *Times* has found it necessary to warn the country that rearmament programs abroad and in this country are not helping recovery but injuring and delaying it. Rearmament creates an entirely fictitious prosperity. England is now spending $7,500,000,000 for rearmament over five years. Hundreds of factories are expanding their plants, taking on workers, operating day and night. When that money is spent, there will be unemployed workers and idle factories unless the demand which will then go up for manufacturers to continue rearmament so that employment and profits may keep up becomes controlling, and a need for still more battleships, airplanes, tanks, heavy artillery, and all the other paraphernalia of modern war is suddenly discovered.

It is a dance of death—economic death—even if war does not come. Here my star witness is again Stanley Baldwin, who said three years before he began rearming England that if the rearmament race were undertaken in Europe, several nations would go into bankruptcy. Yet he swallowed his words, and wound up his career by fastening this terrific program upon England. These are totally unproductive expenditures. They create no great public works, like the TVA or the magnificent bridges that we are getting all over the country, thanks to government funds. A single invention may make utterly useless and antiquated a large portion of the armaments created. But we are told that it is a necessary insurance and that we must no more cavil at the size of the premium than would a business man who insures his plant and inventory. Yet the simple fact is that these rearmament programs make nowhere for lasting prosperity, but bring grave evils in their train.

The most criminal part of the Roosevelt program is the fact that it is not being thought through. The President insists that we are arming only for defense, but asks for offensive battleships, and he cannot deny that there is no comprehensive plan for a defense of the coasts of the United States that anybody has ever heard of. Generals like Smedley Butler and Johnson Hagood have pointed this out repeatedly, but nothing happens. We just pour money out with no plan, no established government policy. We have never settled what we are going to defend or where we are going to defend it; nor have we coordinated army and navy. We even have four government air forces uncoordinated and buying airplanes separately. No business man would dream of embarking on so vast a program without having the objectives and aims carefully worked out by experts; he would go bankrupt if he did. The President, however, gives no sign that he realizes the ramifications of what he is now doing. More battleships and cruisers mean more officers and more men, who become a permanent charge if only because they constantly increase the retired lists—more privileged persons entitled to government support until they die. They mean more shipbuilders and armament manufacturers who feel that the government is committed to support them to the end of time. Those companies which are monopolies, like the one which builds parachutes, have every reason to rejoice, but not the taxpayers, or those who feel that in the long run we must balance the budget, a decent budget which shall take care adequately, as we never yet have done, of the humanitarian needs of the country. To say that we need to arm more against the Japanese is ridiculous, as I pointed out last week on the authority of no less a person than Franklin D. Roosevelt himself. We cannot war upon them with fleets, nor they upon us.

Issues and Men

BY OSWALD GARRISON VILLARD

That War Referendum

BELIEVING that there is much public misunderstanding of the Ludlow war-referendum proposal—a misunderstanding sedulously cultivated in reactionary and military circles and by all who would profit by war—I have endeavored to bring together the arguments against the proposed amendment and the answers to them. If any important ones have been overlooked, it is not intentional but due to necessary space limits.

1. The referendum would be a blow to our whole system of representative government.

Answer: A national referendum in which the people could vote on important issues has been successively urged by Theodore Roosevelt, William J. Bryan, Robert La Follette, Sr., Woodrow Wilson, and, I believe, Franklin Roosevelt. War is the most important of all issues. The referendum is in use in many American states, notably in New York; it has for centuries been in use in the democracy of Switzerland. No injury to representative government arises from the use of referendums.

2. The referendum will cripple our diplomacy and tie the President's hands.

Answer: This is true only if diplomacy and the President cannot function without being prepared to use war as an instrument of national policy—this use of war was formally renounced by the United States when it pledged its name and honor to the Kellogg Peace Pact. The purpose of the Ludlow referendum is to deprive the Executive of the war-making power as far as possible.

3. The President can be trusted not to put us into war; he will know when the cause is just and what the people want.

Answer: General Grant denounced the war in Mexico, in which he served as an officer, "as one of the most unjust ever waged by a stronger against a weaker nation"; he called it "unholy." In the Spanish War, as history now records, Spain surrendered to the United States completely *before* President McKinley went to Congress asking for a declaration of war. The President deceived Congress by withholding the Spanish surrender. James Ford Rhodes and other historians assert that this was done for purely political reasons, to strengthen the Republican Party. Mr. Wilson put the country into war seven times and only once asked consent of Congress.

4. The Congress can be trusted to vote as the people wish because the people are its constituents.

Answer: As shown above, the war-making power, lodged by the Constitution in the hands of Congress, has been usurped by the Executive, who can and does render Congress impotent to exercise its free will by using the prestige of his office, the power of Presidential propaganda, and even, as did Woodrow Wilson in the case of the armed-ship bill, public denunciation of the legislators opposing him as "twelve wilful little men." By the use of army and navy and the diplomatic service the President can maneuver us into a position where there is nothing left for Congress to do but to vote yes.

5. But this state of affairs will not be altered if the referendum is voted because the President will still be commander-in-chief of army and navy and head of the diplomatic service, and will still have the power of prestige and propaganda.

Answer: This is true. A President can put this country into war no matter what laws may be framed, until such time as the American people definitely forbid the resort to war. The referendum will, however, slow up the President, put an additional brake upon him, and impress upon him the desire of the people to reserve to themselves the war-making power. President Roosevelt admitted the present control by the President when he said at Chautauqua on August 14, 1936: "Nevertheless . . . the effective maintenance of American neutrality depends today, as in the past, on the wisdom and determination of whoever at the moment occupy the offices of President and Secretary of State."

6. The President, bearing his tremendous responsibilities for the maintenance of peace, is less likely to be swayed by passion or propaganda than are the people, who may be misled by demagogues using the radio and other means of communication.

Answer: The case of McKinley is again in point here. But the best witness is Franklin D. Roosevelt, who in the same speech at Chautauqua declared that if war should break out again, thousands of Americans would attempt to break down our neutrality, "seeking immediate riches—fools' gold." He continued: "To resist the clamor of that greed, if war should come, would require the unswerving support of all Americans who love peace." He demanded that the nation, confronted with a choice between profits and peace, should answer, "We choose peace"; and he said, "The answer will be clear and for all practical purposes unanimous." He gave us the truthful picture of a President subject, when war nears, to terrific pressure by interested groups, as Wilson was in 1914-17, to put us into war for the sake of profits. The passage of the referendum would relieve the Executive to *some* extent of such pressure. As for the possibility that the people may be misled by propaganda and induced to vote for war, there can be no doubt that that may happen. It is a risk of democracy, and it pertains not only to war but to every election. But at least the parents of the boys then about to die, and the boys themselves if twenty-one, will have voted on their fate.

7. A referendum would advertise the differences of opinion and so encourage possible enemies.

Answer: There has never yet been a war fought by the United States to which there was not tremendous opposition up to the very moment when war was declared—even in 1812. There is much evidence to show that had there been a referendum in the United States in 1917, while the Atlantic seaboard would have voted for war, the people in the West would have voted no. There will always be differences of opinion in Congress as to any war, as well as in the public press.

8. The country may be attacked, in which case (a) there will be no time to take a vote, and (b) the President and the military forces will be weakened if not estopped by the referendum.

Answer: (a) The amendment will not be operative if the country is attacked, and every foreign war in which the United States has engaged has approached slowly; months and years of preparation have preceded the declaration. A vote could be taken today on whether the people of the United States wish this country to go to war with Japan or not. It is preposterous to assert that there would be long delays in ascertaining the people's will by the use of existing or new electoral machinery. A vote could be obtained within seventy-two hours, since by means of the radio the government could notify the remotest hamlet what the question was and when the voting. (b) The referendum will offer no grounds for the army and navy to cease preparing for hostilities. If, as Mr. Stimson declares, the necessity of waiting for a decision "would destroy the initiative and spirit of our personnel," there must be something very wrong with that personnel and its leadership.

9. As Mr. Stimson asserts, "the power and speed of modern naval and air attacks" would make possible in twenty-four hours "a devastating blow upon one of our great cities and its neighboring industrial centers and the landing within a week of 100,000 men . . . "

Answer: This is the purest guesswork. It presupposes the defeat of the fleet, the passing of all mines, the conquest of the coast defenses of the harbor, and ability to force a landing. If one begins by conceding everything to the enemy, one can prove the conquest of Washington in two weeks. Obviously Mr. Stimson is entirely misleading when he declares that an army of 100,000 men could be landed a week after a surprise attack. There is no nation except England which has the merchant fleet to move such a force and its impedimenta quickly. It is absolutely unthinkable that the preparation for such a gigantic undertaking, which must use hundreds of ships loaded with tanks, airplanes, poison gas, heavy and light artillery, plus enormous supplies of ammunition and gasoline, could be hidden. There are only a dozen ships which could move soldiers across the ocean in a week.

10. But naval ships might be sunk and the government could not mobilize the nation for self-defense.

Answer: If every ship in our Asiatic squadron were sunk tomorrow by Japan, we should have plenty of time simultaneously to mobilize and to await the taking of the referendum on whether the American people wished to plunge the country into war to revenge the loss of those ships. Further, the question is an indictment of our military and naval preparations. If our war departments have today no plans for immediate mobilization of the first and second lines of defense in case of attack, then they are entirely incompetent to defend us.

11. Why should we, as Mr. Stimson asks, take up with "untried panaceas" in this critical hour of the world's history?

Answer: We progress only by trying new methods and measures. Our whole neutrality legislation, whether good or bad, is a new venture in diplomacy. There is no precedent for it to be found anywhere; it is a complete reversal of our historic policy. Yet no fair-minded judge will deny that that legislation was passed three times in response to the overwhelming sentiment of the American people. It may be an unsatisfactory device to keep us out of war, but the American people wanted it and were not deterred by the fact that it was an "untried panacea."

12. The referendum would fatally cripple, if not end, the Monroe Doctrine.

Answer: If this is true it presupposes that the American people would decline to fight to protect Central or South American nations from European attack. Is there any reason why they should not decide whether they wish to sacrifice their sons, the national wealth, perhaps our institutions, to keep Germans out of Brazil or the Argentine? They are competent and have the right to pass upon such a question. As a matter of fact, Senator La Follette's alternative to the Ludlow plan specially exempts cases in which there is an attack on the territory of any North American or Caribbean nation.

13. The amendment cannot be phrased to cover every case.

Answer: This argument is true, but it is not controlling. No neutrality legislation can be framed which will foresee every possible contingency, but that is no reason why there should not be the best possible neutrality laws which it is in our power to draft. Mr. Ludlow's referendum is intended for debate and amendment.

14. Could not Executive usurpation of the war power be ended and Congress still left in control of it?

Answer: In the eyes of those who support the Ludlow resolution the war-making power should rest only in the hands of the people because a war today, as distinct from the Civil War, or the war with Spain, would jeopardize the very life of the nation, and destroy our democratic institutions. Modern war involves every citizen, probably the children; even if victory comes, it means staggering debts, world-wide industrial depression and unemployment, complete industrial dislocation through the turning over of a large portion of industry to the war machine. There is every evidence that the country would come out of it with a fascist rule established. The American democracy is the most precious thing in the world today. Only the American people should have the right to decide whether its very existence shall be risked by their going to war.

Issues and Men

BY OSWALD GARRISON VILLARD

COULD anything be more idiotic than the present armament race? If it were not carried on by alleged statesmen, it would be properly characterized as worthy only of morons. It is all of a piece with the horrible incompetence and stupidity which plunged the world, especially the United States, into the Great War. It may be, of course, that there is something radically wrong with me, but when I study the dispatches and letters of Colonel House and Walter Page and the twistings and contradictions and failures of Woodrow Wilson, I am staggered and then horrified that such vital decisions, resulting in the death of 50,000 Americans and the wounding of 250,000 others, should have been in the hands of men so utterly incompetent.

The same feeling of nausea comes over me when I read the details of this naval-armament race now going on. No sooner does England announce that it is building battleships than we follow suit and lay down two. Then Japan makes trouble in the Far East, and we propose to build three more battleships despite the fact that Admiral Sims, commander-in-chief of our fleet during the World War and one of the ablest officers this country has ever produced, publicly stated that in the next war our battleships would all be safely moored way up the Mississippi River. Then along comes Italy and announces that it is going to lay down two battleships which will be more effective ships than any now possessed by any other country, whereupon within three days it is announced from Paris that leading spirits in the government have decided that France will build three more battleships to offset Mussolini's new craft, and that it will continue to lay down ship for ship with the Italians. Just what the Germans are doing nobody knows. They are pretending to be bound by their naval treaty with England by which they have pledged themselves not to have a fleet larger than 35 per cent of the British fleet, but if there are those so innocent as to trust anything that Hitler says, I am not one of them. I wouldn't believe him after what he wrote in "Mein Kampf," and after his subsequent career, if he should stand at the throne of God and raise his right hand and swear to a statement—any statement.

Then there is the Soviet Union. For some unknown reason—perhaps because they have not the necessary facilities in view of our own orders—the American shipyards announce that they will not build any battleships for Russia. Therefore, according to the New York *Times,* the Russians are contracting for huge machinery in England which will enable them to make the necessary armor plate. When this machinery is set up, Russia too will enter the battleship race. When it does I will bet my best suit of clothes that Germany will tell England how sorry it is that it cannot keep its word but it will have to build more ships to meet the Communist menace. The more ships Germany builds, the more Russia will build. As for Japan, there again we do not know what is happening, but according to a dispatch in the *Giornale d'Italia,* three super-battleships, in addition to sixty-three other men-of-war, are being built now or are projected in Tokyo. Meanwhile England is straining every nerve to complete a 1938 naval program which Hector C. Bywater, the well-informed naval correspondent of the London *Daily Telegraph,* believes will include three, four, or five new battleships. Britain plans to send a squadron of at least five battle-cruisers to Hongkong to overawe Japan—a procedure which seems to me just about as futile as to put five British submarines in the Baltic as a threat to Russia.

Speaking of submarines, the race there is also in full swing. It is announced that Italy has more submarines than any other country, but this is disputed by friends of Russia, who say that the Soviet Union has secretly built a far larger number than anybody knows and has enough of them in Vladivostok to make the Japanese extremely uneasy. Then, of course, there is the aircraft-carrier race, and the aircraft race too. The head of our headquarters air fleet, General Frank M. Andrews, sagely wags his head and says that we are falling alarmingly behind European countries in the number of our air pilots—as if that had any bearing whatever on our own defense problem. From London comes the startling announcement that England will soon have no fewer than 12,250 airplanes, more than France, Germany, and Italy together. At least it thinks it will have, but if Artemus Ward were by my side I am certain he would bet all his wife's relations on the Germans producing, when the 12,250 are ready, 1,000 more airplanes than the British General Staff thought Berlin had. Really this is the grandest child's game invented since ticktacktoo, and it has the advantage of being played with human lives and the resources of all the nations.

So once more we have the vicious circle before us. More ships, more armaments, greater expenditures, and then again more ships, more armaments, greater expenditures, with financial bankruptcy and the lowering of the standard of life of all workers right ahead of us. Stanley Baldwin said that another armament race would bankrupt a number of nations and make war absolutely certain. Then he put England into the armament race, and out of gratitude they made him a lord and retired him with all possible honors. Do I hear anybody assert that this is a sane world? If there is any such person he is a liar.

Issues and Men

BY OSWALD GARRISON VILLARD

THE President's latest proposals for increasing the army and navy take us much farther along the road to genuine militarism and in many respects give no additional assurance that the country will be better defended, for the simple fact remains that we are arming without definite plan and without anything like adequate coordination of army and navy. The proposed addition of a force of 75,000 reserves to the regular army will be an important adjunct to our powerful military machine. With few exceptions all military men are propagandists for greater and greater forces and expenditures. The heads of no army or navy are ever satisfied; they are always asking for more. An increase of 2,000 regular army officers will make our army more than ever over-officered in proportion to the number of enlisted men; hence there will be an immediate demand in the next Congress that the number of enlisted men be raised so that there will be troops for these officers to command. Of the 12,777 officers we now have, many are necessarily on detached duty, some of which is valuable and necessary, some of which is not, like the training of high-school boys in the rudiments of military drill. The excuse is that we must have an extra supply of regular officers to command the millions of men we shall raise when war comes again.

It is needless to point out that it is extraordinarily difficult to reduce an army. (It was done in the reorganization of 1870 after the Civil War, when the occupation of the Southern states was growing less important.) Once you have a number of officers they feel that they have a life interest in their jobs and that it is unjust to turn them adrift, perhaps in middle age, when they have been trained for one career and nothing else. Thus the proposed addition to the number of regular officers will in all probability be a permanent charge and make more and more difficult the reduction of the federal budget. Of course the new ships to be built for the navy will also call for more men and more officers. The total force is, or soon will be, three times that of the navy under the administration of Theodore Roosevelt, who was considered a very considerable navalist.

Now if there were a genuine national emergency it would be possible to understand Mr. Roosevelt's action. Since that emergency does not exist, the President cannot complain if he is charged with being motivated by other reasons than the purely military. The dictators abroad have found that increasing their military and naval forces is an easy way to reduce unemployment; it is another way to spend federal money in the expectation of priming the pump again. Like almost all Mr. Roosevelt's actions this one has not been thought through, nor is it in accord with a definite, far-reaching national program. As John T. Flynn and other economists have pointed out, a prosperity purchased by armament expenditure is illusive and dangerous; when the program is completed and the work stops the economic results are bound to be serious.

Certainly, as I have stated on this page before, there is nothing in the Japanese situation to call for this move unless the purpose is to make that situation worse by inflaming it. The news of it will undoubtedly stimulate the Japanese militarists to extra efforts to increase their forces, just as our sending three cruisers to Singapore has been accepted by the government-controlled Japanese press as a deliberate threat to Japan, as has the concentration of British ships at Singapore and Hongkong. Those who are engineering this national policy of rattling the saber appear really to believe that threats of this kind are the only thing that the Japanese militarists will listen to or be moved by. Behind Japan, however, are the dictator states in Europe. I have been shocked in talking with men in high position in Washington to find that some of them actually think that sooner or later we shall have to fight Hitler and Mussolini. If we are to stage another great crusade in Europe to save the world for democracy, the moves just made will obviously not be sufficient for an enterprise which will inevitably bring this country to the verge of bankruptcy and put an end to its republican institutions.

Nothing puzzles me more than the attitude of those who say that we must save the democracies of England and France—and Russia, since Russia is bound to fight with France under the existing treaties. What a joke that will be: American troops fighting not as at Archangel in 1918 to *destroy* Russian communism but to *defend* it, and especially the bloody brand of one Joseph Stalin! And what if in the next year or two France should go either communist or fascist, of which there is a chance? Again, I am dumfounded by the mentality of statesmen who contemplate another war abroad for democracy. They admit the vicious circle of armaments and more armaments, bound in the long run to decrease the standard of living for the workers and creating a dominating military machine. They even admit that if we go into war we may come out of it fascist or communist, and still they insist that we must arm in the present "emergency." They even concede what I have so often pointed out—that, according to Franklin Roosevelt and many military and naval officers, we cannot attack Japan nor Japan attack us. Yet they are for more preparedness, a bigger army, a bigger navy, all of which is a complete confession of the bankruptcy of their statesmanship.

Issues and Men

BY OSWALD GARRISON VILLARD

A WEEK'S stay in Washington has finally convinced me that there is a determined drive on the part of certain persons, some connected with the government, to put us into war with Japan. They are careful to say that that is the very reverse of their purpose, but their words and their acts are precisely such as one would expect if they were part of a deliberate plan to embroil us in the war now going on in Asia. Why else should the State Department be making so much of the fact that one of our diplomats had his face slapped; however humane and chivalrous his motives, he was mixing into something—if the dispatches I have read were correct—that was not his business, which he would have kept out of if he had really understood the duty of a neutral diplomat. Then there was an attempt to play up the rough handling of an American newspaperman, but that fell quite flat. Next came the identical notes of the United States, Britain, and France demanding information about what Japan is really up to in the matter of battleships. I may be wrong, but I would be willing to bet quite a little sum that if Japan should come across with the desired information Mr. Hull's warriors would be the most disappointed men in Washington. I believe that from now on this policy will continue; the government will play up every incident it can to arouse public opinion. Washington newspapermen were freely saying that they expected to see strong action against the Japanese fishermen who are fishing off the Alaskan coast. Their presence provides a wonderful opportunity to rush some cutters and destroyers up there to prove to Japan once more that we are good red-blooded Americans who cannot be trifled with.

When I said this to an official the other day, he replied: "Well, why not? Have we got to take lying down everything those Japs do to us? With the Japanese army and navy out of hand and refusing to obey the orders of their own government, it's up to us to let those militarists know in the only language they can understand just what is likely to come to them." That is exactly the point of view of the belligerent persons I have in mind. When one says to them, "Then you are going to let these militarists lead you into the horror and cost of a war?" they reply that we owe something to our national honor and that it is time we let the dictators everywhere know that we "can still fight if we have to."

Well, if this policy is not changed by an immediate outpouring of public sentiment in opposition, it is only a question of time when we shall come to grips with Japan. Personally I think that a continuation of this policy is certain to infuriate the very Japanese militarists we are seeking to overawe. Those who favor our going to war and are trying to engineer it are setting three months as the necessary time to have enough Japanese "incidents" and work the country up into such a fury that it will be ready to let loose our dogs of war. They "fear" that our ships and sailors will be the victims of other Panay happenings, but when you suggest to them that this is the time to prevent such events by taking our ships out of China they look at you with scorn and repeat Mr. Hull's words that we have rights, responsibilities, and duties in China.

Fortunately this campaign is already running into difficulties; the process of waking up America and making it war-minded is not going as well as had been expected. Many people are speaking out, and acting too. Boake Carter continues his magnificent work on the radio and in his column. Professor E. M. Borchard has just shown up what is on foot in a splendid address under the auspices of the Bronson Cutting Foundation in Washington. Father Coughlin has come to life with a proper broadcast that it is much more important that we take care of the alarming increase in unemployment and suffering here at home than that we undertake the disciplining of berserker Japanese militarists.

The Congress has opened well. That indefensible $800,000,000 armament program is not slipping through so easily and unanimously as the White House hoped. Admiral Leahy has already been nine days on the witness stand, and he appeared to be an extremely unhappy and worried witness when I heard him last week. The revelation that Captain Ingersoll of the navy had been in London masquerading as "Captain Smith" and Leahy's refusal to tell what he was doing there so alarmed Secretary Hull that he answered Senator Johnson's proposed resolution, which the Senate had tabled, before the Senate thought of passing it. Mr. Hull may well say that there are no formal alliances between the United States and England, but he will hardly deny that there have been those long and detailed informal conversations which play so deadly a part at times in international relations. I believe that a perfect understanding exists concerning the role the British navy will play if we go to war with Japan. At any rate Washington is full of stories about the six battleships which the British are to send to Singapore to cut off all Japanese ships at the Straits while we cut the trade routes at Panama and Cape Horn. One of our squadrons, the story runs, is based near the Dutch islands to protect them from sudden raids.

The saddest thing of all is that Secretary Hull cannot see that the day we go into the war all the fine things he had done for peace through his bilateral trade agreements will crash.

Issues and Men

BY OSWALD GARRISON VILLARD

I WISH that these lines might be read by every voter in the state of North Dakota. My reason is that Senator Gerald P. Nye is up for reelection this year with the primary looming quite near at hand, and I should like every voter to realize that the whole country has a stake in that election. For Gerald Nye has made himself not only one of the most valuable members of the Senate, but a great leader in the fight for peace. His loss to the Senate now, when we are being rushed into war by the utterly mistaken policy of the Administration, and especially by Secretary Hull, would be incalculable. The nation needs him, for he has refused to allow himself to be bamboozled by the militarists or by the diplomats whose statesmanship has broken down.

I well remember when Senator Nye first came to Washington twelve years ago. He seemed extremely youthful and callow; he was in fact quite inexperienced in the ways of Washington. He had not held high office before but had made his reputation as a small-town editor. He did not give the promise of Henrik Shipstead of Minnesota or of others who arrived at that time; but as the years have passed, Gerald Nye has made not only a national but actually an international reputation. No more valuable job has been done in Washington in the last quarter-century than the munitions inquiry which Nye headed. True, the idea of it did not originate with him. But he was quick to see the value of the proposal, and he accepted the task when many another would have given a dozen different reasons for declining. It meant an enormous amount of work; it meant that he would be subjected to all sorts of pressure and incur much unpopularity. But he went at the job with an understanding and courage beyond all praise. That alone should entitle him to reelection.

The repercussions of the munitions inquiry had astounding results abroad. It brought about armament inquiries in Canada and Great Britain, and in Canada resulted in regulations giving the government close control of the export of munitions—if my memory serves. In England the inquiry was soft-pedaled by the government and failed to produce the hoped-for action. I have no doubt that the facts uncovered by the Nye committee helped the government of Léon Blum in France to nationalize the munitions industries—the change is reported to be working well and to be aiding French preparedness for war. Here the inquiry made literally millions of Americans aware of the international alliances of the "merchants of death" and enormously stimulated the demand for taking the profits out of war. Its reports are sought and utilized by students of war and peace all over. With war looming on the horizon today, it would hardly be short of a crime if the voters of North Dakota should be misled into keeping Gerald Nye at home.

There is unfortunately some danger of that, for it is to be a three-cornered fight. The Senator may have to run independently. If the men he has exposed and thwarted can contrive it, he will be defeated. Certainly the munitions makers would not be above sending money into his state to defeat him, and the war-makers among us would hail his defeat as a turning of the tide, as proof that America has become war-minded and that therefore they can go ahead with their schemes to have us at war within three months. But it is not only the militarists who would rejoice. They are not the only ones who have found that they cannot control the Senator from North Dakota. Nye was chairman of the Senate committee which ferreted out the Continental Trading Company during the oil scandals. This led to the jailing of Sinclair, the removal of Robert Stewart as president of the Standard Oil of Indiana, the recovery of millions in taxes for the government, and the preservation of oil resources worth hundreds of millions of dollars. Always a liberal and a progressive, he has never let his being a Republican keep him from being independent. He has voted for New Deal measures whenever he could, but he has also courageously criticized the National Labor Relations Board, the NRA, or any other New Deal creation whenever his conscience told him to do so. That is the great thing about Gerald Nye—he votes not as he is told to vote but as his conscience dictates; and that is so rare a quality that it would call for his reelection even if his career had been quite inconspicuous.

Of course Nye has made mistakes. Who has not? Who could find his way through the economic confusion and turmoil of this day and generation, the welter of legislation of every conceivable kind with which a member of Congress is confronted today, without making mistakes? I have had a long and unusual experience with issues and men in this country and abroad, yet I realize clearly how inadequate I should be in dozens of fields if I were suddenly dropped into a seat in Congress and told to help legislate for the benefit of all the people. Nye has really done his best. No one has ever questioned in my presence his absolute courage, sincerity, and honesty, qualities which should win him forgiveness for many more mistakes than he has made. They tell me he has done a lot for his state, getting much federal aid and money. I do not doubt it, but that seems to me far less important than the things I have recited. Liberals everywhere who can help in any way to keep Senator Nye in the Senate should not lose a moment in getting to work.

March 26, 1938

My dear Stanwood:

That is a very fine letter indeed that you sent to the stupid D.A.R. It ought to make a dent, but I doubt if anybody could make a dent in those opaque and un-American minds. Why those who are so proud of their ancestors' service to the Revolution should be the least faithful to the ideas of the Revolution is something that I shall never be able to understand.

You are right. The most horrible thing about the present situation, aside from the torture of innocent people now going on, is the fact that the vile Nazi doctrines are being pumped into children of the tenderest age and that many of them will never be freed from the infection. If there is a God, I am sure he could not possibly devise a punishment adequate to the crimes of the German leaders of today. If war comes again I shall be in favor, if the Germans are beaten, which may easily not happen, of breaking up Germany into the original states and forbidding even a parliamentary union.

Cordially yours,

Mr. S. Stanwood Menken
Menken, Ferguson & Idler
44 Wall St.
New York City

Issues and Men

BY OSWALD GARRISON VILLARD

Retrospect

"WHAT I am opposed to is not the feeling of the pacifists, but their stupidity. My heart is with them, but my mind has a contempt for them. I want peace but I know how to get it, and they do not." Thus spoke Woodrow Wilson to the American Federation of Labor, at Buffalo, on November 12, 1917, six months after the United States had entered the World War. Twenty and one-half years have elapsed since he uttered those words. Let us now examine the record and see how time has dealt with Mr. Wilson's proud boast that he knew both how to accomplish peace and achieve his pacific aims, when the pacifists maintained that war cures nothing, ends no evils but only creates more, and reforms nobody.

The objects of the American entry into the World War were:

1. The destruction of German militarism and autocracy.

2. "The removal, so far as possible, of all economic barriers and the establishment of an equality of trade conditions among all the nations consenting to the peace . . ." (Peace Point 3).

3. "Absolute freedom of navigation upon the seas . . . alike in peace and in war" (Peace Point 2).

4. National armaments "will be reduced to the lowest point consistent with domestic safety" (Peace Point 4).

5. "The peoples of Austria-Hungary, whose place among the nations we wish to see safeguarded and assured, should be accorded the freest opportunity for autonomous development" (Peace Point 10).

6. "A general association of nations must be formed . . . for the purpose of affording mutual guaranties of political independence and territorial integrity to great and small states alike" (Peace Point 4).

7. "For the rights of nations great and small and the privilege of men everywhere to choose their way of life and obedience" (Wilson's war message of April 2, 1917).

This was Mr. Wilson's and the war party's program. Now let us look at the world and see precisely how correct Mr. Wilson was in stating that he knew how to achieve his war aims.

1. No permanent destruction of German militarism was obtained, but there is instead today a more dangerous and aggressive German militarism than ever before, menacing the peace of the world as the Kaiser never did.

2. Economic barriers were not only not removed but were raised to undreamed of heights, plus embargos, quotas, exchange restrictions, and outright prohibition of imports in certain cases. Absolute inequality of trade conditions exists among the nations consenting to the peace.

3. No change whatever was effected with respect to the freedom of the seas; navies everywhere, including our own, are determined in the next war to use unrestricted submarine warfare and to sink ships without warning, precisely as the Germans did.

4. National armaments have been increased to heights never before considered possible. Millions more men are under arms than in 1914. The world's armament bill has risen from five billions in 1931 to twelve to thirteen billions in 1938. The United States is building the largest fleet on the globe.

5. The peoples of Austria-Hungary, "whose place among the nations" Mr. Wilson wished safeguarded and assured, have been split up and Austria has been reduced to a German province by brutal and overpowering force.

6. The "general association of nations" which Mr. Wilson helped to form, known as the League, is hopelessly dead as a political entity. During the rape of Austria it was never even mentioned as a possible means of assuring "political independence and territorial integrity" to that small state. It has lost Germany, Italy, Japan, Austria, will probably lose Spain, and has received the resignation of several South American states. It has been deliberately flouted by the British Prime Minister, Neville Chamberlain, who refused to consider its services in the existing crisis.

7. The present status of the "rights of nations great and small and the privilege of men everywhere to choose their way of life and obedience" is easily demonstrable. We have only to look at Spain, China, Ethiopia, and Austria. All of them are victims of the "force, force without stint" which Mr. Wilson knew in 1917 was the right method with which to achieve peace and to lick the enemy into a law-abiding, peaceful, cooperative member of the family of nations. Many pacifists whom I know have today not merely contempt for Woodrow Wilson; they also have a profound conviction of his absolute stupidity in 1917 and of his utter ignorance of the forces with which he was dealing, which made a catspaw of him.

The pity of it all is that many persons in Washington, in and out of the government, really believe that we shall have to repeat the stupidity of Woodrow Wilson in the near future. They want us to go to war with Japan to save our face in the Orient. They believe that we shall have to take on Mussolini and Hitler because, as they frankly say, England and France cannot possibly conquer the dictators without our aid. Which is just another proof of the wisdom and farsightedness of Woodrow Wilson and the sound basis of his contempt for the pacifists.

Issues and Men

BY OSWALD GARRISON VILLARD

NO ONE can deny that our Japanese policy has undergone a great change. When the hostilities in China began, Mr. Roosevelt took a position similar to the one he had taken on Spain, namely, that American nationals should get out at once. Naval ships were sent to evacuate the American population, and those who remained were told that they did so at their own risk and that if they perished during the hostilities the United States would feel no obligation to avenge their deaths by going to war. When the Shanghai fighting took place, the same policy was followed—at first. Merchant and navy ships were sent, and all Americans were removed except 6,000 who obstinately refused to leave. Some of these were American citizens who had never been in America; others were merchants and traders who told the government that they could not return because they had nowhere to go, no relatives or friends to turn to in the United States who could aid them, and no means of support. The government did nothing about this. In my judgment it should have asked Congress for the means to take those people to the Philippines or to California and to support them there until the hostilities in China were at an end. The few million dollars involved would have been a bagatelle when one considers that on a single day last week the Senate raised the so-called rearmament bill by $140,000,000. If caring for Americans abroad would take even $20,000,000 out of the Treasury, that would only be what war with Japan would cost us every forty-eight hours.

That the attitude of the United States government is entirely different today would, I believe, be admitted in private conversation by all informed officials. While the Administration has wisely recalled the Fifteenth United States Infantry and the extra regiment of marines sent to Shanghai, it has refused to take any more marines out or to recall American warships in Chinese waters, and it has not, I believe, issued positive orders to Americans residing elsewhere in China than Shanghai to get out. On the other hand, Mr. Hull has stated that we should "afford appropriate and reasonable protection to our rights and interests in the Far East." He has also said: "To waive rights and to permit interests to lapse in the face of their actual or threatened violation—and thereby to abandon obligations—in any important area of the world can serve only to encourage disregard of law and of the basic principles of international order, and thus contribute to the inevitable spread of international anarchy throughout the world." Finally he said: "To respect the rights of others and to insist that others respect our rights has been the traditional policy of our country." With this theoretical statement few will disagree, but obviously all depends on the spirit with which these so-called rights are upheld. We have rights in China that we should not have, that Mr. Hull admits we shall give up when, as he says, conditions justify relinquishing them—we and not the Chinese to be the judges of that. But the crux of the matter is whether we shall or shall not maintain those rights, including property rights, at a time of international warfare in China.

In times of stress or strain, earthquakes, revolutions, strikes, floods, and other disasters created by nature or by man, the private citizen often has to resign himself to the loss of rights to which he is clearly entitled. Is there any reason why nations should not similarly be willing in times of international hostilities to waive what are indisputably legal rights? Upon the answer to this question depends in considerable degree our freedom from war. If we are going to take the position that it is a serious offense when one insignificant soldier slaps a consul's face in the midst of a bitter struggle for the mastery of China, or when a Japanese bomb kills a missionary in the course of normal warfare, we are certainly going to make trouble for ourselves and risk our own embroilment. What alarms me about the State Department's new policy toward Japan is its determinedly aggressive character—its inspired publications in the American press, its dispatching of three warships to Singapore, the open statement that we are building up our super-navy against Japan. When the Japanese surrendered on the Alaska fisheries question recently, the announcement of their yielding was accompanied by a statement that the government was going to watch them none the less, a clear intimation—as clear as it was insulting to the Japanese government—that this government does not any longer believe anything the Japanese government says.

Coupled with this has been the refusal of the government to reply to declarations made by the Japanese Prime Minister in the Diet that Japan was willing to discuss the size of battleships again with a view to their reduction, or to comment upon the open charges in the Diet that the American government was building up its fleet specifically against Japan; the Japanese Premier said that in consequence Japan would continue to build up to us. Now it may well be that the State Department places no more faith in Japanese promises than it does in those of Hitler. Nevertheless, the policy now being pursued does not lead toward peace but toward the constant exacerbation of public feeling in both countries; and that is the road to war, a war which there is reason to believe would not be unwelcome to certain members of the State Department who feel that we must let the Japanese know that we propose to dominate in the Pacific area.

Issues and Men

BY OSWALD GARRISON VILLARD

A Problem in Ethics

NEVILLE CHAMBERLAIN has posed a serious problem for students of ethics and morality. He has perhaps deferred the coming of war by making a shameful bargain with Mussolini. He has sacrificed Spain deliberately and finally. He has lent his sanction to the base conquest of Ethiopia. In return, the Mediterranean tension between the two countries is eased and Mussolini gives his approval to the latest British aggression, the new Arabian "protectorate" just set up by the English north of the Red Sea—in other words, a new colony for England at the very moment that perfidious Albion has been asking all the world to concentrate its attention on the wrongdoings of Hitler and Mussolini. So everyone will now judge what has happened according to his own particular philosophy and his ethical standards. There will be some to say that so ignoble a pact should never have been signed, even in the interest of peace; and there will be plenty of others who will point out that this is an imperfect world, that one must be practical, that one cannot hope to achieve the ideal, and that therefore it was the best thing to do.

Actually the pact means little or nothing beyond this recognition of the aggressions of either side. Mussolini promises to get out of Spain just when Franco has about won with Mussolini's aid; and it must not be overlooked that no date whatever is set in the treaty for carrying it into effect. It is all contingent upon the date of Mussolini's final withdrawal from Spain. That may be six months or a year from now. True, the treaty affirms England's intention to keep the Suez Canal open at all times for international use, but to that it was bound anyway. What is most important of all is whether the signature of Benito Mussolini is worth anything. It has pleased him to put his name to this document as he has put his signature to others—only to forget that fact whenever it suited his purpose. There is no truth, no honor, and no sincerity in him any more than in Hitler. I agree with Robert Dell, who has just said that "an agreement with Mussolini's signature . . . is not worth the ink with which it is written." This arrangement with England suits Mussolini for the moment. It will last only so long as he thinks it is to his advantage, and not a day longer.

Curiously enough, this grossly immoral bargain has nowhere been so acclaimed as in Washington. The President himself went out of his way publicly to applaud the accord in a statement read by him at his regular press conference. True, he said that our government "does not attempt to pass upon the political features" of this agreement, but he added that it has seen its conclusion "with sympathetic interest because it is proof of the value of peaceful negotiations." Yet ours is the country which has refused to recognize the theft of Manchoukuo and the rape of Ethiopia and has only recognized the conquest of Austria because of the extraordinary situation of that country. Even before the President spoke, the specially favored New York *Times* reported from Washington that the State Department was rejoicing over the great success of the "realistic policy" of Chamberlain.

What this means is that the State Department now confidently counts upon England's being in a position to decrease its forces in the Mediterranean and send some battleships to Singapore—battleships are always the foundation of Mr. Hull's policy in the Far East. With England threatening Japan at Singapore, our State Department advocates of the mailed-fist policy with Japan—and war if necessary—can be counted on to be more aggressive than ever. I do not know whether it is true that the President, as has been declared, has said that we must have a policy "to scare the pants off Japan," but no further proof is needed that the State Department is ready for "parallel action" with Great Britain in its effort to achieve American dominance in Asian waters. True, the Japanese are obstinately refusing to commit more outrages against Americans, but this may be remedied any day, and even this fly in the ointment cannot keep the State Department from openly hailing the touching sight of Chamberlain and Mussolini guaranteeing each other's swag in the name of peace and harmony.

The American advocates of collective security cannot, however, be as happy about it. They have felt that we must stand by to protect democratic England and France from a desperate Mussolini. They will find it harder now to win the American people to their point of view in the face of the holy alliance of Chamberlain and the Duce. Our people will hardly rush to the rescue of England when England is ready to talk business with the dictator on such terms. If I were an Englishman I might rejoice that the Mediterranean was safe, but I should hang my head with shame that my country more than any other was responsible for the destruction of the fair young democracy of Spain and that it had acquiesced in a wrong against which Glad tone and John Bright, Henry Campbell-Bannerman, and even Palmerston would have protested. If I were an Englishman I should blush to recall how the British peacemakers at Versailles indorsed the new world order of Wilson, in which there were to be no more colonies but only mandated territory. Finally, to me it seems that the price paid by Chamberlain is far too great in dishonor for the slight betterment of the peace situation he has obtained.

Issues and Men

BY OSWALD GARRISON VILLARD

BEFORE me lies a letter I have just received from an old friend in Munich, similar in content to many that have come to me in the last few years. Its burden is that I insist on saying harsh things about Germany which I must know "can only hurt deeply my old friends there." The writer then goes on to say: "I am certain that if you would only come over here and see for yourself, your strong sense of justice would compel you to judge us differently." Here we have again the puzzle of the unfathomable German mentality, which I confess I understand less and less as time passes. The writer of this letter has lived for years out of Germany—in England, the United States, and elsewhere. He has had the opportunity to know other peoples and their backgrounds and especially the Anglo-Saxon way of looking at things. Yet he too repeats this stupid statement that if I would only come to Germany I would quite change my opinion about the great and glorious rule of the Führer, Adolf Hitler.

Unfortunately that letter arrived at a singularly unhappy moment. I had just heard of the death of my noble-spirited, truly patriotic friend Carl von Ossietzky, done to death by years of torture in prison and concentration camp—a torture, it is only fair to say, that was begun under the republic in the pre-Hitler period—for the simple offense of revealing the truth about the way the German government was deliberately dishonoring its signature to the Treaty of Versailles by rearming secretly. This letter from Munich also arrived just after I had been called on by a young Austrian who for opposing the Hitler regime had been arrested in Germany and imprisoned for six months in a concentration camp. His body is a dreadful sight—a mass of scars from daily beatings. In addition, as a result of his injuries he has had to undergo no fewer than sixteen operations since his release. The doctors say that his lungs and kidneys are gravely affected.

So I was not exactly in the mood to be lectured by my friend in Munich. It aroused first my anger and then my pity and then my bewilderment that this intelligent correspondent could really believe that a visit to Germany would wipe out these memories and a thousand others, would make me think well of a government which has openly declared war upon civilization, upon liberty, upon all the humane aspirations of centuries. Of course I should see humming factories, a great army in the making, superb roads, a contented youth. I should behold marvelous changes since the last winter that I passed in Germany—that of 1930-31 when the weak and compromising Brüning was at the helm. I should attend wonderful pageants, circuses, parades. But witnessing these really remarkable achievements of a brutal but able government I should never be able to forget that this government has also declared war upon my own government, that it has appointed a Nazi leader to help wreck our institutions, and that it is spending millions of marks for that purpose in this country every year.

I resent the implication in this and similar letters that a superficial journey around Germany would make me faithless to my democratic faith, my belief that, as Lincoln put it, no man is good enough to govern any other man without that other man's consent.

One thing more: I wish that my German friends would realize that if everything else in Germany were in accord with my political and moral and spiritual ideas, I should never be able to forgive them for what they have done and are doing to the Jews, who have lived among them for centuries and made enormous contributions to the progress and especially the intellectual and artistic advancement of Germany. With an icy cruelty that beggars description they are being robbed of their all, denied the right to work, and turned out to die of slow starvation. After October 1 they are not to be allowed to take part in any business, and as they cannot get a labor certificate there is nothing left but immigration or starvation—and immigration is financially impossible. Never before has a great nation deliberately robbed and tortured more than half a million of its citizens; yet I am supposed to go over and see some stadiums and some happy workers on Strength-Through-Joy trips and forget all this!

I am sorry if stating facts like these hurts the feelings of my German friends, but the fault is not mine. It lies at the doors of the bloody-handed men who have made the Germany of today more feared and hated even than it was during the World War, who have flung ethics, morality, and justice to the winds. All my life I have sought to tell the truth as I see it. I have done so all my life about my own country and hurt many people's feelings. Why should I fail to tell the truth about the Germany of today? My critics were very grateful when I denounced the treatment of Germany at Versailles. I am the same man today and am exercising the same judgment today that I possessed then.

September 22, 1938

Dear Dorothy Thompson:

Thanks from the bottom of my heart for your articles of yesterday and today. Now we see alike. I have [illegible]tten very strongly for The Nation and hope what I have written will get in. I see Hitler bestriding the world, and perhaps the whole world divided into four dictatorships--America, Europe under Hitler, Russia and Japan. What has become of the English conscience and common-sense? At any rate, this finishes the League of Nations and ends any collective securit[illegible]hat would tie us up to a country capable of Chamberlain's monstrous wickedness.

With deepest gratitude,

Ever faithfully,

Miss Dorothy Thompson,
88 Central Park West,
New York City

October 5, 1938

Dear Mr. President:

I should be remiss, indeed, if I failed to tell you how deeply grateful I have been to you for your friendly intervention in the European crisis. As I have written to Secretary Hull, I am sure that there is no more brilliant chapter in our diplomatic history, and I must congratulate you particularly upon the magnificent timing of your dispatches and the extremely clever psychology of the appeal, especially that to Mussolini. That was being a Good Neighbor in the highest degree and I am sure that the American people are unanimously grateful to you for your leadership in this terrible crisis.

I for one have only one other hope, that you will make it clear how horrifying this dismemberment of Czechoslovakia is and the violation of treaties by France and England in order to appease the dictator. Given Chamberlain and the situation he found himself in, I presume that there was nothing else that he could do. He and the world have paid a very high price for the blunders and weaknesses which led up to this situation in which he was finally trapped. I wish that the Congress might pass a resolution of sympathy with Czechoslovakia and that an early invitation might be extended to Benes to visit this country and receive in person the expressions of sympathy which would be as overwhelming, I am sure, as those given to Louis Kossuth when he was brought to this country on an American frigate in the middle of the Nineteenth Century

With renewed expressio s of my sincere gratitude and pride in your achievement,

Faithfully yours,

President Franklin D. Roosevelt,
The White House,
Washington, D.C.

Issues and Men

BY OSWALD GARRISON VILLARD

Dear Mr. Villard: In view of what is happening in Europe, and I agree with what you have recently written in *The Nation* regarding it, has it occurred to you that the world would be a better place today if the Germans had won the Battle of the Marne? Think it over, and perhaps you will do a piece on what you think the state of the world would be today if that had been the case instead of the Allies having been the "victors"—if victors they were.

(*Signed*) E. Y. (formerly of Prague)

THROUGH the mail has come this letter. I confess the thought in it has occurred to me more than once, when I have had a rare moment to think of what might have been. I suppose I rejoiced as much as any spectator at a distance that the French won the Battle of the Marne. We none of us had any idea that that meant the war would last for four years. We were as heartily glad that Paris was spared bombardment as the world is relieved now that for the moment Berlin, London, and Paris have escaped aerial attack. When we consider the present situation of the world, however, it is hard not to admit that the world would be far better off had the Germans won at the Marne.

Here are the facts: Had the Germans won at the Marne they would have taken Paris within a few days. Their advance guard had already seen the Eiffel Tower, and the government of France had moved from Paris to Bordeaux. With Paris in German hands it is difficult to believe that France could have held out or England could have resisted until Kitchener had raised and drilled his millions. Paris is the heart of France, but the Germans would not have stopped there. They would have swept westward to the sea and mopped up all the northern part of France at their leisure; it would then have taken only a small force to capture the Channel ports. Had the war ended then with Germany the victor, no less than 9,500,000 lives would have been saved and an amount of human misery and suffering prevented which no words and no figures can possibly describe. That is the one great outstanding thing.

Next Italy, Rumania, Bulgaria, Turkey, Greece, and the United States would not have entered the war, to say nothing of China, Japan, Cuba, Haiti, and other countries. As a result there would be no fascism today and certainly no bolshevism in Russia—if Russia had made peace immediately after the surrender of France. There would be no Nazis, no Hitler, no Mussolini. There would have been no Lusitania case and none of the thousand sinkings without warning of cargo and passenger ships. While the economic shock of the war would have been great, if it had lasted only three months the present economic prostration of the world would never have come to pass. There would not have been the millions of unemployed all over the globe. We should not have seen the rise of the intense nationalist movements or the drift toward autarchy, or the raising of tariffs everywhere. The world, for better or worse, would probably still be on the gold standard. The Austrian Monarchy would perhaps still exist, and the pitiful old Kaiser, with all his stupidity intact, would doubtless still be reigning.

So much for the credit side. On the debit side we should have an overbearing Germany—just what we have now—a Germany dominant in Europe, with France in its power—exactly as is the case today. The individual German would be so puffed up with pride and arrogance as to be just as unbearable to all civilized people as the Nazis are today. Germany would still be misgoverning its colonies; it would undoubtedly have grabbed a piece of Belgium and added more French territory to German Alsace-Lorraine. Poland would not have been reconstituted, and the Kaiser would probably have helped himself to a good bit of the Ukraine. Undoubtedly military limitations would have been put upon France, its fleet would have been reduced to insignificance, its people condemned to the paying of indemnities which would probably approximate the vast sums they are now paying for their Maginot lines, their increased fleet, their greatly enlarged army, and their huge air force. Europe would be an extremely unpleasant place to live in—just as it is today; and everybody would be wondering where the Kaiser would strike next—just as we are all wondering whether Belgium or Denmark or what is left of Czechoslovakia will be Hitler's next objective. Germany would be well on the road to Bagdad, precisely as it is today.

So there is the picture. I have honestly presented it as I see it. If I have omitted unintentionally any factors on the debit side I hope the readers of this column will point them out to me, for I want to be absolutely just. Finally I want to stress the fact that evil comes with every war, and that the lot of humanity would have been adversely affected whoever had won the World War. Militarism breeds militarism, and mass murder entails more mass murder. It is a pressing question whether those who took up the sword will not perish by it.

December 30, 1938

Dear Mr. Horwill:

I am delighted to get your letter this morning. How little your handwriting has changed in the years; it is just as firm and steady as when we first met! It is so nice to get your views and find that you are in sympathy with mine. I wonder whether the whole gas-mask business was not deliberately part of a scheme to frighten the people so that they would accept the surrender. All the evidence we get here from Germany is to the effect that Hitler would never have fought and could not have. For example, there is an ex-aviation officer here who says that the Hitler air fleet is in very bad shape because of lack of trained personnel. They have magnificent machines, but they are so difficult to handle that, according to this man who was an ace during the war, it will take three years adequately to train pilots to handle them, and they carry so many guns that the problem of carrying sufficient ammunition seems insolmable. More than that, to an American friend of mine residing in Berlin one of the highest party officials said just before the Chamberlain surrender, "We cannot go to war because if we do we shall have to keep 40 per cent of our army at home to hold these people down." All my personal letters and contacts prove to me that Hitler overreached himself with his latest anti-Jewish excesses, and that there is great and increasing indignation throughout Germany among decent people.

The Chamberlain surrender has been a deadly blow to the advo tive security here, and a serious one to

England's standing in America. As one columnist put it, Chamberlain gave nothing away at Munich save honor, good faith and decency. I am glad to hear that a realization of this is penetrating into the British mind. You are quite right, the worst thing in in the world is the absence of leadership in the democracies. Mr. Roosevelt has failed us at so many points that we are almost as badly off . For all the innumerable fine things he has done, and the introduction of social security, for which he deserves a monument, there is a grave question whether he will not leave the country almost a financial wreck, with militarism in an acute form fastened upon us and the way open to a fascist dictatorship. Incidentally, there is no communist menace whatever here. Today the dictators are conquering all Europe for the simple reason that they are so much abler and so much more determined than your Chamberlains and Daladiers, know exactly what their objectives are, and never let up in their drive for them.

My book is done and will be out in March. Constable is bringing it out in England; perhaps I told you that. I wish that you might review it for the Manchester Guardian.

With warmest wishes for a Happy New Year to you and Mrs. Horwill,

Faithfully yours,

Mr. Herbert Horwill,
1, High Grove,
Welwyn Garden City
Herts, England

OSWALD GARRISON VILLARD

OUR MILITARY CHAOS

THE TRUTH ABOUT DEFENSE

1939

ALFRED · A · KNOPF

New York & London

To the American business men and to the liberals who will not see

 Manufactured in the United States of America. Published simultaneously in Canada by The Ryerson Press

FIRST EDITION

Foreword

Although this book was written just before the coming of the Second World War,[1] that horrifying event in no wise affects the soundness of its arguments as to the proper military policy for the United States and, I hope, its conclusions. The necessity of a national inquiry into the whole problem of our defense must now be more patent than ever. If we need the defense forces we now have, all the greater is the wisdom of seeing that they are efficient, coordinated, and economically and properly administered.

There is nothing in the coming of the war itself to call for further preparedness unless the United States should decide to participate, which would be the supreme folly since it would jeopardize the very existence of the Republic and we should certainly reap even less benefit from it than we did from our share in the last Armageddon. Leaving aside all other questions, from the purely military point of view the coming of the present war is to the defense

[1] It was still possible to alter the text during proof-reading; only a few very minor alterations, however, were found to be necessary.

advantage of our country, in that, when it is over, victors and vanquished alike will be exhausted, bled white, depleted financially, economically, and spiritually, to say nothing of the loss of man power. If Italy stays out of the war, and the Allies win, it will be an isolated, jeopardized State and Germany's military power in that event will certainly be ended this time. Even if Germany should win, it could then as readily send an army to Mars as to the United States. Even a conquered Europe would be too dangerous to it to warrant another war and one overseas if its economy and means permitted.

This war has, therefore, *already eliminated America's only possible enemy in Europe for years to come,* just as Japan's warring in China would prevent her attacking the United States even if that were a possible undertaking. Similarly whether Japan wins or loses, her exhaustion after this struggle will long prevent any further military overseas adventures. However deeply and emotionally our sympathies may be engaged—and mine are naturally wholeheartedly with the Allies—this is more than ever the time for Americans to keep cool and to shape our national policies with the one supreme aim of keeping our democracy alive and intact.

OSWALD GARRISON VILLARD

Penned during an air-raid warning period in London, September 6, 1939.

CHAPTER ONE

Our Planless Defense

National Defense: A navy and army adequate for national defense, based on a survey of all facts affecting the existing establishments that the people in time of peace may not be burdened by an expenditure fast approaching $1,000,000,000 annually.

Thus read the national defense plank in the Democratic platform of 1932, on which Franklin D. Roosevelt was first elected President, and which he solemnly promised to uphold. Not many planks in it have been honored save in the breach, and none has been more deliberately flouted than the one just quoted. There has been no survey of the facts

concerning the Army and Navy since Mr. Roosevelt took office. There has been no definition of what constitutes adequate defense and hence no adjustment of Army and Navy to that defense. In time of peace the people, instead of being relieved of the burden of nearly $1,000,000,000 are now being burdened with an expenditure fast approaching $2,000,000,000 annually.

This great sum of $1,735,000,000 for the fiscal year 1939–40 is to be expended without any established defense policy whatsoever to guide this vast outlay. Our military and naval objectives have never been defined, much less our foreign policies, by which the former are supposed to be more or less shaped. Nobody in this country knows today where the defense of the United States is to be, whether in the Pacific Ocean it is a line drawn from the Aleutian Islands to Hawaii and Samoa or Panama or whether the outer defense is definitely to be Guam, Wake, and other far-flung Pacific atolls. On the Atlantic we do not know whether in the event of war we shall stay at home and protect our coasts or send the fleet abroad to seek victory in a mid-ocean or overseas battle. No one has decided whether we shall defend the Central and South American republics from foreign attack or restrict ourselves to protecting our trade routes to South America. The President has declared that we shall fight if Canada

CHAPTER TWO

The United States Impregnable

Nothing is more astounding in this whole defense problem than the fact that some of the highest authorities have declared that the United States is impregnable and today cannot be attacked through the air or invaded from across the ocean. Despite these positive assertions, Congress in this time of national distress, when it has been laying off hundreds of thousands of W.P.A. workers allegedly because of lack of funds, continues to appropriate billions for armaments as if the United States were part and parcel of the continent of Europe and as much in danger of attack as if Washington were as near to Berlin as London and Paris. To expend one dollar unnecessarily or wastefully in this hour of strain, of ten million unemployed, of a rapidly mounting debt, comes pretty close to being treason

to the Republic, for it weakens our democracy and does not aid in its defense at home or against foreign attack. Yet Congress has not stopped to inquire whether these authorities are or are not correct in their statements that the United States is impregnable.

The fortifying of the distant atolls and of the island of Guam—if Congress yields on Guam—is distinctly provocative, and so are many of the inflammatory utterances of admirals and public men. And if, as Major Eliot so emphatically says, war with Japan is impossible, even with all the billions that we have poured out for Army and Navy, why is it necessary to continue these terrific expenditures? They certainly make the American people believe that their treasure is being thus used because of the danger that Japan *might* attack us. That the American people have that impression today cannot be denied, nor can Franklin Roosevelt's assertion in his article in *Asia*, already quoted, that since war with Japan is impossible we should get out of the frame of mind of talking and acting as

if it were, and seek to bring both nations into a friendly attitude toward each other—so far as that is possible today in view of Japan's treaty-breaking and massacring in China.

Japan certainly has the right to look upon us as an aggressor nation. The chairman of the all-important Senate Foreign Relations Committee is Senator Pittman, who has frequently spoken for the Roosevelt administration. On February 10, 1936 Mr. Pittman made a most sensational attack upon Japan and its policies and wound up by saying that since Japan "apparently" will not respect its treaties in the Far East, "there is only one answer, and that is dominating naval and air forces"—a speech widely interpreted, as Mauritz Hallgren has pointed out, as a demand that we prepare actively for war against Japan in Japanese waters. The *New York Herald Tribune* reported that the preponderance of editorial opinion upon it was to the effect that the Senator was "recklessly brandishing weapons in an atmosphere more appropriate to the untamed scenes of his youth [in Nevada] than to the most responsible post connected with American foreign policy, excepting only the White House and the office of the Secretary of State." The State Department, however, not only did not disavow the Pittman speech; it did not express its regret. Japan has felt that our naval maneuvers within short range of her outlying islands were a direct menace to her safety. Since there is no Asiatic naval power except Japan, the mere presence of our fleet in the far Pacific is obviously a move against it. As for the arming of the atolls and the proposal to fortify Guam, that was immediately accepted by the Japanese imperialists and the controlling Army clique as a direct threat.

Curiously enough, although the President has talked of those measures short of war, he has not yet sought to put them into effect except in limited degree. His refusal to apply the existing neutrality law to Japan or to put an embargo on the purchase by Japan of the supplies necessary for carrying on the war with China, notably scrap iron (although inducing our aircraft-manufacturers to cease producing airships for Japan), alone makes possible Japan's successful conduct of her war in China. As Norman Thomas has pointed out, the purchase of Japanese gold on a large scale by our Treasury Department has "made the United States Japan's partner in her criminal Chinese adventure. Even under an imperfect neutrality law the President could have lessened that trade [with Japan] without resorting to collective security. . . . The desire for profit was too strong for the Government and the people." [1] Instead Secretary Hull insists upon our right to intervene in the war zones in China in behalf of trade and property and world order, and the President continues to arm in the Pacific and has countenanced the development of advanced bases which most people believe to be a weakening of our Pacific defense instead of a strengthening. Thus he continues to keep alive in Japan that feeling of hate and fear of the United States which he so strongly deprecated in *Asia*.

Similarly, when it came to peace-time arming by the democracies against the Fascist nations, it was the latter which determined the extent and character of the arming of their rivals. Inevitably these democracies, which in the battle of power politics in Europe reserve to themselves the defense of liberty and individual rights, must approximate the peace-time tricks, stratagems, and industrial organization of their future enemies. They cannot hope to cope with the Fascists unless they construct a military machine as all-embracing, as to both men and mechanics, as those of their rivals. Formerly, when war was merely a matter of some men with guns, a few cannon, ammunition, and some food, it was only necessary to make sure that your muskets were as good as those of your rivals and your men as well drilled. If food was not promptly supplied from the rear, you lived on the country. Today in our mechanized, nation-wide warfare the service of supply becomes all-important. The soldiers at the front are no more valuable than the workers in the rear. Both must therefore be thoroughly prepared in advance to function without a minute's loss of time, and not only the workers. The factories they serve must be thoroughly conditioned in advance for war-time demands upon them. If the owners have to make over their machinery in order to handle war orders, then they must be paid in advance to train at least some of their workers for the eventual war jobs, and to keep on hand the numerous tools and machines needed when the change comes. So runs the story.

That is only a small part of the economic preparation of nations. There follows the piling up of raw materials and foodstuffs, especially those which must be imported from abroad. Naturally, even in peace-time arming, government orders must have the right of way. The greater the preparations for war and the greater the necessity for speed in order to be ready, the more certain the subordination of private business to the rush for armaments. Thus, in Germany today, where restricted finances make possible only the purchase of a portion of the raw materials needed by the whole country, it is the most important factories devoted wholly to rearming that get all they want. Those establishments which cater only to peace-time civilian wants are

given merely what is left over after Army and Navy are served. Hence we have Göring offering the German people the choice of guns or butter. The same choice will inevitably be given to the people of France and of England if the present war continues long, if the statesmen of the world can find no other solution for their respective nations than to devote all their vital energies to the prosecution of the world catastrophe. The same thing will happen in the United States if its present militarization is carried further.

More and more even in the democracies not at war, governments must control and subsidize private industry. The manufacturer is entitled to ask grants from the Treasury if he has to invest more capital to supply the machinery which is to lie idle until mobilization day, unless there is a peace-time use for it. In England prior to the war the Government actively directed capital investment into the channels of war preparation. If the manufacturer is to put capital into plant extension for the purpose of making more tanks, more artillery, more airplanes, more shells, and all the rest, then there is every incentive for him to join those who see in this armament race not a temporary state of affairs —that is, until the Government feels that it is abreast of Germany or Italy or both in armaments— but a permanent and normal condition of national life. That neutral government which decides that it has armed enough and is ready to turn back to peace-time status (save for replacements and the addition to its armament of any new devices for killing) will be brave indeed, for it will be confronted by hordes of outraged manufacturers demanding of the cabinet ministers whether they shall turn out their faithful workers to stagnate on the dole and allow those government-created extensions to their plants and their special war machinery to deteriorate for lack of use when they will be needed if war comes. That will be the moment when some new foreign menace or enemy will inevitably be discovered, or some combination of enemies. Just as in the past England felt itself compelled to maintain a fleet equal to those of any two nations which it might have to fight, so it will be insisted that each particular country's armaments must be ready to take care of at least two hostile air fleets or possible land forces.

In other words, in the "rearming" process—it is really arming, since the democracies were never before armed on such a scale except during the World War—the governments create *vested privileged interests* which will fight against any reduction or dissolution of their businesses, who will insist that *their* products must have precedence over anybody's butter, that their dividends must not be

impaired by any yielding to miserable pacifist ideas or by any weakening of the defense systems. In this attitude they will be backed up not only by their very influential stockholders, but by the labor unions—if the latter should still be active and free at that time. For in every country, especially in England and the United States, organized labor prefers arming to unemployment, or to the charge that it is pacifist and unpatriotic or that it is too selfish and supine to ward off the day when the Russians, or Japanese or Germans and Italians, will enter their country, rape their women, destroy their cities, and run off with the whole national Treasury. In this attitude labor is no blinder than, for example, the American business men who usually make the welkin ring with their denunciations of governmental interference in private business. These captains of industry crave the filling of our half-dozen American shipyards with Government vessels, and cheer unrestrainedly for a great Navy, without realizing that the governmental camel's head is well within the tent and that the end may easily be a Government monopoly, precisely as the American merchant marine is now at last seventy-five per cent in the hands of the bureaucrats in Washington.[1] The greater the preparedness the

[1] The bill pending in Congress authorizing the Government to build warships for the South American countries in American

more inevitable is the harnessing of all industry to the government military machine, the wider open is the road to the totalitarian State.

How fast we in the United States are going in this direction is clearly evidenced by the proposal of President Roosevelt and the War Department in the fall of 1938 that hereafter all our water-power and electric-power developments should be subject to the arbitrary rules of the War Department in order that all future expansion should be in accord with the Army's vision of the function of industry in war-time. Had this proposal carried—and it may yet—all further power developments would have been guided not by the peace-time needs of our industrial development, but by what a group of Army officers may think is best for the military organization of industry after war comes.

navy yards at cost is a most dangerous venture. Intended to keep them from placing orders in the totalitarian countries, this may result in stimulating those countries to build unnecessary warships which will be used against either each other or the United States. Of course no South American country can ever hope to match the Continental navies.

the *Christian Science Monitor* said: "For some time the intelligence unit of the Navy has been working hand-in-glove with the national defense committee of the Daughters of the American Revolution and the other patriotic societies. Presumably the President's order will put an end to this close alignment of a Government bureau and outside groups dealing with controversial subjects." While the President was reported at that time as being "greatly chagrined" by the acts of the bureau, attacks of high naval officers upon peace-loving groups have not ceased. Rear Admiral Clark H. Woodward, Commandant of the Brooklyn Navy Yard, has been constantly reported in the press as violently attacking workers for peace of whom he disapproves.

Some of the utterances of our propagandist generals and admirals might have been lifted bodily out of the teachings of Adolf Hitler and Benito

Mussolini. For example, here is Major General Douglas MacArthur in the *Infantry Journal* for March 1927:

> A warlike spirit, *which alone can create and civilize a state,* is absolutely essential to national defense and to national perpetuity. . . . The more warlike the spirit of the people, the less need for a large standing army, as in such a community every able-bodied man should be willing to fight on all occasions whenever the nation demands his services in the field.
>
> In a free country like our own where everything depends upon the individual action of the citizen, every male brought into existence *should be taught from infancy* that the military service of the Republic carries with it honor and distinction, and his very life should be permeated with the ideal that *even death itself may become a boon when a man dies that a nation may live and fulfill its destiny* [italics mine].

Hitler would certainly say amen to that sentiment, because it can be found almost verbatim in his *Mein Kampf.* General MacArthur is thoroughly consistent. When he became Field Marshal (the first Field Marshal in American history) of the Philippine Army of 18,000 men, he helped not only to introduce universal military service, but to extend that service, again like Mussolini and Hitler, to all boys from the age of ten years up.

General Hanson E. Ely is another American sol-

dier who has absorbed the teachings of the dictators. Speaking to the New York Rotary Club, he said: "We don't prepare for war, but against it. As long as we have reasonable national defense and an adequate army, a good navy and a sufficient air force, so long will we be able to prevent war and no longer. . . . If we had now or could get together . . . more tanks, airplanes, ammunitions than any other country, and faster than any other country, we could lay our cards on the table and say, 'There is our hand, can you beat it?' And there would be no war." This is precisely the philosophy upon which Hitler defends the complete militarization of Germany, which in August 1939 was reported to have 2,500,000 men under arms—and the danger of war was never greater in Europe because every country there was striving to do exactly what General Ely prescribed. General Ely's loyalty to the international policies of his Government can be deduced from his statement to the Exchange Club of New York City that: "We can get around these disarmament pacts and be prepared for the next war only if we adopt some sort of program to maintain industrial preparedness." He was not lacking in his attacks upon peace advocates, calling them "half-baked students in our colleges, led by half-baked presidents," when speaking before the Central Y.M.C.A. in Brooklyn. Utterances like these, made all over the country, could be quoted without end.

It is necessary, however, to cite an article by Captain John H. Burns of the infantry, which appeared in the *Infantry Journal* in December 1928, because it is again as if lifted from the Nazi textbooks, and because there is no reason to believe that this officer was ever rebuked by the War Department:

> The military problem, psychologically speaking, resolves itself into taking every advantage of the herd instinct to integrate the mass. . . . This military processing of civilians is a purely empirical thing, but it is an eminently sound one. It has been handed down from past armies. . . . Constant repetition of the item to be inculcated unsupported by any reasons will have an immense effect on the suggestible, herd-minded human. An opinion, an idea, or a code acquired in this manner can become so firmly fixed that one who questions its essential rightness will be regarded as foolish, wicked, or insane. Suggestion, then, is the key to inculcating discipline, esprit, and morale.

Captain Burns was certainly fortunate in not having been sued by Hitler for violation of copyright; it will be remembered that Hitler says in *Mein Kampf* that the only thing necessary to induce the people to believe a lie is to repeat it often and long enough. Captain Burns is also one with Hitler, the greatest of all showmen and organizers of parades, in saying: "Parades and reviews are great factors in

securing unity. For with pomp and glitter the great unit is massed, and to the sound of rhythmic music, with flags flying and cadenced step, the subunits pass and render homage to their commander. For the soldier not to be conscious and proud of his identity with his herd is, under these circumstances, almost impossible. Finally to express its unity the herd is given a symbol—the colors." All of which sounds as if Captain Burns had attended one of the Nazi party days in Nuremberg and seen its tens of thousands of magnificent banners, and its hosts rendering homage to their commander.

for four years, 1928–32, the Army *Training Manual No. 2000–25* carried this extraordinary definition of American democracy to hundreds of thousands of young Americans who were taking military instruction:

Democracy: A Government of the masses. Authority derived through mass meeting or any other form of "direct" expression. Results in mobocracy. Attitude towards property is Communistic—negating property rights. Attitude towards law is that the will of the majority shall regulate, whether it be based upon deliberation or governed by passion, prejudice, and impulse,

without restraint or regard for consequences. Results in demagogism, license, agitation, discontent, anarchy.

When this choice bit of loyalty to our American democracy and institutions was exposed to public gaze in the press, it was promptly withdrawn. When I printed it, Secretary Dern wrote me a kindly letter asking: "Why pick on a sinner after he has reformed?" The reply, of course, is that it is an alarming state of affairs when, during four years, some officers in the War Department can put such a rank piece of disloyal, subversive anti-Americanism into a widely distributed Government handbook, and that the incident must be neither overlooked nor forgotten by those who cherish their country's democratic institutions.

The development of the Army and Navy intelligence divisions as spying groups on what is happening in civil, economic, and political life is one of the most alarming portents of the whole militarization movement. Originally intended merely to gather military and naval information, they reached out during the World War to run down spies, pro-Germans, "dangerous Reds," pacifists, and others, and set up files, "dossiers," of many thousands of individuals. There is evidence besides that cited above that this policy did not cease with the end of the war and that the Army and Navy carefully watch pacifist, Communist and labor activities.

This has even spread to the National Guard. One of the first witnesses for the prosecution in the recent inquiry into the record of Harry Bridges, the west-coast labor leader, for the purpose of establishing whether he was or was not deportable as a Communist, was a Major Milner, a former National Guard officer of the State of Oregon, who admitted that he had been assigned by the Adjutant General of that state to enter the Communist organization as a spy and stool-pigeon—not the kind of thing that one associates with military activities, or that strikes one as quite compatible with the honor of the uniform.

There is plenty of other evidence that both Army and Navy believe that their functions give them a vested right to guide the thinking of the public not only on Army and Navy matters, but also on questions of national policy, citizenship, the attitude of the individual toward the State, and so on. From the very beginning of the Citizens' Military Training Camp movement there was a twofold objective: instruction in the rudiments of military drill and the inculcation of military and nationalistic doctrines. This is related by Walter Millis as follows:

> And as early as 1913 he [General Wood] had evolved the most subtle of all engines with which he was finally to convert the United States to militarism. There were voluntary citizens' training camps, the

> origin of what was later known as the "Plattsburg idea." It was in the summer of 1913 that Wood opened the first two of these camps with 222 students in all—for the most part college undergraduates. Ostensibly, the camps offered to patriotic young men a chance to equip themselves at their own expense with the military training which Congress had basely failed to provide; actually, General Wood was never under any illusions as to the military value of the experiment. "We do not expect," he wrote at the very beginning, ". . . to accomplish much in the way of detailed military instruction[1] . . . but we do believe a great deal can be done in the implanting of a sound military policy." The camps, to state it more bluntly, were designed from the start to be (as their successors still are today) not practical schools of war but seminaries whence propagandists for preparedness might be distributed through the civil population.[2]

As Mr. Millis says, these opportunities for propaganda are being fully utilized today, and the same is true wherever there are military instructors in

[1] Cf. Major General Hugh L. Scott, Chief of Staff, in his Annual Report for 1916: "Trained youth cannot take the place of trained manhood. Youths make imitation, but not real soldiers."

[2] *Road to War*, by Walter Millis (Boston: Houghton Mifflin Company; 1935), pp. 94–5. Speaking in 1930 of the C.M.T. Camps, Major General C. P. Summerall, Chief of Staff, said in his final report: ". . . it is apparent that the camps do not directly serve to promote any military objective. The chief benefit to the Army lies in the increased confidence in its personnel on the part of the civilian population which has followed from the many contacts incident to the conduct of the camps."

schools and colleges, in greater or less degree. The numbers of young men enrolled in the Citizens' Military Training Camps for a month's training has already been stated—36,365. These youths are naturally attracted by a month's vacation, with its outdoor life, at Government expense. The lectures given in off hours afford the opportunity to inculcate those teachings which the War Department is so eager to have our young men imbibe and through them to reach and affect their families. More than 12,000 officers and men of the regulars are assigned to duty at these camps as instructors, to take charge of supplies, equipment, preparation of food, care of motor vehicles, air mails, etc.

Let us look now at this introduction of military training into schools and colleges. The Reserve Officers' Training Corps is now, in 1939, established in 250 civilian and 60 private military institutions, with an enrollment of 186,757 youths. These boys are trained by 2,067 officers and men of the Regular Army and it is upon them that the Army relies for the bulk of its combatant Reserve officers. On February 4, 1939 the War Department had on file applications from 119 more institutions for the establishment of 37 senior units and 82 junior ones, and it cited these requests, as well as the receipt of 60 or 70 more inquiries, as proof of the growing demand for this kind of patriotic preparation for

war. The reasons why schools and colleges seek military training for their pupils are varied, aside from the desire to serve the Government. Private military academies naturally wish a high military rating and close affiliation with the Reserve Officers' Corps and the War Department. For other institutions, a lure is the obtaining of free equipment and teachers, for whom Congress, and not the college or school, pays. Thus, when there was a rumor spread abroad that the Reserve Officers' Training Corps in the Kansas City high schools might be abolished, the school board protested because "in the three upper classes of the schools here participation in the corps is considered gymnasium credit for graduation. To abolish the units would require an additional five or six physical training instructors, costing salaries annually from $10,000 upward." Moreover, it costs a student less to be a member of the training corps than to be a student in gymnasium work, for the Government supplies the uniform, and the student has to buy his gymnasium shoes, suits, etc.

The cost of maintaining the R.O.T.C. units for 1939–40 will be $4,825,842 through direct appropriations. Actually the cost is much higher—much more than double that—for to this must be added the pay and the allowances of the officers and men assigned to this duty, and the cost of free equipment issued to the units. When Dwight F. Davis was Secretary of War in 1925, he reported officially that the direct appropriations were \$3,818,000, but that the total cost in that year came to \$10,696,504. To-day, when a million dollars additional are directly appropriated and there are many more units to care for, the total cost must come to \$13,000,000 or more. For this the War Department achieves what? Excepting in the military schools and a handful of leading universities, it gives to the students the merest smattering of the outworn squads and company drill, which has shrunk to but little importance in modern warfare—the War Department is this year completely making over the drill regulations. As preparation for trench and mechanized warfare, the drills, notably in the high schools, are worthless. Not even at the great universities can there be adequate provision for training boys under something approaching war conditions; the bayonet drill, so important in war, has been eliminated as something too horrible to teach boys.

CHAPTER TEN

Why the War Referendum

The proposal that there shall be a referendum of the American voters before this country can go to war has again appeared in Congress, a bill calling for a Constitutional amendment to bring this about having been introduced by twelve Senators, among them Bennett Champ Clark of Missouri, Arthur Vandenberg of Michigan, Gerald P. Nye of North Dakota, Robert M. La Follette, Jr., of Wisconsin, and Homer T. Bone of Washington. The measure called forth the usual protests from the White House and the State Department. It was again said that such a referendum would hamstring the Government, tie the hands of the Secretary of State and the President, serve notice that this country may be invaded while the vote is being taken, and that the whole proposal would be a blow at representative government.

There is so much passion on the Government's side and on the part of those, like ex-Secretary Henry L. Stimson, who have strongly denounced it that a factual restatement of the reasons why, according to the Gallup poll, fifty-eight per cent of the American people still favor their being consulted before another war takes place is in order. These grounds are the following:

1. The people believe that President Wilson and Congress blundered when they put us into war in 1917, and they attribute that blunder in large measure to foreign propaganda, the fact that our heavy industries had become a part of the British and French war machines, and that the bankers who financed the British munitions orders here and floated the war loans were determined to get us into the struggle in order to save those investments. No less than 73 per cent of those questioned by the Gallup poll last year voted that the United States had gravely erred in entering the World War.

2. Thoughtful persons are aware that the war-making power lodged without qualification in the hands of Congress by the Constitution has in practice become the privilege of the President. They point out that two private polls taken of Congress before the United States entered the war in 1917 showed that a majority opposed our entering it; these opposing Senators and Congressmen did not

dare to vote against the President's demand because of the hysteria of the moment, the viciousness of the pro-British press attacks, and the President's own excoriation of the "twelve willful men" who defeated his proposal to arm merchant ships.

Sir Willmott Lewis, Washington correspondent of the London *Times,* is the latest commentator upon the development of American institutions to stress the tremendous aggrandizement of the office of the President at the expense of Congress, and the further increase of that Presidential power by the coming of the radio. There is no clearer proof of this aggrandizement than the wresting from Congress of its unlimited Constitutional power to declare war.

3. In addition to leading us into the war with Germany, President Wilson put us into war with Russia, without consulting Congress in any way, sending one American army to Archangel and another deep into Siberia. In addition, he put us into war with Haiti, Santo Domingo, Nicaragua, and Mexico. True, these also were undeclared wars and they have been brushed aside on the ground that they were merely punitive expeditions or military occupations to restore order; but that was not the opinion of those invaded. The Haitians considered that war was being waged against them when in the first year some 3,500 Haitian men, women, and

children were killed by our troops, according to the official report of the head of the Marine Corps, who added to his report his regret that many of these killings were uncalled for.

4. It is now historically proved that William McKinley engineered the country into the war with Spain after that country had surrendered to us at every important point. Thousands of people have read in Walter Millis's *The Martial Spirit* the proof of this, and have also found it in such a standard history as that of James Ford Rhodes. It has made them feel that a political President is not to be trusted with the war-making power.

5. President Roosevelt himself has lent great strength to the movement for the referendum because of his speech at Chautauqua on August 15, 1936, when he declared that it made no difference what neutrality laws might be on the statute books when war came, that the question whether we should or should not go to war would be settled by two men, the Secretary of State and the President, whoever they might happen to be. He did not refer to Congress at all. He declared that when war comes the President is immediately beset by two forces, those "seeking the fool's gold" of war profits made out of supplying belligerents, and the humanitarian forces that seek to keep the country at peace. He besought the country on that occasion to become so

peace-minded that the President could not yield to the seekers after fool's gold, but would keep this country out of war.

6. The public is aware also that because of the President's power over the Army and Navy as Commander-in-Chief and his complete control of the diplomatic service he can maneuver the country to the verge of war and then present Congress with an accomplished fact so that it can do nothing except to register his will.

7. Everyone knows that war is no longer a gentleman's pastime or a matter involving a handful of regulars and a considerable number of volunteers. Today war draws in everybody in the nation, and in European countries, as in Spain and China, women and children are as much exposed to death in it as the men at the front when there are air raids. It engrosses the entire economy of a country, all of its industrial machinery. The advocates of the war referendum feel that since this modern warfare endangers the very existence of the country and that, whether won or lost, it inevitably brings economic disaster to victors and vanquished, the power to make war should be neither in the hands of only two men, the President and the Secretary of State, as Mr. Roosevelt said it is, nor even in the hands of the 627 Congressmen and Senators who constitute Congress.

For the Congressmen and Senators are politicians, swayed by partisan political considerations, subject to the crack of the party whip, always influenced by the patronage controlled by the President, upon which their prestige so often depends. More than that, with the question of re-election always before them, they are subject to the gusts of popular and press passion. They yield readily to the cry that the President knows best because he has better information than anybody else, that our honor is safe in his hands, so rally around the flag, boys, and if you dissent you are a bad American, a traitor, a spineless pacifist, indifferent to the glory of the Stars and Stripes, a pro-Spaniard, or a pro-Filipino, or a pro-German.

8. The proponents of the referendums say that that there is something better than representative government, and that is direct government, and they recall that Theodore Roosevelt, William J. Bryan, Robert M. La Follette, and Woodrow Wilson all advocated the adoption of the referendum by the American people so that they might be able to vote on issues that are naturally lesser issues than those of war and peace.

9. Advocates of this change declare that we entered every one of our foreign wars of our own accord after months and years of debate and discussion; that this country has never been suddenly at-

tacked and has been invaded only once; that many of the leading experts in military and naval affairs and Army and Navy officers declare that a sudden attack is out of the question since no nation could move a large fleet or any army to the United States without the preparations being disclosed months in advance, as were our efforts to send an army overseas in 1917–18.

They laugh at the suggestion that the country could be invaded while a referendum was being taken. They dwell upon the speed with which the youth of America was registered for the draft in a single day by machinery created almost overnight. They will insist, if the referendum carries, that a voting machinery be created in advance. Since the radio instantly brings a Presidential announcement to practically every home and certainly every hamlet in America, they believe that a referendum can be taken in forty-eight hours.

10. Finally, the advocates point out that the referendum is not to take place in the event of an attack or invasion; that it does not make impossible a declaration of war if the country desires it and wishes to send its sons out to die on the field of battle at home or abroad. The referendum will merely assure to the mothers and fathers of America the right to decide whether their sons and perhaps they themselves shall be sacrificed or not.

It is maintained that only those who really pay for a war, the plain people who make the sacrifices, bear the burdens, get no glory or high reward out of it, and then suffer from the economic aftermath of the struggle, are the ones who should decide whether the nation is to fight or not, especially as they have high authority for believing that if the United States goes to war again it will become a dictatorship at once, in order to fight on equal terms with dictators, and will never again become a democracy.

CHAPTER ELEVEN

The Great Need: A National Inquiry

If the facts developed thus far prove anything it is the pressing necessity for an immediate and searching and unbiased inquiry into the whole question under consideration. It has been shown (1) that we have no defense policy whatsoever; (2) that all our expenditures bear no relationship whatever to any established military program; (3) that we are asking the impossible of Army and Navy since we do not tell them what to defend or how and where they are to defend it; (4) that there can be no adequate defense policy set up until there is a decision as to what our foreign policy is to be, until our objectives are defined; (5) that the primary defense question for the United States is whether we are only to defend our shores, or to prepare again to fight abroad; (6) that, because of the failure to define what we shall defend, our policies, notably in the Pacific, vary from year to year, almost from hour to hour; (7) that until that is settled, we are adding to our vast expenditures without the slightest guarantee that those outlays make for a saner and better defense, or that they do not add to the existing unintelligent, wasteful, un-co-ordinated, and undirected system of expenditure and military and naval increase; (8) that there are the gravest faults in the organization of the War and Navy Departments; and (9) that they fail to co-operate adequately; (10) that although no less than seven billions have been spent for defense since the fiscal year 1934–5, the War Department admits amazing shortages in supplies of fundamental importance; (11) that there is no hope of balancing a normal budget without putting a definite limit to the increase of Army and Navy expenditures, now fast approximating two billions of dollars [1] and certain to continue to grow.

It has also been shown that by giving free rein to those who believe in huge armaments the road to Fascism is being thrown wide open, through the subordination of our economic life to the military machine, and that militarism begins to pervade our whole social life. What is even more astounding is the striking testimony produced that the bulk

1 The War and Navy Departments announce that they will ask for a "regular" budget of $1,600,000 for 1940–1.

of our military expenditures, due to fear of foreign attack, are utterly uncalled for and unnecessary so far as any imminent danger to the United States is concerned. All of these circumstances call obviously for a national inquiry—a commission so composed and so directed that as far as is possible the numerous questions to be posed to it shall be definitively answered in the light of the existing American situation. I venture to assert that our democracy is so menaced by our armament developments that there is no more vital need than the immediate constitution of such an inquiry.

Bills have already been introduced in Congress for a commission to be composed of members of the House and Senate only. This will by no means fill the need. Members of the House and Senate Naval and Military Committees are primarily politicians, not without thought of re-election. Moreover, they have been for years exposed to the influence exerted by the Army and Navy and their lobbies, social and otherwise. They are committed to certain policies; they have shown that they were so little interested as not to be willing to insist that a definition of our national objectives be arrived at. Some of them have relatives in the Army or Navy. It would seem, therefore, as if Raymond Clapper of the Scripps-Howard newspapers, and others who have advocated a temporary joint committee of the House and Senate, were not advising a course which could possibly bring the needed results. The Committee on National Defense of the National Peace Conference, however, has voted in favor of the Congressional inquiry, in these words:

> The Committee recommends that steps be taken without delay to clarify the relations between our foreign policies and our national defense requirements in order to avoid a costly and dangerous armament race involving the risk of war.
>
> To this end, the Committee urges appointment of a joint Congressional Committee with full authority to examine the adequacy of existing military and naval establishments, in relation to our foreign policy, the National Defense Act, and other acts relating to the organization of the armed forces, to hold public hearings and receive testimony from officers of the Army and Navy, officers of the Government of the United States, and qualified civilians.

Nor do we need a commission composed of Army and Navy officers, since they are above all others personally involved in any far-reaching decision. Moreover, they are little accustomed to considering broad national policies. To them budgets and the Treasury are there to be milked as much as possible for the benefit of the services, which is quite natural and understandable. The members of Congress are to be preferred to officers, since they have

the duty of providing the funds to be spent. That any commission, however constituted, should have the right to call any officer and as far as possible to ensure him immunity for any statement that he might make is perfectly obvious; whether it will be possible to get the younger officers to express themselves freely as to defects in the organization and what they think should be done is an open question. Military and naval advice, yes, by all means, but not as compelling guidance in all the problems to be thought through. Experts, whether doctors or lawyers or engineers, are all too prone to visualize the problems presented to them from their professional point of view, and are frequently too close to their individual activities to make it possible for them to view those activities in their relation to the whole national problem. There is no desire here to reflect upon military and naval officers. I should take the same position if the question were one of constituting an inquiry into the socializing of medicine, believing that it would not be for the doctors to decide, but for an unprejudiced and unbiased group from the general public.

Then what kind of commission? My answer is: one of outstanding men representing different shades of opinion. It would not do to load the commission with public men already committed to given foreign policies. It would seem as if persons could be found who would be able to bring open minds, like a blue-ribbon jury in an important technical case, to decide the questions involved in the light not of prejudice or predetermined opinion, but of facts and what is best for the country, and especially for the Treasury. If I should be asked to suggest names I should recommend men of the type of Mr. Gerard Swope, president of the General Electric Company, despite the fact that his company is a large contractor for the American, British, and German navies. I should certainly wish to see Senator Bennett Champ Clark, a founder of the American Legion, with his excellent war record, on the commission, although he is a member of the Senate Military Affairs Committee. Others that naturally suggest themselves are Dr. Frederick Keppel, president of the Carnegie Corporation; William Allan Neilson, lately president of Smith College; Frank P. Graham, president of the University of North Carolina; James F. Fogarty, president of the North American Company; Daniel Willard, president of the Baltimore & Ohio Railroad; William Allen White, to represent the press of the United States and the views of the plain people of the Middle West; Norman Thomas, as the representative of the liberal viewpoint and as being of demonstrated statesmanlike quality; Major George Fielding Eliot; the Secretary of Agriculture, Mr.

Wallace; Governor Olson of California; Charles P. Taft of Cincinnati; Alfred M. Landon of Kansas; Edward P. Warner of the Civil Aeronautics Authority; Dorothy Detzer of the Women's International League for Peace and Freedom; Dr. Walter Van Kirk, executive secretary of the National Peace Conference, the clearing house of the peace organizations, which is on record as having endorsed such a commission; and Oscar T. Crosby of Virginia, formerly Assistant Secretary of the Treasury and a graduate of West Point. The defense views of many of these persons are not known to me.

The list could be lengthened indefinitely; the purpose, of course, should be to obtain a strong group before which could be tried the questions at issue. Representatives of the two great labor organizations should be included, but any effort to "balance" the committee by including Jews, Catholics, Protestants, Northerners, Southerners, Republicans, and Democrats and representatives of other parties as such would inevitably mean a weakening of the commission. The temptation to appoint retired officers of the Army or Navy should be resisted. It is believed that a group like the one cited would command the respect of the press, the public, and the Congress. It could certainly call before it men and women of all shades of opinion, and the resulting testimony would be of lasting value, precisely as the proceedings of the Nye Munitions Inquiry have become a historical document of permanent value, constantly quoted from in this country and abroad.

How shall the commission be appointed? One naturally thinks of an appropriation by Congress, with the members appointed by the President. Here the hitch is that we have never had a President more thoroughly committed to large armaments than Franklin Roosevelt. Whether Mr. Roosevelt could be induced to select a commission as unbiased and as representative as the one suggested is open to question. It would seem, therefore, that an alternative plan of the appointment of such a commission and its financing by persons not in political life might be the way out. Here the difficulty is that such a body would not have the right of subpoena and might, therefore, not be able to bring about the attendance of witnesses it should call, notably active Army and Navy officers. To raise the necessary sums to provide essential stenographic, secretarial, and expert service would be far from easy in these difficult financial times, and yet it should not be beyond the range of possibility. Similar commissions, even when privately set up, have exercised very considerable influence upon the development of public opinion. In this case it would undoubtedly be sponsored by men

prominent in public life, such as Nicholas Murray Butler, by the leaders of the peace movement in the United States, by college presidents generally, by public-spirited heads of corporations and prominent clergy and newspaper editors.

Already it is plain that there is a growing sentiment for such an undertaking. For example, the *New York Times*, in concluding a series of seven editorials published from December 12 to December 18, 1938, thought it had stated "the immediate requirements of a sound policy of national defense under the control of a civilian governor." It went on to say:

> At the same time it is important not to lose sight of longer needs and of larger objectives. Without in any way postponing the fulfillment of the immediate and well demonstrated needs of the Army and the Navy, the President could well appoint an expert advisory commission to consider within the next six months the whole question of our probable future needs in the matter of national defense. The goal of this commission should be to recommend for the first time a correlated program for all our defensive forces. . . .

Mr. Popper, in concluding his study of American defense policies for the Foreign Policy Association, writes: "In a crucial period of American history a commission of this type may aid in clarifying the confusion surrounding the subject of national defense. It may suggest changes which would produce a more efficient fighting force with a more definite function." Mr. Popper then puts his finger upon the most important opportunity and duty before such a commission. He says:

> Above all, it may maintain in full vigor proper civilian control over the waxing military machine which the civil arm has created. In a world in which military supremacy and Spartan preparedness tend to become ends in themselves, and the competitive hysteria of the arms race is all too apparent, the preservation of such controls may ultimately prove essential for the soundness of American democracy.

This is precisely why such a commission appears to be the most important move that could be made. Americans are all too prone to think that they may practice the arts of militarism and escape the inevitable consequences thereof, just as they are positive that if their troops should go to war they could not possibly stoop to the atrocities which they freely admit marks the conduct of all other men in war. It is necessary to stress again that if this country embarks on the course pursued by the other great powers it will arrive at the same destination, with the demand that the United States shall become as efficient and as prepared as the dictatorships. There will also be a readiness to accept a weakening of the civilian control of military affairs in order to

achieve that efficiency and preparedness, which again leads us along the path trodden bare by Russia, Germany, and Italy. No military and naval man can be permitted to believe that they, their services, and the necessity of preparing against possible attack are the supremely important factors in the national life of any country. Wherever that philosophy, that exaltation of the military and naval arms of the government, obtains, there the ruin of democratic institutions is at hand.

Similarly, since no military and naval officers the world over are ever satisfied with their armaments or believe that they have reached the ultimate in national defense, the tendency is to develop defense methods and alliances beyond the borders of the country. This is particularly a danger for the United States because of the Monroe Doctrine and of our relations to South and Central America. Before we decide on a policy of protection for other countries the American people should at least be told what that is likely to mean, not only in the way of entanglements, but in outlay of treasure and in the withdrawal of men and machinery from the pursuits of peace. The very fact that even some military and naval commentators are now openly advocating seizing of the Canary Islands, the Azores, and any bases on the African coast where that is nearest to South America if they should be occupied by hostile foreigners is startling proof of how easily we may be led into overseas policies utterly at variance with our original policy of no entangling alliances. It would inevitably plunge us deep into the power-politics game being played abroad and make the temptation to use the Army and Navy as an element in the pursuit of diplomatic ends greater than ever. If a commission of inquiry could help to put the brakes on here, it would certainly be worth any possible cost and far more besides.

Such a commission, if it went below the surface with open mind, could not fail to see that one of the most serious phases of our rapid militarization is that arming is becoming identical with increased worship of the State and the inculcation of the cult of nationalism which has taken possession of the totalitarian nations. Between the exaltation of nationalism and the maintenance of democracy there must always be a conflict. They cannot be reconciled any more than can war and democracy. The greater the worship of the State, the more intense the bitterness and hostility against all those who venture to hold opposing positions, against aliens, against labor organizers, against "Reds," against dissenters of every shade and variety, against free speech, against freedom itself. It detracts public attention from the duty of guarding our democ-

racy from attack, not by piling up armaments, but by making it more than ever efficient, the most just, the freest, and the most democratic of countries. For the most dangerous of enemies to the American commonwealth are not the totalitarian states abroad whose rise has been so rapid, whose decline may be similarly speedy, but those Americans who would exploit the masses and maintain their special privileges by the use of the armed forces, those who frankly say that they favor a large Army and a large Navy to keep the masses in place. It is these who are delaying or thwarting the economic freedom of the masses, who most menace the United States and its safety, and not the foreigners we dislike or despise. These enemies at home are just as ready to sacrifice American institutions for the maintenance of the *status quo* as were the corresponding groups in Germany and Italy.

The right kind of a commission, bent only on really safeguarding the United States, would soon find itself compelled to answer the following question:

What will it avail us to arm to the utmost limit, to subordinate our national and industrial life to preparations for war, if thereby we lose our democratic soul—that soul we are supposed to preserve by pouring out armament expenditures without end?

Appendix

As an example of the way Congress is stuffed with nonsense about the Japanese menace, the following account by me of an executive session of the House Military Affairs Committee is reprinted here. It is based upon the 1936 minutes of that committee, which were, through an error, given out. The minutes contain all the old Japanese yarns to frighten Congress:

One was of a Japanese fishing fleet of 150 vessels based on an island near the mouth of the Panama Canal and being met from time to time by steamers from Japan with fresh replacements. Congressman Dockweiler of California rehashed all the familiar rumors. "Every time our fleet goes out from Los Angeles harbor for target practice it never fails to meet in the open roadstead a Japanese oil tanker standing out there or a Japanese fishing boat. . . . It is always a Japanese boat that is out there, and one commander told me that

when he went up to this [*sic*] craft to advise Mr. Japanese that the United States was having target practice he actually recognized a high-ranking officer in civilian clothes of the Japanese Navy that he had met socially." This happens, he said, every time that our fleet goes to sea to practice—but he did not specify if it was always the same high-ranking officer or the same high American officer who always met him and recognized him, and whether the Japanese wore the same "civilian clothes of the Japanese Navy" or some other kind of clothes.

Mr. Dockweiler next told the horrified and obviously gullible Committee that the Japanese fishing boats "are built in such a way that you can, within a very short space of time, erect a small cannon or machine gun on them"—which is hardly surprising, since there is not a thirty-foot yawl or tug in any American port or summer resort upon which the same thing could not be done in a couple of hours. Worst than that, he said, they "carry a pressure tank sufficient to contain pressure sufficient to launch torpedoes off those boats"—but this valiant Congressman plainly does not know that you cannot launch a torpedo from any craft without a most elaborate torpedo tube.

Mr. Dockweiler's "seein' things" did not stop there. No indeed. There is an equipped Japanese army in California of 25,000 men "that could be under arms immediately if there was any disturbance." His authorities were not the Government of California or of the United States and our secret service, but "the American Legion and our chambers of commerce out there." The

Japanese also "have gymnasiums under the German plan where at nighttime the school children may parade and go through all the motions of military training in the little halls."

Said the chairman, whose eyes were evidently starting from his head: "What do you mean by 'equipped'? Do you mean they have arms?" The dialogue then continued:

MR. DOCKWEILER. How could we stop them from having them, Mr. Chairman?

THE CHAIRMAN. But do they have arms?

MR. DOCKWEILER. We think so.

THE CHAIRMAN. Well.

MR. DOCKWEILER. That is something that would bear further investigation.

THE CHAIRMAN. Now, living in that situation and being raised in it, I assume, Mr. Dockweiler.

MR. DOCKWEILER. Yes.

THE CHAIRMAN. What is your interpretation of the attitude of mind of the authorities, the controlling authorities of the Japanese?

Mr. Dockweiler was not stumped. His "own brother" had been in the diplomatic service for ten years. He was once stationed in Tokyo for a year and a half and was now able to say things he could not in those bygone years. "He has told me many of the stories that I am relating to you. The situation is this: the Japanese have never struck an enemy that was able to

fight back." Which explains, of course, why the Russians never fought any battles in Manchuria in their war with Japan! And so on for pages and pages. Is it any wonder that the shocked Military Affairs Committee voted on the spot for the six new air bases?

The Kaiden Studios

OSWALD GARRISON VILLARD

FIGHTING YEARS

Memoirs of a Liberal Editor

BY OSWALD GARRISON VILLARD

Harcourt, Brace and Company New York

Third printing, May, 1939

Typography by Robert Josephy

PRINTED IN THE UNITED STATES OF AMERICA
BY QUINN & BODEN COMPANY, INC., RAHWAY, N. J.

TO

MY WIFE

AND TO OUR

DOROTHEA MARSHALL, HENRY HILGARD,

AND OSWALD GARRISON, JR.

Then, as today, there was not the slightest effort by Congress to study the military situation intelligently or scientificially;[8] but there was a rush to vote $358,158,361 for the army and $239,632,757 for the navy for the fiscal year 1916-17. "When this measure becomes a law," Congressman Claude Kitchin, the leader of the Democratic House, said prophetically, "thereby putting the arms of the munitions makers into the Treasury to the elbows, with their heretofore undreamed of profits at stake, we can hardly conceive of a power in the nation strong enough to extract them. I fear that the big interests behind this program, with their tremendous and irresistible influence, and their infinite ingenuity will find or make a way to persuade or force the controlling factors of both parties to make perpetual the surrender to them of the Federal Treasury and to place permanently at their mercy the taxpayers of the country."

Claude Kitchin was the bravest of the brave, but there was ob-

[8] For example, the preparedness advocates would not listen to the truth that the German battleships did not jeopardize us because they were without coal capacity to cross the ocean. Secretary Daniels aided in the hue and cry until after the war. In May, 1919, on returning to New York after having seen the German battleships before they were sunk at Scapa Flow, he announced that their bunker capacity proved that they were built for fighting in European waters only. *The Nation*, May 24, 1919.

viously something wrong with him. He could not understand, and publicly said so, why, when the three-year Republican naval program had, on the advice of the weather-vane Secretary of the Navy, Josephus Daniels, been denounced by him and others in Congress as "criminal extravagance and waste," it suddenly became correct and proper two months later when the Secretary and President decided to flop for it. "If such a program was wrong and extravagant then, it is wrong and extravagant now . . ." declared Kitchin,[4] upon whose clear and honest head there descended from then on an avalanche of foul newspaper abuse and, on the part of the New York *Herald*, complete misrepresentation, through an entirely fabricated interview, until his health and career were wrecked. If ever a patriot was murdered by the press it was Claude Kitchin.

On June 23, I had a memorable encounter with members of the Virginia Bankers' Association at the Hotel Chamberlin at Fortress Monroe. The dining room was full of officers in uniform, in addition to the membership; many of the audience were noisy and some overstimulated; there was a wretchedly inefficient toastmaster, and it was stiflingly hot. I had not been speaking for more than four minutes before I sensed the menacing hostility of most of the listeners. Never did I face a harder task; I discarded about a third of my manuscript and finally sat down conscious of complete failure. Instantly there was an uproar and a man who was unsteady on his pins confirmed my feeling by moving that as a result of my speech the association go on record as favoring a

regular army of 500,000 men and 50 more battleships! He was noisily seconded by a number but the toastmaster refused to put the motion. My hosts were obviously greatly distressed and not mollified when some of the diners, chiefly women, came up to speak of what they called my "bravery," as if I might have been expected to run away and refuse to play.

At Middletown, Connecticut, when I re-entered my hotel after the meeting, I noticed a noisy crowd at the front door. When I asked the reason the clerk said: "They are waiting for a pacifist fellow from New York who is making a speech over at the college." I went to my room, moved a rickety bureau before a rickety door, and slept soundly and quite undisturbed. These were experiences that came to all of us dissenters and made us certain that worse was to come, just as it increased our faith in the righteousness of our cause since we did not ourselves feel compelled to intolerance and bitterness. On May 8, President Wilson received a considerable delegation of our group; I did not join it as the President had refused to see me to discuss the preparedness issue and I did not wish to antagonize him by going with the others. He assured them that he thought that New York State was going too far with its compulsory service bills but beyond that made the most unfavorable impression.

In April I astonished my wife by saying to her that I was no longer going on with my Washington correspondence—I had already been working in David Lawrence as our Washington correspondent. He resigned from the Associated Press to join us, thus beginning a career which has carried him far, not without its ups and downs, and with the result that he has now become one of the foremost conservative columnists. There were two reasons why I told my wife that I was no longer going to the White House: the first was that the approaching arrival of our second son made me naturally wish to be at home; and the other was that by then I had completely lost faith in Mr. Wilson. I pointed out there had been no quarrel between us, no breaking off of relations, that our friendship continued, but that despite what he had said to me I was certain then—in April, 1916—he would put us into the war. In that case I should have to take a position of complete antagonism to him and I wanted to stop my regular visits to the White House offices while relations were as good as they were. That did not mean complete cessation of my visits to Tumulty, with whom I constantly corresponded; it meant that I could no longer cooperate with or uphold the President himself.

By that time, or a little later, Mr. Wilson had changed his mind on the initiative, referendum, recall, woman suffrage, the tariff commission, tariffs for revenue only, a permanent diplomatic service beyond politics, the merit system in the Civil Service—from the beginning of his administration he forgot that he had been for years a vice-president of the Civil Service Reform Association and its staunch upholder—on Tammany Hall, on Bryan, on a Continental Army, on preparedness, and then finally, child labor legislation. As for the lâtter Senator Borah was able to show that Mr. Wilson described this legislation in his *Constitutional Government* as unconstitutional and as "obviously absurd extravagance," carrying a congressional power to regulate commerce beyond the "utmost boundaries of reasonable and *honest* inference." If it is only a narrow man whose mind is closed to new ideas, and if a big man does not fear inconsistency, Mr. Wilson by this test was obviously one of the broadest men this country has produced.

During all of that year the blundering in Mexico continued. We neither got Villa, dead nor alive. The entire militia was called out, for what reason no one yet understands unless it was to be a training of the National Guard preparatory to our going to war in Europe. Where Mr. Wilson's handling of this situation was not opera bouffe it became ruthless murder.[7] For example, at two-thirty o'clock one morning Bryan, Tumulty, Daniels, and Wilson decided to intervene in Mexico merely to prevent a German steamer's delivering her cargo at Vera Cruz lest the munitions which composed it be used against us.[8] We had no legal right whatever to stop this ship; we were not at war with Mexico or threatened with war. One of our admirals who witnessed the intervention told me subsequently that "it was as brutal a slaughter as ever disgraced our flag." It cost the lives of four hundred men, women, and children, chiefly boy naval cadets between the ages of twelve and sixteen years. When the bodies of the American dead from Vera Cruz were brought to the Brooklyn Navy Yard the President, who had ended their lives illegally, solemnly mourned their heroic and utterly uncalled-for deaths. Naturally the President failed then or at any time to tell the American people that, despite all this criminal waste of life, *Huerta got those munitions!* No just man, I assert, can read that record and not be convinced of the inefficiency and moral irresponsibility of Daniels, Bryan, and Wilson in dealing with Mexico. Finally, Mr. Wilson was rescued from the mess by our drift into war with Germany

[7] See General Smedley D. Butler's eye-witness accounts of our forcible interventions in Lowell J. Thomas, *Old Gimlet Eye*, New York, 1933.

[8] For Tumulty's prideful account of this see his *Woodrow Wilson as I Know Him*, pp. 150-53. Mr. Wilson's order to Admiral Mayo was: "Take Vera Cruz at once"—without the slightest stopping to inquire what that would cost in lives.

which allowed him to withdraw Pershing, the unsuccessful, from Mexico to become the successful and honored head of the army in France.

During this time the attacks upon *The Evening Post* grew steadily, because of my activities, because we were not anti-German enough, and because we were not deluded by the crass war propaganda. One day I got a letter from two ladies in Stockbridge denouncing me as pro-German because *The Evening Post* had not reported a speech there by a Canadian sergeant who told of a comrade's being crucified by Germans to a barn door. I replied that the sergeant had not told that story in New York City or it would have been reported and I asked for his address that I might obtain his statement. I did not get it but his yarn was extremely effective in inducing young Americans to enlist in the Canadian army which was his purpose. Later I regretted not having kept the names of those ladies in order to have the satisfaction of sending to them the cold-blooded admission in Parliament after the war of Sir Sam Hughes, the Canadian Minister of Defense, that there never was any truth in that yarn but that he had approved of its being widely used for recruiting purposes. What are honor and truth to a statesman?

My refusal to believe those stories of the Belgian children with their hands cut off stamped me clearly as a traitorous pro-German. Nothing else that I know of illustrates so clearly the flight of reason from the herd mind and its utter gullibility in war time. When people told me about those babies—who surely ran into millions—I asked for evidence and got none. I explained that babies with their hands cut off could not live for more than a very few minutes unless there were surgeons present to tie up the arteries, apply dressings, and offset the shock; that I could not see what the Germans had to gain by it when they needed every doctor and nurse and all their surgical supplies for their wounded. This logic earned me only snarls and vicious looks. Then I made matters worse by stating that by my orders our London correspondent had visited a number of hospitals and found no record of any such

Chapter XVIII. The War Madness

SO the great tragedy had come. The country was in the war, in the war it was to win and to lose. The fundamental foreign policy of the republic—to remain aloof from the jealousies, intrigues, and wars of Europe—was thrown overboard. Again the dream of empire, of being the dominating world power was upon us. In the White House Woodrow Wilson more than ever saw himself the dictator of the peace. He at once became the dictator at home with unlimited control of the country's finances; the dictator of the press; the dictator of the farms; of all business, or nearly all; soon of the transportation; and dictator as to who of our youth should live or die—greater power by far than had ever been Abraham Lincoln's. This, we were assured, was proper, for the country was now actually fighting for its life as well as for the democratic doctrine in the world, for everlasting peace, and nobody and nothing must stand in the way of the holiest and noblest crusade since the quest of the Grail.

From the moment we embarked upon that crusade it was marked by a bitterness, a vindictiveness, a rage against all who opposed it, which in themselves should have given pause to those who really believed that out of such passions, out of wholesale murder, would come an all-cleansing spiritual victory. Most of those who dissented and refused to recant, as Rabbi Wise had recanted, and take service with Mars, felt the full force of governmental disapproval or hostility and popular hatred. That was not surprising; we expected misrepresentation, contumely, even persecution, precisely as the conscientious objectors awaited their prison sentences. I am proud to say that I never heard one of our group complain or express self-pity. For a time some of the peace societies suspended all operations, well aware that they were watched and spied upon. Moreover, we were in the war and those of my faith certainly did not want the Germans to win and hoped from our hearts that, if the war must be fought to a finish on the battlefields, our troops would speedily end it. The last thought of any of us would have been to put obstacles in the way. We were determined, however, to ward off the militarization of the country in so far as lay within our power and we were ceaseless in our efforts for a peace of justice and the remaking of the world into a sensible, decent whole. I personally did my uttermost to keep *The Evening Post* and *Nation* free to print as judicially as possible all news of significance, and even to report the undercurrents abroad which did not find their way past the cable censorship.

It was not an easy course to steer, especially as the staff was almost wholly pro-war—intensely so—and much worried lest the pacifist owner get himself and them into serious trouble. There was real fear that the government might move against me or the newspaper, notably when the Burleson censorship was established. That fear was needless; the record soon showed that the Post Office Department was concerned only with arresting small-town editors, suppressing foreign-language publications or little far-Western newspapers, in other words terrifying helpless fry who could not strike back. Since the government knew that the bulk of the people beyond the Alleghenies was not in favor of going to war, the bitterest and most unscrupulous campaign of lies to make Americans hate, to rouse their passions to the boiling point, and to suppress criticism was launched—with the sanction, of course, of the President. Some of the worst speeches of the war were formulated under Mr. McAdoo and sent out by the Treasury in connection with the Liberty Loan campaign. Some of them stopped at nothing. For instance, I heard a passionate and dynamic speaker for one of the Liberty Loans explain in a theatre that he wanted our money—and was going to have it whether we wished to give or not—not for the Red Cross or for the Y.M.C.A. or any field hospital but just to kill Germans, kill them by day and night until there were none left. "The Germans," he said, "are the snakes of the human race and must be stamped out. No, I apologize to the snakes and to the animal kingdom. There is nothing in it so low and vile as a German." It did not seem to me that those in the audience who gave the speaker money did so enthusiastically or even willingly. But that was far less important than the fact that this arousing of blind mass passion worked wholly against any intelligent appreciation of what the war aims ought to be and what kind of a peace should be obtained.

Individually we dissenters soon had the conventional experience of learning who were our real friends and who were not. I soon discovered that half of mine were afraid that I would land in prison and that the other half was afraid that I would not. It was amusing to see how many men got up and left the room if I went into a club and how many others had become too shortsighted to recognize me. Amos Pinchot chuckled with joy in telling me how he had heard one of two men in the washroom of the University Club, who were unaware of his presence, say: "By God, it's come to a pretty pass when a man has to be in the same club with Amos Pinchot and Oswald Villard!" Once I met Talcott Williams on the street. In his most unctuous manner he said: "It must be terribly hard for you. I hear you have seventeen first cousins on the German front line." "That," I replied, "is news to me. I wonder where they all came from. Neither of my father's sisters had children and he never had a brother." This was typical of the attitude of many men, even intellectuals. It was beyond their comprehension that anyone could refuse to agree that the war was the greatest of moral undertakings, bound to result in the regeneration of the world. They could only explain my attitude by my German blood. They thought I was crazy because I revolted against the whole idea that good could come out of the slaughter of millions.

One day a member of the board of directors of the Philharmonic Society came to tell me, the president, that in the board's judgment the time had come for a new head, that "pacifism and music would not mix in war time." The directors' action was entirely proper and the message was tactfully delivered. I should have handed in my resignation when the war began, for the Philharmonic then needed money more than ever as the costs jumped up with the war time and I could not have raised a dollar; indeed, my continuance as president would have cost the society much support. So the directors turned to Clarence Mackay and to other rich and influential persons for the aid that they needed. The society, too, was charged with pro-Germanism and found it necessary to print on its programs in large letters that it had bought Liberty bonds. Before very long one of the most useful women directors led a vigorous fight to prevent the playing of any German music during the war—even Beethoven was to be banned lest its rendering encourage the Germans and dishearten our troops in the trenches! [1] Every concert had to be opened or closed with the poverty-poor music of "My Country, 'Tis of Thee." The national anthem was worn threadbare in those crowded months and if familiarity breeds contempt it must have sunk low in popular esteem.

When I resigned I naturally recalled how on January 17, 1917, on the occasion of the seventy-fifth anniversary of the society, I had addressed the audience in Carnegie Hall and had boasted that our art and our orchestra were unaffected by prejudice, even in the face of war. How soon had this been proved false! On my resigning, the *Musical Courier* declared that in its judgment it would be hard to find another president "to devote himself to the welfare of the organization as unselfishly and enthusiastically as Mr. Villard did at all times, and to fight its battles as stoutly and successfully against financial discouragement and against the insolent attacks of its malignant enemies, chiefly newspaper men trying to manipulate musical quality for their own ends"—pleasant words but giving a picture of my work that I could not recognize and did not merit. Indeed, as I reread these words it is obvious that they were the invention of some other virulent pro-German seeking to enthrone the Kaiser in the White House.

Looking back on those war years it seems to me that I got off

[1] Even the passionately anti-German Owen Wister protested. He denounced this policy as "a mistaken patriotic sentiment." Most of the German symphonies, he pointed out, were written by men who had not shared the spirit of modern Germany. "They wrote the most beautiful music in the world; to banish it from our programs is to make bricks without straw." *The Nation*, November 30, 1918.

very easily. We dissenters suffered most, however, through the pain we caused members of our family. Our children were not spared; my little daughter was constantly asked, with that refined cruelty of which children are often capable, whether she was not ashamed of her pacifist, disloyal and traitorous, pro-German father. One day she burst into my room and in great excitement asked: "Daddy, have I *got* to believe as you do about the war?" "Certainly not, Dorothea, you must believe what you think is right and some day when you are old enough to understand I will tell you just why I have taken the position that I have." "Well, then, I believe that the Germans ought to be killed—all of them—and I am going to say so!" That relief helped a lot to carry her over this most difficult period. At Black Point my elder son, then aged six, manfully fought his way through that first summer of the war, often with his fists.

What caused that summer colony to boil over, however, was the fact that we actually possessed a lovely brown dachshund whose name, worse luck, was Fritz. One of the ladies called upon my wife to inform her that that was too much. The community, she said, found it hard enough to stomach my pacifism but a German dog, by name Fritz, was more than they could stand. Two days later I took Fritz to Thorwood for sanctuary because our children reported that the poor beastie was actually in danger of being stoned to death by neighboring children who were quick to take their cue from their elders. As I stood with him on the platform of the station I heard two of my neighbors say: "Well, I see the Kaiser's leaving us at last," and "it's high time, indeed." Such was the mentality of well-bred men and women in that summer of 1917 when all the country, we were told, was rising in one glorious, elevating, idealistic symphony of patriotic devotion to country and mankind. Needless to say that during that time I found unvarying support from my wife and mother, who never flinched through all those arduous days.

Incidentally the messenger who brought the protest to my wife was a member of one of the most fashionable New York churches and a devout worshiper of Jesus. One day the news came that a young relative of hers, an aviator, had singlehanded bombed and destroyed a German submarine. Her joy and pride were unbounded; he had made good and distinguished himself; he had sent forty-five Huns to one of the most terrible of deaths. They were enemies and that was that. Why not? The Commandment, "Thou shalt not kill," was just then in a moratorium—with God's blessing—and the Scriptures were in cold storage. God was pleased that those forty-five young German "snakes" had been annihilated. As for their parents and families, why, no well-bred patriot thought of them. The amusing thing about this lady was that a distinguished ancestor, of whom she was most proud, was bitterly hated and nearly run out of the United States because he opposed the country's going to war with England in 1812!

Naturally the yarns about me grew day by day. It was reported that I had said that I would not defend wife or daughter if they were attacked by raping Huns; that I had declared that I would fight the conscription of my two sons in that war—their ages of one and six years were not mentioned; that I had affirmed that I would not succor a wounded man if I came across him! I was reported to be in daily communication with the Kaiser—doubtless by the kindness of the Army Intelligence corps and the Department of Justice. The story about my attitude toward the wounded grew out of my opposition to the perversion of the Red Cross into a partisan adjunct of the Allied and American armies, instead of its being permitted to retain its original function, for which it was organized by Clara Barton, as an international, nonpartisan, peaceful organization extending its aid to both sides in every conflict. These experiences were, however, but pin pricks beside the pain of being unable to throw oneself into the stream of war work, to share that utterly mistaken and misguided popular enthusiasm.

For one like myself, who had for some years been in the heart of things, it was hard to see the tremendously reinforced tide of national life sweeping by while one remained stationary on the bank, as it were, and to have the feeling that one must not only refuse to participate but that the great mass of one's fellow-citizens would not wish one to take part.

Although the country had been told there would be no conscription, by June it was adopted and it was elaborately explained to the people that this was after all the most democratic way of dealing with the situation and that Abraham Lincoln had instituted it during the Civil War. The truth was that the army had been planning for it from the beginning and, as General Hugh Johnson has now boasted, had not only prepared the scheme but had actually violated the law in preparing to put it into effect. Moreover, the results of the volunteering showed clearly that the American people were neither overwhelmingly in favor of the struggle nor eager to have their sons fight in the European trenches. Thus was violated what had always been considered, except for the brief period during the Civil War, the fundamental right of American youth to decide whether to give their lives in the service of their country or not. It meant the strangling of the most precious thing in the world, the conscience of the individual, and it opens the way for future infractions of the liberty of the citizen such as universal enforced labor service, an idea which has met with considerable favor since the success of the Civilian Conservation Corps, and the examples set by Mussolini and Hitler, with many American military officers hoping that if that can be put over the way to universal military service will be cleared. The war-time conscription is even used as a justification for compulsory military drill in peace time in many American schools and colleges. In the main, however, the conscription was put over in 1917 with amazingly little friction [7] and with unquestioned ability and has established one favorable precedent. The almost overnight establishment of the selective draft boards showed how quickly new machinery for taking a referendum on such an issue as war and peace could be set up.

As the first war summer dragged on mob violence appeared all

[7] Even the liberal *Survey* printed an article in its issue of December 28, 1918, in which the author wrote that "conscription was necessary, we had to conquer the awful savages and make sure that they cannot murder, torture, ravish and enslave again." The author, a well-known social worker, is still alive to contemplate, as so many others, his complete folly in war time.

over the country. In New York City soldier mobs, with the consent and approval of Mayor Mitchel, broke up Irish and Socialist party meetings—which was one of the causes of his defeat for re-election despite Administration aid. A partial list of the mobbings came to 124 cases between April 1, 1917, and May 1, 1918, yet in only two cases were mob leaders prosecuted and in only eleven cases did the authorities proceed legally against the victims. Whites and blacks were lynched and many tarred and feathered. By April 24, 1918, the Department of Justice reported that 3,465 persons had been convicted or had pleaded guilty to interfering with the operation of the draft, while 181 had been acquitted. Under the general war statutes, 228 additional had been prosecuted and 89 acquitted. By June 8, 1918, the department had prosecuted 1,180 other persons under the Espionage Act, of whom 210 pleaded guilty, 143 were dismissed, 125 were convicted, and 31 acquitted, the remaining 672 cases pending at that time. In addition, 787 were prosecuted under other criminal statutes and, under the act making threats against the President a criminal offense, sixty persons were prosecuted. Those nearly 6,000 cases speak volumes for the alleged unanimity for the war of the people.

Many of the convictions were outrageous miscarriages of justice, later set aside by higher courts. Thus, the officials of the International Bible Students Association in Brooklyn were sentenced to eighty years' imprisonment for an alleged violation of the Espionage Law. The judge, being a loyal patriot, denied them bail, and they were nine months in a penitentiary before they finally obtained bail from another judge. Two months later the judgment was reversed because "they did not have a fair trial." On May 5, 1920, the government dismissed the cases and vindicated these victims of judicial hysteria. The sentences passed were incredible in their severity. In New York three men and one young girl were sentenced by a United States judge to 285 years in jail for circulating legal handbills criticizing our intervention in Russia, which, the court held, obstructed the draft. For saying in an angry moment that he hoped "the government would go to hell," a citizen of Lansing, Michigan, received twenty years in jail and

was fined $10,000. A bad prophet, who said that the Kaiser would win the war, got off with six months in prison. For saying truthfully that the Russians "had more right to feel bitterly against the Americans in Russia than we had against the Hessians in 1776," a New York Assemblyman was indicted for "uttering disloyal, scurrilous, and abusive language about the military and naval forces." [8]

In Los Angeles the Reverend Robert Whittaker was sentenced to six months in jail and fined $1,200 for saying that under certain circumstances he would prefer the ideals of the Bolsheviki to those of the Merchants' and Manufacturers' Association; the Reverend Floyd Harden received a similar sentence for saying he preferred to die with his own blood on his hands rather than with that of a brother! The Reverend Herbert S. Bigelow of Cincinnati, at this writing a member of Congress, was kidnapped and horsewhipped by a mob "in the name of the women and children of Belgium," and left helpless on the banks of the Ohio River; he was long in recovering. Large employers took advantage of the prevailing hysteria to move against their workingmen, particularly if they were members of the International Workers of the World. In Bisbee, Arizona, more than a thousand workers, women, and children were driven from their homes into the waterless desert, and one of the chief officials of the company involved, long the head of one of the great charities in New York, defended this procedure to me. Some of those thus treated were among the 93 members of the I.W.W. sentenced to serve an aggregate of 800 years and fined $2,500,000; their torturers went unwhipped of justice. During all this time the Republican politicians were abusing the President in language which would have landed obscure persons in jail for fifty years. Thus, Mr. Roosevelt said that the President was guilty of "trickery, treachery, and bad faith."

The war spirit greatly encouraged our national lynching habit. Mary Turner, a colored woman, was hung in 1918 merely for saying that if she knew the murderers of her husband, who had

[8] For these and many other cases, see *The Nation*, November 9, 1918, p. 546.

just been lynched, she would have warrants sworn out for them. She was in the eighth month of her pregnancy; her clothes were burned from her; her unborn child was cut out of her body and stamped to death as the mother dangled head down from a tree and she was then riddled by hundreds of bullets. White supremacy and nobility were vindicated once more! Our officials were too busy saving us from the raping Huns to say one word about this proceeding or to punish the fiends who butchered Mary Turner and her child; after all they were just "niggers."[9] Nothing could have been more ironic than the drafting of our Negroes to save the world for democracy when all over the South they were denied every vestige of democracy, taxed without representation, refused a seat in the legislature or any local governmental body, and often denied common schooling.

On January 25, 26, 28, 1918, I published in *The Evening Post* the famous secret treaties. I shall treat later on of Mr. Wilson's denial that he knew anything about them until he reached Paris. These vitally important documents were found in the Russian archives when the Bolsheviki took over the government and were promptly published in full in all of the then existing Russian dailies. Every effort was made by the Allies to keep them out of the United States and to prevent our officials from reading and understanding them. Our great press associations were either too ignorant to appreciate their value, were unaware of the opportunity for one of the greatest scoops on record, or were too subservient to our government to undertake the publication; not even when I published them were they carried by the Associated Press. One day a man walked into my office with a note from Amos Pinchot saying that the bearer had a matter of the utmost importance to discuss with me. He was a Russian, apparently a sailor or stoker. He produced far from fresh copies of a Vladivostok newspaper containing the secret treaties in full; from their appearance the papers looked as if he had worn them ashore between his skin

[9] Between Armistice Day and May 15, 1923, thirty-four Negroes were burned alive.

and his undershirt. He asked a moderate price, received it, and departed, leaving upon my desk the means for me to render what would have been the greatest public service of my journalistic career had the officials in Washington been aware of their duty to their country and if the editors of the United States had had sufficient intelligence and knowledge of what the war was all about to appreciate the tremendous significance of these documents, revealing as they did the hidden policies and the sordid bargains of our hypocritical Allies.

I had the treaties translated and the accuracy of the translation was never questioned. Then, in order to obtain the widest possible circulation for them, I offered them at low rates to the leading newspapers of the country. Only nine took them. They were the Chicago *Daily News*, St. Louis *Post-Dispatch*, Milwaukee *Journal*, Philadelphia *Inquirer*, Pittsburgh *Press*, Baltimore *Sun*, Richmond *News-Leader*, St. Paul *Dispatch*, and, partly, the Hartford *Times* and Buffalo *News*. If there were others which recognized the sensational character of what I offered them, their editors probably felt that there was too much dynamite in the publication or that they might get into trouble with the government, and they also failed to understand what a service to their countrymen they could render by the publication.[10] As it turned out, nobody in Washington asked us any questions about the publication or how we got the documents (I promptly forgot the Russian's name and did not ask him where he was living). The censorship officials were certainly not clever when they failed to understand the importance of these documents and the light in which they placed the Allies. No one who understood them could thereafter claim that the Allies had clean hands or that they had played fair. At the Peace Conference the whole fight centered on how far Mr. Wilson could set aside the underhand bargains contained in those documents.

[10] For a full statement of Ray Stannard Baker's deliberate and misleading belittling of this incident, slurring over the facts, and attributing the publication to "a small group of radicals in New York," see my exposure of him as an historian in *The Nation* of February 14, 1923, under the title, "Ray Stannard Baker's 'Honesty.'"

our invasion of Siberia and the Archangel regions was not war—there we Americans burned villages and killed Russians because Mr. Wilson was so inclined, not because the American Congress had so voted.

Our interest in Russia was not, however, the reason for my clash with the war censorship which took place on September 13, 1918, when we were suddenly notified that our issue of September 14 was unmailable. Utterly dumbfounded, we seized copies and ran them over. The leading editorial was a severe attack upon the Department of Justice, based upon the conservative, pro-war *Tribune's* denunciation of it for having arrested in New York and near by towns within two days no less than 75,000 young men, merely in order to ascertain whether they were draft evaders—less than 3 per cent were found to be such. As our article was buttressed by the fact that the President had ordered an inquiry into this scandalous and high-handed action, and as it quoted from the privileged utterances of two United States senators, we could not see that that article could possibly be the offending one. The next editorial was a criticism of Samuel Gompers's being sent to Europe to report on the conditions of labor there. It was from the pen of Albert Nock who wrote that "the public will get from him [Gompers] at his best merely the kind of information that a sturdy partisan drummer, traveling continually in an atmosphere of sheer bagmanism is able to furnish; and with all that the people can do nothing." Obviously that could not be the trouble. The other two leaders were harmless for they dealt, the one on the possibility of a united labor party, while the other praised highly the pending revenue bill. We then examined an article by Stuart P. Sherman entitled "Carlyle and Kaiser Worship." This certainly was innocuous and so we were stumped. The New York postmaster, Mr. Patten, could throw no light on the matter. He had merely received orders from Washington to impound the issue.

I took the night train to Washington with our counsel, Mr. Wherry, in order to discover what it was all about. I reached Secretary Lane by telephone at breakfast time and he asked me to come to his house at once. He carefully looked over the articles and showed how much cleverer he was than we by putting a finger on the Gompers article and saying: "This is what they are after." It seemed incredible that we had come to such a pass that an American newspaper could not criticize Samuel Gompers but Mr. Lane insisted. Then, when I asked for his advice, he said: "Go straight to the White House and demand to see the President. Do not let yourself be put off by Tumulty or be satisfied with seeing him. You are an American citizen, your constitutional rights have been infringed, and you have a right to know from the President himself if he stands for this. Villard, this is an extremely important matter—of vital interest to the press and the country and you must go to it."

When I reached the White House I found Tumulty so incensed, and so profanely desirous of helping, that I did not insist on seeing the President although I told Tumulty I might yet demand this right. He replied: "Well, first you go down and see that old boll weevil from Texas in the Post Office Department. Tell him what you think of him and if you can't get satisfaction from him come back and let me know." Mr. Wherry and I had a long wait in Mr. Burleson's outer office and the old boll weevil finally refused to see us but sent his solicitor, Mr. Lamar, instead. Lamar came right out with the complaint. It was the Gompers article. Said he: "Mr. Gompers has rendered inestimable services to this government during this war in holding union labor in line and while this war is on we are not going to allow any newspaper in this country to attack him"—thus giving the most perfect proof of the lengths to which a censorship, intended by Congress only to prevent the publication of vital military news or seditious articles, had already been stretched. Argument with one of his small mental caliber soon proved to be impossible. There was no common meeting ground and he did not care what the law said or did not say. Finally he made this offer to me: "If you will tear out that page, which you can easily do, I'll release the issue."

I flatly declined. If memory serves, I told him that that had never been done in our forty-eight years of *The Nation's* history

It is rare, indeed, that a manuscript reaches the editor of any American journal which has pretensions to style that does not call for much revision, even to spelling and punctuation, unless it comes from England. In the New York *Nation* office it has long been a cynical joke that the worst manuscripts come from our college professors.

To meet such kindred souls as I have described has always been one of my happiest and richest experiences—I have encountered them in nearly every country though not in such numbers as in London. Somehow I cannot believe that Tories, or Rotarians, or Imperialists can feel anything like the same deep satisfaction in contacts with their kind. For one thing, there is the joy of being instantly on the footing of an old comrade or friend; we can take many things for granted at once. Our conversation does not start from the usual beginnings; we do not have to probe to ascertain just how we feel before reaching real communion. To be opposed to war; to hold no hate for any peoples; to be determined to champion a better world; to believe in the equality of all men and women; and to be opposed to all tyrants and all suppression of liberty and conscience and beliefs—when one stands on this platform, one has a ready key to priceless friendships. We may not see these friends often; when we do, we begin not just where we left off, but where we left off plus all the joint experiences given to us since we last met by our keen mental and moral participation in the world's events. We are up-to-date in our emotions when we begin to talk. I have a friend in Europe today from whom I hear irregularly; no one need tell me how Ethiopia burned into his soul, how he suffers for Spain by day and night, and how earnestly he has opposed every Hitlerite aggression on his fatherland. He is one of the fellowship of those whose country

is the world, with which fellowship, I insist, there is none to compare.

To see English public opinion at work then was a highly instructive experience but a disheartening one, for it became apparent that it was just as difficult to deal with the reactionaries in a small and compact country like England as in our own enormous and so diversified republic. The liberal elements, including Mr. Scott, were then quite fearful that the completeness of Lloyd George's victory would strengthen the direct-action forces and lead to serious labor troubles. They were much concerned over the mutinous conduct of large bodies of the returned troops, like those at Folkestone, where thousands paraded, defying their officers and

bearing signs reading: "We Will Not Fight in Russia" and also demanding their immediate discharge. Not one word of these demonstrations was printed in the London press but the Cabinet knew of them and the danger of their spreading all over the country. Undoubtedly these demonstrations, together with the outspokenness of the Liberal and Labor press, plus Wilson's refusal to go along, kept England from the folly of a hopeless holy war to purge Russia of the Bolsheviks.

When the New Year came in I felt I could make no better use of the day than to devote part of it to visiting a friend, Hubert W. Peet, a conscientious objector, in the hideous Pentonville prison. He was allowed to see his wife only once a month and permitted only two short letters during that period. Knowing him to be a Quaker, a man of deep religious convictions and high spirituality, I expected to find him calm and serene, for I remembered hearing how cheerfully my grandfather and the other Abolitionists and the early Quakers had borne their various incarcerations. Mr. Peet showed clearly how grave are the effects of imprisonment even upon men whose consciences are clear, who are guilty only of obeying their consciences and following in the footsteps of the Savior. The severance from all family ties, the complete change in one's habits and work, the deadly routine of endlessly sewing upon mailbags, which was Mr. Peet's task, the intellectual isolation, all took a heavy toll. He did not, of course, complain or express the slightest self-sympathy but the strain on his nerves was evident enough. Thus all over England and in the United States were men of the very finest type martyred even when not tortured by the shocking cruelties practiced in Alcatraz and at Fort Leavenworth. No one could foresee, on that New Year's Day, 1919, that in fifteen years no fewer than thirty-five of those British conscientious objectors would have seats in the same Parliament. The badge of dishonor turned in their cases to honor. So stupid and so wasteful of precious human material are governments!

I took the familiar way to my aunt's; I carried a small satchel filled, even without access to my trunk, with smuggled goods. We met with the deepest emotion for she had written me in 1915 that I must never set foot in Germany again else I should be dealt with severely for my disloyalty to my German traditions and ancestry in taking sides with the Allies. But whatever attitude she may have meant to take with me, blood and deepest affection proved stronger than national feuds. The agonizing past, with all its bitter, hateful differences, dropped away as she came, weeping, towards me. . . . I was the same, but she! War, suffering, and undernourishment had taken their toll. This pitifully thin, trembling, almost tottering woman hardly suggested the extraordinarily erect, vigorous, distinguished aristocrat who was my aunt; the one who was always beautifully gowned, always equal to any situation, whose title *Excellenz* seemed not a title but a description. The world she loved and adorned had crashed. She who had known royalty and courts was now like a pitiful child confused. Again and again she asked what it all meant, why this terrible disaster? They had been told for more than three years that victory was assured; why had all the world turned against them? Why had the Kaiser and the kings fled? The very ground seemed sinking beneath her feet. "Why, why, why?" she kept asking me, her nearest of kin.

It was on February 21 that things happened right in front of the quietest hotel in the quietest street in Munich. Upon that day the Landtag, which was to decide the fate of Kurt Eisner, finally met in its building diagonally opposite to the Baselerhof. I presented myself to the guard and demanded admittance. In vain. I must have a pass and the passes had all been issued. I asked to see the official in charge. His astonishment was great. A representative of the American press at this historic opening session of the first democratic Landtag in Bavaria— "Well, really, Mein Herr!" What papers had Mein Herr with which to identify himself? "Here is my American passport; here is my Paris pass admitting me to the Peace Conference as an American correspondent, here my visiting card." "But what is there to show that you are

connected with *The Nation?*" I tried to explain a rather intimate connection; apparently it only made matters worse to have me declare that I was both editor and owner. Suddenly the official's face lighted up. Something about the name on my passport attracted him. "Are you by any chance," he asked very earnestly, "the son of Henry Hilgard Villard, the benefactor of the Palatinate?" I replied that I was. He rose to his feet, solemnly shook hands with me, and said: "I used to live in the Palatinate and your father's son can have everything here that it is possible for me to grant. This is your ticket to the journalists' box for the session already under way." I left the room fairly dazed by the extraordinary coincidence that this official should have been one of the few men in Munich still to remember my father's name and deeds; I seemed to feel his spirit watching over me.

The journalists I found in the box in the gallery, directly opposite to and looking down upon the platform upon which the officials sat, were astounded when I appeared. A colleague from America? Why, there were hardly three Americans in all Munich. The correspondent of the *Frankfurter Zeitung*, Doctor Fritz Wahl, kindly pointed out the various dignitaries. That minister on the right was a locksmith's apprentice only a little while ago. Timm, the Minister of Education, on the left was a tailor's son and long a public schoolteacher. Minister Auer, about whose head the storm was particularly raging, had left school at eleven to be a herdsman for eleven years. Yet this was aristocratic Bavaria. Then there was Rosshaupter, to whom the independent Socialists and Communists were as much opposed as to Auer; both were charged with being reactionaries and too kindly to the old order. Several women delegates came in. "Think of that in Bavaria," said my coach, "woman suffrage in hidebound, priest-ridden, old Bavaria. Then there is Professor Quidde, the chief of the Bavarian pacifists, of whose efforts to stop the war you must have heard in America. Now they are all here except Kurt Eisner." A moment later a very young man, as pale as a sheet, walked feebly to the platform. "That," said the voice by my side, "is Fechenbach, Eisner's secretary. What is wrong? Something must have happened to Eisner." At that moment a soldier dashed into our box; calling down to the platform he shouted: "Kurt Eisner is murdered; Kurt Eisner has been shot." And to prove it he held up the bloody eyeglasses of the liberator of Bavaria.

It is almost impossible to describe the scene when the house grasped the import of the news. Ever since I have felt that I could gauge the shock that there must have been in Ford's Theatre when the audience realized that Abraham Lincoln had been shot down. From every part of the house and the gallery came cries of "shame" and of horror. For a few minutes there was utter confusion. The galleries were more vocal than the members of the Landtag. Even the journalists joined in. "Adjourn, adjourn," they cried and then rushed for the telephones. Finally the temporary president called the meeting to order and in a cool, calm voice announced the assassination of the President and declared the meeting adjourned for one hour. The news that the assassin was the young Count Arco-Valley intensified the gravity of the situation. The bitter hatred of Eisner cherished by the middle classes, the aristocrats, and the officials, and carefully fanned by a capitalistic press, had vented itself. More than one of the journalists declared that there would be bloodshed that night and that bolshevism would come to Bavaria.

"I pity the anti-Eisner press tonight," said one, "there will not be a stone left in the building of the *Münchner-Augsburger Zeitung*." "You'd better get away," declared my Frankfurt friend to his wife, "things are going to happen." Here I was betrayed by my New England conscience. Remembering that I had a luncheon engagement with two leaders of the peace and suffrage movement, Anita Augsburger and Lida Heimann, I tried to telephone. The booths were all occupied by frantic newspaper men calling the capitals of Europe. I decided to go across the street to the Baselerhof and cancel the engagement. In five minutes I was back but it was too late—journalist passes were no longer of any avail. I and others stood about disconsolate, but a Viennese correspondent thought we should miss nothing and went off advising us all to stay indoors that night. "Tonight blood will flow."

I also ran across the only American officials in Munich, Doctor Haviland H. Field, who was there as the representative of the American Peace Commission, and a young lieutenant I met on the street, who turned out to be the military courier for Doctor Field. The latter, an eminent biologist, had lived for years in Switzerland and was, therefore, thoroughly conversant with European affairs but his nerves appeared badly shattered by the happenings in Munich. Residing as he did, in the Vierjahreszeiten on the same floor with the twenty or more hostages imprisoned there after the shooting of Eisner, he was mortally afraid lest some other crime bring a mob storming into the hotel. "Just think how terrible it would be," he said, "if in raiding the hotel to get at those generals and aristocrats the mob should accidentally kill me. It would dreadfully inflame the relations between the United States and Germany." I ventured to suggest that he might move around the corner into the Baselerhof or into a suburb, as some Germans were urging him to do, but without result. A few days later he telephoned me and asked me to come to see him. He was then definitely of the opinion that he must leave at once lest there be a grave international incident and he asked me, since I was going to Berlin anyhow, if I would accept a commission to represent him on a tour of investigation into food conditions which he was to have made. I agreed to go to Weimar and Dresden on my way to Berlin and Doctor Field provided me with an official letter with instructions what to do and where to report and he duly notified the authorities in Dresden of my coming. For all of this I was extremely grateful to him since it gave me a sort of semi-official status and might, I thought, be useful in mitigating the punishment which I was certain awaited me on my return to Paris for my deliberate violation of the President's orders forbidding American pressmen to enter Germany.

My journey from Munich to Weimar instead of taking seven hours lasted for twenty-four, four of which I spent sleeping on chairs in the station restaurant at Jena. The railway system was shot to pieces. As on the trip from Lindau, the coaches were battered and dirty and in Munich there was the same crowding into the cars to get seats. The aisles were jammed by people standing or sitting on their luggage. There was, of course, no pretense of keeping to a schedule. But, long as the trip was, there was never a moment when it was not of profound interest. What more astonishing piece of luck could I as a journalist have had than to find late that night that one of my fellow-travelers had been an officer of the guard on the train which took Lenin across Germany and into Russia when he was set loose to begin his contribution to world history? From this young man I got at firsthand the whole story of the way Lenin and others were penned up in a car like wild animals and never permitted to leave, and how the officers and men were sworn to secrecy. No one was allowed to know who was in the car or what the whole move signified. Even more thrilling were the conversations around me that went on all day and to which for hours I was a silent listener. The minute the train left the station in Munich the debates began. Why had Germany been beaten? Was it true that the German army had misbehaved in France and Belgium? How guilty was the Kaiser? Everybody was a stranger to everybody else but that made no difference. No one held back. Others crowded into the coupé to listen or take part in the debate.

The most striking figure was a man who told us that he was a peasant leader, a rather distinguished one I afterwards learned, a man of deep religious feeling. It was he who wanted to know why it was that the churches of the world had failed so completely. Why had the German churches blessed the war and told them it was righteous and fine to kill their enemies when the churches in France and England and Italy and the United States had done the same thing? How could anyone respect churches that behaved this way? How could any intelligent man believe that God approved of the action and policy of these various national churches? As for himself he was perfectly certain that, if war came again and the churches repeated their actions, religion was

doomed. He would never again take part in a war no matter what or how occasioned, he who had done so much to rouse his people to the support of their government during the struggle just ended. For him the only way out was complete pacifism and disarmament. There was no disagreement. Then I spoke up and asked if an American might say amen. The astonishment was almost ludicrous. An American in Germany—in that train? They could hardly believe it, and when they found out that I was a journalist without hate, save for the war and the governments that brought it on, a torrent of questions poured over me which it took hours to answer. They ceased only as one by one my fellow-travelers got out, leaving me the opportunity to hear the lieutenant's story of his part in a great historic episode which the German government had as much cause to regret as any other incident in the whole struggle.

Weimar was jammed with soldiers, hundreds of troops brought from Berlin, together with many Berlin policemen—you could not enter the town or buy a ticket for Weimar at any station in Germany without showing an official *laissez-passer*. I had already ascertained that there was not much interest in Germany in the National Constitutional Assembly which was drawing up the constitution destined to be finally destroyed by an ex-house painter then doubtless still in his lance corporal's uniform. The Assembly was like the Paris Peace Conference in that its proceedings were much too long drawn out; it often proceeded as if it could discuss every proposal *ad infinitum*, just as if Germany were not on the edge of chaos and ruin and actually fighting the Spartacan movement to bolshevize the country. There was, of course, much unreason in some of the criticisms. The long-drawn-out negotiations in Paris made people feel that they were in the position of a criminal awaiting sentence and that there was no use planning for the future until the sentence was pronounced. The radicals were, of course, bitter that the Weimar convention had not proclaimed a Soviet Republic or at least socialized all German industries, as if that were possible. But I found some real reasons for criticism and discovered that the faults of the Assembly were largely the faults of the Ebert-Scheidemann government. I was amazed at the number of old men present, or of men more or less closely connected with the old regime, like the notorious Doctor Bernhard Dernburg, Count Posadowsky-Wehner, Doctor David, and others. I thought the *Journal de Genève* was not far wrong when it described the Assembly as "a sister of the defunct Reichstag," though I could not go so far as to agree that President Ebert was using "precisely the language of Wilhelm." Certainly the Assembly made no impression of vigor and force upon a casual observer like myself. I wrote that it was curious to hear in that Assembly "the old stories of terrible outrages upon women and children bobbing up again upon this side of the line from this new field of war [Poland]. The enemy always makes it his special business to outrage women and butcher children—no matter who the enemy is."

At Dresden I was received at the station by a group of officials who bowed low before me as if I really represented the destructive Big Four in Paris. They put me into one of the three automobiles of which Dresden then boasted and took me to the food bureau where I was again shown the official ration for a day—eight or nine unidentifiable morsels supposed to be food, which anybody could have swallowed at one gulp. Together they did not cover more than half the palm of one hand and on this a human being was supposed to exist for twenty-four hours. Not one pound of meat was distributed in Dresden during that week. Of course the people made getting other food their chief concern. They bought, bribed, and stole. Anyone whose second cousin's brother owned a farm some twenty-five miles away counted himself one of the most fortunate of men. The food officials knew this yet strove sincerely to make the people live upon nothing. They were an earnest set of men, borne down by the weight of their responsibility and actually unable to see anything ahead but the collapse of society if food did not come in soon. They told me that the returned soldiers felt the lack of food most for they had been well fed before the armistice.

"Who," I noted, "hears today in Paris of the freedom of the seas? Who, when he reads of the Saar basin, recalls the fine phrase about 'no punitive damages or annexations'? If there are today four Napoleons setting up new governments and redrawing the map, at least the Great Emperor spared the world the hypocrisy of clothing his acts in language to charm—and to be discarded at will." I found that some of our foremost representatives in Paris had lost all interest in the League of Nations which seemed to me "foredoomed to failure by the insincerity of many of those who have accepted it, by the exclusion from it of the representatives of two-thirds of Europe and all the black races."

The strongest American and British advocates of the League no longer offered any argument for the plan save that it was a half, or a third, of a loaf. "Try it," they said, "and out of it may come something worth while." My indignation was especially aroused by Mr. Wilson's agreeing to join England in giving a permanent guarantee of protection and treaty of alliance to France, for that meant, among other things, our keeping in being a great expeditionary force. "This action," I wrote, "will give the *coup de grâce* to his own creation [the League] and it is no longer worth discussing by serious-minded Americans."

The handling of Russia was one of the most striking evidences of the Big Four's folly and worse. The French policy, voiced by M. Pichon, the French Foreign Minister, was warmly approved even by some Americans, notably Simeon Strunsky, always politically unrealistic in his correspondence for *The Evening Post*. It was to encircle Russia "with a wall of bayonets." That was complete stupidity, if the idea was to prevent the spread of radical doctrines to Europe, for new ideas overleap every materialistic barrier ever erected. It was an excellent plan of Mr. Wilson to dispatch Bullitt and Steffens to Russia, but what did it avail? Their report was completely ignored because it did not picture the situation in Russia as the Big Four wished it portrayed. Furthermore, its existence was even deliberately denied. Of all the many falsehoods of statesmen I have chronicled in forty years, none was more unblushing and flagrant than Lloyd George's evasion in the

House of Commons on April 16, of the fact that he had full knowledge of the Bullitt mission into Russia and had even met Bullitt. I, being then in New York, was able to nail this on the spot by the statement in *The Nation* that Lloyd George not only knew about it but had invited Bullitt to breakfast with him.

When Bullitt arrived in New York he asked if I was a mind reader. "Nobody knew anything about that breakfast," he said. "How did you find it out?" I reminded him that he was to have breakfasted with me on the morning that the Lloyd George meeting took place. To my chagrin I woke up that morning after nine o'clock, already nearly an hour late for my appointment with Bullitt. As I jumped out of bed I noticed a slip of paper under the door. "Sorry I can't breakfast with you," it read, "but I've got to breakfast with L.G.—Bullitt." That was the explanation. I must add that in his testimony before the Senate Committee on Foreign Affairs Bullitt charged Lloyd George with being guilty of "the most egregious case of misleading the public" when he said in Parliament that no approaches or proposals had been made by the Soviet chiefs to the Entente. Soon after Lloyd George's whopper, Bullitt said, Philip Kerr called and apologized for Lloyd George's action, stating that the British Premier had found on his return to England that Lord Northcliffe and others had prepared to oust him if he recommended Soviet recognition!

Wilson flatly refused to see Bullitt, as he had refused to see me, using the old excuse that his mind was a single-track one, that it was then absorbed with Germany and that therefore he could not interest himself in the Russian situation! [3] Nothing more completely revealed Mr. Wilson's inadequacy for his Paris tasks, his mental tergiversations, his habitual refusal to face raw facts, than the treatment of Russia. On January 18, 1918, he had declared that our policy toward Russia would be the "acid test" of our good will. One of the fourteen peace points called for "such a settlement of all questions affecting Russia as will secure the best

[3] Testimony of William C. Bullitt before the Senate Foreign Relations Committee, September 12, 1919.

and freest co-operation of all the nations in the world in obtaining from her an unhampered and unembarrassed determination of her own political development and national policy. . . ." Thereupon Russia was invaded from three directions by American, British, French, and other Allied troops. When the temporary all-Russian government at Omsk begged General Graves not to send American troops further into Siberia, that officer replied that "the policy to be followed by our troops in any country is one to be determined by the Executive." He was quite correct. Congress had yielded its war-making power to the President; the full responsibility for this wanton invasion of a country with which we were at peace will for all time rest squarely upon Mr. Wilson's shoulders and upon his head lies the blood of the Russian and our own soldiers murdered in his private war.[4]

Some time after, when Nansen made his Russian food relief proposal, the Big Four accepted it but made it a cardinal prerequisite that the Soviet government cease fighting! Of course, all the fighting in Russia at that time was being done by Allied and American soldiers, or by counterrevolutionary troops, instigated, financed, and supplied by the Allies as Lloyd George frankly admitted to the House of Commons on April 16—a policy *The Nation* properly characterized as "combined burglary and starvation, coupled with pious phrases." The result of all this horrible blundering and international criminality was the defeat of the Allies and the United States at every point, the establishment on solid ground of the Soviet Republics and their miraculous rise to the position of the world's greatest power next to the United States. Such was the intelligence of the four men who were dominating Europe and by the middle of March were utterly ignoring

[4] In the summer of 1929, when in Nishni-Novgorod, the writer and others unexpectedly entered a classroom in a "People's House" in which some boys and girls were being taught the use of the army rifle. As soon as the instructor noticed that we were Americans he stepped to a large wooden map of Russia and pressed two buttons. Immediately the lines occupied by our American armies in Archangel and Siberia were outlined by tiny electric lights. Russia has not forgotten 1919 if the American public has.

the delegates of all the other nations who were kept in Paris merely in order to sign, like the Germans, on the dotted line!

Among the lesser delegates and diplomats the regret grew hourly that a quick and satisfactory peace, based upon a few principles and the original Wilson terms, was not obtained by January 15 as it easily could have been. Germany would gladly have signed a treaty, which could have been drafted—as Mr. Lansing insisted—in twenty-four hours, to comprise the following points: the League of Nations; cession of Alsace-Lorraine and the German colonies; the surrender of the German fleet; the reduction of the army to a gendarmerie organized only as police to maintain order; the razing of the Rhine fortifications; and a pledge by Germany to pay indemnities, to be determined later, in order to make good the destruction in France and Belgium. With that signed, the blockades could have been lifted and the normal processes of life restored. That was the vital need. Rasped nerves would have been quieted; undernourishment ended; revolutions would have been checked and at the same time the Allies safeguarded. It was all so simple, but too simple to be within the grasp of the four great minds. After such a treaty had been agreed to, the Big Four could have settled down to details and to revising the map if they had to do so.

These are not *post facto* views of mine. I published them all at the time. But what is vastly more important, they were the beliefs of practically all the lesser American officials in Paris. The fight which our ignored Peace Commissioners, and Hoover, Lamont, Baruch, McCormick, Henry P. Davison, and many others and some British officials put up to save Europe seems to me the one bright chapter in the whole dismal story of chicane, intrigue, selfish aggression and naked imperialism which gave the lie to all the pretense of noble aims with which we and the Allies had carried on the war. So keenly was the extent of the betrayal of American ideals recognized in our own official ranks that in May no less than nine attachés of the American Peace Commission resigned in a body in protest.

the Communist Party had not only called the meetings on **January 2, 1920, which Mr. Palmer's federal agents raided all** over the country, but had actually written the *very portions of the Communist platform* upon which the government based its prosecution of the men it duped! In other words, the government manufactured the crime and then sent men to prison for doing what it had induced them to do.

Judge Anderson declared from the bench that "it is perfectly evident to my mind that the government owns and operates at least part of the Communist Party." But his wrath did not stop there. It was proved before him that one man had been arrested on January 2, 1920, on a warrant which was not even issued until January 15 when it was telegraphed from Washington. Judge Anderson declared that the whole procedure of the government "seems to have been carried out on the theory of hang first and try afterwards." When Mr. Palmer's representative tried to defend the action of the government, the Judge replied:

> I wish you would show me one case in which the Department of Justice has the authority to arrest persons and hold them two weeks without warrants. A more lawless proceeding is hard to conceive. Talk about Americanization; what we need is Americanization of those who carry on such proceedings. I can hardly sit on the bench as an American citizen and restrain my indignation. I view with horror such proceedings as this.

When Judge Anderson asked Mr. Palmer's representative how he dared arrest a person without warrant, the reply was that he was acting under direct instructions from his superiors in Washington. To this Judge Anderson replied: "Any citizen with a knowledge of Americanism should resign when given such instructions." It was no wonder that *The Nation* exclaimed: "And there at last is the note of real Americanism! Massachusetts has again brought forth a man to voice, under the shadow of Faneuil Hall, the old traditions, the old liberties, the most sacred of our American rights. That there is a Judge Anderson to brand the Department of Justice as it should be is enough to stir the pulses." [4]

[4] *The Nation*, May 1, 1920, p. 569.

Between 5,000 and 6,000 people were seized in those January 2, 1920, raids, among them girls of fourteen, sixteen, and seventeen years who were arrested as "criminal anarchists" and women prisoners were poured into Ellis Island until the Commissioner of Immigration protested that it was neither sanitary nor decent to send any more. In Detroit more than one hundred men were kept in a bull pen 24 by 30 feet—a procedure "intolerable in any civilized city" the Mayor of Detroit wired to Washington. Not only were all known Communists arrested but any visitors found in their homes were seized because, said the police, if they were not Communists they would not have gone there! To defend these wholesale arrests, unparalleled in our history, the Department of Justice gave out solemn statements that the Communist and Communist-Labor parties were bent on overthrowing the government by force. It naturally neglected to state that both of those parties had held organizing conventions in Chicago in the previous summer without the slightest interference by the government. Mr. Palmer forgot, of course, to add that advocacy of communism was not a crime unless accompanied by a deliberate attempt to overthrow the government by force.

The authenticated cases of torture, sadism, and crime, committed by agents of the Department of Justice and condoned or encouraged by the department, would take several chapters to recite. They prove that Sinclair Lewis need not have written a book to show that *It Can't Happen Here.* He need only have cited the Wilson-Palmer record to show that it did happen. Much has occurred under Adolf Hitler in Germany which could be paralleled by official misconduct in this country during this period. One could really believe that the dictators were patterning after us if one were not aware of their sublime ignorance of everything outside the boundaries of their own countries. Mr. Palmer and his officials were denounced in a report signed by Dean Roscoe Pound of the Harvard Law School, five other teachers of law, and six attorneys of high standing. Writing in *The Nation,* Captain Swinburne Hale stated the case of the committee—that there had been "one thousand and one criminal acts" which had been "in-

tentionally and purposely done to terrorize the foreign working population." He said that he did not refer to the thuggery "which beat Oscar J. Tywerewski to a pulp in the presence of five invited newspaper reporters" and then terrorized them into silence and officially whitewashed the affair; nor to the suffocation nearly to death of three men "in the steam room" of the Hartford jail; nor "to the broken body of fifty-year-old Professor Lavrowski whose crime was teaching algebra in Russian instead of in English"; nor to the forgery of Gaspare Cannone's name to false testimony after filthy words and beatings had not broken him down; nor to the wholesale blackjacking of 300 Russians at once at 133 East 15th Street, New York City; nor did the committee especially dwell on the horrible case of Andrea Salsedo and Roberto Elia, held in eight weeks' secret confinement in the offices of the Department of Justice in the Park Row Building, New York City, and their daily physical and mental torture until Salsedo jumped from a fourteenth-story window and smashed to pieces on the pavement below. Horrible as these things were, what concerned the committee was the criminality of the Department of Justice itself and the fact that these things could happen with the knowledge of Washington and without the punishment of a single wrongdoer.

It is not surprising that on June 12, 1920, we urged the impeachment of Palmer, who, by the way, called himself a Quaker, for misuse of government funds to conduct a personal press campaign against free thought and free speech, for violation of the Constitution in certain deportations, for betrayal of common decency as Alien Property Custodian, and for his failure to check profiteering or other law violations by the trusts. As Custodian alone he was a disgrace to America. Naturally he fathered a sedition law proposal which read that whoever "threatens to commit . . . any act of . . . *hate* . . . against the person or property of any officer . . . of the United States . . . shall be deemed guilty of sedition"! This certainly parallels the present German ruling that any judge may deem any act treason to the State. Of course not even the subservient Congress could stand for this proposal though I am sure Wilson would not have objected.

We had little aid from the press in this fight which was one after my heart since it enabled us to champion the oppressed, the tortured, the innocently convicted.[5] The Associated Press frequently refused to carry the news of what took place and to accept protests against lawless officials. The independent weeklies were as outspoken as we and, of course, the Baltimore *Suns*, the New York *World*, and the St. Louis *Post-Dispatch*. The most powerful newspapers like the New York *Times*, *Tribune*, and the Chicago *Tribune*, either kept silence or approved. True, when Charles E. Hughes and other conservatives protested against the ousting of five Socialists from the Assembly in New York some of the newspapers followed suit. They had nothing to say about the conviction of twenty Communists in Chicago for the crime of being members of their legal party. When the Sterling Bill was introduced, which would have made impossible the mailing of Lincoln's first inaugural because it contained this sentence: "Whenever they [the people] grow weary of their existing government they can exercise their constitutional right of amending it, or their revolutionary right to dismember or overthrow it," some of the conservatives began to stir uneasily; they even realized that this would make impossible the mailing of the Declaration of Independence. Such was the government-created terror that swept over the land.

We liberal editors were actually denounced with increasing bitterness for fighting for the preservation of our institutions, and so we of *The Nation* set ourselves to printing as able and informative a journal as possible, without regarding the question of cost. I am proud of those fighting issues, whatever their errors.[6] They were not wholly given over to the battle for liberty. Indeed, we

[5] In Waterbury, Connecticut, a boy was arrested and sentenced to six months' imprisonment for no other reason than that he said to a customer in a clothing store that Lenin was "the most brainiest man" produced by the war, a sentence some of us succeeded in getting quashed. *The Nation*, April 17, 1920.

[6] In my absence the staff on August 28, 1920, printed a blast that bowled me over when I saw it—an editorial headed: "Take Every Empty House." Because of the great shortage of homes this course was urged upon the mayors of our cities. This leader, I admit, bordered on the hysterical.

printed numerous special issues, devoting one to the railroads with two conservative railroad presidents, Messrs. Lovett and Loreé, contributing, and we gave eighteen and one-half pages in one issue to the educational problems of reconstruction; under Carl Van Doren our special book issues were at high-water mark. On July 19, we scored a "beat" by printing a secret government dispatch sent from Tokyo to Colonel House by Arthur Bullard, one of the star reporters in Russia of Mr. Creel's bureau of misinformation. This dispatch told the brutal truth about Kolchak and his unbelievably bloody performances in Siberia—a dispatch which made disgraceful our American support of that monster. Exactly how this and some other dispatches reached me I did not know and do not to this day, for Max Eastman, the intermediary, has never revealed the secret; I found them on my desk one morning. It was at once announced that the Department of Justice would take us in hand but nothing happened beyond the visit of a very dumb sleuth. When Eastman was threatened with arrest—he had read one dispatch at a public meeting—he stopped any further governmental action by giving out a statement that he hoped he would not have to expose other secret documents in his possession beyond those relating to the Siberian adventure. The Wilson crowd did not want any more truths to leak out. I am convinced that the publication of this material compelled the withdrawal of our troops from Siberia.

We devoted much of our editorial space to the fight against the peace treaty and our entering the League of Nations. We gave especial attention to the betrayal of China on the Shantung issue and we "deadly paralleled" Mr. Wilson in issue after issue, giving one whole supplement to citations from his speeches before and after entering the war, not forgetting to print an extraordinary account of Metternich as the predecessor of Woodrow Wilson and recalling the fact that even after his downfall Metternich said: "My mind has never entertained error." To the Progressive senators in Washington we gave aid and counsel. I saw a good deal of Senator Borah at this time and our friendship developed most satisfactorily until it was ended overnight in 1928 when Hoover was making his first campaign for the White House and I innocently asked Mr. Borah in *The Nation* how he could reconcile two statements. The first was made in 1919, when he told the Senate that Herbert Hoover was unfit to be trusted with the expenditure of $100,000,000 for relief in Russia, and the second, which he had just made, was his assurance to his countrymen that Herbert Hoover was the man best fitted in all the United States to be President—a laughable assertion, indeed, in view of Mr. Hoover's subsequent record in office. When Washington correspondents took up my editorial and asked Mr. Borah to answer the question and reconcile his inconsistency, he frankly said that he could not. He remains to this day an enigma; gifted with extraordinary talent, a great fighter in opposition when his indignation is aroused, he should have been the dominating personality in American political life and could assuredly have found his way into the White House had he had stability of purpose, made himself a leader of the liberal forces, and consistently stuck to his platform.

Naturally we of *The Nation* made much of Woodrow Wilson's confession in his St. Louis speech of September 5, that: "The real reason that the war that we have just finished took place was that Germany was afraid her commercial rivals were going to get the better of her, and the reasons why some nations went into the war against Germany was that they thought Germany would get the commercial advantage of them. The seed of the jealousy, the seed of the deep-seated hatred was hot, successful commercial and industrial rivalry." This was not only what many had thought from the beginning but was a confirmation of what Eugene Debs had said in his speech declaring it to be a capitalist war, for which he was then in Atlanta Penitentiary, Mr. Wilson refusing, with utmost vindictiveness, to release him despite the fact that Secretaries Lane, Lansing,[7] and other members of his Cabinet urged that the great Socialist leader be pardoned.

At this time, too, there came up the question of the secret treaties which still will not down and was only recently aired again in

[7] Letter of Robert Lansing to the author, Nov. 7, 1919.

connection with the Nye Committee's investigation into the munitions makers. Naturally because of my having printed those treaties in *The Evening Post* I have had a deep interest in this question. As I see the evidence, there is no question whatsoever that Wilson deceived the Senators of the Committee on Foreign Relations who called upon him at the White House on August 19, 1919. In that interview the President stated, in reply to a question from Senator Borah, that his own knowledge of the secret treaties "came after I reached Paris. . . . The whole series of understandings were disclosed to me for the first time then." Senator Borah asked: "Then we had no knowledge of these secret treaties, so far as our government was concerned, until you reached Paris?" The President replied: "Not unless there was information at the State Department of which I knew nothing." Senator Johnson then asked: "Was the United States government officially informed at any time between the rupture of diplomatic relations with Germany and the signing of the Armistice of agreements made by the Allied governments in regard to the settlement of the war?" To this the President replied: "No; not so far as I know." When Senator Johnson asked him whether or not an official investigation had been made by our government to ascertain whether there were "treaties of territorial disposition," Mr. Wilson replied: "There was no such investigation."

Now how was this possible? Not only was *The Evening Post* read daily in the White House but, as I have already stated, the secret treaties were syndicated in nine other daily newspapers as far West as St. Paul and were then reprinted in pamphlet form and put on sale on the newsstands in New York, Boston, Philadelphia, Chicago, and especially in Washington, as well as other cities. More than that, two copies of the treaties were mailed to every Senator and every Congressman, and copies mailed to the White House. The latter, of course, may have been thrown away by mail clerks without an understanding of the seriousness of their import. But it would certainly seem that if there were a vestige of efficiency in the State Department at that time some official would have been sufficiently interested to read and study anything as widely circulated as these treaties. Yet Mr. Lansing had to make the humiliating confession to the Senate on August 11, 1919, that he did not know *until February, 1919,* when the Peace Conference was well under way, of the secret treaties between Japan and the Allies as to the Pacific islands and Shantung, a statement that again gave the lie to Arthur Balfour, who in the House of Commons stated that President Wilson had been kept *fully informed* by the Allies as to what was going on.

But there is further evidence than this. Lincoln Colcord was one of the journalists in the special confidence of Colonel House in the period leading up to the war. Writing in *The Nation* on May 17, 1919, Mr. Colcord said:

> Did President Wilson, in the summer of 1917, know about the secret treaties of the Allies? Beyond question, he did. When Mr. Balfour was in America in the early part of that summer, Colonel House requested him, on the score that we were now in the war, and that President Wilson ought to see what we were fighting for, to send copies of all the secret treaties to Washington on his return to England. Mr. Balfour gladly consented. I heard this statement in September *from Colonel House himself.* At that date, Mr. Balfour had submitted no treaties to Washington, and no further request for them had been made at the British Foreign Office.

Again, on September 13, 1919, Mr. Colcord said that in the summer of 1917 he was a member of a group "that had constant access to the highest sources of information. This group at that early date based its conception of American policy in the war upon a knowledge and understanding of the secret treaties. I should be untruthful, indeed, if I did not state that the initiative in the formation of this conception emanated from the Administration." Mr. Colcord then declared that: "On the 28th of June, I think it was, Foreign Secretary Balfour, in answer to interpellations from Liberal members, made his notorious statement on the secret treaties: 'By these treaties we stand—our national honor is bound up in them.' This statement I had the pleasure of bringing to the attention of the *President and Colonel House by letter,* enclosing

the newspaper clippings of the incident and pointing out very fully its bearings." Mr. Colcord then continued:

> I could multiply the instance by hundreds. Our journalistic group was in constant communication with Colonel House; every item of news regarding the secret treaties was at the disposal of the Administration. I can recall dozens of conversations with Colonel House about the secret treaties going back as far as the summer of 1917, and I remember how again and again during that season, and during the following winter, we urged upon the Administration the danger of the course that was being followed by America; the unwisdom of leaving the secret treaties unrepudiated. . . .

If the President was really in ignorance of all of this activity inspired by Colonel House, then he must have lived in an airtight chamber. Is it conceivable that the Colonel constantly discussed these treaties with Lincoln Colcord and others of the group, of whom William C. Bullitt was a member, but failed ever to discuss the matter with the President? Of course he did not. More than that, Lincoln Colcord assured me at the time that I printed his article, which he called "Black is White," that he had in his possession a letter from Colonel House thanking him for two copies of the secret treaties in the pamphlet form and stating that he was enclosing those pamphlets "in the private mailbag for the White House tonight and you know the President alone has the key to this bag." Yet in the face of all of these printed facts Senator Carter Glass continues to denounce and to revile anyone who declares that the President was fully aware of the secret treaties before he went to Paris. If, however, the defenders of Wilson are right, they cannot deny that he who held at Paris the brief for humanity, the greatest brief ever accepted by any man, failed to take the most important step to win his cause, namely, to learn his case, to ascertain the background and the facts which he was to plead before the eyes of the world.[8]

[8] "It does not seem important which of the various versions of President Wilson's acquaintance with those treaties is the correct one—whether he knew their contents, as did other citizens who bought the ten-cent pamphlet giving their text in full, and considered them irrelevant; whether he did not know them and there-

Naturally when the end of the treaty fight came and the Senate defeated it we rejoiced wholeheartedly. We felt with Colcord that the "honor of the United States has not been betrayed." We regretted that it was not rejected squarely upon the ground of its inhumanity, of its betrayal of solemn pledges given by the American government during the war, and of its flouting of the great program for world reorganization formulated by Woodrow Wilson in the Fourteen Points. We were sorry, too, that the defeat was largely due to a "group of partisans, most of them narrow nationalists with no adequate vision of the true internationalism which the future holds in store for the world." But we rejoiced that the country had been saved from "acquiescing in a treaty which embodies so gross a breach of faith with the American dead in France and the Americans living everywhere who took at full value and held in honor the assertions of the President that we were in the war to safeguard democracy and advance the cause of human liberty."

To our associate editor, Arthur Warner, came the opportunity to investigate the Boston police strike and to print, as early as December 20, 1919, the facts about Governor Calvin Coolidge's connection with it—facts officially confirmed by James J. Storrow of Lee, Higginson & Company, the conservative head of the Citizens' Committee appointed by Mayor Peters. The truth was that at the crucial time of the strike Calvin Coolidge either refused to face the issue, or disappeared, being "reported to be in the western part of the state." There never was a word of truth in the claim that he ended the strike by the firmness he displayed and by his calling out the state militia—it was actually summoned by Mayor Peters. As the Storrow committee put it: "By Thursday morning order had been generally restored in the city. *On Thursday after-*

fore proceeded in ignorance; or whether he was aware of their existence but brushed them aside without comprehending their significance. The unfortunate fact remains that the secret treaties became the basis of the 1919 peace treaties which the United States was instrumental in enabling the Allies to write, treaties deeply infected with the germs of future wars." Professor Edwin M. Borchard, *Neutrality for the United States*, New Haven, 1937, p. 47.

noon, the Governor assumed control of the situation." Yet Calvin Coolidge rose to the Presidency because of the absolutely false press reports of this strike.

I reported the 1920 Republican National Convention at Chicago and made my contribution to the defeat there of General Leonard Wood, by publishing his record in *The Nation* of May 29, which statement was widely circulated in pamphlet form. After the nomination of Harding by the convention I moved forward on the journalists' platform and sat among the Massachusetts newspaper men. When Calvin Coolidge was nominated for Vice-President they laughed heartily, thinking it a great joke. When the convention adjourned I went to the Congress Hotel. There in the lobby stood Robert L. O'Brien of the Boston *Herald* and Richard Hooker of the Springfield *Republican*. The air was blue about them and they were saying most uncomplimentary things about Coolidge, O'Brien insisting that Coolidge had never attained any honor on his merits. He said: "You know, Villard, I have known all our public men since Grover Cleveland's time. This is the worst man I ever knew in politics." He then turned to Richard Hooker, and using the Quaker form, said: "Richard, I will bet thee a dinner that Harding will die and Coolidge become President."

For us of *The Nation* that campaign soon became "a choice between Debs and dubs." We felt that no self-respecting liberal could vote for Harding and that what we were witnessing was the spectacle of the old Republican bosses again in complete control of a subservient party and defying all aspirations for reform and progress. Both Cox and Harding were second-rate editors and speedily showed their intellectual inadequacy for the White House. Cox himself was of course better than Harding though a graduate of the politics of the same State; at least it was a cause for thanksgiving that both Mitchell Palmer and McAdoo were defeated for the Democratic nomination. Nobody close to Wilson could have been chosen. Indeed, nobody except Mr. Wilson himself should have been asked to shoulder the burden of the mistakes, the follies, the wrongs, perpetrated by the President and his subordinates, but no Democrat could have won. Franklin Roosevelt made an able campaign for the Vice-Presidency and again and again avowed his lifelong fealty to the League of Nations for which, during his Presidency, he has not been willing to lift a finger.

Soon after the inauguration of President Harding, the "Marionette," I passed through Chicago and as was my wont called upon an old schoolmate of mine who had been in the Ohio Legislature with Harding and the "Ohio gang," and later was a judge until his removal to Chicago. Closing the door of his office, he asked me what I knew of the Harding Cabinet. I told him that I was acquainted only with Hoover, Hughes, and Weeks. He astounded me by telling me that the government had been turned over to a set of third-rate, small-town grafters, that Washington had never fallen so low. He stated that he had played poker night after night with these Ohio men and had repeatedly fought them, and that some of them were open grafters known by everybody as such. It was the first time that I had heard of Jess Smith. Indeed, my friend's horror at what had taken place and what was to come seemed to me so unbridled that I all but dismissed it from my mind and failed to take journalistic advantage of the tip. A couple of years later he was proved correct at every point.

One extremely valuable experience I owe to the temper of those times. I lectured in Cincinnati on January 30, 1921, before the Wise Center and my address attracted no particular attention; it dealt with existing conditions in Europe and what part I thought the United States should play. I returned to repeat the address on February 12 to a joint meeting of the City Club and the Women's City Club. As I stepped off the sleeper from Chicago I was met by two agitated men who, after ascertaining who I was, said: "We must hurry off as fast as we can." That struck me as odd but my attention was arrested by a large group of policemen. "What are they here for?" I asked. "To protect you from being mobbed," was the answer. At the Sinton Hotel I was almost mobbed by a large group of reporters and photographers and found that for the first and only time my name had figured in streamer headlines across the front pages of the morning papers.

For all this I was indebted to Miss Ruth Harrison, the Reverend Frank H. Stevenson, a Presbyterian clergyman, and the Bentley Post of the American Legion. Mr. Stevenson had stated in the pulpit, after citing my record as a Bolshevik, that "an aroused people should be as prompt in muzzling him as they were in stopping the illiterate discourses at the Communist headquarters on Vine Street." Miss Harrison had presented a petition to the clubs bearing one hundred signatures asking that the invitation to me be revoked; eighty-six members resigned from the Women's City Club and twenty-eight from the men's. The Cincinnati *Tribune* declared of me: "He did what he could to make the entrance of the United States into the war a failure abroad and a calamity at home. He still preaches his damnable doctrines," and it added that there were "momentous occasions in a nation's life, where to tolerate other than one universal opinion, conviction, judgment, is to tolerate treason. . . ."

My address was scheduled for immediately after the luncheon hour. I was not allowed to have my lunch with the members. As I stood by the window of an office overlooking the street I saw fine-looking, well-set-up young men entering a music store across the street and then reappearing on the floor above where they crawled on hands and knees to the windows and peeked out. That prepared me for what happened, particularly as I had noticed only two policemen at the door. When I began my lecture I stood on the rostrum facing the entrance to the large room; I could look through it into another room and then through the hallway beyond to the entrance door of the club which had glass panels and was at the head of a flight of stairs from the street. I had been reading my probably rather dull picture of the situation in Europe for about fifteen minutes when the mob came across the street, the two policemen stood aside, and the Legionnaires and others charged up the stairs. A group of club members headed by a courageous American, Guy Mallon, three of whose sons had been in France, threw themselves into the breach, slammed the door, and the fight was on.

The door was forced, the glass broken, and one man badly cut.

The invaders pushed in step by step, finally entering the second room where the fight went on until they were repulsed. All of that put my powers of concentration to a real test, for only the chairman and I could see what was happening. It was a real battle and all my reporter's instincts made me wish to watch it yet I had to go on with my talk; as a pacifist I could not even hesitate. Meanwhile the audience was much disturbed by the noise and confusion and the chairman called down from the balcony behind us asking that a riot call be sent in. In no time at all the police cars were there with their sirens shrieking, which so disturbed the audience that many, among them Adolph S. Ochs of the New York *Times*, who sat in the front row, jumped to their feet and turned around, so that I had to stop. As soon as the police restored order and drove out the mob I asked the audience to sit down and took particular satisfaction in reading every word that I had come to voice. Then we adjourned, the chairman said some pleasant things to me, I found a friend's car waiting for me in a near by street, and I was driven to the home of a relative of my wife's in Wyoming not far away. There I spent the evening until the chief of police, who said that he would not guarantee my life if I tried to take a train from Cincinnati as the Legionnaires were patrolling the streets looking for me, sent an open car with three plainclothes policemen to drive me to Dayton where I took the sleeper to New York.

With the Legion in the rush into the club were some Covington roughs belonging to a semisecret order of patriots akin to the K.K.K., which was believed to have been responsible for the tarring and feathering of Herbert Bigelow. It was their intention to seize me when I arrived and give me the same treatment; only the fact that no one knew from which direction I was coming saved me from disappearing immediately upon my arrival unless the police had prevented. While the press gave columns and columns to the riot, not one newspaper, so far as I am aware, printed a word of my address or condemned the mob. Ten years later I was again asked to speak in Cincinnati and, being politely applauded when I arose to begin, could not forbear contrasting that friendly

greeting with the one in 1921 and lamenting the press's loss of interest in me; I had not even made the first pages. A columnist, "Cincinnatus," writing in the Cincinnati *Post*, said of me: "He returns as a prophet who was despised and now comes to some honor; for the multitudes of prostrate citizens testify to the villainy of the war and of the peace." Not a Legionnaire peeped; the Reverend Mr. Stevenson was dumb, and the Constitution remained inviolate. I am sincere in expressing my gratitude for that riot experience. It was a test that I am glad to have faced, an occurrence I would not have missed.

If this chapter gives a most disheartening picture of our national leaders and the national life in 1920-21, I have only recorded the truth. To such political depths had our republic been reduced in three years as a result of our zeal to slay Huns and make the world safe for democracy! Mr. Wilson insisted to the end that his policies would be upheld; we prophesied the almost unanimous election of Harding "by disgust." Governor Cox was rejected by more than 17,000,000 of his countrymen, of whom 919,799 voted for Mr. Wilson's prisoner, Eugene Debs. The end of a heartbreaking era had come.

Chapter XXVI. Liberty in the Caribbean and Elsewhere

NOT only domestic issues stirred us deeply in those days. When we looked at what was happening in the Caribbean, it was difficult to exercise self-restraint. If Russia was the "acid test" of our unselfishness and benevolent intentions in Europe, Haiti, Santo Domingo, and Nicaragua certainly should have been the "acid test" of our fair play and democracy in the Caribbean. It afforded a genuine opportunity for leadership, good will, and consistency toward the lesser American republics for Woodrow Wilson and his subordinates, William J. Bryan, Josephus Daniels, and Robert Lansing, yet every one of them originated or participated in the most brutal and bloody attacks upon the Haitian Republic without the shadow of a tenable excuse.[1] It was never alleged that a single American had been injured there or a dollar's worth of American property destroyed. The reasons given for this wanton attack upon a helpless little republic were: (1) that there were lawlessness and disorder in Haiti which we could not permit in any country in the neighborhood of the Panama Canal; (2) that unless we rectified internal conditions foreign intervention might result, especially as (3) both France and Germany claimed a special interest in Haiti because of their investments there; and (4) there was a

[1] For the established proofs of this statement see "Conquest of Haiti and San Domingo" by Ernest H. Gruening in New York *Times's Current History Magazine* for March, 1922; "The American Occupation of Haiti," Foreign Policy Association Information Service, Vol. V, No. 19-20, November 27-December 2, 1929; "The Seizure of Haiti by the United States"—a report by twenty-four well-known lawyers, 1922, Foreign Policy Association. Also hearings of the select committee of the Senate on Haiti and the Dominican Republic, October 4, November 16, 1921, Government Printing Office; also the report of Major General George Barnett, October 13, 1920; "Conquest of Haiti" by Herbert Seligmann, *The Nation,* July 10, 1920; Letter of Major General John A. Lejeune, *The Nation,* July 24, 1920.

special danger after the outbreak of the World War that Germany might make Haiti a base for its submarines. The Haitians properly replied that the occupation was plainly illegal for international law conferred no authority upon the United States to intervene as Haiti had injured no Americans, defaulted on no debt, violated no obligation to the United States. There is unhappily plenty of proof that the internal disorders in Haiti were provoked or intensified by the State Department and American citizens in order to advance the interests of the National City Bank and other American enterprises in Haiti.[2]

On December 13, 1914, the government of Woodrow Wilson embarked upon its hypocritical and bloody course. Without warning anyone, American marines landed in the Haitian capital, went to the Haitian National Bank and carried off $500,000 in gold by force, in pursuit of an arrangement entered into by Secretary Bryan and the American directors of the National Bank of Haiti, which bank was owned by the National City Bank of New York. This was surely an extraordinary business for the anti-Wall Street William J. Bryan to engage in! Naturally Haiti protested against this violation of its sovereignty but no answer was ever vouchsafed, doubtless because no defense was possible. The excuse given in Washington was "fear of revolution." The actual pretense for the subsequent intervention was a mob's dragging President Guillaume of the Haitian Republic and General Oscar, commander of the garrison of Port-au-Prince, out of the French legation and cutting them to pieces. The night before these two officials had murdered between one hundred and two hundred Haitians of the better class charged with fomenting revolution, after having lodged them in jail. The mob was determined to have its revenge and had no grievance whatever against the French legation.

This incident was just what Mr. Bryan and Mr. Lansing had been waiting for. A lieutenant and nine men of the French navy

[2] See James Weldon Johnson: "Government Of, By, and For the National City Bank." *The Nation,* September 11, 1920.

having been landed on Haitian soil to guard the legation, this impressive military demonstration was portrayed as an *infraction of the Monroe Doctrine!* The next day a regiment of American marines was put ashore and there began an occupation which did not end for nineteen years and, like interventions elsewhere, did infinite harm to American prestige and our business interests in the Caribbean, Central, and South America. A puppet government—a perfect pattern for the Japanese in Manchukuo—was set up, a constitution favoring the United States forced upon the Haitians, their legislature being dissolved by Colonel Smedley D. Butler, who now freely says that in Haiti he was "doing the dirty work for the National City Bank." Admiral Caperton on September 8 telegraphed to Captain Durrell, commanding at Cap Haitien: ". . . treaty situation looks more favorable than usual. This has been effected by the exercise of *military pressure* [italics mine] at propitious moments in negotiations. Yesterday two members of the Cabinet who have blocked negotiations resigned. . . . Am therefore not yet ready to begin offensive operations at Cap Haitien but will hold them in abeyance as additional pressure." The authorship of this shameless constitution was first credited to Franklin D. Roosevelt, then Assistant Secretary of the Navy. The Associated Press reported on August 18, 1920, that, speaking at Butte, he had said that he "had something to do with the running of a couple of little republics. The fact is I wrote Haiti's constitution myself. . . . Until last week I had two votes in the League Assembly myself." He added that the United States controlled about twelve votes of little American republics in the League of Nations. This report he denied on September 2. Two weeks later Mr. Harding quoted that part of the Associated Press interview relating to Haiti and Santo Domingo which Mr. Roosevelt had not clearly denied. Mr. Roosevelt then telegraphed another denial.[3]

What happened after American control was complete was subsequently told by Major General George Barnett of the Marine Corps—all honor to him.[4] This officer, who refused to allow his uniform to keep him from telling the truth, declared that 3,250 Haitians were killed and that he regretted that many of these deaths were "practically indiscriminate killings." From 1915 on *The Nation* almost singlehanded fought the battles for these unfortunate victims of Woodrow Wilson's democracy and Josephus Daniels' piety. Only three days before the Barnett report appeared the New York *Times* had attacked Mr. Harding for denouncing the American policy in Haiti, charging that he "got his information about conditions in Haiti from a weekly paper in this city which, if not actually bolshevik, is so near it that the distinction is not visible to the naked eye." When Major General Barnett told the truth, and confirmed our allegations, the *Times* did not apologize to us but changed its position and whined that "the American people have not had the details. They have not known what was going on"—an interesting admission from the newspaper which daily boasted, then as now, that it gave "all the news that's fit to print." Even then it did not bring out the fact that the truth was suppressed in Haiti by the strictest kind of a censorship clamped down by the navy.

[3] *The Nation*, October 6, 1920. The A.P. correspondent insisted that he had telegraphed the truth.

Some effort was made to break the force of Major General Barnett's revelations and the previous admission by Major General John A. Lejeune that "some officers and men have failed, at times necessitating court-martial and other punishment," by pointing out that a Lieutenant Brokaw, who was guilty of horrible atrocities, had been placed in an insane asylum, but Josephus Daniels offset this by reinstating a captain who had been found guilty by a court of having given orders to shoot all prisoners.[5] From the moment in 1920 that I was visited by a committee of the admirable *"Union Patriotique"* formed to liberate Haiti, the present President Stenio Vincent being a member of the delegation, we redoubled our energies. Herbert J. Seligmann, Lewis S. Gannett, James Weldon

[4] The New York *Times*, October 14, 1920.

[5] See *The Nation*, October 20, 1920, p. 436.

Johnson, Ernest H. Gruening, Mrs. Helena Hill Weed, and others went to Haiti for us and brought back the truth or bore the brunt of the fight in the columns of *The Nation.* Doctor Gruening, then managing editor, especially deserves honor; he speedily made himself an authority on Latin-American affairs.

Even the New York *World* failed us in this Haitian fight; it was too closely tied up with the Wilson Administration. Our repeated proofs, our widely circulated pamphlets were ignored by the dailies which believed the gullible—or worse—Josephus Daniels when he declared that "with a few exceptions, the officers and men carried out in letter and spirit the order to set an example in helpfulness and kindness in the discharge of a difficult duty." The character of the slaughter of the Haitians was clearly revealed by the fact that while our marines killed no less than 3,250 men and women—a strange "example of helpfulness and kindness"—the American loss was only *one officer and twelve men.* This was completest proof that it was not war that was waged in Haiti. An illustration of the way error persists was demonstrated at the Williamstown Institute of Politics in August, 1924, when I quoted the figures of Major General Barnett. Two admirals, H. P. Jones and Harry McL. P. Huse, rose and denounced me as a slanderer of the navy and marine corps, Jones saying that it was the "most monstrous and unpatriotic statement" he had ever heard from an American!

Santo Domingo fared somewhat better at Mr. Wilson's tender hands but its government was for a second time deliberately seized by our marines. One week after Haiti had ratified our treaty at pistol point, so that we could have complete military and financial control of Haiti, a similar draft of a treaty was laid before President Jiminez in Santo Domingo—only to be emphatically rejected. Mr. Daniels waited patiently for six months and then his opportunity came. On May 4, 1915, during a revolutionary disturbance, without notification to the Dominican government, marines were landed near Santo Domingo City. On May 13, the American minister told the Dominican government that the subsequent author of the slogan that we went into the World War

"for the rights of nations, great and small . . . to choose their way of life and of obedience" [6] was about to land a large force of marines to occupy the capital. The Minister threatened in good Japanese style that these marines would bombard the city and fire upon the natives "without restriction" if there was the slightest opposition. On June 5, the Minister gave formal notice that the American Receiver General of Customs, an official who had been appointed under the treaty of 1907, was to take over all the finances for the government. For five years thereafter the United States—in the name of liberty—held Santo Domingo in "the iron bondage of martial law." Meetings were forbidden, the press completely censored, and protesters against American rule court-martialed; one of them was Fabio Fiallo, a well-known poet, whose imprisonment aroused the anger of intellectuals throughout Central and South America. The Dominicans we killed we called bandits; the Dominicans called them patriot martyrs. It is only fair to say that the marines did a far better job in Santo Domingo than in Haiti, but when they left the Dominicans refused to ratify the acts of our military government, which included loans bearing interest ranging from *9 to 19 per cent!* Our efforts on behalf of these two republics were warmly seconded in Washington by such men as Senator Medill McCormick, who spoke out splendidly in the Senate, Senator Borah, Senator King, Senator Norris, and others—King so effectively that he, a United States Senator, was excluded from Haiti by the marine officers as late as 1927 on the ground that he was an "agent of the *worst elements of disorder*"! [Italics mine.] Senator McCormick headed a commission appointed by the wicked President Harding, which held hearings from May, 1921, to June, 1922, to review the acts of the noble President Wilson. I still stand by my statement to that committee that our intervention in the two republics constituted "the blackest chapter in American history in the Caribbean"—though that was saying a great deal. The commission condemned the forced labor inflicted upon the Haitians by the American occupationary forces and ex-

[6] Woodrow Wilson War Message, April 2, 1917.

pressed "chagrin at the improper or criminal conduct of some members of the Marine Corps." It reported that, besides Lieutenant Brokaw, another guilty officer was dead and a third had been dismissed. It then condemned the efforts of individuals and committees "to bring into general disrepute the whole American naval force in Haiti," instead of pointing out that the fault lay far less with the marines than with the Democratic Administration which placed them in circumstances the bloody outcome of which could be foretold by any person familiar with the history of colonization and imperialism.

President Hoover in 1930 sent a commission to Haiti, headed by W. Cameron Forbes, which included my warm friend, James Kerney, ever benevolent and ever desirous of doing justice. The commission highly praised the then commander of Haiti, Major General Russell, for his "wholehearted and single-minded devotion to the interests of Haiti as he conceived them [*sic*], his unremitting labor, and his patient and painstaking efforts to bring order out of chaos. . . ." But it found: "Race antipathies lie behind many of the difficulties which the United States military and civil forces have met in Haiti. . . . The failure of the occupation to understand the social problems of Haiti, its brusque attempt to plant democracy there by drill and harrow, its determination to set up a middle class however wise and necessary it may seem to Americans—all these explain why, in part, the high hopes of our good works have not been realized." Kerney wrote me on April 10, 1930: "The United States has spent approximately $23,000,000 in Haiti in the last fifteen years and has done nothing to fit the Haitians themselves for handling their affairs." Finally, in August, 1934, the American troops left Haiti and the republic was restored.

I look back upon these crusades on behalf of our Caribbean neighbors with unbounded satisfaction. They alone seem to me to have justified all the time and money I put into *The Nation.* I firmly believe that if we, and the *New Republic,* the Senators I have named, and such public-spirited men as Louis Marshall, George W. Kirchwey, Charles C. Burlingham and Professor

Zechariah Chafee of Harvard, had not appealed to the American conscience the occupation of the sister republics would still be going on. When I visited Haiti for the first time, in 1937, I sought some letters of introduction to people in Haiti only to find to my great surprise on my arrival there that my wife and I were received as guests of the republic and generously entertained by President Vincent. I had supposed that by that time all that *The Nation* had done for Haiti had long since been forgotten—basing my judgment on the length of time the average American remembers with gratitude any favors done him by a newspaper man.

In Nicaragua our military forces were the agents of New York bankers who had invested $15,638,700 in that little republic. We occupied it for the third time in 1912, again giving a false reason for our mission—that we were there to protect our Nicaraguan canal rights. By the time we began to evacuate, in 1932, our protection of the bankers' $15,648,700 had cost us $6,076,000. During all those years we killed hundreds, probably thousands, of the Nicaraguans and lost some precious American lives also—and never caught Sandino any more than Pershing caught Villa in Mexico. It was altogether a disgraceful and utterly uncivilized episode and like our other invasions was bitterly resented throughout Central and South America. *The Nation's* part in the Nicaraguan affair became dramatic when at the beginning of 1928, Carleton Beals, whom I had sent to Nicaragua to report the truth, reached Sandino. He was the first American and also the first bona fide newspaper correspondent to talk with Sandino after he took the field against the marines. Beals underwent considerable risk and hardship to reach Sandino's headquarters as he had to travel overland from Mexico City through Guatemala, San Salvador, and Honduras, and then halfway across Nicaragua. Naturally our marines were furious. They had been unable to locate Sandino but this American interloper held them up to ridicule and laughter by calmly walking into Sandino's camp. As Beals left him Sandino said to him: "Do you still think us bandits?" "You are as much bandits," Beals replied, "as Mr. Coolidge is a Bolshevik." "Tell your people," Sandino flashed back, "there may be bandits in Nicaragua but they are not necessarily Nicaraguans."

Sandino authorized Beals to make public the following terms, upon the acceptance of which he pledged himself to lay down his arms and never take them up again in any domestic struggle and never to accept any public post or salary: First, immediate withdrawal of our marines; second, the appointment of a provisional president, a civilian, who had never been President or a candidate for the Presidency and, third, the supervision of elections by Latin-Americans. These were certainly fair and moderate and just terms, but our marines continued to keep their puppet President in office and to hunt in vain for Sandino as if he were a wild animal. Beals's articles were brilliantly written and gave a most vivid picture of conditions and of the futility of the marines' occupation.

In 1920 *The Nation* undertook another venture which also brought down upon it and its editors a torrent of abuse. Doctor William J. L. M. Maloney, a brilliant young Irishman residing in New York, who had served as a surgeon with the British army and been severely wounded and, for a time crippled, at Gallipoli, suggested the formation of an Irish commission by *The Nation* to call attention to the dreadful situation in Ireland at that time because of the bloody rule of the Black and Tans. The indefensible acts of these hastily recruited British mercenaries had led to similar reprisals by the Sinn Feiners and all who thought the status of Ireland at that time an impossible one. In view of the subsequent establishment of the Irish Republic and the alteration of the relationship of Ireland to the narrow thread which now binds it to Great Britain, without any American protest or excitement, it is hard for me to understand why that Irish commission roused such passionate anger among the ruling classes, especially the "society people" in New York, Boston, and Washington. I suppose that we were then still so near to the war that it seemed an effort to reflect upon the British who were still our dearly beloved Allies. Even from warm British Liberal and Labor friends I received pained and shocked letters at this interference in a purely domestic British affair.

Long ago it was said: "One who molds the people's beliefs ought to have the wisdom of a sage and the inspiration of a prophet and the selflessness of a martyr." Still more is asked of the editor of today. In addition to the economic pressure upon him, his lot is made extraordinarily difficult because never in the history of the press has such all-embracing knowledge, such rapidity of judgment, such surety of vision been demanded of leader writers. From every corner of the world comes news, often of extreme significance in its bearing upon events fifteen thousand miles away. There is little or no time for careful consideration. When I joined *The Evening Post* we often found ourselves hard put to it in summer to discover subjects enough to fill the daily editorial page. Today, politics having become economics and economics politics, and the world standing on its head, a journal needs a large staff of specialists and expert legal advice to be had for the telephonic asking. Fortunate indeed were the Abolitionists and other early reformers, for their causes were simple and understandable of all men. Slavery presented a plain issue and yet that was threefold: it was an economic problem, a vital political problem, and, most important of all, a burning human problem. It has often seemed to me that one of the foremost reasons for the failure of nations to progress faster, and of the intelligent peace-loving minorities in all countries to make themselves potent, is that the multiplicity of reforms, of issues, and of news events the world over, bewilders the multitudes, just as it often dries up the sympathies and paralyzes the enthusiasms of the reading public. The human mind cannot react simultaneously to horrors in Ethiopia, slaughtering in Spain, and indescribable massacres in China. The wellsprings of human emotion are inevitably sucked dry.

Although the demands upon the editor are beyond any one man's powers today, the rewards of a free journalist remain of the greatest. We now know well what happens when the editors of a country all lose their freedom under government control. Of all the prostitutes in the world such editors are the most contemptible because they deliberately and knowingly lend themselves to misleading and poisoning the identical people their newspapers were meant to enlighten and inform. Under freedom, the education of the unchained editor never stops. He acquires knowledge every day, whether he wishes to do so or not. The very studying with expert eye of the day's dispatches adds to his store of facts, gives him a deeper background, and—if he has within him the possibility of growth—a wider and wiser perspective. That is one of the chief attractions and one of the great rewards of the profession—the joy of intense intellectual absorption in stimulating and exciting tasks which put the editor behind the scenes of politics and in touch with the men who work the governmental machinery.

I have repeatedly asserted that one who has had the joy of saying in print just what he thinks and feels, of breaking a lance on behalf of any cause in which his heart was enlisted, never relinquishes this privilege happily but always with deep regret. That privilege has been the great boon which inherited means bestowed upon me. They gave me the opportunity to be my own master; they enabled me to write as I pleased without ever having to wait upon another to get his orders. The ability to roam the world in order to see for myself the kinship of all peoples; the power to aid in some slight degree the suffering, the oppressed, the victims of prejudice, of injustice, and of cruelty everywhere; above all, the freedom to say one's soul is one's own: these are the sole justifications of wealth that I have been able to discover. In darkest days friends have asked me how I could still be optimistic—undaunted. I have replied: "Being one of the most fortunate of men I have no right to be other than one of the happiest."

Still it has been far from easy to retain one's courage when bitterness, hatred, and medieval cruelty have entered into men's hearts and brute force at this writing rules the world. Much of the great promise of my youth has been dispelled.

But a vital sustaining fact is that the world is witnessing the greatest, the most overwhelming, proof of the futility of force in the settlement of national and international problems and that fact millions are admitting. Never did it occur to me in 1917 that within twenty years the bulk of our countrymen would agree with us who declared that we could not win the war and that our entry into it was the greatest blunder in American history. But there the fact is; poll after poll tells the tale. Never could there be under heaven a more complete demonstration that you cannot shoot virtue or democracy into human beings nor kill sufficient to make the survivors forswear militarism and mass destruction. It is not because we can say with undeniable truth in 1939: "We told you in 1914-1918 what would be the exact outcome of the World War," that our spirits remain steadfast, but because of the proof that the principles of human conduct, the ethics, derived from Christ himself, which we championed, for which some of us were martyred in prison, have been completely justified.

We see that the prophecy that they who take up the sword shall perish by it may yet come true of the nations which sought in 1914-1918 to establish peace on earth by unparalleled human destruction. We are of the opinion that the present armament race, if it does not result in war, will do almost as much injury to the economies of the nations taking part in it as war itself; that the devoting of such large portions of a nation's revenues to the making of munitions opens a direct way to the regimented, totalitarian State. We believe that if the democracies seek to maintain themselves by war they will inevitably emerge from it as fascist States. But we think in all sincerity that sooner or later the madness of the present hour will pass and the nations realize that armaments offer no security whatever, but the reverse; that the road they are now following leads not to safety, nor glory, but to despair.

The list of our successful causes we are prone to forget because the unsuccessful press us on every side—yet it is there. We have seen kings and kaisers, who seemed beyond question enthroned, fall overnight. We have witnessed the disappearance of one prejudice after another, the breaking of social chain after chain, the removal of injustice after injustice. We have seen caste lose its hold even under the dictators. We have beheld the complete change in the status of women; a Hitler has tried in vain to restrict them to *Kinder* and *Küche*, though not to the church. Women can and do conquer as much of the industrial world as they desire and they have penetrated deeply into the professions in all enlightened countries. They have captured advanced positions in their assaults upon the archaic laws which have held them in bondage—with some redoubts still to be taken. Woman now knows that her body *is*, or should be, her own; that she has rights as to her children and, in some countries at least, owns her own property free from the control of her husband. The establishment of her right to vote, and to participate in government in as many countries as have yielded it, insures the inevitable spread of her political power when the present period of darkness has passed. Even in Turkey the veil, which had seemed perpetual, was abolished, with the fez, by one stroke of the dictator's pen; Turkish women have literally overleaped centuries in twenty years, and now find themselves almost in the status of their sex in progressive countries of the giaour.

Best of all has been the marvelous alteration in the relations of men and women, their having been freed, even in Germany, from the incredibly degrading assumption that if a young man and woman found themselves together they could have but one thought and aim—a relic of the age-old theory that the woman existed solely for the gratification of the man. With this has come the growing recognition, especially in the Anglo-Saxon countries where it was particularly needed, that in this field, as in relation to the liquor traffic, individuals cannot be made moral by law.

February 13, 1939

Dear White:

I was greatly pleased with your letter because I did not like that review as well as you did. I still feel that it was inadequate in its prase of your craftmanship. Looking back I think that was not only due to lack of space but to the compelling interest of your analysis of that extraordinary man. I enclose the latest characterization of him which has only just come to me—I did not see it when it was printed. Had I known it I think I should have been tempted to steal it for my book.

Yes, you are right, these public men are entirely two-sided. Wilson was another whose bad side, however, steadily took hold of him after he obtained power, and I am convinced that we shall be extremely fortunate if Roosevelt does not put us into war. I saw him a couple of weeks ago and he is in a state of complete jitters about Hitler and said the most fantastic things about what Hitler could and probably would do to South America. For example, that he had 1550 bombers who could fly from Berlin to Rio Janeiro in 26 hours, this at the very time that his chief admiral, Leahy, had testified that there isn't a bomber in existence that can fly 1400 miles loaded. An expert with whom I have talked about this idea of F.D.R.'s said he thought it was the craziest thing he had ever listened to. I think that F.D.R. now realizes that the New Deal is stopped, that he is not making a dent on the unemployment situation, that the present tremendous spending is doing very little to restore prosperity and that he has lost control of Congress. I found Ickes and all the lesser officials that I talked with quite despondent about the outlook for 1940 and the prospects for a continuation of liberal government.

February 28, 1939

General Rt. Hon. Jan C. Smuts,
Doornkloof, Irene,
Pretoria, South Africa.

My dear General:

I greatly appreciated hearing from you, and thank you warmly for your kindness to the Peers, who have written me with enthusiasm of your kind reception of them.

I have often wished that I could have the privilege of talking with you about the dreadful situation into which the world has blundred as a result of those fatal decisions made in 1919 in Paris.

This has been recalled to me during the past months because I have been writing my Memoirs, which are shortly to be published here and later in England, in which I have paid my respects to you--with criticism of your attitude on the color question. I hope that you will forgive me for that. The statement that you gave out in explanation of your signing the Peace Treaty has stood marvelously the test of time. You and Nansen stand out to me, among all the men of that period. I have never ceased to regret that the peace making could not have been in the hands of the Second Internationale at Berne, which I attended at the end of January 1919. If those men and women could have made the peace the World would never be where it is today. The outstanding fact about that gathering was that hardly a single man there, outside of Kurt Eisner of Bavaria, held office. They were free, untrammeled, and bore no responsibility for what happened in Europe.

But it is of no avail to look back. The Allies have now been vanquished without the firing of a shot by a man who could never rise above the rank of Lance Corporal in four years of fighting. I have been recalling Woodrow Wilson's proud boast on Armistice Day that German militarism was dead forever and the rhetorical question which ran to the effect who now would dare reestablish that government of autocracy and militarism. I simply cannot understand the base surrender of Chamberlain and Daladier. It is so short-sighted from their own point of view to have another dictatorship along the British life line of the Mediterranean. It is so hopelessly stupid and unrealistic that one wonders whether the thing will end with a most complete abasement of both England and France. Did you ever believe that we should live to see a country kill some two hundred British seamen without any protest from Great Britain? Yet that is what Franco did, and Nelson did not rise from his grave.

Our own situation here is extremely difficult. The President has done many fine things, but he is now losing his grip, and there is every indication that we shall have a conservative reaction at the next election. The fault lies with the President himself. He is a very bad administrator and coordinator, and many of the reform bills that he has put through are so badly drawn that the work must be done over again. Yet he still holds the imagination and loyalty of the great bulk of the workers, indeed of about 51 or 52% of the entire people. But we still have some ten million unemployed, and all the vast spending of the Government has not succeeded in bringing about restoration. Now he is terribly upset about the situation in Europe, and we shall be lucky if he does not put us into war, as men of power are so apt to do when they need something to distract attention from domestic failure. You will understand the terrible anxiety that I am under when I tell you that both of my sons are of military age and unmarried, and therefore would be among the first drafted. The simple truth is that the one man who is winning in the world today, conquering us all, is General Field Marshal Stupidity, as the Germans say, against whom the gods fight in vain. Well, I agree with you that we are well on our way to a new society. For us older men what comes is of less importance, but for the younger generation! Fortunately, in this country, the younger people are extraordinarily serene and hopeful, wiser than we were, and refusing to accept us at our own value, or to respect our damaged authority. For one thing, they have never known anything different than a world of wars and horrors, and they seem to expect little else.

My wife and I are going to England this summer, if conditions permit, and it would be a great joy indeed if we should find you there. Of course, I hear about you and of you constantly from the Clarks. If there are finer people than they, I do not know them.

With renewed thanks and warmest regards, as always,

Faithfully yours,

Issues and Men

BY OSWALD GARRISON VILLARD

WHATEVER may be the outcome of the battle in Congress over the neutrality question, it seems as if we might all rejoice in the independence displayed by Congress in dealing with this issue. I know that here I am touching on a difficult subject. On the one hand there is the belief that if a President and his party are to accomplish anything there must be party acceptance of the President's program and policies; on the other hand is the demand that the legislator shall not subordinate his conscience and his own beliefs to the will of the party leader. Where the happy medium lies is always a parliamentary problem.

To my mind the battle that we are witnessing redounds to the credit and honor of democracy and not to its discredit, as so many of my friends seem to believe. That Republican and Democratic Senators alike are thinking for themselves on this issue and voting without regard to party positions seems to me to constitute one of the triumphs of democracy, particularly welcome at this hour as a complete demonstration that we *are* a democracy and that our government is not dominated by one man, and I shall hold to this belief whether my side wins or loses. The only regrettable feature about the fight thus far is the assertion by the Administration that what it regards as the unfavorable vote in the House of Representatives has given aid and encouragement to Hitler and Mussolini; that the Administration has heard from abroad that Hitler and Mussolini are radiantly happy that complete power has not been given to the President to decide who shall buy munitions and military equipment from us if war comes abroad. That statement seems to me an unworthy one. When an Executive has to try to dragoon legislators into his way of thinking by assuring them that they are playing into the hands of foreign foes, he is very hard up. It reminds me too much of the way McKinley insisted that those of us who opposed our Philippine aggression were encouraging the Filipinos in their resistance to us and therefore we, and not he, were responsible for the loss of a good many valuable American lives.

Similarly, in the propaganda years before we were misled into the World War, we were constantly being told that we must not do this or we must not do that because if we did it would play into the hands of the Kaiser. In the former case we anti-imperialists refused to allow ourselves to be kept from telling the truth about what was going on in the Philippines, and our opposition to it, by the obviously biased statements which came from military men that they had found documents on Filipino dead citing anti-imperialist statements in the United States. So today the duty of a Senator or a Congressman on this question of neutrality is, in my judgment, to vote what he thinks will keep this country out of war without stopping to consider how Hitler or Mussolini may view his action. He has taken an oath to vote according to his conscience and his best beliefs. He did not swear to take the position he deemed right *unless* it might lead some foreign statesman to form a certain opinion. There is no such proviso in the oath.

As for the actual effect of our neutrality legislation upon the European dictators, I beg leave to doubt whether they are really concerned with what our Congress is doing. Common sense tells me that they are wrapped up in their own game and the threats to them of the so-called democracies. They are vastly more excited about the British efforts to form a close military alliance with Soviet Russia than they are with what our policy will be toward the belligerents if another war should come. Germany and Italy are staking everything they have on a quick and successful war, a sudden destruction of London and Paris. They know perfectly well that if it is a long war Britain and France will get supplies enough from somewhere to beat them; indeed, it may be that the Allies will defeat the dictators merely by staying on the defensive and just starving them out, as was done during the last struggle.

Speaking of the hopeful workings of democracy, as illustrated by what is happening in Washington as I write, let me call attention here to Arthur Garfield Hays's excellent book "Democracy Works." It has already been favorably reviewed in *The Nation,* but I want to stress its value because I meet so many people who are beginning to wobble about our democracy in their fear of Hitler and Mussolini, without realizing that in yielding to that fear they are giving victory to the dictators. I like Art Hays's clear, frank statements, his summary of what we have accomplished, his frank admissions of our faults and weakness, and his confession that he has no panaceas to set us right overnight. I welcome particularly his statement that our democracy is capable of working out new policies to fit new situations, and that is precisely what I think that our Congress is doing in regard to neutrality. The present neutrality law was epoch-making, for no other country ever undertook such a policy. I believe that it will stay—and go far toward keeping us out of war.

Issues and Men

BY OSWALD GARRISON VILLARD

SO WAR has come again, with all its horror and misery. We witness once more the breakdown of the theory that peace may be established or upheld by force. It seems as if that lesson ought to have been learned from the rise of the Germany of Hitler and the collapse of the Treaty of Versailles, with its complete demonstration of the futility of Wilson's proud assertion that German militarism was defeated for all time. Yet for four years now the so-called democracies have been engaged in a mad race against Italy and Germany to pile up enough armaments, call out enough soldiers, and construct enough airplanes to overawe the other fellow. Each side was certain that if it could only be strong enough to terrify the other side there would be no war. Military men the world over have declared—none more emphatically than our own—that if a country piled up arms enough nobody would dare attack it.

Now we see the inevitable outcome. We see the demonstration of the truth of Lord Baldwin's statement that if an armament race began again in Europe it would bring war and not peace. We see once more complete reliance on military force to solve the problems of nations and establish the perpetual peace for which all except the militarists and the Nazis long. Once more we shall be told that this is really the war to end war, and that if the Allies do not win it, democracy will be finished for all time, whereas if our friends win and properly make over Germany, the Kingdom of God will reign on earth. All this will greatly stir people, but it will be just as far from the truth as the similar slogans of 1914-18. The world will not be made over by force; nor will militarism be destroyed in this way; nor will Germany be purified of the unspeakable Nazis and their even more horrible doctrines. Salvation cannot come that way; it can only come with a general recognition that war must be done away with lest it do away with our modern civilization.

The unfortunate and discouraging thing about it all is that human beings will not learn. The surviving numbers of the three million Americans who were called on to fight for their country during the World War have forgotten the feeling of outrage with which they returned from France, realizing not only the horror but the futility of war, and have yielded to the renewed militaristic propaganda. They have again come to believe that the United States must squander boundless treasure upon preparations for war in order to keep a possible enemy from our shores, must so terrify him by piling up our might that he won't think of attempting to raid us. They will not be affected by the results abroad; they and many other deluded Americans will believe with our militarists that if England and France had only started their rearmament a few years earlier, Hitler would never have dared to attack. The folly of it screams to high heaven. Dictators are never awed by the amount of armament piled up by the other fellow. They are driven into war by the nature of their own government. When their economic situation becomes bad, they have to do something to distract the attention of the deluded people from what is happening at home. There must always be scapegoats, if not Jews and Communists and pacifists at home, then the nations which are trying to encircle the country. Against them the dictator gladly takes a chance to win all or lose all by one desperate throw of the dice, or else he imagines, like Louis Napoleon, that he can defeat the enemy even with smaller resources and a smaller army because of his greater cleverness and efficiency.

The outcome is now on the lap of the gods. It will be harder to know what is happening and where the truth lies than in the last war, for the censorship is bound to be more complete, more destructive of the truth. The practice of deceiving their own people and the world at large has been carried to greater lengths by the dictator states than ever before; it has become the normal course with them, not the abnormal. It will become the normal attitude of the democracies now that war is at hand. Hence it is the duty of all good Americans to take everything with a grain of salt and not to permit themselves to be stampeded by their natural desire to see England and France win. Of course we all want to see Germany defeated; on that issue the American people are united as never before, the only dissenters being the disloyal German-Americans of the Fritz Kuhn, German-American Bund type. But that does not mean that we should let ourselves be drawn into the struggle, that we should again become the catspaw of the Allies. If the war lasts long enough, we are only too likely, with the present President in th White House, to be drawn in again—perhaps by lure of what Mr. Roosevelt has called "fool's gol But if America keeps sane and really wishes to serve humanity and civilization, it will absolutely refuse to enter a European war again on any plea whatever.

Issues and Men

BY OSWALD GARRISON VILLARD

The United States and the War

London, September 8

TO ALL of us American correspondents over here it seems as if the United States were taking this war far more excitedly and tragically than the people of this country, whose amazing calm I have already stressed in this correspondence. We are told that various American admirals and generals have, as usual, burst into print to declare that the only lesson for the United States is that it must arm at once, still more. It must not be content with the $2,000,000,000 voted by the last Congress but must add another billion just as soon as Congress reassembles. There is certainly not the slightest reason for this unless the United States intends at once to enter the war. Actually, from the purely military point of view, the security of the United States has been increased by the outbreak of war. And the longer war continues, the safer the United States will be, if it ever was in danger. For with each day that passes, the exhaustion of the contestants will become greater—through the piling up their debts, the sinking of their ships, the ruination of their trade, the steady impoverishment and demoralization of their peoples.

But, I can hear the admirals and generals saying, what if Germany wins? Will not Hitler then promptly come over and conquer us and South America? The answer is emphatically no. Hitler has not enough ships in the German merchant marine to move even a hundred thousand men with the necessary arms and supplies, and his navy is insignificant in strength in comparison to our own. If he wins, he will have an exhausted people, half-starved and ready to rebel at any suggestion of further conquest. And all Europe will have to be held down by huge German forces. Hitler certainly will not be able to take over the British navy and use it against us. He will never get his hands on it; any more than the English got the German navy at the end of the last war.

If Hitler loses the war, there will have been removed the one country in Europe that could be considered an enemy to the United States. The only possible enemy remaining is Japan, which at the moment is so disgusted with Germany for betraying it that it will be less inclined than ever to start hostilities with us. And once more, for the hundredth time, I wish to stress the fact that Japan cannot physically make war upon us nor we upon Japan. On this page I have repeatedly quoted opinions of high naval and military officers to this effect, including the positive opinion of the commander-in-chief, Franklin D. Roosevelt himself, uttered when he was not in office and not in a position to indulge himself by playing with and commanding a huge fleet. Will somebody mention a third nation which might in any way menace the United States? Certainly both France and England will have been bled white if this war lasts any length of time; and Italy will never be in a position to menace the United States. And why should it? Its eyes are on Africa. It wishes to dominate the Mediterranean. It could no more attack the North American Colossus than it could undertake an expedition to the moon. Moreover, Mussolini, like Hitler, is a scoundrel who has to hold down his subjects by force.

No, the truth is that if reason and logic, and not sentiment, hysteria, and self-interest, were applied to this question, the American army and navy would take the lead in advocating disarmament—always provided that we are not going to be so insane as to go to war in Europe again. I am even hoping that my friends the editors of *The Nation* will now turn about and join me in exposing the needless waste of the terrific military expenditures we are now making, to say nothing of the steady militarization of the country. I hope they will also give a great deal of space to recording the very important movement under way over here, led by the London *Times*, the Manchester *Guardian*, the *New Statesman and Nation*, and many distinguished individuals, to bring about a prompt statement of Allied war aims. If these aims are just, they will be the best possible propaganda to drop within the German lines.

So far, every proposal that I have seen calls for the scrapping of the League of Nations and the building of a Federal State of Europe; it is believed that the continent cannot continue to live and develop in an atmosphere of crisis after crisis, war alarm after war alarm. In this the United States can help enormously, and it has already been suggested that President Roosevelt be asked to sound out neutral opinion everywhere on the form the new order should take. Here is a better opportunity for American leadership than any to be found in wasting more money on absolutely needless armaments. My fellow-countrymen can sleep in peace. They are not being got out of bed, as we are here, by the air-raid sirens, and there is not the slightest danger that they ever will be. They are not awaiting the inevitable destruction of life and property in the city in which they live. Let them be calm, and work for a new world and a decent one.

Issues and Men

BY OSWALD GARRISON VILLARD

England, America, and the War

London, September 15

WHAT of the attitude of England to the United States now that war has come? Well, there is thus far a most commendable absence of any visible effort to propagandize. Sir Frederick Whyte has been appointed head of the American division of the Ministry of Information, which has been established in the magnificent new Senate Building of the University of London, but I am assured on high authority that there is not the slightest intention this time to send over a group of paid propagandists to convert the Americans. This decision is due in part, I believe, to the realization that it is totally unnecessary to do any converting, that the American people, with the exception of a few disloyal German-Americans, are solidly anti-Hitler, and in part to the realization that Americans have not forgotten the British sins in the last war. Certainly the only people who can prejudice the Allied cause in the United States this time are the Allies themselves. It would be the height of wisdom for the British government to announce that no paid propagandists will be sent over; if it does not, veteran British lecturers, like S. K. Ratcliffe, who have been interpreters and never propagandists, may find that their activities are misunderstood.

It is even more important that the English should not feed us atrocity stories this time. Some horrible stories of the effects of the war upon Poland are naturally coming through—justified and truthful reports I believe, for you cannot wage war with the present high-powered killing weapons, airplanes, and such, without laying everything waste. But we most assuredly need no false Lord Bryce reports, no yarns of crucified Canadian soldiers, of babies with their hands cut off and nuns with their breasts removed, to make us oppose Hitlerism and give our sympathies to the Allies. If anything of the kind should start, it would become a serious boomerang. What the ministry should send over to the United States, if it sends anything, is facts. It ought to give all possible help to the American correspondents here to get the truth—as much as may be printed without injuring the military situation. It ought to do everything in its power to make the American, as well as the British, public believe that the British bulletins and communiqués are absolutely true and not deliberately falsified as were the figures of shipping losses in the last war. I am happy to say there is every evidence thus far of a desire to do this very thing. At least, the government has not concealed the unhappy fact that it has had very serious losses of ships since the war began, and that they are continuing.

It goes without saying that the people here hope that the President will have his way with Congress, and bring about the amendment of the neutrality law; and I have no doubt that many of them are praying that if the worst comes to the worst we will again send an army. Yet many say to me frankly that if they were Americans they would be in favor of the law as it stands, and against American intervention over here. I had an interesting talk with a taxi driver in Salisbury a few days ago, a veteran of the last war who is awaiting his call as a member of the reserve to go again. Obviously of superior education—he said that the last war had ruined his chance of becoming a mechanical engineer—he asked if we were not coming in to help. When I asked him if he thought we Americans ought to underwrite the blunders and stupidities of British diplomacy every twenty-five years, and if in that case he didn't think we ought to have some say about the formulation of British foreign policy, he replied, "Of course you should." When I have half jestingly suggested this to people of importance in this country, and asked whether we should not have at least two ministers in the British Cabinet, to my surprise the suggestion has been taken rather seriously.

Similarly, when I have pointed out that the isolationists truly believe that the best way for the United States to help the Allies and the world is to keep out of the present struggle and to remain a great reservoir of democracy and of material means with which to rebuild the lost continent of Europe, they have unanimously declared that that was an entirely defensible point of view. I am more than ever of this opinion, for I see British democracy vanishing day by day. Parliament is rapidly becoming a group which meets once a week to hear a report from the Prime Minister of the progress of the war, to listen to criticisms from the two opposition leaders, Greenwood and Sinclair, and to ask a few questions. The power has gone to the Cabinet and the Prime Minister, and what has been done here to make over industrial life in the last two weeks would make startling reading. In 1914 "Business as usual" was the slogan. This time the government has played havoc with numerous industries, the reason or the excuse being that the danger of air raids necessitates it. Well, any war would bring changes. How radical they are going to be this time depends on the length of the struggle.

Issues and Men

BY OSWALD GARRISON VILLARD

London, September 25

WHATEVER else the war has done in its first three weeks, it has wiped out the last traces of Woodrow Wilson's interference in European affairs. He who boasted that he knew how to get peace and that his mind had only contempt for the pacifists because they did not know how to get it, and who remarked on the first Armistice Day that no one would dare to say that German militarism, then in the dust, would ever be resurrected, should have lived to see what is left of the elaborate structure raised at Versailles. Poland has followed Czechoslovakia into the discard; the red flag of communism has advanced halfway across Poland—that red flag round which the Big Four at Paris threw their "sanitary cordon of bayonets." Germany has now torn up the last bit of the Treaty of Versailles. Not even the poor Tyrolese, who by fiat of Woodrow Wilson were wrested from Austria and delivered over to Italy, are where he placed them—at least, Mussolini is supposed to be expelling them from their historic homeland and settling them in Austria. The League of Nations is so dead that in all the discussion of the new war aims going on in the British press no one has even suggested that it be revived. Yet Wilson considered it his cleverest stroke that he insisted on putting the Covenant of the League into the treaty of peace in order to insure its adoption and its continuity. Some historians of the future may portray Wilson as the leader of the first attempt to organize the world, but they will always describe it as a completely unsuccessful experiment, which lasted only twenty years.

For this sad outcome the Allies bear the heaviest share of responsibility. The French sabotaged the treaty when they marched into the Ruhr, and the British calmly violated it when they made their naval bargain with Hitler in 1934, for which they are now paying a terrible price in treasure, ships, and men daily being sunk by the submarines Sir John Simon gave the Germans permission to build. Of course one still hears here that it is America's fault that the vision Wilson held has come to naught. That veteran journalist, A. G. Gardiner, writing in an evening newspaper, brings out the old charge that we wrecked the League by not taking part in it. This is based upon the amazing assumption that if we had joined the League it would have been perfect. We and England, the argument runs, would have dominated it and the world and invariably done the right thing—kept the French in check, prevented their going into the Ruhr, spanked Mussolini for killing the orphans of Corfu, and chased the Poles out of Vilna. It is only necessary to state it to show how preposterous it is. Can any sane American imagine Harding, or Coolidge, or Hoover sending liberal, enlightened, internationally minded statesmen to represent the United States? They would certainly have sent men of the type of Charlie Dawes, Andrew Mellon, Frank Kellogg, and the weak and ineffective Norman Davis, and it is impossible to believe that any of them could have measured up to the task.

Now that Hitler has finally wrecked the whole edifice of Versailles, what of the future? This brings us squarely to the question of the war aims. Mr. Chamberlain has just given his word that the British government is committed to the formation of a stable international system having as its object the prevention of war and the just settlement of international disputes by peaceful means. So far so good. But this must be supplemented by detailed proposals, and before very long, if the neutral nations and Germany are to be convinced that England has learned the lesson of the failure of 1919. If a peace offer does come from Germany, the English and the French must be ready with something more than a flat refusal to consider it. That will be their opportunity to make a real proposal for the definite reorganization of Europe.

Two striking facts emerge from the discussion of war aims. The first is that Europe cannot continue to live as it has been living, going from one alarm and one crisis to another, and carrying a burden of armaments which will be financially impossible after the debts of this war have been piled on top of the unliquidated debts of the last. Secondly, one hears on all sides the belief that Europe must be reorganized on federal lines. For this idea, great credit must be given to Clarence Streit. By no means all who have read his book favor his proposals, which are full of dubious points. His great achievement is that he has made the thinking people of England read and discuss and ponder his demand that the nations be organized this time, not on a national basis, but after the example of Switzerland, the United States, and the Soviet Union. I am happy to record the fact that several officials of the government with whom I have talked are keenly aware of the absolute necessity of a sane new order; they even see that there must be economic disarmament and an entirely new deal as to colonies. How far up that feeling extends I do not know. That it exists anywhere in government circles is most encouraging.

Issues and Men

BY OSWALD GARRISON VILLARD

London, September 19

NOW that the full measure—or very nearly so—of Stalin's and Molotov's perfidy has been revealed, it must be pointed out that they did much more than stab Poland in the back and abandon the anti-dictator front. They dealt a deadly blow to their Communist movement, and to its friends at home and abroad, of which they will not hear the last for many a year. Many persons besides myself, without being themselves Communists, have wanted to see the Russian experiment tried out fairly and squarely. When I testified before the New York State Reconstruction Commission in 1919, I said that it seemed to me most fortunate that the Russians were ready to try a system which has been urged for mankind ever since human beings abandoned their communistic method of living in the earliest ages. I came back from Russia in 1929 deeply impressed by the extraordinary progress made in industry, on the farm, and in every walk of life, and thought it thrilling that a state was trying primarily to serve its workers and not its privileged classes. Ever since then my faith that communism was being fairly tried out in Russia has been waning. I could not believe that a government based on the ruthless dictatorship of one man, that had to be kept going by wholesale purges and by the starvation of millions of people, as in the Ukraine, could give communism the chance to show whether or not it was the way out of our decaying capitalism.

Now I am hopeless of any good coming out of the experiment. Three months after Molotov said that Russia was not going to desert the anti-aggressor front it joined the aggressors, and used the precise language of Hitler and Goebbels in so doing. The *Pravda* editorial which gave the show away might have been written in Berlin, or even lifted bodily out of one of Hitler's tirades. Today Molotov is congratulating the army on its "heroic deeds," these being its valiant march over a prostrate neighbor with whom Russia had signed a non-aggression pact. After all those fine speeches that Litvinov used to make at Geneva, speeches that I and *The Nation* frequently called the only civilized utterances in international politics, the Russian government has revealed itself as a common despoiler and robber. If any group in America again puts out a statement urging me and the rest of their fellow-citizens to think differently of the Russian dictatorship than of the others, I shall refuse most emphatically. It is not only just as bloody as the others, but just as crooked, treacherous, and criminal. At the very time that Litvinov was demanding that the League of Nations enforce sanctions against Mussolini for making war on Ethiopia, some of us called attention to the fact that the Russian government was calmly lining its pockets by selling gasoline to Italy for its planes and tanks. That, we now know, was the true measure of its sincerity and honesty.

I have heard many pacifist-minded Americans defend the great Russian armies on the ground that Russia had suffered so much from the military intervention without declaration of war of the United States, Japan, Great Britain, and the others that it was justified in preparing to defend its frontiers, especially after the appearance of Hitler. But when the Russian army began to number millions, I for one began to have my doubts, though it was only to be told that this great army was the one force that could possibly save democratic Europe from domination by Hitler and Mussolini. When the undeclared war in Mongolia began several years ago I found myself extremely disturbed, but I was assured that the guilt was solely Japan's and, moreover, that the diversion was helping China and so helping democracy. Then, after having thrown away heaven knows how many Russian lives, Stalin made peace with Japan, and abandoned China. And now he is rescuing the Polish minorities and forcing Latvia and Estonia to give him whatever of theirs he wants. Soon, I suppose, he will be taking Bessarabia away from Rumania. If Hitler wins the war, he and Stalin will divide the swag in Rumania precisely as they have done in Poland.

It is not certain to what extent Stalin has damaged the military prospects of the Allies. The British government is undoubtedly worried about what he actually proposes to supply Hitler. Some people think he will give a great deal of help; others are sure that he can deliver very little, and will ask a high price for whatever he contributes. One military expert with whom I have just talked thinks that Hitler, knowing the character of his fellow-criminal in Poland, will have to leave at least forty divisions there to prevent the Bear from walking in on him and to hold down the Poles. Stalin has four million men in arms! But whatever happens now, Stalin, I repeat, has dealt his cause a blow from which it will not recover for generations and has greatly strengthened the enemies of communism the world over.

[*Mr. Villard is now in Germany, but will not send us any articles on conditions there until he is outside the country.*—EDITORS THE NATION.]

Issues and Men

BY OSWALD GARRISON VILLARD

The Hague, November 13, by Cable

THE grave state of anxiety which has dominated official diplomatic circles here has been modified somewhat by the receipt of a very polite message from Hitler that he will personally examine the mediation proposal of Queen Wilhelmina and King Leopold and answer soon. It is not believed that he would reply in these terms if he were contemplating an immediate move against the Dutch. This may seem a slight reason for the sudden optimism, but there is in fact a great sense of relief. According to one story going the rounds, to which considerable credence is attached, the Belgian King was asked by a very prominent German what would be the attitude of Belgium if Hitler should insist on access to the sea at or near Flushing in southern Holland. The King, it is said, went at once to The Hague, and the joint offer of mediation resulted. Another story, confirmed by an important banking source, asserts that Hitler personally favored an attempt to obtain control of the Dutch coast but was held off by the Foreign Office, which feared the effect on neutral opinion.

The German press campaign attacking Holland for not opposing British interference with its shipping and declaring that their inaction made the Dutch unneutral really alarmed the diplomatic corps by its resemblance to the press attacks on the Czechs and Poles. Fortunately the attack died down suddenly, but the belief persisted that Holland might suddenly face an ultimatum. All this led Mr. Gordon, the American Minister, to publish again Hull's appeal to all Americans to leave the country unless their stay was absolutely essential. Additional cause for alarm has been found in the German shooting outrage at Venlo on the border, the violations of Belgian territory by German fliers, and the heavy concentration of German troops on the frontier—130,000 between Gladbach and Aachen. At the request of the government these facts have been carefully concealed by the press. Only one story has appeared so far, in one daily, giving the German denial that any invasion was threatened. Hence the cafes are crowded with people who are gay and happy—in marked contrast to those I have just seen in Germany.

After the Munich explosion some observers were of the belief that Hitler might need quick foreign action somewhere to distract attention from domestic conditions. This theory I am convinced is false. I believe the Foreign Office officials in Berlin were sincere when they assured me that they had no desire to arouse Washington, other neutrals, and world opinion by repeating the errors of the last war. Incidentally they insisted they were not guilty of the Athenia sinking; strictest orders had been given to avoid another Lusitania. Any threat of America's entering the war would further depress the spirit of the Germans, which is already so low that an officer on leave from the front remarked publicly in Frankfort, "The spirit of the people is devastating at home; it is much better at the front." Again, while it was easy to put over atrocity stories about the Poles, it would be harder to arouse hate against the Dutch, who are quite inoffensive and cannot be blamed for not wanting to antagonize the British, who might completely stop Dutch shipping. An attack on Holland would convince many Germans of the truth of Allied assertions that Hitler menaces all small nations in Europe. Hence it is my belief that Hitler will not attempt it unless he later finds himself in great straits. The complete confidence of the German military that they can smash England completely by next spring will also make against hasty action now. The only possible excuse that would go down with the German public would be absolute military necessity, as in the case of the Russian alliance, regarding which many if not most important business men believe the price paid was too high. Many workers are uneasy over Polish events and the treatment of Jews. The rape of Holland now would solidify their antagonism.

There is still another source of uneasiness here in Holland. It is feared that the Dutch colonies, which are rich and prosperous, are great temptations to Hitler. He could not seize them now even if he invaded Holland, but if the war ended in a stalemate or in his victory he could then take them, thus getting better possessions than the pre-war German colonies. This may seem fantastic in New York, but it is a true measure of the state of Dutch nerves before the joint peace move.

The Low Countries are certainly in a worse fix than they were in the last war, and they believe themselves entitled to be heard on stopping the war. They are convinced a long war means ruin for all, not the freeing of Europe from Hitlerism; the only victors would be the Communists. This fear is shared by many diplomats. Today the situation probably boils down to whether three men can devise a face-saving method of starting conversations without appearing weak or beaten. On that question may hang the lives of millions of human beings —even the survival of European civilization.

Issues and Men

BY OSWALD GARRISON VILLARD

Collective Security Must Come

London, December 1

ONE of the few encouraging facts about the war situation is that here in England one finds universal recognition of the fact that if the Allies win there must be a new order and collective security in Europe if the Continent's civilization is to survive. The man in the street or perhaps one sitting next to you on the bus tells you that Europe cannot stand a continuance of the armed peace of the last five years. Only yesterday I was astounded to have an American army officer say to me that collective security must and will come because "the soldier has become too costly for any country to support." I had never expected to hear those words from an active officer of our army, but he assures me that he has been preaching the doctrine of collective security for some years. Reams and reams of white paper are being covered here by people writing on peace terms and on how Europe should be rebuilt if it survives this war. And there seems to be a pretty general recognition that if the nations will not or cannot outlaw war, they must find a collective way of guaranteeing peace. Preparedness for such wars as this one costs more than any nation can afford.

Ever since my return from Germany I have been eagerly asked what the surviving liberal, anti-Hitler forces there are thinking about the future. I have had to reply that I never heard the subject of a reorganization of Europe mentioned. The people of this stripe I talked with were all too much absorbed in the war and their actual living conditions to have time to think about what might come after. As for France, I hear that the one idea there—and my information comes from very important sources—is to deal with Germany, if the Allies win, in such a way that France will never again be invaded from the east. That is the collective security that they want. They are saying that this is the third attack since 1870 and that if they win, it will be the last. This time they are going to be thorough about it. They will take the left bank of the Rhine, will favor splitting Germany up into at least two states, one Protestant and one Catholic, and see that this time Germany's disarmament is permanent. This, by the way, is in accord with what one German I had just met said to me abruptly as we were parting: "The only way to deal with us Germans is to disarm us. Give us guns and we shall always be a menace because we like to be soldiers and to fight." Plainly, it will be extremely difficult to hold the French in line for anything else than a peace which they trust will make forever impossible the domination of Europe by German armies. They have learned nothing and forgotten much!

Here there continues to be a great deal of favorable discussion of Clarence Streit's plan for the federalization of Europe. It is admitted that the League of Nations is dead save for its Labor Office and its humanitarian activities. So the solution is rightly sought in a new machinery which will avoid the errors of the League, foredoomed to failure as it was by being tied up to that body of death, the Treaty of Versailles. The merit of Mr. Streit's proposal is in its suggestion for a federal union in which all nations would have equal status; its weaknesses and faults are many—he does not even define democracy before using the word as a touchstone in picking out the states which he would have lead the way to a federal union of the world. But he must be given credit for having made people everywhere think about a new world order.

The difficulties in the way of collective security are endless, as the French attitude shows. The other day when I was urging one more restatement of the Allied peace aims for the purpose of encouraging the peace movement within Germany a British officer said to me, "But there are great difficulties in doing that." I replied, "I am aware of them all and probably know more about it than you do since I have just been on the other side of the fence in Germany. But is it not the task and duty of your statesmen to find the way out? Who else will, just now?" He admitted that I was right. What frightens one over here is the conviction that it will be harder to get a wise and just peace than in 1919 because there were no such madmen as Hitler, Stalin, and Mussolini to deal with then, and no such hostile economic systems to reconcile. But what is even more alarming is the dearth of statesmen equal to the tasks which will confront the peace-makers if the Allies win. One almost regrets that there is no one with the forcefulness of Clemenceau or the adroitness of Lloyd George as one scans the horizon for anybody who gives promise of having the stature needed for the superhuman job ahead. But then the realization comes again that for all their ability these leaders of 1914 were the architects of our present misery. The only comfort, I repeat, is that everybody I have met here is aware that the Europe of 1934 to August, 1939, cannot be reestablished when the war ends.

Issues and Men

BY OSWALD GARRISON VILLARD

The Latest Anti-Jewish Horror

The Hague, November 20

THE flood of war news has I fear blanketed the latest developments in Hitler's crusade against the Jews. I refer, of course, to his determination to jam them all into a small piece of Polish territory which is to be called a "Jewish State," but which is to be nothing else than a huge concentration camp and charnel house. During my stay of nearly four weeks in Germany I could obtain very little news about this beyond the fact that heart-breaking deportations were going on in Austria and Moravia. Now some of the facts have leaked out here, but the German people will doubtless be kept in ignorance of them—as usual. Hitler himself seems now obsessed with the idea of moving minorities. He first undertook to move the Tyrolese Germans, with Mussolini's blessing. His "recall" of the Baltic Germans was the next step. Now comes his decision to dump all the Jews possible into a territory at present described as "from Nisko on the River San to a point southwest of Lublin." The deportations began in the Czech Protectorate, from which 150,000 were to be moved by October 17, and are to be continued by the removal of 65,000 from Vienna, 30,000 from Posen, and 200,000 from the rest of the Reich—all that remain of the 600,000 living in Germany when Hitler the Fiendish took charge.

Lest anybody ask at this point why it is not a good thing to set up a Jewish state where the Jews can be safe and by themselves, let me say that before these people are moved they are to be robbed of all their wealth except 300 marks, and they will not be allowed to take any furniture or equipment of any kind with them. Into a space of eighty by one hundred kilometers 1,950,000 people are to be jammed, without working capital, without tools or habitations, unable to do business even with the contiguous territories. How they will live until their first crops or how they will till the land without tools or animals is not explained.

One has only to contrast these barbarities with the way that the German papers say the returning Balts are being received to realize that they are unnecessary and deliberate. The Balts are welcomed by the Red Cross, by special reception committees, by government officials; they are taken with marvelous efficiency to homes all in readiness for them. They are to be paid for the property they left behind and are to be given the necessary tools and implements and working capital to start life anew. But the Jews are treated literally as no German would be allowed under the law to treat a dumb animal. I have seen a letter sent by an Aryan German from a town in Moravia to an American official begging him to get the American government to intervene. He said that he was a loyal German but that he could no longer remain silent. He declared that a train of cattle cars—the Jews are allowed no others—had stood for twelve hours in the station of his town. The weather was cold, and there was of course no heat. There were no toilet facilities. No food or water was provided. He said that the moans and groans of the older people could be heard blocks away. German laws forbid such treatment of cows or swine or dogs.

Meanwhile, the remaining German Jews sit around waiting for their turn in the cattle cars. In Vienna, the Dutch papers report, eighty-two Jews, thirty-six of them women, have committed suicide in the last two weeks. That is what Hitler likes to hear. He can steal everything they leave. He would have Jews murdered out of hand, I have no doubt, if he dared. It would certainly be more merciful if he did. I have no means of knowing how much of this news has reached America or what can be done about it there, but I am sure that a tremendous wave of denunciation from non-Jews, led, let us say, by the Quakers, might help, because the Germans are particularly anxious just now not to draw America into the war. I recall those wonderful mass-meetings at the time of the Kishinev massacres in Russia, one in Carnegie Hall with ex-President Cleveland speaking. If ever a similar outcry were called for, it is now.

One other piece of bad news I must give. It is widely believed in responsible circles in Germany that part of the bargain with Stalin calls for the application of the Nürnberg laws to Russian Jews, and that this will be done within six months from the signing of the pact. It is not thought that such laws will actually be put on the statute books. Stalin will simply give certain orders; that will be enough.

[*Since this article was written, a report has been received from the Netherlands that 40,000 Jews have already been herded into the "Jewish State" under such shocking conditions that typhus is rampant. A later dispatch, from Paris, indicates that the plan for the Lublin "reservation" has been abandoned in favor of a larger reservation of mixed Polish and Jewish population.*—EDITORS THE NATION.]

WITHIN GERMANY

With an Epilogue
ENGLAND AT WAR

BY

OSWALD GARRISON VILLARD

D. APPLETON-CENTURY COMPANY
INCORPORATED
NEW YORK LONDON
1940

This book was published in Great Britain under the title *Inside Germany*

PRINTED IN THE UNITED STATES OF AMERICA

PROLOGUE

INSIDE GERMANY TODAY

I must say frankly that the Germany I have liked so long seemed to me utterly unhappy and depressed. I found none of the elation and enthusiasm which marked Germany's entry into the War of 1914, only the profoundest wish that the war might end soon.

Prominent Nazi officials, notably Karl Hermann Frank,

Deputy to the Protector of the Czech Protectorate, Baron von Neurath assured me that the people were as one man behind the Fuehrer, and would die for him and the country, but I do not hesitate to say from my own experience that this is nonsense. My trouble in Germany was to find men outside the Army and official circles who were a hundred per cent Nazi. The others were of all shades of opinion, and many of them were wholly anti-Nazi. Workmen spoke out against Hitler and his Government with a frankness that astounded me—and terrified me for their safety. I found only one or two who really wanted to fight for Hitler in this war. Some even declared that the ruling group in Germany had made the war for their own purposes.

Undoubtedly the Germans are patriotic and will fight in defence of their country. Undoubtedly many of the younger men in the Army and Navy are eager for the war and believe the anti-British propaganda, but the bulk of the people look and seem worn, tired, depressed, and in some cases, hopeless. Never, I am sure, did a people go less willingly into war, and never was one started with so little zeal for it on the part of the older people and the bulk of the workers.

The German people appear depressed because they lack all freedom, because the older ones remember the sufferings of the last war, and groan when the food cards reappear, because they long for peace and quiet and are utterly tired of living from one crisis, one alarm, one war to another. They are unhappy because they are confused. One day they are told that they must send their sons to die

in Spain, fighting against the Bolsheviks, and next they learn that their saviour is that scum of the earth, Stalin. One moment they were told by Hitler that the Poles were a great people, and that the relations between them and the Germans were entirely satisfactory, and the next minute they were asked to send their sons against such vile people, such murderers as these horrible Poles. Not one moment of quiet or freedom from the fear of war have they had since the Nazis came to power.

Most of the people I met were utterly opposed to the robbing and rotting out and driving out of the Jews. It is true that they do not speak out against this as they should, but how can they when the Government has the power to commit them to prison or concentration camps without trial or even an accusation, and to keep them there indefinitely? *"Wir sind nur Sklaven"* (we are nothing but slaves), said more than one to me, and yet these *Sklaven* are expected to further the imperialistic aims of Hitler and his inner group, to conquer England so that Hitler may dominate the world.

Well, after having been in both England and Germany I feel certain that Germany will not win this war. Freedom, human decency and dignity forbid it. Humanity and justice and morality forbid it. I am no churchman, but I believe profoundly that there are morals and ethical values and imponderables, and that the side on which these are to be found will win in the long run. This may sound idealistic, perhaps even "churchy," but it is my honest belief.

It is a great relief and happiness to be back in England, to find a free, cheerful, determined, and conscience-clear people. I could not say that they are happy, because no people can be happy in modern war, but one does see bright and cheerful faces, and I am astounded again, as I was before I went to Germany, at the unanimity of sentiment, the quiet calm determination to see the thing through to the bitter end, that Europe again may have peace and quiet, and an orderly way of life, and responsible governments that will abide by the laws of nations and of all common morality.

The English have no doubt about the outcome, but they are not boastful, nor vainglorious, and they are not, like the military in Berlin, fixing the exact hour when they are going to smash their enemies. They know that they may be in for a very bad time indeed, but they are ready to face it without flinching. They are not terrified—not by all the sinkings that are now taking place, nor by the German planes that occasionally fly over parts of Great Britain. I found myself constantly saying, "These are a very great people. They have made mistakes in the past; like other nations they have often done injustice to other peoples; but at heart the Englishman and Englishwoman is sound, and that is what makes the atmosphere of London today so fine and makes me so confident."

I wish I could tell you exactly in words how great the difference is between the two countries at this moment. There is so much more life in the streets here. People do not sit in the cafés looking utterly despondent. One does hear laughter, and see the soldiers' good fellowship, camaraderie, even a readiness to joke, which I missed entirely in Germany.

Finally, I want to assure my German listeners that I have *not* heard *one* single Englishman say that he wished to dismember Germany or that he thought the German people ought to be crushed and humbled. Nothing of the kind. The British people are not hating the German people. They have no quarrel with the mass of Germany. Their quarrel is with her present ruler. They do not wish to deprive Germany of her place in the sun. They are not thinking in imperialistic terms. They are not seeking the domination of Europe, and they do not believe that their Government is. They want a peaceful and ordered world and for that idea they and their soldiers are willing to die. And you in Germany who may be listening to me will, I hope, take these words of mine to heart, for freedom, democracy, the liberty of the individual, and the dignity of every human being are still the finest, most vital and most important things in the world.

I did not find one man or woman outside official and military circles who defended the treaty and alliance with the Russians. Army men merely said: "It was an absolute military necessity, so what is the use of discussing it? We could not fight this war with an enemy in our rear." That was also the reason why Poland had to be smashed completely before hostilities with England and France began.

These officers did not deny that if war came with Russia the Kremlin's possession of half of Poland and of the air and naval bases ceded by the Baltic States would cost the Germans dear. They merely insisted that the alliance with Stalin was a necessary evil.

Foreign Office officials also defended it on the same ground, but one of them said that, after all, the Bolsheviks and the Nazis had many common aims. Men in private life did not conceal their alarm and wondered what secret terms were contained in the treaty. Few had heard that 6,000 Communists had been released from prisons and camps by Hitler after the treaty was signed, for the news of that was not published.

Berliners, who are renowned for their wit, now speak of Stalin as *unser neues, liebes Vetterchen* ("our new, dear little cousin"). In Frankfort there was quiet amusement that Hitler's *Mein Kampf* has been ordered to be withheld

from circulation by the public libraries there—until a new edition, with all scurrilous references to Russia and the Bolsheviks withdrawn, is published. The menace of Communism, now widely felt, is not, however, regarded as a laughing matter—far from it. Hitler's anti-Bolshevik propaganda has done its work too well to be forgotten by order over night.

Many people said to me that instead of fighting one another, England and Germany should be presenting a united front to the Russians. There is the gravest doubt as to the amount of materials and food that the Russians will be able to furnish. I heard of one official, charged with inaugurating trade under the new treaty, who was already in despair at the slowness and bad business methods of the people with whom he had to deal. That the drift to Communism is unmistakable and rapid and would have come had there been no treaty will be shown later.

As for the food conditions I did not meet one person, whether Nazi or bitterly anti-Nazi or in-between, who was not certain that the Germans could hold out for two or more years, and this was also the opinion of American and other neutral observers. They will suffer and complain bitterly, but they will have enough food to exist on—if rationing works out as promised—unless something unexpected happens.

I was astonished at the unanimity of this sentiment and the forcefulness with which it was argued by men who were praying for the downfall of Hitler and his whole crowd.

VII

WHAT may prove to be the final act of the incredibly brutal and cruel tragedy of the Jews in his power which Adolf Hitler has staged is now going on, and without receiving the attention of the world as it should, because of the pressure of war news. With practically no publication of the plan in the German newspapers, Adolf Hitler is going ahead with the creation of a so-called Jewish State, located in Poland, near Nisko, on the San, south-west of Lublin. A stretch of land, about eighty by one hundred kilometres in size, has been set aside, enclosed by a barbed-wire fence, and only Jews will be allowed to live therein. Into this small territory are to be jammed no less than 1,940,000 Jews. What is to become of the Poles who have inhabited this region is not stated, but it is said in various quarters that the land is exceptionally poor. Whether it is poor or rich, this mass migration by force has been begun now, in the dead of winter, and in a manner that cannot be interpreted as anything else than a determination to create, not a Jewish State, but a most horrible concentration camp, which can certainly become nothing else than a habitation of death.

For these unfortunate people are forbidden to leave with more than 300 marks. They are permitted to take with them only such handbags as they can carry. All the

rest of their belongings, the furniture in their apartments, the rest of their means, their jewels—everything is stolen from them as is the usual custom of these men who declare that they belong to the purest and noblest strain of humanity the world has yet seen. No preparations are made for the reception of the exiles; they are simply to be dumped down and left to shift for themselves. If they cannot find shelter in the deserted homes of the evacuated Polish peasantry, why, they can freeze to death, or build new homes, without means, without materials, without tools, without anything. How they are to subsist when they get there no one knows. How those who survive until the spring will obtain seeds and farming tools and cattle and horses no one can imagine. It is impossible to conceive any more barbarous cruelty—and that cruelty is deliberately calculated.

One has only to look at what Hitler is doing—if indeed one can believe the reports—for the 800,000 people who have chosen to migrate from the Baltic States to Germany, to see what could be done if decency and fair play ruled instead of the purest sadism. These Balts are being moved in fine steamers and met by reception committees and representatives of the Red Cross; are given excellent temporary accommodation if their permanent homes are not ready for them. The German papers have been outspoken in admiration of German efficiency and speed in moving so many thousands of people in the middle of a great war. It has been stated that these newly arrived Germans will be given all the necessary equipment to start life anew, and that eventually they are to be reimbursed for all the property they have left behind (there seems to be some hitch, as the negotiations with Esthonia for a quick liquidation of the emigrants' property are reported to have ended in a deadlock). For the Jews nothing is to be done. Behind the barbed-wire fence they are to live or die under circumstances which would not be permitted in any civilized country if the victims were cattle or dogs.

Not only are 1,500,000 Polish Jews to be confined there, but to them are to be added 150,000 from the Czech Protectorate, 65,000 Viennese, 30,000 from Posen and West Prussia, and 200,000 from the rest of the Reich. This means that every remaining Jew in Berlin and elsewhere will be forcibly interned. People of the greatest refinement and culture are to meet the same fate as the Polish Jewish peasants. Perhaps these figures for the Reich are a little too high, for according to the latest report of the Reich Association of German Jews, as published in the *Rotterdamsche Courant,* the number of Jews in Germany has fallen from 500,000 in 1933 to 185,000 on October 1st, 1939. Of these, some 77,000 are men, and 108,000 women, of whom no fewer than 95,000 reside in Berlin. A majority of the whole number is totally without means, and subsists on the capital remaining to those who were well-to-do or wealthy.

No one is allowed to work except some able-bodied men who have gone to labour on farms; they report, by the way, that they are kindly received and humanely treated by the farmers. Otherwise not a penny of earned income comes to these people. There they sit, forbidden to be in the streets after 8 o'clock at night under penalty of arrest,

without anything to do, with only two repaired synagogues available in Berlin for religious services, and with practically no places of entertainment open to them. On the holiest day of the Jewish religious year they were called out of their synagogues, a year or more ago, made to return to their homes, and to give up their radios—without compensation, of course, so that they are deprived even of that means of passing the time. The hour was deliberately chosen, of that there is printed proof. Such schools as remain for the children are hastily created organisations, and not even these exist in small towns and villages where only a few Jews are left. Under such conditions these unfortunates sit in their homes, and every time the door-bell rings, they expect that the order to prepare for immediate departure for Poland, and what they consider certain death, has come.

The forced migrations began on October 17th. The first to go were those from the Czech Protectorate, the second from Austria, the third group from Posen and West Prussia, and the last from the Reich, the movement being in charge of the Gestapo. There were being taken out of Vienna every week some two thousand men, women and children, but at the end of October one such transport comprised only fourteen hundred persons, according to information given to the *Allgemeen Handelsblad* of The Hague, because so many had sought to escape this fate through suicide or flight. "In the last fourteen days," its Berlin correspondent reported on November 10th, "in Vienna alone 82 Jews have committed suicide, of whom 36 were women." Nowhere were the deportations pushed more vigorously than in Moravian Ostrava, where already many Jewish-owned houses are standing empty.

What this actual evacuation means in terms of human suffering I learned from a letter sent to an American official by an Aryan German residing in a certain town. Writing to this official, this German asked whether the United States could not be induced to protest against the horrible cruelty of the transportation. He stated that a trainload of cattle-trucks containing these unfortunates had stood for twelve hours in the station of the town in which he resided, that they were without food or conveniences of any kind, and no heat. He declared that the moans and groans of these desperately wretched sufferers could be heard a long distance from the station. He declared that he was a loyal German, but that he could not keep silence in the face of such horrible wickedness. I repeat that, of course, not one word of this can appear in a German newspaper. The public is therefore utterly unaware of what is being done, and individuals will not believe the truth when it is told to them.[1]

[1] "According to a Warsaw message published in the Amsterdam paper, *De Courant*, on November 27th, forced labour has been introduced in the Jewish 'reserve' for all men below 70 and all women below 55. Work continues for 12 hours daily, with only half an hour's rest for the mid-day meal. Rations consist of potatoes and black bread. Hundreds are said to be dying from spotted typhus, pneumonia, and from the effects of exposure. Many have had to sleep in the open. A handful of Jewish doctors are doing their best to master the typhus epidemic, but owing to the appalling conditions are fighting a losing battle. The German medical officers of health are refusing to give any assistance, and are merely advising that the cases of typhus should be isolated in camps. Fears that the epidemic may sweep westward into Germany are growing." *The Daily Telegraph and Morning Post*, November 28, 1939.

What adds to the general confusion of these strange migrations is that Russia and Germany have just signed an agreement for the repatriation of German citizens in Soviet-occupied Poland and Soviet citizens in the German-occupied section, and that at least 500,000 Jewish refugees, of whom 350,000 have received Soviet citizenship, are now reported to be in Lemberg, the chief town of the Soviet-occupied Polish Ukraine. Hitler is currently reported to be migration-mad; ever since he hit upon the idea last winter of moving the Germans out of the Italian Tyrol his mind has occupied itself with the shifting of minorities out of the regions in which they are to be found, and reuniting them with people of their own race. But with the Jews the motive is to get rid of them without loss of time, and without the slightest regard for what may become of them after they have reached their destination. It goes without saying that Hitler would not thus treat cattle on the railroads, for such cruelty to them is forbidden by strict laws.

I suspect that there is an ulterior motive behind all this. It is altogether probable that one reason why these poor people are stripped of almost everything before being thrust into this charnel house is so that Hitler may point to them when they die off of hunger and cold and say: "See, I told you these were a parasite people who could only live by battening on Gentiles. I gave them territory on which to build their own State, and see how utterly they have failed." I did not dare, for their sake, to call on more than a very few Jews while I was in Germany, lest I injure them. But I found that they were entirely aware of what transfer to this "State" meant. Their one request of me was that I make known to the English and American Jewry just what this proposal signifies, and beg them not to be misled. They pointed out that even if this "State" were adequately prepared for the migration, it still could have no economic future, since it will be surrounded on all sides by hostile communities, who will doubtless not be permitted to do business with such unfortunates as may survive within the barbed wire. I have no hesitation in saying to my German friends that if the Hitler Government were in every other respect a model one, I should still consider it utterly damnable, because of what it has done to Jews who had the misfortune to come within the power of their despot.

Issues and Men

BY OSWALD GARRISON VILLARD

AGAIN the President has demanded of Congress increased appropriations for army and navy. He asks $271,999,523 more in this fiscal year "for the proper observance, safeguarding, and enforcing of the neutrality of the United States and the strengthening of national defense." The total for the two defense services in the budget for 1940-41 is the enormous sum of $1,800,000,000. I presume that we may take the Kansas City *Star's* comment, that "the national-defense statement was reasonable," as representing the average opinion of it. Yet it was not reasonable, for all army and navy appropriations are unreasonable as long as they are not based upon a thorough study of the problems of national defense and a clear understanding of the possible enemies of the United States by whom it could conceivably be attacked. I know that there is less need of great defense expenditures today than there has been for many years. It is gratifying to note the number of Congressmen who are demanding an accounting of these items.

I have not just come from the belligerent European nations without knowing that they are far less able to attack the United States today than they were when war came in September, and that the last thing they are thinking about is attempting it. Even if Hitler should win this war, Europe would be prostrate for years, and a victorious Hitler would be surrounded by enemies who would welcome his getting embroiled in a war with the United States. I asked a British major general in London just before I left whether he had ever heard of a European military or naval officer who thought that an attack upon the United States in any form was feasible. "Preposterous," he said, "absolutely preposterous and impossible. No one dreams of such a thing." This officer has been stationed in the United States and knows our military conditions and our chief military leaders.

Since I have been for years demanding that calm logic and not hysteria should control our military policy, I was delighted lately to receive additional support for the proposal I advanced in my little book "Our Military Chaos" that there should be an immediate inquiry by an unbiased group, preferably civilian and non-Congressional, into just what dangers, if any, confront us. Thus, General Hugh Johnson, while saying that he cannot support many of my conclusions, strongly urges my principal recommendation, "which is that we need an impartial, non-partisan, extra-governmental commission to look into this question." He cites General Marshall, Chief of Staff, as having just said that in spite of the billions we have lavished on the War Department our defense is not 25 per cent effective. General Marshall charges this to the historians of the United States, who, he says, have always represented us as being victorious in our wars and have failed to record our defeats. But General Johnson points out that there are other culprits. He says: "I would shudder to see a careful compilation of comparative unit costs—per soldier or per ton of shipping—as between our own and the armies and navies of all other nations. It would shock the country." He concludes: "A commission of inquiry is imperative. If it finds that this column and Mr. Villard's book are wrong, it will be a splendid vindication which I, for one, would welcome. If it finds that we are only partly right, the country ought to know it."

Writing in the New York *Herald Tribune*, Major George Fielding Eliot, who approaches the problem from a different point of view than mine, said on January 4: "It is plain that we cannot continue as in the past making plans for defense without some definite idea of what we are going to defend; the army and navy cannot decide what they need until they know what they are going to have to do with it. The point is well taken that the major decision of this sort which now confronts us is whether we are going to prepare for the defense of the Western Hemisphere, or whether we are going to plan for military adventures overseas." But Major Eliot desires a permanent Committee of National Defense with Congressional representation to study particular problems, to straighten out our "tangled defense scheme," and to command "a greater degree of public confidence when heavy expenditures are called for." I still feel that the first inquiry should come from an absolutely independent commission without Congressional or military or naval members, since these are bound to be biased if only by reason of their training.

It is quite characteristic of President Roosevelt that his new budget shows an increase only for national defense. He does not succeed in justifying it; he could not if he would justify the increases in the army and navy and coast guard which he ordered at the outbreak of the war, an action which struck foreign observers—I was in England at the time—as absurd and inexplicable. He cannot justify the 300-mile safety zone around the Americas, which is utterly impracticable and ridiculous. Does he expect British and German warships which may begin an action 302 miles from us to stop fighting when they cross the 300-mile line?

Issues and Men

BY OSWALD GARRISON VILLARD

SOMEBODY asked me the other day what I would do in the matter of mediation in the present war if I were President of the United States. I replied that I would offer mediation on even Mondays, Wednesdays, and Fridays, and odd Tuesdays, Thursdays, and Saturdays, with all Sundays thrown in for good measure. In other words, I favor continuing mediation. I should also, were I Mr. Roosevelt, immediately ask the Pope to join me in getting the heads of Italy, Spain, Switzerland, Holland, Belgium, Denmark, Norway, and Sweden to sign a joint request to the belligerents that they once more state their peace terms, without recriminations and without self-laudation—just in the fewest words possible. It would then be possible to see whether they should be invited to send representatives to discuss, together with representatives of the neutral states, the question of a settlement.

I know that there will be strong dissent from some of those who read these words. I have had the reasons against such a move stated to me over and over again in Germany, Holland, England, and the United States. In London a high official thought the difficulties in the way of even formulating exact terms very great. I replied that I knew more difficulties than he did, because I had just been in Berlin and had heard the matter discussed there. But whatever the obstacles, right-minded men everywhere I went were of the opinion that one more effort should be made to see if the Allies and Hitler could not be brought together. The alternative is a knock-out blow inflicted by one side or the other, or a stalemate with all Europe going to pieces from economic and financial exhaustion. The fighters will lose nothing if the President makes this effort. They can go right on bombing and sinking ships and guarding both sides of the Rhine. If the effort comes to nothing, the military situation will not have been changed.

Naturally the first objection is, "But how in the world could you get Hitler to consider setting up small Polish and Czech states—no sane man believes that it would be possible or desirable to reconstitute the old Czechoslovakia, and Poland cannot be restored without a war with Russia?" To this my answer is that no man can foretell what Hitler will do, but that I am more than ever convinced that there is a split both in the German army and in the German Foreign Office and that considerable elements in both of them would like peace negotiations for various reasons. Hitler and his generals must also be aware of the total lack of enthusiasm for the war, even opposition to it, on the part of the bulk of their fellow-countrymen. The officer in the Frankfort tram who said openly one day, "Why, the spirit of the people in this city about the war is devastating. It is better at the front," revealed a great deal. I do not know whether those dissenting governmental and military forces, plus the attitude of the public, are sufficiently powerful to induce Hitler to consider terms which would be a profound humiliation and defeat for him. Nor does anyone else know. I am only urging that the method suggested above be resorted to in order to ascertain this.

More than that, I am convinced that if such an offer were made by the Pope, President Roosevelt, and the heads of the countries I have enumerated, it would not be possible for Hitler wholly to suppress the news of the move. If he did try to conceal it and it leaked into Germany, it would do him a tremendous amount of harm and increase the ill-will of the majority of his people toward him and the war. Similarly, I cannot think of any better anti-Hitler propaganda than to publicize his refusal to reply to an offer from such sources. The news would be bound to get into Germany and would immediately raise the question why he had taken this extraordinary attitude against such important mediators.

Of course much would depend upon how confident the pro-Hitler generals are that they will win the war next spring. Undoubtedly many military men and a great many civilian officials believe that they will win easily. The stake that Hitler and his gangsters are playing for is the domination of the European world. They may be willing to gamble their lives and the success of their party on the chance of rising to a height of power never before achieved in the history of Europe. On the other hand, if they lose they lose everything; they will be lucky if they get off with exile like that of the Kaiser at Doorn. That is the exact situation. The question each reader of these lines must decide for himself is whether he thinks that this statement of the case warrants one more effort being made before such blood-letting takes place that no further effort to stop the war will be possible until a knockout blow has been delivered or all Europe is completely finished. I hope that no reader will overlook the fact that Germany can no more be cleansed of Hitlerism and National Socialism by forces from the outside than it was purged of militarism by the Allies and the United States in 1918, when our joint efforts, plus the Treaty of Versailles and the inflation, produced a vastly more dangerous militarism than that of the Kaiser.

Issues and Men

BY OSWALD GARRISON VILLARD

If This Be Treason—

I AM guilty of another crime—at least so I am told. I had thought there wasn't another in all the category of wrongdoing which could possibly be attributed to me of which I had not already been declared guilty by somebody. Now it appears that I have sold out to the British, that I have been taken into camp by them—all because I have been praised and flattered for having published in London a certain article that gave pleasure to large numbers of people. Some warm friends have told me that I have become "much too friendly" to the British and have asked what the reason is.

Well, here is my explanation. In the first place, I have been in Germany and seen the Nazis in their stronghold, and after that I am prepared to embrace the Patagonians. In the next place, having something that might be described as human sympathy and perhaps even understanding of people, I was profoundly moved by the bearing of the British masses when the war came. I was in England at the time. My emotions *were* stirred. Why should they not have been, and why should I not have expressed those emotions on leaving the country. The words of mine that appealed to many persons were in praise of the plain people who are England. I said that there would always be with me hereafter "the quiet faces of those without uniforms, without titles, the plain people who carry on; who have nothing—yet if they have sons everything—to lose; who must pay and pay and pay, for these are England—the England that must be made free of war, free of fear, free of injustice—for them after the war must be built the England that is to come, better and finer than ever before." If that spells surrendering to the powers that be in Great Britain, to the specially privileged, I must indeed plead guilty to having been taken into camp.

Of course I have not changed my pacifist position. Of course I have not taken back one word of the many criticisms that I have written in past decades about British imperialism. I am just as much aware that the British Empire was built up by wholesale piracy, by the theft of lands, by cruel and unceasing wars. I said freely in England that this war was the result of a contest between idiocy on one hand and insanity on the other; that I thought 40 per cent of the blame for it rested squarely upon the last three British Prime Ministers. But all that is now over the dam. Whether they wished it or not, and many of them did not wish it, the rulers of England have actually come to occupy a position where they are defending everything that is decent in the life of nations. Naturally, since the war is here, is going on, I want with all my heart to have the Allies win—I am as much concerned for the future of France as for that of England. That does not mean that I therefore condone all the sins of the past, that I can excuse the incredible stupidities of British foreign policy at Versailles, and after, or that I no longer desire peace. It does mean that I think that everything that is honorable and possible should be done to save the British people from the threatened results of their leaders' mistakes.

Can any good come out of this war? I have never believed that any good can come out of war beyond temporary relief. It would be a fine momentary gain to purge Germany of the present government and to reconstruct a Czech and a Polish state. But, as I have said before, the real sanitation of Germany, the cleansing of the land of the horrible sins of which its rulers have been guilty since Hitler rose to power, must come from within. Only the Germans can do away with the Nazis and their totalitarian state. If, as so many people believe, this war is but one phase of a world-wide proletarian revolution, even that may not be accomplished. We tried purging Germany of militarism in 1917-18, and we know just what we got. At least we knew then that there were liberal forces in Germany to which the Kaiser's government might yield its power. We have no such assurance today; Hitler has destroyed them. And because resort has been had to war, England is risking everything upon the outcome of a struggle which may be lost by the blunder of a single general, as the Germans lost the Battle of the Marne, or of a single admiral, or of a war minister.

But the faces of those quiet English people continue to come back to me; they are my chief concern. It was not they who set up concentration camps in South Africa; nor was it their grandfathers who instigated the opium war in China. I feel akin to them since half of my ancestry is purely British. They have their faults, heaven knows; they still have their caste system, their lords and ladies. They have not yet seen to it that full justice is done to Ireland. Still, these are the people whom I would do anything—short of war—to help preserve. If this be treason, if this means that I have been purchased by the friendliness of my treatment in England, please make the most of it.

Issues and Men

BY OSWALD GARRISON VILLARD

BEING still beset by thoughtless people who believe that I favor an immediate peace with Hitler on Hitler's terms and—incredible as it may seem in any person capable of raising fifteen cents to buy *The Nation*—think it necessary to tell me that a murderous anarchist's word is not to be trusted, I rejoice to have received an admirable Englishman's admirable statement on this whole question of immediate peace negotiations. Charles Roden Buxton comes of a long line of Englishmen distinguished for their public service, their humanitarian point of view, and their intense interest in foreign affairs. Few Englishmen have known as much about Southeastern Europe as he and his brother, Lord Noel Buxton, both of whom during the Versailles days were conspicuous for their desire for a reasonable and decent peace and for just treatment of the Germans. In "The Case for an Early Peace" Charles Buxton has put together all the arguments for and against exploratory negotiations for peace in so calm and reasoned a manner that his seven-page pamphlet has compelling value for all who wish to think this vital question through.

Mr. Buxton begins by expressing his respect for those who think that if the Allies should make peace now "it would give us no security against future aggression by Germany." To those who feel that the war must be prosecuted to the bitter end and until the elimination of Hitler, he says that we who think otherwise have the right to call upon them to prove two things: first, that secure peace is *not* possible at an early date; and, second, that "a secure peace, or at least a better peace than is now attainable, *could* be attained at the end of three years, say, of war." He himself believes that "the probability of attaining a reasonably secure peace at an early date is so great that an attempt should be made to attain it; that the settlement after three years of war, whichever side were the victor, would be a worse settlement than could be obtained now." With this second point I especially agree. If the war goes on for three years and the Allied peoples are reduced almost to beggary and are infuriated by the destruction of their cities, the chances of a humane, intelligent, and far-sighted peace that will really bring about the establishment of that completely new order in Europe which Chamberlain says he wishes will be slim indeed.

But beliefs are one thing, and the arguments on which they are based another. What are Mr. Buxton's arguments for his position? He contends that Hitler's speech of October 6 last outlining certain terms was not his last word but obviously merely the beginning of negotiations. Very soon, if approaches were made, Mr. Buxton thinks, the Allies would reach the stage of negotiation not with Hitler alone but also with powerful neutral states, whose signatures would guarantee the settlement finally reached; they would necessarily be interested in *maintaining* that settlement because it would in part be their own creation. He assumes of course a genuine conference in which there would be give and take, and in which the interests of Italy and Russia, and also of the smaller neutrals, would be taken into consideration.

Why does Mr. Buxton think that Hitler would be willing to consider peace at a time when the Germans are confident, as they seem to be now, that they are winning the war? He believes that if complete war with the Allies comes soon, it will make Hitler much more subservient to Russia than he is now and far more so than he wishes to be. "Russia would be able to do almost what she pleased." Mr. Buxton feels sure that if Hitler were faced with the possibility of a just and universal settlement, such as the Dutch Premier called for on January 3, he would not dare to compel his people to go on fighting if the only points at issue were the establishment, for example, of a Polish and a Czech state. As to that opinions will differ—naturally; I came out of Germany thinking that it was by no means impossible. It depends for one thing upon the morale of the German people and the strength of their opposition to the war. Finally, Mr. Buxton makes the unanswerable point that a new European order is the only possible guaranty against aggression and the brigand morals of which Stalin and Hitler are the distinguished exemplars.

Those people who think that all would be well if only Hitler could be eliminated, if Göring could make the peace, are utterly deluded. Who could take the place of Hitler save a military despot? And what guaranty would there be that such a man's word was any better than Hitler's? No, the only guaranties worth anything *on either side*—for I have not forgotten all the broken promises, American and Allied, since the Armistice—will inhere in the peace itself. And after even a year of bloody total war a reasonable peace will be out of the question, whether the Allies win or lose. Such a war will end in the destruction of the German Empire or of the British Empire, and neither will mean lasting peace or a new order. No, let us make one more effort for a negotiated peace before going on to a vindictive dictated peace and complete economic disaster.

Issues and Men

BY OSWALD GARRISON VILLARD

TO MY mind the most sensational aspect of the German publication of the Polish documents relating to the utterances of American diplomats is the calculated attack upon the United States. When I was in Berlin last fall, Foreign Office officials assured me again and again that they had not the slightest intention of drawing the United States into the war. "There will be no Lusitania case in this war and no Belgium," they said; and they insisted that they had not sunk the Athenia. I attributed their courtesies to me, when they knew of my hostility to the Nazi regime, as another evidence of their desire to cultivate American public opinion. Now they have plainly had a change of heart and are ready to attack the United States, to link us with the Allies, and to antagonize our public and our press.

The explanation can only be that they believe we are now hopelessly tied up with the Allies and that they feel so strong and certain of victory that they are ready to take us on also. They are obviously riding high. They believe that they have the mastery of the air and are winning on the sea; they are making better headway against the British blockade than they had hoped and are inflicting extremely heavy losses on Allied and neutral shipping. Hence their aggressiveness and confidence, which are unlike anything seen in Berlin during the last war. These Nazis believe in forcing the fighting all along the line, and one must record the fact that as yet they are showing none of that fatal misunderstanding of the psychology of other peoples that is usually characteristic of Germans. The English press admits that the German broadcasts to England are making headway even among the British troops.

From an entirely reliable source I have recently heard of a conversation which took place on New Year's Day between an American business man, the head of a great company, and Hermann Göring. They have known each other since Göring's residence in Sweden after the last war. "You Americans are coming into this war," said Göring to his visitor. "No," was the reply, "our people are 80 per cent against our going in." "You are wrong," said Göring; "the latest polls show as high as 95 per cent against going in, but you will be in next fall just the same." This bears out the theory that the Nazis feel there is no longer any use in trying to keep us out and are therefore willing, as the Polish revelations show, to abuse us. On the other hand, their American advisers may have told them to go ahead on the theory that the disclosure of the way our diplomats have been siding with the Allies may discredit Roosevelt with the peace-loving American public and increase the determination of the masses to keep this country out of the struggle. It is too early yet—I am writing this in Los Angeles before the publication of the second promised batch of documents—to tell what effect these publications will have in Washington, but coming as they do on top of the calculated indiscretion of the American minister to Canada, they furnish dynamite for Congress, or would if there were an effective opposition. How Senator Borah would have welcomed this opportunity to cut loose!

That the Germans chose the moment they did for the publication of the Polish documents—almost the very day that Sumner Welles was reporting to the President on what he had learned abroad—shows clearly that they were determined to offset the effect of his recommendations or to blanket his return by overshadowing it. Undoubtedly they have had these papers in their possession ever since the surrender of Warsaw and could have published them months ago; this again would seem to argue that they have recently changed their policy in regard to the United States. That they are substantially correct reports I do not doubt, for Mr. Bullitt has made no concealment of his passionate advocacy of the French and English cause. His speeches in France have at times, it seems to me, gone beyond the bounds of diplomacy. I have no doubt that he has been doing his best to influence Allied policy behind the scenes. There is nothing inherently improbable in the extracts from the Polish documents which have appeared here except the orders to Joseph Kennedy in London which are attributed to Mr. Bullitt.

The outstanding facts are that Germany is now on the war path against us and that Washington, according to the headlines, is seething with indignation. Let those who wish to keep this country out of war take notice. Mr. Kennedy, as everyone knows, is opposed to our getting into the war, but with Mr. Roosevelt and Mr. Bullitt it will be a very different story if things go badly with the Allies. One thing I can record about my trip across this continent by motor. Nowhere did I see the slightest indication in press or public of any desire that we should enter the war. The tremendous applause given to Taft and Dewey whenever they attack Mr. Roosevelt's attitude toward the war shows clearly what the American people want.

For the Nation

ISSUES AND MEN

Bt Oswald Garrison Villard

Hitler Wins In Washington

Adolf Hitler and his doctrines have had a good week in Washington. The Senate has voted a navy bill which calls for $963,797,478—just when Congress has been declaring that it did not have money enough to appropriate the sums necessary for relief. Next, Admiral Taussig has lifted the banner of naval expansion right manfully in his arms and planted it squarely on an impregnable base in the Philippines, and come out for an unbeatable fleet and all the perquisites. Once more we are to let the Japanese know who are their masters and who is going to dominate in Asiatic waters hereafter. And Franklin [illegible] Roosevelt paid Hitler the greatest compliment of all by serving notice to the representatives of the [illegible] American Republics assempbled in the beautiful Pan-American building in Washington that we "shall meet force with force" if anybody assails anyone in the Americas.

Adolf must have felt a considerable pride when he read these items in Dr. Goebbels's confidential reports. For he certainly can claim that his philosophy is making great strides in the American republic. It was plainly fear of him that was responsible for the size of that naval bill which carried with it authorization for two 45-000-ton battleships and a couple of cruisers—battleships now cost about $90,000,000 to $100,000,000 apiece. Not that it alarmed Hitler. He knows that the provision of those ships has no bearing whatever on the present war since they cannot be laid down in any ship yard for some time to come, and will take from five to seven years to go into service after they are started. He is sure moreover that Goering is right when he tells him that before the month of July is over his airmen will have proved that the battleship is as dead as the dodo and can no longer be an instrument of national policy. But whether Goring is right or wrong, there is no doubt that when Hitler read Admiral Taussig's words his heart rejoiced within him. Were it not for the Admiral's possibly Semitic name one could almost hear the Fuehrer saying: "There is an officer after my own heart. He is unafraid. Why, he even dares to name the potential enemy, Japan, instead of resorting to the usual subterfuge of speaking of 'a Pacific power'. That will stir the Japanese admirals not a little. It brings the possibility of war between Japan and the United States much closer because of course the Japanese will spread Admiral Taussig's words before evry man and woman in Japan who can read as proof that the United States is moving on Japan. How nice it would be if war should come now between Japan and the United States and how it would help me by keeping American airplanes and money and supplies at home!"

But after all the words of the President must have pleased Hitler most, for in them he of course sees a departure from previous American policy -the readiness of the United States to assume the responsibility of defending all of South and Central America. True, the Monroe Doctrine carried with it from the start an implication that the United States would prevent colonization or alienation of land on the American Continent by force. But this is in a sense a new doctrine in this new world. It means that the United States will now definitely adopt the doctrine of a nation in arms and forget all about the century and more during which its word was sufficient to protect all the Americas. It means that America, too, is definitely committed to the Hitler doctrine that force is now all that counts in the world. Naturally Mr. Roosevelt means that force will only be applied if injustice is done and some one is attacked. But Hitler, too, says that, just as the English have always maintained that their airforce was only for defence-even when they were bombing to bits hill tribes in Afghanistan which no more wanted British protection than the people of Denmark desire the kindly guardianship of Adolf himself. The language of those who put their faith in force is always the same-and their acts in the long run are the same, too.

At any rate, the United States will not fall behind in the race to detroy civilization by arming, arming and arming. The Congress will see to that. It will not take the time to ascertain whether battleships are really of the past or not; it will pay no attention to the miltary officers who say that this is not the way to get efficient and adequate preparedness. It will lay down no national policies so that the army and navy may plan intelligently and not in the dark. It will not pass a law forbidding naval officers, and army men too, from alarming the public without first submitting their remarks in advance and obtaining governmental permission as is the case in every other country. It will declare its fear of war with Japan and do nothing to prevent the open declaration of governmental officials that we are preparing and must prepare to fight the Mikado's people. It will say we must be safe and then by steadily increasing -unnecessarily according to many experts-the army and navy will undermine the democratic foundations of our own land.

Force against force-that is what the world has come to and the more nations adopt it the more it will please the dictators who know better than any one else that democracy and great military forces cannot live permanently side by side, that inevitably the military will come out on top. Security? That is of course what Congress and the American people want. What a pity it is that in their eagerness to get it they cannot stop seriously to inquire whether the means they are adopting will not destroy the very thing they wish to save; whether even in this dreadful welter of force in Europe there is not the possibility of great and noble leadership in another direction, especially when the peace of force -or exhaustion-has come. Meanwhile, let our churches go on preaching that it is the spirit of Christ which conquers, and nothing else.

Issues and Men

BY OSWALD GARRISON VILLARD

A SAINT on earth died the other day, a man really too good for this kind of world. Of course I refer to George Lansbury, perhaps next to Gandhi the most outstanding pacifist in public life anywhere. I suppose that death was not unwelcome to him. At least he may not have wanted to carry on now in enfeebled health in a world which is so deliberately bent on self-destruction and will not read the simple and plain lesson of its war folly. It is only two years since he personally went on a mission of good-will to Hitler, Mussolini, and the heads of the French and other governments; I do not remember whether he got to Stalin or not. Yes, even Hitler received this benign and kindly old man, though Germans have been condemned to a lifetime of servitude merely for holding to Lansbury's Christian belief that the Commandment "Thou Shalt Not Kill" applies to all times and all conditions. When I was in England last fall he was apart from the great currents of life in his country, all of which, except a small group similarly conscientiously opposed, stood behind the government in its belief that Germany can be purged of Nazism by guns and unlimited bloodshed. But he died as true to his faith as ever did a Christian martyr.

"Member of Church of England; teetotaler; non-smoker; twice in prison"—thus Lansbury described himself in "Who's Who." He went through fire during the last war years, in and out of prison, but he was one of those men whom prison could not mar or break. Once when he was on a hunger strike in jail, he wrote, a prison chaplain rebuked him "for injuring my body by voluntary starvation because it was the temple of the Holy Ghost." At once Lansbury asked him if he were a Protestant. The chaplain said that he was, whereupon Lansbury replied: "If it had not been for Latimer and Ridley allowing their temple of the Holy Ghost to be burned in defense of their faith you could not have been a Protestant at all. You would not have come into my cell to talk this nonsense to me." But not his religion or anything else could dim his sense of humor; he recalled in his Memoirs the joyous interruption "shouted at canvassers for a school-board candidate who was in favor of secular education: 'They want to rob us of our bloody religion.'" This reminds me of what Augustine Birrell once said—that "the trouble with Lansbury is that he *will* let his bleeding heart run away with his bloody head."

None the less, however much his heart ran away with his head, he was, as was once pointed out in the London *New Statesman and Nation*, "immensely shrewd in practical affairs, and a most astute political fighter." Yet he would not remain at the head of the British Labor Party when it plumped for the sanctions against Italy in connection with the invasion of Ethiopia because he thought that would be inconsistent with his devotion to the doctrine of non-violence. Nobody hooted or sneered at him when he took this position, not even the most dyed-in-the-wool reactionary Conservative. Everybody respected and honored him, and the *New Statesman and Nation* spoke the truth when it declared that "George Lansbury is the only name that is known in every town and village of Great Britain." He was so simple, straightforward, and lovable, so completely uninterested in what happened to George Lansbury, so unwilling to conceal his lack of boyhood education, his humble origin, and his years of working as an ordinary laborer that one naturally thought of him as the "purest Christian in all England."

How few examples we have had of men who were willing to sacrifice the prestige of high office and a good salary by putting conscience above preferment! Too many like Ramsay MacDonald have salved their conscience by convincing themselves that they were indispensable, that they must not leave their party in the lurch in time of national crisis. Moreover, in Lansbury's case he knew that he had to turn the party leadership over to a man who was not so able; Clement Attlee is today nothing like the leader His Majesty's Opposition should have when the nation, as Winston Churchill has just admitted, is in greater danger than ever before. But Lansbury's intellectual honesty was crystal clear. So he gave up the leadership at seventy-six, without recrimination, without bitterness, without a sign of self-pity.

Afterward he went on as full of the zest of life and as certain of the correctness of his doctrines as Gandhi himself. How can such men as these be downcast? They have only to look around to see in a crumbling world about them the justification of all they have taught and preached. True, the militarists and believers in force are on top. And more and more people, even in our own country, are ready to put their faith in armaments, believing that if a nation only has enough arms, even if it is driven to the point of bankruptcy, it is safe. The world is giving that theory its final test now. Is it any wonder that an American general said to me that no country is now rich enough or big enough to support the soldier?

Issues and Men

BY OSWALD GARRISON VILLARD

WALTER LIPPMANN has got the jitters again. More than three years ago, when it looked as if war was near in Europe, he declared that, if it came, the only way we could safeguard our neutrality would be to mobilize three million men at once and set them down on our shores. With incredible naivete and the lack of realism that is so often astonishing in this man who has been for so many years writing for the press, he actually set forth (see my Issues and Men of January 16, 1936) that this would be the surest way to prevent the rise of a great war party in the United States, demanding war as did Theodore Roosevelt and Leonard Wood in 1915-17, and the surest way to keep us out of war. It never occurred to him that an army of three million men, after it had made all the sacrifice of drilling for months and months, would be just crazy to get going and do something.

Now Walter Lippmann declares that our duty to America requires us to prepare to make over our state according to the Hitler model, especially if the Allies are defeated. Of course he does not use those words, and if he reads these of mine he will say that he never said anything of the kind. Yet what he calls for is none the less exactly that. This is what he actually wrote:

> Isolated in a world that envies us and despises us, we too shall have to become a nation in arms. We too shall have to have conscription; we too shall have to regiment capital and labor in order that we may be able to build the ships and the airplanes, and the guns and cannon without which we shall be harassed and intimidated, threatened and blackmailed by the coalition on both sides of us.

He elaborated further in these words:

> The next thing to do is to adopt a program of national defense of vastly greater scope than that which is now in operation. The experience of Great Britain should be a lesson to us that it is not enough to appropriate money to buy what the existing facilities can supply: it is necessary to create new shipyards, new airplane factories, new plants for the production of guns and other implements of war. There is needed a larger investment of new capital: it is not safe to let the aircraft industry, for example, wait for its expansion upon subsidies from the Allies.

Precisely. I have done him no injustice. Carry out this program, plus universal military conscription and the complete reorganization of American industrial life to make it part of the American military machine, as German industry has been made part of the German military machine, and you have the totally militarized state which can only lead to Fascism or National Socialism. What he wants America to do in order to protect our democracy is to undertake the very way of life which is most inimical to the continuance of republican institutions. If we take his advice we shall destroy democracy in order to defend it, destroy it by injecting into its veins the very poison which has proved fatal to it in so many countries abroad.

I find myself wondering whether Walter Lippmann would not admit that I am right, that the remedy may be as bad as the evil of conquest by the dictators, or lead in the last analysis to the same end, and say that he prefers to take the risk. I find many people caught in this dilemma. The minute the total war began they too cried out that we must arm at once, at all costs. They too forgot all their horror over Franklin Roosevelt's unbalanced budget, their bitter indignation that he was anxious to lift the debt limit still higher. And when I asked them what they were planning to do to safeguard democracy, they admitted the weight of argument on my side but added helplessly: "But what else can we do?"

Of course if Walter Lippmann had anything really to contribute to the defense problem of the United States except mere emotion and an incredible ignorance of military affairs, he would have recommended that we keep cool and quiet and ascertain why it is that we have no defense policy and that therefore our expenditures bear no relationship to any military program, and why we do not tell our army and navy what to defend and how to do it. He could then have pointed out (1) that the primary defense question for the United States, one that is still unsettled, is whether we are only to defend our shores or are to make ready to fight abroad; (2) that all our military expenditures are unintelligent, wasteful, uncoordinated, and often misdirected; (3) that there are the gravest faults in the organization of the War and Navy departments, and that they fail to cooperate adequately and will not function in war time. Why, he might have asked, is it possible for Major General Arnold to have told Senator Lodge that only one hundred of our thousands of airplanes are today fit to go into action in Europe? Just raising these questions and seeking the answers would have contributed more to a sane defense policy than all the wild words he has penned so far. But now that the President has come to this position, he will be the more certain he is right.

Issues and Men

BY OSWALD GARRISON VILLARD

THE President has not yet taken the American public into his confidence in regard to his defense plans. He has not told them how large a standing army a fleet of 50,000 airplanes will call for, and he has given them no indication of what will be the cost of keeping up such an air armada. More than that, he has not told them whether he now for the second time favors a two-ocean navy, or whether he is going to advocate universal military service. As for the financing of the whole tremendous enterprise, that is only just beginning to be a subject of discussion. It is characteristic of the President's method that the financial aspect is entirely subordinated—first commit yourself to a program and then see how you can pay for it. This may be good politics, but it is neither statesmanship nor good finance.

The President has just announced the composition of a civilian board to supervise the carrying out of the industrial side of the armament program—a useful idea. Perhaps he felt the universal disapprobation of the idea that these matters should be left to Frances Perkins, Harold Ickes, Harry Hopkins, and Henry Morgenthau. But none of this goes to the root of a successful defense program. Nor will that program be furthered by such misleading statements as those of his address to the public of May 26. For example, he said then that the navy in 1933 had only 1,127 useful aircraft and that at present it had 2,892 planes on hand or "on order." It appears that no fewer than 1,100 of these planes are on order, and, according to Phelps Adams of the New York *Sun,* "it will be many months under present production schedules before those 2,892 planes that the President mentioned will actually take the sky." In 1933, the President said, we had only 355 anti-aircraft guns. Now, he said, we have 1,700 modern anti-aircraft guns "on hand and on order." Actually very few of these guns are on hand. Similarly the President spoke of 1,600 modern infantry mortars being "on hand or on order." Yet today the army possesses only 3 modern six-inch mortars and 163 modern eighty-one-millimeter mortars! Finally, the 1,700 modern tanks and armored cars which the President cited simmer down to but 114 new armored combat cars and 485 lightly armored scout cars now on hand. Is this being fair with the public?

Granted that the President now intends to speed up these programs to the fullest possible extent, the most important thing will still remain to be done. There can be no efficient military defense of the United States until the War Department is overhauled and modernized. Let me recall once more what General Johnson Hagood has said about the War Department:

> It is so involved that no Secretary of War has ever been able to understand it, and no Chief of Staff, however well qualified, has ever been able to keep it under control or to know just what was going on among his subordinates . . . no human being, no archangel of heaven, could operate a machine which is as badly constructed and as complicated as the War Department is under existing law. It is too big. It is top-heavy. It has too many independent agencies working at cross-purposes to each other and with no fixed line of authority or responsibility.

The General has solemnly warned Congress that "if we became involved in a serious war in which we do not have allies to keep things going while we get ready, the War Department would collapse as it did before." In his book he recalled that in 1917-18 America spent a billion dollars on the manufacture of artillery and artillery ammunition, but that not a single shot was fired from an American gun by an American on the western front, except from some railroad cannon of the navy's.

If the President really wanted efficient defense he would not only insist upon the reorganization of the War and Navy departments and put at their head efficient and able men in place of such lightweights as Woodring and Edison; he would go before Congress and demand that the Congressmen and Senators who have insisted for political reasons on maintaining 420 posts, barracks, and forts recede from their position in the interest of an efficient army. He might also inquire why it is that, as the present Chief of Staff, General Marshall, has just testified, it costs the United States $21 to maintain a soldier for every dollar that foreign countries spend for the same purpose. Of course one reason is that the United States pays decent wages to its soldiers, whereas foreign nations pay only a few cents a day. But that is only part of the story. Much could be saved by business methods.

The President must know these things or he is not competent to head a defense program. He must know that if we are to fight the Germans, we must put our organization on a business-like basis, free from politics. But I fear that John T. Flynn is correct when he writes that it looks to him as if the President were merely throwing a smoke screen around his failure to put the unemployed to work and to restore prosperity.

June 12, 1940

Dear Will White:

May I make a most friendly protest against your lending your name to such an advertisement as has appeared all over the country, which it appears was written by Robert Sherwood, who is so passionately for the Allies as to be, it seems to me, almost beyond reason. What I object to is his statement: "Anyone who argues that they will wait is either an imbecile or a traitor." There are millions of Americans who are not Fifth Columnists, nor imbeciles or traitors, who do not agree that we are going to be "alone in a barbaric world", and that we are in jeopardy. We may be wrong, but we are entitled to be treated as just as loyal, just as sincere, and just as earnest Americans as Sherwood or anybody else. You know that-- I do not need to tell you. I am sure that you never saw this advertisement; but I beg of you to make sure that no more such statements appear over your name; your reputation is too precious to

Yours always faithfully and devotedly,

Mr. William Allen White,
Emporia, Kansas.

THE EMPORIA GAZETTE
W. A. WHITE, EDITOR AND OWNER
K. W. DAVIDSON, BUSINESS MANAGER
EMPORIA, KANSAS

June 14, 1940.

My dear Villard:

Your letter gave me a bad night and this morning I come to you saying "mea culpa". What happened does not justify it but perhaps I can explain what happened, and you are entitled to an explanation. And it will have to rest until I can make some kind of a public restitution and acknowledgment. First let me tell you what happened.

I have known Bob Sherwood for many years since the old days when he and Gibson were on "Life". I have always respected his patriotism and his broad temper. A copy of the advertisement was sent to me by airmail but it came late in the afternoon and I glanced it over most carelessly. It seemed all right. I expected to go over it more carefully in the morning. Late in the evening by long distance telephone I was asked about it. The time was short and I said to Clark Eichelberger, whom I also have always respected, "Have your read it carefully?" He said yes. Then I said, "I'll take you and Bob Sherwood for it. Go ahead." There my foot slipped.

Now I must find some way to disavow the sentences which I disapprove to do so if possible without seeming to discredit the things that I do approve which is most of the advertisement.

Getting a tremendous stack of mail every day I separate it into favorable and unfavorable, and to the unfavorable letters I reply with this form:

> "I have your kind letter and have read it with great interest. There are, of course, two opinions held honestly by intelligent people in the United

States. One is that to help the Allies keeps the war in Europe rather than to wait until the Germans conquer Europe and turn their greedy eyes westward. The other opinion is your opinion and many fine, wise people hold it. There being two sides, perhaps the best thing each of us could do is to respect the honesty and integrity of each other's opinions and realize that there must be differences if there is progress in the world.

All that you say I had considered before taking my position and felt that on the whole I was right, yet now without doubts as probably you have in holding yours.

With kind personal regards, I am"

I must find someway now to present the tolerant view embodied in this form a statement of general circulation. That I shall do and I shall do it soon. I shall wait a few days for an opportunity, a news peg to hand it on, but as soon as possible I shall present that tolerant view and try to give it the same wide circulation that the advertisement had and also make it clear that I do not approve of the intolerance in the advertising. Perhaps I should make a bold disavowal now without waiting. Nettle grasping might be brave--but, and you will say but me no buts. Yet I am going to wait for the kind of a chance I want. If it does not come "Festus I plunge"!

And now I want to tell you that I do appreciate your letter. Without it I shouldn't have understood much of the violence with which the advertisement was received. For as you may imagine I am tremendously busy and am trying to conserve every ounce of my strength and your letter was, I know, honest, friendly criticism of a wise and just friend.

With warm personal regards, I am

Most cordially yours,

W. A. White

Mr. Oswald Villard,
20 Vesey Street,
New York, New York.

June 13, 1940

Dear Freda:

After reading your last two issues and particularly your coming out for universal military service, I want to notify you at once that I cannot continue to write for The Nation and that I will wind up my connection of forty-six years with a valedictory next week. I could not possibly seem by continuing to contribute articles to approve in any way your extraordinary and, what seems to me, your insane course. It is, as you know, a complete and absolute break with all the traditions of The Nation, of which there is nothing left now but the name. Some day perhaps I shall have some explanation as to how Freda Kirchwey, a pacifist in the last war, keen to see through shams and hypocrisies, militant for the rights of minorities and the downtrodden, has now struck hands with all the forces of reaction against which The Nation has battled so strongly. There is now, of course, no reason for buying The Nation when one can read Walter Lippmann, Dorothy Thompson, the New York Times or the New York Herald-Tribune.

You know that I have often been correct, as the record shows, in my forecasts of what certain national and international policies will produce. I want to go on record to you now as saying that the policies you are advocating, if persisted in, will destroy the New Deal, subjugate labor, and enthrone reaction, precisely as did our last adventure into war in 1917, which finished the New Freedom of Wilson. Our active intervention in the war will only mean the prolongation of a struggle which in any event, as I found out during my four months abroad, can only bring about complete economic disaster. Harold Ickes told me when I last saw him that we were bound to have our dose of Communism and Fascism. I do not believe that this is inevitable unless we go into the war. It should, of course, be fought against by the right means by day and by night. But if it comes you and The Nation will bear a heavy share of responsibility for it, and you will be wailing because of the new crop of Mitchel Palmers and J. Edgar Hoovers who will be doing to death the causes for which you have stood.

I shall touch very lightly upon these things in my valedictory, since I do not wish to start a controversy or to injure The Nation by doing so. I would strongly advise that as little publicity as possible be given to my resignation in the interest of yourself and The Nation. I want to part amicably with you, though with profoundest regret that you have, according to my beliefs, prostituted The Nation, and I hope honestly that it will die very soon or fall into other hands.

Sincerely yours,

Miss Freda Kirchwey
The Nation
55 Fifth Avenue,
New York City

Issues and Men

BY OSWALD GARRISON VILLARD

FOR the last time* I wish to write a few words about the new military policy of the United States—if one may dignify the mad rush to spend money for defense with the name of policy—words based upon a lifelong study of military affairs in America and in some parts of Europe. The present drive for arms, which *The Nation* now so whole-heartedly espouses, is based obviously on the theory that sooner or later we shall have to fight the dictators who have at this moment apparently won the war in France—I am sure that they cannot win in the long run. If that is the prospect before us, then what we are doing amounts to nothing at all. Hitler has achieved his victories by creating literally a nation in arms, in which every single phase of industrial and economic life is subordinated to the military machine. If the Allies are now losing this war, it is because they failed to do the same thing, failed to sacrifice democracy, freedom of the press, the right to criticize the government, personal liberty, to arming so that they could successfully fight the dictators in their own way. If we are to have any hope of success in the military field against these same dictators, Hitler and Mussolini, we too must go the whole hog. It will mean farewell to democracy. But that does not appall a great many Americans. They are so certain of the menace of victorious dictators abroad that they are willing to have this Republic go down fighting.

In order to compete with Hitler and Mussolini, if they survive five or ten years longer, which I for one do not expect, we shall want universal military service. Since Hitler makes his boys serve six months in a work camp and two years in the army, ours, in order that we may have better soldiers, should work nine months in a labor camp and spend two and a half years in the army. An officer of the General Staff in Washington who is giving special attention to anti-aircraft guns told me a year ago that America was not rich enough to buy the anti-aircraft guns needed to protect our 7,000 miles of coast from air raids, to say nothing of defending Alaska and Hawaii and the Panama Canal. That is of course nonsense. If we are going to plan to beat Hitler in the Hitler way, then the United States will certainly raise the money to protect itself. We should have one anti-aircraft gun for every ten feet of our 7,000-mile coast, and we should have thousands of them protecting our cities, as I saw them protecting factories and even apartment houses in the Ruhr last fall. We should have at least five times as much coast defense as now and make it fifty times as efficient. Our regular army should comprise at least 2,600,000 men, aside from the aviation forces, which already are to be brought up to 1,600,000 under the Roosevelt program. We ought, indeed, to go farther and make America really air-minded; no American boy physically capable of flying should be given the right to vote on coming of age unless he could prove on registering that he was a certified pilot or trained to enter the ground force, in addition to having served his two years with the colors. That should make Hitler sit up.

As for the navy, I still believe in the defense afforded us by the Atlantic Ocean, but as the masters of America no longer do, it is obviously ridiculous to talk of a two-ocean fleet. It should be a five-ocean fleet if we are to sleep comfortably at night and not in terror of Hitler. How otherwise could we ward off Hitler if he suddenly appeared off the Chilean coast with 2,000 bombers and a fleet composed of the German, French, British, Italian, Danish, and Norwegian warships, plus the Swedish probably? It would be manifestly impossible for our Pacific fleet, if it were then as now protecting Hawaii and Samoa from the Japanese, to get to Chile in time to prevent its subjugation in a *Blitzkrieg*. So we ought to have a great fleet in the South Atlantic and one in the South Pacific, one in the North Atlantic and one in the North Pacific, and a fifth based on Greenland and Iceland, for of course we should annex those islands promptly if we are going in for 100 per cent defense. Finally, we should train 2,000,000 women annually to protect us from parachutists, fifth-column workers, and labor malcontents; of these women many should naturally be trained for ambulance and hospital work.

I hope no one who is really militaristic now and determined to defeat Hitler will object to this program on the ground that the cost will be prohibitive. That argument will not weigh with Mr. Roosevelt, who has never allowed his policies to be affected by any financial consideration whatsoever. And don't pay any attention to anybody who may remind the President that at Buenos Aires he said that arming "builds no permanent structure and creates no consumer goods for the maintenance of a lasting prosperity," and that "nations guilty of these follies inevitably face the day either when their weapons of destruction must be used against their neighbors, or when an unsound economy like a house of cards will fall apart." Times were different then.

* Mr. Villard's last regular contribution to *The Nation* will appear next week.—EDITORS THE NATION.

June 28, 1940

My dear Holmes (I do hope we can drop the formal Mr.):

Your letter touched, as you can understand, a deep chord in me. Of course what we are facing is the end of the world that we have known, which we have striven to better, and the temporary relegation into the background of all our ideals. What makes it the sadder is that more than ever we are right. What has happened has justified us on every point in our protest against the use of force as a means of settling human disputes, but today no one will listen to us.

Have you ever read the Life and Letters of Franklin K. Lane? There is a marvelous passage written when he thought that he was going to die. He was very close to his end, but came out of the operation and they let him think that he was safe, so that he recorded the struggle within him and finally his coming to the point where he could say "I accept, I accept." I think we are very much in the same position. We have got to accept it howewer bitter the paim, however overwhelming the disappointment, me particularly at the end of my long life. Then we must put it aside, face the fact that this is a totally different world, and seek to readjust ourselves. I can take a certain sardonic pleasure in sitting back and laughing at the Lilliputians learning nothing, seeing nothing, hearing nothing, and trying to reestablish a finished world by the old methods which produced its destruction. That this is the end of capitalism as we have known it I have no question. We in America may escape for a time, but that what we are witnessing is a tremendous economic convulsion the world over I cannot doubt. I found

Ickes in Washington (this is private to you) feeling that we had got to go through our dose of Fascism or Communism. He said it was because the French and English had so botched this whole war business, but they aren't the only botchers. Ickes and the President, and all the New Dealers have given us the coup de grace. I am thankful I never voted for Franklin, much as I was tempted to, for I knew and said both times that this was what he would do to us. I can see myself now voting the Republican ticket, which I swore I would never do, for the great, overwhelming issue is getting him out of the White House.

This week I broke with The Nation after 46½ years of contributing or editing or owning. The apostasy of Freda Kirchwey, the turning over of that historic journal to the very opposite of all the things that it has stood for, is one of the greatest tragedies of my life, for she was one of the most steadfast, most pacifist and most radical members of the staff during the last war and for many years thereafter. Letters of protest are beginning to pour in on me, and I do not doubt on her, but it is final and irrevocable.

What I find is that in most cases I have no longer the power of persuasion. Our minds are absolutely closed. In my own family I cannot convince all. My elder son who is starting his career in life extremely well and is marrying today a lovely girl, is ready to fight, and I cannot encourage the younger one to be a conscientious objector because I think the protest will be of no avail whatever and will not even be published if we go to war. I should be willing that he sacrifice himself and his life if thereby some good would come of it, but as Jerome Chaffee of Harvard has pointed out, when we go into this war by act of Franklin Roosevelt no one will be allowed to know the number of conscientious objectors, their names or their whereabouts, so of what avail would be the protest. In any event, I have never tried to influence my younger son because the decision could only come from him. Either way it is a decision for life or death, perhaps both.

Well, it does put us to our trumps; it is the greatest test of character that could come to us, and we must meet it with all the power and philosophy that we can and above all be cheerful. We who are now in the loneliest of furrows ought to get together more and I do hope that in the Fall this will be possible. I have not been well and am going now to the country to see if I can build up this summer. I am still writing for a small syndicate of newspapers, some fifteen, and I am deliberately beginning a Life of Wendell Phillips to go alongside of my John Brown, to seek to escape what is happening and to refresh my soul with another study of the finest and truest and most successful group of Americans that ever lived.

Yours in warm affection and fellowship,

Mr. John Haynes Holmes,
26 Sidney Place,
Brooklyn, New York.

P.S. I wrote to Mr. Smith that I did not feel that I could take hold of the India Committee now. The reason is that it will be misinterpreted as a stab in England's back; because Gandhi himself has deemed it wise to put off Satyagrahi, and because it will infuriate our crazy fellow citizens and therefore injure India. Let us be patient and wait a few months to see what will happen. Later on we may be able to go full speed ahead for India.

Issues and Men

BY OSWALD GARRISON VILLARD

Valedictory

IT IS nearly forty-six and one-half years since my first contribution appeared in *The Nation*—January 11, 1894. In it I reported my observations of the Spanish army deep in mud in Melilla, North Africa, during an armistice in one of the periodic wars between the Moors and the Spaniards. It is a coincidence that my last articles have dealt with the greatest and most calamitous of all wars. At any rate, it is the differences of opinion which have arisen between myself and the present editorial board as to the relation of the United States to the catastrophe in Europe which has led me to ask for the acceptance of my resignation. Since January, 1933, Issues and Men has been a weekly feature of this journal, and during that time I have had the luck never, in sickness or in health, whether I was here or in Europe, to miss a single issue.

That in the nature of things this series of articles was nearing its end is obvious. I regret all the more, therefore, that my retirement has been precipitated at this time by the editors' abandonment of *The Nation's* steadfast opposition to all preparations for war, to universal military service, to a great navy, and to *all* war, for this in my judgment has been the chief glory of its great and honorable past. As I said in my address at the recent Seventy-fifth Anniversary dinner, I have realized that times change and also the views of owners, and that with new editors come new policies. My own making over of *The Nation* when I became editor in 1918 pained many of its devoted readers. Yet I can truthfully claim that under my guidance it held to the fundamental principles of the founders and was conducted in their spirit, in fullest support of their correct conception of what the liberal world should be.

They knew war, many of them at first hand, and their detestation of it was beyond any yielding to such a pitiful, craven fear of the modern Napoleon as is now sweeping over the United States. They founded this journal within three months after Appomattox for the purpose of championing the freed slaves and helping to steer the country back to the ways of peace, to the Bill of Rights, after four years of bloodshed. To them and to me war was never anything else than "the sum of all villainies," out of which at best only an occasional modicum of good could come; in modern times it only engenders worse evils than those sought to be ended by mass murder. To permit *The Nation,* for which some of us labored and sacrificed so heavily for so many years, now to become recreant to those ideals and beliefs, embracing for the purpose of saving our democracy the very evils certain to destroy it either in peace or in war, is the privilege of the present ownership. But it has made impossible the continuance of a relationship which would be as unfair to the editors as to myself and the public.

That I end my regular contributions with deep regret everyone will understand. For better or for worse I put into *The Nation,* especially during the years when I was solely responsible for it, 1918-1933, the best that I had to offer for our country's welfare and advancement. Whether that contribution was worth while others have judged and will judge in the future—perhaps when the history of these times is written by men marveling that a Hitler beyond seas could so have swept the greatest republic from its moorings. I can only ask that there may be recorded then the causes that were successfully championed by my predecessors, by me, and by my many associates. I hope, too, that there will be just recognition of the efforts of the many men and women who have written in these pages with complete honesty and sincerity, just as their consciences dictated. At least the record is there, for as long as there are critics to examine it, of a free and untrammeled journal.

I have no doubt that the present hysteria will pass and with it the fear which has already gravely endangered the liberties of America and led to steps which will as inevitably wind up the New Deal as our entering into the first World War finished Wilson's New Freedom, now totally forgotten, and made inevitable the coming of Harding, Coolidge, and Hoover—reaction at its worst. I believe, too, that the present editors will some day awake to a realization that the course they are now proposing will inevitably end all social and political progress, lower still further the standard of living, enslave labor, and, if persisted in, impose a dictatorship and turn us into a totalitarian state. America is to be safeguarded, not by guns and warships that may be rendered valueless overnight by new inventions and new tactics, but only by greater economic and industrial wisdom, by social justice, by making our democracy work. That the United States has the genius, the power, the resources, and the vision to accomplish this I cannot question, if only it is not again betrayed in the White House and by the politicians.

With this statement of a veteran journalist's faith in his country this long record closes.

Should Britain Now Talk Peace?

By Oswald Garrison Villard

REALLY this question should read: "Should England *have* talked peace with Hitler?" For Viscount Halifax's reply to the man who is threatening England with "the worst destruction ever seen by mankind" closes the door, or apparently does so. Even before the British foreign minister spoke, Hitler's speech met with only cold contempt in England. "Discussing peace" with Hitler means to Englishmen, or at least the great bulk of the British people, a shameful peace, dictated by a Hitler flushed by his unparalleled victories over Poland, Norway, Denmark, Holland, Belgium and France. It means talking with a man whose word has again and again been proved to be utterly worthless, whose whole philosophy is the practicing of deceit, trickery, fraud, corruption and violence to attain his most abominable falsehoods, calumnies and vilifications, not only of the English people, but of the British leaders. It has continuously demanded the total destruction of the British empire. Yet Hitler now unblushingly says to them once more that really he has always liked and respected the British and the British empire and that therefore he kindly and generously gives them one more opportunity to save their skins, their wives, children and their whole country from destruction.

Neutral Voices for Peace Spurned

That the answer would be what it has been was a foregone conclusion. On last October 6 Hitler made a somewhat similar speech in which he announced his readiness to talk peace, and that offer was contemptuously spurned by the Allies. This did not meet with approval among the neutrals, with the result that the King of Belgium and the Queen of Holland made their own appeals to the warring powers to discuss the possibility of ending the war, which appeals were rejected on both sides. Again, this left the neutrals wholly dissatisfied. On January 3 the Dutch prime minister, Jan Van De Geer, made a "New Year speech" in which he declared that he looked with the profoundest anxiety into the future; that the only hope that he had came from the fact that certain voices were being raised in Europe and America demanding a reconsideration of the situation, and particularly a re-examination of all the events of the last twenty years and of the international reactions resulting from the last war. This, he said, should be done. But no one listened to the premier's effort to save Holland from its impending fate.

Then and since then English officials have steadily taken the position that they cannot treat with Hitler because they have no guarantee whatsoever that any treaty or agreement made with him will last any longer than it suits his convenience or his malign purposes, and no one can deny that there is plenty of justification for that attitude. In this position England's government and her writers in the press are backed by an extraordinarily unanimous public opinion. Even that fact, however, does not necessarily establish the correctness of the British policy in refusing to respond to Hitler's latest speech. When I entered the home of one of our foremost diplomatic representatives in Europe last fall, when the war was in its third month, he said to me: "I am for a shameful peace if necessary, because the alternative is too terrible to contemplate." I presume that as he looks at Norway, Holland, Belgium and France today he feels justified in his attitude; the alternative has proved more horrible than most of us here in America can realize.

The Dutch legation in Washington has just issued a bulletin which lies before me. It recites that: "The crime against Rotterdam was a deliberate, fiendish assault on unarmed, undefended civilians. . . . The result was the greatest mass destruction the world has so far known. In the seven and one-half minutes the planes were over the city, thirty thousand people died—four thousand unoffending men, women and children per minute. Seventy thousand others were maimed and injured. Not even the forces of nature have ever been so wantonly cruel. Not even the volcanoes of Pelee and Krakatoa took such a horrible toll of life in so short a space of time. Two groups of twenty-seven planes each were responsible for this display of barbarism. They dropped one-thousand-pound bombs."

Why is it that the British are ready to risk similar destruction not merely in one of their cities but in many? The Germans told me in November what their program was and everything that they foretold has come true, as I reported it afterward, with the exception of the fact that Spain is not yet in the war, and that England was not destroyed by the 15th of July as they prophesied. They assured me that when they cut loose with the full power of their thirty thousand or more airplanes and their great fleet of submarines and fast motorboats, not a single British port would remain undestroyed except the city of London itself, which they swore they would not bomb because of its priceless monuments of the past and because of the effect such bombings would have upon neutral and especially American opinion. Thus far London seems to have escaped.

What Determines Britain's Choice?

Is the British readiness to face such possible destruction due to its belief that, despite its inferiority in bombers and pursuit planes, it can hold off the German attacks and repel any possible invaders? Or is it due to a mental and moral determination to die rather than to surrender to an enemy as utterly despicable and merciless and wicked as Hitler when their island constitutes practically the last citadel of free institutions in Europe?

Both beliefs have played their share in this decision. The British have now three million men under arms in England, Scotland and Wales. Since the débacle in France they have achieved military wonders in preparing for attacks. Characteristically their morale has risen steadily with each reverse; at last they have come to a realization that they are up against the most ruthless and most efficient military machine the world has ever seen. They are not afraid and they are not deterred by the fact that it is obviously impossible for them to achieve a military victory. The most that they can pray for is to hold off the threatened wholesale destruction of England until winter brings some amelioration, in the hope that the threatened famine in Europe, war weariness on the part of the German people, and the Russian threat in the Balkans will next winter force a truce and peace on honorable terms. Indeed I suspect that many Englishmen will see in Hitler's speech not an attempt to be magnanimous, but a sign of weakness. There can be no doubt whatever that the popular response in Germany to the "glorious victories" has been nothing like what the Hitler gang had hoped and expected; there is plenty of trustworthy evidence that the German people are depressed and not elated, and that they dread beyond all else, as they did when I was in Germany in November, a continuation of the war.

Preserving a 'Life Above Life'

As to the public feeling in England in regard to negotiation, the readiness to go on and face the worst is universal except among those groups that either sympathize secretly with Hitler and fascism, or are of the conscientious belief that all war is wrong, that there must be no compromise with it whatsoever, and that any peace terms are preferable to such things as happened in Rotterdam. Both of these groups together constitute only a small minority. Perhaps it is because the British are lacking in imagination and are unable to visualize what happened in Poland and Holland and France; perhaps it is because of their own dogged characteristics, but today they prefer to take the risk of losing everything. There has been no more consistent pacifist in England for the last thirty years than Emmeline Pethick-Lawrence, wife of the well known member of Parliament and of the former Labor government, F. W. Pethick-Lawrence, also an ardent worker for peace. Writing to *Peace News*, the organ of "Dick" Sheppard's uncompromising "Peace Pledge Union," she said:

> And now that nemesis has fallen upon us all, we have to adjust ourselves to the new situation. We have to meet the full shock of our fate as a nation and overcome it—not by negotiation, for that way is for the present moment closed; not by surrender, because that would be dishonor, but by wholly accepted sacrifice and by an immovable will to win back our lost rights of determining our future so that having learned our lesson, and been purified by suffering, we may as a united people enter in the end on the path that will lead to a new world, based on a new justice, whereby class privileges and economic inequalities will be swept away, and all may enjoy, on the same terms, the bounty of the earth.

In a long letter to the *New York Times*, R. H. Tawney, English writer and Labor leader, declares that Labor has entered the British government and submitted to the loss of rights, the deprivation of privileges and liberties which no one dreamed that it would give up without [illegible]ht, because the working people of England are [illegible]g "to preserve a way of life which we value above li[illegible]. [illegible]e mean to leave it to our children, even if, in order to save it for them, we ourselves must be knocked out." This is not said by Professor Tawney and others in any spirit of braggadocio or mock heroics. It is, I repeat, sincerely felt by the British people as I observed them during the first thre[e] months of the war and since; even then they were saying that it was a "horrible job," but that it had to be done, "so let's get on with it."

And still I am not convinced, any more than I was in October, that some effort should not be made now to see if Hitler has or has not come to his senses; to see if he has any terms to offer which Englishmen might feel that they could accept or at least discuss further. That was not only my attitude last October, but that of numerous neutral diplomats. We felt that the fighting could continue, if that was desirable, while the possibilities of peace were being explored; that the stakes were so enormous that no stone should be left unturned to stop the horrible destruction of human values and human life. Even if one does not want to touch Hitler with a forty-foot pole, he is, unfortunately enough, the representative of a great people (many of whom, as I found out when in Germany, opposed the war and wanted it stopped), and as such it is necessary to deal with him. I cannot see how anything could have been lost by the British by an inquiry as to what he had in mind, what kind of Europe he visualized, what terms of peace he proposed. Since he made the advance no one could accuse England of weakness in asking; German raids over England could continue and English raids over Germany if that is desirable. The destruction of England is so horrible to contemplate that, though it may not come to pass, surely humanity alone dictates that everything should be done to avoid the possibility of this disaster, which will be a disaster not only to England, but to all the world, to all who have profited by the heritage of free men and free institutions.

The Arbitrament of the Bomber

When I returned from Europe I was asked by one of our highest officials if I had found trace of a movement in Holland headed by the queen against making any resistance to Hitler if he attacked. I replied in the negative. He rejoiced. I said: "Surely you would not want them to fight when they told me they could not possibly hold Hitler off for more than four days, which would be of no practical military value whatsoever?" He said: "Yes, I would." I said: "Are you not forgetting the horrible suffering that will result, what will be done to men, women and children, without any compensation in the way of holding up Hitler?" He refused to reply although I twice put the question to him. Sometimes I think that that is one of the worst faults of men in high office when it comes to making war. They cannot visualize the cost in the misery and suffering of others when they are safe and sheltered.

So I think England should have inquired then and should do so now. Against my puny judgment must be set the fact that, as I have said, the great bulk of the British people are behind their government and ready to submit their very existence to the arbitrament of the bomber.

Humanitarians

MEN rue the hosts that flood and storm have slain,
Red conflagrations, and black tidal waves.
And then, with gun and bomb, we dig more graves
Than the blind earthquake and the hurricane.

STANTON A. COBLENTZ.

EMERGENCY COMMITTEE TO DEFEND AMERICA FIRST

General Robert E. Wood
Chairman

National Headquarters
1806 Board of Trade Building
CHICAGO

R. Douglas Stuart, Jr.
Director

August 16, 1940

Mr. Oswald Garrison Villard
20 Vesey Street
New York City, New York

Dear Mr. Villard:

America is not yet at war. The danger of being precipitated into the war increases daily. I am writing you to ask you to serve as a member of the National Committee which is being formed to counteract the forces leading this country toward war.

General R. E. Wood has accepted the Chairmanship of this Committee in an effort to promote the interests of America First and to express the real desires of the majority of American people.

For your convenience I am enclosing a list of persons who have already agreed to serve on the Committee. Our endeavor is to bring together all American poeple who see eye to eye on these principles regardless of differences on other matters. The work of the Committee will be absolutely non-partisan.

I do not need to emphasize the urgency of giving effective expression to this point of view. The American people must be immediately shown the necessity of keeping their heads and Defending America First. They must be made aware of the danger of getting into the war by the backdoor.

It is important that the Committee have your support. Your name stands for something that will give confidence to thousands of Americans.

The enclosed prospectus outlines the Committee's principles and objectives. I hope that it will meet with your approval.

Sincerely,
R. Douglas Stuart, Jr.
R. Douglas Stuart, Jr.
Director

August 21, 1940

Dear Mr. Stuart:

I shall be very glad, indeed, to join your Emergency Committee to Defend America First on the basis of the names and principles submitted to me with your letter of invitation. I must reserve, however, the right to differ if it appears necessary with the Committee as to what constitutes "an impregnable American defense".

I am ardently in favor of keeping this country out of war and ready to give time to that purpose and am constantly devoting my pen and my voice to the cause.

Very truly yours,

Mr. R. Douglas Stuart, Jr.,
Emergency Committee to Defend America First
1806 Board of Trade Building,
Chicago, Ill.

September 24, 1940

Mr. R. Douglas Stuart, Jr.,
America First Committee
1806 Board of Trade Building,
Chicago, Illinois.

Dear Mr. Stuart:

I notice in one of your publications that you say that Fascists, Communists and Pacifists are not wanted by your Committee. I think, therefore, I should call your attention to the fact that I am and have been for many years a pacifist. This is so well known that I assumed that you were informed of it when your invitation came to me. There seems also to be some misunderstanding in your office as one of your assistants informed a visitor when she called attention to this fact that "when you are getting up a national committee it is impossible not to get some objectionable people on especially if they force themselves on." Naturally if I am objectionable you cannot wish me on the committee. As for forcing myself on, you are aware I am sure that I knew nothing about this committee until you wrote me and I never asked to join.

For your information I my add that I am heartily in sympathy with the program of the committee, but as I think I wrote you in accepting your invitation, that I should probably differ with you as to what constitutes a prepared America and an impregnable defense. I agree with the second, third and fourth clauses of your principles and I am wholly and enthusiastically in favor of your five objectives and should be happy to serve you along these lines by speaking over the radio etc, should you so desire. But if the fact that I do not believe in the theory of force should make me ineligible you will please regard this as my resignation.

One thing more as to my position. I realize that the bulk of my fellow citizens are in favor of military defense and therefore I am not only not opposing it, but am devoting the experience of a lifetime of study of military affairs in this country and in Europe to urging that whatever defense we decide upon it ought to be effective and not jeopardize the liberties of the American people or our democracy. It may interest you to know in this connection that the Christian Science Monitor of September 14 stated that : "The most forceful and comprehensive summing up of the Republican case against the futility of Mr. Roosevelt's defense program is that of Oswald Garrison Villard in a letter to the editors of the New Republic."

Yours very truly,

America First Committee

NATIONAL HEADQUARTERS * 1806 BOARD OF TRADE BUILDING * CHICAGO

TELEPHONE WABASH 6996-6997

R. DOUGLAS STUART, JR., DIRECTOR

National Committee

AVERY BRUNDAGE
JANET AYER FAIRBANK
JOHN T. FLYNN
HENRY FORD
BISHOP WILBUR E. HAMMAKER
GEN. THOMAS HAMMOND
JAY C. HORMEL
GEN. HUGH S. JOHNSON
CLAY JUDSON
KATHRYN LEWIS
ALICE ROOSEVELT LONGWORTH
HANFORD MacNIDER
THOMAS N. McCARTER
RAY McKAIG
STERLING MORTON
DR. ALBERT W. PALMER
WILLIAM H. REGNERY
EDWARD RICKENBACKER
LESSING J. ROSENWALD
EDWARD L. RYERSON, JR.
LOUIS TABER
OSWALD GARRISON VILLARD
MRS. BURTON K. WHEELER
DR. GEORGE H. WHIPPLE
GEN. ROBERT E. WOOD

September 26 1940

Libby
Detzer
KEEP AL OUT
... WAIL ...
C ...

Mr. Oswald Garrison Villard,
20 Vesey Street,
New York, N. Y.

Dear Mr. Villard:

Many thanks for your letter of September twenty-fourth.

It is an interesting fact, that this Committee about one week ago, came to the conclusion that we had been wrong in excluding those persons who do not believe in the theory of force. The enclosed material will show you this policy has been changed.

Frankly, the Committee sought to avoid the smearing to which Libby's Committee has been subjected. For this reason, when the Committee was launched, we attempted to get the punch across before the opposition punched us with that brand. In other words, by professing ourselves not to be pacifists, we hoped to escape that label.

But last week, as I have said, the Committee realized that it was a mistake to exclude those whose objectives so closely approximated our own. Of course the Committee adheres to its belief that force must be used to repel any invader from our shores.

I hope this clarifies our position and convinces you that you are completely eligible to work with this Committee, and it is important that this organization should not be "torpedoed" by resignations of members on the National Committee.

As far as the misunderstanding, for which one of my assistants was responsible, I wish to apologize for her mis-statement. It was perfectly ridiculous. Obviously there is no person on the National Committee who is objectionable to those persons who put them on the National Committee. I do hope you will excuse this unfortunate mis-statement. It was probably made by some voluntary worker in the office, who was not sufficiently acquainted with the organization.

I hope I will hear from you many times with advice or criticism. If you are ever in Chicago I would greatly enjoy the pleasure of meeting you.

Sincerely yours,
R. Douglas Stuart Jr.
R. Douglas Stuart, Jr.
Director

The Wrong Way to Prepare

By Oswald Garrison Villard

IT IS now clear, even without Mr. Knudsen's almost hysterical appeal to the Machine Tool Manufacturers' Association urging them to speed up production because of the "terrible urgency of the situation," that the preparedness program has bogged down. The army admits that a number of its camps are nowhere near completion. The whole conscription program has now been altered several times and it is not clear how many more times the raising of levies will have to be postponed in the next few months. This need surprise nobody. Haste always makes waste. Given our army setup, the hysteria and fright of the administration from the President down, the constant changing of plans, and the fact that the country as a whole is in no such state of panic as the government, nothing else was to have been expected. The condition of the war department alone was certain to insure confusion. Last spring it was content with an army of 800,000 regulars. Today, the Foreign Policy Association reports, the plan is for an army of 4,000,000 men of all categories, regulars, national guard, conscripted men and reserves, to be available for immediate service for hemisphere defense or an intercontinental war in Europe.

Undoubtedly the army is in better shape than it has ever been. By that I mean that there are many able officers in it and the material going into the ranks has never been surpassed in all its history. But how it is going to handle those men, what use it is going to make of them, and how modern the training will be which is to be given to them, is something that is far from being known. Indeed, Hanson Baldwin has gone so far as to say that conscription may easily prove to be a real detriment, and not an aid, to the preparedness which the country needs. He believes with George Fielding Eliot that such large forces are not necessary. They bear out a dispatch from London printed last summer in the *New York Sun* which quoted some of the leading military men in England as saying that they could not understand why President Roosevelt wanted conscription; that his demand for it showed that he had "not learned the first lesson of the war," namely, that it is no longer a question of masses of men but of tanks, bombers, planes of every kind, submarines, anti-aircraft guns, anti-tank guns and innumerable other mechanical devices calling for large numbers of technicians and above all for huge armies of men in factories and shipyards.

Prior Decisions Required

Further proof of this is the news that has come from a reliable source in Berlin that the German army is now being 65 per cent mechanized. Only two weeks ago one of our generals assured me in Washington that Hitler's troops were only 25 per cent mechanized and that I must not make any mistake, the chief reliance of a nation must still be upon masses of infantry. The very next day the other news came through. Until the objectives of our preparedness program are clarified, until we know just exactly where we are going, how many men we are going to keep under arms, how many in reserve, how many we are going to mechanize, and how large an airfleet we are really aiming at, we shall not have taken the first real step toward military preparedness.

You cannot ask officers to prepare when you do not tell them what they are to prepare for. If they are to develop a landing force for Japan it means, unless my lay intelligence is at fault, different categories of ships and different preparations from those necessary for putting an army into Europe. I have been told that moving an army to South America would present a still different problem from the other two. But even as to South America the plan changes constantly. Mr. Roosevelt has declared that we will defend not only all of South and North America, but the waters adjacent to America just so far as our interests dictate.

Unanswered Problems of Strategy

The army, on the other hand, several months ago abandoned the idea of total hemisphere defense and declared that it was interested only in that portion of South America above the Brazilian bulge. This territory it must control, it maintained, in order to preserve the Panama Canal. Everything to the south of us is being built around that precious Panama Canal which is held to be absolutely vital to us so that the fleet may be transferred from one ocean to the other. So we have taken the British bases in the Caribbean primarily to protect the Panama Canal, and we have actually authorized the construction at an enormous cost of a second and a third set of locks to be used only by the navy, so that if bombers put one set of locks out of commission there will still be two more for naval purposes.

Obviously, however, when the two-ocean fleet is built the Panama Canal will no longer have this tremendous military value which is now attached to it by some, in fact by most officers. There are dissenters, however. Hanson Baldwin of the *New York Times,* for example, refuses to believe that we should be fatally hamstrung should the Panama Canal be destroyed. The English are getting on very well in this war without the Suez Canal. Undoubtedly it adds to the cost and length of time of transportation to India. Still, they are doing it, and we could move our fleet around Cape Horn if we had to, precisely as the Oregon came around in 1898. To which the reply is that while the fleet was coming around the enemy might do us a deadly injury.

What we propose to do in regard to Japan if we go into this war is equally veiled in doubt. It is certain, however, that Japan will declare war upon us; she is bound to do that by the terms of her adherence to the Axis pact. Here there are two schools of thought among army and navy officers and experts. One believes that we should carry the war to Japan at any cost, if only to protect the Philippines. The other declares that this is impossible and unnecessary, and that the thing to do is simply to blockade Japan and to get England to join us in boycotting and cutting off all trade with her. That, it is stated, will bring Japan to her knees in a few weeks' time.

With us at war with Japan, no Japanese vessel could cross the Pacific going eastward. They would have to go around the Cape of Good Hope or through the Malaccan Straits, which might easily be blocked by a fleet based on Singapore. Mr. Roosevelt himself wrote in an article in *Asia* in 1923—it was reprinted in 1934—that we could not make war upon Japan or Japan upon us because of the distance between us. George Fielding Eliot has stated in one of his books that it would take the navy two years at the cost of many lives to reach Guam with 100,000 men, and then only, he says, would the "real show" begin.

Total Lack of Policy

I cite this merely as another instance of the total lack of clear-cut aims and policies, or a general agreement on what is to be done if we go to war, or what we are to prepare for if we stay out. Instance after instance of the same weakness in other fields could be cited. There seems to be a great deal of testimony that the British are disappointed in our airplanes which they say are not up to theirs, not modern, with very faulty landing carriages. It is explained that our planes are built to land on cement runways, and that there are precious few cement runways available when you are fighting in a war. Here again is an instance of equipment not being fitted to the use to which it is to be put. When it comes to the question of transportation, we have not begun to think about it. The navy has been buying up our best ships as rapidly as possible for transport purposes. England is purchasing the ships that it can get from the Maritime Commission.

Some years ago the navy declared that in the next war it would need something like 675 merchant vessels, tankers, auxiliaries and so on. That will make a big hole in our fleet. How many will the army need? Nobody knows or can even guess, because here again the army does not know what it will be called upon to do. Shall we prepare a fleet of transports to carry a million men to Brazil? Well, that will call for no less than 12,000,000 tons of shipping, as each soldier and his equipment call for no less than 12 tons. Actually we had 11,470,177 in our whole merchant fleet on July 1, 1939. We have added several hundred ships since then, and sold several hundred.

Planning and Brains Needed

If we take out those that the navy wants it is probably very close to the truth to say that we may not have even half the tonnage necessary to transport a million men to South America. For the total figure of shipping includes vessels of every type and all sizes. To get together a fleet to carry even half a million men is a stupendous undertaking; Major Eliot and Mr. Baldwin declare that at the outset of the war England with all her great merchant fleet could have transported only 200,000 troops to the United States, and that no two other nations combined could have done any better.

It all comes down to a question of planning and brains, and it is right here that Hitler has won his victories. He was certain that the war of masses was over and that the day of aerial warfare had come. He retired every one of his older generals and in accordance with Göring's counsel put all his strength into airplane production. He knew what he was planning to do and what forces he would need and he bent the whole economy of the nation to that end. We shall accomplish nothing like this unless we, too, bend every energy to the carrying out of a preconceived modern plan, and the first requisite is entrusting the carrying out of the plan to vigorous, competent men who have forgotten all about the First World War, trench warfare and mass movement. The difficulty is that the war department has never been modernized. Major General Hagood declares that no secretary of war has learned to know the war department, and to control and coordinate it.

Undoubtedly on the supply side we have made progress, but here the failure to give a head to the Defense Advisory Commission has been a great mistake. I heard on very good authority in Washington that that body complains that one of the bottlenecks threatening full speed production is the desk of Franklin Roosevelt; that there are many papers piled up there awaiting decision. There are even those wicked enough to insinuate that one reason for the delay is—political considerations, which would certainly seem to be uncalled for now that the election is over. The appointment of the new four-man "Super-Production Commission" is obviously a long step in the right direction.

Are We Going In?

Finally, the great clarification needed is the decision whether we are going to get into the war or not, and if we are going to get in whether we are going to get in sternforemost without a declaration of war, without a vote by Congress, without giving the mass of the American people who have repeatedly shown their overwhelming opposition to going to war again a chance to make their wishes felt. If we go on resorting to such subterfuges as "leasing" ammunition, tanks and so forth to Great Britain, we shall certainly be actively in the war before very long.

The greatest danger of all is that in the haste and excitement of the mad rush to prepare, those responsible for our future will fail to take heed of what will happen to us if we go into the struggle. The unanimity of opinion among our big business men that we shall become a totalitarian state, that we shall be bankrupt, and that it will cost us sums of which the world has never dreamed, is startling. But that does not weigh with those of our patriots who are screaming that we shall be lost if England is, that it is our sole defense, and that we must stop at nothing to save the British, not even at sacrificing ourselves. With them there is no use arguing.

But there still is time for public opinion in the United States to let the Roosevelt administration know that it is overwhelmingly opposed to our committing suicide in trying to give to England help which we are in no position to give. Certainly if the people are put into the war they will go reluctantly, unwillingly, involuntarily, and more than halfheartedly, into a struggle which Captain Rickenbacker, our wartime flier who is now president of the Eastern Airlines, declares will last a minimum of three to four years and a maximum of five to six, and leave us a dictatorship with a debt of somewhere between $150,000,000,000 and $200,000,000,000.

The Pattern for War Is Repeated

By Oswald Garrison Villard

THE PATTERN for war which is now being worked out under our very eyes seems to me in many ways the most astounding repetition of history in recent times. There are certain differences, of course, as was inevitable with the two presidents concerned. But in the main what we are witnessing is the story of 1915-17 over again. Indubitably the British have a far better case for American sympathy than in the earlier war, despite the fact that the stupidity and shortsightedness of their statesmen ever since the making of the Treaty of Versailles are in very considerable measure responsible for the coming of the Second World War. Again, there has been no such appeal to American emotion as that caused by the murder of American citizens bound for Europe on the Lusitania and other vessels.

Finance and Business Hold Back

The attitude of big business is another exception. In the last war the Morgans and others were openly expressing their eagerness to have us enter the war, and had a tremendous financial stake in our getting in. Today big business is not eager for what President Roosevelt called at Chautauqua the "fool's gold" of war profits. The head of the United States Chamber of Commerce, James S. Kemper, has repeatedly warned American business that involvement in a war would probably lead to national bankruptcy and that the European dictators came into power in consequence of national bankruptcy. He has asserted that participation in war might change "our whole social and economic system."

What Mr. Kemper has said has been echoed by a number of other business leaders, with the result that they are dubbed "appeasers." Undoubtedly the fear of socialism as well as of bankruptcy and of revolution, and fear of the repetition of the post-war economic depression, have a great deal to do with the attitude of big business men. They burned their fingers before and have lost much more during the long continued depression than they made during the First World War. Whatever may come out of the present campaign to put us into the struggle, it will be impossible in the future to blame international bankers or international business men.

No Counting of the Cost

In other respects, however, the pattern is almost precisely the same. Just as many of the intellectuals, particularly on the eastern seaboard, lost their balance and were carried away by their emotions a quarter-century ago, so the intellectuals of today are traveling the same road. Indeed, they are open to a greater indictment than in the last struggle. This time fear has really laid strong hands upon them. It is astounding how many men, even some who risked imprisonment in the last war by their opposition, are now declaring that this war is an exception. The leaders of much of this rush to war are university professors; some of the political science faculties are unitedly for our entering the war at once, and are no more counting the cost in human suffering and misery than they were in the last struggle.

These academicians are blithely combating the idea that if we go into the war we shall be a totalitarian state; they are upbraiding persons like the writer who think that we shall come out a dictatorship and point to the fact that we did not lose our democracy after the last war as proof of the correctness of their attitude. Yet I do not hear a single one of them ever evidence by a single word that he is even thinking of what our entry into the war will mean in the toll of human existences ended in early youth, of the thousands who may be immured for life in veterans' hospitals, hopeless wrecks, as is the case today, or even mention the horrible sufferings that those who are wounded and survive are called upon to endure. Those things are written down as among the sacrifices, and apparently the lesser ones, that America must cheerfully make in order to preserve democracy.

There are still other familiar threads in this pattern for war. Again the mass of the people is opposed, as every Gallup poll has shown. Again it is a minority, rich and powerful, which is taking the lead, and again chiefly in the east. It is once more fashionable to enter war work. The Back Bay and Park Avenue have again struck hands in their zeal to wrap bundles for Britain, to send overcoats and ambulances and to knit innumerable garments. They have the power to organize and the means and the time for it. They are the ones who hold bridge parties and balls, and their husbands cheerfully pick paper stars, at $10 a star, off the practically nude Gypsy Rose Lee—all for dear old England.

No one can charge the idle rich with being idle now, any more than was the case after the sinking of the Lusitania. They and the college professors, and the editors of liberal journals, and numerous other groups are showing what minority pressure plus organization can accomplish. They are bound to impose their will in this matter upon the country even if the Gallup polls continue to show that 85 per cent of the American people are opposed to going to war, precisely as the small pressure group that put over conscription gave a most brilliant example of what money, quick organization and knowing the ropes in Washington can accomplish with the aid of some of the most powerful newspapers in the country.

A Familiar Newspaper Technique

The newspapers as a whole are reacting just as they did twenty-five years ago. The more radical peace groups with their less influential leaders and membership are lucky when they get a couple of sticks of type on the twenty-third page. Verne Marshall gets the first pages partly because he is himself a newspaper editor, partly because he understands publicity, and partly because those opposed to him think they can best dispose of him by featuring some rather rash statements that he makes, his ineptness, and the record of the man who, he says, is his chief financial backer. The America First Committee has fared well because of the prominence, especially in the business world, of its leader and some of its members. No newspaper is apt to ignore the head of Sears, Roebuck and Company. But the cartoonists are again given full swing to portray the alleged dangers to America and to bring out the wickednesses and cruelties and stupidities of the dictators. Only a few dailies are really striving to keep the country at peace, at least in the east. The southern press, too, is distinctly belligerent. All these papers lend themselves readily to the "smearing" of opponents by describing them as appeasers and fifth columnists or even German agents.

In the last pre-war campaign for American participation we did not have these particular names and adjectives, which are themselves the product either of the last war or of the actions of the British statesmen up to the time of the coming of the present one. In 1915 and 1916 the terrible offense was to be a pacifist. It is now considered one of the gravest offenses to be unwilling to fight to save England. Here, however, the present pattern deviates. It is now a disgrace to be an advocate of America first. I heard a Harvard professor the other night treating the America First Committee as if its members were convicted fifth columnists and traitors.

It used to be considered a matter of course that Americans should stand for America first. Those who stood for the League of Nations, for internationalism of the true cooperative type, were denounced by the Lodges and their allies as bad Americans. Of course the opposition to those who stand for America first now is not due in most cases to a desire for a real cooperation of all nations: America simply must not be put ahead of England. A committee called "America and England First, Plus France If It Does What We Wish," would probably be beyond attack.

Resort to Calling Names

As in the previous instance, passion and bitterness and name-calling are all on the side of those who want us to go to war. It has always been an interesting fact that that is the case even when no wars are on. If then you oppose large armaments you instantly are confronted by a vindictive desire to punish you and to hold you up to scorn. Your motives are suspect and any committee which relies upon public contributions must show that it is not receiving aid from men who prior to the present war, or the last war, were dealing with the "Huns." When war comes there will be the same mobbing of all who dare to stand out against the President's policy, but it will be worse this time because President Roosevelt is now setting the example. These words he used in his message to Congress: "The best way of dealing with a few slackers or troublemakers in our midst is, first, to shame them by patriotic example, and, if that fails, to use the sovereignty of government to save government." Such words are unprecedented in our history. It was the first time that a President of the United States has threatened to use the power of the government in peacetime to suppress criticism and dissent—this in a democracy!

Similarly, the President's statement at one of his press conferences that there would soon be Liberty bond issues and that those bonds would be made the test of the loyalty of all persons with means to subscribe for them, opens the door to a repetition of the dragooning of persons for bond purchases, notably in the west and northwest, which disgraced our conduct of the last war. This time there will thus be presidential sanction for these acts, which in certain sections of the country led not only to actual torture but occasionally even to murder, to horse-whipping, tarring and feathering. I know of a man who had actually fought at Gettysburg and until Appomattox who was the victim of such violence. If the President realizes the effect on the mob emotions of the thoughtless which his statement may have he was guilty of what comes perilously close to being incitement to violence. If he did not realize it, the more's the pity.

'The More It Is the Same'

To list all the other parallels would take a great deal more space than I have at my disposal. There is the same amazing assurance that we shall win the war if we enter it. There is the same raising of every kind of fear of the enemy and his power, and the same taking counsel of those fears. There is the same mad arming as in 1916-17, and I fear the same welter of inefficiency. There is the same lack of definite objectives, the same ignorance of what England plans to do if it wins the war, of what kind of world it will seek to create if it triumphs in the struggle. There is the same readiness to go in without, so far as can be seen, any effort toward a clear understanding of how the war is to be jointly conducted. I think that before long we shall have a sensational dismissal of German consuls to parallel the dismissal of the Austrian ambassador, the German military and naval attachés, and finally Bernstorff himself in 1916-17.

All of this duplication of patterns for war brings up a fundamental question, that of minority rule. Again the masses of the plain people are unable to make their wishes felt. They cannot organize suddenly, or raise large funds, or become vocal, or win support by the bulk of the conservative press. Anyone who, like myself, has spoken to audiences on the side of calmness, a rational view of events, a clear understanding of what war will mean to us, will agree with me that inevitably someone in the audience asks in deeply troubled tones, "Well, what *can* we do about it since there is no referendum upon war?" One feels hopelessly ineffectual when one lists once more the few ways of making public opinion felt—letters to the President, senators, congressmen and the newspapers; mass meetings, the forwarding of resolutions, talks on the radio (when there is no money available for such talks) —that is all that one can say.

I have long wondered whether this is not the fundamental weakness of democracy, this inability of the masses to do what rich, powerful pressure groups can achieve. The dissenting peace-lovers or anti-conscriptionists or opponents of large armaments simply cannot make their wishes known and controlling even where they are in the vast majority. Here is a rock upon which the ship of state may be foundering and democracy being riven asunder. Here is something to my mind far more ominous than the presence among us of spies and agents of dictators and fifth columnists generally. For we can deal with the latter if we wish; there is no immediate remedy for that lack of majority rule which theoretically is supreme in the United States.

January 29, 1941

Dear Colcord:

I send you a copy of a letter that I am sending to the Boston Transcript in regard to the Churchill interview. My private opinion is that Griffin tells the truth and that it is just another case of a public man's welshing when what he said got too hot for him.

After the barrage of Morgenthau and Marshall yesterday I do not suppose there is much hope left. The proposed amendments to the Lend-Lease Bill do not improve it, of course. F.D.R. will have his own way just the same. All the people I meet of our faith are perfectly hopeless. On the short Chicago-Detroit trip that I have just made, which ended in my passing out in the middle of my Detroit lecture, I found everybody certain that war is at hand. I talked to a great audience of Jews and found 80 per cent of them against me. They feel that if we do not get into the war Hitler will get over here and put them in concentration camps, so they are taking the direct road to anti-Semitism and militarism. Did you see President Hutchins' magnificent speech? But that don't offset the Lamonts and the officials.

Best greetings,

Faithfully,

Please return the enclosed as
it is my file copy.

The Betrayal of Our Democracy

By Oswald Garrison Villard

IF FUTURE HISTORIANS are called on to write ponderous tomes on "The Decline and Fall of the American Empire," they will surely have to devote some important chapters to the part that deliberate hypocrisy will have played in the undermining of our American institutions. I am moved to this thought first by the testimony of Mr. Willkie before the Senate committee dealing with the lend-lease bill, when he brushed aside his severest campaign criticisms of Franklin Roosevelt as certain to lead us into war and disaster if reelected by declaring that those things were said in the heat of the campaign and were therefore not to be taken too seriously. His own undermining of his spoken word by this admission constitutes such an indictment of himself that he will be alone to blame if every time he speaks hereafter someone rises in the audience to ask whether he has just talked campaign bunk or something that he wishes the audience really to believe.

Authoritative Testimony

But if we are going to be put into the war now, the other side will not be able to cast a single stone at Mr. Willkie. Before me lies an article by Arthur Krock, the chief editorial correspondent of the *New York Times,* who usually speaks by the book, and has twice been favored by President Roosevelt with information for articles not given to any other reporter. In his article Mr. Krock brushes aside the hypocrisy of the government's past assurance that it had no intention of putting us into war by saying that official opinion has now swung to the point where it is no longer willing to deal in subterfuges and compromises such as giving the British a new American destroyer for every British destroyer brought to our harbors for repairs, or by exchanging two or three heavy British battleships for certain of our smaller vessels needed by the British for north Atlantic convoys. Since the navy, he says, continues to object to the sale, gift or transfer of any existing war craft and "official opinion grows in opposition to both schemes on the ground that they are subterfuges and that time for realism has arrived," it is now "the official disposition to look at the case squarely, forget the hopes, promises and *political deceptions of the past,* and provide direct means to meet whatever situation may arise." The italics are mine; they are the crux of the statement. They mean that Mr. Krock has discovered that the administration is ready to lay aside the mask of hypocrisy and deceit.

Hence, he says, the convoying of supply ships by our navy this spring is being faced as more than a possibility and he quotes two statements made by officials who, he says, believed, or tried to believe, in "short of war" solutions. The first is: "What's the sense of producing weapons to fight Germany that never get there?" The second reads: "When a nation sets out on a policy, approved by the people, it must pursue it to the limit of effectiveness." That is, effectiveness in aiding Britain is to supersede honor and simple decency and honesty in the relations between Mr. Roosevelt and his cabinet and the American people. In order to make sure (as if that could be done) that American supplies will reach England, the most solemn pledges of the Democratic national platform and of the President himself are to be broken and forgotten.

Breach of Faith

The "political deceptions" of which Mr. Krock speaks are now to be cold-bloodedly brushed aside, doubtless in the hope that the American people will be so excited by the alarmist speeches being made every day by ex-ambassadors like Mr. Bullitt and members of the cabinet that they will forget the solemn assurances of the last campaign. Finally, Mr. Krock concludes: "An official Washington seems at last resigned to make whatever application is found to be necessary," the reference being to an aphorism in which the national danger is likened to a "drunk" who may do anything and has to be handled accordingly.

In more than forty years of journalism I cannot recall a more shocking case of breach of faith with the American people than is involved in this statement of Mr. Krock's as to what the situation is at this hour. When Mr. Wilson was elected on the platform, "He kept us out of war," in 1916, and then put us into war in 1917, it was alleged on his behalf that the situation had tremendously changed between November 1916, the time of the election, and April 1917. There can be no such allegation this time. There is nothing in the situation today that is different from that during the presidential campaign. If the shipping situation is more ominous, on the other hand we must not forget the magnificent victories in Greece and Africa.

The conclusion is inescapable that, as I and so many others wrote and said during the campaign, Mr. Roosevelt deliberately deceived us at that time and that he had then and still has the full intention of putting us into the war. Now Mr. Krock's words confirm, if they are correct, the position taken by us during the campaign. I wonder, knowing Mr. Krock and his high ideals as I do, that he could bring himself to write such a terrible indictment of the administration, even though he felt it his duty as a good reporter to portray the facts as they are.

What Will the Reaction Be?

I find opinions differing here in Washington as to how the American people will accept the fact of our being put into the war after Mr. Roosevelt's positive assurance that "American men and American ships will never be sent abroad." The wife of a senator who has been reading her husband's enormous mail, more than 95 per cent of which is opposed to the lend-lease bill, tells me that she is certain that a tremendous wave of indignation and outrage will sweep over the country when war comes. Another friend who had been working all day with three officials of the government told me, to my surprise, that they were all three outraged at what was going on and at the evident determination of the President and his cabinet to put us into war.

My own newspaper judgment coincides with the view of some Washington correspondents I have talked to, that the country will accept war without the slightest enthusiasm, in the same spirit of sullen, unhappy resignation in which the French and German people went to war and without that marvelous, grim determination of the British to see it through. But of one thing I am certain and that is that this impending open duplicity of the Roosevelt administration will have a profound and most unfortunate influence upon our own democratic institutions. Mr. Roosevelt denounced Mussolini when he went to war last June for having delivered a stab in the back. Whether consciously or unconsciously, he will deliver a dreadful stab in the back to our American democracy if he breaks his word with the American people and goes to war.

Treachery to Democracy

How can democracy survive such treachery? I asked myself that question in 1917; I asked it many times before and I have asked it every year since. My mind goes back now to an incident that took place at a tariff reform dinner here in the city of Washington some years ago. A distinguished senator from a New England state was one of the speakers, as I was. He made a typical politician's address—"on the one hand and on the other," balancing deftly on the top rail of the fence. I made an out-and-out free trade speech, pulling no punches. The senator, when I finished, excused himself and left to meet another appointment. As he left the table he stopped and whispered to me: "I agree with every word you have said. That's exactly how I feel, but if I should say that I should be defeated for reelection." It was all I could do to restrain myself and keep from yelling after him, "Curse you, it's just because of hypocrites like you that democratic government is cracking in America." This, be it remembered, was before the rule of Hitler, when the führer was on his way up. Even then the danger to our republic was apparent enough.

The reader may say, "Well, it has always been so, from the earliest days of the republic." Possibly, but the reader must remember that the stakes today are vastly greater, that the dangers facing democracy are without precedent in their gravity, that the machine age and the tremendous industrial development of the United States have made this intellectual treachery to the democracy vastly more serious than similar dishonesty even during the days of the fight to free the slaves.

There is one appalling statement quoted by Mr. Krock, namely, that the "people have approved" the government's policy of all-out aid to England. The people have not approved it. They have had no opportunity to vote on it; the evidence is that the vast bulk of the letters received by senators both for and against the lend-lease bill are opposed to the government's present policy while eager to aid England. The administration has just as much right to say that the people approved the voting of conscription last summer when they obviously did not. Pretty soon we shall be told that the people are overwhelmingly behind President Roosevelt in taking us into war and that they understand that the situation has changed and that he has reluctantly, weeping endless tears of regret, found himself compelled to take us into war.

I can see Harold Ickes (who has just revealed to an audience in Boston that this is now a war to save Christianity) assuring the country that 90 per cent of the American people stand behind the President in using, to quote Woodrow Wilson, "force, force without stint," against the Huns. One will be just as false as the other. Christianity will not be saved by more war. On the contrary, it will be endangered as it has never been before. It was Lloyd George himself who, a few years ago, speaking to the annual convocation of the Welsh church, warned his hearers that if the churches of America and England allowed another world war to come they might just as well lock the doors of those churches at the outbreak of the war because they would never be used again after it was over.

But it is the plight of democracy that most appeals to me today. How can one expect the American people to have faith that their institutions will survive when they find that the politicians in office are just as untrustworthy as is Mr. Willkie on the outside? Hopelessness, despair, misery, indifference, loss of faith—these can be deadly fifth columnists indeed, far more deadly than the so-called "appeasers" and the futile American adherents of Stalin the butcher, yes, even more dangerous than the agents of Hitler, the mass murderer, however skillful and insidious those borers-from-within may be. For if you take from the American people their belief in the soundness of their government and their institutions you have no reason to expect them to repel attack from the outside or the inside. You will not be able to enlist their enthusiastic support of efforts to reform our state and make over our institutions and cure our economic abuses and wrongs and injustices. They will simply say, "What is the use, what is the use?" and let everything go at that—grateful like the decent downtrodden anti-nazi Germans if they are let alone and given a day's work and their daily bread.

Are We to Rule the World?

By Oswald Garrison Villard

THE QUESTION WHETHER we are to rule the world and make that the real objective of our interference in the imperialist war now going on is being squarely presented to the American people, notably by Henry C. Luce, who is today perhaps the most influential of all our magazine publishers. His pamphlet entitled *The American Century* has been endorsed by Dorothy Thompson again and again; she says she is not sure that this will not prove to be a historic piece of literature. In its essence it is a demand that America seize this opportunity when Europe is rapidly committing suicide to take the leadership of the world, to formulate in what is left of this century its policies and to impose our will upon the globe.

Lest any reader think that this is an exaggeration, may I point out one fact which has been overlooked even by critics of Mr. Luce's extraordinary effusion? Thus, he advocates not just freedom of the seas, but freedom of the seas "for ourselves and our friends." Could anything be more revealing? In 1917 Woodrow Wilson put us into war on behalf of freedom of the seas for everybody, for all the nations of the earth. The English did not like that, but they swallowed it with a mental reservation that Mr. Wilson would not get it, though they assured him they were all for it. At Versailles nothing further was heard of freedom of the seas.

The New American Imperialism

But now this new historical American imperialism, born of the earth-shaking events in Europe and the sudden panic fear which has overtaken the descendants of Lexington, Valley Forge, Antietam and Gettysburg, is frankly determined if it wins this war—and it has no doubt of its impending victory—to make of the oceans of the world an American possession for the benefit of "ourselves and our friends." As a veteran journalist writes to me after reading these words in Mr. Luce's paper: "Shades of Theodore Roosevelt, Captain Mahan and John Hay! Did any of these, the first in his wildness, the second in his ignorance, the third in his cynicism, ever dare that! That's not mere imperialism, it's imperialism plus aggression. You would have to go to *Mein Kampf* for a parallel."

Now let no one think that this proposal of Mr. Luce's is just an impossible fantasy. We have now entered into partnership with Great Britain for better or for worse. We have joined hands with her to beat Hitler. This time we are going to be the senior partner in the enterprise—that is, if it goes on any length of time. For we are going to furnish the ships and the money and the munitions and the food and the hundred thousand articles which go toward outfitting the modern army, to say nothing of the tanks, the motor trucks, the tractors and the airplanes. If this war lasts two years England will be hopelessly in debt to us—even if we do not ask any money return. She will be in debt to us morally and actually may owe to us the very continuance of her free existence. Under those circumstances she will do what we tell her. If we decide after our victory that henceforth the world is to be ruled by the British and American fleets and that nobody else is going to be allowed to have a warship, why Mr. Luce's desire will have been accomplished. The oceans of the world will be closed seas to any who are not our friends—or our subjects—whenever we wish to close them.

An Ambassador's Dream

Mr. Luce isn't the only man who has been toying with this idea of a dictated peace for the world. Hitler is determined to impose a *Pax Germanica* upon all of Europe and the Mediterranean countries, if not upon the whole world. On December 1, 1939, I talked with an important American ambassador in Europe who assured me that the Allies would have air superiority by March 1940, that that would end the war, that Stalin would then be ordered out of Poland and that the world would then be peaceful and serene, with a peace dictated by the British and French air forces, none other being allowed, world without end. Oh, yes! I forgot to add that before the peace was established three or four German cities were to be utterly destroyed down to the last house, so that the Germans would for once know on their own soil what war is like. With this act of justice completed we should have, he was certain, the benefits of a successful war to end war.

Frankly, that kind of world doesn't appeal to me. Nor does Mr. Luce's world ruled by a combination of English and American wisdom and statesmanship. Of course I know that we Americans and the English are the noblest people on earth. As a loyal American that has been dinned into me on every Fourth of July, in every election campaign, at every patriotic rally. Have we not always called this God's country? And have we not known that we were God's chosen people? Is not the complete proof of God's favor this glorious and fantastically rich country which he has turned over to us? Mr. Luce plainly has imbibed this belief and this philosophy of life. "We and our friends"—and today our friends are practically only the English—are to rule the seas. But we, God's anointed, shall make this our century and our world.

The English May be Obstinate

Mr. Luce thinks the British people are worth risking our national existence to succor, but I am sure that when it comes down to it, he knows in his heart that we Americans are much wiser and nobler and purer than the English. We shall save the British, but let it not be forgotten that this is to become "the American century."

Of course there are some obstinate Englishmen who will be slow to admit this. Contemplating the glorious fight which they have put up against overwhelming nazi forces, they are not unnaturally thinking very highly of themselves and their magnificent demonstration of the power of a spirit which has risen above unparalleled destruction, misery and wanton and wicked slaughter. But even before this war there were some Englishmen who were just as certain that they were the chosen people of the world as we have been sure that God has selected America for special, well deserved favors, or as Hitler is convinced that the Germans are the finest and greatest human beings ever seen, destined to control everything, with all the other inferior races as their servitors and slaves.

Doing God's Work

There is Lord Beaverbrook, for example, the British newspaper magnate, who is today saving Great Britain by the magnificent work he has been doing as the head of British aviation production. Speaking a few years ago at a meeting held at Putney, as reported in the London *Daily Express,* in the course of a debate upon the customs union within the British empire, this great statesman said: "I absolutely assert that in advancing a policy of a customs union in the British empire we are doing God's work."

"When you say," asked an auditor, "that you are doing God's work, does God admit that one man is a foreigner and another is his brother?"

"Certainly," replied Lord Beaverbrook. "Why did God raise up the British empire? Why did God raise up the Israelites? Why has God maintained the British empire during the tempests and trials of centuries? Why has God made us the greatest, finest and most powerful people in the world?" (Loud applause.)

Of course the audience applauded. What patriotic audience would not? What patriotic audience anywhere would not expect to be told by every statesman and politician appearing before it that his auditors belonged to the greatest, finest and most powerful people in the world?

Good and Bad Dictators

Well, again I stubbornly record my dissent. I do not think that this world was made to be ruled by Anglo-Saxons, by any two nations or any one nation. Of course I should prefer to be ruled by Americans or next by the British if one country is to dominate the world by sheer force. But it would be no time at all before the assumption of that power would destroy the country using it, morally, intellectually and finally physically. President Alan Valentine of the University of Rochester correctly observed, in testifying against the lend-lease bill, that the difference between a good dictator and a bad dictator was only a matter of time. He was right in thinking that the longer a despot rules the worse he gets. So with any country which might assume the domination of the world. Its very certainty in its own superiority, its being the chosen of God, will bring about its destruction. The megalomania of Hitler and his absurd belief that God created Germany to dominate the world will in time wreck his government even if he should win this war. If any world domination were attempted really in a spirit of moderation, of justice, and of the desire to rule fairly and equitably, it would inevitably deteriorate and fail. That is the unfailing lesson of all history.

Still we shall continue to be deluged with appeals to take over the management of this erring world. Already we are being told that it wasn't our fault that the Treaty of Versailles went wrong, or Mr. Wilson's. It was all the wickedness of the other participants in the making of the peace. They would not listen to our wisdom and give us our Fourteen Points. No, they took their own way, and now look what they've got!

So this time, plainly, the thing for us to do is not to ask anybody's cooperation in making the peace. We shall make it ourselves. We shall be the most powerful nation, militarily speaking, with by far the greatest armada the world has ever seen, and we won't stand for any Lloyd George business at the making of this peace. We shall tell them all where they get off. God's country is on top and proposes to stay there. The William Allen White Committee will of course fall in line without a moment's hesitation. Did not Mr. White himself write: "It is the Anglo-Saxon's manifest destiny to go forth in the world as a world conqueror. He will take possession of all the islands of the sea. He will exterminate the peoples he cannot subjugate. That is what fate holds for the chosen people. It is so written. Those who would protest will find their objections overruled." Yes, it was William Allen White and not Adolf Hitler who penned these astonishing words.

God's Chosen People?

So let us begin planning now to rule the world. Let us do away with the various self-constituted committees which are setting up a program for the world that is to be. Let us tell Mr. Streit to desist from planning his Anglo-Saxon union. If Adolf Hitler wins there will be no such union, and if we win our government will attend to that itself and dominate everything. What is left of England and the dominions will stand as loyal satellites. We may even have to take over India, but why not? If we are going to extend our rule over all the Pacific why should we not make over Asia?

And—heart-warming thought—how readily then we shall be able to eliminate the bolsheviks! With the rest of the globe in our hands, we can simply and easily blockade them, shut them off from all contacts by mail, telephone, telegraph, radio, railroads and shipping. We shall make them live to themselves alone. What they cannot raise or create they will not be able to buy until they have reformed their ways and become as fine a democracy as some of those we are now going to support, such as Greece and Turkey.

Indeed, the more I contemplate Mr. Luce's historic piece of literature the more certain I am that if we follow his lead this nation is going to have the time of its life. We shall raise our boys not only to be soldiers and sailors, but as great transoceanic bearers of our culture and religion to the outermost places of the world, as were the leaders of the legions of Rome when they conquered England and most of Europe. If that doesn't produce the millennium, why—but of course it will. God's chosen people cannot go wrong. They will produce a world that will make heaven seem shoddy indeed.

President of the World?

By Oswald Garrison Villard

I SEE that the *New Republic* has printed, over the initials which it uses to cloak the anonymity of its Washington correspondents, "T.R.B.," an article announcing that President Roosevelt is no longer President of the United States but President of the World. That seems like going a little bit far. Both Mr. Hitler and Mr. Stalin, and the Japanese government, might dispute that claim. There could, of course, be no righteous dissent if this correspondent had called Mr. Roosevelt President of America and England, for that Mr. Roosevelt now is. He who pays the piper calls the tune. If what the President says as to the needs of England is true then the destiny of England is in his hands. He can tell Mr. Churchill what to do and what he cannot do; the *New Republic's* writer says that the President himself ordered the unwilling English to let the Red Cross food ships through the blockade and that he has personally demanded that they sell the Viscose Company back to Americans, which was something that the British refused to do throughout the last war during which they held on to their American companies.

If it is true, and I believe that it is, that the President sent seven dispatches in nine days at the time of the fall of France to Marshal Petain instructing him what to do with the French fleet, it would certainly not be surprising if he told Mr. Churchill from time to time what to do in a military and naval way. If England's situation gets worse it will be the more dependent upon us; it will need more American ships, more American money, ammunition and supplies, and eventually American men. Every time Mr. Churchill asks for additional aid he will go deeper and deeper into our debt and become more and more a tool of the White House. Undoubtedly if England gets into a terrible jam Mr. Churchill will make a formal offer of union now with the United States, precisely as he did to France.

It must not be forgotten—as I find most people have, and as I am sure Mr. Clarence Streit will be anxious to forget—that Winston Churchill offered a complete union to France in his last desperate effort to keep France from surrendering. He even proposed that Frenchmen and Englishmen exercise a joint citizenship, which was about as close to being a complete merger as one can imagine short of complete amalgamation. If he finds himself in the last ditch there is nothing that Mr. Churchill will not do to induce us to take over complete responsibility for the fate of England. That we shall join forces with Canada, if England goes down, is a foregone conclusion.

When we look at Europe I admit that there is considerable ground for "T. R. B.'s" contention that the President is already President of the World. Certainly he is on his way to becoming that. What could be a more incredible departure from every American tradition, what a more complete break with all our history, than the announcement the day after the overturn in Yugoslavia that under the lend-lease bill the United States was ready and willing to back the new Yugoslav government in every possible way?

Incitement to War

Talk about George Washington's advice against entangling alliances! This must make Washington turn in his grave not once but many, many times as he marvels that his countrymen have so completely forgotten his solemn warning against European alliances as to have hurled themselves into support of a revolutionary government before it had even been thirty hours in the saddle. Discretion might have dictated waiting at least a few days, but Sumner Welles was Johnny-on-the-spot. The President was off in the Caribbean and Mr. Hull was away, so the acting secretary of state had an immediate note delivered to the new dictator of Yugoslavia telling him that the United States treasury was open to him, provided he would go to war, or to put it more delicately, "oppose aggression." Mr. Welles could have put his note into far fewer words: "Come and get it."

This seems to me a distinct incitement to war. The new Yugoslavian government has wisely taken the position that for the present it will neither repudiate nor affirm the agreement with the Axis which led to the revolution, and that it proposes to maintain neutrality as it had steadily been trying to maintain it up to the time that it surrendered to Germany. But in his haste to strike a blow at Hitler in our undeclared war upon him, Mr. Welles went farther than General Simovitch, with the idea of frightening Hitler off by letting him know that the United States stands squarely behind the young King Peter. Who shall say now that we are not a European power, at least by our acts? Who can deny that if this goes on we shall soon have a fine group of satellite states all being helped to victory by the money of the American taxpayer? Greece, Yugoslavia, and Turkey if she comes in. Already we are using the horrible plight of Spain and our surplus food to play politics there by letting Spain know that our altruism and beneficence will end on the day that the dictator yields to the Axis, and of course every move we make in regard to free France is with the purpose of keeping Petain and Darlan from striking hands with Hitler. Could we really be in any deeper than we are?

Power Politics Above Principle

Undoubtedly we would be willing to pat Japan and Russia on the back and ask them what they would like us to serve out to them in the way of money and supplies if they, too, should suddenly break with Hitler. Washington has already lifted in part the embargo against Russia and is doubtless much miffed that the Russians don't seem to be the least bit moved thereby ("T. R. B." bemoans the fact that the Russian ambassador has deliberately failed to keep two appointments with the state department). We are no longer applying any yardstick beyond our one demand that the country in question shall oppose Hitler. The government may be a dictatorship as in Turkey; nonetheless we rush to force our bounty of money, ammunition and planes upon the Turkish dictator. This new government in Yugoslavia certainly has claims to be a popular one, brought into being by public opposition to the alliance with the Axis, but whether it will not shortly become as much a despotism as its predecessor we cannot even wait to see. Everything is being subordinated to lightning-like moves to check Hitler. Only it is reported that our administration has grown lukewarm as to China. Something has gone wrong over there; the President's special envoy, Lachlan Currie, seems to have brought back a discouraging report, perhaps that Chiang Kai-shek is not belligerent enough. Who knows? Not we, the American people.

Again, we are told that Germany's declaring a blockade around Iceland has brought us to the verge of the war since the edge of that blockade is only a few miles from Greenland, and Greenland is within our new American zone of operations in the Atlantic since it is included in our "neutrality zone." Of course that German action was a mere form since, as the English promptly pointed out, the Germans have been sinking ships in those waters whenever they saw them. On the other side of the globe some of our warships have suddenly turned up in Australia and New Zealand. Under Secretary Knox's voluntary censorship of the press, we were not allowed to know that they were on their way there, but news of their arrival is freely given out, together with a full account of the warm reception given them, in order to impress Japan. If they do not continue their voyage to Singapore I shall be very much surprised. The point is that if Mr. Roosevelt is not yet President of the World there are few parts of the globe in which he is not showing his hand.

The New Role of World Dominator

"T. R. B." says that one reason for the President's voyage to the Caribbean (during which his accompanying destroyers have made a mimic attack upon "his yacht"), in addition to his natural and proper desire for a rest, is that he needs at this time to adjust himself to the great new role of world dominator that he must now play. A chapter has been ended. The New Deal and the first two terms are well in the past. He is no longer to concern himself merely with the welfare of 130,000,000 people, but in the name of their safety to mold the progress of the world in the quest of security for democracy. Naturally he wants time to think a little bit about this trifling new task. He must set his thoughts in order; he must plan what the next steps are to be, how his world domination is to take shape. It is reported that he still believes that he may be able to keep us out of a formal war by frightening Hitler.

Navy to the Mediterranean?

Will he now send our navy into the Mediterranean? We are told that it is obviously ridiculous to turn America into the arsenal of democracy if we cannot deliver the products of the arsenal and that therefore we must convoy the transports, at least halfway across the Atlantic. But if the arsenal of democracy is now to furnish weapons and ammunition and aircraft and food and clothing and all the rest to Greece and Yugoslavia, can we proud Americans permit any ships convoying these goods of ours to be sunk in the Mediterranean by German and Italian submarines on the loose? Obviously not. Senator Glass, the 83-year-old fire-eater from Virginia, is all for convoying our ships at once. What right has Hitler to dare to interfere with the will of the American people?

Well, the trouble is that it is not the will of the American people, but of Mr. Roosevelt and his subservient cabinet. I know that not all public men in Washington are happy about this. I had a long talk recently with one of the most distinguished, holding one of the very highest positions, who is so utterly outraged by all that is going on, by our having become a part of the European war, by our meddling in every situation as it arises, that he is seriously debating whether he will not resign his high post and his financial security to sound a trumpet call for a new line-up. Probably he will at the last moment find himself unable to do so. But that his conscience is troubling him, and his patriotic feelings as well, he did not attempt to deny. I was much struck by one thing he said, probably because it has been my own feeling for so many years, voiced by me when twenty-four years ago we were similarly on the verge of going to war.

A Troubled American

His point was that we had held a mirror up to the rest of the world by keeping ourselves free from all the age-old struggles of Europe, and had set our high standards of what a great and peaceful country ought to be—something different from the run of European nations, something better and finer, a nation deeply engrossed in working out its own democratic experiment so that all the world might profit thereby. He has not fallen for the belief that it is absolutely necessary for us to plunge headlong into the tragedy of Europe to preserve our democracy. He feels that our own institutions will not survive our entrance into the war if it lasts any length of time. He is not for our having a President of the World in the White House, although he is indebted to the present occupant thereof for preferment. He does not thrill to the thought that our American President is or is about to become the dictator of the world, for he sees in it no honor, but rather the abandonment of all that gave us our tremendous moral influence throughout the world. He does not believe that Hitler has compelled the abandonment of our historic way of life.

The disheartening thing is that the American public does not seem to realize what is going on, or if it realizes it is not moving. Americans have become apathetic. A keen observer told me the other day that he found as he went about the country that the plain people would not talk about the war and our policies until they found out how you stood. They sense that the time is already here to be chary of expressing their own beliefs, but when they trust you, he says, it invariably comes out that they are bitterly unhappy. I have found youth similarly apathetic outwardly. The young men are without enthusiasm for conscription. They are listlessly accepting it, which is hardly the spirit out of which one makes zealous soldiers. They know that something is wrong, that we are on our way to a new order, however different from the new order of Stalin and of Hitler. I have found them an extraordinarily able and attractive and thoughtful generation—I mean the one now in its twenties. My only criticism is that they do not know how to take a stand, how to make themselves felt. It is true, also, that they do not yet fully realize how much they are going to be the pawns of the first President of the World if we fight.

California

April 29, 1941

Dear White:

I hope you got my telegram from Denver telling you how deeply touched I was by your most interesting and touching letter. Had I known you were in such a jam and Mrs. White so ill I should not, of course, have printed one word about you and I am extremely contrite. But as I wrote you, the humor of it appealed to me. You are right in saying that Flynn should have emphasized that it was an early opinion and was not to be taken too seriously. I wrote at once to the Christian Century that I was disturbed to find that some people thought my quotation from you represented your present point of view and that I had not deemed that possible in view of your leadership in the fight against Hitler.

What you tell me about the situation in the Committee is very illuminating. I have never believed that Clark Eichelberger was a sincere man and there is no doubt whatever that many of the members have been in favor of going to war from the very beginning. It is only three years since Herbert Agar, by the way, wrote a syndicqted column heartily approving of my attitude against America ever being committed to another war and saying that if his readers were urged in that direction they should remember the things that he quoted from me! Never were people swept from their intellectual moorings as in this crisis and never was there a stranger mixup; the old lines have been crossed in every direction.

As I wired you I hoped that you could speak out against convoys, but you have the best of reason for not doing so. After all, the most important thing now is your lovely wife's health and I hope with all my heart that she is coming along well and that your mind is wholly at ease about her and that you yourself are entirely well again. I shall be back in New York by the 15th of May and hope that I may find a letter from your secretary telling me how you both are getting on.

It will interest you to know that I am simply astounded at the unanimity out here against our going to war. One encounters this in every walk of life and if the President insists upon putting us into the war, he will find that he will not be backed by a majority of the people, not even if he puts on the screws and establishes concentration camps for the dissenters. I am sure he would never carry California if the election were tomorrow, and if Lindbergh should come out here, I believe that he would get tremendous ovations everywhere. Indeed, I think F.D.R's. attack on Lindbergh outrageous beyond description and I believe without parallel in our history. When any man in high office takes advantage of that office to denounce a private citizen merely because the citizen disagrees with the official's view of what American policy should be, he proves that his heart is bad or that he knows that his cause is bad. I have said this to several audiences in connection with Ickes' smearing of me and they have applauded enthusiastically. Ickes in Chicago called me a fellow traveler with Hitler, when he knows that there isn't a man in the American press who has stood more rigidly against the dictators and been more bitter in denunciation of Hitler than I. I am having an interesting correspondence with him and have demanded an apology, but I do not think that "howling Harold" will give it. Naturally anything that I may say in rebuttal will be seen only by a handful, where the denunciation was read by hundreds of thousands. And this is the man whom I have defended through thick and thin as a great and honest public official, despite a loose tongue and other weaknesses! There is no getting around it, American public men cannot "take it" when it comes to criticism. Isn't it amazing that Roosevelt and Ickes should be trying to suppress criticism by tarring all who differ from them just at a moment when Winston Churchill has been asking for the creation of a loyal Opposition composed of "gentlemen" who will criticize him and his conduct of the war and thus make him more effective in carrying it on.[2] There is an editorial subject for you!

With all good wishes and unending affection for you both,

Faithfully yours,

OGV

There Can Be No Unity

By Oswald Garrison Villard

IF THIS COUNTRY goes to war there will be less unity, in my judgment, and more opposition than in any previous American war venture. That this is the case is shown by every poll. More than that, it is demonstrated by the actions of the administration. Its members have been determined to put this country into the struggle abroad for some time and have taken step by step the road to war. They have held off from undertaking convoys only because they were aware that American public opinion did not stand behind them. That is why on April 25 Secretary Knox and Secretary Hull made their most determined effort to frighten the American people into approval of the convoy system and the President, while disagreeing with his cabinet members but favoring patrols, declared that American ships would be protected on all the seven seas. The administration will never achieve unity this way. The bulk of the American people are not going to be frightened into approval of the war policy.

To Gag Opposition

My old friend and former co-worker, David Lawrence, now editor of the *United States News,* tries to attribute the strikes on defense projects to the fact that "no unanimity of public opinion prevails on the urgency of production for defense." Until the American people think that we are really defending ourselves in aiding England, he says, it will be impossible to get labor and capital to pull together and "to persuade the people to put national defense first and their accustomed pursuits second." He does not want to choke off dissenters, but he wants the President to give another one of his fireside chats and in it to call upon every governor, every mayor, to create a national psychology "which would give fewer and fewer audiences to those who are attacking the nation's foreign policy."

But many, many others are for clapping on the gags now. The secretary of the navy and the President are doing it so far as our ships and our sailors and our marines are concerned. Those newspapers are attacked by the President which dared to print the news of the arrival of a British battleship in New York. An aviator is to have his license revoked for the crime of having flown over that battleship when it lay at anchor in New York, so that a photographer could take a picture of it. (Pictures of it appeared in many newspapers, and in *Life.)* Secretary Ickes, using the perfect Hitler technique of "smearing" all who dare to disagree with the administration, has dubbed all of us who are in opposition fellow travelers of the nazis. Of course he knows a great deal better, but this incident merely illustrates anew the determination on the part of the administration to beat down all opposition and to compel unity by force.

They will never achieve it. They may lock up the dissenters and fill concentration camps as they please. They may browbeat the masses into silence and they will undoubtedly make the daily press as subservient organs of the White House as the journals of their respective countries are of Hitler, Mussolini and Stalin. Still, they will not achieve unity. Outwardly it may appear so, just as outwardly in Berlin and in Rome there appears to be no opposition to the dictators. But men's minds and consciences simply cannot be enchained.

Force Cannot Change Minds

Men may be broken by incredible torture and by confinement itself, yet can anyone doubt that Hitler has not made a single sincere convert of the poor victims of his fiendishness in his concentration camps? Some may have recanted for the moment under duress, but wherever they go there is within them the reinforced knowledge that what Hitler stands for is the destruction of everything in life that free men hold dear, that makes for decency, for the dignity of the human being. After my last visit to Germany I came out convinced that 65 per cent of the German people were opposed to Hitler, and that has been confirmed to me by some remarkably interesting testimony from an American woman who has just returned after three years in Berlin.

So if Hitler has not been able to make the bulk of the German people think as he wishes them to think, it will not be possible for any power in America to change the 83 per cent majority against our going to war into a 100 per cent unity in favor of our joining in and warring against Germany and Japan. They may represent the dissenters as nazi sympathizers if they please; they will know that it is not true. The American people are overwhelmingly opposed to everything that Hitler, Mussolini, Stalin and the Japanese stand for. The dissenters are as devoted to American institutions as are their libelers. They are merely indulging in their constitutional rights to dissent and to oppose policies at least until those rights are abridged by the national law-making body. They are following a most sacred American tradition, one that is deeply embedded in our history. There has not been a single war in which there has not been dissent.

Opposition to Other Wars

In *Oliver Wiswell* we have had a striking new picture of the way in which the country was split during the Revolution. In the second war against England in 1812, some of the foremost men in the country, including the first chief justice of the United States, were absolutely opposed to America's going to war with Britain. Unity? There was no thought of it. Nor was there unity in the war with Mexico. Abraham Lincoln and the whole conscience of the north, the abolitionists, together with many of the clergy were entirely opposed to that American aggression and the theft of such great stretches of territory from the Mexicans (a regular Hitler deed) at the behest of the slave power.

In our war against Spain the anti-imperialists could not, it is true, stop our warring upon the innocent Filipinos, whose sole offense against us was that they objected to our buying them and their islands from the Spaniards. Those of us who protested then were "smeared" as friends of Aguinaldo. We were told that our protests encouraged the Filipinos to resist our soldiers. Nonetheless, the McKinley administration did not dare to suppress the most outspoken press opponents of its policies, and in the end that anti-imperialist campaign checked for a generation our sudden plunge into imperialism.

In the last World War there were huge minorities in complete opposition to the war policy. Indeed, it is an open question whether, if a war referendum could have been held at that time, there would not have been a clear majority against our going into the war. There was every evidence in the middle west and in the south that that was the case. What was then done to smash all who refused to conform has been told and retold. It made life a hell for literally millions of American citizens of foreign birth, aside from the German-Americans; Norwegians, Swedes, Danes—all were subject to the tender mercies of mobs. And when it came to extracting Liberty loans it was a holiday for hoodlums who liked to point their revolvers to show their superiority and to pay off old grudges.

But it was never possible for Mr. Wilson to achieve unity. He sent Eugene Debs to Atlanta penitentiary for saying the very things as to the origins of the war which he himself after its conclusion gave as the reasons for its coming to pass, and up to the moment that he left office he refused to pardon Debs. That act of the President's alone made impossible the unity he sought to achieve. It strengthened in the heart of every friend and follower of Debs the belief that that war was unrighteous, that it must be unrighteous, else such abuse of authority, such violation of the right of conscience, such vindictive vengeance against a great and noble man could never have occurred.

That is what the mere approach of war does. It stirs men to anger and hate, to bitterness and rage, to profound acts of injustice and wrong. It makes men who have power eager like Mr. Ickes to use it upon those who dare to question their wisdom and the righteousness of their cause. They burn to crack down upon the other fellow. Swearing their allegiance to democracy they proceed to strike it down on the ground that this period in our history is the exception; that rights must be suspended, to be restored in the years to come when the victory has been won.

The Need for an Opposition

Can all this make for unity? On the contrary. It heals nothing; it only divides. It makes sores; it shakes the faith of multitudes in their country and its institutions. And they think those thoughts whether they can voice them or not. Why this intolerance should always be in the United States is not easy to explain because we have the Anglo-Saxon tradition. Right in the midst of the life-and-death struggle in which he and his government are engaged, Winston Churchill suggested in March that an official opposition be formed in the House of Commons. He urged that "a sufficient body of gentlemen constitute themselves an opposition" so that "they could be definitely recognized as such." There you have the real Anglo-Saxon tradition of fair play, the earnest desire to preserve democracy and parliamentary efficiency in wartime.

This action of Mr. Churchill's is the more remarkable because he, too, has appealed for unity both during and after the war. In Washington, on the other hand, so the private news services report, there is already a demand that unfavorable speeches made in the Congress, whether in the Senate or the House, be suppressed. That would, of course, be the highest treason to our American ideals. One's mind goes back to Abraham Lincoln's opposition to the war upon Mexico. He spoke out on the floor of the House and asked some rather uncomfortable questions of President Polk which the President never seemed to be able to answer. It is perfectly true that this led to Lincoln's being successfully "smeared" by the local Ickeses of his day, with the result that his career in Congress came to a prompt end. But that is less significant than the fact that he did stand up in Congress and say what he believed, and that in doing so he was exercising his democratic rights and helping to put brakes on the administration whose infamous war upon our southern neighbor Ulysses S. Grant called "one of the most unjust ever waged by a stronger against a weaker nation."

The Road to Dictatorship

As Daniel Webster put it in that admirable statement printed by The Christian Century recently: "There are men in all ages who mean to exercise power usefully; but they mean to exercise it. They mean to govern well; but they mean to govern. They promise to be kind masters; but they mean to master. They think there need be but little restraint upon themselves." That is the historic story, and not only is it the right but it is the duty of Americans who would preserve their liberties and their institutions to refuse to be silenced. Otherwise the tremendous powers now exercised by the President will be unchecked and uncontrolled. When that comes to pass Americans will ask why they must fight even so abhorrent a dictator as Hitler if they have a dictator themselves. I know well the argument that we had a dictator in 1917-18 and yet the republic was restored. Again I reply there is no comparison as to what was going on in the world in those years and what is happening today. There were no dictators then, and the world is full of them at this hour.

No, there will be no unity in America if we go to war. A profound sense of injustice will abide with a majority of Americans. They will feel that they have been tricked and betrayed, and they will continue to think it unless the President orders the removal from all libraries and all sources of information of the speeches and the promises that he made during the last campaign. Unity in the face of the wrong of war? Never. Ethics, religion and morality forbid it, as well as our history and our traditions. Sooner let us haul down the American flag and hoist the swastika. The minute such unity comes, democracy dies. For that unity will be compelled, regimented and forced by bayonets, so far as that is possible. A democracy setting out to conquer despots without an opposition? That is unthinkable. The very essence of liberty is the right of free men to protest at any and all times the acts of their rulers.

Shall a Minority Decide Our Fate?

By Oswald Garrison Villard

I HAVE just returned from a nearly five weeks' trip to California and I have come back convinced that the Gallup polls have understated, if anything, the opposition of the middle west and west to the President's plan to put us into the war. Everywhere, if one gets under the upper crust of the very well-to-do and their idle women who love to knit and welcome the job of making bundles, and gets past the college faculties and the Anglophiles, there is an overwhelming antagonism to our going into the struggle.

A physician in California gave me case after case of patients who had turned to Lindbergh because of Roosevelt's attack upon him, and he assured me that he did not know a single man or woman who wanted war. A clerk in a shoestore burst out when I suggested that taxes would soon be much higher and said, "Yes, and if we go into the war the whole middle class to which I belong will be wiped out." A retired army officer introduced himself after one of my meetings, declared that he was more than one hundred per cent with me in my opposition to going into the war, and that he did not know a single army officer who believed that we should enter the war or that we were in any degree prepared to do so. An active officer insisted that the whole thing is going "rottenly"; he, too, is against our going into the war. A third officer wished he could bring me before all the service clubs in his town.

Youth Against Intervention

At Berkeley, California, the local daily featured a speech by Mark Mathews, president of the New York city junior chamber of commerce, printing in large black type these words: "America's young men, including the entire personnel of 1,000 junior chambers of commerce, will defend to the death this country from any threat of armed invasion, but they have no desire to become nameless crosses on some European battlefield. They have greater ambition than that."

As for the young men who are being conscripted, the universal testimony was that they were going resignedly, but without a particle of enthusiasm. One mother in Los Angeles told me that her son and three other young men who were visiting him broke into loud hurrahs when a fifth member of the group reported by telephone that he had just been rejected by the army surgeon because he had a bad heart, varicose veins and bad instep. "Isn't he the lucky devil!" was the joint opinion. At Madison, Wisconsin, I addressed a magnificent audience of fifteen hundred students who applauded most enthusiastically at the conclusion of my part in a debate with one of their university professors who thinks we are already in the war, and that therefore any criticism of the President's policies or the lease-lend act is treason and helpful only to Hitler. At another Wisconsin college there has almost been a break between the students and the faculty because the latter tried to prevent Senator Wheeler from appearing on the campus, and the students insisted that they had the right to hear him and gave him a magnificent reception.

The Student Mind

I have seen no more touching piece of writing than one called "Another Lost Generation" by Sarita Henderson, editor of the *Daily Californian,* the organ of the undergraduates of the University of California at Berkeley. Writing her final editorial as editor she says:

> The transition experienced during the year has demanded of students a deep-rooted change in the philosophy of a lifetime. We have been schooled to distrust force, appeals to emotion, and the catchwords of easy patriotism. We have been impregnated with the knowledge that war is the greatest enemy of democracy. With stunning suddenness, the signals have been switched. Within a year, gunpowder and shells are urged upon us as the panacea for the ills of mankind. The state above the individual, national unity above personal liberty, the means and ends reversed, but the same goal—democracy.
>
> The result has been confusion and a conspicuous lack of enthusiasm for war. Skepticism for the "just" cause, for the process of war to end war, for the rationality of fighting to defend democracy has been burned into the minds of this year's seniors. The irony of Versailles and the disaster of the League of Nations has bred a deep distrust in the humanity and rationality of men who drain the bitter dregs of blood and fury. Small wonder that when the same prospect is urged upon us, youth asks for some tangible assurance of its results.
>
> With singular blindness, our elders remonstrate with us for our "cynicism," our "moral irresponsibility," our lack of idealism.
>
> But the one straw which should keep idealism afire is the hope of rebuilding a better world. It is our task and it lies in rejection of the treachery and duplicity of a world which has made war inevitable. It must be rooted in a solid basis of social and economic justice and a transformation of knowledge into action. A determination to carry this task into completion may yet preserve us from becoming another lost generation.

At the University of California in Los Angeles there is a professor who in a letter to the editor of the college daily said in his anger that there was no war enthusiasm among the undergraduates: "All men die and death is only morbid and gruesome to those who have nothing to live for. Sheer existence apart from purpose is meaningless." That brought out some stinging rebukes from undergraduates as well as from the editors whose editorial position he had ventured to criticize, calling them mawkish, maudlin and sentimental because they wished to live and not to die in battle.

The Voice of the Middle West

But the most striking proof of the position of the middle west is to be found in a poll of the *Indianapolis News.* It was only by accident that I discovered it, buried on the fifteenth page of a Washington daily, when it should have been on the very first page because of its sensational character. The *News,* which is the most influential paper in Indiana, published a ballot with two questions on it. The first was, "Are you in favor of the use of the United States navy to convoy ships carrying war supplies to

Great Britain?" The second read, "Do you favor the United States entering the war and sending our troops abroad?" On the first question the vote was no less than 92 per cent against convoying to 8 per cent for; on the second question the vote stood 95 per cent against and only 5 per cent for. I cannot recall so overwhelming a vote in any other newspaper poll. Yet so far as I can ascertain no New York paper has played this up, nor the fact that in some New York movie houses there is not a clap for Mr. Roosevelt's picture and enthusiastic demonstrations when that of Colonel Lindbergh has appeared. This has been true in one of the largest and most central movie houses in New York city.

In the south they are more belligerent. In Texas some towns are taking Lindbergh's name down from streets named after him, and some school boards are removing his picture so that their schoolchildren shall not be contaminated by looking at the representation of this "copperhead." But even in Florida, the state of Senator Pepper, the Gallup poll does not claim that more than 35 per cent is with that great man. If my long journalistic experience teaches me anything it is that the country is overwhelmingly opposed to going to war, and I am not overlooking the Gallup poll which stated that a majority would favor going to war if it were the only hope of saving England.

War Pressure from the Administration

All of which brings me squarely to the question as to whether certain officeholders, headed by the President and his cabinet, and a small minority of intellectuals, of people ready to sacrifice their own country to save England, of sentimentalists, of college professors and college presidents (with many honorable exceptions), can put this country into war, whether declared or undeclared, in opposition to the wishes of the mass of their fellow citizens. That is the great question that confronts us. This is supposed to be the country in which the will of the majority rules, and that majority today absolutely refuses to believe that we cannot preserve our institutions and our four freedoms unless we go to war on the side of England. They do not agree with the hysterical Secretary Knox that this country is "in mortal peril" because of Hitler's successes. They stand with the secretary of commerce, Jesse Jones, Mr. Knox's colleague, who says that we are not in the slightest danger of invasion. They will agree with the opinions of Hanson Baldwin, the military expert of the *New York Times,* who, in his new book, *United We Stand,* writes: "The author does not know a single responsible military or naval officer or government official who believes that this nation is threatened by direct invasion, even if Germany wins. . . . Invaders can reach this country only by ship or by plane; armies cannot swim to victory. . . . By air the problem is even more difficult, and Colonel Lindbergh, as all military observers know, was perfectly correct when he said that the United States could not be invaded by air."

But the President is apparently determined to disregard the will of the majority, and we have the astounding statement of Mrs. Roosevelt, the erstwhile pacifist, that her husband never promised to keep this country out of war always. Even Mark Sullivan has had to rebuke her and say, "This statement, incidentally, is seriously incorrect." Many newspaper and official observers in Washington are convinced that the President's recent indisposition can be directly connected with his Boston pledge, and the dilemma in which it has put him. They believe that the administration has another grievance against Adolf Hitler —that he will not sink an American vessel or make some overt attack upon us so that the President can declare war openly and ask Congress to do so.

Consult the Will of the People!

This situation goes very deep indeed. If the war party triumphs it will be a bad blow to our democracy, a doubly serious one. In the first place, it will breach, as I have said, the doctrine of majority rule. In the second place, it will make millions of Americans lose faith in their institutions and their President. I doubt if Hitler himself could aim a graver blow at us short of war. It has long been plain that the Constitution has been nullified insofar as it confers the power to declare war upon the Congress. That power is now vested in the President. If Mr. Roosevelt puts us into an undeclared war, as he has intimated he might, he will of course not consult Congress at all and will thus gravely weaken the stability and the integrity of our organic law. It is no excuse to remind the public, as he does, that we had two undeclared wars in the first years of this republic, one with France and one with the Algerian pirates and corsairs.

Never was there a greater need for a national referendum such as was called for by Theodore Roosevelt, William Jennings Bryan, Woodrow Wilson and Robert M. La Follette, to mention only a few statesmen who have favored it. Why should we be dependent now upon private polls for information as to the wishes and opinions of the American people? Mr. Roosevelt, the politician, would certainly be profoundly affected if a vote of the people could be taken today and the results were broadcast throughout the country. He would find it far more difficult to get around than his Boston speech. How he thinks he can whip the American people into an enthusiastic support of war I cannot understand; not even his marvelous showmanship, or the verbal terrorism of his cabinet officers, or his own oratorical ability can accomplish that. Certainly there is vastly more opposition to our going to war this time than there was in the fateful April of 1917. If that can be shoved aside and disregarded, we are well started on the road to totalitarianism.

July 3, 1941

Dear Mr. Webster:

I am very much pleased that you and Mr. Flynn should wish me to join the New York Chapter of the America First Committee. My difficulty is this: I resigned from the national committee because of that plank in the platform which calls for complete armament and defense, because I believe that that is not necessary to protect the United States and that complete militarization is but little short of war and an evil influence upon any country. Again, I am honorary and practicaly action chairman of the Keep Us Out of War Congress, and I think that I should not complicate this situation by joining your committee. As it is, I am cooperating with you in every way, and if I can serve you at any time I hope that you and Mr. Flynn will call upon me.

With renewed thanks,

Sincerely yours,

Mr. Edwin S. Webster, Jr.
America First Committee
515 Madison Avenue, New York City

Who Rules America?

By Oswald Garrison Villard

WHETHER one man or the Congress shall rule this country is the issue now squarely before us. Are there any limits to the power of the President as commander-in-chief, or not? Has the chief executive the constitutional right to send troops out of the Western hemisphere when the Congress has specifically voted that he shall not? Can he establish bases in Ireland, the Azores, the Canary islands and even capture Dakar if he wishes on the ground that in his judgment America's safety demands it? If he can do these things he has nullified the constitutional provision that Congress alone shall have the power to make war, besides defying the plain intent of the Congress that we shall not go beyond the Western hemisphere in our so-called defensive measures. These measures are now plainly no longer determined by our own defense need, but by the President's desire to give all aid to England. He has admitted that he recently said that Iceland was not in the Western hemisphere.

What Did the Founders Intend?

If this is not usurping ungranted powers, then it must be that the founders of this country intended that the President should be a military dictator. Why should they have specified that Congress alone shall have the right to declare war if they thought that the President should also have the right to send our army and navy overseas and into any war of which he approved? At the time the Constitution was written the United States had practically no navy and no army worthy of the name. The drafters of that great document could not have visualized any President's sending a great fleet and masses of men to take over a foreign country situated in a legally delimited war zone without the President's consulting Congress and in the face of the indisputable fact that the bulk of his countrymen were entirely opposed to entrance into that war. That would have seemed to them impossible. But that is what has happened now. The President has confronted the governing body with an accomplished fact and now virtually says to that body, "What are you going to do about it?"

Well, if all the members of Congress were free of party shackles and of a pitiable but unjustifiable fear of Hitler's ability to attack us, they would vote those troops out of Iceland. If the President can get away with this, there will be nothing whatsoever to prevent his confronting Congress with other accomplished facts—a naval base in Ireland or Scotland or the seizure of the Azores or any other Atlantic port or island which he fancies is essential to our safety. Senator Taft was absolutely correct when he declared that every argument put forth by the President to explain his acts in Iceland applied just as cogently to England, or Ireland, or Portugal.

Mr. Taft could not have overstressed the transparent pretense of the whole proceeding. In the first place, Mr. Roosevelt deliberately gave the impression that he had to rush American troops to Iceland to protect us from attack. He had heard that Hitler was meditating a move upon the island; he could lose no time, and of course could confide in no one until our soldiers had arrived. Had he done so, Hitler might have attacked and got ahead of him. But it soon appeared on Churchill's own statement that the British garrison which the prime minister had considered ample to defend Iceland was still there and that he has no immediate intention of removing it. Then why all this haste and secrecy? Did the President also have secret information that the British garrison was too weak to ward off the attack which someone had told him Hitler was going to direct from his position on the battlelines in Russia?

Convoys the Real Purpose

Thus it became plain that the real motive is to be found in the other reasons given by Mr. Roosevelt for his action. These were the safeguarding of ships bearing supplies to England and relieving the British garrison. That, of course, is his real purpose. The President has agreed to Secretary Knox's position that we are going to "clear the Atlantic of the Germans." Under the pretense of safeguarding the United States, the American planes based on Iceland will patrol the sea, together with American naval vessels. Under the President's instructions they will take "any measures necessary" to protect the line of supply between the United States and Iceland—and England. To my mind this is just as much an act of war as if we relieved the British garrison at Gibraltar or the anti-aircraft forces which are protecting Scapa Flow.

Now I am well aware that the President can cite other instances in our history where a President has used his powers to invade other countries and to use force in them, and has been allowed to do so by Congress. Such was President Wilson's naval attack upon Vera Cruz which took many lives and accomplished precisely nothing. Such was our invasion of Haiti. But I cannot recall that even in those cases Mr. Wilson strove to justify his acts by declaring that he was using his constitutional powers as commander-in-chief. He said he acted as President of the United States. That term "commander-in-chief" has had a tremendous fascination for Franklin D. Roosevelt ever since he took office. In fact he is the only President so far as considerable research has been able to establish who has signed himself as "C.-in-C." I have asked Mr. Tumulty if Mr. Wilson ever used that title, and Mr. Tumulty says that he did not. There is no case on record in which Abraham Lincoln signed himself commander-in-chief, even though he was actually exercising that function in ordering movements of the Union army.

Anti-War Majority Grows

But after all, these men occupied the office of President when war was on. We are not in war, and the President has no right to assume that we are going to be in the war until war is legally declared by vote of Congress. In the present state of public opinion, he does not dare ask for such a vote. The latest Gallup poll shows that 79 per cent of the people oppose the United States' entry into the war now, as against 76 per cent a month ago, or before the Russo-German break. The President is aware of these figures. One of the tipster services out of Washington declares that the government cannot get over the "apathy and indifference" of the American people, and its inability to "sell" the war to them. But the President is going right ahead to put us in through the back door. He thus violates his sacred pledge to the American people not to send their sons into a foreign war. He has sent them into the foreign war when he has stationed them alongside combatant troops of the British empire, who, if the President is right, are in daily expectation of an attack by their enemy. I can recall nothing in American history sadder than this betrayal.

It is obvious that our Constitution is weak in that the powers of the President as commander-in-chief are not properly defined. George Washington would have known what they were. He would have put himself under the orders of the Congress and would have consulted with it as to every move. I suppose there will be protests that war is different today and that you have got to act with the utmost secrecy. To this I reply that that merely brings up the issue as to whether this is a democracy or a dictatorship. It is quite possible that by acting in the open the waging of war would be harder for us, perhaps more costly, but that is one of the prices we pay for being a democracy. If that is to be disregarded *before* we go to war then of course we must expect to hear of other accomplished facts. Then anybody like Senator Wheeler who deems it his duty to let the American people know something of what is going on behind our backs must expect even worse treatment than the abuse and vilification which are now being given him.

That Veil of Secrecy

By Oswald Garrison Villard

NO ONE can find serious fault with the "startling" peace aims formulated by Mr. Churchill and Mr. Roosevelt with such theatrical secrecy. There is nothing "startling" about them. They are, as far as they go, a close parallel to the Fourteen Points of Wilson which were so effective in breaking down the German morale in 1918. And they are, moreover, only an elaboration of the peace terms outlined by Anthony Eden a few weeks ago. It is so hard to see why these aims could not have been formulated by letter or cable that one cannot help wondering, as does the *St. Louis Post-Dispatch,* whether we have been told all that took place on the Prince of Wales. What else was discussed and what other agreements reached?

The President enjoys startling people like a smart aleck schoolboy, and so he has reveled in keeping the press in the dark, leaving his newspaper retinue behind and having a "historic" meeting at sea. Arthur Krock points out in the *New York Times* that the President tried as far back as 1936 to have a meeting on the high seas with the dictators, Hitler and Mussolini, as well as with the other heads of nations, and that he toyed with the idea again in 1939. His itch for showmanship is insatiable. But that showmanship should not conceal the fact that this was a thoroughly bad way to do a good business.

It is the dictators' way; it is a poor copy of the Hitler-Mussolini meetings on the Brenner and elsewhere. It is also the dictators' manner because of the secrecy involved. That is as un-American as anything could possibly be. No American president has ever so flouted the right of the American public to know where its chief executive is and what he is about. Our presidents have, in the main, lived and acted in the open. If it was safe for Mr. Churchill to cross the ocean in the Prince of Wales then it would also have been safe for him to land in Canada and meet the President at Toronto or Buffalo or at the White House. As it is, the press, the public and Congress have no means of penetrating further into the veil of secrecy behind which the President is more and more hiding all his acts relating to the war. Never was there such a need for a question hour in Congress like that in the British Parliament when the executive must answer questions publicly—except that an answer can be refused on the ground of public safety.

Nothing is more disturbing in this whole critical situation than the fact that the executive branch of the government is working behind a veil of secrecy. Congress, as everyone knows, has not voted any censorship, yet an even more rigid one is enforced than during the last war. Obedience to that voluntary censorship has been made a test of loyalty and patriotism, and newspapers which for a time gave news that the American people should have—as, for instance, that a number of British warships are being repaired in this country—were denounced both by the President and by Secretary Knox.

It was behind this veil of secrecy, of course, that Iceland was occupied. It had been on the boards for some time. Positive statements have been made that American troops and advance parties had been going to Iceland for two months, but the American people were not allowed to know about it, nor can they be told today how many troops are there, and whether the British forces will or will not retire, and, if they are going, when. This is the third war that I have lived through in which this country has participated, and I can recall nothing like it.

More Seizures Contemplated?

It is true that modern war and the existence of fifth columnists and spies, and the easy means of communication, demand methods different from those of the past, and perhaps greater secrecy in hiding troop and fleet movements. But this country is not at war, and therefore the facts of what is actually happening should not be hidden from the American people unless our democracy has already been abandoned. We Americans are thinking people and not unintelligent, and as long as the republic is a republic we have the right to know what our government is doing. In no respect has Congress failed us more at this time than in its refusal to demand the whole truth and nothing but the truth. It is a pathetic spectacle that Congress presents in thus laying itself open to having suddenly sprung upon it accomplished facts, like the seizure of Iceland.

Newspaper men in Washington write freely that the Portuguese islands will be taken next. Everybody knows that Dakar would have been seized by now were it not for the fact that we cannot get that harbor without bloodshed and without attacking our once beloved allies, the French. Occasionally the veil is lifted, as when it was announced that two of our heavy cruisers had arrived in Australian waters, coupled with the hypocritical statement that they are on a "practice cruise." Of course their whereabouts was disclosed in order to add to the anxiety of the Japanese, if they are anxious. It is just one more move in the whole bankrupt Roosevelt-Hull policy of trying to stop Japan, first by appeasement and second by naval threats.

An Assault on Constitutional Government

That the President enjoys all this is beyond dispute. Not only the boyishness in him, but his lifelong, absorbing interest in naval affairs make him revel in what is happening. He is extending his powers as commander-in-chief beyond anything ever done by any previous chief executive. He issues orders as commander-in-chief, and he signs himself "C. in C.," which neither Abraham Lincoln nor Woodrow Wilson ever thought of doing. I am sure that he is fascinated by the game he is playing in moving American vessels all over the globe, both merchant and naval. From one point of view it is well if you are going to war to have a president who understands naval matters, but to have one who assumes dictatorial powers *before* we are in war, behind a veil of secrecy which he has himself imposed, is an extremely grave assault upon constitutional government in the United States. That it is done lightheartedly, flippantly, almost in a mocking manner, adds to the offense.

The first result is that the people as well as Congress are reduced to practical helplessness. This is intensified by the absence from Congress of any outstanding figures competent to cross-examine and dissect what is going on. I am constantly reminded of the great fight made by Carl Schurz and Charles Sumner when General Grant sought to have Congress annex Samana Bay in his second term. He tried to put it over in exactly the same way. An unnamed foreign power was seeking, he said, to purchase this harbor, and of course if it got a foothold in San Domingo it would menace the United States. The acquirement of this territory was advocated by army and navy officers, according to General Grant, but the Senate refused to concur and the project was defeated. One reads today with incredulous eyes that there is no adequate cross-examining of the generals and admirals and diplomats who appear before the committees of Congress. No wonder General Marshall jubilantly exclaimed that the war department had asked for much more than it thought it would get and that for the first time in our history Congress voted not only all that was asked but more besides!

The truth is that we are already witnessing the breakdown of the system of checks and balances which has been so loudly acclaimed for a hundred and fifty years as the most original achievement of American constitutional development. The Supreme Court is now packed, not with "nine old men" out of step with the times, but with seven men appointed in the confident belief that they will do exactly what the President expects of them. Worst of all, Congress abandons not only its vitally important duty of being the watchdog of the treasury and scrutinizing at all times every proposal for national expenditure, but has abandoned all control of national policies, especially in foreign affairs. Naturally Mr. Roosevelt goes ahead developing his personal government and acquiring more and more power, so that I, for one, believe that Mussolini told the truth when he said that if the United States goes into the war it will not only prolong it for three or four years but it will teach the totalitarian states what a real totalitarian state looks like.

October 21, 1941

Dear Henry Mencken:

I got great happiness out of your latest book which I have just reviewed for the Saturday Review of Literature. Whether it is because of my own background and training, I do not know, but I fell pretty hard for it as you will see, and I have no sympathy with Lewis Gannett's stupid notice in the Herald-Tribune, and one or two other stuffy affairs that I have seen. It took me back to my all too brief repertorial days in Philadelphia which, by the way, merited well the dig that you gave to it. The newspaper situation in Philadelphia in the 90s was just about as rotten and crooked as anything could be, and they were damned bad journalists, too.

Well, doing that job gave me a genuine longing to see you again and have a good talk with you. The first thing you know I shall be asking if I can drop in on you on my way to Washington. We can weep together not only over the Nation, which has become a journalistic disgrace aside from any of its views, but also over the ease with which the present road to war has been initiated and built. Yet the fact remains that the bulk of the people is absolutely unmoved. There is where democracy breaks down when fellows in the White House and Congress can put war over against the will of the majority.

Good luck to you always,

Faithfully yours,

Mr. Henry L. Mencken

The Death of Our Humanity

By Oswald Garrison Villard

I CANNOT REFRAIN from quoting here from a letter which appeared in the *Wall Street Journal* of November 1, because it illuminates the point I wish to make in this article. Here it is:

> The greatest sacrifice in war is not the giving up of one's life. Sooner or later all mortals have to do that. It is [made by] those consigned to the purgatory of "No Man's Land," those who pay in soul-wracking instalments the supreme sacrifices of war—the legions of maimed and disabled men, many of whom can neither be claimed by the dead nor the living. The writer—who does not pose as any war hero—happens to be one of those retrieved from the "No Man's Land" of the last war. He spent seven years in hospitals; two years without getting out of bed. Seven long years in which he saw hundreds of fine young Americans wasting away from diseases and wounds incurred in the World War, who finally were carted off to the graveyard. They in truth paid the full measure of supreme sacrifice!
>
> The World War was fought, we were told, to make the world safe for democracy. We are now well along the road to losing our democracy.
>
> The present war, we are now told, is to make the world safe for religion, apparently including communism—*mirabile dictu!*
>
> The World War failed to end war just as this or any other world war will fail to end war. War generates war and no lasting world peace will ever come from the battlefield. The present war, if it engulfs America, will complete the process of destruction of democracy and instead of preserving religion will likely end it, too.
>
> The President, his cabinet members and other high executives of the government and its legislators on Armistice Day should take a tour of the hospitals still housing the wrecks of the last war. Then they should multiply these hospitals by the hundreds and these war victims by the thousands and figure what they will help to reap when they sow the seeds for the new crop of maimed and disabled. When they come to gaze upon the wrecks that come out of the new war, then let them be ready to say: "I helped to do this to my fellow countrymen!"
>
> "VETERAN OF THE WAR TO END WARS."

Breakdown of Imagination

Not a day goes by but that I am shocked and horrified by the inability of people with whom I come into contact to visualize just what war means, to understand to what it is they are condemning hundreds of thousands, perhaps millions, of boys when they insist that we shall go to war to destroy Hitler and Hitlerism. We seem to have lost completely the ability to feel for others. Our hearts are shell-shocked. Our minds no longer react to the simplest humanitarian feelings and instincts. I suppose it is because we have so long supped on horrors. Sometimes I have said that perhaps it is just as well, because if we could visualize and realize and personalize the suffering which exists in the world today we should probably all go insane—that is violently insane, since few of us are any longer normal.

Nonetheless I bitterly resent the attitude of those older people who, from Mr. Roosevelt down, are ready to condemn a considerable part of their fellow Americans to the horrors of the battlefields and of the veterans' hospitals with their wrecked lives. I echo the sentiment of the writer of this letter that he wishes the President and his cabinet could be taken through those veterans' hospitals. Two years ago my friend Oscar Ameringer, that dauntless fighter for peace and progress, told me almost with tears in his eyes of his having just visited a couple of these hospitals. Said he: "The sights that I have seen there of human wrecks are beyond description. Nothing that was accomplished by the war, or that could be accomplished by any war, would make up for the misery of a single one of those men who have not only been robbed of their lives, but condemned to the torture of the most horrible of existences."

The Other Fellow Dies

Yet every day I meet men and women, particularly women, who want us to go to war, who want no such letter published as the one at the head of this article. Safe in their homes, usually without sons or relatives to suffer, they are insistent that Americans shall go out and die to save England and to stop Hitler. They denounce the flabbiness of the young men and young women in our universities who are so overwhelmingly opposed to war. These misguided youths, they hold, are cowards and shirkers. What has become of their virility, their manhood, their patriotic readiness to give their lives to their country, even as their ancestors died in our previous wars? When I try to bring home to them what war means, when I ask them how they can possibly consent to the subjection of human beings to such torture, they say that that is pacifist, "Miss Nancy" stuff, that Americans ought to be glad to give their lives and go to veterans' hospitals as wrecks for the sake of their country. They wax eloquent about their preferring to die rather than live as slaves on their knees before Hitler. But usually it is the other fellow whom they wish to have make the supreme sacrifice. They are, I repeat, unable to visualize to what they are condemning others or their hearts are dead and cold within them.

Only the other day I met a man who was a captain of artillery in France during the First World War. He is just as bitter against our going into this war as is the writer of the letter quoted above. He told me that on the ship returning from France he saw "150 caged men"—shell-shocked victors of the Argonne and the advance to the Rhine. It was his duty to go by their quarters every day. The horror of it has remained with him until this hour. They were animals, he said, trying to climb up the sides of the ship, rolling around on the floor, without a vestige of humanity left. Yet he told me that when he now protests against America's committing this crime again against its own citizens he is ostracized in his club. He is rich, a successful business man. His record for courage and devotion to his country can be questioned by nobody. But he is ostracized because he dares to voice today sentiments with which everybody was agreeing when the troops came back from France in 1919-20. What must be in the mind of such a man when he compares the President's Armistice Day speech this year with those words of another American President, spoken in that pier-shed at Hoboken as he faced those rows and rows of flag-covered coffins, with the tears coursing down his cheeks, "It must not be again! It must not be again!"

The Noblest of Crusades?

On the other hand, here is a young Yale professor, a highly intelligent, able, sincere young man, who waves all this aside, partly because he has never seen war or its aftermath, and partly because he is obsessed with the idea that he is going to be a slave if Hitler is not defeated. He is convinced that Hitler will win if we do not throw into the scales every single thing we possess. He is ready for bankruptcy and/or a debt never before seen in this world, and he does not care how many lives it will take to march to Berlin. He cannot comprehend any world in which Hitler continues to rule, and he is therefore 100 per cent behind the President. He thinks that even if Hitler does not attack the United States, the minute he has conquered England and Russia—if he does—we can live in the world with him only by being just as militarized as he and spending more money and more of our riches on armaments than the Germans can possibly bring together for that purpose. Therefore, he says that this is the noblest of crusades to save the world for liberty, law and human decency.

This young professor has no question about the return of our liberties after the war. His is the familiar cliché that we have been through a lot of other wars, that even Lincoln was depriving us Americans of our liberties before the Civil War ended and yet we have maintained our democracy nonetheless. He is not moved by the retort that we have never been in a war like this total war before, which before we are in it brings the complete subordination of our industrial life to the government.

Difficult as it is for me to understand this point of view, what troubles me is the inability of this young man to realize the tragic cost of war in human suffering and wreckage. Is it just the size of the canvas upon which this horrible world struggle is being painted that is responsible, or has education failed again? Have the movies that have familiarized us with destruction all over the globe drained the last drop out of our reservoirs of human sympathy?

Psychologists Needed

I suppose that these are the real explanations. I admit that even in domestic horrors we have never been able to visualize the suffering of the individual and his family. True, we are all shocked when a submarine goes down in peacetime and we know that sixty or seventy men are entombed without hope of escape. But when it comes to doing something to stop the loss of more than 35,000 lives and injury of hundreds of thousands on our roads in the course of a year, there again the magnitude of the figures seems to stop us from turning our whole attention to preventing this loss of life. Yet this occurs every year with an ever increasing toll of victims. Here is certainly a field for the psychologist, and for all who are concerned with mass emotion. Perhaps they will be stimulated by the fact that the American people have refused to be stirred by the loss of life on the Reuben James. They can go mad, as Brooklyn did recently, over a victorious ball club, but they no longer react to great loss of human life, they are no longer stirred by mass violations of the law, "Thou shalt not kill."

It is this situation, I suppose, which is partly responsible for America's failure to understand what is happening in the world today. I find everybody praising the magnificent stand of the Russians, but no one trying to visualize just what Russia looks like where the armies have swept over it, the scorched earth foul with the wreckage of obscene corpses, with the ruined paraphernalia of modern mechanized war. I well remember what the earth looked like at Verdun when I was there soon after the Armistice. It was something foul, revolting, green, yellow, evil. On the Ypres front they were pulling cannon and skeletons out of mire twenty feet down, and that mire was unlike anything I have seen in years of travel. It reflected the baseness and vileness of what human beings had done to it.

Hitler's Guilt—and Ours

Today I read the most touching letters from Greece of the sufferings there. No word gets out of Yugoslavia; we do not have to believe that 350,000 have been butchered there under nazi rule to know how unbearable conditions are. From every European country the dread news comes. Yet we are to go in and add to all of this sort of thing. We are to prolong it, we are to increase the sum total of human sufferings which today men's minds can no longer measure. It is all not our fault but Hitler's. His is the blood guilt. All of this is due to the fact that people have sunk to Hitler's level and think there is no other way except to put brute force against brute force. The average American is resigning himself to our becoming a purely militaristic state whether Hitler wins or loses the war. In one case we have got to arm to meet him if he attacks, in the other to hold the Germans down forever.

The worst of this is that it leads our statesmen to believe that they fulfill their duty to their country and to humanity if they just see to it that we have armaments enough to satisfy the generals. It relieves them of any sense that they must find a way out of this human wilderness, that they must set themselves to working out a peaceful world with justice to all. It deprives them of a compelling urge to build a new state of society to lead in the direction of international law and government. It enables them to repeat the banal idiocy that there is now no time to think about anything else except destroying Hitler. Their problem seems to them to be only to wipe out that horrible man and then all will be well with the world. They too have lost the power either to feel or to see.

The Christian Century -- Not used Dec 1941

WE TAKE UP THE SWORD

By Oswald Garrison Villard

So the decision has come and we are at war. What the President's policies have made inevitable has come to pass. It is hard to believe that any portion of the world will now escape the effects of the vast totalitarian revolution which has shaken the very globe itself. Where this first step will lead us no man can even guess, nor how long the war will last. It is now not only a total war, it is much more of a world war than the last, and it is now all one, the war in China, the slaughter in Russia, the daily massacres on the sands of Libya. Who now will be able to check its spread? Who can give us the assurance that it will burn itself out before all humanity is prostrate? The only certain thing is that the war has engulfed us. Soon we may be fighting against Germany, Italy, France, Finland, Hungary, Rumania, heaven alone knows how many others.

In this most solemn of hours there is at least the satisfaction that the first overt acts came not from us but from the Japanese. The duplicity, the black treachery, the foul criminality of their attacks upon the forces of this unwarned country at the very moment when, with complete perfidy a special Japanese ambassador was in Washington sparring for time, so that their submarines, aircraft carriers and battleships might be taking up the positions assigned to them -- all of these abominations will certainly unite the overwhelming body of Americans behind the Administration. What could possibly be more stupid than these acts of the Mikado's militarists? We used to think that nothing could surpass the opaqueness of the German mentality, but the Japanese have gone the Germans more than one better. Not only have they taken just the course to rouse and embitter the country to a great height of passion, they have thrown away their own standing in the court of public opinion and in the final tribunal of history. They have conferred upon the United States the moral advantage and thereby sealed their own doom. They have made it impossible today for anyone to stress the shortcomings of our own policies and to adduce on their behalf their undoubted difficulties. These would be beside the mark. They are ancient history for us. War always means that statesmen have blundered and failed, but those bombs rained on our ships and men and women and children in Hawaii clean the slate for the bulk of our citizens today.

That this means a complete interruption of the progress of American life is as obvious as it is unutterably tragic. From now on the whole effort of the government will be to solve as difficult a military problem as could possibly be devised. Never in human history, at least since the coming of steam, have nations separated by 7,000 miles of water been able to battle successfully with one another. Franklin Roosevelt himself said as late as 1934 that we could not fight with the Japanese nor they with us, and Admiral Sims died believing that even the thought of war with Japan was out of the question. It still remains to be proved that they were wrong, for the distances are the same, and the islands have not moved, nor the rest of the geography changed, nor the tides and the fogs of the ocean. True, the submarine has enormously increased the range of its murderous activities, and the aircraft carrier has been developed and the bomber, too, but no such raids as those which Japan has staged will shake the will of the American people or be anything else in the final solution than a grave military incident.

Only the other day one of our admirals went to a very important personage to beg him to avert hostilities with Japan. He said it meant years of war, that he still could not see how we could conquer Japan. We had not enough bases in the Pacific, he declared. True, we could send our aircraft carriers to lie off the coast of Japan and release their deadly broods. But that type of ship, he said, was the most vulnerable, the best target for dive bombers, with its wide decks. He could not see his way out at all. But opinions do change. It was only in June, 1939 that Major George Fielding Eliot, who has now been demanding war, wrote an article entitled: "That Impossible War With Japan." He said that it would take us a full year to fight our way to the island of Guam with any considerable force. Lately he has felt that Japan is the weakest link in the Axis chain, and that the United States could do nothing better from the military point of view than to war on the Mikado's fleet and keep Japan so busy that its present pressure on Siam, Singapore, the Dutch East Indies, New Zealand and Australia would be immediately relieved. It is to be hoped that his forecast will prove to be true.

But where all of this leaves Great Britain it is hard to say. Mr. Churchill must be anxious indeed lest the flow to England of munitions and cannon, and airplanes suddenly diminish. Men of my age can recall the panic terror which swept over the Atlantic seaboard, then totally unarmed when we entered the war with Spain, and how much of fear there was in the last war of the German raids that came, but proved unimportant. Shall we not see those demands for protection repeated now? Undoubtedly Japan is serving well her German master by this move. It means that no more American war ships will leave the Pacific. It may mean that many cargo boats must be taken through the Panama Canal that would otherwise be serving the British on the Atlantic. It presents to us the same possibility of fighting on two fronts which Adolf Hitler dreaded so much until he made the disastrous blunder of attacking Russia in the mistaken belief that it would collapse under his blows in a few months' time. Can we possibly now supply Russia and China and England and the British in Libya and on the Red Sea, and equip our own army which is now to be raised to 2,000,000 men? Truly we are in for amazing events and incalculable happenings and developments. Before these lines appear in print the whole vast conflagration may have become more lurid, may have spread much further, with the Japanese assailing Russia.

What we are now witnessing is beyond all else a test of the philosophy that has brought the whole world to this pass--that only force can meet and overcome force; that when war comes Christianity may properly be scrapped; that in war the end justifies the means; that by wholesale murder one may purge the world of its sins, or at least that part of it which would wreak its will upon the rest of the world without mercy, without the slightest restraint, with a cruelty on a scale the world has never seen before. Since the test had to come--if one takes a fatalistic point of view--it is at least satisfactory that no one can deny the validity of this test of the belief that superior prowess and arms can make everything right and restore a wholly disordered humanity to a sane, normal and peaceful life. True, the world as we know it may go down in the process of establishing the facts. On the other hand, if it does survive it must surely be certain that this war will bring with it a complete regeneration. I for one have the faith to believe that after so incredible an ordeal the nations of the world will come together, admit their complete exhaustion, acknowledge their own faults, and willingly join in a proper "new order" which will be at least somewhat in line with the Commandments, with the simple elements of human decency hitherto considered the cornerstones of civilization.

But today we face something so vast and so inscrutable that no man is wise enough even to venture to sketch what the future will hold. Yet I see no reason for hopelessness nor despair. if one has simple faith and honest belief that the world will find that it must return to those ethical principles, those methods of life embodied in the greatest of human personalities. It is the road to destruction upon which the world is now thrusting itself; The way back will remain open.

The Betrayal of the American People

By Oswald Garrison Villard

ONCE more before it is too late I wish to make my protest against the casuistry, misrepresentation, evasions and concealment by means of which the President and his cabinet are edging this country into the war. These are strong words, but they are justified and I accept full responsibility for them. I have never until recently believed what some columnists have written, that this administration is without faith in the American people. I have not wanted to believe it, because I still feel myself deeply beholden to Franklin Roosevelt for the sound New Deal legislation he has placed upon the statute books. I well know, for example, from many contacts what the old-age pensions mean to untold Americans. Nonetheless, I am now convinced that the deliberate withholding from the American public of vital information by a "voluntary (!) censorship" and the refusal to tell Congress what is going on behind the scenes, although we are not legally or constitutionally at war, can be explained only as due either to a failure to trust the public and its elected representatives or to a realization that what is going on behind the scenes will not bear the light of day.

The thesis that it is necessary to engage in this concealment and withholding of information in order that the "enemy" shall not know what is being prepared, I reject *in toto.* Only Congress has the right to authorize many of the actions now being taken. Moreover, I suspect that the German embassy and its spies know a great deal more of what is going on than do the American people. But if that is not the case, it would be far better for the future of our institutions to have a few facts penetrate to Berlin than to establish the indefensible precedent that any time when he thinks that an emergency has been created a future President may begin to withhold news, facts *and the truth* from the American people whose steward he is.

Good Faith Made Suspect

That much of the present situation arises from the insincerity of the President's campaign promises only makes things worse. He obviously did not mean what he said in October 1940, for he is now doing what he said he would not do, sending American boys into the European war—and some to their deaths—on our warships and our merchant ships. Mrs. Roosevelt's shocking casuistry in seeking to justify this on the pretense that it is not a foreign war in which we are engaged since it has "come to us," is so false and so mischievous as to make suspect every word of every public man hereafter. Jesuitical is the only word which can apply to reasoning like this—with my apologies to the modern Jesuits.

For some decades it has been easy for me to get on well with people whose views differ from mine. I, having long preached tolerance, have tried not to be intolerant. My difficulty today is that while I can be tolerant and on good terms with those who sincerely believe the opposite of what I do, I find myself raging when the other side carries on without intellectual honesty and straightforwardness. To my mind those who are trying to get this country fully into the war are on the road to complete destruction of our democracy. I can respect them when they candidly state their reasons and act in the open. But I cannot respect any man or woman who says one thing and plans and means another, who uses devious ways to achieve ends. I cannot respect those who form, for example, committees to defend America by aiding the Allies when their real purpose is to get this country into war. For all of this degrades our political life to the level of the Germany and Italy and Russia of the dictators, who suppress, lie and falsify in order to deceive those of their people they do not murder.

Fighting the Devil

All this deceit is justified in Washington by the hoary old assertion that to beat the diabolical fellow you are going to war with you must use his tools and his methods. The theory is that you have the highest moral sanction for doing temporarily, until you lick him, the very things you are going to war to punish him for. Then you will resume your former virtues, look upon your throwing overboard all your standards of right and decency as a necessary sacrifice on the altar of righteousness, and proceed to be as self-righteous and victorious as ever. Probably few of my readers have heard that when we went to war with Spain in 1898 to punish her for her abominable cruelty to the Cuban people and to the Filipinos, her use of concentration camps, her destroying of crops and villages and the constant application of that most diabolical torture, the "water cure," Prof. William Graham Sumner of Yale uttered a solemn warning to his countrymen. He told them that they would soon be doing, if they went to war, the very things that we had condemned in the conduct of the Spaniards, and that the spirit of cruelty and oppression we had set out to exorcise by military force would in turn enter into our own souls.

Professor Sumner was denounced as a vilifier of America, but everything that he warned against came to pass within a year, when we established concentration camps in the Philippines, burned the Filipinos' crops, ravaged their country, killed men, women and children, and applied the water cure torture so frequently that more than eighty officers and men of our army were tried for administering it, or for other abuses and murders of unarmed Filipino prisoners. Middleton Murry has just voiced the same thought in England in saying that "there is no escape from the inexorable necessity which drives England on to become the thing she fights."

What has stirred me particularly just now is fresh evidence of the falsity of the President's fundamental assertion that the United States is in physical danger, strongly supplemented as it has been by Secretary Knox and others of the cabinet. *Uncensored,* that able little four-page anti-war weekly published in New York, has dug out from the records of the "secret session" of the Senate foreign relations committee the testimony of Admiral Stark on just this question as to whether the United States was in any danger of invasion. As no daily newspaper to my knowledge has touched this I reprint it here.

Admiral Stark's Testimony

Referring on October 21 to the proposal to arm merchantmen, Senator Murray asked Admiral Stark: "You think it is a defense measure completely?" The admiral replied: "Yes, I do." Immediately after this there followed this colloquy between Admiral Stark, who is our most important naval officer since he is the head of naval operations, and Senator Hendrik Shipstead of Minnesota:

Shipstead: When I asked you about the battles of Narvik and Crete, you said you thought it was very hazardous to get ashore with troops. Do you think that those experiences have minimized the danger of invasion of the United States?

Stark: Unquestionably; yes, sir. They would minimize it anywhere. If England could maintain distinct air superiority, it would make any landing very hazardous.

Shipstead: Do you mean in England?

Stark: Anywhere.

Shipstead: But it would also apply to the United States?

Stark: Yes, sir.

Shipstead: The invasion of the United States has been put far in the background from where it was before that was demonstrated at Crete and Narvik?

Stark: Yes; but I think it was pretty far in the background anyhow, because they have got to come a long distance by sea. It would take a perfectly enormous amount of tonnage, and they would have to knock the navy out first even before they got to the air.

Shipstead: So there is not much to this talk that we hear about an invasion of the United States by Germany so long as we have plenty of bombers and the men to man them?

Stark: And so long as we have a naval force.

Shipstead: But, after all, they would have to sink our navy?

Stark: Granted your hypothesis that we have a powerful navy and superiority in the air, I think no one can invade us.

Of course many another officer, admiral or general, and numerous civilian writers on military topics have taken this position. But here is the head of the navy officially stating to the most important committee of the Senate that there is nothing to the whole bugaboo of possible invasion. Any honest man who reads this testimony can hereafter only assert that, since we have a very large and efficient navy and plenty of airplanes, while we may be in danger of a possible ideological attack upon us by Hitler, we are not in danger of a physical one.

Fanning the War Spirit

I hope it will be remembered that this is the position that I have taken in this series of articles from the very beginning. On top of this testimony of Admiral Stark comes the statement of Herbert Hoover in his superb speech of November 19 that "the dangers to the United States and England from Europe are less than they were a year ago." He added: "Yet during this past year we have seen a steady rise of war psychosis among our people." He correctly stated that the four great weapons to arouse war spirit are "exaggeration of fear, the stimulation of hate, the challenge to courage and the appeal to ideals." This is exactly what has been happening in Washington. Official circles have exaggerated fears that were baseless at the outset, they have stimulated hate, and they have appealed to American idealism from these false premises.

When before have we had a President denouncing a miscreant, an international brigand, in the language which Mr. Roosevelt has used in his references to Adolf Hitler? Certainly the annals of the state department will, I believe, produce no parallel to Mr. Hull's unbridled attack upon the Germans with whom we are still technically and legally at peace. This applies also to Mr. Hull's attacks upon the Japanese. There was a time not long ago in international relations when such utterances by responsible statesmen would have been considered immediate reason for the withdrawal of ambassadors and breaking of relations. Woodrow Wilson, I believe, never went as far as Mr. Roosevelt in personal attacks upon the Kaiser, although twenty-four years ago the latter was just about as much a personification of the devil as Hitler is today.

Moral Victims of War

Any effort to be consistent with our own record in international affairs is deliberately abandoned. We have forgotten that we made England pay heavily for fitting out the commerce destroyer Alabama in her ports. During the Civil War our minister to England, Charles Francis Adams, wrote to Lord John Russell, the British foreign minister, that if the ironclad rams, which were then on the point of leaving England to serve the Confederacy, were allowed to depart, that meant war, and England detained them. Today we not only give warships to England, but fit out and repair her ships to make war upon another country with which we are technically at peace. This is only one instance. If our intervention in the affairs of Europe without a declaration of war does not jeopardize the Monroe Doctrine for all time, it will be simply because no one is powerful enough on the ocean to challenge us.

All this again brings up the question whether the vile spirit of Adolf Hitler has not already begun to enter into our own souls. Certainly we have already begun to use the phraseology of the dictators. We have taken Iceland and Dutch Guiana into "protective custody." We are sending "tourists" in civilian clothes to war zones, and we are sending military missions to Russia, to Egypt, to China and, it is said, to a number of other countries. We are deliberately assuming that since the Germans are beyond the moral pale we can do anything we please; the mere fact that we are doing it makes it just, right and noble.

It is not even thought necessary for the government to explain when one of its statements is proved untrue, as when the President said that our troops had gone to Iceland to take over that country from the British troops, and the British troops are still there, with a British general commanding our American soldiers. So unimportant have the American people become in Mr. Roosevelt's eyes that it is not worth while for him to explain what has happened since he made his original statement to change the situation in Iceland and his plans for assuming control of that country. If truth is the first victim when a nation goes to war, certainly morals and ethical standards are the next.

July 14, 1943

1

Dear Barnes:

George Kneller, who spent the night here last night, advised me to send you the enclosed pamphlet when I told him that I was endeavoring to find someone who would contribute to a widespread distribution of it. He suggested that possibly Mrs. Seton Porter might be interested, but that at any rate you would know. So I am writing to inquire.

The danger of Am rican domination of Germany is very great, and as England is also training men to govern that country there may be quite a conflict for the overlordship of the Germans. Raymond Clapper told me that the leading men in the State Department were convinced that the record of the German Republic showed that the Germans were totally unfit for democratic self-government and never would be otherwise. He was astonished when I told him that there were many fine things in the record of the Republic, and that that the Allies were fully fifty percent responsible for the breakdown of the experiment. He, of course, had never heard of my "German Phoenix" which is perhaps the only account of some of the achievements of the Republic which is in existence anywhere that I know of. And I venture to say that none of the Berles, Welleses, and other lights of the State Department know any more about that Republic than does Clapper. I suppose it is a forlorn hope to try to stop the plan for American elevation of the Germans, but I think we ought to do what we can.

I hope you are well; I know you are tremendously busy for I see the results of your labors.

Cordially yours,

Mr. Harry Elmer Barnes

Head On for Imperialism

By Oswald Garrison Villard

THIS MAY BE a war for the Four Freedoms, but it is rapidly becoming a war for other things as well. At least we are not going to let any chance to garner some rich pickings pass us by as we wend our triumphant way toward the new world order. Take the case of the five globe-trotting senators and their statements to the secret session of the Senate. It is now published on their behalf that they did not attack England and the English. Far from it. They were, it appears, merely green with envy at the marvelous British governmental efficiency in planning for postwar economic business with their left hand while battling for liberty and the rights of the individual everywhere with the other. The senators' criticisms were directed at our own government. It is asleep at the switch. It is too concentrated on its moral aims. It needs alert salesmanship lest all the good plums be gobbled up by the British while we fight on. One must not let the other fellow pick up all the good things that line the road to glory.

Even when it comes to the new league of nations, whatever its form may be, we are being told that we need to participate in it not merely for idealistic reasons, or to achieve permanent peace, but in order to feather our economic nest as well. Here, for example, is Raymond Clapper, of the Scripps-Howard newspapers, telling us that there are discussions now going on in Washington which, he says, "may lead to government and private partnership in the development of Middle East resources." He begins by explaining that "we are running out of oil," not tomorrow "but perhaps in thirty years or so, perhaps in the lifetime of the younger generation." We have, he adds, 10 per cent of the world's oil and we are supplying "70 per cent of the world's production. No diagram is needed to show where that leads." The five senators are also worried about this and think that England might supply more oil for the war from her Persian fields.

Mr. Clapper also thinks that our government has been too absorbed in other aspirations, and puts it this way:

> Our oil people have been more farsighted than our government has been. They were lured by the search of profits, and it has carried them far out into the world where we as a government would never have ventured to look for even such an essential resource as oil. Whether we have oil or not means the difference between our being a first-class power or a third-class power, but nothing has been done except what the pursuit of private profit has stimulated. American companies have enormous holdings in the Middle East. We have a quarter share in Iraq oil. We have a half share in Kuwait, all of Bahrein oil and all of Saudi Arabia, which is a concession of 244,000 square miles leased by Standard Oil of California and Texas Company jointly.

Mr. Clapper rejoices that "there is more American-controlled oil in the Middle East than we have in the ground in the United States, but the trouble is that it is privately owned oil," and that disturbs Mr. Clapper greatly because "we have usually taken the attitude that if private American capital was involved the operation was just a bit sinister and certainly nothing that should be the concern of the American government—and never would we be sending marines out to protect Standard Oil." But oil, he stresses, "is an essential national resource and our national interest is deeply involved." So the only thing left is for the United States government to jump in and go into the oil business overseas, as it is now preparing to do!

Uncle Sam in the Oil Business

There have been times when the government wasn't very friendly to Standard Oil and the Texas Company, but now, by Jove, when our national prestige is at stake and the future of our automobiling, Uncle Sam knows what to do. He will strike hands with these ancient domestic foes and take part of their Arabian holdings to assure us of bigger and better oil supplies when the next generation grows up. If anybody protests that this is socialism with a vengeance, our government going into private business overseas and destroying private enterprise, individual initiative and the American way of life, why he is just a carper who doesn't realize that we live in new times. The policy for America from now on is to take any oil field or foreign harbor or Atlantic or Pacific island that we deem essential to our national safety. If anybody doesn't like it, he may go back where he came from.

Next there is Persia. We are doing a grand job there in developing the Persian harbors and sending 1,500 tons a day of lend-lease supplies to Russia over the Persian railway in American cars, pulled by American locomotives, run by American engineers. Our Persian army of occupation has completely rebuilt the railroad, strengthened it, put in sidetracks, increased the water supply, rebuilt highways, as well as wholly rehabilitating the two Iranian harbors and the near-by Iraq one on the Persian gulf. We have taken over practically every activity of the Persian government except on the educational side. We control army, constabulary, finance, health, commerce and other things besides, and the word of our representatives is law. Neither the shah nor the national legislature can veto our decisions.

The American flag waves over a large portion of southern Persia and now the demand is that we shall not get out of there without some share in Persian oil. The difficulty is that about 95 per cent of the Iranian oil supply goes to Russia and to England. So our oil magnates insist that we must not come away from there without getting a look in. For what are we staking Russia and England? To the Four Freedoms, of course, but the palm of the left hand itches. What if butting in here will inevitably mean a serious involvement with Russia and England in fear of whom Persia asked us to take over? Well, let Uncle Sam demand his share, go into the oil exploitation business himself, and neither England nor Russia will dare to keep us out.

Trouble Ahead in the Caribbean

Last week it was reported that all the leading men of the American oil industry were down in the Caribbean and Venezuela looking over the situation there. But in those fields there is no room for any outsider. Pretty much everything in sight that is not already held by foreign companies has been gobbled by the Standard Oil of New Jersey which told the whole story in a recent report to its stockholders—one of the most amazing industrial documents I have ever read. Such a wealth of resources as that company has acquired overseas alone justifies Wall Street in singling it out as the leading oil stock in the market today.

Talk about your international complications! If the time ever comes when the inhabitants of the countries involved decide, as Mexico decided, that they want the right to their own natural resources there will certainly be a great furor in this hemisphere. Perhaps our government may take over there also so that it can legitimately send in marines when trouble comes. The Caribbean is now definitely an American lake, precisely as so many of our public men and writers like Mr. Clapper declare that henceforth the Pacific and Atlantic oceans must be American lakes so that we shall never again face the slightest danger, imaginary or otherwise, to our national security.

Manifest Destiny

So there we are in the middle of this idealistic war well on the road to becoming an imperialistic power interfering in concerns of others and grabbing natural resources all over the globe. We are to have permanent conscription and a seven-ocean navy, the largest ever dreamed of in the world, and a merchant fleet of 50,000,000 tons owned by the government and presumably run by the government, or directed by the government if it is in private hands, entirely in the interest of national policy, to be prepared for our next wholesale effort to save the world for democracy or from other countries, white or yellow, which we may have to put in their places. A prominent American who has just returned from Russia and stopped over at many American encampments, including some in Persia, on his way going and coming, declares that at every stop American soldiers asked him if he didn't think that we should have to fight Russia next.

Henry Luce's "American Century"? Certainly we aren't going to put in all this effort, spend all this treasure and all these American lives without getting something out of it, are we? It is already evident that Russia is coming out of this war the most powerful country in Europe and Asia. We have got to be the great power in the western world. What a pity it is that Admiral Peary is not alive to continue the campaign he conducted for so many years to carry the American flag right straight down to Cape Horn. That, he said, was America's manifest destiny. Can anyone doubt it now? The South American states have delivered themselves to us. We now have airfields, military bases, naval ports of call all over Central America and in the northern part of South America. The new Pan-American highway is to be a magnificent artery of commerce—and also for tanks, self-propelled guns and armored trucks. And there are our parachuters and the greatest air force in the world. Long live the American empire!

The New Leader A WEEKLY PUBLISHED SINCE 1923

328

Seven East Fifteenth Street, New York 3, N. Y.

Telephone ALgonquin 4-4622-3

February 29, 1944

Mr. Oswald Garrison Villard
78 East 79th Street
New York, N.Y.

Dear Mr. Villard:

In his recent book, As We Go Marching, John T. Flynn says that Roosevelt -- and the exigencies of war -- are leading us down the road to Fascism. Drawing a parallel to Italy and Germany, Flynn claims that the stupendous national debt, unbalanced budget, huge public borrowing and tremendous public expenditures bring a greater concentration of power in the government and regimentation of the economic life of the country. The consequences, he states, are monopolies, militarism and war.

Do you agree? Are we marching down the same path to disaster that European nations followed? Or where are we marching?

Would you set down your opinion in a short statement, under 500 words if possible, for a symposium The New Leader is conducting?

Sincerely,

Daniel Bell
Daniel Bell
Associate Editor

afoe

March 3, 1944

To the Editor of the New Leader,

Dear Sir:

In reply to your inquiry as to my opinion of John T. Flynn's book "As We Go Marching", I am entirely in agreement with Mr. Flynn's thesis, and I believe that his book proves it beyond question. I admire this volume especially because Mr. Flynn does not attack President Roosevelt or any special group in the community. He builds his case on the fact, which cannot be questioned, that in all aspects of our government finance we are doing precisely what Italy and Germany did on their road to Fascism. I agree that the stupendous national debt, unbalanced budget, and vast public expenditures inevitably mean Fascism in one form or another, certainly complete regimentation of the national economic life. I believe that if there had not been danger of the war in Europe Roosevelt would have turned to conscription, preparedness and militarism as the only way to save himself from his disastrous conduct of the New Deal. Please remember that I am a New Dealer and have supported every liberal reform of Mr. Roosevelt's that I possibly could, especially all his measures for the improvement of the lot of labor. But I thought in 1940, and I think now, that there is no such urgent need in all America as his retirement to private life.

March 6, 1944

Dear Charles:

I must not leave for Puerto Rico tomorrow without sending a word to you and Mary, if only to tell you of my joy in meeting you each week in Life. A woman asked me the other day how much I thought you were paying Life to print these articles. I asked her if she hadn't noticed that Henry Morgenthau had just announced that he expected more income by far on the next income tax day than the Treasury Department had counted on, but I don't think I quite convinced her that you are not a multi-millionnaire. At any rate, it has been grand to see those weekly pictures of you on your vacation. I hope you have had a real rest; the trip before me is in a response to an appeal from the island to help the independence cause. I told them I did not know whether I conscientiously could, for I still am not clear in my mind as to how such a little island could live if it were cut loose from the American tariff system. But they maintain in the most interesting wat that actually they are being bled to death by their association with us.

I need not say that I have read your book with care and admiration and gratitude. You will guess where I cannot go along, or, if you would prefer, would rather not go along. I am sorry you open the door to any suggestion that war may be helpful or desirable, and your feeling that a league of nations is not possible shakes me when I want to believe the contrary. I shall continue to work for at least an association of nations as the only hope of the world's escaping another disaster. Washington is determined (confidentially, I got this from Harry Hopkins) to be a great imperialist nation with naval bases , airfields, army garrisons all over the world, and especially in Formosa to make the Japs behave. And of course the largest navy in the world. I asked him if there had been any talk of disarmament at Teheran or Cairo by international agreement. He said: "Why, no, no admiral or general favored it." - as if any admiral or general ever would. Then he added "nor did anybody else" which placed Stalin because he had just been talking at length about him. Altogether the outlook for the future is such as warranted Archibald MacLeish's saying at Freda Kirchwey's dinner, according to the Times, (I was not asked to be present) that when "liberals meet in Washington these days, if they can endure to meet at all, to discuss the tragic outlook for all liberal proposals, the collapse of all liberal leadership and the inevitable defeat of all liberal aims. It is no longer feared, it is now assumed that the country is heading back to normalcy, that Harding is just around the corner. ..." Well, what did the idiots think they were going to get? I have written an article asking MacLeish this question. What is the use of writing history when people can't even learn by the lessons of twenty-five years ago? I wish I could have another evening with you to tell you of much that I have heard, and especially to help if I could to clarify the military situation. The editor of the Wall Street Journal is betting that there will be no second front and quotes General Harbord as saying that we will not invade until 1946. Kiplinger this week says that the army is running everything in Washington, and that the whole conduct of the Government in every line is now keyed to the invasion. English publications admit that it is the most desperate adventure ever undertaken, and that if it doesnot succeed in the first rush and settles down like our stalemate in Italy, the effects will be disastrous and will result, as one puts it, "in startling and revolutionary changes in Europe." Italy is starving behind our lines, the conditions so horrible that Montgomery's veterans of two years' fighting in the desert are actually nauseated at what they see. But of this not a word in the American press. One Time reporter has said over the radio that we are now hated in Italy worse than the Fascisti, but the conspiracy of silence as to what is really going on is complete. However, we can write much more freely in this war than in the last, for which I give thanks.

My warmest greetings to you both, and I shall hope to see you in New Milford in the Spring, gas permitting.

Ever faithfully,

Mr. Charles A. Beard

xxxxxxxxxxxxxx 79 East 79th Street

February 21, 1945

Dear Robert:

I was glad to get your letter of January 21, and happy to write you again as you wish. I can't give you a wholly good report of myself. That is, I have been wretched all winter, and am just up from a two weeks' siege with grippe. But I have made marked headway because the doctor is now very much pleased with the heart condition, thinking that my latest two weeks in bed have done me a good deal of good by the enforced rest and quiet. How the heart will stand up if I begin to renew my activities, even in a very slight degree, is a matter of experimentation. I am still being drugged. I am thinking somewhat of getting away, but bless me if I can afford it with these taxes. However, as I am dipping into my capital anyway this year I might as well sell another bond. Both Bermuda and Costa Rico seem very alluring, but there are all sorts of obstacles to be overcome to get out of the country. However, I don't believe it will be so much longer. I cannot see how the Germans can hold out longer than a couple of months at most, though I think the Russians will find it not so easy to take Berlin as other places. I can't bear to read of the slaughter of our men on Iwo; I can't believe that anything we may get out of this war is worth the losses we have had, now over 800,000, the ruined lives and the intense human suffering. I am not thrilled at all by Dumbarton Oaks or Yalta. It is the same old swindle. What hope is there in a world order to be upheld by the dominant forces of England, the United States and Russia. I will bet the few normal remaining teeth I have that soon after you and I have passed off the scene the country will be called upon by some cheap poor white, like Harry Truman, to save the world from bolshevism and preserve the Christian religion, and of course the country will be just stupid enough to fall for it again. Do you know that the Germans and we have both been working on the splitting of the atom in order to produce a Uranium bomb five of which of a ton each will probably be able to destroy all of New York? I understand that the OWI no longer permits the press to mention the work Uranium. God bless us all.

Thanks again for your help at the Cosmos with the boy. He is still in Paris working very hard for the American Air Forces. I don't know when I will ever get down to Washington again, but if I do I will let you know. I will try not to have another heart attack while there and throw myself on your mercy again.

Always faithfully,

Mr. Robert L. O'Brien,
The Highlands Apartments
Connecticut Avenue,
Washington, D.C.

After Victory—Europe's Death Agony?

By OSWALD GARRISON VILLARD

WHATEVER the future holds in store for us, every decent human being under heaven must be grateful that the use of wholesale murder to achieve a new order in Europe is now at an end, and must pray that similar news will soon come from the Pacific.

Villard

Every one who has a spark of humanity left in his soul must feel that the ending of the horrible slaughter of human beings for five and one-half years is beyond price. Never since the Middle Ages have women and children, as well as unarmed men, the aged, the sick, the miserable everywhere, been so brutally and ruthlessly destroyed.

To have this finished transcends everything else, for, whatever may be the superficial belief that by arms and violence this guilty earth can be purged of its sins, history teaches that no paradise, no Kingdom of Heaven on earth, can be established in any such way. The road to salvation does not lead through rivers of blood.

Today, in the hour of victory, we are confronted with the question whether the death agony of Europe can be stopped even by the German surrender, whether there will be any survival of the democratic processes where they previously existed. Yes, the situation is just as serious as that and so grave that it is of the utmost importance that even in this moment of national rejoicing, when the parents of our men at the front are on their knees giving thanks for this respite from their agony, it be kept steadily before the American people lest they forget it, lest the demand for additional sacrifices should find them totally unprepared to make them.

Quite aside from the war in Asia, the aftermath of victory in Germany and the occupied countries will make greater demands upon our resources, upon our statesmanship, upon our ability to adjust ourselves to and to overcome difficulties greater than we have ever before encountered.

Economy Is Destroyed

Look at what the German situation is: We are occupying a country with its urban life completely shattered, its factories destroyed, its homes in a number of cities 90 per cent obliterated, their local transportation lines out of business, even their electric light systems gutted, every normal civic process at an end and all government officials under grave suspicion, or expelled, or dead.

Almost every bank is wiped out; only one insurance company survived the last war and the inflation and that one has undoubtedly gone on the rocks this time. The owners of homes have no redress; the holders of mortgages have no security left; the owners of stocks and bonds must dig them out from under tons of rubble—if they can; the beneficiaries of the insured may whistle for their money as most of those did who were in similar circumstances in the 1920's.

As for government bonds, they are worthless. The survivors of perhaps 12,000,000 men enlisted in the war forces must seek now to find civilian jobs when the entire industrial machinery is prostrate or destroyed. The tax-gathering machinery, what is left of it, will seek to squeeze blood out of rubble. On top of all this there will be the division of all Germany into 4 parts, governed by different forces, with different ideals and different aims, with Austria being torn loose to be set up again as a separate entity—this time, apparently, under Russian domination.

Then there is the chaotic condition of the manpower of the land, plus the seven millions of slave laborers and military prisoners. How many Germans are to be turned over to Russia for forced labor there? How many of the 368,000 German prisoners we have will be kept by us, and how many by England and France?

Will they be paid enough to support their families or will they get as little as Nazi Germany paid its victims? What will become of the millions of Russians now pouring, not all toward the East but some toward the West? An American military government officer, just returned, declares that the most trying experience he had was facing freed Russians, some of whom actually begged on their knees not to be returned to Russia.

You Can't Please Everybody

Washington Star

Food? There is the gravest problem of all. Like all the problems set forth above this affects not merely Germany, but all of Europe. It has been worst of all in Holland. The Assistant Secretary of War, Mr. McCloy, who has just returned from the battlefront, declared Apr. 26 that food stocks in the sectors captured by the Allies which he visited will be exhausted in from 30 to 60 days. Everywhere in Germany, he said, he saw "complete destruction" and "dissolution of society—complete collapse of the social and political economy."

From Russian-occupied Poland also come alarming reports: "There is chaos and a complete lack of plan; the organization of city governments is failing; there is complete economic stagnation in many localities, and there are mass arrests and deportation."

Almost no news comes out of the Balkans because of the Russian blackout, and what does leak out is all of the same purport—dire misery, lack of food and clothing, lack of housing, destroyed cities and towns, hopelessness and complete dejection. As for Italy, the danger of a terrible upheaval is perhaps greatest of all there.

I hope that no reader will accuse me of having printed the above facts in order to create sympathy for the Germans. I am always in favor of aiding miserable human beings whatever their virtues and sins, but that is not the purpose of this article. It is, I repeat, only to call public attention to the fact that we are facing the greatest of difficulties in all Europe, that we are lacking in ships to transport the food to Europe, and the organization to distribute it and to manage the territories we have taken over, and that this is a vital problem for the welfare of the United States as well as Europe. Thus, a dispatch from Gen. Bradley's headquarters in Germany reports that AMG simply does not have the manpower or qualified, trained personnel to govern Germany.

One major, one lieutenant, and one warrant officer are trying to administer 200 square miles with a population of 200,000, including 63 towns and villages and four displaced-persons centers with 5,000 persons in each center.

An effort is being made by the Ninth Army to train men for this purpose, but they are to be given only a 2 weeks' course of instruction! The British general who completed the capture of the Ruhr district has notified the Germans that 2,000,000 within that district will die of starvation in the next few months if they do not exert themselves to the uttermost to replant their ravaged fields. He cannot, of course, offer them tractors or animals or tools or seed. These they must conjure up themselves. And so it goes.

Challenge To America

And behind it all is the spectre of the coming Communism. As Judge Samuel Rosenman has just reported to President Truman, after his trip to Europe by order of President Roosevelt:

> **"United States economy would be deeply affected unless northwest Europe again resumes its place in the international exchange of goods and services. Furthermore, a chaotic and hungry Europe is not fertile ground in which stable, democratic, and friendly governments can be reared."**

Representatives of England, Canada, and the United States have just stated that "either the United Nations must find the answers to the food problem or millions of persons will meet disillusionment and disappointment following in the wake of victory. . . ."

So America *must* gird itself to give all the food that can possibly be spared, for the burden will fall upon us. We must supply the working teams that are now waiting to feed and build up the starved Dutch and to aid in every way those Hollanders who, occupying one-sixth of Holland, have been robbed of their land by the wicked flooding of their country by the Nazis.

No other nation but ours can do this. England will cooperate, but we alone have the resources and the financial strength to prevent all of Europe from becoming an absolute chaos, with people tearing themselves to pieces in their efforts to get food and keep alive. We alone can prevent what we are witnessing from becoming the death agony of all Europe.

THE PROGRESSIVE, MONDAY, MAY 28, 1945

Our 'Generous' Program For Germany

By OSWALD GARRISON VILLARD

SO OUR ARMY has decided to be very tough with Germany and, supremely aware of its own virtue, has laid down the terms upon which it will deal with that portion of the German people fate has delivered into our hands. First of all, Secretary Stimson tells us that Gen. Eisenhower's deputy, Lieut. Gen. Lucius Clay, who is apparently to be the real ruler of American Germany, is a "tough-minded soldier," who was "handpicked by President Roosevelt for the direction of our occupation." Next he assures us that any activities by underground organizations "will be ruthlessly suppressed."

Villard

That pledges us to treat any German "patriots" conspiring against foreign military occupation precisely as the Germans treated the Polish, Danish, Norwegian, French, Belgian, and Dutch underground forces—with violent punishments and shootings at sunrise. What in our hidden Allies was noble virtue naturally becomes a crime when done by our former enemies. That is running true to form. We went to war with Spain in 1898 to stop her use of concentration camps, her cruel burning of villages, her infliction of the water-cure torture, and other little embellishments of Christian war, and within a year or so we were smart enough to use all these devices.

Control Of Press, Education

When I heard a movie commentator say a couple of days ago that "the only good Jap is a dead Jap," I recalled how Gen. Sheridan originated this saying in connection with the Sioux, and how our soldiers in the Philippines applied it to their enemies in 1899 and 1901, though no Filipino ever harmed a hair on an American's head before we began subjugating them "ruthlessly" to our will. We play this game well.

To return to our newly conquered, just so that the Germans may understand that they are up against a hard peace, Gen. Eisenhower has fixed the death sentence as a possibility for more than a dozen crimes. If the military courts do not order hanging or shooting, imprisonment may be ordered up to 10 years and fines not exceeding $10,000.

Already the Germans face a food ration of only 1,006 calories a day—3,000 is the daily allotment for the American soldier. Let the "beasts" live on that and nourish themselves on the memory of how much food their armies stole from the rest of Europe.

Next, Secretary Stimson tells us, Gen. Clay will control "all forms of public expression in Germany," including "newspapers, radios, magazines, motion pictures, etc," and will establish "an unbiased and truthful press and radio system"—precisely as we have them at home, as everybody knows. Next, we are to take over education and all schools will remain closed until pre-Hitler German text-books, or new ones edited by us, can be introduced to lead the children along proper paths.

Then, in order to make the Germans realize how wicked they are, there is to be no entertainment for them of any kind, no movies, no music, nothing. According to a dispatch to the New York *Times* from Munich on May 15, there are to be no mails whatever so that they cannot gloat over any discovery that they have surviving relatives in other cities. Telephone communication is likewise forbidden, "the curfew is strictly enforced and travel by any means, except on foot or bicycle, is prohibited." The railroads are being repaired "but not for the benefit of the German civilians."

For the present "all shops, except those offering food, remain closed." Censorship, Mr. Stimson assures us, "will be solely on the basis of military security"—in which case there may be no censorship whatever since it is difficult to imagine any hostile military activity, but we shall take no chances. In addition, the non-fraternization order imposed on United States troops is reported to be "functioning to a point near perfection" at Munich.

There will be "an over-all Intelligence Section," an American Gestapo, to "maintain general supervision and surveillance over the entire de-Nazification program, and it is to carry on the elimination of Nazis from all industry, labor unions, etc., down to the last Hitler follower. The number of Nazi criminals who will face our courts and those of our Allies is now fixed at a figure which may be 6 million—a figure that might stump others less tough than ourselves and the Russians, but we shall fix them all right and let not one guilty Nazi escape, however many years it may take.

There will be a small task for the Economic Division—there will be 12 major divisions of our supervisory government. It will have only to supervise the problems of food, agriculture, forestry, fuel, mining, price-control, rationing, public works, utilities, internal and foreign trade, industry, conversion and liquidation, and requirements and allocations. All this we shall also take in our stride and in carrying out the program we shall see to it that we have no intercourse whatever with the Germans, but only exercise remote control.

All of this plainly marks a new epoch in human relations. No other nation on earth has ever attempted anything like it before, but we shall do it successfully and efficiently. This is so certain that I regret to see evidences, even in some official quarters, of an effort to weaken our plans.

Thus, the Army Medical corps opposes non-intercourse on the ground that that will send up the venereal sick rate by 100 per cent since sexual intercourse between our soldiers and the German women cannot be stopped, and our soldiers will avoid going to the prophylactic stations rather than to face a fine of $65 by admitting their transgressions.

Death For Dissenters!

And here is Rep. Clare Luce of Connecticut, coming back from Germany and making the discouraging statement that "death, destruction, starvation, disease, political chaos is now indescribable and will become far worse before it is better." That, I submit, is uncalled for pessimism in view of the Stimson plan I have recorded above. Let no one seek to weaken our morale by dwelling on the fact that Germany may prove a difficult problem because there will be 3 other governments in the Reich, with Austria already torn from it and reinstated as a republic.

Any man who suggests that we may not be able to cooperate amicably with the Russian, the French, and the British co-administrators of our conquered territory is plainly a pro-German to be watched and denounced. No one but a potential Nazi could have any question as to the correctness of this program of ours. Can any real American doubt that through it we shall win the love and gratitude, the respect, and the admiration of the Germans? Can any one fail to visualize that in the Germany of the future statues to Mr. Stimson and Gen. Clay will stand in every one of the German cities over which the American flag now flies? And that by such demonstrations of our generosity, our kindliness for their own good, our Christianity, we shall win all the German millions under our control to immediate adoption of American ways and methods?

July 16, 1945

Dear Charles:

This is just to report that the Villards finally arrived here two weeks ago and have since been very busy opening the larger house which has been more or less closed for four years. Mrs. Villard came with me to keep an eye on me and to help our daughter-in-law who leaves for her third accouchement a week from today, and our grandson. My daughter is also here, and as my younger son and his wife are due for a week today, the whole tribe will be here with the exception of our elder son who is studying the air damage in Southern Germany for the Army Air Force--I have just seen some incredible pictures of it being privately circulated in Washington for the Air Force officers. The wreckage is horrible beyond words and makes me more than ever unable to see the slightest moral justification for what we have done, however great the incentive. How can anyone doubt that the world will pay a terrible price just for the destroyed wealth all over Europe? Yet we sail on serenely without giving much of any thought, at least among the public, to the tremendous economic punishment which will confront us. I must say, however, that the Congress is much more concerned about the immediate future than is the public.

I am under no illusions about the San Francisco Charter, but like Norman Thomas and other dissenters, I have decided to accept it with reservations and not to oppose its passage. This time I don't want fools and knaves to say that we have wrecked the league by not going in. I am sure that you are as delighted as I at the change in the atmosphere of Washington. A Congressman writes me today: "You will be surprised to know the change in atmosphere here in Washington since Roosevelt died. A certain unexplainable relief has come not only to those who were opposed to Roosevelt politically, but even with the Democratic Party, except the extreme New Dealers. Truman has a certain political sense which will be used to the advantage of our country, I am sure, and he has also had the advantage of understanding the psychology on Capitol Hill. I daresay he has almost as many supporters in the Republican Party today as within the Democratic Party."

Do tell me how you are and whether you have your strength fully back. I have bad days and good ones and am now trying to stop my loss of weight which for years I longed to achieve! I have often wanted to go to the telephone to ask you how you are, how Mary is. Have you made any headway toward the new house? Later on I certainly hope to be able to call upon you, but gasoline is much scarcer for me than last year so that I can't move around very much.

With most affectionate greetings to you both,

Ever faithfully,

P.S. I turned up the enclosed article yesterday
and thought you might enjoy looking it over. You
were very right in some spots, but like myself,
F.D.R. and so many others, we were ignorant, weren't
we, of what a tremendous fighting machine the Japanese
could develop?

Dr. Charles A. Beard
New Milford, Connecticut.

August 7, 1945

Dear Dorothy:

A letter from Hubertus Loewenstein gives me the grand news that you are just as outraged by the Pact of Potsdam as I. I have written as strong a denunciation of it as I possibly could hearkening back to my similar denunciation of the Treaty of Versailles and prophsying that it means the destruction of Europe and of course it cannot be put through, anarchy and chaos will stop it. To think that there should be anybody in Washington capable of accepting the proposals of Vansittart and Morgenthau! That reveals the utter ignorance which controls there and proves how utterly unfit we are to deal with the problem we have undertakem, as you and I have known we were from the beginning. Stupidity and ignorance are destroying this world. I don't get any hope out of the British election on the foreign side, but I am happy that Churchill is out. Attlee is small, but intrinsically a decent and very modest man.

And now we have the atomic bomd to top it off. That means either the end of war or the destruction of humanity. I have known about it for a year and a half, as I presume you have, and I know how desperately frightened the scientists working on it and in similar fields have beem lest the Germans get ahead of them and win the war. I hope you will bring out the news published in today's Times that three German Jewish scientist discovered the principle and refused to give it to Hitler. How wicked the Jews are! I should invite myself up to see you if I could travel, but I have been a semi-invalid ever since last October when my sorely abused heart went on a strike. I can do some writing, but not much, have had to give up my little syndicate of newspapers and find it very hard to place any articles. Either the magazines don't want me or my hand is slipping--probably both. But I do feel the need of communion with understanding people who really know Europe and I feel terribly isolated. I would give a lot to be able to head for your domain.

Affectionately yours,

Miss Dorothy Thompson
Twin Farms
South Pomfret, Vermont

World Disarmament Now!

By OSWALD GARRISON VILLARD

SOON after Franklin Roosevelt took office as President he declared that we had "nothing to fear but fear." That was when the country was facing economic collapse. Today, in the face of unparalleled victory in the greatest and worst of all wars, there is nothing so plain and so astounding as the fact that almost our every national act is dominated by fear—fear primarily of our beaten and utterly smashed enemy.

O. G. Villard

Twelve of our returning generals have just declared jointly that Germany cannot recover and be dangerous militarily for 100 years, and Japan's complete and abject surrender is before us with the loss of all her empire. Still fear of their revival controls us. Even the revelation of the atomic bomb and its monstrous use in slaughtering men, women, and children by the hundred thousand has not set us to yip-yipping in good old American style that we are top dogs for all time.

On the contrary, the President on his return from Berlin announced early in his speech that we shall hold all the bases we have captured which we think necessary for our safety and acquire at once such others as we may think we need to protect us. The brutally vindictive and self-injuring terms which we and the Russians and British have forced on the Germans without any popular mandate, or the vote of a national assembly, reveal only too clearly that no matter what our generals say or how great the destruction of Germany, we are primarily actuated in everything that we are doing in Europe by fear of a beaten Germany, and secondarily by a passionate thirst for vengeance.

It does not occur to anyone in authority that this is hardly the hour for calm and rational thinking when our nerves are still jangling, when our emotions are deeply stirred, when we can think only of our wrongs, when the grief of unbearable losses presses down upon so many of us, when we dwell upon the wickedness of those who but yesterday were destroying our precious young manhood.

We want to act at once, to assure ourselves this very minute that it cannot happen again, that our children's children shall not have their Gethsemane a few years hence, with up-to-date atomic bombs wiping out whole cities at one blast. No voices are raised to urge deferment of definite decisions as to postwar policies, to make sure that we are really taking the right road and advocating the proper methods to bring about that permanent peace which every humane person must desire from the bottom of his heart.

* * *

FEAR still prevails. Those who believe that safety lies only in the drilling of every young American are still demanding universal military service. The Navy will not think of abandoning its plans for a 500,000-man fleet, and Secretary of War Stimson talks of keeping at least 3,000,000 men indefinitely in the Army to hold down the Germans and Japanese, to garrison the innumerable islands and bases the world over upon which we are to display our flag.

In other words, we are definitely committed to the militaristic theory that we cannot be safe even after our stupendous achievements and the demonstrated fact that no country on earth can compete with us as a fighting nation, excepting Russia, if we do not have armed men with tanks, airplanes, V-1 and V-2 bombs, atomic missiles all over the seven seas ready for some marauder to drop down from the skies.

Nobody is to be trusted, and no one is to remember that we shall soon have among us 7,000,000 veterans of the most successful armies in the world's history. We are to have no faith that the United Nations organization will soon police the world and safeguard air and sea and land.

Instead, we read Stalin's announcement that he is founding no less than 12 new naval academies and building a vast fleet like our own— to hold the Germans down and control the Baltic and the Dardanelles—and we shiver. We are convinced that our only hope of freedom in the future is to share the secret of the atomic bomb with no one but Great Britain. We may not be very happy about it and its indescribable wholesale destruction of life. It may trouble our consciences at night. It confounds the clergy. But still, we say, "How much better that we should be blotting out the vile Japanese than that they should destroy people as good and kind and brave and humane as we. Let us put our faith in this weapon and keep millions of men in the Army and Navy for all time. Won't it be vastly cheaper than six months' expenditure in the next war?"

* * *

NOW I submit that none of this is worthy of the grandeur of the opportunity for world leadership which has come to us, nor of the tremendous military achievements we have behind us. If we are going to lead the world into the paths of peace, the first thing to do is to recognize that today we have nothing to fear but fear, that our sole purpose should be, with the aid of the atomic bomb if you please, to make certain that the world has seen the last war.

This is the last hour, when the blood of our precious youth has only just ceased to flow, to be planning for the next struggle, or even to shape our national policies on the theory that war is inescapable and that, with all its horrors, an atomic war in which five bombs may destroy the whole city of New York is certain to come. It is the time to insist upon finding other roads to safety—and there are plenty—and above all, to move immediately for complete disarmament by *all* nations.

Already voices are beginning to be raised along this line. For example, the Rev. Bernard Iddings Bell of Providence, R. I., lately president of St. Stephen's College, in a sermon at Trinity Church at the very head of Wall Street, took the opportunity to say the following wise words:

"Mr. Truman, Mr. Attlee and Mr. Stalin should show one another and the rest of the world that they mean business by beginning immediately the demobilization of their armed forces, the scrapping of their armaments and by ceasing to train more peacetime conscripts." That is the way certainly to prevent any possibility of a third global struggle for power.

That it will be extremely difficult to compel our Government to rapid demobilization is obvious enough. From the very beginning of the war we have overmanned it. For the first time in our history we gave an absolutely free hand and an unlimited exchequer to the Army and the Navy and they went the very limit in demanding everything that they had ever thought of in their wildest dreams of military power.

Whether there was or was not justification for a lavish use of manpower in outlying posts and stations, there can be no excuse whatsoever for failure to demobilize the Army and Navy now with all possible speed to a sensible level. Of course the Army doesn't want to do that. Its officers, who have risen from low rank to positions of high command, have no desire to return to the slow peacetime methods of promotion and their regular grades.

America Demands The Truth About Pearl Harbor

By OSWALD GARRISON VILLARD

THE decision by Congress to conduct a comprehensive investigation into the diplomatic and military developments leading up and through the Japanese attack on Pearl Harbor Dec. 7, 1941 has rightly won the enthusiastic approval of the entire nation. The original determination of the Truman Administration and the Army and Navy brass hats to squelch a civilian inquiry was vetoed by the people themselves who were shocked by this brazen attempt to keep the whole truth from coming out.

O. G. Villard

It is heartening, however, that once forced by pressure of public opinion to abandon their strategy of silence, concealment, and whitewash, the Administration decided to go all the way. Majority Leader Alben Barkley, author of the investigation resolution, promised that the inquiry would be conducted without partisanship or favoritism toward **"any responsible official, military, naval, or civilian, high or low, living or dead."**

There is much still to be told—much that was not included in the reports of the Army and Navy which were dumped so hastily on the nation recently. We do not know yet why we were caught so tragically asleep at Pearl Harbor when the late Mr. Roosevelt, as President and Commander-in-Chief, had what seems to be positive advance information that the Japanese were going to strike when and where they did.

Nor do we have the answers to many other vital questions which are needed not only because the nation is entitled to the whole story of the Pearl Harbor disaster, but perhaps more important, as Dr. Charles Beard pointed out in his superb article in The Progressive a fortnight ago, because the lessons to be learned from the diplomatic and military mistakes of the Pearl Harbor episode can have a profound influence in the shaping of our foreign policy and defense programs.

That the newly published 144,000 word reports have advanced our knowledge of the situation is happily true. It is something to have men in Army and Navy uniforms censure not only the active commanders, but go out of their way to criticize the Chief-of-Staff, the active head of the Navy, and the Secretary of State.

The careful analysis of what took place to be found in the Army report is welcome indeed. But that is not enough. There is still much light to be thrown. As the *Wall Street Journal* has pointed out:

"It is perfectly possible to recite all the facts in a given case without revealing the truth. There is room for suspicion that the Pearl Harbor reports . . . do just that. One thing the reports bring out clearly. The attack at Pearl Harbor was no surprise. It was so little of a surprise that Washington knew within the range of a few hours when the attack would occur."

Months in advance, as far back as January, 1941, the State Department was put on notice by Ambassador Grew that important circles in Tokyo declared that the Japanese were planning a sneak attack upon Pearl Harbor. It was promptly discounted in Washington, partly because it was doubted in the Tokyo Embassy itself by some of Mr. Grew's aides, and the Army and Navy promptly pooh-poohed the idea on the ground that if the Japanese were planning anything of the kind it would be the last thing that would leak out. We need to know more about this.

* * *

NOR is it a satisfactory alibi to put the responsibility for the disaster upon the system. Of course the Army and Navy system was hopelessly antiquated. In my book *Our Military Chaos*, printed in 1939, I pointed out that our defense was planless, that the War and Navy Departments were inefficient and wasteful, and that there was totally inadequate cooperation between the Army and the Navy.

I quoted a major-general—anonymously of course—who said that if war came there would be grave danger of the Army and Navy air forces colliding in mid-air because neither would know what the other was going to do—a charge completely borne out when war came by the fact that it took the two services from Dec. 7, 1941 to the middle of April, 1942, to meet and agree upon a joint defense of the Atlantic coast during which time we lost the bulk of our tanker fleet.

Nor is it an adequate defense to say that the Army and Navy chiefs were "dulled into a buck-passing attitude by long fear of political attacks," as does George Fielding Eliot in the New York *Herald-Tribune* of Aug. 31. When was there a time when the Army and Navy chiefs did not pass the buck? When was the period in our military history when those chiefs were really on their toes and working night and day for up-to-date military and naval forces? I never heard of it, and I have been writing Army and Navy comments longer than I dare admit—including 21 years as Army and Navy Editor of the New York *Evening Post*.

Diogenes Looking For An Honest Report

* * *

GRANTING the system was deficient, two great questions remain: first, were Gen. Short and Adm. Kimmel professionally competent, and second, and even more important, were they given sufficient information to enable them to get a clear picture of the actual situation? This is where the State Department is dragged in. In defense of Secretary Hull his hitherto unpublished letter of Sept. 28, 1944, has been released at last to prove that the Army Pearl Harbor board's charge that he "touched the button" which started the war, by his ultimatum to Japan on Nov. 26, 1941, is not true.

That it is true is the belief of multitudes of Americans who do not agree with Mr. Hull that it was not an "ultimatum." Mr. Hull now says that it was a very generous offer that he made, giving the Japanese "substantially the economic and other advantages they sought in Asia, provided they would give up their aggressive policies." This is in itself a remarkable confession of appeasement. Actually, however, the document, which Mr. Hull says was not an ultimatum, *demanded* that the Japanese *give up all their conquests* and retire largely to their homeland. If that was not an ultimatum, what on earth could be?

Furthermore, Mr. Hull does not bring out the fact that after sending this document he assured Viscount Halifax, the British Ambassador, that he was then through with the Japanese and that the whole matter was in the hands of the Army and Navy, that diplomacy had ceased to function. Yet that he had taken this stand was no more communicated to the commanders at Pearl Harbor than was the fact that he had sent the message of Nov. 26 to Japan.

Whether it was an ultimatum or not, it was a crucial document. Yet Adm. Kimmel and Gen. Short were told nothing about it, just as the American public was kept in total ignorance of the gravity of this provocative document which did help to bring on the war, until long after Pearl Harbor. There is no more vital point than this.

Historians will have to take sides on it for all time to come if they undertake to find out just how much the United States was responsible for the war and how much the Japanese, and whether Oliver Lyttleton, a Minister in the Cabinet of Winston Churchill, told the truth when he blurted out that everybody knew that Mr. Roosevelt was pushing Japan into war.

* * *

NOW obviously it was beyond the scope of the Army and Navy courts of inquiry to go into these matters in detail. Yet these matters are fundamental if we are to have the true picture of what occurred and who was responsible. The army court was thoroughly justified in going as far as it did, but it shied off from the question as to the actual responsibility of the late President of the United States.

After all, Mr. Hull was the President's subordinate, and Mr. Roosevelt was to a considerable degree his own Secretary of State. He must not be spared. We need a vigorous civilian inquiry—and the Congressional investigation must be just that—to carry this probe right through to the bitter end and let us know exactly why it was that our Government was playing a double game with the Japanese and the American public.

* * *

WHEN Pearl Harbor took place Mr. Hull sent for the two Japanese envoys who had been talking peace to him while their fleet was approaching Pearl Harbor for its dastardly attack, and blistered them with language of a character never before heard in the Department of State, according to contemporary reports. The fact that he himself had been continuing to talk peace to these same Japanese envoys for all the days after he had told Viscount Halifax that the matter of peace or war was no longer in the hands of the diplomats, but rested solely in those of the Army and Navy, he has never stressed in any letter that I have yet seen. Was this any more ethical? Certainly nothing brought out in the Army report shows that Gen. Short and Adm. Kimmel were any more made aware of the ending of negotiations than was the American public. Nor is the fact borne out that the task force which was sent to relieve and strengthen Midway Island was told—according to a publication permitted by the censor and the Navy Department—to sink any Japanese ship that might happen along, with all on board, so that no word would get back to Tokyo that Midway was being strengthened.

Still another alibi offered for the Army and Navy is the familiar one that they did not have the materials on hand to enable them to carry on war efficiently. That is undoubtedly true. There was only one radar set, and that was being used less for protection than for the instruction of untrained officers and men. Airplanes were coming in from the mainland without ammunition and entirely unprepared for attack.

There were not enough planes to carry on the necessary air reconnaissance and the Navy court upholds Adm. Kimmel in abandoning it because of the lack of the proper planes and for other reasons. But here again Gen. Marshall knew early in 1941 that there were rumors from responsible sources in Tokyo that Pearl Harbor might be attacked. Why did not the War Department drop everything else then to protect Pearl Harbor?

The whole theory of the War and Navy Departments from then on was, however, that Japan would not attack Pearl Harbor until the war was well under way and that the immediate danger point was not Hawaii, but lay in the Southwestern Pacific in the direction in which the Japanese advance on Malaya, Java, etc., did develop. Final judgment on that policy cannot be passed by Army and Navy officers. It calls for rigid cross-examination by civilians determined to get at the truth at any cost.

* * *

AS for the professional efficiency of Adm. Kimmel, there is certainly room for question whether even with the partial information given to him he was justified in concentrating the whole fleet in a small harbor when he was aware that he was without adequate air protection or sufficient anti-aircraft guns. But the Navy Department knew that he was doing this, knew that under orders issued in September, 1941, there would always be a large portion of the fleet in Pearl Harbor—probably two-thirds—and it did not fully warn him of the danger even after it knew in advance that there was risk of a submarine attack; actually Japanese midget submarines entered and safely left Pearl Harbor undetected days before Dec. 7.

Whatever this officer's merits or demerits, he is entitled to a real day in court, and as one who believes that both he and Gen. Short have had an extremely raw deal in being compelled to wait for three and three-quarters years in a state of professional suspension and contumely, I think that the least that should be done for them is to give them the opportunity to appear before an unbiased committee of Congress accompanied by counsel and free to tell the whole truth and nothing but the truth. That I have been urging for a long time. The hour has now come when they should be clearly vindicated, or their errors of judgment set forth beyond any question.

* * *

WE need an inquiry which will spare nobody, which will deal with Secretary Hull, Secretary Stimson, and the late Secretary Knox without gloves, and uninfluenced by the fact that they have played distinguished roles in the winning of the war.

We want to bring out into clear light the whole question as to whether the stupid system of separate Army and Navy ought not to be ended at once—President Truman has just approved of this—and whether it is possible to devise any system of national defense in which the chiefs do not pass the buck and free themselves from blame for the failure to give the country efficient, economical, enterprising and progressive measures of defense by placing the responsibility upon Congress or the public.

Let us for once end Army and Navy buncombe and have the whole truth!

Showdown In Korea

By OSWALD GARRISON VILLARD

WHAT is the explanation of our Government's attitude toward Korea, its hesitancy in promising the independence promptly to be given to the Philippines and other victims of the Japanese? Why is it that the Declaration of Cairo, which said that all the peoples conquered by the Japanese should be restored to their previous national allegiances or be set free, limited its reference to Korea by the words pledging a "free and independent ... Korea ... *in due course*"? Why is it that the Russians have taken the northern half of Korea while we occupy the southern, and that our commanding general, Lt. General John R. Hodge, made the incredible blunder of announcing that he intended to administer our zone of this unfortunate country with the present Japanese officials, including the Governor-General, Noboyuki Abe?

O. G. Villard

That he was immediately compelled to back down from this position by Gen. MacArthur and protests from Washington, did not wholly assuage the feeling of the aroused Koreans who have demonstrated in large numbers in their capital Seoul against this incredible American attitude of continuing in office their hated conquerors.

The prompt overruling of this stupid general, who could have saved the whole situation if he had explained at once that he was going to get the Japanese out as rapidly as possible, does not conceal the fact that our Government has lacked faith in the Koreans' ability to govern themselves in view of their long period of subjection and exclusion from office and administrative functions during the 40 years' rule of the Japanese.

The Administration seems quite willing that Thailand (now renamed Siam) should go its own way, but it doubts whether the Koreans are immediately fitted to assume the full responsibilities of independence and self-government. It is known that President Roosevelt insisted from the beginning of our entrance into the war that Korean independence must be a war objective, and, it is believed, that the first government should be an international one to be administered jointly by the United States, China, and the Soviet Union.

It is explained for him now that he felt that if they were not given such an international control the Koreans might readily be taken over by some nearby Power, presumably Russia, on the ground that it could not adequately govern itself and menaced the frontiers of this other country.

* * *

THIS brings us right up against the fundamental principle of democracy—which is whether a people demanding freedom shall be held in leash until some other people think that they have qualified for government according to the latter's standards, or whether they shall be given a chance to strike out for themselves to sink or swim on their own.

Almost nobody in Great Britain thought the American colonies could govern themselves when we won our freedom, and it would be amusing to turn back to the jingo newspapers of 1898-1900 and pick out the innumerable statements that appeared, when we were slaughtering the Filipinos, burning their fields, destroying their villages, and putting thousands of them into concentration camps, seeking to prove that anybody who thought that the Filipinos would ever be capable of governing themselves was simply idiotic.

William Howard Taft, when Governor General of the Philippines, was denounced, ridiculed, and abused from one end of the United States to the other because he began filling offices with natives, and what is worse, actually practiced social equality with them and governed them as if they had some rights in formulating plans for their own future. All those who favored independence for the archipelago were denounced as hopeless idealists and the chief denouncers were naturally the Army and Navy officers who were serving or had served in the islands.

What is at stake is the vital principle that self-government does not mean good government and must never be construed as meaning that. It is nobody's business to say of any people who have been held in tutelage that they cannot govern themselves. Give them a helping hand, yes; loan them officials, as we have loaned trained American administrators to Iran, yes; induct them in the most modern ways of financial management, yes; help them to establish an efficient constabulary, yes; aid them with advice and counsel in every way on a big brother basis—of course.

But the way for a people to learn to govern themselves is to start right in and make their own mistakes. Heaven knows we made plenty in this country in the days immediately following the Revolution, and heaven knows that we have been making the gravest of mistakes and have been far from living up to our democratic doctrines ever since. But the right of a people to misrule themselves is as sacred as any right to government which measures up to British, American, German, Dutch, or French standards. The Koreans are absolutely entitled to start right in now and find the way to good government by blundering as much as they please. These are the principles which should have governed our relationship with Korea from the beginning of this war, and it will take more than pious promises of the kind made last week by President Truman to convince the people of Korea and Asia.

* * *

INSTEAD, the representatives of the Korean Provisional Government and of the Korean Commission, whose headquarters are in Washington under the leadership of Dr. Syngman Rhee, have been cold-shouldered by the State Department, and deliberately kept at arm's length.

The excuse for this has been that there were several groups representing the Koreans, and that there was no adequate proof that any group of Koreans actually represented the Korean people as a whole, or any considerable part of them. It is intimated, too, that one of these various groups is strongly influenced by Moscow and should, therefore, not be encouraged.

Hence, the hesitancy in the Cairo Declaration; hence, the occupying of the northern part of Korea by the Russians and the southern part by the United States.

To this the reply can be made that the United States might have picked one of the groups and placed itself squarely behind it and done its uttermost to make it ready to take over as soon as the conquest was completed and then to leave to a democratic plebiscite among the Koreans the question as to who should be the permanent leaders.

Not at all. The State Department preferred to drift. It is not necessary to cite the fact that in other cases some of its officials have leaned to the imperialistic, or even totalitarian side, as in the handling of Franco in Spain. It is sufficient to point out that the Department was not interested enough to prepare plans in advance for a government to be set up immediately on our taking over.

As in the case of Japan itself, the sudden, unexpected ending of the war found us unprepared to deal with the immediate situation. The Washington Koreans and their Chungking brethren of the Provisional Government had been put off and brushed aside as typifying problems which could be duly handled when the Japanese collapse came. Now it is here and Gen. Hodge finds himself compelled to carry on with enemy officials, while our Government tries to make up its mind what he should do and how rapidly he should appoint Koreans. Plainly he had no instructions to guide him when he took over the task of civilian administration for which not one general in 50 is fitted. So far as is known, no civilian experts on the Korean situation have been sent to him—there are some, even though they are not in the State Department, and they could have been enlisted long ago for the emergency.

* * *

WHO are the Koreans? They are a highstrung, sensitive, proud people, who to a remarkable degree remember their past. They have not forgotten that they were the first people to have a national flag, a printing press, and even an ironclad navy as far back as 1592, when they defeated an early Japanese effort to enslave them.

It is not true that they have supinely accepted Japanese rule. Close to half a million have fled the country rather than submit. Thousands upon thousands have been thrown into prison by the Japanese, for "thought crime" and other thousands executed. Still, in 1919 the Koreans declared their independence. Again the Japanese executed many of the passive protestors and no less than 11,000 demonstrators were flogged.

More than that, in this war they have supplied a Korean force to the Chinese Army, and there have been Korean troops serving with the Russian Red Army. In addition, there has been a steady underground movement against the Japanese comparable to the French and other resistance movements. The desire for independence has never for one moment died down in Korea. The spirit of liberty has steadily swayed these gifted and able people who now number no less than 25,000,000.

If the United States is going to be true to its own ideals and live up to its pretended objectives in this struggle, the military phases of which have ended, we must royally and generously stand by the Korean people. If not, we can blame no one if we are charged with Anglo-Saxon hypocrisy, with deceit, with weakness, with inefficiency, with the failure to stand by a country that is, and will continue to be, a key to peace in Asia.

It is of enormous importance that Korea shall be reestablished as a free, independent, buffer state which shall stand between China and Russia, between China and Japan as a memorial to the integrity of the American effort to purge Asia of Japanese domination.

The very fact that the Russians are in Northern Korea and have long been accused of a desire to take over the whole of the country, dictates a quick declaration of America's permanent policy in what was for so long known as the Hermit Kingdom. The best answer to Russian aggression whether planned now or not, is for the United States to come right out and say that it will not consent to any other fate for Korea than complete and absolute independence, and that it proposes to see to it that this is accomplished, and that it is not to be deterred from setting up a national government immediately by fear that the Koreans may be insufficiently experienced in government to carry it out.

We did tremendous things for Iran at the beginning of our participation in the war, and even before. We loaned eight officials under Dr. Arthur C. Millspaugh to take over complete financial control. We put an Army medical officer in charge of health matters, including water supply, and especially charged him to deal with sanitation problems in the leading cities of Teheran and Ispahan.

We can put Korea on its feet in no time at all, by friendly, sympathetic cooperation. Let us lose no time in giving this help to Korea and getting American and Russian troops out of there at the earliest possible moment. The Koreans don't need to be policed by American and Russian army corps; they can take care of themselves. This is the least that we can do in honor and decency for our Korean ally and in partial redemption of our pledges.

October 2, 1945

Dear Henry Mencken:

I have been wanting for some time to write you and tell you how happy I was to see those fine reviews of your book, and to know that it was at least released, but I have had a couple of bad turns and have fallen behind on correspondence as well as reading and writing articles. It has been a mean summer for me, except that I have had the joy of having long visits from our children and my grandson, a very nice little three-and-a-half-year-older who gave us unending joy. I have thought of you often, aside from your book, and longed for an opportunity to talk things over with you. We are certainly in one hell of a mess and are already beginning to properly pay for our folly in going into the war. I am appalled by the fact that none of the men now handling affairs in any country, except Russia, seem capable of dealing with the situation. Truman is certainly a good, kindly Rotarian trying his best, handicapped by his professional loyalty to FDR, and wholly without the vision and the understanding, and, I fear, the strength, to stand up to Uncle Joe. As for what they have done to Germany in their folly, there is no need to comment on that. They are in an awful mess there, self-created at Potsdam, and every day that passes will make the situation worse for our generals. I get a real Schadenfreude out of it. Think of putting a sensationalist and self-exploiting ignoramous like Patton in charge of Bavaria, and under him a second-rate Irish-American journalist, who has already had to be removed!

Fortunately there are some sane voices. They tell me Ernest Lindley is beginning to see the light, and the London Economist is doing magnificent work, and so is Dorothy Thompson. I have taken a few pot-shots at the enemy in The Progressive, for which I still write every other week, and of course Frank Hanighen and Felix Morley are doing a grand job with that little Human Events. I wish they could expand it into a first-class weekly. The New Leader is also doing good work, whihe The Nation and New Republic are simply nauseating. Imagine my Nation unable to criticize Stalin to any extent, and keeping silent as to the revelations with regard to Roosevelt's role at Pearl Harbor and his part in fleecing Mr. Hartford! I wish I could feel that the Pearl Harbor inquiry will do the right thing, but I am afraid they have picked nonentities and good party Democrats who will shield the saviour of the world.

I expect to be up there until November, but what my winter plans will be I can't tell until the expert decides what will be best for me. I am having the usual experience with the doctors; one group says it is the liver which is affecting the heart, another votes for the gall bladder, and a third said it was a ruptured diaphragm. The heart seems to be the victim, but not the originator of the disturbance, but they can't seem to find out the criminal and deal with him properly.

Well now the great question is what will the mustered out men do to us. What is your guess?

With warmest greetings,

Ever faithfully,

Mr. Henry L. Mencken
1524 Hollins Street
Baltimore, Maryland

Shall We Have A Monstrous Navy?

By OSWALD GARRISON VILLARD

TAKING a lesson, perhaps, from the collapse of the campaign for universal postwar military service, which it and the Army were hoping to have voted by Congress while the war was still going on, the Navy is now rushing its demand for the greatest permanent fleet ever seen on this globe. It is asking for no less than 1,079 ships to be manned by an enlisted force of 500,000 men, by 50,000 officers, with a reserve officer force of 50,000 more, and there are signs that the Congressional naval committees are looking with favor upon the proposal. The Navy brass hats have hit upon these figures by adopting the century-old slogan of the British Navy, which was, "A fleet large enough to defeat any combination of navies that may be brought against us." This policy is now openly advocated in Washington.

O. G. Villard

The Navy has also filed a long list of the bases, large and small, which it wishes to retain throughout the world. It is asking for 18 battleships, 82 cruisers, large and small, 24 big carriers, 10 light, and 79 escort carriers, 367 destroyers, 296 destroyer escorts, and no less than 200 submarines. About one-third of this vast force is to be kept in full operation and the rest held in reserve. It is navalism beyond anything the world has ever seen, and the American taxpayer is expected to foot the bill without any complaining and with genuine satisfaction.

* * *

THIS incredible program is being put forward in the face of the atomic bomb on the ground that it is dictated by "the lessons of the present war." If you ask naval men whom we are arming against so prodigiously the private answer is Russia, and of course the "danger" to us of the British fleet is also counted in. What could be more preposterous than that? The British people know that twice in 25 years we have come to their rescue to save them from defeat, and they know that we released in the second war the greatest industrial power in the world against which, if they were pitted against us, they could make no headway whatsoever.

The only fleet remaining in the world which might at some time constitute a threat is plainly the Russian —Stalin has just announced that he is going to create 12 naval academies to provide officers for his new flotilla which we and England have aided him in building up during the war by giving him various second-hand vessels, cruisers, destroyers, and at least one British battleship. There will be no German fleet, no Japanese, and, it is to be hoped, no Italian. What is left of the French ships will certainly never constitute a menace. It will certainly be generations before that country will sufficiently recover from the effects of this war to threaten our safety.

Even if it were certain that at some future time there could be a British, Russian, and French combination against us, it is nothing less than idiotic to build our future naval force on this, for the great outstanding fact is that the atomic bomb has knocked every military and naval armament into a cocked-hat. All the Navy can say on this subject is that it will not give its judgment of the role that the atomic bomb will play in future warfare until it has "made some tests and experiments." As one commentator has pointed out, a large Navy would be "an interesting target" for future bombing fleets provided that "the aggressor did not simply choose to ignore it."

When bombs capable of the most terrific destruction can be carried in an individual's pockets; when the head of a country controlling these bombs will be able to destroy a nation at one blow by pressing a button on his desk and releasing automatic bombers, what good will be 1,079 warships? And how valuable will the outlying bases we propose to seize as part of our postwar booty be in the light of the fact that the Germans were on the verge of bringing out a plane that American officers think would have been able to cross the Atlantic in 17 minutes? When Maj. de Seversky declares that we are facing such remarkable new developments in aviation that in 10 years' time not one of our great superliners will be of any value whatever?

* * *

TODAY our Army has a bomber which can be guided by television from a plane 15 miles from the objective, and a bomber with a range of 5,000 miles is an accomplished fact. Just how far our Army has gone with rockets it is not possible to say, but it is a fact that it has picked up a number of valuable ideas and nearly finished weapons from the Germans. Is it not, therefore, the height of stupidity for the Navy to say now, at this stage of the military and naval evolution brought about by the past war, that we are in a position to plan for the future what we shall do if we continue to put our national faith in huge armaments?

I leave out entirely the question as to what moral attitude we should take toward the criminality of the use of the atomic bomb—I think history will say that our unleashing it when it was not necessary for the immediate defeat of Japan was without doubt one of the greatest blunders of all time. It was so short-sighted as to give any thoughtful man the creeps when he thinks that Mr. Truman and Mr. Stimson and their associates were so amazingly without vision as to spring this missile on the world and to divide it at once into two camps, those who possess the bomb and those that do not.

One group of the young scientists who helped to make the atomic bomb admits frankly that they are frightened "to death of the very thing that their genius had produced," and are saying that we cannot possibly keep the secret of it for more than five years, perhaps only two.

Plain common sense should tell Congress that this is no time to listen to the demands of the Navy or to lay out any definite program whatsoever for the future of our naval might. The Navy should certainly not be encouraged in its present effort to induce 30,000 of its war-trained officers of the reserve to become regulars. What is called for is surely an interim program until the Government of the United States makes up its mind on the fundamental question as to whether it will lead the world toward disarmament and do everything in its power to bring Russia into line, or whether in the face of the atomic bomb it will continue its big Navy policy.

Until that decision is taken in Washington every other move is beside the mark. We are either going to seek to play a big imperialistic role along old-fashioned lines, revelling in our naval superiority, dominating Germany, Japan and Italy, settling the fate of Tangier, Libya, Eritrea, Korea, the Near East, and endless other countries, or our leaders will realize that this is an atomic world and that it has been entirely altered since we dropped the first atomic bomb on Hiroshima.

After that issue is decided we can turn if we wish to such questions as battleships, carriers, submarines, bombers, and automatic weapons, and settle once and for all the question of establishing one defense department under one head, instead of an Army and Navy with their separate air forces, not to speak of innumerable other problems.

Unfortunately Congress is certain to be influenced by the opportunity for patronage and jobs. Literally hundreds of thousands of young officers in the Army and Navy want to continue in the services because they have never known any other employment, having been taken right out of college. Probably a majority of them have married and have at least one child to support. They have no desire to be turned adrift, many of them, because they would not know which way to turn, and whether they could or could not achieve at the outset of a business career enough of a salary to support their families.

Even more important is the fact there is tremendous pressure being brought to bear upon the public to continue our armaments. Gen. Wainwright, who has lately seen the world only from the inside of a Japanese prison camp, declares we must under no circumstances weaken our present forces. His right hand aide and general declares in a series of signed articles, widely promulgated, that we must not stop short of destroying every single Japanese, that there will be no peace on the earth until we have wiped out the last of our Asiatic enemies!

These men are sincere, but deluded. They have not been made to face and to study the new problems created by this horrible new weapon which we have devised, which, as has been said, may have opened up the whole question of life itself and put in the hands of a few people the power to destroy the whole universe. They are living in the world as it was when they surrendered. The sense of the terrible indignities put upon them by the Japanese, in violation of all civilized warfare, is hard upon them. But talk they will, and do, and the danger is that the public and the Congress will follow them without in the remotest degree facing the actual facts of the new life in which we live.

Let it instead listen to these wise words of Admiral Spruance:

"We can't maintain the present-size Navy; it is too big, too much of a strain on the country. Some ships, if modern, probably will be kept in reserve; some will be sold if there is any use for them, and some will be scrapped. . . . We have gotten along without bases on the coast of Asia this time. I take it that it would be ill-advised in the present state of world opinion to take bases in China. I don't think it necessary. . . . I don't think we would want our coast controlled. I think that applies to China and Russia. We want to see that Japan is not in a position to start on a rampage again. But we must not do anything to prevent the resumption of friendly relations. . . ."

* * *

THERE is still another factor which is molding public opinion in the wrong direction. I dislike to refer to it, but it is necessary. There are many men in the services of high rank who are calling for a huge Army and Navy because their own future is at stake. For example, there is a story going the rounds of a young Air Force general who called his staff of 28 officers around him and said that he had been ordered to send home 25 and that he would not obey the order for the reason that if he did he would probably be mustered out himself and returned to his low rank as a captain in the regular Army.

I hope that this story is not true, but I know that the question of holding on to the high ranks bestowed upon junior officers in the course of building our huge Army is affecting some men and automatically and subconsciously must affect the officers who suddenly find themselves facing the loss of high pay, rank, and distinction and going back to routine garrison duty in subordinate positions. That is human nature. Naturally they are preaching the necessity of the United States being armed as never before, and if there were no Russia to talk about as our future enemy, they would create a Russia, or would even tell us that if we did not keep up our great Army and Navy we should someday be overwhelmed by threatening forces marching up from South America, or by yellow hordes from Asia.

As to the bases, there is not the slightest need of haste in deciding what our permanent policy will be, we can occupy them as long as we please and give them up tomorrow if we see fit. Even from the militaristic point of view, until we know whether the San Francisco Charter will survive, whether or not Europe will go down into chaos and anarchy, whether or not Russia will continue her triumphant advance toward the Atlantic, we should certainly not decide as to how much we are going to weaken ourselves by spreading armed forces throughout the Pacific and along the Atlantic coasts.

I say weaken deliberately, for we should never have been in this war with Japan if we had not made the enormous blunder of conquering the Philippines and so becoming involved in Asiatic problems indefinitely, and some of them of a very nasty kind, such as the present British use of Japanese troops to hold down the Indo-Chinese for France, the natives of the Dutch East Indies for the Dutch. That is dangerous blood which is being shed there!

* * *

FOR a long time I have felt that the world was dying more because of stupidity than from any other cause. The Allies were so stupid they let Hitler arm Germany; the British gave them authority, in violation of the Treaty of Versailles, to build a Navy one-third the size of theirs. We sold weapons and necessary supplies for war to Japan and Germany, and so did England and France up to the very moment of the declaration of hostilities, and France even after that by using Belgium as a middle man in dealing with the Germans. Can we not take to heart some of these lessons?

Can we not at last say to our militarists, see where your policy of armament has landed the world! Don't give us the old lie that this happened because the United States, England, and France were not sufficiently armed to deter the dictators. Just recall Calvin Coolidge's words to the American Legion when he said that: "No amount of armaments ever kept a country out of war or assured it victory after war came." History has proved him to be correct over and over again. It is our opportunity to turn over a great new leaf in the book of history and to start the world along another line than self-destruction. Shall we do it, or shall we plan to put all our reliance upon the biggest Navy in the world, and the "greatest and most efficient Army"?

'Our Lunatic Policy In Germany

By OSWALD GARRISON VILLARD

THE words in the title of this article were used in a debate in the British House of Commons, on Oct. 26, to describe what we and Russia are doing in Germany. It was a memorable debate for many reasons and it would stand out if only because it showed the British at their best—that the bulk of them are of such spirit that they refuse to gloat over or to humiliate a conquered opponent, whether in athletic contests or in dreadful war.

O. G. Villard

Putting aside the terrible punishment which England received at the hands of the Germans, the Commons, under the leadership of the new Foreign Secretary, Ernest Bevin, made it plain that the English are horrified by the misery and starvation in Germany today and the worse conditions which are sure to come unless immediate drastic measures are taken by the Allies.

No less than 14,000,000 homeless, starving wanderers are now stranded in Germany, utterly destitute and without shelter. They "are being," to use Mr. Bevin's words, "driven, some one way, some another," while about 10,000,000 displaced persons are waiting to be moved from Germany back to Italy, France, and elsewhere. Other speakers not only denounced Russia and the United States, but declared that the "greatest catastrophe the human race ever experienced is at hand unless aid is promptly furnished."

Mr. Bevin himself warned the world that if the United Nations Relief and Rehabilitation Administration does not at once receive the $1,800,000,000 it is asking of Congress, it will face disaster in its undertaking. Hard hit as England is financially, Mr. Bevin announced that it was ready to do its share—pay one per cent of its national income to UNRRA and to go it alone if no one else is humanitarian enough to contribute.

* * *

WHEN one Conservative member said that he "did not care two pins what happens to the German women and children," the Commons, described by Herbert Matthews of the New York *Times* as "emotional, highly strung," cried out "shame." Even this inhuman Conservative, however, urged relief for Germany and warned that "disease can spread like wildfire."

Michael Foot, a leading Laborite, declared that "it is still our duty to show that this country is the foremost champion of tolerance and decency."

Mr. Bevin began his speech by wishing that there were more parliaments like the Commons in other countries to debate this terrible subject in the freest terms and, referring to his visit to Berlin, said: "As I watched, I felt, my God, that is the price of man's stupidity and war. *It was the most awful sight you could possibly see*," (my italics)—this in reference to the throngs that were pouring into Berlin from Poland and Russia.

Sir Arthur Salter, an independent member of Parliament, who also testified as to the conditions in Berlin from personal observation, told the horrible truth when he asserted that "if, as is now thought, millions during this Winter freeze and starve, this will not have been the inevitable consequence of material destruction and world shortage of material." Of course not. It is the inevitable consequence of cruel hard-heartedness, of the "insane policy" of vengeance and revenge of the French, Americans and the Russians, and of the British until now.

It is the inevitable consequence of merciless Allied leaders condemning millions to death by arrogating to themselves the right to order the lot of these people without the slightest regard for any decent economic, humanitarian, or ethical considerations. Never was it made clearer that the fate of nations cannot be arbitrarily placed in the uncontrolled hands of three, or 10, or 20 individuals—especially when their spirits are tainted by war hates and the surpassing bitterness of needless war losses of precious lives.

Only the rarest person in the world can be trusted with such power. But Mr. Bevin proved himself an exception—at least he has not yet been in his present office long enough to lose his compassion, his humanity, his sensitiveness to suffering, his understanding that no matter what the sins of the Nazis have been, no decent Christian man sits by and sees people dying and condemned to die without trying to do something about it, unless he determines to egg it on in the manner of a Henry Morgenthau.

I wonder if we in America have in office a single man who might be as big and magnanimous as Ernest Bevin, who even added to his passionate plea his admission that the whole dividing up of Germany into zones had now proved to be another mistake. How often does so high an official in any land admit that his government has erred, and erred crassly and horribly?

* * *

PERHAPS Mr. Bevin saw in Berlin in those desperate throngs coming in from Poland, as did Charles Bray, a London reporter, a despairing woman "trying desperately to force milk from her milkless breast—a pitiful effort that only left her crying at her failure. . ." to feed "her two whimpering babies."

Undoubtedly Mr. Bevin referred to the horrors of the trains with the dead and dying arriving at the Stettiner station seven days enroute from Poland without food or water—in one cattle car "four or five were dead already, another five or six were lying alongside of them given up as hopeless by the doctor, and just being allowed to die."

No less than 25,000 of these utterly pitiful people had reached Berlin in a single day. Yet up to Sept. 1, the Allies have given no help to the Social Welfare Organization which, with a staff of 33 and 220 helpers, has been trying to offer relief to the best of its ability, or in any other way sought to deal with these dying victims of organized Allied cruelty. Yet Gen. Eisenhower and the three associated heads of the other occupying forces must know exactly what is happening if Ernest Bevin saw it, but their hearts are unwrung. All that Gen. Eisenhower has said that I have seen is that it will be a bad Winter and that he looks for "some trouble" for his troops—American bullets, perhaps, as an antidote for starvation and the insanity of the starving.

Nor, so far as I am aware, has any American correspondent in Berlin cabled the horrifying stories of what is going on that have been appearing in the London *News Chronicle* and the Laborite *Daily Herald*. Indeed, one of our illustrated weeklies in giving the pictures of one of these terrible trains has commented cold-bloodedly that bad as the situation is, it is not likely to arouse sympathy among the Allies. It had not counted on the underlying fineness and generosity of so many of the plain people of England.

No American newspaper that I have seen has brought out the fact that most of these victims are not Nazis from the cities, but harmless peasants torn from their land on which they and their forebears have lived industriously and peacefully until their government forced them into war.

But it was Churchill who told the House of Commons that it would be all right to uproot these 5,000,000 in East Prussia and stuff them into what was left of Germany, for the Allies had certainly killed that many Germans and these expatriates could take the places of the dead—let us thank heaven that we have Attlee and Bevin in charge of England and not Churchill.

* * *

BUT America? America sits back and does nothing. Congress delays in voting anything to the UNRRA, and the Republican minority thinks that only $550,-000,000 should be voted instead of the $1,800,000,000. Because of our "insane policy," the mails are still closed from the United States to Germany—it was only last week that the Germans were permitted to send letters from one zone to another if they wished to inquire, for example, whether their relatives in other cities were alive or dead. But no American today who has an anti-Nazi friend or relative in Germany can send one dollar or a parcel through the mails to help them to live.

Well, frankly, I prefer the methods and morals of the Middle Ages. In the Thirty Years War you knew what would take place; when the invading army captured a city it frankly and openly looted the town, stole everything it could get its hands on, raped all the women and usually set fire to a large part of the city. That was in full accord with the "laws" of war as they existed at that time.

But we do everything in such an unctuous, self-righteous, holier-than-thou way, that it is nauseating. In the name of democracy and peace on earth, numbers of our soldiers have helped themselves to whatever they could ship or carry home.

Our Government, like that of the other Allies, has seized all the public moneys upon which it can lay its hands and in addition it compels the Germans to contribute to the support of our troops, though fortunately, unlike the Russian Army, ours is not living oft the land.

We help ourselves to private property, just as did the conquering troops of Tilly. We throw private individuals out of their homes to make way for our officers and men—our and the French and the British commanders have just made a present of the great Krupp factory to the Russians, thereby cutting out the heart of the Ruhr and condemning many thousands of Germans to unemployment and starvation.

And the average American says: "Good, serves them right; they asked for it and now they are getting it." Just as if the thousands of workers in Krupps, who voted the Socialist or Communist ticket against Hitler as long as they could, or the peasants from German Poland, are responsible for Hitler's misdeeds!

* * *

WELL, I for one don't want to be held responsible because of Roosevelt's misdeeds at Cairo, Yalta, and Teheran. I refuse to share his guilt, just as I denounced Potsdam as a terrible crime which is already beginning to revenge itself much sooner than the most optimistic among us had dared to hope. I want Congress to vote that $1,800,000,000 to the UNRRA, with all its faults, right straight off; I want it to utilize every possible ship, every carrier and every battleship that has any carrying space on or under its decks to send food and supplies to Europe.

I want this because it profoundly affects not only the good name and reputation of the United States, but because it will render a service to our country if we can ward off the catastrophe in Europe. We shall pay a terrible price for it—if we do not—an economic price, but also a human price. The world is too small for such a disaster to come to one part of it without the other being affected, and, as the Conservative Member of Parliament said, diseases spread like wildfire.

I want to see us help the Germans because if we do not, we must renounce every claim to being a Christian nation. Lloyd George told the Welsh Church some years before this war began that if the churches of England and the United States permitted another World War to come they might just as well lock their doors in advance because there would be no use for them afterwards. There will be waning use for them in this country if they do not take the Christian attitude toward all Europe—Belgians, Dutch, Greeks, Danes, French, Italians, Germans, and the miserable people everywhere.

* * *

MY plea is, of course, not merely for the Germans—heaven forbid! What Americans refuse to realize is what I have so often written before, that whether you detest Germany or like her, that country is the industrial heart of Europe and you cannot destroy it and have millions of her people die of hunger and cold without injuring all the adjoining nations directly, and ourselves indirectly.

It is enlightened self-interest for which I am appealing, as well as right doing, and if the readers of these lines feel as I do I trust they will write immediately to their Congressmen and Senators for action now. Together we can make it impossible for Englishmen to rise in the House of Commons and speak of the "lunatic policy" of the United States.

The Coming Collapse Of The Potsdam Pact

By OSWALD GARRISON VILLARD

IF Adolf Hitler had conquered a country and robbed it of all its ships, we know what we of the Allies would have said of it. "Wicked criminality" would have been the mildest of our epithets. But our dividing the German merchant fleet among ourselves is righteous and just. "They asked for it when they went to war and they got it." "Besides, what we have done to the Krauts is as nothing to what they did to the countries they conquered. Think of those concentration camps! They can feel themselves lucky we have left them anything. So we are not going to allow them to use anything they can ever utilize for war again. And, after all, we divided up the surviving German ships in 1919, didn't we? So what are you grousing about?"

O. G. Villard

Well, we did take Germany's naval and merchant fleets from her after the first World War, but it never occurred to us to say to this great maritime nation: "Because the Kaiser and the militarists went to war and violated Belgium, you'll never sail another ship." This particular bit of vengeance we reserved for 1945, the Potsdam declaration and the enforcement of the Morgenthau-Vansittart Plan. We base it squarely on the theory that merchant ships are capable of being turned into cruisers, just as it is possible to drop light bombs from passenger planes.

Again, just like commercial pilots, merchant ship officers can be used by the Navy after war comes and so—off with their heads. No more aviators and no more mariners for the Huns. They must stay on land, and be thankful we permitted that.

* * *

THUS another important source of revenue and employment is stripped from the 75 million or more Germans who are not only supposed to support themselves on a minimum scale of living, but are to support four occupying armies, after losing most of their heavy industry and 25 per cent of their agricultural lands, to say nothing of the seizure of mineral wealth. Yes, indeed. We are going to make the Krauts understand this time that they lost the war.

Now the fact is that the German merchant fleet played a very small role in both the World Wars. A few ships became ocean raiders in the fashion of the Confederate cruiser *Alabama* during our Civil War. Undoubtedly the German occupying troops in Norway were largely moved there by transports and subsequently considerably supplied by them.

In the Mediterranean some German ships and the Italian merchant fleet supplied the Axis armies in North Africa. But the sum total of the war service of German cargo vessels is certainly a relatively small part of the total German military picture. For the most part the fleet was interned in foreign harbors, or kept close in shore in the hope of preserving the ships.

In 1938 that fleet comprised only 2,328 ships of 4,243,888 gross tons which was, by the way, 1,216,000 fewer tons than were at the Kaiser's disposal in 1914. Still we are going to take no chances and those great German shipyards which were not destroyed by bombing are closed down for good and all. It is back to the land—if they can find vacant spots—for all the thousands of skilled shipbuilding artisans.

Hereafter all German imports and exports are to be carried in Allied ships—a nice little victory plum for our British, American and French shipping magnates. But are there going to be German exports and imports, I hear some one ask? Yes, there are. Well, how does that happen? Why, the Potsdam Pact specially provides for them.

Thus, it is stated that: "In working out the economic balance of Germany the necessary means must be provided to pay for imports approved by the Control Commission in Germany." Again, it is specified that the sums required for this trade shall be first levied against the export profits. There is to be a so delicately adjusted scale of foreign trade that, the instant it shows signs of bringing in more money than the Germans need for their minimum cost of living, either the trade will be curtailed or the Allies will have a greater surplus from the enslaved German labor for Allied reparations.

But these exports and imports are never to be carried in German ships—for fear lest 25 years from now the Allies will again be so stupid as to allow the Germans to imitate Hitler, reintroduce conscription, and proceed to rearm and turn over the bulk of their industry to war purposes without any protests and even with the connivance and cooperation of Allied statesmen and Allied Big Business, as happened before World War II.

* * *

THE Germans are natural-born seamen and they built up their merchant fleet long before they had a navy by sheer individual enterprise, ability, and initiative. They were very proud of the fact that up to World War I they were given no subsidies to speak of by the Government except mail payments. German order and discipline were in evidence on all the vessels. Their trans-Atlantic ships were as popular with Americans and others as the British, and if anything their safety record was superior.

When we began to reconstitute our merchant fleet from 1919 on, we gladly manned our vessels with German cooks and stewards and some seamen—with due respect to the law requiring a large percentage of American citizens. In the Far East the Germans pioneered and built up a number of excellently run lines that took the cream of the trade from the less enterprising British—right in those Asiatic waters which England regarded as especially her own preserves.

It cannot be said, therefore, that the decision to deprive Germany of her water-borne trade has met with any opposition in British or American shipping circles. Far from it. "To the victors belong the spoils."

The American merchant fleet has had to be bolstered by one subsidy after another, so that it has been largely mortgaged and supported by the Government. The competition between us and England is going to be fiercer than ever as soon as things settle down, for the latter is practically bankrupt and more than ever needs to obtain revenues in foreign currency and credits by shipping services all over the world. It gives one a comfortable feeling under the belt in such circumstances to know that one's chief competitor has been eliminated for all time so that he will never even carry his own products again.

"Never again," are, of course, ridiculous words to us in a world such as ours of 1945. There were many permanent or semi-permanent provisions in the Treaty of Versailles—they collapsed to the last one. I have just been talking with two American experts on the Potsdam agreement who have recently returned from Germany. They both told me—separately—that in their opinion **the whole effort to carry out that document will collapse within a year certainly, and quite possibly in six to eight months.**

Just to state the economic problem posed by the pact is to show its utter impracticability. Lewis Carroll's Mad Hatter could not have conceived anything more impossible.

* * *

January 2, 1946

Dear Mr. Hutchinson:

I am enclosing herewith a review of Alexander Leighton's bad book "The Governing of Men," which is appearing in the Yale Law Review, as Professor Eugene Rostow of the School has asked me to bring it to your attention. This I gladly do and hope that other editors will deal equally roughly with this half-way Nazi.

Next may I tell you that a group of us are trying to get together a committee of twenty-five, which Dorothy Thompson, Clarence Pickett, Norman Thomas and others have joined, to be composed of editors and clergymen, to bring additional pressure to bear upon the President to open up communications with Germany. The Lutherans are seeing him this week but when you read the enclosed letter from him to Senator Wheeler you will recognize the necessity of keeping after him. I think it is a shocking epistle, just a complete revelation of what an utterly conventional, middle-class American Legion mind he has. I think he has no understanding whatsoever of the actual situation. I don't believe that he ever read or heard of Bevin's magnificent speech or that 50,000 English people have asked the Government to cut down on their food rations so that the Germans can have enough to live on. You will notice that he says we must not be "unduly cruel." Will someone please tell me what constitutes "duly cruel?" This letter to Wheeler must be kept absolutely confidential and it is only for your eyes and Dr. Morrison's eyes. I know you hate to bothered about delegations but if we can pull this off and the platform which we shall submit to him is satisfactory, would not one of you join this delegation? Clarence

Pickett is most eager for it and I would rather have his approval than anyone else's as he knows exactly what is going on, and each hour's need. May I have an immediate airmail reply? We are, of course, getting a strong Catholic delegation and I am hoping to see Fosdick this week but may not be able to do so as he is leaving town for a short vacation. We should like him to head the group. It is the Post-War World Council which is pulling the men together. I am afraid it will be beyond my strength to take part as I am still not allowed to travel.

Next I write to inquire whether you would be interested in a short article on the Javanese situation? I think it is very essential to bring out the fact that the American people are being fooled into believing that the Japanese stirred the natives up and that the Dutch have been wonderful rulers, far superior to any others. This is unfortunately not true. The natives have fought repeatedly for their liberty and when the Japanese took over the country, they released some one thousand four hundred Indonesians who had been in a horrible jungle concentration camp since 1926 - such as were left of them. I don't know how you feel but nothing has roused such angry passions within me to the extent fostered by our helping England and the Dutch in Java and our treatment of Korea. Have you noticed how publications like the New Statesman in England speak now as a matter of course of America being embarked upon a most dangerous imperialistic course?

If you have had all of that subject that you want, how about my doing something more for you on the extraordinary situation of the bargain between us and England? I have never read such editorials as are appearing in England about the injury we have done to them by making them this huge loan! They think it means absolute slavery to us, yet they would not have felt so if we had made them a present of it. Oh that Lewis Carroll could have lived to this day!

P. 3

I hope that all is going well with the C.C. and believe that as soon as you can go out for more circulation you will get it. I hope the paper embargo is near the end.

With best New Year's wishes to all of you,

Sincerely yours,

Mr. Truman's Military Blueprint For America

By OSWALD GARRISON VILLARD

PRESIDENT TRUMAN signalized his complete adoption of the Army's plan for a merger of the Army and Navy, with the Air Force elevated to the same rank as the older services, by another appeal for universal conscription in peacetime, in which he made the monstrous mis-statement that in his belief the conscription proposal "has met with the overwhelming approval of the people of the United States."

O. G. Villard

The very next day the American Farm Bureau Federation voted unanimously against conscription, on the ground that it "is foreign to the American way of life" and "leads to regimentation, a militaristic point of view and future wars." It thus joined the National Farmers Union, the AFL, the CIO, and virtually all the rest of the whole labor movement, the great mass of the churches, and no less than 100 civic and educational organizations in militant opposition. If this proves that the American people are "overwhelmingly" on President Truman's side, I don't understand the meaning of words.

But when it comes to the merger of the services, the President is on firm ground. Some of us have been urging this for many years. If the President had wished to point up his arguments even more than he did, he could have reminded Congress of the facts being brought out in the Pearl Harbor inquiry. There the defense of Hawaii was divided between the Army and the Navy. While it is not true that there was a deliberate failure on the part of Gen. Short and Adm. Kimmel to cooperate, and there is no proof of any hostility between them, it has been brought out that sometimes the Army did not notify Gen. Short because it expected that the Navy would, and vice versa.

* * *

HOWEVER, the most striking example of what the lack of cooperation did to us is to be found in what happened on the Atlantic coast. The war began on Dec. 7, 1941 and it was not until the middle of the following April that the Army and Navy got together and decided to cooperate in the defense of the coastline from German submarine attacks.

During that time of non-cooperation and playing their own games, we lost the bulk of our tanker fleet, partly because the Navy was so stupid as to let the ships come up the coast within sight of shore, their regular route, instead of sending them out to sea and thus avoid the submarines. Whether because of the merger in April, or for some other reasons, our ship losses began to decrease from that time on.

As the war in the Pacific progressed, the unprecedented happened. Admirals were put in charge of joint Army and Navy operations, and generals given complete control of joint Army and Navy task forces. Anybody who would have said five years ago that that would take place would have been deemed a candidate for a madhouse, yet the exigencies of the war compelled it and everybody was for it.

As for the other reasons given by President Truman, of course we should have integrated, strategic plans and a unified military program and budget. Enormous savings can unquestionably be made through unified purchasing and control of supply and service functions. The President admits—with much moderation—that there has been a great deal of waste in both the Army and Navy because of duplication, but he correctly says that "the extent of waste through lack of coordination between the two departments is very much greater than the waste resulting from faulty coordination within each."

Mr. Truman added: "If we can attain as much coordination among all the services as now exists within each department we shall realize extensive savings." He next touched on the waste of personnel. Protests are now being heard every day against the calling out of too many doctors in the war so that hundreds of them have been given no medical work at all, but have been utilized as supply officers and in other non-medical capacities, to their own professional detriment and with great injustice to the civilian communities at home, many of which were deprived of both doctors and nurses. Had there been one department of defense this obviously could not have occurred, at least not to the extent to which it went. Again, there was no rhyme or reason in the maintenance of twin research organizations, nor for the struggle between the Army and Navy to head off each other in obtaining the best possible officers from civil life.

* * *

AS for the air services, the President has erred in declaring that the Navy shall continue to have complete control of its Air Force instead of insisting upon one unified air command. There is no reason for this. The Air Force will always be wholly made up of specialists—bombers, navigators, fighter pilots, transport captains, balloonists, etc., etc., and men can early be designated as specialists in naval warfare and trained as such. Here Pearl Harbor affords another illustration. Neither the Army nor the Navy at that station knew what the other service was doing in carrying out its patrolling duties, which is one of the reasons why the approach of the Japanese fleet was not detected. It is, of course, true that you can have military inefficiency—and you probably will—if you have unity of the services as well as when they are divided. Every war we have ever fought has resulted in tremendous unnecessary expenditure of lives and of treasure, and that will be the case in the next war unless there is efficient supervision of the Army and Navy and a determination by whoever is in the White House that as long as we have the armed services they shall be ably and efficiently administered, economically carried on, and kept up-to-date.

We talk about the dry rot and the backwardness and lack of enterprise in the civilian bureau. They have always been exceeded within the War and Navy Departments, the Navy especially having always been ruled by cliques and, up to the coming of this war, so dominated by the brass-hats that every informed person knows that advancement has been won only by standing in with the admirals—and their wives.

Unification is so plainly called for by every consideration that it is worth while to examine the arguments raised by the Navy in opposition. Their chief charge is that the merged forces will be dominated by the Army, and that so much military power will be vested in the head of the joint services as to constitute a grave danger to our democracy and our liberties.

The answer is that our democracy and liberties are very much menaced now with a divided command and the Army's and Navy's reaching out for power which has just led the House to vote an additional 9,000 regular officers for the Army. As long as they exist, armies and navies constitute a danger to their people—witness the domination of German life by the officer class, the Franco army rebellion in Spain, the innumerable revolutions in South and Central America due to the armies.

If we gave the American Army and Navy their way completely, they would dominate our whole civilian life

—the conscription proposal is but one more step in that direction. How far they will be allowed to go depends again largely upon the Presidents in the White House and whether the Congress will effectively control the Army, the Navy, and the Air Force.

That there is a domestic military danger for us today is obvious. It comes from the fact that this is the first war which we have fought in which the Army and Navy were given complete control. Undoubtedly many will say that that is the reason why it was the best fought war by the best equipped and best-drilled Army and Navy that we have ever had. The point is that President Roosevelt failed to control policies and to share responsibility with his Cabinet, which was never called together for its constitutional purpose of giving him *advice*, but only to receive his fiats.

Of course in a war the carrying out of military strategy and tactics should be dominated by the military—subject always to revision by the controlling civilians—but they should never be allowed to suggest or control political policies. It is a tremendous break with all our American and democratic traditions to read that the day before Pearl Harbor the American and the British navies agreed by themselves upon a joint plan for the attack upon Truk when we were still at peace.

* * *

AS for the subordination of the Navy to the Army, the President points out that the military commander-in-chief shall alternately be an air man, or a representative of the Navy or the Army, and that such a chief cannot serve for more than two years. The Army would be just as entitled as is the Navy to point out that it, too, is being deprived under the Truman plan of having its own representative in the Cabinet, and that it is losing some of its prestige when it becomes but one member of a triangular departmental set-up.

Certainly the Navy with its undersecretary will be completely on a par with the Army with its undersecretary and with the Air Force and its controlling civilian. It is my belief, after writing on military and naval affairs for nearly half a century, that if this plan goes through, in five years no one in either service will think of going back to the old waste and disorganization, rivalry, and jealousy provided always that efficient men are put at the head of the new department—men who are not bent on constant military and naval aggrandizement as is the case now, but on producing efficiency and with huge savings to the American people.

Despite the credit that must be given to the President for coming out for this plan, in the face of the tremendous naval opposition and the determination of men like Sen. Walsh of Massachusetts and Rep. Vinson to block the proposal, it is regrettable that the President should be so deeply concerned with military and naval matters and should not see that his effort to extend conscription to peacetime and to maintain the largest Army and Navy in all the world (Russia probably excepted) makes against the success of the UNO, against the coming of peace, and for a war with Russia.

After every great war which we have fought the effort has always been to reduce our military establishment to the lowest possible limit. The plan now is to continue to dominate the world by the armed forces of the United States, Great Britain, and Russia. If that is maintained, the UNO will die like the League of Nations. The rest of the world will certainly not tolerate anything of the kind. In other words, the emphasis is all wrong, especially with the President. He sweeps away the atomic bomb which probably makes armies and navies quite useless. He throws away the enormous veteran reserve of nearly 12,000,000 which we will have for from 12 to 15 years, by saying that we must not call upon them again. He refuses to recognize that we have only one possible enemy, Russia, and not a single fleet on the ocean to cause us to be on our guard.

* * *

AS is the case with most statesmen, even in the face of the V-bombs, the atomic bomb, and the new giant super-bomber, the XB-36, which will have an operating radius of 5,000 miles and is to make non-stop flights from Tokyo to New York and back "as a matter of course," the President does not vow to make war with Russia impossible by world reorganization, but continues to place his faith upon force.

He long ago accepted the stupid and false assertion that we won't have any influence in international councils unless we have a huge Army and Navy. It is not reason, or justice, or fair play, or economic freedom to which he would turn in this dire emergency, but just to force, force, and more force. So let us be grateful that at least the President wants one efficient, coherent, well organized, economical military machine.

The Shame Of The American Press

By OSWALD GARRISON VILLARD

MADISON, WISCONSIN, MONDAY, FEBRUARY 4, 1946

THE record of the American press during World War II and in the half year which has followed the end of hostilities is replete with sordid distortions of the truth. It is a record of shameful suppression, of too easy acquiescence in censorship, of apologizing and covering up for the mistakes of the military, of fanning hatreds against whole peoples even when the war was over, and of miserable incompetence and inadequacy in reporting the occupation of conquered countries and the struggle for freedom in colonial areas.

O. G. Villard

Neither the military censorship nor the Government is wholly to blame for the lengths to which the American press has gone in the unprecedented campaign of hate and the spreading of atrocity stories under big headlines. The writer of this article would be the last to wish to suppress the horrors of Dachau and Buchenwald—indeed he was bringing them to public attention in *The Nation* very soon after those fiendish places were established, when it was almost impossible to get the daily newspapers interested in them.

It was obvious that Gen. Eisenhower did just the right thing in having proofs of this unparalleled barbarism photographed and shown to the high-ranking German prisoners and to as many other Germans as possible. But our press has dwelt so continuously on these stories as to achieve what seemed to many its deliberate purpose of making Americans think that most of the victims of the horror camps were Americans, and that our men in German prison camps were starved and maltreated in accordance with a general policy of the German Government. An interesting example of this was afforded when the American Red Cross reported officially that "99 per cent of the American prisoners of war in Germany have survived and are on their way home"—a remarkable record for the best of prison camps and one vastly superior to the ghastly showing of our prison stockades North and South during the

Civil War.

This extraordinary showing was made when we were bombing German supply and communication lines and millions of homeless civilians were roaming around the country. It was not allowed, however, to make any impression upon our public. Thus, the dispatch reporting it appeared under these headlines in the *Herald-Tribune* which "buried" the statement as to the safety of our prisoners under the Hitler item:

HITLER ORDERED U. S. AND BRITISH FLIERS KILLED

But The Army Refused, Says The Red Cross, Because Allies Followed Geneva Rules

No dispatch more clearly belonged on the first page of our newspapers, for none could possibly have meant so much reassurance and encouragement to the children, parents, and wives of the many thousand American prisoners within the German lines. I have yet to meet any one who read this dispatch and only one or two who had seen the official statement of Provost Marshal General Archer L. Lerch that, while some individual German camp commanders were violating orders and mistreating American prisoners, he was **"convinced that in general the Nazi Government was trying to treat Americans with strict if not generous legality."**

What was the New York *World-Telegram's* top headline on this story? Here it is: "Are We Coddling Prisoners?" It is only fair to add, however, that the second headline, bigger and blacker, read: "Army Blames German Crackup for Mistreatment of Yanks"—also quite misleading. But it, too, was not front page stuff. Nor, so far as I am aware, were there any editorial comments upon these two official testimonies that, with defeat overwhelming them, and their country literally collapsing about them, the Germans made an honest effort to treat our prisoners decently, while ill-treating and murdering by wholesale the Jews, the civilian "slaves" and military prisoners of other nationalities.

* * *

NOR have I seen any denial on this side of the Atlantic of the charge made by Allan Wood, a front correspondent of the London *Express*, that *"the most amazing thing about the atrocities in this war is that there have been so few of them. I have come up against few instances where the Germans have not treated our prisoners according to the rules, and respected the Red Cross.*

"I have seen much of the way in which human chivalry is kept alive amid all the sickening bestialities of war; though, of course, I have rarely been permitted to mention the chivalry when it was on the German side. . . . And even if the censor does not object, the newspapers exert their right, under our system of a free press, to suppress anything which contradicts their policy."

His last statement is, of course, true of newspapers everywhere. Certainly our press could not find time or place to record a remarkable piece of cooperation between an American and a German surgical team during the December break-through of the Germans when they operated side by side on German and American wounded alike, with the battle going on around them. Nor has our press reported that the records show that the German surgeons did their best, with limited and decreasing means, when our wounded fell into their hands. Its duty was plainly to create hate and ill-will—not to hold the scales even and report objectively.

Again, our newspapers have unitedly taught the American people that the Germans had our obliteration bombing "coming to them" because they "began it." Not a daily has, I believe, brought out the fact that an English official, J. M. Spaight, formerly the "Principal Assistant Secretary of the Air Ministry," published in 1944 a book called *Bombing Vindicated* which not only declares that England began the "strategic" bombing of Germany *before* Germany bombed England, but that the English should be proud of having done so. Mr. Spaight writes:

"Because we were doubtful about the psychological effect of propagandist distortion of the truth that it was we who started the strategic bombing offensive, we have shrunk from giving our great decision of May, 1940, the publicity which it deserved. That surely was a mistake. *It was a splendid decision.* [Italics mine] It was as heroic, as self-sacrificing, as Russia's decision to adopt her policy of "scorched earth." It gave Coventry and Birmingham, Sheffield and Southampton, the right to look Kiev and Kharkov, Stalingrad and Sevastopol, in the face. Our Soviet allies would have been less critical of our inactivity in 1942 if they had understood what we had done."

Since this book was published by a former official, who was legally bound not to reveal government secrets without permission, and had passed the strict British censorship, it cannot be asserted that it was the idle allegation of a minor officeholder. But not one of the great corps of American correspondents in London cabled this sensational charge.

THROUGHOUT the obliteration bombing our press helped the Government to maintain the lie that we were only doing "precision bombing." As late as Feb. 22, 1945, the Associated Press carried Secretary Stimson's official statement that it was absolutely false to say that we were doing any obliteration bombing whatsoever. Twelve days later, Mar. 6, the United Press reported from London that "more than 1,100 RAF planes bombed Germany last night, most hitting the key railway and defense hub of Shemnitz in an obliteration raid. . . . Though Shemnitz has been bombed repeatedly by Allied air armadas, *including an American formation yesterday* [my italics], the new attack was ordered because the city was still not devastated to the extent of smouldering Dresden (!) the Ministry said."

Obviously this gave the lie direct to Secretary Stimson. Who cared? Not the press, which had rallied as one man to denounce some 18 clergymen and publicists who protested against this obliteration bombing as contrary to all laws of war and the decencies of humanity.

* * *

PAGES could be filled with the deliberate misrepresentations of war events by order of the military. Thus, when our great bombing raid upon Schweinfurt turned out to be a disaster, the press helped the Allied governments to lie about it, even though the enemy knew exactly what had happened. In fact the German statement of fully 100 planes shot down has recently been borne out by the admission that the American Air Chief called in the reporters after the raid and admitted the losses were staggering. He said that it could not be printed because that would injure the morale of our fliers—just as if our surviving airmen did not know that many more than the 60 bombers, which the Air Chief insisted should be printed as missing, had not returned.

The result was, therefore, only to fool the American people. Similarly, the first raid over Ploesti in Rumania was wholly misrepresented. Surely united action by the press would have compelled the airforce and the Administration to stop this useless lying. The newspapers also spread abroad the Churchill falsehood that the outcome of the Dieppe raid was quite satisfactory, coupling this with misrepresentation of the losses, every detail of which the enemy well knew since he possessed the dead and the prisoners.

On the other hand, it is to the credit of the censorship and the New York *Herald-Tribune* that the latter printed on July 25, 1944, a most revealing dispatch from Richard L. Tobin, its correspondent at Supreme Headquarters, as to the constant suppression and falsities of the press agents of the airforces. Nonetheless, that daily continued to print biased and fallacious military reports with little or no warning to its readers, save in the case of its deadly editorial analysis of Gen. MacArthur's misleading official bulletins on the conquest of Leyte. Probably the editor would say that it was not their duty to if they clearly marked the official sources of these bulletins.

At this writing our newspapers are plainly failing to give to the public any real picture of the catastrophic and brutally inhuman conditions in occupied Germany, conditions resulting from our misgovernment of that country, its division into four parts, and the incredible savagery and ferocity of the expulsion of millions of people from Czechoslovakia, Poland, the Sudetenland, and elsewhere, and the violation thereby of the agreement in the Declaration of Potsdam that "the transfers . . . should be effected in an orderly and humane manner."

I have seen in no American daily so horrible a picture of the Russian atrocities in Danzig and East Prussia as has been published by F. A. Voigt, the outspoken editor of the London *Nineteenth Century and After* in his issue of November, 1945, based upon 17 statements by eyewitnesses of what happened in Danzig, and detailed reports by two British officers, and one from a British officer who toured the Sudetenland in September, plus numerous reports by clergy, doctors, and others who witnessed this fearful hegira. In fact I doubt if any reader of the American newspapers anywhere has the faintest idea that Danzig was destroyed down to the last building, and that the women were raped, sometimes 30 and 40 times, by the drunken Russian soldiery.

If, as most observers believe, we are now in the most dreadful Winter in modern history, with millions condemned to die from cold and starvation, and this comes as a surprise to the American people when it happens, the fault will be with our dailies, with some fine exceptions, like the New York *Times*, which recently gave the bulk of two pages to portraying conditions all over Europe.

Even then, however, it did not give a true picture of the existing sufferings and wholesale deaths. When Ernest Bevin, the British Foreign Minister, told the Commons what he had seen in a railroad station in Berlin as he watched the trains bringing the dead and dying people from Poland who have been guiltless of any hostility to either Russians or anyone else, he said: "As I watched, I felt, my God, that is the price of man's stupidity and war. *It was the most awful sight you could possibly see,*" [my italics]. Yet in New York the *Times* alone featured the story as it should have been featured. Beyond its readership few people, I venture to assert, have the slightest knowledge of this extraordinary debate in the House of Commons in which its members upheld the British Government in its determination to do everything possible to succor the Germans who but a few months ago were seeking to destroy the greatest of cities and the British people.

* * *

WHAT it all comes down to is whether the press, even in wartime, has or has not a transcending duty to its readers and to its country to interpret objectively the facts, to regard its own Government with suspicion from beginning to end, to consider itself as being charged with the final responsibility for the truth and for that freedom of utterance which the press usually demands, and for the preservation of American institutions.

The question now is whether, after five years of lying and half-truth telling, the dailies, with censorship ended everywhere, will put aside hate and the blind upholding of Washington policies and cease their slanting and editorializing of the news, in favor of giving the people the truth so they can be intelligent citizens in a free society.

xxxxxxxxxxxxx 79 East 79th Street

21

February 6, 1946

Dear Charles:

I am very hungry for a talk with you and if you are accessible would beg for an appointment. It would do my soul good to get your reaction to some of the things that are happening. I wonder, for example, if you feel as worried as I do about the situation in Washington. There are times when I wonder if there isn't going to be a general collapse there for lack of leadership. Certainly the way the tide has swung against Truman in this section of the country is as extraordinary as it seems to be deserved. Four times you and I have seen a President die in office, yet I suppose we shall go on being just as stupid about selecting Vice-Presidents as we have been since the days of Lincoln and before. I have had a copy of a letter from Truman to Senator Wheeler on the question of opening up Germany to free intercourse with the rest of the world. It is without question about the worst letter I have seen from the White House, certainly since the days of Harding. Such incredible ignorance of what is happening is really beyond belief. The truth is we have a highly militaristic, lower middle-class, back-slapping American legionnaire in the White House who has given free rein to the militarists, and we are being made over under our eyes into a tremendous military imperialistic Power--exactly what we went to war with Germany to prevent their becoming!

The only cheerful news I have heard, and that is a very great bit of cheer, is that you are doing a book on the Roosevelt Administration and are already far along in it. How you can produce at the speed that you do away from libraries and apparently without secretarial help is beyond my limited mentality to understand. I am sure you will do the greatest possible service to the country by writing this book, but I warn you that it will be soft-pedalled or attacked by the press. My friend Prince Loewenstein has done a big, discursive book on the German people, published by the Columbia University Press. It obviously has its faults, but it has been absolutely ignored by the daily newspapers with the exception of the Chicago Tribune and Sun--the Herald-Tribune has a review on the hooks, but can find no room for it. The S. E. L. printed an unworthy attack upon it. Altogether he is heart-broken that three years of labor is to practically go for naught.

I am sure also that you must be very disappointed at the botching of the Pearl Harbor inquiry. The Times has plainly had but one purpose in its comments, to whitewash FDR, and all its news has been handled from that point of view, it seems to me. The testimony is not yet being printed. I tried, for example, to get the Stark statements which seemed to me of the utmost importance, but they have not only not been printed, but no date has been fixed for their being issued. Yet the press report of the testimony entirely proves--if I read it aright--how completely Roosevelt used the voluntary press censorship to put us into the war without a declaration by Congress. What an opportunity you will have when you get to that. It was Hoover who told me about your book and that he was begging you to include the first year of the war in your first volume. I sincerely hope you will and can.

As for Europe, the news of the food situation is ghastly and I don't wonder that Truman is to give us a statement about it today. This morning the Times announces that the British food ration has now been lowered beneath the war standard. A friend who has just returned from two months in France and Germany says that living conditions are worse in the former than in the latter, and that there is acute suffering. Even Anne O'Hare McCormick admits in her correspondence that our treatment of the expatriates/going into Germany equals the crimes of Hitler, and the Austrian Wiener Zeitung has denounced the Allies for "brutality and extreme cruelty" in the treatment of German-language populations being forced through Vienna to Germany without food clothing or medical care, in direct violation, of course, of the hypocritical Big Three announcement that the movement of populations would take place without any cruelty or ill treatment. It makes one utterly sick and hopeless to read of these things and to realize that there is not a single powerful voice raised in the United States in protest. Hoover understands, Alf Landon has spoken out splendidly, and so have a number of individuals, but nothing happens. Hoover told me weeks ago that he would reconstitute his Feed Germany Committee in ten days; there is no sign of it. I am sure that we shall pay a terrible price for our part in this wickedness. But who cares among the public? "They asked for it, didn't they?" Dorothy Thompson, by the way, is paying a high price in being forced off the radio and in losing newspapers for her column because of her admirable stand.

As for our militarization, I presume you have noticed that the National Guard is to be increased from 300,000 to 750,000, which means billions of expense in itself since there are no National Guard armories in which men may be trained for modern warfare, or even given regimental drill of the old-fashioned kind. It is very sinister that the army now says openly that these State organizations will no longer be allowed to be such, but will be entirely federalized, and that the State troops will be created out of the temporary organizations set up for the war which militarily speaking are worth nothing at all. In addition, we are to have 2,000,000 men in the army from July 1, and a million in the navy and Marine Corps, and huge costly reserves. It is a dreadful spectacle that both the President and Congress have given the army and navy their heads completely. Vinson and Walsh are the merest erand boys for whoever is at the head of the navy, and again the country is either unaware or totally indifferent, or fails to understand. And learning nothing from our Philippine experience,withthe Japanese war as a result, we shall annex all the bases in the Atlantic and the Pacific that the army and navy want. Poor Iceland is desperately struggling to make us live up to our pledge to get out, but we still have a garrison there big enough to be commanded by a brigadier-general, we are working vigorously with the government of Iceland to let us stay there permanently, and not a word of it gets into the newspapers. It is very hard, dear friend, to keep one's spirit up in the face of all this utter destruction of the finest American traditions and ideals.

You will be glad to hear that I have gained steadily for the last two months--since coming to town, and that the doctor today gave me permission to travel as far s Washington to see our new granddaughter. But it is hard for me to accomplish what I ought to be doing--which makes me again look at you with the frankest and most unblushing envy. I hope you are having a good winter at Tryon. It has been a miserable one here and very bad in Connecticut according to our farmer and his wife. Our younger son, Oswald and his wife ave left for California by trailer, which trip is to include a three weeks' holiday in Mexico, and they were wise enough to have taken the precaution of pulling their own sleeping quarters after them because they have been notified that there was no possibility of getting accommodation in Palo Alto where they will spend a year and a half while he finishes his work for his Ph.D. or Doctor of Science. Henry, the elder is spending this week-end in Amherst with his wife to see if they can pick up a house for them to live in next Fall when he returns to his professorship.

Forgive this screed, and believe me dear sir and madam, to be your most obedient serv't,

Mr. Charles A. Beard
Pinecrest Inn
Tryon, North Carolina

Are We Arming For War With Russia?

THE Associated Press reports that the Army has "secretly" disclosed to the House Military Affairs Committee the plans it has made for a postwar National Guard. It is to have an initial strength of 425,000 enlisted men with an eventual total of 750,000, as contrasted with the prewar figure of approximately 300,000, which was, however, hardly realized. The proposal will mark another most important step in the rapid militarization of the United States if the Congress accepts it. The National Guard would be "a first-line reserve component of the postwar military establishment capable of immediate expansion to war strength, able to furnish units fit for service anywhere in the world, trained and equipped:

O. G. Villard

"A. To defend critical areas of the United States against land, seaborne, or airborne invasion.

"B. To assist in covering the mobilization and concentration of the remainder of the reserve forces.

"C. To participate by units in all types of operations, including the offensive either in the United States or overseas."

That is not all. While the language of the dispatch is not clear, it appears from its statement that "State units of the Guard would continue to perform their normal tasks of maintaining law and order" but "under competent orders of the State authorities." It would appear from this that the present temporary State organizations, hastily raised for service during the war, are going to be retained as State organizations by the kindness of the War Department.

If this interpretation is incorrect and the above reference is to the enlarged National Guard, it would seem as if it could hardly be ordered about on State duty by competent authority if it were in service overseas for the Federal Government or entrenched on the Pacific coast.

* * *

THUS we are more than ever face to face with the fact that we have here another clear-cut encroachment of Federal authority upon a State domain. That has been many years in coming, but no one has heretofore suggested that the National Guard should be wholly and completely federalized and made ready for instant overseas or domestic service. As the dispatch says:

"The National Guard will be considered an integral part" of the Army of the United States. The training is to be both in the armories and in the field, and that will mean of course that a large body of regular Army instructors will be required, and that more will be expected of National Guard officers than they have heretofore been able to give and remain in civil life.

This is plainly another illustration of the way the Army is utilizing the postwar feeling of the moment to develop an enormous military machine. We have been told that the postwar Navy and Marine Corps will aggregate a million men, and that the Army must have 1,500,000 men after July 1st next, if the nation is to carry out its sacred obligation to scatter garrisons all over the world and to impress upon the other nations that our international policies (whatever they may be) are backed up by overwhelming might. It will be recalled that President Truman has several times said that only force counts and that we would lose our prestige overnight if we should let our Army and Navy sink to unimpressive levels. We are not to put our faith in the righteousness of our cause. To quote his exact words:

"Until we are sure that our peace machinery is functioning adequately, we must relentlessly preserve our superiority on land and sea and in the air. . . . That is the only way we can be sure—until we are sure that there is another way."

As a cynical veteran remarks in the *Atlantic Monthly* for February: "First get all set for another war, then talk peace. . . ."

* * *

BUT of course the Army will not be satisfied with the National Guard as a reserve. It is merely adding it to the great reserve of officers—some 50,000, perhaps more than 200,000—the Reserve Officers Association is demanding "an active reserve of *400,000 officers*" (italics mine) and the Army will hardly oppose that, and the reserve of at least 500,000 enlisted men it hopes to build who will be paid an annual retainer to keep in touch with the War Department.

The Associated Press dispatch quoted above says that there is no mention in this National Guard proposal of universal peacetime conscription. If the War Department has thrown up the sponge on that, that is certainly something to be thankful for, but it will undoubtedly mean that the War Department will do everything in its power to have the Congress accept the American Legion "compromise" which would compel our youth to serve either in the National Guard or in some other military organization.

Now this National Guard proposal illustrates how completely our Washington brass hats are thinking in the terms of the war just ended. Like the Navy they are deliberately minimizing or brushing aside the atomic bomb. They are paying little or no attention to the fact that we shall soon have commercial and military planes flying at the rate of a thousand miles an hour, and that the continent has already been crossed in a trifle over three hours.

The National Guard is to be trained in the same old armories—we can look forward at once to a demand for hundreds of millions of dollars to expand them, bring them up to date, and make it possible for them to house 750,000 men instead of 300,000. It will have the same old teaching, will be indoctrinated in the same way, and will doubtless be told that they must be ready to go overseas on a minute's notice, V-bombs to the contrary notwithstanding.

Probably they will be told of Admiral Halsey's statement to the Senate: "We want to win wars, and we want to fight them on enemy ground. That makes us all invasion-minded. That calls for an overseas movement as the first step in our air, ground, and sea offensive."

They will certainly not be told of the incredible revelations we have been getting from the Pearl Harbor inquiry as to the utter inefficiency there of both Army and Navy and their failure to keep each other and themselves adequately posted as to what was going on.

WHATEVER the Army may propose in regard to the National Guard, the brass hats know perfectly well when they talk with one another in private that, leaving out all question of the new atomic warfare, it will be impossible to make any National Guard forces ready to move at once overseas unless they are made full-time troops.

Modern warfare is so largely a technical affair and changes so from day to day that only the professional soldier can be in any way kept up to date. Six months after any soldier is retired or discharged he is a back number unless he is given refresher training. Naturally the Army wants the public to believe that the day after we decide upon invading another country the National Guard will all be on board ship in San Francisco or New York. Actually the equipment and moving of 750,000 National Guardsmen, plus the bulk of a regular army of 1,500,000, plus 500,000 Marines will take weeks and weeks, if it does not utterly swamp the transportation lines of the country—I have purposely omitted reference to the 500,000 men in the Navy and the proposed hundreds of thousands of reserve officers, and the large regular reserves both the Army and the Navy propose to have. And what will the enemy be doing in the air while this vast mobilization of millions of men is being rushed through to the utter disorganization of civilian life and the hampering of industry's change from peacetime to wartime production?

Now if the Congress of the United States were true to our historic American traditions it would tell the Army not only in regard to this National Guard plan, but to all the other vast enlargement schemes, which as they now stand will withdraw at least 3,000,000 able-bodied men permanently from the industrial life of the United States, that these are questions for the Congress to decide and not military men.

It can judge better than any prejudiced generals what the American military policy should be. The latter cannot for a moment forget that raising the National Guard to 750,000 men will make room for a lot more generals, both of the regulars and of the National Guard—of the latter 13 officers have become generals in the Federal service since 1940.

That principle is so securely established in England that I have seen not one single British military or naval proposal for large increases of their services since the war ended. Across the border, in Canada, the Government has officially announced that the regular army will be reduced to 25,000 men! It, too, is on the American continent and is far weaker in national resources and wealth than the United States. But it is going right back to the old American theory that it does not need a large force to keep itself safe. Even in France Gen. de Gaulle was unable to put through his plan for a large standing army.

In his case the pecuniary condition of France and the need of workingmen to rebuild her industries were responsible for the refusal of the French Government to accept the proposal for an 835,000-man Army, Navy, and airforce and to limit the services to only 495,000 men. Here we do not consider finances. As in the case of almost all its other proposals, the War Department apparently attached no estimates of its cost to its National Guard plan. Why should it care what it may cost? Congress has not put on any brakes and has not closely supervised expenditures. Just now the Navy, with Army approval, is actually presenting a fleet of warships to China and not a word of protest has been heard, while the Army announces that it is going to raise a great united national army for China by keeping there a large corps of American officers and enlisted men as trainers. If Congress permits such outlays why should the war services concern themselves with costs?

AT bottom the truth is that all of these moves are preparations for our coming war with Russia which, however, neither the Army and Navy nor the White House will admit. No other explanation is possible. Gen. Eisenhower assured Congress that he knows from his European experiences that "there exists no fear of our motives in keeping ourselves strong." Oh yes? Just let him interview the Kremlin and ask what they are thinking about our military moves.

If there is no danger of an early war with Russia, then why are we preparing to militarize ourselves and to spend approximately eight to ten billions of dollars annually to keep up that force which President Truman declares is necessary?

If it is not Russia for whom we are arming, then the only answer is that the armed services wish to keep us militarized for their own particular benefit, for there is no other possible foe in sight.

THE PROGRESSIVE, MONDAY, MAY 13, 1946

Crushing A Dire Conspiracy

By OSWALD GARRISON VILLARD

OUR ARMY in Germany and Austria has distinguished itself again and won another great victory over the forces of evil. Not long ago it struck against the enemy at night, silently, swiftly, with cyclonic force—and arrested no less than 1,000 Germans suspected of pro-Nazi thoughts. As the official report put it, this was the "culmination of a 10-month-long combined operation" to crush "the first major attempt to revive Nazi ideologies."

O. G. Villard

At the same time it was revealed that the dastardly leader Artur Axmann, a one-armed, 30-year-old former German youth leader, and "about 200 other leading personalities of the movement, which was designed to establish a new Nazi hierarchy, had been in the United States and British custody for several months." That's the way to do it—nip the conspiracy in the bud, grab the leaders who dare to think as we do not wish them to believe, and rush all their depraved followers to jail and keep them there indefinitely without trial.

* * *

IT WAS Gen. Edwin Sibert, the chief intelligence officer, who revealed the dreadful facts to the press. He declared that these thousand kraut miscreants had not been guilty of any overt acts whatsoever—the Army was doubtless too smart to let that happen!

In the beginning it appears the rascals did dally with some dangerous thoughts as to sabotage possibilities, but, as the General put it, "the aims of the movement were long-term and not concerned with sabotage." They were just guilty of evil planning as to what they would do when the Americans and other occupying troops march out of Germany a decade or two hence.

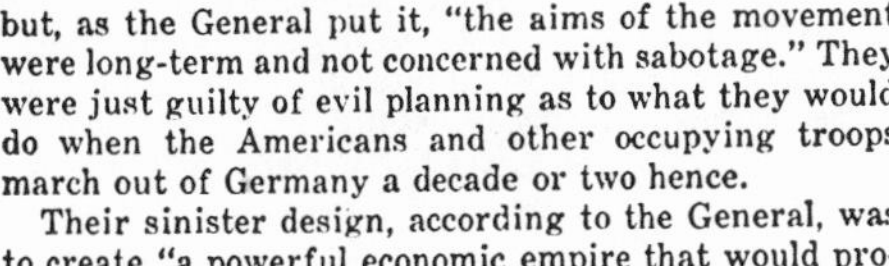

Their sinister design, according to the General, was to create "a powerful economic empire that would provide cover and backing for the second phase—long-range, subtle influencing of German politics along the Fuehrer principle." The subtlety of this undertaking alone reveals the perfidy of Herr Axmann—what a fitting name for a brutal Nazi Fuehrer! Had he had the virtues of a good Anglo-Saxon he would have done his plotting without guile, right out in the open.

But what can you expect of Nazis? Why, this miserable set of Huns not only committed no overt acts, they actually let themselves be taken without a fight. The dispatches report that while no less than 200 towns were raided by the 7,000 of our gallant troops who participated in this magnificent achievement, and "gunfire exchanges reportedly occurred in several towns and villages," the Nazis were so white-livered and such poor shots that "no reports of injury had been received" from a single one of the 200 battlefronts.

Yet these desperadoes were "taken into custody for questioning in connection with the most dangerous threat to Allied security uncovered in occupied Germany since the war." Still they did not fight. They were content to do all their fighting by thought control. But as Gen. Sibert modestly said to the press, his agents had "disguised" the earlier arrests so carefully that not a single person on the primary target list had escaped the trap.

Then, in token of his magnanimity, he told the news hawks that "some of those taken into custody might be found to have been unaware of the real intention of the ringleaders and, if so, would be released after investigation." I am glad to record that there is no confirmation of the report that most of those arrested have already been released to continue thinking what the Japanese called their "dangerous thought" against our American security.

At any rate, here we have another illustration of the true American principle of law enforcement: arrest everybody you suspect and then release the innocent—just as Mayor O'Dwyer in New York City has been scooping up hundreds of dangerous gamblers for "protective custody" or as "vagrants" to be held as long as possible. But the ringleaders in the Nazi plot will not be allowed to go free, no indeed, for here is Gen. Sibert's careful report of the deviltry they were up to:

There were two movements, the one headed by Axmann, and the other one by Willi Heidemann. Willi was plainly the more dangerous for, in May, 1945, he was discovered to be directing the recruitment of faithful Nazis who under his guidance were to be given jobs in a giant business network and sometime in the future were to "direct the revival of Nazi principles in the German Government."

"Convinced that sabotage was not feasible, Willi built up his nefarious business enterprises"—when he knew perfectly well that we are absolutely opposed to the reconstruction of any German business—"and extended them into the British zone." He actually went to the shocking lengths of opening "branch offices of five firms in many major cities of the two zones" and he "staffed them with former high-ranking Hitler youth personnel." I submit that hanging will be too good for him.

Two other leaders—another Willi, namely Willi Lobel, and a candidate for the gallows named Budaeus—started another movement in North Germany, but the American cavalry, excuse me, our counter-intelligence officers, galloped to the rescue as always. They soon discovered in their researches that there were numerous "embryo subversive elements at work" and they put their net on the leaders in embryo. Surely Hitler and his SS could not have done a better job. We have not only got all the leaders, we have put the fear of divine wrath in their hearts, certainly wherever the German-descended Sibert surveys the scene.

* * *

TAKE for instance this story of one Nazi plotter, or better plottress, as cabled to the New York *Times*. Four counter-intelligence agents, not stopping to ring the bell or to knock, smashed at night the front door of the residence in which Trudi Sommers, with her 25 years of Nazi decadence heavy upon her, dwelt with her parents. She was "a dark-haired girl *suspected* (my italics) of having made contact with the ringleaders of the anti-Allied plot."

The four agents got her out of bed. Did she show her overbearing, dictatorial, inner-born Nazi aggressiveness and sullen defiance? Not she. Instead, under the watchful eyes of the four armed agents "the girl dressed slowly and without betraying any emotion. When she was ready to leave with the raiders she calmly shook her wizened father's hand and left without a word. No questions were asked." What clearer proof could there be of her hardened criminality than her producing a "wizened father" and a mother "with a shawl around her shoulders" to try to move her adamant captors? No more than Maj. Andre did she move her brave American captors.

Hereafter those critics who have been attacking the slowness of our denazification policy in Germany will, we trust, keep their peace. The Army has in one night purged a thousand minds and made tens of thousands of Nazis recognize that, having improved upon Hitler's back-number and slovenly methods, and having our own concentration camps in which to place suspected criminals for indefinite periods without trial, they might as well give up dreaming idle dreams and thinking evil thought about the future.

The Stars and Stripes are on top in our zone and don't you forget that we shall not permit anybody to think under our flag the thoughts we don't want them to have, or to plan anything for the future except an exact duplication in Germany of all our American institutions.

* * *

I SINCERELY trust that no pacifist-inclined reader of this journal will snort and talk about our having gone to war with Hitler in order to head off the very thing we are now doing ourselves. If there is such a person, let him understand that after all we are dealing with Huns, that when you are in Rome you must do as do the Romans, and that after all you must trust the Army, for, as Congress has been told ten thousand times since the war began, the Army is there on the spot; it knows best what is needed; it is trained for the job, and its Siberts and McNarneys are steeped in the true American spirit. They know perfectly well that the Four Freedoms may be all right for America, but are certainly not intended for Huns.

P.S. The saddening thought comes to me, if King George III had only had a Sibert, instead of some muddle-headed Hessians, to apply himself to removing the "dangerous thought" of the American colonies, we might still be a part of the British Empire and there would have been no world wars because the Germans would never have dared attack us.

THE PROGRESSIVE, MONDAY, OCTOBER 21, 1946

DYNAMITE IN THE DARDANELLES

By OSWALD GARRISON VILLARD

THERE are five outstanding facts in the highly important Dardanelles dispute.

The first—carefully hidden by ourselves and our Allies—is that the Allies of the first World War promised to give to Russia exactly what the latter is asking now.

O. G. Villard

Second, the British position is frankly imperialistic and based primarily upon its "need to protect the Empire's lifeline."

Third, the United States has declared in true imperialistic fashion that this country is deeply concerned as to who controls the Straits and proposes to have an important say in the decision.

Fourth, it is a matter of life and death for the Turks since they are determined to go to war rather than let Russia interfere with their sovereignty, establish military bases on their territory, and obtain control of the Dardanelles.

Fifth, the Russians give every indication of meaning business and appear bent upon forcing the issue to a settlement now when they are at the height of their strength and power. The outcome will certainly tell the rest of the world just how much truth there is in Stalin's latest pacific statement with his assurance that the Third World War is not in sight.

CURIOUSLY enough, the Russians have not made effective use of the first fact just cited—that the Allies of 1914-18, excepting ourselves, agreed to give to Russia that precious control of the Dardanelles.

This promise was actually embodied in one of the

secret treaties that Woodrow Wilson assured Senators on his return from Paris that he had never heard of until he reached Paris, although the author of this article published them in the New York *Evening Post* and nine other newspapers, put them on sale in pamphlet form, and mailed copies to the White House and to every Senator and Congressman.

Actually as early as March, 1915, the Russian Minister of Foreign Affairs, Sozonoff, telegraphed to the Russian Ambassador in Paris that the British Government had joined France in complete agreement that Russia should annex, when victory came, "Constantinople and the Straits." The Allies were asking the world to believe that their sole aim was to safeguard democracy and to end war. Instead they were planning so selfish and imperialistic a division of the spoils as that now being witnessed on an even larger scale in Europe.

When, however, the peace came, to the horror of the Allies the Bolsheviks governed Russia. So the noble Allies forgot all about their promises to the Tsar and the Bolsheviks, being then opposed to aggression of any kind, made no demand for their fulfillment. Nor would it have helped them if they had, for they soon found themselves at war with the upholders of democracy.

There the record is, and today the old Allies, plus the United States, are united in saying no to the Russian demand for the booty promised in 1915. Of course the Russian proposal of today is not quite as bald as that. Stalin merely demands that the only Powers having anything to do with the Black Sea shall be the Black Sea States—Russia, Turkey, Rumania, and Bulgaria. He is actually so ungrateful as to ask England and the United States to keep out on the ground that it is none of our business.

His quarrel with Turkey is that the latter wants to do all the controlling and defending of the Straits herself, while Stalin insists not only on being a partner in the enterprise, but being given the three Turkish areas of Kars, Ardahan and Batum (excepting the harbor of Batum), all of which adjoin Russian territory. Stalin pretends that he cannot understand why Turkey should not wish to bring to her side the enormous Russian Army, and—in a few years—the great fleet Stalin is to create, for the manning of which he is setting up no less than 12 naval academies. Turkey realizes full well that any such partnership with Russia means the early gobbling up of its whole country, especially as Bulgaria and Rumania are now merely Russian satellites.

NOW it may be that among the readers of this article there are some old-fashioned Americans, and perhaps a few of those strange creatures think the United States should stay at home, make its own people happy and its Government work honestly and efficiently. If that is the case, they may be indignant that we should now be mixing in to the Black Sea imbroglio. Actually it can be said for the Truman Administration that we have been in it up to our necks for sometime. Thus, in 1936 the United States was a party to the Montreux Agreement governing the Dardanelles for a period of 10 years. It was then that we definitely involved ourselves in this problem which might easily precipitate the Third World War.

That agreement limited the control of the Dardanelles to Turkey, Russia, Bulgaria, and Rumania, but then of course Rumania and Bulgaria were not under Russian control. Under the Montreux Agreement the Straits are open to merchant vessels of all countries, to warships of the Black Sea Powers, except when Turkey is attacked or believes herself in danger, while other foreign men-of-war are not to use the Straits except with the consent of the Black Sea Powers.

These are certainly not unfair terms for the navigation of the Straits, and the Allies are now ready to agree that there shall be added to the existing agreement a stipulation that foreign warships shall be permitted to pass through them when directly in the service of the United Nations. That, too, is unexceptionable. But what our interference means is that our first line of defense, which Mr. Roosevelt defined as being on the Rhine, has now been extended to the Dardanelles, thousands of miles away from our shores, precisely as in the Pacific we have placed it in the Philippines and even nearer to Japan.

Moreover, we are saying this in an increasingly menacing manner which cannot but rouse enmity and fear in Moscow. Thus, Secretary Forrestal on Sept. 30 in a formal statement said that units of the United States Navy were in the Mediterranean and would remain there to support Allied policy in Europe and "to protect United States interests and support United States policies in the area."

The same afternoon the State Department issued a less menacing, but nonetheless clear, announcement that we had a definite interest in the Dardanelles and did not accept the Soviet position. So now the world knows that if an explosion comes there, we Americans will be on the front line with atom bombs in our coat pockets.

England is admittedly gravely alarmed by the Russian attitude, primarily because of the militant tone taken by Moscow in its proposals to Turkey and the continuation of the anti-Turkish propaganda in the Soviet press and radio discussions, ever since the Soviets in March, 1945, denounced the 1925 treaty for permanent Russian-Turkish friendship.

NOW it is true, as Forrestal has said in defense of our position, that we have often had American warships in the Mediterranean—a great-uncle of mine served a number of years there nearly a century ago. The exploits of some of our naval officers in attacking pirates and the Algerian Government are known to all schoolboys. But it is surely out of the question to compare those minor activities with the deliberate injection of the United States into major European and Mediterranean politics and our sending our best battleship and newest airplane carrier to Greece and elsewhere as an open warning and threat to all who oppose our American and British policy, especially in view of the hostile attitude of the Russians toward the Turks.

If Russia should attack Turkey, either directly or by stirring up local revolutions like those which took place in Persia, the British will find themselves in a most dangerous position.

It is not possible to see how England could survive another such struggle without the assurance at least of immediate American aid, including the atomic bomb. How far would she be willing to go to protect that "lifeline of the Empire" when she has given independence to India and is retiring from Egypt? How much will then remain of the British Empire in the Far East, and will it be worth risking the fate of England itself to fight another war for it? Such a decision should surely come from the British people themselves and not from any Cabinet, whether Labor or Conservative.

WHATEVER England's policy may prove to be, it seems as if the United States should recommend internationalization of the Dardanelles, preferably under the aegis of the United Nations—if that organization survives. Any other arrangement is an invitation to war. As for Mr. Wallace's declaring that we should be "horrified and angered" by any Russian counterproposal that we demilitarize the Panama and Suez Canals and put them under international control, I believe that the American people would not be horrified but would think such an action a great step forward for world peace.

That plan is something which would make our generals and admirals tear their hair and shriek to heaven for help, for some of their fattest jobs have to do with the Panama Canal. It would, however, be a wonderful proof to the world if we took such action of our genuine desire not to play the role of the victorious great Power, but to set a true example of moving toward peace, international sanity, and cooperation. Incidentally, it must be pointed out that Henry Wallace, with his usual disregard for facts, made a misstatement when he said that we were demanding "the internationalization and the defortification" of the Dardanelles. Neither is true.

I know well the difference between the Panama Canal and the Dardanelles and the Suez Canal. But the internationalization of these waterways together with the Danube and the Rhine is an absolutely realistic proposal, however much generals and admirals may storm against it. It would remove a great cause of international jealousy and reduce the so-called necessity for the arming of certain nations by that much.

THE whole thing hinges on Russia. It is much to be feared that what Stalin wants is less the actual control of the Dardanelles than the return of Kars and Ardahan which the Bolsheviks surrendered to Turkey by treaty in 1921, in addition to the two military bases on the Straits which Russia demands for herself—all this that Stalin may be in the best possible position to dominate Turkey.

But after all, compared to many other problems this is one of the simplest to confront the United Nations. If our statesmen and those of other countries cannot work this out peacefully, what hope is there of settling without bloodshed the even graver and more threatening problems?

November 11, 1946

Dear Mr. Rubin:

Thanks for your note. I hope you liked the article on the British Press. I offer you two other subjects in reply to your request. First, "The Opportunity Before Robert Taft", to show what he might do in the way of leadership, and second, an article on Governor Dewey. You could have the latter first if you prefer. I think there should be a quiet examination of Dewey as a candidate for the Presidency. It would bring out his extraordinary personal unpopularity even among men who agree that he has been a good Governor. Still another subject is the way we are doing away with the Potsdam Pact, as evidenced by the report in today's Times that the Russians are ready now to consider the unification of Germany in return for a price. That Germany would have had to be rebuilt I have had no doubt whatsoever. It was only a question of time. There are again reports from Belgium and Holland that the present condition in Germany must be ended they are suffering so severely from their loss of trade and coal from the Reich. Let me know what you think of these and whether they have or have not been preempted.

People talk about the difficulty the Republicans will have in choosing a candidate, but who will the Democrats ~~will~~ have if they discard Truman? The suggestion of Wallace will tear them wide open. For the first time in my life I voted the straight

Republican ticket, and so did four other Democratic members of my family. We all felt that it was a crucial election even if only going from the frying pan to the fire, that the dafety of the Re-public demanded the ending of Democratic mistule.

Please not that I am moving to New York on the 18th and that all mail thereafter should be directed to 20 Vesey Street, New York 7. Please notify your circulation department.

Cordially yours,

Mr. Morris H. Rubin,
The Progressive
Madison, Wisconsin

P.S. I dined with the [illegible] Yale University Press on Saturday evening. He brought up of his own accord my review of the Beard book and said that he liked it immensely--a tip for your advertising department!

OSWALD GARRISON VILLARD

FREE TRADE-FREE WORLD

ROBERT SCHALKENBACH FOUNDATION

NEW YORK, N. Y.

To those four great apostles of free trade:

JOHN BRIGHT
RICHARD COBDEN
WILLIAM LLOYD GARRISON
and
HENRY GEORGE

PRINTED IN THE UNITED STATES
FIRST EDITION

CHAPTER I

★

NO PEACE WITHOUT RADICAL TARIFF REFORM

THERE can be no lasting peace in this shrinking world unless there is freedom of trade. Yet in the face of the unparalleled disaster of the Second World War the Allied nations failed utterly to profit by the lessons of the bungling at Paris in 1919, which made the second catastrophe inevitable, and to take immediately the straight road to reconstruction and economic rehabilitation by the freeing of trade from all possible restraints and barriers everywhere. History has, therefore, repeated itself. Politics, nationalism and the bitter war hatreds roused by the sadistic German crimes against humanity controlled such efforts as were made toward a peace, precisely as had been the case in Paris, save that the condition of Europe has been far more menacing than the combined hunger, disorder and economic chaos that marked the end of the First World War. Undeterred by that, the major Allies wrote the already discredited and abandoned Potsdam Pact as if determined to increase the misery of all the war-ridden peoples and to make them, whether allies or enemies, suffer as long as possible. The result was a steady sinking of the standard of living, the increase of famine in Europe, the placing of England in the greatest jeopardy of its entire national existence, and the increasing destruction of the normal economic life of Germany, the powerhouse of Europe.

reciprocity, lower tariffs, and the removal of trade obstacles, the failure to call together the International Trade Conference at Geneva for two years after the cessation of hostilities is proof enough of the general lack of understanding that there can be no permanent peace as long as there is economic warfare, not to say anarchy; that there is no possibility whatever of the world's returning to the antebellum tariff systems and making life economically bearable for the survivors of the world's greatest catastrophe. Neither Mr. Churchill nor Mr. Roosevelt was a man of economic knowledge and understanding; neither foresaw that the splitting up of Germany into four parts created an economic abortion which made it necessary for their governments actually to keep their ex-enemies alive at a cost to the American and British taxpayers of hundreds of millions of dollars a year. Hence, by January, 1947, it was discovered that merely to make it possible for Germany to support itself would cost the Anglo-Saxon partners one billion dollars in the next two years—provided the reconstruction was immediately and vigorously undertaken.

At least it should have been pointed out that all the magnificent plans discussed during the war for disarmament, for a world police force, for an international currency and control of exchanges, for banishing famine by a world granary, for supervision of immigration, for freer access to raw materials, lead directly to world economic union. Every effort should have been made to co-ordinate these proposals and to show their relation to each other and the whole economic problem.

If it is alleged that this is a counsel of perfection, and that it was impossible because of war hatreds and Russia's attitude alone to bring the nations together at once, the answer is that Secretary James Byrnes, to his lasting credit, advanced in April, 1946, a proposal that *all European countries abolish their tariffs for a period of five years* to expedite the economic recovery of the Continent—a plan which should have been offered immediately after the surrender and pushed home with all the power of the United States Government as the most important issue of the hour. Instead, it was dropped and the International Trade Conference at Geneva was put off until April, 1947. When it came to organizing the United Nations at San Francisco, every emphasis should have been laid upon the restoration of the economic health of the world as the supreme issue—instead of which there were excluded from the first deliberations not merely the defeated enemies, but even neutral nations, such as Portugal, Switzerland and Sweden and political plans had the right of way.

The Allied failure to regard the tariffs as a major menace to future peace was the more remarkable because the Second World War was portrayed not only as a crusade for democracy, but for the abolition of special economic advantages, for the freedom of the individual citizen from encroachments by the State upon his personal liberties and his life from cradle to grave. Yet in no other field than this

one of international trade have there been more determined efforts to compel the individual to yield to special privilege, to limit his freedom of action on nationalistic grounds, to tax him to make great profits for favored manufacturers or favored agriculturalists. The champions of liberty and of the rights of the private citizen said nothing in their war propaganda about the role played by tariffs in bringing on aggression and war. They did not feature the slogan, "If goods do not cross boundaries, armies will,"[2] nor, even while the cannon were still being fired, make the most determined plans for a clean sweep of trade obstacles.

Today, free markets and international competition are the best safeguards for the health of a nation and its greatest protection against that totalitarianism which continues to split the world apart, despite the victory of the United Nations. They are the best antidote to those who, opposing a sound and absolutely just economic system, are leaning toward the suppression of true industrial liberty, and even upholding international cartels and monopolies as the road to international welfare. Under-Secretary of State for Economic Affairs, William L. Clayton, has declared that bilater-

alism in trade is the economic counterpart of fascism and nazism. Even if this is an exaggeration, there can be no doubt that it creates new rivalries, new jealousies, international wirepulling, the use of economic weapons for political purposes, and may even transfer to the economic field those balancing alliances which, in the political field, have led to endless hostilities.[5]

The convening of the conference for an International Trade Organization on April 15, 1947, was plainly a recognition of the above truths and was of supreme importance. Naturally, the United States was compelled to be the all-important factor at Geneva if only because of the injury done to the whole world by our past tariff procedures, to say nothing of our having the only well-stocked treasury on the globe. Again, world trade is the keynote to peace and we have the largest share of it. Before World War II, our productive capacity was the largest among the nations, amounting to 40 per cent of the world's total and 50 per cent of the world's ability to produce steel which is the basic material in an industrialized economy. Where other manufacturing plants were to a greater or lesser degree worn down or destroyed during hostilities, ours were tremendously expanded and modernized. These enormous productive facilities must now serve, not as the arsenal of

[5]Mr. Clayton might well have cited these words of William Lloyd Garrison reported in the Boston *Journal* of April 21, 1869: "For the cause of human liberty covers and includes all possible forms of human industry and best determines how the productions thereof may be exchanged at home and abroad to mutual advantage. Though never handling a tool, nor manufacturing a bale of cotton or wool nor selling a yard of cloth or a pound of sugar, he is the most sagacious political economist who contends for the highest justice, the most far-reaching equality, a close adherence to natural laws, and the removal of all those restrictions which foster national pride and selfishness. . . . . There is nothing intricate in freedom, free labor, free institutions, the law of interchange, the measure of reciprocity. It is the legerdemain of class legislation, disregarding the common interests of the people, that creates confusion, sophisticates the judgment, and dazzles to betray."

democracy, but as a vast storehouse and power plant which give the best, if not the only, hope of a swift industrial reconstruction the world over. If our business and political leaders are but wise enough to recognize the unlimited opportunity that the dire needs of humanity offer to us, there will be no need to fear that we shall have to abandon part of our industrial production or to dread great unemployment.

The greatest stumbling block to free trade remains the spirit of nationalism among the countries of the world. They will not apply the lesson of the vast free trade markets within Russia and the United States to their own situation and so they allow their trade, external and internal, and their whole economic condition, to be crippled and choked because the flag which flies over them is different from those of their neighbors. It has been the easiest trick of protectionists everywhere to wrap themselves in the banner of their country and to appeal to the selfishness, the ignorance and the fear of the masses of their people in whom have been sedulously cultivated the doctrine that the foreigner has but one object in life and that is to take the bread from their mouths. Always they are told that with just a little higher tariffs they will be safe and protected. Yet that elysium is never won according to protectionists. On the contrary, tariffs have gone higher and higher under American leadership, and hidden behind the tariffs have been great combinations of capitalists and laborers, politicians and masters of privilege concerned only with their personal welfare and not with national or international situations.

Now, however, the world has caught up with them. The great wars which were inevitable under the capitalistic high tariff system have produced a condition of chaos, misery and want and have compelled manufacturers and statesmen everywhere to realize the interdependence of all traders and of all nations. In the face of beggary and starvation, with one nation after the other on the verge of bankruptcy and all the governments grinding down their people by higher and higher taxation it seems extraordinary that the old slogans, the pretended altruisms of the protective tariffs, can still hold anybody enthralled. Certainly this would seem to be the last hour, the final moment, for freeing humanity from this legalized exploitation, for leading it into a real association of nations—an economic brotherhood out of which will arise, once it is tried, the closest ties between all the peoples of the world and the greatest assurance of peace, that will open the road to a real parliament of mankind and to that world community for which the greatest minds have striven for centuries.

CHAPTER XI

★

TARIFFS, PLANNED ECONOMIES AND DICTATORSHIPS

CAN THE United States do business with countries whose economic systems differ radically from our own? This is an oft-repeated question today and a crucial one in view of the rapid drift toward highly controlled and elaborately planned economies, if not Communism. Indeed, on its answer may possibly depend the future peace of the world. It is especially vital to this country since it is seeking to lead the nations in reconstructing the war-ruined economies, in raising the standard of life everywhere and in building up international trade to a level never before attained, as the best means of preventing further economic radicalism and of heading off further wars. How, the query runs, will it be possible for our free economy to trade with Soviet Russia or the United Kingdom in view of the governmental controls of business, imports and exports in both countries? The answer that it *is* possible can best be illumined by an examination of the foreign trade policies of the countries in question. Perhaps the most realistic answer was given by Secretary Vinson who, when he was head of the Treasury said: "We've got to take the world as it is."

The deep-rooted tendencies toward self-contained nationalism created by the First World War had developed because of economic controls and political pressures into economic blocs by the coming of World War Two. They were greatly accelerated by the necessities of that global struggle and, whether we like it or not, the blocs and economic controls are an important part of the world structure today.

Moreover, it is not only state-controlled economies that impose restrictions on trade or use them for noncommercial purposes, but capitalist nations as well can, and do, erect these barriers and even use them for political ends. Thus the American Government became very skillful in preclusive buying of materials and in other aspects of economic warfare during the hostilities. It is, of course, obvious that we cannot set ourselves up in judgment on, or attempt to interfere with, the internal affairs of countries that have been forced by dictatorships into economic planning. Professor J. B. Condliffe points out that "by 1947, the Soviet economic system will have been in existence for thirty years . . . . A whole generation has grown up which has never known any other way of life." Moreover, the State trading monopoly which controls external transactions is also "an integral and essential element of the planning of domestic production and employment. It cannot be modified without imperilling the whole structure of the Soviet economy."[1]

It is Professor Condliffe's correct belief that the best hope of bringing these totalitarian or socialistic countries into close trading contact with the Western world is to set up an effective multilateral trading system which it will be to their interest to deal with.

[1]Gunnar Myrdal, "The Reconstruction of World Trade and Swedish Trade Policy" (a pamphlet published December, 1946), p. 26.

By its very nature, freedom of trade is out of place in a dictatorship or a state ruled wholly by planned economics. Free trade guarantees freedom to the individual trader—the freedom to buy in the cheapest market and to sell to his fellow-citizens at the price he and they agree upon, without first having to obtain the consent of his all-ruling government. It must be held in mind, however, that different countries where state planning exists offer different problems. Whereas the autarchical policies followed by the German Fascists in the 1930's were a direct deterrent to those aiming at a high level of international trade and were used as a means of achieving self-sufficiency or even world domination, there are other countries where both the form of planning and the motivation differ from those of Hitler's State. Where this planning is not aimed at self-sufficiency or world control, and seeks to raise the level of international trade, it is obvious that, despite our own preference for individual initiative, for uncontrolled production and distribution, we shall be able to trade with countries of a different type. It must, however, be noted that a forthright examination of the economic realities existing in the world today reveals many difficulties for the free trader to face.[2] That

[2]"Even the European governments most eager to see their countries' foreign trade move back toward normal were handicapped by the disorganized condition left in the wake of the war—the destruction of productive facilities, the exhaustion of supplies, the disruption of transport and distributive channels, the scrambled ownership of industry, and inadequacy of foreign exchange assets, the internal financial confusion, and often also the unsettled status of the gov-

does not mean that this ideal should not be most vigorously pursued as it should have been from the day of peace. It does not detract from this need to say that today we are facing a world wholly different from the one of John Bright, Richard Cobden, and the other great classical free traders.

Let us take the United Kingdom as the first example. All the planning measures undertaken in the field of international trade and in domestic affairs by the government of that country since the war, have had only the one aim of increasing that country's foreign trade in order to head off bankruptcy and starvation. It was, therefore, it was alleged, impossible to allow trade to develop of its own accord, and there must be further and further restriction of imports as the only way to conserve dollars and save the British Empire. Gunnar Myrdal, lately the Swedish Minister of Commerce, whose country has been traditionally devoted to free trade, pointed out to the Swedish Economic Society on December 5, 1946, that: "An advanced and active trade policy on an international scale is required merely to create the possibility of trading at all, and still more to expand it to a volume corresponding to commercial possibilities—which is the real purport of free trade." He added: "The modern doctrine of free trade is in fact, very different from its predecessor." His own country has been compelled, almost at pistol's point, to enter into an agreement with Russia to give that country a loan which is a huge one for so small a nation and to supply goods over a period of years which may prove to be beyond the power of even as able and industrious a people as the Swedes.

ernmental regime itself . . . . a large measure of governmental control and even direct official intervention in foreign trade arrangements seemed unavoidable, at least for a time."—Henry Chalmers, "Current Trends in Foreign Trade Policies," reprint from *Foreign Commerce Weekly*, February 9, 16, and 23, 1946.

When it comes to Russia, the best hope of maintaining peace with that war-ravaged country is not only to give it loans, but to build up normal trade between our two nations. There is no doubt that a main purpose of the "iron curtain" which secludes Russia from foreign observation is to conceal the horrifying extent of the damage done to Russia by the Germans, and the suffering and need of the people. There is an overwhelming lack of consumer goods of the type which are best produced in the United States. Economic interdependence, as well as the success of the United Nations, requires peacetime commercial and cultural intercourse between us. Russia can do, and has done, business with us in the past, not to the extent, however, of her needs or of our potentialities. An increase in trade would give great benefit to both of us and might well serve as an indirect stimulus to trade in many different parts of the world.

With our expanded productive facilities requiring additional customers, particularly in the capital equipment field, we are in an excellent position to supply Russia's needs. The problem of increasing trade between the two countries will not be easy to solve, particularly if political considerations are to govern all the moves of the Washington Government. But if a large expansion of multilateral trade could be organized around the United States and British spheres of trade influence, the U.S.S.R. could develop greatly increased markets for oil, lumber, furs, minerals and grain. That any commercial relationship of the democracies to Russia will call for endless patience, tact and forbearance, need not be stressed. It seems certain, however, that the lower the tariffs, the wider the world markets and the greater diversity of trade there is between them, the easier should be the relationship of Russia to the other trading nations, particularly if they stress multilateral agreements.

Another development which seriously makes for restriction of trade and limits freedom of enterprise is the international monopoly, or cartel. How it works can be illustrated by the apportioning of the world prior to the war between such great manufacturers of electrical lamps as the American General Electric, the German Siemens interests and the N. V. Phillips Company in Holland, etc. Their agreement bound each signatory not to enter the domain of another or to permit any other similar business in their respective countries to do so. Professor Walton Hamilton's remedy for the cartel is "clearly to sterilize the political frontier; to remove the barriers which hold industries to narrow and artificial markets; to tear down the dams which hold back the forces of an expanding economy. . . . . If, however, tumultuous industry is to continue to beat against obsolete national boundaries, mankind—in a world of scarcity susceptible to war—must take the consequences."[4] While the prevailing opinion in the United States, and especially in government circles, is largely against cartels, it cannot be denied that there are marked differences of opinion. Some officials, as in the Department of Agriculture, lean toward international government agreements in order to keep up world prices on vital commodities.

The Department of Justice, on the other hand, has been strongly opposed to cartels of every kind, especially the former Assistant Attorney-General, Thurman W. Arnold, who believes that these combinations were largely responsible for the Second World War, and in his judgment would lead again to mass killings if they are revived and developed. Assistant Attorney-General Wendell Berge, who is now in charge of the antitrust division of the Department of Justice, is also bitterly antagonistic and has declared that "one might as well urge that a railway wreck promotes transportation as to urge that a cartel agreement promotes trade." He

[4]"Cartels, Patents and Politics," *Foreign Affairs,* July, 1943, p. 593.

has stated, however, that for political reasons government participation in some cartels is justifiable and has said that "as an economic matter it makes no difference whether an agreement to restrict trade is private or governmental. As a political matter, I would agree that if we are going to have such agreements, with their widespread economic diseases, they had better be the responsibility of the government, if only because the governments which make such agreements can be changed by voters."[5] Yet he is also of the opinion that government control of private monopolies would require such a degree of interference with private industry as to place in jeopardy our whole free enterprise and private property system.

The undemocratic functioning as well as structure of cartels is well described in the following:

> In the case of cartels, treaties are made for private not public, ends. The consequences of their acts may be vital to society, but their aims are framed with reference only to their own welfare. In the purview of cartels, the whole world economy is an area of exploitation. From this perspective they determine spheres of influence and divide hemispheres by treaties which require no consent either from the public or from legal governments.
>
> When, for instance, the United States enters into a treaty with a foreign nation, its acceptance must be ratified with the advice and consent of two-thirds of the Senate, in the light of national policy. When a monopoly enters a cartel agreement, which equally affects the foundations of our national economy, no voice can be raised to question or approve. In fact, it is characteristic of cartel agreements, which, because of their economic importance, may be of greater moment than political understandings, that they are arrived at secretly and maintained in silence. There are

[5]Address to the Export Managers Club of New York, *The New York Times,* May 17, 1944. See also the lengthy address of Congressman Jerry Voorhees on "Peace or only an Armistice; the Menace of German-Controlled Cartels," in the House of Representatives, May 21, 1945.

no "open covenants, openly arrived at." There could not be, for otherwise it would be too evident that cartel agreements transcend any standard of national interest.[6]

Before the Second World War, it is further stated, "Germany, through international cartels, built up its own production and assisted the democracies in restricting their production in electrical equipment, in drugs, in chemicals, in basic war materials, such as magnesium and aluminum. International cartels with the active assistance of American interests have operated to deprive us of markets in our own hemisphere by giving them away to Germany."[7]

Cartels may be, as the English aver, an inevitable outgrowth of modern capitalism, but there can be no denying that they point toward totalitarianism at home and to the most serious consequences in the international field. This has led to the suggestion, among other remedies, that there be established an international forum or court to which countries lacking raw materials may turn for protection from international monopolies. The true remedy, however, lies in the striking down of tariffs, the freeing of the seas, the opening up of the backward areas to all countries alike, and the complete encouragement of merchants everywhere to trade without restrictions of any kind. Meanwhile, a refusal on our part to trade with planned-economy countries would result in moves against us in the form of blocs, tariffs, quotas, hostile exchange manipulations, and all the other measures of economic warfare distinguishing the interwar period and leading to World War II. There has never been any question that the tariff was the mother of American trusts, and it has without doubt been the mother of trusts abroad. What is more natural than that these trusts should strike

[6]Joseph Borkin and Charles A. Welsh, *Germany's Master Plan: The Story of an Industrial Offensive* (New York: Duell, Sloan & Pearce, 1943), pp. 154–55.

[7]*Ibid.*, introduction by Thurman Arnold.

hands and seek to divide up the entire world among themselves? If we are not to see the establishment of global business organizations almost powerful enough to defy their own governments, then we must certainly plan counter-measures without loss of time, notably the immediate acceptance of the principles of the International Trade Organization including the protection and advancement of backward regions.

CHAPTER XXIII

★

OUR TARIFF HISTORY

Our tariff history begins the day after the first Congress of the nation was organized. A bill was brought in by James Madison of Virginia, the leading member of the House of Representatives, imposing duties averaging about 8 per cent on sugar, molasses, tea, salt, glass and other imports. Madison urged it as a means of securing revenue to meet the country's financial obligations, and its protection features were not stressed though its preamble described the bill as "an act for the encouragement and protection of manufacturers." It is interesting to note that this bill, like many others in our subsequent tariff history, brought its own type of corruption with it. Importers who had large quantities of goods en route from Europe managed to secure a postponement of the day when the act was to go into effect until after their cargoes were landed, meanwhile putting up the prices of their goods to the new tariff level.

Alexander Hamilton, the spiritual father of the American tariffs, always looked upon them as merely temporary measures. Said he in 1791: "The continuance of bounties in manufactures long established must always be a questionable policy; because a presumption would arise in every such case that there were natural and inherent impediments to success." The original idea was that protection should be granted only to newly established industries, whose development, or whose security, was threatened by artificial or accidental causes. John Stuart Mill, long one of the patron saints of American tariff reformers, approved of this policy in principle.

So the infant industries of the thirteen struggling, just united American colonies were to be aided by the government in meeting European competition only until they could stand on their own feet. Actually, however, when these infants had grown nearly to their present gigantic proportions, some of them being the largest and richest on earth, they demanded and received higher protection than ever before. Hence, instead of being a minor fiscal problem, the tariffs became for generations a dominating force in American political life and, as already stated, some national elections were purchased by slush funds raised by tariff beneficiaries. Presidents have actually been elected or defeated as they favored or opposed high tariffs, notably President Cleveland when he sought re-election in 1888. The original excuse for their establishment having disappeared, other arguments were brought forward, such as the assertion that prosperity depends upon selling all you can to foreigners and buying just as little as possible from them in order to keep your money at home. Then the alleged danger from European "pauper labor" began to appear, and with it the pretense that our standard of living depended upon the exclusion of foreign goods and not upon the diligence, intelligence, natural skill, freedom of movement, and adaptability of American workers in a country of unlimited opportunity and almost unlimited riches.

The tariff of 1816 served a genuine purpose in protecting our infant industry from the dumping of British goods. As well as covering iron, glass, leather and woolens, the bill provided protection for the then most advanced American industry, cotton, which was in fact its greatest beneficiary, for no imported cotton could be rated under twenty-five cents a yard according to the tariff schedule. Even this bill proved inequitable and favored certain segments of the population disproportionately. As McDuffie of South Carolina pointed out, the tariff on cotton favored the manufacturer at the expense of the farmer, to which John C. Calhoun replied that the protective tariffs were not intended to benefit the manufacturers, but "to bind the different sections of our country together in a mutual dependence which would be the surest guaranty against disunion." Thus the growing nationalism in the country tended to make the country plan for economic self-sufficiency rather than aim at favoring new industries. As industrialization called for more and more imports of materials from abroad—it was achieved in the first instance by machines and technical skill imported from Europe—and as technological progress made evident the essential interdependence of the many different areas of the world, the original tariff ideas proved difficult to maintain in the face of the demands of the specially privileged.

In 1824 and 1828 tariffs were voted containing numerous increases in rates. In 1830, however, the duties on molasses, tea, coffee and cocoa were lowered in order, extraordinary as it now seems, to reduce the federal revenue.[1] There were also tariff bills enacted in 1832 and 1833; by July 1842 a general level of 20 per cent was reached. In September of that year the duties went up again, not because of a public demand, but because the politicians sought an issue. The act of 1846 is often described as a free trade measure and it continued until 1857 when a still further lowering of duties was made, this being the period of our greatest success with our shipping. Nonetheless, the protectionists alleged not only that the lowered tariffs had induced the crises of 1837 and 1839, but that the 1857 tariff reduction had brought on the terrible depression of that year. Actually, the crises of 1837 and 1839 were due to different causes—bank troubles, the in-

[1]Prior to 1861 customs duties furnished 90 per cent of the government's total income; in 1912 the percentage was 45, from 1921 to 1930, 13 per cent, and in 1932, 15 per cent.

flation of the currency, Jackson's financial blunders, and general conditions of speculation and of too expanded credit.

Similarly, the crisis of 1857 was also primarily due to other causes than the tariff, such as speculation, panic, depression and banking errors. Yet it was called by one of the prophets of protection "the terrific free trade crisis of 1857." Despite this, there was little belief that the great foreign trade in which the country was engaged at that time was a detriment to its economic life; during the year ending June 30, 1860, nearly twenty-four thousand vessels left the harbors of the United States, of which almost thirteen thousand were American, bound for more than seventy destinations. No less than four million tons of goods were sent to Canada alone, more than three-quarters on American ships.

It was the coming of the Civil War which gave the protectionists their opportunity and definitely fastened the modern protective system upon the country. The passage of the Morrill Tariff Act of 1861 was primarily due to the desire for increased revenue to meet the expenses of the war, and so were the enactments of the tariffs of 1862 and 1864. When the conflict was over, however, they were to a considerable degree maintained. Thus, the stamp of high tariffs was indelibly put upon our economic policies with vitally important effects upon the remarkable industrial development of the country in the post-Civil War political and economic life, bringing with them numerous evil results.

During the Grant Administrations a "marriage of the tariff and the bloody shirt" (by the latter the severe reconstruction policies toward the South is meant) enabled the industrial areas of the United States to dominate the country. The twenty-five years from Appomattox to the voting of the McKinley tariff act in October 1890 were years of a mad race for wealth and power, the building of huge fortunes as a result of tariff benefits, the growth of business combinations and trusts, and the complete domination of the Republican Party by the protected manufacturers, whose purchase of votes in Indiana and elsewhere "in blocs of five" was one of the scandals of the Presidential election of 1888. The McKinley tariff raised the wool and woolen schedules and the rate on steel rails; the duty on refined sugar, a domestic monopoly entirely controlled by the Havemeyer interests, was placed at half a cent a pound, though raw sugar was put on the free list.

It must not, however, be thought that these years were without voices raised in protest. In 1882, in the Senate of the United States, James B. Beck of Kentucky spoke of the "enormities of the present high protective system," which Senator Morrill of Pennsylvania and his "co-monopolists" wished to "whitewash."

This Senator also pointed out that then, as in 1876, the farmer who furnished nine-tenths of our American exports and sold them at world prices "cannot buy with the money he gets in the market where he sells the things he must have, without paying 45 per cent at least more than they are worth, or than the man who has them for sale asks for them. I never could see how that protected American labor . . . . ." He then gave the following admirable definition of what protection is, which ought to be in every American household:

> The protection (so-called) is a Congressional license to a few influential corporations or wealthy combinations to extort from the American farmers, laborers, professional men and their families a large percentage of their earnings, not to support the government, but to enrich people who have no right to take anything from them, *and call that protection*. It is the protection the wolf gave the lamb.

When Grover Cleveland entered the White House in 1884 he admitted that he was utterly ignorant of the tariff problem which he had never had to face in his previous career as sheriff, mayor and governor of New York State. He promised, however, to take the matter up thoroughly and when urged to announce his candidacy for a second term declared that he would do so only on a platform which would contain a plank advocating a tariff for revenue only. This he put through in the face of the correct warning of his Cabinet and his party advisors that it would mean his defeat—he preferred defeat to remaining silent on this question. When President Harrison succeeded him, the passage of the McKinley tariff took place with the result that this measure, which its author boasted was "protective in every paragraph and American in every way," frightened even some of the apostles of protection. Two years later, the then Secretary of State, James G. Blaine, sponsored a number of reciprocity treaties with nine Latin-American republics, the Spanish islands of Cuba and Puerto Rico, the British West Indies and the German and Austro-Hungarian Empires. These laws admitted some products of the countries cited without duty in return for free entrance of some American goods into their markets. Although this policy ran directly contrary to the Republican protectionist theories, Mr. Blaine was able to secure Congressional support for it.

On Mr. Cleveland's re-election in 1892, in part because of popular dissatisfaction with the high protective duties, he insisted that his party should live up to his tariff-for-revenue plank which was repeated in its platform of that year. But when he tried to induce Congress to pass a radical tariff reform measure he made the discovery, as did Woodrow Wilson later, that the old line of cleavage between the political parties, according to which the Republicans were the sole advocates of high protection and the Democrats of low tariffs and free trade, had begun to change. The South had always been strongly for low tariffs, but when it began to be industrialized its Democratic leaders turned in the other direction. While the House of Representatives responded to Mr. Cleveland's appeal by passing a fair tariff reduction bill, named after Congressman William L. Wilson of West Virginia, the Senate made 334 changes in it and ruined it for Mr. Cleveland and the tariff reformers. The President refused to sign it but allowed it to become a law on August 27, 1894, without his signature. He was betrayed by Democratic Senators headed by Senator Gorman of Maryland. President Wilson experienced a similar betrayal when he endeavored in 1913 to make a revision by passage of the Underwood Tariff Bill.

After Mr. Cleveland's retirement from office and the election of President McKinley, the Republicans, more than ever devoted to the tariff, passed the Dingley Act at a special session of Congress in July, 1897. This law reimposed duties on wool and hides and put higher tariffs on silk, linen, chinaware, metals and sugar. Its effect on the American working man's standard of living appears from the fact that in the first ten years after its enactment the price of raw materials increased 50 per cent, and of manufactured goods 32 per cent, while wages in more than four thousand establishments rose only 19.1 per cent.[2] During this same period, the profits of the large manufacturers of wool, woolen goods, cotton, shoes, farm machinery and many other commodities rose enormously—thanks to the labor of their working men who had to buy their necessities at the tariff-inflated prices of the market.

Early in his career, Theodore Roosevelt favored the lowering of tariffs, writing in November, 1882, that "though elected as an independent Republican, I hardly know what

[2]Muzzey and Krout, *American History for Colleges* (New York: Ginn & Co., 1933), p. 185.

to call myself. As regards civil service reform, tariff reform, local self-government, etc., I am quite in sympathy with Democratic principles."[3] Two years later he wrote: "As regards the tariff I am, as was my father (a life-long Republican) before me, a bit of a heretic when looked at with Republican eyes." In the same letter he said: "Political economists have pretty generally agreed that protection is vicious in theory and harmful in practice; but if the majority of people in interest wish it and it affects only themselves, there is no earthly reason why they should not be allowed to try the experiment to their heart's content. The trouble is it rarely does affect only themselves." Once he declared that the country would finally go on a free trade basis, stating in 1883 that the time was "surely coming when the protective tariff would be swept away as in a torrent."[4] As in many other cases, however, political expediency and personal ambition made Theodore Roosevelt change his beliefs or subordinate them to what he readily persuaded himself was the public's weal or the public's desire.[5] Finally, in 1907 in his Annual Message he declared that the protective duties needed revision and promised in the 1908 Republican platform that this would be done by a special session of Congress.

President Taft, in accord with this promise, summoned a special session on March 15, 1909. Congress, however, understood revision to mean revision upward in the interest of the privileged tariff beneficiaries. The latter were completely satisfied; they had their own way and the ultimate

[3]*Ibid.* [4]*Ibid.*

[5]William Roscoe Thayer, long an intimate personal friend and an admiring biographer of Theodore Roosevelt, wrote that on the tariffs he "was less satisfactory than on any other [subject]." He added: "To those of us who for many years regarded the tariff as a dividing line between the parties, his stand was most disappointing . . . . greatly to our chagrin, he did nothing." *Theodore Roosevelt, An Intimate Biography* (Boston: Houghton Mifflin & Co., 1919).

consumer was unheard. The tariff, however, soon became very unpopular with the result that President Taft endeavored to negotiate the 1911 reciprocity treaty with Canada which met with the defeat recorded elsewhere.[6] There is no doubt that the high duty set by the Payne-Aldrich Act contributed considerably to the defeat of Mr. Taft which was, however, foreordained by the split in the Republican Party headed by Theodore Roosevelt. Despite President Wilson's determined fight for tariff reform, his party steadily weakened in its historic opposition to high duties. Indeed, the platforms on which Alfred E. Smith in 1928 and Franklin D. Roosevelt in 1932 ran for the Presidency really committed the party to a new tariff position.

When the Republicans returned to power after the second Administration of Woodrow Wilson they passed two tariff bills, the Fordney-McCumber Act of 1922, containing the highest duties up to that time coupled with certain prohibitory ones to protect new industries, and the Hawley-Smoot tariff of 1930. The Fordney-McCumber law marked two departures in our protection policies. First, the ad valorem duties were made assessable on the foreign value of the goods or their export value at the port of shipment, whichever happened to be higher. Second, the law laid down the principle that the fundamental aim of American protection was equalization of the cost of production between our products and competitive foreign articles. Thus it was intended that the tariff should be a flexible one regulated by costs of production abroad, and the Tariff Commission was created to ascertain the differences at any time in American and foreign costs, to investigate complaints by foreigners of unfair practices on our part, and to draw up new schedules of rates when it deemed revision necessary. For the first time the President was given the power to proclaim

[6]See Chapter XII, pp. 125–26.

new rates based upon the Commission's information, though that was not binding upon him. Actually, as has been pointed out, for many years the Commission achieved nothing but the raising of a few unimportant rates and it never lowered any of consequence.

When President Hoover signed the Hawley-Smoot tariff, the protective rates were again raised to the highest point in our history, its schedules topping those of the Fordney law as a whole by nearly 7 per cent. This monstrous measure was approved by Mr. Hoover although no less than a thousand trained economists, financiers, editors and public men protested against it and prophesied that it would strike a deadly blow at American prosperity. They especially pointed out that it would inevitably bring about reprisals by foreign nations. They were entirely correct. Even while the bill was in process of being passed twenty-six nations officially protested against some of its schedules and when it became a law no less than fifty nations took official action against this country by reprisals such as embargoes, quotas, special import duties, higher tariffs and other strangling devices intended to exclude or to limit severely the importation of American goods. Mr. Hoover also had before him when he made this fatal decision, the protests of the international conference of the bankers of the world in London against the postwar tariffs everywhere, and especially in Europe. They deplored particularly the erection of tariff barriers by the various new nations created by the Treaty of Versailles and accurately prophesied the coming of the unprecedented international depression of 1929.

Nothing could have been more mistaken than the statement by General Winfield S. Hancock when a candidate for the Presidency on the Democratic ticket in 1880 that the tariff is a purely local issue. Actually, the making of an American tariff has become an act of war against foreign countries and is so considered. It is bound to have repercussions in every other nation in the world. One direct example of this was reported in 1890 by the American Consul at Chemnitz, Germany, who, speaking in his official capacity, declared that the McKinley tariff had lowered the standard of living throughout Saxony, for the employers there who produced many goods, notably china, for export to the United States, cut wages to reduce costs after the appearance of the McKinley schedules in order to get their goods into the United States. The American protective system more than anything else has been responsible for dividing the whole world into national compartments surrounded by high tariff walls and placing every obstacle in the way of the normal processes of trade. Our present change of front and eager advocacy of lower tariffs everywhere is only a small atonement for the injury we have thus done to the world at large.

COVENANT WITH DEATH

By OSWALD GARRISON VILLARD

"A COVENANT With Death and an Agreement With Hell," the Massachusetts Anti-Slavery Society in 1843 dubbed the U. S. Constitution because it made slavery legal and possible. I am tempted to apply these words to the Potsdam Pact. It has been and still is a Covenant with Death because under it many persons are and have been condemned to death and millions to utter misery. I maintain that it was an Agreement with Hell to separate Germany into four zones; to authorize wanton destruction of wealth-creating industrial properties when all Europe was crying for goods and reconstruction; to make almost impossible the recovery of our Allied and friendly nations, France, Denmark, Holland, and Norway, if not Belgium.

O. G. Villard

I should be willing to leave the Germans entirely out of the picture and then I should still say that it was an Agreement with Hell, for the pact is a deadly blow at the sanitation of Europe, at the efforts to head off a third World War. I maintain that I am correct in this attitude because obviously our Government has now undertaken to scrap the pact, and as a first step it is putting through the amalgamation of the British and American zones. There can be no question that it would draw the Russian and French zones into the consolidation if the stupidity, the intransigeance, and the inhumanity of those two countries would make it possible.

Precisely as was foretold, the Americans and the British have now discovered that Germany is the industrial heart of Europe, that, whether one likes its people or hates them, believes that they are capable of resurrection or thinks of them as perpetual enemies of peace and order in Europe, there is no getting away from the truth that a sick Germany means an ailing and disabled Europe. If anybody doubts this, let him observe that the Prime Minister of Holland has announced that his country is trying to bring about a union of four or five of the smaller states to bring pressure to bear upon the Allies to end this whole German business, to throw open the frontiers to travel, to mails, to business, so that Dutch men of affairs can cross the boundaries to see if they cannot buy the goods which Holland must have in return for its exports.

THE utterly unnatural barricades on the frontiers must cease, the waterways must be opened up and the railroads, too, so that *normal relations* may be restored. I italicize those two words because that is all that is asked. For centuries Europe has been a cockpit set aflame either by the French or the Austrians or the Germans, and after every holocaust the old economic order has had to be restored. If it is to be blocked definitely now it can only mean widespread economic disaster, national retardation, and retrogression.

I suppose that this statement will once more be met by the retorts one hears from the irreconcilables, the non-Christians among our Christians with their continuing patter: "Well, the Germans began it, didn't they, and they must pay for it, mustn't they?" The other day I heard two speakers addressing the Foreign Policy Association in New York. They bitterly criticized the economic set-up of Germany; they attacked the system which is costing us at least 200 million dollars a year, which compels us to give the Germans just enough food to keep the great bulk of them from dying of malnutrition and the diseases incident thereto.

Both made it perfectly clear that we were robbing ourselves by this crass international stupidity, but both found it necessary to say that it must not be thought they were against a hard peace, oh dear no. Not one single word of sympathy for suffering human beings, however innocent or guilty, escaped their lips. Indeed, one of them, after reciting the terrible conditions, hastened to declare that he was in favor of the Germans undergoing a long purgatory, as if anything in the way of purgatory could exceed what the mass of the German population is now enduring.

Neither apparently had ever heard that one should love one's enemies as oneself, nor who it was that gave utterance to that sentiment. Neither had ever heard that it is mercy and magnanimity and forgiveness which redeem and pacify, and not revenge nor hate nor torture.

So now we are off on a new tack. What is the first thing we are told? That just to put the British and American zones on their feet economically will take three years and cost the United States and Great Britain $500,000,000 each—a terrible burden for nearly bankrupt Britain to shoulder.

What could be more ironic than this? First we destroy the German cities, with three exceptions, and gloat over the thoroughness with which we have wiped out the workingmen's quarters and the industrial districts. Then when we march in and occupy the conquered land we add to the destruction by blowing up great plants, or, as in the case of the English and French and Russians, either dynamite important works or move them away bodily so as to destroy the industrial power of the country lest it start another European war 50 or 100 years from now.

The price for that is not only the billion dollars that we must pay during the coming three years, but the far larger sums which it has cost us, the French, and the Russians to maintain our troops as guards in the year and a half of our occupation. The English say that it has been costing them 80,000,000 pounds a year to do all this; there are those who declare that this is not the real figure, that the true total has been decreased by charging against it the value of the goods and properties which they are taking out of the country. Whatever the sum, it is an enormous part of the financial loss which has driven England to borrow $4,750,000,000 from the United States and Canada, and led Stafford Cripps to say recently that if England could not speed up its production enormously, he did not know what would happen when the loans were used up, and that they were going very fast.

FORTUNATELY, there are numerous other signs that sanity is returning. The readiness finally to begin the discussion of the peace terms is one. It is true that the mistake has been made of choosing Moscow as the scene of the discussion—which was doubtless considered an extremely foxy move to fan Russian vanity and induce her the more readily to go along.

However cynical one may be as to what may come out of it, beyond question it will be a great gain just to discuss peace for the conquered, which means peace and freedom of movement and restoration in Western Europe. Next, there is Winston Churchill's splendid appeal at Zurich for a European union on tariff and other lines—he even endorsed the Coudenhove-Kalergi proposals to this end which that remarkable man has been advocating for some 20 years or more. It might easily have prevented the coming of the second World War. This may have to be considered.

In our own conduct of German affairs there has been an entire change of spirit. Secretary Byrnes voiced the demand for a restored and efficient Germany in his Nuernberg speech. Gen. McNarney, our military commander, has directed the abandonment by our troops and officials of the policy of hate, always a disgrace to us, with which the occupation officially began. Next, he has allowed some American men and German women to be married and to leave for the United States.

Another great advance has been ending of all political arrests and detention of Germans by the Counter Intelligence Corps which sometimes led to midnight arrests of thousands of men and women upon whom no warrants were served, against whom no definite charges were laid, but who were many of them interned for months without trial in the concentration camps which we are maintaining all over Germany for prisoners, refugees, and displaced persons.

Greater efforts have been made to put food into Austria and some more into Germany. It would almost seem as if humanity were returning when one reads that Gen. McNarney has stopped, at least temporarily, the proposed seizure in Munich of 1,000 more homes of Germans for the use of our military. The dispatches reported that the city government in Munich was in the greatest alarm at this excess and was begging the citizens not to undertake public demonstrations of protest lest they lead to violence.

How grave this evil is appears from the simple fact that whereas when the fighting ceased there were 45,000 habitations left in the city of Frankfort to accommodate 425,000 people, the American military has seized for its own use no less than 23,000. Yes, 425,000 people to be accommodated in 22,000 apartments and separate houses, with refugees pouring in from Eastern Europe destitute of everything!

Finally, a Berlin dispatch says that by Jan. 1 13% of the military and civilian personnel in the AMG in Germany will be relieved from duty there, and 22% more will be recalled by June 30—there are 26,000 British civilian employes living in their zone, in addition to all the military, when England rules India today with only 1,500 white officials. Mr. Patterson, Secretary of War, still demands that we shall keep 160,000 men for our occupation tasks in Austria and Germany, and 170,000 more for service in Japan and Korea.

THE other steps that should be taken at once besides the immediate reduction to the very minimum of our military garrison and civilian employes are the opening up of the mails so that we Americans may at least help to get the truth before the Germans by mailing them American newspapers, periodicals, and books as much as we please. How ridiculous it is to have the Society of American Editors appealing for freedom of news and news communications and saying nothing about this exclusion of American journals from the place where they are needed most, to have the State Department spending large sums for informatory broadcasts and consenting to the continuation of the censorship of all mails to Germany and from Germany, as if the fighting was still going on, with stupid officers striking passages out of private letters to American citizens!

We need greater and greater food shipments, and more and more coal. To use President Harding's classic phrase, we need the "return to normalcy." Only in that way can we approach peace and harmony in Europe and lift up peoples' hearts both in the countries we have conquered and in those so abused and repressed by the Germans. Only by moving in this direction can there be real assurance that there will not be clashes between us and those we oppress. And, what is more important, only by moving along these lines will it probably be possible for us to get Germany on a self-supporting basis by 1950. Let us stop punishing the Germans in order to punish ourselves.

Let us complete the scrapping of the Potsdam Pact at the earliest possible moment. We can do away with this Covenant with Death, if the new Congress determines to do so.

March 5, 1947

Dear Irving:

Many thanks for your letter. I am so glad your silence is broken. I am delighted that I shall figure in the 100th anniversary issue of the P-D. Will you be sure to see that I get a copy of the paper. I wish that the P-D could give a real honest to goodness review of the Morgenstern book which has been shockingly mishandled hereabouts. Every book criticizing FDR gets the same treatment. Unless I am mistaken, so far the Saturday Review of Literature has not even mentioned the book, just as it made no comment on my "The Disappearing Daily." I would have bet $1,000 to one cent that the Times and Herald-Tribune would damn it, and they did. Moreover, their daily reviewers, Gannett and Prescott ignored it completely. If it had been laudatory of the war and FDR it would have been spread all over the paper. Why, oh why, can't the P-D play its old role? I know what the first J.P. would have done.

No, I have never heard from Capt. Peter Hart, but I shall look him up the first chance I get and see if we can't go to lunch.

We are in the middle of the most terrific happening, perhaps, in all our history--our taking over of Greece and also Turkey. I enclose a confidential memorandum which you are to show to nobody else, the origin of which you must not even guess at and you will please destroy after reading, though it only confirms information already in the press. Where in the world will this venture not lead us? Just as the Spanish War took us from Cuba into Asia, who can foretell in what this will not involve us? The effects may be very marked a hundred years from now. It is like the breakdown of the British Empire! It is the beginning of the pay-off for our going into the war. Again, no one can forecast what the final bill will be. As other countries are hovering on the verge of disaster one must ask how many more and how much can we really put up to keep the world afloat. Yesterday I talked with a highly placed colonel who told me that far more important for us than Greece was Turkey, for it is through Turkey that the army is planning its campaign in our next war, since by striking up from the Eastern end of Turkey we can cut into the weakest portion of Russia--provided we fight our way through the Caucasian Mountains.

Look in the next Progressive, but one, for my piece "Russia Rules the United States"--they may, however, change the heading. The one on the breakdown of England in the last I hope you will also see. Last week was a bad one for me as I had a cold and was laid up more or less for ten days. Right in the middle of it I received an order from the Readers Digest to turn in within a week an article against conscription. You can imagine how pleased I was, not merely because of the emolument or the power of its great circulation. Anything that makes a 75 year-older think that he isn't, after all, a total back number means a lot to his morale!

My affectionate best to you and your wife.

As ever,

P.S. Do make the P-D send you on here for important work for your centennial issue. That is a fine editorial in the enclosed Tribune. Some of the best editorial writing I have ever seen is being done on that paper and subjects being treated that are deliberately overlooked here and ought to be discussed by every paper. Gosh, how I hate to admit that there is good in the C.T.! I had already read your editorial on J.P.Green before your copy came and had liked it--indeed it stood right out of the page.

March 11, 1947

Dear Norman:

I think we can all agree in the Post War World Council that no more important question has come before us than this one of the attitude we should take in regard to the Greek situation. I write in advance of the President's address which may modify or intensify the situation, and I must confess frankly that in all my years of commenting upon world events in the press I have never been so puzzled as to what attitude liberals opposed to war should take.

If I were to be guided solely by my instinct I should say under no circumstances let us go beyond helping to keep the Greeks alive through such an agency as the Red Cross. My reason also heads me to a considerable degree in this direction. I fear most of all the more distance consequences. The money side seems to me of no importance, but if we get into Greece through the government the army and navy will lose not one minute in urging military occupation. Again, the question as to whether we should support the present regime or any regime would at once present itself with the State Department, I am sure, clamoring for control of whatever government might come out of our intervention. As an army officer of importance told me last week, the army feels that our control of Greece and of Turkey is essential. Correctly or incorrectly, he stated that the army was planning its war against Russia with Turkey as the all-important means of approach, with its million fresh soldiers and what he called its easy approach to Georgia and the Caucasus--he asserted that Spain would be the all-important base for our operations. I have the strongest feeling that it will be no time at all before we place troops in Greece to protect her borders and to keep out the Communists.

With the foreign situation steadily getting worse we shall similarly be called upon after taking over Greece and Turkey to hold up Yugoslavia, Czecho[illegible] and any other countries, and that this will go on--always in order to head off Russia--until we have the whole burden of Europe upon us. As for Russia, I am strongly of the opinion that she cannot possibly fight us now or for years to come, and feel that there is considerable evidence of serious unrest at home--about the reported mutinies in the army we have not enough evidence as yet. Nonetheless she will be more than ever hostile if we break completely with the past and actively take England's place as the dominating force in all Europe. I am afraid there is a great deal of truth in Lawrence Dennis's assertion that all Russia "needs is to have us continue our present bipartisan foreign policy and further involve ourselves in foreign interventions, failures and costly disasters. This indefinitely prolonged crisis will not only help Russia and Communism, but will reelect Truman."

If we take Greece and Turkey into our"protective custody" that will not alone keep us from being affected by Russian propaganda. That will be carried on steadily whether we occupy two or six European countries.

On the whole, therefore, I would recommend that the PWWC confine itself to urging humanitarian policies in Greece and Turkey alone and make it absolutely clear that we shall not interfere in domestic politics; that we regard it strictly as a humanitarian action to be carried out by the present relief organizations and make the positive statement that our action is not in any way to be taken as a move against Russia. If we once get mixed up with the Dardanelles and similar problems no one can in his wildest fancy guess where we shall finally land. Having seen the United States go into Cuba to rescue it from tyranny and wind up in the Philippines on the other side of the globe, and after fifty years in a war with Japan in consequence, I feel intensely on this point.

With great regret that I cannot attend the meeting on Thursday,

Faithfully yours,

Mr. Norman Thomas

Russia Rules America

By OSWALD GARRISON VILLARD

YES, RUSSIA does rule the United States Government at this moment. You may not believe it, but just look at the record and see for yourself. All our foreign policies are now dominated by fear of that country. Every single move is dictated by the Russian angle. Why is it that the Government today is actually asking the leaders of both parties to assent to our taking over England's dominating role in Greece and Turkey? Why, simply and solely because of its dread that if the collapsing British Empire gives up its interference in the affairs of those two countries, Russia will move in.

O. G. Villard

What a prospect that opens up for us! It is bad enough that we are now definitely mixed up with the exploitation of oil in Iran and Saudi Arabia, that the Government is playing oil politics in that distant section of the globe. Now we are actually being asked to take the leading place in what was for generations the most dangerous tinder-box in the Near East.

I have just been going over a map of Europe with a distinguished soldier who has pointed out to me that in a war with Russia, which he thinks inevitable within eight or nine years, Turkey will be of enormous importance to us—in fact will be the key state for us, since American armies working up from Turkey could strike into the weakest portion of Russia. "In addition," he said, "Turkey has a splendid army of one million of the best kind of fighters."

TRUE, it is reported that our reply to England says that we will not send troops to Greece and Turkey, but who can tell what will happen once we have been projected into a situation like that? Apparently we are to assume the guardianship and the financial responsibility for these two countries, and if we don't send troops, I'll wager my best hat that in no time at all the U. S. Army will be insisting that Greek and Turkish armaments be standardized according to our own so that there may be full interchange of weapons and ammunition, as has now just been arranged with Canada.

This is only one evidence of Russian control of our affairs. Are we fighting for air bases in Iceland and talking of buying Greenland? Well, lay both of these policies to our fear of the Russians.

Why are we keeping 100,000 troops in war-wrecked and disarmed Japan, and 90,000 more in the Philippines? Is anybody so innocent as to think that the War Department expects an uprising in Japan or the Philippines? Of course not. They are there to impress Russia with the fact that we still have great military strength.

We don't dare take our troops out of Southern Korea lest the Russian Army march down out of the North, which it is now treating as a conquered country. Never before in peacetime have we had a larger Army than 15,000 men in the Philippines. The natives would like our Army to go home. We have presumably given them their independence and now they want to enjoy it, but those 90,000 troops are as fixed in their posts as are the 200,000 troops we have in Germany.

The latter are costing us a huge sum of money, are more and more disliked by the Germans, are certainly not needed to preserve order because the American Military Government is developing constabulary as rapidly as possible, and with Germany totally ruined and starving the idea that there could be a serious revolt against us is of the stuff of which nightmares are made.

TWELVE victorious U. S. generals who returned in 1945 from Germany certified over their joint signatures that Germany was so destroyed that it could not become militarily dangerous for a hundred years, and that has been confirmed again and again by other civilian and military observers. But both our military and naval men are thanking God for Russia. It not only gives them an excuse for being, but enables them to demand the militarization of the United States on a scale never before dreamed of.

Look at South America. Why is it that we are pushing for military alliances with every one of the Central and South American republics? Why, they are to fight with us when we are attacked and prevent "any enemy" from establishing airfields, or rather bases, and operating against us from there. "Any enemy" means Russia—of course, for there is not another Power on earth that could possibly threaten us.

In this year of peace the Army asks that it be given 14 times as much money as in 1939. It has in service no less than 565 generals and it is safe to say that they and all the General Staff officers are devoting their days and nights to planning the war with Russia when they are not spending their time endeavoring to put over universal military training.

The Byrd expedition to the Antarctic, the military maneuvers in Canada and above the Arctic Circle, are all aimed at Russia. If Russia dominates the State Department it certainly cracks the whip over the War Department.

So with the Navy. There is not another fleet on the ocean to threaten us. The English fleet is far inferior, but if it were equal to ours, it could be no threat in view of the break-up of the British Empire before our very eyes, and because no human being, even if England were rich and prosperous, could conceive that a war between the United States and England were possible.

Our fleet is larger than all the other fighting navies put together, and my Army friend undoubtedly spoke for his service when he said that it must be kept up because in the war to come we shall have to attack Russia by way of Sicily, Norway, Denmark, the Adriatic, the Black Sea, wherever there is a water approach to Russian soil. Can anyone doubt that if Russia were to blow up tomorrow because of an internal combustion, because of a rising by those downtrodden and abused and victimized subjects of Stalin, there would be no excuse for maintaining a large Navy? The finest navy telescope couldn't discover another "menace" anywhere.

Take our situation in Asia. Why did we hang on in China as long as we did? Because we were warned that if we did not keep troops there Russia would filter in and try to make permanent the occupation of Manchuria which Mr. Roosevelt so stupidly and shortsightedly granted to Stalin.

Even our attitude toward developments in Indo-China and Malaya and the Dutch East Indies appears to be colored by the Russian peril. Indeed, Hitler was never considered such a menace as is now the Russian colossus.

THE worst of all this is that we have abandoned the historic policy of the United States in carrying on its foreign relations on a basis of ethics, morality, and justice, without any show of force, in favor of the military belief that the only thing the Russians will listen to is force, force, and force, and that the same is true of the smaller nations like the Balkan states and all others.

On this theory we must show our fleet everywhere;

otherwise we shall have no influence upon what is going on. I assure my readers that this is no exaggeration whatever. That is what Congress is being told. Secretary Marshall himself has been quoted as saying to committees of Congress on military affairs that if the Army and Navy appropriations are cut one dollar he will be hurt in his efforts to put through a peace with Germany at Moscow. That is also the reason given for the Army's continuing propaganda for universal service to which I have already referred. We need it not only for self-defense, but, we are told, to impress other nations with our military strength. Well, I have been writing on foreign affairs for so many years that I carry straight back to the time when we had no fleet whatever and our Army totalled only 25,000 men. We had five modern cruisers and no coast defenses to amount to anything when President Cleveland challenged the might of the British Empire and protested against its policy against Venezuela in 1895 on the ground that it was undertaking to breach the Monroe Doctrine.

England could have sent its fleet into any American harbor with complete impunity. According to Gen. Marshall, Mr. Truman, and the present advocates of the blood and iron policies which distinguished Bismarck in his building of the German Empire, we should have been utterly humiliated because Mr. Cleveland couldn't parade a single battleship or heavy cruiser, much less a submarine or torpedo-boat destroyer, as they were then called. Instead, a Conservative British Government, that of Lord Salisbury, yielded to the weight of Mr. Cleveland's arguments, the Venezuela dispute was referred to arbitration, and its final settlement rocked neither country.

TAKE the case of Cleveland's attack on the Russian Government for the Kishinev massacres of the Jews. We still had no armaments and not an American citizen was hurt or suffered the loss of a dollar of property in those killings. But the Czar's Government backed down and the pogroms ceased. There you have a second example of the moral influence and vast strength of the unarmed American people. There are numerous others.

Never, I venture to assert, was the prestige of America higher than at that time. The very fact that no one could accuse us of being militaristic or imperialistic, and that we reached out into no other spheres than our own hemisphere, strengthened us enormously in the eyes of the conventional imperialistic and militaristic Powers. They knew we were unselfish, that we were jeopardizing nobody, interfering in nobody else's concerns, being absolutely aboveboard and that we powerfully influenced world opinion. It was not until William McKinley and Theodore Roosevelt came into the White House that we had to have secret diplomacy and embark upon overseas adventures and bloodshed.

Now we have not only got to keep our German and Japanese enemies alive, we still owe many millions of Lend-Lease dollars to our possible enemy, Russia, who has every reason, in regarding our military preparations, to be terrified by our threats. Now we are going to take over the job of managing Greece and Turkey.

Some of my readers in and out of uniform may like this kind of America that we now have, and may enjoy being embarked upon foreign policies that are leading us heaven only knows where, but I frankly don't. I am ashamed and humiliated by it, by the sacrifice of those magnificent ideals we held when we were utterly opposed to militarism and war and refused even for a time to annex Hawaii.

It was a great American age; it was an age of peace and relative happiness—when no one thought or planned for a world to be dominated by either Russia or the United States, when we planned our own policies and they were not formulated as today by a corrosive fear of one rival state. America's moral influence can yet do the job of helping to build a free, democratic world—a job for which the military is totally unequipped—if we abandon our reliance in force and place our faith in the ideals which made us great. Red imperialism can be checked by democracy—not more imperialism.

March 28, 1947

Dear Irving:

A cousin of mine, Theodor Engelmann in Munich, (I don't know whether he came to see you but he knows about you) has written begging for some help. The black mark against him is that the damned fool joined the Nazi Party; he thought it was necessary, I suppose. His wife also joined the Red Cross as a Nazi and one daughter got a Nazi job, so now they are out and trying to live. He speaks English, Spanish, French, Dutch, Latin and Greek--the last two would be especially valuable, I know! He is 68 but "well preserved." I am not particularly eager about helping him, but, after all, there are three women in the family who are freezing and starving, so I wonder if you have any suggestion as to how he could get a job. I understand the ban is off those who were merely party members and not active in any way.

When I read the editorial inthe P-D on this criminal venture into Greece and Turkey I could see poor J.P. not merely turning in his grave, but shrieking as well with ghostly yells. The man who fought the Panama, Philippine, Nicaragua and Haiti invasions, what would he not have said to this direct declaration of war on Russia? I really felt like weeping myself. For Truman it was the cleverest thing he could have done and he will now take the usual measures short of war that will land us in the struggle. I suppose you hav noticed that Stalin has not received Marshall, though giving a long interview to Bevin. The Communists are said to be very happy over the calm, cool indifference with which Truman's fulmination was received.

With most affectionate greetings,

As ever,,

April 2, 1947

Dear Mr. Rubin:

I was dismayed when that article came back, not that I want to challenge your editorial judgment this time, but only because it means such ann effort gone wrong when I have so few reserves. I cann't send you another this week because I am simply buried under the"final, final" revision of my tariff book--which no publisher has yet committed himself to bringing out. That must be finished within the next two or three weeks, and I also have promised a long pamphlet to Human Events by April 15, about which I wrote to you.

You say you are overburdened with foreign matter. My reply is you ought to be on this Greek-Turkish affair because it commits America definitely to a worldwide course of vicious imperialism, if it does not take us into the third war. But passing that, what would you say to a longish article on our shipping situation, asking whether we must subsidize or nationalize. I wrote it for the Readers Digest which played its usual trick of being much interested in the suggested and then holding the article for a long time and finally returning it. While it has its international aspect it is a domestic subject, but if you don't want it or have had all you can carry on this subject, say so, please. I will bring it up-to-date, of course with a new and rather amusing lead--our patriotic shipbuilders who are so insistent upon subsidies and building ships and are stampeding to put vessels, 145 so far, under the Panamanian registry so as to avoid the LaFollette shipping law and other shipping controls, to say nothing of the unions. You can't beat these patriots try as hard as you may

By the way, you have never answered my queries as to whether you want me to write on Taft or not. Did I tell you that Dick Neuberger hopes that I will--Mrs. Kimberley says I did. It will interest you to know, by the way, that Wallace is getting enormous audiences. Madison Square Garden was crowded to the doors and many turned away, and the same thing happened in Philadelphia two weeks ago. But the way the damned Republicans have fallen for the patriotic dodge again puts us right back where we were in 1940, and Truman has only to sit back and laugh and play the same game again. Probably he will soon be asking the newspapers for another voluntary censorship in the best F.D.R. manner.

Sincerely yours,

Mr. Morris H. Rubin
The Progressive,
Madison, Wisconsin

June 16, 1947

Dear Mr. Hutchinson:

The news in this morning's paper moves me to send you at once my warmest congratulations on your succession to the editorship of The Christian Century. I earnestly hope that, if the paper situation permits, you will now be able to push the circulation rapidly, for the paper ought certainly to have the much greater readership which it has so well earned. There is a unique opportunity before the C.C.--if it will make no further compromises with the war gods, and find no excuse for World War III. Two years ago I said--without irreverence--that the slogan for that would be "Save Jesus from Joseph". That is what it will undoubtedly be,otherwise phrased. I think you will receive an early mimeographed copy of the pamphlet which I have just written on our militarization of which I told you. I hope it will seem convincing to you.

Meanwhile let me congratulate you and the Christian Century again on your accession to the leadership and your wise choice of Harold Fey as managing editor. If you can see at any time a way in which I can help please let me know.

Sincerely and cordially yours,

Mr. Paul Hutchinson,
The Christian Century
407 South Dearborn Street
Chicago, Illinois.

Why Should Russia Fear Us?

By Oswald Garrison Villard

WHEN Stalin and his admirals and generals look across the ocean to the United States, they have every reason to believe that this country is preparing for war as never before and that its target is the Soviet Union. Were they in doubt, they would only have to look back to the years immediately following World War I and reflect how relatively quickly we disarmed then, how free we were from any effort to spread our military and naval power throughout the world, how we even invited the Naval Disarmament Conference to meet in Washington. Today the United States is being militarized with a speed never dreamed of, although the public continues largely unaware of what is going on. And the objective is plainly the Russian Bear.

I

This is what Stalin and his military men observe going on under the American flag today:

An army of 1,070,000 men as contrasted with one of approximately 300,000 just prior to the last war. Of this total, 400,000 constitute the airforce, for which new machines are being developed with unlimited funds and all possible engineering ability.

A continuance of production of atom bombs for army and navy at an enormous expense.

A navy reported to comprise 2,691 ships and able to defeat the combined navies of all the rest of the world, with 1,750 additional vessels in reserve for emergencies. Congress is just voting $344,000,000 for new destroyers, submarines, cruisers and aircraft carriers, plus a special appropriation of $3,000,000 for two experimental submarines fitted with the latest German devices. The total cost of the navy in the coming fiscal year is to be $3,500,000,000, with the naval airforce seeking more money than the entire cost of the navy prior to the war. The army and navy employ 1,100,000 civil service employees. Its commissioned officers from ensign to admiral number 48,445, and the total force is 500,000 men for the next fiscal year.

The largest merchant fleet in the world, totaling more than 25,000,000 tons, controlled by the government, which permits no ship to be built until its plans have been passed upon by the Maritime Commission with a view to the usefulness of the ship in the event of another war.

The maintenance of many wartime bases, even in Irak, with our government making special efforts to retain landing fields and bases in Greenland and Iceland.

Enormous military and naval activity in the Aleutians and in Alaska, and heavy artillery being flown to the latter.

Military and naval maneuvers in Canada and in the Arctic and Antarctic, and the fitting of some submarines with special equipment to permit operation under ice fields. For the first time Admiral Byrd's expedition to the Antarctic has been financed by government instead of by private funds. A carrier and a number of government vessels are making special Arctic equipment tests.

The army's demand for control of no less than 4,500,000 square miles of land and sea in order to protect the 500 square miles of the Panama Canal Zone! The canal defense system is to begin 1,200 miles away from the canal and include Bermuda and bases in the Azores and Brazil, and then, following a line through northern South America to Peru, is to swing northeast to Guatemala from the Galapagos islands.

The maintenance of an army of 96,000 men in the Philippines where the United States never had more than 25,000 troops prior to the war, and forced cession by the Philippines of enormous new bases for army and navy, all of which arrangements are obviously aimed only at Russia.

The refusal of the United States to place its recent conquests in the Pacific under United Nations trustee agreements, the only other nation holding out against such agreements being the Union of South Africa. Ex-Secretary Ickes charges that the navy's insistence on having the former Japanese islands as "strategic areas" was due to a desire to avoid "inspection, criticism and publicity" of the navy's administrative methods by keeping them "top secrets."

The President's demand for the arming of Latin America with American weapons, and American military and/or naval missions stationed in each of the 21 republics. The bill now pending for this move gives President Truman the right to train soldiers, sailors and airmen of the nations of the western hemisphere, and the right to withhold reports on the details of what is being done by us militarily south of the Rio Grande if he considers that a public disclosure would be contrary to the public interest! This plan has been sanctioned by General Marshall as secretary of state, despite objections from civilians within his department.

The introduction of high politics in army and navy planning. Thus the policy and strategy group of the plans and operations division of the Army General Staff, and the navy's politico-military affairs section in the Office of Naval Operations, are concerned with questions of "high political policy," as Blair Bolles has said in a report of the Foreign Policy Association. Both services aim at control of our foreign policy.

The complete domination by army and navy of scientific research in the United States, for which the government expended $1,250,000,000 in 1946. Of this sum, $1,125,000,000 was spent by the army and navy, which are invading the college campuses in numerous directions. Five thousand students especially picked from the high school graduates of the country will hereafter be sent annually to 52 colleges and universities for training as officers of the navy, in which they will be committed to serve for from 15 months to two years. The number of R.O.T.C. units in high schools and colleges steadily increases.

The army and navy, for the first time in our history, entering into close relations with industrial corporations and supervising the building up of great stockpiles of rare, war-needed materials, the maintenance of a large number of "stand-by" plants to be kept in service or in immediate readiness for service in case of war, and the stimulation of many committees to act with the departments for the various vital industries.

The establishment, if the pending bill for the merger of the army and navy passes, of a National Security Council consisting of the secretary of state, the new secretary of national defense, and the assistant secretaries in charge of the army, navy and airforces. There is also to be a war council comprising the four "military secretaries" and the officers in charge of the army, navy and airforces, backed by the national general staff.

The trebling of the National Guard so that it will total 600,000 men, and the creation of an enormous pool of manpower through unlimited officer and enlisted men reserves of the army, navy, marine corps, and so forth. The war department expects that these reserves will be made up of between eight and ten million men, all of whom will have had some military training.

The demand for universal military training, despite the fact that the President's Universal Training Commission declared that even with this system 12 of our largest cities could be destroyed overnight under modern conditions of warfare.

II

If Stalin and his ministers and generals read the speeches being made in this country they are aware that one public address after another includes direct attacks upon the Russians. Thus Gen. Curtis LeMay, the head of the army's air research department, has publicly declared that the airforce is now totally inadequate to protect the United States since it is ten years behind the Russians in research. (How this secret information as to Russian progress in air research has reached General LeMay from behind the iron curtain has not been explained.) The Russians will also have noted that both President Truman and General Marshall have emphatically insisted that universal conscription is absolutely necessary to enable the United States to carry out its foreign policies and have the weight in international affairs to which it is entitled. On April 6, 1946, Mr. Truman said that "only so long as we remain strong can we insure the peace of the world."

As for the Greco-Turkish policy, now known—perhaps only for a little while—as the Truman Doctrine, the Russians are well aware that we are not arming Turkey because its people are in want or distress or are being attacked by guerrillas, but because, since the Montreux agreement of 1936 governing the Dardanelles, we have taken the position that America is directly involved in the government of that strait and does not propose to have Russia dominate it. It is obvious that we are arming Turkey against nobody else than Russia. Indeed, it is the belief in some army circles that Turkey will be our main avenue of land attack upon Russia when the war, which the army considers inevitable, comes. The idea is that there are no natural obstacles between the two countries and that it will be easy for an invading force, with or without atomic bombs, to push into Georgia.

The army also has its eyes upon the Turkish army whose size is variously put at 750,000 to 1,000,000 men The Turks have always been excellent fighters. As an American officer of considerable rank stated to the writer of this article, "We want the aid of that Turkish army." In addition, Russia is well aware, though Mr. Truman has not told the American people of the facts, that up to May 24, 1944, according to Winston Churchill, $80,000,000 worth of British and American arms were given to Turkey to try to get her to enter the war on our side, of course without success.

III

As for President Truman's address to Congress asking for the approval of his Greco-Turkish invasion, it need only be pointed out what the reaction would have been in this country had Adolf Hitler made any such move or used any such language. The President's address was so open in its hostility to Russia as to have warranted that country in recalling its ambassador from Washington or demanding a categorical explanation of the American objective. Similarly, Mr. Truman's utterly undiplomatic outburst when asked in his newspaper conference about the Russian communization of Hungary—in which he declared it "a terrible outrage" and added that this government would not "stand idly by"—ranks as an unprecedented attack by the head of one great nation on the action of another in a third country. It certainly justifies Russia in making every defensive preparation possible.

That the Hungarian coup was an alarming and indefensible move must not be allowed to hide the fact that we have gone back with a vengeance to the shirtsleeve diplomacy of the 1890's and early 1900's. But that time, when we took off our coats, we dealt with minor powers in a world that was in no such unsettled condition as now. What would we say if Stalin were to retort in kind and say just what he thinks of our Turkish move?

xxxxxxxxxxxxx 79 East 79th Street
x
21 January 22, 1948

Dear Freda:

Mabel Miller has told me that you were wondering how I felt about Henry Wallace. Needless to say there is much in his platform that appeals to me. I believe that he is dead right in saying that the Truman policies are taking us straight into war. As John Foster Dulles has intimated, foreign policy is being dictated by military men (he excepted Marshall curiously enough), and that military men must not be allowed to formulate national programs. Some of Wallace's articles I find myself entirely sympathetic to, and I could not go along with your attitude--after having supported LaFollette--that a third party must not be organized without large labor support.

My difficulty is that I don't trust ~~xx~~ Wallace himself and consider that he is in a thoroughly inconsistent position in opposing war now when he cooperated with FDR in putting us into the Hitler war in violation of the constitutional provisions as to warmaking, and by means of the greatest deceit of the American people on record in our history. I also remember his telling people at the time of the economics of scarcity, that he didn't believe in killing the little pigs, etc., but that he had to do it. His failure to defend himself for breaking his word to Baruch is another thing that destroys my confidence in his mental integrity. Doubtless I am a back number in still believing in intellectual integrity and moral decency, but that I do. Hence, I don't see any resting place for me when the campaign opens.

Sincerely yours,

Miss Freda Kirchwey
The Nation
20 Vesey Street, N.Y.

August 25, 1948

Dear Irving:

Many thanks for your two letters written on the bus -- how glad I am that you take that conveyance instead f driving yourself! Also, I have yours of the 30th of July from Fort Riley. I am glad if you are happy in keeping your fingers on the military pulse. I even won't quarrel with you for taking a foreign decoration in violation of the Constitution but I frankly would like it much more if you were out of the service. You will surely admit that the progress of our militarization is very rapid and very serious. I wish you could make sometime an elaborate study f the so-called Merger Law which Senator McCarthy rightly said will within twenty-five years turn over the whole Government to the defense services. I suppose it would cost you your reserve commission to do that but it would be a highly patriotic service. The present conscripti n will al o be a grand target for you if you were free to analyse it but I suppose the P.D. as well as your commission would forbid.

I am glad th t you are going to vote on the side of the protestors, As I think I've written to you there is a great deal in the Wallace program and the Wallace speeches of which I heartily approve but since he does not hold the scales even and regard to Russia and I have no faith in the man himself, I cannot go into his camp, so I suppose I shall drift back into voting for Thomas. So far, I have refused to join the Non-Socialist Committee which backs his canidacy. The truth is that I cannot get up much interest in this campaign. In part it is because I am so very miserable and am not allowed to write, and part because I do not think that it makes much difference whether it is Truman or Dewey, so far as the saving of Europe is concerned. I have just read Dulles' speech with great care and have smiled at the editorial of the Times which so nearly denounces him for his pacifism but falls back on his defense of our preparedness and our conscription to preserve his standing with the public That is just the trouble with him for me. He is very able and certainly very religious but I just can't enthuse about these good churchmen who blow hot and cold on the subject of war and war preparations. I have found him very cold ordinarily and I recall a couple of nice talks I have had with him when he really warmed up. His brother Alan is much more attractive but a goodgdodldoflacsnob; have you heard that there is a good deal of Washington gossip to the effect that Alan will be sent to London as Ambassador--I can't quite believe it. John gives an enmrmous amount of time to the Federal Council of Churches and is really a very religious man. I don't think reporters will ever cheer for him when he is Secretary of State. He desires that office because his grandfather, John W. Foster, and his uncle, Ronald Lansing, had it. I suppose you saw the map that the Chi.Trib. printed the other day giving all the states of the Union to Dewey in the coming election with the exception of a handful of Southern States awarded to the Dixiecrats. But somehow I can't feel that it is necessarily a walk-over. How much depends on the Russian situation while the bulk of Labor seems certain to go for Harry, but among the people I meet there is no one who has a good word for him. My elder son will vote for him, however under protest in preference to Dewey.

I had heard about that broadcast but wasn't sure that I came out of it with flying colors or not, just as I am puzzled by something that has recently appeared in the Harvard Alumni Bulletin. I have submitted it to a number of people and can't get a clear cut verdict as to whether it is a knock or a boost.

It is an article on Laski's book, comparing him to Tocqueville and Bryce, the editor says, "Unlike them, he is not really the detached foreign observor at all. He is an adopted American in the thick of the fight. He is, despite his background, a most American liberal, in the tradition of the young Orestes Brownson, Theodore Parker, Oswald Garrison Villard and Henry Wallce." The question is whether the inclusion of Wallace's name does not rule the rest of it out. What does your editorial mind say? It is the more amusing because the Bulletin for thirty years refused to take any note of me to cite or review any of my books and generally barred me from its columns as a bad Harvard men. Well, whatever I am, I am having a very bad time for my sins. Mrs. Villard had a major operation on the 8th of July from which she emerged triumphantly and my brother broke his left hip and is still in the hospital. I spent ten days in New York while Mrs. Villard was in the hospital, lost five pounds, and came back utterly exhausted and so weak that there are times when I cannot walk over a hundred yards. The heat has a most depressing effect upon me. As it is, I have no strength whatever. I take endless medicines but there is no ability to get at the real trouble. My heart is greatly improved and there is a growing belief that a blocked gall bladder is not so very important if it does not give rise to intense pain. The Battle Creek doctors said frankly they do not know what is the matter, besides the number of my birthdays. So I am almost house-bound and am lucky if I get in a short automobile ride. Now why can't you take pity on me and really come to see me when you come on to your O.B.E. It would be an act of great kindness and would be tremendously appreciated. Besides, I should so like to have you see this lovely place before it is sold this fall. I can't swing it any longer, for various reasons, among them that Mrs. Villard does not come up any more and the children only make brief visits. It will be a terrible wrench to give it up after twenty-five years but everything has to come to an end sooner or later, even a Truman administration.

It is hard for me to let so many subjects pass by me; for example, there are many wonderful magazine subjects that I'd like to do and wish you would. The important one is the way that important policies in Washington are now outlined by subordinates. Congress no longer decides policies, unless for example, the chairman of the Maritime Commission and other admirals decide what shall be the Mercantile Marine Policy of the U.S. Come and see me and we will have a wonderful couple of days together. There may not be many more chances!

My warmest regards to the family and best of greetings to you,

Affectionately yours,

OGV/pr

Mr. Irving Dilliard
St. Louis Post Despatch
St. Louis, Mo.

Charles A. Beard, Patriot

By OSWALD GARRISON VILLARD

OF ALL Americans known to me, Charles A. Beard was the one the country could least afford to lose. Here was an absolutely devoted patriot, whose pen was dedicated to the truth and nothing but the truth. He never, during his nearly 74 years, yielded to compromise, or remained silent in the presence of what seemed to him a national error. Fear of the consequences of any position he might take was unknown to him.

This he demonstrated beyond cavil when, in 1917, he resigned his professorship at Columbia University in protest because an insincere president and a war-mad board of trustees dismissed from the faculty two men whose sole offense was their exercise of the free-born American's right to oppose our entry into World War I. Beard himself was no pacifist; he did not share the opinions of his two colleagues, but he knew well that their dismissal was the gravest blow struck at academic freedom up to that time. Many another on the faculty shared his views, but they thought of their families and remained silent.

Beard, with his wife and two children, went forth fortified and ennobled by this sacrifice to principle, and he found no difficulty whatever in supporting them by the might of his writing. To the American people he has bequeathed no less than 34 books, many of permanent economic and historical value, which have been studied by hundreds of thousands throughout the land and have profoundly affected the teaching of history.

That many of them have stirred the fires of controversy is true. That merely emphasizes their power, the vigor of his presentation, his moral earnestness, his readiness to strip from national heroes the imaginary garments of righteousness with which others had clothed them, his bitter hatred of cant. Not that he was a muckraker—far from it. His aim was always to present the facts as he found them; whether others agreed was of little or no importance. Yet, when there was some political or personal action that deeply aroused him, his indignation flashed fire.

An example was his ringing protest against the ventures now underway to write the recent history of the United States in accordance with purely official views. Especially was he rightly stirred by the voting of $139,000 by the Rockefeller Foundation to enable Prof. William L. Langer of Harvard to write an officially favored history of World War II in order to head off another "debunking journalistic campaign" such as "followed World War I." Dr. Beard pointed out that Prof. Langer had been given "exceptional access to materials bearing on foreign relations" as the Carnegie Foundation boasted, "access," Dr. Beard stressed, "to secret records withheld from other scholars and inquirers."

It is no wonder that he asked whether recent history is to be portrayed by persons well-subsidized, under Government patronage, or by those who, seeking the truth, desire to set forth the picture without official favor or favoritism, and without subsidies from a source which decrees in advance that the resulting book shall be a favorable description of the acts of the governmental officials in and before the war years.

Dr. Beard's critics, on the other hand, charged him with likewise writing with prejudgment. Indeed, the Associated Press in its obituary account of his career contained the editorial allegation (taken, if memory serves, from a hostile review of his *President Roosevelt and the Coming of War 1941*) that Beard "employed his powers of analysis to interpret hindsight." That is false, for never was a book more carefully buttressed by documents and official facts. However outraged Charles Beard felt about that betrayal (which some of Roosevelt's ardent followers now freely admit*), nothing could have induced him to suppress or alter facts, or to gloss over moral wrong-doing.

But, after all, Dr. Beard's reputation does not hinge upon his latest work. His scholarship and high historical standing do not depend upon his recent books nor upon the allegation that he was ruled by partisanship. As the New York *Herald-Tribune* has pointed out, he is widely believed "to have affected the course of teaching and the interpretation of history as no other man of his generation." His *The Rise of American Civilization* and his *Economic Interpretation of the Constitution* each sold more than 175,000 copies and are required reading in many colleges. His and his wife's *Basic History of the United States* likewise aroused controversy and stirred the historical stand-patters and warmakers by its excoriation of the acts which put us into World War I. It had an enormous sale.

He had favored our entry into the war in 1917—but his critical and honest mind revolted when he ascertained how we had been led into it. He opposed our taking part in World War II with a remarkable prophecy as to the insecurities and tensions

OSWALD GARRISON VILLARD is the dean of the nation's liberal journalists, as Charles Beard was the dean of American historians. For many years Mr. Villard edited The Nation and The New York Post, and he has long been a fighter, with his pen, in the vanguard of liberal causes. Among his many books are "Prophets True and False," "Fighting Years," "The Disappearing Daily," and "Free Trade — Free World."

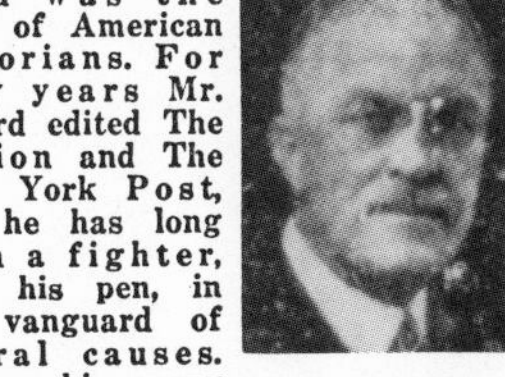

*Thus A. A. Berle, Jr., a veteran adviser of F. D. R., writes in *Life* that Roosevelt's promise to the American people not to send their sons into a foreign war "was a low-water mark in Presidential morality; but the President won the election."

which would inevitably follow our winning of it. Equally correct were his and his wife's forecasts years ago that we should soon have such a sociological and political upheaval as was embodied in the New Deal. They could always look far ahead.

It is, of course, impossible to write of Charles Beard without speaking of his wife, Mary Beard. Their life partnership, their complete and ideal comradeship, and their literary collaboration can only be matched by that of Beatrice and Sidney Webb in England. She has written valuable books of her own, and to all his books she gave a faith and a sympathetic aid that surely helped to mold every one, not merely those that bear her name as well as his.

Such happiness as was theirs comes to few people, and surely still fewer lead such stimulating and interesting lives—or have pioneered in so many directions. It is greatly to be hoped that Mary Beard will finish the uncompleted second volume of her husband's examination of the way we were deceived into World War II.

It is related of him that he very often began his lectures with these words: "Let us examine the assumptions . . . ." That was the key to the mental attitudes of both husband and wife: they always sought the bases of statements and policies in a spirit of scholarly skepticism which has put this country profoundly in their debt.

Infallible they were not, of course, as they would have been quite ready to admit. That Beard shifted his policy on the role of economics in history is true; never was his mind so rigid as to forbid a reappraisal, a reexamination. But no man can say that he ever abandoned a principle or yielded to any pressure to modify his views.

One had only to appeal to him on behalf of a wrong—his reaction and anger at the injustice were immediate. This was one of the traits which marked him as a true democrat, for his sympathies knew no bounds, least of all nationalistic ones. That alone should have made it impossible for his critics to charge him with being an "isolationist" in the derogatory sense. He wanted his country to be isolated from a futile, needless war, whose outcome, a lost peace, he so clearly foresaw. He was isolationist in his rage against those who put us into the hopeless maelstrom of centuries-old European rivalries and bloody power politics. But when it came to sound international cooperation not based on power politics, of course Charles Beard was for it like any other intelligent, far-sighted man.

He was a great democrat because he so profoundly sympathized with labor and the underdog, because he never lost faith in the American democracy, or yielded one iota to the false doctrines of the present age. Our drift into a militaristic state was no more acceptable to him than would have been an appeal to become a fellow-traveler, to subscribe to the abominable doctrine that the individual is merely a pawn of the state.

People criticized him for one thing or another; a petty Lewis Mumford might try to prevent the award to him of the highest honor of the American Academy of Arts and Letters, its gold medal bestowed only once in 10 years. But no one could challenge for an instant his fundamental loyalty to our institutions, because it is doubtful whether any other American had so profound a knowledge of our Constitution, of the history of our nation, of its basic tenets, of its wonderful possibilities for human happiness never yet realized. He was intellectually a one-man "arsenal" of democracy, a giant in his forever-shining liberalism.

II

One of my happiest memories will always be coming upon Charles Beard, with all his charm and friendliness, on the veranda of his home at New Milford, Conn., interrupting his reading or discussion to look across the Housatonic far below us to the eternal hills toward the sunset. Sage and philosopher, statesman and patriot, he knew what lay beyond those heights, as he knew every element that entered into the long history of the little New England town just beyond his sight and of his big farm some miles away.

I thought of him then as kin to Jefferson, similarly drawing inspiration from the natural beauties of Monticello. Their faith was unshakable; their belief in the innate possibilities, yes, nobility, of the individual alike. They were inwardly serene and at peace, for they had both found spiritual joy and the ultimate satisfaction. They were truly masters of their souls. They used their superb powers for the welfare of all.

October 7, 1948

Dear Friends:

It is so long since you have heard from me that I am really ashamed about it but I have been so miserable, so weak and so unable to carry on with my old ways, that my correspondence has suffered greatly. My working hours are reduced to four or five a day, I am still forbidden to write articles and urged not to write many letters The difficulty of the situation is that not one of the many doctors I have consulted can tell me what the trouble is. Two heart specialists say that that organ is in much better condition and that the gall bladder is not making any trouble. Other specialists are equally cheerful, but when it comes to telling me just what is causing this increasing weakness, why, they just don't know. My seven weeks in the sanitarium in Michigan ended with the doctors saying that frankly. I can only hobble a couple of hundred yards and return.

But the purpose of this letter is not to recite my clinical symptoms but merely to let you know that I often think of you both and wish that I could have imitated my secretary of thirty-three years, who resigned last spring, went on the retired list and then took a trip to England! The report she brought back was very vivid in and entertaining, and so was Francis Nielson's, after his first visit to G.B. for ten years or so. They treated him royally, even the sons of former friends now in the Great Beyond. He almost wept in telling of the decayed look of those portions of residential districts that had escaped the bombings. Cripps' optimism over here has encouraged people a good deal. I know F.W.H.'s feelings about it, but it really looks as if he would be P.M. after all, in view of the ill health of Bevin, Atley and Morrison.

Meanwhile, the Russian situation gets stead'ly worse and our militarists here are attacking her openly in the most flagrant way. I have no respect for Henry Wallace and could not vote for him under any circumstances but he is telling a gret many truths about the aggressive attitude of our government toward the Soviets, as to which Vishinsky has told the truth. It is heart breaking that every proposal made by the Russians is sneered away by our big Press Barons as ridiculous, wholly untrustworthy, etcetera, etcetera. Well, I haven't much faith in the Russian's word but I should favor court martialing any general or admiral or official who attacks Russia and Ishould have infinite patience in giving them the opportunity to show whether there is sincerity behind their proposals or not. The military critic of the Times, Hanson Baldwin, has just made a violent attack upon the Secretary of War because of his outrageous denunciation of the Russians.The truth is, that we have a headless Government and that under officials have no hesitation in enunciating Governmental policy without any authority. This Congress advocated under F.D.R. and failed to carry out the historic policy of controlling the executive. The collapse of F.D.R.'s reputation here is something astounding. I am afraid you'd be very much disillusioned if you were to read the statements made about him by his former intimates and office-holders, Miss Perkins, Ambassador Berle, Hull, Burnes, etc. etc. each avows his great admiration for F.D.R. as a political leader and then sticks in a stiletto and turns it around, Berle going the furthest.

I had a nice long talk with C.C.B. when I was in New York for a day last week. He was in excellent form though he complains bitterly that he can neither see nor hear and said that he'd never had so lonely a summer in his life because not one of his grandchildren could visit him, and he has no one to talk politics with at Black Point, except Alice Ford and Philip McCook, and the latter is a lightweight. He was overwhelmed by telegrams and letters on his ninetieth birthday and by much publicity,and he was misquoted as saying he was going to vote for Truman which he is not.going to do. I enclose an extract from John L. Lewis's proper characterization of Truman as the weakest president we've ever had. Just now, with this great crisis on us, he is roaming around the country as no President ever did before, for campaign purposes, and boasting that he will be re-elected. F.D.R. certainly hit us a terrible blow when he chose that man to be his successor. As Walter Lippmann and others have pointed out, the conduct of foreignal affairs hase been completely turned over to Marshall and three or four others as has never before happened in our history. His reelection seems to me unthinkable and the possibility that he might be chosen would be too ghsastly for words. In St. Louis they are betting fifteen to one against his reelection! Like C.C.B. I have no love for Dewey and I have a great deal of sympathy for Col McCormic 's saying that it may be as hard to get Dewey out of the White House as it was to stop Roosevelt. The Chicago Tribune came out yesterday for Dewey on the ground that he was "the least worst" of the candidates! How this business of going to war produces statesmen and solves the problems of peace! If ever the doctrine of pacifism approved itself it is now when there isn't a statesman in France, Italy, Spain, Germany, England and the United States. Now our Government says openly that the whole underlying principle of our foreign policy is reliance upon force, and the military state is here with hundreds of thousands of officers. When I think that war to end militarism I indulge in a sardonic laugh. Why, the Kaiser was a mere kindergarten espouser of militarism compared to what is going on in Washington now and the whole economy of the country is being hooked up to the military machine. Don't think this is extravagant language, I can justify it a hundred per cent.

As for my family news, my wife had a serious abdominal operation on July 8th and came through triumphantly and is is much better condition in every way with nothing to becloud the future. She has still not been up here but is planning to come soon. It has been very slow for her to regain her strength. Our children are all well and the sons particularly happy in their professorial activities. Our daughter appears to have made up her mind definitely to stay in Washington. It is now more than three years since I have been there, something that has never happened before since I left the University, and my old friends are rapidly passing off the scene.

With warmest greetings to both of you, and the hope that you are both well and able to carry on fully, and with warmest regards,

Faithfully yours,

S.K. RATCLIFFE

October 23, 1948

Dear Irving:

Thanks for your note and the clippings which I greatly enjoyed. I hope, with all my heart, that you can see me when you come on. I had hoped to stay here until Thanksgiving but there is quite a possibility that I shall move to New York definitely by the fifteenth. I am going down on Monday in order to vote and to see the heart specialist . It is quite possible that they will have a different program for me. The truth unfortunately is that I am steadily losing ground and getting weaker and weaker. That wouldn t be so bad if someone could only tell me what is the matter and I could feel that we were moving on the enemy, but all the doctors admit they don't know what the trouble is, and their only advice is to try more medicine, more doctors and more visits to hospitals for "looking over." But enough of that.

Your revelations as to Greene are startling. I knew he was pretty bad but had no idea that he had made such a cesspool out of Illinois. I am not too sold on Professor Douglas whom I knew years ago when I first went to the <u>Nation</u>. I have a feeling that he has shifted his moorings a number of times. Sometimes I think it might be just as well if the Senate were to go Democratic, but unfortunately there is an unanimity now on what seemed to me the worst policy, UMT Arming Europe, etc., and threatening Russia, etc. If only Henry Wallace were intellectually honest and really trustworthy, I could subscribe in the main to his platform, and on Germany he is bad as the worst with the usual total failure to understand. I do hope you are right about Missouri and that if we must get Dewey he will go in with a big sweep.

L McAm 1323 (903)

I will keep you posted as to my movements,

Affectionately yours,

OGV/pr

Mr. Irving Dillard
St.Louis Post-Dispatch
St.Louis, Missouri

November 9, 1948

Dear Norman Thomas:

Replying to your memorandum of November 2, I am greatly distressed at the suggestion that the Post War World Council be given up. I admit the overwhelming difficulties of the situaion both at home and abroad, and yet I feel the need more than ever for an organization of that kind. One of the worst features of the re-election of Mr. Truman is that it gives free play to the militarists who have controlled him so far. It is significant that he took Admiral Leahy -- that evil genius - with him to Key West. The proposals that we shall now spend billions upon rearmament for all of Western Europe either directly as is already sure to have been the case with some French divisions, or through our new Lend - Lease. If we now undertake the insane policy of trying to conquer the victorious Chinese Communists we shall be in war over our necks and the military influence will permeate every phase of American life. Well, of course we do not wish to be a one-issue organization.-- This military one should be the leading one and of course be held up with international disarmament. There are other organizations devoting themselves to the federalization of Europe but we too should throw ourselves behind the movement and if we cannot all agree on working for Free Trade we can at least strengthen the defense of the Reciprocity Treaties which probably would have gone by the board had the Republicans won.

The difficulty, of course, lies in finding the right person to take hold and if only an effective executive could be got I am sure that the organization could be made to grow rapidly. My difficulty in making these suggestions is that I cannot back them up by the promise of personal aid since I am steadily losing strength and immobility. I can no longer walk even a block and attendance at any meeting is out of the question. And because of several import nt drains upon me I cannot promise the considerable financial support I have given in the past, and yet it does seem to me that by certain energetic advertisements in such mediums as the Saturday Review of Literature, it might be possible to turn up some person who would take hold. To close down now seems to me like desertion under fire.

Sincerely yours,

OGV/pr

Mr. Norman Thomas
Post War World Council
112 East 19th Street
New York 3, N.Y.

XXXXXXXXXXX
x
21

79 East 79th Street

April 5, 1949

Dear Irving:

Those were find editorials that you sent me and warmed my heart to think of the P-D getting on the right track again, but, oh dear, there is such a lot to catch up on. I could not put the signing of the North Atlantic Pact on my television last evening, for to me it marks the final blow to our beloved Republic, and the establishment of a complete military State. It gives you all the bigger targets to attack, and I am perfectly certain that if the American people only knew the facts they would rise overwhelmingly against what is going on. By the way, have you seen Milton Meyer's article in the current Harper's on the Chicago Tribune? I have never known anything more completely devastating. But I still et a good deal out of that paper when one can rely upon its statement of facts. How could McCormick or his chief editorial writer let an article like that get into the paper? In this connection I think you will be interested in Sprague Holden's letter herewith (please return)/ Thanks to an introduction from me to John Knight he worked his way up to first editorial writer under Bingay, and then, also on my advice, went into teaching. He is quite right about the decay of the editoreal page. I read a number of comments fromall over the country on the North Atlantic Pact. They were dreadful; total ignorance and stupidity. So I think it is fortunate that you are back and holding the fort as far as you cam.

You will be glad to know that I am better, though a new symptom--loss of breath--is not very encouraging or comforting, but I have gained strength and a couple of pounds in weight, and feel more vigorous. I cannot, of course, make any summer plans as yet.

Most affectionate greetings to you,

As ever,

Mr. Ewing Dilliard,
St. Louis Post-Dispatch
St. Louis, Missouri